MW01618462

THE TRADITIONAL POTTERY OF PAPUA NEW GUINEA

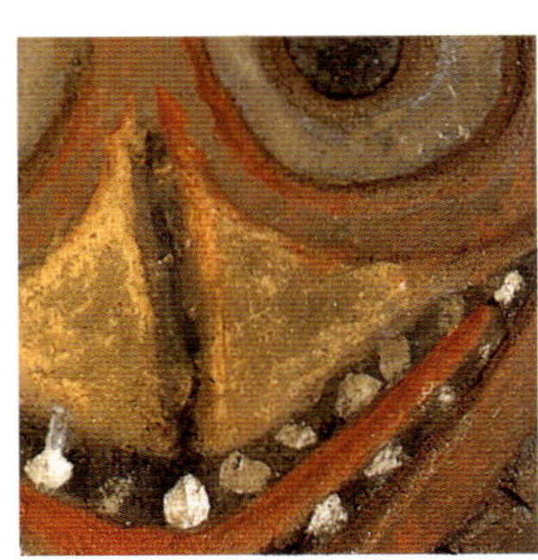

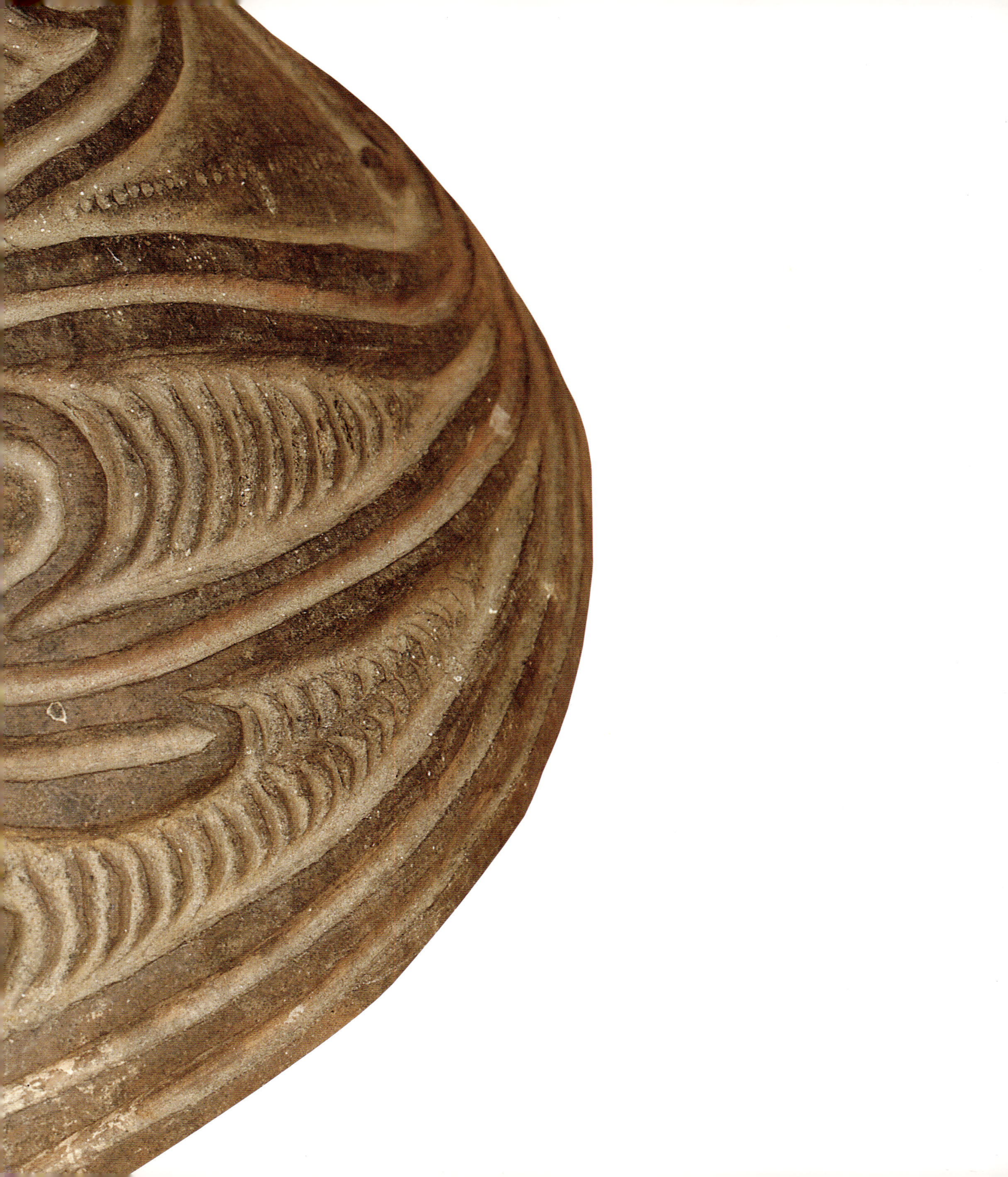

THE TRADITIONAL POTTERY OF PAPUA NEW GUINEA

PATRICIA MAY   MARGARET TUCKSON

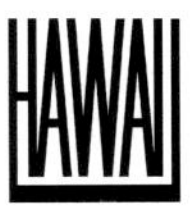

UNIVERSITY OF HAWAI'I PRESS
HONOLULU

Contents

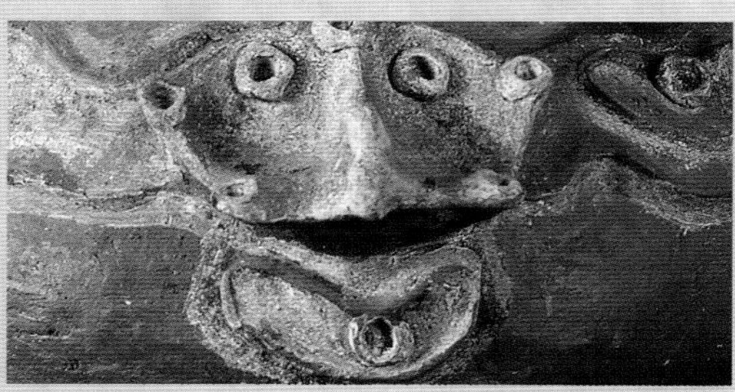

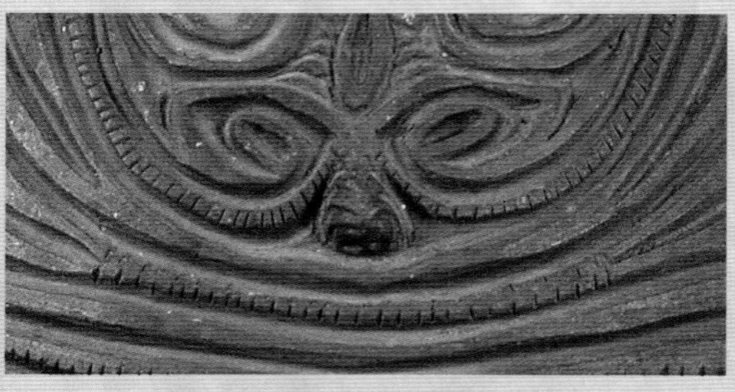

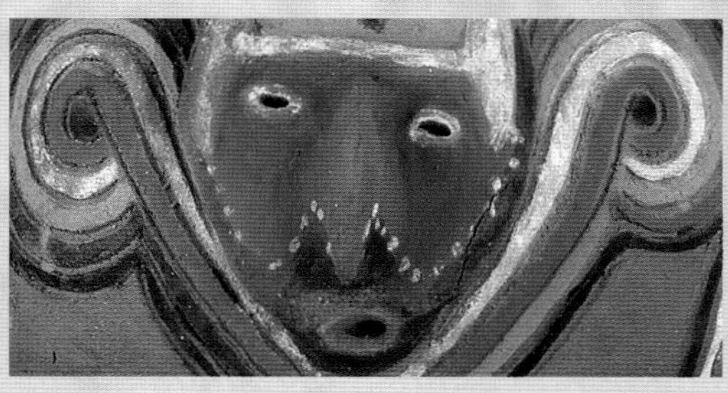

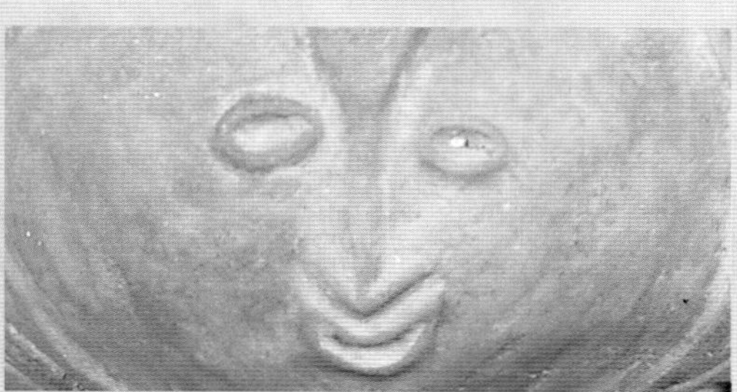

A CHP Production

Published in North America by
University of Hawai'i Press
2840 Kolowalu St
Honolulu, Hawai'i 96822

Produced and published by
Crawford House Publishing Pty Ltd
Adelaide SA 5000, Australia

First published 1982
Revised edition 2000

Designed by Jarrod McCauley
Jacket and preliminary page design by Travis Crawford
Jacket and preliminary page photography by Ranid May
Endpaper art by R.J. May

ISBN 0-8248-2344-3
Library of Congress Cataloging-in-Publication Data has been applied for.

Printed in China by Everbest Printing Co. Ltd

04 03 02 01 00 5 4 3 2 1

Foreword

This book is a unique achievement. It is the product of a decade's labour and collabo ration – in the field and in museums and libraries – between a potter and an art historian. They have produced the most comprehensive coverage of a significant but poorly known aspect of the material life of people in Papua New Guinea.

Earthenware pottery is, or was once, produced by hundreds of communities in Papua New Guinea for their own use and for trade to many groups who do not make it. Despite the inherent fragility of these pots, thousands of them have found their way into collections around the world. For the most part, however, the art of the potters has taken second place to that of the woodcarvers, weavers, painters and other artists of the region whose products fill museums and flood the commercial markets. The artistic and linguistic diversity of Papua New Guinea is widely acknowledged, but rarely does this acknowledgement include the diversity and richness of its pottery and the skills of the potters. This book goes a long way to rectify this situation.

We now have archaeological evidence that pottery may have been first made in the Papua New Guinea region around 5000 to 6000 years ago, and was certainly being made in the islands by 3300 years ago. How the present-day pottery industries relate to those of the past remains a matter for much research, but in some areas there is clear evidence for continuous production of pottery over several thousand years. This book is not, however, a 'history' of pottery making in the region. It is a review of recent times, drawing upon information from the last century as well as from the personal observations and experiences of the authors in the 1960s and 1970s.

The authors have described as many pottery industries as they could identify. Over many years, they personally visited almost every one; only in a few cases did they have to rely upon information from other people. This extensive fieldwork gave them unique opportunities to see how potters go about their business, what they produced and how their products are used. The authors present this information by provincial areas and provide an invaluable introduction to the techniques of forming, decorating and firing the pots, as well as the various forms produced. The excellent maps show how irregularly distributed is the potter's craft in this part of the world. The verbal descriptions are strongly supported by a wealth of outstanding photographs taken by the authors themselves. These illustrations are not just about pots, but show people making pots, firing pots, and using pots. Consequently, the book is as much about the potters as it is about their products. Many of the pots described are not anonymous objects, as we all too often experience with objects in museums, but relate to people with identities and personalities.

Why re-issue the book? Simply because it is still the most complete compendium of the traditional pottery industries of Papua New Guinea ever written. It is highly unlikely that anyone will ever repeat this task. In some areas the craft is changing or declining under the pressures of cultural change through economic and social development. Innovation and change are inevitable, as the archaeological history of the people of Papua New Guinea clearly demonstrates over many thousands of years. The emphasis of the book is on 'traditional' pottery at particular times and places, yet it acknowledges the changes that have taken or are taking place. It is not a single 'snapshot' of them all at one point in time. One of the major strengths of the book, then, is that it is an irreplaceable and largely unrepeatable record of those places and times. While some pottery making industries described in this book, such as those of Aibom, Madang and around Port Moresby, were already well known before the authors began their project, there were also many industries for which there were few or no records, written or otherwise. This book places them literally, 'on the map'.

No other authors could have produced such a volume. Between them, Patricia May and Margaret Tuckson have seen more Papua New Guinea pots – in the field and in collections – and spoken with more village potters than anyone else in the world. Their knowledge and experience are incomparable. In 1972, when I joined the Australian Museum in Sydney, I suggested to Margaret that she and I should collaborate on producing a book about Papua New Guinea pottery. By that time, however, she and Patricia had already agreed to collaborate and in retrospect, we are fortunate that this was so. They brought to the task the insights of a highly-skilled potter and teacher, and the discernment and attention to detail of an art historian. The result is a classic in its own right. As a spectator to its production, I realised over the years how massive a task Patricia and Margaret had taken on. It is a sign of their dedication and commitment that they persevered, making special field trips to check the accuracy of information or to track down yet another potting community about which they had heard but not visited. Much of this travel was done in canoes, small boats and on foot, rarely in comfort. Their aim was not just to see pots, but to meet and talk to the potters themselves, and to record their activities. In addition to these field trips, Patricia and Margaret also spent many hours working through published records and visited museums around the world to ensure that they gathered as much information as possible. Reducing this vast body of information to a single volume was an intimidating task, but one which they completed as few others could have done.

During the revision of the book and as part of the preparation for an exhibition about PNG pottery, the three of us spent more than twelve hours in the storerooms of the Australian Museum. We looked at over 400 pots of all kinds from most of the industries discussed in this book. Many of these pots came from the various expeditions undertaken by the authors, who also contributed outstanding examples of the potter's art to the collections of the National Museum and Art Gallery of Papua New Guinea. Their dedication to their task thus provides for posterity not just an illustrated, written record, but a tangible one as well. The book ensures that a wide readership around the world now has access to two parts of that record. It is also a fitting tribute to the thousands of potters in Papua New Guinea, past, present and future. For that reason alone, it merits re-publication as a celebration of their achievements.

As I noted above, this book does not present a 'history' of pottery making in Papua New Guinea. Since the original publication of the book, there has been an enormous increase in archaeological studies within the New Guinea islands, especially in the Bismarck Archipelago, and in selected coastal areas of north New Guinea. There are several reports of the discovery of pottery in contexts dated between 4000 and 6000 years ago on the New Guinea mainland, though these remain to be confirmed. The most widely accepted date for the earliest pottery yet recorded is around 3300 years ago or slightly earlier, with the appearance of Lapita pottery in the Bismarck Archipelago and north Solomon Islands. This remarkable pottery is extremely rare on the New Guinea mainland, where many pottery industries probably had very different origins. The relationship between this Lapita pottery and many recent industries remains arguable in most areas. In many areas people stopped making or using pottery after the end of Lapita pottery; the reasons for this are not known. The cultural history of the region has undoubtedly been complex. Readers who wish to know more about this history, and especially about Lapita pottery, should turn to P.V. Kirch's book *The Lapita Peoples: Ancestors of the Oceanic World*, and to *The Island Melanesians* by M. Spriggs, both published by Blackwell (Oxford) in 1997.

Jim Specht
Australian Museum

Preface

We began this survey of the pottery industries in Papua New Guinea in 1965. It is our intention to provide a record of these industries, many of which, already barely known to the young people of the village, will inevitably become extinct within a generation. We hope to stimulate the interest and pride of both the established potters and the young people in whose hands lies the fate of the country's ceramic traditions. We wish also to bring before a wider public this aspect of Papua New Guinea's heritage.

It has been our goal to write as comprehensive a survey as possible of the existing pottery industries in Papua New Guinea. We have not attempted to provide a description of other industries in this South-west Pacific region, namely those of Irian Jaya, Vanuatu, New Caledonia and Fiji. We have, however, described those of the adjoining Solomon Islands.

Two preliminary comments must be made on sources and arrangement of data. At the commencement of this study there was little information available on the pottery of Papua New Guinea. Margarete Schurig had published a valuable survey, in German, in 1930, but her information was derived entirely from secondary sources and it contains many errors and omissions. A few industries, mostly in Papua, had been recorded elsewhere in some detail and several others mentioned briefly in more general accounts. Since then, a number of other industry studies have become available. We have attempted to give due weight to all these sources; nevertheless many of the industries described here are recorded for the first time. Jointly or individually, we have visited all of the industries (though not all of the villages) except the Watut River valley, Sinasina, Mailu, some parts of the Sepik and the Solomon Islands. Our field trips took us over hundreds of kilometres of land and sea by small aircraft, canoe and launch, four-wheel drive vehicle, motor bike and foot. We endeavoured always to observe pots being made as a normal pursuit within the community. When this was impossible due to seasonal inactivity, absence of clay resources, social restrictions (such as periods of mourning for important members of the community) or declining or defunct industries, we were obliged to rely on demonstrations and data gathered from informants.

In many cases our visits were brief and, where information is incomplete, we have summarised the situation as well as was possible; there are obviously many areas which need further study – in some cases it is needed urgently.

It was our original intention to organise our information by stylistic regions. As data accumulated, however, it became increasingly obvious that such a classification would be highly subjective and largely speculative. It is clear that over the centuries, through movement of peoples and through trade, there has been a mixing of styles. Forms have been adapted, decorative schemes and motifs have been borrowed and probably also there have been changes in technique. The effects of such mixing are especially apparent in the pottery of the inland Sepik. Other changes in particular styles may have been brought about by innovative individuals or by a progressive loss of skills. One tentative attempt to classify pottery industries according to stylistic traditions (apparently on the basis of archaeological evidence and similarity of form and decoration) has been made by Bulmer (1970). Useful as this suggested classification is, in our opinion it merely demonstrates how tenuous such a classification must be. Additional archaeological evidence (including clay analyses) will help us to understand how present industries have evolved but in the meantime stylistic classification on the basis of present information remains highly subjective. Instead, therefore, we have organised our information according to present administrative divisions (provinces) of the country and, within each province, largely according to language group. Names used for provinces in the text and maps are current at the time of writing. It should be mentioned, however, that changes are being made, for example, Northern is now Oro Province and West Sepik is now Sandaun Province. We must add that linguistic research, too, is in its infancy: our language data represents the position as best known at the end of 1977 and *The Village Directory* (1973) has been used to standardise all village names. In the text, words from the local vernacular are in italics and pidgin words are in quotation marks.

In overseas museums there are a number of Papua New Guinea pots, many of them collected earlier this century and often poorly documented. Some of these have been illustrated in museum catalogues and in books on Papua New Guinea art and, for the most part, we have endeavoured not to reproduce these. Many of the pots illustrated here were photographed in the field. Some pots are from private collections. There are also illustrations of vessels in museum collections, many of which are of pots collected for them by us. We are grateful to those museums, institutions and private collectors who have given us permission to reproduce the illustrations. Acknowledgements, registration numbers and photographic credits are given at the end of the book.

Preface to this edition

This book was written almost two decades ago, following roughly a decade of extensive fieldwork. In the intervening years many of the potters recorded in this study have passed on, and a number of pottery industries – some already in advanced decline in the early 1980s – have died out. Further linguistic, prehistoric and ethnographic research has also modified, somewhat, our understanding of the boundaries and characteristics of the histories and cultures of some of the peoples we have recorded. Political changes have led to the renaming of two provinces (West Sepik to Sandaun and Northern to Oro).

The first edition of the book has been out of print for some years, yet demand for it has continued, reflecting its position as the only work of its kind. We are delighted that Crawford House Publishing has not only recognised this need but has provided us with the opportunity to reissue the book.

In preparing the book for reprinting we have not attempted the impossible task of updating the text, which remains essentially as it was when first published in 1982. We have, however, made a few minor amendments in the light of comments received from colleagues, and have added appropriate text where recent research or new information suggests modification of certain passages is needed.

We have also made additions to the "Bibliography" of significant studies published since 1982.

In making revisions we are grateful to Jim Specht, Christian Kaufmann, Ron May, Helen Dennett, Richard McMillan and Pam Swadling.

Acknowledgements

We are grateful to so many individuals. First, we wish to acknowledge our debt to the potters of Papua New Guinea for their generosity, hospitality and assistance. In particular, we thank the following potters: Oma of Vanimo, Murupen Galuk of Mindiri, Regina Teraku of Kaiep, Yousi Sisi of Samap, Langwe and Levetmeri of Koiwat, Imat Ragun of Zumim, Tamaok Aijakiel of Tumleo Island, Telefi of Ali, Kesesa of Garaina, Rose Mary Gorewa of Emo, Lydia of Wanigela, Grace Kaware of Oreresan, Doris Wesley of Tubetube Island, Lea and Maila of Wari Island, Delilah and Lily of East Cape, Kesaya, Estelle and Meliani of Panaeati Island, Etele of Brooker Island, Kaspar Hananumbo of Paliama, Liton Pilu of Yabob and Bangamali and his wife at the Maprik High School Cultural Centre.

Others to whom we are indebted are Gabriel Wafewa of Soandogum, Blakia of Bikei, Kingsley Dikuwola of Taboina, Mukar Sumak of Madang, Domaia Kilo of Wari, Linda and Salome Isaka of East Cape, Russel Sailasi of Tubetube, Lamak Katit of Fulumu, Mongi of Misima, Banyan Pilikesa, Nistila Kola and Sinela of Panaeati and Yese Laufailedi of Fergusson Island.

Like most researchers working in Papua New Guinea, we could never have completed this study without the cooperation of government field officers and the various missions. We thank especially Sister Helen Roberts of Wanigela, Sister Joseph Mary of Yule Island, Sister Aileen Lawrence of Oro Bay, Sally Green of Margarida, Father Nobbs of Tangu, Father Brian Bailey of Alotau, Father Syd Smith and Alf Smith of Samarai, Bob Solberg of Ranara, Father and Mrs Martin Chittleborough of Popondetta, Reverend and Mrs Grey of Alotau, Father Tom Ritchie of Lumi, Bob Conrad of Maprik, Dr Braun of Madang, Desmond Clifton-Bassett, Desmond Pike, John Sergeantsen, John Quinn, Max Orchard, Mike Cockburn, Mary Hickson, Noel McGuigan, Caspar Yaman, Moses Semeon, Tony and Jenny Maddern, Bruce Murray, Chris Butler, Martin Kerr, Bob Mitten, Michael Data, Bogahohia, Bob Wilson, Lady Rachel Cleland, Peter Lincoln, Joel Bradshaw, Leslie Conton and Dale Ratliff.

There are a number of other people whose helpfulness greatly facilitated our task. Among them are Brian Egloff of the Museum and Art Gallery of Papua New Guinea; Christian Kaufmann of the Museum für Volkerkunde, Basel; Pamela Swadling and Harold Ellwand of the University of Papua New Guinea; Douglas Miles and Peter White of the University of Sydney; Jocelyn Powell of the Botanical Gardens, Sydney; Sue and Hartmut Holzknecht of the Markham Valley; Jan Grocott, Fay O'Sullivan and Susan Faircloth of the Institute of Applied Social and Economic Research; Tau Manega of the New Guinea Research Unit; Henry Isa and Anna Craven of the Solomon Islands Museum; Father Z'Graggen of Madang; Reverend and Mrs Karl Holzknecht of Lae and Ron Perry.

While nearly all those whom we contacted for information were helpful, the kindness and assistance of some deserve special acknowledgement. These include Jeanetta Douglas, Renata and Percy Cochrane, Dr Price, Albert Mispel, Dick Hueter, Nigel Oram, Muriel Larner, Geoff Ellworthy, Gabrielle Johnson, Geoffrey Irwin, Margaret Stevens, Ziska Schwimmer, Don Tuzin, Ian Hughes, Don Laycock, John Terrell, Elspeth Young, Nancy McDowell, Dave Eisler, Angus and Linda Hutton, Paul Greenaway, Robin and Carolyn Hide, Helen Dennett and Helen Broadhurst. For their assistance during field trips we thank Lynn Hosking, Sonia Farley, Helen Broadhurst, Barbara Barclay, Annette McDonald and Malina Reddish.

We thank, too, the Craft Board of the Australia

Council, Institute of Applied Social and Economic Research (now the National Research Institute) for financial assistance, and the Institute of Papua New Guinea Studies and the English Department of the Australian National University for logistic assistance.

For valuable help with technical problems, geology and clay analysis, thanks are extended to Russell Hill, Owen Rye, Lloyd Hamilton, Lindsay Anderson, Brian Davey and Michael Tuckson.

We are especially indebted to Traudl Junge and Nora Romot who translated Kaufmann (1972), Schurig (1930) and other articles and source material. (A copy of the English translation of Schurig has been lodged with the Australian Museum, Sydney.) Thanks are also due to Heidi Spiegel, Hildegard Anstice, Hildegard McLauchlin, Elisabeth Slater, Wendy Nathan, Bunny Hauser, Rose Kirth and G. A Bauer for their help with translation, to Louise Utteridge for her help with typing and to Verna Spicer who typed the final manuscript.

Our deepest gratitude goes to our mentors Jim Specht of the Australian Museum, Sydney, and Ron May of the Australian National University for their advice, support, encouragement, perseverance and endurance during the eight years it has taken to complete this volume. Margaret Tuckson wishes to acknowledge also her very great debt to her late husband, Tony Tuckson, for his encouragement and understanding.

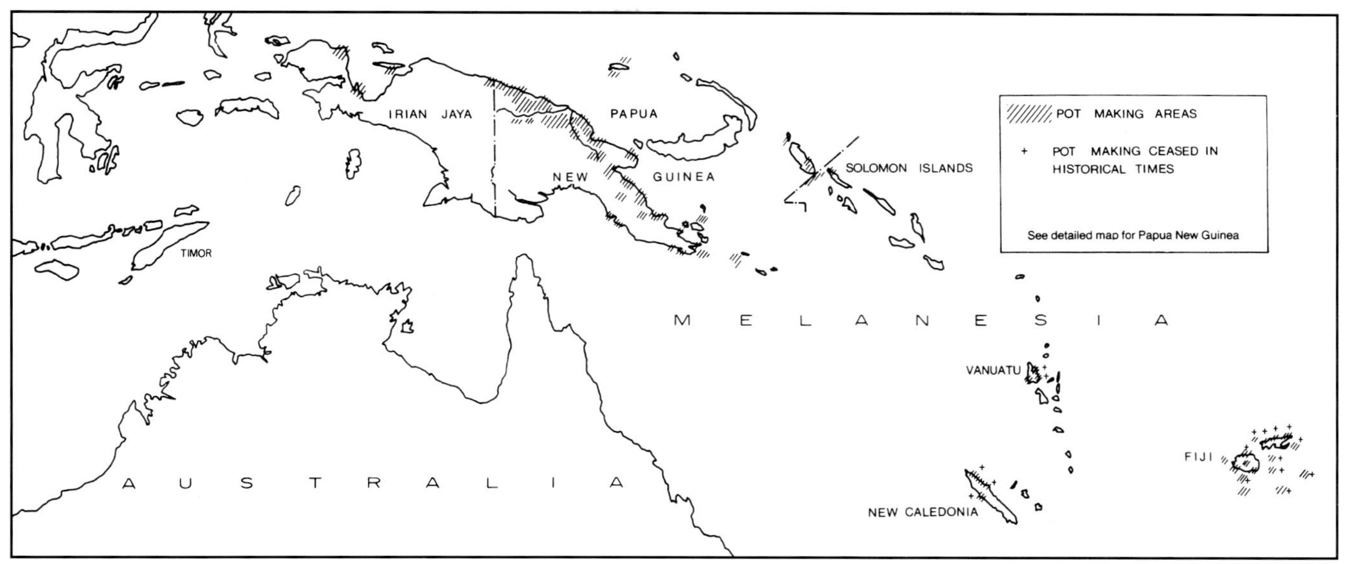

MAP 1: Distribution of pot making, Southwest Pacific

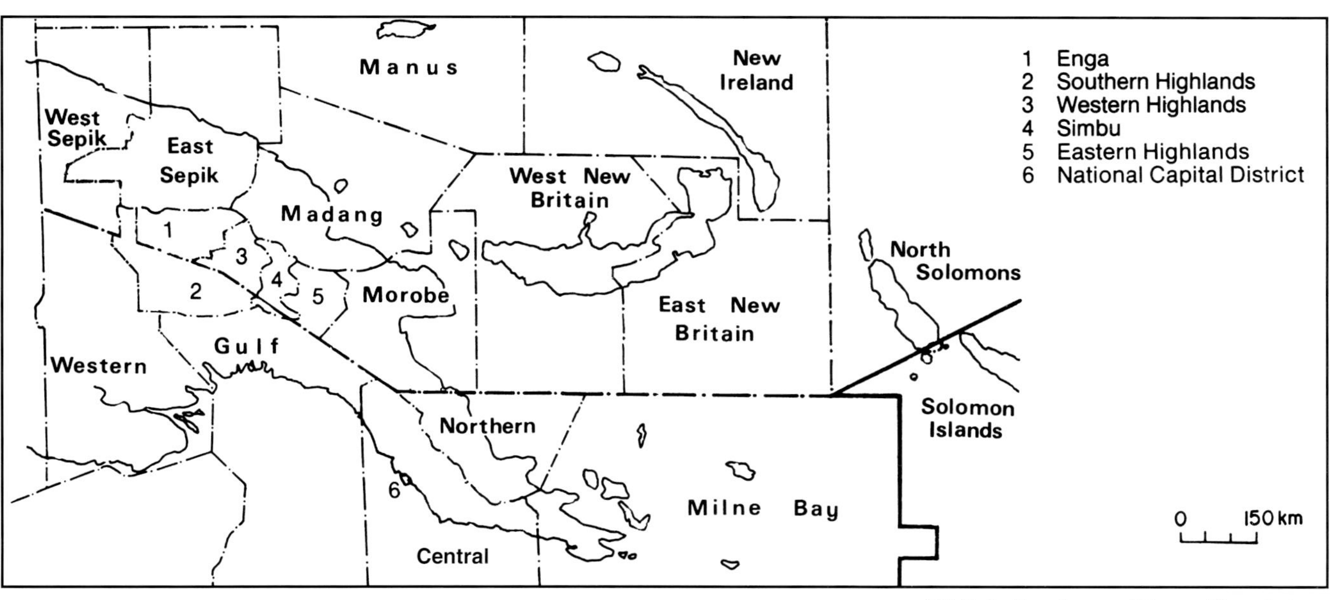

MAP 2: Provinces of Papua New Guinea

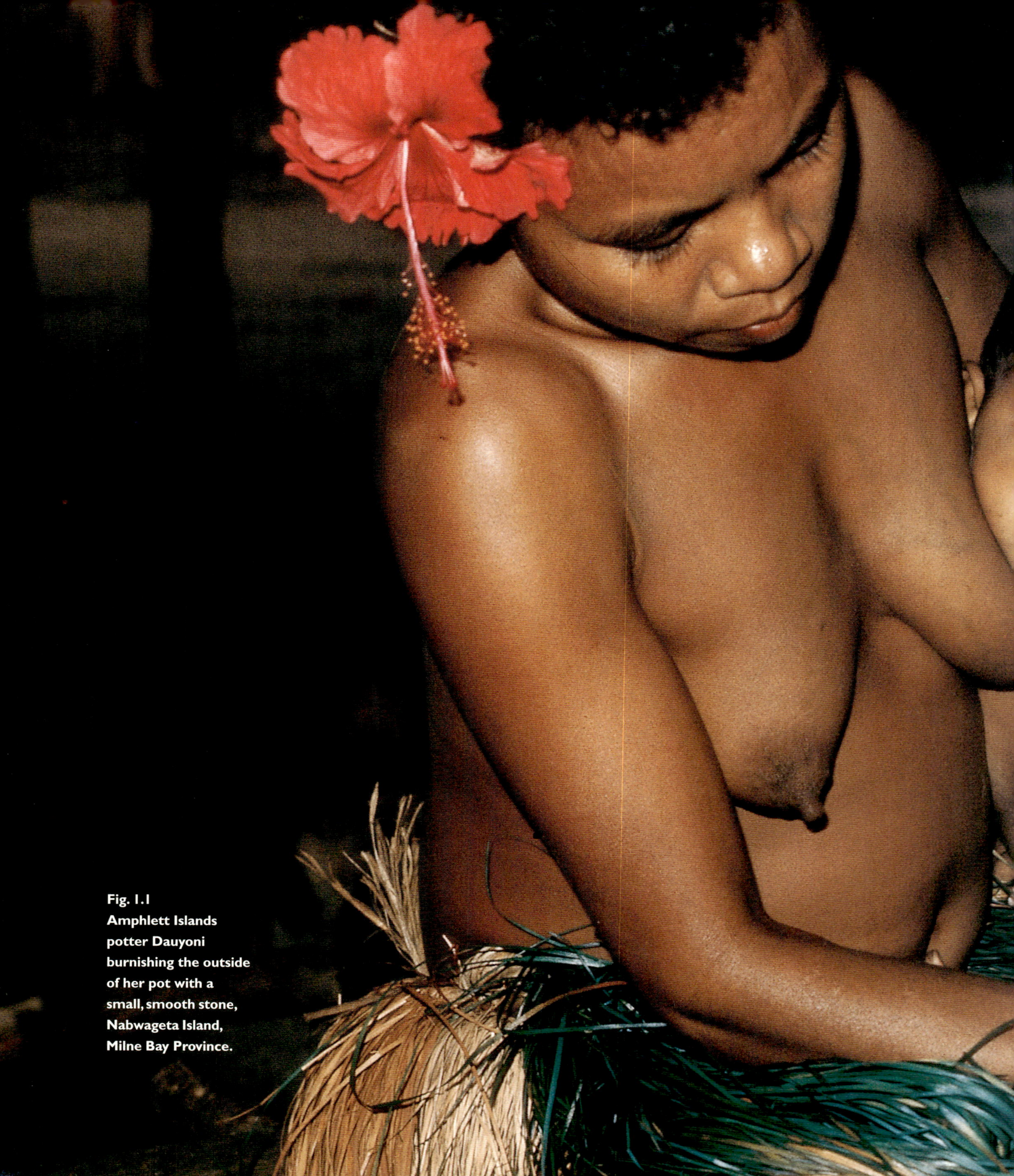

Fig. 1.1
Amphlett Islands potter Dauyoni burnishing the outside of her pot with a small, smooth stone, Nabwageta Island, Milne Bay Province.

1 Introduction

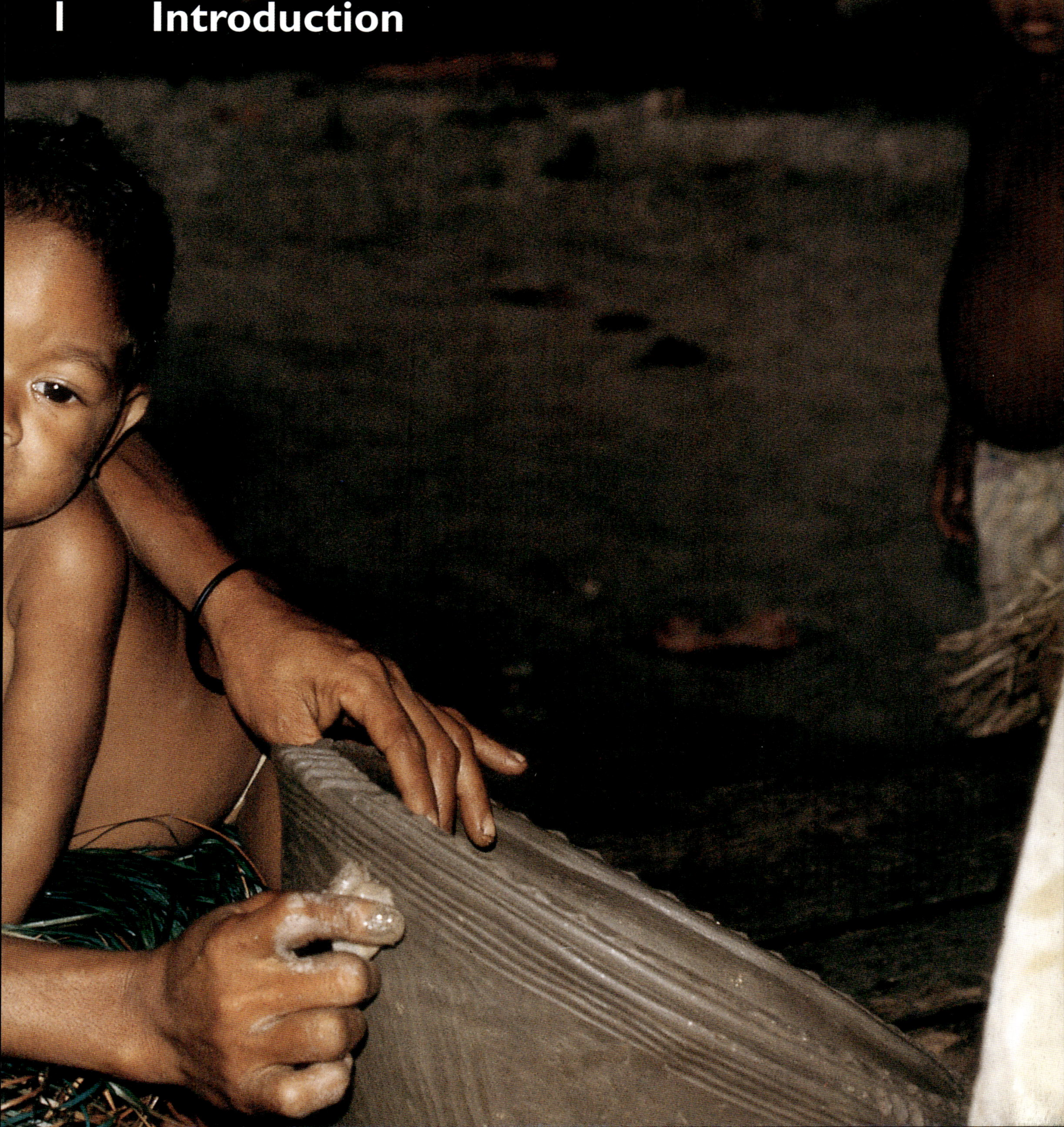

Papua New Guinea occupies the eastern half of that large dinosaur-shaped island directly to the north of Australia; it includes the islands of the Bismarck Archipelago, the D'Entrecasteaux Islands, the Louisiade Archipelago and the northern Solomon Islands. The country, which became independent in 1975, is the amalgamation of former colonial territories: New Guinea, a German territory which came under Australian trusteeship in 1920, and Papua, previously British New Guinea and from 1906 an Australian protectorate. From 1949 to 1975 the two territories were administered as a single unit. To the west and occupying the remainder of the island is Irian Jaya, a province of Indonesia and formerly Dutch New Guinea.

The indigenous population of Papua New Guinea, totalling approximately 4.4 million (1996), is predominantly Melanesian. These people are divided into about 800 distinct language groups, and political units (lines, clans, tribes) are typically small. The languages of Papua New Guinea are divided into two broad categories: a minority of language groups, nearly all of which are spoken by coastal or near-coastal people, is classed as Austronesian (a class which extends throughout the Indo-Pacific region and includes the Polynesian languages); the remainder, a grouping of diverse languages spoken by mostly inland groups, is loosely termed non-Austronesian. It is generally believed that the Austronesian speakers are relatively recent arrivals.

Human settlement on mainland Papua New Guinea has been dated to 25000 BP (Before Present); it may be longer. The country was probably colonised by successive waves of migrants from South-East Asia. The first settlers are thought to have been hunters and gatherers but by at least 7000 BC domesticated wild plants and plants introduced from Asia were being cultivated in the Central Highlands.

There were sporadic encounters between coastal people and European explorers, and probably more regular contact with Malayan fishermen and traders, but European colonisation proper did not begin until the final years of the 19th century. European administrative and mission stations and plantations were largely confined to the coastal fringes of the mainland and the larger islands and although several remarkable exploratory ventures were made into the interior, the Central Highlands were not penetrated until the 1930s. Large areas of the country remained unknown to outsiders until well into the 1950s. Some small nomadic groups have been contacted for the first time as recently as the 1970s.

The traditional cultures of Papua New Guinea are Stone Age; metal was unknown before European arrival. The only fabrics were beaten bark cloth and, in a few parts of the highlands, aprons of knotted string and fur. Agricultural systems were simple but in conjunction with hunting and gathering yielded a comfortable subsistence to most people. There appears to have been little movement of people; the migrations that did take place were probably the result of warfare or local scarcities of resources. Although there are several notable instances of trade links extending over considerable distances, in most 'pre-contact' communities social and economic relationships seldom reached beyond fairly immediate neighbours.

At the time of European contact, as now, pottery industries were distributed over a fairly restricted area of the country a number of villages along the north coast in what are now the Sepik, Madang and Morobe provinces; villages along the lower and middle Sepik River and its tributaries; the densely populated area between the Sepik River and the north coast, up to about 125 kilometres from the border with Irian Jaya; numerous inland villages of the Madang Province; the Markham and Watut valleys; the northern and south-eastern coasts of Papua and the islands of the Milne Bay Province; and a small number of villages in the Eastern Highlands, Buka and Bougainville in the North Solomons (Map 3). In large areas of the country, notably (with one exception) the heavily populated highlands, the whole of western Papua and the islands of New Britain and New Ireland, there was no pottery making even though suitable clays exist. Some pottery was carried by trade to the west of New Britain and across the Papuan Gulf but, despite extensive trade links between the coast and the highlands, pottery formed part of this trade only in a few areas of the Eastern and Central highlands. In these 'potless' areas people cooked on a direct fire or in earth ovens or sections of bamboo; they carried and stored water and such commodities as oil and sago in bamboo and gourds, as many village people still do.

Archaeological evidence, however, has established the existence of pottery industries earlier than those existing at the time of contact, industries unknown to present inhabitants and often with no clear stylistic continuity. On Watom Island, near Rabaul in East New Britain, and on Ambitle Island, off New Ireland, have been found sherds which recent analysis has linked with the Lapita ware first identified and systematically studied at a site (Lapita) in New Caledonia and since found at coastal sites in Vanuatu, Fiji, Tonga and Samoa. It is now generally believed that the Lapita potters were the first inhabitants of some of the South Pacific islands and that they colonised New Caledonia and Fiji as early as 3000 BP. On Watom, the Lapita potters appear to have disappeared at least 2000 years ago. To the south-east, archaeological sites on Buka have yielded sherds of red-slipped pottery, apparently related to the Lapita ware, which have been dated as early as 2300 BP. Associated archaeological evidence indicates continuous settlement but an abrupt change in pottery styles (and in the range of stone artifacts) about 750 years ago. Similar red-slipped pottery has also been found on the central coast of Papua, at Yule Island and at sites near Port Moresby. It, too, has been dated before 2000 BP but around the same time as the sudden change in pottery styles on Buka the Papuan red-slipped tradition was replaced by one which has been identified with Massim styles and is now generally believed to be ancestral to modern Motu pottery.

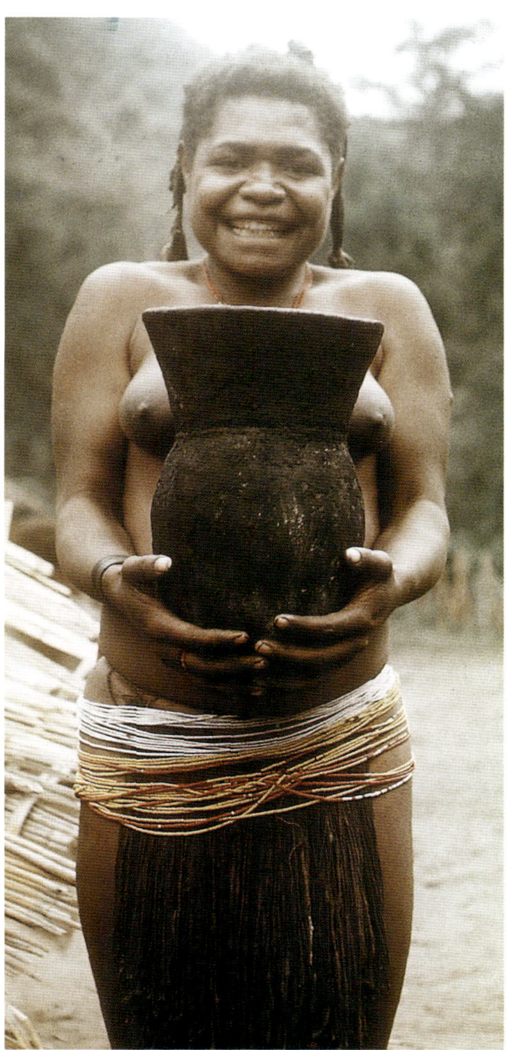

Fig. 1.2
A Henganofi girl with a Rawa trade pot, Eastern Highlands.

Simple vessels decorated with incised patterns, applied nubbins and strips and occasional zoomorphic forms as handles, which have been linked to prehistoric ceramics found in Vanuatu (where they disappear about 1000 BP), have been found at several sites in Papua New Guinea, including Watom (dated to around 800 BP) and sites on New Ireland, Buka and Bougainville.

Figs 1.3 to 1.7
Paddle-and-anvil technique.

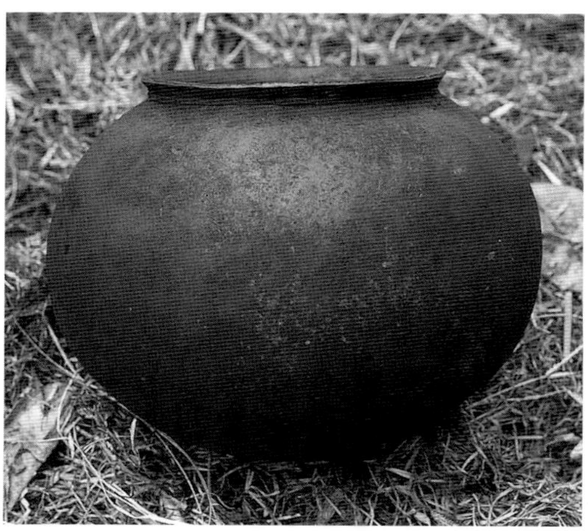

Fig. 1.3
Pot used for cooking, *matapwei*, or water storage, *pwentung*, M'Buke Island, Manus Province.

Early this century, at Collingwood Bay, quantities of large-bellied, thick-walled pots and bowls decorated with grooved curvilinear patterns were excavated from burial caves and niches; identical pottery has since been found at Dyke Ackland Bay and on Goodenough and the Trobriand islands. Recent research has placed this tradition at around 1000 to 500 BP but has also identified in the same area an earlier tradition consisting of vessels with impressed or incised triangular patterns. An unusual pedestal dish (illustrated in a museum catalogue, Papua New Guinea National Museum and Art Gallery, 1977) resembles wares from the Philippines and Taiwan. A wide range of sepulchral pottery found in the Cape Rodney area, tentatively dated to 500 to 1000 BP, indicates at least two

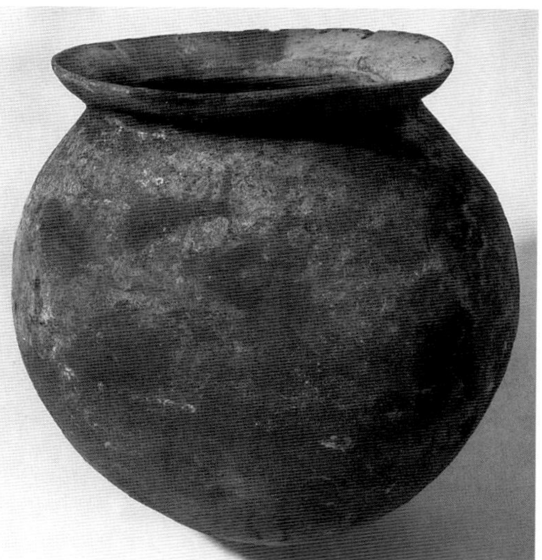

Fig. 1.4
Motu cooking pot, *uro*, collected in the late 1800s, *h* 32 cm.

ceramic traditions apparently related to Massim prehistoric and historic ceramics.

At a broader level, it has been suggested that the Lapita tradition and others derived from it are part of a larger South-East Asian tradition, the Sa-Huynh-Kalanay, whose origins are in China. Others have pointed to close affinities between some Papua New Guinean pottery and that of the Japanese Jomon culture. At present, however, such relationships remain speculative.

To date, most of the information about Papua New Guinea's prehistoric pottery, apart from that of the Watom and Buka sites, has come from the Collingwood Bay, Massim and central coastal Papua regions. Little work has been undertaken, for example, in the Sepik provinces which now exhibit such rich and varied pottery traditions. Archaeology is still in its infancy in Papua New Guinea, further research is necessary to improve our understanding of existing pottery traditions and to provide information concerning the movement of peoples and the evolution of Papua New Guinea and Melanesian cultures.

The technology of pottery making in Papua New Guinea is relatively simple. Basically, two techniques are employed, coiling and paddle-and-anvil, although there is a number of regional variations. As in many other 'simple technology' cultures, the potter's wheel and the kiln are unknown among traditional potters (Map 4).

The paddle-and-anvil technique is used exclusively by a number of localised coastal and small island groups in which the potters are women. In the majority of cases these groups are Austronesian. Exceptions are Vanimo, Leitre, Terebu-Samap, Pila, Korak-Tavaltae, Nasioi and Buin. Although there is some variation in the starting methods used by these female potters, the main technique, the form and the functional range of the vessels are markedly similar. Paddle-and-anvil vessels are all round-based and full-bellied. Those of the north coast potters, those of Manus and those of the Motu and Roro on the south coast are nearly always spherical or sections of spheres. The pottery made by the coastal women of Madang and the Huon Peninsula, on the other hand, generally comprises restricted vessels with distinct shoulders and necks but these, too, are round-based, full-bellied

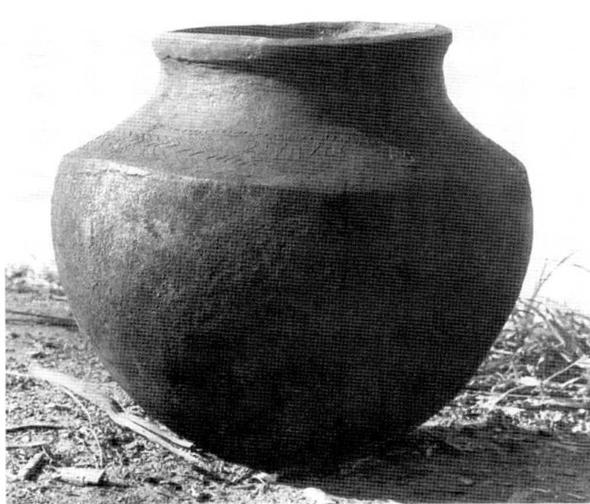

Fig. 1.5

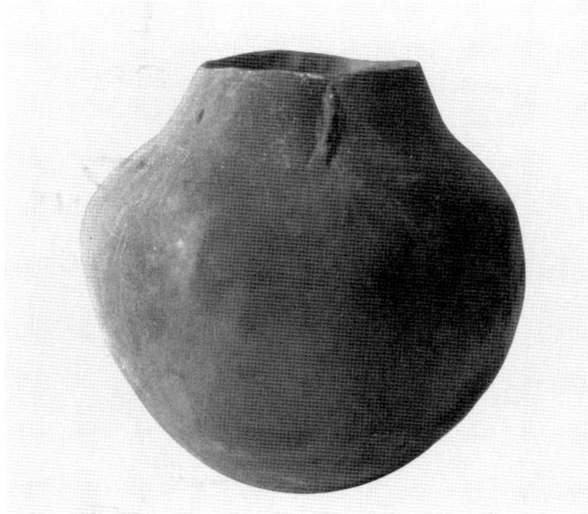

Fig. 1.6

Fig. 1.5
Korak cooking pot, *komnan*, Tavultae village, Madang Province, *h* 29 cm.

Fig. 1.6
Pila cooking pot, *senai*, Madang Province, *h* 19 cm.

and typically 'female' in form. Most are light and thin-walled. The similarities in technique and form, and in language, suggest that these female potters are part of a larger tradition. On the basis of language and geographical distribution this is a more recent tradition than that of the inland makers of coiled pottery.

With coil-made pottery the situation is more complex. In the great majority of cases coil pottery is made by men (this includes all the inland Madang industries, the highland Agarabi, and in the Sepik, the Bungain, Kamasau, Muniwara, Urimo, Boiken, Mountain Arapesh and the Ole and One potters of the West Sepik Province), or by both men and women (most of the remaining inland Sepik industries and the Guhu-Samane of Morobe Province) using the spiral coiling technique. The pots in figures 1.8, 1.9, 1.20, and 1.22 are all examples of coiled pots made by men from widely separated areas. There are, however, several groups spread over a wide geographical range among whom spiral-coiled pots are made by women only. These include the Ngala, Keram River, Porapora, Wosera and Buna industries of the East Sepik Province; Rao, Bosman and Josephstaal of Madang Province; Salamaua of Morobe Province; and the women of Miadeba on Normanby Island. Nearly all the industries (the few exceptions all being women potters) belong to inland villages and, with the exception of the two Salamaua villages, Miadeba, a small inland Madang group and the potters of Siwai, all are non-Austronesians.

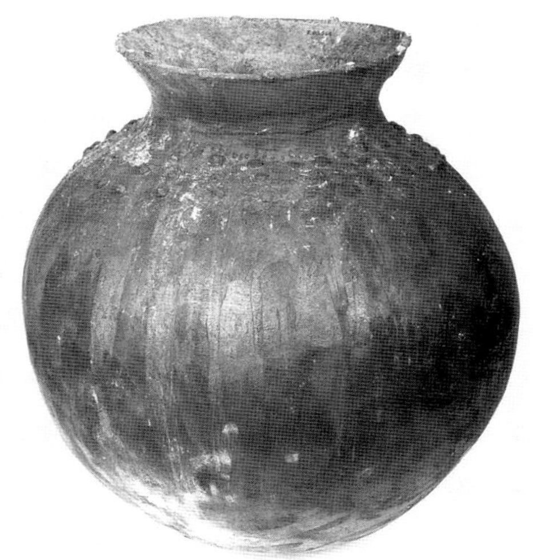

Fig. 1.7
Cooking pot, *uro*, made by Buta from Gitua village, Huon Peninsula, Morobe Province, *h* 34 cm.

Coiled vessels are made for a number of purposes, functional and ritual. A wide variety of forms, restricted and unrestricted, is made but these are generally characterised by pointed or nipple bases. They tend to be thick-walled, heavy (exceptions: Bau, Kwanga and Kombio) and often, especially in the case of simple cooking pots, crudely made.

In the Milne Bay area and Northern Province (overlapping into the Morobe and Central provinces) a different tradition of coiling emerges. From East Cape to the south, pots are made by spiral coiling completed by ring building and in all cases they are made by women. To the north, as far as Manau in Northern Province, pots are made by spiral coiling (or, in the case of the Amphlett Islands, slab building) and completed by beating, again always by women. Two cases of women

Figs 1.8 to 1.10
Examples of coiled pots made by men from widely separated area.

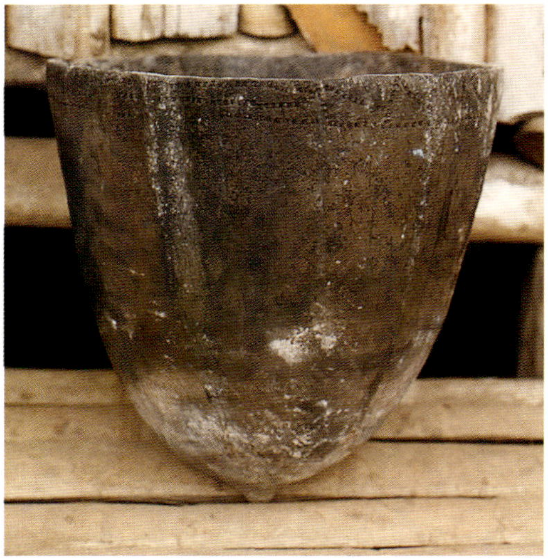

Fig. 1.8
Waria cooking pot, Morobe Province.

making pots by spiral coiling completed by beating also occur in Madang Province. The pots made by the Milne Bay women are, with one exception, round-based, although generally unrestricted, and thin-walled; the range of forms and functions is limited. Stylistically they are unmistakably 'female' pots, having a closer affinity to the paddle-and-anvil pottery than to the pottery of the mostly inland, largely male 'pure spiral coil' industries. It is perhaps not surprising, therefore, to find that nearly all these coil potters are Austronesians. The exceptions are the deviant Bosman, a few inland villages behind Wanigela, the Mailu at the western extremity of the spiral coiling-ring building group and the

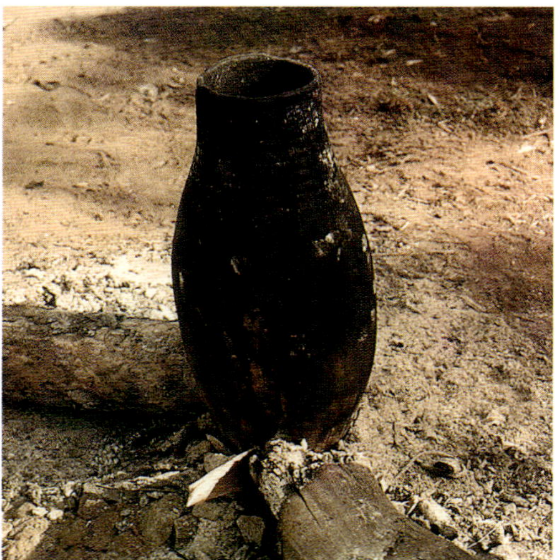

Fig. 1.9
Peka cooking pot, Madang Province.

Binanderean language groups which constitute the northern extremity of the female spiral coiling-beating technique. The linguistic deviation of the Mailu, whose pots conform to the general pattern of southern Milne Bay pottery, clearly requires a particular explanation. However, the simple unrestricted pottery of the Binanderean groups contrasts with that of the spiral coiling-beating industries farther to the south in being thick-walled, often crude and generally with a perceptible pointed or nipple base. Stylistically as well as linguistically, therefore, the affinity of the Binanderean potters is with the pure spiral coil potters to the north rather than with the tradition of northern Milne Bay.

Two industries stand out sharply from this general pattern: the Austronesian potters of the Markham Valley (the Azera) and the non-Austronesian potters of Aibom. In the Markham, men make the pots by spiral coiling completed by beating. Apart from the limited use of a paddle by one small inland Madang group, this is the only instance of men using beating to finish their pots: yet, despite a similarity of technique with the northern Milne Bay and Northern Province women potters, the Markham pots are unmistakably 'male' pots, round-based and restricted but heavy, with (at least in the past) a variety of forms and a rich and complex repertoire of decorative elements. The Markham potters are, with the Ham group of inland Madang, also unique in being an Austronesian group which is inland and in which men are the potters. At Aibom, women make a wide range of heavy, ornate vessels by ring building although men decorate certain pots. From several points of view, these two industries are perhaps the two most interesting in the country and fortunately they are probably the two most active.

Pottery may serve a number of functions. To the individual potter and to the pottery making community, the production of pottery may fill a need in personal use or exchange, it may meet a ritual requirement and it may be a means of artistic expression or of gaining individual or collective prestige. When pots are traded, their importance in cementing social relationships may be as great as their importance in terms of economic exchange.

Most of the pottery made in Papua New Guinea has an immediate physical function; the majority of industries, in fact, produce only utilitarian pottery. All pot making groups produce simple cooking vessels which display a variety of forms, from the wide-mouthed, unrestricted vessels of southern Milne Bay to the narrow, elongated, ellipsoid pots of the inland Madang Kokon-Peka and their neighbours. In a few places, more complex cooking vessels are, or were, made: divided vessels at Wanigela, on the Amphlett Islands and Brooker Island; a vertical *bain marie*-style double pot and a horizontal double pot, both made until recently by the Azera. Old pots no longer considered suitable for cooking are put to a variety of uses, such as mixing dyes and storing clay, and they may eventually serve as containers for pig food. At villages along the Keram and Yuat rivers, at Aibom, Manus and on the north-west coast, a flat or flattish sago frying dish is made. The Yuat villagers also make a perforated pot in which to smoke meat and fish. Small pots used for preparing magical substances have been found among the Azera, Kwoma and Porapora and may have occurred elsewhere in the past.

Serving bowls and individual eating bowls, reserved specifically for this purpose, are common around the Sepik River and in inland Sepik villages but are not found elsewhere. They are usually elaborately decorated (by men) and are often associated with 'haus tambaran' ritual. Vessels for storing sago are made by most of the pottery groups on the Sepik River and its tributaries, the coastal potters of Kaiep-Terebu-Samap, Vanimo and Tumleo, the inland Boiken, the Kwoma and the Motu. The most famous are the large and striking vessels made at Aibom. Surprisingly, not all the sago-eating pottery groups use sago storage vessels; some keep their sago in leaves or 'limbum' baskets, despite the fact that this is clearly less efficient. The list of places where porous clay vessels are made for storing and also for cooling water is surprisingly small: the Motu and Roro villages, Panaeati, Brooker, Wanigela, Yabob-Bilbil-Mindiri, Dimiri and Manus (figs 1.11-1.15). An oil storage vessel is made by the Kwoma. Other unusual utilitarian objects are the fire hearths made at Aibom, the pot supports made along the Keram and Yuat rivers, support dishes (plates) used for manufacturing pots in southern Milne Bay and on Tumleo Island, and the clay hand drum ('kundu') made by the Azera.

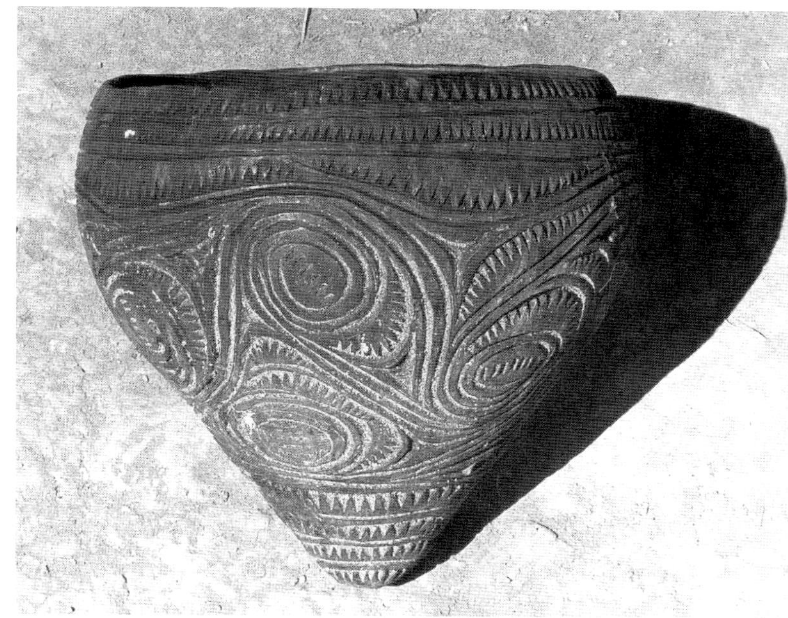

Fig. 1.10
Kwoma ceremonial eating vessel, *aumar*, East Sepik.

Apart from these last three, the only other clay vessels which are not containers are ritual objects made by non-Austronesian potters and, with the exception of a phallic object from the Ramu, all come from the Sepik. These ritual objects comprise the ridge tiles of Aibom, the heads and, yam altar objects of the Kwoma and Mayo, the animal and human head models of Dimiri-Yaul-Marawat and the ocarinas of Dimiri-Yaul-Marawat and the Wosera. Although the basic pot form of the Aibom ridge tile and the Dimiri models now sold to tourists may be made by women, decoration is done exclusively by men; in the past the men may well have been also the makers. As mentioned above, the serving and eating bowls which are exclusive to the Sepik are associated with 'haus tambaran' ritual and amongst the Abelam disused cooking pots are inverted over the highest point of the 'haus tambaran' (figs 1.18, 9.121).

Outside of the Sepik and the Ramu, the only ritual use of pottery other than in the preparation of magical substances appears to be in a funereal context. At Cape Rodney, at Collingwood Bay, on the Trobriand and Woodlark islands, at Nuamata Island north of Goodenough Island, at Panaeati and in the Markham Valley, pottery has been found in prehistoric (and, in the last two instances, recently used) burial caves (figs 1.19, 1.21, 6.2).

Fig. 1.11
Motu water pot, *hodu*, Central Province, *h* 30 cm.

Fig. 1.12
Water pot, *ulunbwal*, Panaeati Island, Milne Bay Province, *h* 23 cm.

Fig. 1.13
Yaul water pot, *latambu*, Dimiri village, East Sepik Province, *h* 23 cm.

Fig. 1.14
Water pot, *yu-bodi*, Yabob village, Madang Province, *h* 21 cm.

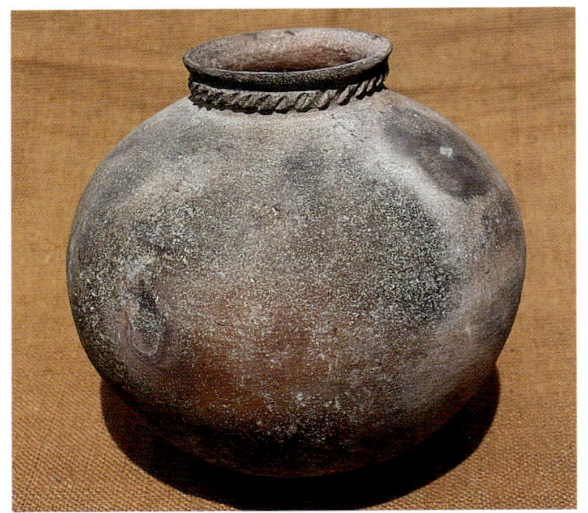
Fig. 1.11

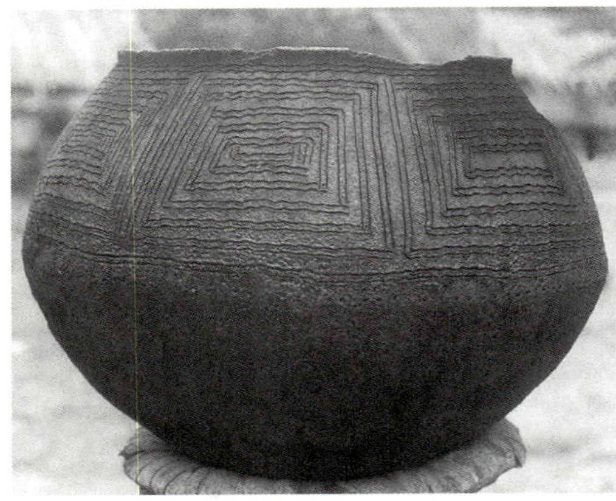
Fig. 1.12

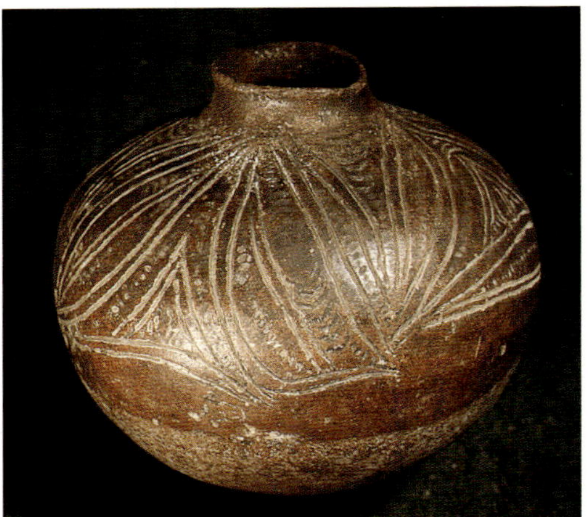
Fig. 1.13

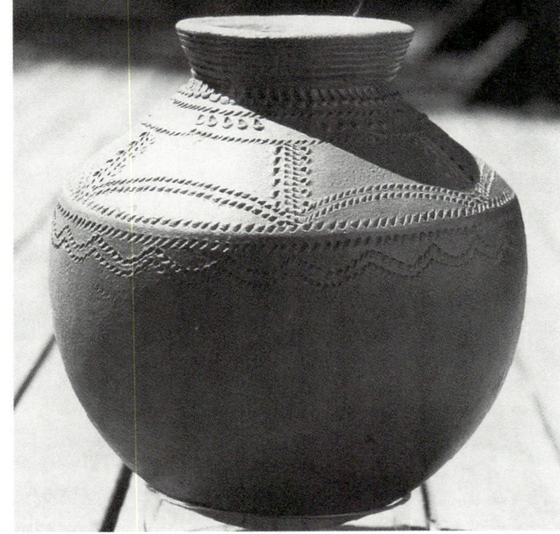
Fig. 1.14

In a few places sun-dried, unfired clay objects are made. The ocarinas and other objects made by the Sinasina people are discussed in Chapter 7. Other interesting uses of sun-dried clay appear in the over-modelling of skulls in the middle Sepik and, previously, in East New Britain, and as an overlay on basketry masks from the middle Sepik, Yuat River, Sepik grasslands and a few Boiken villages. We have not, however, included them in this survey.

Thus it is clear that there is some relationship between technique and form but the correlation is not strong. Paddle-and-anvil vessels are all round-based; pure spiral-coiled pots typically have pointed or nipple bases but the Milne Bay potters start their pots by spiral coiling and produce round-based pots. Spheres and sections of spheres are typical shapes of pots made by the paddle-and-anvil method but the potters of Pila make restricted vessels with necks not dissimilar to those of some inland Madang pots made by spiral coiling. The coil potters of Dimiri-Yaul-Marawat make spherical water storage jars which at their best closely resemble in shape those of the paddle-and-anvil potters at Tumleo, Kaiep-Terebu-Samap, the Motu, Roro and Manus. An almost universal generalization here is that pots made by men (including the only male Austronesian potters, the Azera and the Ham) are thick-walled and heavy, exceptions are the delicate pottery of the Bau group (inland Madang) and Kombio eating bowls. A similar generalisation does not hold for women's pottery. Although nearly all the pots made by paddle-and-anvil techniques and those of the Milne Bay (including always Mailu and Collingwood Bay) women have a feminine *delicatesse*,

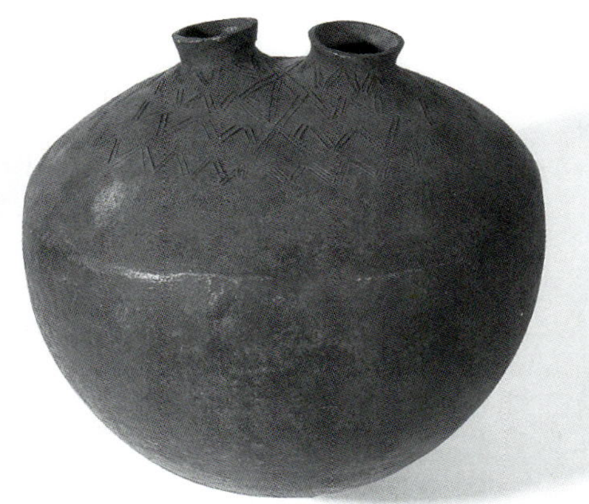

Fig. 1.15

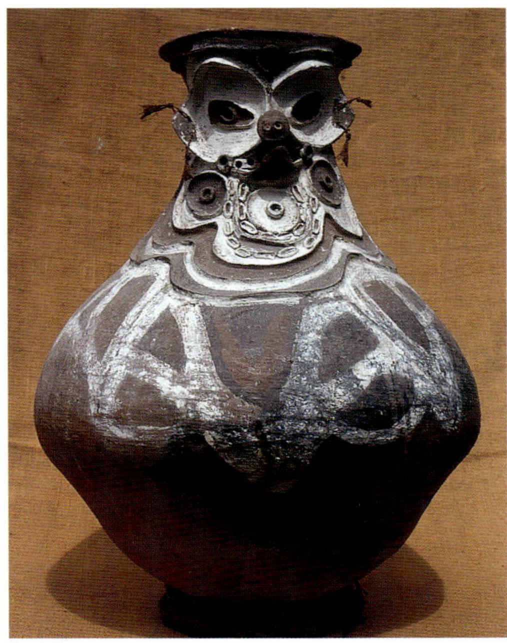

Fig. 1.16

Fig. 1.15
Double-mouthed water pot, *chepoung*, Admiralty Islands, Manus Province, collected by Captain Farrell in 1887, *h* 27 cm.

Fig. 1.16
Sago storage jar, *damarau*, with applied and painted decoration, Aibom, Sepik River, *h* 108 cm.

the same cannot be said of spiral-coiled pots made by women, many of which are heavy and crude. And at Aibom, women make the thickest-walled, heaviest pottery in the country. Finally, while the variety of forms produced by the coil potters is undeniably greater than that resulting from the paddle-and-anvil method, this is at least partly due to the greater variety of traditions among coil potters, many of whom produce only simple, unrestricted cooking pots.

Outside the Sepik, the Markham Valley and Milne Bay, decoration of pottery is generally restricted to simple incised, impressed, punctate and applied patterns around the neck and shoulders and the use of partly exposed coils (see Chapter 2). Such design motifs as do occur are either geometric or representative of forms occurring in nature. This is not to deny the beauty of some of these simple designs: the exposed coils of the Bau pots, provide one of the most attractive schema in Papua New Guinea (fig. 1.22). Simplicity of decoration is particularly true of paddle-and-anvil pottery, perhaps lending weight to the suggestion of Kidder (Shepard 1971: 244), that '... in general, undecorated wares are more pleasingly shaped than those that bear ornament, particularly applique'.

The decoration on Milne Bay pottery is somewhat more elaborate, particularly in southern Milne Bay where combs are used to create continuous chains of geometric and curvilinear patterns on the upper body of the vessels, in the Amphlett Islands where applied strips are further elaborated by stippling and impressing and at Wanigela where the major portion of the exterior walls is covered by applied, impressed strips or incised, grooved and impressed lines. Motifs here are also geometric or natural. In all these cases decoration is an integral part of the potter's art.

More complex decoration is to be found only when men make and/or decorate the pottery. In the Markham Valley, as well as using a wide repertoire of incised, impressed, dentate stamped and applied decorations, Azera men make pots decorated with modelled heads of birds and animals and the 'head' of a fighting stick. In the past human genitalia were also represented. If these once had a particular ritual significance it is no longer known

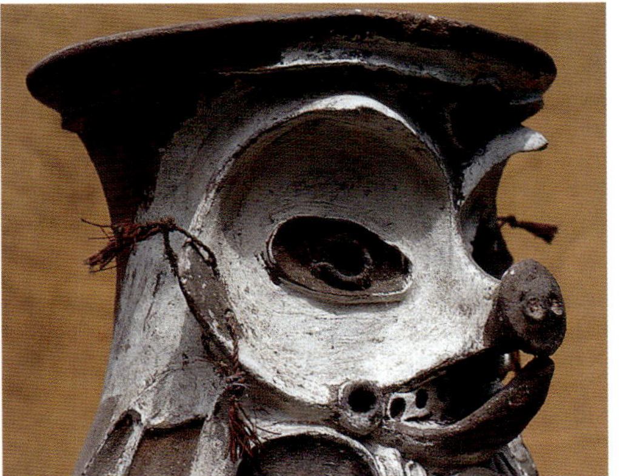

Fig. 1.17
Detail of sago storage jar, *damarau*.

Fig. 1.18
Abelam cooking pots, *au*, inverted over central post of a 'haus tambaran', Halik village, East Sepik Province.

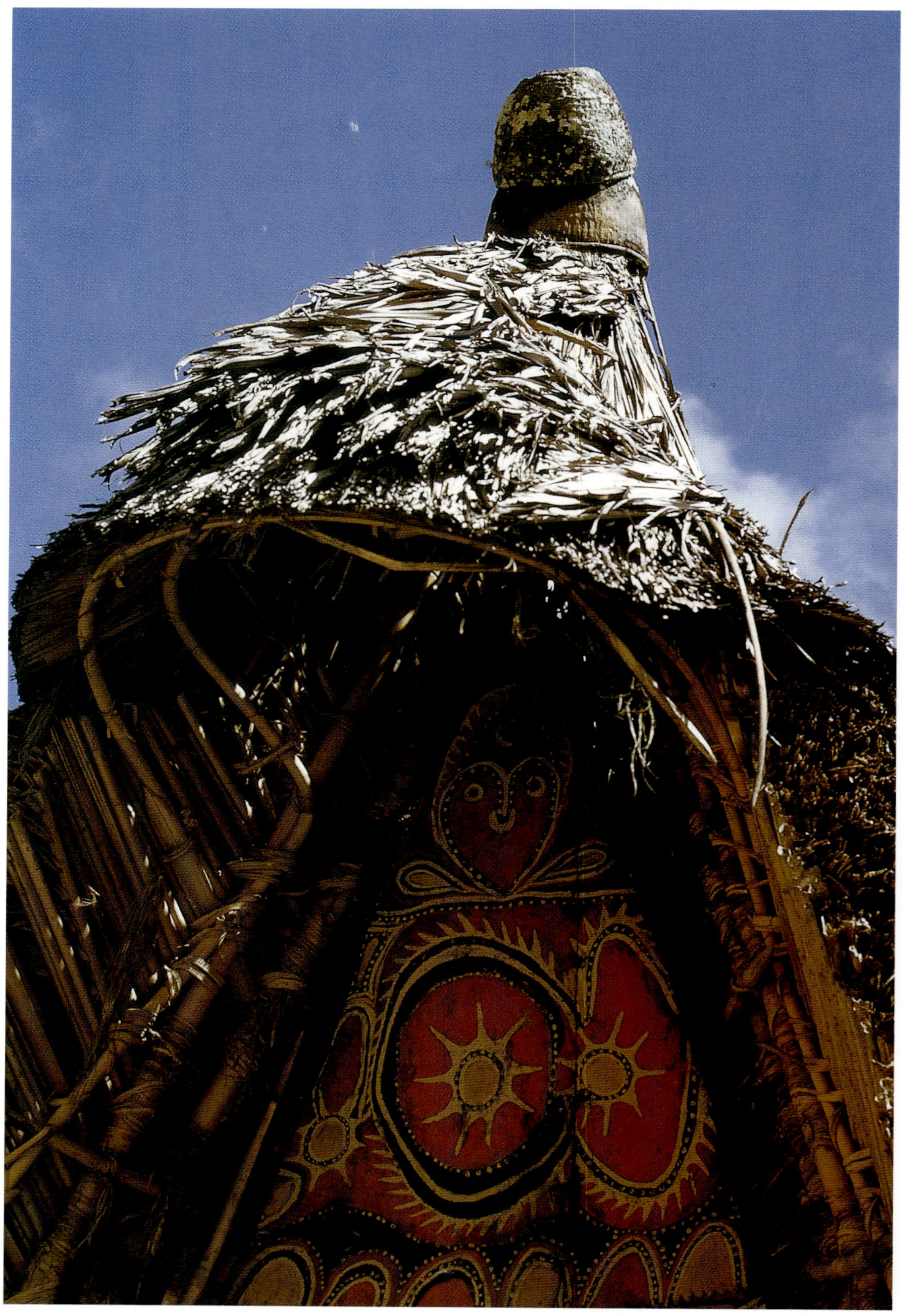

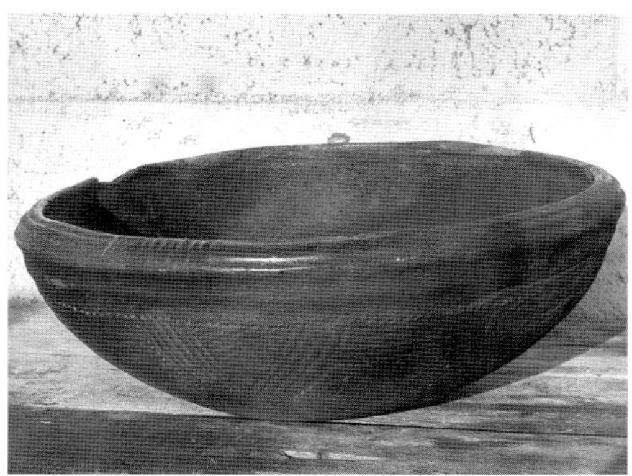

(or admitted) but it is a generally observed rule that only meat may be cooked in pots with heads. Apart from their pottery, the Azera do not have an especially rich artistic tradition, although the head motif is repeated (or used to be repeated) on fighting sticks, adzes and bone knives used to peel bananas. Among the villages of the Sepik River and the inland Sepik on the other hand, highly decorated pottery is part of a rich and varied artistic tradition which encompasses utilitarian as well as ritual objects. Decoration includes incised, carved and applied designs and, unique to the Sepik industries (except for Humboldt Bay and Buin), post-firing painting. Decorative motifs include geometric forms, representations of natural objects, the faces or other attributes of spirits or culture heroes and objects of religious significance. The same motifs are found in wooden carvings and on painted 'pangal'. In several groups, notably the Kwoma, Mayo, Abelam and Wosera, pottery plays an important part in ritual. In Chapter 9, the authors have attempted to describe Sepik pottery within its broad social and artistic context but an adequate presentation of this relationship would require far more detailed discussion than is possible in this work and greater knowledge of Sepik iconography than presently exists.

In many pot-producing societies pottery is a specialised craft and exceptional skill brings corresponding economic re ward or social status. In the pottery making communities of Papua New Guinea, however, most men and/or women in the community traditionally make pots and still do in those communities where the industry is active; although outstanding skill is usually recognised it seldom brings anything in the way of additional economic reward or elevated status. Within the pottery community, people seldom seem to acquire the pots of other than their immediate kin and trade with outside groups is a communal affair in which one person's pot is equal to another's. Sometimes people can identify the maker of a particular vessel by the quality of workmanship or by 'signatures' of design but very few instances of individuals or clans having exclusive rights to designs were found. The conventions of tradition, in pottery as in other art forms, tend to discourage individuality or innovation.

In the past, pottery was widely traded. Pots were a common item in both social and economic exchanges and it is not uncommon even today to find the pottery of two or more industries in a single village. Pottery played an important part in three major maritime trading systems: the *hiri*, the *kula* and its extensions, and the complex system of the Vitiaz Straits (see Chapters 3, 4 and 6). Sometimes it was distributed through middle-men. It is notable, however, that, with the exceptions of the pottery imported into the Eastern Highlands from the Markham Valley and from the distant Rawa people, and that brought into northern Chimbu from the Peka group, pottery did not reach the highlands along with other coastal goods which were common enough at the time of European contact.

Since European contact, the introduction of more durable aluminium and enamel pots and pans and the inhibiting impact of missions and others

Fig. 1.19
Old burial pot from Nuamata Island, off Goodenough Island, Milne Bay Province.

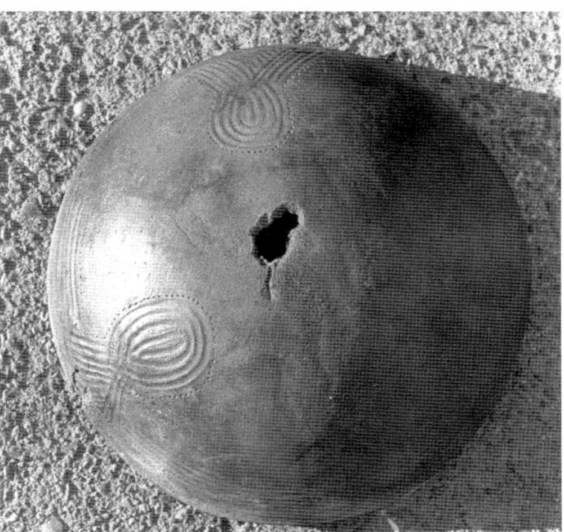

Fig. 1.20
Base of the old burial pot from Nuamata Island.

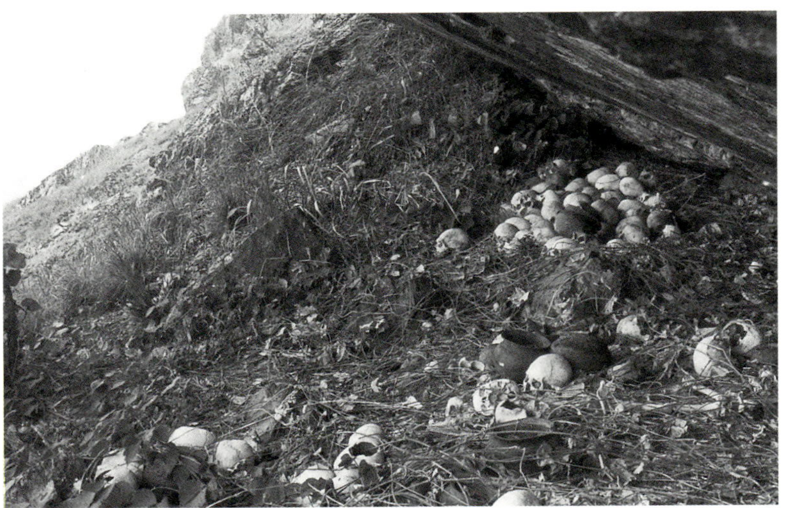

Fig. 1.21

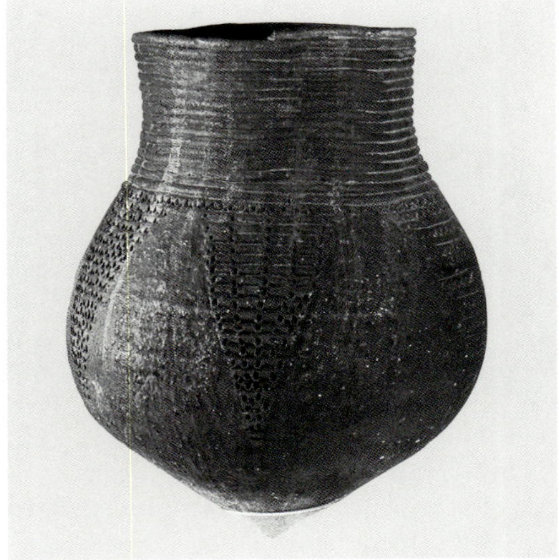

Fig. 1.22

Fig. 1.21
Skulls and pots in a burial cave in the Kraetke Mountains, Markham Valley, Morobe Province.

Fig. 1.22
Bau cooking pot, *avar*, Fulumu village, Madang Province, showing exposed coil decoration with typical last coil adornment broken off, *h* 36 cm. Compare with Paparam pot (fig. 9.89).

Fig. 1.23
Chalice made for use in the Catholic church, Aibom, East Sepik Province, *h* 16 cm.

on pottery making with a ritual significance, many pottery industries in Papua New Guinea have been in a state of decline: fewer pots are made and some types are not made at all, decoration has deteriorated, the meaning and significance of decorative motifs has often been forgotten and, as older people die, the knowledge of pottery techniques is frequently lost. There are exceptions, where pacification has opened new avenues for trade or where industries (such as those of the Azera and the people of Wari Island in Milne Bay) have expanded to fill a void created by the demise of neighbouring industries. There are also a few instances in which industries have flourished in response to the demand of resident collectors or tourists or in which strenuous efforts have been made by missionaries, school teachers and others to 'revive' lapsed or flagging industries. In one or two cases, well-meaning outsiders have tried to 'modify' traditional styles, improving clay preparation or firing techniques, flattening bases or adding legs, in an attempt to make pots more attractive to foreigners.

However, in the face of Western influences, the traditional pottery of Papua New Guinea has been remarkably resilient, maintaining the integrity of its artistic and technical traditions.

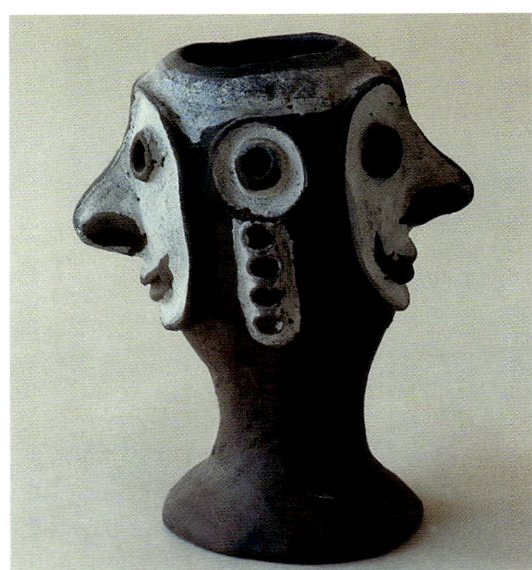

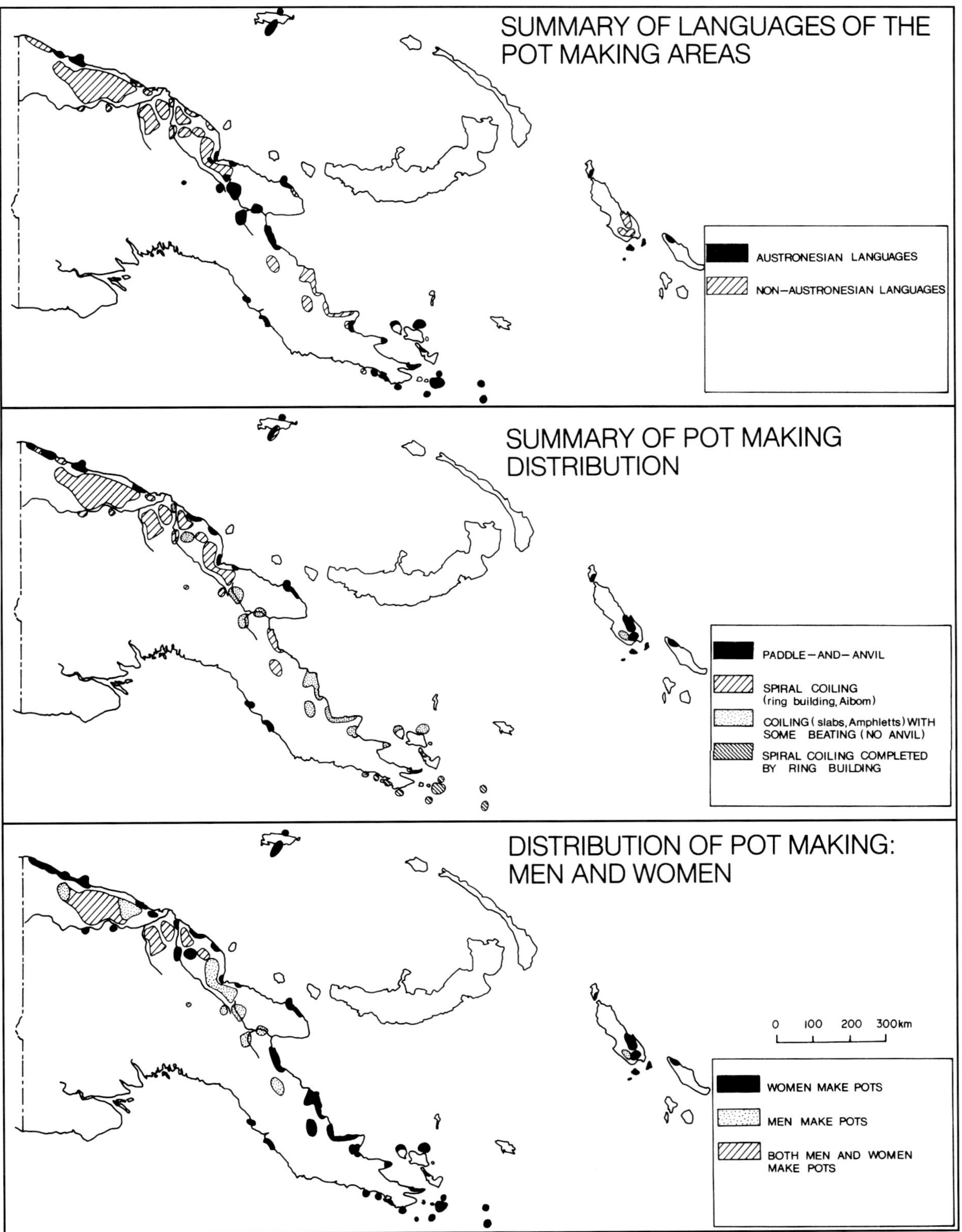
SUMMARY OF LANGUAGES OF THE POT MAKING AREAS
AUSTRONESIAN LANGUAGES
NON–AUSTRONESIAN LANGUAGES
SUMMARY OF POT MAKING DISTRIBUTION
PADDLE–AND–ANVIL
SPIRAL COILING (ring building, Aibom)
COILING (slabs, Amphletts) WITH SOME BEATING (NO ANVIL)
SPIRAL COILING COMPLETED BY RING BUILDING
DISTRIBUTION OF POT MAKING: MEN AND WOMEN
0 100 200 300km
WOMEN MAKE POTS
MEN MAKE POTS
BOTH MEN AND WOMEN MAKE POTS

TECHNIQUE TABLE

Pot-making industries	Coastal or Inland	Province	Map Symbol	Technique
VANIMO	C	West Sepik	■●	Ball of clay flattened to disc, beaten to dish shape. Strips added for larger pots – *paddle-and-anvil.*
PINO (Leitre area)	C	West Sepik	●	Starting method similar to Vanimo? – *paddle-and-anvil.*
ISI (Leitre area)	C	West Sepik	■	Ball flattened to disc, beaten to dish shape, slices of clay added – *paddle-and-anvil.*
TUMLEO ISLAND	C	West Sepik	●	Lump pounded open with fist, beaten with knuckles, neck formed by beating – *paddle-and-anvil.*
KAIEP TEREBU and SAMAP	C	East Sepik	●	Ball pounded open with long stone, *paddle-and-anvil*, one thick coil added for neck – *paddle-and-anvil.*
HUS ISLAND	C	Manus	●	Ball flattened to disc, beaten to dish shape. Neck formed by beating – *paddle-and-anvil.*
M'BUKE-TIMOENAI	C	Manus	◆●	Start as for Hus, coils added for larger pots – *paddle- and-anvil.*
PILA KORAK	C	Madang	●	Ball pounded open with long stone, deepened by throwing in a round stone – *paddle-and-anvil.*
YABOB, BILBIL and MINDIRI	C	Madang	●	Ball opened with thumb and rim formed while turning on hand, deepened by throwing round stone – *paddle-and-anvil.*
SIO-GITUA-SIALUM	C	Morobe	●	Ball beaten to a cone, beaten around a round stone – *paddle-and-anvil.*
MOTU-RORO	C	Central	●	Lump opened with hand, walls dragged up with fingers, rim formed with fingers – *paddle-and-anvil.*
BUKA	C	North Solomons	■	Ball beaten to dish shape, handfuls of clay squeezed on – *paddle-and-anvil.*
NASIOI	C and I	North Solomons	■	Round base beaten, slabs joined – *paddle-and-anvil.*
BUIN	I	North Solomons	■	Ball beaten to a cone, hollowed with a stone, *paddle-and-anvil*, strips joined – *paddle-and-anvil.*
SIWAI	I	North Solomons	◆	Round base beaten, coils added – *paddle-and-anvil.*
BOUGAINVILLE STRAIT	C	Solomon Islands	■	Round base beatento shallow dish over a stone, strips joined – *paddle-and-anvil.*
CHOISEUL ISLAND	C (and I?)	Solomon Islands	■	Round base beaten to shallow dish over a stone, slabs joined – *paddle-and-anvil.*
RAWO (Leitre area)	C	West Sepik	▼	Lumps beaten to dish with coconut shell, finished with fingers. *Coils* added for larger pots only.
SISSANO	C	West Sepik	▼	*Coiling* (details not known).
LUMI	I	West Sepik	▲	Spiral *coiling*, hand smoothed.
NUKU	I	West Sepik	◆	Spiral *coiling*, hand smoothed.
KOMBIO-YAMBES-URIM-URAT KWANGA KWOMA-MAYO	I I I	East Sepik East Sepik East Sepik	◆ ◆ ◆	Spiral *coiling*, hand smoothed. Spiral *coiling*, hand smoothed. Spiral *coiling*, hand smoothed.
ABELAM (MAPRIK) ABELAM (WOSERA) SAWOS	I I I	East Sepik East Sepik East Sepik	◆ ◆ ◆	Spiral *coiling*, hand smoothed. Spiral *coiling*, hand smoothed. Spiral *coiling*, hand smoothed.
AIBOM	I	East Sepik	○	Dish base squeezed and pinched, *ring building (coils).*
NGALA	I	East Sepik	▼	Spiral *coiling*, hand smoothed.

Pot-making industries	Coastal or Inland	Province	Map Symbol	Technique
BUNA	I	East Sepik	▼	Spiral *coiling*, hand smoothed.
BOIKEN	I	East Sepik	▲	Spiral *coiling*, hand smoothed.
BUNGAIN, KAMASAU, MUNIWARA-URIMO	I	East Sepik	▲	Spiral *coiling*, hand smoothed.
MOUNTAIN ARAPESH	I	East Sepik	▲	*Coiling* (details not known).
YAUL/BANARO/ KAMBOT	I	East Sepik	◆	Spiral *coiling*, thinned by scraping, hand smoothed.
ADJORA	I	East Sepik	◆	Spiral *coiling* (details not known).
BOSMAN	I	Madang	◇	Spiral *coiling* – *paddle-and-anvil* (hand as anvil).
JOSEPHSTAAL area	I	Madang	◇	Spiral *coiling* – *paddle-and-anvil* (hand as anvil).
RAO	I	Madang	▼	Spiral *coiling*, hand smoothed.
TANGU	I	Madang	◆	Spiral *coiling*, hand smoothed.
MIKARU	I	Madang	◆	Spiral *coiling* (details not known).
WANUMA	I	Madang	◆	Spiral *coiling* (details not known).
INLAND MADANG area	I	Madang	▲	Spiral *coiling*, hand smoothed.
AGARABI	I	Eastern Highlands	▲	Spiral *coiling*, hand smoothed.
AZERA-WATUT	I	Morobe	◆	Spiral *coiling* – *paddle-and-anvil* (hand as anvil).
KELA-SIPOMA	C	Morobe	▼	Spiral *coiling* – *paddle-and-anvil*? (hand as anvil?).
GUHU-SAMANE (WARIA)	I	Morobe	◆	Spiral *coiling*, hand smoothed.
POPONDETTA area	I and C	Northern	◇	Spiral *coiling* – *paddle-and-anvil* (hand as anvil).
AMBASI	C	Northern	◇	Spiral *coiling* – *paddle-and-anvil* (hand as anvil).
MANAU	C	Northern	◇	Spiral *coiling* – *paddle-and-anvil* (hand as anvil).
DYKE ACKLAND BAY	C	Northern	◇	Spiral *coiling*, inside thinned by scraping – *paddle-and-anvil* (hand as anvil).
WANIGELA and CAPE VOGEL	C	Northern	◇	Lump spread down, out and up to form large base, spiral *coiling* – *paddle-and-anvil* (hand as anvil).
GOODENOUGH ISLAND	C and I	Milne Bay	◇*	Spiral *coiling* – *paddle-and-anvil* (hand as anvil and paddle alone).
AMPHLETT ISLANDS	C	Milne Bay	◇*	Slabs, squeezed rolls – *paddle-and-anvil* (hand as anvil and paddle alone).
MIADEBA, NORMANBY ISLAND	C	Milne Bay	▼	Spiral *coiling* onto a ball of clay.
EAST CAPE	C	Milne Bay	◡	Spiral *coiling* and ring building.
DAWSON ISLAND	C	Milne Bay	◡	Spiral *coiling* and ring building.
ENGINEER GROUP	C	Milne Bay	◡	Spiral *coiling* and ring building.
PANAEATI ISLAND	C	Milne Bay	◡	Spiral *coiling* and ring building.
BROOKER ISLAND	C	Milne Bay	◡	Spiral *coiling* and ring building.
WARI ISLAND	C	Milne Bay	◡	Spiral *coiling* and ring building.
BONARUA ISLAND	C	Milne Bay	◡	Spiral *coiling* and ring building.
SILOSILO BAY	C	Milne Bay	◡	Spiral *coiling* and ring building.
KAU KAU	C	Milne Bay	◡	Spiral *coiling* and ring building.
KONEMAIAUA	C	Milne Bay	◡	Spiral *coiling* and ring building.
BONA BONA ISLAND	C	Milne Bay	◡	Spiral *coiling* and ring building.
MAILU ISLAND	C	Central	◠	Spiral *coiling* and ring building, brief *paddle-and-anvil* (hand as anvil).

* Formed upside-down

MAP 4

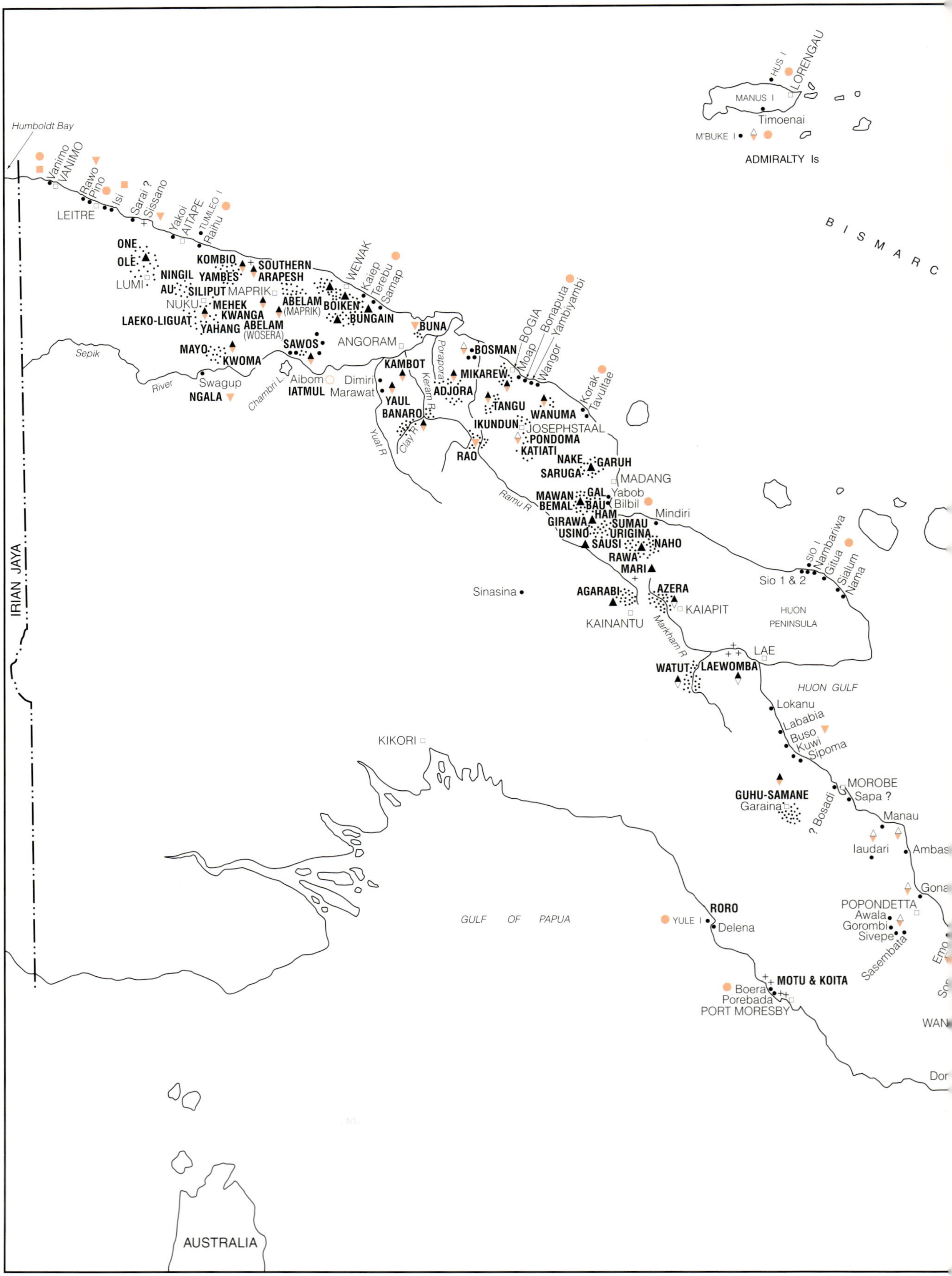

HUS I
LORENGAU
MANUS I
Timoenai
M'BUKE I
ADMIRALTY Is
BISMARC
Humboldt Bay
Vanimo
VANIMO
Rawo
Pino
Isi
Sarai ?
Sissano
LEITRE
Yakoi
AITAPE
TUMLEO I
Raihu
ONE
OLE
LUMI
NINGIL
AU
KOMBIO
YAMBES
SOUTHERN
ARAPESH
SILIPUT
MAPRIK
NUKU
MEHEK
KWANGA
ABELAM
(MAPRIK)
LAEKO-LIGUAT
YAHANG
ABELAM
(WOSERA)
WEWAK
Kaiep
Terebu
Samap
BOIKEN
BUNGAIN
BUNA
SAWOS
ANGORAM
MAYO
KWOMA
Sepik
River
Swagup
NGALA
Chambri L.
Aibom
IATMUL
Dimiri
Marawat
KAMBOT
YAUL
BANARO
Yuat R
Clay R
Keram R
Porapora
BOSMAN
BOGIA
Bonaputa
Yambiyambi
Moap
Wangor
MIKAREW
ADJORA
TANGU
WANUMA
Korak
Tavultae
IKUNDUN
JOSEPHSTAAL
PONDOMA
KATIATI
RAO
Ramu R
NAKE
GARUH
SARUGA
MADANG
MAWAN
GAL
Yabob
BEMAL
BAU
Bilbil
HAM
Mindiri
GIRAWA
SUMAU
USINO
URIGINA
SAUSI
NAHO
RAWA
MARI
IRIAN JAYA
Sinasina
AGARABI
AZERA
KAIAPIT
KAINANTU
Markham R
SIO I
Nambariwa
Gitua
Sialum
Nama
Sio 1 & 2
HUON
PENINSULA
LAE
WATUT
LAEWOMBA
HUON GULF
Lokanu
Lababia
Buso
Kuwi
Sipoma
KIKORI
MOROBE
Sapa ?
GUHU-SAMANE
Garaina
? Bosadi
Manau
Iaudari
Ambas
Gona
POPONDETTA
Awala
Gorombi
Sivepe
Sasembata
GULF OF PAPUA
YULE I
RORO
Delena
Emo
MOTU & KOITA
Boera
Porebada
PORT MORESBY
So
WAN
Dor
AUSTRALIA

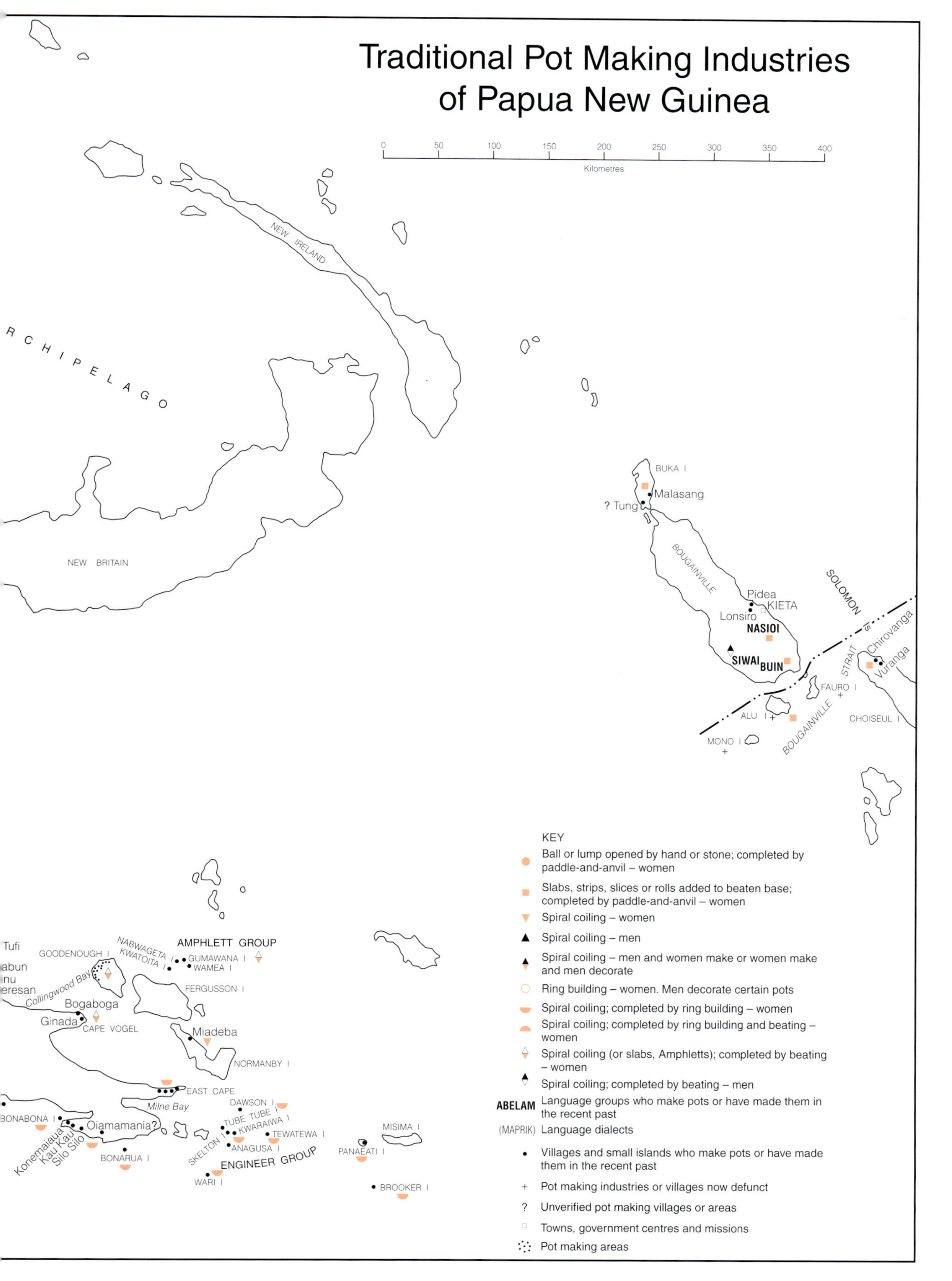
Traditional Pot Making Industries
of Papua New Guinea
0
50
100
150
200
250
300
350
400
Kilometres
NEW IRELAND
ARCHIPELAGO
NEW BRITAIN
BUKA I
Malasang
? Tung
BOUGAINVILLE
Pidea
KIETA
Lonsiro
NASIOI
SIWAI
BUIN
SOLOMON Is
Chirovanga
Vuranga
STRAIT
FAURO I
ALU I
CHOISEUL I
MONO I
BOUGAINVILLE
KEY
Ball or lump opened by hand or stone; completed by paddle-and-anvil – women
Slabs, strips, slices or rolls added to beaten base; completed by paddle-and-anvil – women
Spiral coiling – women
Spiral coiling – men
Spiral coiling – men and women make or women make and men decorate
Ring building – women. Men decorate certain pots
Spiral coiling; completed by ring building – women
Spiral coiling; completed by ring building and beating – women
Spiral coiling (or slabs, Amphletts); completed by beating – women
Spiral coiling; completed by beating – men
ABELAM Language groups who make pots or have made them in the recent past
(MAPRIK) Language dialects
Villages and small islands who make pots or have made them in the recent past
Pot making industries or villages now defunct
Unverified pot making villages or areas
Towns, government centres and missions
Pot making areas
Tufi
abun
inu
eresan
GOODENOUGH I
NABWAGETA I
KWATOITA I
AMPHLETT GROUP
GUMAWANA I
WAMEA I
Collingwood Bay
FERGUSSON I
Bogaboga
Ginada
CAPE VOGEL
Miadeba
NORMANBY I
EAST CAPE
Milne Bay
DAWSON I
TUBE TUBE I
KWARAIWA I
TEWATEWA I
SKELTON I
ANAGUSA I
ENGINEER GROUP
WARI I
BONABONA I
Oiamamania?
Konemaiaua
Kau Kau
Silo Silo
BONARUA I
MISIMA I
PANAEATI I
BROOKER I

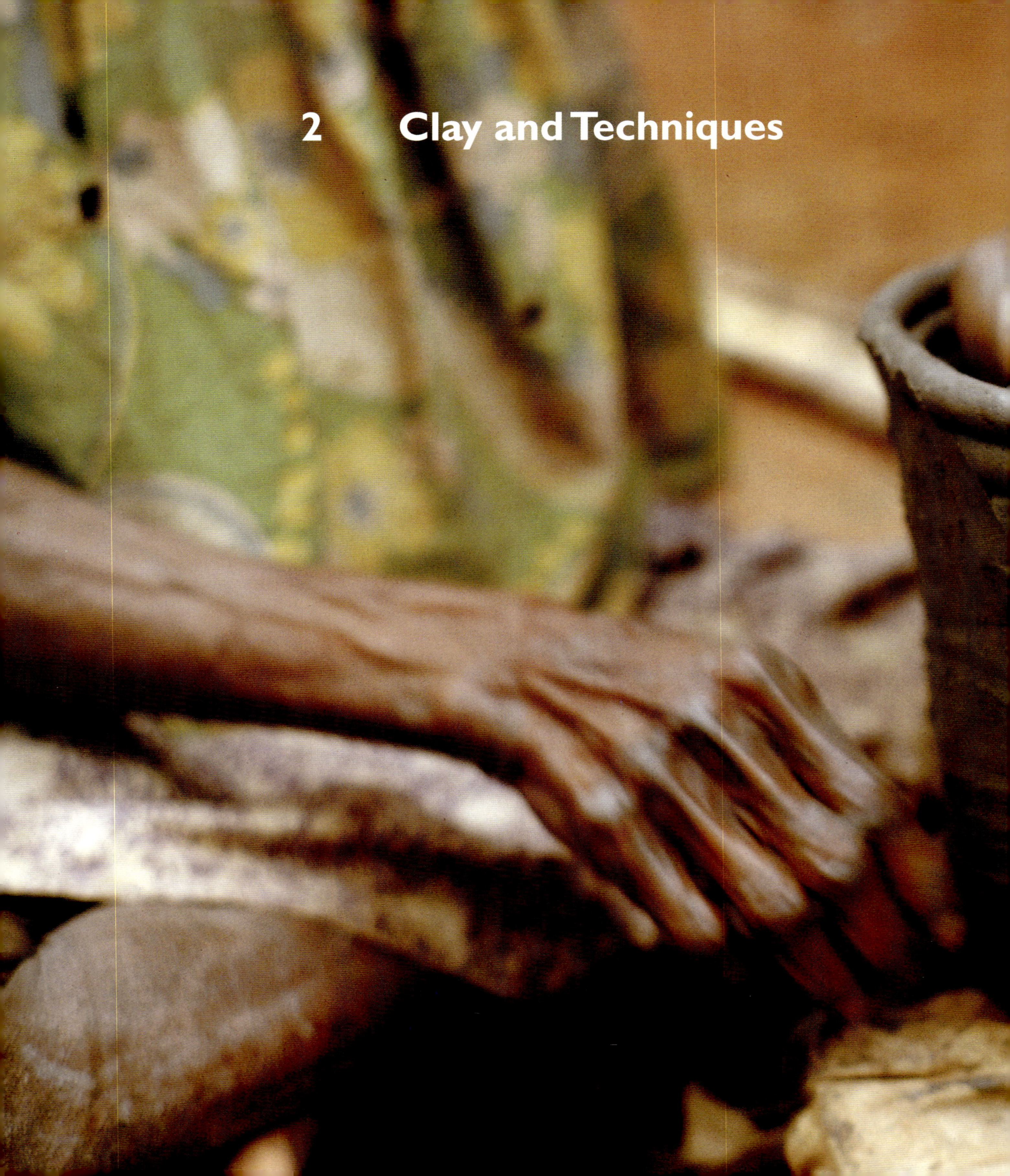

2 Clay and Techniques

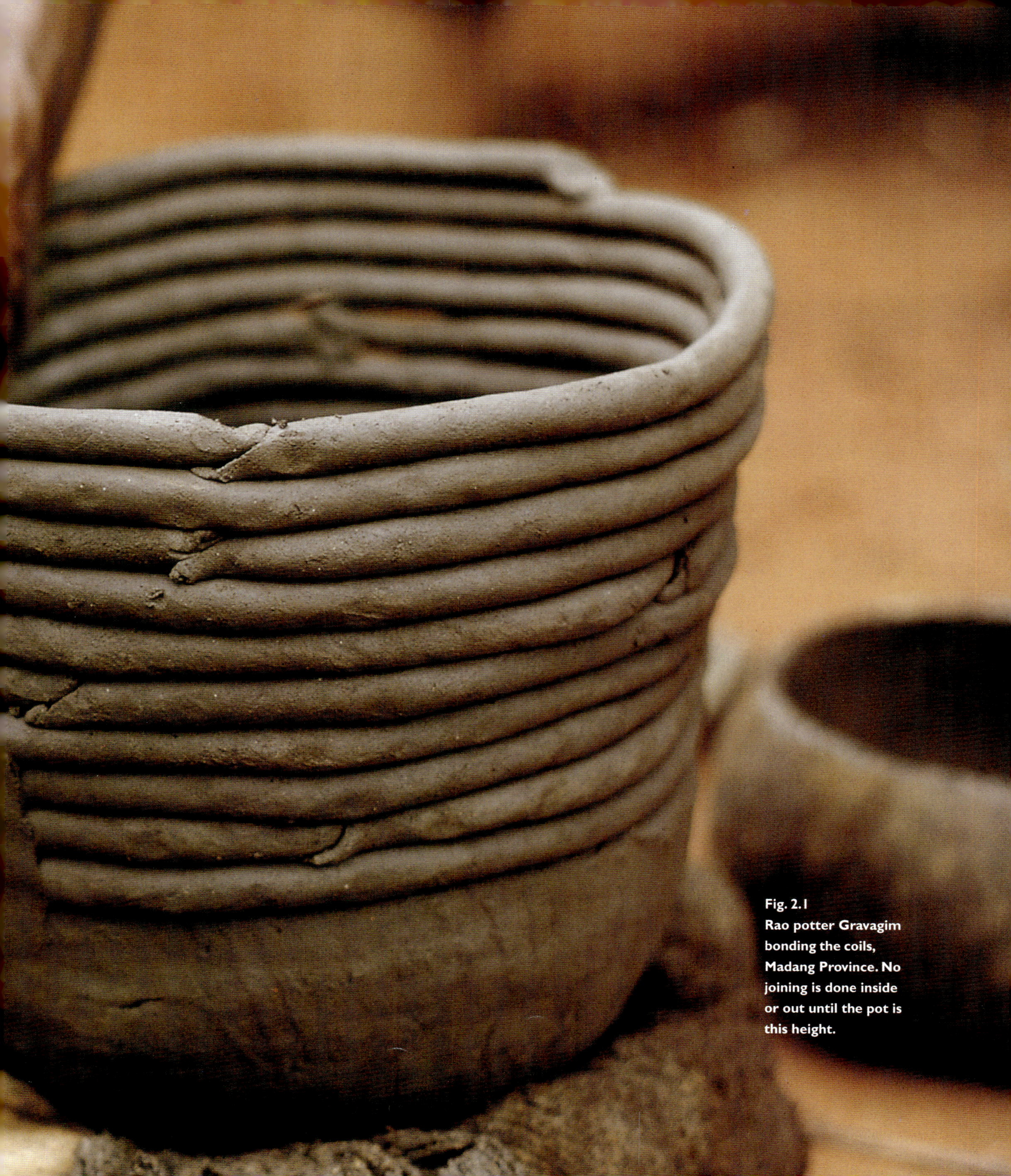

Fig. 2.1
Rao potter Gravagim bonding the coils, Madang Province. No joining is done inside or out until the pot is this height.

Papua New Guinea is on the eastern end of a string of folded mountain ranges which run from the Himalayas through the Malay Peninsula to tail off in the islands of Milne Bay. Intensely folded by earth movements which still continue to some extent, these ranges form a rugged central backbone to the island, contrasting with the wide and stable coastal plain of the south-west which is an extension of the more ancient Australian shield. In the north are mountains of lesser stature and between them and the main range is a great trough where the Sepik, Ramu, and Markham rivers flow.

Fine grained, intermediate to basic rocks and sedimentary rocks, with large areas of limestone, are found throughout most of the island. Alluvium covers large areas of the south-west and north-west. Acid intrusions, arkose and sandstone occur in small areas. Widespread volcanic activity has produced lava and ash deposits which, along with the alluvium and sedimentary rocks, are important sources of clay.

Clay mineralogy

To date, few deposits of materials (such as kaolin) suitable for a ceramic industry have been found in Papua New Guinea. As a result of the wet conditions strongly hydrated minerals, which are often poorly crystalline (such as halloysite or allophane), develop rather than kaolinite (Hill 1977). Clays of the montmorillonite group, smectites, could be expected also and analyses of clays have shown that they are commonly used by the traditional potters. A few clays contain halloysite together with smectite, illites, and in some cases mica, have been found in minor proportions in some of the clays. Several of the clays have included allophane and a few chlorite. Kaolinite has not been positively detected in any of the clays analysed by X-ray diffraction but other tests do indicate its presence in minor amounts.

The basic clay characteristics, such as plasticity and firing properties which are determined by the clay minerals present, are greatly modified by the natural non-clay minerals. These are known as accessory minerals, or impurities; they occur in various proportions and grain sizes and comprise the non-plastic component of the clay. Clays low in these materials are often too sticky to work and are said to be too tight or too fat. Non-plastics must be added. They are variously referred to as temper, filler, backing, opening material, aplastic, rough stuff or, inaccurately, grog. Non-plastic is a good descriptive term for a material which does not possess plasticity itself; temper can be another, more open, clay usually containing a high proportion of non-plastics. The term 'clay body' will be used to describe a blend of clay with one or more other materials.

Most potters in Papua New Guinea make no additions to their clay. The few results available of grain size distribution tests on untempered clay samples show a high to average natural non-plastic content, ranging from fine gravel (grit) size through coarse and fine sand to silt. About 60 per cent non-plastics could be considered average. A montmorillonitic clay used by the men of Komas in the inland Madang area has as much as 82 per cent non-plastics; this, surprisingly, is a reasonably plastic clay to use. Various D'Entrecasteaux Islands clays tested for Lauer all showed at least 65 per cent non-plastics. The accessory minerals of these natural Papua New Guinea clays include quartz, calcite, feldspar, limonite, haematite, mica, and fragments of all of the three geological classes of rocks: igneous, sedimentary and metamorphic.

Tempered clays

Potters throughout the world temper their over-plastic, or 'fat', clays with many different materials but a limited variety is used by the potters of Papua New Guinea. Most use beach sands which include shell and coral carbonate sand, volcanic sand with quartz and minor magnetite sand. As far as is known, only three groups of potters use river sand. Specht (1972) reports the only use of a tuff, a semi-consolidated lithic tuff, at Buka Island. On Tumleo Island is the only known case of a 'disintegrated rock' used as a temper. It contains a small proportion (9 per cent) of clay mineral, a smectite, but its main part is a fine gravel to fine 'sand' fraction composed of shell fragments, quartz, gypsum, feldspar, hematite, and geothite. This temper, together with another clay, is added to the basic clay and forms the most complex clay body in the country.

In at least three areas two or more clays are mixed together. At Brooker (Utian) Island a red clay is mixed with a black clay containing three times the proportion of coarsest particles (White and Hamilton 1973). The black clay therefore acts as a temper. At Aibom two, and sometimes three, clays are combined but as these clays have not been tested the reasons for this are not known.

Lauer (1974) recorded an interesting story about the use of clay on the Amphlett Islands. The local Government Council in charge of the traditional Amphlett clay source on Fergusson Island decided, in 1967, to charge the Amphlett people SA6 per basket of clay. The Amphlett islanders boycotted the clay and searched for new supplies. Several were found in the Amphlett group as well as others on Fergusson Island, but none was as satisfactory as the original. The potters experimented with mixing the clays together but never tried adding sand or other temper; as Amphlett potters had not traditionally used temper it seems they had no understanding of its possibilities. No analyses are available of the new clays so it is not known if they were lacking in sufficient non-plastics but, because the problems were mainly drying and firing cracks, it seems likely. Lauer reports that the standard of finish of the pots and the decorations also deteriorated. Happily the Fergusson Island people relented and the Amphlett potters are using their traditional clay again.

Tempering and heat resistance

In Sepik areas, where elaborate carving is carried out on clay serving and eating bowls (among the Boiken, Sawos, and Kombio-Yambes people), a finer clay is selected for the carved pots than for cooking pots. At a Kombio village it was stated that if the fine clay was used to make cooking pots they would break when used. The texture of their cooking pots showed that a rough gravelly clay had been used and this would certainly be unsuitable for the refined carved decorations. McMeekin (1967) suggests that the repeated cycle of sudden heating and cooling that a cooking pot must withstand necessitates, among other factors, an open-textured clay body with good thermal shock resistance.

Rye (1976) is studying the problems related to heat resistance and tempering using carbonate and sea water additives. He has found that calcite is also widely selected as a temper for low-fired cooking pots in other parts of the world, in spite of its apparent dangers. Calcium carbonate decomposes during firing and swells on uptake of water at any time after firing. Rye suggests that coastal potters such as the Motu, who add calcite sand as temper and use only sea water for wetting their clay, probably do so with good reason. His speculative explanations of the successful use of calcite are, first, that the presence of salt may increase vitrification during firing (this would produce a stronger fired clay which could perhaps hold against the pressures of expanding calcium hydroxide) and, second, that the vitrification would close off some of the pores against the entry of water to the calcium oxide.

Other Papua New Guinea potters who seem to have overcome the problems of the presence of

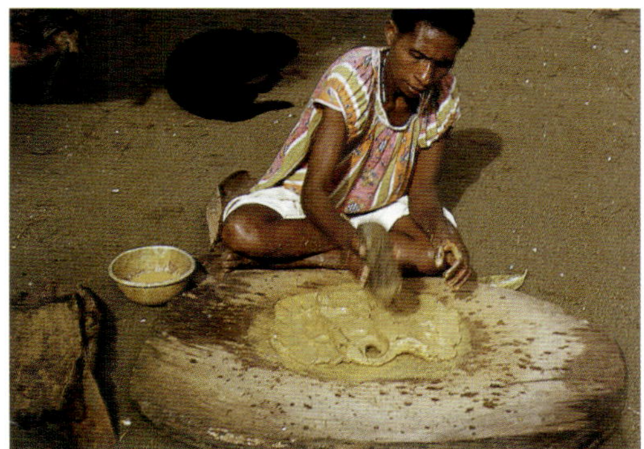

Fig. 2.2
Regina Teraku of Kaiep village, East Sepik Province, pounding sand into the clay on a traditional board made from the buttress root of a tree.

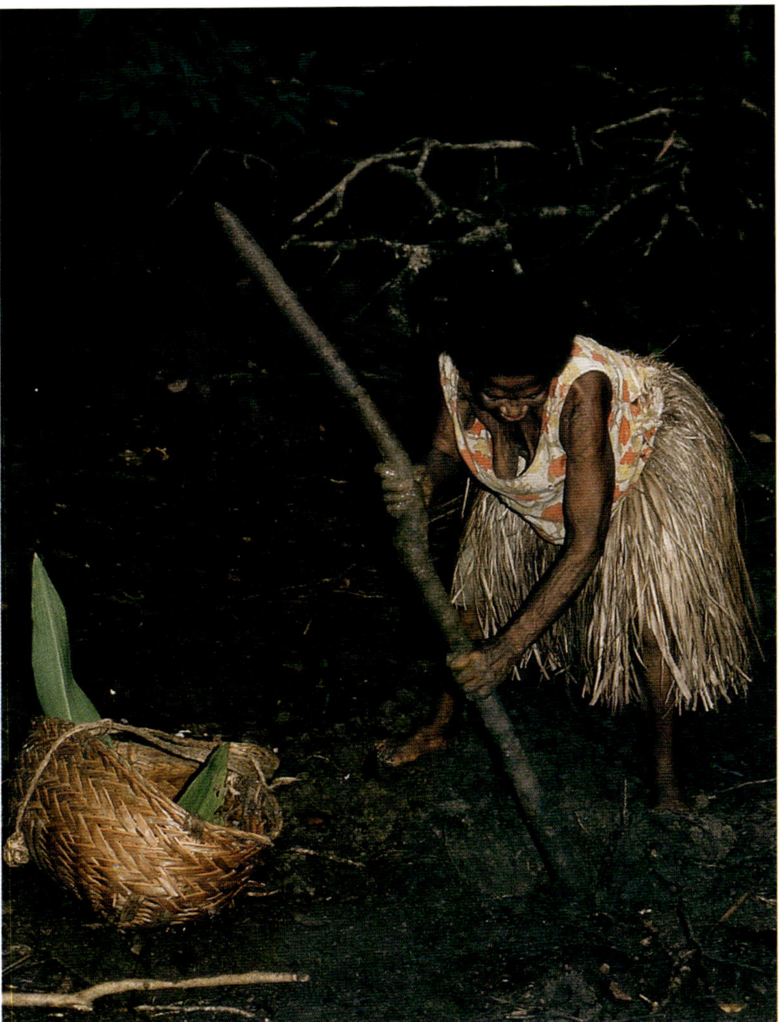

Fig. 2.3
Itsinamu of Waladau village digging clay at Wewiateha, Silosilo Bay, Milne Bay Province.

calcite in their clay bodies are potters from Hus Island, who add coral sand to their clay: M'Buke whose beach sand temper contains some limestone; Tumleo whose temper includes shell fragments; and Mindiri who add a beach sand with a minor proportion of shell grit. Dickinson and Shutler (1971) record the use of many calcareous tempers from coastal sands in the western Pacific islands.

In some areas, such as the Engineer Islands of Milne Bay Province, potters insist on using fresh water to soften their clay, declaring that if salt water touched the clay the pots would break during firing. The reasons for this belief have not yet been explored although, as Rye (1976) suggests, the potters no doubt have good reason for their preference.

Clay colour

Unfired clay colour is due primarily to two classes of 'impurities' carbonaceous matter in colloidal form and iron compounds. It can vary tremendously. A very small amount of the finely divided carbonaceous material will colour a clay grey to almost black. The iron compounds impart colours which vary from buffs, yellows, browns and reds to greys. These raw colours are not necessarily retained after firing because the carbonaceous matter is mostly decomposed and many changes take place in the iron compounds; for example, dehydration of limonite turns it from a definite yellow to a brownish-red.

The clays used in Papua New Guinea are usually yellow browns to greys with some black browns. Only two or three are of a reddish-brown colour. No white clays are used but a paler yellowish-grey clay is used on Buka Island. Where samples were available, wet clay colours given in the following chapters are from *The Standard Soil Colour Chart.*

Clay preparation

Methods of gathering clay are more or less uniform throughout the country but clay preparing techniques vary considerably. Very little equipment is needed at any stage. Traditionally, clay was loosened from the pit with a pointed digging stick; now a sharpened iron bar, a bush knife or a spade is often used. Clay is usually found at a depth of at least 30 centimetres below the overlying leaf mould and soil. It is taken back to the village in the particular carrying vessel of the area: a string bag lined with green leaves, carried on the woman's forehead and hanging down her back; a square bucket-shaped container made from the tough flexible leaf-base of one of the various types of black palm; or a basket woven from coconut leaves which often has a long handle so it can be worn around the forehead.

For clay preparation, some coastal and river villagers use long shallow wooden troughs; they are the sides of discarded dugout canoes. In some villages old whole canoes become containers for soaking clay, as at Aibom and Mindiri. Another common clay working board is made from one of the plank-like buttresses which occur on several types

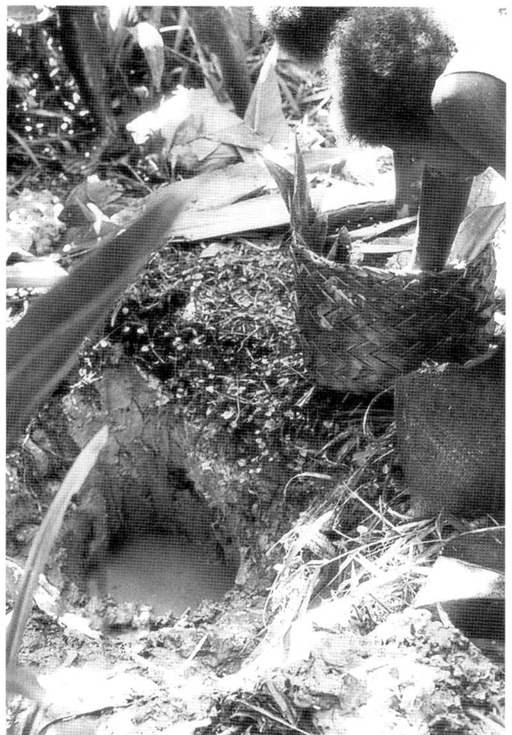

of jungle tree: these are a suitable thickness (about 3 to 5 centimetres) in their natural state and only have to be cut from the tree in a rough square or oblong shape. They are still used widely although milled timber is sometimes substituted where available. A very useful working surface which frequently acts also as a mat for the potter to sit on is the same pliable leaf-base used for the carrying baskets, in Pidgin, 'limbum'.

Clay is usually dug in the wet season: the potters say it is too hard to dig in the dry. In some areas it comes naturally wet from sago swamps. If not for immediate use it is often patted into football-sized balls and left under the house where it dries out. Some potters keep their clay moist and ready to use by wrapping it in green leaves or storing it in an old clay pot or wooden bowl.

In all except two areas, the larger pieces of foreign matter in clays – roots, stones, oversized grit, coral pieces or shells – are removed with the fingers. At Yabob-Bilbil-Mindiri they were traditionally extracted with the teeth. The Tumleo potters are unique in their use of a cane sieve to eliminate the larger grit and stones. Some of their raw material is first crushed and then sieved dry; some is soaked and sieved with a great deal of water. The wet-mix method helps plasticity. The dry material assists the mixing of the sticky mass. In recent years the Tumleo potters have been introduced to wire sieves; Yabob and Bilbil were also shown the sieving method and are the only other groups to use the wet preparation technique (figs 9.94, 9.195).

The normal method of sorting out the rubbish from the usable material is to press out pieces of clay between thumb and fingers, throwing aside unwanted bits as they are detected. On Tubetube Island the pressing out is done on the end of a lump of clay; this action also begins to knead the clay into good condition. The stickiness of the clay makes it difficult to get rid of the bits and the Bilbil potters give this as the reason for pulling the bits out with their teeth and spitting them out. The potters of Boera, near Port Moresby, probably have to discard more rubble than do others; their clay, dug just behind the beach, is full of whole and broken shells which must be removed.

In many areas wet clay is beaten or pounded with a stick or heavy stone. At one Sepik village, clubs which exploit the natural shapes of roots or branches of trees are used; the side of the knobbly end is the beating surface. The side of a long stick may also be used for beating; for pounding, the end of a stick is used. At Koiwat an adze-shaped wooden pounder is employed. An interesting adjunct here is the 'limbum' sheet on which the clay is prepared. It is folded over on top of the clay and rocked back and forth, leaving the clay compacted and ready for further flattening. This is a very thorough and efficient method and is used in a few other Sepik pot making centres. At some coastal

Fig. 2.4
A clay source for Hus Island potters, located in a swamp on Manus Island. The clay basket is woven from coconut leaves.

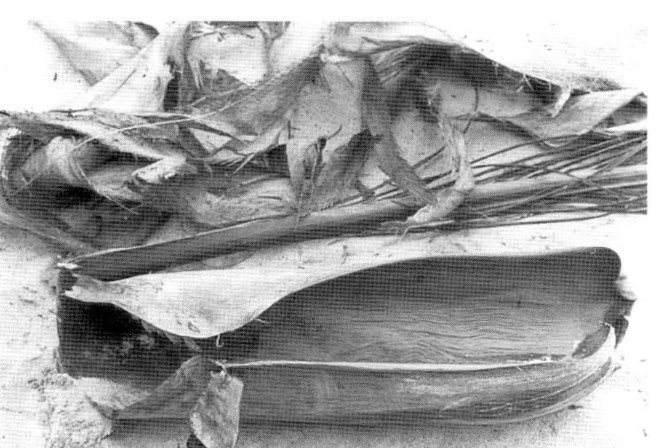

Fig. 2.5
'Limbum', the leaf-base of a black palm, used for the preparation and carrying of clay, Tumleo Island, West Sepik Province.

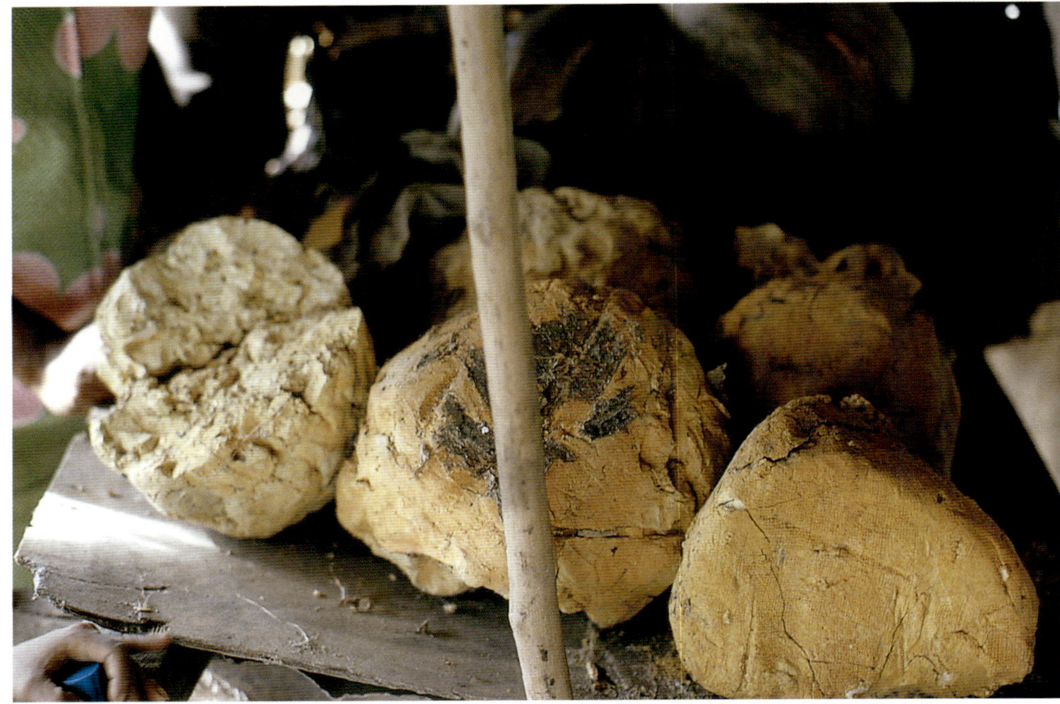

Fig. 2.6
Dry clay stored under a house, Hus Island, Manus Province.

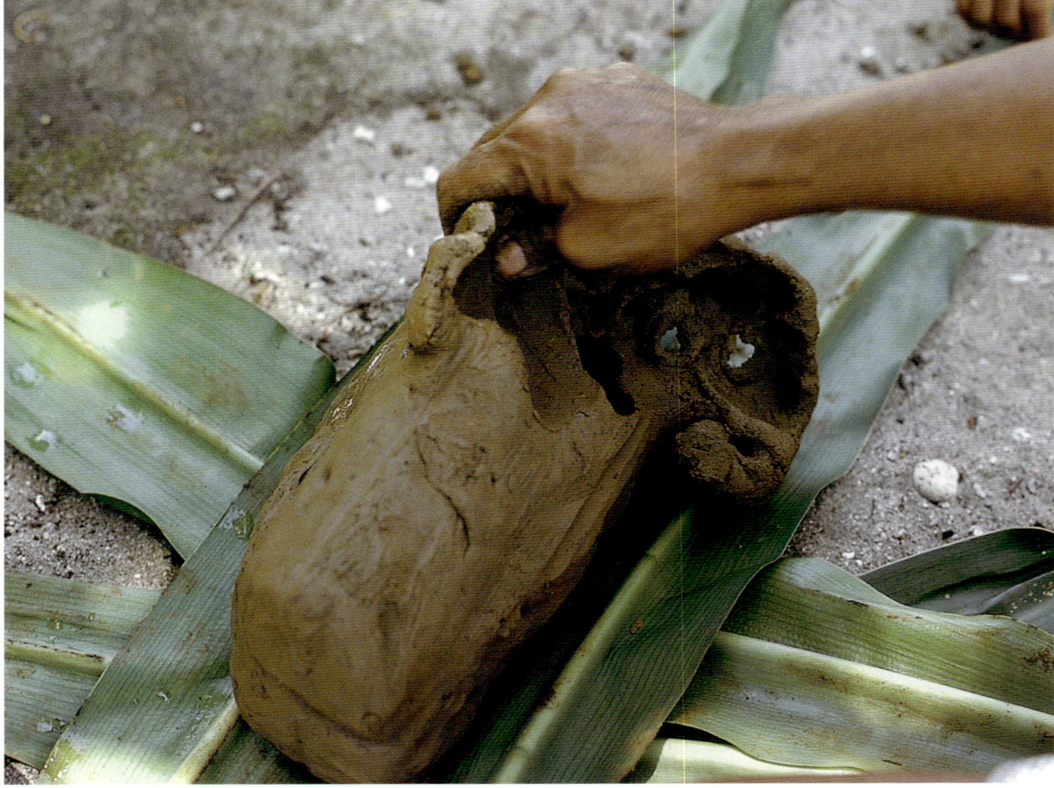

Fig. 2.7
Doris Wesley removing grit from the clay, Tubetube Island, Milne Bay Province.

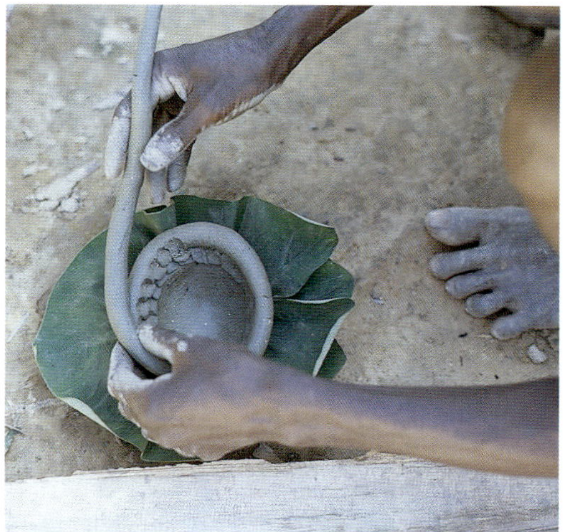

Fig. 2.8

Fig. 2.8
Spiral coiling at Ali village, West Sepik Province. The potter is Telefi.

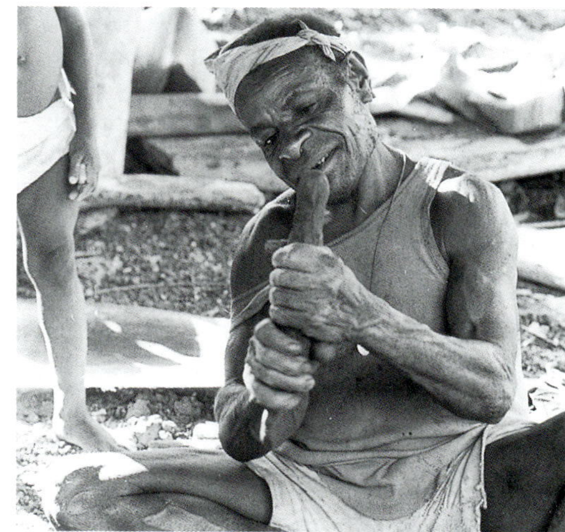

Fig. 2.9

Fig. 2.9
Kaspar Hananumbo preparing rough rolls of clay prior to rolling them into thin coils, Paliama village, Inland Sepik.

areas long stones are used instead of sticks and sand temper is pounded into the clay on a traditional wooden board. At Bilbil a similar method is used on a board, handfuls of clay with sand are flattened to almost paper-thin discs by using a rounded stone. These discs are then soaked in water.

All Papua New Guinea potters adjust their temper-clay mixtures by feel, judging when correct workability has been achieved. Most coil potters achieve the final conditioning of the clay by firmly squeezing it into short thick rolls, ready for making coils. The majority of the paddle-and-anvil potters finish their preparation with kneading which is done either in the shallow trough or on the traditional board. In all areas observed the potters used their clay in an exceptionally soft condition.

Pot making techniques

As previously stated, the Papua New Guinea potter uses either the paddle-and-anvil or the coiling method. However, there are distinct regional variations in methods of 'starting' and 'finishing'. Starting methods consist of coiling, forming from a lump or ball; slab building (and strips, slices and rolls) and, rarely, pinching. Finishing methods are paddle-and-anvil, paddle alone and hand smoothing. There are many variations within each of these categories.

Coiling refers to the technique of building up the walls of a vessel with long rolls of clay. The main differences in coiling are related to the way in which the rolls of clay are applied. In the case of spiral coiling a roll of clay is fed spirally onto itself; each new coil starts where the last one finishes. In ring building on the other hand, one roll or, in some cases, two or three rolls must complete a circle for each layer. (Strictly speaking, this is not coiling but in common usage 'coil' has come to signify the roll of clay and 'coiling' although inferring a spiral, is extended to ring building.) The clay rolls for both of these coiling techniques may be thin (from 5 millimetres to 1 centimetres) or thick (up to 4 centimetres).

A combination of spiral coiling and ring building is employed in the villages of southern Milne Bay. The pot is started by spiral coiling in a shallow clay forming dish, which also acts as a turntable, until it is 6 to 10 centimetres high and is then completed by ring building (fig. 2.11). In the inland Sepik (except at Aibom), inland Madang, Ramu River, inland Morobe, Kela-Sipoma area and in Northern Province

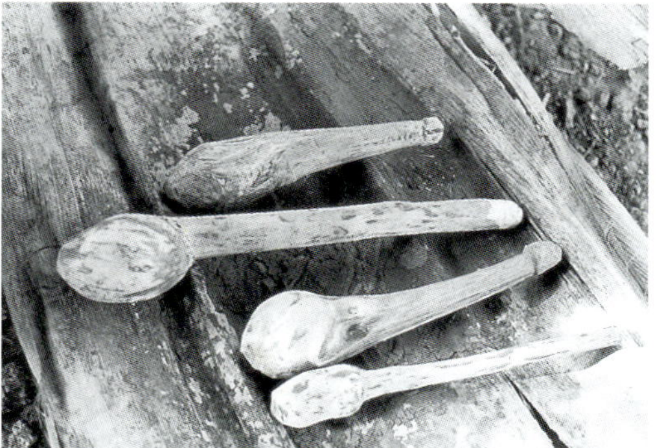

Fig. 2.10
Kaspar's clay beaters, Paliama.

coastal and inland areas, the spiral coiling technique is used. At Aibom the base of the pot is formed from a squeezed-out lump of very soft clay and thick rolls of clay are added in rings to form the walls. This is the only case of ring building without the spiral coiling start (figs 9.49-9.53).

Only a few examples of coiling are found along the coast and these are mostly in conjunction with related inland coiling groups. They occur in the Northern Province in about seven groups from Manau south to Dyke Ackland Bay, among the Kela-Sipoma of Morobe Province and at Rawo on the north coast, where coiling is carried out by people who have migrated to the coast from the hills.

Three unusual methods of starting a coil pot are found in south-eastern Papua. At Miadeba, on Normanby Island, coils are built up on a ball of clay. At Wanigela and Cape Vogel coils are added to a curiously pinched and scraped-up base. On Goodenough Island the pot is coiled upside down (see Chapter 4). A method of squeezing on handfuls of clay to raise the walls is used on Buka Island and on the Amphletts. From one to several handfuls of clay complete a circle, depending on the diameter of the pot. It is difficult to categorise this technique: it can hardly be termed coiling. The pot is completed by beating.

In several other areas beating completes coil pots but it does not involve so much thinning and shaping as does the pure paddle-and-anvil technique described below. The potters of the Markham Valley and the nearby Watut Valley use a technique of thick spiral coiling partly shaped with a paddle which is also used to compact the base. Some support is given inside by the hand but no anvil is used. On the lower Ramu, in the Josephstaal area and throughout the Northern Province pots made from thinner coils are beaten and smoothed with a paddle, again with the hand rather than an anvil, inside. At the Amphlett Islands and Goodenough Island the shaping and smoothing of the outside of the pot are completed with a paddle while the pot is still upside down. A minimum of beating with a stick only, is employed on Mailu Island to help fill a hole in the base of the upturned pot.

Traditionally, a board for rolling coils was made from the leaf-base of the sago palm, which is readily available in many pottery areas. A bush knife is used to hack the whole leaf from the base of the trunk and it is cut to varying sizes, up to about 130 centimetres long and about 40 centimetres wide. In most areas the thick ridge at the back is then sliced off to enable the board to be more or less flattened, and the needles of the wild sago are removed with the bush knife. The result is an ideal board for rolling coils: it has a slight natural curve and a smooth, slightly absorbent surface.

A convenient brief name for this leaf-base board is 'pangal'. 'Pangal' refers also to the narrower part of the leaf frond which is used in the construction of house walls. Both parts are used as fuel for firings. The wide flattened part, often incorrectly referred to as sago spathe, is also used for bark paintings and the painted facades of the 'haus tambaran' in the Sepik area. At the Bosman villages on the lower Ramu, the potters traditionally used a much narrower and thicker sago leaf board and on Goodenough Island a split sago frond was used.

Fig. 2.11

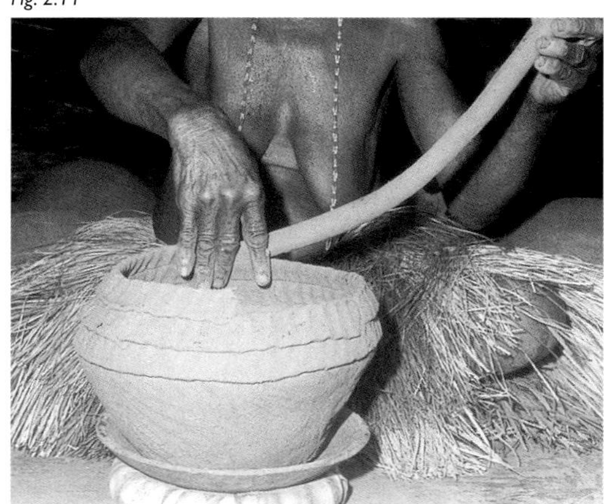

Fig. 2.11
Ring building on Panaeati Island , Milne Bay Province. The pot sits in a fired clay support on a pandanus leaf ring.

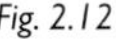
Fig. 2.12

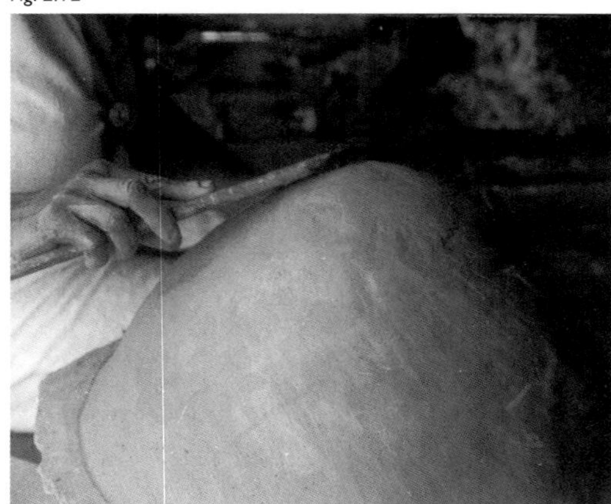

Fig. 2.12
Mattledi Alaba compacting and smoothing the outside of the pot with a paddle, Goodenough Island, Milne Bay Province.

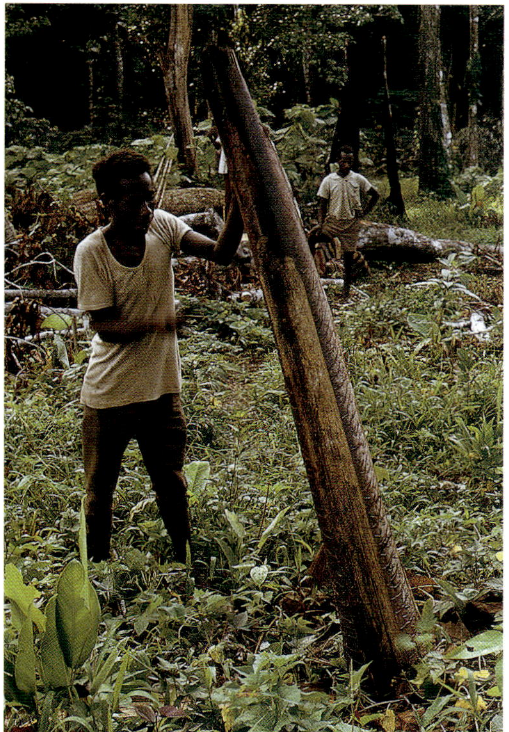

Today sawn timber boards or three-ply are sometimes substituted.

Another aspect of coiling is the manner in which the coils themselves are produced. The most usual method is to roll them out on a board with the hands; first, however, a pile of rough rolls is usually produced by squeezing and turning in the hands. In the areas in which the authors observed the rolling of coils, all potters used only the heel and palm of the hand, never the fingers, to achieve coils of a uniform thickness and they used only one hand. The length of the rolled out coils varies from about 50 to 120 centimetres. This method of forming coils is used in the inland Sepik (except at Aibom), the Ramu River, inland Madang, by the Binanderean potters of the Northern and Morobe provinces, and at Goodenough Island, East Cape and Brooker and Panaeati islands in Milne Bay Province (fig. 2.15).

The principal alternative method of making coils is to roll them between clasped hands with a back and forth and slight rotating action. Usually, as in most of southern Milne Bay, the potter is sitting on the ground and the hands must be held at or a little above shoulder height to allow enough space for the coil to dangle out from the bottom of the palm of the hands. The Wanigela women, however, stand while rotating the coils and also while joining them. At Aibom the thick rolls are formed by squeezing as well as rolling between the hands while the Azera and Salamaua potters produce rough rolls by squeezing only. As in southern Milne Bay, their hands must be held high while turning and extending the clay. The Azera and Aibom rolls are smoother and more even than those of the Lokanu (Salamaua) women (Figs 6.5, 6.31).

There are some variations in the methods of supporting pots during coiling construction. Mostly the rudimentary vessel is held in one hand, sometimes supported against a knee, while more coils are rolled with the other hand. In many cases, when the pot becomes too large to hold easily it is placed in a ring-support or ring-cushion. This is usually made from partly dried banana leaves and leaf sheaths or from pandanus leaves. Three or four layers of the material are first formed into a ring then more strips or bundles of leaves are bound over and over the ring, overlapping each other to form a thick firm cushion with a hole of varying size in the centre. On Gumawana Island the potters use grass rings. It is common to lie a green taro leaf or a piece of a banana leaf across the ring-cushion before resting the pot in place. Schuster (1975) suggests that this is to enable the pot to be lifted off easily if necessary. It is probably also to help prevent the ring pressing into the soft base of the pot. In addition to accommodating the round or pointed bases of pots during construction and decoration, the ring-support acts as a turntable, the

Fig. 2.13
Theodore making a coil rolling board from a sago palm leaf-base, 'pangal', Mansep village, East Sepik Province.

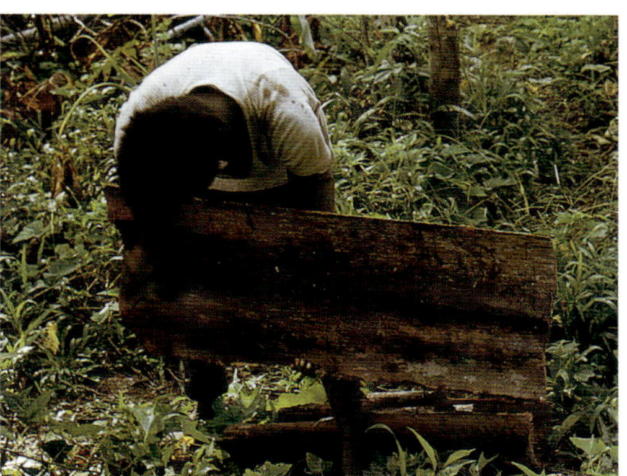

Fig. 2.14
Theodore flattening the 'pangal', Mansep.

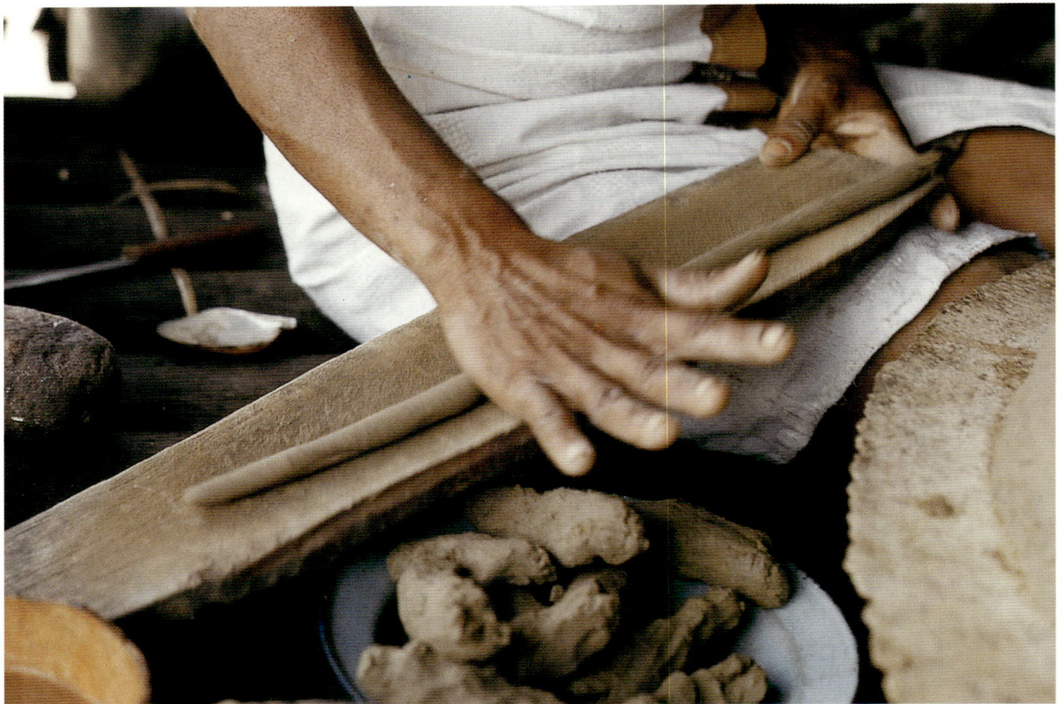

Fig. 2.15
Mattledi Alaba rolling a coil with the heel and palm of the hand only, Goodenough Island, Milne Bay Province.

potter turning it to bring the pot into the most convenient working position. It is also used, in the Markham Valley, for example, to hold pots on their sides for the purpose of finishing the base. In the Kela-Sipoma villages, in the Mari area and in the Eastern Highlands in the past, pots were supported in a hole in the ground. In southern Milne Bay the pots are formed and turned around in a shallow, round-based clay dish; on Mailu Island a half coconut shell is used for the same purpose.

Coiling can be carried out with the pot turning in either a clockwise or anti-clockwise direction, depending on whether the potter is right or left-handed. It can depend also on whether the coil is being applied overlapping inside or outside.

The methods of joining a coil to the one (or ones) below vary. The majority of potters feed the coil on with one hand while the thumb of the other hand bonds it to the coil below by pressing some of the clay down across it on the inside of the pot. In some areas the thumb is pressed down across two layers of coils. Only in the middle Ramu at Nodabu was a potter observed laying the coils on spirally, making no joins until the pot was about 15 centimetres tall: at this stage the coils were all bonded inside and out by dragging the thumb down from the top to the bottom. Another variation was seen at Garaina and other Binanderean villages; each coil is pressed directly down on top of the one below it with the forefinger leaving a dimpled row of impressions in the top coil. At Goodenough Island the thumb and forefinger are used to pinch coils to those below. The Aibom method of joining is unique: the thick roll is placed overlapping the one below and the thumb moves quickly upwards, pressing firmly against the hand which supports outside, smearing much of the soft clay across the join and leaving the wall of the pot several centimetres higher.

The curvature of the walls of coiled vessels is achieved in various ways: by positioning the coil on either the outer or inner edge of the coil below it; by pressing outwards with the fingers, thumb, shell or coconut piece during bonding and smoothing of the coils inside the pot and likewise pressing inwards with the outside supporting hand: or, rarely, by a pressing and scraping action carried out with a narrow wooden beater.

In nearly all areas final smoothing of joined coils is done by wiping the pot all over with wet hands.

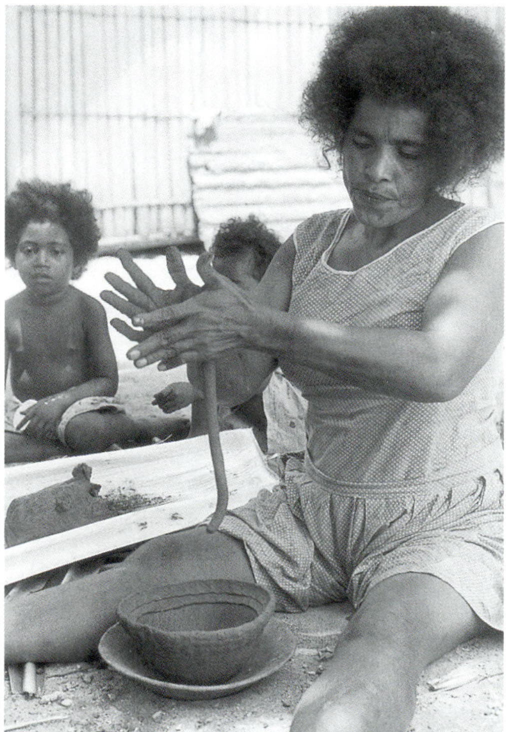

Fig. 2.16

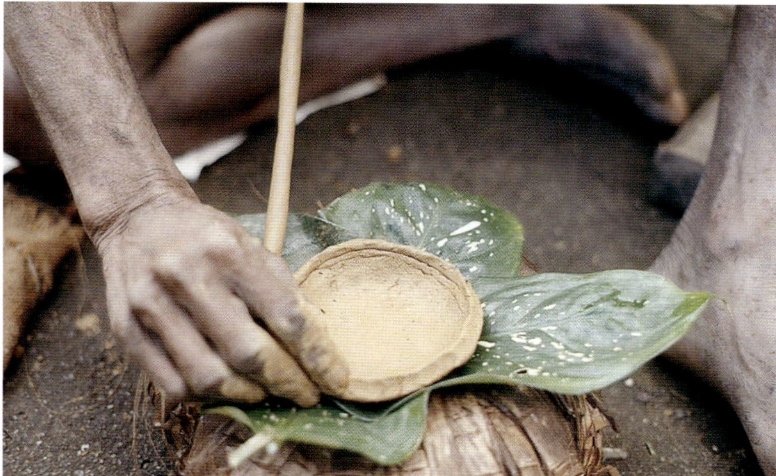

Fig. 2.17

Some coil pots need particular treatment to finish the base. At Aibom the bottoms of large pots and frying pans are thinned by scraping or planing with a sharp shell ring, leaving a very open texture which probably helps prevent base cracks and absorb the shock of repeated contact with flames during cooking.

Paddle-and-anvil has become the accepted term to describe the technique by which a pot is shaped and thinned by the impact of a beater on the outside wall against a hard object held on the inside. In order to shape and thin the pot the 'anvil' is generally moved firmly towards the inside wall with each beat of the 'paddle' against it. Paddle-and-anvil is essentially a finishing technique. It is sometimes not carried out until the basic form has been set aside to become firmer (fig. 2.19).

Except where the hand or fist is used, the anvil is always a smooth stone. It can be spherical, ellipsoid or a rounded, flat form. In other countries it is sometimes a fired clay object shaped like a half-sphere with a handle. 'Paddle' implies a wooden shape widening out from the handle but often in Papua New Guinea it is a straight piece of wood of even width. Several beaters of various widths and surfaces are used at different stages. In general, a narrow-ridged stick is used to commence the thinning of the walls; the rough surface grips the clay and helps force it upwards. Wider, smoother paddles are used for finishing. In all cases the two implements are kept moist by dipping the paddle into water and rubbing over the operative surface of the stone, thereby ensuring that water does not also get on the hand holding the stone, causing it to slip.

The base of paddle-and-anvil vessels may be formed in many different ways. Perhaps the quickest method is that used by the Motu potters of the Port Moresby area: they open up a soft pug of clay

Fig. 2.16
Doris Wesley of Tubetube Island, rolling a coil, Milne Bay Province.

Fig. 2.17
Kesesa joining a coil to the one below by pressing downwards, Garaina, Morobe Province.

Fig. 2.18
Wari Island potter smoothing a finished pot with wet hands, Milne Bay Province.

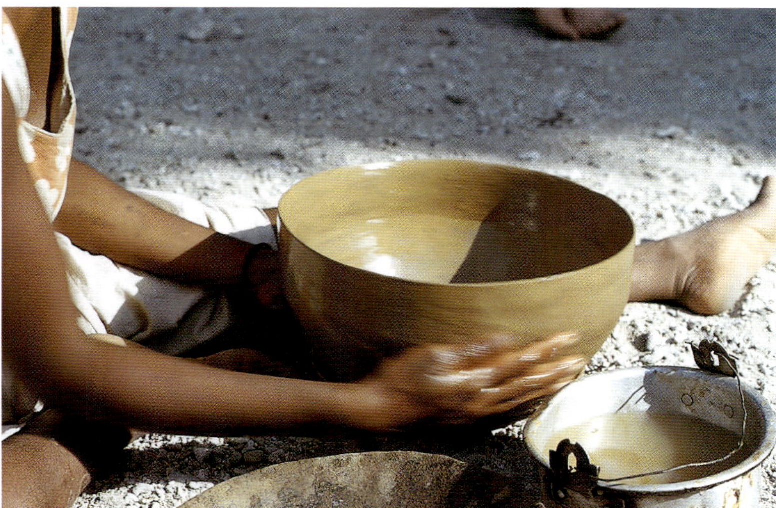

by plunging a hand into the centre and dragging the clay upwards to form the walls. At the villages on the coast near Wewak and at those near Bogia a ball of clay is pounded open with a long stone. Yabob-Bilbil-Mindiri also use this technique when forming a particular type of pot. At the Tumleo group of villages the opening is achieved with the fist but it seems that traditionally a stone was used there, too. The Bilbil group have a starting technique which employs the principle of spinning the pot, achieving almost a thrown look. A ball of clay is opened with the thumb of one hand while it is spun quickly around on the other hand. Next, wet fingers are held on the outside forming a flange which becomes the rim of the pot. When firmer, the opening is enlarged by tapping into it with a small smooth stone. At the coastal villages on the Huon Peninsula, a cone of clay is beaten up around a stone anvil and completed by paddle-and-anvil.

The method of flattening a ball of clay to form a disc and then beating it into a dish shape to start the pot is used by many of the paddle-and-anvil potters. At Vanimo, and at Hus Island in the Admiralty Islands, the vessel is then completed with the usual paddle-and-anvil but on M'Buke Island (also in the Admiralties) coils are added to the base to build up the walls before beating. At Rawo, near Vanimo, a coconut shell is tapped into a ball of clay to form the dish shape. At nearby Leitre slices of clay are added to the same sort of base while at Vanimo slices are only added when larger pots are made.

Yet another series of preliminary forming methods for paddle-and-anvil pots is employed in the Solomon Islands. Round, shallow bases are beaten out in slightly varying manners, similar to those of Vanimo. As has been mentioned, at Buka handfuls of clay are then squeezed onto the base to build up the walls; the Nasioi and the Choiseul islanders beat slabs, often on a large flat rock which are then beaten together onto the base. The Buin potters and the Shortland islanders used to add beaten strips of clay and the men of Siwai add coils. All are finished by the paddle-and-anvil method.

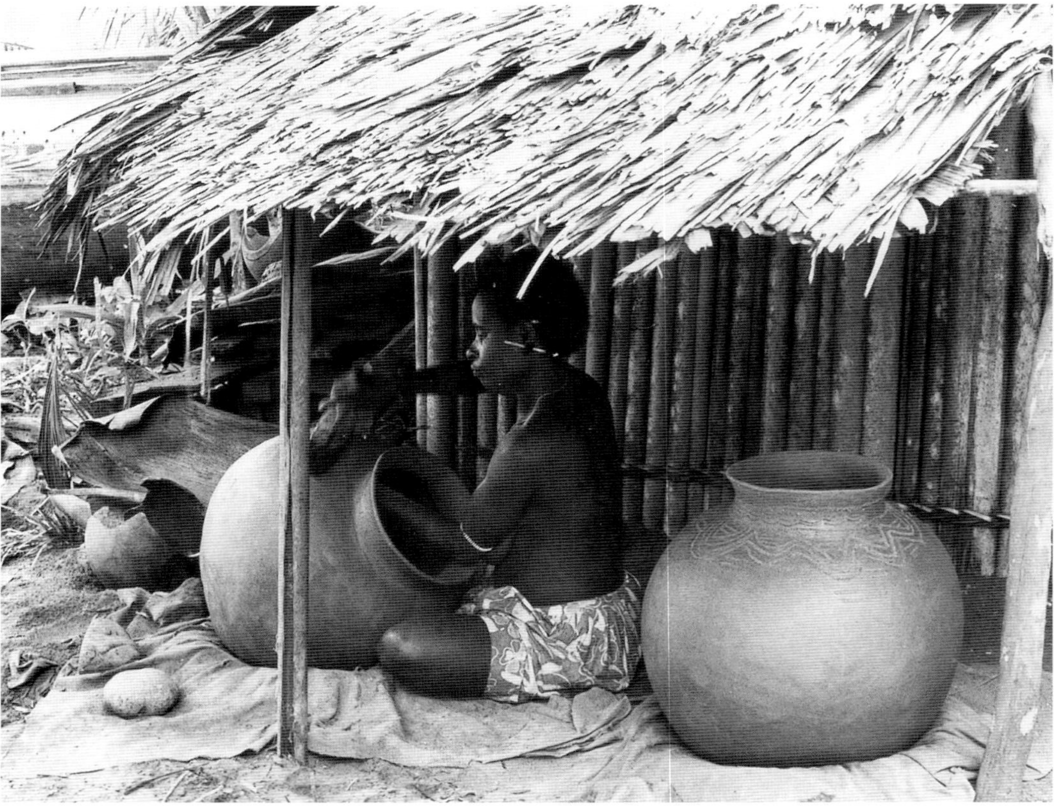

Fig. 2.19
Paddle-and-anvil technique, using a wide smooth paddle at Kaiep village, East Sepik Province.

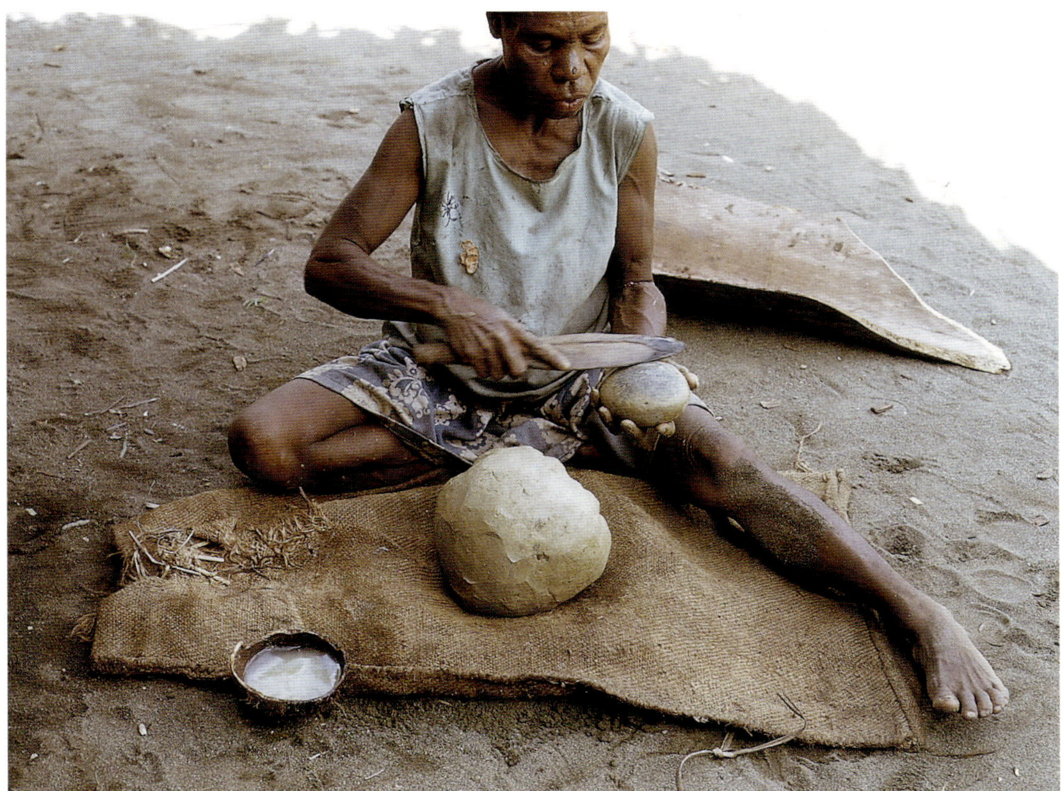

Fig. 2.20
Moistening the stone with a wet paddle, as is done by all paddle-and-anvil potters. Terebu village, East Sepik Province.

Some variation is apparent in the methods of finishing the paddle-and-anvil pots but the wide differences in forming the basic shapes are of principal interest for comparison. Sometimes the growing pot is supported on the lap or between the feet but in many areas it sits sideways on a ring-cushion; at the coastal villages near Wewak it is settled on its side in a hollow in the sand.

To swell out the full spherical form of the paddle-and-anvil vessels, the most common procedure is to beat from the base gradually around and upwards and then to start at the base again repeating the movement a little further around the pot. The only exception observed was at Moap village near Bogia, where the beating is carried out from the top down and around to the base. The final smoothing is carried out in a gentle sliding-beating action performed with a wet paddle, usually the widest one in use.

Both coil and paddle-and-anvil potters use various methods to level the top edge. The most frequent technique is to slice off the high points with a fibre of coconut or bamboo and to smooth the edge again with wet fingers. Some coil potters use the tips of the thumb and forefinger to push the clay from high spots around to lower spots. An unusual technique of clipping with a shell is used on Tubetube Island.

Repairing techniques used by paddle-and-anvil potters were observed at the Motu villages, Vanimo, Tumleo and Kaiep. They were almost identical in each case. The continual dampening of tools is a precaution against cracking but inevitably some cracks appear. If the crack is caused by a pebble it is removed and then often the crack is pushed further open. Clay is manoeuvred from all around the crack by beating gradually towards it until the two edges can be overlapped and beaten firmly together. Clay sliced off from thick spots or high top edges is usually beaten back into thin or low spots. At Vanimo a potter was observed excising a sliver of clay down each side of a crack reversing the pieces and beating them back into the space (figs 2.25 and 2.26).

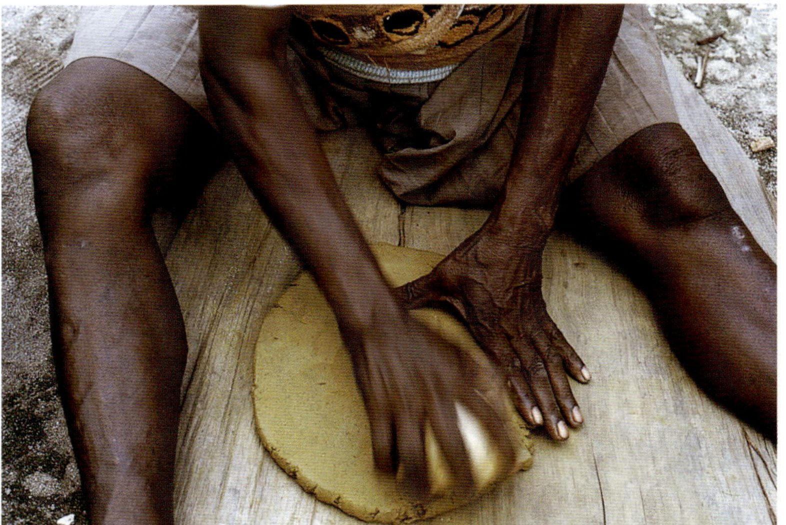

Fig. 2.21
Oma pounding a ball of clay flat to form a paddle-and-anvil pot, Vanimo village, West Sepik Province.

Fig. 2.22
Victoria Bobi beating slices of clay on to the walls of the pot, Isi village, Leitre, West Sepik Province.

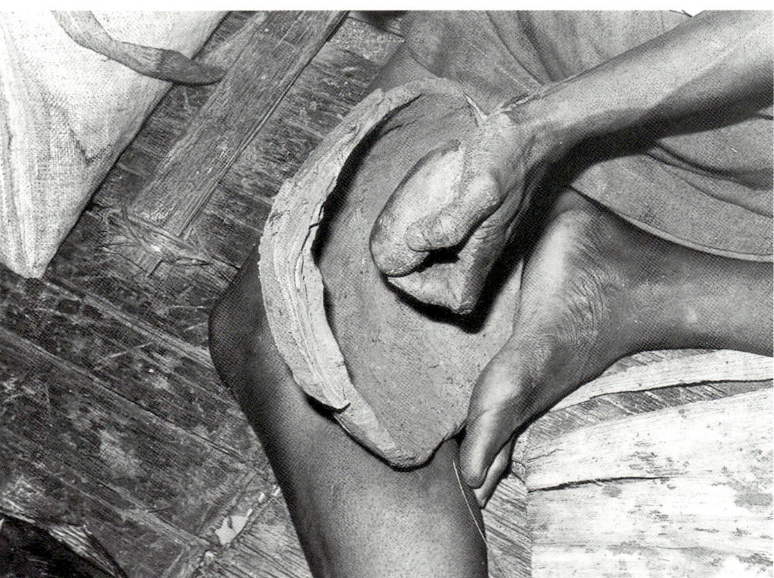

Correlation of forming techniques and tempering practices

A correlation between tempering practices and forming techniques amongst present-day potters in Papua New Guinea and islands in the south-west Pacific has been made by Key (n.d.). He suggests that potters who use the paddle-and-anvil technique use tempered clay while those who use the coiling technique use untempered clay. Evidence gathered by the authors supports this to a certain extent only. There are two coiling groups known who do add sand (river sand), namely Dimiri and Swagup in the Sepik. Unfortunately, no clay or temper samples from here have been tested but Kaufmann (1972) reports that the Swagup clay is very 'fat'. Of the pure paddle-and-anvil potters only one group, Sio-Gitua, does not add sand but there are many potters who use mixed techniques, combining coils, slices or slabs with paddle-and-anvil: some of them add temper and some do not. Further, Rye and Tuckson (in preparation) conclude that there is no technical reason why different techniques should need different tempering. Therefore, it is possible that the partial correlation observed between technique and tempering is due instead to varying cultural-traditional origins. Alternatively, it could be environmental: coastal people have easy access to sand and finer clay while those who inhabit alluvial valleys use coarser clay.

Archaeologists have been attempting to make similar correlations for prehistoric pots and sherds but only certain aspects of the pot and the pot making process are preserved. Key used a petrological microscope to observe sherd texture and so identify the temper used by prehistoric potters. He worked on the assumption that added tempers are usually 'well sorted' (even) sand-sized particles whereas natural non-plastics are 'poorly sorted' and usually have a higher proportion of sand and silt. He proposed that, by observing the size of temper particles in a sherd, it can be determined whether the pot was made from tempered or untempered clay. He could then deduce from this whether it was made by the coiling or paddle-and-anvil technique.

More recently, Rye (1977) has shown that X-ray examination of sherds can provide direct evidence of forming methods by revealing preferred orientations of mineral grains, voids and other inclusions in the sherds, which result from different characteristic pressures applied to the clay in different forming techniques. Thus, by knowing present-day pot making techniques and studying X-rays of contemporary pots, comparisons can be made with prehistoric sherds.

Decoration

Some pots are decorated while still damp or, at least, after only a short drying period. The applied

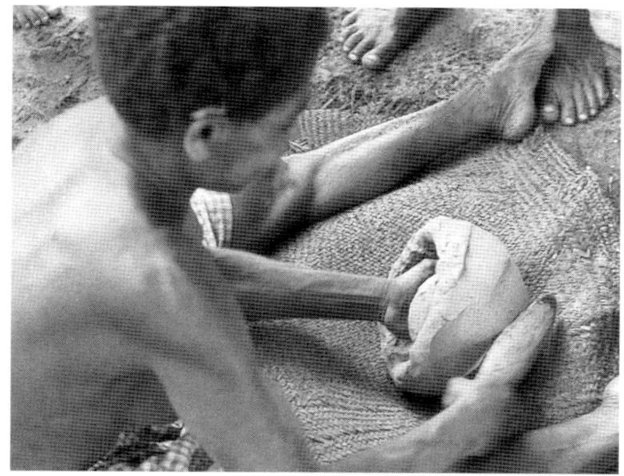

Fig. 2.23
A mat-covered hollow in the sand in which the pot is supported while being formed and dried. Regina Teraku of Kaiep village, East Sepik Province, is the potter.

decorations of Aibom and the Azera, the coil marking of inland Madang, the combing of Milne Bay Province, the incising of Wanigela, Vanimo, Kaiep and the Bilbil group are all carried out at this stage.

The only decoration completed during construction of the vessel is the type of finger drag technique used on cooking and storage pots at Paliama and other Boiken and Abelam villages. The gouging and carving of the Sawos, plains Boiken, Abelam and Washkuk groups must be done at the firm, leather-hard stage of drying.

Many pre-wheel potters use a polishing technique known as burnishing; it is usually carried out on the leather-hard clay when the pot is firm enough and the surface not sticky. A mirror shine can be achieved by rubbing vigorously with a round, hard object. Papua New Guinea potters use either a smooth pebble, the back of a shell, a piece of coconut shell or a large seed from the matchbox bean, *Entada phaseoloides*. This achieves a smooth, attractive surface, practical for eating or serving, and it also seals the surface to some extent. Reche (1913) mistook, it seems, the burnishing of Koiwat-Kamanggaui eating bowls for fine-grained slip which he thought had been applied with the fingers or a spatula, the strokes pointing nearly always from the bottom up towards the rim. Burnishing is easier and so more frequently carried out on a non-sandy or pebbly clay but a polish of some sort can be achieved on any clay (fig. 9.27).

Firing

All pots must be thoroughly dried before firing. Some are put in the sun: this seems a drastic measure but the high humidity in Papua New Guinea is probably the reason it is possible (sun combined with a dry wind would almost certainly cause drying cracks). Many potters dry their ware under the house or on the floor or shelves inside the house. In Lumi and inland Madang the pots are bound in split cane and hung from the rafters of the houses. Here they become smoked which is believed to strengthen them. In most cases the pot remains supported on the ring-cushion during drying. The length of time considered necessary for the pots to become dry enough for firing varies from a few days to several months. Many pot makers will only fire their pots during the dry season (fig. 9.55).

All firing of pots in Papua New Guinea is done in open fires (bonfires) and it is very rapid. It takes place on the ground in or near the village or on the beach. There is some variation in the methods of forming the fire but in nearly all cases there is fuel both underneath and over the top of the pot or pots. One or two long sticks are used to move pots in the fire and to remove them when the firing is finished.

Some potters preheat their vessels before firing mostly by holding burning fronds inside the pot or by placing them on a low fire before transferring them to the main fire when almost too hot to hold. At Buka Island pots are set around the fire to warm, with their thicker bases towards the heat. These precautions enable the water, and consequently the steam to escape more slowly limiting the risk of bursting or cracking in the early stages

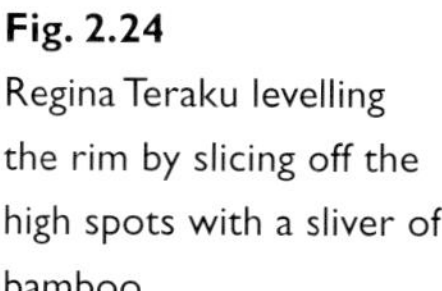

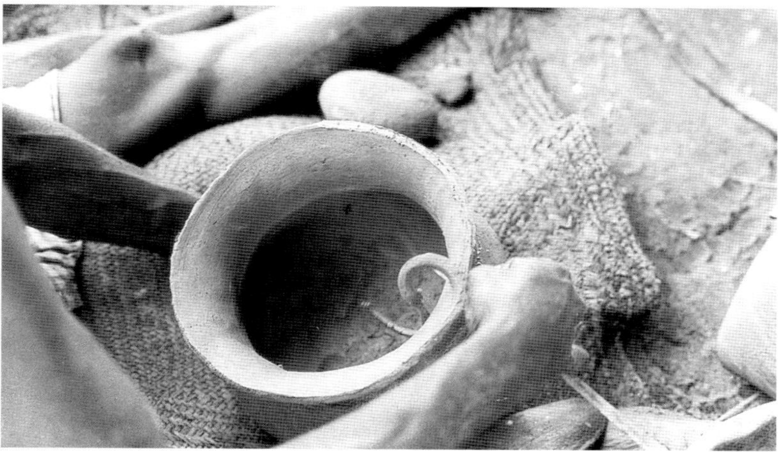

Fig. 2.24
Regina Teraku levelling the rim by slicing off the high spots with a sliver of bamboo.

Fig. 2.25
Repairing a crack by overlapping and beating, Tumleo Island, West Sepik Province.

Fig. 2.26
Beating strips of clay into thin areas of the walls, Tumleo Island, West Sepik Province.

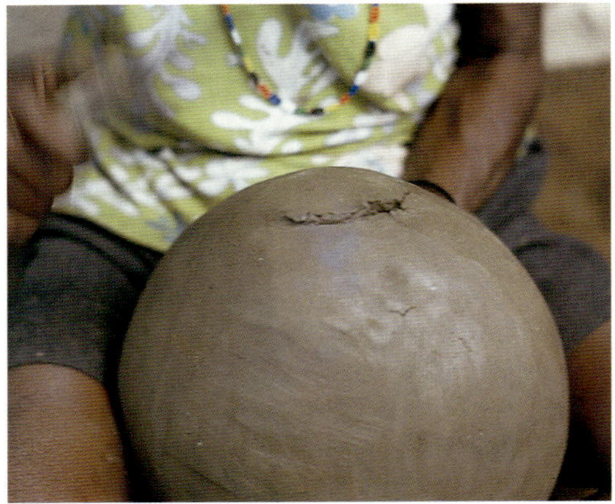

Fig. 2.25

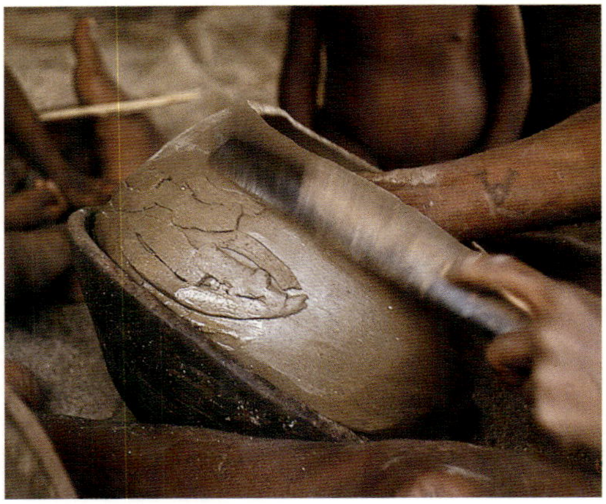

Fig. 2.26

of firing. Fine hair cracks over the surface of pots can also form if the firing is too rapid. The most interesting and practical method of preheating, observed at Ali village in the Lumi area, is to construct the firing platform over a recently used cooking fire; the pots are gradually warmed before the fire ignites. These low-heat preliminary firings deposit soot on the surface of the pot so it is often said that the pots are blackened first rather than preheated. But the blackening has no functional significance since the carbon is mostly burned away when the main fire reaches 600°C.

In many groups no preheating is carried out and at a village in the Ham group of inland Madang the fire is lit at the top of the structure and the pot plunged straight into the flames. These different treatments must have evolved through trial and error, the potters discovering what their own particular clays could withstand (fig. 8.29).

Firings have not been observed or recorded in all areas but of those witnessed the most common method is to make a platform of criss-crossed wood on which the pots are placed in rows or in a haphazard pile. The rest of the fuel is leaned against and on top of the pots. In some villages only one pot is fired at a time, as in southern Milne Bay, but more generally from about three to twenty pots will be fired together.

Fuel varies with availability. From research carried out by Lauer (1972, 1974) in the D'Entrecasteaux Islands, it seems that sago fronds have a higher combustion rate than split logs. Split timber is used in conjunction with sago or coconut fronds in most areas. Details of the particular fuel used and of the construction of fires will be found in the description of each area.

The duration of firings is fairly uniform; on nearly all occasions when firings were timed they lasted only about half an hour. Lauer, however, reports some firings on Goodenough Island which lasted only ten minutes: if further fuel was added it prolonged the firing up to forty minutes. The Azera

Fig. 2.27

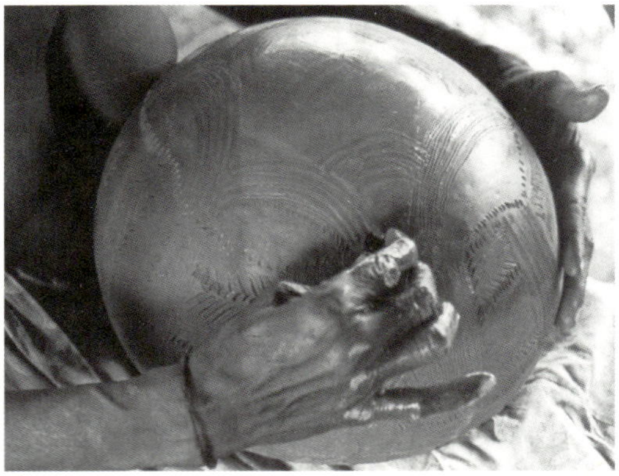

Fig. 2.28

Fig. 2.27
Lydia decorating with a shell on a still wet surface, Wanigela, Northern Province.

Fig. 2.28
Bangamali incising into the leather-hard clay with a flying fox bone, Saragum village, inland Sepik.

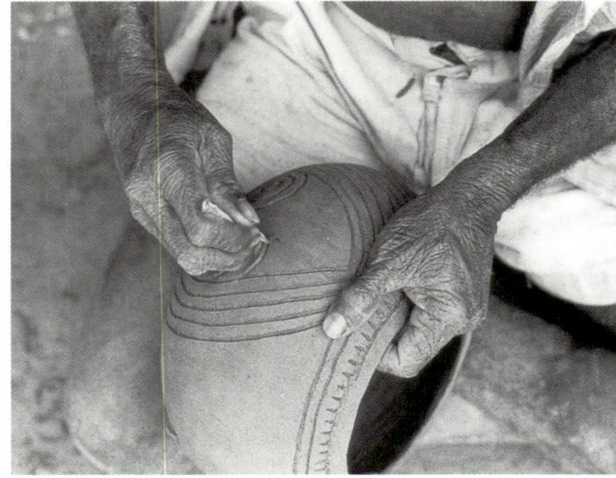

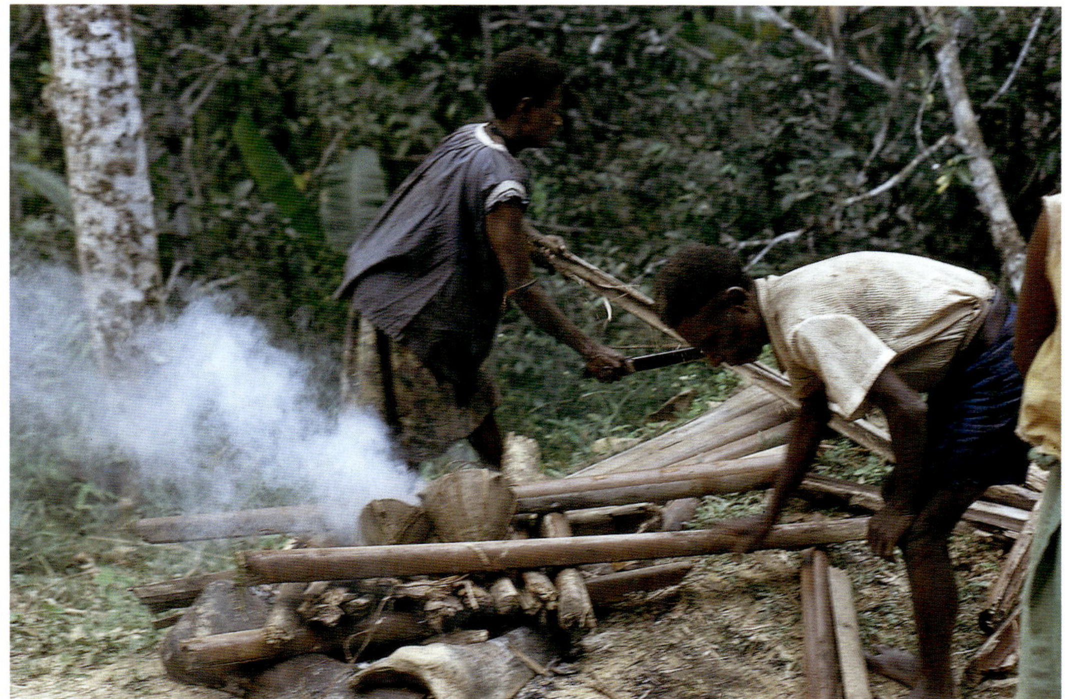

Fig. 2.29
Preheating by firing over a recent cooking fire, the 'pangal' begins to smoulder. The potter, Telefi, and his wife firing at Ali village, Lumi, West Sepik Province.

potters fire their wares for about an hour. At Meno, Kaufmann (1972) reports pots being left in a fire for over two hours, although the peak temperature is reached within ten or twenty minutes. The fine clay eating bowls of Koiwat are also fired very rapidly: a firing filmed by Kaufmann (1974) took only fifteen minutes. The Koiwat clay has only an average proportion of non-plastics, mostly of fine sand fraction, and the surface is compacted by burnishing inside and out; this makes such a rapid firing surprising indeed.

Lauer recorded firing temperatures at Goodenough and Amphlett islands with a pyrometer and three thermo couples giving readings from three areas of the fire. (Seger cones are not suitable for temperature readings in open fires.) At Goodenough Island the pyrometer readings showed that usually the temperature rose most quickly and was greatest at the top of a fire; it was more even at the bottom. An amazingly quick rise of temperature was achieved in one of the Goodenough Island firings: to 880°C in four minutes. This was also the highest temperature recorded here and was from one of the ten-minute firings. On the Amphletts the firings recorded by Lauer took longer on the whole: one lasted for thirty minutes, another for fifty-three minutes, and the top temperature here was 918°C, reached in twenty-six minutes. A higher temperature, 926°C, was also recorded in this area. The only other figures available for firings in Papua New Guinea are from Irwin's recent work on Mailu Island (Irwin 1977). His top temperature recording (1018°C) is surprising but was unusual: of seventeen firings monitored in the same manner as Lauer, the next highest was 947°C.

With results from only these two areas it is impossible to say if these are representative temperatures for the country as a whole. The lowest temperature reported by Lauer is about 720°C for two Goodenough Island firings. It is possible that some temperatures lower than this do occur but a temperature of at least 600°C is essential (it needs to be above the temperature at which the particular clay minerals decompose, that is, lose their chemically held water). One mineral present in many Papua New Guinea clays, montmorillonite, decomposes at a temperature of 678°C (Rye 1976). Pots, or parts of pots, fired below these decomposing temperatures could revert to clay if filled with liquid or left in the rain. Pottery fired to a sufficient

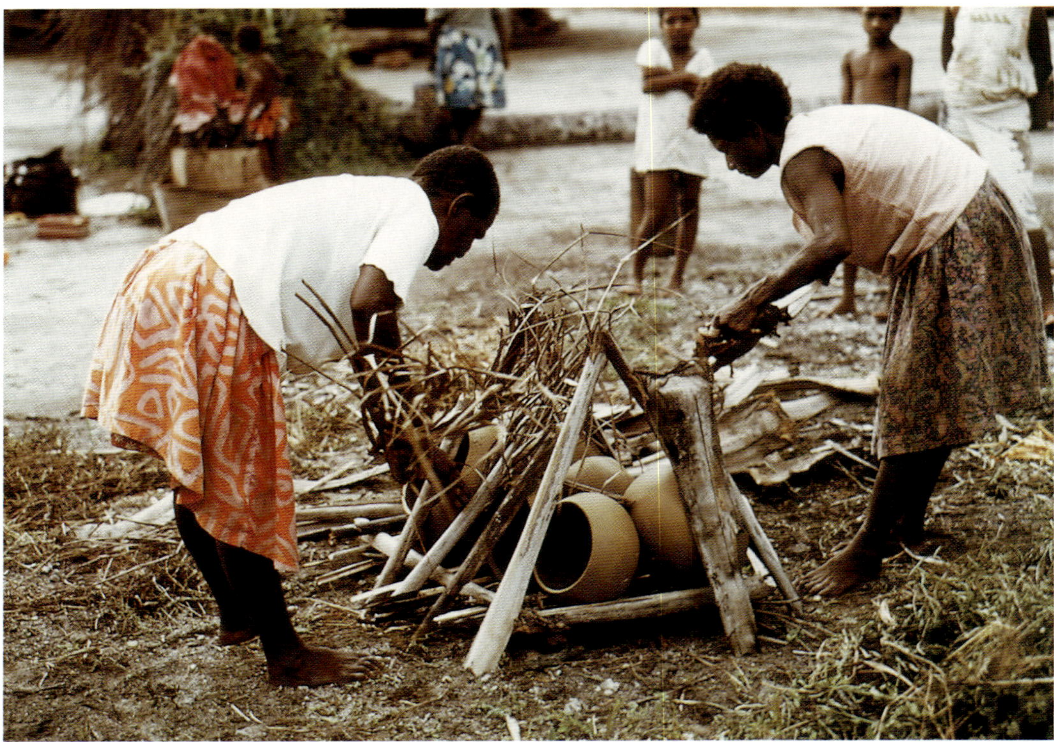

Fig. 2.30
A typical firing construction using coconut palm fronds. The potter, Oma of Vanimo village, West Sepik Province, is helped by friends.

temperature is known to have been buried for thousands of years without disintegrating.

Firing tests carried out on some of the clays collected in the field showed a possible firing range far above the temperatures reached in an open firing. Of thirty-two clays tested the lowest vitrification point was 1100°C; most were 1200-1250°C; three were about 1300°C and one was a surprising 1500°C. As the top temperatures reached in open firings are between 900° and 1000°C there is no risk of over-firing and so distorting the clay. The firing of these Papua New Guinea clays well below their vitrification point is, of course, the reason for their porosity.

The rate of breakage during firings is not known overall but none was witnessed in the fourteen or so firings observed by the authors. Lauer (1972) records that no pots broke in firings during his stay on the Amphlett and Goodenough islands and Irwin reports the same for Mailu Island. On Mailu, Rye also witnessed twelve firings with no breakages.

There are frequent and sudden changes of atmosphere in an open firing so that it fluctuates from oxidising to reducing conditions. Oxidising results when there is sufficient air amongst the fuel; if it is tightly packed or if piles of grass are covering the fire closely there will be reducing conditions. This will result in grey to black areas on the pots, where the ferric oxide content of the clay has been reduced to a lower form. But when full combustion of the fuel is taking place many of these darker patches will be oxidized again and will return to buff or red colours. When the temperature is dropping below 750°C and partly burnt fuel remains in contact with the vessel, localised black and grey areas will appear and are referred to as smudging (Shepard 1965) or carbon inclusion. This is caused by colloidal carbon penetrating the still porous vessel; stable black pigment is deposited, as well as some loose carbon on the surface. On some red clay pots buff yellow patches will show also, caused by a momentary neutral atmosphere. It is difficult to assess the exact causes of these flashings of colour because, although temperatures above 300°C are needed before the reducing gases act on the ferric oxide, it is hard to know, for instance, if a black area on a pot is due to reduction or to smudging. It is suggested that if it is solidly black in colour it is smudging. During a firing many factors affect the colours produced from the several different forms of iron oxides: these, along with other aspects of pre-wheel pottery, are discussed in Shepard (1965).

Most Papua New Guinea potters prefer their pots to be unblemished by these uneven patches and often turn their pots over in the still-hot remains of the fire: a red glow combined with air helps eliminate the patches. They also understand the necessity for quickly removing the pots from the fire, before the temperature drops too far and causes smudging (fig. 2.32).

Pueblo potters of America and others deliberately create black pots by controlling the formation of carbon. Some broken pots show a black or grey core. This arises in rapid, low temperature firings where there is not enough time or heat for either an earlier reduced area to be re-oxidised or for carbonaceous material to burn out.

How long do the low-fired pots last? They are, of course, fragile and easily broken if knocked or dropped but the people, even children, are accustomed to handling them with care and so they can be in use for many years. At Tubetube Island it was said that people replace their cooking pots after three or four years because food tastes better in a newer one; old pots are used for soaking clay. On Mailu Island the people say they only use the cooking pots for about three months.

Sealing and painting

Potters using low temperature, open-fired processes use a wide variety of vegetable materials to finish the surface of their pots after firing. Generally, the pores are sealed only temporarily; use in cooking and storing in a smoky environment will eventually seal the pots further. These sealing coats are not glazes, which are coatings of glass-forming materials that have to be subjected to the appropriate heat to melt them and form permanent impervious surfaces on the pots. There are combinations of materials which would do this at bonfire temperatures but the results would not be satisfactory since remaining fuel and grit would become embedded in the glaze as it solidified on cooling.

Traditionally, no glazes appear to have been tried in Papua New Guinea but several different sealers are used. They are usually applied immediately after

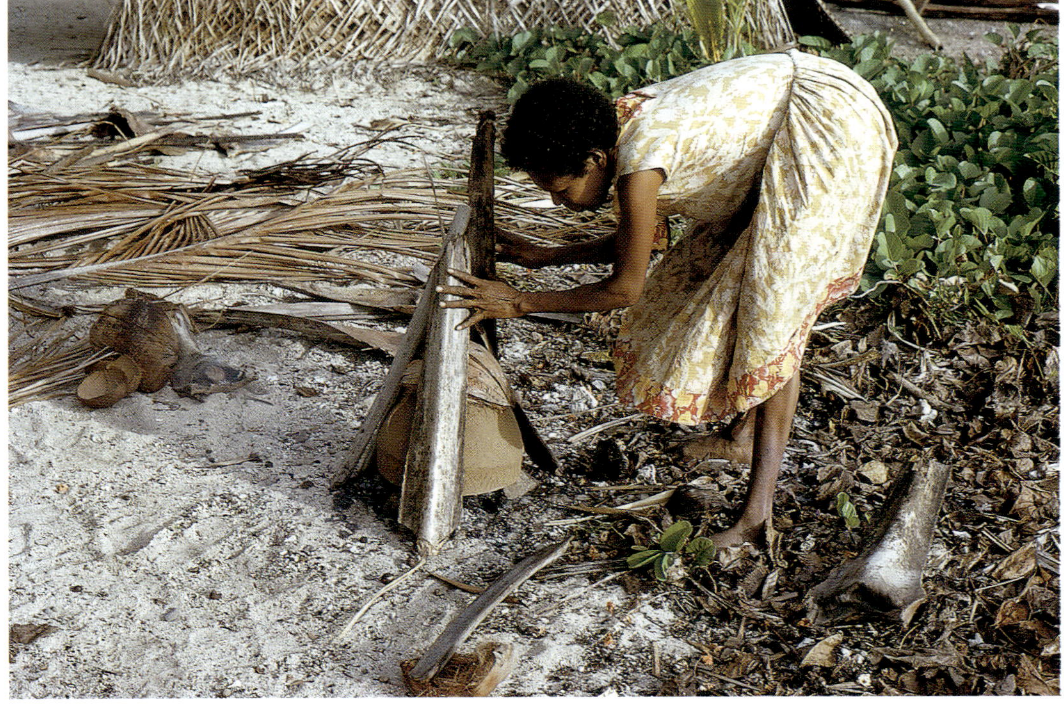

Fig. 2.31
Deidi firing a single pot on Tubetube Island, Milne Bay Province.

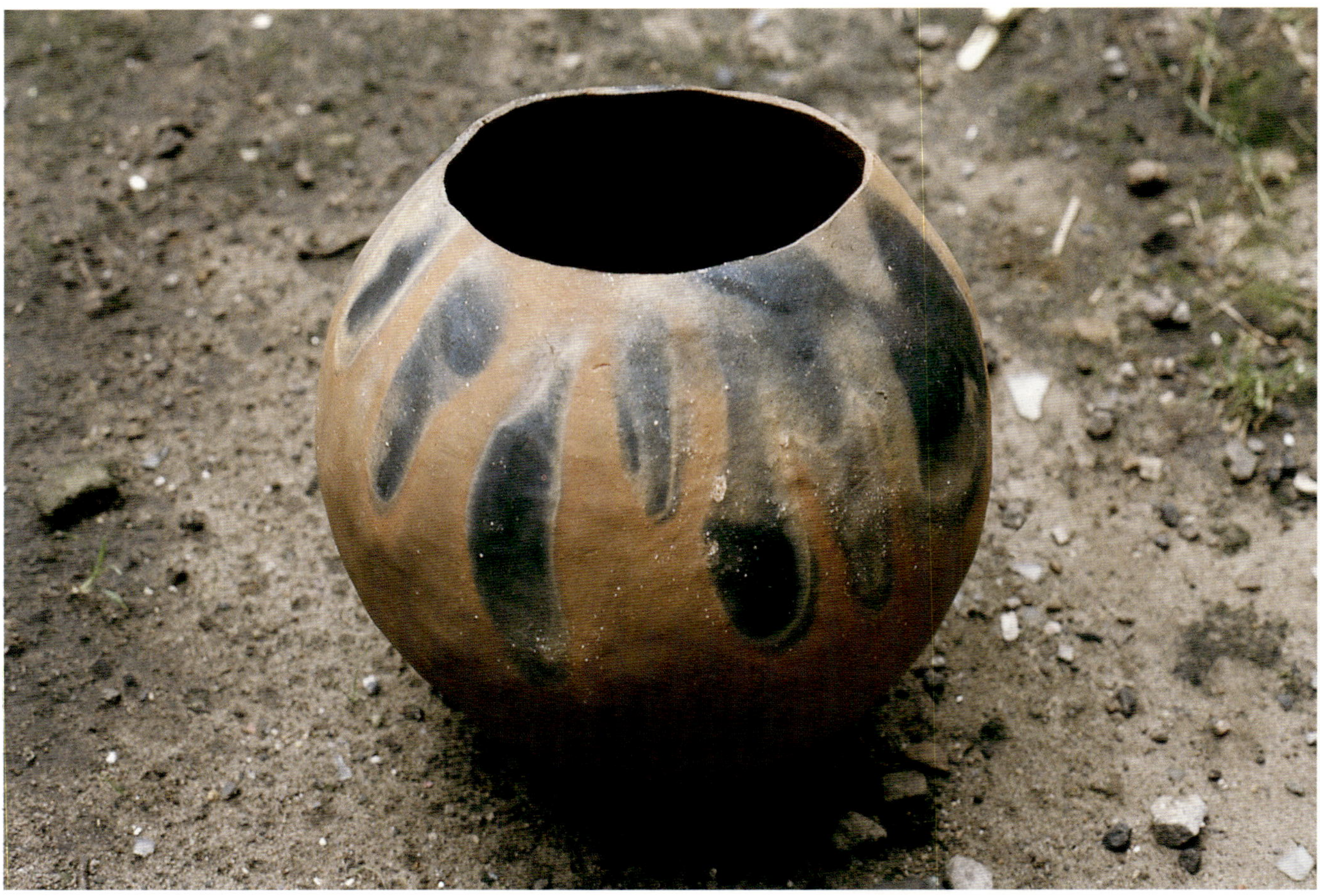

Fig. 2.32
Pila cooking vessel showing reduction and smudging marks, Yambiyambi, Madang Province.

firing. The most common sealer is sago solution. Sago flour, produced from the trunk of the sago palm, is stirred with boiling water to make a solution similar to, but thinner than, that of sago porridge. It is splashed over the pots with a bunch of leaves or the husk of a coconut, leaving the pots shiny and richer in colour. In some cases, pots which would not seem to need sealing are coated with sago: the big fire hearths made at Aibom, for example, are seen glowing and shining from the treatment although fire would burn off the sealing the first time the hearth was used. Perhaps this is just to impress trading partners (fig. 2.33).

At Kaiep village, on the northern coast, young green pawpaws are boiled in new cooking pots before they are used, the pectin forming a sticky coating. In the past Motu potters and Alu Island potters rubbed the inside surface of banana skins or leaves of native passion vines on the hot pots. The Nasioi potters of Bougainville and the potters of the Admiralty Islands rub the split-open fruit of the putty nut tree, *Maranthes* (*Parinari*) *corymbosa* over the cooling surface to make it stronger. This also stains the pot an uneven brown colour. In some parts of the Solomons, after sealing with the putty nut a short extra heating is necessary to eliminate its toxic effect. This should not be mistaken for a second firing.

The sealing of pots is often seen also as a test. Some people use the new pot to cook vegetable scraps which are fed to the pigs. If the pot does not crack and holds liquids satisfactorily it is ready for use and can be traded or sold. Markham Valley potters appear to be especially fussy about this testing; they insist that a pot must be tried two or three times. Boiling water from an old pot is poured into a new one and yam, bananas and other vegetables are boiled to almost nothing, leaving the pot sealed.

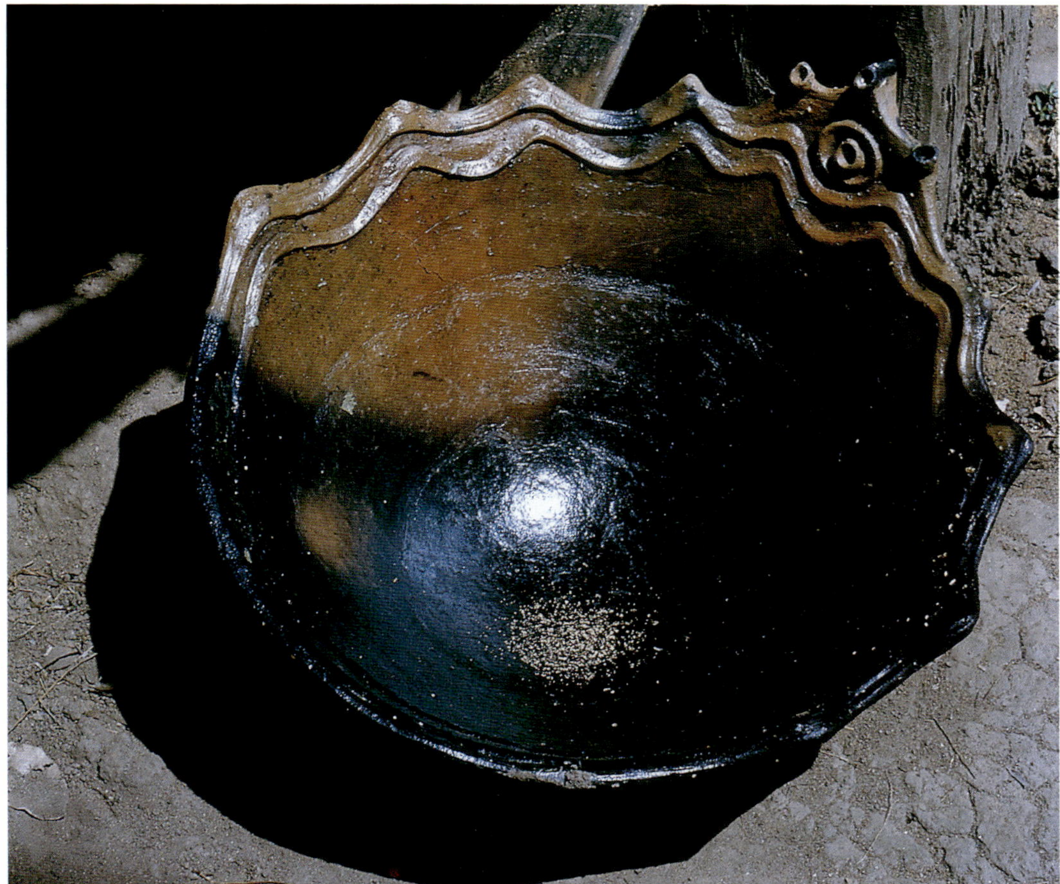

Fig. 2.33
A recently fired hearth still shiny from application of sago starch solution, Aibom village, Sepik River.

In Milne Bay Province, a small amount of oily coconut milk is boiled and swirled around inside the pot before it is traded.

Pots for carrying and storing water do not need to be sealed; the seeping of the water through the porous walls keeps it cool. A Manus Island man now living and working in Port Moresby recalled that he has not had such a pleasant cool drink of water since the days when he drank from the family water pot. At Yabob-Bilbil, however, water pots are sealed with sago solution or tree resin. Here also is the only case of a clay slip application on the pots (discussed in more detail in Chapter 8) before firing; this helps seal the surface. In Fiji, a much shinier, solid looking coating than any in Papua New Guinea is achieved by rubbing the gum of the kauri tree on the hot pot after firing.

Except at Buin, the only colour used by the potters of Papua New Guinea as decoration is that painted on the pots after firing. The traditional colour range is limited to yellows, reds, white, black and, in a few cases, grey. The main sources for yellows and reds are the iron minerals, magnetite, haematite and limonite, which occur in a variety of rock types and are widely distributed. Haematite and limonite come in hard form, as softer earthy ochres or as the colouring in clays: all three forms can provide pigments. Some potters obtain a brighter red from the red pulp surrounding the seeds of a shrub, *Bixa orellana*, and in the Wosera area the burnt roots of a tree are said to produce a reddish hue. White comes from white clay, soft crushed coral or lime which is usually made by burning shells and is in constant need for betel nut chewing. Black is from charcoal, black earth or clay. Softer materials can be mixed in a half coconut shell or a tin but the harder ones must be rubbed on a wet flat rock to produce the colour. A binder is

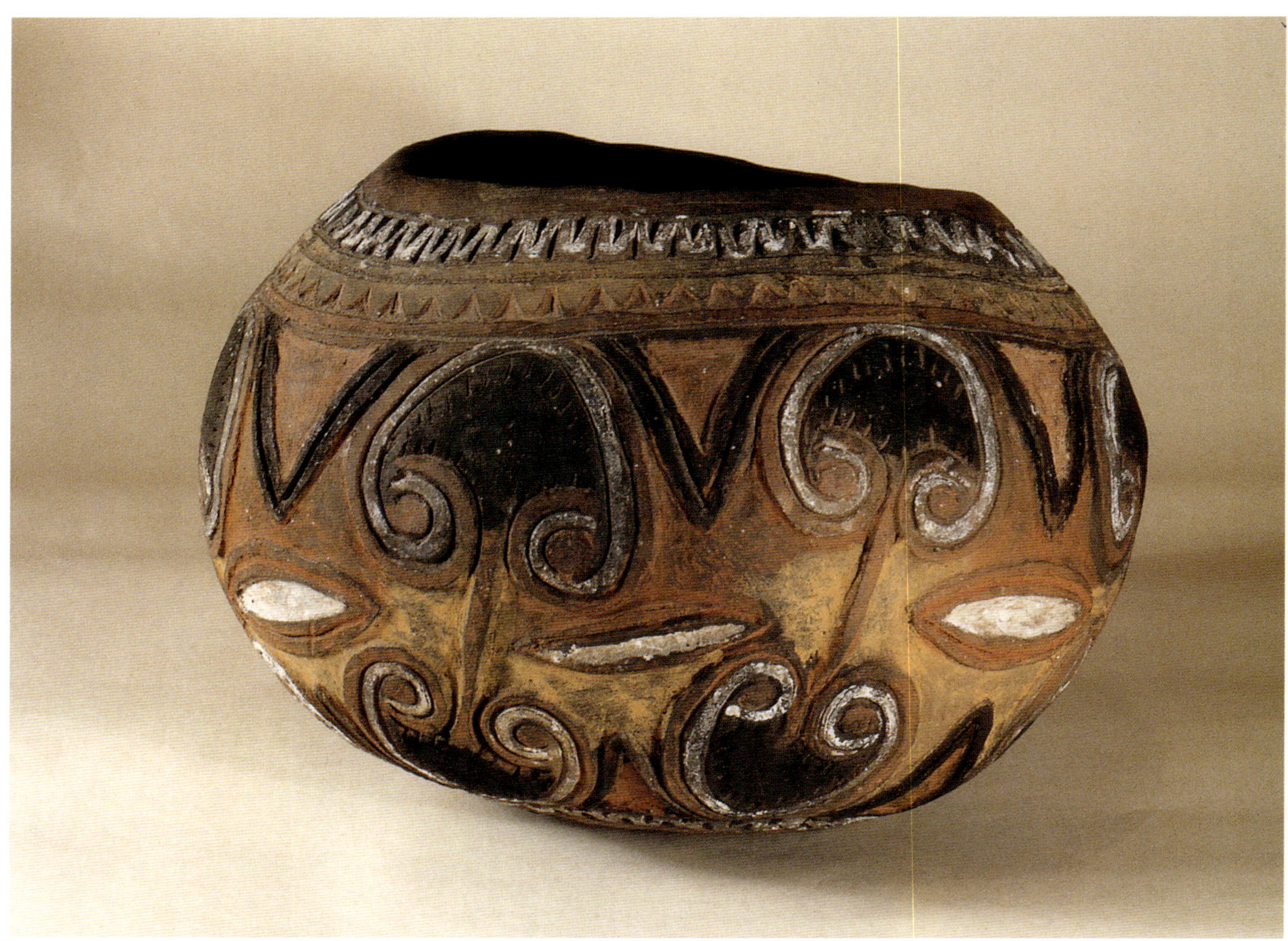

Fig. 2.34
A ceremonial bowl painted with white clay, yellow ochre and red ochre or red paste from seeds, on the fire-blackened surface, Wosera, Inland Sepik.

necessary to hold the paint on the pot and improves the flow of the pigment during application, but it is sometimes dispensed with. Among binders observed in use were the sticky sap of the breadfruit tree which was obtained by slashing the trunk and then mixed with *B. orellana*; the juice of the stem of the 'tanget' *Cordyline fructicosa*, a plant with coloured leaves which are much used for decoration, was mixed with red ochre; and the green leaves from the 'tulip' *Gnetum gnemon*, a tree used for many purposes, were chewed with charcoal and lime by a Yangoru potter and the resulting juice spat out into a half coconut shell. Brushes for the application of pigments are made by fraying or chewing the ends of small sticks or bamboo.

Painted decoration is rare outside the Sepik provinces. At Gitua a few pots are decorated with some pigment in conjunction with strings and feathers tied through holes in the rim but this is probably only for the tourist trade in Lae. Some inland Madang pots with pigment decoration have been found in the highlands. Terrell (1976) reports pots painted before firing at Buin the only exception to the rule. A yellowish-tan slip is applied with a finger.

The Sepik pots, eating bowls and large serving bowls are mostly painted for ceremonial occasions. In all cases the painting is combined with either carved or applied decoration. At Aibom, feast pots and the applied faces on sago storage jars are painted and swirling designs often flow to lower parts of the pot. The house post pots are sometimes elaborately painted. Kwoma ceremonial objects and pots are painted in conjunction with both applied and chip-carved decoration. Sawos, plains

Boiken and Wosera serving and eating bowls are also painted (fig. 2.34).

In the Humboldt Bay area of Irian Jaya large areas of the round pots are swathed in flowing designs painted, mostly in white, directly on the surface of the vessels and not combined with carving or applied decoration, although there can be a small area of incised lines around the rim.

These post-firing colours are of a very temporary nature; even when well held on with a binder they rub or wash off easily or become discoloured from smoke in the houses, dust or mud splashing on them when stored under a house. They must be repainted for use on ceremonial occasions.

In the Motu villages pots are sometimes stained with a dye made by soaking mangrove bark in water which is splashed on the hot pots straight after firing. This turns the buff coloured clay to a patchy dark purply brown colour which becomes more permanent as it soaks into the pores of the clay. In some cases today trade store paints are used but it is very rare to see colours other than the traditional.

The surface appearance of pots can tell much about their treatment during production and use. Newly open-fired pots range from buff colours, like those of the Amphlett Islands, to terracotta, as at Yabob, or dark brown at Kalabu (Abelam). The colours of all fired pots cannot be given because, in many cases, the only samples seen were discoloured from use or storage. Rye (1976) observes, however, that pots made from clay mixed with fresh water fire to a terracotta colour and tend to have distinct changes from red areas to smudged areas while those made with clay mixed with salt water (if fired above 700°C) become a yellowish to whitish colour, although later the surface may become 'scummy' as, for example, with Motu pots. A pot that has not been cooked in but has been kept in

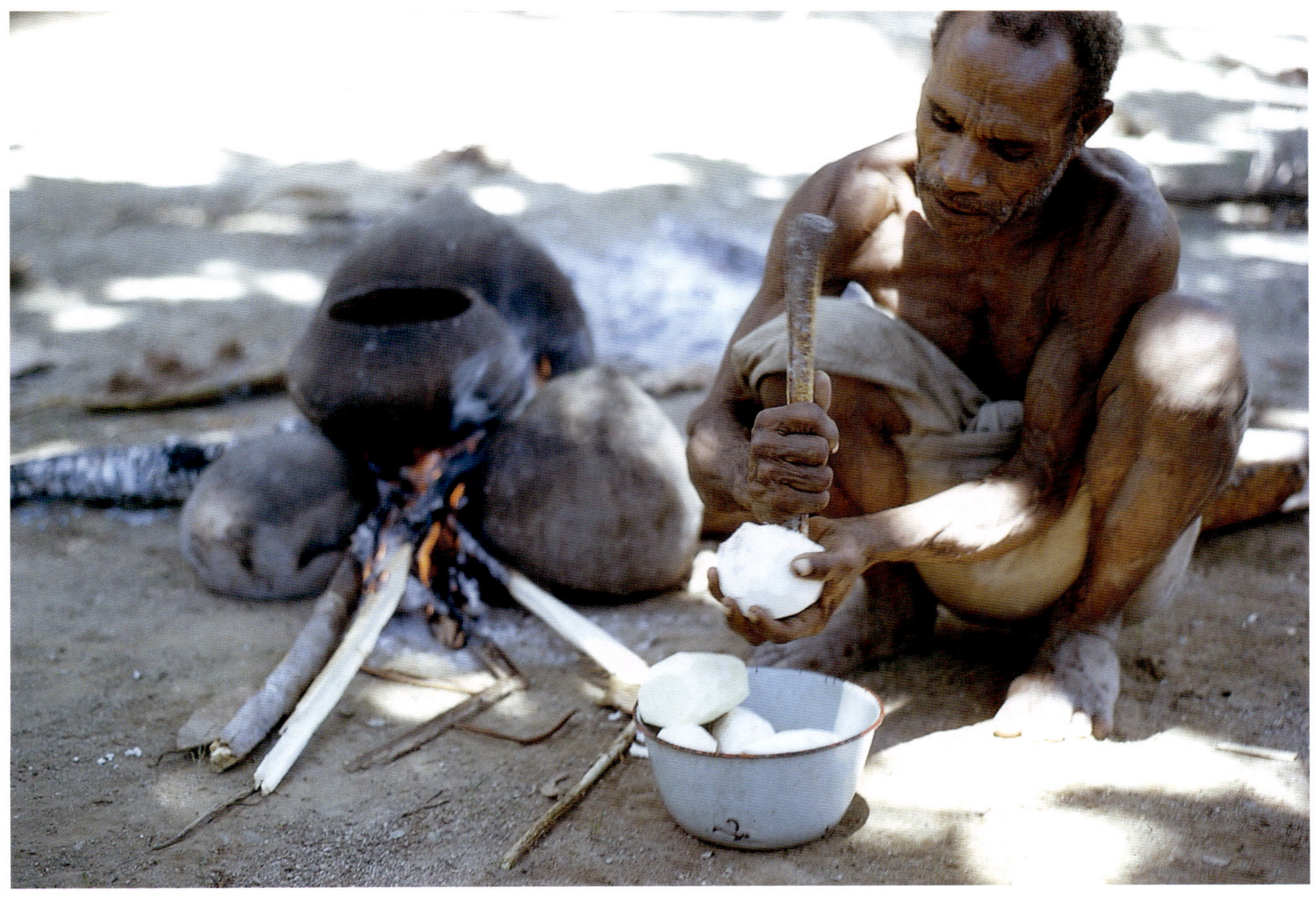

Fig. 2.35
Ham cooking pot in use, supported on three upturned pots, at Buru, Madang Province.

the house for some months will be covered in a deposit of carbon, the result of smoky fires which are kept burning most of the time for cooking, for smoking fish or meat and for discouraging mosquitoes. The black carbon will be either a thin coating or encrusted according to the degree of smokiness and the amount of exposure. It will be all over the pot but thicker either inside or outside depending on whether the pot was upside down or right way up on the rack. In ascribing uses to pots mistakes have been made by assuming that a blackened pot is a cooking pot. Also, early reports of pottery in Papua New Guinea have sometimes referred to certain areas as producing only black pots. A pot that has been used on the cooking fire will be blackened right up the sides but a light greyish colour on the base where the fire has been hot enough (approximately 600°C) to burn off the carbon. Cooking pots are supported over the fire either by three rocks, broken pots or fired clay supports, or by burying the bottom quarter of tall pointed pots in the ashes. Where pots have been stored, for years perhaps, underneath a house they collect dust and rain splashes mud on them. In Soandogum and adjoining villages, where pot making has almost died out and most people now use metal and plastic bowls, the dust of years settles on the deeply carved pots, sometimes giving them the appearance of having been painted a dirty grey colour. If this is washed off, traces of red or yellow ochres often appear.

Over the centuries the potters of Papua New Guinea have come to know their raw materials and evolve their techniques. Through trial and error, intuition and common sense and with no help from advanced technology they have produced wares well suited to their various purposes.

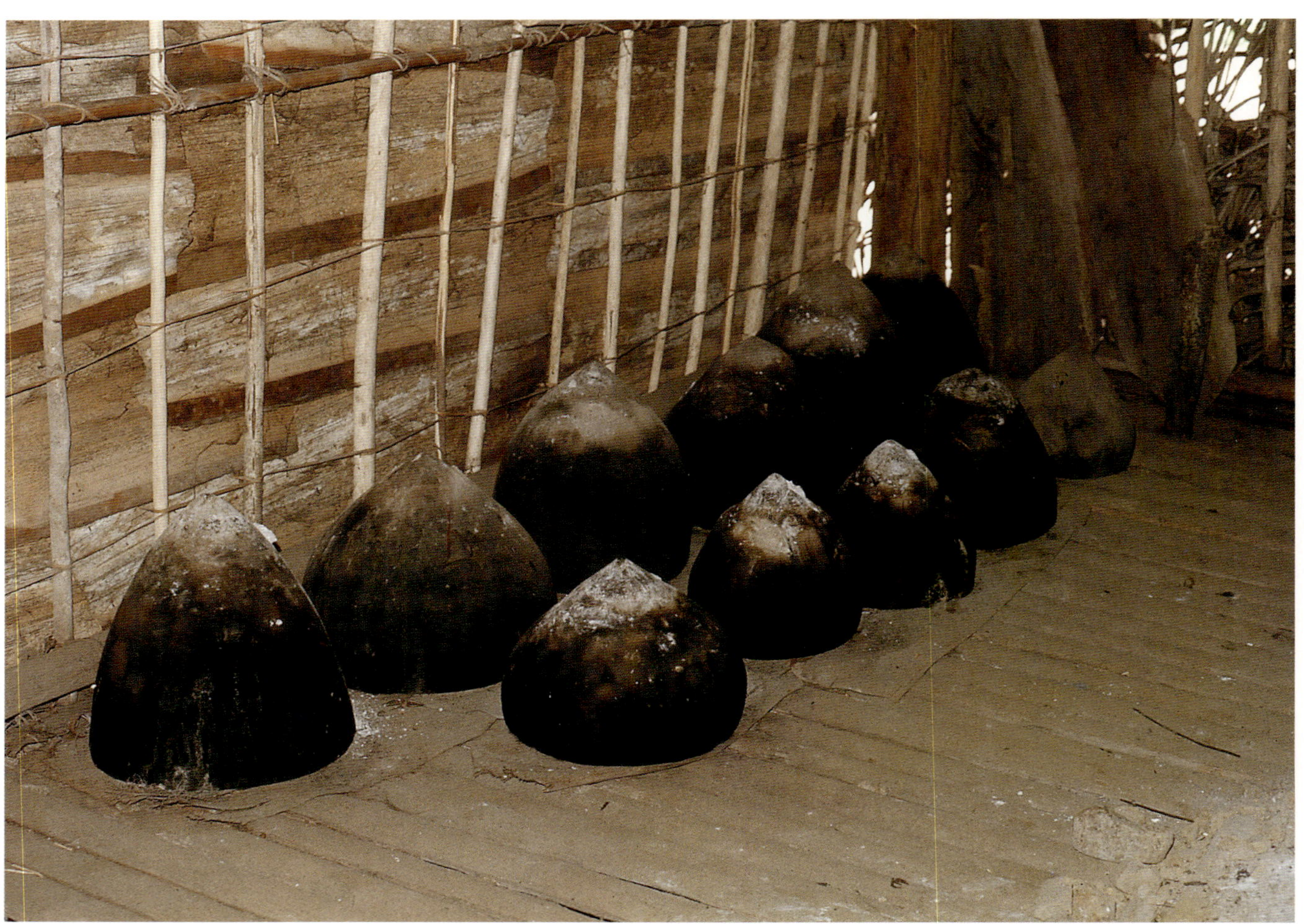

Fig. 2.36
Josephstaal area cooking pots with their bases burnt clean of carbon from the heat of the cooking fire, inside Yavaki's house, Waititangu village, Madang Province.

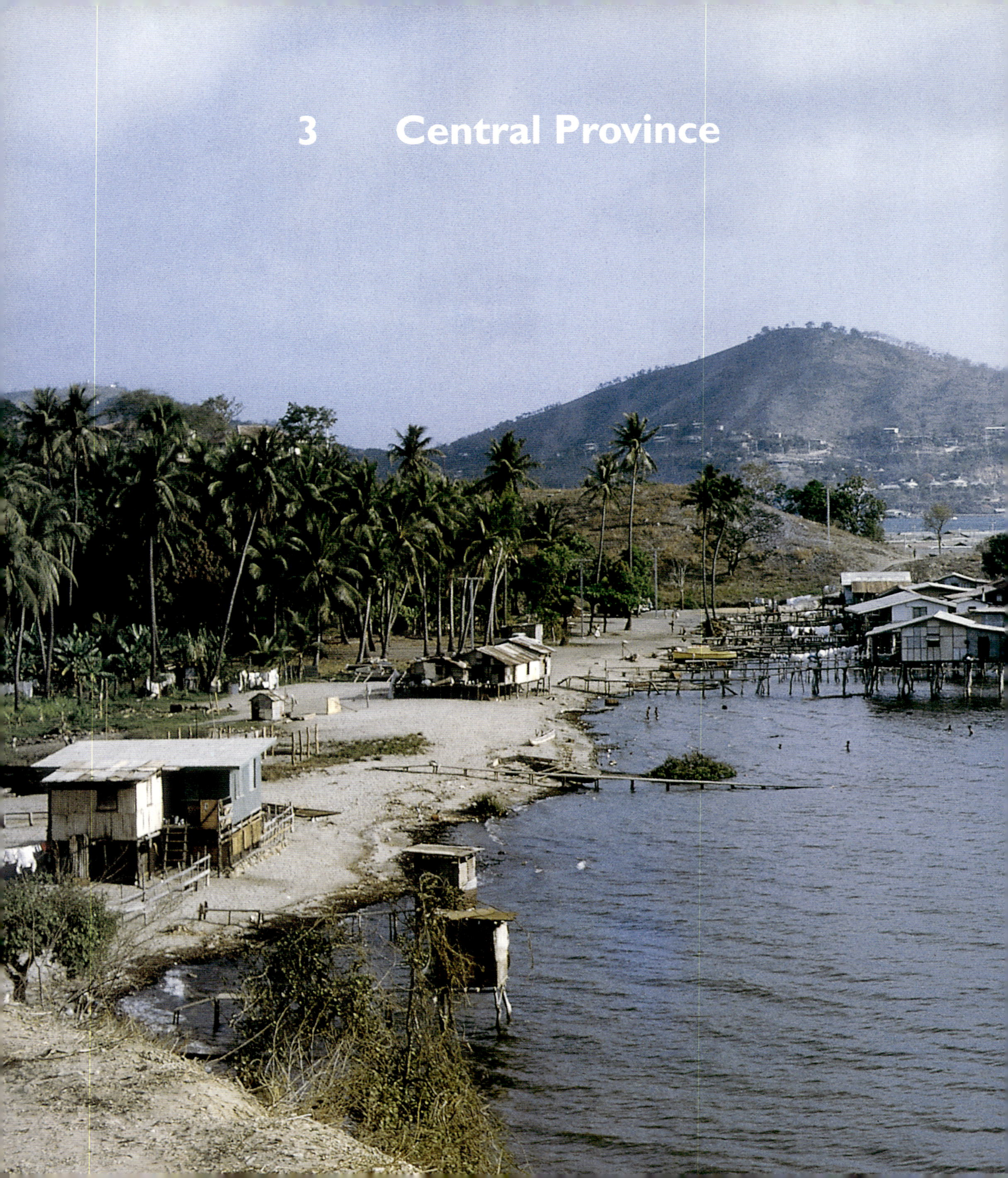

3 Central Province

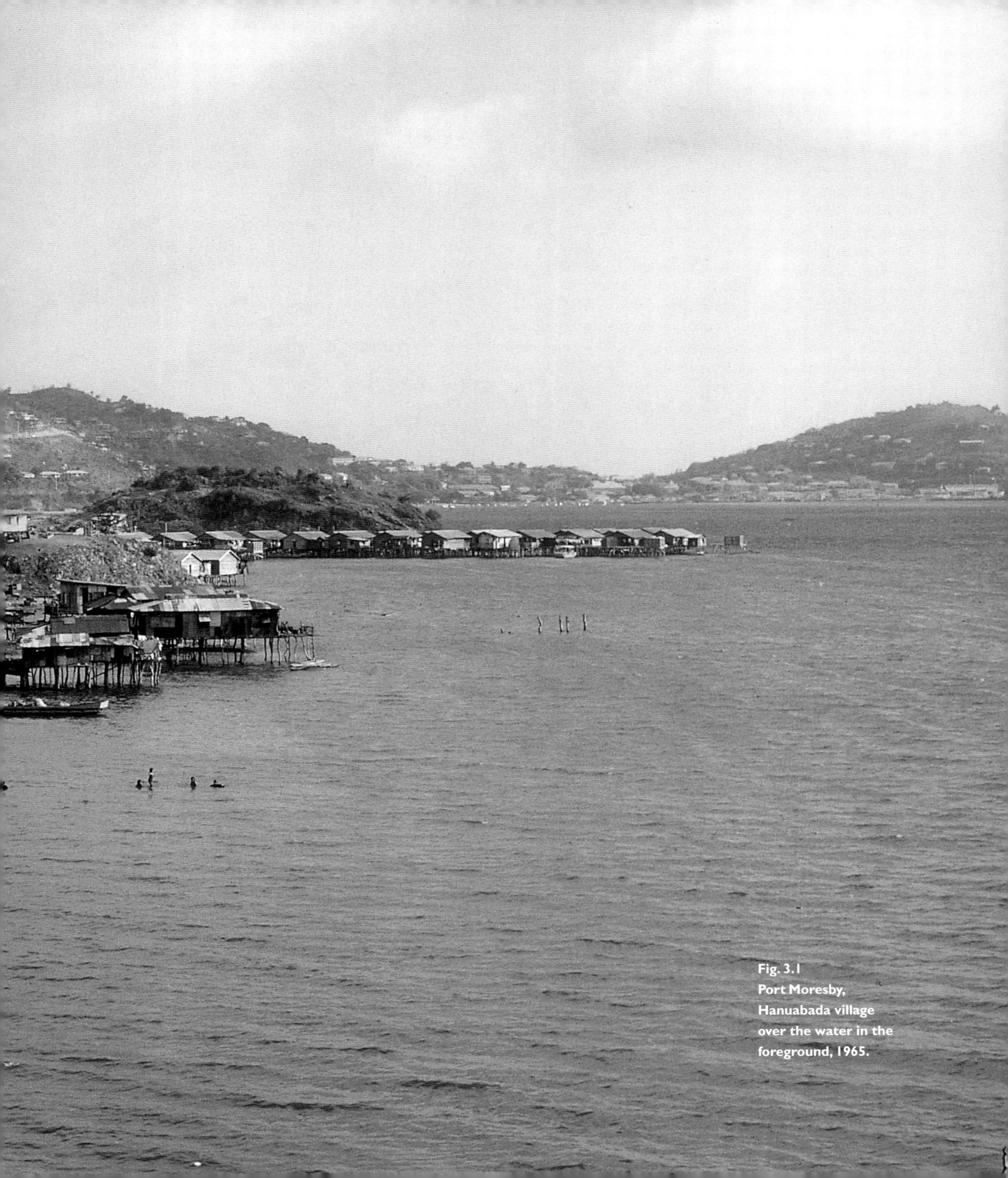

Fig. 3.1
Port Moresby, Hanuabada village over the water in the foreground, 1965.

Central Province is a narrow stretch of land which extends along the south-east coast of the mainland. It is bounded to the north-east by the Northern Province, to the south-east by Milne Bay Province at Orangerie Bay and it extends north-west to the Gulf Province. The main mountain mass is the Owen Stanley Range, which separates the Northern Province from the Central Province and continues out along the tail of Papua to become submerged in the waters of Milne Bay.

The bulk of the population lives in villages along the coast and is a mixture of Austronesian and non-Austronesian speakers. All the pot making groups of Central Province are coastal Austronesians except the Mailu people who live in and around Amazon Bay and speak a non-Austronesian language. For subsistence, the coastal people have their own small gardens and also rely on fishing.

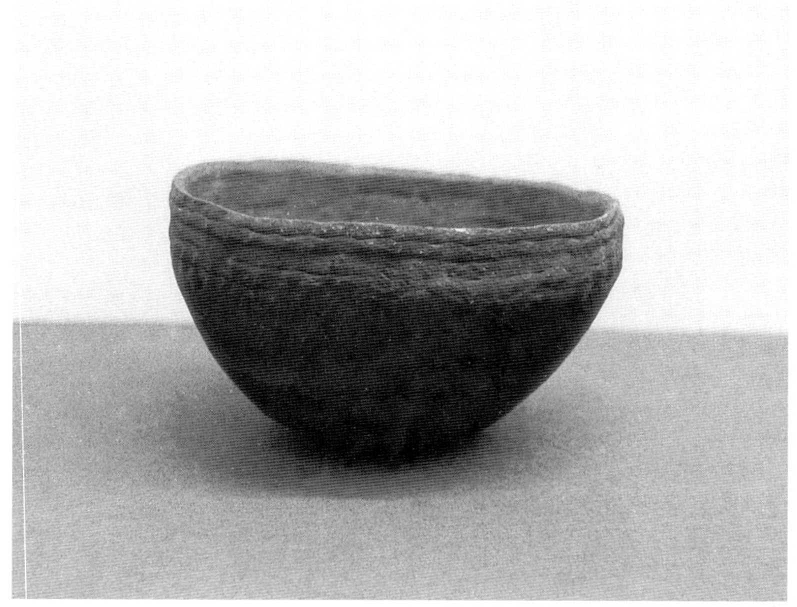

Fig. 3.2
Old bowl with unbonded coils adorning the rim, collected by the *Chevert* Expedition, 1875, at Hall Sound near Yule Island. Possibly made by the inland Hakeko people, *h* 9 cm.

The other people of the province are mostly mountain dwellers who live in small hamlets, growing taro and sweet potato as their staple food; they are non-Austronesian. Trade alliances between the mountain and coastal dwellers are necessary for exchange of commodities. Pottery, shells, shell jewellery and fish were eagerly traded for betel nut, dogs, dogs' teeth, bird feathers, yam and taro from the mountains.

There are, or were, five pottery industries in the province and they are restricted to the coast. The potters are women. The two predominant industries are those of the Mailu people who live on Mailu Island in Amazon Bay and the Motu people who live around Port Moresby. A third industry is the Roro, which is actually an extension of the Motu, and a fourth, a now defunct ancillary to the Motu industry, was that of the Koita people who live adjacent to the Motu. The Mailu potters use the spiral coiling and ring building technique completed by very minimal beating. Although they are located in Central Province their pottery is an extension of the industries of southern Milne Bay. The Motu, Roro, and Koita pots are hand formed, completed by paddle-and-anvil. A fifth industry, that of the Maopa-speaking people of Dorama village in Cloudy Bay, has been reported by various sources including Chalmers (1857) as making pots in the Motu fashion for local consumption. An anthropologist who lived among the Maopa for several years reports that there was in the early 1970s no evidence of a continuing tradition.

An 1894 report by Sir William MacGregor, then Administrator of Papua, claims that pots, 'crude clay dishes', were made by the Hakeko tribe. They lived inland on the Vailala River which empties into the Papuan Gulf between Kerema and Orokolo. A pot, obviously coil made, collected at Hall Sound in 1875 and now at the Macleay Museum, Sydney,

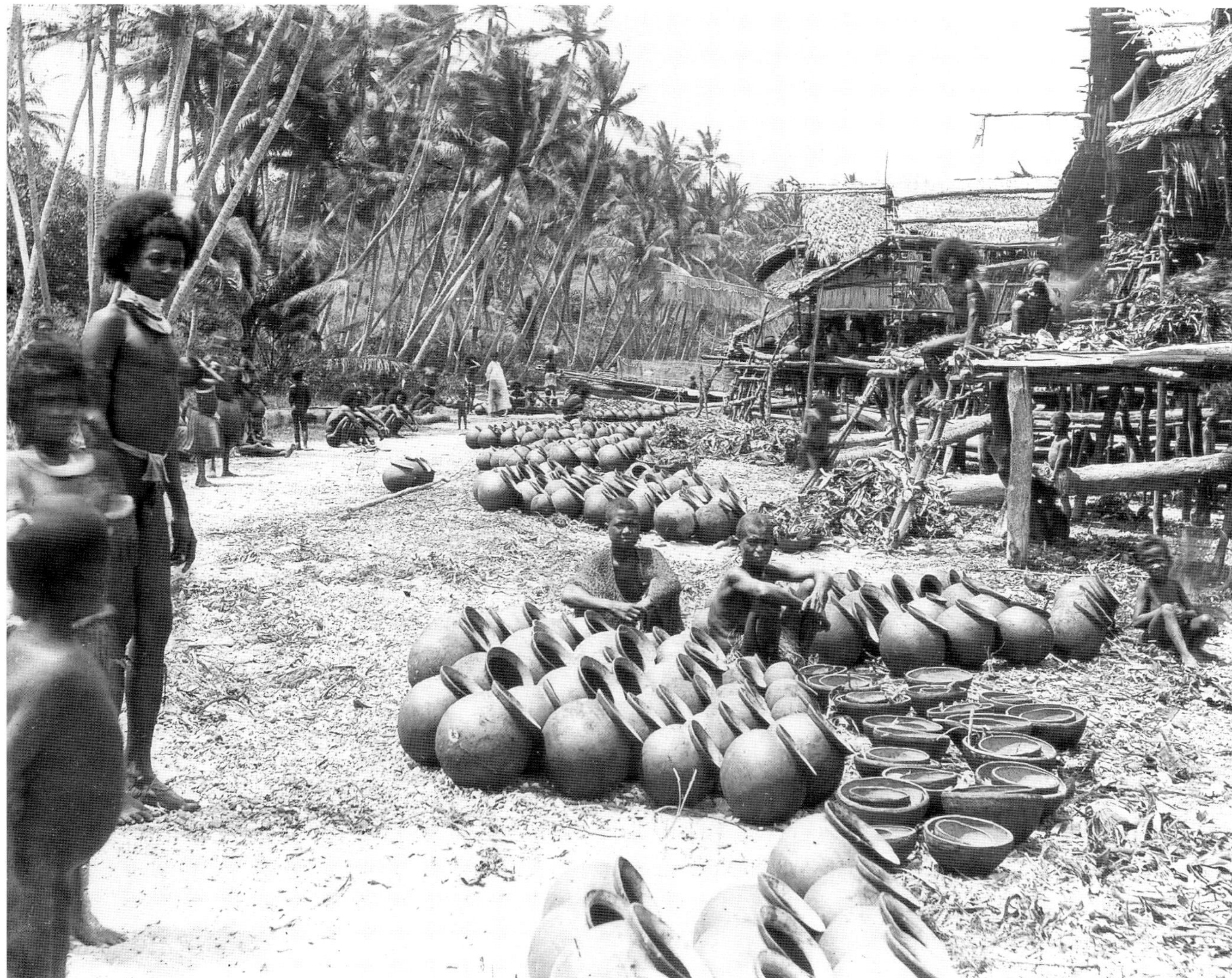

Fig. 3.3
Hundreds of Motu pots on a beach, ready for a *hiri* trading voyage in the late 1800s.

could possibly have been made by the Hakeko. The authors found no other mention of coiled pots in the Central Province (fig. 3.2).

The extensive trade in pots along the south-west coast of Papua, from South Cape to the Gulf area, was conducted predominantly by the Mailu and Motu. The Mailu carried clay pots to South Cape and to the Aroma people to the north-west. The Motu sphere of influence extended south-east to Hood Point and north-west to the Gulf of Papua. The Roro and, at one time, the Koita traded pots to the Gulf area but in a small way when compared to the Motu. There is still occasional trade with traditional partners.

Data on the Mailu people and, fortuitously, on the pottery industry has been recorded by both Malinowski (1915) and Saville (1926). More recently, Irwin, an archaeologist, spent about a year on Mailu Island studying the contemporary pottery industry and its prehistory (Irwin 1977).

Mailu

The Mailu comprise a group of about 5 000 people inhabiting coastal areas between Cape Rodney and Orangerie Bay and speaking Magi, a non-Austronesian language (Dutton 1973). Pottery is made on Mailu Island which is about 8 kilometres to the

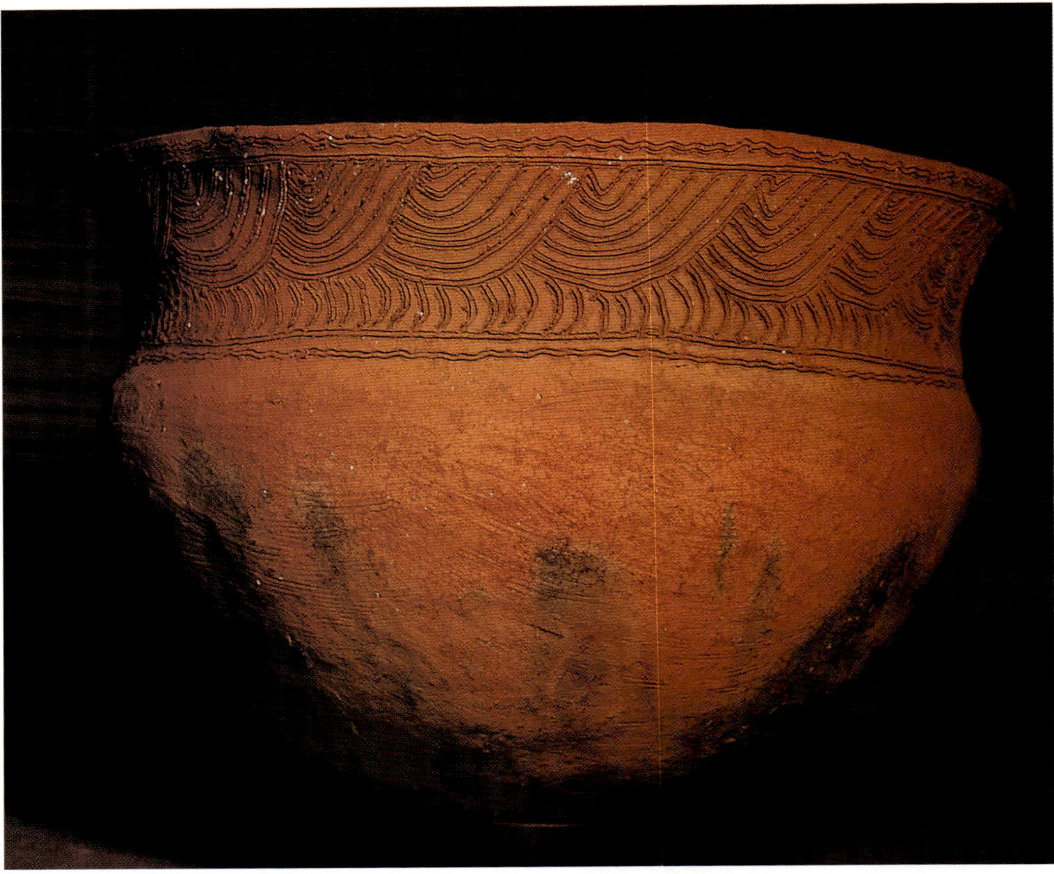

Fig. 3.4
Mailu Island cooking pot, *om, h* 30 cm.

south of Amazon Bay although in the past a small number of Mailu women living along the mainland also used to pot.

In contrast to the denuded and dry hills of the Motu, the Mailu area is lush and the fertile soils yield an abundance of foodstuffs: bananas, taro, sugar cane, yam, sweet potatoes and fruits, and the alluvial flats and swamps provide sago. Plentiful timber supplies wood for canoes that the Mailu men are skilled in making. The sea affords fish, shellfish and shells that are used for trade and personal adornment. The bush supplies small game such as wallabies, bandicoots, bush pigs, birds and cuscus.

On Mailu Island the major vegetable foods are bananas and taro; these are supplemented by fish and game from the mainland. Those villagers that have Mailu Island pots cook in them; others bake in stone or ground ovens. Pots are a popular commodity and, with pacification through government controls and the influence of the missions, the Mailu islanders expanded their trade. Until recently men, women and children used to go on several major trading expeditions each year. The women potters took along clay and made pots on board the canoes during the day, firing them on the beaches at night. In Malinowski's time, although the Mailu people had sufficient food for subsistence and timber for canoes they traded to obtain shells, pigs and betel nut from the Aroma and from exchange partners at South Cape they obtained green axe blades, dogs and such items from the Massim area as bowls from the Trobriand and Woodlark islands. The Aroma had arm shells but the Mailu craftsmen were expert at grinding them down so that they fitted higher up on the arm, which increased their value.

The South Cape area, Bonabona Island and Suau served as clearing houses for goods coming from the D'Entrecasteaux Islands and Mailu. It was

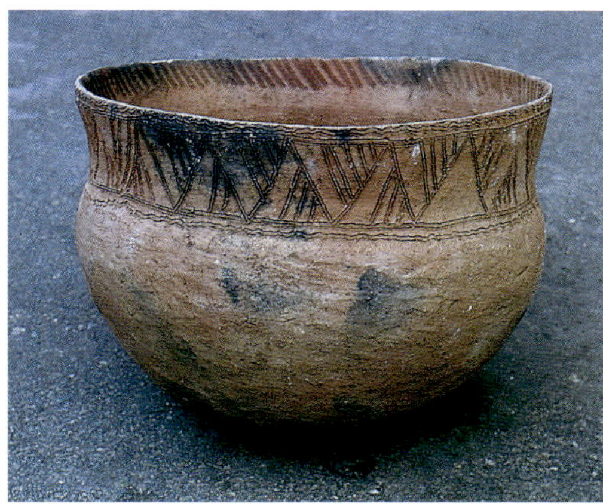

Fig. 3.5
Mailu Island cooking pot, *om*, with the decoration both inside and outside of rim, *h* 22 cm.

through the Suau people that items found their way from Mailu to the Massim and, conversely, especially through an overland route to Mullins Harbour. The hinterland bush area provided bird feathers and bamboo while Bonabona supplied the typical decorated wooden plates of the Massim in return for boars' tusks, shell discs, shell armbands and, of course, clay pots.

Johnston (1974) reports that today pots are transported from Mailu to Margarida, the nearest patrol post, where they are sold or traded to people from the hinterland in return for large string bags of foodstuffs. Although token or hospitality voyages are still taken by Mailu people to the Suau, trade in pots has declined considerably and the mainland people are using mostly aluminium saucepans. Recently, a few Mailu pots have been brought to Port Moresby for sale to the expatriate market. These dramatic red-coloured, boldly decorated and well-shaped vessels are snapped up quickly by discerning buyers.

On Mailu itself, the pottery industry is still active and many pots are in constant use for cooking. There were more than twenty women making pots when Irwin was there. The women gather the heavy black clay from the grass-covered alluvial flats behind the village. Saville reports several taboos concerning the clay and pot making: great care is taken that the clay and the clay pits are in no way polluted by foreign matter such as garbage or liquids from cooking food.

> The diggers themselves ... are very careful never to drop fish bones or coconut milk on the leaves covering the pots when cooking or spill gravy, or let any refuses connected with cooking come near the clay-pit, lest all the pots should crack in making! [Seville 1926: 146]

Taboos apply to making the pots also. The woman potter must not cook, eat or touch food, especially fish, until the pot has been completed.

Tools used in the manufacture of the pottery are rings of twisted banana leaves, called *poni*; half coconut shells used to start the form (rather than the disc-shaped clay turntables employed by some of the Milne Bay potters); a container for salt water; a decorating tool, called *porri*, a comb made of coconut midrib or black palm; and a shell used for scraping and smoothing.

The vessels are all cooking pots, *om*. They are spherical, restricted with everted rims. The only report of pots being used for magic is Malinowski's observation that the Mailu were headhunters and heads were boiled in a pot which was later broken and cast into the sea. The people were not cannibals but smoked and dried the heads after boiling and kept them as trophies.

After the few impurities present are removed the clay, *keedakeeda*, is moistened with salt water only. Saville mentions that sometimes the women submerge the entire load of clay in the sea in order to wet it. Between their hands they prepare a number of sausage-shaped rolls, 2 centimetres in diameter and 40 centimetres long and start coiling with one of these rolls half way up the halved coconut shell. After this the coconut shell is placed on the ring-support and subsequent coils, placed almost perpendicularly, are added to form a pot which is roughly cylindrical in shape. The rings of clay are smoothed and scraped with the palm of the hand and a shell. The shaping of the body of the vessel is achieved by outward pressure on the cylindrical form while scraping. The top portion is slowly pressed out to form an everted, flaring neck and rim area. During this process the pot is kept moist by dipping the fingers and shell into salt water and gently rubbing the surface. While the pot is still wet a two-pronged comb is used to impress decorations along the outside and on the interior rim area. The pot is then dried in the sun, just long enough to harden it a little (figs 3.6, 3.7).

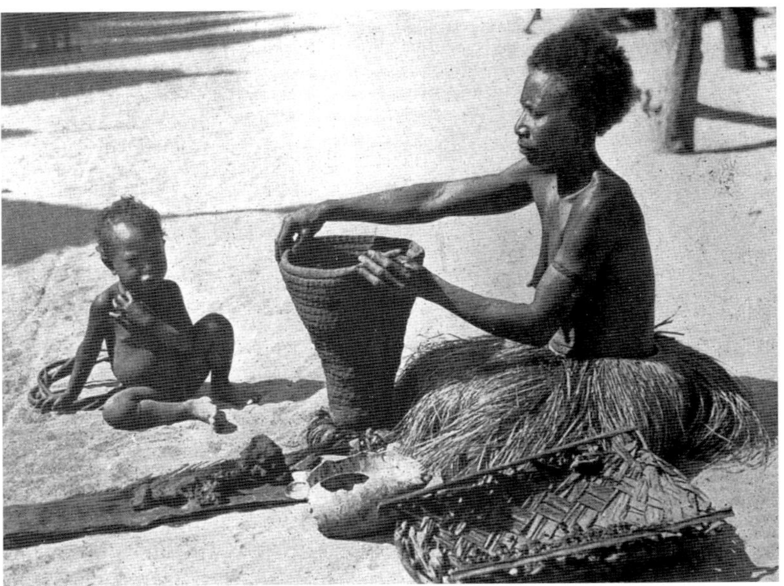

Fig. 3.6
Mailu Island potter, 1921. Coiling when the pot is still a tall cylinder.

Fig. 3.7
Mailu Island potter in 1921. Completing the pot after it has been bellied out.

When firm, the pot is removed from the coconut shell and placed upside down on an old grass skirt. The coils, previously hidden against the inside of the coconut shell, are now smoothed with the thumb pad and then beaten briefly towards the hole remaining in the base. No anvil is used and any piece of wood suffices as a paddle. Irwin (1977) reports a round, flat piece of clay placed over the hole and then bonded and smoothed thoroughly inside and out with the shell. The pot is now put

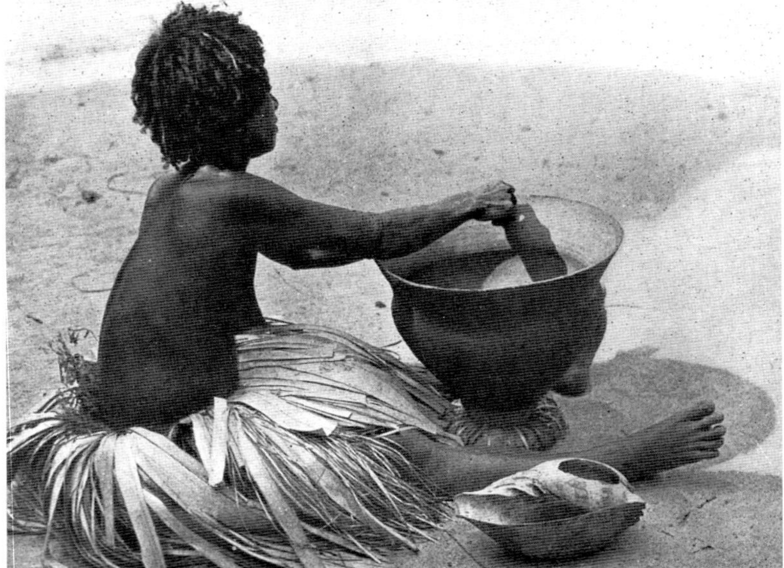

in the sun to dry. The only other instance of a base hole having to be filled when the pot is removed from its support occurs among the Motu potters. They do this by the paddle-and-anvil method and no further clay is added.

According to Irwin, Mailu potters say they can fire pots successfully on the same day but they prefer to leave them to dry for at least another day or two. Saville reports another scraping of the base inside and out, which the potters say is a precaution against cracking during firing. The firing takes place on the foreshore, always in the evening (as at Panaeati) and only when there is a wind to fan the fire. Firstly, however, there is a preheating: burning coconut leaves are tossed inside the vessel until they are consumed and then the base of the pot is held against the fire for about sixty seconds. Irwin describes the rubbing of the base, both inner and outer, at this stage, using the rounded side of a shellfish operculum. Steam produced by the preheating would dampen the clay a little and this action could effectively fill any cracks. These two stages are sometimes carried out twice before firing.

The pots, fired singly, are placed upside down on three rocks in the embers of a fire. Fuel consists of lengths of coconut midribs, some husks and sometimes spathes: thin pieces are placed nearest the pot while the leaf-bases are stacked in pyramid fashion around it. The wide butts are always set at the base, forming a sort of funnel for the flames and so keeping the main heat directly on the pot. The fuel usually needs to be ignited with a bundle of burning coconut leaves. After the pot has been on the fire for about twenty minutes the potter pushes aside the unburnt fuel and lifts the pot off with two sticks: the falling temperature is still as high as 500 to 700°C and sometimes over 800°C. The vessel is left to cool.

Firing tests and observations by Irwin give details of rate of temperature rise, highest temperatures and comparisons of temperatures at different parts of the vessel. He demonstrates the amazing ability of the women potters to control the temperature of their fires by applying extra coconut leaf torches at intervals and by rearrangement and addition of fuel. He shows, too, that at the precise moments when his pyrometer recorded small temperature drops, the potters would remedy this. Also, they were able to

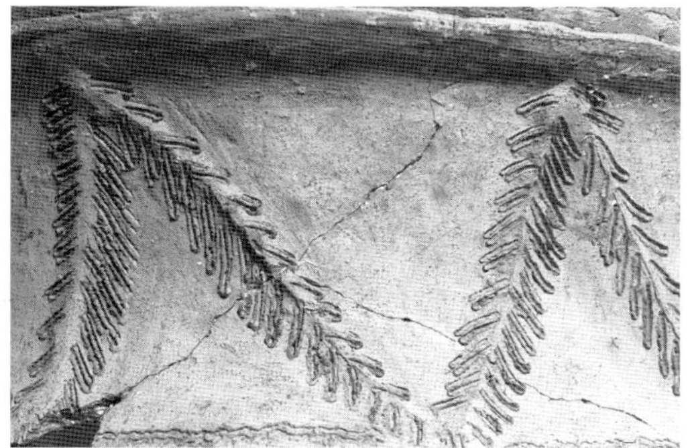
Fig. 3.8

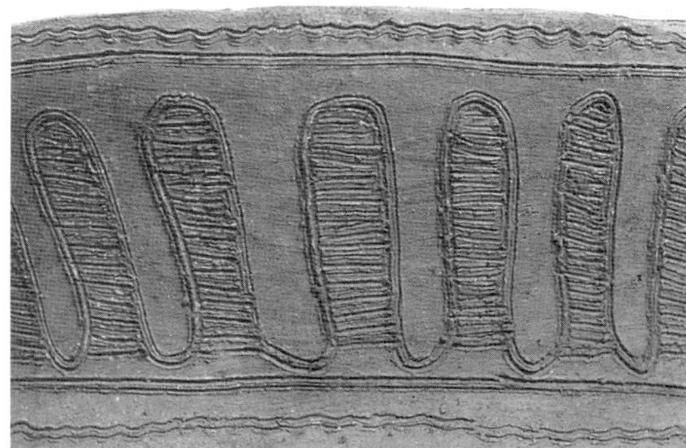
Fig. 3.9

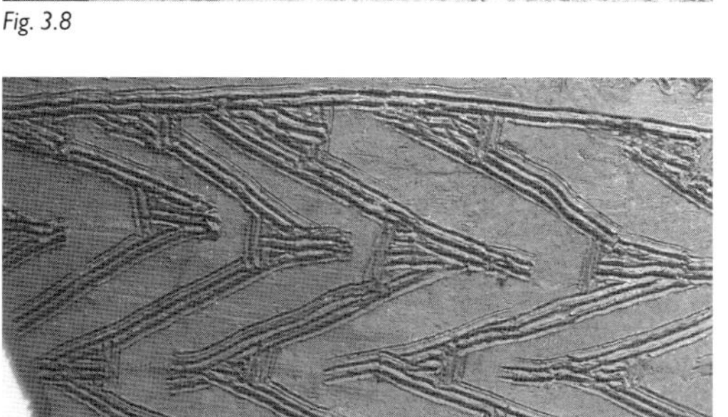
Fig. 3.10

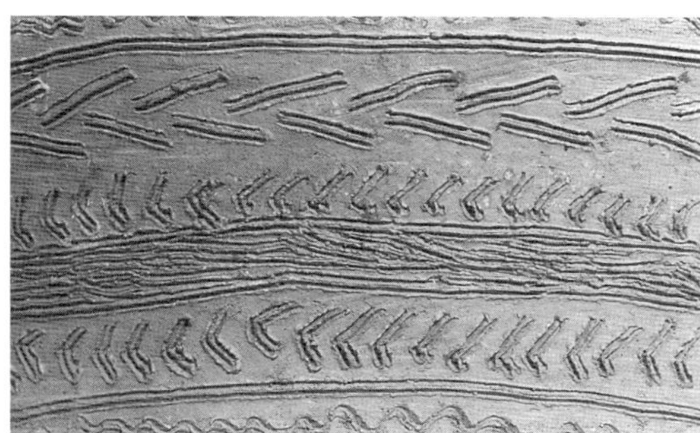
Fig. 3.11

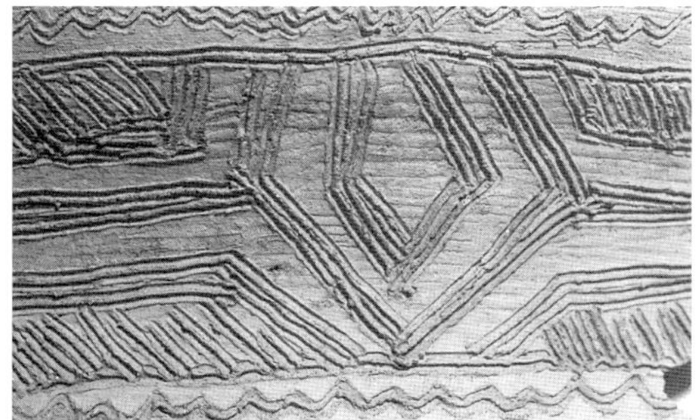
Fig. 3.12

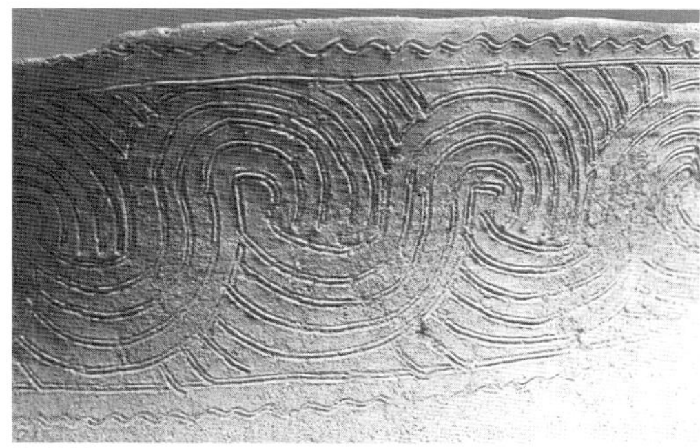
Fig. 3.13

Figs 3.8 to 3.13
Combed decorations on rims of Mailu Island cooking pots from an early 1900s collection.

judge the time when temperatures at all parts of the pot became more or less equal during cooling. At this point the pot was removed, thereby minimising stress on the pot walls. In seventeen firings the highest temperature recorded by Irwin was 1018°C; this was for the exterior base of the pot, which proved to be the hottest part in all firings. The lowest temperature recorded for the base was 811°C whereas the temperature range for the lip of the vessels was 540 to 670°C. The top recorded temperatures for firings on Mailu Island, 931°C, 538°C, 947°C and 1018°C are higher than those recorded by Lauer in the Amphletts. Irwin's temperature graphs show also that the glowing embers under the pots, before the new fuel was ignited, gave temperatures of 50 to 150°C. Preheating of the inside of the vessels was difficult to monitor but appeared to be between 300°C and 400°C.

Irwin found a uniformity in the potters' performance in all aspects of manufacture, including firing. No breakage of pots during firing was observed. This efficient industry seems doomed, like others, to fade out because young women are not learning the craft.

Decorative patterns, generally geometric but some curvilinear, are incised into the top quarter of the vessel. The design, which starts at the rim, usually consists of a scalloped horizontal line running around the circumference, beneath this is a broad band of repetitive designs, offset by a border, at the inflection point, of another scalloped line. Designs are also incised along the interior rim. Saville records the names of designs and their meanings. Representations of some of the designs are as follows: a frigate bird, shield pattern, a design taken from Massim canoes, a lizard tail, clouds standing in line, a frog's hind leg and foot and various patterns taken from women's tattoo marks and bamboo knives.

Motu

When the first Europeans settled in the Port Moresby area in 1873 the Motu people, inhabiting villages extending along the coast for 128 kilometres around Port Moresby, were essentially a maritime people; the women in the main villages of Hanuabada, Elevara, Tanabada, Boera, Porebada, Lealea (Rearea) and Manumanu were prolific potters and the men were sailors. The strip of coast was barren and infertile and during the six-month dry season the gardens on the hillsides overlooking the sea seldom yielded sufficient food to support the people. This necessitated the spectacular and dangerous annual trading voyages known as *hiri,* when thousands of pots were transported on large sailing canoes to the people of the Papuan Gulf in exchange for sago. An account of a *hiri* voyage is given by Captain Barton in Seligmann

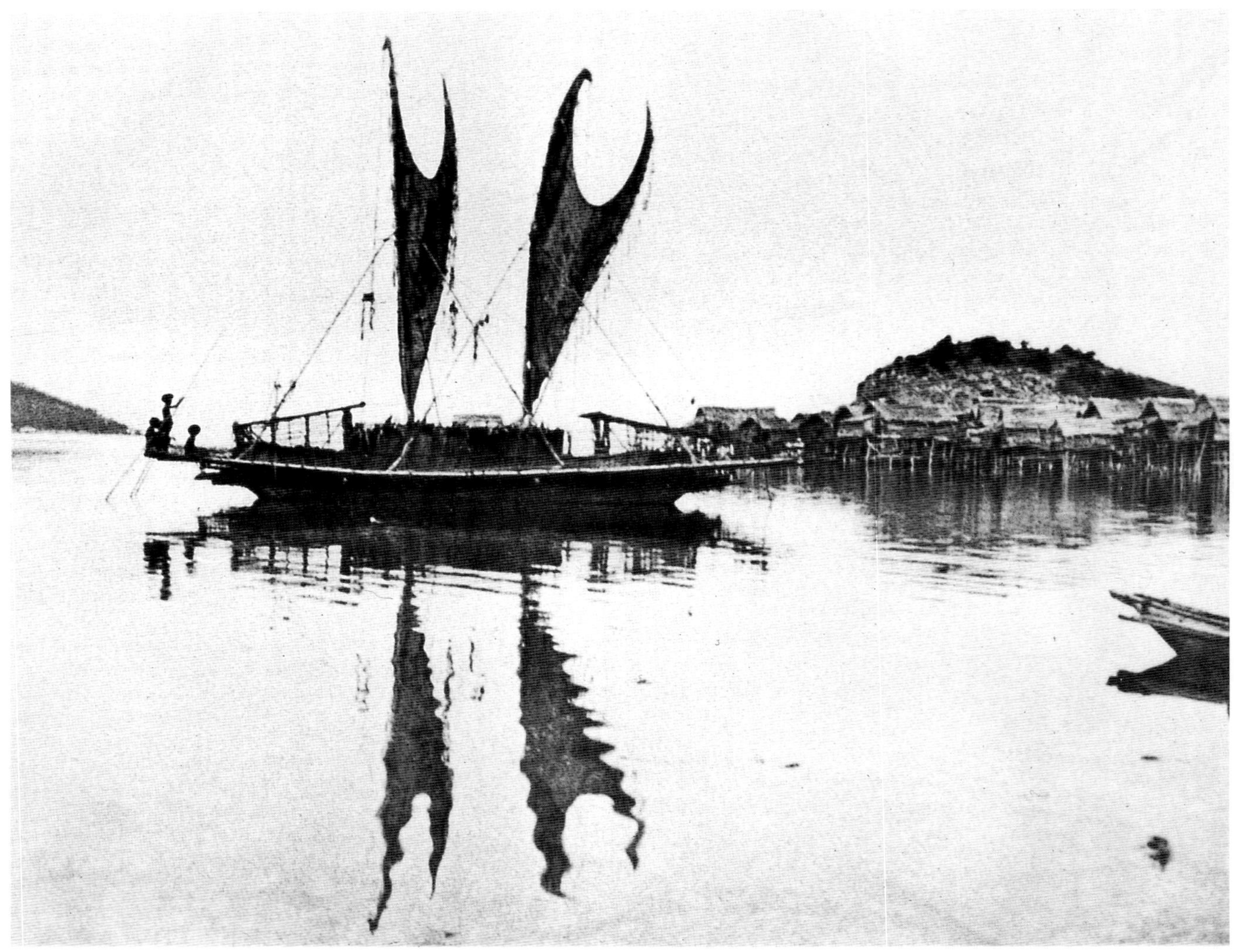

Fig. 3.14
Motu trading boat, *lagatoi,* ready for a trading voyage, *hiri,* to the Papuan Gulf in the early 1900s.

(1910). Williams (1932-33) gives an account of trading voyages going in the 'contrary direction' from west to east. The *hiri* voyages were a significant factor linking people of different languages in a network of ceremonial and economic exchange.

While pot making was women's work and local business was conducted by the women, who either took canoe loads of pots up the rivers to inland villages or walked there, carrying three to four pots at a time, the men acted as their agents in the *hiri*.

The organisation of the voyages, the making of the pottery, the construction or overhauling of the *lagatoi* (the sailing canoes), the sojourn in the Gulf area and the return were all subject to ceremony, ritual and magic.

In April or May certain of the leading men would decide it was time to organise the equipping of the *lagatoi*. The organiser, called *boditauna*, enlisted a partner, *doutauna*, and by prearrangement they were joined by their respective crews. The overhauling and caulking of the dugout canoes began in August and was followed by the lashing together of four to eight canoes to form a raft with a high partition built in the centre to hold the cargo of pots. Sometimes two platforms were built at either end as well. Finally, two masts made from small mangrove trees with spreading roots were lashed firmly to the crossbeams. Meanwhile, in the village the sail captains made the 'crabclaw' shaped sails by sewing plaited mats together and attaching them to mangrove poles. One of the largest *lagatoi* recorded by Barton consisted of fourteen dugout canoes, measuring 18 by 16 metres, which returned from the Gulf with 34 tonnes of sago. In his day, the usual size of a fleet was about twenty *lagatoi*.

The voyages were generally undertaken in September-October, before the south-east trade winds finished. The *lagatoi* were given sea trials and finally loaded with their cargo of pots, shells, shell ornaments and necklets. An average size four-hulled craft would carry a complement of about thirty men and 1000 pots stowed away in the partitions and in the dugouts. Depending upon wind and sea conditions, the voyage would take from three to five days to reach the closest trading partners. During the trip only certain foods could be eaten and these were always cooked in a special pot and served from a special clay serving bowl. At the end of the voyage these vessels were ritually broken and thrown into the sea.

While the men had been preparing for the voyage, the married women had been occupied with making the clay pots for the trip. Each crew member of a *lagatoi* was responsible for taking along the pots belonging to female members of his household; he was also socially obliged to uphold special kinship relationships with other households and to offer to carry pots made by other females. Each woman received a bundle of sago in return for her pot. This custom ensured that households lacking males going on the *hiri* could still obtain the necessary supply of sago to see them through the lean months.

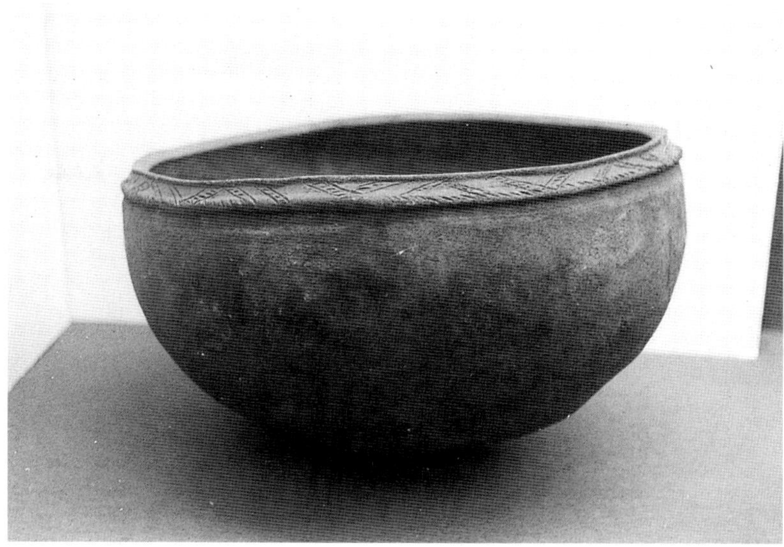

Fig. 3.15
Old Motu bowl collected by the *Chevert* Expedition, 1875, at Hall Sound near Yule Island, *h* 16 cm.

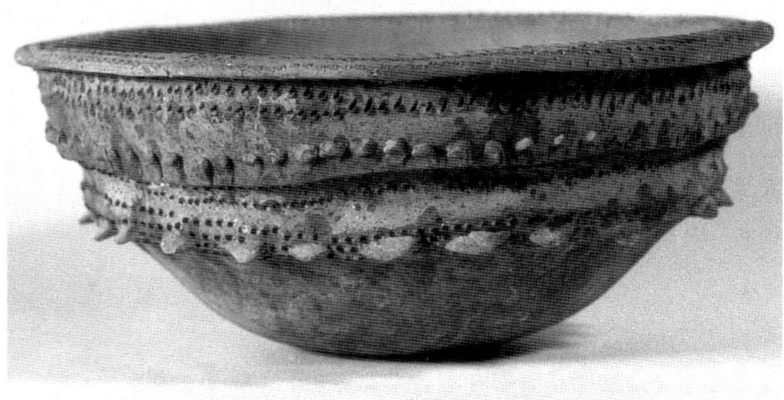

Fig. 3.16
Old Motu bowl collected in the early 1900s, *h* 10 cm.

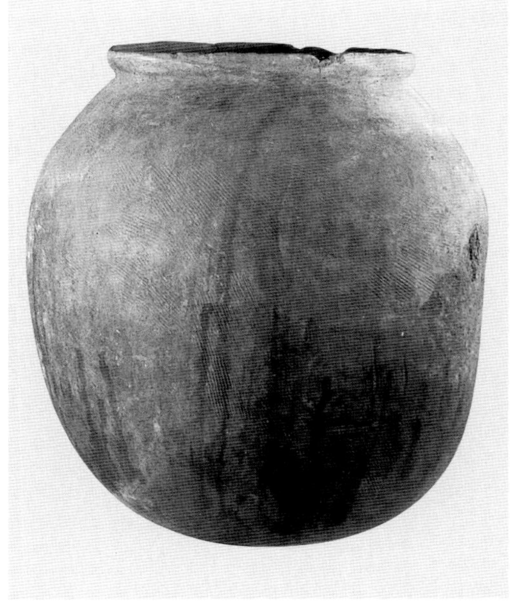

Fig. 3.17
Old Motu sago storage jar, *tohe,* from Manumanu village, *h* 56 cm.

Before the pots were loaded onto the *lagatoi* they were ritually brushed with banana leaves. A short booklet for children by P. Cochrane tells of the magic performed by a sorcerer, *babalau* to ensure the safety of the voyage.

> He carried three things, a broken piece of clay pot, a string bag full of fearsome relics, and some banana leaves. The men drew back from their work and the *babalau* prepared his magic: He placed the broken pot on one end of the *lakatoi*, and put his string bag beside it From the mysterious contents of the bag he chose some pieces of cassowary claw, the snouts of several garfish, and some very dry pieces of the root and bark of a secret tree. He stirred the mixture well, and lit it. A thick black smoke arose and, mumbling charms all the time, the sorcerer smoked the outsides of the *lakatoi* all over ... to make doubly sure of wind, weather and tide, the sorcerer now wrapped small bundles of the green leaves of a bush plant in pieces of banana leaf. These small bundles he pushed firmly into the square holes in the bulwarks. [Cochrane 1961]

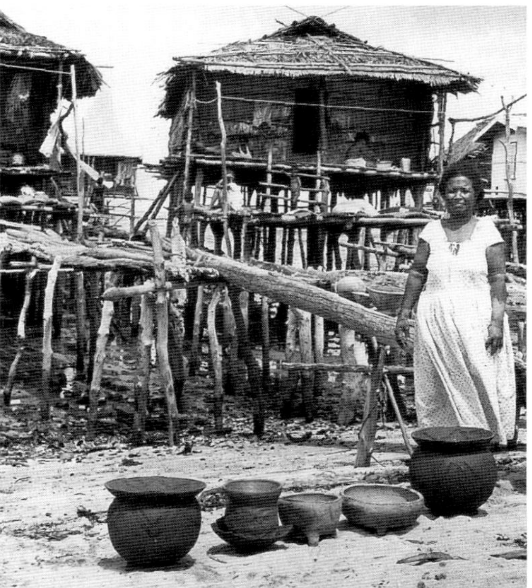

Fig. 3.18
Non-traditional Motu pots and flower pots, and one unfinished pot, at Porebada village.

Upon arrival, the Motu and their hosts engaged in ceremony and material exchange. While the Gulf people (the Elema) prepared the bundles of sago the Motu men outfitted and rebuilt their crafts with large logs supplied by their hosts. When the weather was favourable (about November) the reconstructed *lagatoi* and their cargoes of sago returned home.

Captain Barton's description of the *hiri* lists seven types of pots classified by shape and size but a study of the Motu pottery industry at Manumanu and observations of three *hiri* voyages in 1954, 1957 and 1958 by Groves (1960) update our information. Groves lists only six types of vessels still produced by the paddle-and-anvil method in Manumanu. The pots on the whole are all restricted spherical vessels except for one dish type. Besides cooking pots and sago storage vessels, a water container is also made. Named types are: *uro*, a large, wide-mouthed cooking pot measuring about 25 to 41 centimetres in diameter and about 41 centimetres high; *tohe*, a larger version of the *uro* used for storing dried sago; *hodu*, a narrow-necked spherical vessel used for carrying and storing water; and *nau*, an eating plate in the shape of a shallow, circular dish. There is also a small basin with legs, *ituru,* for holding tattoo dye. Three other types of pots mentioned by Barton were taken on the hiri trading voyages but not used commonly in the villages.

From Groves's report in the 1950s, Manumanu women made thousands of pots during three seasons and the *hiri* voyages were still conducted, although not annually. Hanuabada women no longer

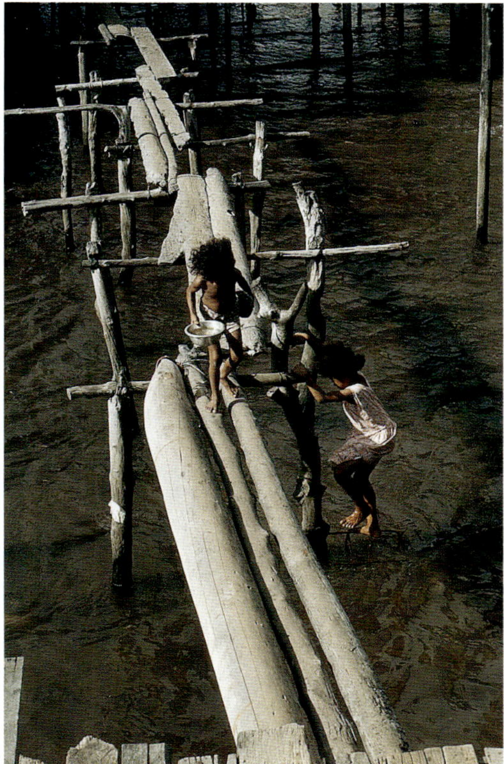

Fig. 3.19

made pots and already in Boera and Porebada traditional trading practices had been replaced by new marketing procedures: *Hiri* voyages by Boera, Porebada and Manumanu people (the Roku and Koderika villages of the Koita people also engaged in a *hiri* in 1954) continued spasmodically in the late 1950s and 1960s.

Local trade was still prolific. The Mekeo, Maiva, Doura and Gabadi still exchanged vegetables for

Fig. 3.21

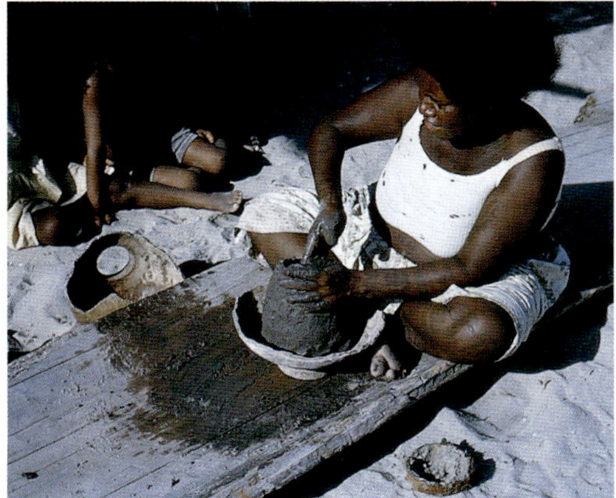

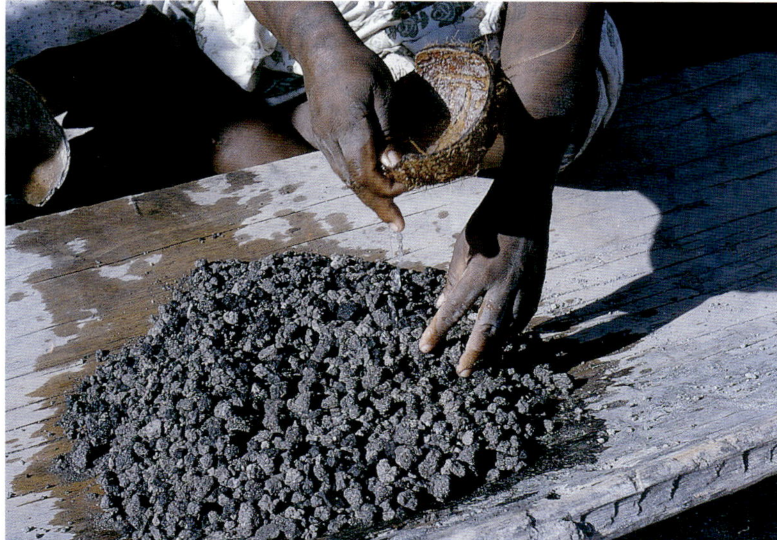

Fig. 3.20

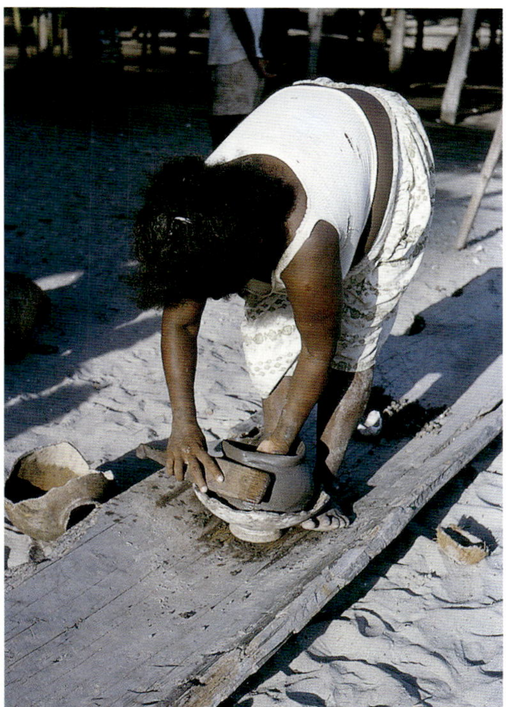

Fig. 3.22

coastal pots. Middle-men distributed the pots further inland and also further west in the Gulf.

In 1977 the prospects for the continuation of the industry were bleak. Only Boera and Porebada are still producing a few pots. Aluminium saucepans have almost entirely replaced the traditional clay

Figs 3.19 to 3.22
Techniques at Porebada and Boera villages, 1965.

Fig. 3.19
Girls fetching sea water for their mother to wet her clay at Porebada.

Fig. 3.20
Motu potter, Vagi Raho, trickling sea water on the dry clay from a half coconut shell, Boera village.

Fig. 3.21
Vagi Raho dragging up the soft clay from inside the rough cylinder, supported in a broken pot neck, Boera.

Fig. 3.22
Vagi Raho beating the soft pot briefly before setting it aside to become firmer, Boera.

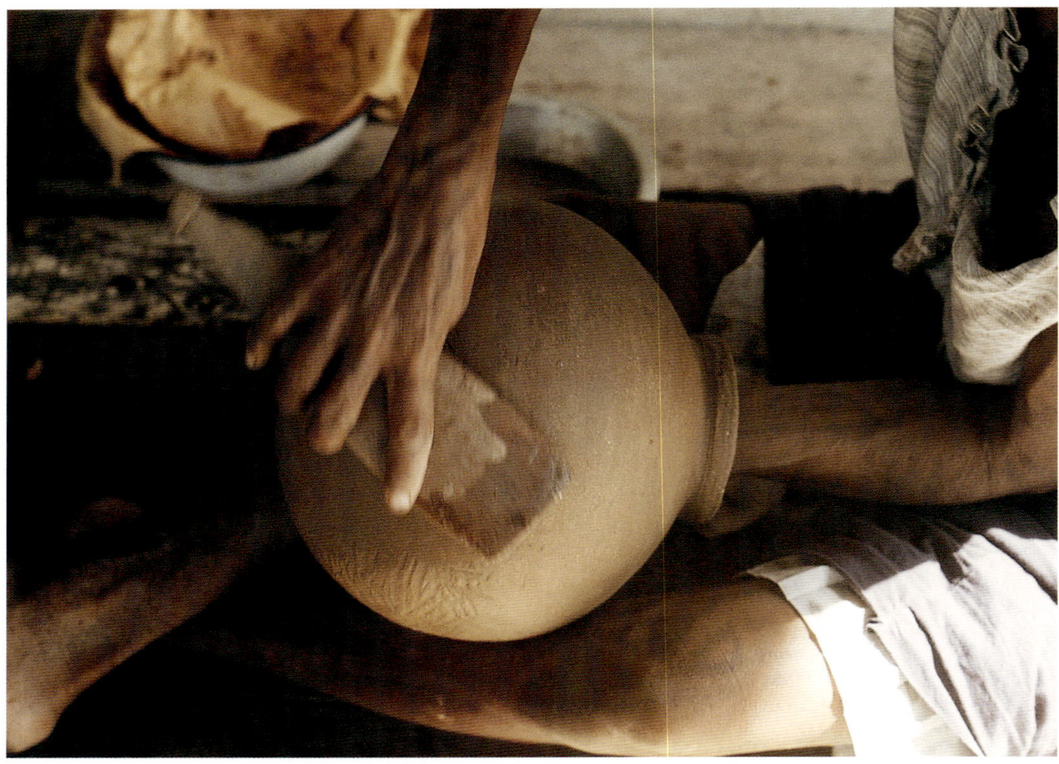

Fig. 3.23
Kari Lohia at the final stage of beating, using a smooth paddle to eliminate the texture from the ridged beater, Porebada village.

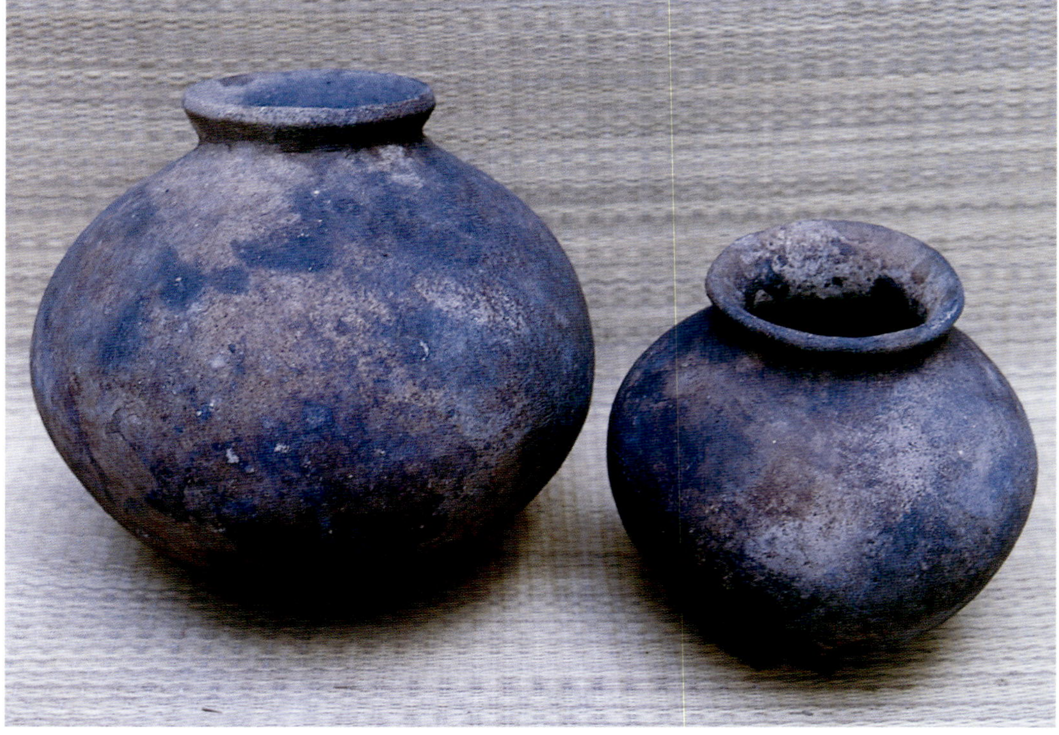

Fig. 3.24
Small Motu water pots, *hodu,* stained with mangrove bark soaked in water:(left) *h* 18 cm; (right) *h* 14 cm.

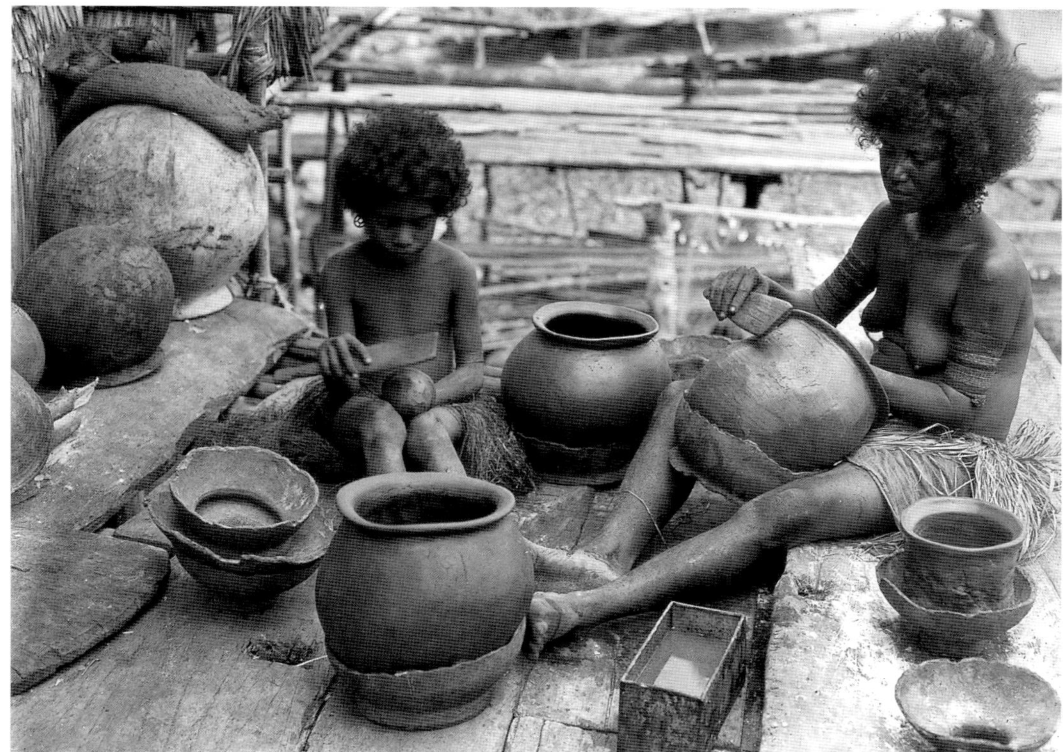

Fig. 3.25
Motu cooking pots, 1921, at four stages of construction.

pots. The proximity of Port Moresby and the rapid changeover to cash economy have disrupted the old trade relationships. Johnston (1974) reports that Manumanu villagers have not made pots since 1959; apparently they used to gather their clay from Lealea village but the Lealea people decided to charge for it and the Manumanu women immediately lost interest. Recently a few water pots and cooking vessels have been seen in use at Lealea, Porebada and Boera. Old sago storage jars are still in use at Manumanu, where they are stored on the verandahs. Flower pots intended for sale to residents of Port Moresby are now produced in Boera and Porebada. These modified *uro* have perforated holes in the bases and sometimes stand on three legs. The quality has deteriorated and one strongly suspects that many are made by non-potters who are trying to profit by selling to indiscriminate consumers. On the other hand, some excellent high quality water pots and cooking pots are also offered for sale.

As for the *hiri* voyages, Ryan (1970) points out that the disruption of trade brought about by World War II (the Motu villages were evacuated) and the increasing involvement of the Motu in wage labour in Port Moresby, which lessened their dependence on trade for subsistence, made these journeys less important.

> Toaripi men still occasionally make a trip to Port Moresby in a big double-hulled canoe, but they spend more time in migrant settlements visiting their relatives than they do in the villages of Motu trading partners. If they sell sago it is for cash, not clay pots. [Ryan 1970]

The method of making pots does not appear to have changed at all since Captain Barton's days. The women potters of Porebada and Boera dig their shell-laden clay from pits behind the beaches. At Boera it is a yellow brownish-grey colour when dry. This clay contains far more coarse material that must be discarded than any other clay seen in Papua New Guinea. There are numerous whole shells and shell fragments and some quartz, sandstone, basalt and clay pellets. Amongst the finer non-plastics are also some obsidian, jasper, tourmaline and mica.

Fig. 3.26
The rims of two broken magic pots, *ra'a*, Tseria, Yule Island.

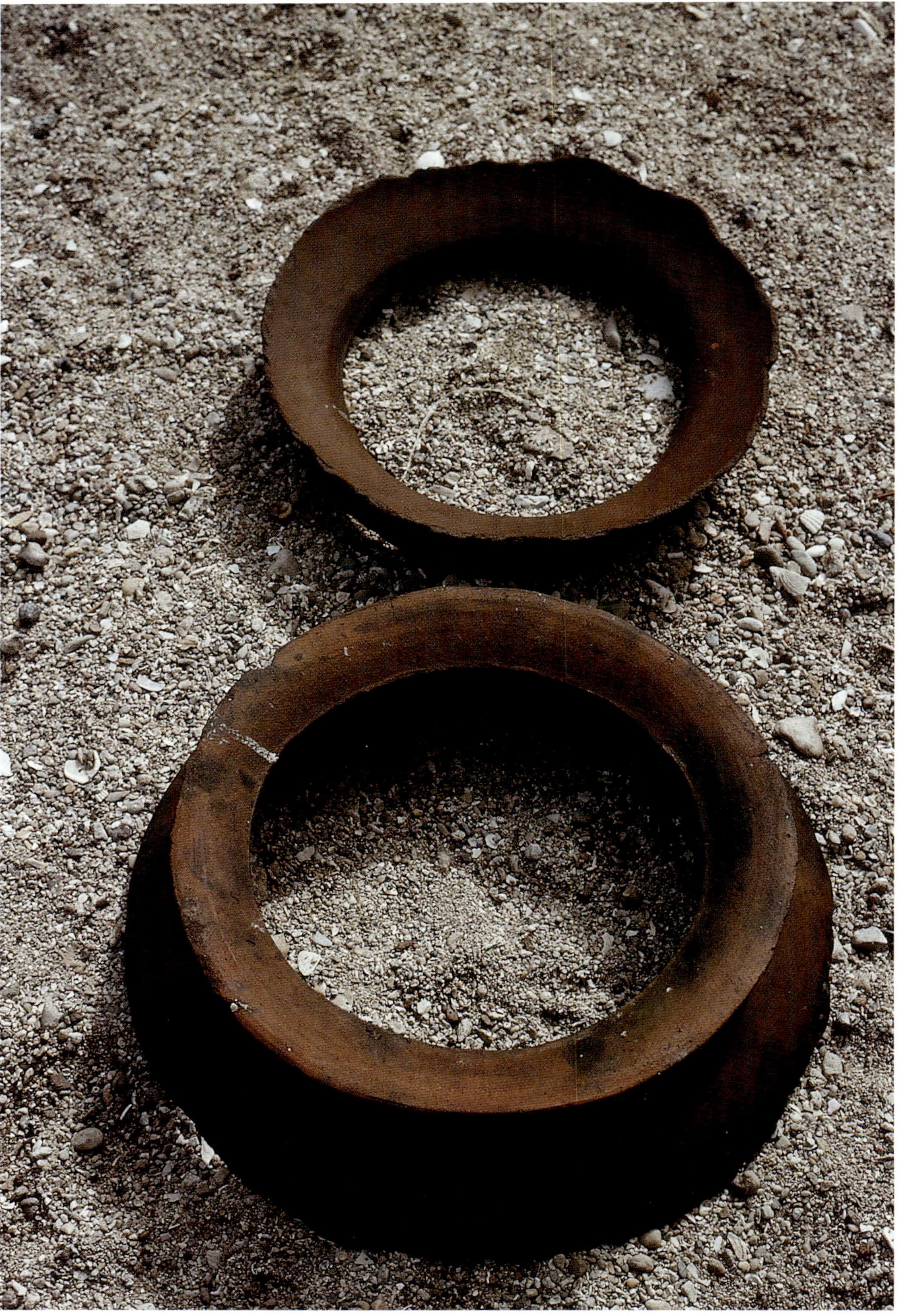

The clay mineral is a smectite (28 per cent) but when the potter has eliminated much of the coarse stuff this percentage would be somewhat higher, making the non-plastic content about average.

Each woman fetches clay when she needs it and carries it back to the village in a string bag, hessian sack or rice bag. She empties it out onto a curved plank taken from an old canoe hull and it is left there to dry. While on the plank, the clay is broken into marble-sized pieces with the fingers or with a heavy shell or stone. Shells and other large impurities are discarded. Sea water, never fresh water, is then sprinkled onto the dry clay, which soaks it up quickly. It becomes workable almost immediately and is left to soak while beach sand from under the surface is collected. This is added in unmeasured proportions while the potter kneads the mixture until she feels it is right. The clay is now black-brown in colour, very soft and with good plasticity. The potter then forms several spherical pugs of clay. Taking the first of these, she compacts it further by firmly patting it and then places it in the base or the neck piece of a broken pot which serves as her turntable. She pushes a depression in the top of the sphere then, plunging one hand into the very soft clay, she drags it up, continually turning it around until the rough walls have formed a cylindrical shape. After smoothing the outside with her hands, she forms the rim of the pot by running a wet hand around the top edge with the thumb inside the pot as it is quickly turned around and around with the other hand. This rim is made to the exact size desired and evened out until it becomes symmetrical. The pot is now briefly beaten.

At this stage the pots are set out in the sun to become firmer. Next, the pot is cradled in the potter's lap and a smooth, round stone is held inside the vessel, with a wooden beater held in her other hand she strikes the wall with both implements. After repeated beating and moving, the pot walls are swelled out and evenly thinned until an almost perfect sphere is formed. A second paddle with a ridged surface is used for further beating and a third without ridges is used for final wet smoothing of the shape and especially for eliminating most of the pattern formed by the rough beater. Smoothing of the inside of the neck area is done with a shell. Early in the beating stage the potter must beat over the hole which has remained in the bottom because the vessel sits on the turntable while being formed. The beating stones are treasured possessions and passed on from mother to daughter. Today, although many of the women no longer make pots they still treasure and keep their stones (Figs 3.19-3.23).

Before the vessels are put into the sun to dry for about an hour they are decorated very simply with geometric incisions made by a shell. When the women are ready to fire their pots they first wipe over the surfaces with a hand moistened with salt water. Then they preheat the pots by burning dry coconut fronds over them. The pots are removed and properly fired by setting them on a fuel bed of coconut fronds and leaf stems; more fuel is stacked over them. When the pots are fired and still hot they are splashed with a solution of mangrove bark soaked in water which brightens their red or buff colour, making them purply brown (fig. 3.24). Water vessels are sealed by further treatment: they are rubbed with starchy, sappy leaves and plants. For further strengthening, the water pot may be cooked on a fire for about fifteen minutes; water is then added to the hot vessel. This process is repeated until there are no leaks.

Roro

The third major pot producing group is the Roro-speaking people, Austronesians, who live in Hall Sound about 128 kilometres north-west along the coast from Port Moresby. The Roro have settled on Yule Island and along the adjacent mainland at Delena, Poukama and a few other coastal villages. Archaeological and documentary evidence indicates that the Roro are relatively recent arrivals to this area. The Motu were at one time inhabitants of Yule Island and the Roro people, originally living near Bereina, were pressured by the Waima group and began to settle near the sea. The Motu, also under pressure, moved back south-east along the coast close to what is now Port Moresby. At some time prior to European settlement, the Roro established themselves on Yule Island and along the coast. They learned how to make pots from the Motu. According to legends the Motu women kept their pot making skills secret but somehow the Roro women, either through spying or intermarriage,

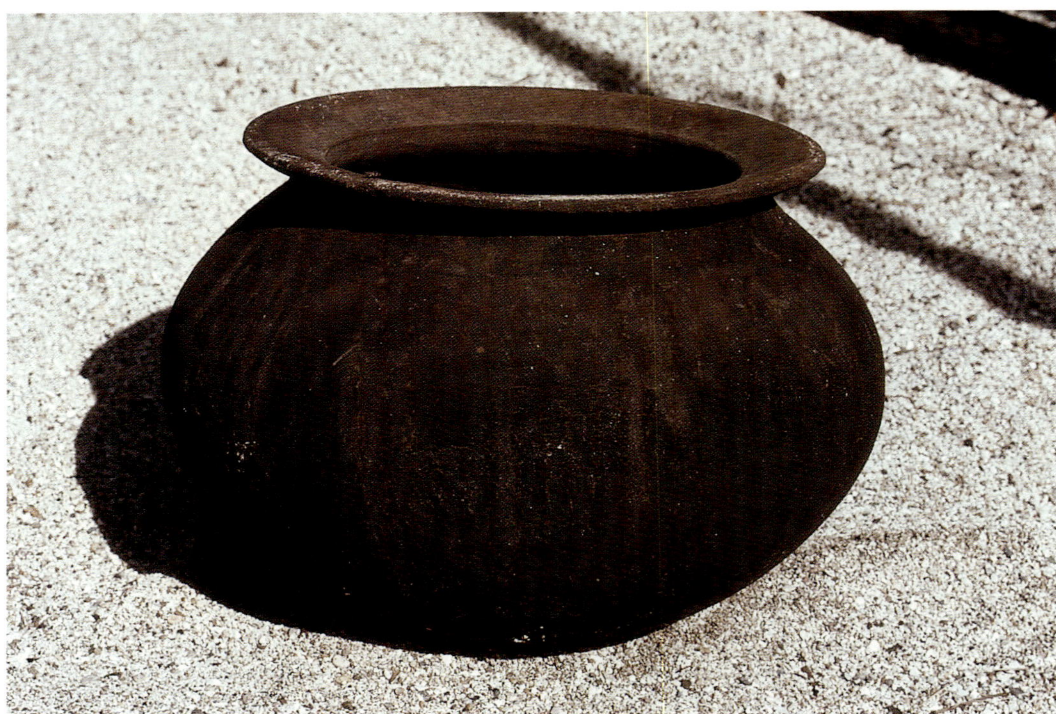

Fig. 3.27
Yule Island cooking pot, *ororo*.

were taught the skill several generations ago. One village on Yule Island, T'seria, is still producing a few pots while Poukama and Delena villages, which have been reported in early literature as centres of pot making have practically ceased activity. During the authors' 1976 visit to Yule Island and Delena only one woman was reported to be still making pots at Poukama; about five women still make them occasionally at T'seria.

Important detailed literature on the Roro includes general ethnographies by Haddon (1900) and Seligmann (1910), a description of population movements and oral traditions by Chatterton (1968) and Vanderwal's thesis (1973), which describes various aspects of the prehistory of Yule Island. No thorough description of the pottery industry has been attempted to date.

Roro trade in pottery was not as extensive as that of the Motu but there was an equivalent to the Motu *hiri*, called by the Roro *harima*. The pots were taken by canoe to Kerema in October and November and were exchanged for sago. Vanderwal reports his disappointment in November 1969 at missing by one day the *hiri*-type trip of a schooner from T'seria village to Karema village in the Gulf. The last trip before this had been in 1938. In 1969 about 350 clay pots were taken aboard to be exchanged for sago. Locally, a few pots were traded inland with the Mekeo people for feathers, dogs' teeth, betel nut, taro and bananas.

The generic term for pots is *uro*. There are several named vessels: the *ororo,* a restricted spherical pot with a flattened everted rim used for general cooking purposes (fig. 3.27), about 25 to 30 centimetres high, with a rim 5 centimetres wide: the *eiei,* a smaller version of the same type, about 9 to 12 centimetres tall, used for individuals or children; the *puou*, a water-carrying vessel the appearance of which is exactly like the *hodu* of the Motu; the *tohe,* used to store sago and shaped like the *ororo* but larger with thicker walls and less rim area; and the *sihu*, a small dish-shaped vessel with an inverted lip, used now to hold cinders for lighting 'smokes' and other fires.

Another category of vessel which looks exactly like the common *ororo* but has never been used for cooking is the *ra'a*, a magic pot kept by sorcerers and some women to store magic paraphernalia. These pots do not appear to be in use now (if they are, it would never be admitted) but the rims of broken ones have been carefully preserved and are kept in the houses. The magic pots are broken by the widow when her husband dies (fig. 3.26).

Decoration consists of impressing rather simple herringbone and vertical marks, called *ari ari*, along the flat top surface of the everted rim of the *ororo* and around the neck area of the other vessels. The designs are taken from clan marks and every woman potter has her own selection of designs, many of which are repeated in tattoo marks on her arms, chest and thighs. It is quite probable that potters belonging to the same clan will decorate their pots with similar designs.

The technique of production is that of the Motu hand building finished by paddle-and-anvil. There are ample clay deposits along this coastal region but the women from T'seria get their clay from behind their village. Sand temper is also used here and black sand is collected from the mainland beaches near Poukama. Salt water is used to moisten the clay; rubble is removed by hand. The clay is worked by the hands until ready for use. The vessel is started in a broken pottery base or in the everted rim and shoulder of the water pot. The tools of the potter include several paddles used for beating and shaping called *baha* and *yahuahu*, round stones called *pitara*, and shells used in decorating, called *yabe*. Large pots are dried under the houses for about three days. Firings are multiple and fuel consists of coconut husks, leaves, fronds and split hardwood. The pots are preheated in the sun for several hours before being fired. There are thus few variations on the Motu techniques.

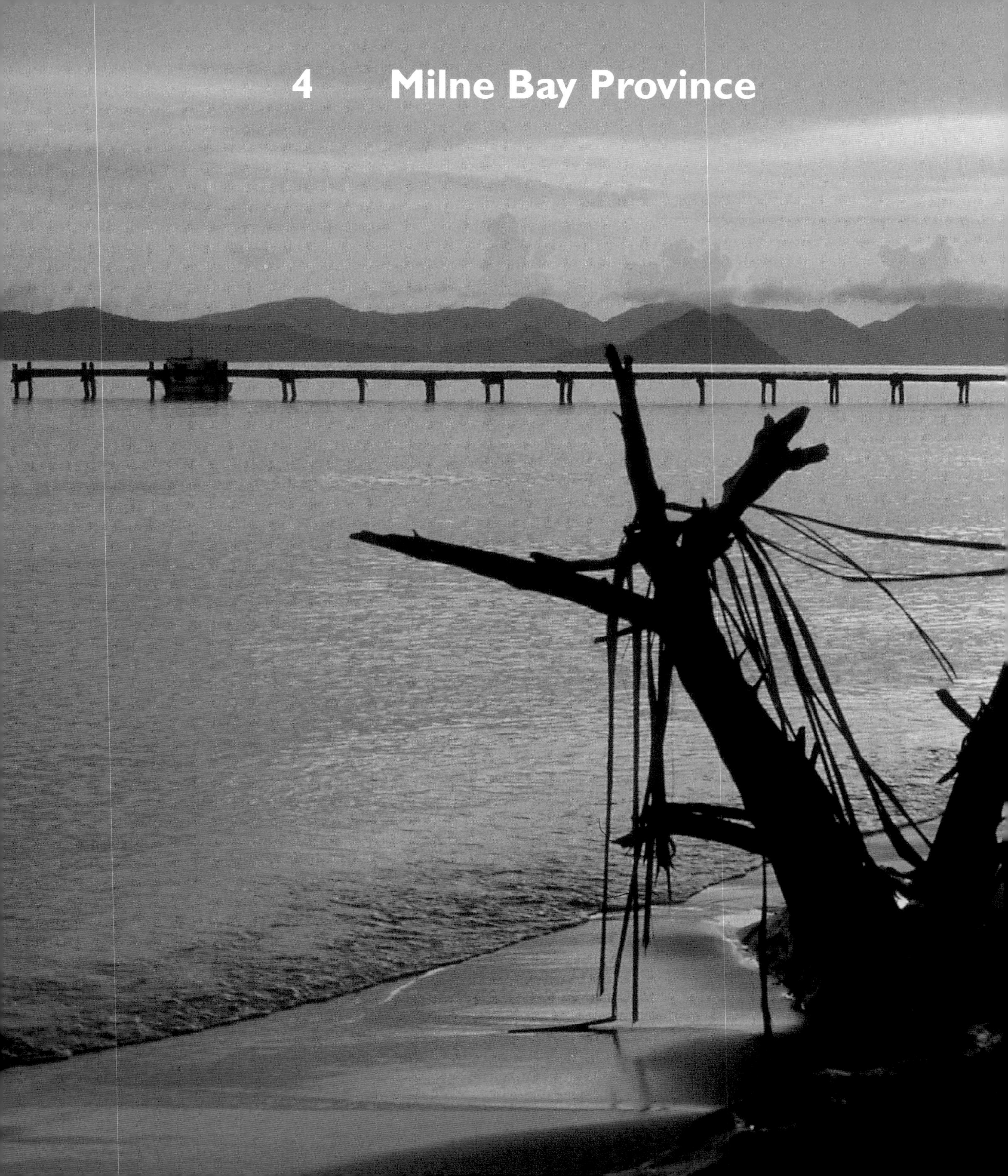

4 Milne Bay Province

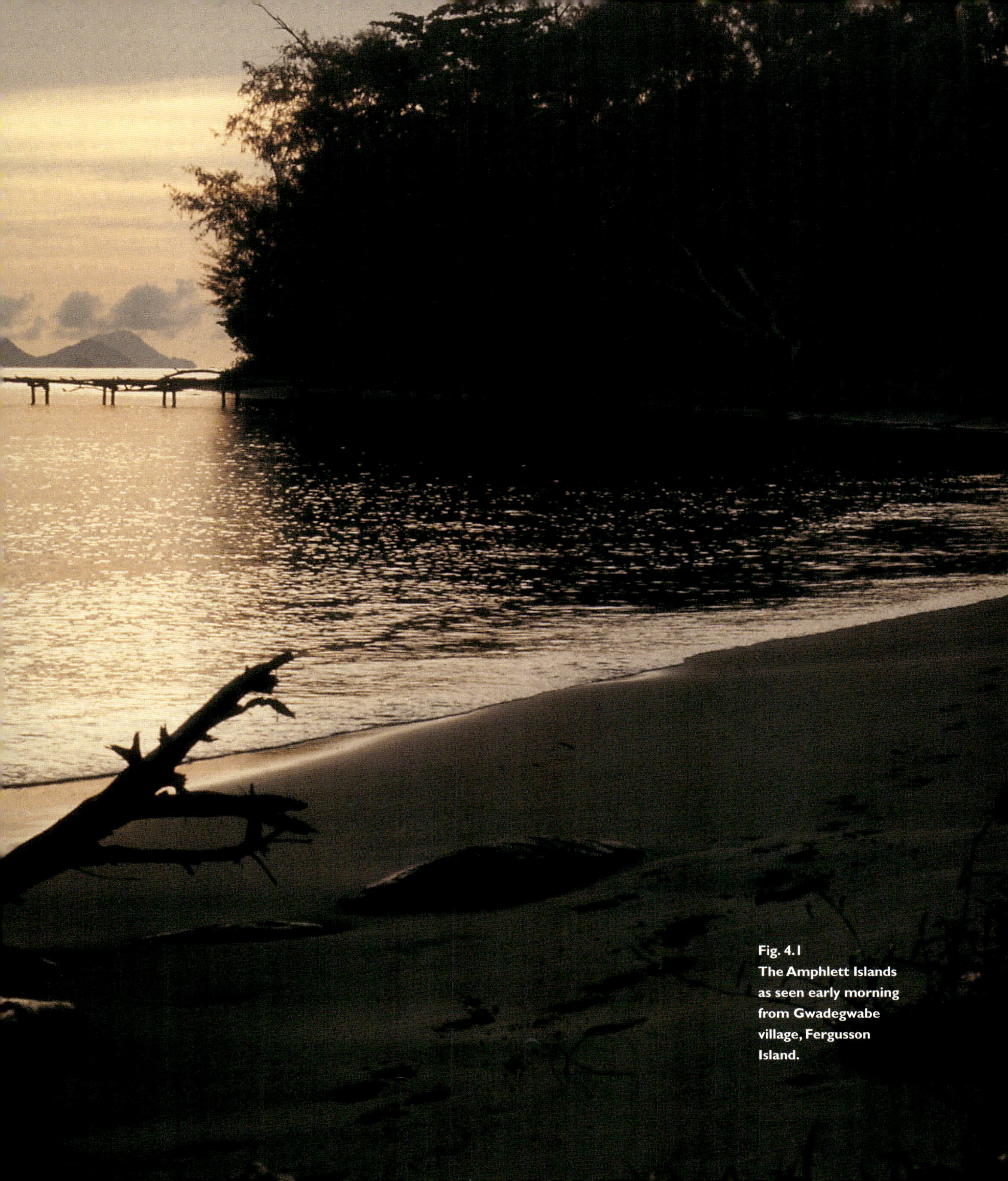

Fig. 4.1
The Amphlett Islands as seen early morning from Gwadegwabe village, Fergusson Island.

MAP 5

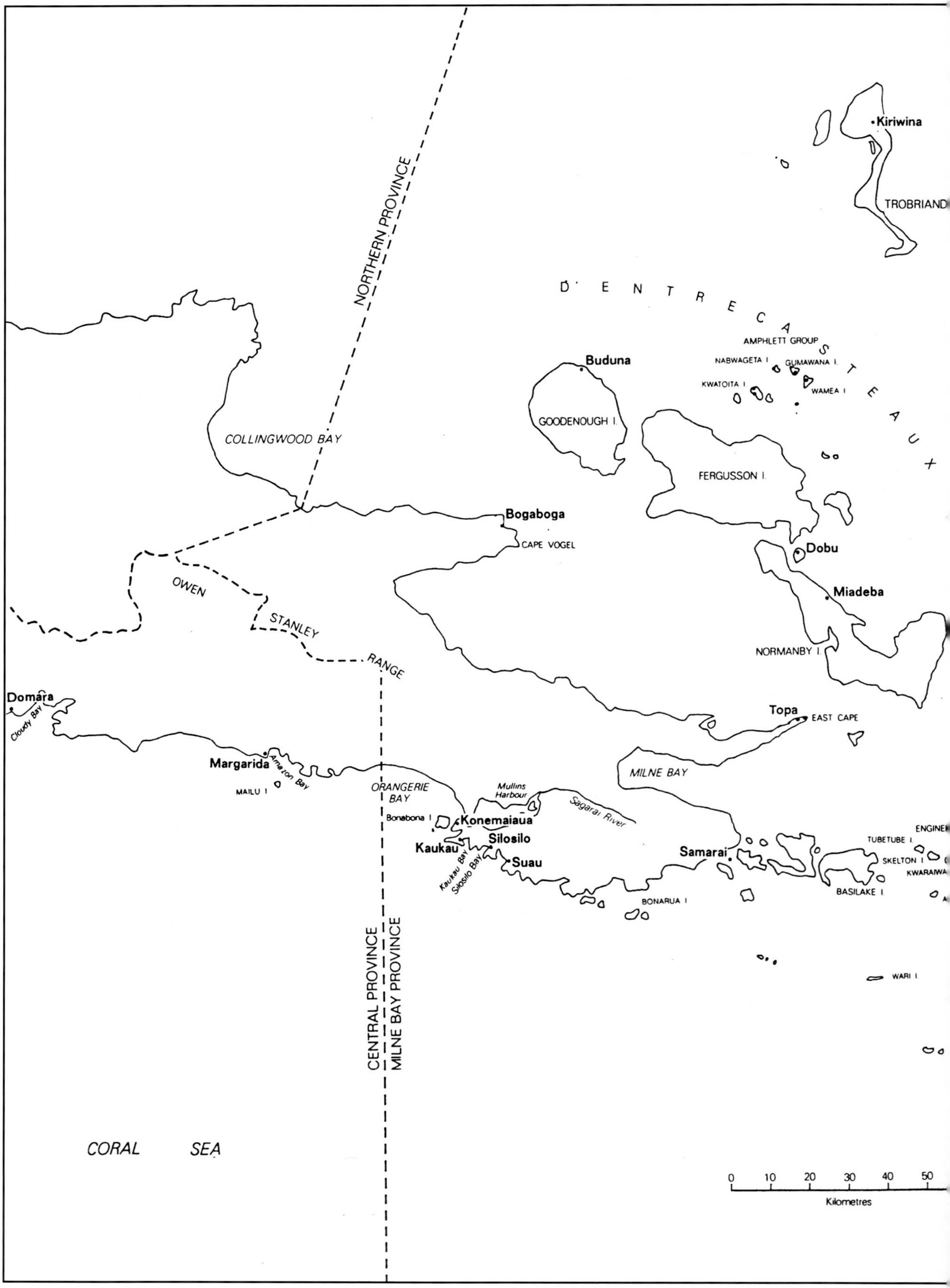

NORTHERN PROVINCE
Kiriwina
TROBRIAND
D'ENTRECASTEAUX
AMPHLETT GROUP
NABWAGETA I.
GUMAWANA I.
KWATOITA I.
WAMEA I.
Buduna
GOODENOUGH I.
FERGUSSON I.
COLLINGWOOD BAY
Bogaboga
CAPE VOGEL
Dobu
Miadeba
OWEN STANLEY RANGE
NORMANBY I.
Domara
Cloudy Bay
Topa
EAST CAPE
Margarida
Amazon Bay
MAILU I.
ORANGERIE BAY
Mullins Harbour
Sagarai River
MILNE BAY
Bonabona I.
Konemaiaua
Silosilo
Kaukau
Kaukau Bay
Silosilo Bay
Suau
Samarai
ENGINEER
TUBETUBE I.
SKELTON I.
KWARAIWA
BASILAKE I.
BONARUA I.
WARI I.
CENTRAL PROVINCE
MILNE BAY PROVINCE
CORAL SEA
0 10 20 30 40 50
Kilometres

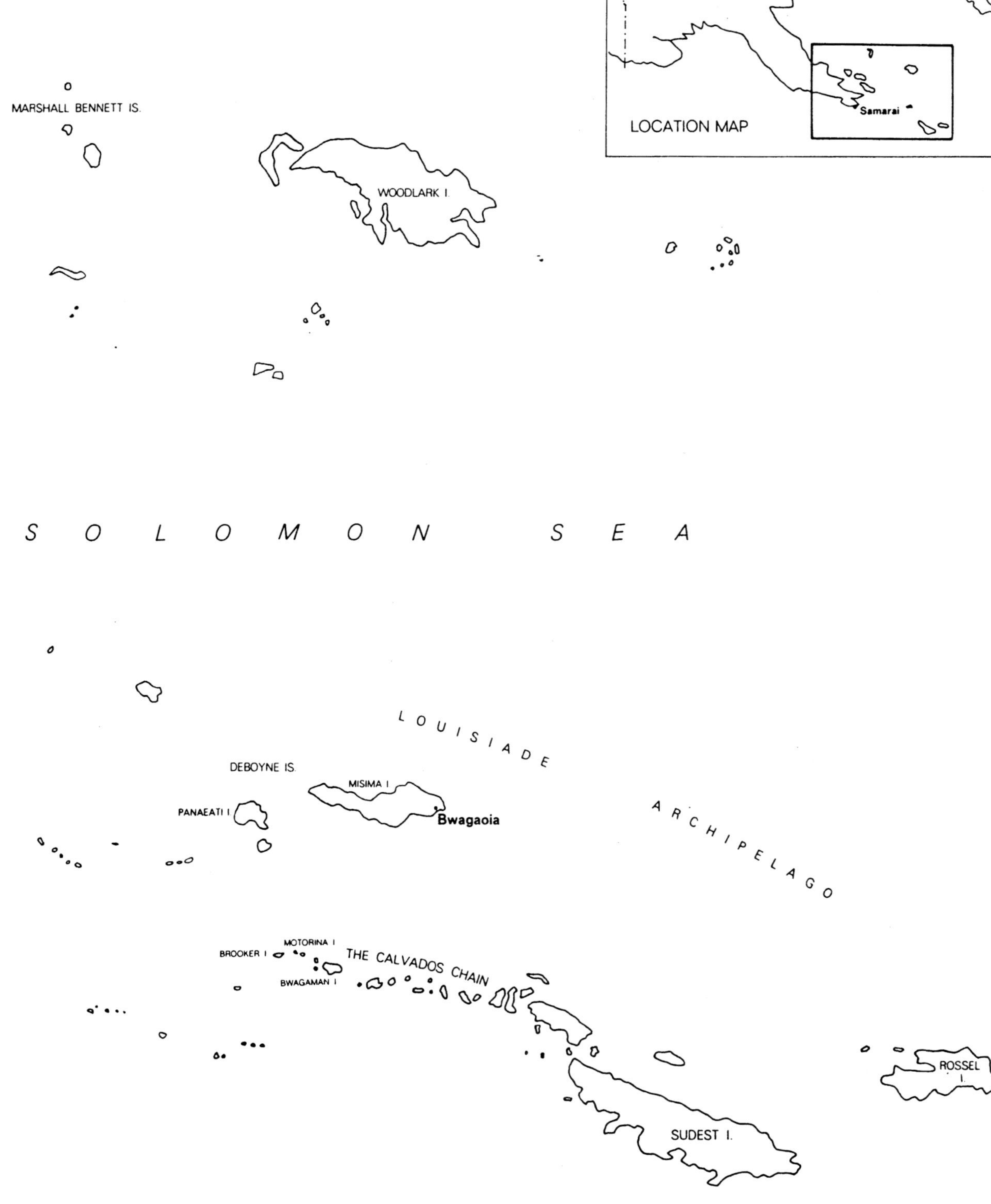

Milne Bay Province
LOCATION MAP
0
200
Kms
Samarai
MARSHALL BENNETT IS.
WOODLARK I.
SOLOMON SEA
LOUISIADE ARCHIPELAGO
DEBOYNE IS.
MISIMA I
PANAEATI I
Bwagaoia
BROOKER I
MOTORINA I
BWAGAMAN I
THE CALVADOS CHAIN
ROSSEL I.
SUDEST I.

Fig. 4.2
Sabito scraping up the clay from the two joined slabs. Her daughter watches and learns. Nabwageta Island, Amphlett group.

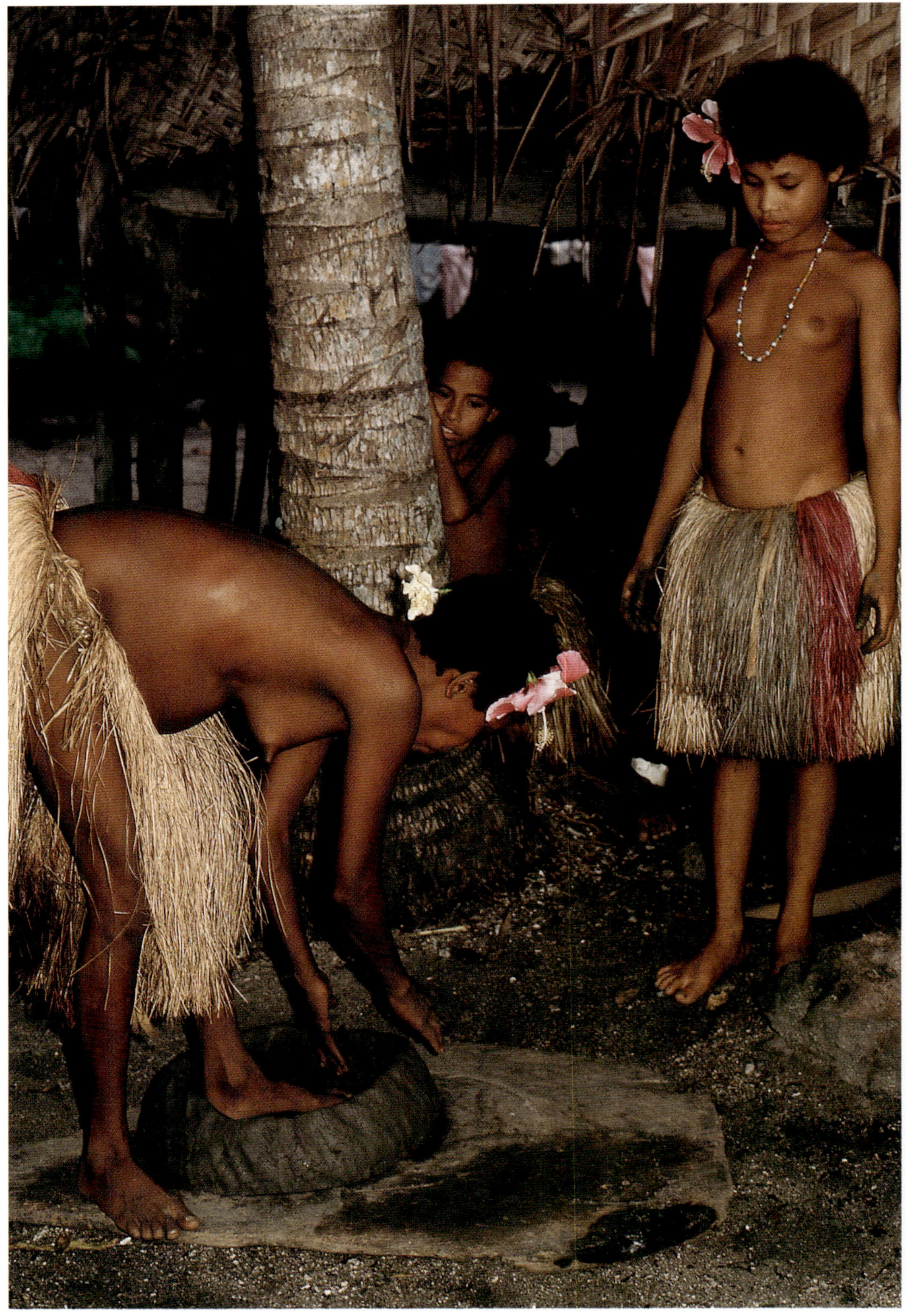

Milne Bay Province, comprising the south-eastern tip of the mainland and hundreds of islands, coral atolls, archipelagos and reefs, is one of the most prolific areas of pottery making in the South Seas. The mainland portion is distinguished by a backbone of mountains, the Owen Stanley Range, which extends into the sea and reappears as islands off the south-east coast, the D'Entrecasteaux Islands. The three largest islands are Goodenough, Fergusson and Normanby; the smaller islands include Dobu and the Amphletts. The inhabitants are Austronesians.

Goodenough Island is one of the most mountainous in the world; it is basically oval in shape, with mountains reaching as tall as 2460 metres. There are few reefs except on the north coast. Small alluvial plains rise from the sea on the north-east and eastern shores, where most of the population has settled in hamlets scattered along the coast. The Amphlett group comprises twenty-eight small

Fig. 4.3
A family from Nabwageta Island, Amphlett group, setting off to Fergusson Island to gather clay.

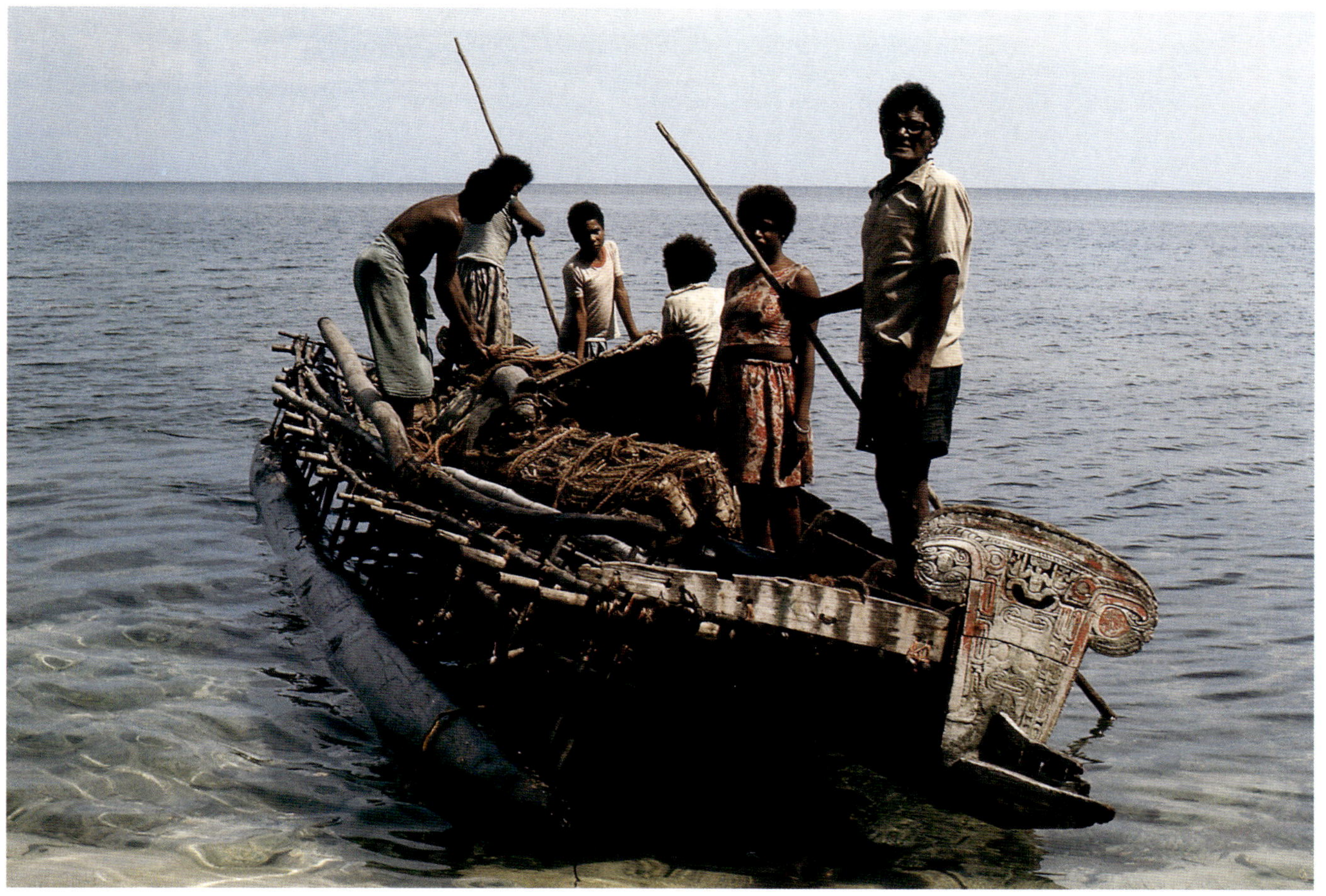

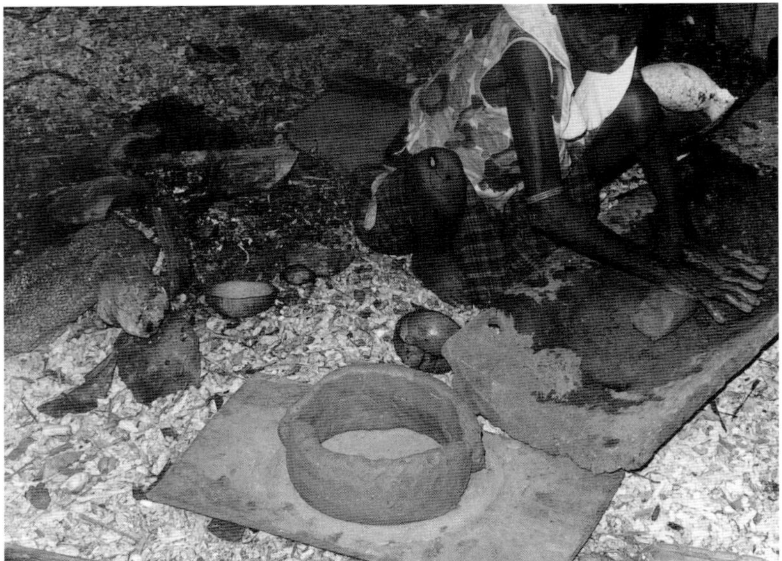

Fig. 4.4
A potter preparing more clay to add after the two slabs have been joined, Nabwageta Island, Amphlett group.

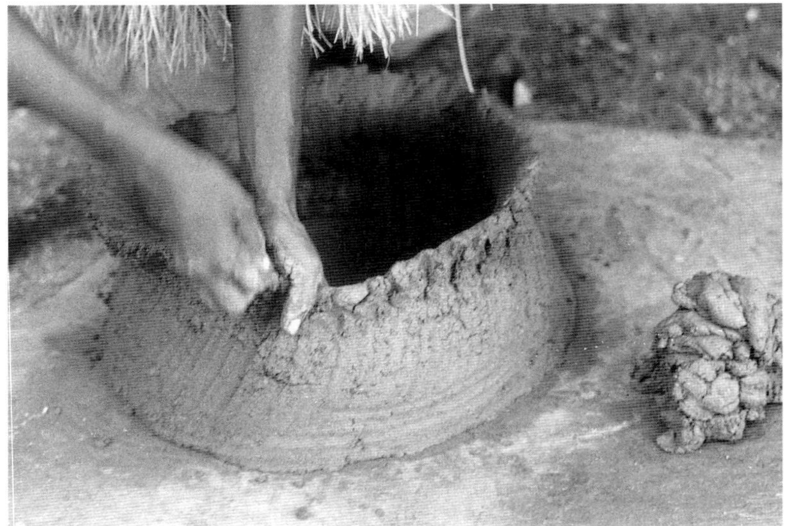

Fig. 4.5
Sabito scraping up the clay after the slabs have been joined, Nabwageta Island.

islands, four of which – Gumawana, Nabwageta, Kwatoita and Wamea – are populated permanently. Fergusson Island is noted for its thermal springs, extinct volcanoes and once lush forests. Normanby is separated from Fergusson by a narrow stretch of water called the Dobu Passage and Dobu Island lies between the two.

South-east of the tip of the mainland lies a long chain of islands and barrier reefs known as the Louisiade Archipelago. The coral islands, scattered atolls and rugged reefs make this group scenically beautiful but navigationally hazardous.

Two famous anthropologists, Charles Seligmann (1873-1940) and Bronislaw Malinowski (1884-1942), carried out scientific expeditions to mainland Papua and Milne Bay. Seligmann stayed at Wagawaga and Tubetube islands where he gathered data on commerce and the extended trading expeditions of the islanders. Malinowski, whose study overlapped Seligmann's, carried out research on the Trobriand Islands, located north-east of the D'Entrecasteaux group, and extended Seligmann's observations on trade and specifically what Malinowski called the *kula* ring trade. His results were published in the monumental study *Argonauts of the Western Pacific* (1922) in which he described *kula* as the system of ceremonial exchange between the people of neighbouring islands who depend upon one another for indispensable items such as sago, dried fish, yam, betel nut, wood for canoes, and pottery. The *kula* was an overt expression of social relations between these trading partners. Expeditions were made by canoe to other islands, either to give or to receive two valuables, the trochus shell arm ornament and the spondylus shell necklace. The exchange routes between the islands were fixed, as were trading partners, and exchange was based on very definite and complex rules, with the result that the necklaces circulated clockwise, always being traded to the north, and the arm shells travelled anti-clockwise, to the south. Malinowski stressed the important aspect of the *kula* as being this exchange of the two articles, emphasising the political and social organisation which brings together different and rival groups in a symbolic and ceremonial exchange. There are also exchanges of foodstuffs and other commodities of vital economic importance. While many areas like Woodlark Island, the Trobriands and the D'Entrecasteaux group are self-sufficient in terms of food production, other islands, volcanic in nature or coral formations having little fertile topsoil, are unable to supply their entire food requirements and certain other necessary commodities; these people have specialised in the production of trading products such as pottery and canoes. In Malinowski's time the *kula* incorporated nearly all the islands off the south-eastern coast of Papua and included the south-eastern portion of the mainland. More recent research by

Fortune, Belshaw and Lauer has established the existence of other independent ceremonial trade rings and regular trade routes.

With the coming of the Europeans and the development of a cash cropping economy, the necessity of maintaining seasonal commercial exchange has lessened. People on the islands are now able to buy food and other commodities from trade stores and new markets have become available in areas that before had been hostile territory. But certain items are still widely traded today, including pottery, betel nut, yam, sago, basketry, wooden bowls and jewellery. The pottery industries described by Seligmann and Malinowski are flourishing and subsidiary *kula*-type rings linking the network of islands in Milne Bay Province and including the Papuan coastal villages are maintained by periodic trading expeditions. In the outlying islands of the Trobriands, Amphletts and Engineer group, *kula* canoes are still used but in general the motor and diesel have replaced the sails and wind of the island mariners.

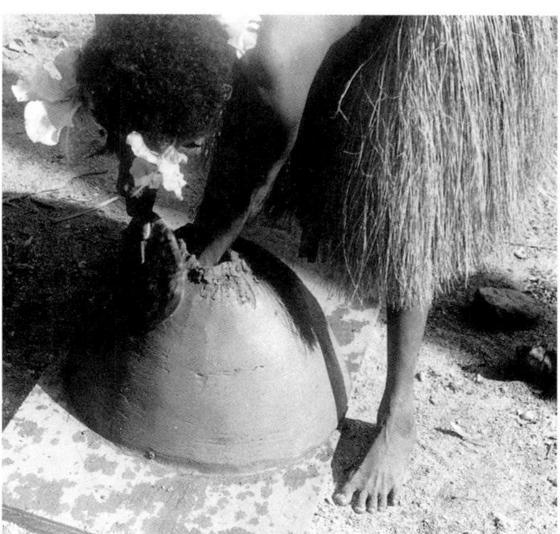

Fig. 4.6
Sabito shaping and smoothing with the paddle, Nabwageta Island, Amphlett group.

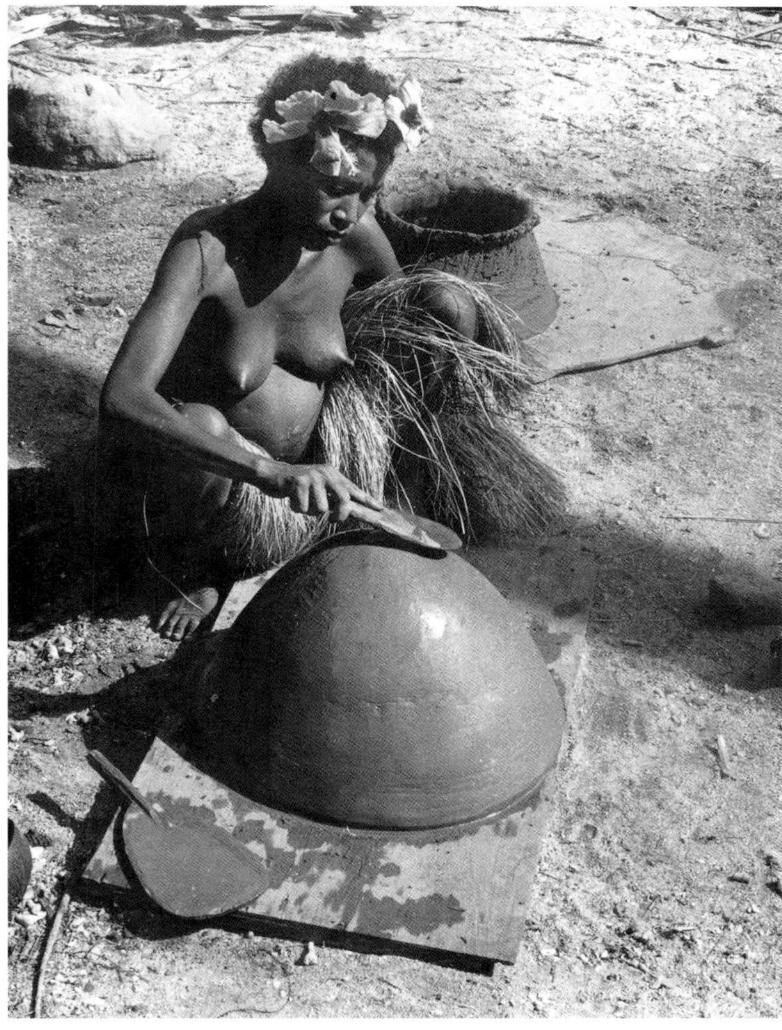

Fig. 4.7
Sabito carrying out the final smoothing after another pot has been started, Nabwageta Island.

Amphlett Islands

> The strongest and best decorated pots in the Possession are made on the islands of the Amphlett Group whence they are traded in two directions, northwards to the Trobriands and southwards and eastwards to Milne say and the neighbouring islands. [Seligmann: *The Melanesians of British New Guinea*, 1910]

Pottery from the Amphlett Islands is highly praised and valued by nearly all the people living on the islands off the south-eastern coast of Papua. Now, although metal cooking pots are readily available at trade stores and are used in many households, clay vessels are still made in great numbers and widely traded. The people agree that food cooked in clay pots tastes better than that cooked in aluminium and the acquisition of pottery still involves voyages to or from the pottery centres, affording desired social contact with other islands and with the mainland of Papua. The following description of pottery and techniques of Goodenough, Amphletts and Normanby islands is a compilation of data recorded by Peter Lauer in a number of

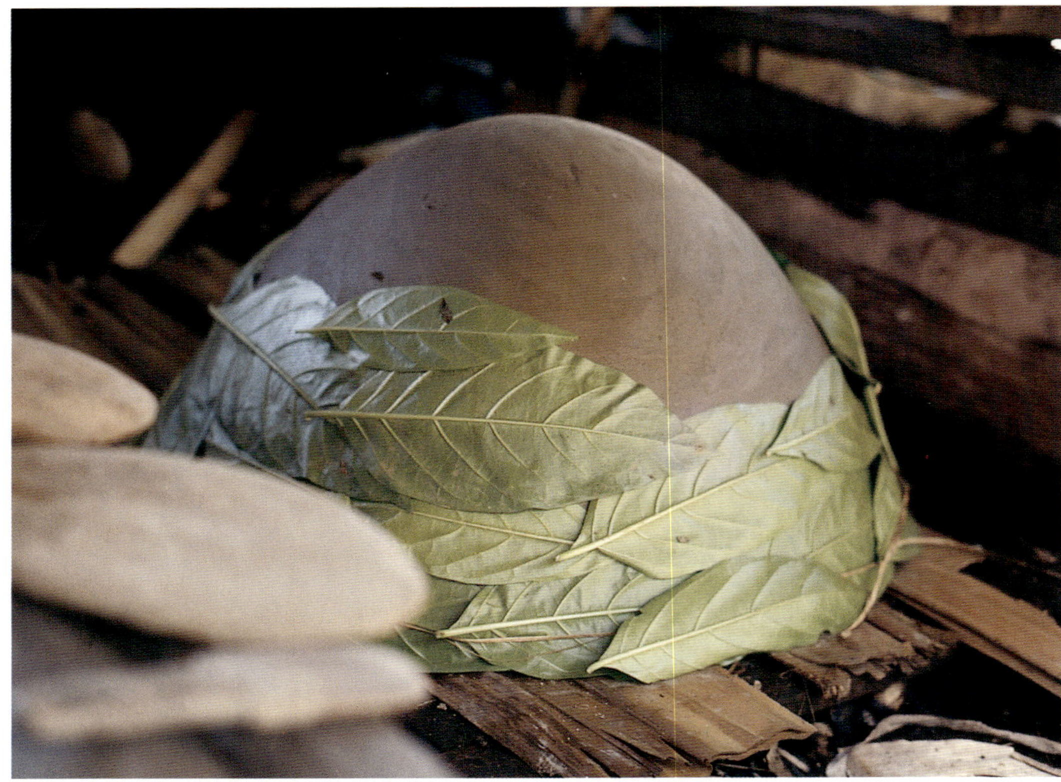

Fig. 4.8
Green leaves keeping the rim damp on a drying vessel, Gumawana Island, Amphlett group.

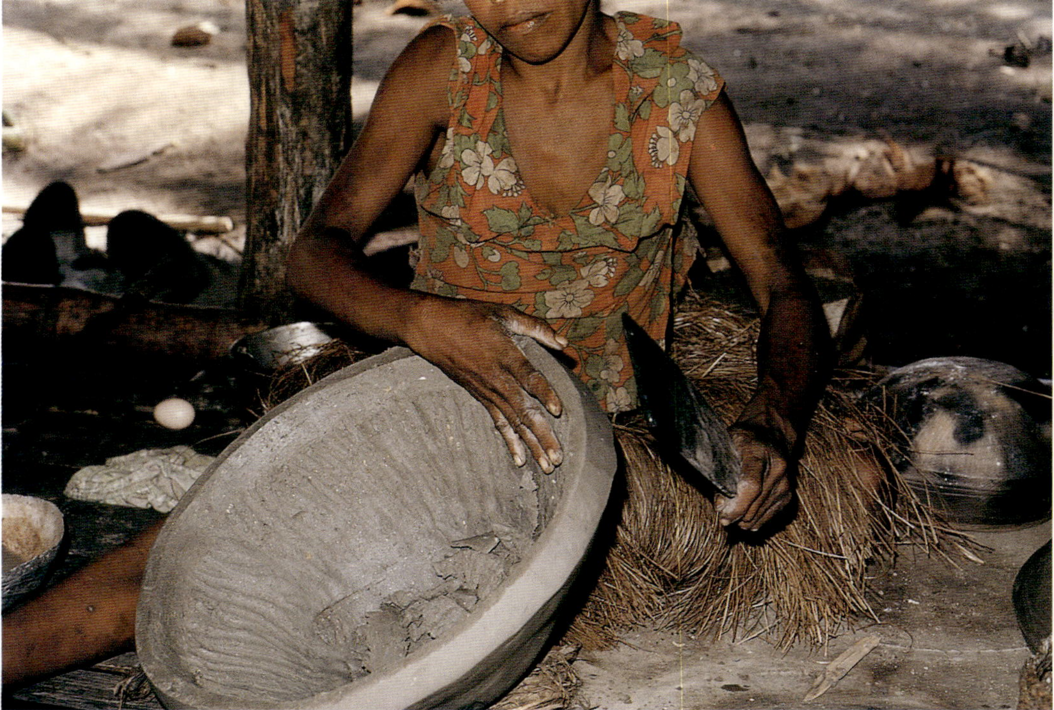

Fig. 4.9
Leesi beating over the rim of a leather-hard pot. Scraped marks show the beginning of the thinning process, Nabwageta Island, Amphlett group.

publications and information gathered by the authors during a field trip to the area.

Practically all women older than about fourteen years who live on the four inhabited islands know how to make pottery. Although the manufacture of pottery is women's business, men traditionally participate in two important aspects: they are responsible for gathering the clay and for the distribution of the finished vessels destined for sale and exchange.

According to the legends of the Amphlett people the knowledge of pot making originally came from Kiriwina in the Trobriand Islands, where the people first emerged from a cave named *obuwaga* to settle all the Trobriand group. Eventually, a group of migrants left the Trobriands to settle on Gumawana Island, taking clay and the art of pottery with them. The clay was deposited at Tumonomono, a high point on the island. At the hamlet of Kitautauna lived Namaleo and her husband Tolalabena. One day, a dispute arose and Tolalabena accused his wife of sleeping with Tolosipupu, a man from Gumawana village. Tolalabena accused Tolosipupu in front of the entire village and the two men came to blows. Tolalabena was defeated. He left Gumawana Island with his wife and migrated to Fergusson Island, to a place called Yayevana. Namaleo filled her basket with clay and took it to her new home. Ever since, the clay on Gumawana has been unsuitable for making pottery and the men of the Amphletts have had to obtain their clay from Yayavana. Usually, when the men sail to Goodenough Island on pottery exchange voyages, they stop off at Yayavana on the return trip and fill their canoes with clay from the pits. The clay is distributed to the families of the men who took part in the voyage and helped quarry it.

There are several clay pits at Yayavana, starting with a large deposit located at the bottom of a steep hill. The clay from this site is dark grey-blue in colour and is mainly used to make large pots called *nokuno* and to supply the applied decorative elements on other types of vessels. Two other sites further up the hill contain a reddish clay used in making smaller pots. The men remove the topsoil, loosen the clay with a digging stick and pack it quite solidly by pressing it down with their feet into baskets made from coconut fronds. Each basket can carry about 40 kilograms of clay. The baskets are then loaded onto the canoes and transported home. Here they are distributed, covered by a mat of grass and stored under the houses, sometimes for as long as six months.

The Amphlett potters use a technique of pot making unique in Melanesia. Essentially, the vessels are built upside down, starting with the rim and finishing with the rounded bottom, in a technique combining slabs and rolls of clay for the main body and paddle beating to smooth and shape the body and finish the rim.

The clay contains less than 35 per cent of clay minerals, which consist of kaolinite and chlorite; the non-plastics include talc, quartz, feldspar, some blue-green hornblende and muscovite mica.

The potter prepares the clay on an old canoe hull, breaking the hard dried pieces with a large pebble, adding fresh water and working it in with her hands until the clay becomes sufficiently plastic. It is then kneaded and shaped into a large lump that is rolled on the trough into a cylindrical shape. Stones, roots and grit are removed during this process.

The clay, now ready for building, is divided into two equal parts and rolled into thick cylinders, their sizes varying according to the size of the intended vessel. From these cylinders are formed two flat, elongated slabs of clay which are set on edge on a flat wooden base to form a circle. Their ends are then joined together. Additional clay is placed in

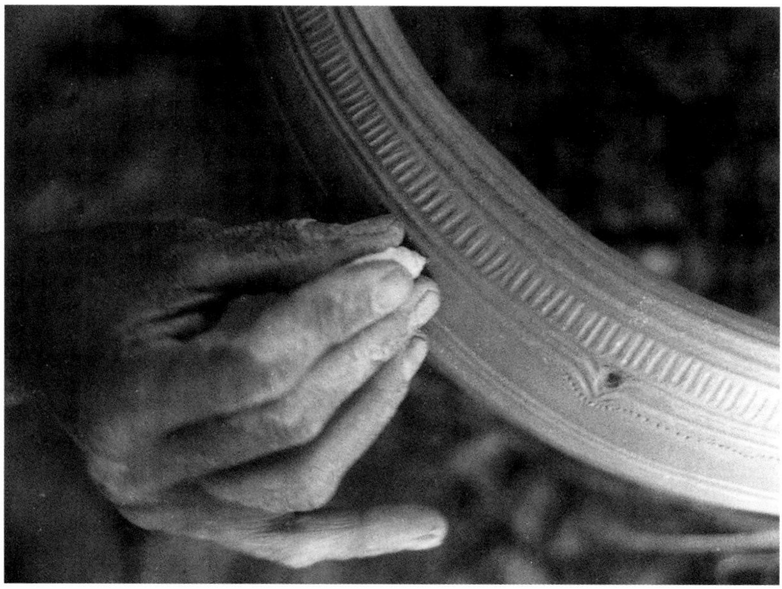

Fig. 4.10
Decorating a *nosipoma* with a shell, Nabwageta Island, Amphlett group.

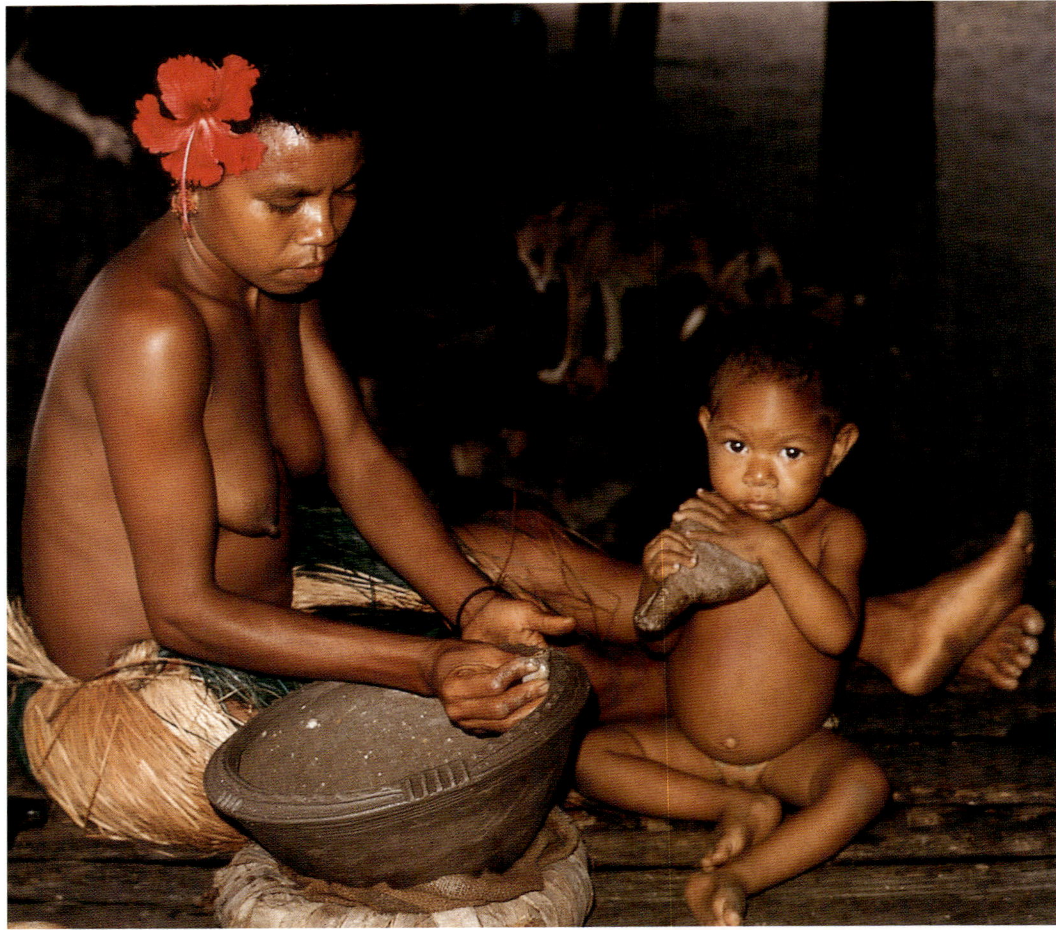

Fig. 4.11
Dauyoni decorating her pot with a small shell, Nabwageta Island.

the centre of the circle. While supporting the interior sides of the circle of clay with her left hand, the potter, holding her right hand in a half-closed fist position, scrapes the clay upwards from the outside to form a constantly growing, upward and inwardly curving vessel wall. In order to carry out this technique, it is necessary for her to move around the pot. Short rough rolls of clay are taken from the middle lump, added to the top edge of the wall and thoroughly bonded by scraping. Finally, the vessel attains a dome shape with a small hole in the top centre. The potter then smooths the outer wall by beating with a moistened paddle in a downward motion: she supports the vessel wall from within by thrusting her left arm through the hole in the top. To close the top and form the base of the vessel clay is dragged towards the opening and distributed evenly while the finger is slowly extricated; the base is then beaten with the paddle until a rounded shape is achieved. Irregularities of the outer rim are removed by the paddle (figs 4.4-4.7).

The vessel is left in the shade to dry for one or two days until it reaches a leather-hard condition. The rim may be protected by a covering of green leaves or moist cloth to prevent it drying too quickly (fig. 4.8).

The leather-hard vessel is removed from the wooden base: a grass ring is placed on the bottom of it and it is then inverted so that the pot comes to rest on the ground right side up. The lip is smoothed and trimmed with a wooden stick and rounded by a rubbing motion of the fingers. The characteristic Amphlett rim is shaped by beating the rim towards the centre of the vessel with the paddle, with blows directed downward while the left hand supports the wall from within. When the lip attains the proper size and evenness it is trimmed again with a wooden knife and smoothed with the flat side of a paddle. The vessel is then ready for decoration which, for most types of vessels, is applied to the rim area; the lip usually remains unelaborated except in the case of the *nofaewa* which is generally decorated also along the shoulder (figs 4.9, 4.10).

Decoration of the pots consists of grooving, applied designs and stippling. Impressed parallel lines or grooves are made on the rim area with the edge of a large flat bean seed which is held between thumb and index finger. Excess clay, pushed up by the grooving motion, is smoothed over the design by the potter's index finger. Applied design is achieved by rolling a number of thin strings of clay, each 3 to 4 millimetres wide and 15 centimetres long, which are then applied horizontally along the upper edge of the groove or as separate design motifs. Stippling of the applied coils, grooves and lines is achieved with the serrated edge of a shell. When the decorations have been completed, the interior wall of the vessel is very carefully scraped with the edge of a shell. It has been purposely left thick until now to withstand the pressure exerted by the decorating tools. When evenly thinned it is burnished with a small stone or the smooth side of a slipper shell in a quick, arching, up-and-down movement below the shoulder and in a horizontal direction above the shoulder. The outside has already been burnished with the large smooth seed while the pot was still upside down. The distinct marks left by this process assist in identification of Amphlett sherds (fig. 4.12).

Pots are dried in the open air for a further two to three days. The fuels used for firing are dried coconut husks and fronds and split wood. The source of greatest heat is the wood, the husks being used for kindling. The vessels, singly in the case of larger pots or compositely when they are smaller, are fired in the open air, usually on the sand when a slight breeze is blowing. First, dried coconut husks are lit then a grid-type framework of wood is placed over them. The vessels are placed upside down over the wood. Dry coconut fronds are stacked in a pyramid over and around them. By this

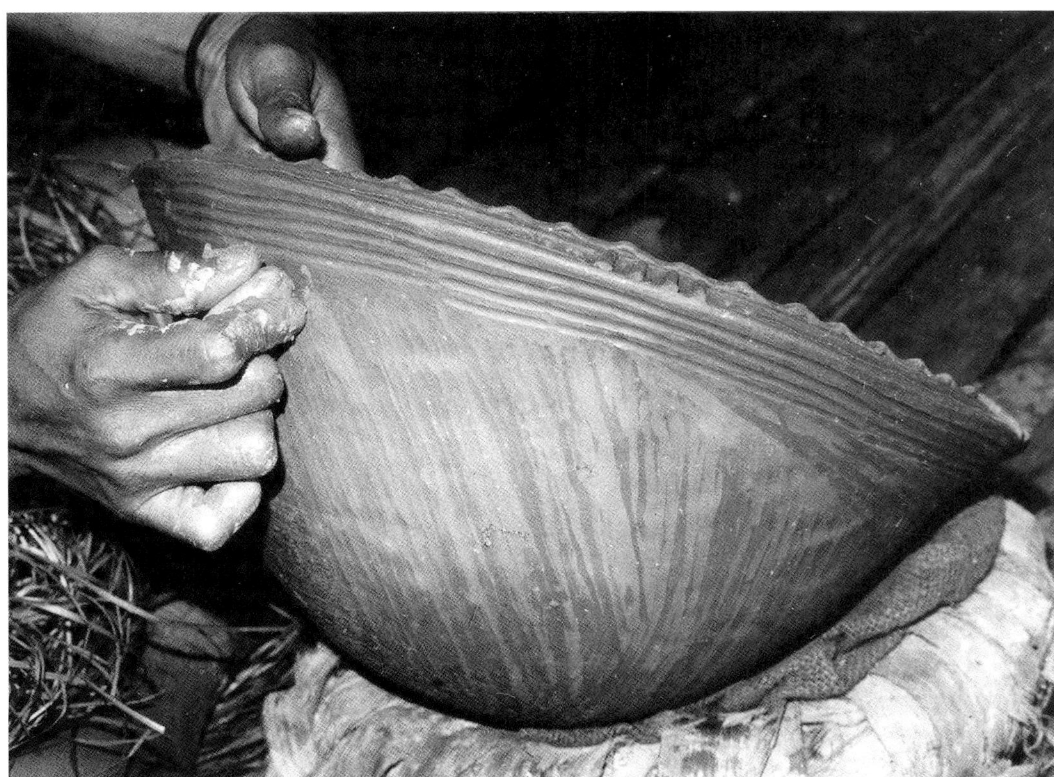

Fig. 4.12
Dauyoni burnishing with a small, smooth stone, Nabwageta Island, Amphlett group.

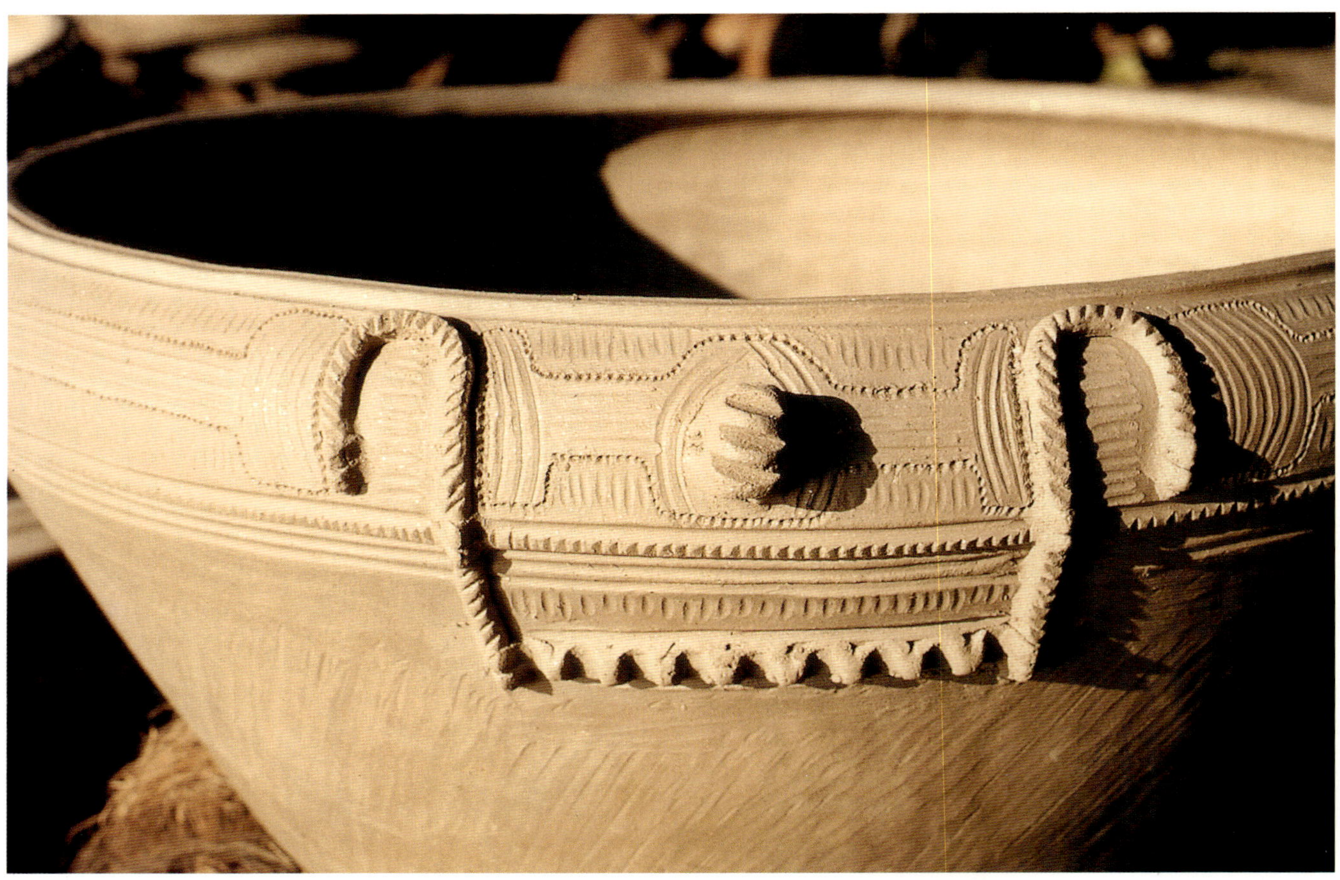

Figs 4.13 to 4.17
All from Nabwageta Island, Amphlett Islands.

Fig. 4.13
A *nokuno* drying in the sun.

time the wood has started to burn quickly and the potter watches the firing closely in case she has to replace coconut fronds which slip or protect the fire from sudden increases of wind. The potters believe loud noises can break the pots and strict silence is observed. The firing process is completed after some forty minutes. Two sticks are used to remove the vessels from the heat before the temperature falls and causes discolouration. They are turned right side up and left to cool. If small cracks have occurred in the rim these are sealed with the sap from a plant during the cooling off period. Coconut juice is usually added to the hot vessel to seal it.

The temperatures of several firings were recorded by Lauer: the average temperature was 700 to 800°C the highest 918°C. In order to produce an unsmudged surface it is important that the vessels be removed from the heat before the temperature falls. Amphlett pots are noted for their flawless, reddish-pink colour when properly fired as well as for the thinness of their walls and their aesthetically pleasing decoration. They are also famous for the speed with which food can be cooked, a very important factor in areas where there is little fuel.

There are seven named types of vessels produced by the Amphlett islanders, each of which is characterised by size, shape, function and decoration. In general, the basic form of the pots is a round-based, cone-shaped container with an inward turning rim. The types and some of their distinguishing characteristics may be described as follows. The *vaegatoina* and *nofaewa* are identical in shape and characterised by an inverted rim area separated from the upper body by a marked shoulder. The *vaegatoina* is an everyday cooking pot while the larger *nofaewa* is used during feasts for boiling yam and taro and has a greater range of decorative elements and greater complexity of design. The *kaokao* (no longer made) and *nokuno* are both

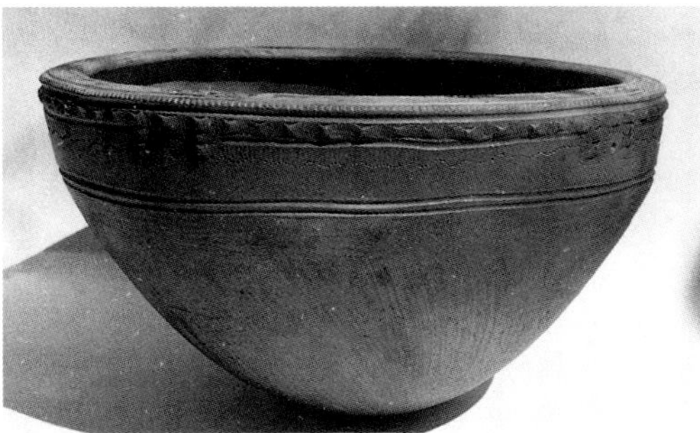
Fig. 4.14

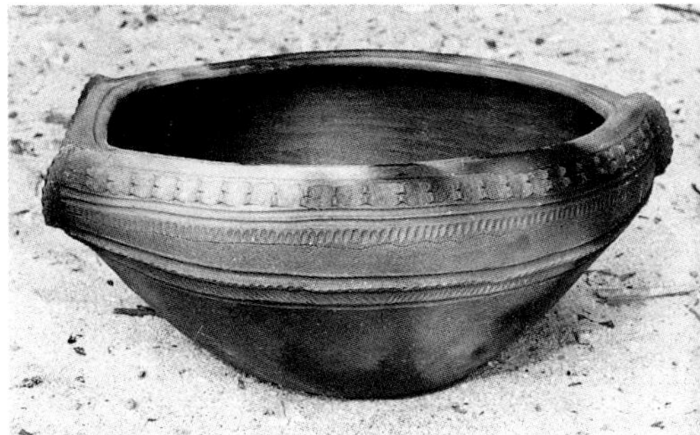
Fig. 4.16

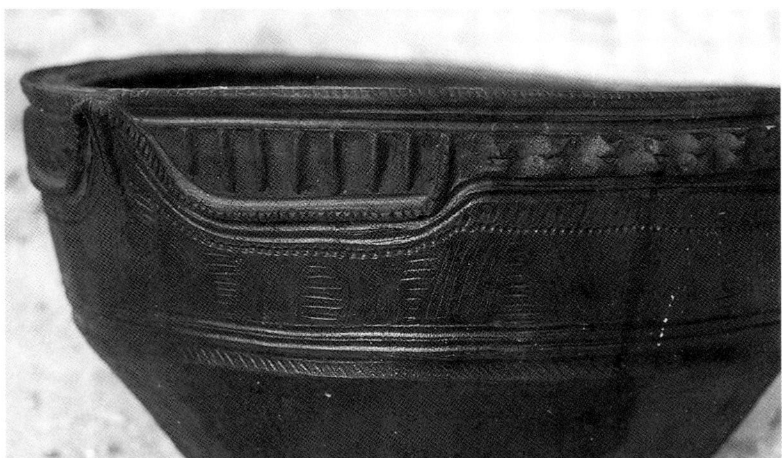
Fig. 4.15

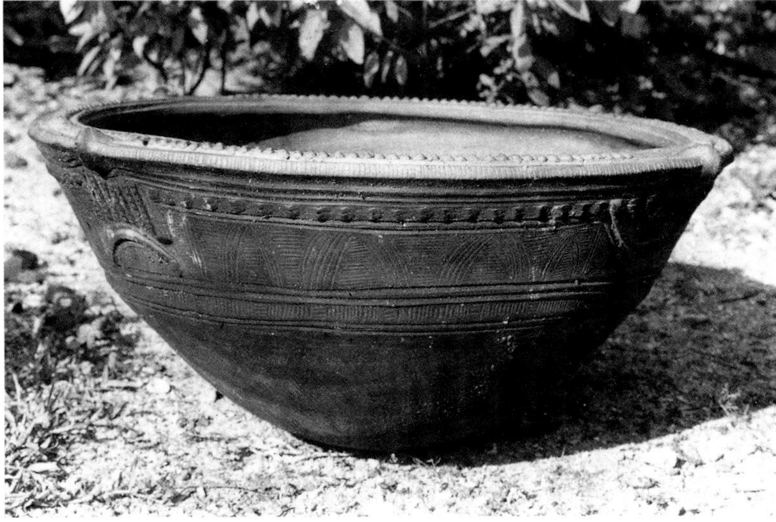
Fig. 4.17

distinguished by a rounded shoulder and inward arching rim; the *nokuno* is large enough to be used for food preparation during feasts and is decorated on the upper body and rim by symmetrical stippled parallel grooves that run in different directions, applied rolls of clay forming U shapes and applied semi-circular discs of clay. The *nosipoma, aidedeya,* and *alimanu* have composite forms and are similar in size but the most striking differences between them appear in the treatment of the rim and involve the absence (*nosipoma*) or presence of two (*aidedeya*), three or four (*alimanu*) protrusions spaced at equal intervals around the circumference. Lauer (1974) describes a divided cooking pot used on Goodenough Island to separate foods such as fish and vegetables but he makes no mention of one from the Amphletts; a newly-made one was collected by the authors at Nabwageta Island in 1975 and the name given for it was *wabodapaina* (figs 4.14-4.18).

Goodenough Island

On Goodenough, the population is concentrated on the small alluvial plains along the north-western shores. The seven major hamlets where pots are produced are Buduna, Kikwanaura, Monunaoya, Vedakala, Wisalu, Manuebeleya and Yauyaula. Almost all the adult women in these hamlets know how to make pottery: it is still widely used and especially valued for ceremonial occasions. Pottery plays an important role in the village economy; as an item of trade with the neighbouring non-potting peoples, it ensures additional food supplies when the villagers' stock runs low. There is, however, no trade with people other than Goodenough islanders. While the individual skill of particular potters is recognised within the pottery community, potters and their families do not achieve greater status nor do aesthetically or technically superior pots bring higher prices.

Fig. 4.14
Feast or common cooking pot, *nofaewa, h* 17 cm.

Fig. 4.15
Common cooking pot, *aidedeya.*

Fig. 4.16
Cooking pot shaped like a European boat, an unusual *aidedeya* made by Negode, *h* 20 cm.

Fig. 4.17
Cooking pot, *alimanu, h* 25 cm.

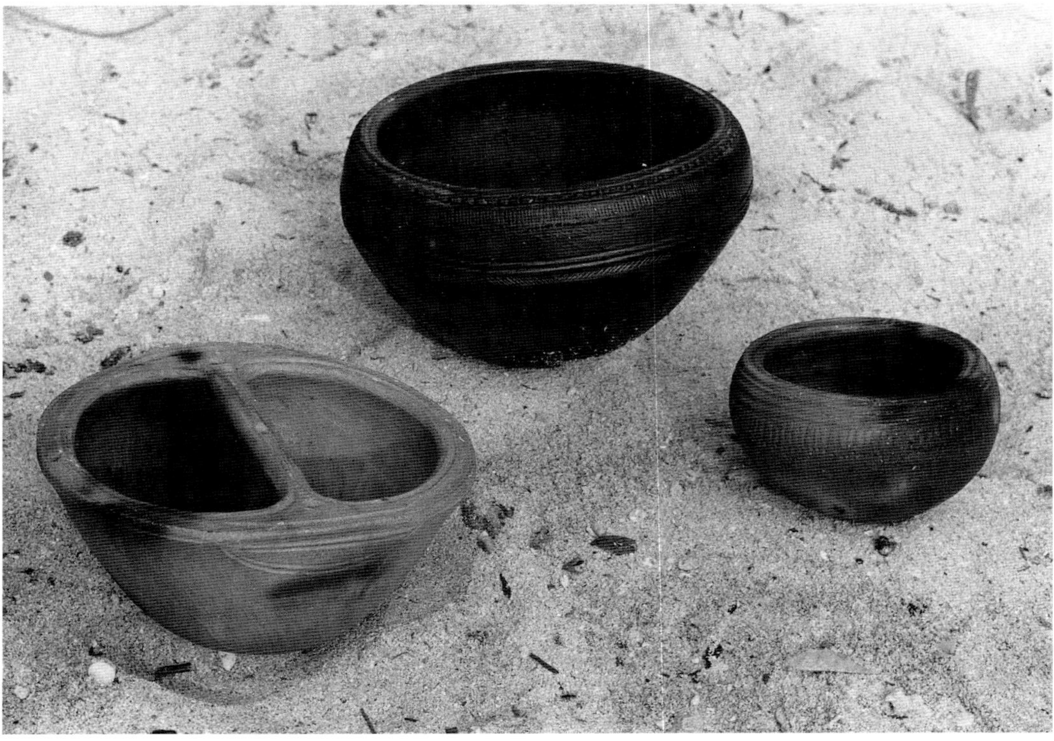

Fig. 4.18
Three cooking pots from Nabwageta Island, Amphlett group: (left) *wabodapaina*, *h* 9 cm; (centre) *nosipoma*, *h* 13 cm; (right) *kaokao*, *h* 9 cm.

Three types of cooking vessels are made, with local variations. Basically, the vessels are round-based and conical with an inward turning rim. One is round, one oval and the third has a partition dividing the interior into two parts, which allows separate cooking for different foodstuffs. The local word for pottery is *tage*: there are no specific words to describe the three different types of pots.

The Buduna potters, helped by men and children, gather their clay from pits about 2 kilometres away. Grass and topsoil must be cleared first, then the grey clay is dug out with a traditional digging stick or a bush knife. Like the Amphlett clay, it has a low proportion (less than 28 per cent) of clay minerals made up of allophane and kaolinite; it also has some smectite. Fresh water is mixed with the clay before it is kneaded between thumb and fingers.

The tools and techniques are similar to those of the Amphletts. The Buduna potters are the only other group in Papua New Guinea to form the vessels upside down but, instead of starting the form with slabs, thin coils are used. Short thick pieces are formed from the prepared clay and many coils are rolled out to finger thickness on a 'pangal' or a board and set aside in an unusual manner. The potter picks up both ends of the coil and places it in its U shape in a dish. The outline of the mouth of the pot (ultimately the top of the vessel) is marked with a wet finger on a board. The first coil is laid on the damp marked circle and spiral coiling is continued upwards and inwards. Each coil is pinched onto the one below, overlapping on the outside. As in the Amphletts, only a finger remains in the central hole which is filled by dragging clay up to it with the little finger. The pot is then bonded and smoothed. When the pot has become leather-hard, the shape is perfected by gentle beating with the wooden paddle. Later it is turned right side up and the edge is levelled with a shell or knife and the inside is thinned by scraping with a shell. The rim is beaten inwards in the same manner as on the Amphletts.

Decoration, which consists of grooving, stippling and appliqué, is achieved with the same techniques and tools as in the Amphletts except that the grooves are more shallow on the Goodenough vessels. Archaeological analysis of old pots shows that while a wide range of applied and incised motifs was used there is now more emphasis on grooving. Old Buduna ware reveals intricate and complex arrangements of stippled designs; the designs of recent Buduna ware are simpler and lacking in detail. This points to a decline in the standards of the Goodenough pottery while, conversely, the modern Amphlett pots have gained in the skilled quality of the decorations. Goodenough pottery has been found widely distributed on the island but today it is restricted to the northern aspects of the island. Lauer suggests that while the markets for Goodenough pottery were wider in range in the past, the present restriction of its distribution may have led to a loss of quality. Another consideration is that Goodenough Island did not participate in the *kula* ring trade. Since contact, traditional *kula*-linked centres have given way to less restricted marketing patterns and the Amphletts, who monopolised the pottery trade to the Trobriands and to Dobu Island, expanded their markets to include other islands, especially Goodenough. Goodenough Island pottery therefore no longer has a monopoly and quality has declined.

Firing in the Amphletts and on Goodenough Island differs in that the absence of wood on Goodenough has led to the substitution of sago fronds, although stories refer to the wood of a special tree which should always be used for firings. The number of vessels to be fired together is limitless. To fire four pots, two ribs of the coconut fronds are placed parallel on the ground, about 1.5 metres apart. Two more ribs are laid in rectangular fashion over this frame. Dry coconut leaves are placed in the centre and lit. Then short fronds are further laid over the rectangle and the vessels are placed upside down on the platform. Sago fronds are stacked around the pot and the fire is lit with coconut leaves. Firing takes from fifteen to twenty minutes and vessels are removed from the fire with a long stick. Both fires attain a high degree of heat but the sago fire produces a shorter firing period with a more rapidly rising and falling temperature.

Lauer suggests that there is little doubt that these two separate pottery industries belong to the same tradition because of the similarities of technique, form, decorative elements and legends relating to the origins of pot making.

Like the early population of Goodenough Island, who emerged from a hole in the rock on Gauyaba, the first settlers of the Amphletts came out of a similar hole in Gumawana Island. In both Goodenough and the Amphletts there were later immigrants who came with pottery, though the legends are clearer on Goodenough about the earlier inhabitants' ignorance of ceramics. The origin of the Goodenough

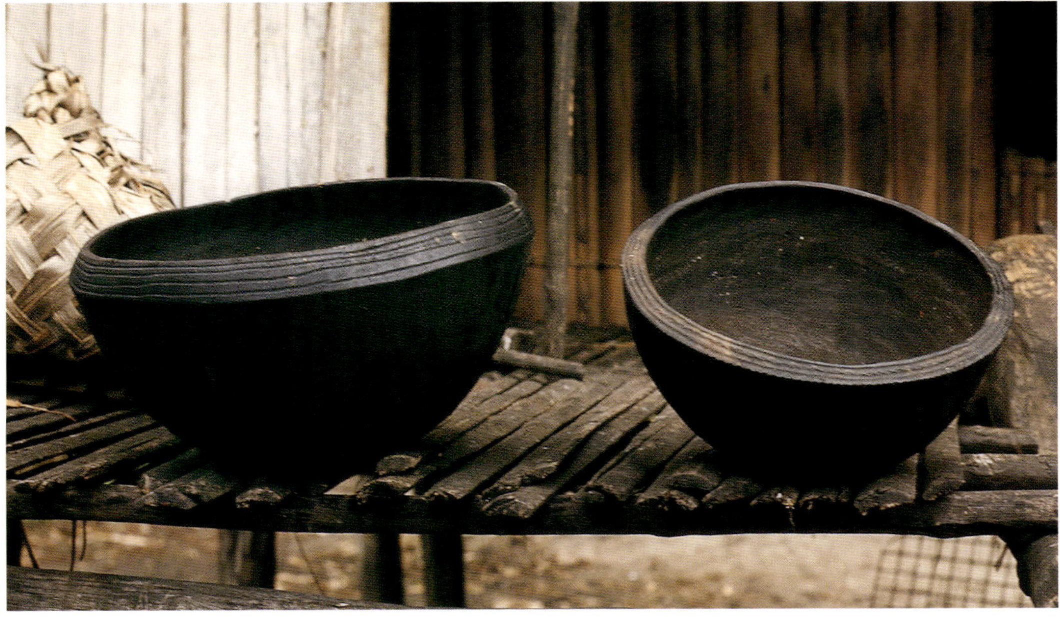

Fig. 4.19
Two used cooking pots, *tage*, made by Draima, Buduna village, Goodenough Island: (left) *h* 21 cm; (right) *h* 16 cm.

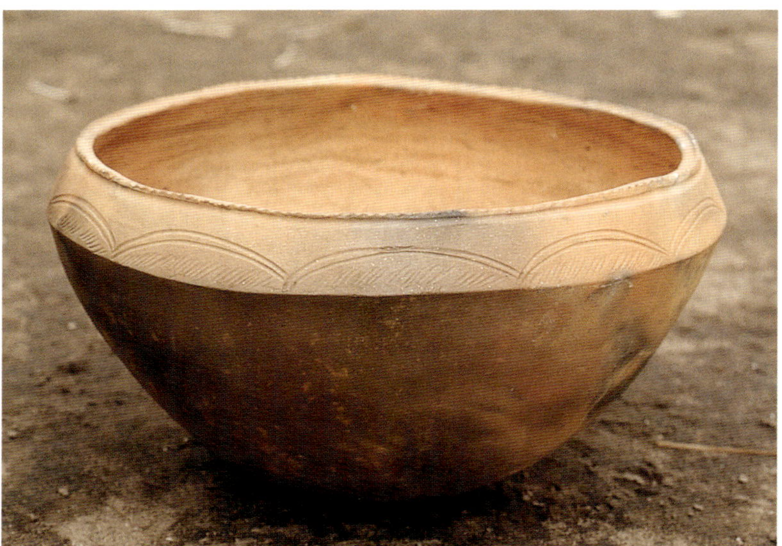

Fig. 4.20
A new, unused cooking pot, *tage*, Sivesive hamlet, Goodenough Island.

immigrants is not specified, the Amphlett immigrants, allegedly from the Trobriand Islands, are said to have brought with them the clay from which good pottery can be manufactured. [Lauer, unpublished manuscript]

Normanby Island

The third pottery producing area of the D'Entrecasteaux Islands is Miadeba, located on Normanby Island. While other pottery producing centres of Milne Bay – Goodenough, the Amphletts, Wari and Tubetube islands – attracted early attention from ethnographers, Miadeba went unnoticed and unrecorded until Lauer's description (Lauer 1971). One reason for Miadeba's anonymity is that it is not today and, judging by information, was never in the past a prolific industry and produced vessels only for local use.

The Miadeba people inhabit ten hamlets on the eastern shore of Normanby Island and the four surviving potters recorded by Lauer live in four of these: Matamalala, Bosiawana, Auwalai, and Wauvauto, all of which are situated on a coral peninsula. Only one type of vessel is produced, a conical pot with a direct rim and 18 to 40 centimetres tall. This vessel, used only for cooking, is simply decorated by incised parallel wavy lines running around the interior and exterior portion of the upper rim. Occasionally, lugs (small lumps of clay) may be applied to the extreme vessel walls on opposite sides. The only clay pit in use today is near Matamalala village; the clay is greyish. The potters do not store clay in their hamlets but gather it when they are ready to build a pot. The only tools used are a digging stick for extracting the clay from the pit, a mussel shell for scraping the vessel walls, a grass ring for support of the vessel and a small shell used as an incising tool.

For most of the process the vessel is constructed in the potter's lap. Fifteen to twenty rolls of clay 2.5 centimetres in diameter are carefully prepared and set aside. The base is made in a curious manner: one side of a clay ball 10 centimetres in diameter is beaten with the potter's hand until she obtains a flat circular surface; the first coil is then pressed down by her thumb onto this surface in circular fashion. The index finger acts as guide. The next strip is joined to overlap the first by about 2 centimetres. Subsequent coils are added to the lower ones at a larger radius and thus the vessel wall grows continuously upwards and outwards. The coils are smoothed together with the thumb and the index finger. Clay is pushed up from the bulbous base to fill in the cavities between the strips. If there is any clay left, it is simply removed. The base is then rounded by beating it with the flat of

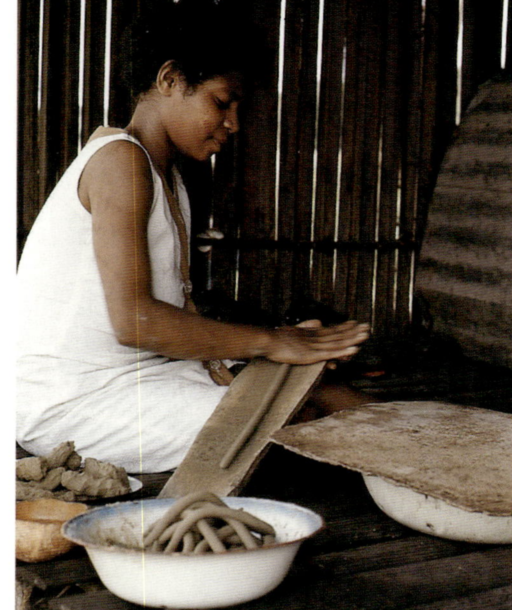

Fig. 4.21
Mattledi Alaba rolling coils, Dayakakona village, Goodenough Island.

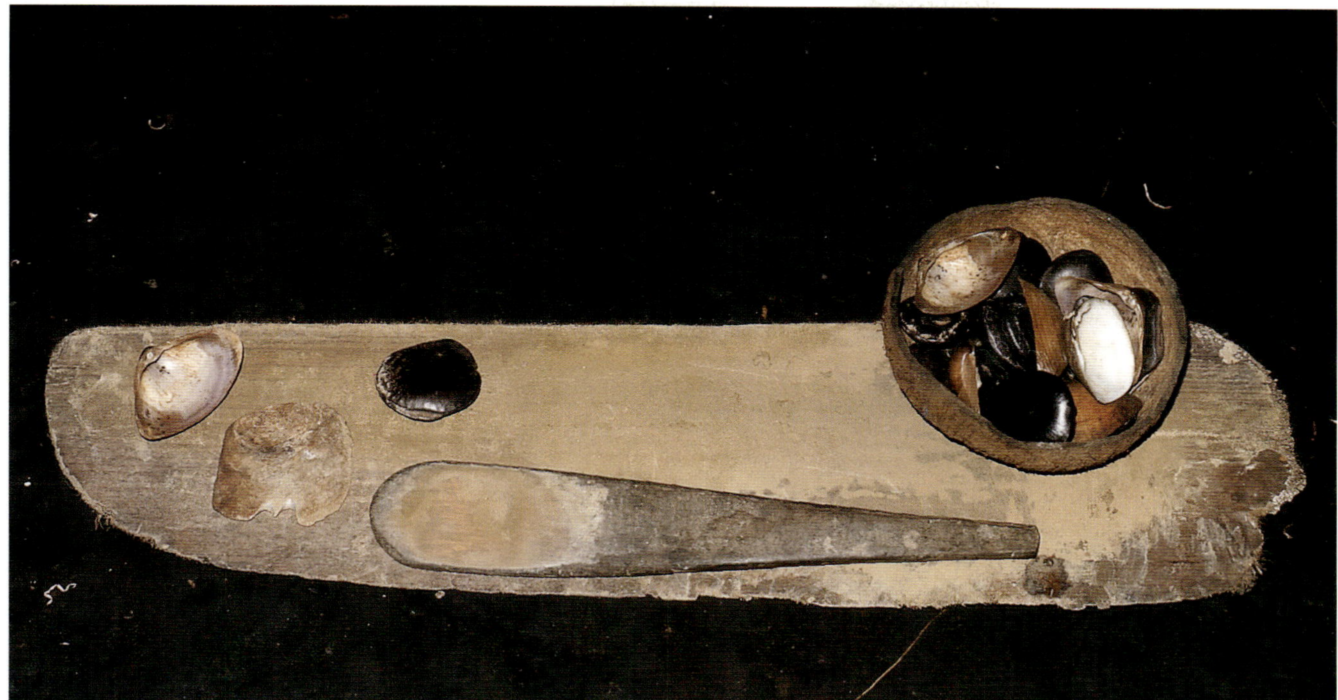

Fig. 4.22
Potter's tools – black bean seed used for burnishing and decorating, Sivesive village, Goodenough Island.

the hand and the walls are scraped, rubbed and thinned with the index finger and the concave side of the mussel shell.

When the pot becomes too awkward to hold in the lap it is transferred to a grass ring on the ground and the potter walks around the vessel, building the walls until it reaches the required size. After the pot has been decorated it is taken to a house to dry and after two or three days the vessel's bottom is thinned with the shell scraper. It is then left to dry for two or three weeks. Vessels are fired separately, upside down in open fires with charcoal and wood for fuel. The fuel is stacked upright around the pot to form a pyramid. Firing takes from fifteen to twenty minutes.

These techniques, the upside down building of pots in the Amphletts and Goodenough islands and the method of coiling onto a ball of clay at Miadeba, are very unusual by world standards and may even be unique.

Southern Milne Bay

At the end of the mainland two peninsulas, East and South Cape, jut out into the sea to flank Milne Bay. To the east and south-east are located the islands of the Louisiade Archipelago. A widespread pottery industry extends from the tip of East Cape to include the islands in and near the Engineer group, some islands of the Calvados chain and some areas of the southern mainland and offshore islands.

Wari Island, south of the Engineer group, is today the centre of this industry. Islands of the Engineer group on which pot making takes place are Tubetube, Kwaraiwa and Skelton. Anagusa and Dawson are close by. Panaeati, north of the Calvados chain, and Brooker are also potting centres. Active potters who have migrated from Wari and Tubetube produce pots on or near the south coast at Bonabona Island, Konemaiaua, Kaukau and Silosilo Bay. The tip of East Cape is another centre of activity.

Conflicting reports have been received by the authors about pot making on the coast between Cape Frere and East Cape. It is possible that pots similar to those of East Cape are made at least at Taupota. Reports of pots being made in recent years on Tewatewa Island on the eastern side of the Engineer group are unconfirmed. The people at

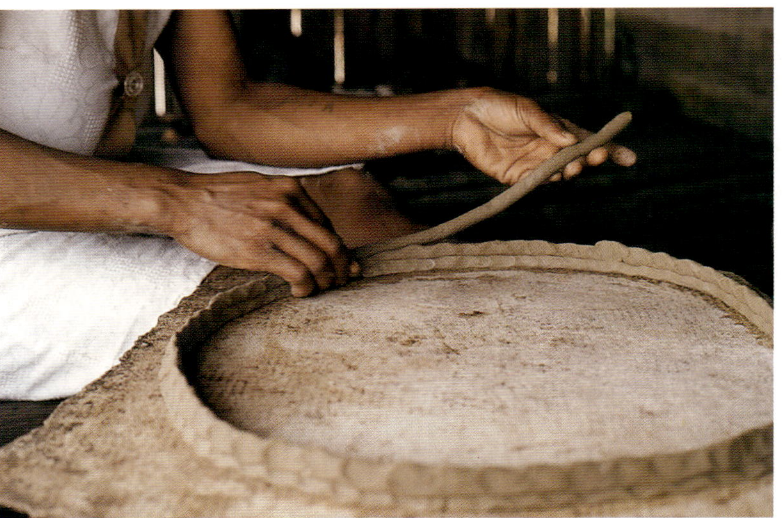

Fig. 4.23
Mattledi Alaba forming a pot upside down. Early stage of spiral coiling, Dayakakona village, Goodenough Island.

Fig. 4.24
Mattledi Alaba filling up the hole in the base of the pot, Dayakakona.

Wagawaga on the southern shores of Milne Bay give contradictory evidence as to whether they made pots in the past or not. Seligmann (1910) reports seeing locally made pots along with imported vessels from Tubetube, Wari and the Amphletts but there are no locally made pots at Wagawaga now. Along the northern coastal area of Milne Bay Province pottery is made at Cape Vogel villages in a style similar to that of pottery made in Collingwood Bay (see Chapter 5).

The most common vessel made in the southern Milne Bay industries is generally composite in shape, thin-walled, with a rounded base, a definite shoulder (usually marked at the inflection point with a horizontal design) and a neck, usually decorated, which can be straight-sided, restricted or unrestricted. It is difficult to distinguish the origins of the vessels by form or even use of design elements. In his study of the exchange pottery found in the Amphletts, Lauer admits that Tubetube and Wari Island pottery could not be distinguished by himself or the local population (Lauer 1970b). The authors also confess to being unable in all cases to distinguish vessels from given places, although pots from Wari, East Cape, Panaeati, Brooker and Mailu (Amazon Bay) can be readily identified.

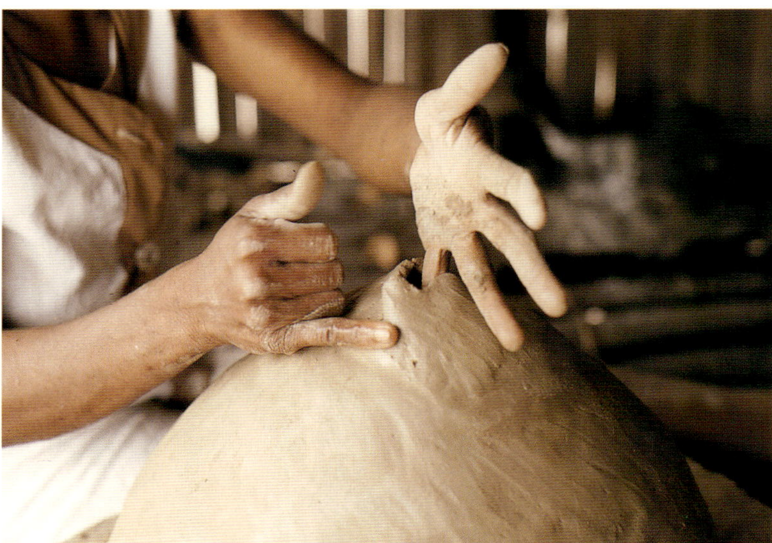

All the pottery in southern Milne Bay is made by women and their technique is spiral coiling finished by ring building. Most of the islands have their own clay deposits but several prefer to buy or exchange clay from Wari because it is considered to be superior in quality.

Tubetube (Slade) Island

Tubetube Island in the Engineer group seems to have been the dominant pot producing island and the most active in trading in the *kula* ring during Seligmann's time. The women of Tubetube still trade a few pots but are making them primarily for local consumption. They trade or buy Wari pots (in order to help the Wari people during periods of food shortage) in exchange for commodities from other islands.

On Tubetube pots are called *gulewa*. Clay, *bwatano*, is dug from the side of a hill about 1 kilometre behind the village and is carried back in baskets common to the whole of Milne Bay. The brown clay is high in smectite, with a little illite (mica) or possibly halloysite. Some talc is also present. It is a very gravelly, sandy clay with a great deal of feldspar and a little quartz. It is only moderately plastic. Men or women may gather the clay. If the clay is too dry it is put into an old pot with fresh water and left to soak for several days. When soft, it is patted into a lump and wrapped in green leaves. The potter then works the clay from the end of the lump through her thumb and fingers, removing stones and roots. The arms are held at shoulder level and a handful of the compacted clay is rolled between the hands with a slight rotating action, thus producing a thin coil about 1 to 2 centimetres in diameter and 70 centimetres long. This is then coiled spirally into a cone shape and rested against the inside slope of a shallow dish, called *kepekepe*, which is made especially for the purpose of supporting the vessel during manufacture. The right hand guides the coil to overlap with the layer below while the left thumb presses it downwards, slightly flattening it. The potter leaves regular thumb impressions on the coils inside. She works sitting on the ground, adding the coils to the far side of the pot and turning the *kepekepe* in a clockwise direction. Each roll is joined spirally in this way until the pot is about 10 centimetres high; the coils are then joined more thoroughly inside and out with a downward action of the fingers. This pressure from the fingers inside helps swell the shape out. The lower portion of the vessel eventually takes the form of the inside of the *kepekepe*.

From now on the vessel is built up in rings instead of spirally; the same joining method is used and as the pot becomes wider two rolls fit exactly around the top edge. At this shoulder point the next layer is overlapped on the outside instead of the inside. When full height is reached the pot is scraped inside and out with a shell to remove irregularities; excess clay is then scraped down to the shoulder of the pot on the outside and formed into a ridge which is smoothed between wet thumb and forefinger. The top edge is levelled by clipping it off with a mussel shell. The distinctive Tubetube rim is achieved by applying a final coil overlapping on the outside. Finally the pot is smoothed all over with wet hands and the backs of the hands are wiped against the pot until a thick slurry is formed. White and Hamilton (1973) refer to this as 'self-slipping'. No sea water must be used at any stage of manufacture because the potters believe that the pots will crack if clay comes into contact with it.

The pot is decorated while still wet. The only tools used are small combs, *kelekele*, made from sago palm bark or midrib. The potter's simple but most effective method of levelling the ends of the prongs is to hold them briefly against a glowing stick from a fire, blowing gently to make the stick glow more. This also burns off stray whiskers and presumably hardens the prongs. The combs, about 7 centimetres long and 1 centimetre wide, have from two to six prongs. The potter makes squiggly lines with rapid movements of her hand while turning the pot around on its *kepekepe* with the other hand. Lines are marked first around the top circumference of the pot and above the shoulder point, then the design is filled in in sections in the space between. Lastly, small indentations are made on the ridge at the shoulders.

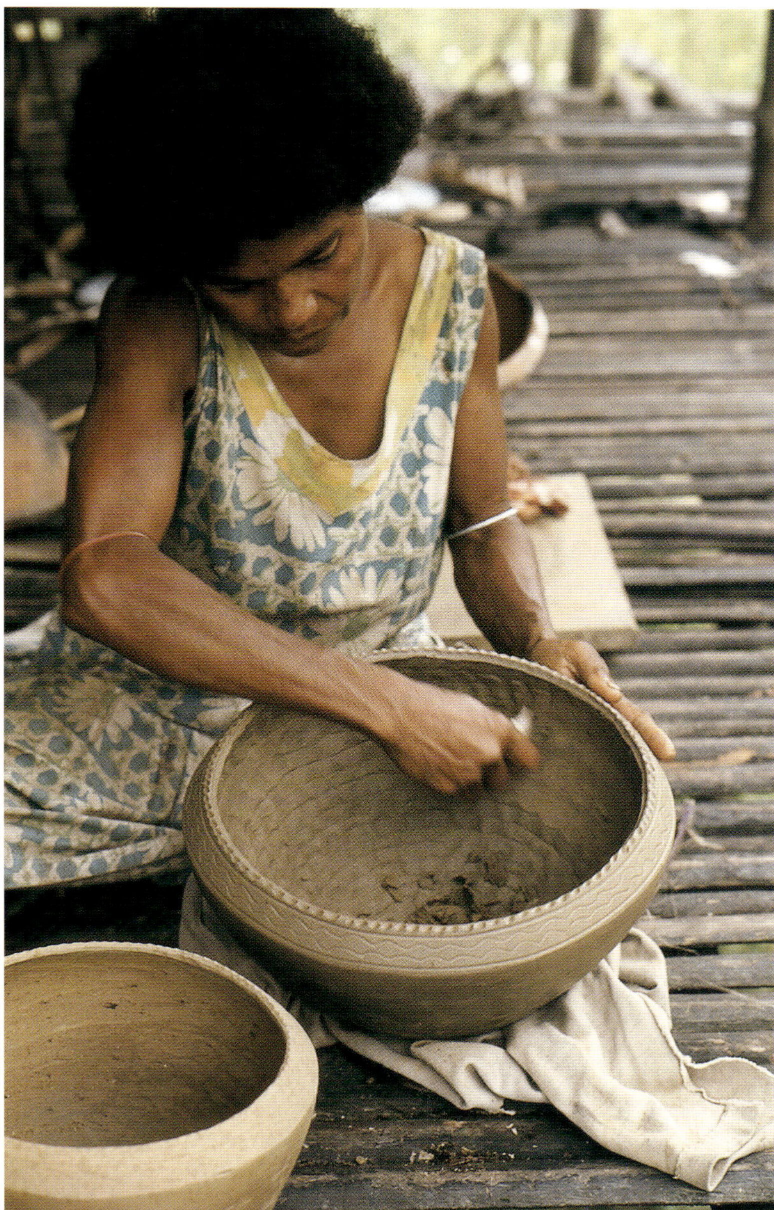

Fig. 4.25
Argoleta Frontin thinning the walls by scraping with a shell, Buduna village, Goodenough Island.

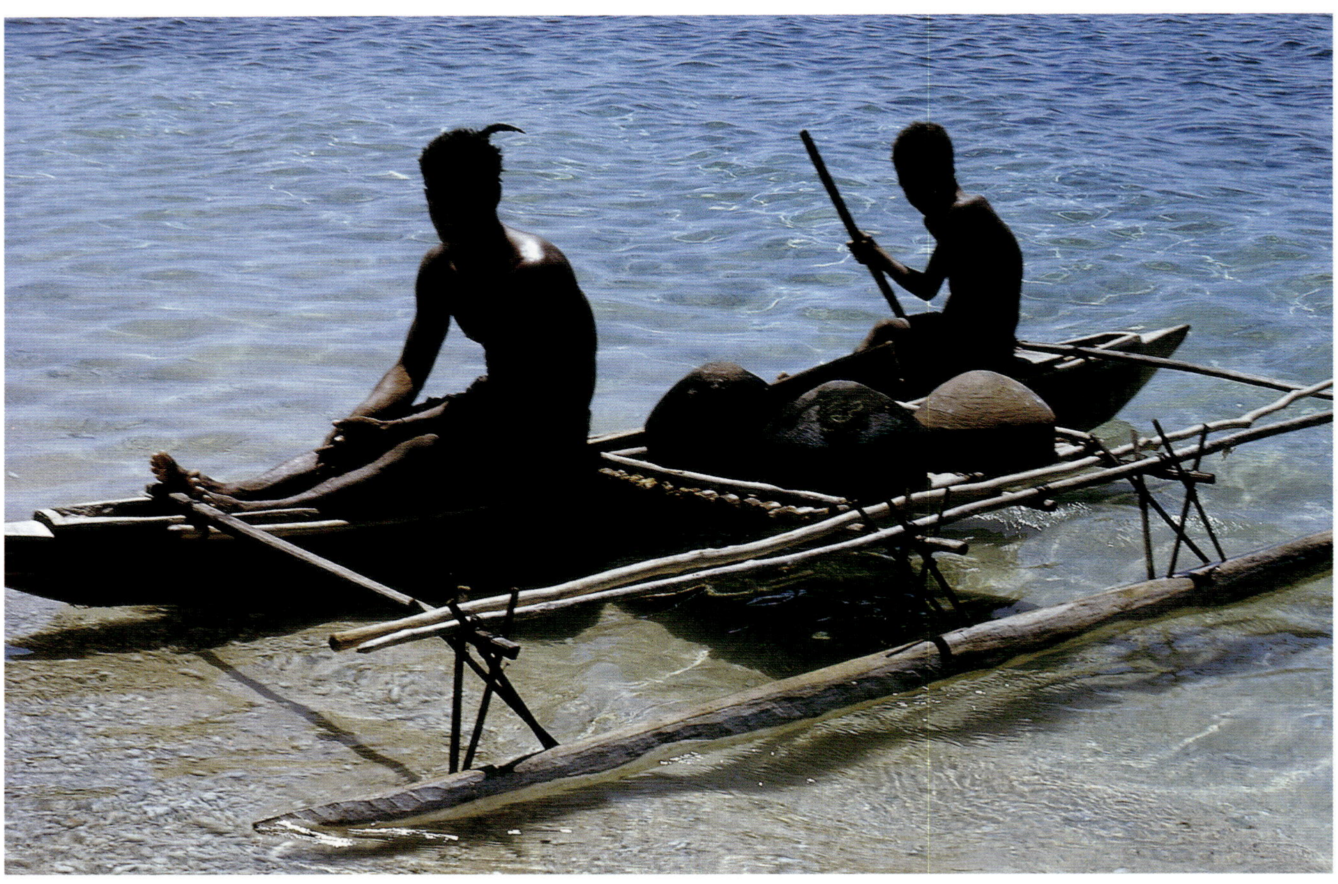

Fig. 4.26
Wari Island pots being delivered to Tubetube Island from a larger boat offshore.

The pot, still sitting in the *kepekepe* is dried for a few days. Then the potter scrapes the base of the pot with a shell and finishes it by polishing with the wet back of the shell and with her hands.

When the vessel is completely dry it is fired at any time of the day on the sandy flat behind the beach. If there are several pots they are fired one after the other on the same fire. The fuel consists of coconut palm – husks, shells, fronds and leaf-bases; the fronds are hacked into approximately 100-centimetre lengths with a bush knife. If it is available, other wood can be used with the coconut material. Firstly, a small fire is made. After this burns down a pot is placed upside down over the embers, with its rim supported on three rocks. This acts as a preheating method, for while the potter stacks the fuel around the vessel it is gradually warmed by the embers. Coconut husks are put on top of the pot and fronds and leaf-bases are leaned against it with their wide ends at the bottom, which acts as a chimney. Extra fuel is placed on the windward side. Bundles of burning dry leaves are pushed under the fuel since not enough heat remains in the embers to ignite it. The fire burns for about thirty minutes; during the last ten minutes or so the potter lifts back falling pieces of burning fuel with two long sticks. When the fire is nearly out the pot is lifted off by the end of a stick and is left on the sand to cool. Firing marks show on the pot where fronds have rested against them. Later, a small amount of coconut cream is boiled in the pot to seal it. New pots are tested by being used a couple of times for cooking before being traded or sold.

Wari (Teste) Island

Wari is about 4 kilometres long and 1 kilometre wide. Over the years it has become practically denuded of trees; the land is dry and the population must import much of its food.

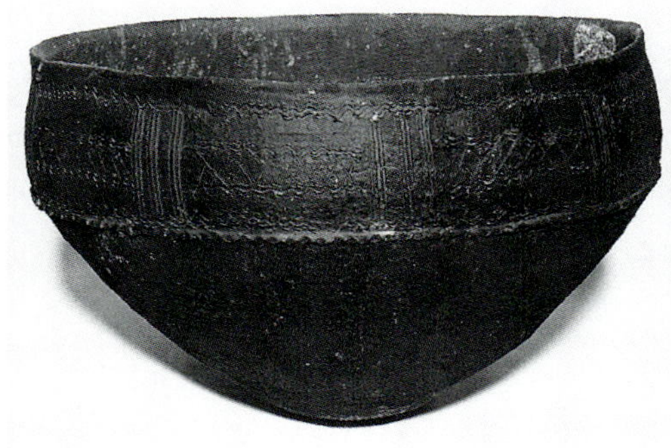

Fig. 4.27
A typical cooking pot, *gulewa*, Tubetube Island, *h* 22 cm.

A story told by Iairo Lasaro, a history student at the University of Papua New Guinea, describes the migration to Wari Island of a group of people belonging to the Badilabedabeda clan from Badilau Island, off Normanby. These people, carrying a ceremonial pot, stopped off at Nuamata Island, where they stayed a short time. Still carrying the clay pot, symbol of the knowledge of pot making, they travelled on until they arrived at a small island close to Basileke, where they fought and split into two groups. One group migrated to Wari and the other group to Bonarua Island, close to the mainland.

Cyril Belshaw, a Canadian anthropologist, spent some months on Wari studying the economic and social development of Wari and outlying islands (Belshaw 1955). His data has contributed to the studies of trading relations between the islanders in Milne Bay, the *kula* ring and the subsidiary trading rings. In 1935 as reported by Belshaw, Wari pottery was traded to the mainland and to islands such as Tubetube, Basileke, Wagawaga, Suau, Normanby and Samarai. Today, Wari is producing pottery for trade on a much larger scale. In 1973-74 the authors found that Wari pottery was traded as far as East Cape, Alotau, Kwariawa, Skelton, Anagusa, Dawson, Wagawaga, Bonarua, Dobu and the Trobriand islands. Formerly, the Trobriand islanders depended on the Amphletts, East Cape and Normanby Island for their pottery; recently, however, the Amphlett islanders have sought markets closer to home and the Trobriands have had to depend upon the rare *kula* visit for their Amphlett pots (Lauer 1970a). The Trobriand islanders are therefore eager to receive Wari vessels from the middle-men on Dobu and Tubetube. Wari vessels have a reputation in Milne Bay for being superior ware. Evidence of this superiority in quality and appearance is provided by the fact that most households, even those on islands where pots are made, have several Wari vessels on hand.

Pots, *gulewa*, are distinguished by the local people by size only. The vessels range from a small pot, *kikidoydoy*, about 10 centimetres high, to a larger pot, *unsansan*, the average height of which is about 22 centimetres. The shallow dishes used for building pots are called *nibaniba*.

Decoration of the exterior walls begins at the shoulder point and stops a few centimetres short of the rim edge. It consists of parallel wavy lines made by incising tools (two, three and four-pronged combs), forming vertical and horizontal set patterns repeated in separate registers around

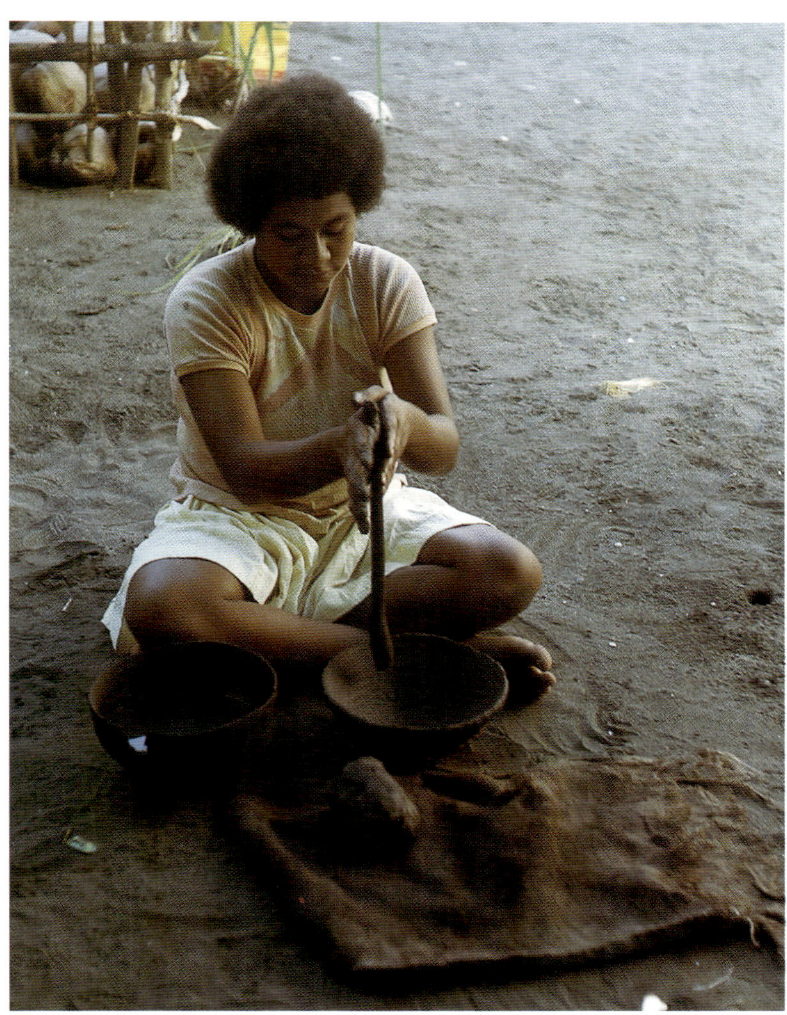

Fig. 4.28
Maila of Wari Island rolling a coil. The same technique is used on Tubetube Island.

Fig. 4.29
Ring building: Maila of Wari Island overlapping a coil on the outside as is done on Tubetube Island.

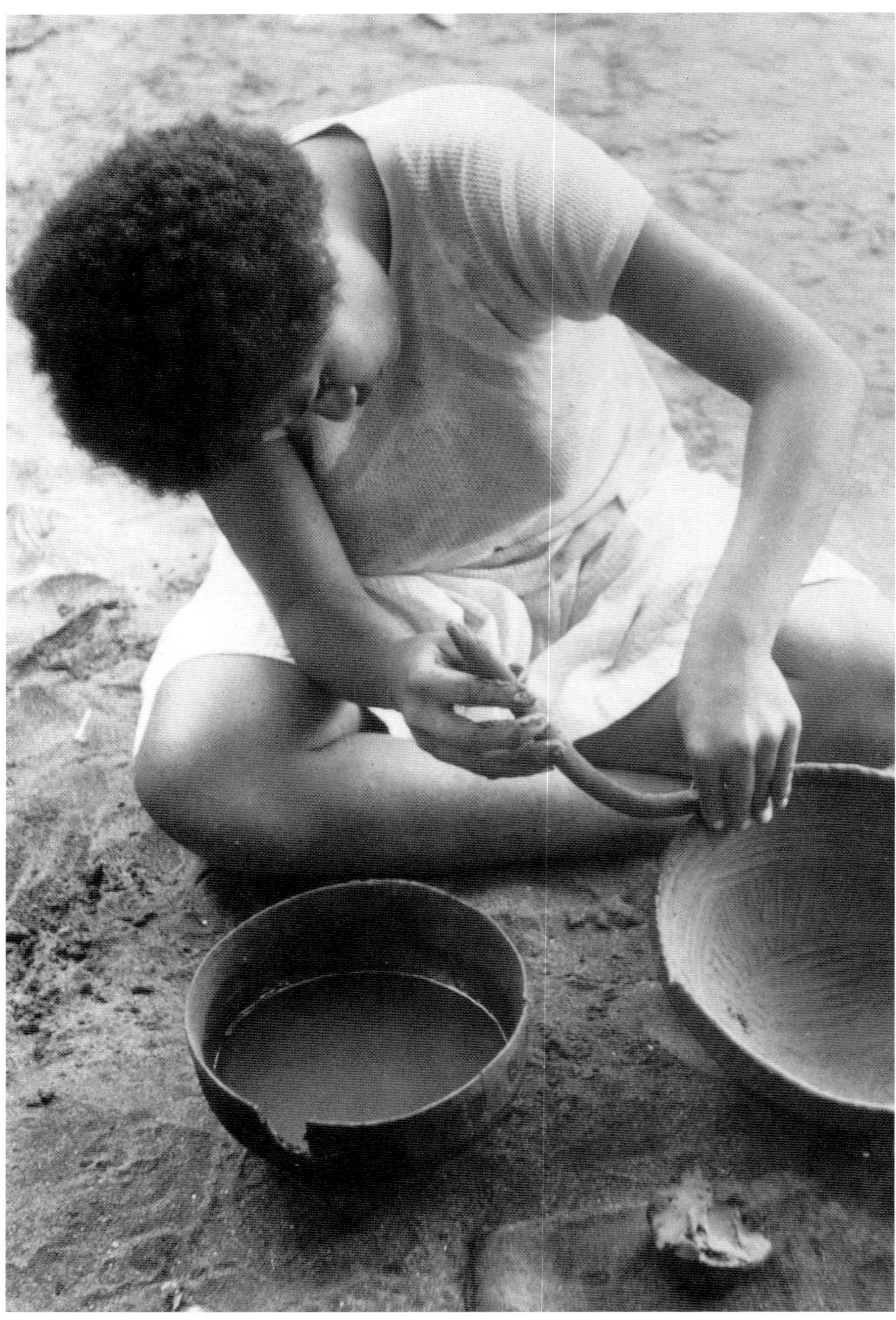

the circumference. Each series of design elements had a name in the past and in some cases informants were able to identify both the name of the design and its representation of a particular aspect of nature, for example, a cross-section of a leaf, a net sinker, a butterfly. The shoulder point itself is defined by gouge marks made with the end prong of the incising tool or the exterior edge of a mussel shell.

The incising tools, *boyaboya*, are made from a species of black palm wood which is not found on Wari but must be imported from Basileke Island. The two-pronged comb is called *kaysilisililobe* and the four-pronged comb is called *kayatayatata*. In many cases the potters seemed uncertain as to the names and meanings of the designs.

Clay, *dubadubais*, is collected by women from the other side of the island. N. Peterson (1971) reports that there were two kinds of clay on Wari, one red and one black. Tests carried out on Wari clay used by the Anagusa women showed the black clay to be very similar in composition to the Anagusa clay. Techniques of production are almost identical to those used on Tubetube although no excess clay is scraped down to the shoulder to form a ridge. Wari vessels are quite distinct, generally having vertical or nearly vertical necks.

Skelton (Naruaruari) Island

About five women still produce pots, *guliawa*, here for local use and trade. Pots are taken to Samarai and sold in the local market, to Basileke Island and traded for sago, taro and betel nut and to Sideia and Normanby islands. Water carrying vessels used to be made but are no longer produced. It would seem that the water pot is now obsolete in all these islands except for Panaeati and Brooker but that it was traditionally made several generations ago in most of this area. The Skelton people import pots from Tubetube and Kwaraiwa. None of the informants could name or identify the design of the vessels.

Kwaraiwa (Watts) Island

Some of the older women still make pots here. Nonetheless sago, yam and taro are exchanged in return for Wari pots. The authors have been unable

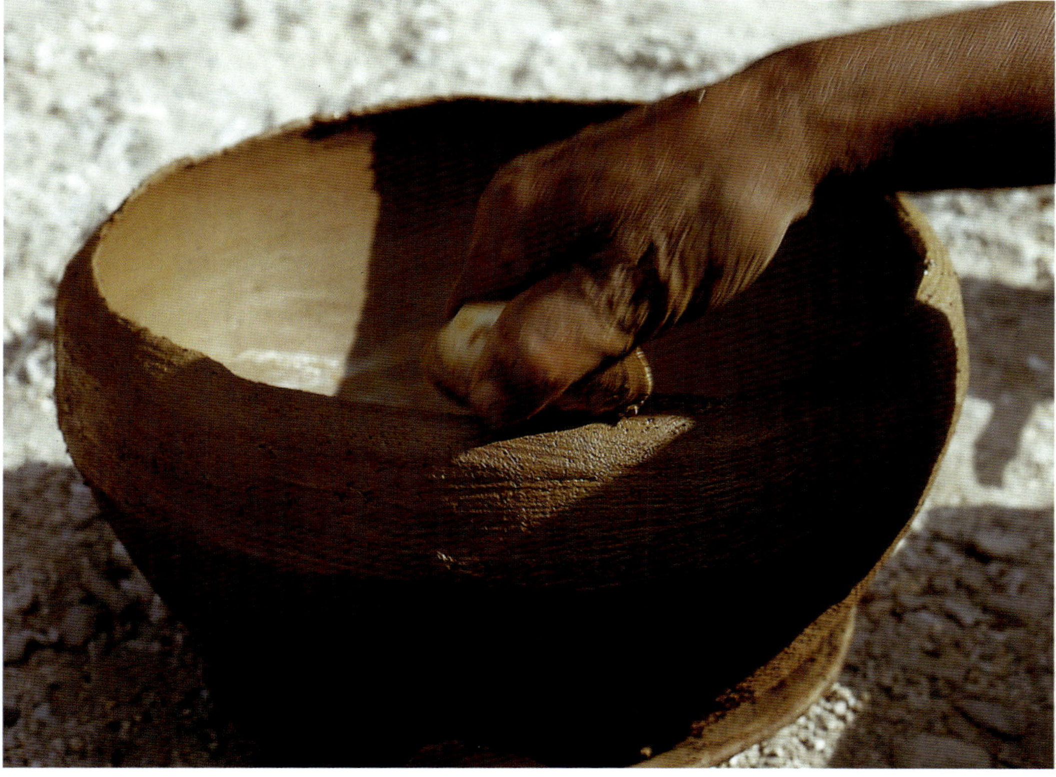

Fig. 4.30
Tubetube Island. Clipping top edge of the pot with a shell to level it.

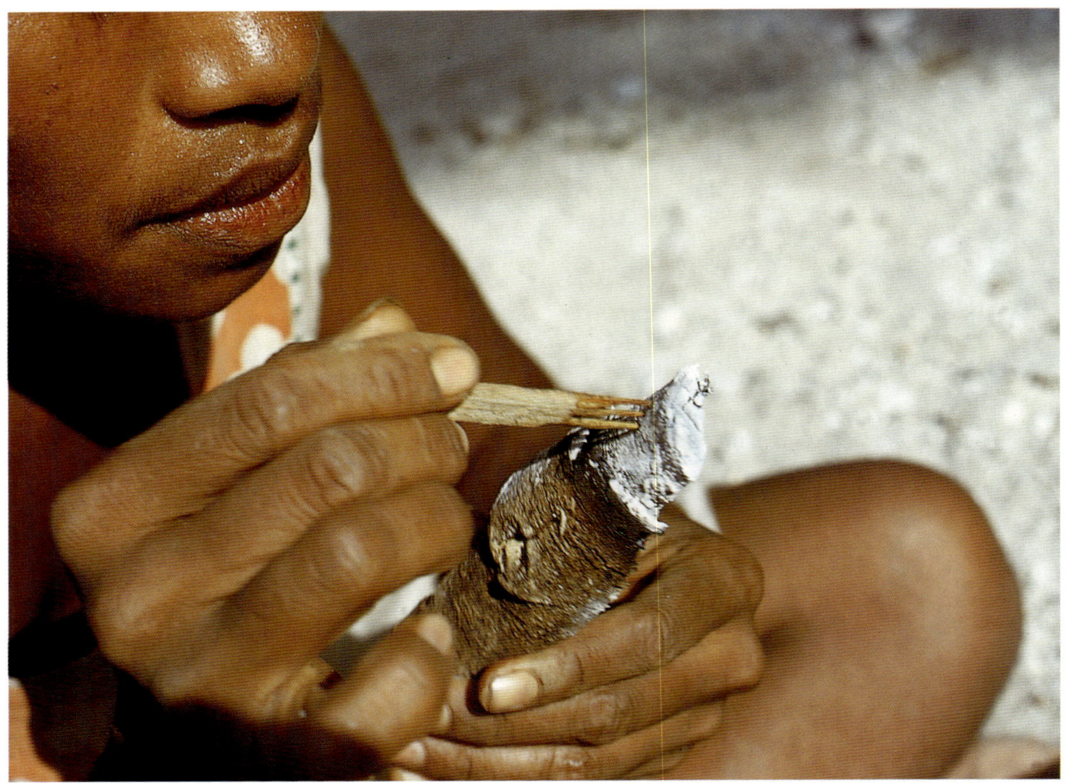

Fig. 4.31
Tubetube Island. Kempe holding a newly cut sago bark decorating comb against a glowing coal to burn it off level.

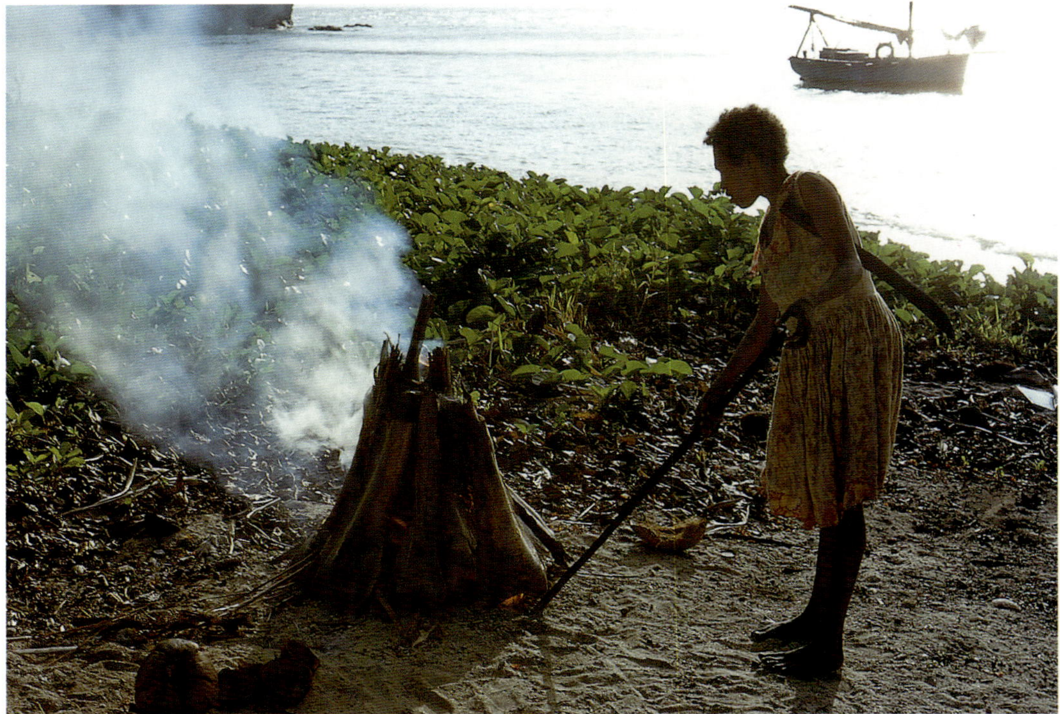

Fig. 4.32
Tubetube Island. Deidi firing a single pot in the late evening.

to establish a separate Kwaraiwa style. The black-brown, sandy clay has a little smectite and illite or possibly halloysite; among the non-plastics is some feldspar. Plasticity is fair. Although aluminium saucepans are used in everyday cooking the authors were fortunate to be on the island during a feast and twenty or so clay vessels were in use at the time.

Anagusa (Bentley) Island

Anagusa is an isolated island which lies south of the Engineer group. It has been settled by migrants from Normanby and Wari islands and it is not surprising that the pottery style and techniques are identical to those of Wari. About five women still make pots. There is a clay deposit on the island but the women prefer to use Wari clay. The local clay, however, seems to be similar to Wari clay and has good plasticity. It is black-brown and sandy in texture. The clay mineral content is divided between smectite and illite or possibly halloysite.

Dawson Island

Along with Kwaraiwa, Dawson is one of the few islands in Milne Bay visited by the authors where very few aluminium saucepans were in use. Dawson is a small, isolated island north-east of the Engineer group and has little contact with the mainland. It has not been fervently missionised, does not have a trade store and relies on its large trading canoes and trade visits to the Amphletts, Tubetube, Wari and Panaeati for exchange of goods and hospitality. Each household owns from four to six pots imported from Wari, Panaeati and the Amphletts but some locally made vessels are still in use. Pottery has not been made on Dawson since the late 1960s and the clay source, located on the

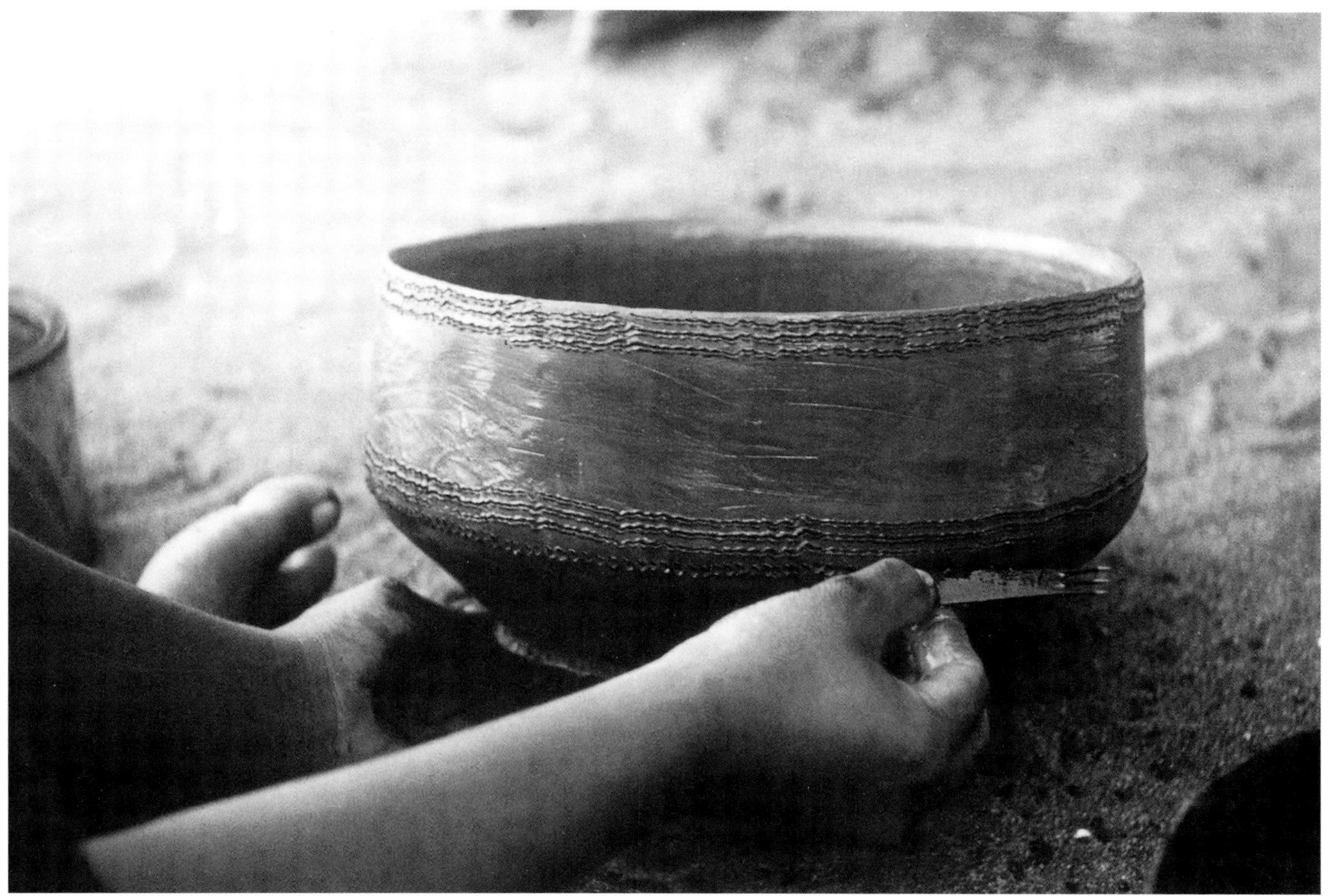

Fig. 4.33
Maila of Wari Island decorating soft wet pot, using the end of a three-pronged comb to mark the bottom row of nicks which typify a Wari pot.

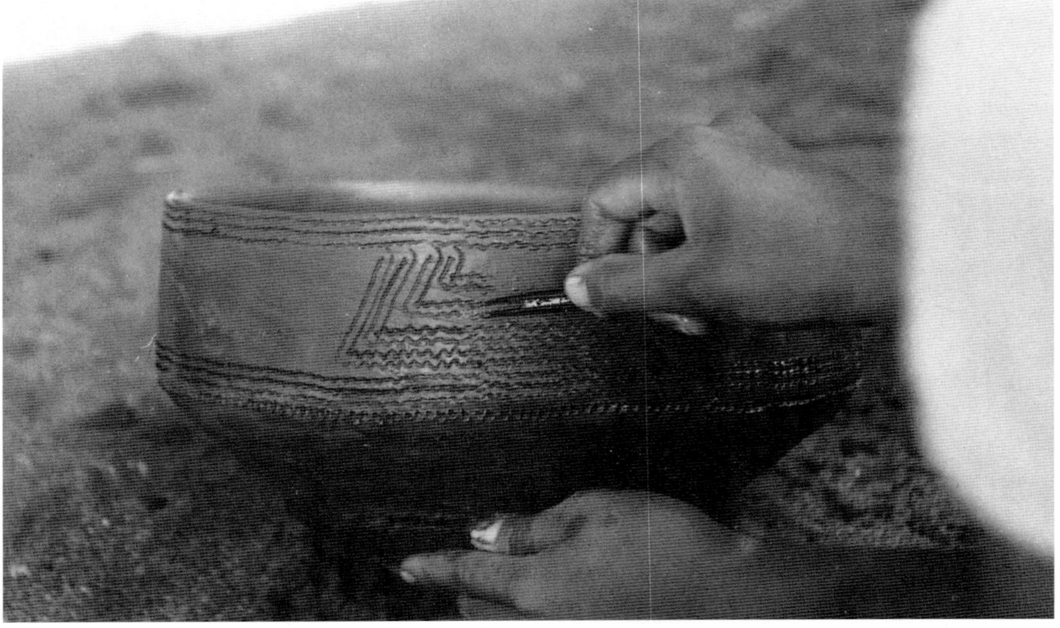

Fig. 4.34
Maila of Wari Island decorating using a two-pronged comb as is done on Tubetube Island.

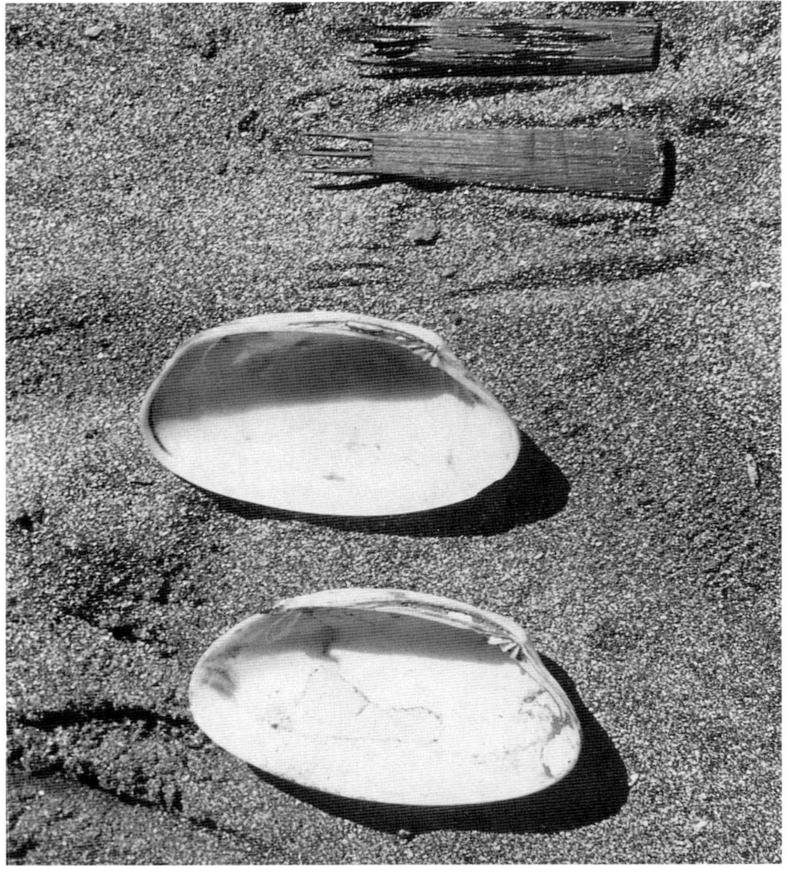

Fig. 4.35
Potter's tools, Wari Island. The same tools are used on Tubetube Island.

uninhabited side of the island, is now overgrown and inaccessible. The people say that the clay was not very good and they preferred to collect clay from Tubetube. One vessel here was similar to Wari vessels but deeper in proportion, with vertical walls. It was a huge pot measuring 51 centimetres high and 49 centimetres at the mouth.

Panaeati and Brooker (Utian) islands

The two pot producing islands in the south of the Louisiade Archipelago, Panaeati and Brooker, have to be considered an extension of the southern Milne Bay industry because of similarity in vessel form, decoration and technique of manufacture. Their vessels can nonetheless be distinguished from those of the other islands although it is harder to differentiate between the two.

Literature on the two islands is limited. In 1969 White and Hamilton (1973) recorded the manufacture of seven different types of pots on Brooker. The Panaeati industry was described very briefly by Tindale and Bartlett (1937), the latter having collected eight pots for the South Australian Museum, Adelaide. Since these reports, a description of the role of pottery in the trading practices of Panaeati and Brooker has been recorded by Stuart Berde

Figs 4.36 to 4.39
On Kwaraira Island

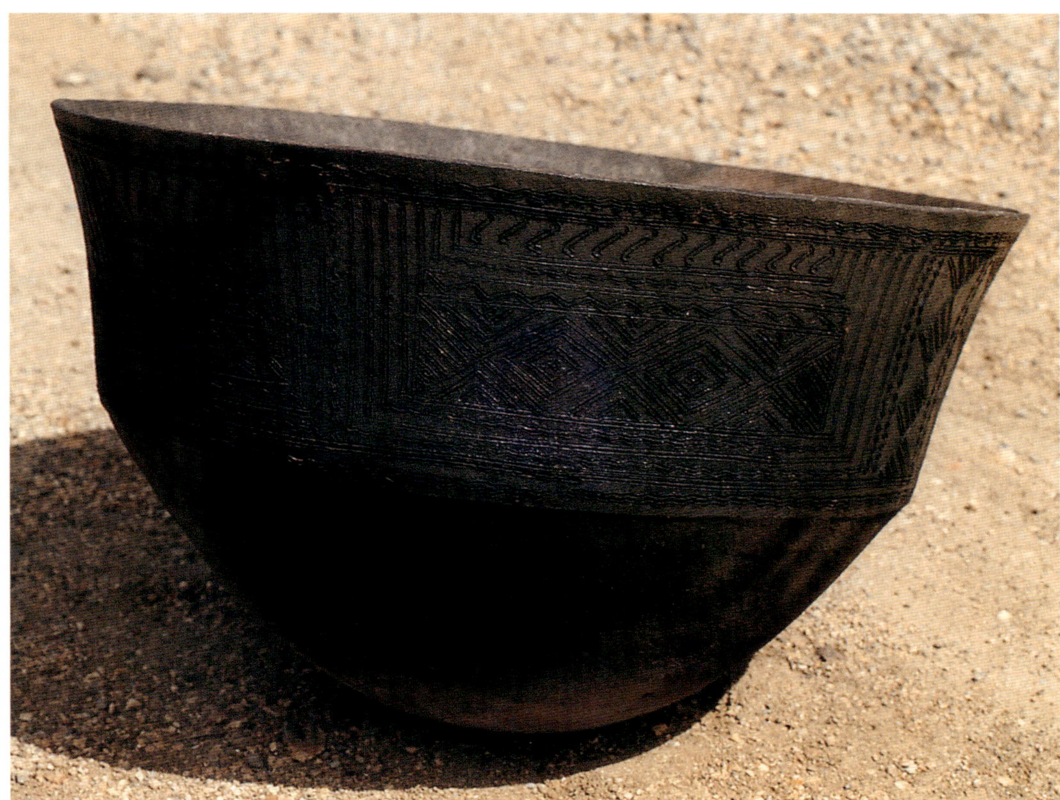

Fig. 4.36
Cooking pot made by Edna Senade, *h* 28 cm.

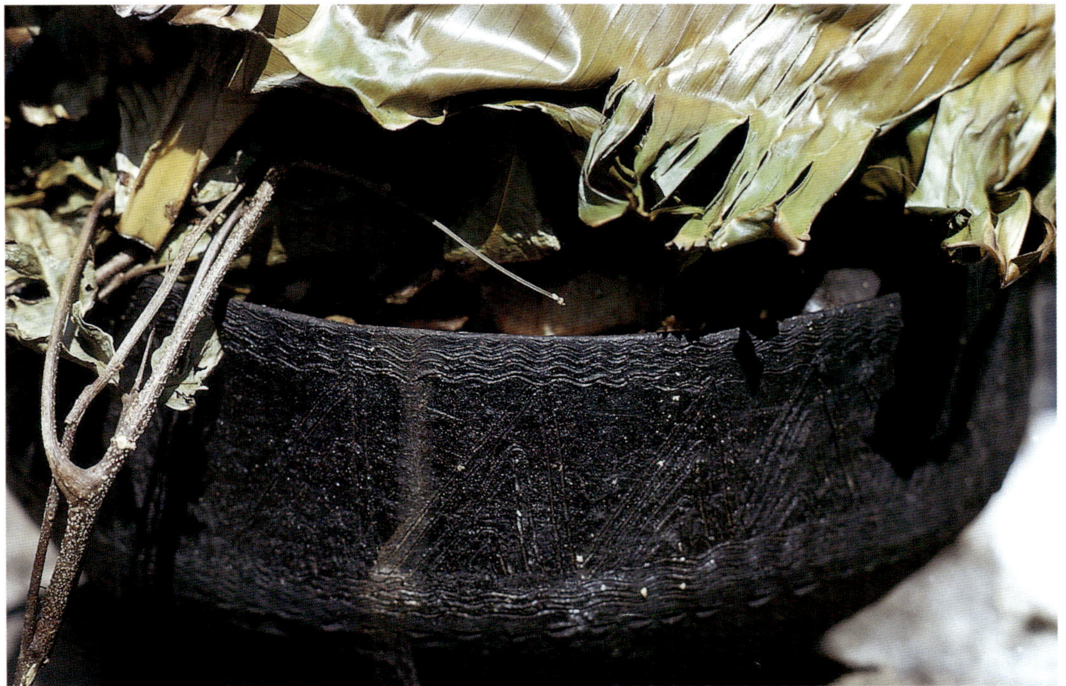

Fig. 4.37
Food being prepared for a feast in Wari Island cooking pot.

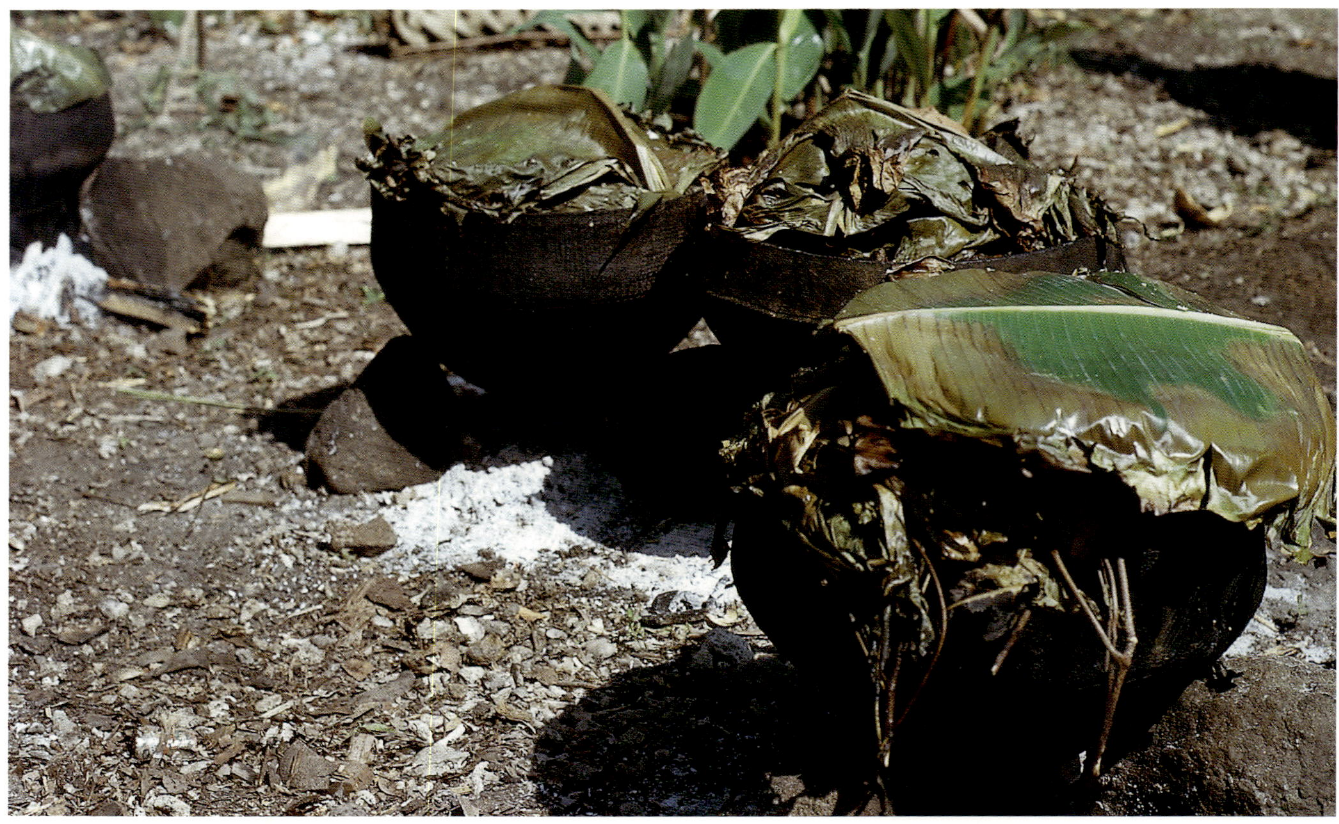

Fig. 4.38
Food being prepared for a feast.

Fig. 4.39
Ceremonial sago paddle in use. Mashed banana, sago flour and coconut milk being cooked in a large feast pot.

(1974). The authors made a field trip to this area in 1976.

Panaeati, an island in the Deboyne group, is about 5 kilometres wide and 8 kilometres long and is located west of Misima. South-east of Panaeati stretches the chain of islands called Calvados, which includes Motorina, Bagaman, Kimuta and Brooker. South of these lie Rossel and Sudest islands. These islands located in the southern portion of the Louisiade Archipelago, while participants in the *kula* ring trade, have had a thriving subsidiary trade which was independent of the main *kula* traffic and followed local trade rules. Each island developed a speciality in certain traded items. Misima, Motorina and Sudest have sago for export. Rossel Island manufactures shell jewellery. Panaeati has a monopoly over the building and trading of canoes (its primary resource is hardwood trees). Pots played an important role in the 'hospitality' side of trade transactions. According to Berde, Panaeati pots were given for betel nut, foodstuffs and sago

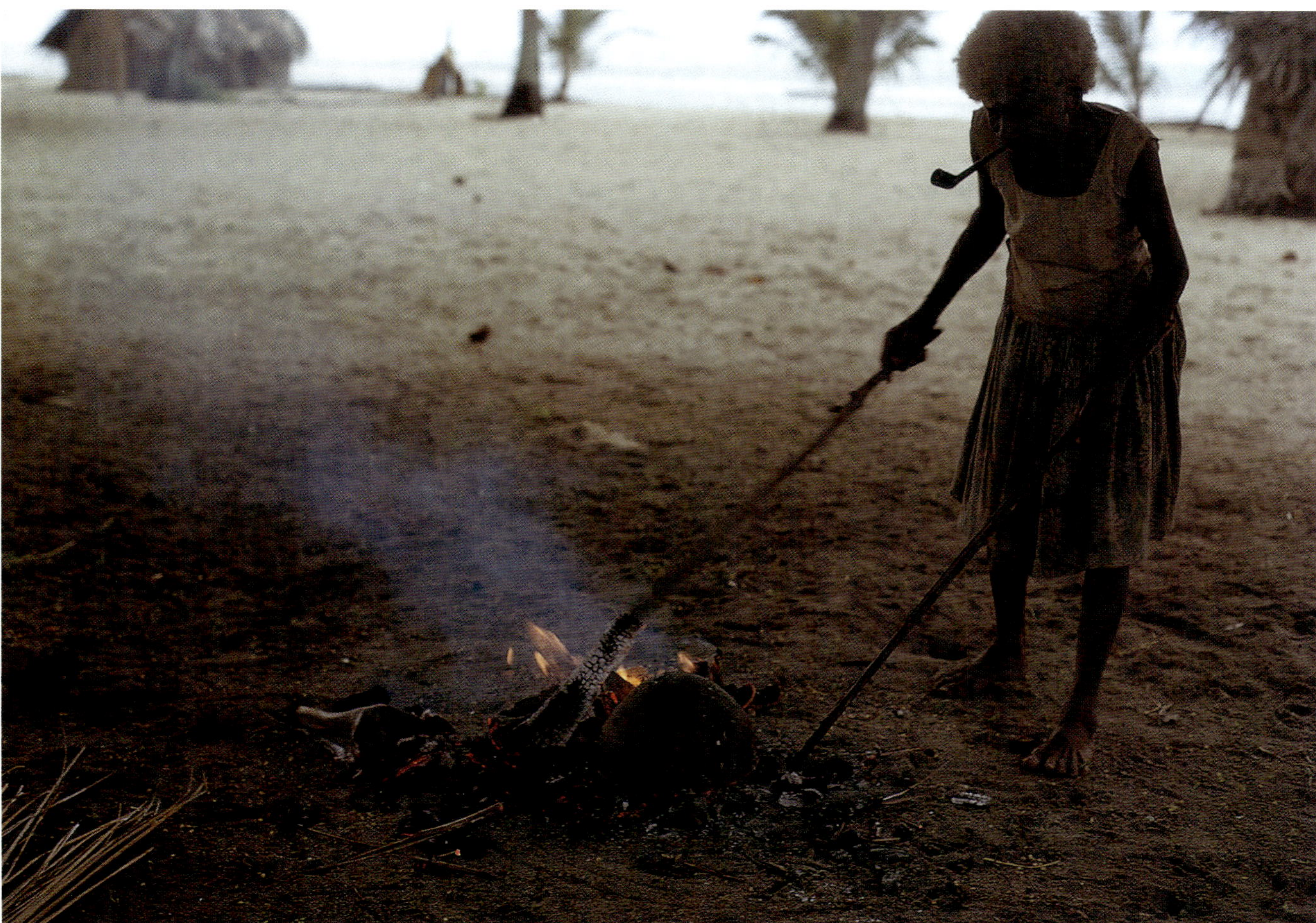

as 'forerunners to more serious transactions', pigs, wealth items and cash in exchange for the most important item, canoes. Before mission activity reduced hostilities between island groups at the end of the 19th century, pots were made on Panaeati mostly for local use but, with an increased flow of trade and a growing preference on nearby islands for food cooked in clay pots instead of earth ovens, Panaeati men took to the seas to trade their canoes and the pots of the women (Berde n.d.).

While Panaeati has a long pot making tradition, the women on Brooker Island took up pot making at some later period. Pottery export from Brooker to most of the islands of the Louisiade Archipelago developed around 1900 and Brooker has now replaced Panaeati as the primary pot exporter. According to Berde, Brooker vessels have a reputation with the islanders for being superior to those from Panaeati because the clay is better and the pots last longer. While Panaeati pots are regularly traded to Misima (the Panaeati people claim they originated in Misima but Misima has no clay) they were also traded as far west as the Engineer group. Brooker, on the other hand, trades pots mostly within the islands of the Calvados chain. In 1974 islanders living in the Engineer group always referred to Panaeati as the source of pots.

Berde implies that Panaeati women are not such active potters as the Brooker women but a field visit to both islands in November 1976 showed the reverse. About eight to ten women on Panaeati were making pottery and working in groups at the 'club house', a large bush materials house where the women get together to make mats or pots and the men work together on woodcraft or other activities. A hospitality and trading visit was being

Fig. 4.40
Salome firing one of her pots, moving it to burn off carbon deposit, Anagusa Island.

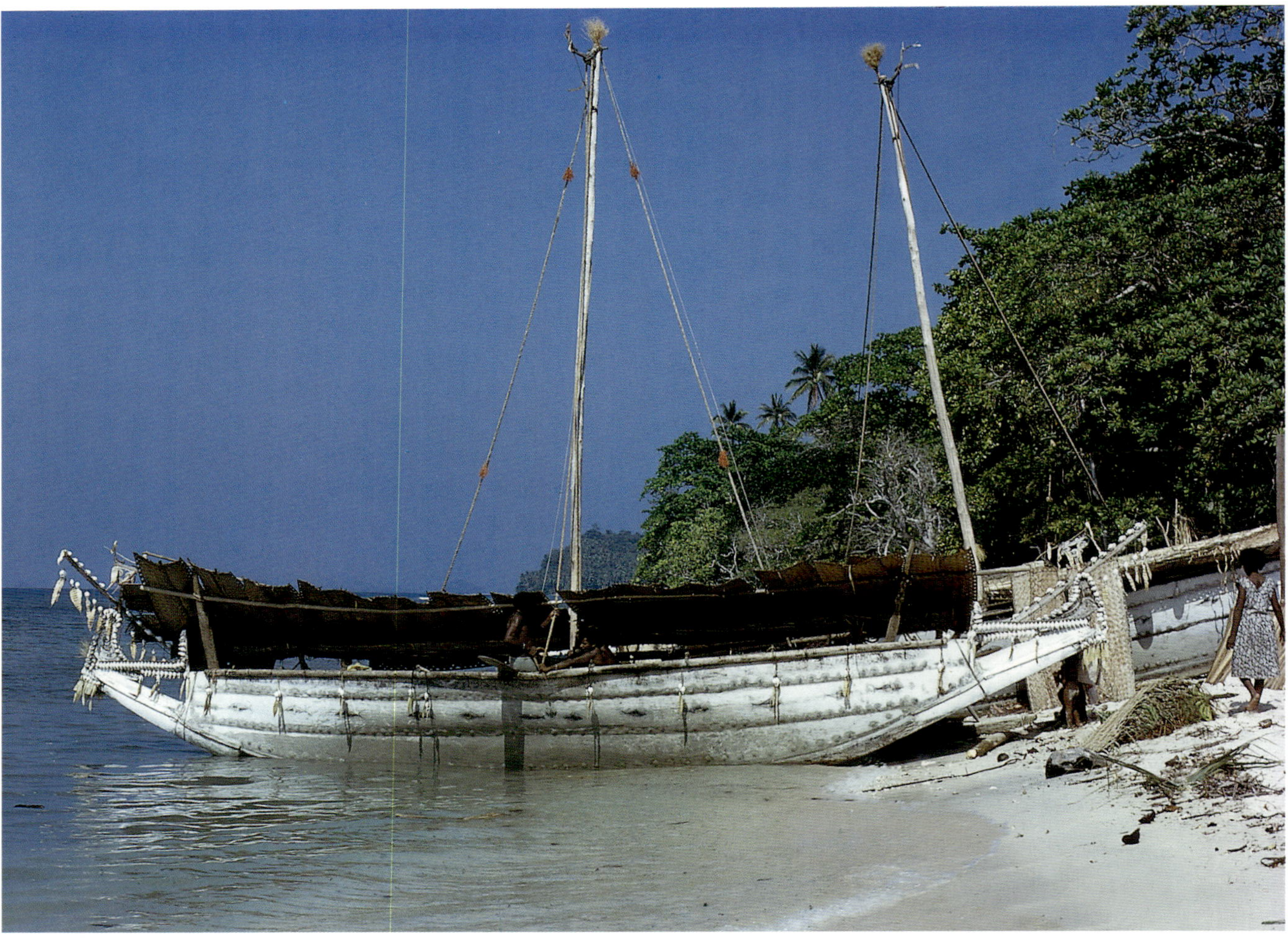

Fig. 4.41
Dawson Isand *kula* ring trading canoe at Kwaraiwa Island.

planned to Bwagaoia on Misima. One of the motivating factors for the planned trip was the scarcity of stick tobacco on the island; Bwagaoia has several trade stores. (This is one of the few areas in Papua New Guinea where in 1977 tobacco was still preferred over money.) On the other hand, little pot making activity was seen on Brooker Island at this time.

Panaeati vessel forms are composite and can be restricted or unrestricted. While there are a number of types of vessels the distinguishing Panaeati type (which can always be recognised when seen on islands where it has been traded) is a wide pot with a rounded base and a rather dramatic neck which flares outward. The neck, usually decorated, is very deep in proportion to the lower body. The restricted vessel also has a deep-proportioned neck but it is inverted; this is a reflection of its function, which is to carry and boil water. Vessels are named for their functions. The pots, *ulun*, are: *ulunligaliga*, a common cooking pot about 40 centimetres high used by individual households; *ulunbwana*, a large vessel about 60 centimetres high used as a community cooking pot; *ulunsabaia*, a cooking pot about 60 centimetres high reserved for feasts and mourning rites and never put to common use; *ulunmoni*, a large pot about 60 centimetres high used for cooking sago; *ulundelevega*, a small pot about 12 centimetres high used as a serving or eating bowl, for storing dry food and for cooking sago cakes. Another type differing in shape is the *ulunbwal*, a water pot (discussed above) which is about 30 centimetres high. While a traditional form, the *ulunbwal* is no longer used or made on a large scale. Round plastic floats are now used for carrying water.

Tindale and Bartlett reported that pots were used in a funeral context and describe small pots taken from a burial cave which were thought to be used as food containers for the dead, and larger pots which contained bones and skulls. This burial practice is no longer observed.

The clay on Panaeati is found in the middle of the island and comes from a single hill that rises to about 215 metres above sea level. The mustard coloured clay is dug from the base of the hillside and brought back to the hamlets in large baskets, *agoa*, where it is kept until needed inside the houses, usually in cracked pots covered by banana leaves. A temper is added which consists of very finely ground red coloured rock. The women and girls gather the clay and prepare it in work groups. After the larger pieces of grit are removed, the clay, crushed rock and fresh water are worked together to form lumps weighing about 0.5 kilograms; these are worked into rough rolls and then into coils on a flat board, *imutmut*. The coils, *mutmut*, differ in length according to the intended size of the vessel and are about 3 to 4 centimetres in diameter. The pot is started by spiral coiling and completed by the ring building technique. After about six levels of rings have been built, the pot is transferred to a clay dish, *kapikapi*. The technique from then on is comparable to Wari and other Milne Bay industries. A bivalve shell and pearl shell are used to smooth and shape the walls and to trim the rim (figs 4.43-4.48).

The decorations are added while the vessel is still wet. The potter continually uses fresh water to moisten the outside walls, ensuring that the clay remains wet. The designs are made with two and three-pronged forks called *erereli* (fig. 4.49). While

Fig. 4.42
Detail of decoration on an old feast pot, *bwana*, made by Ludi Nokok of Abalomaloma village, Panaeati Island. Collected in the 1930s, *h* 30 cm.

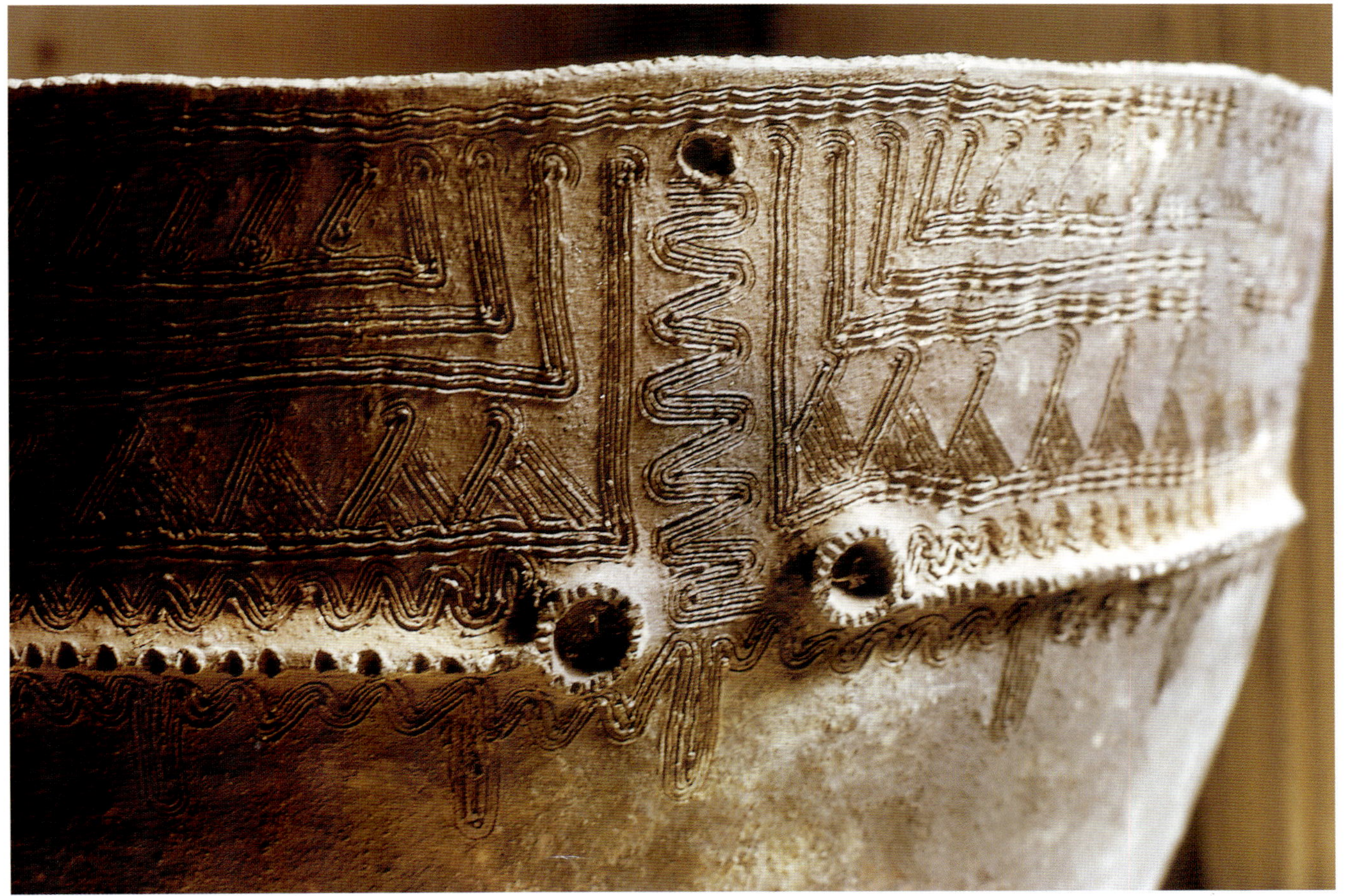

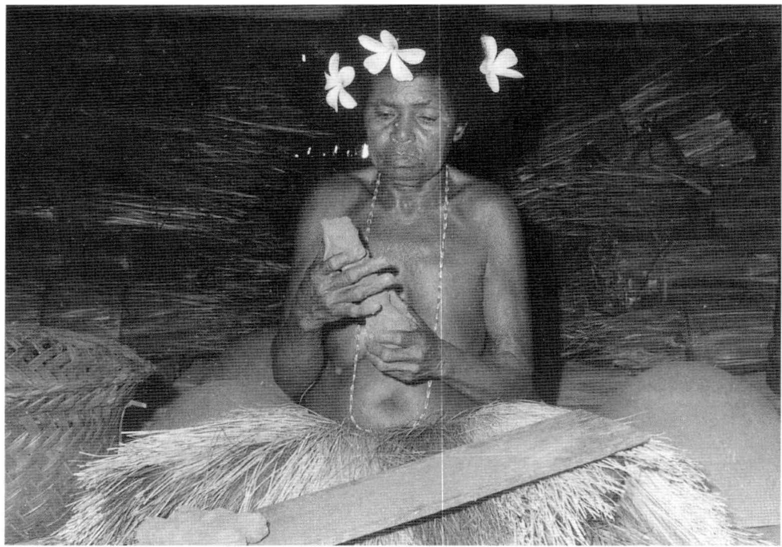

Fig. 4.43

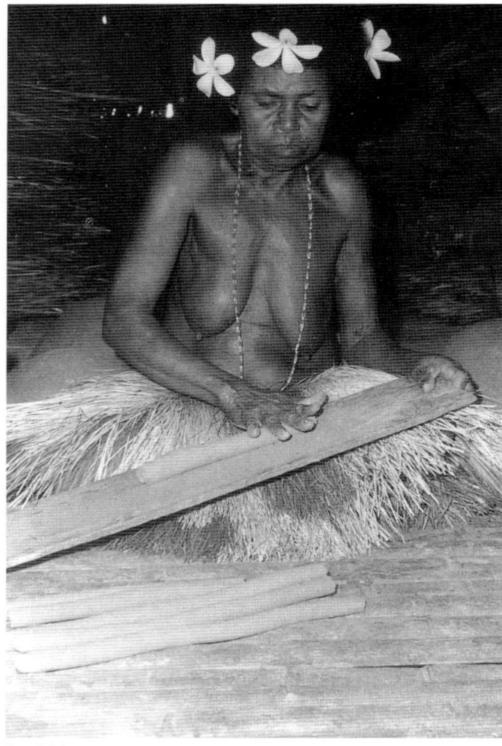

Fig. 4.44

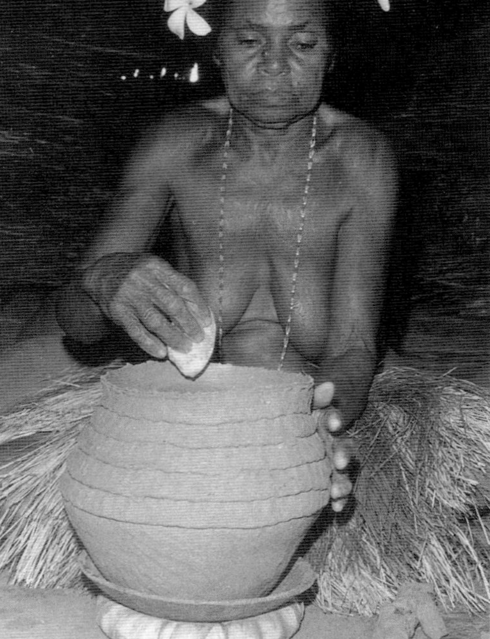

Fig. 4.45

Figs 4.43 to 4.49
All from Panaeati Island.

Fig. 4.43
Keseya making a water pot: squeezing rough rolls prior to rolling them on the board.

Fig. 4.44
Rolling a coil.

Fig. 4.45
Clipping and shaping the top edge with a shell.

the design motifs are shared by all the potters, each woman has a favourite and the people can identify the potter by the designs. Unfortunately, only a few women can name or even remember all of the designs once used. While about five designs were given names, the older ladies had explanations for only three of them. A common triangular design called *bebebi* is a butterfly; others were *monad*, the sinkers (shells) used on fishing nets, and *mati*, fish. Judging from the decorations seen on pots in the households of the long string of hamlets and those found on sherds, the selection was much greater in the past and many designs are no longer used. When the decorations are finished, the potter goes over the outside walls with the moistened pearl shell and the pot is set aside on a ring-support to dry for three to five days before firing.

Communal firings are done usually in the late afternoon or at night, because the sun is too hot for the women (not the pots). Firing techniques are similar to the rest of Milne Bay but there is some variation. Fuel consists of split softwood. Five or six lengths of wood are set afire and over these other lengths are laid in a horizontal position. The pots are fired singly. To preheat them they are held upside down in front of the fire for about fifteen seconds. The vessel is then placed rim down on three chunks of coral. Wood is stacked in several layers in a pyramid around the pot and more is added during the firing which takes about twenty

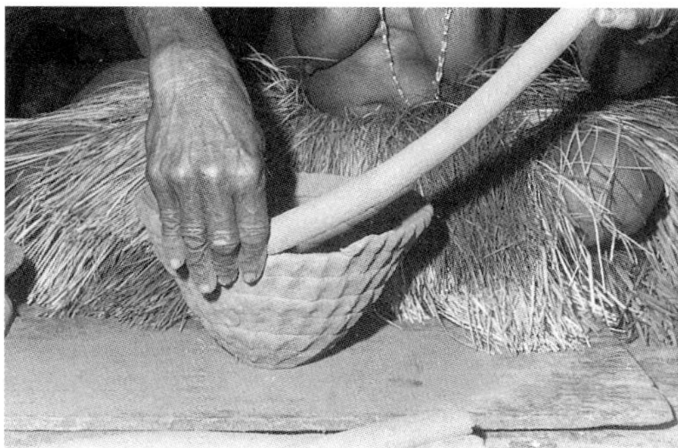

Fig. 4.46

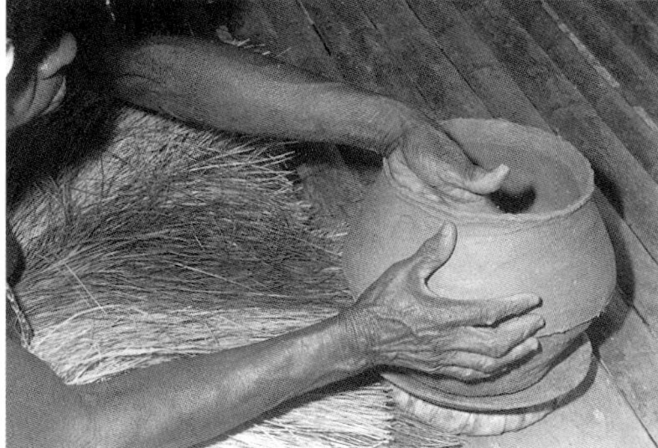

Fig. 4.48

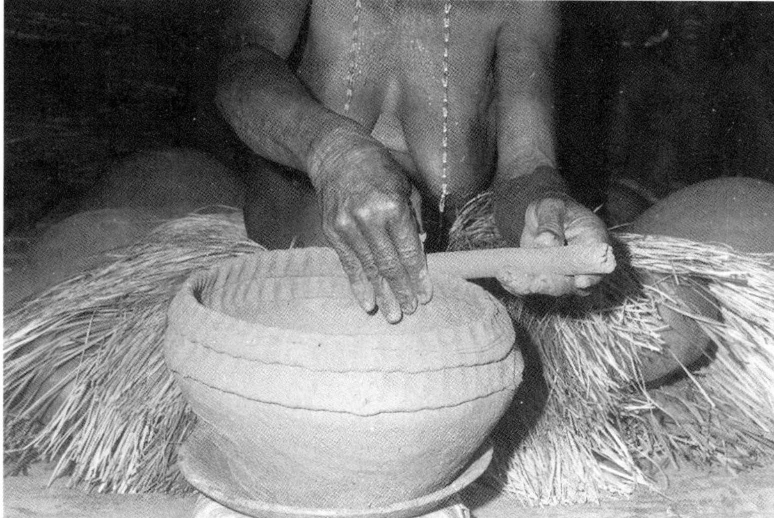

Fig. 4.47

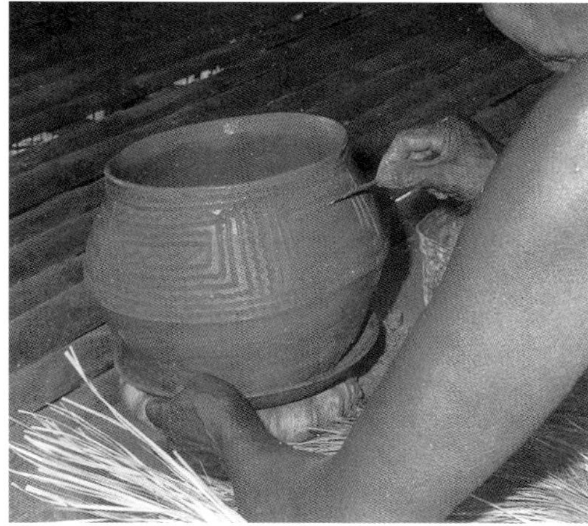

Fig. 4.49

Fig. 4.46
Applying a coil, overlapping at an early stage.

Fig. 4.47
Applying a coil, overlapping on the outside.

Fig. 4.48
Smoothing and shaping the rim with thumb and fingers.

Fig. 4.49
Decorating with a two-pronged comb.

minutes. When the fuel has burned off, the pieces facing the wind are removed and the side of the pot which is behind the breeze is left to fire a little longer. Two sticks are used to roll the pot off the fire; when it touches the ground it is caught by another woman who turns it with a stick and sets it right side up to cool. It is bright orange when it is removed and it takes about one minute to cool down and lose the transparent glowing colour. It can be sealed at any time after it has cooled by cooking starchy vegetable matter and coconut milk together.

The pots on Brooker are similar to those from Panaeati in shape, although the different clays used on the two islands produce pots with different textures. Brooker pots appear more coarse, while Panaeati pots are finer textured and probably more fragile. There are a few variations in technique, vessel shape and the naming of the pots. The Brooker women call all pots *ulunligaliga*. Vessels with special names are: *ulunbwal*, a water carrying vessel which is used commonly on Brooker (unlike Panaeati, where it is almost obsolete), the form and decorations being exactly the same as those seen on Panaeati; *ulunsagede*, a type not seen at Panaeati, which has a restricted neck, an inverted rim and a pronounced corner point, its angle of inflection making it comparable to vessels made at East Cape; *ulunabgabom*, a simple unrestricted vessel with slightly outward flaring neck and decoration covering the upper area from a few centimetres below the rim to the shoulder point; *ulungurekeke* (*keke* means small), shaped like the *ulunabgabom* but only about 10 centimetres high; *ulunsiel*, shaped like the *ulunabgabom* but larger, about 23 to 32 centimetres high, and with a slight outward flaring rim; *ulunbwana*, an unrestricted vessel used for feasts which has a hemispherical base and everted neck, the junction between the two

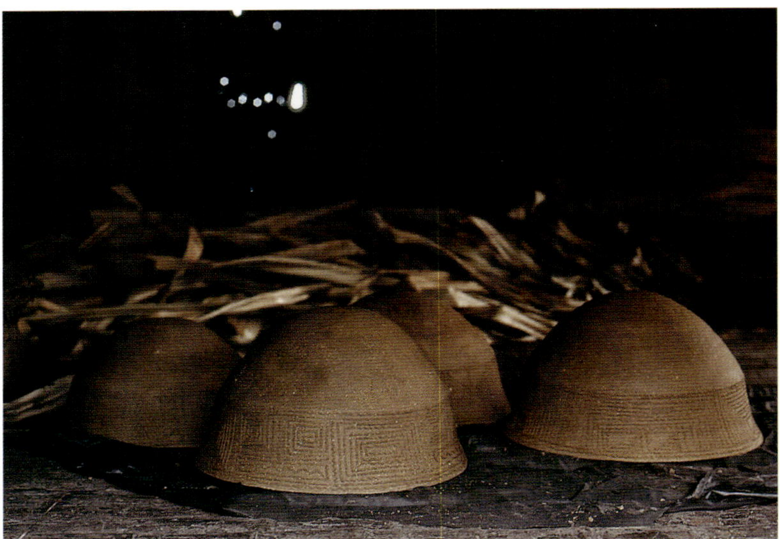

Fig. 4.50
Pots drying, Panaeati Island.

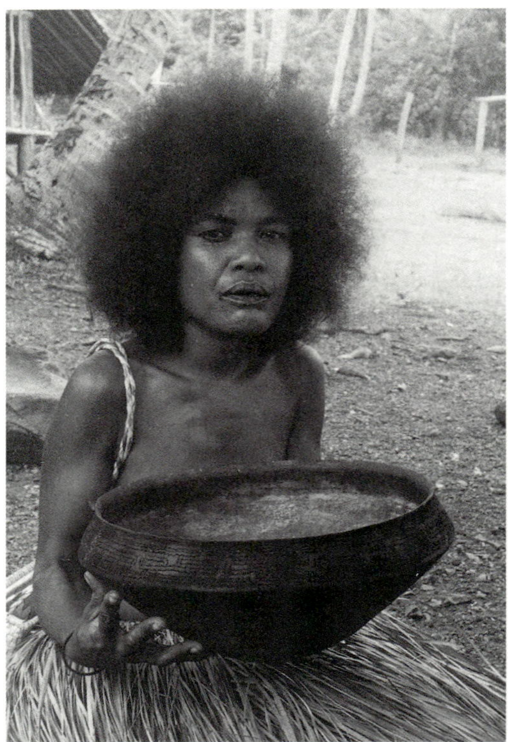

Fig. 4.51
Etele holding an *ulunsagede*, Brooker Island.

being marked by a ridge running around the vessel; *ulunmorni*, used for cooking fish at feasts and shaped like the *ulunbwana* but with a projecting ridge which encircles the vessel at the corner point in the form of a scroll. White and Hamilton (1973) also describe the manufacture of an unrestricted vessel whose interior was divided into sections by partitions. This unusual type is seldom made today, although similar ones are made at Goodenough and the Amphletts.

As recorded by White and Hamilton, equal proportions of a red and a black clay are kneaded together. Both clays have widely ranging particle sizes but the black has about three times as much nonplastic material and so acts as a temper. The percentage of clay fraction in the black clay is very low: only 10 per cent. The clay mineral is montmorillonite; there is much feldspar and some quartz. The building technique observed by the authors is the same as that used at Panaeati.

SOUTH COAST INDUSTRIES

Cooking pots are produced along the south coast of Papua from Bonarua Island, near Suau, west to Bonabona Island, situated in the eastern part of Orangerie Bay. (Mailu Island, located on the west Papuan coast in Amazon Bay, Central Province, also makes similar pots but this industry is discussed in Chapter 3.) It has been reported to us that pottery is made at villages in the Buhutu valley which is situated between Mullins Harbour and Milne Bay but this has not been confirmed.

Bonarua (Brummer) Island

Bonarua Island, lying about 10 kilometres off the southern coast, is a long narrow strip. Local legend tells how an eagle picked up a snake and flew up into the sky with it but it was too heavy and the eagle dropped it into the sea, where it became Bonarua Island. Pots were once made here; according to legends the settlers, members of the Badilabedabeda clan, originally came from the same source near Normanby as do the Wari people.

There is active trade between the island and Wari. People bring pots to exchange for sago which grows on the mainland. Several generations ago, pots were made by Bonarua women in a style similar to that of Wari. This industry is now defunct; a few older women retain skills but are inactive. It is reported that one of these women now lives near her gardens on neighbouring Horioea Island and still produces a few cooking pots. The clay source is at Iloilo on the mainland, opposite the two islands.

Silosilo Bay, Konemaiaua, Kaukau, Bonabona Island

Some aspects of pottery activity in Silosilo Bay were described in 1975 by Hosking and Dikuwola (1978). A number of women, living in eight villages located on the bay, are still producing a few cooking pots mainly to be used in exchange for goods with Mailu, Wari and Tubetube. Formerly, plenty of pots were made for local use and trade.

Although a technique almost identical to that of Wari is used throughout this area, there is a variation in vessel shape. Most of the Silosilo pots are deeper in proportion; they are simple unrestricted or restricted forms, conical or ellipsoid, and do not have a shoulder (a definite change of direction between the shoulder and neck). They are also more round-based than Wari vessels. The general cooking pot is called *gulewa* (as at Wari) and a sago cooking vessel is called *odo'odoi*. A pot used especially for cooking fish is *ialaledu* and a deeper, very large vessel called *laulaueli* is used during feasts. A pot with an inverted rim, *batu mo'do*, is used to cook tough meat. The *salaki gulewana*, a Mailu-inspired shape, is used for cooking pig at feasts and the little clay dish used to support the base of a pot during forming is called *nibaniba* as at Wari.

The women from Silosilo villages collect their clay, *gulewa*, from a swampy area a few metres behind the shoreline. The clay is yellow brownish-grey, with a few streaks of yellow ochre running through it. It also contains white and black sand-sized particles that give it a sandy texture. The clay mineral is a smectite, with a little mica. There is a substantial quantity of feldspar and some quartz. It is dampened with fresh water and transported in baskets lined and covered with leaves. Care is taken to protect the clay from salt water while it is carried from the pit to the village by outrigger canoe. The *nibaniba* is sometimes supported on a stiff cane ring, *ui*. A shell tool, *kolukolu*, is used for scraping, smoothing and thinning the vessel walls. Decoration consists of incising with a shell or pronged comb, also called *kolukolu*, the top third

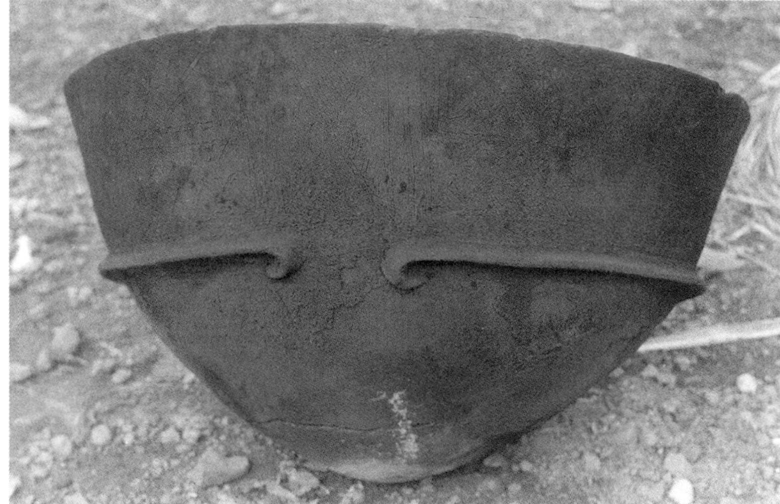

Fig. 4.52
Ulunmorni, a feast pot used for cooking fish, Brooker Island.

Fig. 4.53

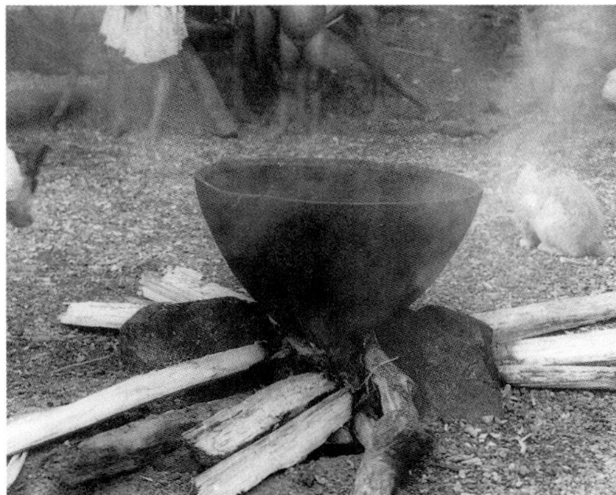

Fig. 4.53
East Cape cooking pot, *habaia*. Compare with Fig. 4.52.

Fig. 4.54

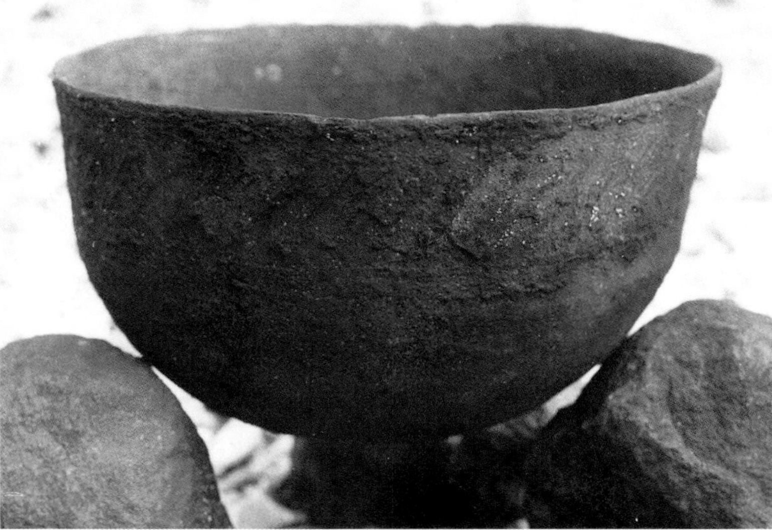

Fig. 4.54
A very old Bonarua Island cooking pot encrusted with carbon from much use.

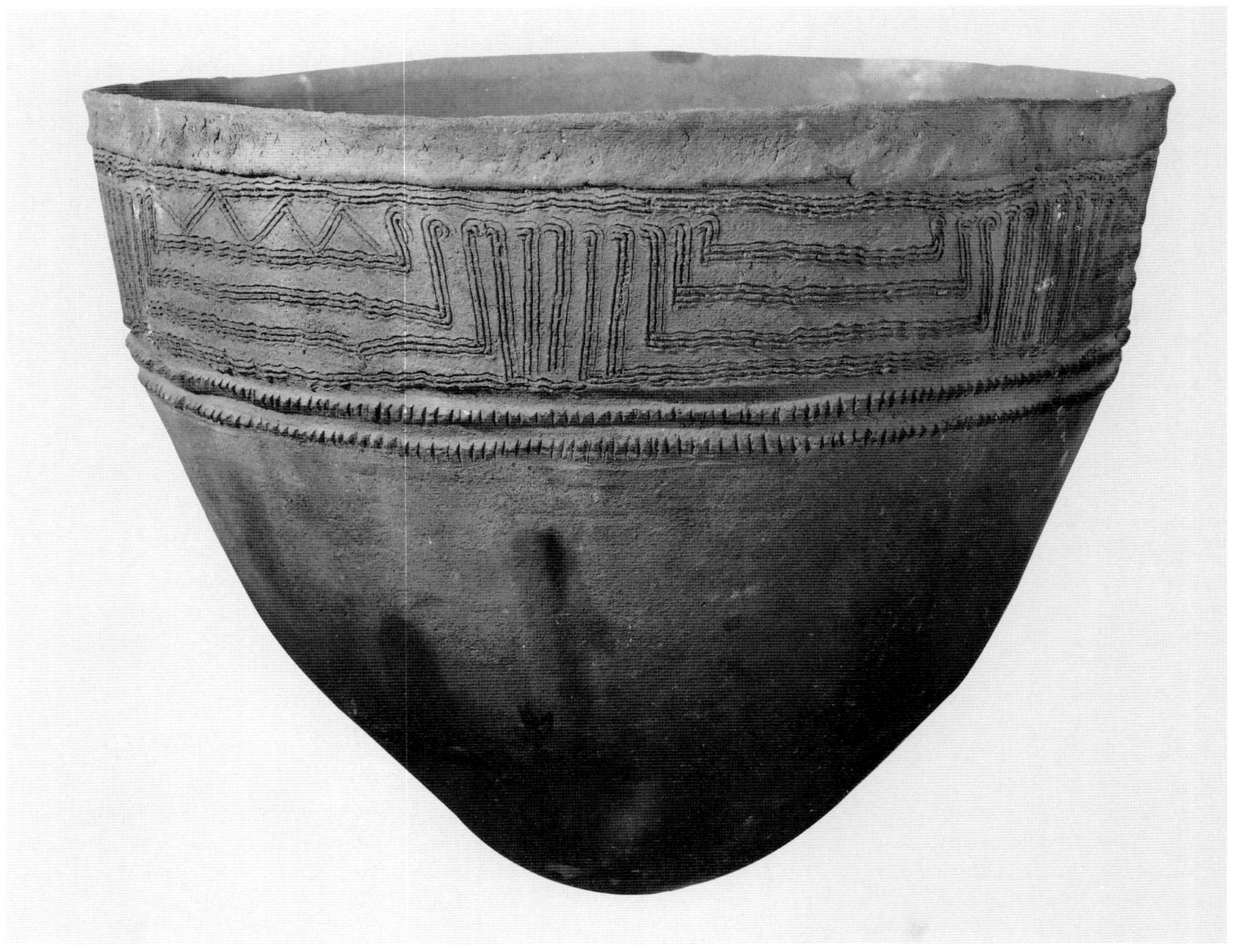

Fig. 4.55
Feast pot, *laulaueli*, Waladau village, Silosilo Bay, *h* 34 cm.

portion of the pot. Today any sharp pointed objects, including hairpins, are used. There is no correlation between the designs used and the vessel shapes.

Two legends concerning pottery are recorded here, as told by the Suau people.

How the clay pot and the fire came to the people of Silosilo Bay

During the season when the men went into the bush to hunt pigs the women prepared their food for their return. At Gedigedi village lived a witch who was the only woman who possessed clay pots and fire to cook with. Every day the witch prepared the food for the hunters by placing it in the sun. She also prepared her own food by peeling vegetables and putting them in a clay pot and cooking them with the fire which she took from her anus. In order that the men would not learn her secret, when she finished eating she would put the pot and fire back into her anus and prepare their sun dried food. One day the men discovered some of the food that the witch had mistakenly left amongst their sun dried food. They ate it and decided she had a special way of preparing it. They wanted to know how she made it taste different so one man hid himself in a corner of her house when the other men went out hunting. When the men had gone, the witch took her pot and the fire from her anus and started cooking. The man watched her and rushed out and grabbed the fire

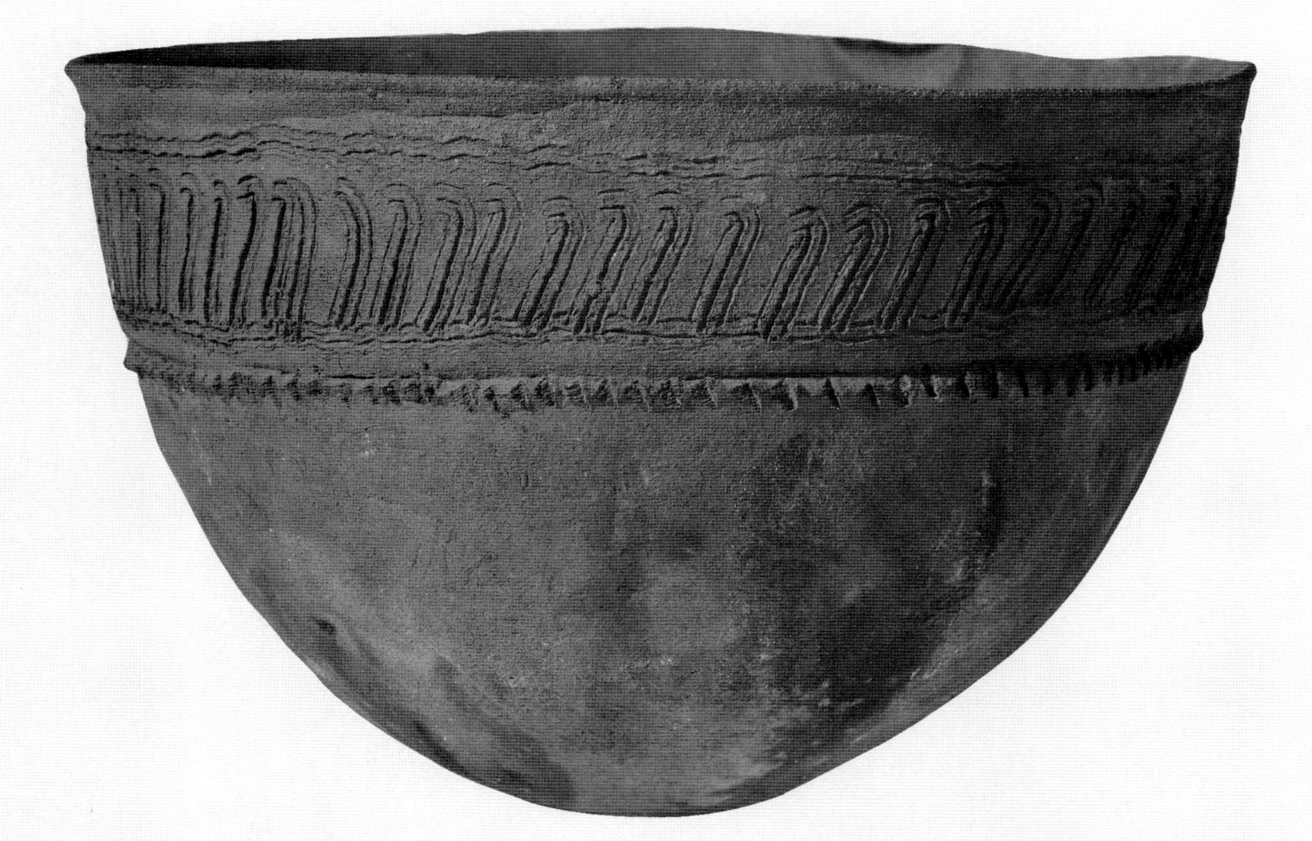

Fig. 4.56
Cooking pot, *gulewa*, made by Elema of Taboina village, Silosilo Bay, *h* 18 cm.

and took it to the other men. They then took it to their villages and in this way fire was given to all the villages of Silosilo Bay.

The women in the villages, wishing to cook food the way the witch did, went to her and threatened to kill her if she did not tell them her secret. So she showed them her pot and how to make it. The women went back to their villages, made pots and taught other women. Today, the people use fire and clay pots for cooking instead of drying their food in the sun as they used to do long ago.

How clay was brought to Weweyateha in Silosilo Bay

Long ago there was nowhere to get good clay in Silosilo Bay. One day the women decided to ask the witch women to help them. The witches surveyed the Milne Bay area at night, seeking the best clay source. They finally found a good source on the island of Wari. During the night the women flew with the witches to Wari Island. They filled their baskets with clay and flew home. They landed at Aloalo village on Waybumari Bay (next to Silosilo Bay) where they planted the clay. From there it grew bigger and bigger so they transferred some of it to Weweyateha which is where the women of Silosilo get their clay (Hosking and Dikuwola n.d.).

The same tradition is found in the other villages: Kaukau in Kaukau Bay, immediately to the west of Silosilo, in Sikokolo and Suabili on Bonabona Island and in Konemaiaua. The clay for Bonabona Island comes from the Nigonigo River at Suaeabina on the mainland. As at Silosilo, these industries are declining (fig. 4.58).

East Cape

Another pottery producing area, administratively referred to as East Cape and comprising several villages, extends along the coast of a peninsula in

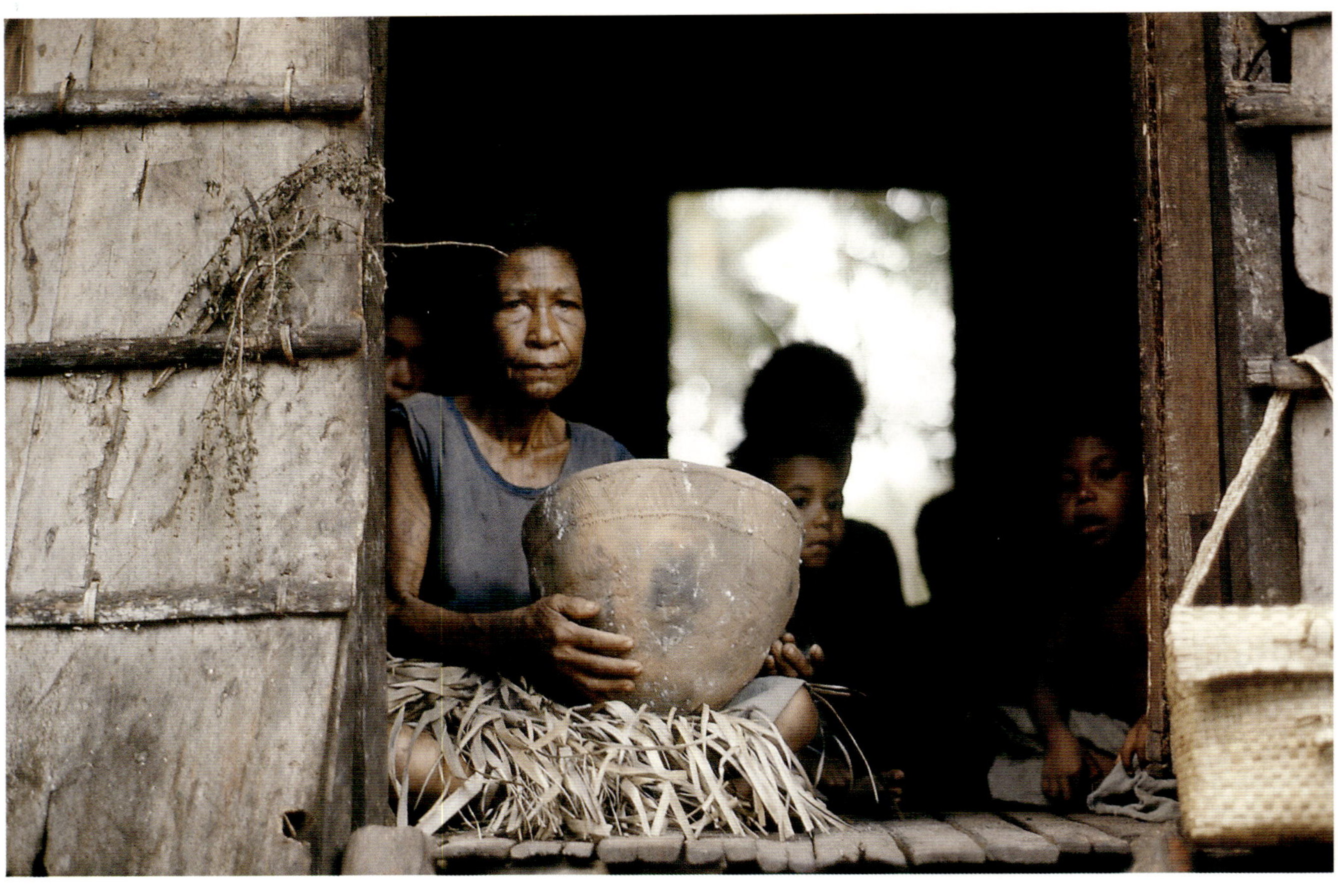

Fig. 4.57
Dileta with a cooking pot, *gulewa*, made by her, Taboina village, Silosilo Bay.

Alotau district. The traditional pot making villages are Kehelara and Topa. The gardens of East Cape produce tapioca, sweet potato, bananas and coconuts but because of a long dry period and the poor condition of the soil the East Cape people find it difficult to subsist on their own crop yields. The women potters produce enough vessels to supply their own needs and for trade with Normanby, Nuakata and Dobu islands in return for yam, taro and betel nut and pandanus leaves (which the East Cape women use to make Polynesian-type mats, a craft taught them by the mission). While East Cape pottery has been sighted at Wagawaga, Samarai, Alotau and Dobu, major trading partners are localised compared to Wari/Tubetube and the Amphletts and, unfortunately, as in so many of the pottery industries which only produce vessels for local markets, manufacture has started to die out. However, the women potters go to the local school once a week to instruct the young girls in pot making. A factor contributing to the decline in production is the popularity of Wari Island vessels. Trading voyages are made to Wari to collect pottery in exchange for Polynesian chestnuts (*Inocarpus edulis*) which grow at East Cape and undyed bush string that is favoured by the Wari islanders for making grass skirts. Wari vessels are also brought over by schoolchildren attending the mission school at Kehelara to help pay for their stay and as hospitality gifts.

Most of the adult women make pottery. The method of production is the combination of coil and ring building techniques. There is one clay source located behind one of the hamlets and anyone may gather the clay. Pots are made at any time during any season and only enough clay is gathered for use on one occasion by those potters living within easy walking distance. A digging tool is used to extract the clay from the ground. The clay is wrapped in banana leaves and carried back to the potter's house in baskets woven from pandanus leaves. The yellow brownish-grey clay is sandy and contains little grit. The dominant clay mineral is smectite, with some mica or possibly halloysite. Plasticity is good; fresh water is added until it becomes malleable. Salt water is taboo. Stones are removed with the fingers and, with a hammer-shaped tool, the clay is pounded out on wood taken from the side of an old canoe. The clay is then kept in a covered container until ready for use.

There are three types of vessels produced at East Cape. The first, called *nauwokatulatama,* is a basin-shaped pot with a rounded base, a distinct shoulder and a decorated neck area (fig. 4.62). It is similar to Wari/Tubetube pottery except that the base of East Cape pots is much thicker and the shoulder forms a distinct angled corner point, while the shoulder on Wari-type pots is more rounded.

This difference is brought about by technique. The potter, having rolled out coils on a board (not between the hands as at Wari and Tubetube), starts coiling in her hand and levels each coil by pressing her thumb downwards in a flattening process; subsequent coils are added, overlapping the flattened surface by only about 1 centimetre, and the walls of the vessel grow very slowly upward and outward. When the walls reach a height of about 13 centimetres the potter holds the pointed base in her left hand and smooths the outside coils with downward strokes of her index finger. She then slaps the point of the base with the palm of her hand to flatten it. The vessel is next placed on a fired clay dish, *kepekepe*, made especially for the purpose of supporting the pot during manufacture.

From this stage the coils are laid in rings instead of spirally, the potter pinching off the excess clay when it has completed a circle. When the vessel attains the desired height, the potter changes technique by placing the next ring at a right angle, on the inside of the previous level instead of on the outside as before. This ring is flattened but in an upward and inward direction and, since the coils are now flattened up instead of down, the area above the shoulder point is noticeably thinner than the body and the area below has thicker walls. This creates the distinctive shoulder point at the juncture of the body and the neck. After about five rings are added, the interior of the pot is smoothed. The clay is scraped downward with the index finger, then smoothed further with the sharp edge of a shell which has been moistened in fresh water. Excess clay is deposited in the bottom of the pot.

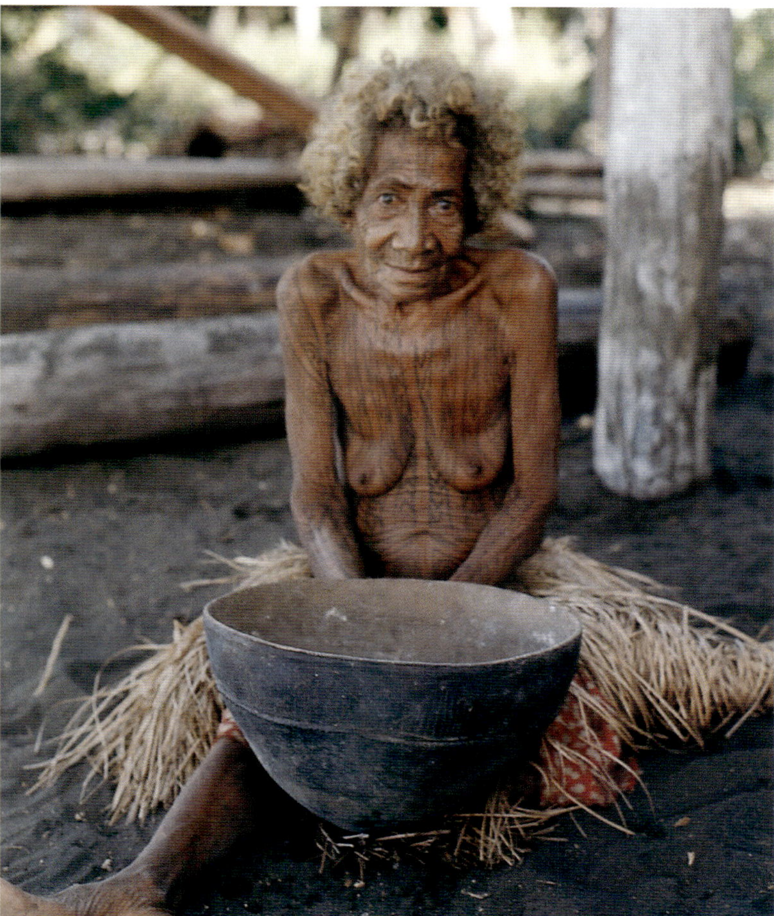

Fig. 4.58
Suabili village, Bonabona Island. Bonio, one of the last potters on Bonabona, in 1975.

To form the lip the potter collects the excess clay from the vessel and makes two rolls which are joined at the top. Then, gently supporting the lip with her left hand held on the outside, she lightly rubs the inside with the rounded edge of a shell, wetting it when necessary. The outside walls are then smoothed with the thumb and two fingers. The vessel, still resting in the *kepekepe*, which is balanced on a metal ring, *katakatapa* (traditionally this was a coil of grass), is left to dry under the house for three or four hours.

A variation of the *nauwokatulatama*, in which the coils between the lip and shoulder are not smoothed, is called *oguperopero*. Both are cooking

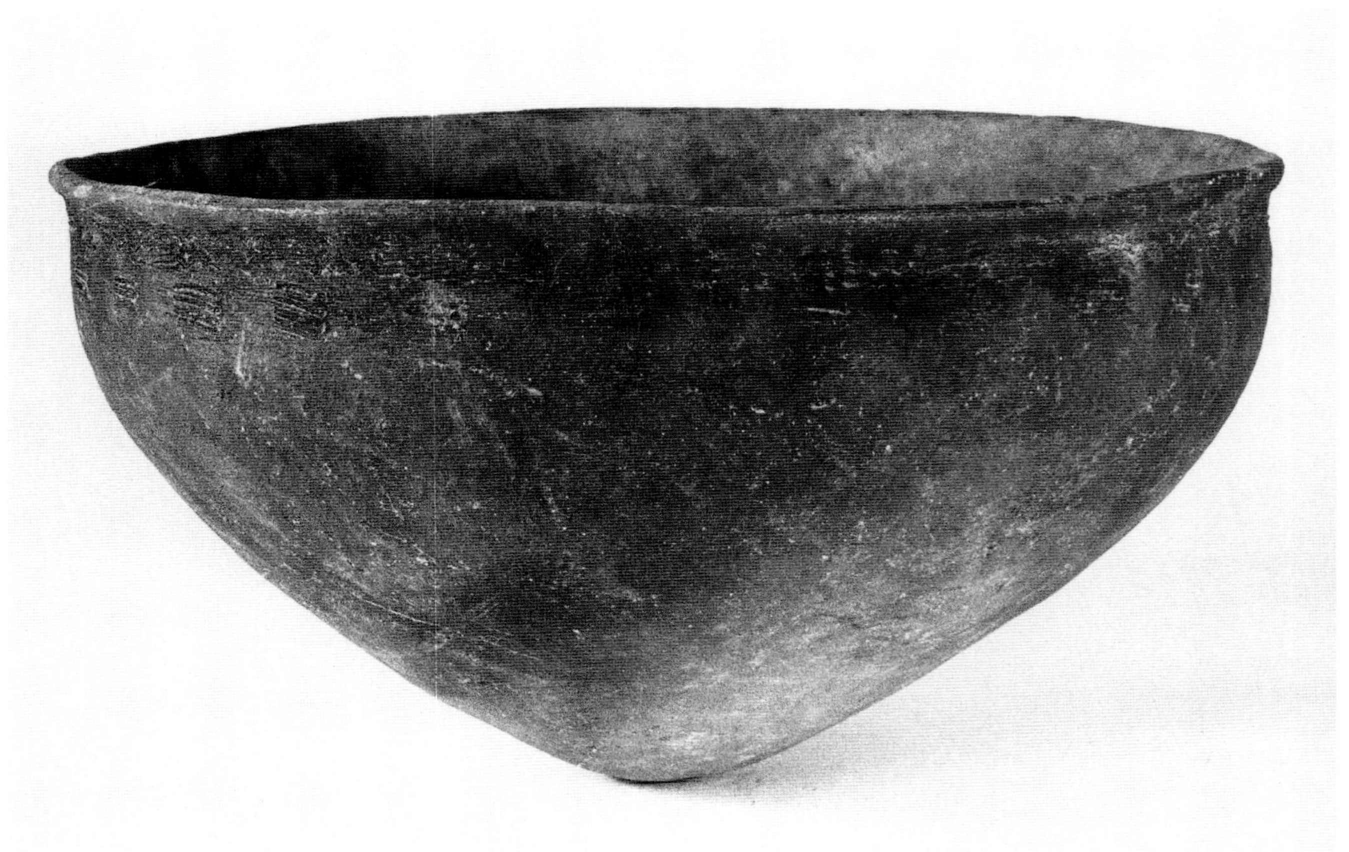

Fig. 4.59
A typical East Cape *habaia* collected at Wagawaga village, *h* 16 cm.

pots. The smallest pot sighted was 16 centimetres high and the largest measured 45 centimetres tall.

A third type, the *habaia*, which is used specifically for cooking soups, is unrestricted and has little or no decoration. The smallest *habaia* seen belonged to a child and was 10 centimetres high; an average-sized *habaia* which was 16 centimetres high was used by a household and the largest one sighted was 26 centimetres high and used only on special feast days. Another named vessel, the *nakikei*, is a small pot (about 12 centimetres high) related to the *habaia* and used by children, individuals or a small number of people. It is a simple unrestricted vessel decorated by applied knobs spaced evenly around the top rim.

Decoration, consisting of panels of incised designs, is applied to the *nauwokatulatama* on the neck area, above the shoulder and a few centimetres below the edge of the rim. Designs include triangles, rectangles or combinations of the two, made with a multi-pronged tool called the *animigiluma* and single impressions made by the serrated edge of one half of a bivalve shell. On the *habaia* the corner point of the shoulder is generally marked by horizontal impressions made with the shell. Simple designs on the *oguperopero* consist of vertical bands of incised lines usually running around the neck or under the lip.

The design motifs are limited in variety but are particularly distinctive due to the preciseness and fineness of the marks made by the *animigiluma*, which, unlike the combs used in the other related industries, can have as many as twelve prongs. Following is a description of the techniques used in decorating the *nauwokatulatama* with a six-pronged *animigiluma*. After the vessel has undergone preliminary drying under the house for three or four hours, more excess clay is removed from the inside and outside walls with the edge of a shell. The entire surface is then smoothed and rubbed with

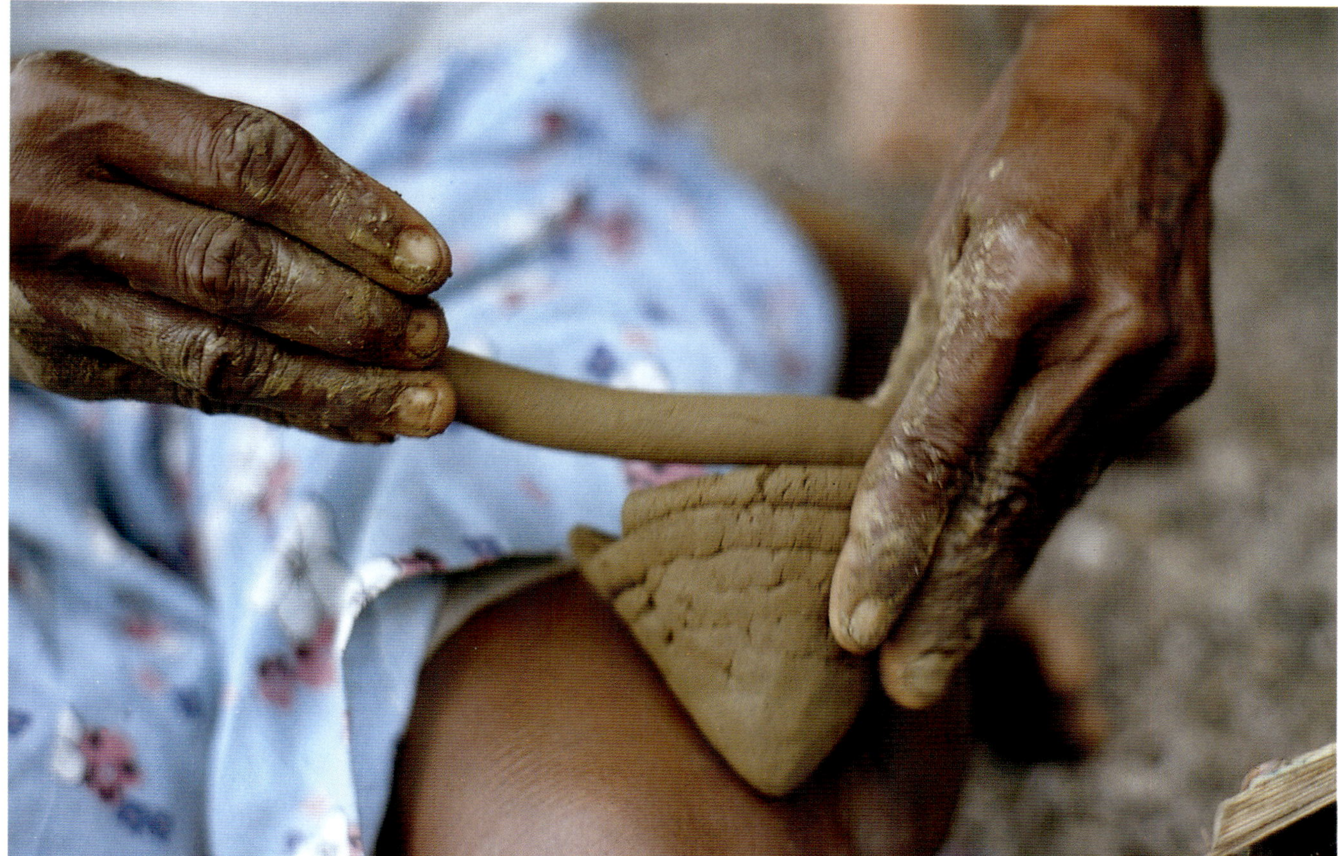

Fig. 4.60
Coiling; supported against the knee, East Cape.

the back of the shell or with the potter's fingers dipped in fresh water. In this process much of the distinct shoulder disappears and impurities are removed with the back of the fingers or a moistened thumb. The corner point of the shoulder is then marked with the serrated edge of a shell in a running scalloped motif. A six-pronged comb is taken up and used to mark the outside neck area below the everted rim. The topmost prong hits the overlapping underneath portion of the lip and leaves little gouged marks while the other five prongs make a very fine running motif of wavy parallel lines. A second set of parallel lines is incised just above the shell-impressed design at the corner point leaving the smooth area between the two parallel sets of lines. When the decoration is completed the pot is left to dry in the shade for a week before it is fired.

Firing techniques are similar to those used on Wari/Tubetube. Fuel consists of dried coconut husks, fronds, palm spathe, wood chips and several varieties of wood. The vessel is placed upside down on three hearth stones over the glowing embers of the coconut shells, wood chips, dried fronds and some of the wood. Bundles of fronds, leaf-bases and split wood are then piled around the vessel to form a pyramid and dried coconut husks are stacked around the pyramid. After the fuel burns down the pot emerges from the ashes a reddish colour with a few smudge marks. Vessels are fired singly and often crack on the interior wall and sides during firing. This high incidence of cracking is probably the result of a fault in the composition of the clay. Indeed, a household survey of vessels in two hamlets revealed that many of the pots were cracked and broken along the rim.

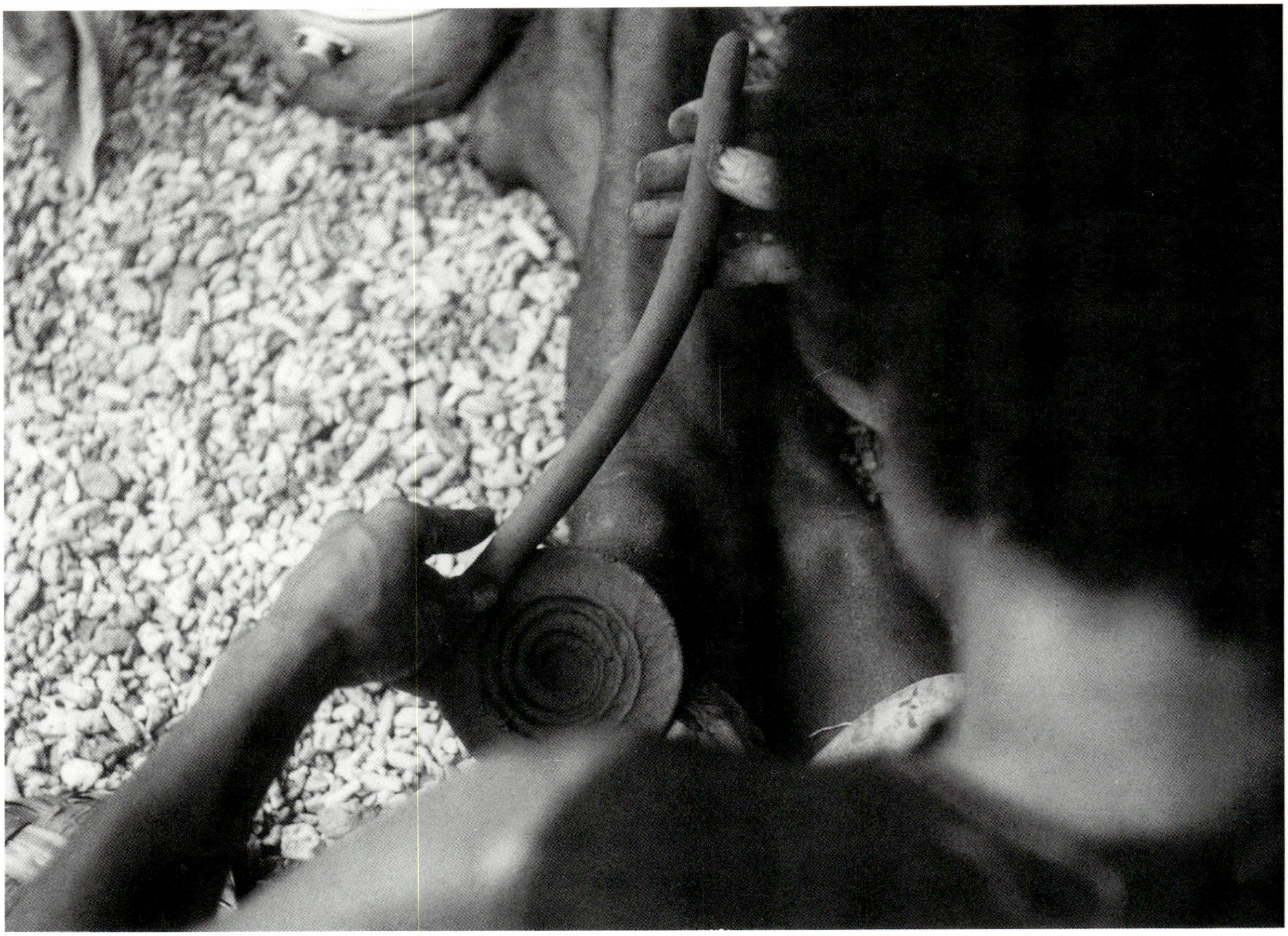

Fig. 4.61
Pressing a coil spirally down onto the one below, East Cape.

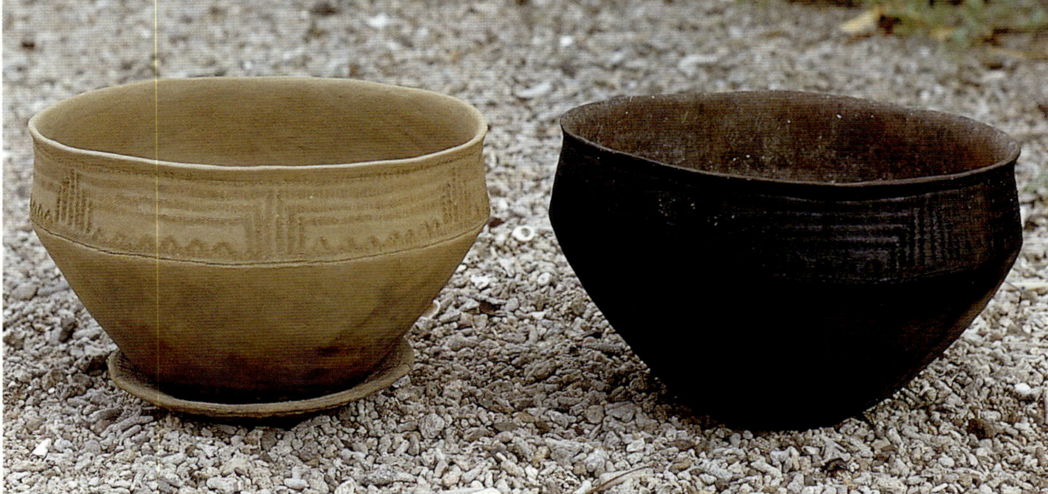

Fig. 4.62
Typical *nauwokatulatama* and a new pot drying in the support dish, both made by Lili Sikalu, East Cape.

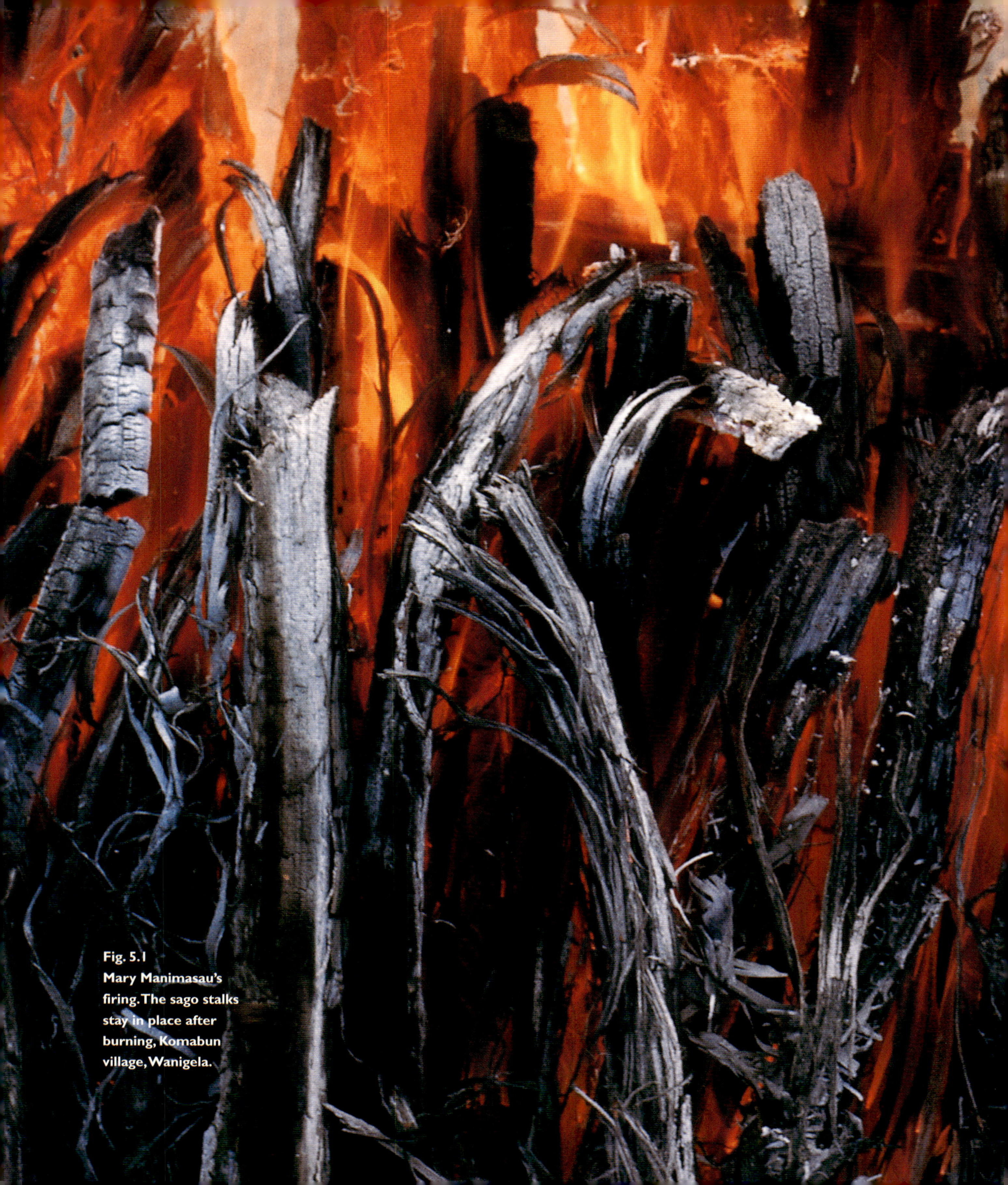

Fig. 5.1
Mary Manimasau's firing. The sago stalks stay in place after burning, Komabun village, Wanigela.

5 Northern Province

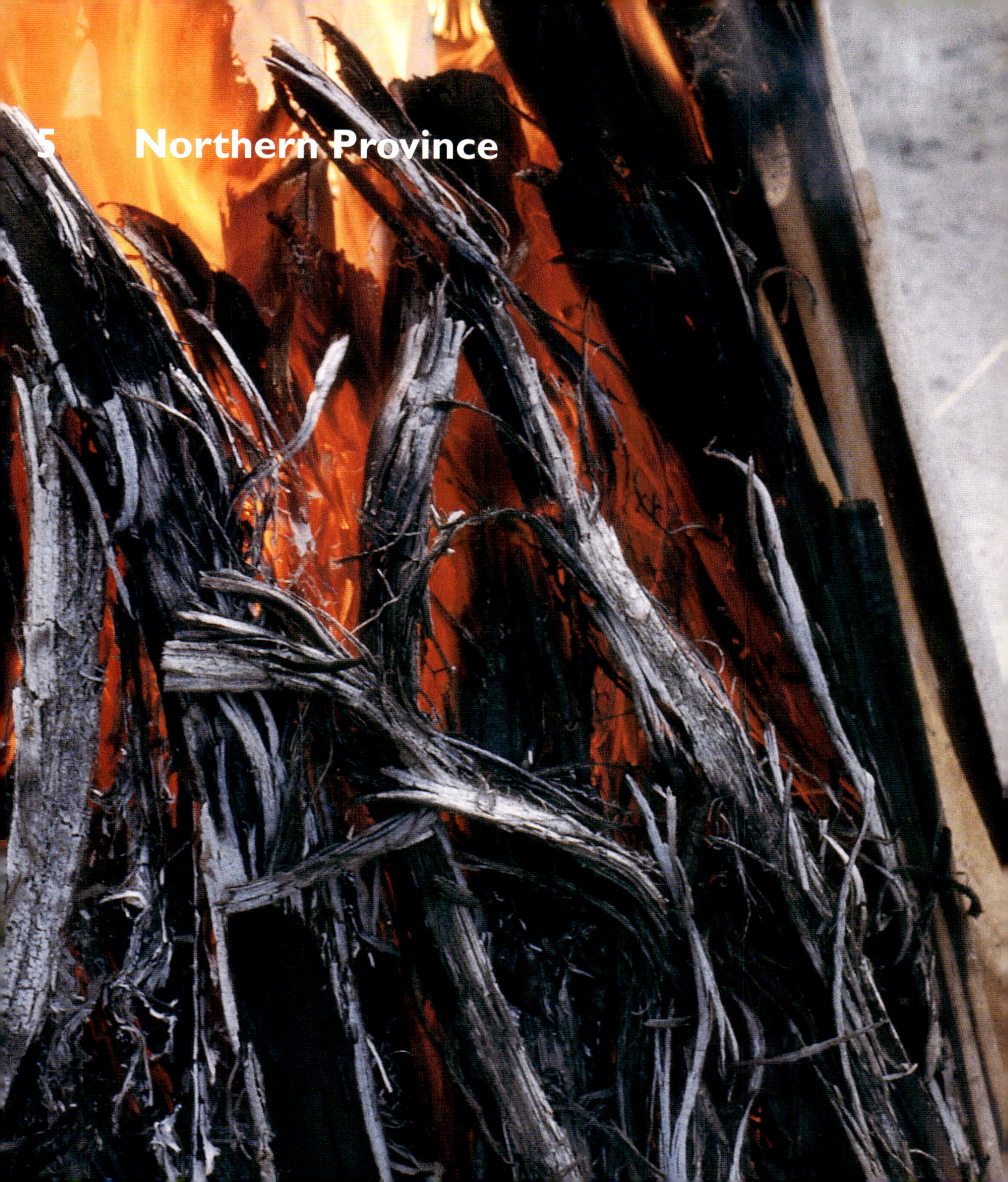

Northern Province is situated in the northeast of the mainland. It stretches from around the Waria River in the west, where it borders Morobe Province, to the eastern extremity of Collingwood Bay, where it merges with Milne Bay Province; to the south it borders Central Province in the Owen Stanley Range. In Northern Province, to a greater extent than in any other province, the language groups and pottery traditions overlap the administrative boundaries.

At this time five pot making areas may be distinguished in the Northern Province: Manau, and the Mambare and Gira rivers; Ambasi; the Popondetta area; Dyke Ackland Bay, including Oro Bay; and Wanigela and the related areas, Tufi (Cape Nelson) and Cape Vogel. A sixth industry, now defunct, was located at Gona in Holnicote Bay.

These divisions, however, do not define exactly areas of differing styles. More research is necessary before style regions can be established and this will be difficult: there are few Northern Province vessels in museum collections and very few pots are in evidence in the villages of most of these areas. Waddell and Krinks (1968) saw as many as six pots in one household in 1964 but today those that remain are rare and valued as heirlooms. Assessment of style provinces is complicated further by the copying of neighbouring styles.

All of the above areas except Wanigela belong to the Binandere language family. This is the family of languages referred to by Williams (1930) as Orokaiva but Dutton (1973) reserves this name for only one of the many Binanderean languages, that spoken by the people of Popondetta and the Mount Lamington area. Four of the Binanderean languages occur in Morobe Province; their pot making has been described in Chapter 6.

Throughout the Northern Province pots are made by women. The technique is basically one of coiling, with a paddle used for extra joining and consolidating of coils and for smoothing with a gentle patting and sliding action. This is the only area where coils are added to a simple pinched and patted base and where the same technique is used on the coast as well as inland. The only major variation in technique is at Wanigela.

Throughout the province pot making has declined and unfortunately very little thorough study and recording was done during the period when it was flourishing. More recent material has been presented by Ziska Schwimmer (1967) and Egloff (1973). Schwimmer gives information concerning clay sources and the number of potters active at the time but her description of technique is scanty and she does not discuss styles. Egloff gives a detailed account of pot making at Wanigela.

Binanderean pot making in the early 1900s was described by F.E. Williams (1930) who was then the government anthropologist. His description holds for all the 'Orokaiva' although the vernacular terms are those of the Aiga (Dutton's Aeka), which he observed.

> *Pottery* (*Obu*). The yellowish clay used for pottery is not found in all parts of the Division, and the collecting of it may mean a long journey. It is brought home in a wrapping of moist leaves, and beaten out on a large flat board (*obu-iri*) viz. the flange of a forest tree. The club is a piece of plain wood called *obu kungabu*.
>
> When the clay has been thoroughly pounded the woman commences to work with her hands. First she fashions a small saucer-like base (*obu-atu*). Then, taking a small lump of clay, she rolls it with the heel of her hand on a broad strip of bark which she holds in her lap for a rolling-board. Thus treated it becomes a long thin strip perhaps a quarter of an inch in diameter. This she coils around the rim of

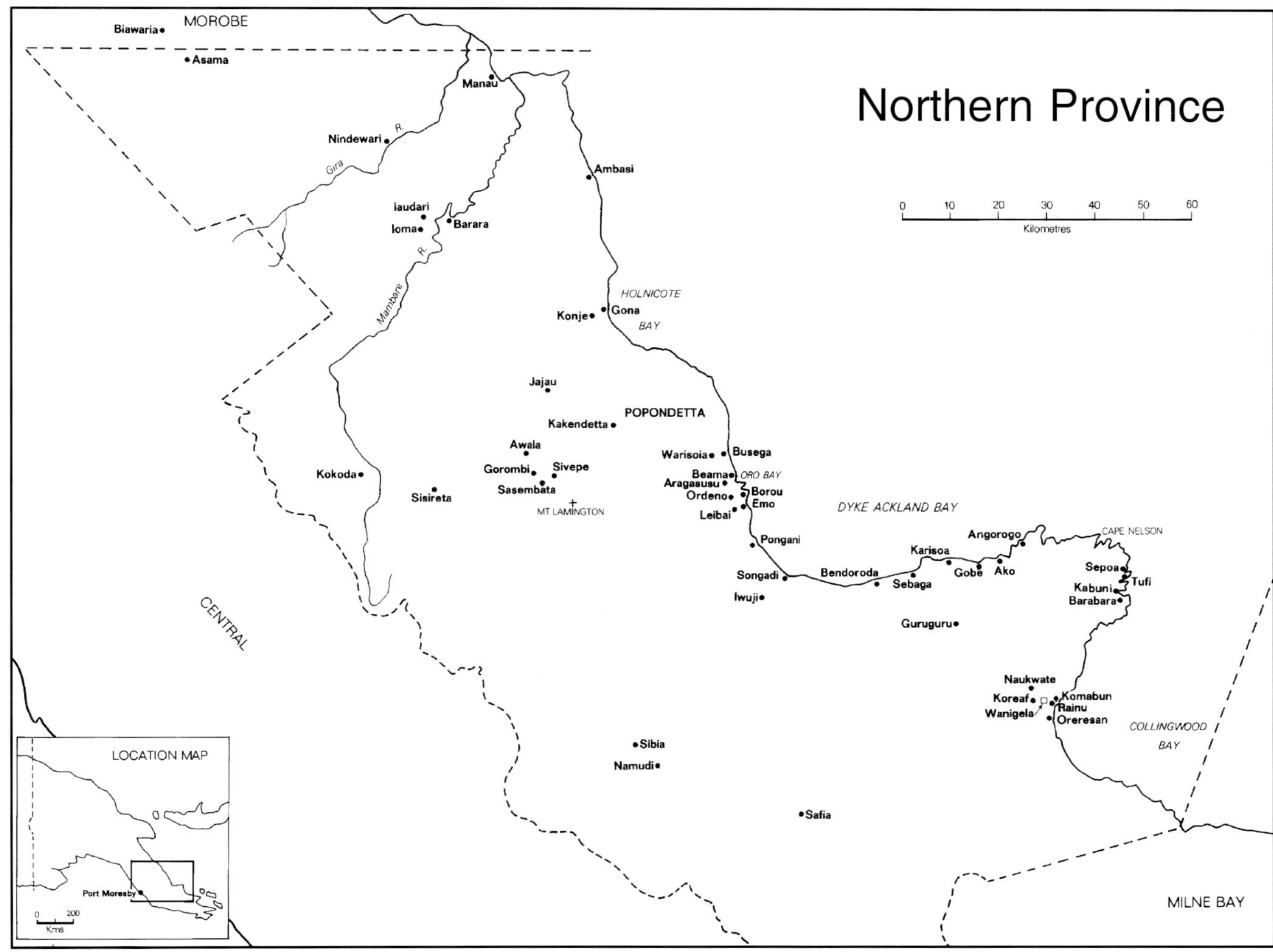

MAP 6

the *obu-atu*, and thereafter continues to roll strips and coil them one above the other so that the pot gradually grows and widens. Each coil is pressed home with the thumb and tapped lightly with a small baton (*tavi*). When three or four have been applied the potter moistens them with a few drops from a broken gourd of water by her side, and with the baton pats or smooths out the grooves on the outer side. She does the same more carefully on the inner side with the smooth surface and the sharp edge of a river shell-fish.

The completely fashioned pot is set aside till several are ready and may be burnt together. In shape it widens towards the mouth, which forms a good circle. Instead of being semi-globular the vessel shows a slight tendency to narrow down to a point at its base, so that its form has been compared to the more pointed half of an egg.

The modern pot is often devoid of ornament. Sometimes it has a few incised markings: sometimes raised pinched markings. Neither possess much artistic value. On the river Gira (and on certain earlier fragments from near the mouth of the Opi, where I understand pottery is not nowadays made) I have seen overlaid markings (formed by pressing on small strips of clay while the pot is in making) which have more artistic possibilities. They are called *bubuko* (the same word being used for the raised cicatrice sometimes seen on the arms and breasts of women). [Williams 1930: 76-7]

A photograph in Williams (1930: 79, Plate XVlla) shows a woman beating clay to a very thin sheet

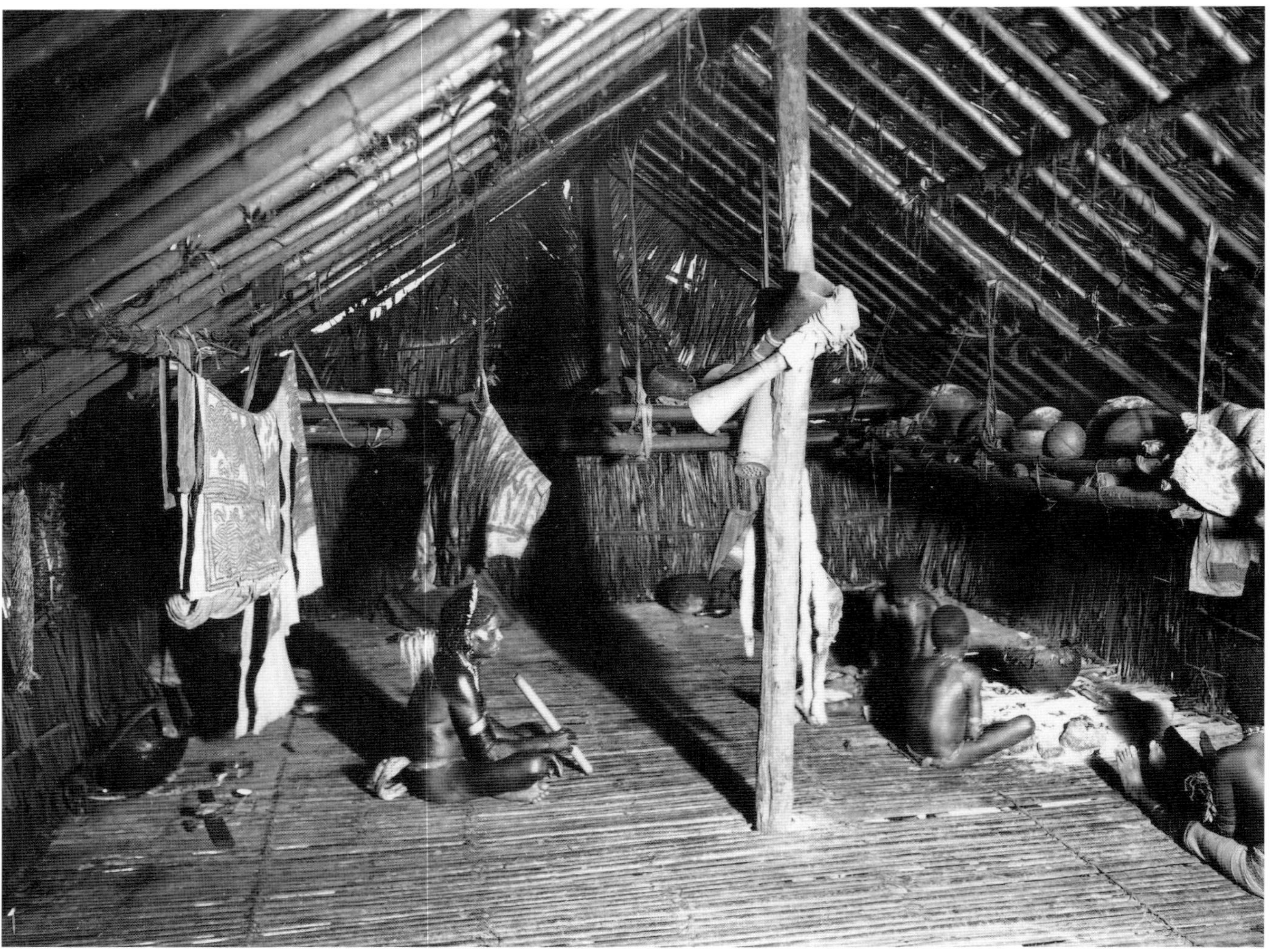

Fig. 5.2
Interior of a Northern Province house, May 1921, showing tapa cloth and pots.

on a thick board. She has a round stick of about arm's length and approximately 4 centimetres in diameter which she uses in a horizontal position, flattening the clay with its whole length.

Williams does not describe a firing but information from Schwimmer and from local informants in several villages suggests that it is more or less similar in all areas. Any available wood and sago palm leaf stalks are criss-crossed into a platform on which the pots are rested and then covered with more fuel. Half way through the firing a stick is used to turn the pots over. The firing is reported to take about an hour; this perhaps includes the preparation. The vessels are lifted off on the end of a stick and, when cool, fern leaves are boiled to 'sweeten' the pots. This is probably another method of sealing and strengthening but perhaps it does also impart a pleasant flavour.

Nearly all Binanderean cooking is done in clay pots but sometimes hot stones are used. Pots of food are taken on expeditions and were even taken when the purpose of the journey was warfare. Leaves and coconut husks are burnt on large pieces of broken pottery to produce a saline ash for cooking.

Pots are important in bride price transactions; in fact bride price in the Aiga language is *dorobu*, a compound of *dora*, wealth in the form of ornaments, and *obu* pots. After the initiation of boys and girls, the initiate's maternal uncle receives from the initiate's father a pig and from his mother a gift which frequently includes a pot. When a person dies, part of his or her property is destroyed and

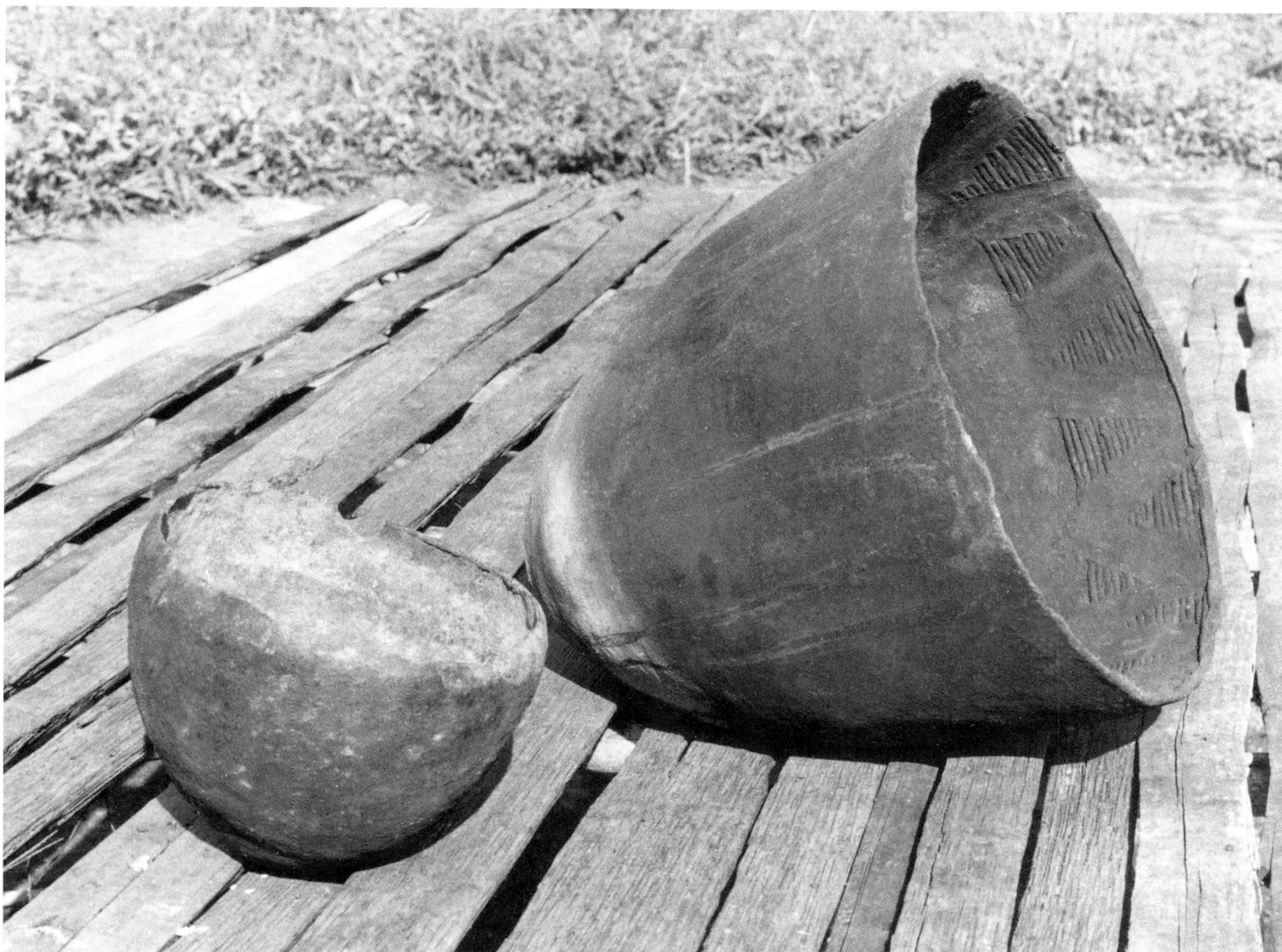

Fig. 5.3
Two cooking pots, Sivepe village, Popondetta area. The larger is Ambasi style, possibly made in the Gona area, *h* 43 cm; the smaller was made at Sivepe, *h* 20 cm.

pots may be smashed in a display of grief. A widow wears a hood of bark cloth or netted string and around her neck mementoes of her dead husband, including sometimes a piece of the pot in which she cooked his food.

Pots also feature in Binanderean legends of creation:

> One of the best known of Orokaiva legends concerns a man-monster named Totoima who was in the habit of slaying all whom he met. His sister (or wife), however, while at work in her garden cut her finger on a leaf of sugar-cane and caught the blood in a leaf of taro. Wrapping this up she hid it away in a pot where it was transformed into two children, or, as other versions say, a great number of boys and girls. These children grew up, and with the assistance of their 'mother' managed to dispatch the tyrannical Totoima, after which they waxed in numbers and became the Orokaiva people. It is only in some versions of the story, however, that these miraculous children born in the pot are made the nucleus of the Orokaiva. The legend necessarily presupposed a previous population on which Totoima could practise his persecutions, and in the more usual version the remnant of these people came flocking in from their hiding places to devour various parts of the monster's body, and in consequence acquire the several dialects of the Orokaiva tongue. As for any light which this legend might throw on the provenance of the people, it may be said that, although the knowledge of the tale is widespread as

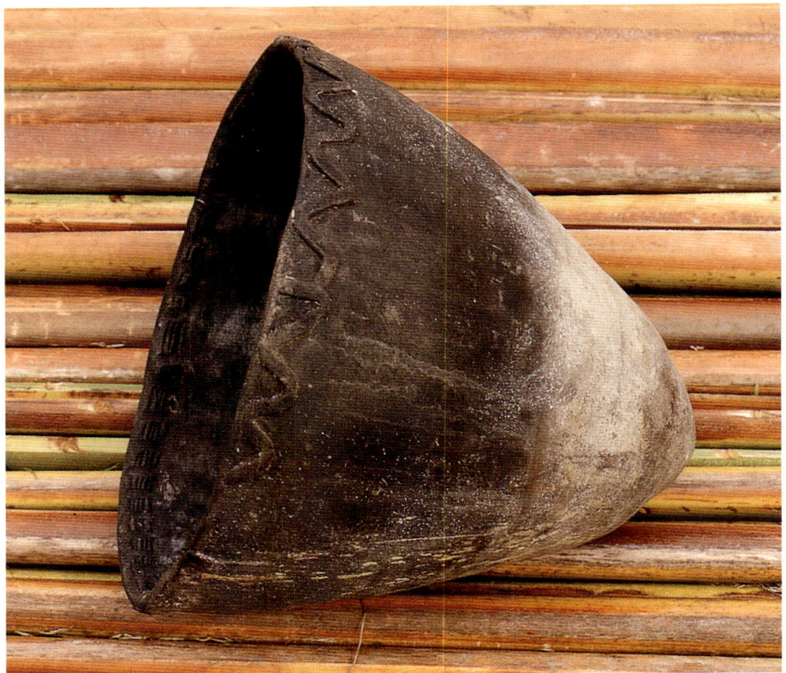

Fig. 5.4
Ambasi-style cooking pot made by Elsie Rorowi, an Ambasi woman, at Konje village, Gona.

the actual depredations of Totoima are supposed to have been, it is associated especially with the river Gira, where the scenes of the monster's dramatic downfall are pointed out. [Williams 1930: 155]

Manau and the Mambare and Gira rivers

Manau, a village of the Binandere language group, is on the small section of coast that faces north, near the mouth of the Mambare, the largest river in the Northern Province. It is an isolated area accessible only by boat. From Schwimmer's report we know that it has an extensive deposit of a particularly high quality plastic clay and that there are numerous clay sources on the Mambare and Gira rivers. One deposit about 1 kilometre from Manau mission station is at least 0.8 hectares in size and at least 0.6 metres deep. Manau clay is almost free of large rough impurities and is considered by the potters to be ready for use. Key (n.d.) reports that it contains a great deal of fine silt quartz and has rounded fragments of schist and some epidote. The clay minerals are montmorillite (smectite) and allophane.

Some 35 to 40 kilometres upstream on the Mambare River are Barara and Iaudari and on the Gira River, about 30 kilometres inland, is Nindewari. These are the only other pot producing villages listed in the Binandere language area. In 1967 the young women of the Women's Club at Iaudari conducted an active industry, using the technique described by Williams. The style of Manau and Iaudari pots is evidently the same and is similar to that of Ambasi pots. Vessels produced in recent years are of only average quality but they are produced very quickly. There is little decoration.

Ambasi

Near Ambasi Anglican Mission, on the coast south of the Mambare River mouth, is another isolated group of about sixteen villages where the Ambasi language is spoken. They also can only be reached by boat. In most villages some of the women are pot makers; women who marry into other Binanderean groups, north to Iwai'ia village and south to villages in the Gona area, continue sporadic pot making activities. Ambasi women in the Gona area now have to collect clay from Ambasi when they wish to make cooking pots.

The technique of two Ambasi women living in Konje tallied exactly with observations made at villages in the Mount Lamington area and with Williams's account. The bottom of a large flattish-based wooden dish was used for preparing the clay; the same was used for rolling out the coils. As shown in an *Annual Report of Papua* (1914-15) traditionally a 'pangal' was used; no doubt this is what Williams described as a 'broad strip of bark'. The Ambasi women's method of firmly pressing down on top of the coil, spreading it and leaving a fingermark pattern, is identical to that used by their Binanderean language family neighbours to the north, the Waria. Both Williams and Schwimmer describe the use of a small wooden baton (paddle) to tap each coil into place. This is an unusual procedure for coil potters and is not carried out by the Waria. Elsewhere a paddle is used for consolidating and smoothing when the pot is complete or nearly so. The Ambasi women used quite a large round-headed paddle with a narrow handle which had a small crosspiece near the end for better gripping.

Deep cone-shaped pots are produced and some are very large; pots up to 50 centimetres high were seen at Gombe, Jenaga and Konje in the Gona area. A distinctive feature of these pots is their unusual decorative treatment. For a depth of some 4 to 10 centimetres inside the top edge coils are left showing, flattened by the method of placement but not bonded. The rows of visible coils are sometimes crossed in zig-zags with a finger or stick and mostly appear with a small angled-in rim. One example had an applied wavy line around the outside top portion combined with finger-marked coils inside (Figs. 5.3, 5.4).

These conical pots with decoration inside the rim were seen at several villages around Mount Lamington. It was established that they were Ambasi pots that had come as presents from the coastal villages around Gona. Although the inland people have made pots, too, it is said that originally only the coastal people were potters and that they taught the inlanders the skill.

Gona, Holnicote Bay

Gona, situated on a wide bay, is about 15 kilometres north-east of Popondetta. It seems that about a generation has lapsed since the people here made pots and when they did it was with clay from Ambasi because there were no local sources. One Gona informant stated that their forefathers had come from Ambasi and it is said that when the Japanese landed at Gona in 1942 many people from there fled up the coast to Ambasi.

Pots illustrated in the *Annual Report British New Guinea* (1898) as 'Gona Bay Pottery (north-east coast)' are Wanigela-style pots and almost certainly would have been traded. Another pot illustrated in the same report is more of a mystery. It is said to come 'from Waututu (north-east coast)'. Waututu does not seem to exist now but there is still a Waututu Point. The pot is entirely different from any made recently anywhere in the Northern, Morobe or Milne Bay provinces. It is a simple, straight-sided, thick-walled vessel with a round base. It appears to be about as high as it is wide and has incised decoration in a band around the top outside edge. It is so long since Gona area people made pots themselves that it is difficult to establish a style for them but it seems their pots were similar to those of Ambasi. The 'Waututu pot' is so different it is more likely to have been an import. But from where?

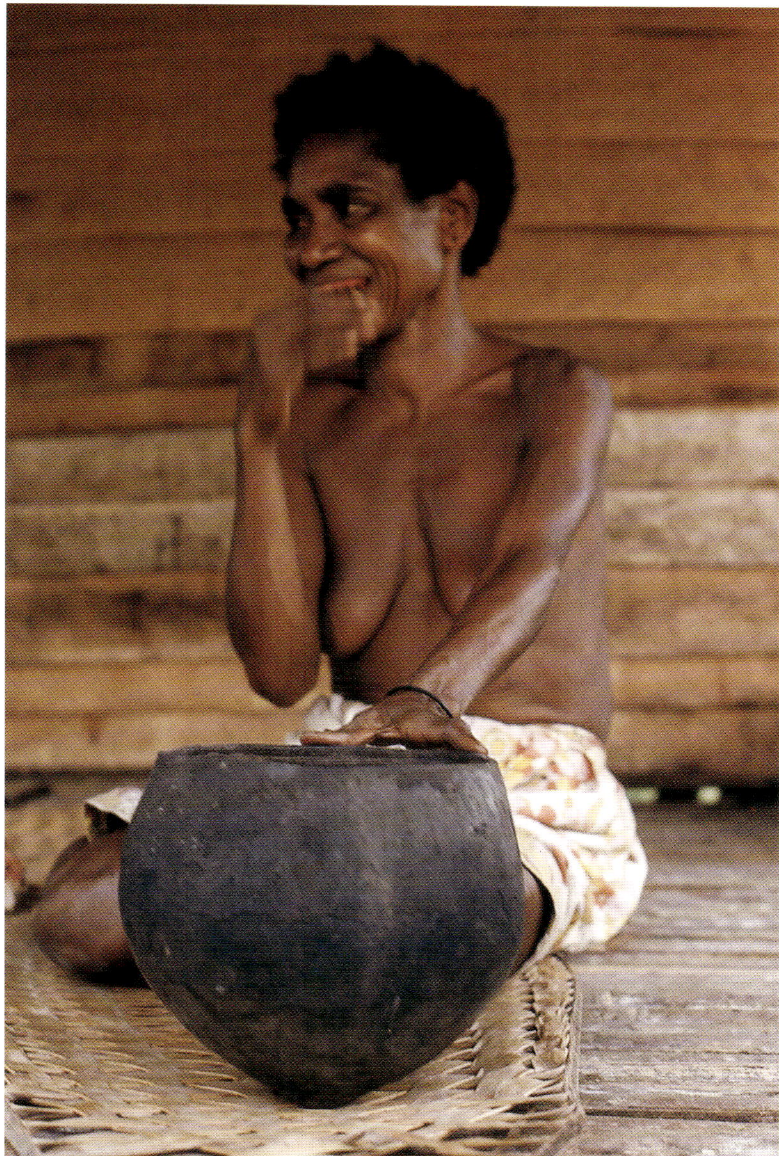

Fig. 5.5
Mary Outa with a Garombi cooking pot made for her by her grandmother, Natalie, Garombi village, Popondetta area.

Popondetta area

Villages of the Orokaiva language group whose inhabitants are known to have produced pots in the recent past are Sivepe, Sasembata, Garombi, Awala and Jaiau on the north-west slopes of Mount Lamington; Kakandetta, close to Popondetta; and

Busega, Aragasusu and Warisoia, south-east of Popondetta towards Oro Bay. It is highly probable that there were more in pre-contact days. It is difficult to determine how long ago the pot making ceased but when Ziska Schwimmer was there in 1967 pots were still made occasionally.

The main clay source was on Awala village land, about two hours' walk from Sasembata and Sivepe, but in recent years Awala has been extended and the clay pit is now in the middle of the village and no longer available. There was also a small deposit at the hamlet of Pusahambo. Schwimmer (1967) reports that the clay from this area, in contrast to that from Manau, needed to be worked for about half an hour and that the traditional board used here for pounding the clay was a very hard fine-grained wood, *puga* (*Pangium edule*). Erik Schwimmer (1973) mentions the use of rough leaves for scraping pots.

A wide variety of forms was produced; more often these inland pots were restricted forms whereas the Ambasi pots are nearly all unrestricted. The Orokaiva name for clay pots is *obu*, as in Williams's Aiga language. Many of the Orokaiva vessels are plain but some have simple incised marks around the outside top and others have the Ambasi-style decoration of unbonded and finger-marked coils inside the rim.

Little trading seems to have been carried out in this area, at least for many years, although pots are offered as hospitality items to people living inland. At Kakandetta two women still know how to make pots and they used to get clay from a creek bed close by. Their pots were similar in shape to those of the Ambasi. A wide assortment of pots was seen at the villages near Oro Bay. One woman at Warisoia village still makes pots occasionally in the dry season. Her clay source is nearby. At Aragasusu three locally made pots were seen; these were more similar in style to their closer neighbours at Emo and Pongani. Pots sighted in this area were from Wanigela, Emo, Pongani, Gona and Panaeati Island

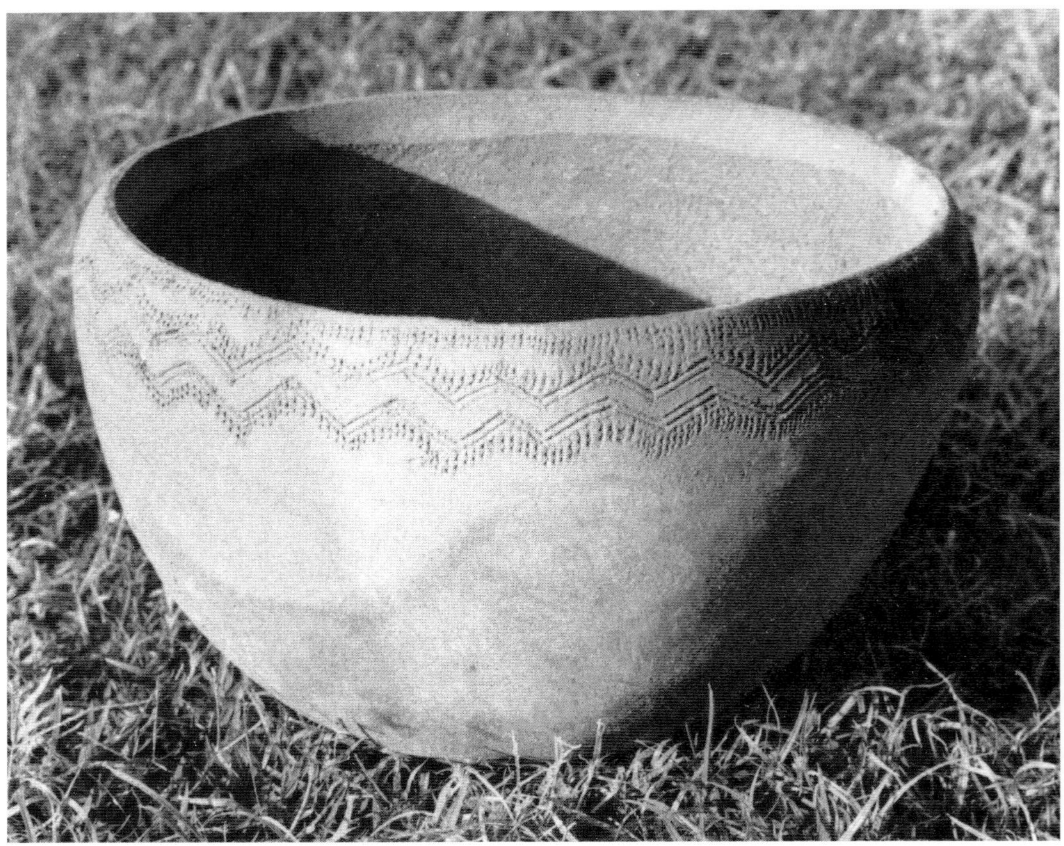

Fig. 5.6
Cooking pot made by Anastasia Rajara of Pongani village, Dyke Ackland Bay, showing the inside scraped surface, *h* 18 cm.

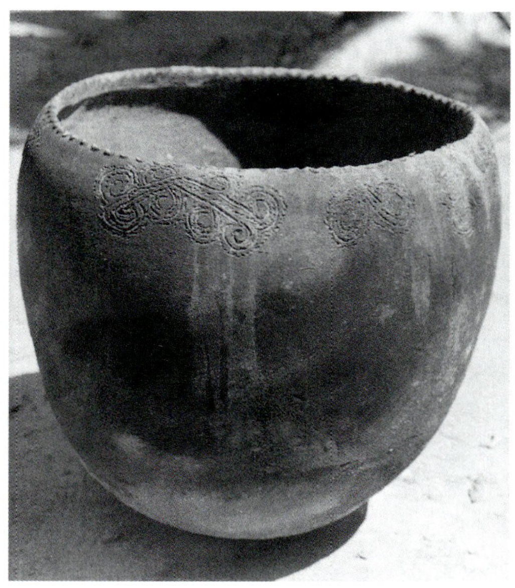

Fig. 5.7
Sago storage or feast pot made by Rosa Mary Gorewa of Emo village, Dyke Ackland Bay, *h* 32 cm.

in Milne Bay. There was even an Azera pot brought back from the Kaiapit area by a schoolteacher. Descriptions of techniques given at some of the villages were identical to those of other Binandere groups.

More detailed research is needed here before all evidence disappears.

Dyke Ackland and Oro bays

Dyke Ackland Bay lies between Oro Bay and Tufi, south-east of Popondetta. There are six different languages spoken around the bay: Notu, Gaina, Baruga, Dagoro, Yega and Kainte, all of the Binanderean family.

The best known pot makers of this area are the Notu-speaking inhabitants of the coastal villages of Pongani and Emo. Only cooking pots are made at Pongani now, while larger sago feast pots are still

Fig. 5.8
Detail of decoration on a cooking pot made by Grace Jenny Kaware of Oreresan village, Wanigela.

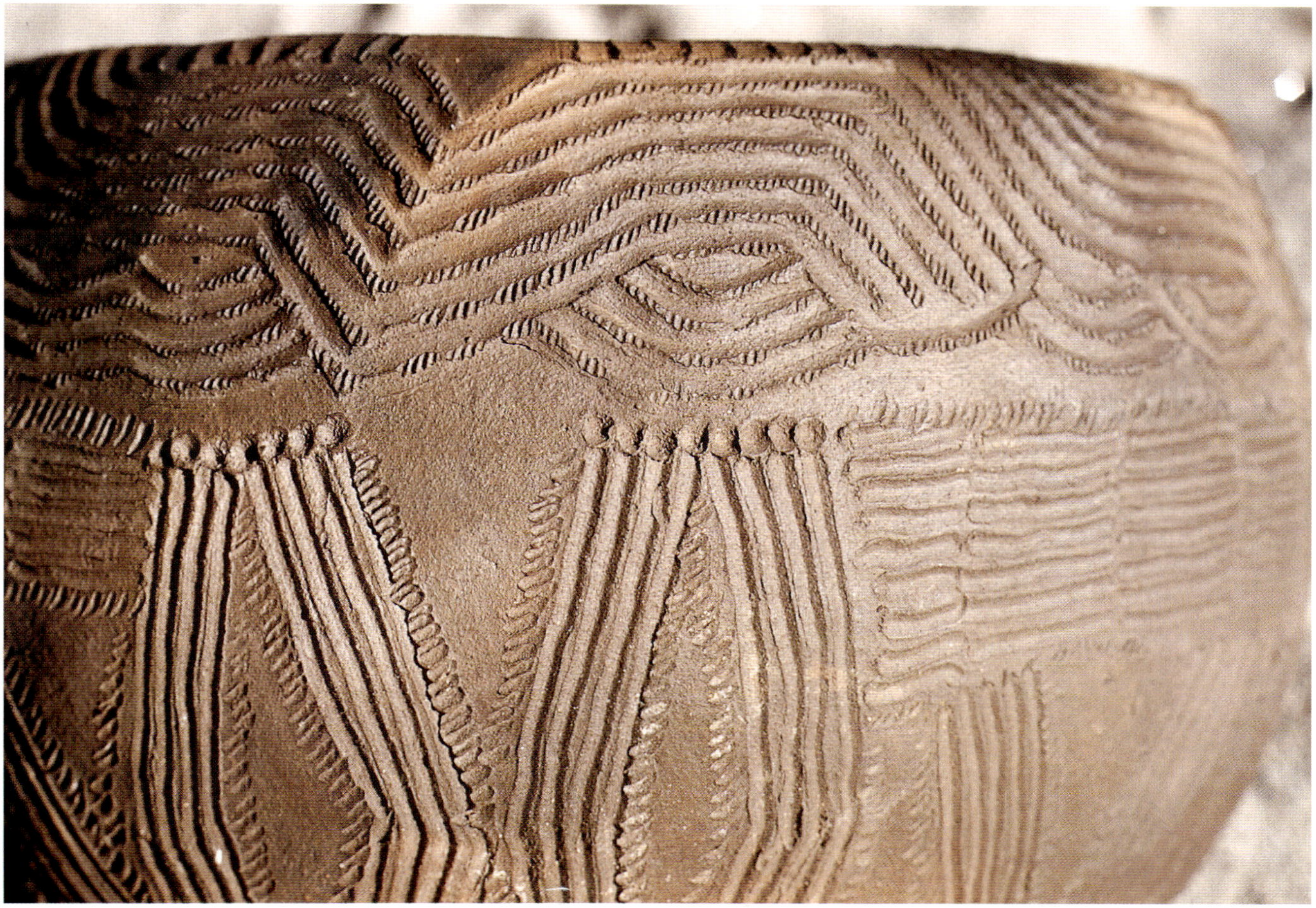

being made at Emo (Figs. 5.6, 5.7). Clay used for Pongani pots gives them a different colour and character from any others of the area; it is sandier in texture and more orange in colour. The workmanship is rough. The form varies from semispherical to spherical, with pointed to flattened bases; all are restricted forms. One particular element which seems to be unique to Pongani and perhaps to Emo is the thick, inward-angled rim which is always smoothed in contrast to the scraped surface of the interior of the pot. Decorations are mostly incised, combed or impressed, using shells, and confined to the upper third of the pot. Simple geometric half circles, zig-zags, straight lines, wavy lines and rows of small marks are made. One feast pot with applied coil decoration was sighted at Pongani. Everyday cooking pots are generally about 13 to 18 centimetres high. Another locally made feast pot from Pongani was 35 centimetres high with a 34 to 38 centimetres wide mouth. Feast pots at Emo were a similar size.

The clay source for Pongani is many hours' walk away at Kopoe. Emo women and some Pongani potters get clay from Baoro, near Leibai village, about three hours' walk inland from Emo. A pot making demonstration was observed at Pongani. Fresh water is used to dampen the clay. The forming technique is similar to that used in other Binanderean villages but the base is not formed first; the first coil is simply set in a circle on a board and subsequent coils are added in the normal manner. Coils are bonded by downward dragging and smoothing with the fingers and, when firmer, the inside coils are joined and then scraped with a shell before the pot is turned over for beating. A wooden beater is used to close the still-soft hole in the base of the pot. The inside is scraped with a shell and, surprisingly, it is not later smoothed to seal the gritty open texture.

At Emo, about twenty women know how to make pots. One of the most prolific, who is considered by the other women to be the best potter, is Rose Mary Gorewa of Tatarie hamlet. As well as making traditional cooking pots and large feast pots she is creating new shapes for sale to tourists and others. No data was collected on drying, firing or trading but prestation seems to be a custom in this area. Pots found at Pongani were from Iwuji, Gobe, Leiba and Wanigela.

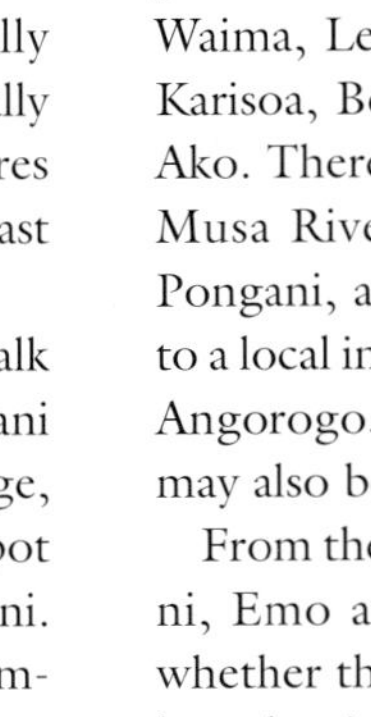

Other villages in this area where it is reported from several sources that pots are made or where pots have been produced in recent years are Beama, Waima, Leibai, Borou, Ordeno, Iwuji, Songadi, Karisoa, Bendoroda, Sebaga, Gobe, Beporo and Ako. There is also a report of pot making on the Musa River, about 50 kilometres inland from Pongani, at Safia, Sibia, and Namudi. According to a local informant, the Karafe-speaking people of Angorogo, Barabara, Kabuni and Sepoa villages may also be pot makers.

From the limited number of pots seen at Pongani, Emo and Beama, it is difficult to establish whether there is a style variation between the villages but it can be said that the Pongani-Emo pots are distinct from those from Ambasi. The influence of Wanigela pottery can be seen in the whole area although in general the workmanship is inferior. It was reported in 1975 that Wanigela potters had married into the inland village of Guruguru where they found good clay and had introduced the skill of pot making. Such intermarriage could explain the Wanigela style in Dyke Ackland and Oro Bay pots.

Fig. 5.9

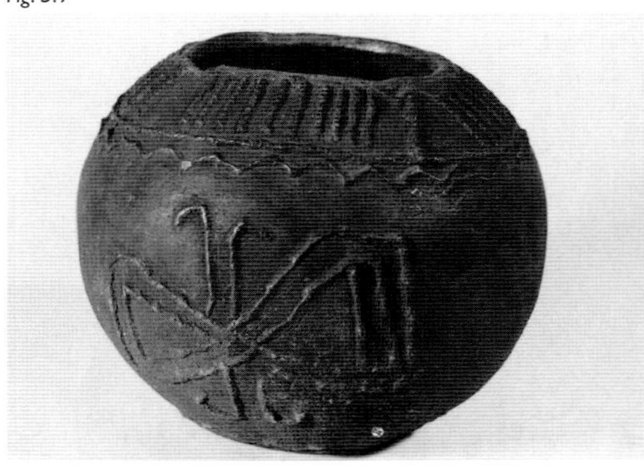

Fig. 5.10

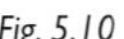

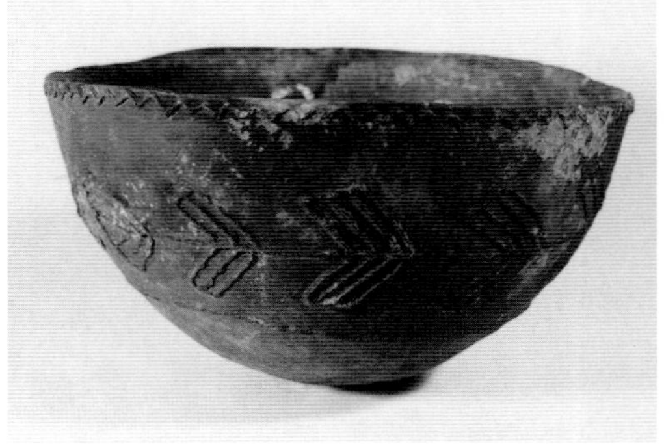

Figs 5.9 to 5.12
Pots collected in the Wanigela area 1904-07.

Fig. 5.9
Old pot of unusual shape, function unknown, *h* 16 cm.

Fig. 5.10
Old pot, probably a serving bowl, *h* 16 cm.

Wanigela

A distinctive type of pottery is made at what is commonly referred to as 'Wanigela', an area of land on the coast of Collingwood Bay between Cape Nelson to the north and Cape Vogel to the south and consisting of a complex of three coastal villages, some hamlets and two inland villages. Pots are produced by the women from the Austronesian-speaking coastal villages of Oreresan (Arifama-Miniafa language), Rainu and Komabun (Ubir language) and the inland non-Austronesian villages of Koreaf and Naukwate (Onjob language). In spite of the variety of languages the same tradition of pot making prevails.

Pots are traded with inland people for feathers, reptile skins and tapa cloth and with the coastal people along Collingwood Bay for Fergusson Island obsidian, shells and canoes. The tapa cloth, made by women in the inland villages, is decorated by the Wanigela women and re-traded or sold for cash. The mission at Wanigela has for some time been aiding in the marketing of pots and tapa cloth, which are transported to the coastal people and to Port Moresby for sale to artifact shops and tourist centres.

Research on the Wanigela pottery industry has been carried out by Egloff (1971, 1973), who excavated archaeological sites around Oreresan and Rainu and reported on contemporary pot making at Rainu, and by Key (1968, 1973), who briefly describes the industry, concentrating on clay analysis. A report by Scott and Segman (1968) describes a collection of Melanesian ceramics acquired by the Buffalo Society of Natural Sciences; some of the vessels described are wrongly attributed to Gona Bay and Cape Nelson, as has been noted by Egloff (n.d.) who suggests that they originated in Wanigela and were probably transported to Gona mission by mission boats. Egloff (1973) reports that in 1905, P. Pock, a Viennese doctor and P. Money, a lay missionary at Rainu, made a collection of sherds and specimens which are now housed in the Australian Museum, Sydney, and the South Australian Museum, Adelaide. These specimens and Money's records and photographs of the manufacture of vessels indicate a similar method of production but a slight change in vessel form and decorative elements (Figs. 5.9-5.11).

Three vessels recorded in 1905 are no longer made. *Simum*, a container used for storing water in the house, was tall, ovoid and with two or more handles; the entire surface was decorated with impressed applied strips called *sanos* (Fig. 5.12). *Kepkep* was a food-serving vessel made of two small bowls joined together; a variation consisted of an ovoid vessel with a partition dividing the interior into halves. *Sewaf*, a boat-shaped vessel with a handle, was not often made but was used as a water dipper, possibly for filling the *simum*. Some twelve Wanigela pots were wrongly accessioned at the time of collection in the Brisbane Museum. They were illustrated by Edge-Partington (1898) who says 'probably from the neighbourhood of the Mambare River, N.E. coast'.

Many cooking and water pots are still in use in spite of the influx of billy cans, enamel bowls and metalware. The principal effect of European vessels

Fig. 5.11

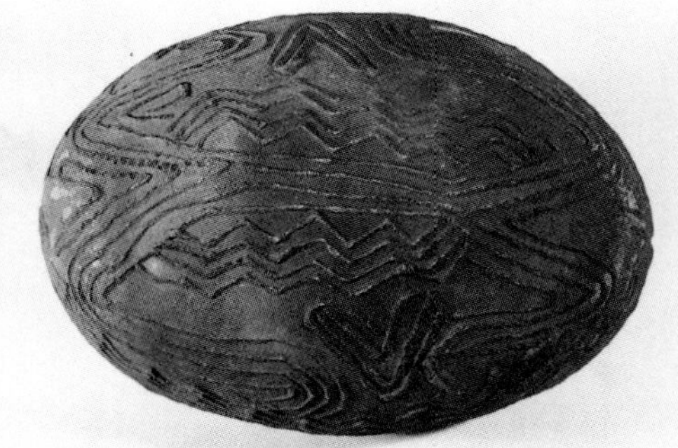

Fig. 5.12

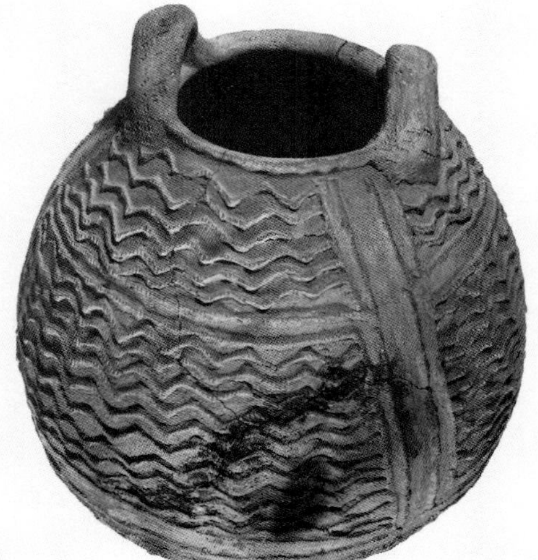

Fig. 5.11
Old ovoid bowl with decoration on the base, *h* 15 cm.

Fig. 5.12
Old water pot with two handles, *simum*, collected in the Wanigela area 1883-87, *h* 22 cm

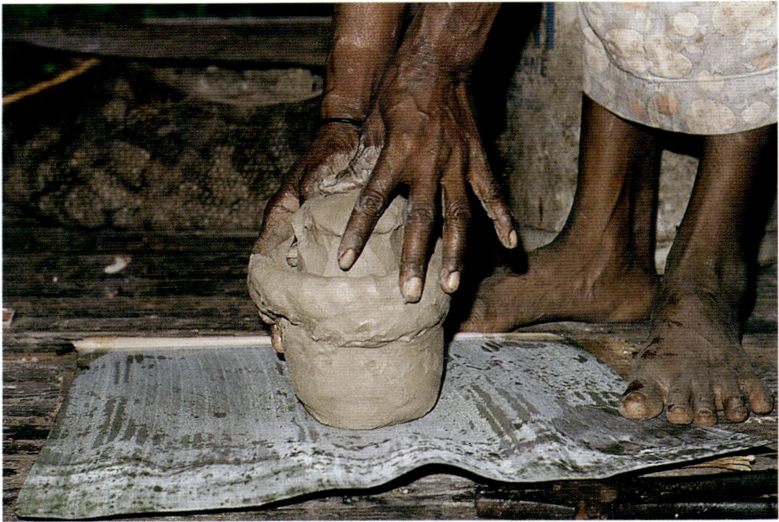
Fig. 5.13

Fig. 5.13
Lydia, pushing down clay from a cylinder to form a ring at the bottom for a cooking pot, Komabun village, Wayug hamlet, Wanigela.

Fig. 5.14
Grace Jenny Kaware scraping up clay from the thick ring to form the walls, Oreresan village, Wanigela.

Fig. 5.15
Grace Jenny Kaware scaping up clay from the inside of the walls, Oreresan.

Fig. 5.16
Grace Jenny in a tapa cloth skirt, rolling a coil, Oreresan.

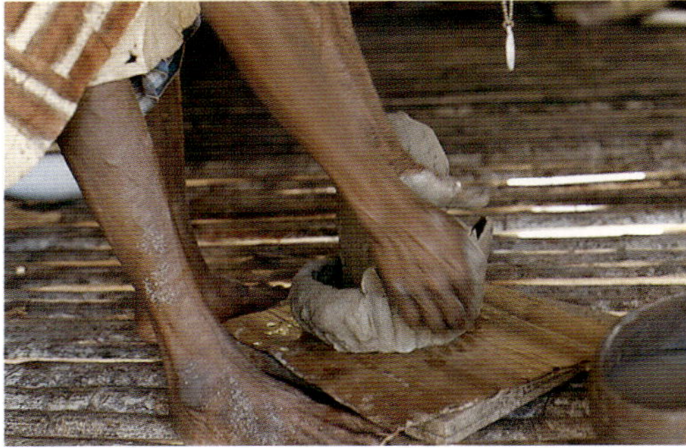
Fig. 5.14

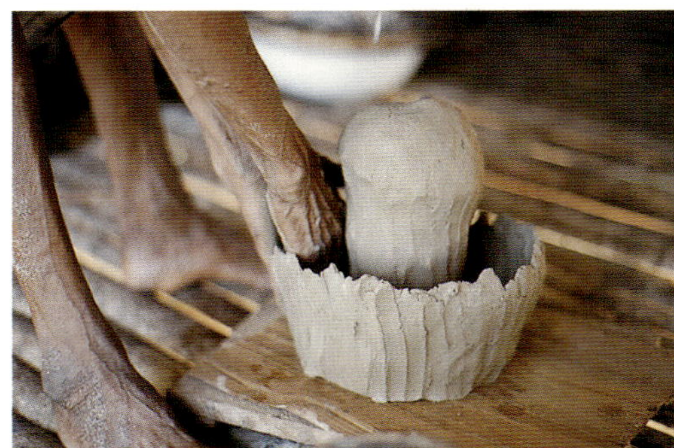
Fig. 5.15

has been to limit the range of forms in use. During the last ten years or so, one basic form has been made commonly for both cooking and holding water. Nowhere else in the country is such a wide-mouthed pot used for storing water. Larger vessels of similar shape are used less frequently for feasts and open bowls for serving cooked food. Wanigela pots are of an even thickness and are popular because their thin walls enable food to be cooked quickly. The types of pots produced today have been recorded by Egloff (1973) whose research centred on Rainu village; the local terms are therefore in the Ubir language. The cooking pot, *babiaf*, is used for general cooking, its average size being 22 centimetres high and 24 centimetres in mouth diameter; it is spherical with a round to slightly flattened base and restricted simple form. The pot used for water, *serau susu*, is essentially the same pot as the *babiaf*. The *kiriwas* is a bowl or cup which was traditionally used as a small eating bowl; it is the same form as the *babiaf* but much smaller and has been replaced by European utensils. A pot used for feasts, the *sabed*, can be either restricted or unrestricted, with a round to slightly flattened base. A serving bowl, *ramo*, is used commonly or at feasts. The *ramo* used during a feast is decorated with special clan markings. It is semi-spherical, with a round or slightly flattened base.

Cracked or chipped pots have many uses and are given separate names. A flawed *babia* is used to

Fig. 5.16
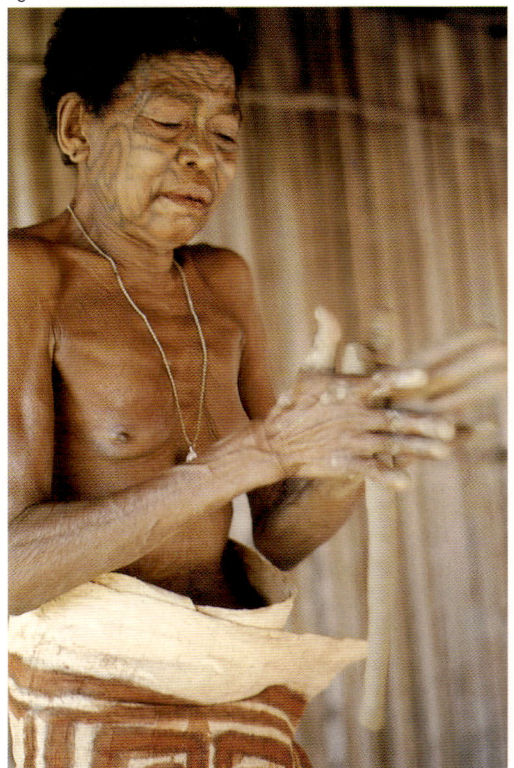

hold clay; if used to hold shells, chickens or other things it is called *nosif*. An old *kiriwas* or any small container is used to hold the potter's tools and water. Large sherds from any vessel are called *rewage* and are used as food plates for feeding dogs and pigs.

Over the past seventy years the main change in decoration has been the decrease in use of applied impressed lines, *sanos*. These are often used to cover the entire vessel, including the base, but now are usually found only on the top quarter or third portion of the outside of the pot. The remainder of the walls of modern pots as well as some of the early ones are decorated with incised or grooved lines, shell impressions and punctation marks.

A recent innovation is the production of vases used to hold flowers in the mission church. Some are made for tourists but they are not very successful because the low-fired clay is naturally porous. The vases are reminiscent of the early water pot, *simum*, but have flat bases. It is interesting that here a flat-bottomed vessel is a likely progression resulting from the forming process (the pots start as flat-bottomed forms, a unique process in Papua New Guinea).

Key's report (1968) on Wanigela pottery concentrated on clay and its properties. Some of his

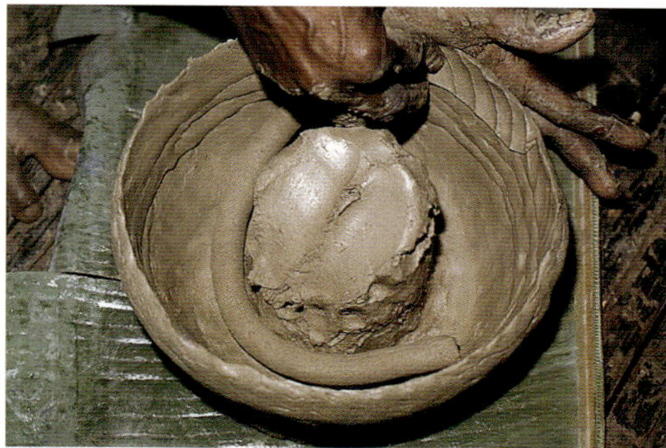

Fig. 5.18

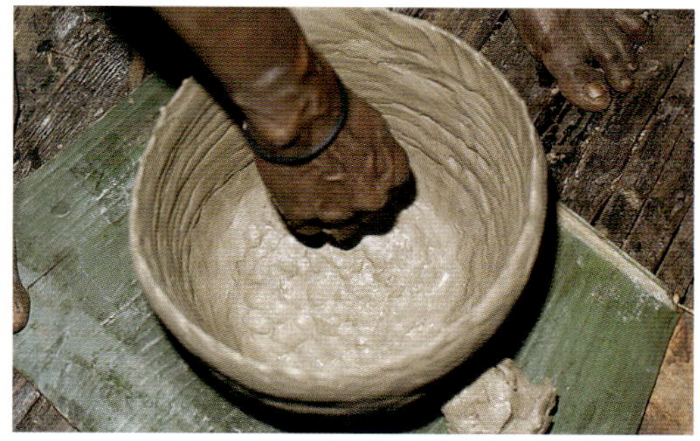

Fig. 5.19

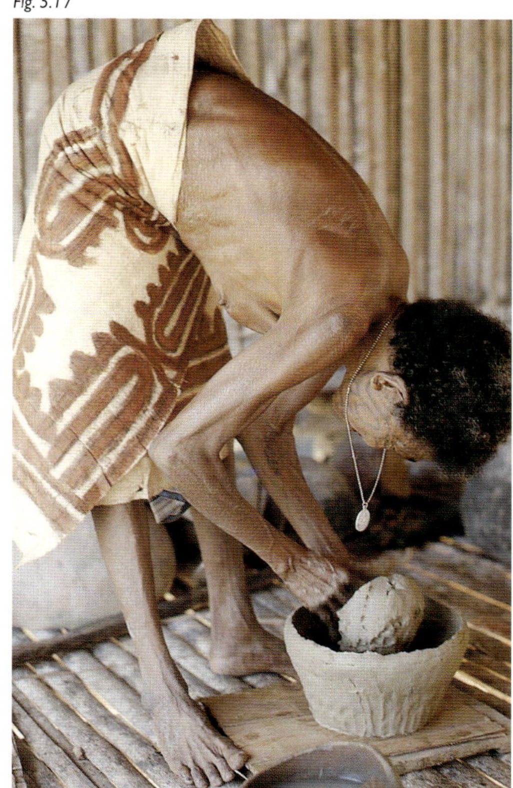

Fig. 5.17

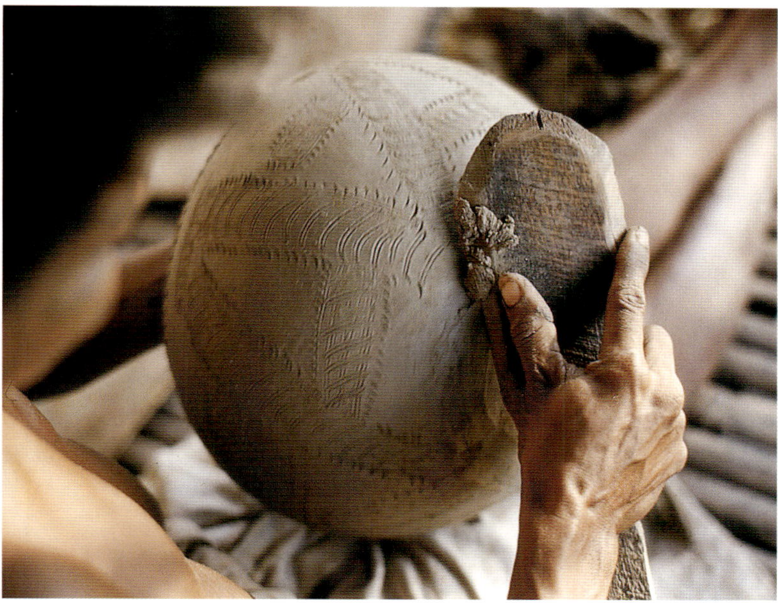

Fig. 5.20

Fig. 5.17
Grace Jenny adding a coil to the pot, Oreresan.

Fig. 5.18
Lydia pressing another coil on to the top edge. Clay is pinched off the column to form the coils, Komabun village, Wayug hamlet, Wanigela.

Fig. 5.19
Lydia consolidating the base with her knuckles after all the clay from the centre has been used, Komabun.

Fig. 5.20
Gladys scraping the ridge off the base, Komabun.

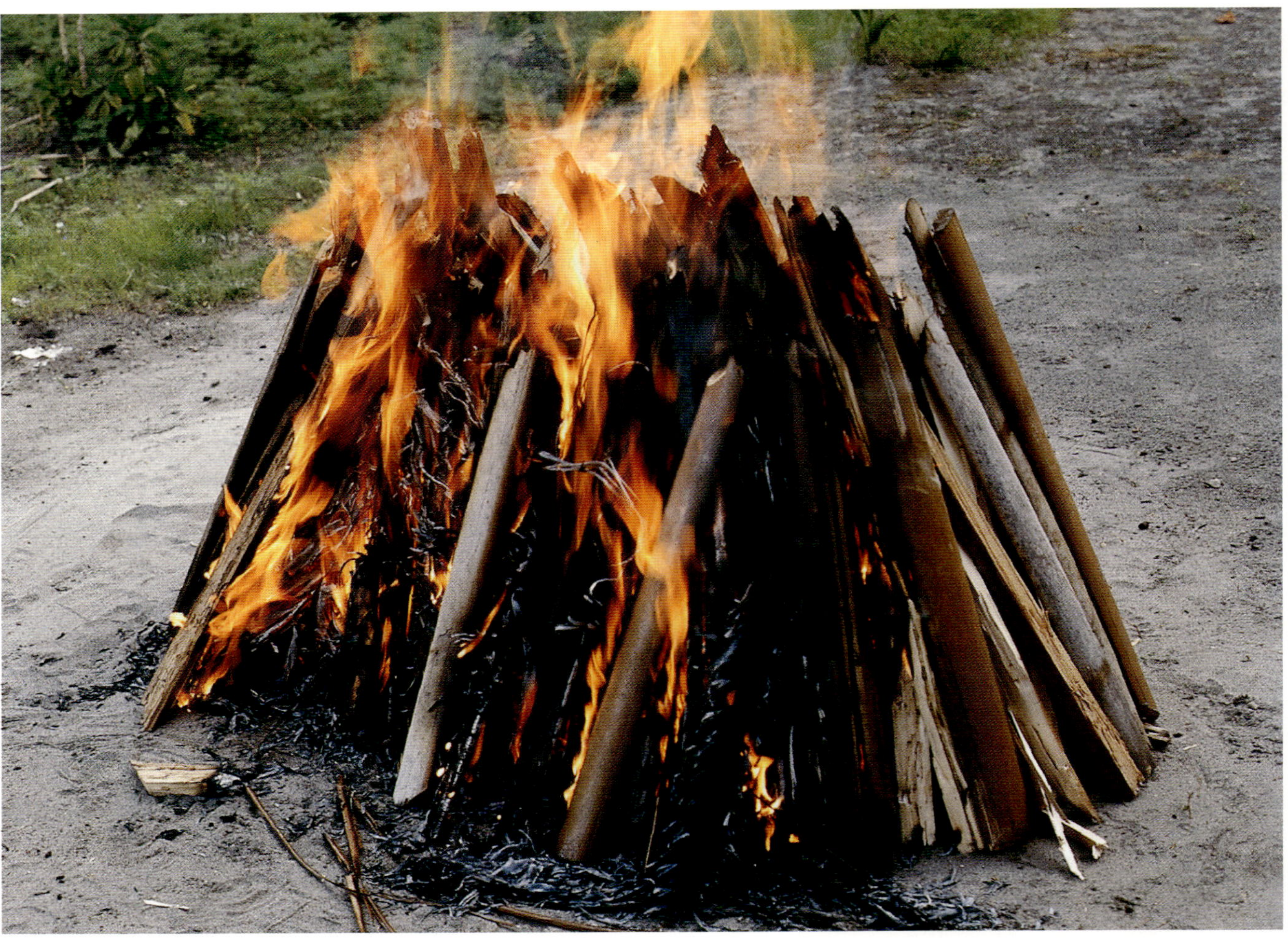

Fig. 5.21
Mary Manimasau's firing using sago fronds and some split wood, Komabun village, Wanigela.

findings are as follows. The clay source for Wanigela potters is a pit at a place known as *potet* which is 2 to 3 kilometres inland from the beach villages. The clay comes from an unusual sedimentary deposit about 65 metres above sea level on the lowest slopes of the extinct volcano, Mount Victory, and is derived from an intermediate volcanic ash. It consists of, on average, 63 per cent clay, mostly kaolinite and a little montmorillonite, with 37 per cent silt and sand-sized particles. These particles are extremely poorly sorted, which would give a good tightly packed material, but the high percentage of silt and sand ensures a clay that will shrink without setting up undue stress at any point even though the shrinkage results in a 15 to 20 per cent loss in volume. An average content of 4.7 per cent organic matter helps give it good plasticity. The impurities in the clay are mainly fresh feldspar fragments. Fragments of glassy, sometimes devitrified porphyritic hornblende and andesite are also a major component. There is also a small percentage of mica.

The word for clay is *naukwat* and is the same as the generic term for ceramic vessels. The clay, when it is brought back to the village, is stored in a *nosif* or sometimes in a tin, covered with a green leaf or a damp piece of cloth and stored under the house or on the verandah. Equipment and tools used in the manufacture of pots include a thin board or pandanus leaf mat on which to support the vessel, a damaged pot or any small container to hold the water, a wooden beater (various shapes) and a variety of bivalve and univalve shells used for scraping, smoothing, shaping, cutting and decorating.

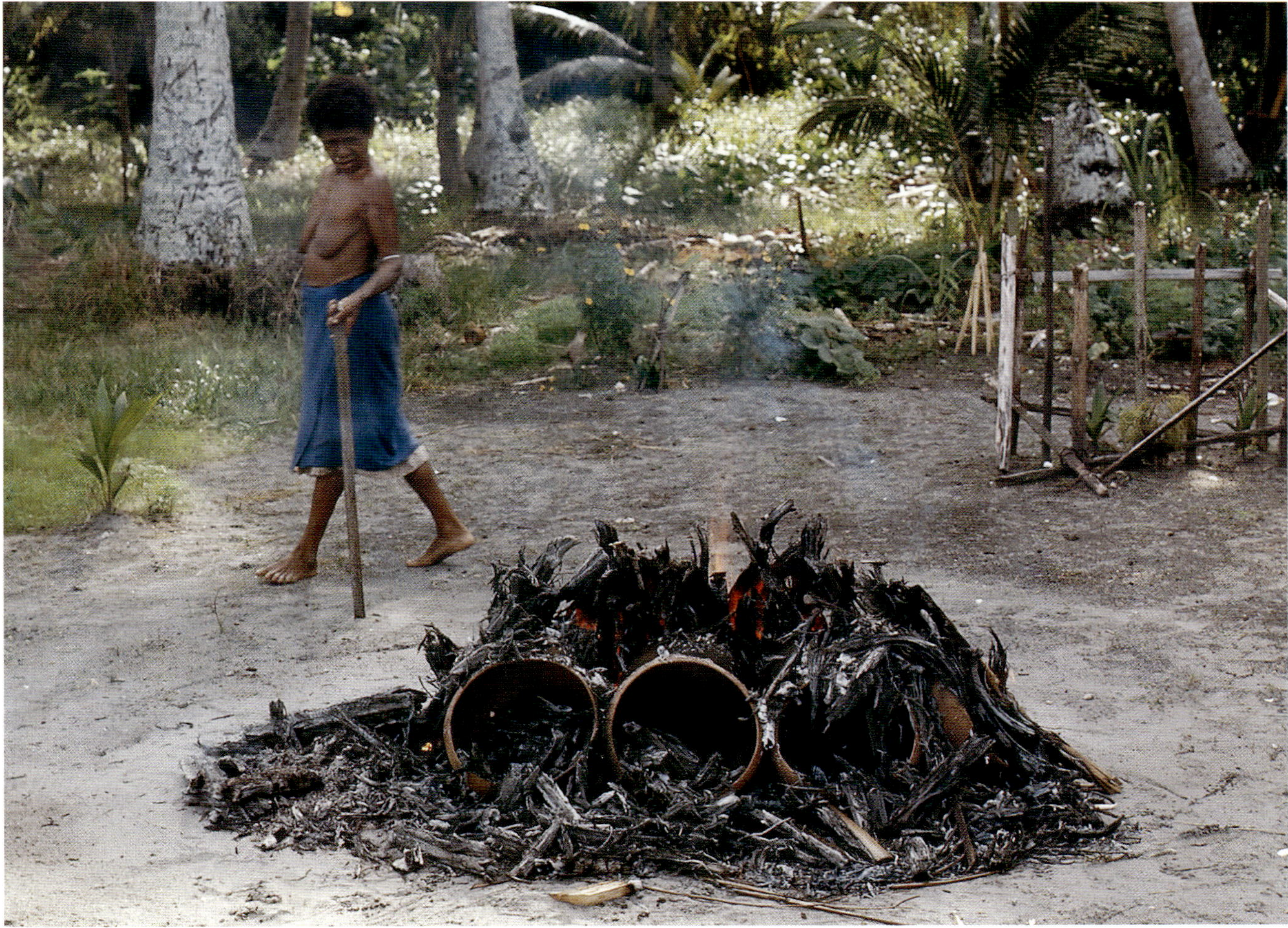

Fig. 5.22
Mary Manimasau watching her firing, Komabun.

The women work either on their verandahs or on a covered platform near the house. The clay is kneaded with the hands and small stones and roots removed. A small amount of fresh water is kneaded into the clay to bring it to the right consistency. No temper is added. Four or five lumps of clay are banged and rolled into pugs about 30 centimetres long and 15 centimetres in diameter and made ready for the same number of pots. A pug is stood upright on a support and the potter stands above it. With her thumbs she pushes clay down from the sides of the pug forming a thick roll of clay all around its base. This is now scraped out and up with the fingers, which spread the roll of clay into a flat-bottomed, straight-sided dish shape, with the high piece still standing in the centre. The top edge of the dish is levelled by pinching and smoothing. The potter next pinches off a piece of clay from the top of the pug and prepares it for rolling by pinching it into a small rough dish shape. She then rolls it between her hands held at shoulder height. When the roll dangles a few centimetres, she turns it up the other way and completes the rolling, making a coil about 60 centimetres long and 2 centimetres thick.

One end of the coil and the forefinger of her right hand are now dipped into water. The coil is laid down inside the dish around the pug and the wet end is lifted up to the top inside edge of the pot and applied, overlapping the one below, with an upward pressure of the forefinger. The three other fingers lift the coil into position and the thumb presses outside while the left hand also supports the exterior walls. The coil is flattened and thinned by this process and so raised to about

3 centimetres. One potter was seen to complete a ring with a single coil; other potters either fill a gap with the start of the next coil or make a short one to complete the last layer before starting the next. Thus it seems the method can be either ring building or spiral coiling (Figs. 5.13-5.20).

After each coil is pressed into place, the potter runs the back of her fingers around the inside to smooth it. When several coils have been added and bonded, she scrapes the outside and inside with a mussel shell, *wairarak* (*Batissa violacea*) and smooths both with a wet shell; the shells are always kept clean and wet while in use. While the pot becomes firmer the potter has a smoke or may work on another pot.

When the central pug of clay has been made into coils, the potter consolidates the inside base by tapping it with her knuckles. Further scraping and smoothing are carried out with the mussel shell, the vessel at this stage being a rough flat-based cone shape, wider at the top. It is now left again to dry a little. Next, the inside is smoothed with another bivalve shell and then the bellying-out of the form is done with the larger mussel shell until a thinner spherical form is produced. After another break the potter cuts the uneven lip of the pot with a small bivalve shell. Then, after the pot has dried for one or two hours, it is ready for decorating.

The decoration of a cooking pot usually takes twenty to twenty-five minutes. With the pot still sitting upright on its board the potter stands over it and decorates the entire exterior of the vessel. Each potter uses a wide variety of designs with her own identifying signs. Various grooves and crescent-shaped marks are made with the tip of a small univalve shell (*Polinices* sp.). The ridged exterior edge of the lip of a bivalve (*Cardium* sp) is used for making parallel line impressions. The pot must become firmer again before the potter proceeds with the applied decoration. Small rolls of clay about 2 to 3 millimetres in diameter, called *fotu*, are applied in wavy zig-zag or short parallel lines around the top of the pot. After they have been worked onto the vessel walls they are impressed with the ridged back of the same bivalve used to make the parallel line impressions on the lower walls.

Again the vessel must harden, this time until it is firm enough to be turned upside down but still sufficiently malleable for the base to be shaped. Sometimes excess clay is first scraped or cut away from the outer edge of the flat bottom, using the sharpened side of a wooden paddle, *fefef.* These pieces of clay can then be used to patch and fill holes left by any discarded pieces of grit. The paddle is now beaten firmly against a fist held inside the pot to act as an anvil and each stroke finishes with a sliding action from the outer edge to the centre of the base. The pot and paddle are both kept moist. When the base has been rounded it is scraped with the side of a *waifus* shell (*Melania juncta*), and the interior base is smoothed with the lip of the mussel shell. Finally, some potters smooth the base with wet hands, forming a slip which remains as a fine clay layer finish. In some cases the decoration nearest the base must be touched up and extended further under the now curved surface.

Pots must dry in the house for one to two weeks before being fired. A potter makes from two to four pots a day and will fire them when from four to twenty vessels are ready. During the drying period the potter collects firewood while tending her gardens in the bush. Coconut husks and fronds and uniformly split wood are used as fuel, *nowei.* Three kinds of wood are used: *mumur*, *aurab* and *wawau.* A raised platform of wood is made just large enough for the number of pots to be fired. The pots are placed back to back in two rows with the bases touching. The firewood is stacked in pyramid form around and over the pots.

Firing usually takes place in the cool of the evening or morning when there is a light breeze. The fuel is lit with a palm frond, first on the upward side of the stack and then on the downward side. If more than six pots are to be fired, two or more people will light the fire at the same moment to ensure even firing of all pots. The wood quickly bursts into flames and extra fuel is added where a pot becomes uncovered. After about twenty minutes the wood is burnt to embers and the pots are removed with a long stick held inside the opening or with two sticks under the base. They are left to cool while the potter inspects them for flaws, which are few. If any bursting or spalling has occurred it will have been detected against the sound of the wood crackling; the most common fault appears to be thin spalls from the base.

The pots are taken into the house and put on a rack over the cooking fire, where they are smoked for several weeks until they have a slightly shiny brown appearance. Some informants spoke of pots being soaked in a freshwater lake for about a week before smoking. One of Egloff's informants stated that if a pot has dark 'fire clouds' after firing it can be dipped in salt water and refired. This is supposed to lighten the dark areas.

Cape Nelson and Cape Vogel

The authors have heard from European residents and nationals in the vicinity that there is some pot making activity in the Tufi area, Cape Nelson, but conflicting information makes it difficult to establish whether this is so. If scattered pottery making does exist it is likely to be the result of Wanigela women having married into families in the area. More research is necessary for Dyke Ackland Bay and Cape Nelson.

However, it is a fact (Egloff 1973) that vessels similar in style to those of Wanigela are produced in the Austronesian villages on the eastern extremity of Cape Vogel, to the south of Collingwood Bay. This is in Milne Bay Province but is included here because of the similarity of the pots. Egloff records Bogaboga as the pot making village; other villages reported are Ginada, Mukawa and Rausewa but no confirmation is available. The Bogaboga pots are thicker-walled than those at Wanigela, but with a definite thinning a few centimetres below the rim. The Bogaboga claim to have learned the craft from their traditional trading partners in Wanigela but admit that their product is inferior. The manufacturing process is identical.

Two examples of pots from Bogaboga are illustrated in Egloff (1973) but whether they are typical forms is not certain. The cooking pot *naukwaikwa* is more shallow than its Wanigela counterpart; it is semi-spherical with a rounded base similar in shape to the Wanigela *ramo*. The bowl used for feasts, *rama*, is much larger than the cooking vessel, with a round base and an unrestricted orifice.

6. Morobe Province

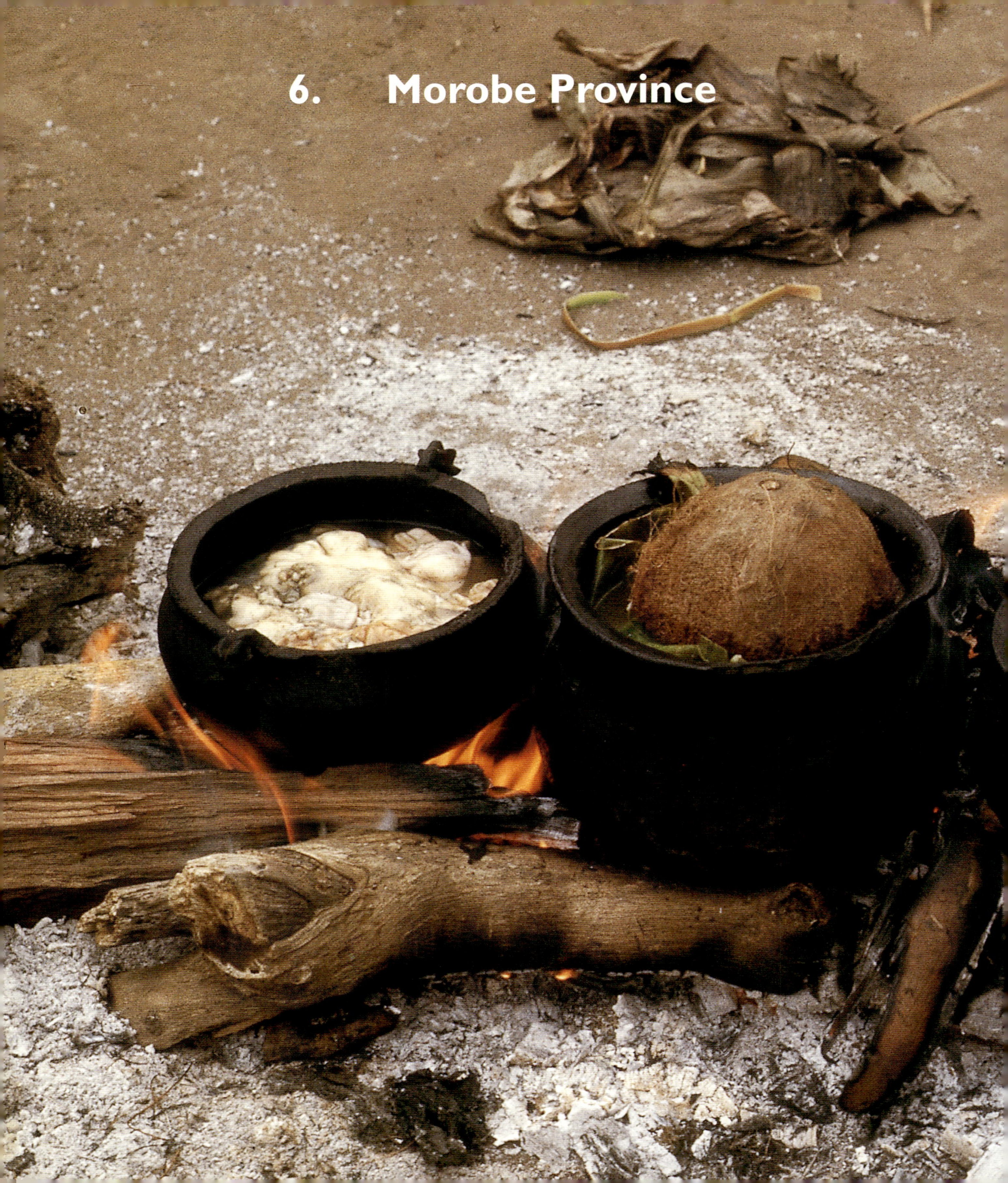

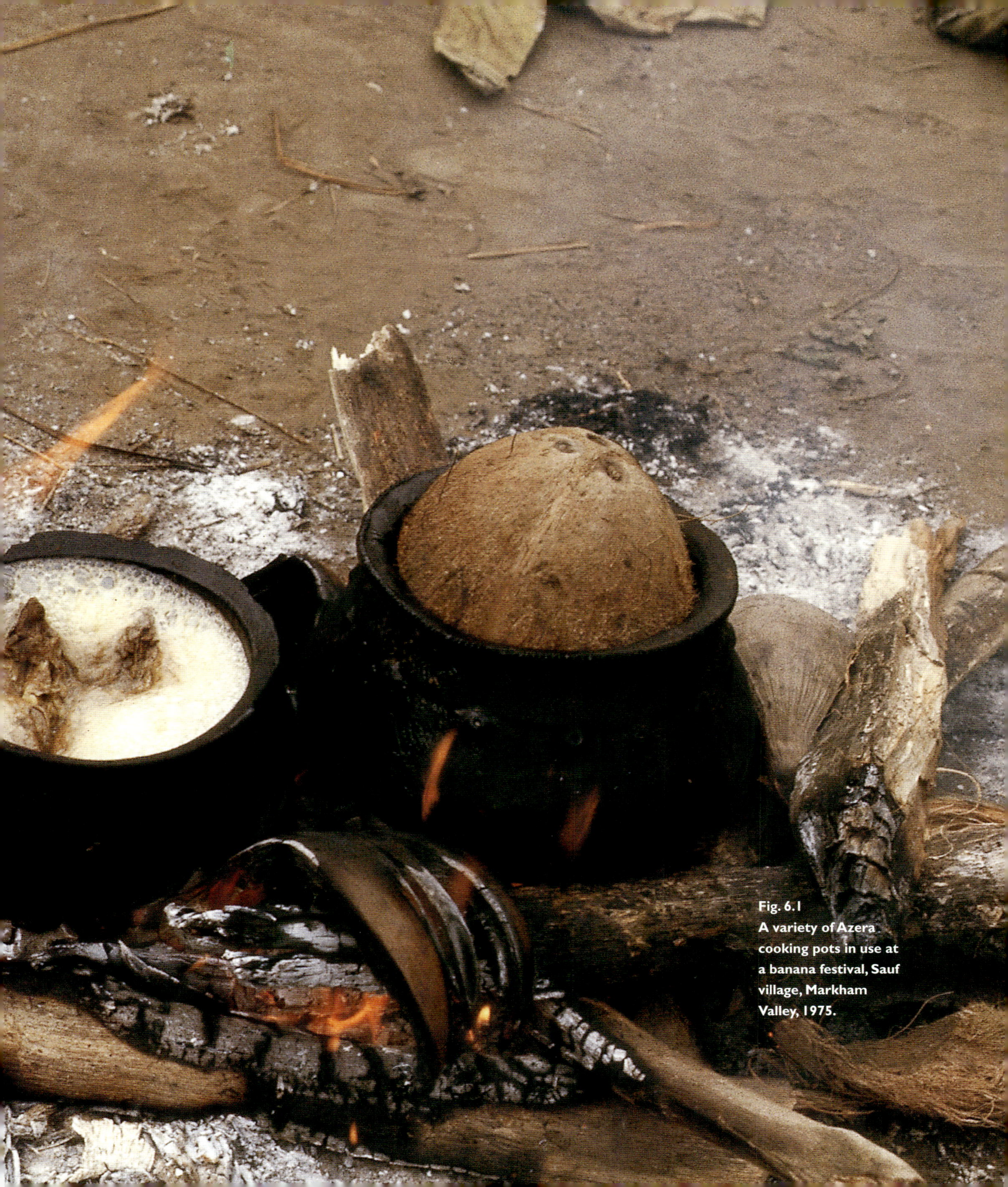

Fig. 6.1
A variety of Azera cooking pots in use at a banana festival, Sauf village, Markham Valley, 1975.

MAP 7 (opposite)

The coastline of Morobe Province extends for about 400 kilometres and includes the Huon Peninsula, Huon Gulf and the Vitiaz Strait. The largest town, Lae, is the provincial headquarters, the largest port in Papua New Guinea and the gateway to the highlands, connecting the highland provinces to the coastal region. The Markham Valley, stretching from Lae about 120 kilometres north-west to the foothills of the Eastern Highlands, is a broad flat area with grassy plains; foothills and mountains flank the north-east and south-west sides. It is about 30 kilometres across at its widest point. In full flood, the Markham, fed by the Ufim, Erap, Leron and Maniang rivers as well as by countless other watercourses, cuts a channel up to 4 kilometres wide as it races down to Lae and the sea. The southern portion, that area lying south of the Markham Valley, is mountainous but contains several river valleys where people have settled. The Watut, Waria and Wau-Bulolo valleys have all attracted gold prospectors.

Morobe Province is divided both geographically and linguistically by the Markham River. The Sarawaged and Finisterre mountain ranges, lying north of the valley, have been settled by non-Austronesian speakers, groups of whom extend into Madang Province where the men produce coiled pots. Other non-Austronesian pot makers who live south of the Markham are people who have settled around the Waria River, which is close to the western borders of the province.

Austronesians live in the whole of the Markham Valley, the area south towards Bulolo, including the Watut Valley, the coastal area south of Salamaua Peninsula to within about 50 kilometres of the Morobe patrol post, and north of Lae in the Huon Peninsula and the islands of the Vitiaz Strait (Tami and Siassi groups) (Hooley and McElhanon 1970).

With the exception of the group along the Waria River, all of the pot producing groups in Morobe are Austronesian-speaking. Both men and women make pots; the women potters live in the coastal areas and the male potters live in the hinterland. The two coastal pot producing areas are Huon Gulf, south of Salamaua Peninsula, and Huon Peninsula at Cape King William (König Wilhelm). Inland, there are two groups of male potters both belonging to the Azera family: the Azera language group living in the upper Markham Valley near Kaiapit, and the Amari language group, close relations of the Kaiapit Azera, occupying the headwaters of the Markham near the Umi River; the second group comprises the men of the lower Watut Valley.

In the past other Azera groups, the Wampar and the Mari, also produced pots but these industries are now defunct. The Wampar people (also known as Lae Wampa or Lae Womba) comprise two groups, one of which lives in the middle Markham Valley, from the Leron River to about 30 kilometres from Lae, and the other which has settled along the Wampit River, with Gabensis and Wampit as the two former principal pot producing villages. The Wampar pots were similar to the Kaiapit vessels, although heavier and cruder. The Mari (Garamari) people inhabit villages in the Ramu River plains but are now administratively part of Madang Province. Their pots were open, conical vessels, closer to the Ramu style than to that of their Azera neighbours; they are discussed in more detail in Chapter 8.

During the period of German colonisation of New Guinea (1884-1917) the Sepik, Ramu and Markham rivers, the hinterland of the Huon Gulf, Astrolabe Bay and other remote areas were explored and mapped and German missionaries, explorers and ethnographers methodically recorded material cultures and collected artifacts for European

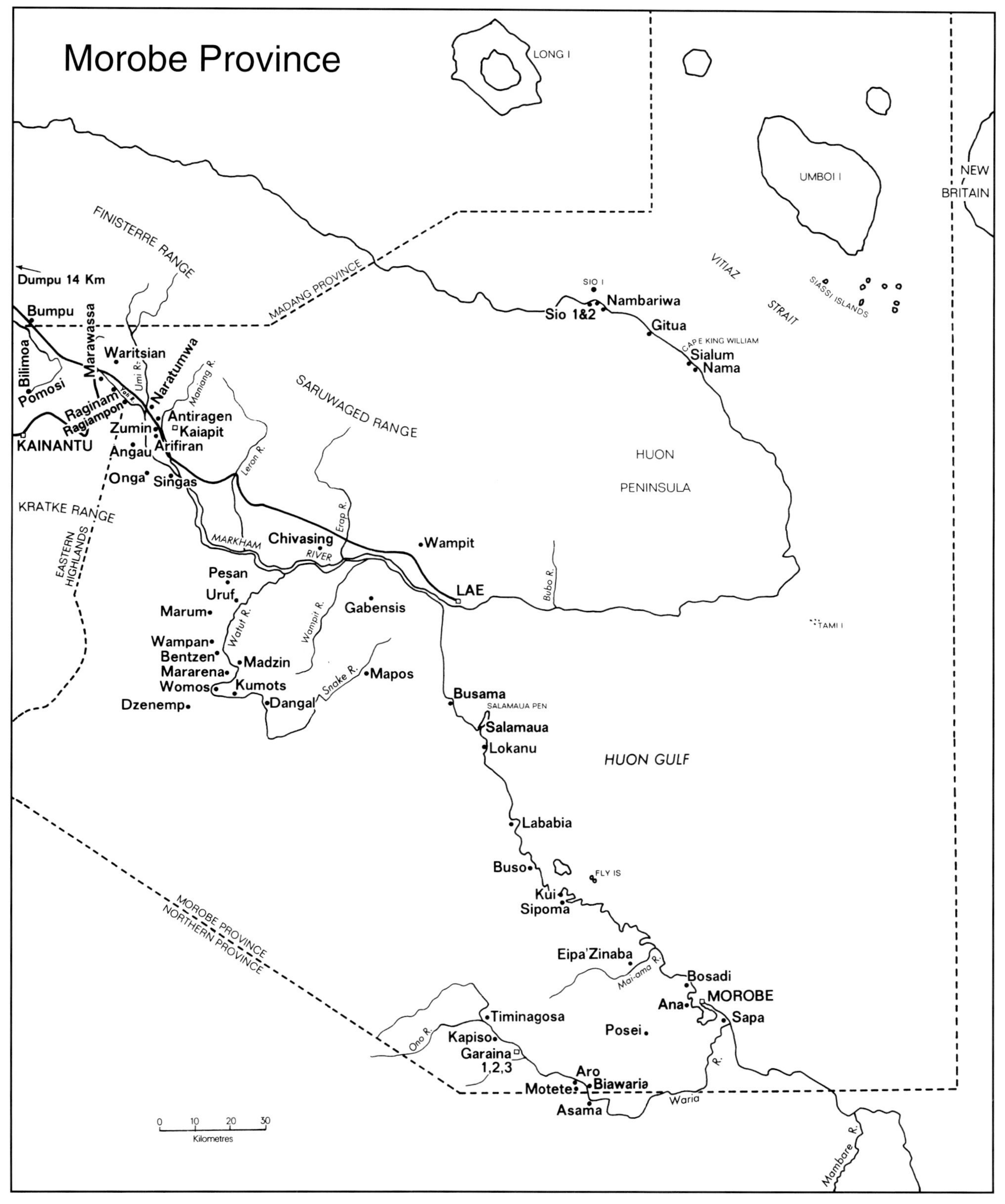
Morobe Province
LONG I
UMBOI I
NEW BRITAIN
VITIAZ STRAIT
SIASSI ISLANDS
FINISTERRE RANGE
Dumpu 14 Km
Bumpu
MADANG PROVINCE
SIO I
Nambariwa
Sio 1&2
Gitua
CAPE KING WILLIAM
Sialum
Nama
Bilimoa
Marawassa
Waritsian
Umi R.
Naratumwa
Maniang R.
Pomosi
Raginam
Ragiampon
Antiragen
Kaiapit
Zumin
KAINANTU
Angau
Arifiran
SARUWAGED RANGE
HUON PENINSULA
Leron R.
Onga
Singas
KRATKE RANGE
EASTERN HIGHLANDS
MARKHAM RIVER
Chivasing
Erap R.
Wampit
Pesan
Uruf
Marum
Gabensis
LAE
Bubo R.
TAMI I
Watut R.
Wampit R.
Wampan
Bentzen
Madzin
Mararena
Womos
Kumots
Snake R.
Mapos
Dzenemp
Dangal
Busama
SALAMAUA PEN
Salamaua
Lokanu
HUON GULF
Lababia
Buso
FLY IS
Kui
Sipoma
MOROBE PROVINCE
NORTHERN PROVINCE
Eipa'Zinaba
Mai-ama R.
Bosadi
Ana
MOROBE
Sapa
Timinagosa
Posei
Ono R.
Kapiso
Garaina
1,2,3
Aro
Biawaria
Motete
Asama
Waria
R.
Mambare R.
0 10 20 30
Kilometres

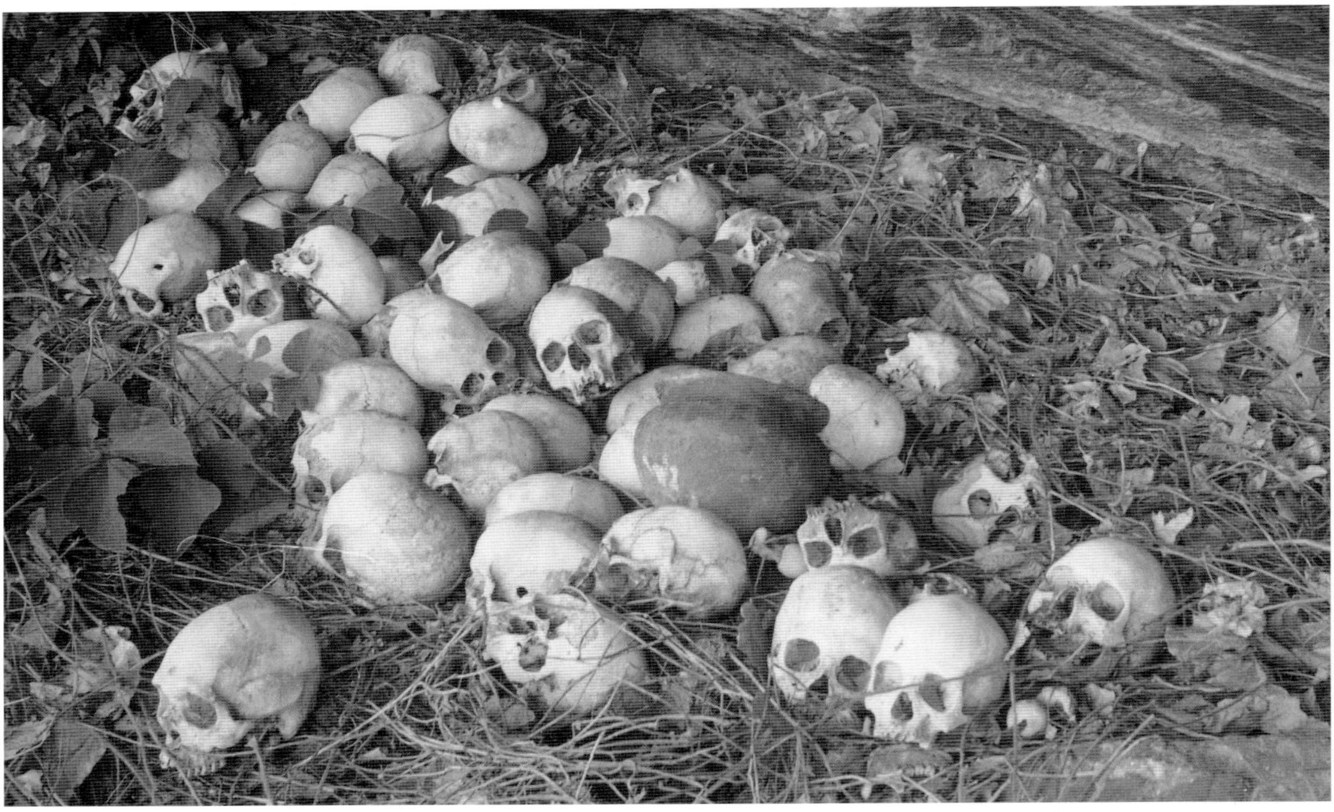

Figs 6.2 to 6.4
Azera pots from a burial cave, Markham Valley.

Fig. 6.2
Skulls and pots in a burial cave, Kraetke Mountains, Markham Valley.

museums. Neuhauss published in 1911 a volume that records the pottery industries of the Wampar, Salamaua and Kelena (Gitua-Sio) centres, along with invaluable photographs of pots and brief descriptions of techniques of manufacture and firing. Another German, Karl Holzknecht, a Lutheran missionary, historian and linguist, has published (1957, 1977) a thorough account of Kaiapit Azera pottery. Specht and H. Holzknecht (son of Karl Holzknecht) (1971) have described pottery found in archaeological sites located in the Markham Valley floor in the Amari area; this has helped to date the Azera industry as being at least 800 years old. Hans Fischer, a German ethnologist, has discussed some aspects of the pottery industry located in the lower Watut Valley (1962). The coastal pottery areas of the Salamaua Peninsula and Cape King William have been briefly described by Neuhauss, Groves (1934-35), Vogel (1911) and Hogbin (1947); more recently Specht has carried out field work at Gitua-Sio and collected vessels there for the Port Moresby Museum and the Australian Museum, Sydney. The authors have made brief field trips to all the pottery industries in Morobe Province, with the exception of the Watut area, and have made a detailed study of the Azera.

Kaiapit Azera

In the upper reaches of the Markham Valley, from the Leron River to the Ramu River valley, a group of tall Melanesian people has settled. They speak the Azera language and number about 18 000; they are grouped together into units based on common origin, genealogy and intermarriage. The origin and cultural history of the Kaiapit Azera and the Wampar has yet to be clarified but sources indicate that the Wampar came from different directions – one migration came from the Wampit Valley while another movement came down the Markham and settled in the middle valley – and that the Kaiapit people came from beyond the Markham Valley, entered it and followed it up, diversifying along the way (H. Holzknecht 1974). The Azera are hunters and agriculturalists and in the past were feared by neighbouring groups for their warlike activities.

A group numbering about 8000 has settled in the Umi-Maniang Valley plains and the foothills of the Kratke Range; they live in some eighty-five villages. They lead a peaceful existence, harvesting bananas, taro, yam and sweet potato. The tall grass of the plains offers cover for bush pigs and other wild animals and birds which supplement domesticated fowl and pig in their diet. The Azera are fortunate in having coconut palms and their predominantly starchy food is enriched by coconut milk, ginger and a wide variety of greens. Many of the people have now taken up cash cropping and other entrepreneurial activities and the major industries are cattle and peanuts.

In some, but not all, of these villages men have specialised in making pottery. In the past pottery figured strongly in exchange with neighbouring groups and today there is an increasing local demand for Azera pots, especially since other neighbouring pot making groups have allowed their skills to die out. The people in the Markham Valley have been remarkably reluctant to change over to metalware and there is a predominance of Azera cooking vessels in the households of the Wampar (lower Markham and Wampit groups), the Mari, the Lae, Huon Gulf and Mumeng people. Previously, Azera pots were traded into the highlands as far as Kainantu.

While pottery is still traded and given in bride price payments in some areas it is also sold outright, especially to expatriates, boosting the cash economy of those clans fortunate enough to have male potters as members. Any man, given motivation and ability, can become a potter and gain status within his own community as such. Certain of the older men are renowned for their pot making and can be called master craftsmen. Younger men who display ingenuity in marrying successfully a variety of imaginative decorative non-traditional elements to the traditional forms are also respected. Expected high standards and the demand for clay vessels as exchange items have thus far maintained the quality of pots except in one or two cases where potters have succumbed to commercial rewards and are producing tourist items – ashtrays, miniature clay drums, quixotic animals – and cooking vessels which are hurriedly manufactured and easily breakable because the post-firing, sealing and strengthening stage has been omitted.

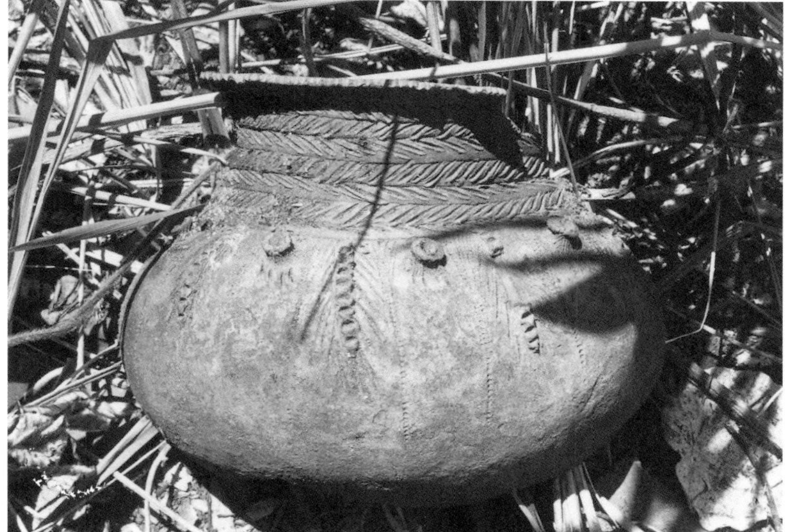

Fig. 6.3

Besides the importance of pottery in trade and bride price payment, it also figures strongly in the ritual and customs of the Azera. There are taboos surrounding the gathering of clay. The casual handling of certain vessels by outsiders is frowned upon (a host will always carry the eating vessel to a guest and it is considered taboo for the guest to pick up the vessel himself). Certain vessels are decorated with representations of male and female genitalia. Men are reluctant to discuss these pots and, since

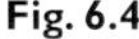

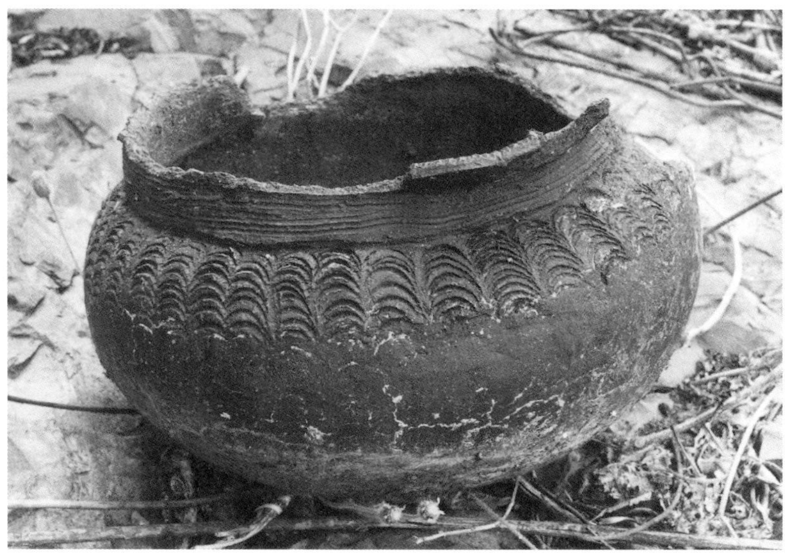

Fig. 6.4

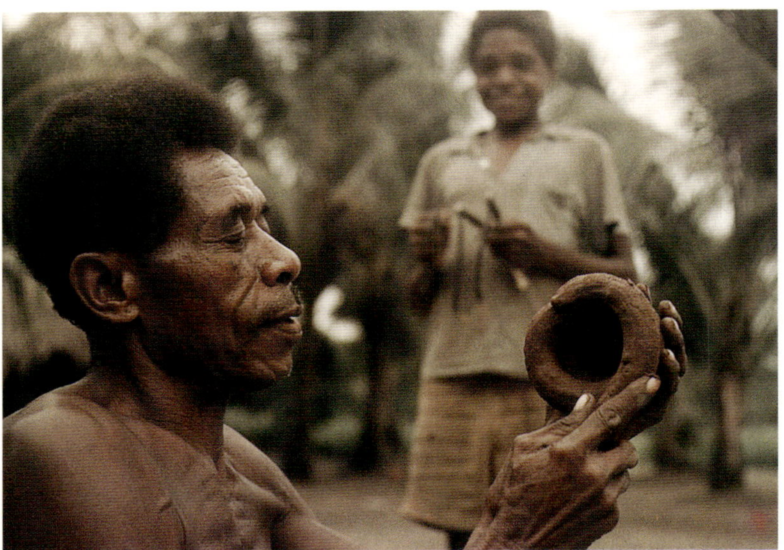

Fig. 6.5
Imat Ragun coiling, Zumin village, Markham Valley.

the Church has been opposed to this type of decoration and the function of the pots within the society, they are seldom made. There is a small sorcery-medicine pot, *gur isim* (small pot) or *gur asam* (ginger pot); it is a simply decorated vessel used for cooking herbs and soup or for preparing coconut oil (the basis of most magic spells) but the men are reluctant to discuss it.

Vessels are also used in a funeral context. The bones of the deceased are taken to the foothills of the Kratke Range and placed under projecting rocks or in caves; the possessions of the dead, including their pots, are displayed around them. Unfortunately, the burial caves have been vandalised and there are only a few broken pots remaining. Judging from the pots sighted in a number of caves, the shape and decoration of the older vessels have been modified by more recent potters. While the same decorative elements are found on the cave pots, they have been combined in schemes not seen today. Outsiders are not taken casually to view the caves; permission must be sought from the landowners. The burial pots are protected national cultural property.

Pottery was traditionally made in a number of Azera villages, including Antiragen, Zumim, Sauf, Arifiran, Anga, Singas (in the central group), in villages in the Onga and Guruf groups, in some villages of the Sangan group and in Ragiampon, Ragitsumang, Raginam, Wankung, Ragigumpuan and Marawassa in the Amari group. In other words, pottery was made in all villages along the south-western edge of the valley which had access to clay pits. Due to marriage links, groups that did not formerly make pots now have access to these sources of clay and there are pot makers in villages that previously did not have them.

Renowned master craftsmen used once to go on long trips to other villages, to visit, socialise, gossip and make pots for a client; now that access to the clay pits is less restricted, pottery making skills have spread and this form of social and economic exchange has declined. However, Ragun, one of the master potters from Zumim, undertook such a journey in 1974. He travelled on foot to Gabensis on the Wampit River, where he stayed for several weeks and made pots for his hosts. In return he was paid in food and cash.

Clay deposits are located in the foothills of the Kratke Range, on the south-western side of the Markham River. The clay may be gathered only by members of the group with rights to it but nowadays it may be purchased or traded. There are taboos and ritual connected with the clay gathering: only married women who have not yet had children can gather the clay and only at certain times. Young girls may accompany the women but usually they do not help in extracting the clay from the ground. They should wear traditional dress,

Fig. 6.6
Imat smoothing and shaping with a coconut shell tool, Zumin.

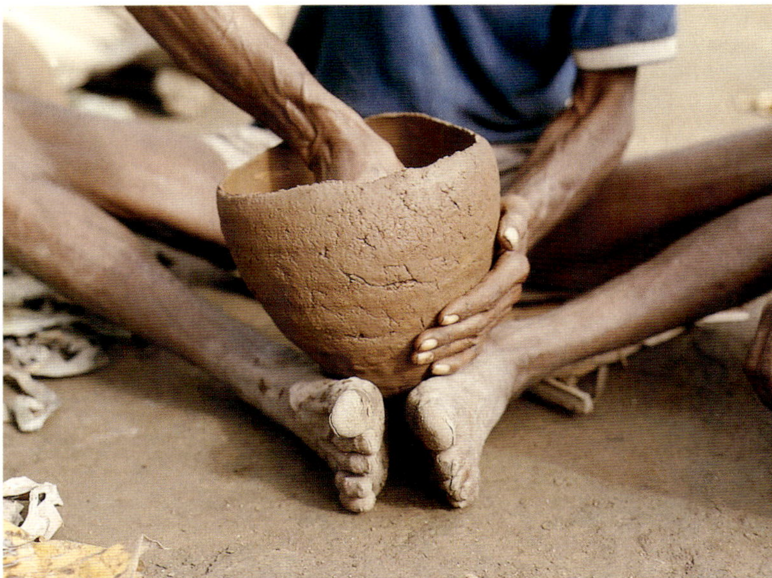

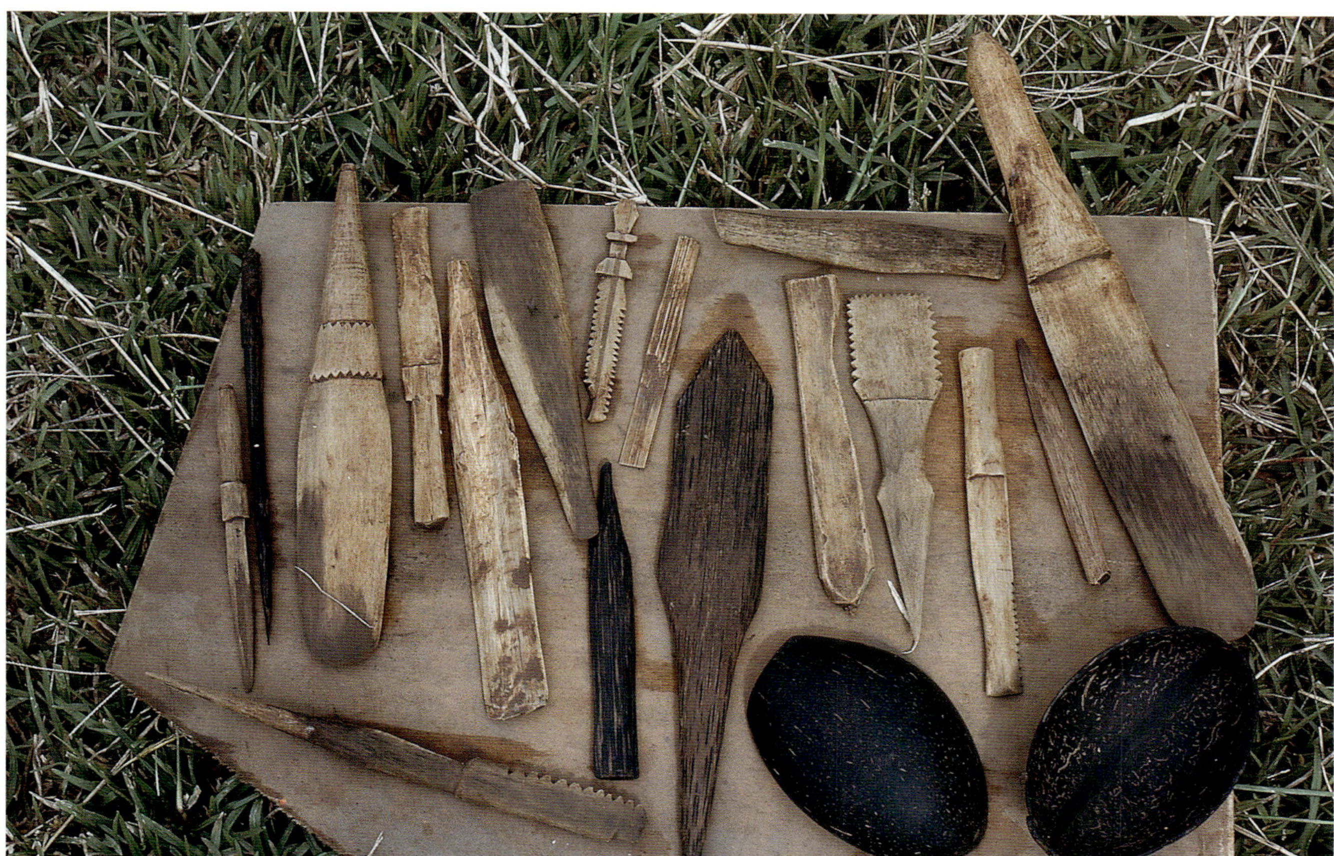

may not smoke or chew betel nut and they must speak in their own language (they may not speak pidgin). No outsider should be allowed to witness the actual digging of the clay.

The clay is wrapped in green banana leaves and brought back to the village where the women prepare it for use. It is dark reddish-brown, of a sandy consistency with some gravel. About 6 kilograms of clay are prepared at one time. The woman places the pug on a flat board, *afit,* which has been moistened with water and beats it with a paddle, *tipa,* which is also moistened, until it spreads into a flat sheet which is folded into a lump again. This is repeated for about forty-five minutes and stones and grit are removed during the beating. When the clay is malleable and most of the impurities have been removed it is wrapped in green banana leaves and stored under or in the house.

The male potter takes a lump of the damp clay and kneads and works it for a short time. He then makes three to five (depending on the intended size of the pot) sausage-shaped rolls and sets them aside. The potter forms a long coil about 3 to 4 centimetres thick by squeezing out a roll between his hands. Holding this in his left hand, he quickly and rather roughly feeds the coil onto itself upwards and outwards. He smooths the coils together on the outside by a downward movement of the thumb. When the vessel reaches the desired height it is placed between the potter's feet and held while he smooths the interior walls with a moistened piece of coconut shell, *umpi,* working from top to bottom in a circular motion. As the walls are thinned they are simultaneously drawn upward and outward and this gives the vessel its characteristic Azera shape (Figs 6.5, 6.6).

Fig. 6.7
Imat Ragun's tools, Zumin village, Markham Valley.

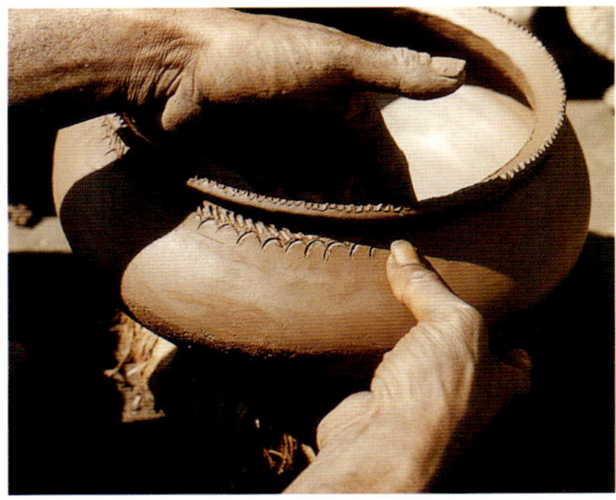

Fig. 6.8
Amaram making a row of thumbnail marks, Zumin village, Markham Valley.

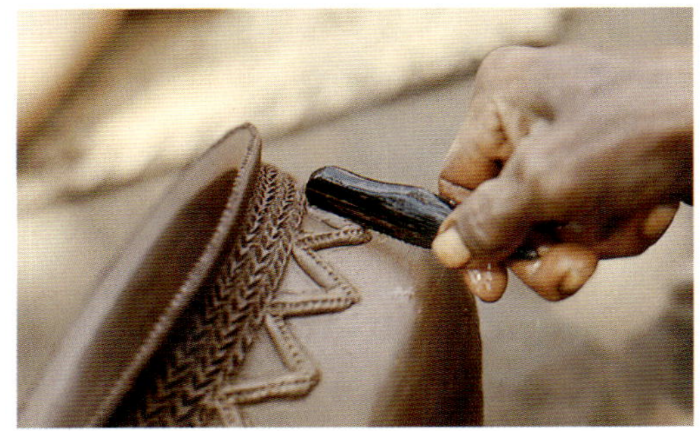

Fig. 6.9
Imat Ragun making the lizard's teeth, *sinap nifon,* with the special tool, *sinap,* Zumin.

The pot is then transferred from the ground to a support, *madzam*, a ring shape made from part of the banana plant which is covered with a green banana leaf; here it is further thinned and shaped. Finally, the upper portion of the exterior wall is beaten with a wooden paddle, *gai isa gur*, while the potter's hand supports the vessel on the inside. When the upper edge of the vessel is about 0.8 centimetres thick the top edge is trimmed by a sliver of bamboo and then smoothed with a wooden tool, *upuf*. To form the rim another wooden tool, *tangang ringan*, is pressed onto the interior edge in a gentle outward patting motion, until the edge is angled over about 1.5 centimetres and the lip starts to flare out. Finally, the rim is smoothed with wet fingers. The vessel is left to dry in the shade for about an hour-and-a-half. Then it is once again smoothed on the interior walls by the *upuf*. It is finally set aside on the ring for another thirty minutes before the decorations are applied. After the decorations have been applied and the vessel has again dried for about thirty minutes the base of the pot is perfected by scraping, beating and smoothing.

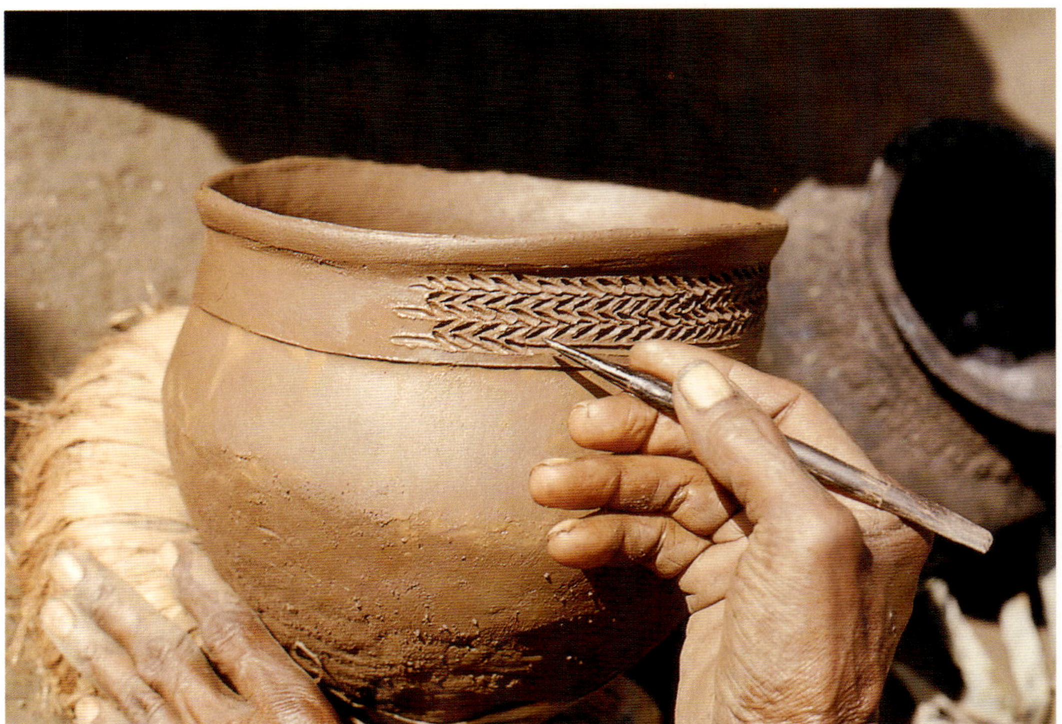

Fig. 6.10
Imat making decorative centipede's tracks, *gaif*, Zumin.

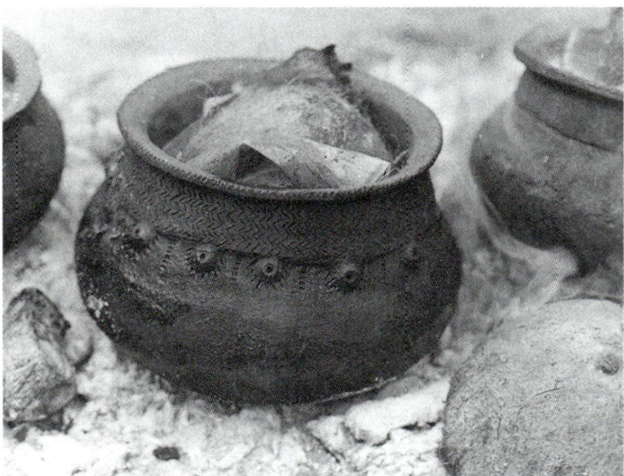
Fig. 6.11

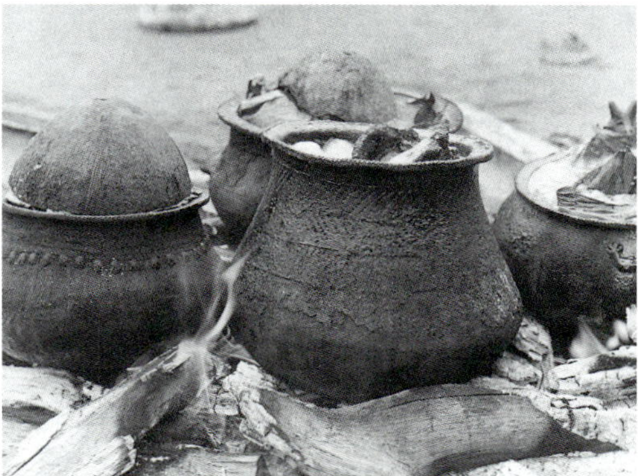
Fig. 6.12

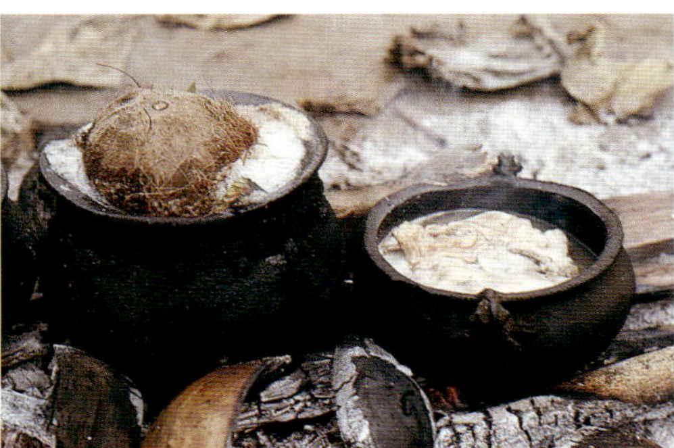
Fig. 6.13

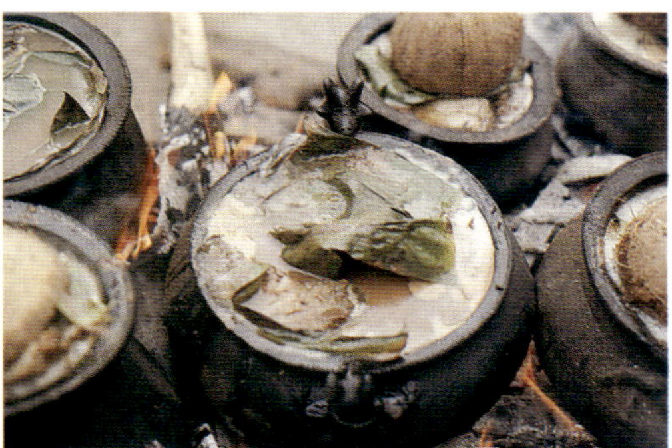
Fig. 6.14

Fig. 6.15
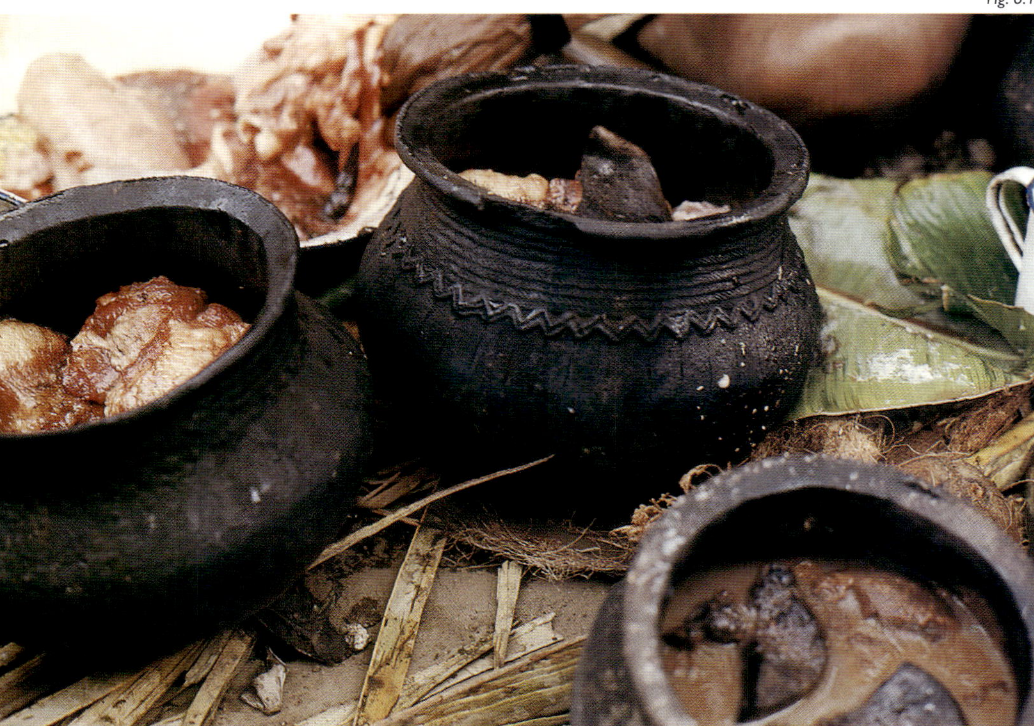

Figs 6.11 to 6.15
Pots used at a banana festival, Sauf village, Markham Valley, 1975.

Fig. 6.11
Gur banga, decorated with applied nubbins representing hornet's eyes, *wampop maran.*

Fig. 6.12
A group of Azera cooking pots. The three *gur banga* in the front row can be used for meat while the pot at the rear is a *gur bantun.*

Fig. 6.13
Food cooking in (left) *gur banga* and (right) *gur aniang.*

Fig. 6.14
Gur aniang with flying fox heads, *gangant gudzun,* decoration.

Fig. 6.15
Pig meat ready to be cooked in a *gur banga.*

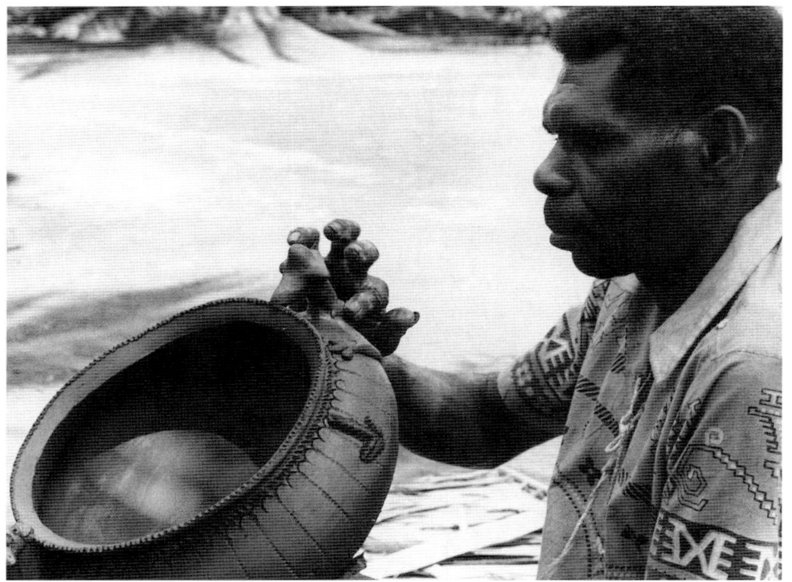

Fig. 6.16
Amaram joining on a flying fox head, Zumin village, Markham Valley.

Pots are dried for two to three weeks before being fired. Traditionally, firing was women's work although men might occasionally fire certain ritual vessels. Split hardwood and coconut fronds are used as fuel and a number of pots can be fired at a time. The firing lasts about one hour, which is uncommonly long, but there are several stages. The pots are placed upright on the burning wood and small pieces of wood are placed on top of the vessels but never inside. After about twenty-five minutes the pots turn black and are then turned on their sides and fired for another twenty-five minutes. When they begin to turn slightly rusty in colour they are taken off the fire and cooled slightly. River water is then poured into the cooling pots and stirred with a stick. The pots are still hot enough to evaporate the water. When they have cooled they are a brick red colour.

Tradition requires that the pots are not sold or traded before being tested. Yam or ripe cooking bananas are cooked until soft and this seals the pot. For cooking, the wide-based pots sit directly on the fire. The thick bottom holds the heat so efficiently that food bubbles long after the pot has been removed from the fire.

Decorations consist of lip notching, incised linear patterns, dentate impressions made by carved tools, thumbnail impressions, comb incising, punctation marks, applied relief consisting of rosettes, nubbins and strips usually dentate stamped, and applied modelled representations of birds and

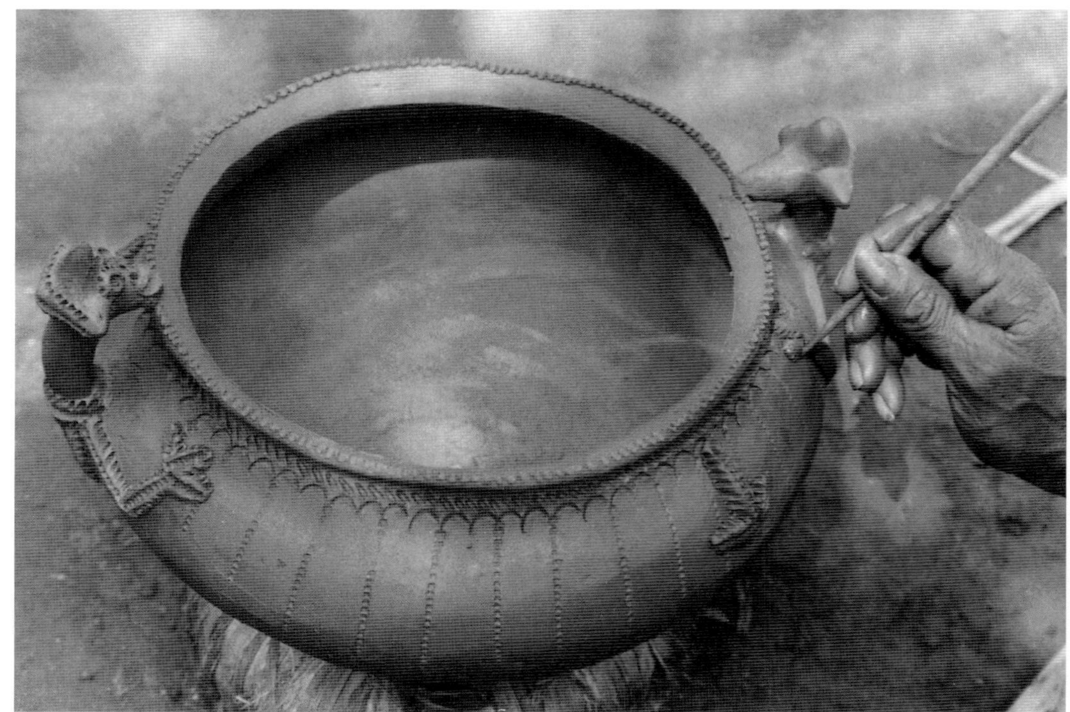

Fig. 6.17
Amaram marking the heads on a *gur aniang*. Crescent marks are thumbnail impressions; slanted dashes running around the neck just under the rim are *gaif* (centipede's tracks); parallel stamped marks running down the shoulder are *sinap nifon* (lizard's teeth). Zumin village.

animals. Two unusual tools are used for decorating, a flat paddle-shaped wooden implement, *upuf*, smooth along one edge and serrated along the other, used for indenting; and *wampup maram* (hornets' eyes), a pencil-shaped piece of black palm with one pointed end and one end carved with two concentric circles used for embossing. A paddle is used for indenting ridges around the necks.

Simple decorations consist of rows of lines arranged in various patterns representing certain characteristics of animals, insects and birds. Some are identified as follows: *sampai oran*, giant snake bones; *rima sasia gin*, track or hand of a ratlike creature; *ira fagan*, mouse footprints; *sinap nifon*, teeth of a monitor lizard; *sima sasia gin*, a kingfisher's feather; *gaif*, mark of a centipede. More elaborate decorations consist of applied coils which are then embossed, impressed or indented with one of the decorating tools. The most characteristic mark is that of the concentric circles which represent *wampup maram*, hornets' eyes. Other embossed marks are *uwing ragin*, the intestines of an earthworm, and applied nodules or rosettes which represent *gantisison*, the seed pods of a coconut, and *sisunifab*, the breasts of a pig. The three-dimensional models of animal and bird heads will be discussed.

Classification of vessel types is complicated by the fact that the Azera name vessels according to size, function, shape and decorative elements. Basically, there are five broad categories of pots produced. Karl Holzknecht also lists several other types which are no longer made although it is certain that a few of the older men still retain the skill.

Firstly, there is a general cooking pot, ovoid, with a rounded to flattish base, restricted, with a definite neck area and a rolled or everted rim. The common cooking pot used for vegetables has three names, based on size: *gur pari* is the largest pot, about 40 centimetres high; *gur bantun* is a medium-sized pot, about 20 to 30 centimetres high; *gur angkiang* is the smallest, about 10 to 20 centimetres high. A fourth pot is known by the generic term for vessels in which meat can be cooked, *gur banga*: it usually has a deeper neck area. The everted rims are notched at regular intervals. The neck may be left unmarked or is marked by parallel horizontal lines. Usually the corner point of the shoulder and neck is defined by punctate marks extending down to the bulge of the belly. This area can also be marked by parallel line incisions, applied rosettes or nubbins and dentate stamped designs. These marks represent some aspect of nature and have specific names. Sometimes the common cooking pot will have more elaborate relief decorations. On the vessel sides strips of clay are superimposed in various patterns and then decorated by dentate stamping.

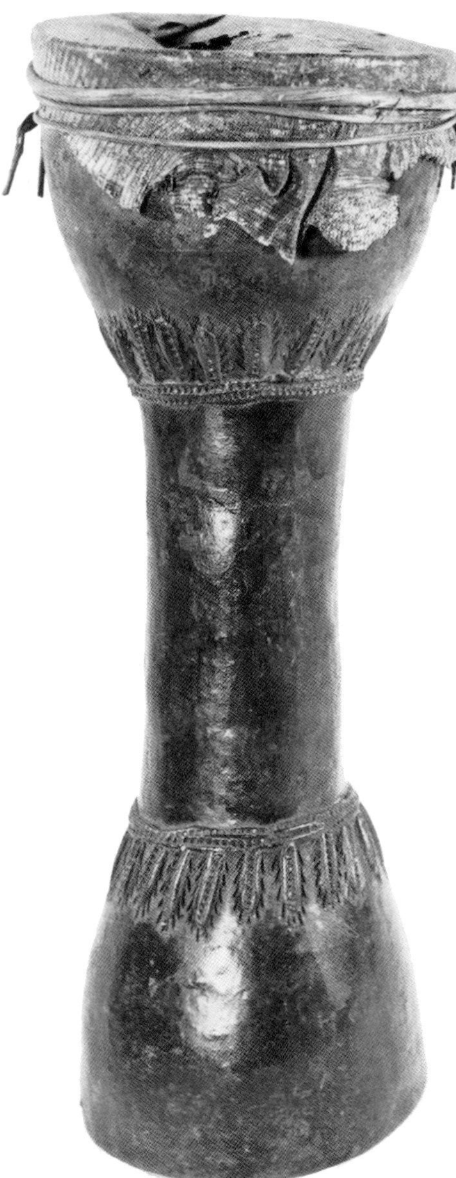

Fig. 6.18
Clay drum called *simpup gur.* Applied decoration is called *bunga bunga nizun* (a kind of grass seed). Zumin village, Markham Valley, *h* 36 cm.

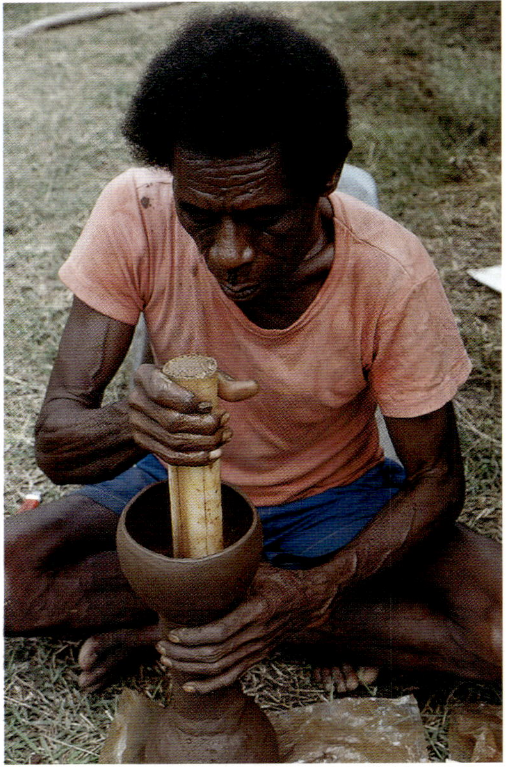

Fig. 6.19
Imat Ragun working a banana core up and down to join and smooth the inside cylinder for a clay drum, Zumin village, Markham Valley.

onto the interior walls. The modelled head can be variously decorated by incised or indented marks around the collar or by the addition of arms and legs radiating out from the joint of the neck and the outer wall of the vessel. Heads (*gudzun*) of creatures commonly depicted include: *angang*, bush fowl; *pri pri*, small bat; *nguk nguk*, pigeon; *utsungiang*, bird; *simimpi*, tortoise; *inkiring*, bush fowl; *wagiats*, frog; and *gangant*, flying fox

A third type of object still made by a few of the older men from Zumim, Onga and Antiragen is a hand drum, *simpup gur*, shaped like an hourglass and covered at one end by a lizard or snake skin. This drum is the only major musical instrument made from clay in Papua New Guinea (Fig. 6.18). Minor instruments include a small sun-dried clay ocarina made by the men from Sinasina in Chimbu Province, a round clay ocarina made by the Wosera people in East Sepik Province and a zoomorphic ocarina made by the male potters at Dimiri-Marawat.

The hand drum is made from two normally shaped vessels of the same size. When they are leather-hard the potter takes one and, using a bamboo knife, carefully cuts a circular hole in the base.

The second type of vessel is called *gur aniang*, *aniang* meaning meat. This is the generic term for all pots with handles (modelled heads). They are used for cooking meat although vegetables may also be cooked in them. The body is basically the same shape as that of the common cooking pot but the profile of the neck and rim differs in that the meat vessel has little neck and is characterised by the addition of two confronting modelled clay forms representing animal or bird heads, arranged on opposite sides of the rim and projecting over the edge. The decorative marks and relief designs are otherwise a combination of those used on the cooking pots. While meat and vegetables can both be cooked in the *gur aniang*, the only common cooking pot used for cooking meat is the *gur banga*.

The handles are added after the decorations have been applied. Two holes are cut in opposite sides of the vessel with a small bamboo tool. The potter models the heads from two small sausage-shaped pieces of clay. Firstly, the eyes, ears, and projections of the head are formed then the ends of the forms are inserted through the two holes and smoothed

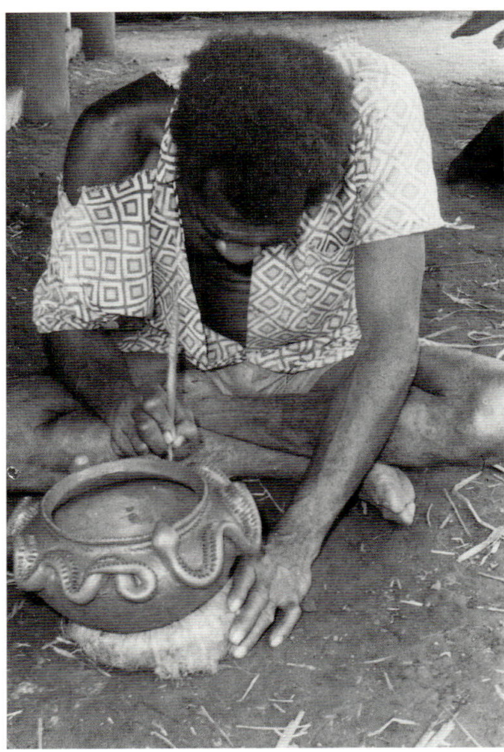

Fig. 6.20
Amaram decorating a 'snake pot', *gur miu*, Zumin.

The rim and hole are then trimmed by a sliver of bamboo, *itia*. Next, a long coil is wrapped around the cylindrical inner core of a banana plant (about 60 centimetres long and 30 centimetres wide). The palms of the hands pat this coil into shape, thin it and lengthen it. When the shape is about 20 centimetres high, it is strengthened by gentle tapping with a moist paddle. The banana core is carefully eased off and the clay cylinder is fitted into the circular base hole of the vessel. Extra clay is added to bind them together. The banana core is worked up and down inside to shape further the connecting cylinder and to ensure the joint of the vessel and cylinder is not clogged with excess clay (Fig. 6.19). The interior is further scraped and thinned by the *umpi*. The base of the second vessel is opened up in the same way, shaped by the banana core and joined to the rest. The banana core remains in the drum while it is set in the sun to dry for about twenty minutes. The cylinder is then scraped and smoothed and decorations are incised on or applied to the areas where the cylinder fits into the inverted vessels. After the *simpup* has been fired, a lizard skin is fitted over one opening and attached by a gluey sap extracted from a tree.

A fourth type of vessel, the previously mentioned *gur isi*, is shaped like a cooking pot. The average height is 8 centimetres. It is simply decorated with incised parallel lines running around the neck and additional simple incised patterns. Karl Holzknecht identifies this pot with war magic. He says it was used to boil up roots and leaves which were used to decorate the spears and faces of warriors preparing to fight. It is now used for cooking ginger.

Holzknecht lists four other types of vessel which are no longer produced. These are: *gur untu untu*, a double-lipped pouring vessel; *gur omant fagan* (taro foot), a small pot similar to the *gur untu untu*; *gur zadgub bangin*, a double pot with a connecting piece; *ibanggai*, a shallow bowl-shaped vessel. The Amari also used to make a double-storeyed cooking pot called *mara ampi mara aba*: *mara ampi* means generosity and refers to the top portion, and *mara aba* means meanness and refers to the bottom portion.

While the majority of the older potters continue to use traditional designs, the younger men are imaginatively adding to the repertoire of forms. One *gur aniang* sighted had four rim projections made up of the modelled figures of a man, a woman, a frog and a tortoise. Other pots have snakes writhing around the middle or coiled around the neck. These snake pots, called *gur miu*, are a speciality of two potters, Amaram and Impagai, from Zumim village. Younger informants insist that these pots are traditional but they seem to have appeared on the scene only within the last ten years. The Azera have an interesting story which may have inspired these bizarre and very untraditional-looking vessels. The story as recorded by S. and H. Holzknecht is as follows:

> A family of renowned rainmakers who lived in Zumim claim that a porcelain dish was found just after some Europeans had passed through the area. They turned it over and rain started. When it was turned upside down the rain stopped. It is said that a snake guards it and that only the rainmakers can approach it.

It has not been determined whether only people from that rain making group mentioned in the story are allowed to make the 'snake' pots. It is still believed that individuals have the power to make rain. When there is a bad drought in Amari people visit Zumim and take cowrie shells and money to particular people there for them to make rain.

Nowadays, unusual combinations of traditional appliqué designs are made with somewhat baroque results and these extremely elaborate examples often end up being sold to expatriates through artifact dealers. The quality of craftsmanship is high in most cases. In 1976 a young man from Zumim returned to his village and, with the aid of the Office of Business Development, set up a kiosk trade store and pottery workshop along the Highlands Highway. Young men are serving as apprentices to three of the master potters and are making small vessels about 6 to 12 centimetres high to sell to tourists and travellers. The prices of these pots are very high in comparison to the local exchange prices but, if successful, this grassroots experiment could bring good economic returns to the people. On the other hand it is to be hoped that this activity does not disrupt the traditional role of the pottery in exchange and sale to the local consumers.

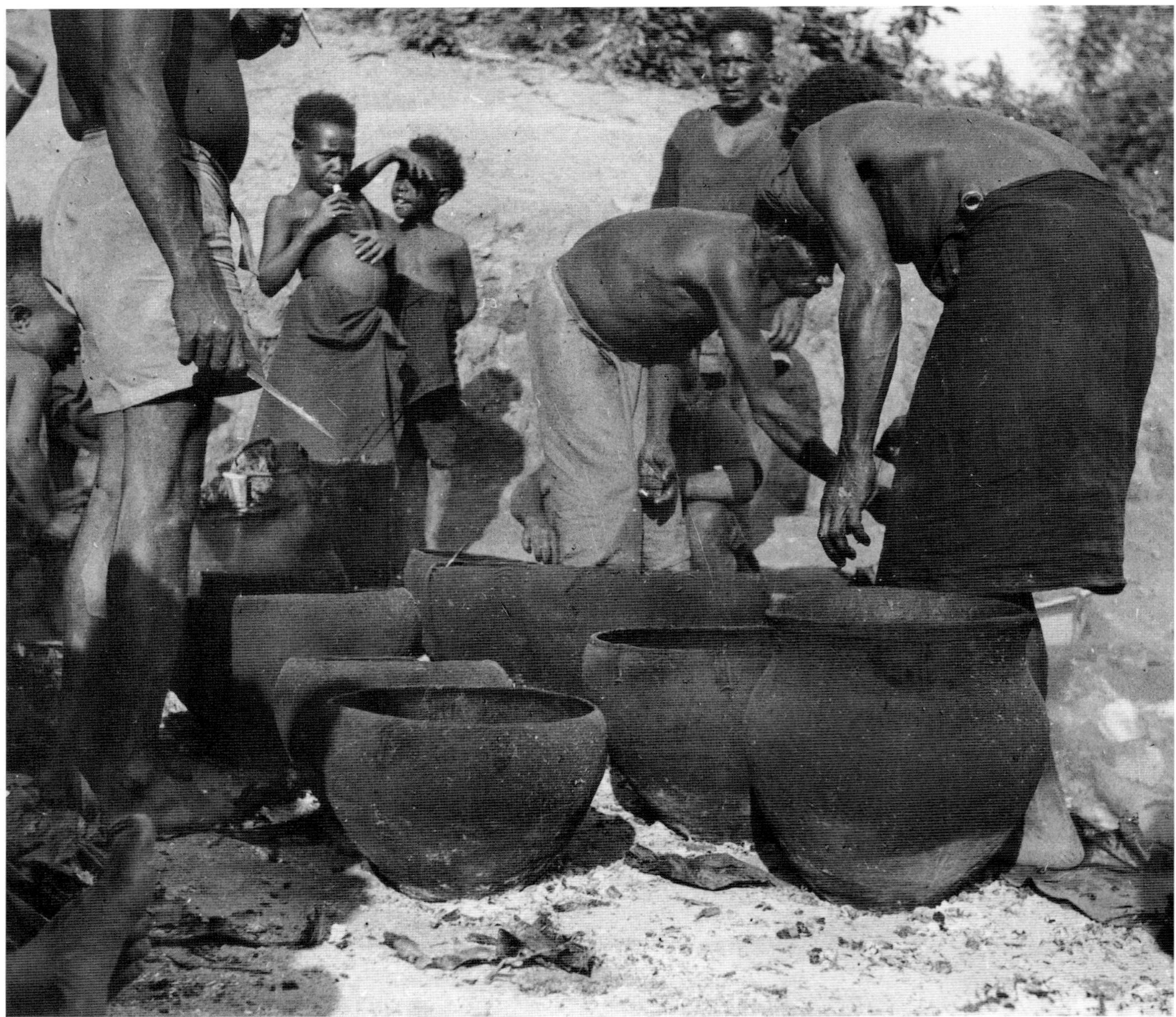

Fig. 6.21
Preparation for a feast, Mapos village, Morobe Province. The tall pot, front row, is probably a Watut pot. The others are Salamaua pots traded up from the coast. The feast is offered as reparation for damage to someone's garden by a pig.

The Azera potters stand out in a number of respects. They are, along with the Ham-speaking people of Madang, the only male Austronesian potters. They are unique among male potters in using the coil technique combined with beating with a paddle (with the minor exception of one small non-Austronesian group in inland Madang, where men and women combine coiling with use of a paddle). Their tools, decorative motifs, and nomenclature for pot types and designs are the most sophisticated in the country. Pot making is a thriving, growing industry. While practically all other pot industries are on the decline, the Azera have spread their sphere of influence until they now dominate traditional pottery markets previously supplied by centres of activity that are now defunct.

Watut

Prehistoric and present-day pottery from the Watut River valley has been described by Hans Fischer (1962). The inhabitants, Austronesian speakers

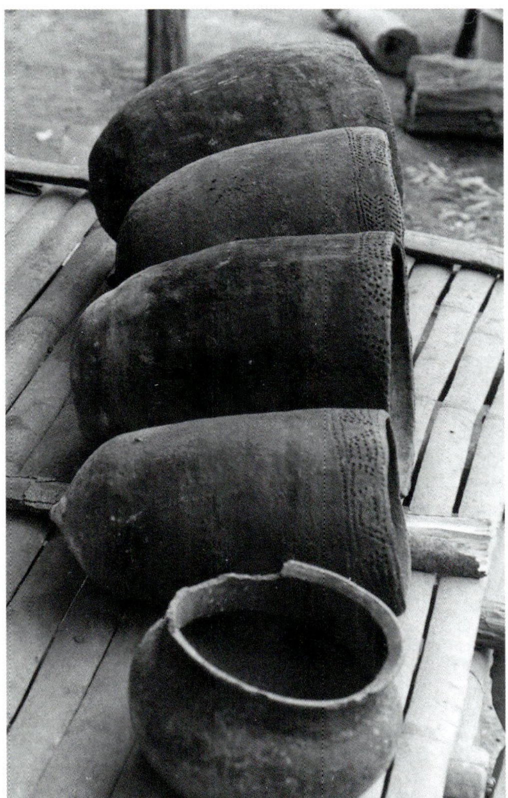

belonging to the Azera family (Hooley and McElhanon 1970), are divided by Fischer into three groups: northern, central and southern.

The northern group, geographically closest to the Markham Azera people, lives in the villages of Pesan, Wampan, Uruf and Morum. Their pots are similar in form to those of the Kaiapit Azera. Only one type of northern vessel is described and it is a cooking pot made by men in the coil technique and finished by beating.

The central group, which lives in Mararena, Madzim and Bentsen, also produces vessels like those of the Azera. The pots are shallower, more spherical and the bases are usually rounder (although occasionally pointed); the neck area is less deep and the everted lip is set off as a distinctive part of the vessel; the lip is flattened and tapers inward. Decoration consists of scalloped or toothed indentations on the lip and simple rows of parallel lines or a herringbone motif on the neck area.

The southern group, living in Wawos, Kumots, Dzenemp, Maralanko and Dangal, produces a different type of vessel. It is deep, has a sharply pointed base and an ellipsoid body with a sharply defined shoulder and a restricted neck which flares outward and has a direct rim. Decoration consists of punctate points encircling the inner edge of the rim, indented ladder or triangular designs around the neck area, a line of herringbone motifs defining the area between the shoulder and the neck and, occasionally, incised triangles marking the shoulder.

Clay is available to everyone. During the wet season it is collected, carried to the villages wrapped in leaves and left for a few days. Fischer's description of the techniques used tallies closely with the methods of the Azera potters except that coils of clay are rolled out onto a wooden board here. The base is formed by the first coil which is spirally fed onto itself. Moistened hands are then used to smooth the coils both inside and outside. The vessel is placed in a ringed support and further coils are added. The neck is formed by beating a stick on the outside against the hand held on the inside; the rim is cut off with a bamboo knife. The pot is dried for about one hour and decorations are then added. The repertoire of shapes and designs is less complex and varied than that of the Kaiapit Azera, even among the northern pots which so closely resemble some Azera types. Applied coils, nubbins, rosettes and modelled forms (those elaborations of decoration that characterise the sophisticated Azera wares) are lacking.

Fig. 6.22
Waria cooking pots, *toka apu*, in Garaina village. A traded Markham Valley pot is in the foreground.

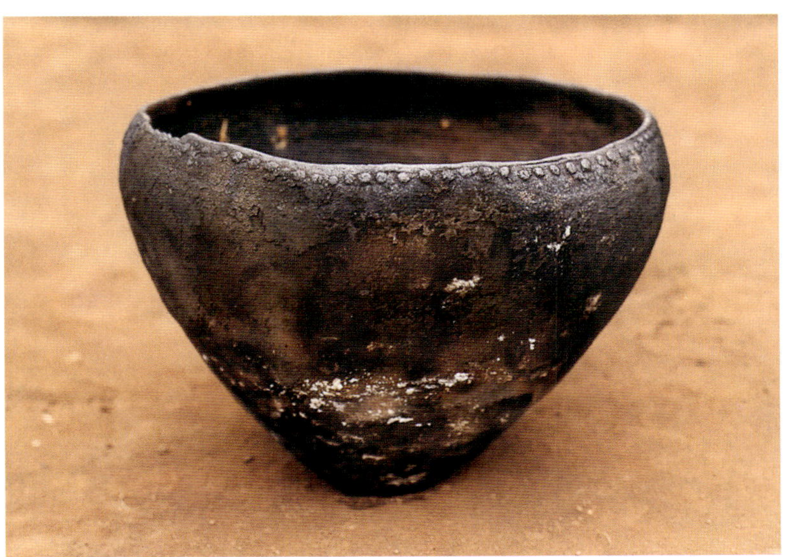

Fig. 6.23
Salamaua form of cooking pot made at Bosadi on the coast and traded to Garaina, *h* 27 cm.

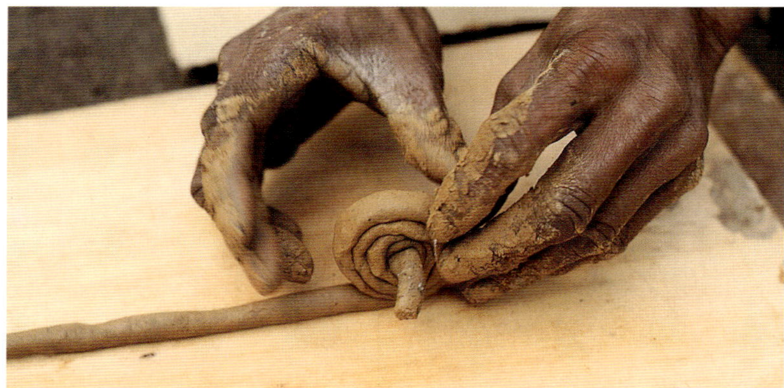

Fig. 6.24

Fig. 6.24
Waria potter Kazeze forming the base of his pot. The nipple of the pot will be formed from the end of the coil. Garaina village.

Fig. 6.25
Kazeze smoothing the base around the nipple, Garaina.

Fig. 6.26
Kazeze pressing a coil down on the one below, Garaina.

Fig. 6.25

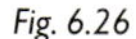

Fig. 6.26

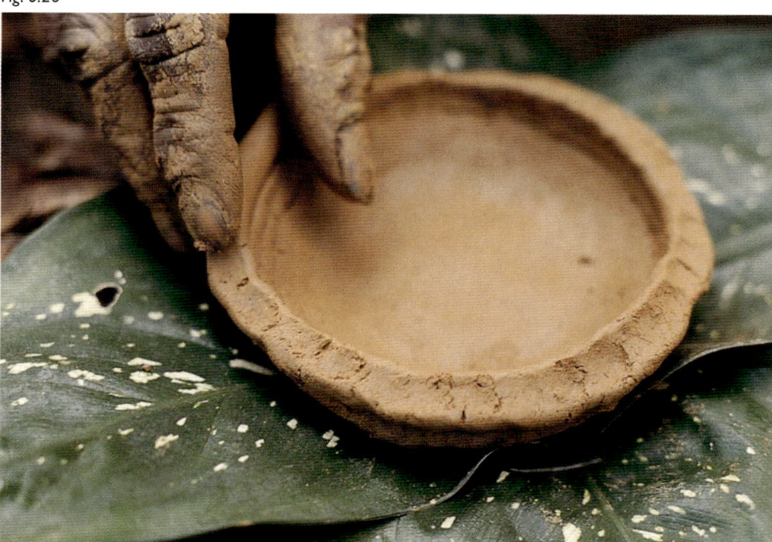

Fischer's archaeological finds, while more richly decorated than today's pots, correspond to the recent pots of the central Watut group and confirm a continuing tradition. He has also found sherds of Azera vessels in the northern portion of the valley, which seems to confirm the theory that a group of Azera people settled there in the past. However, there is still a possibility that Azera pots were traded in.

Waria

Garaina is a sub-district in the Waria Valley in the south-west corner of Morobe Province. There is only one early report of pot production in this area: Neuhauss (1911) reports pots from a village he calls Jacuna (not known now) one-and-a-half days' journey up the Waria River but the pots he illustrates appear much more like Ambasi pots than present-day Garaina pots. To the authors' knowledge, there was only one Garaina-style pot in a museum collection before 1975. This is a small vessel in the Australian Museum, Sydney, collected in 1957 at nearby Kunimaipa by Dr Margaret McArthur.

There are several villages on the upper Waria River and its tributaries the Bubu and Ono, the inhabitants of which still make coil pots, although activity is now infrequent. These villages – Garaina 1, 2 and 3, Kapiso, Timinagosa, Aro, Motete and, to the south, Biawaria, Bakeri (hamlet) and Asama (in the Northern Province) – belong to the Guhu-Samane language group of the Binandere family but are often referred to as the 'Waria'. Several other villages in this area may be pot making centres. Pots are made by both men and women but now mostly by men. Pot making seems to have originated in the southern villages and spread to the others. The Binandere family is widespread in the Northern Province.

Ten kilometres inland from the coast on the Maiama River is another Guhu-Samane group which speaks a different dialect. This includes the people of Eipa'Zinaba, where the women are said to make pots from black clay collected near the coast. The form of Eipa'Zinaba pots is much the same as that of the inland Waria although a simple applied decoration of wavy lines and knobs around the top appears to be a variation.

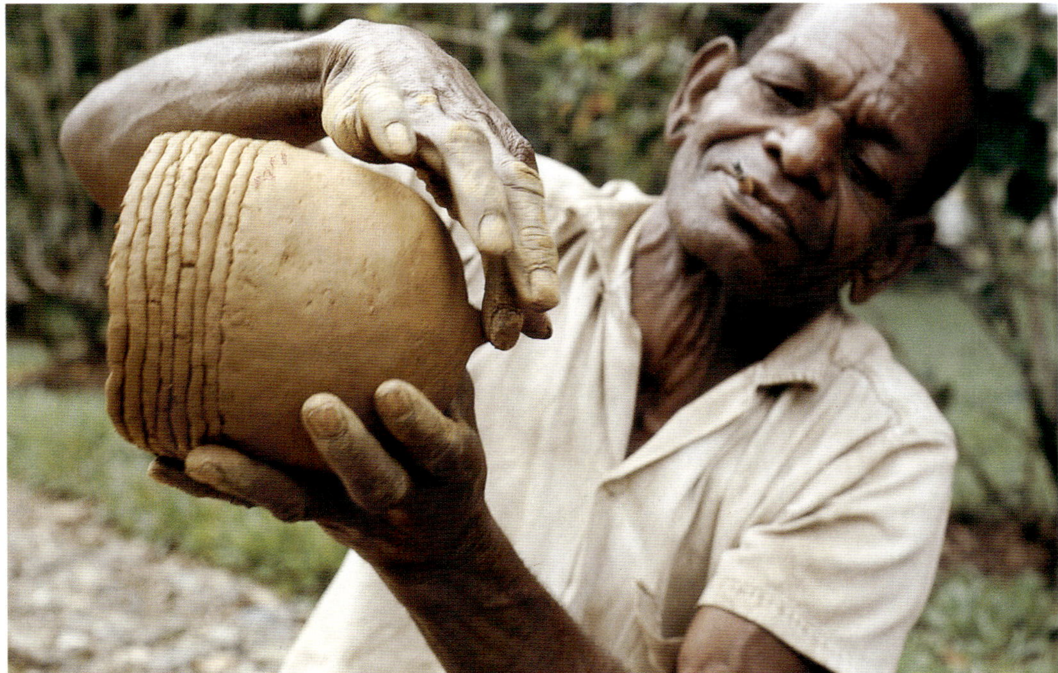

Fig. 6.27
Waria potter Kazeze checking the nipple base, Garaina village.

Fig. 6.28
Kazeze decorating with a matchstick, Garaina.

The Waria people make only cooking pots, *toka apu*. They can be restricted or unrestricted, straight-sided or slightly flared, and the bases are rounded with nipple points. They are generally about 36 centimetres high (Fig. 6.22).

There are, in this southern part of Morobe Province, other language groups (all of the Binandere family), the members of which are reported to have made pots: the Zia form a group which extends from the mouth of the Waria and Wuwu rivers up to Iema, about 40 kilometres up the Waria and south into the Northern Province; the Yekora form a small group just south of the Morobe patrol post in the villages of Sapa, Ana and Posei; and the Suena occupy the area around the Morobe patrol post. A pot from the Suena village of Bosadi, seen at Garaina, was wider-mouthed than Waria pots and had small knobs of applied clay below the rim; it resembled the Lokanu vessels. It is possible that people from all the coastal villages used to make pots but now have difficulty in obtaining good clay. South of the Zia, near the mouth of the Mambare River in the Northern Province, the people of Manau, another Binandere group, are potters.

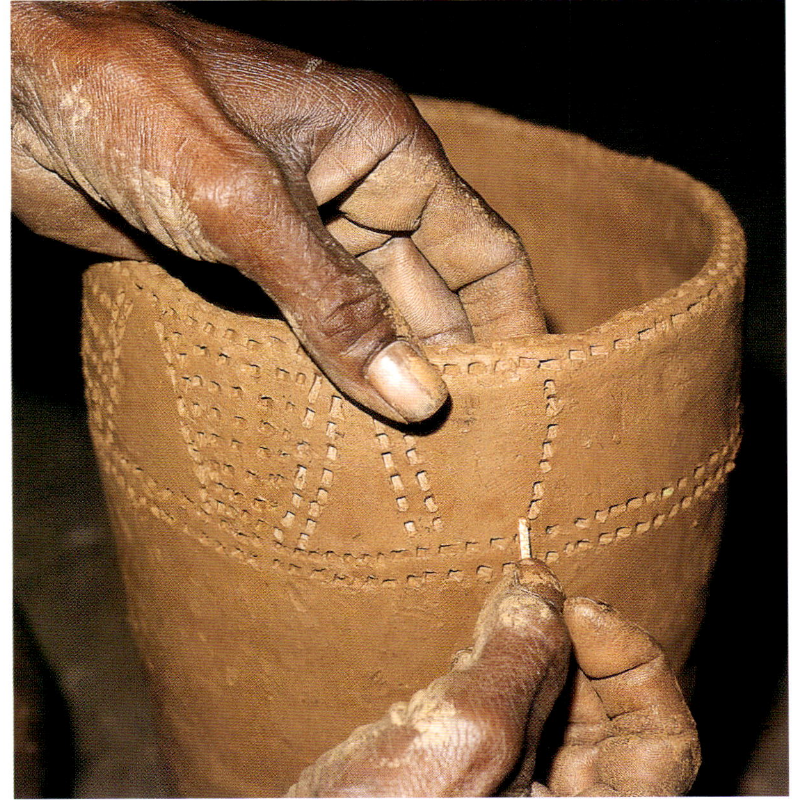

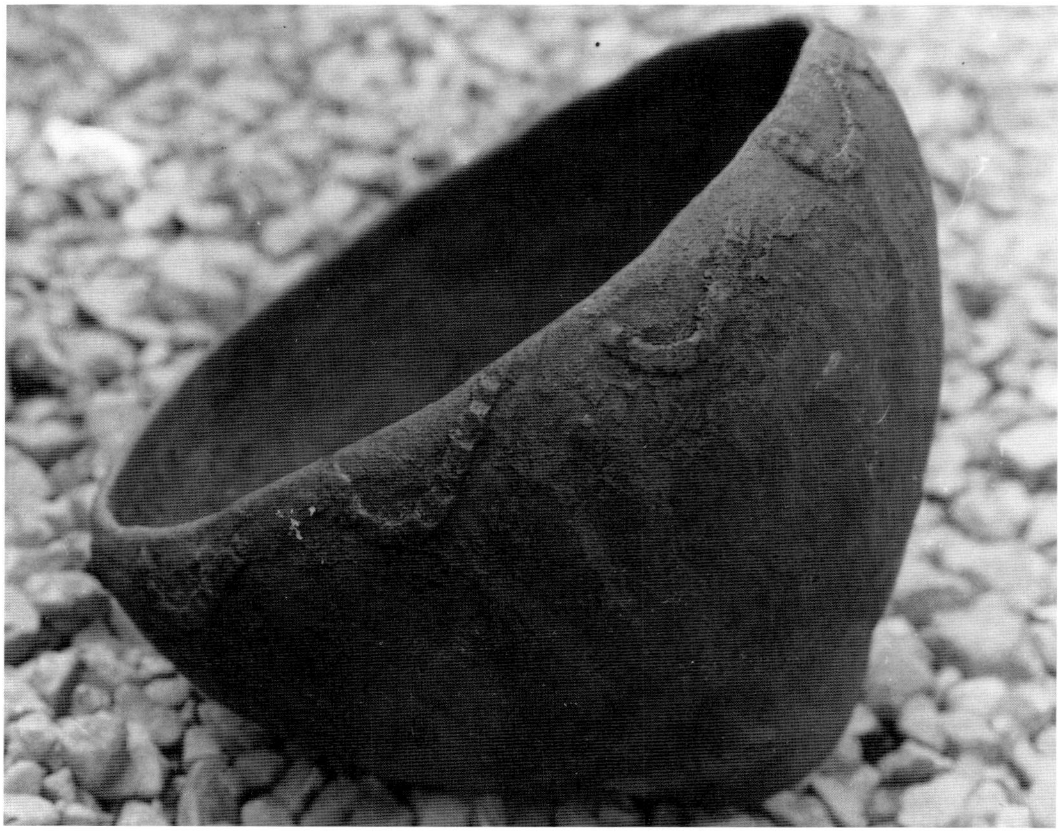

Fig. 6.29
Lokanu cooking pot, *uli,* with typical haphazardly applied and impressed decoration, Salamaua area, *h* 23 cm.

The inland Waria get their clay, *nenunga,* from various sources on the Bubu, Ono and Waria rivers and from near a volcanic hill, Tomano, about one hour's walk from Garaina.

Sometimes people bring the clay to the potters and are paid for their services with finished pots. The clay is brownish-orange, very sticky, with plenty of grit and stones which are subsequently removed.

Pot making was observed at Garaina 2 (Figs. 6.24-6.28). Prepared clay is squeezed into a short thick roll; about ten rolls are made to start with. Coils, *toka*, are rolled on a 'pangal', or board, with the palm of the hand until they are approximately 8 millimetres thick and 35 centimetres long. To allow enough clay for the knobbed base, the coil is doubled over at right angles to the remainder of the coil and then rolled along over this piece until the whole coil has formed a flattish disc with a protruding tail. The potter now joins the coils and models the extra piece into a rounded nipple, *kopina*. Another coil is joined spirally onto the outer edge of the now shallow dish by pressing it down firmly. This flattens and spreads the coil, making the wall of the pot some 2 centimetres wide. This is a very slow building process, each coil raising the walls by less than 1 centimetre. After the first few coils are added the pot is transferred from the hand to a pandanus leaf ring-cushion which has fresh lily leaves placed across it. When eight or so coils have been added they are again joined, this time with a small flat tool made from a piece of outer skin of sugar-cane. The tool is dragged down across the coils which are then smoothed. No water is used. If the clay is softer than usual the pot must be put aside to become firmer. An unusual aspect of the technique is that the potter, after joining the new coil to the end of the last one, lays it all around and then goes back to pinching it on. Every now and then the pot is held aloft to check the shape; it is pushed and smoothed to eliminate bumps and the nipple is remodelled if necessary. When the desired height is attained, final smoothing on the outside

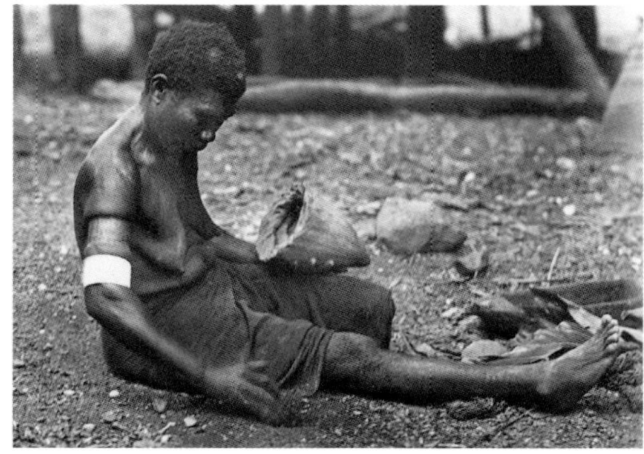

is done with the back of the sugar-cane tool. According to one informant, an incantation is traditionally uttered during pot making and the potters used to be secretive about the procedure of making pots and children were kept away. This is denied by other Garaina informants.

Pots are decorated with a piece of square-cut, double-pronged sugar-cane, *zapu*, with a piece of grass or now sometimes a matchstick. Decoration is limited to the top 5 to 6 centimetres of the outside of the pot including the rim. Most common are geometric designs of dotted zig-zag lines of punctations made by dragging the two-pronged stick (comb) and pressing it in at regular intervals. Some pots have unsmoothed coils left showing in zig-zags and some are marked with a stick or finger and the top triangular areas are filled in with stabbed decoration. It is said that each potter has his own design. The mark made by Kazeze is called *supu* and is the mark made by ducks' feet in the soft ground. The pot collected in Kunimaipa in 1957 has a different decoration: two lines of simple vertical deep incisions around the top 4 centimetres. There is no information concerning pots from the other areas mentioned above.

Pots are kept inside the house to dry for at least two weeks before firing and only one pot is fired at a time. Fuel can be a hardwood, *korizo*, or a softwood, *horahora*, and the bark of a tree, *taperua*. Four layers of wood are placed criss-cross fashion to form a platform. After the fire is lit underneath, the pot is placed on its side on top of the wood; small pieces of fuel are placed inside it and lit. During the firing no fresh wood is added but burning pieces are placed around and over the pot. A long stick is used to turn the pot at regular intervals until one revolution is completed; then it is lifted off. The firing takes about half an hour for a medium-sized pot, a little longer for a larger pot.

Ashes are removed from inside the pot by wiping it with taro leaves. A hollow is made in the centre of the glowing ashes, the pot is placed there, more wood is added and sealing is effected by boiling in it water and taro leaves. For cooking, pots are stood with their knobbed bases buried in the ground and the fire is built all around. Such vessels are still highly regarded and are said to be able to tenderise even the toughest pig. Traditional trade in pots was usually restricted to the language group, including the coastal Guhu-Samane.

Figs 6.30 to 6.32
Techniques photographed at Lo Kanu (Lokanu) village, Salamaua area, in the early 1900s.

Fig. 6.30
Woman potter making a hole in the ground in which to support the pot while it is being formed.

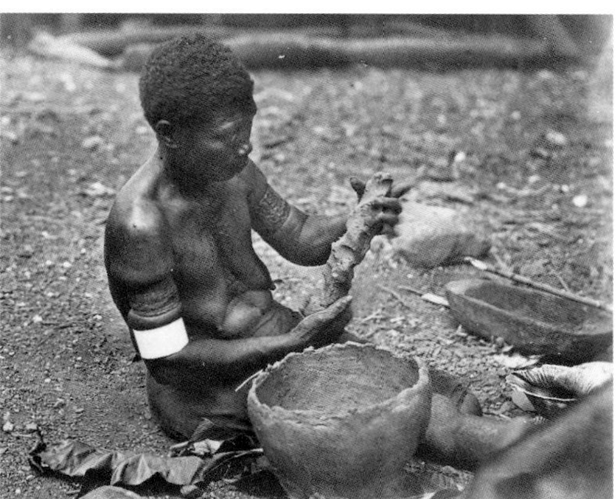

Fig. 6.31
Squeezing out a thick roll of clay to add to the top edge of the pot.

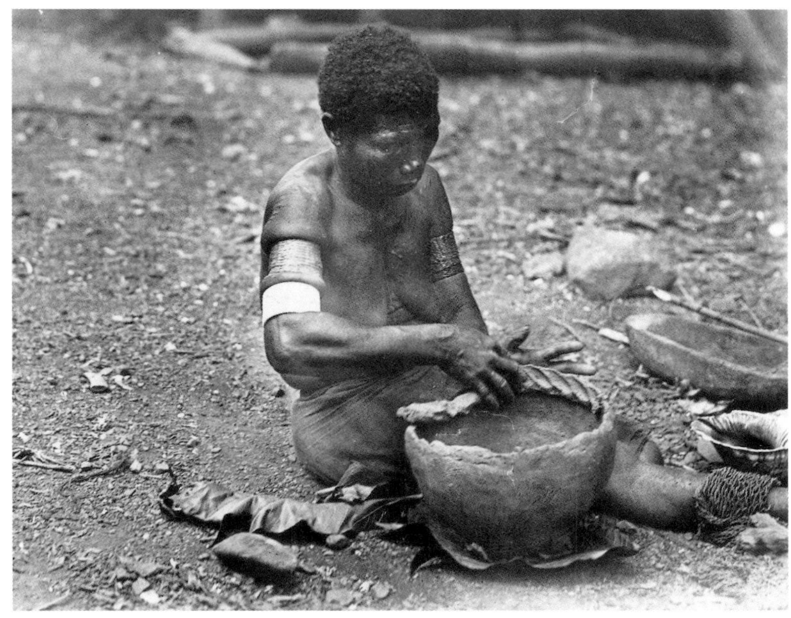

Fig. 6.32
Woman potter pressing a soft roll of clay on the top inner edge of the pot.

Fig. 6.33
Cooking pot, *uro*, made by Bonan from Gitua village, *h* 39 cm.

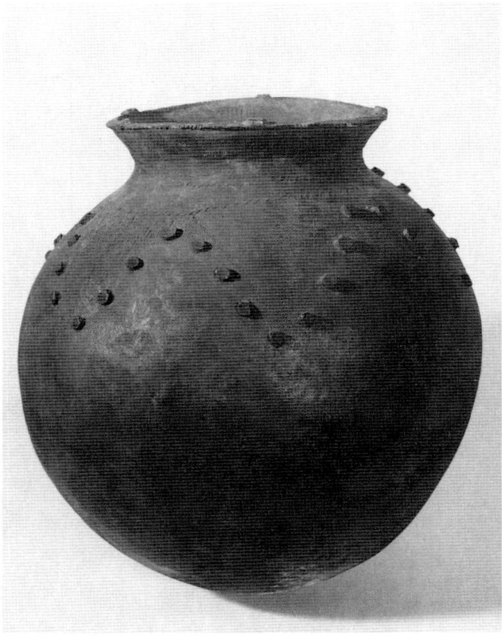

Salamaua (Kela-Sipoma)

Coiled pottery made by Austronesian-speaking women was until the last ten years produced in a group of coastal villages south of the Huon Gulf. These villages are located south of Salamaua and the industry has been referred to by Papua New Guineans as the 'Salamaua' industry. The pot producing villages were Lokanu, Lababia, Buso, Kui and Sipoma. Karl Holzknecht reports that the people of Keila, just north of Salamaua, also made pots in the past but this activity has long since been abandoned. The name Kela has been given to the language group which extends along the Morobe coast from Salamaua to Buso and Kui; inhabitants of Sipoma, however, speak the Sipoma language (Hooley and McElhanon 1970).

There are unconfirmed reports of other villages farther south near the Morobe patrol post and the mouth of the Waria River where pots similar to those from the Salamaua area are made. Albert Lewis (1951), who visited the area as leader of the Joseph N. Field South Pacific Expedition in 1909-13, and Ian Hogbin (1947, 1951) have written what are at present the most thorough accounts of the Salamaua industry. Further data has been collected by the authors during field trips in 1974-76.

This industry produced plain cooking pots, called *uli*. These vary greatly in size, ranging from small pots used by individuals and families to huge feast pots. The vessels are conical with pointed bases and slightly inturned rims; they are fairly thick and heavy. The top sections of the pots may be decorated with simple applied designs that can be incised, impressed or pinched. Punctate marks and applied nubbins are also sometimes found (Fig. 6.29).

The only clay deposit is located on Uliawa Island, one of the Fly Islands, which are about 5 kilometres off the coast opposite Kui village. Uliawa, or Ulangawa as it is called in Sipoma, lies within Sipoma territorial limits and not only must others ask Sipoma people's permission to use the clay but Sipoma women must clear their own needs with one of the older women in charge of the clay.

Ulangawa is known along the coast as 'Sospen' Island, 'Sospen' being the pidgin term for pot, and the names Uliawa and Ulangawa come from the words for clay and pot – *uli* (Kela) and *ulanga* (Sipoma) – and for hole or pit – *awa* – thus, 'claypit island'.

Men are responsible for collecting the clay and they travel to the Fly Islands in canoes equipped with empty petrol drums (presumably large baskets in the past) for the clay and enough food to last a few days. There are three varieties of clay: green-grey, red-brown and dark brown. It is dug from deep holes with digging sticks or spades and put in baskets which are hauled up to the top; large pieces of grit and other impurities are removed before the clay is dumped into the drums. When the men return to the village, the clay is formed into large balls and stored under the houses for future use.

The spiral coil technique is used and the women form the pot entirely with their hands, using neither tools nor supports. Neuhauss, however, describes the use of a small flat piece of wood or turtle shell for final beating of the base, which has become distorted by the weight of the pot. No subsequent reports mention this and the people of Lokanu do not remember it. Sipoma people agree that they used to beat their pots with a wooden paddle but that turtle shell would not be heavy enough.

The clay was prepared by the women, who broke it up into containers of fresh water and left it to

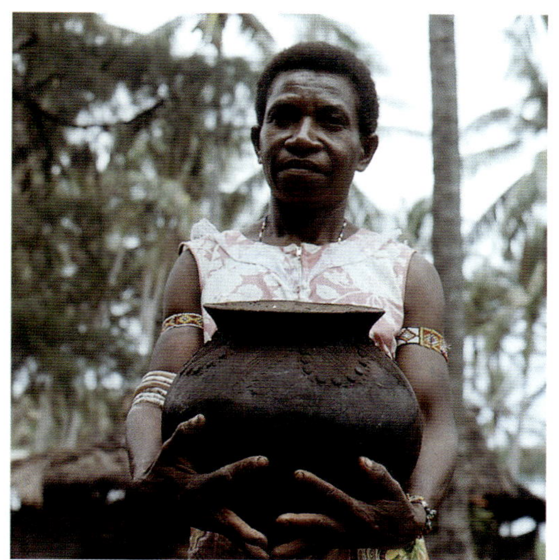

Fig. 6.34
Woman with a cooking pot, *keva*, at Sialum village..

soak overnight. Next morning all remaining impurities were removed from the softened clay. Rough rolls about 16 to 30 centimetres long were squeezed out, sometimes by a helper. Spiral coiling was used to form the thick pointed base which was held in the hand. When the vessel reached about 17 centimetres high it was placed in a hole lined with green leaves. The pot was rotated in a clockwise direction while the walls were continually built up by the addition of coils. Smoothing both inside and outside was done with wet hands. Neuhauss reports that women potters walked around the pots to join and smooth the coils, which would certainly be necessary for very big pots.

Drying was started in the sun and completed on a rack over the fire in the house. Pots, fired one at a time, were set upside down on a small platform of sticks or split wood about 5 centimetres thick, with more fuel stacked up against the pot to form a pyramid. Firing time is not known. To test the pot before use, taro peelings were boiled in it and the people say that if the water becomes discoloured the vessel must be broken. Pots approved for cooking were used a few times by a family to make quite sure they were strong enough to be traded. Sago storage pots are not needed in this area because the sago is wrapped in leaves and roasted on an open fire or smoked on a rack in the house.

Hogbin (1947) and Harding (1967) supply most of the information concerning the trading of pots in this area. Salamaua cooking pots were in demand right around the coast to the Tami Islands just south of Finschhafen and the Tami traders carried them to places as far away as the Siassi Islands. Each village or group of villages contributed some particular item to the trading cycle: Tami islanders, who have little land, had become experts at carving wooden bowls; Labu lagoon villagers produced baskets made from the reeds in the lagoon; the north coast people of the Gulf supplied mats for bedding, rain capes and string bags; Busama provided foodstuffs, especially taro, from their garden lands; and sago was grown around Keila. In earlier times, Lutu on the Salamaua Peninsula supplied adze blades.

The coastal villagers trade with the people from the hinterland. Pots are exchanged for tobacco, yam, sweet potatoes, dogs' teeth, bows and arrows, betel nut and birds' feathers. The Busama people trade with the Buang of the Snake River, several kilometres away in the mountains. The Buang people have never been potters and the Busama act as middle men by passing on Lokanu pots to the upper reaches of the Snake River; the lower river people obtain pots from the Watut area. A special study of this area was made by Girard (1956) and from her report comes details of the traded pots and photographs of them in use at a feast at Mapos village (Fig. 6.21). For the Buang, pots have always been precious objects and are valued for bride price payments. Formerly pots were received in exchange for dogs' teeth, bark cloth and large string bags. In the gold mining days the Buang were in demand

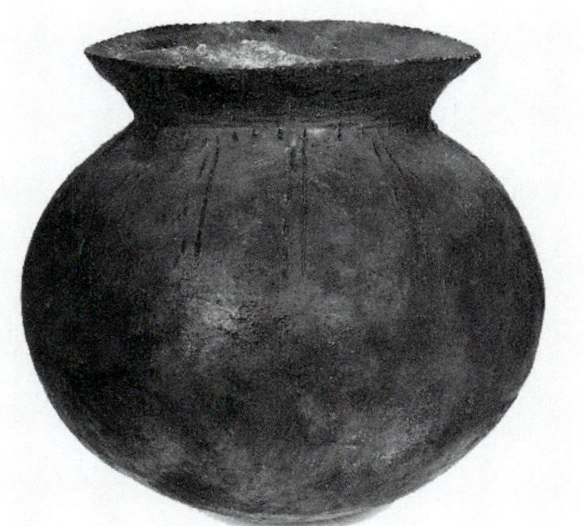

Fig. 6.35
Cooking pot, *kulo*, from Sio, *h* 23 cm.

as labourers and so cash payment for traded goods was often possible.

Each community restricted its voyages to its own section of the Huon Gulf. The potting villagers usually sailed only as far as Busama and their pots were then distributed by the Tami islanders. It appears, however, that Lokanu people might sometimes have sailed all the way to the Tami Islands. The pot makers also traded to the south but the extent of their travel is not known. In early times large canoes sailed as a fleet; there seems to have been a special immunity from attack by traditional enemies while on a pot trading expedition. In post-contact times the dependence on numbers was lessened and small boats would set off alone or in pairs. Men were the traders; women sometimes accompanied them but were never involved in either gift exchange or bartering.

Sio-Gitua

Paddle-and-anvil pottery was produced traditionally by Sio-speaking people on Sigawa Island (Sio), at Nambariwa on the coast and at Gitua (Kelanoa, Kelana). During the last fifty years this industry has expanded to several other Sio settlements on the mainland and to Sialum and Nama, extending along 75 kilometres of coastline.

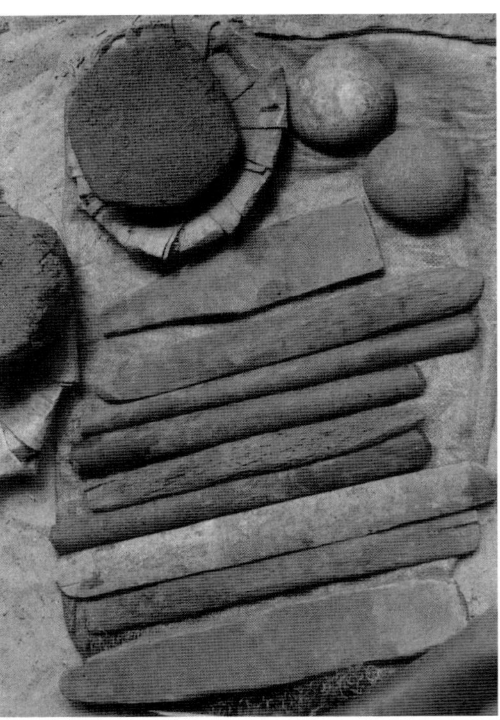

Fig. 6.36
Potter's tools, Sialum village.

A study of archaeological sites and of both the historic and modern industries was carried out by Jim Specht in 1973. Previously, brief information on the pottery had been collected by Neuhauss (1911), Vogel (1911), Groves (1954), Bodrogi (1961) and Harding (1967). The following description of the industry is based mainly on Specht's report. The authors have visited only the Sialum industry.

Sio Island, known locally as Sigawa Island, is situated some 300 metres off the north coast of the Huon Peninsula in the Vitiaz Strait. It is a small barren island and in about 1964 population growth necessitated a move to the mainland, where the villages of Balambu, Laelo and Basakalo (grouped as Sio No. 1), and Lambutina (Sio No. 2) were founded. Nambariwa is a separate village an hour's walk to the south-east. Sigawa Island now supports only a few pigs.

Pottery was started in Sialum about forty years ago by two Sio women who married Sialum men and by a Sialum girl who learned to make pots while living in Gitua. In the past, women from the three traditional centres who married into other villages or lived away from home were not allowed to pursue the craft but there was no restriction on women who married into Gitua or the Sio villages.

The original potters of the area are all Austronesians who speak the Sio and Gitua languages. The more recent potters of Sialum and Nama are non-Austronesians, speaking the Sialum language. The Sio people claim to have come from the coast to the west; Gitua origins are said to be on the Siassi Islands, a group of small islands between the Huon Peninsula and New Britain. The first home of the Gituans was a small limestone island where, it is claimed, survivors of a voyage from Siassi drifted and settled. This island, close to the present village, was destroyed by a violent storm several generations ago.

The north and east coasts of the Huon Peninsula are formed by a series of limestone terraces consisting of coral fringing reefs. Several major rivercourses drain the mountainous hinterland of the Finisterre Range and carry in their beds pebbles of rock types foreign to the limestone coast; these are used by the potters as tools for pot making.

Cooking pots only are made; coconut shells and bamboo are used for storing food and water. The style variation between the villages is minimal. The vessels are spherical, with thin walls, round bases, restricted necks and everted rims. At Sio, pots, *kulo*, usually come in two sizes, small and large, with heights ranging from 14 to 32 centimetres. Gitua pots, *uro*, are made in three sizes, small, medium and large, with heights ranging from 12 to 38 centimetres. Sialum pots, *keva*, have a size range similar to those from Gitua. The small pots hold food for two people, the medium pots are used for a family and the largest are for cooking pork and other food at feasts.

Decoration generally covers only the part of the pot above the shoulder, including the neck, the rim interior and the lip. The lips of most pots are notched and the designs on the neck and rim interior consist of rectilinear geometric arrangements of straight lines, slash and stab marks, and relief or applied elements used in a repetitive pattern. Gitua terms for decoration were as follows: perforations (rare), *pura*; applied knobs, *binoro*; incising and lip notching, *boma*. The term *nongo* refers to decoration in general.

There are two clay sources which have been used recently by the Sio villages. One, *lakakulu*, is just west of Balambu in Sio No. 1, several hundred metres from the sea. The clay is taken from below the surface of a grassy area and has grass roots and other vegetable matter through it. It is a compact black clay with an average clay mineral (smectite) content but very poor plasticity. A high proportion of the non-plastics is pyroxene with some shell and pumice fragments, quartz and obsidian. The other source, *kukolo*, used by both Nambariwa and Lambutina potters, is on the south bank of the Kwaling River upstream from Nambariwa village. There are several large pits about 50 centimetres deep. The clay taken from under the surface is grey-black, that taken from the base of the pit is yellow-brown. These two clays are mixed together in an unknown ratio and produce a satisfactory potting clay.

Gitua also has two clay sources. One, *kukumei*, is located near the village on the south bank of the Roto River. The grey-brown clay is quarried from small pits dug into the upper section of the south bank just below the topsoil. A sample analysis showed a very low clay mineral (smectite) proportion of 20 per cent. The non-plastics include white shell fragments, sponge spicules, olivine and quartz. Almost half the clay comprises a fine sand fraction and the plasticity is very poor. It is not surprising that this is not the main clay source for Gitua. A brown clay, *kembere*, from the north bank of the Sazom River between Gitua and Sialum, is more often used.

The Sialum source is the north bank of the Sakat River near Nama, about 300 metres inland from the beach. The brown clay is dug from 25 centimetres below the topsoil and is used by the potters of both Sialum and Nama. The potters use string bags to carry the clay back to their villages. An average bag of clay would be enough to make about five small to medium-sized pots, or four large ones, and it is kept hanging outside the house from ten days to a month until well weathered. No temper of any kind is added to the clay. These are the only paddle-and-anvil potters in Papua New Gui-

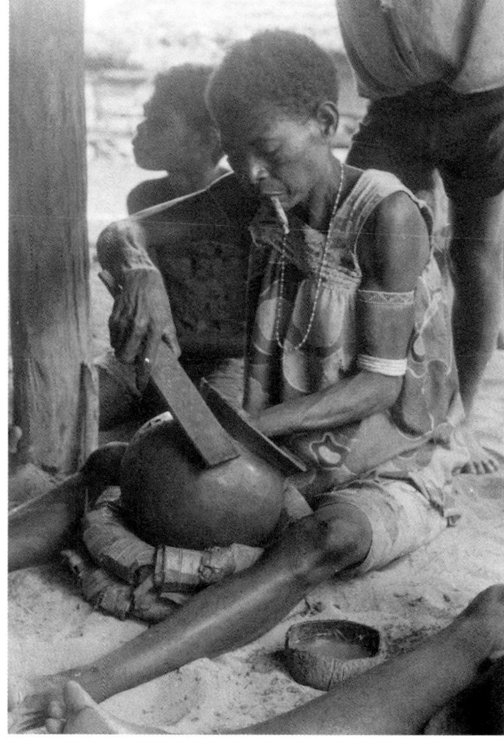

Fig. 6.37
Beating almost completed, Sialum.

nea who do not add temper to their clay. The clay is softened with salt water, kneaded and made into balls ready for forming.

Equipment used is a bailer shell to hold sea water, ring-cushions of varying diameters and made of sago leaves at Nambariwa and of pandanus leaves at Gitua and Sialum and, for Sio potters, a large slab of stone as a working surface (at Gitua a flat board of wood is used). Tools consist of one or more smooth pebbles for use as anvils, specific ones being required at different stages of formation, and a range of wooden paddles (beaters). The number of paddles each potter uses varies considerably. At Gitua the generic name for paddles is *poepoe* and there are four named paddles, which vary in weight as well as shape: *vagaranga*, rough-surfaced heavy paddles made from the grained wood of the areca palm, unshaped except for trimming to the required width and used for heavy initial beating; *poepoe*, finer-grained wood with a smooth, narrow working surface, used in the second stage of beating; *yalunga*, broad, flat and thin, spatulate in form, occasionally with designs carved on the handle, made from a hardwood tree, used for final beating of the body and base and sometimes used to notch the lip; *talinga*, very narrow, thin paddles used to finish the rim and neck and sometimes to notch the lip. The paddles range in size from 25 to 40 centimetres in length and 2 to 10 centimetres in width (Figs. 6.36, 6.37). For decorating, thin sticks are cut when needed and discarded after use. These are called *nongo* at Gitua, the same name as given to the designs.

The paddle-and-anvil technique is similar in some stages to that used at Korak in the Madang Province. Worthy of note is the use by Sio potters of a flat stone slab for the preparatory stages of the work; this method is not used anywhere else on the mainland but is employed in the Nasioi region of Bougainville and south of there on Choiseul Island in the Solomon Islands.

Only women are allowed to make pots but men may watch, touch the clay and visit the clay sources without restriction; they also carve the wooden paddles used to beat the clay. Before marriage girls learn the craft from their mothers or other female relatives. Generally the older women are considered the experts.

The Gitua and Sialum potters use the heaviest wooden paddle to beat one of the balls of prepared clay into a solid cone shape. The top, the widest end of the cone, is beaten upwards around a stone anvil held inside. As the cone is turned, the wall thus formed is beaten back down into a solid cone again. This process is repeated several times, gradually increasing the size of the cone, which begins to assume the shape of a pot. Several stone anvils and paddles can be used at this stage. Lighter paddles are used to thin the walls as the pot grows bigger and the narrow beater is used to form and smooth the rim and neck. The pot is now placed on the ring, either between the potter's legs or to one side, and is slowly turned as it is beaten evenly all around from the base upwards. Occasionally a wet hand is rubbed over the surface of the pot. For the final beating and smoothing the widest paddle is used.

After wiping the pot with wet hands, decorating is begun by notching the lips with the edge of one of the lightweight paddles. Then the designs on the rim interior, the neck and the upper body are incised. Knobs are formed with the fingers and pressed first onto the lip and then onto the body of the pot; they are then tapped gently with the finishing paddle.

With the exception of the initial preparation the method used by a Sio potter is much the same. Two balls of clay are beaten separately on a wet stone slab, first into cones, then into flat discs, back into balls, again into discoids and finally beaten upwards into cup shapes. This is to help eliminate stones or roots and, presumably, to work the clay into a more manageable condition. The cup shapes are set aside overnight and once again beaten from one shape to another, finishing as solid cones which are banged together and then beaten on the slab into a single cone which has a blunt base. Nowhere else in Papua New Guinea is such an elaborate conditioning of the clay carried out. The cone is then transferred to a ring-cushion and a wet stone anvil is thrown into the centre to open it out. From here the technique follows a procedure similar to that described for Gitua.

At several stages pots are set aside to become firmer and before firing they are dried for four days to a few weeks. For firing at Gitua, where fuel is in short supply, slow-burning logs are used and the remaining coals help cook the evening meal. Thin sticks, coconut fronds and split bamboo are added to the fire but no furious flames are allowed. One pot at a time is turned slowly around until all sides are sufficiently fired. Pots are tested by boiling food scraps in them; the resulting blackened pots, if sound, are then available for sale. At Sialum several pots are fired together and coconut milk is cooked in the pots to seal them.

Sio-Gitua pots are important trade items today, just as they were in the past. Harding (1967), in describing the trade of the area, says that although much had changed in the way of life since the German annexation 'the trading system by a seeming miracle survives'. Siassi islanders are the main traders; they take pots across the Vitiaz Strait to New Britain and to other smaller islands, down the coast of the Huon Peninsula and to the Tami Islands. They also used to overlap with the Bilbil traders on about 160 kilometres of the Rai coast. The Siassi islanders traded directly with the beach villagers who in turn traded with inland groups bounded on the south by the Sarawaged and Finisterre ranges.

To the Siassi islanders pigs are the most valuable trade item and the aim of most of their voyages is to procure, firstly, pigs and, secondly, other goods that can eventually be exchanged for pigs. Of lesser importance are dogs and wooden bowls. Taro is the most important of the many food items exchanged, followed by sweet potatoes, fish and coconuts. Pots are considered wealth objects in some areas and play an important part in bride price transactions. In the inland villages of Umboi Island, for example, great quantities of hoarded pots from Sio and Gitua can be found.

Sio, the most populous area in the trade system, is a main stopping place for the Siassi traders. Some of the mountain people have strong trade alliances with the Sio, exchanging items such as staple foods, pigs, dogs, string bags, bows and arrows for pots, fish and coconuts. Trade within the hinterland villages follows channels established by marriage. Sometimes women are exchanged for coastal products such as pots.

Both Sio-Gitua and Madang pots reached the western part of New Britain through the Siassi traders. No pottery is made anywhere in New Britain and an extraordinary belief came about that pots were exotic products of the sea. The Siassi islanders played on this by saying that pots were the shells of deep water mussels (Harding 1967).

7 The Highlands

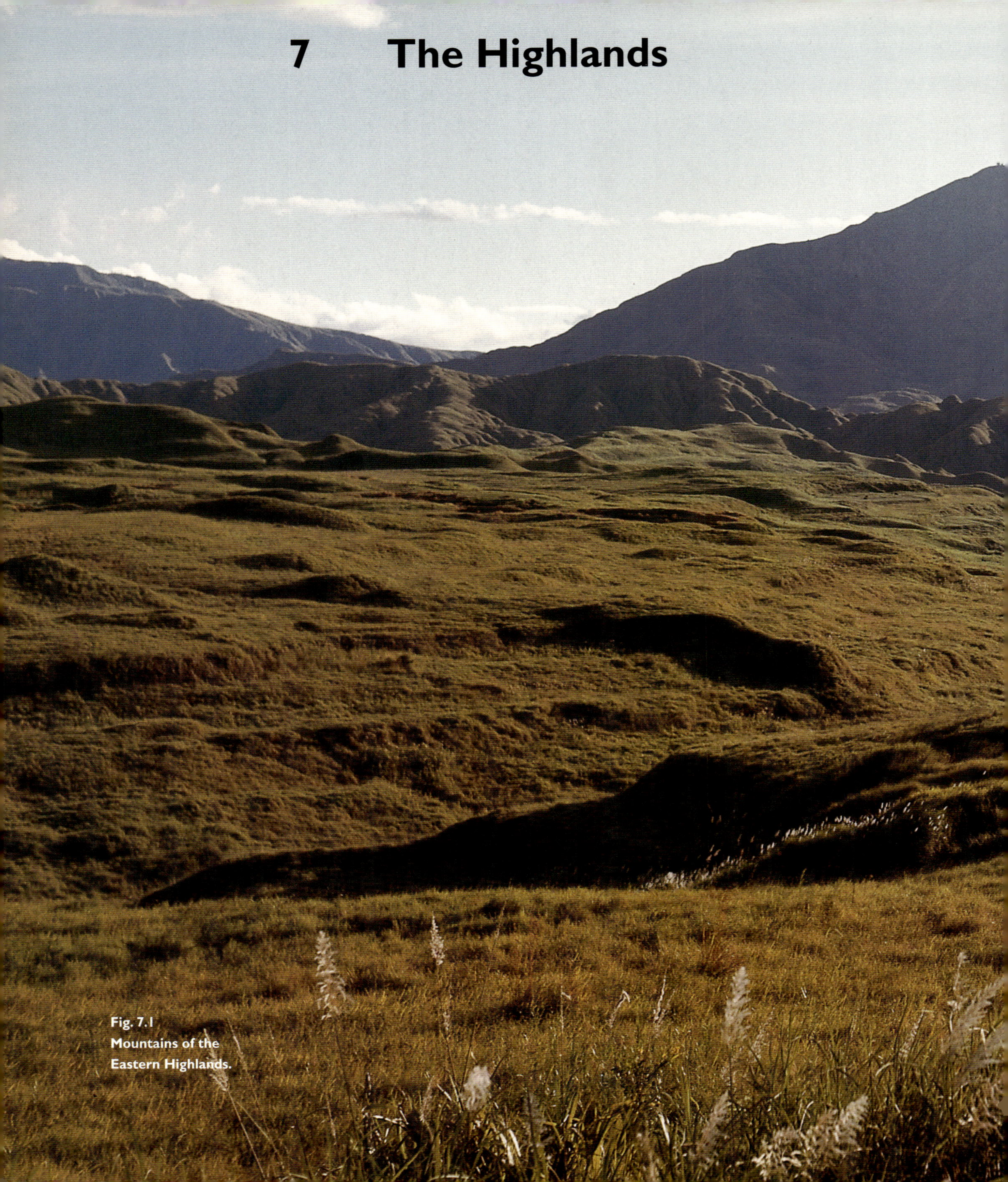

Fig. 7.1
Mountains of the Eastern Highlands.

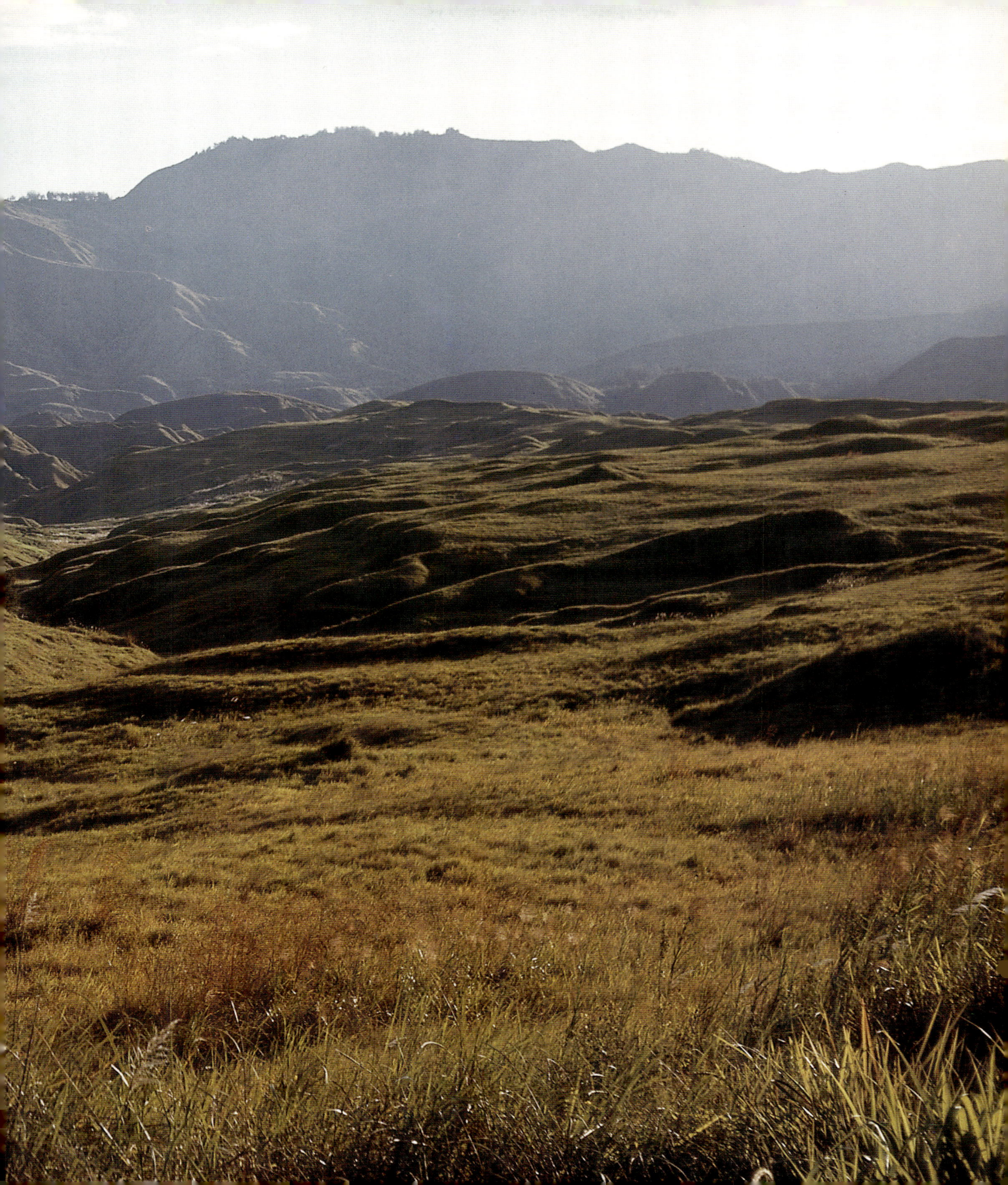

Running down the centre of the Papua New Guinean mainland is a string of high mountains whose fertile valleys are fairly densely populated by groups of non-Austronesian people. The highlands embraces five provinces: Eastern, Western and Southern highlands, Chimbu and Enga. The people of these highland provinces are mostly agriculturalists whose principal subsistence crops are taro and sweet potato. European contact with the highlands did not come until the 1930s although some European goods had, through trade, found their way into the highlands before this. The Australian administrative presence was not firmly established in the highlands until well into the 1950s.

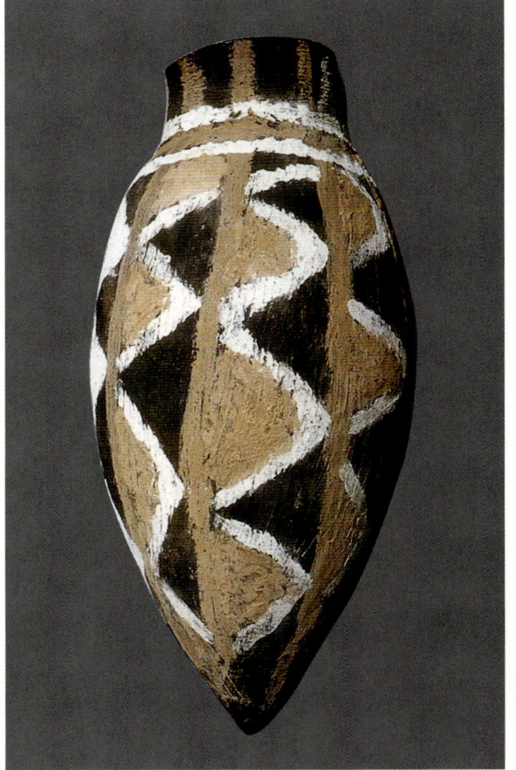

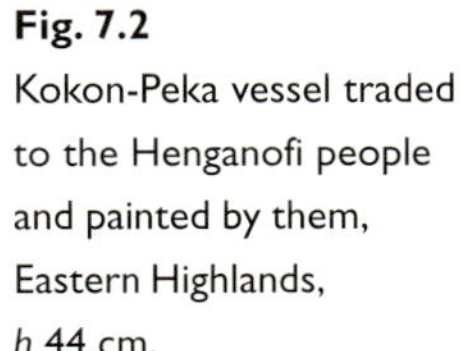

Fig. 7.2
Kokon-Peka vessel traded to the Henganofi people and painted by them, Eastern Highlands, *h* 44 cm.

The highlands are remarkably lacking in pot making communities. There is only one area where pots were made in the recent past among some of the villages of the Agarabi people who live in the mountains of the Ramu-Markham divide in the Eastern Highlands Province. One other area, the Kundiawa district of Chimbu Province, which is inhabited by the Sinasina people is noted for a sun-dried clay ocarina made by men. It has popularly been called a 'pig whistle'.

Pottery trade to the highlands has been fairly restricted when compared with the flow of shells from the coast. Azera vessels from the Markham Valley were traded into Eastern Highlands Province. Rawa pots were traded with the Benabena people and transported across the Ramu River into the Eastern Highlands. They have been found in the Dunantina Valley, in the Agarabi villages and in Henganofi (fig. 7.3). The Benabena people were probably the principal distributors (see Chapter 8). Kokon-Peka pots from the low mountain ranges overlooking the Ramu River plains were traded to the north of Chimbu Province and are commonly found in the area around Bundi (fig. 7.2). This trade has been described in detail by Hughes (1971). Madang coastal pots were traded on a small scale into Goroka and Chimbu.

Agarabi

It is difficult to account for the isolated occurrence of pot making among the Agarabi. Stylistically, the pots are most closely related to the inland Madang coiled pots and the pointed-based, deeply proportioned pots of the southern group of Azera speakers in the Watut Valley. Oral tradition suggests that the Agarabi people had their origins in the Markham Valley and were pushed up the valley into the mountains. This would place them geographically, at some time, close to the Madang coil potters.

Muriel Larner, an Australian planter and potter living near Kainantu, has recorded a legend about the first pot. It was told to her by a man from Pomasi II.

> One day an old man from Pomasi walked down towards the river. He found a spring welling up from the ground. Fascinated, he sat and watched the bubbling water and eventually fell asleep. While he slept the 'Dream Man' came and told him to dig up the ground, roll it into snakes, make a saucepan, dry it in the sun and cook it in a fire until it was strong. On waking, he dug up the clay, took it back to his village and did as the Dream Man instructed. When the first pot was completed he was a little uncertain of the magic or poison and feared he might die from the food cooked in it. So the first lot of sweet potato that was cooked was fed to the pigs and dogs. When they did not die he cooked more; this he tried himself, and when he too did not die, another batch was cooked. This was then given to the family.

Watson (1955) has also recorded an origin story in which a culture hero named Mani taught a woman, Banenano, to make pots.

Agarabi vessels were never widely traded although we found several in the Dunantina Valley and Watson (1955) and Coutts (1967) report a limited trade with the neighbouring Kamano, Tairora and Gadsup people. Since these pots are large, unwieldy and heavy this may not seem surprising, although Rawa vessels were carried to neighbouring groups in the Eastern Highlands from the far away Finisterre Mountains.

According to Watson (1955), in the 1950s pottery was still being made in the following Agarabi villages: Pomasi I and II, Bilamoia, Anonantu, Unantu, Punano, Akinakenu, Asipuia and Ajamoentenu. Today the industry is virtually defunct although in recent years a few of the older men have demonstrated pot making at the Kainantu Council exhibition at the Agricultural and Cultural Show held every two years in Goroka. Two possible reasons for the decline in this industry, apart from the universal replacement of traditional pottery by trade store china and metalware, are the efforts involved in obtaining clay and the absence of a strong demand for Agarabi pots. Some older men in the villages claim they know how to make pots.

Only one kind of vessel seems to have been produced: a cooking pot, called *kabe*, deeply proportioned, ellipsoid, with an everted neck and a pointed base. Watson (1955, 1977) describes a number of vessels found in the Eastern Highlands. Some she ascribes to the Agarabi and Kamano, for others she hesitates to designate a provenance. Almost certainly, however, her illustrations are of vessels from Agarabi, Rawa and the Azera. Decoration consists of incised slashes, perpendicular or diagonal to the lip, and incised, gouged or punctate patterns marking the lower neck area around the inflection point. Sometimes tool impressed patterns of continuous wavy lines are found, the tool being a crudely fashioned multi-toothed piece of bamboo (Figs. 7.4, 7.5).

Several clay sources were cited by informants from Bilamoia II and Pomasi I. One source is located many days' walk away in the lowland grass country along the Ramu River. The Pomasi have the rights to clay which is located in a valley several ridges away from their village. They say that the Bilamoia people used to buy the clay from them

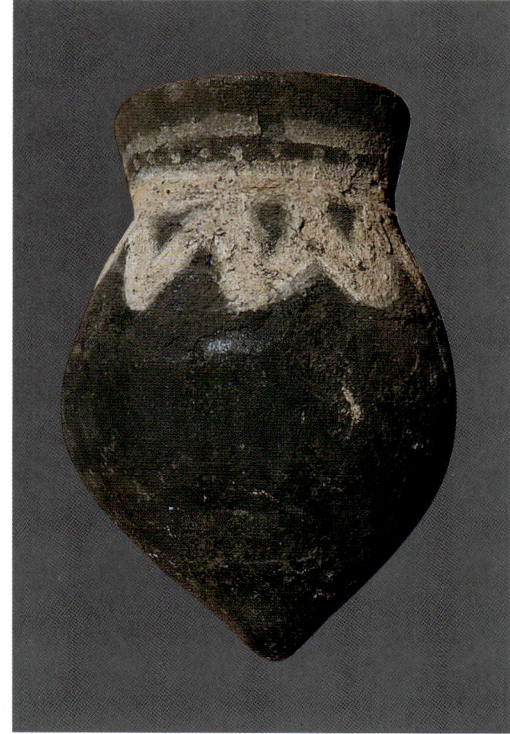

Fig. 7.3
Rawa trade pot, painted, collected in Henganofi, Eastern Highlands, *h* 27.5 cm.

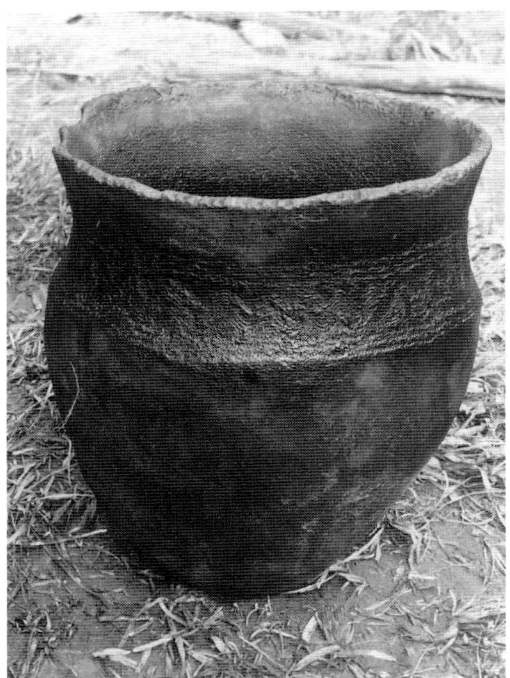

Fig. 7.4
Agarbi cooking pot, *kabe,* at Tuta village, Eastern Highlands, *h* 32 cm.

and that disputes have arisen in the past over this. The Anonantu people have their own clay but it is reputed to be too 'soft'. Watson (1955) mentions that clay comes from Lake Evadetton, a lake to the north of the potting villages.

Men and women went together to excavate the clay, *pipi trate*; the men broke the hard ground and the women, as is usual, carried it back to the village. In the village, women broke up the lumps with a stone and removed little pieces of grit. A large amount of water was added to the coarse material. It took between one and two days to prepare the clay for use.

Fig. 7.5

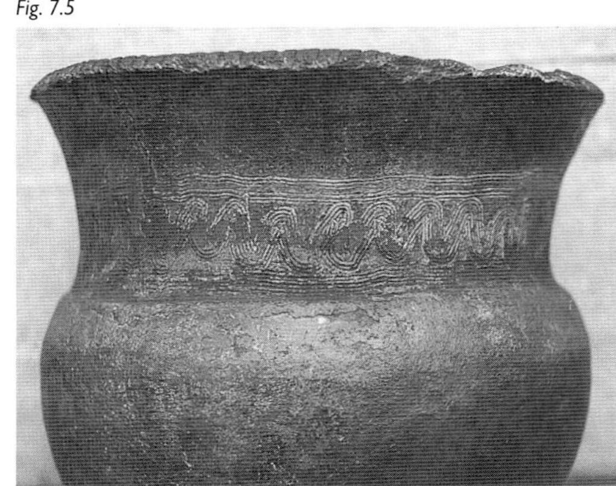

Fig. 7.5
Detail of an Agarabi pot, *kabe,* showing decoration made with a multi-toothed bamboo tool.

The only tools used for manufacturing the pots were a piece of coconut shell used for cutting away surplus clay, scraping and smoothing and a bamboo knife for removing excess clay on the bottom. The technique of manufacturing was coiling. To start the form, the potter made a hole in the ground and lined it with green leaves, usually banana. He then took a pug of clay the size of a football and made coils about 2.5 centimetres thick and of varying lengths. The first coil was started in the hole in the ground. A great deal of water was sprinkled onto the vessel during the building process. The form, including the neck, was shaped and smoothed by the piece of coconut shell. Decorations were applied with the bamboo implement and then the vessel was inverted and the roughly shaped base was finished. Surplus clay was cut away with the coconut shell and the bamboo knife. Finally it was smoothed once more. The vessels were put out in the sun to dry. A small pot took about a week to dry and large ones took up to two weeks.

Pots were fired singly. The fuel used was split hardwood arranged in a grid shape. The pot was set upright on the fuel and grass was laid along the top. The authors have no data for firing times. While still warm from the firing, the vessel was sealed and rubbed with a solution of banana, taro and sweet potato. The first two batches of food

Fig. 7.6

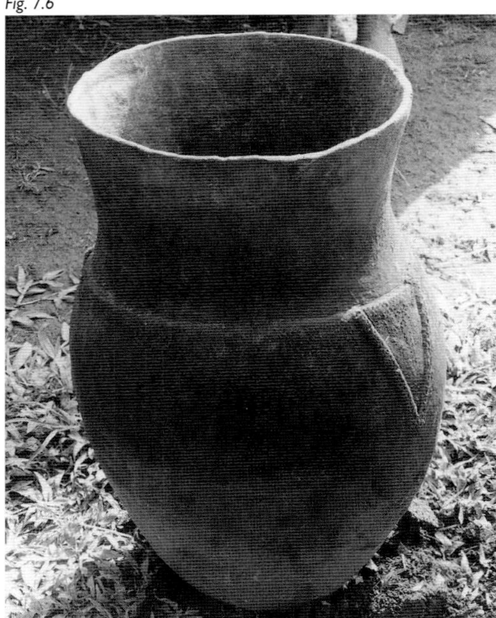

Fig. 7.6
Rawa cooking pot at Tauta village, Madang Province. Compare the form with the Agarabi vessel (fig. 7.4).

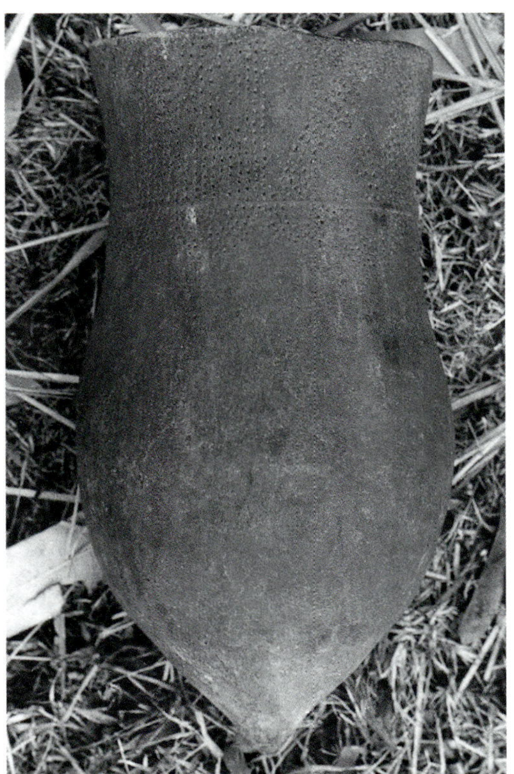

Fig. 7.7
Rawa cooking pot at Sankian, a Mari village, Madang Province, *h* 37cm. Compare the form with Agarabi vessal (fig. 7.4).

cooked in the pot were discarded as described in the legend.

The Agarabi vessels have affinities with the elongated pots made by men in the Watut River valley (see Chapter 6) and in the mountains of Madang Province, especially the Rawa vessels. A comparison of Rawa and Agarabi pots shows a similarity in general shape and size. Agarabi pots are large, about 35 to 40 centimetres high, about the size of the larger Rawa vessels, which were seldom seen outside the Rawa area because they were not traded as regularly as the smaller ones. Most details of manufacture, some firing procedures (the split fuel arranged in a grid shape) and comparison of vessel shapes suggest that the Agarabi industry may be an offshoot of the inland Madang tradition. The Agarabi, however, have one unusual aspect of technique, that of starting the coils in a depression in the ground, which they share with the Mari (Madang) and Kela-Sipoma (Morobe) industries. Decoration affinities with the Markham Valley Azera vessels can be seen in the marking of the lip and in the use of a multi-pronged comb.

Sinasina

In the Sinasina area of the Kundiawa district, around the Kamtai patrol post, men make clay ocarinas, *morimuge*. These are generally flattish triangular or round shapes with three holes, a mouth and two finger stops, which are arranged to resemble a pig's snout: hence the term 'pig whistle' commonly applied to them. The authors have also seen small prisms apparently made as playthings for children. The ocarinas vary in size but are typically about 12 centimetres in length (or diameter); the prisms somewhat smaller. Both are made from a local clay which is bluish-grey and has good plasticity. The ocarinas are made by moulding the clay over grass with sticks set in for the eyes and mouth. When the clay is dry the grass and sticks are pulled out. The objects are left in the sun to dry and, although not fired, they become very hard and brittle, especially along the edges. Occasionally they have been mistaken for stone objects. After drying they are usually carved with a sharp piece of bamboo or a knife in simple geometric linear patterns, portions of which are coloured black, traditionally with charcoal (Fig. 7.8).

According to informants the ocarinas are not used in any ritual context nor, as some have suggested, for calling pigs; they are 'playthings' for young men and are used to attract girls. Nowadays, primary school children in the area produce crude but quaint 'pig whistles' for sale to tourists along the Highlands Highway.

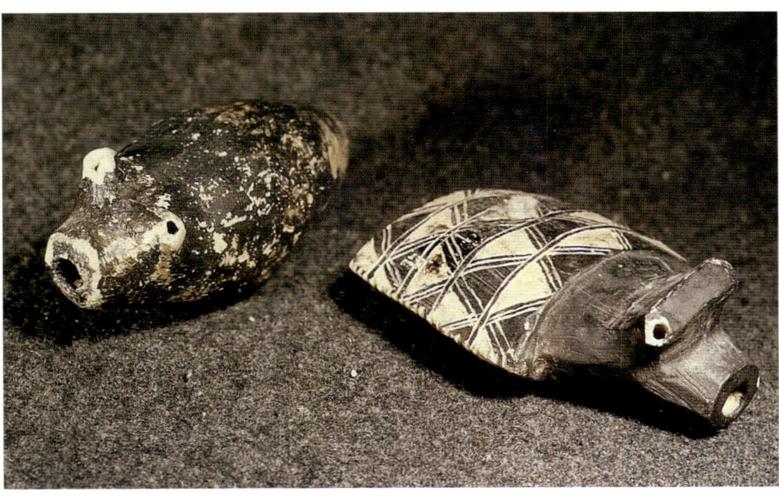

Fig. 7.8
Ocarinas or 'pig whistles' from Sinasina, Eastern Highlands, *l* (left) 9.5 cm; *l* (right) 12.5 cm.

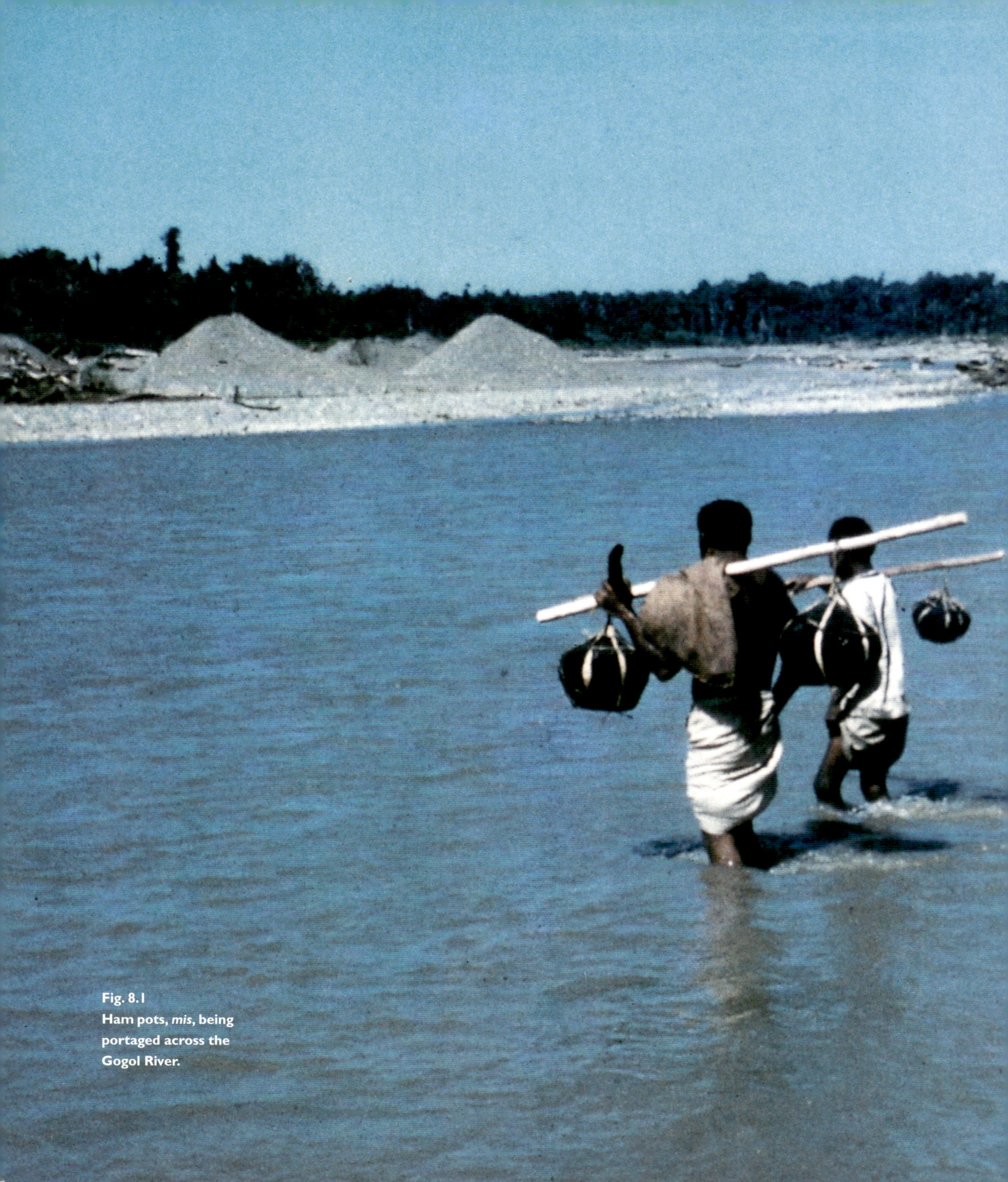

Fig. 8.1
Ham pots, *mis*, being portaged across the Gogol River.

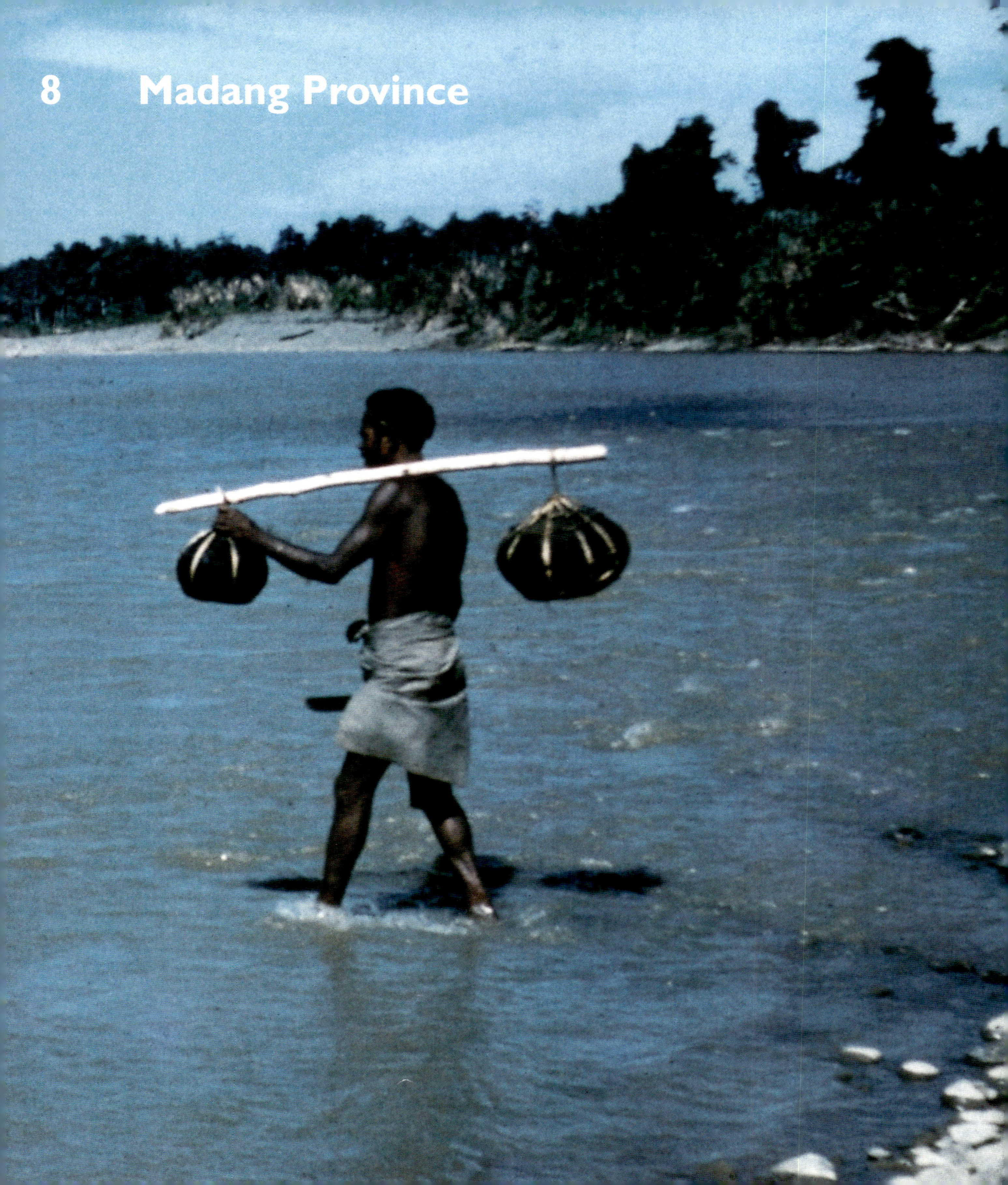

8 Madang Province

Madang Province
(North)
0
10
20
Kilometres
Sepik River
Porapora R.
Keram
R.
EAST SEPIK PROVINCE
RAMU
RIVER
Guam R.
Sogeram
R.
HANSA BAY
MANAM I.
KARKAR
ISLAND
ADELBERT RANGE
BOGIA
JOSEPHSTAAL
Kaian
Awar
Nubia
Mangai
Dongon
Goinbang
Makarup
Tiap
Tongbur
Pir
Moap
Bonaputa
Yambiyambi
Wangor
Dongwanam
Ariangong
Wasamb
Ni'out
Ruonganan
Riknang'tien
Barien
Wanar
Rurunat
Korak
Tavultae
Bingo
Tokain
Mindivi
Tsumba
Nagrabu
Pakingabu
Bamfu
Pondoma
Angasa
Kisila
Katiati
Wabriatau
Wanuma
Magila
Sengrusengru
Komiarum
Kosilanta
Ikarinagra
Ilebeguma
Sabu
Nodabu
Baibu
Kragabu
Watubu
Annaberg
Moibu
Jitubu
Litibu

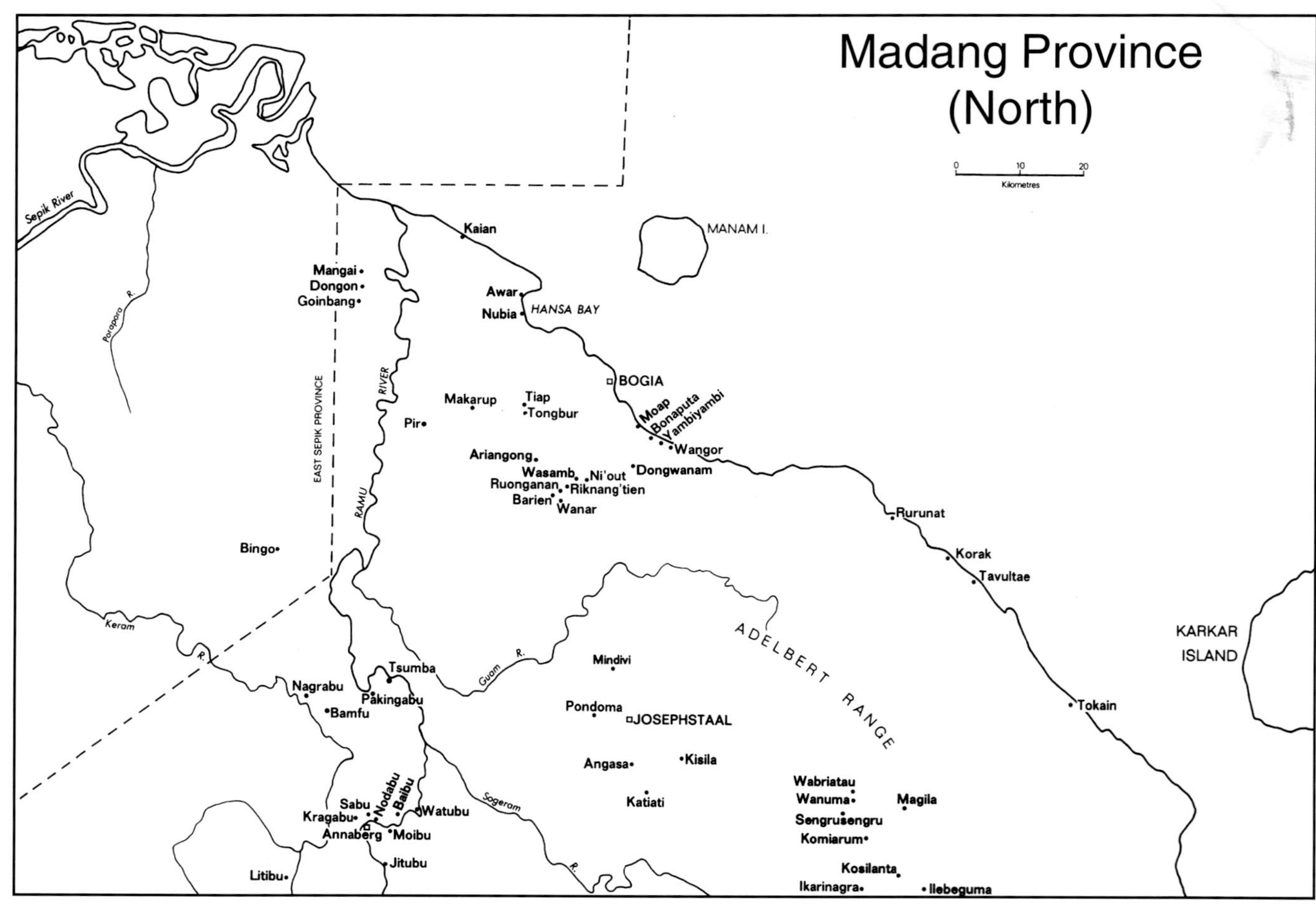

MAP 8

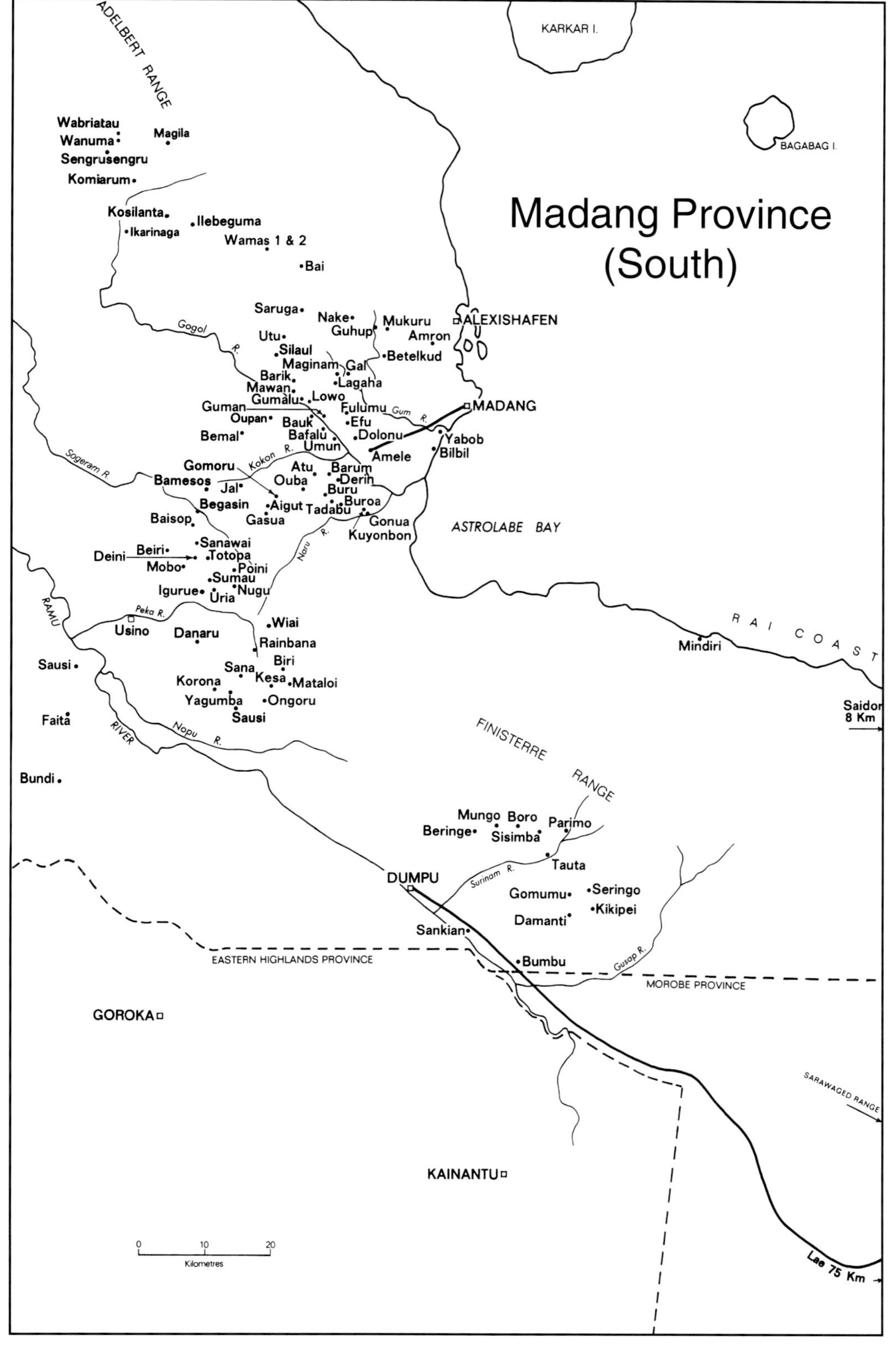

Madang Province
(South)
KARKAR I.
BAGABAG I.
ADELBERT RANGE
Wabriatau
Wanuma
Magila
Sengrusengru
Komiarum
Kosilanta
Ilebeguma
Ikarinaga
Wamas 1 & 2
Bai
Saruga
Nake
Guhup
Mukuru
ALEXISHAFEN
Amron
Utu
Silaul
Betelkud
Maginam
Gal
Barik
Lagaha
Mawan
Gumalu
Lowo
Guman
Fulumu
Gum R.
MADANG
Oupan
Bauk
Efu
Bemal
Bafalu
Dolonu
Yabob
Umun
Bilbil
Amele
Gogol R.
Sogeram R.
Kokon R.
Gomoru
Atu
Barum
Bamesos
Ouba
Derin
Jal
Buru
Begasin
Aigut
Buroa
Tadabu
Baisop
Gasua
Gonua
Kuyonbon
ASTROLABE BAY
Naru R.
Sanawai
Deini
Beiri
Totopa
Mobo
Poini
Sumau
Igurue
Nugu
Uria
RAMU
Peka R.
Usino
Wiai
Danaru
Rainbana
Sausi
Biri
Sana
Kesa
Mataloi
Korona
Yagumba
Ongoru
Sausi
Faita
RIVER
Nopu R.
Bundi
RAI COAST
Mindiri
Saidor 8 Km
FINISTERRE RANGE
Mungo
Boro
Parimo
Beringe
Sisimba
Tauta
DUMPU
Surinam R.
Gomumu
Seringo
Kikipei
Damanti
Sankian
Bumbu
Gusap R.
EASTERN HIGHLANDS PROVINCE
MOROBE PROVINCE
GOROKA
SARAWAGED RANGE
KAINANTU
0
10
20
Kilometres
Lae 75 Km

A wide range of pottery is made in Madang Province. On the coast women make spherical pots by the paddle-and-anvil technique and the inland men make coiled pots.

COASTAL POTTERY

Yabob and Bilbil are the best known coastal potting villages because of their proximity to Madang township; however, Mindiri (previously known as Mediseh or Medize), on the Rai coast across Astrolabe Bay from Madang, has the same tradition of pot making. All the people from these areas are Austronesian speakers.

North of Madang there are two more coastal groups of women pot makers, both non-Austronesians. Korak and Tavultae, the only two Korak-speaking villages, located within a few kilometres

Fig. 8.2
Trading boat in Astrolabe Bay, 1905.

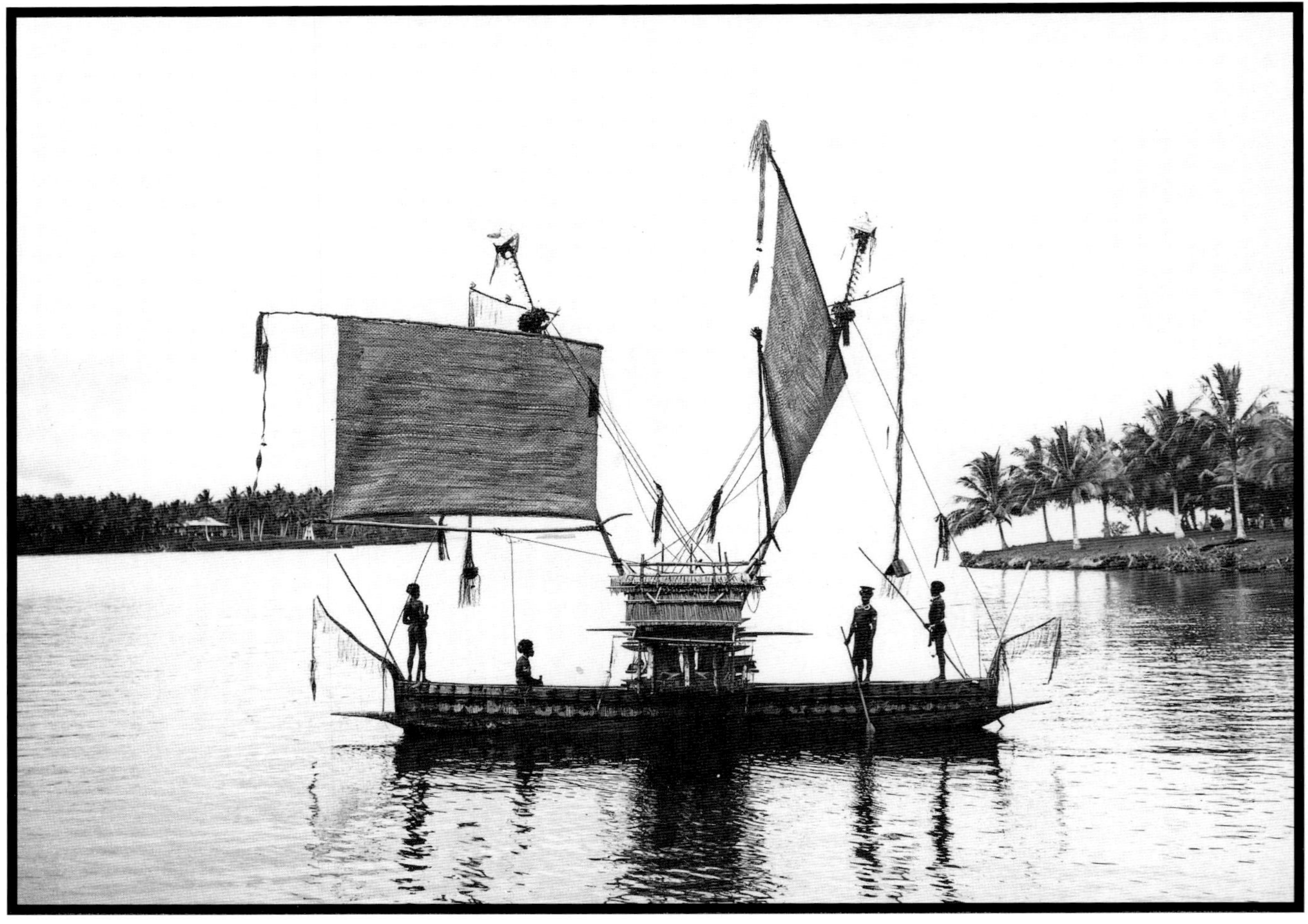

of each other, make pots similar in form to Yabob-Bilbil but they are much thicker, heavier and rougher. In contrast to these solid pots are the thin, quite delicate pots made by Pila-speaking women from four villages farther north, not far from Bogia.

Several early explorers and missionaries reported other villages on the coast north of Madang where pot making took place. Schurig (1930) mentions Matukar, about 35 kilometres north of Madang, Tukain (now Tokain) opposite the southern end of Karkar Island, Togain shown on Karkar Island on Schurig's map and Korat which appears to be the present-day Korak. The present people of Matukar are adamant that they have never been pot makers and the Tokain no longer make pots; no one knows of a Togain village on Karkar Island although some of the Tokain people speak the same language as the people of the southern half of Karkar and may have produced pots on the island in the past.

Yabob, Bilbil and Mindiri

Yabob is on the coast about 4 kilometres south of Madang and Bilbil is a further 41 kilometres south. In recent years Yabob people have been living in four different places; Yabob, on top of a cliff overlooking the sea: Morelan hamlet, on the water's edge below and a little closer to Madang township (often known as Yabob-down-below); a few on Yabob Island; and some in Yabob hamlet, on Jomba (or Moreg) Island.

The Yabob and Bilbil people hold the traditional pot making rights in the area; women who marry into another village may not make pots. Even in a village such as Siar, into which many Yabob and Bilbil women have married and where there are suitable clay deposits, pot making is taboo. Conversely, women who marry into Yabob-Bilbil may learn to make pots there.

Between 1871 and 1883 the young Russian scientist, Nikolai Mikloucho-Maclay, lived among the people of the southern coast of Astrolabe Bay, now known as the Maclay or Rai coast, and his diaries (Maclay 1975) contain many references to the pots traded and used in this area. By the early 1900s more records had been made of the Madang area by German anthropologists and missionaries (Finsch 1888, 1914; Krieger 1899; Hagen 1899: Neuhauss 1911; Werner 1911; Schafroth 1916; Dempwolff and Kunze 1926) and also by the Hungarian Biro (1901).

In these early years pot making mostly took place on Bilbil Island (at that time Bili Bili Island) but also on Yabob Island and, according to Finsch, on Jomba Island and Bilia Island (Eickstedt Island) in Madang harbour. Dempwolff mentions Gapen and four more unnamed villages which, it seems, were all on Bilbil. Clay had to be gathered from the nearby mainland where the pot makers had the rights to land. Before German annexation the Bilbil people had a dominant position among the coastal tribes but after 1884 their mainland area was taken over and they suffered various indignities. In 1904 a planned revolt was discovered; some of the ringleaders were shot, the people of Bilbil were banished to the mainland and their villages destroyed. According to Werner, some founded a new settlement at Bahor near the Gogol River. In 1907, after further problems, the remaining populations of Yabob and Bilbil and some of the islands were exiled to the Rai coast. It seems that there are no records of whether they made pots there but it is possible that these Bilbil people started the pot making of Mindiri; it was not reported by Maclay on the Rai coast during his time there up to 1883. After the outbreak of World War I the territory was occupied by the Australians and the Bilbil people were allowed to return to their ancestral islands where they continued their pot making.

As in most other pot making areas, the craft declined with the influx of European goods. However, during 1966-67 some impetus was given to it through the interest of a young teacher in Madang, Janetta Douglas (nee Smith). She encouraged the women to continue to make pots, assisted with marketing to surrounding villages and to Australia and organized visits to one of the Yabob villages, which stimulated a tourist trade in pottery. This created an income for the Yabob women, who had lost much of their original land through the growth of Madang township and were unable to grow surplus garden products to sell or trade.

In July 1967 a training centre at Yabob was started in a temporary workshop by an International Labour Organisation consultant, Jorgen Petersen.

Young men were trained to use kick wheels to produce a variety of European-style pots; the women were encouraged to continue with their traditional techniques and forms but were shown new methods for preparing clay and how to build and fire with a simple wood-fired kiln. Later, in response to the enthusiasm shown by the Bilbil people, another temporary workshop was built there. A few problems were encountered, mostly at Yabob: some of the women started to earn quite large incomes, larger than the wages of some of the men working in Madang, and this caused jealousies. On the whole, however, the higher-fired pots were in great demand and output and sales increased substantially. Apart from smaller pots made for tourists, the women confined themselves mostly to traditional cooking pots and later water pots with one, two, or three mouths. With the exception of the higher firings, the only other change made was, at Petersen's suggestion, the addition of three small knobs of clay on the rounded base of the pots to enable them to stand on a flat surface. Among those outsiders who were watching the project with interest opinions differed as to the wisdom of this change: the pots looked stiff and unnatural sitting upright and some observers felt that it would be preferable to supply rings made from some natural material, such as pandanus leaves, for those who wanted their pots to sit steady. After Petersen left, the output of hand-thrown ware dwindled although the women continued producing high standard pots, sometimes using the kilns and at other times firing in the traditional manner.

Mindiri, accessible from Madang only by boat, is situated on a small peninsula in Pommern Bay. The steep hillsides behind the village build up higher and higher into the towering mountains of the Finisterre Range. It is an isolated pottery centre; there are no reports of any other pot making activity along the coast of the Huon Peninsula until one reaches Sio Island and Gitua (now in Morobe Province) on the eastern end.

Mindiri is quite a small village but there are still about eight women who make pots and two or

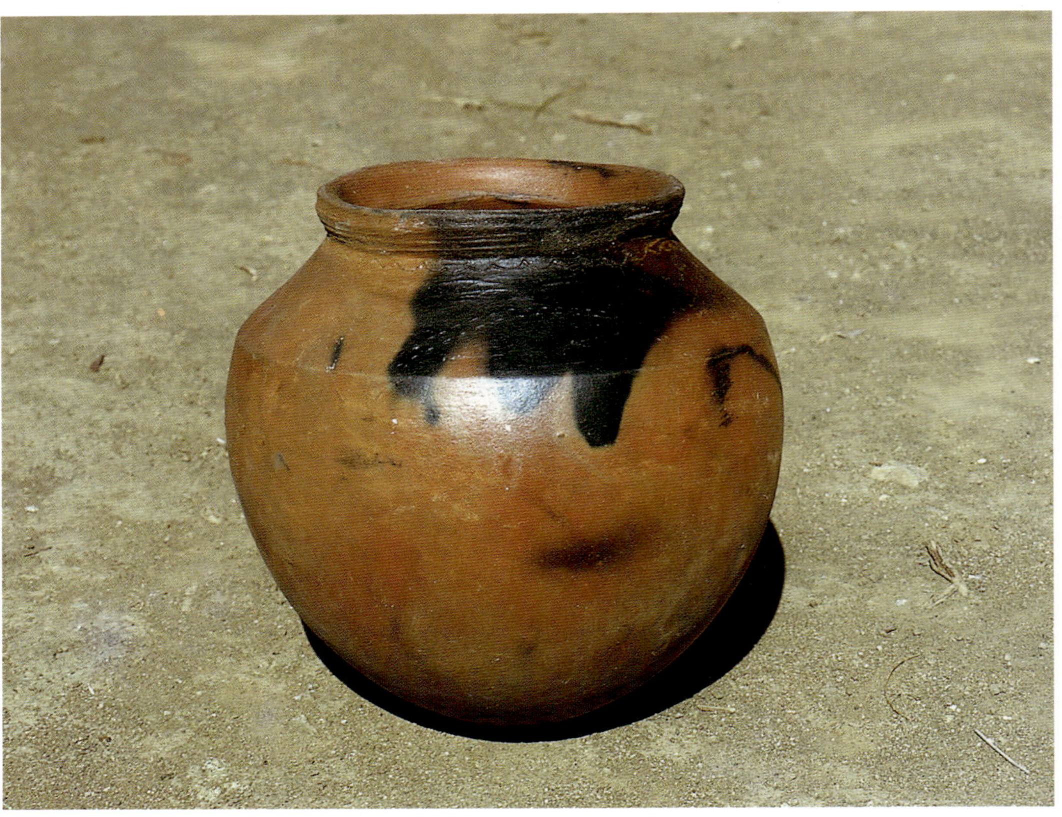

Fig. 8.3
Yabob cooking pot, *bodi*, traded to Amron village, near Alexishafen.

three younger ones are learning There are the same restrictions on pot making in the area as at Yabob-Bilbil. Quite recently, a Mindiri girl married a man of another Rai coast village and went to live there; she found good clay but was forbidden to make pots and the village people were told that they would never be able to get pots from Mindiri again if the embargo was broken.

Before German settlement, Yabob and Bilbil were part of a vast trading system, including places as far afield as the volcanic Manam Island north of Bogia and the Siassi Islands off the north coast of the Huon Peninsula in the Vitiaz Strait, about 300 kilometres from Madang. Yabob-Bilbil pots also found their way to New Britain through the Siassi Island traders.

The complex Vitiaz Strait trading system overlapped with that of the Rai coast. Harding (1967) has thoroughly described the trading of this whole area, including the Huon Peninsula around to Tami Island (see Chapter 6). Finsch (1914) reports that Yabob-Bilbil people carried their goods to Cape Rigney on the Rai coast but Maclay found that they travelled as far as Sio (at that time Sigawa Island) and Krieger claims they traded as far as Finschhafen although this is denied by present informants.

Each village had something particular to contribute: some provided outrigger canoes, grass skirts, wooden bowls, necklaces and other tribal regalia, drums, pigs, dogs, dogs' teeth, taro, yam and pots; others acted as distributing centres for inland trading routes. Certain coastal villages held the monopoly of bartering with specific inland villages but Krieger states that only the Bilbil people had won the privilege of bypassing the coastal middle-men in order to trade directly with mountain villagers of the Hansemann and Oertzen ranges, located directly behind the coast. During the north-west monsoons the Bilbil men set sail along the coast in their outrigger canoes to barter their pots. Finsch shows a drawing of a canoe under sail having a covered cabin formed of 'pangal' and with a row of pots on top. The same style of canoe was built by all the Vitiaz traders but the Yabob-Bilbil boats had the addition of a tall, elaborately carved S-shaped piece which was fastened to the prow boards. The boats always carried a large pot sherd full of smoking embers used for cooking food on the long journeys and water pots covered by lids of half coconut shells. It is said that a special clay lid, *awan*, was also used. In those days ten large cooking pots could be traded for one large canoe, and one pot purchased a wooden bowl from the mountain people behind the Rai coast, a grass skirt or a small pig.

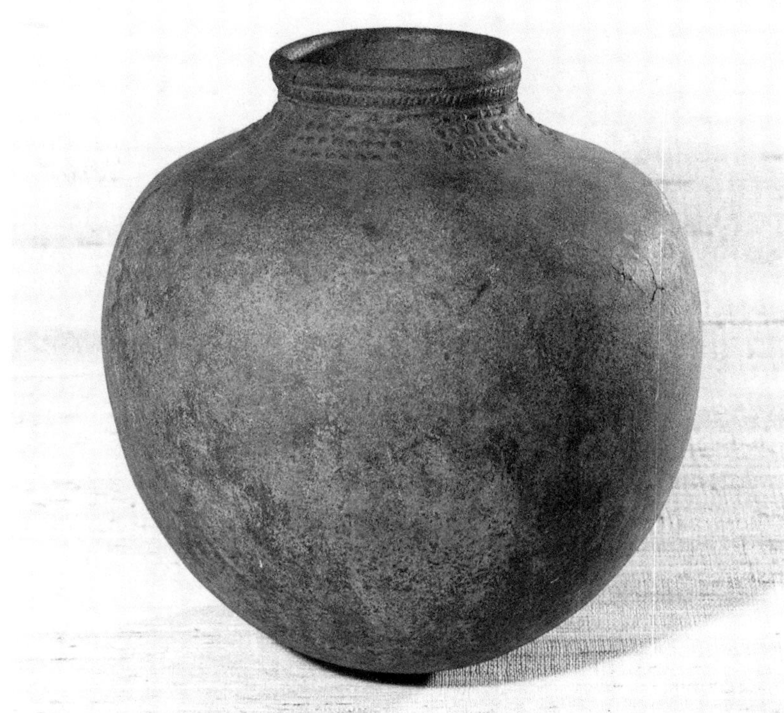

Fig. 8.4
Old water pot, collected by Mikloucho-Maclay in the 1870s.

The Bilbil people were renowned seafarers and fluent linguists, speaking many of the mainland languages. In fact, children were sent for prolonged stays in other villages to learn as many languages as possible for use in trading transactions. The Mindiri were also active traders. They seem to have held the monopoly on the sale of pots at one stage, and probably acquired it during the period of Bilbil's banishment. A story is told by Douglas (1967) of how the Yabob people were jealous of this and planned to put a stop to it they invited the Mindiri people to their village for a feast then massacred the visitors while they slept. The survivors back in Mindiri continued to make pots but were only allowed to trade with villages close by. Some antagonism remains and the Mindiri still only trade with nearby coastal villages and with mountain people

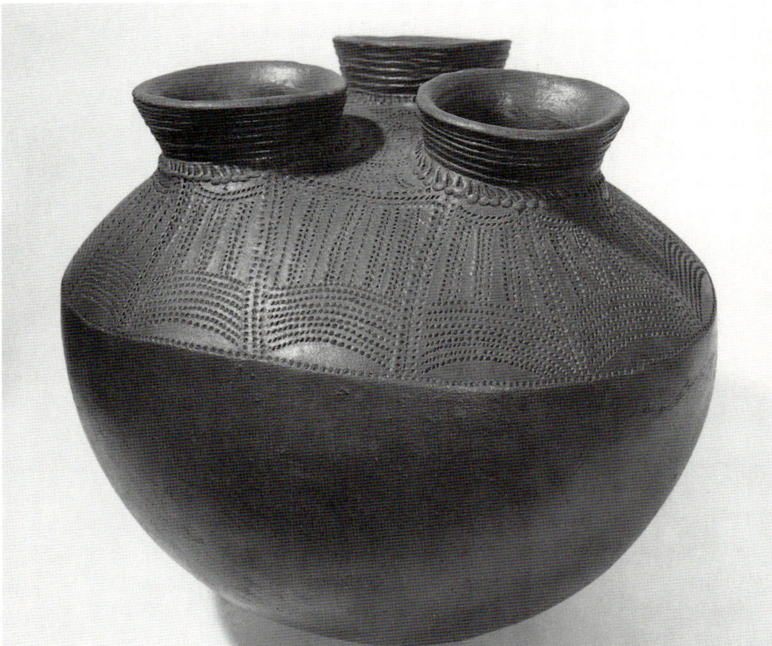

Fig. 8.5

Fig. 8.5
Three-mouthed water pot made by Liton Pilu, Yabob village, *h* 28cm.

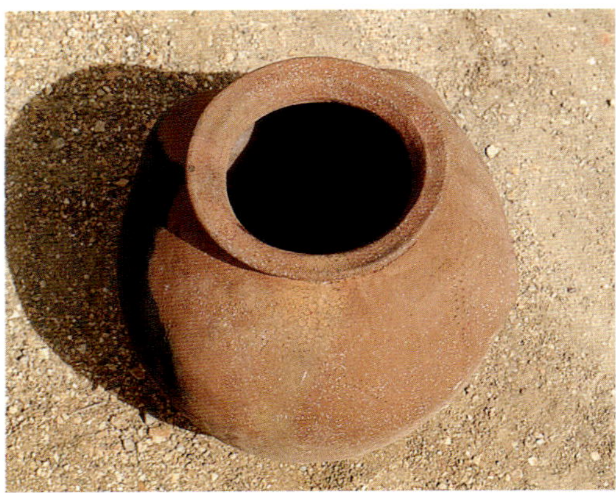

Fig. 8.6

Fig. 8.6
Mindiri cooking pot with four bulges in the upper body, *bornda, h* 25 cm.

who mostly come to Mindiri to get the pots they need. Villagers in the Finisterre Range make wooden bowls and trade these, betel nuts, tobacco and bows for pots and shells.

With the increased availability of European utensils and the disruption of traditional trading systems, the sea-wide distribution of pots has ceased, although Yabob-Bilbil pots are still traded up the coast as far as Matukar and inland into the mountain regions. Maclay writes of the many feasts he attended and describes one at the village of Gorendu.

> The other side of the area was occupied by two rows of logs placed parallel. On these were placed large pots a foot to a foot and a half in diameter. I counted 39 such pots. In addition there were five pots of even greater capacity also standing on two logs in which the 'buam' (sago) was boiled. [Maclay 1975: 124-25]

He tells also of two villages near Alexishafen whose inhabitants were cannibals and from whom he enquired about special utensils for cooking human flesh. The answer was that ordinary pots were used and it was served in the usual wooden bowls.

The typical Yabob-Bilbil pots are distinct from other paddle-and-anvil pots in that they have a sharp corner point at the shoulder, are composite in contour and redder in colour. Mindiri pots are very similar to those of Yabob-Bilbil but they are heavier and the clay is coarser in texture. Also, many of them have unusual rounded swellings around the shoulder. The Yabob-Bilbil made this type of pot in the past (Finsch 1911) but they are rarely made today. An example of an older form not made today can be seen in a vessel collected by Maclay in 1877, now at the Macleay Museum, Sydney University. The pot has a high round shoulder and applied nubbins decorating the neck area (figs 8.3, 8.4).

Fig. 8.7

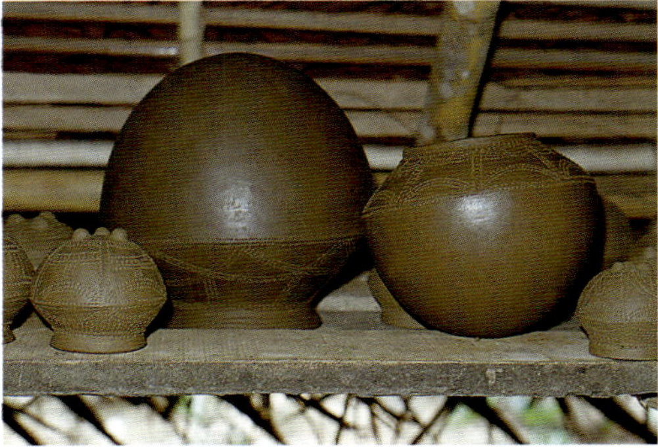

Fig. 8.7
Pots drying at Yabob. Pot without a neck is a *magob*; small pots with three knobs (feet) on the base are made for tourists.

Fig. 8.8

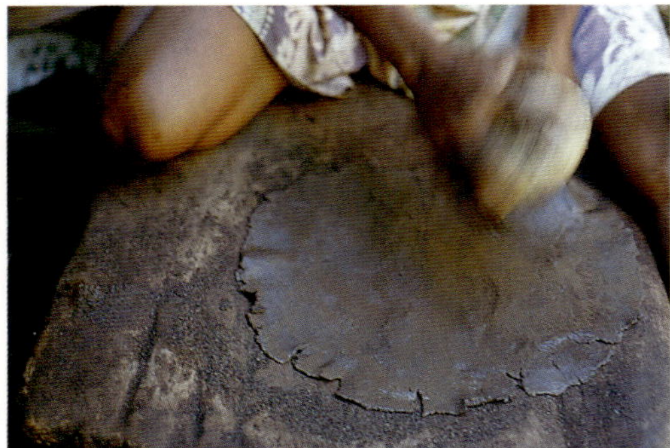

Fig. 8.8
Clay preparation at Mindiri village: pounding beach sand into the thin sheet of clay.

There have been changes in form and decoration over time but sherds collected by Brian Egloff in 1975 around Madang and outlying islands indicate a continuing tradition which is at least five hundred and fifty years old.

Four types of vessels are made at Yabob-Bilbil. Firstly, *bodi*, a common cooking pot about 30 centimetres high is a restricted composite vessel with a rounded base, spherical belly and a corner point forming a sharp-angled shoulder. The neck is short, the everted rim is slightly thicker than the walls of the pot and has three or four ridges underneath it on the outside and a definite ridge on the inside. A variation of the *bodi*, called *daum*, has Mindiri-style bulges. Secondly, *yu-bodi*, a water storage and carrying vessel, is shaped like the *bodi* but is taller and narrower and has a smaller mouth. Some examples have sharp corner points while others are more rounded. A variation has two necks and is perhaps derived from the two-necked vessels of the Admiralty Islands. Traditionally, a water pot is owned and used by a particular person. Petersen introduced a three-necked vessel and it has been suggested that the three necks are for use by grandfather, father and son. Thirdly, *magob*, a sago cooking and storage pot, is a restricted vessel, round-based and with a sharp-angled corner point and shoulder and a large mouth. The rim is slightly thickened. Cooking pots with broken rims can be cut down to become *magob*. A recent innovation in the traditional *magob* is the addition of three feet to the base and holes in the bottom; this is designed for tourists and is intended for use as a flower pot. The fourth type of vessel, infrequently produced, is the *bodi palan*, a round-based sago frying bowl. It is made by reshaping (cutting down) a broken *bodi* or *magob*.

The Mindiri range of vessels is almost identical to that of Yabob-Bilbil. The cooking pot, called *bornda*, is similar to the *bodi* but generally lacks the sharp-angled shoulder. Characteristic of the *bornda* are the bulges located below the shoulder and running around the widest portion of the vessel. It was explained at Mindiri that the bulges, used as a form of decoration, were inspired by a four-cornered jungle fruit, *gabar*, and that this name is given to the decoration. Sometimes the pot itself is called *gabar*. Mindiri traditionally made water pots, *badin*, but they have not been made since World War II. Their form was identical to the Yabob-Bilbil *yu-bodi*. They also manufacture the sago cooking pot, *magob*.

Yabob has two sorts of clay: a reddish-brown clay is gathered from a pit located about fifteen minutes' walk inland; a darker one comes from a swamp farther away. Women usually collect clay in groups of eight or more; they work it into large balls and carry it back to the village. The Mindiri pit is located about 1 kilometre south-east of the village. About 20 centimetres of black soil is first removed

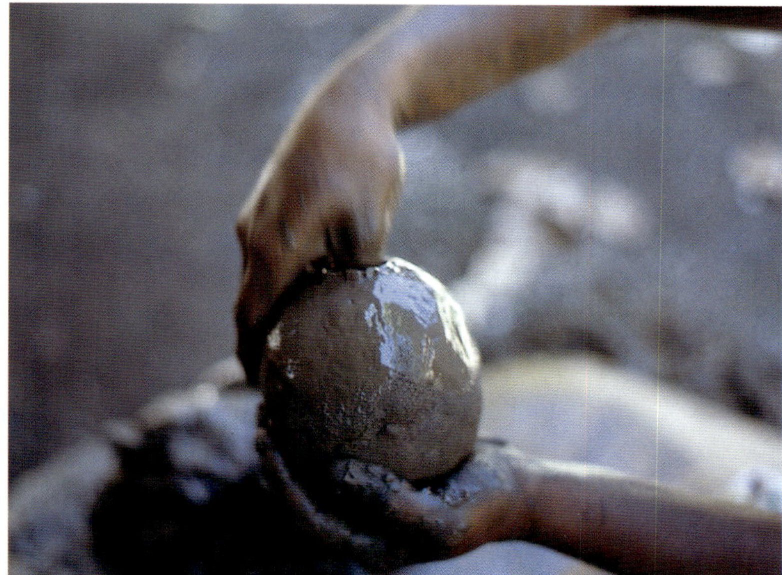

Fig. 8.9
Forming a hole in the centre of a ball of clay, Mindiri.

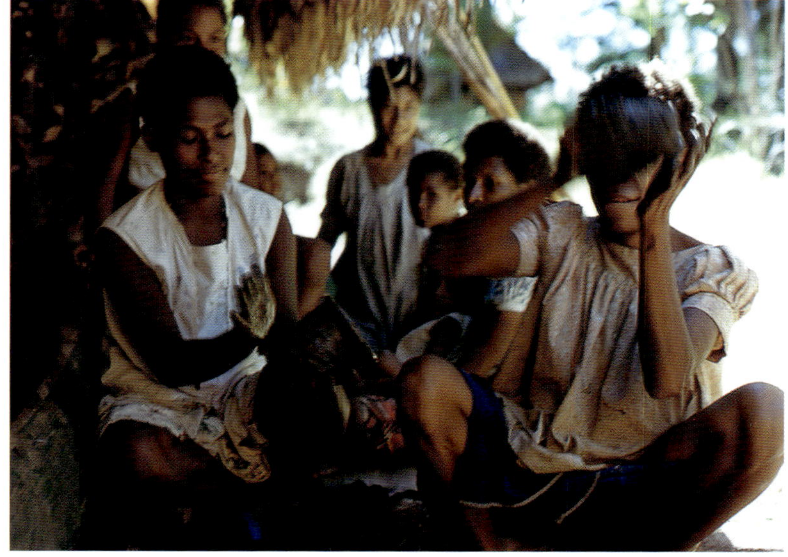

Fig. 8.10
Murupen (left) adding clay to partly formed pot. Elizabeth (right) spinning the ball to form the hole in the centre with her thumb, Mindiri.

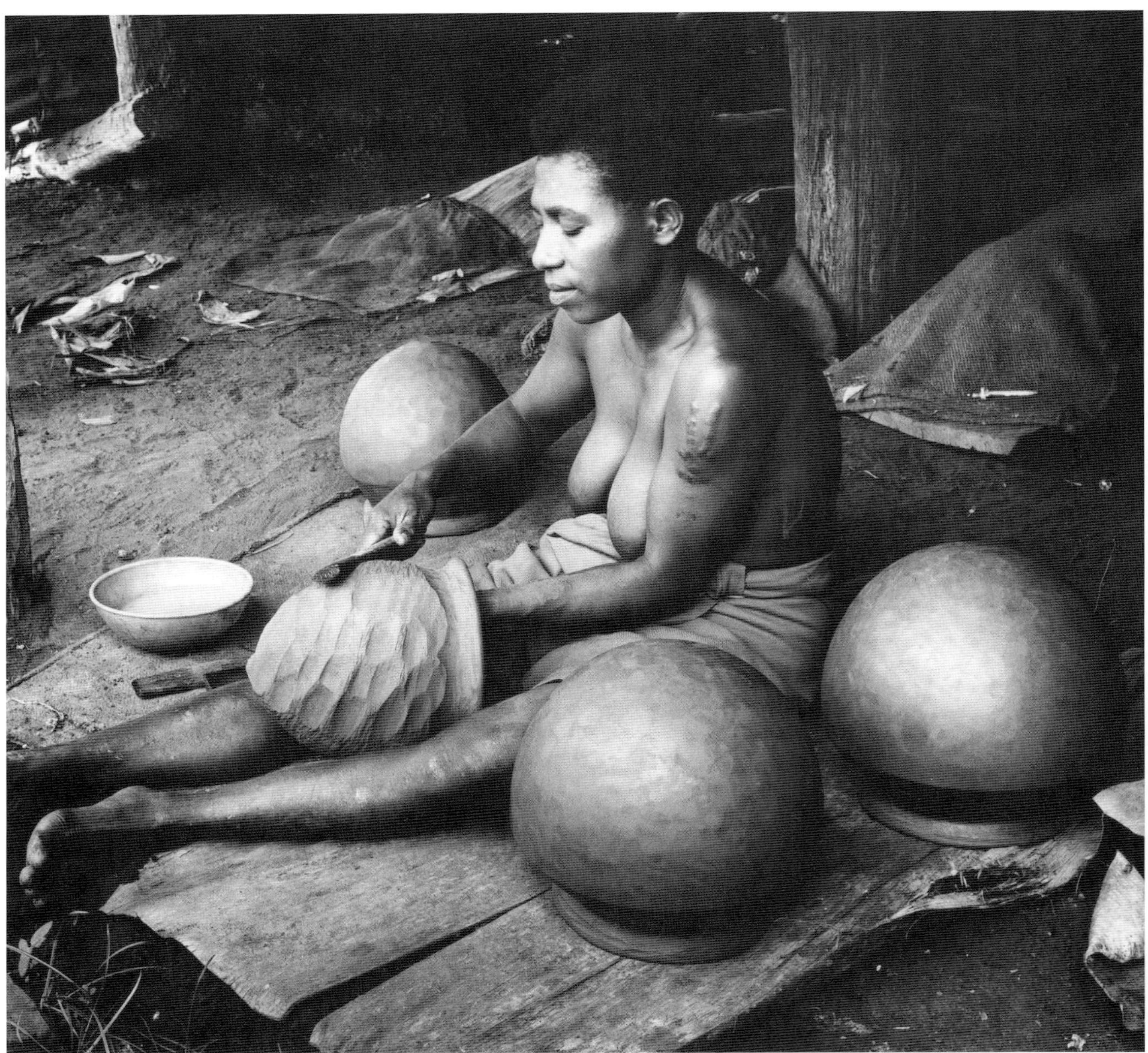

Fig. 8.11
Gensemy beating with the narrow beater at an early stage of forming, Yabob village.

from the top before the hard black clay is excavated. It is a compact smectite clay and tradition calls for people to be ceremonially marked on the face with it if they are visiting the pit for the first time.

Yabob clay is stored under the houses and kept moist with damp bags. Clay preparation used to be the same at all three villages and took place in three stages. At Mindiri the same procedure is still followed and a traditional board, *kambau*, is used. Initially, beach sand is sprinkled on the board and the clay, which has been softened in water (fresh water at Yabob, salt water at Mindiri), is pounded on it until it is almost paper thin. More sand is added during this process. The sheets of clay are then soaked until they are soft enough to be squeezed through the fingers. Any uncrushed grit is discarded. The clay is drained on piles of sand, usually under the house (fig. 8.8).

After the black and white beach sand has been added to the Mindiri clay it is a black brown colour with white specks from the sand's shell grit content; these are clearly visible after firing. The 35 per cent non-plastic content of the clay from the swamp changes to 62 per cent after the sand addition. The remaining non-plastic portion of the clay body is quartz, magnetite, haematite and a trace of brown zircon. The clay mineral is smectite. The Bilbil clay body is very plastic and is grey yellowish-brown. It has a low smectite content, high quartz and some feldspar.

Finally, the potter kneads the clay and extracts small stones with her teeth. Since the International Labour Organisation project, Yabob and Bilbil potters have dispensed with the pounding stage and now soak the clay in drums then sieve it into another drum through wooden-framed wire sieves. Excess water is ladled off after the clay settles and the sloppy mass is put out onto piles of sand to drain. Some Yabob clay body collected after this sieving showed no gravel and few coarse sand-sized particles but plenty of fine sand. It is certainly finer than most of the unsieved clays.

There are three types of tools used at Yabob-Bilbil-Mindiri: anvils, paddles and decorating tools. The anvils are smooth round river stones called *piti* (at Mindiri they are called *pot*). These stones are believed to possess magical properties that drive out the evil spirits from the clay and are prized possessions handed down by the women to their daughters-in-law after they have been initiated into pot making. Yabob-Bilbil have three kinds of paddles: *darib* has a rough, naturally ridged surface, *hohoi* is narrow and very smooth and *dardral* is wider, flat and smooth. Mindiri uses four kinds of paddles: *trsenieng* is a ridged narrow piece of wild palm tree, *tabalbalieng* is a narrow beater, *pallatieng* is another ridged beater and *talunieng* is a smooth flat beater. Small tools for decorating and making the ridges under the rims of the pots are made from black palm, split bamboo or stems of grass. They are shaped to a fine point for incising and are rounded for ridge making.

The prepared clay is patted into a large egg-shaped lump. The top is carefully moistened and smoothed and the right thumb is plunged into the centre. The lump is skilfully spun around anticlockwise in the palm of the hand until an opening has been formed. The fingers of the right hand are now held inside the hole and the thumb and forefinger overlap onto the outside while it is moved more slowly and deliberately in a clockwise direction. The hole widens and the flange of the top of the pot is formed by the extended forefinger running firmly underneath its edge. The opening becomes shallower as well as wider and finally there is a smooth symmetrical rim on top of the lump of clay. With the exception of Motu pots, the appearance at this stage is entirely different from that of any other paddle-and-anvil form (figs 8.9, 8.10).

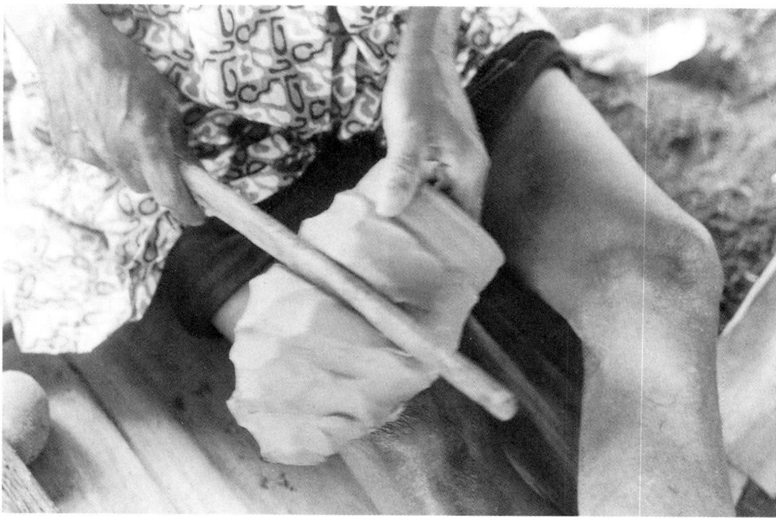

Fig. 8.12
Lalo making a water pot, Yabob village.

Any hollows or cracks on the top are plugged up with clay and more clay is patted onto the outside of the pot. There seems to be a limit to the amount of clay the potter can manage for the spinning stage: if a large pot is to be made the necessary amount must be added at this stage so the whole firms up to a uniform consistency for the next stage. If a particularly large pot is planned this rimmed lump is put down into a soft, roughly hollowed out ball on the potter's working board and joined to it with the fingers. Several pots will be made to this stage and then put aside under the house from two to five days until they are quite firm.

Next, the potter supports the pot across one thigh and with a round smooth stone she taps the centre top of the pot, gradually hitting more firmly as a hole opens up until eventually she throws the stone into the opening to make it deeper. When

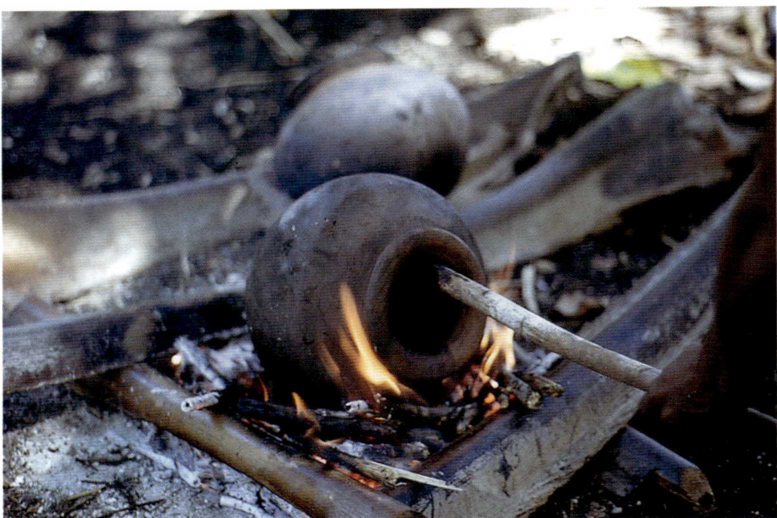

Fig. 8.13
Preheating ready for firing, Mindiri village.

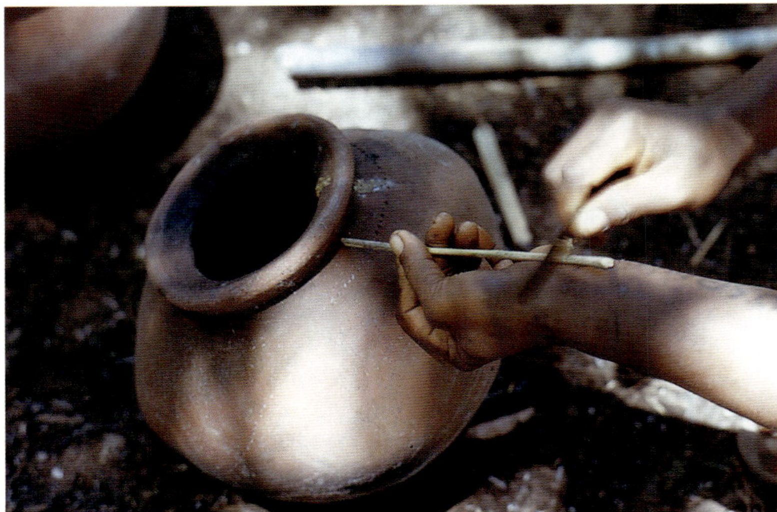

Fig. 8.14
Scraping the bark off a twig to make *dim* to fill cracks in the fired pots, Mindiri.

the hole is large enough to contain a hand holding a stone the normal paddle-and-anvil process begins, commencing with a ridged beater. All the beating is carried out with the pot supported in the potter's lap and at several stages the pot is put aside to become firmer before the final smoothing with the wide paddle (figs 8.11, 8.21). The rounded swellings on Mindiri pots are formed by leaving thicker clay in this area and by pressing the stone more firmly inside while beating around it. Biro and Kunze recorded the use of a small coconut instead of a round stone for opening out the pot.

The *magob* is formed without the spun neck from balls of clay stiffened overnight. The top of the ball is thumped open with a stone until the normal beating process can complete it. The top edge is trimmed level with a knife and the rim gently beaten into shape with a paddle. A different method is used to form a water pot. On a lump of clay longer than that used for a cooking pot a small rim is spun and put aside to get firmer. Next, all the clay below the rim is beaten with the narrow stick to compact it. Then the potter, beating with the sharper edge of this stick, separates the neck from the rest of the pot (fig. 8.12). The bottom part is widened into a shallow bowl shape; the neck piece is opened up by tapping with the stone from underneath the neck (this is necessary because the neck of the water pot is too narrow to be opened from the top). When the stone has formed an opening right through, the inside of the neck is trimmed with a sharp stick. The two pieces are joined by using the fingers to drag the clay down from the top half to the bottom. The neck is now just wide enough to allow a hand containing a stone to enter while the paddle-and-anvil process is used to finish the pot. The two and three-mouthed water pots are made by forming several necks, each on its own piece of clay; these are cut off and left to firm before they are joined to a pot which already has one neck.

The characteristic ridges under the rim, known as *bili*, are formed by pressing the decorating tool against the neck while turning the pot around. Small raised parts are also made by pushing up bits of nicked clay with quick movements of the wrist while the pot is slowly turned. Sometimes small marks are impressed around the neck with the end of a small piece of curved bamboo. Simple designs are nicked into the shoulder area.

Completed pots are stored under the house until they have turned a yellowish colour or, in the case of the black clay, until it is a dull grey. Then they are dried in the sun for a time before a clay slip, *mein*, is applied. This is made from a dark yellow fine-grained clay which is soaked in water, stirred, applied to the pot with a piece of fibrous coconut husk, rubbed all over the outside with a circular motion and finally spread and smoothed with the potter's hands. The inside of the rim and neck are also slipped. It fires a redder colour than the clay of the pot and helps seal the surface. The slip must be dried in the sun for about three hours before the pot can be fired. At Mindiri the slip is made from a reddish-orange clay and before firing the pots are always left on a rack over the house fire for about a month after the slip is applied.

Pots are preheated on a small fire made from bits of wood and coconut fronds. They are turned constantly with a long stick and become covered with black soot, indicating a temperature below 600°C. A bigger fire is carefully constructed by placing four rocks at the corners of a square about 1 to 2 metres in size; dry coconut ribs are placed in a square on the rocks and split bush timber pieces up to about 1 metre long are put inside the square, leaning on the cross members, sloping inwards and meeting in the middle of the square. More fuel is put in the centre and coconut leaves and fronds are put under the cross members. Up to twenty-four of the warm pots are placed in the middle and burning ingots are used to light the coconut leaves, which burn rapidly. Large bundles of grass are criss-crossed over the pots. No more fuel is added during the firing. After about fifteen minutes the potter makes a careful inspection; if she sees large areas of black marks on any of the pots she turns them over with a stick. After twenty-five to thirty minutes the fire dies down and the pots, which are covered with a thick layer of ash, are removed and allowed to cool before being wiped all over with a sago solution. The colour of the fired Mindiri pots is a grey reddish-brown and there is a tendency for small cracks to appear on the surface. The Yabob pots are a reddish-orange colour. Water pots are treated with an additional sealer called *dim* or *dimi* in the Bilbil language. *Dim* is also used as a caulking compound in the construction of the trading boats and is a sticky milky substance that comes from the bark of a huge tree (*Glochieden* sp). The water pots are left in the sun until this sealer dries. Traditionally, before a cooking pot can be used it must be covered with the blood of a pig. The repair of the cracked rim of a pot, hot from firing, was observed at Mindiri. A substance similar to *dim* was applied to the crack with a knife and then pushed well in with the fingers. The Mindiri potters call this substance *blabil*: it is probably from the same tree as *dim*.

A most interesting comparison of techniques can be made between Yabob-Bilbil and Orelan village of East Timor, the latter method having been recorded by Ian Glover (1968) during archaeological field work. At Orelan the opening is first produced by pounding a wet coconut shell into the pug of clay. Following this, the same method of forming the rim is employed: the pot is rapidly turned in the left hand while the thumb and fingers of the wet right hand produce the everted rim. Here also a clay slip is applied to the leather-hard pots. None of these processes has been found elsewhere in Melanesia.

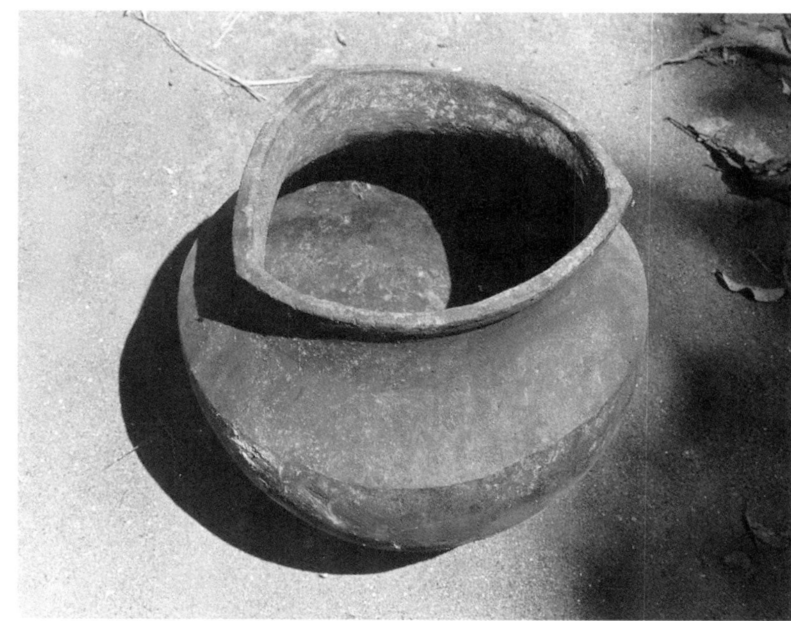

Fig. 8.15
Cooking pot with a three-cornered rim, *komnam*, Korak village, *h* 30 cm.

Douglas (1970) has collected some legends from the Yabob and Bilbil people concerning the origins of pot making and rituals related to pottery.

> A Yabob islander named Burag looked up one night from the beach and saw not ordinary stars but the eyes of the proud star maidens who lived in the sky. He wished he could marry one of them. A little bird, 'Kidi Kendi', who was perched on the prow of a canoe, agreed to fly up and bring one back for him. And so Honpain arrived but Burag was terrified because she was so beautiful and had such light coloured skin and many necklaces and seeds attached to her skirt which tinkled when she walked. He was afraid the villagers might want to kill her so he hid her in his father's attic. Many days went by before his father heard the jangle of Honpain's jewellery and found her. The father decided to prepare an

enormous feast before telling the Yabob people, and when it was ready he called them all on the 'garamut' and told them they must look after Honpain and make her happy. Honpain and Burag were then guests of honour at the feast and later were married and had a son called Talo.

Honpain quickly learnt the ways of the other village women and in return taught them how to make and fire clay pots which they could use for cooking or carrying water.

When her son was about six years old the other children started teasing him, saying he was not really a Yabob boy and that his ancestors lived up in the sky. Honpain became more and more despondent as she and her son were virtually ostracised by the villagers.

One morning Honpain gathered all the clay pots she had drying under her house and put them beside piles of wood and grass. When the sun was high in the sky she stacked the wood and her pots and lit a giant fire in the centre of the village. When she placed the green grass on the fire a blanket of smoke enveloped the entire village and into this climbed Honpain with her child clinging tightly to her back. Burag's father tried to persuade her to come back but she replied that she was going back to her father. Burag was called but it was too late, she had climbed up a rope which had been lowered down from the sky by her father; Burag shook the rope and called to her to come back but the rope suddenly fell back into the fire breaking all the pots except one, which was a two-mouthed water pot.

Today the Yabob women can still show visitors the beach on Yabob Island where this story took place and the pot sherds on the site where Honpain

Fig. 8.16
Cooking pot with a three-cornered rim, *komnan*. Testing heat of pot ready to seal it with coconut milk and vegetables, Tavultae village.

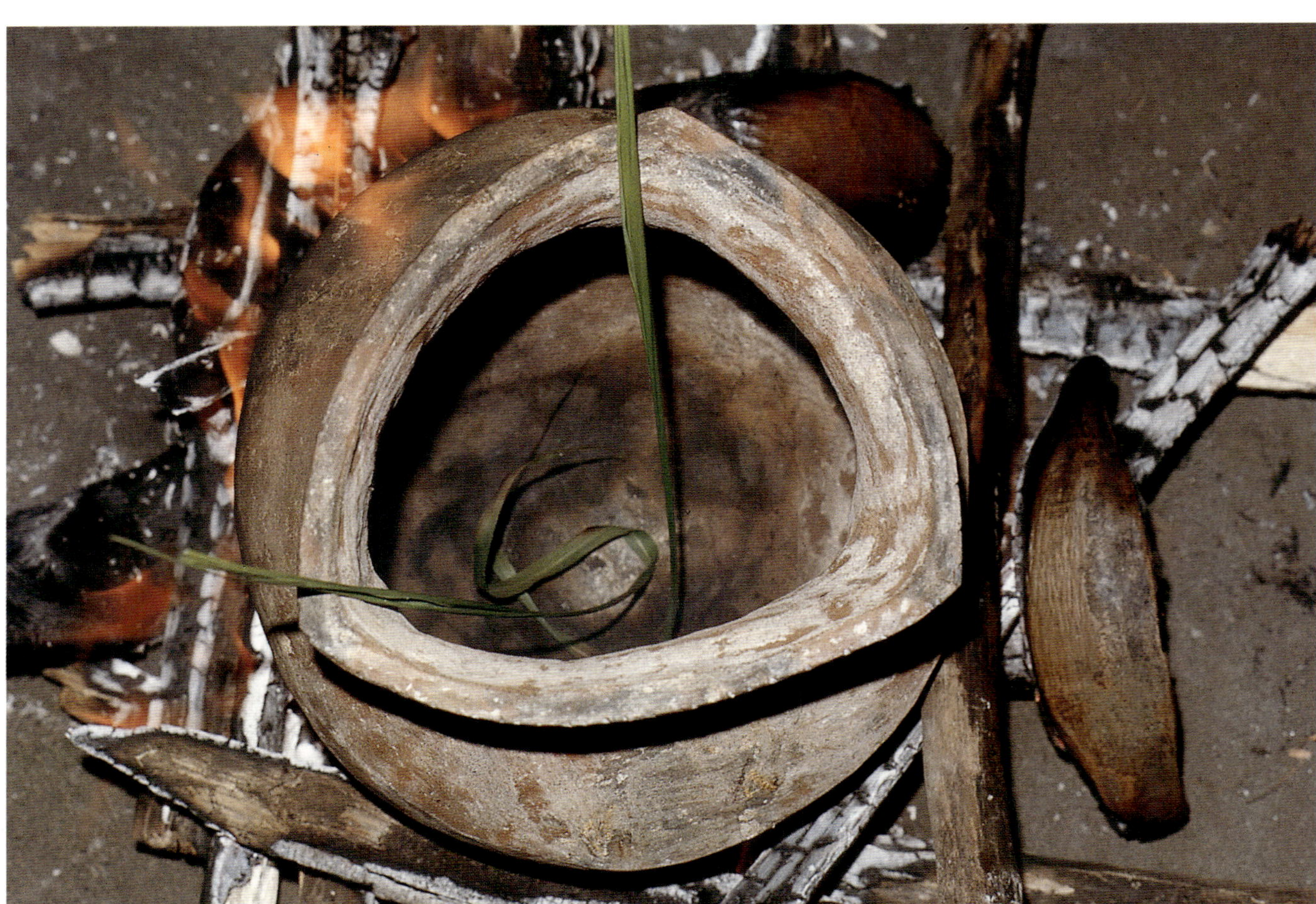

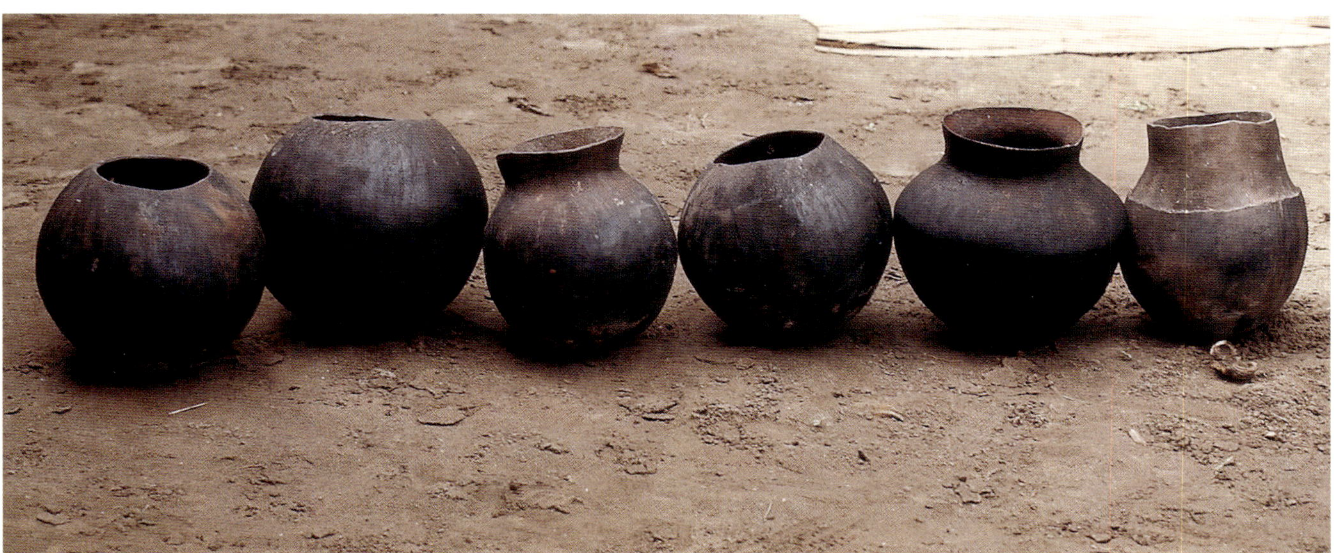

Fig. 8.17
Six Pila cooking pots showing variation of form, Moap village.

lit her last fire. The Yabob women potters still cling to some of the traditions developed from this legend; pots must never be made after the sun goes down behind the trees and breaking a pot after dark is the same as hitting the head of Honpain.

A Bilbil legend retold by Douglas is the story of Ninggur.

> Once upon a time a man named Ada, his wife Liliki and their daughter Sion arrived on Bilbil Island where they found good clay for making pots.
>
> Sion had two sons called Ninggur and Taimbur whose jobs were to barter their mother's cooking pots for food. Although Ninggur was able to carry many pots without breaking them and sell them to surrounding villages, Taimbur was only able to sell half the number and broke many; he couldn't understand why Ninggur could sell so many more pots so he offered to buy Ninggur's secret of success in exchange for some yam. This made Ninggur very angry. The two argued and Ninggur is said to have sailed away, taking all the clay of the island with him. Before he left he told Taimbur he would not go far away and that the people of Bilbil would be able to see him on a cloudless day. The Bilbil villagers were angry that Ninggur had gone, because he was a rich man and because he had taken their clay from them.
>
> Eventually they found good clay on the mainland near where their village is today and continued to make pots. The true Bilbil pots are said to have a more pointed base than Yabob's and are sometimes known as Ninggur pots, but they are made the same way as Yabob or Honpain pots. Ninggur lives, they say, on the bald mountain like an upturned cooking pot – clearly visible from Bilbil on a clear day – and has changed his name to Gurgur.

Korak

Continuing north-west from Yabob village, about half way between Madang and Bogia on the coast opposite the northern end of Karkar Island, are two villages where pots are produced on a small scale. The people of these two villages, Korak and Tavultae, speak a non-Austronesian language, Korak

The potters here are women and the technique is paddle-and-anvil but pot making is dying out quickly. Only a few of the older women can still pot and the standard of workmanship and decoration has deteriorated. Cooking pots, *komnam* alone are made. Water was gathered and stored in bamboo tubes, coconut shells and gourds. The industry appears to be, and perhaps has always been, fairly localised. Neighbouring villages will occasionally request some pots when needed but there is no evidence of trading in pots although the authors have seen Korak vessels to the south at Tokain.

In form the cooking vessels are related to those from Yabob-Bilbil. They are restricted, spherical bodies with a definite corner point between the

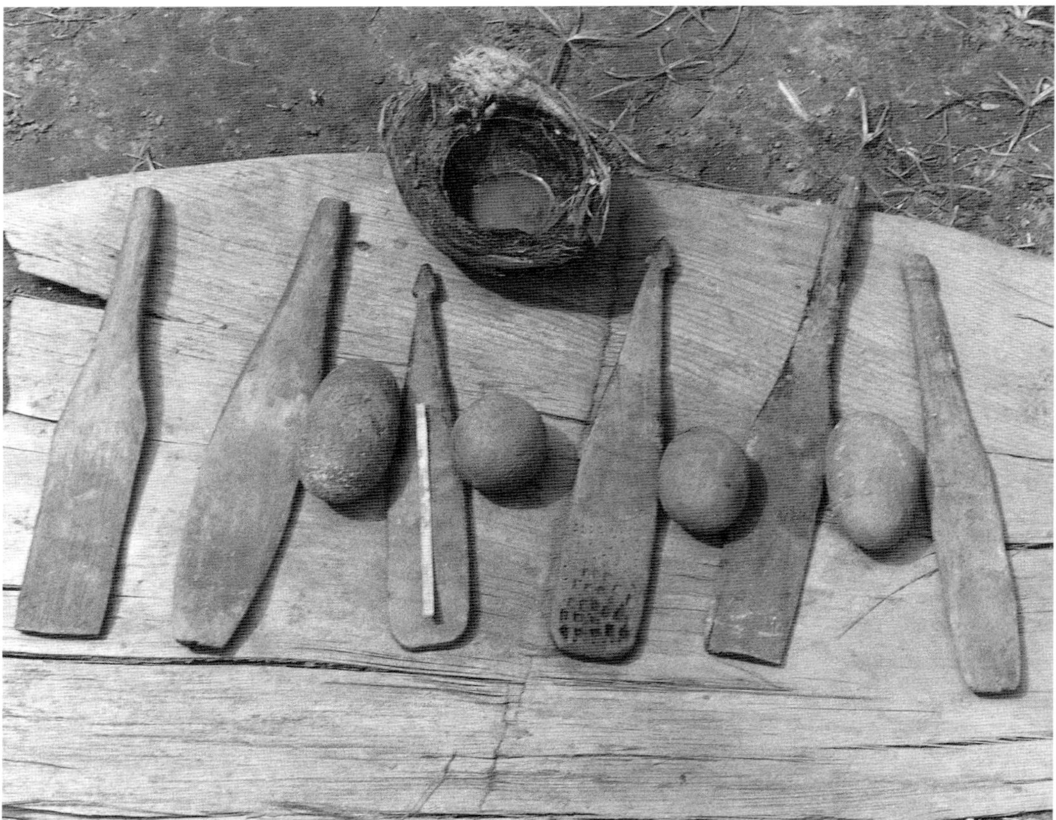

Fig. 8.18
Pila potter's tools, Moap village.

Fig. 8.19
Damwanai beating with a carved paddle which leaves a raised pattern, Moap.

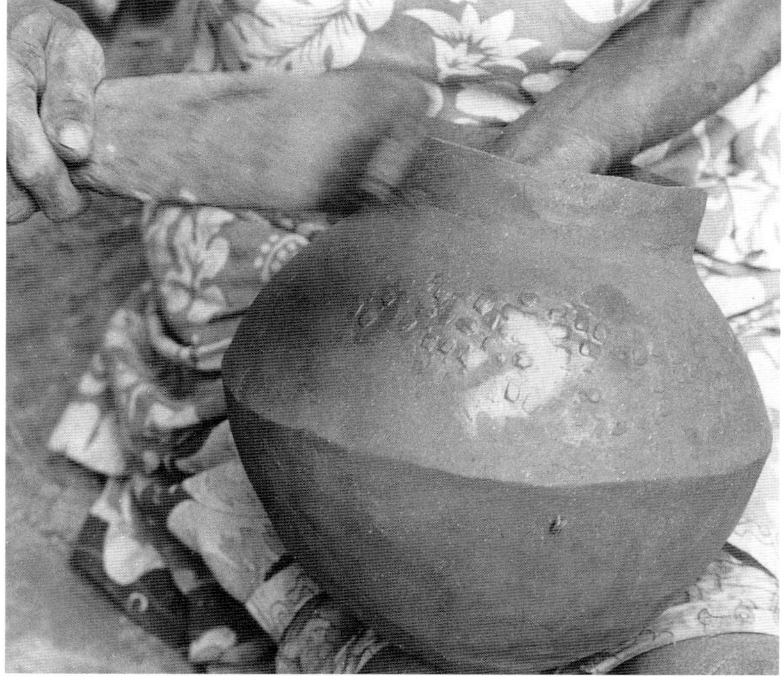

belly and the shoulder. The necks are everted and have a thick rim. In recent years, a variation on the shape of the rim and the mouth has evolved. The general shape of the vessel remains the same but the mouth has a triangular shape and each side of the triangle is slightly convex on the outside of the rim. The vessels are usually about 25 centimetres high although formerly enormous pots large enough to hold about 18 litres, were made. Some of the older vessels in the villages are of handsome form and proportion but all are thick and heavy in comparison with the Yabob-Bilbil pots (fig. 1.5).

The clay source at Tavultae is about 1 kilometre inland, across the coastal road in a jungle area near one of the gardens. The Korak clay is located about an hour-and-a-half's walk from the village and the four or five women here who know how to make pots say they are too old to carry the clay from its source. Like the cooking pots, the clay is called *komnam*. It is yellowish-brownish-grey and free of grit and coarse sand particles. It is prepared on a sheet of 'limbum'; black sand is added and salt water is sprinkled on the mixture, which is kneaded first with the feet and later by hand. It has excellent plasticity.

A lump of clay is patted into a round ball which is pounded open with the end of a long stone called *mandung*. (The only other potters using this method of opening a ball of clay are the women of the Moap villages north of Korak, the women of the Kaiep group near Wewak and those of Yabob-Bilbil-Mindiri who use this method for their neckless pots, *magob*. These three groups of potters are not separated by any other coastal potters but other aspects of their techniques are different and the forms of their pots are dissimilar. When the opening is large enough the round stone, also called *mandung*, is held inside with one hand while the narrow wooden beater, *aus*, is used on the outside. While she beats it the pot is supported by the woman's feet and she is very adept at manoeuvring the pot with them. Final beating is carried out with the wider beater, also called *aus*, and the shape of the neck is achieved by beating it with the narrower of the two paddles.

The pot can be treated with a sealing solution any time after it has been fired and has cooled. The outside is rubbed with a peeled green banana and this leaves an uneven whitish smear. The empty pot is put directly into the fire and tested by placing pieces of grass inside it. When they begin to scorch where they touch the bottom, the pot is ready for sealing. The grass is removed and coconut milk is added. When it sizzles more coconut milk, green vegetables, sweet potatoes, cooking bananas and taro are added: these may be eaten when cooked. This is one of the few areas where the cooking pot sits amongst the firewood with no supports; the thick heavy pot not unduly round-bottomed, remains steady enough.

Pila

There are four villages in the Pila group: Moap (Moapwiket), Bonaputa, Yambiyambi and Wangor, about 20 kilometres south of Bogia. None of these villages has been reported in early literature but Bonaputa was mentioned in Petersen's report although no details were given.

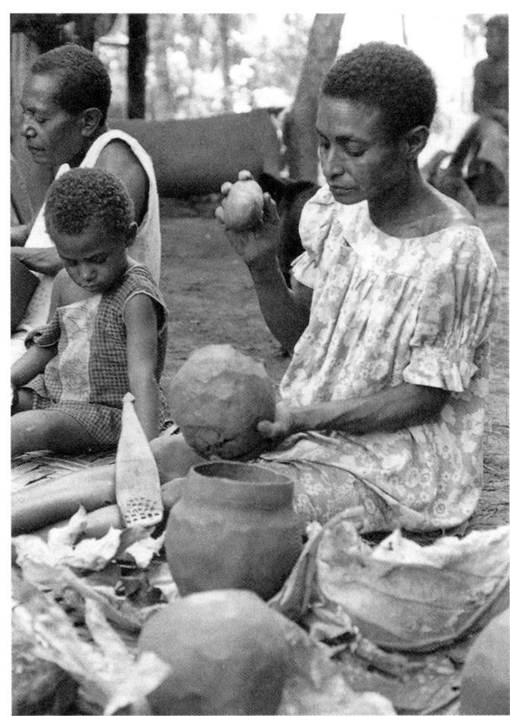

Fig. 8.20
Pila potter Raramai opening up a pot by pounding with a long stone, Moap.

Pot making is flourishing in all of these villages except Wangor. Nine women make pots at Moap, five at Yambiyambi and six at Bonaputa. Young women learn how to make pots but until after their child-bearing years they are only allowed to help with preparation. If they make a pot before this, it is believed it will break.

Cooking pots only are made and although the technique is very similar to that of Korak-Tavultae the pots have an entirely different character. They are thin, especially towards the rim, light and much freer in shape than any other paddle-and-anvil forms in Papua New Guinea. They are also less symmetrical. All are round-bottomed; some are spherical or ellipsoid with no neck; others are restricted with a rounded shoulder and neck; others are a little more the shape of a normal paddle-and-anvil pot with a shoulder still rounded, a neck and an everted direct rim. One pot observed had a curious ridge between the shoulder and neck formed by beating the clay from below upwards toward the neck and leaving it as a defined uneven line (fig. 8.17).

The general name for pots is *koamun*, very close to the Korak word. The two main variations are

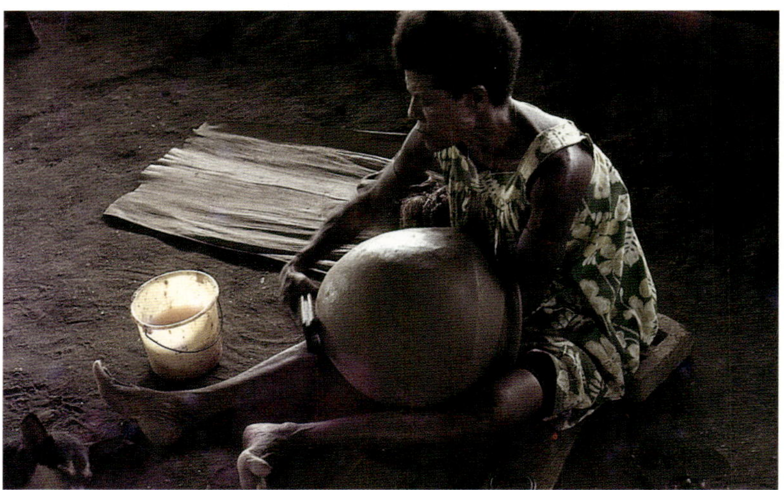

Fig. 8.21
Final beating of a cooking pot, Yabob village.

senai, a restricted round-based spherical or ellipsoid shape, either neck-less or having only a marginal neck; and *semanat*, spherical or ellipsoid with a shoulder and neck and everted rim. The general size of these cooking vessels is about 23 centimetres tall with a mouth diameter of 13 to 14 centimetres.

Most vessels are undecorated but a few have simple incised lines, *sisik*, sometimes criss-crossed immediately below the lip: some have applied nubbins evenly spaced around the pot below the lip. Some pots sighted were decorated above and below the shoulder with a carved paddle (the only contemporary occurrence of carved paddles used for decoration in Papua New Guinea) which left raised, roughly square, round-cornered, closely packed marks. Each rough square carved into the wooden paddle was about 5 millimetres square and among the rows of shapes are scattered smaller holes. This particular paddle was the only one seen; presumably there are others, the patterns of which vary. All decorations are called *sisik* (figs 8.18, 8.19).

The four villages get their clay, *wambui*, from near Yambiyambi. It is a hard, compact yellow brownish-grey clay when dry, with low grit and sand content. It is dampened with fresh water although sea water is permitted; when wet it is a black-brown colour and has high plasticity. A lump of soft clay is worked flat in the hands and coarse white sand, *solov*, from nearby beaches is patted into it. The sand shows as white specks in the dark clay.

Each woman uses only one beater, *tatav*, another unusual aspect of this paddle-and-anvil group. It is a medium-weight paddle with a smooth surface and a narrow handle, knobbed at the end for better gripping and wider at the beating end. It is

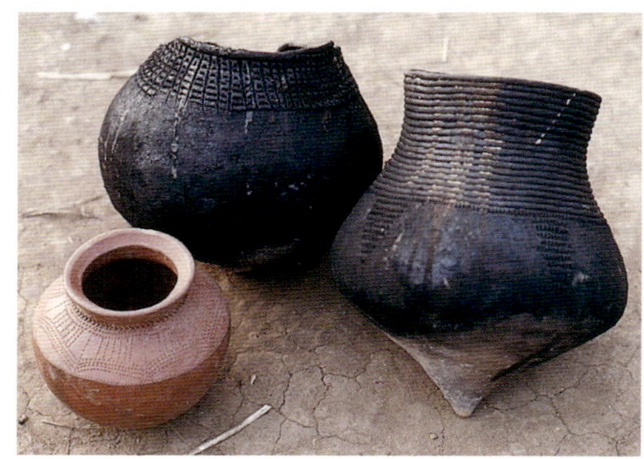

Fig. 8.22
Group of cooking pots, Dalum village: (left) Bilbil; (back) Ham; (right) Bau.

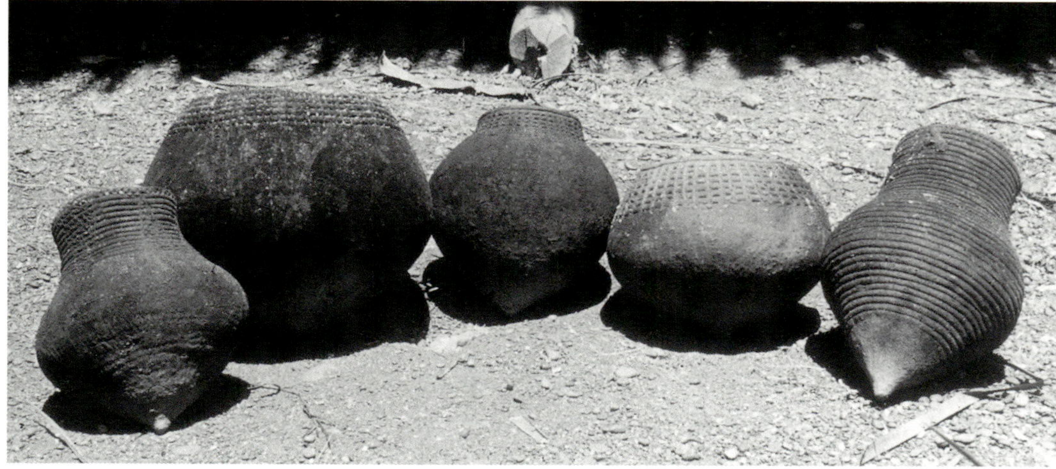

Fig. 8.23
Cooking pots from Bau and Ham people, Tenmile village, near Madang: (extreme left and right) Bau; (centre) three Ham pots.

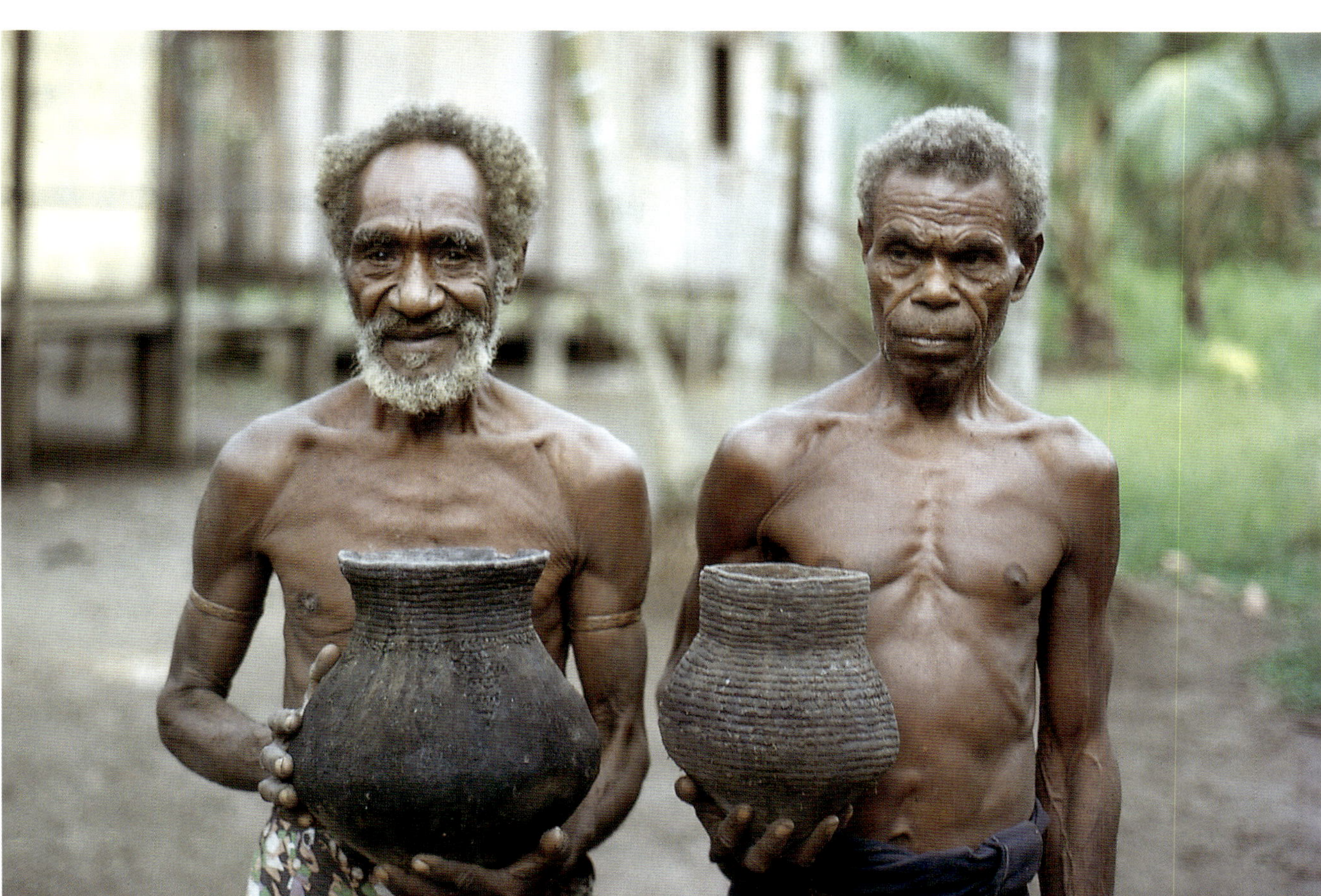

Fig. 8.24
Two Bau cooking pots, *avar*, at a Baimak village.

about 7 centimetres wide and 35 centimetres long. Both ends of the paddle are used. The carved paddle used for forming, shaping and decorating is called *tatav sisik*. Two smooth stones, called *pat*, are used, one ellipsoid for opening out and the other rounder to act as the anvil. A small piece of thin bamboo (today sometimes a razor blade) is used to cut and level the top edge.

A ball of clay about the size of a grapefruit is patted and the long stone is tapped into the centre of it. When the clay is opened up the stone is pounded into the hole and later the round stone is thrown in, as at Yabob. During the whole of the forming the pot is supported in the potter's lap while she sits on the ground with legs outstretched and feet crossed. Pots are set aside to become firm. An unusual aspect of the beating is that the potter holds the long stone inside the neck to thin the top of the pot first, with a downward beating action pressing excess clay to the bottom of the pot. Later the round stone is used for finishing the lower part. The neck shaping is achieved by beating with the narrow end of the paddle. The top edge is cut level with the bamboo tool and smoothed with wet fingers before the whole of the outside of the pot is smoothed with wet hands.

Decoration is carried out as soon as the forming is complete except when the carved paddle is beaten over the surface, sometimes altering the shape slightly. The incised patterns are made with a small pointed stick. Pots are dried upside down or on their sides under the houses.

Vessels are fired singly or sometimes two or three at a time. They are put on a small fire first, turned frequently then put on a larger fire and covered with more wood. No particular timber seems to be preferred. When ready, after approximately half an hour, they are lifted off with a long stick.

Fig. 8.25
Male Ham potter squeezing out a rough roll of clay, Gonoa village.

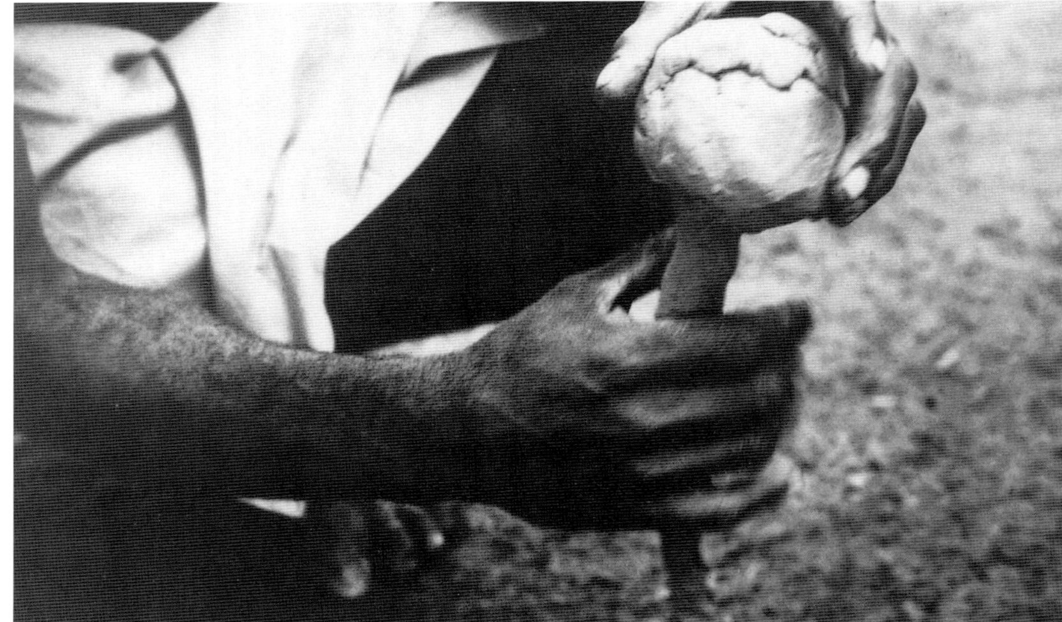

Fig. 8.26
Beginning of spiral coiling: the thin disc of clay has been pinched out to remove grit, Gonoa.

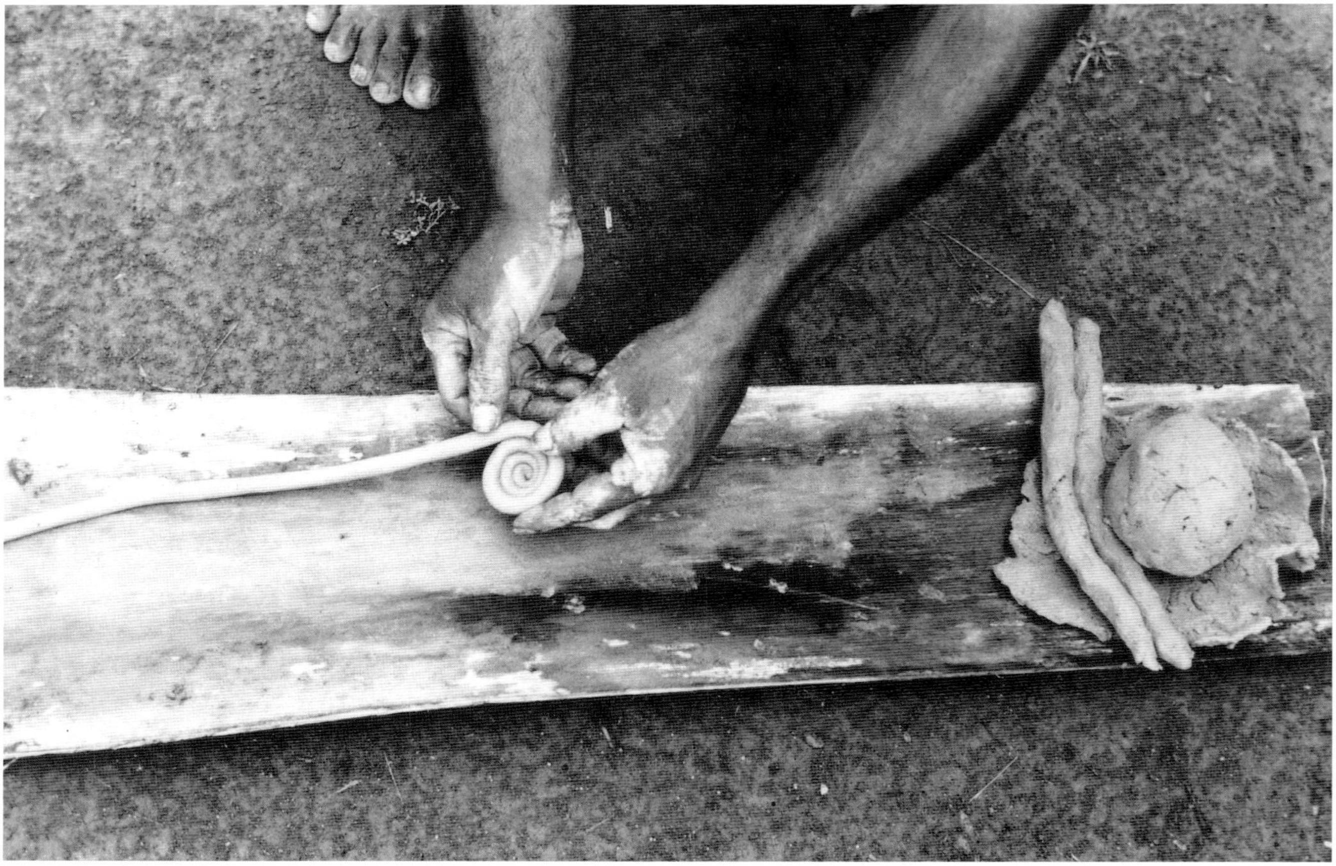

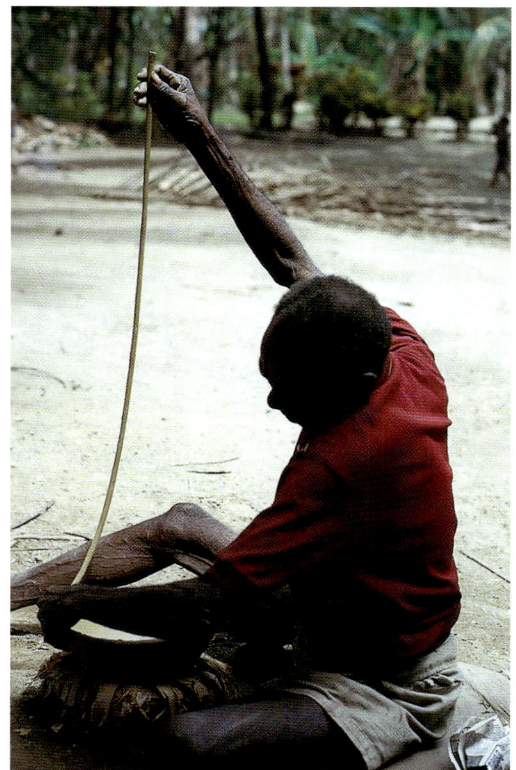

Fig. 8.27

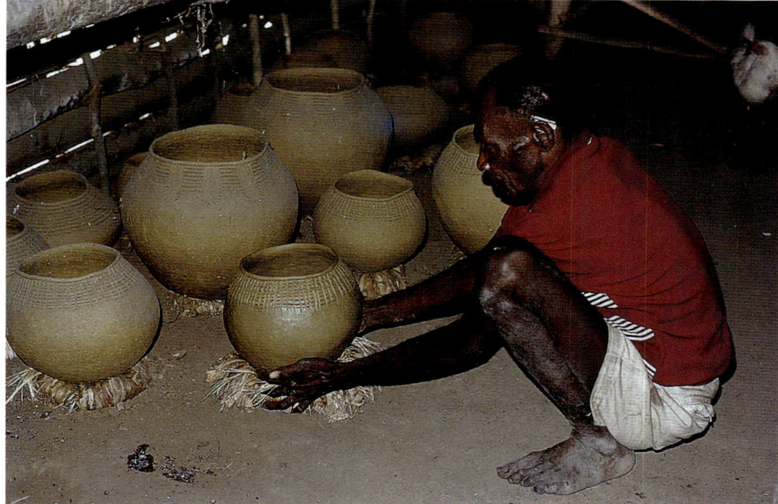

Fig. 8.28

When necessary, the pot is sealed using a method similar to that of Korak-Tavultae. The base is said to be red hot before water is poured into it and the food used in this first cooking is considered fit only for pigs and dogs.

Pots from these four villages are traded far along the coast: north as far as Awar and Kaian, south as far as Rurunat and inland to Donkouam and Bar. Pots are exchanged with the mountain people for wooden bowls, one large pot for one bowl.

INLAND POTTERY

Coil making activity in the inland mountains and rivers of Madang Province is widespread. The area can be divided conveniently into inland Madang south and inland Madang north. The limits of the southern groups more or less follow the linguistic boundaries of the Madang Super-stock: from north of Alexishafen inland, west towards the headwaters of the Gogol River, from there south to the Ramu River near Usino, down the Ramu to a few kilometres south-east of Dumpu and back to the coast near Saidor. The northern groups start from the Wanuma and Josephstaal areas, go north to Tangu and the Bosman on the lower Ramu and then west to the Rao group of the middle Ramu. These are all non-Austronesians.

A similar, but not identical, method of coiling is used throughout, in the southern group by men only. In the northern groups both men and women make pots, with the exception of two groups on the Ramu River where women only make them. A surprising addition to the coiling technique in the Bosman and Josephstaal villages is the use of a wooden beater at the final stage of making. There are many style changes and some variations in the

Fig. 8.27
Ham potter Kori Lama adding a long coil to his pot, Malu hamlet, Buru village.

Fig. 8.28
Kori Lama putting pots, *mis*, in his shed to dry, Malu.

Fig. 8.29
Firing: the unheated vessel is put straight in the flames in the top of a 60cm high square stack of wood, Malu.

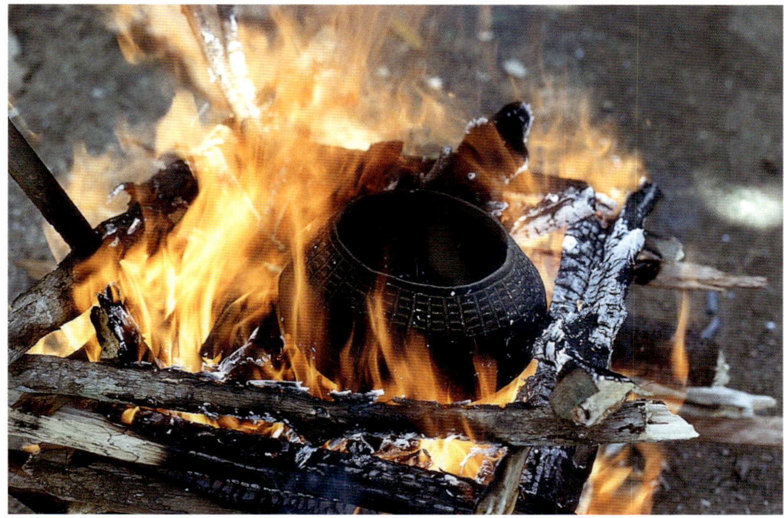

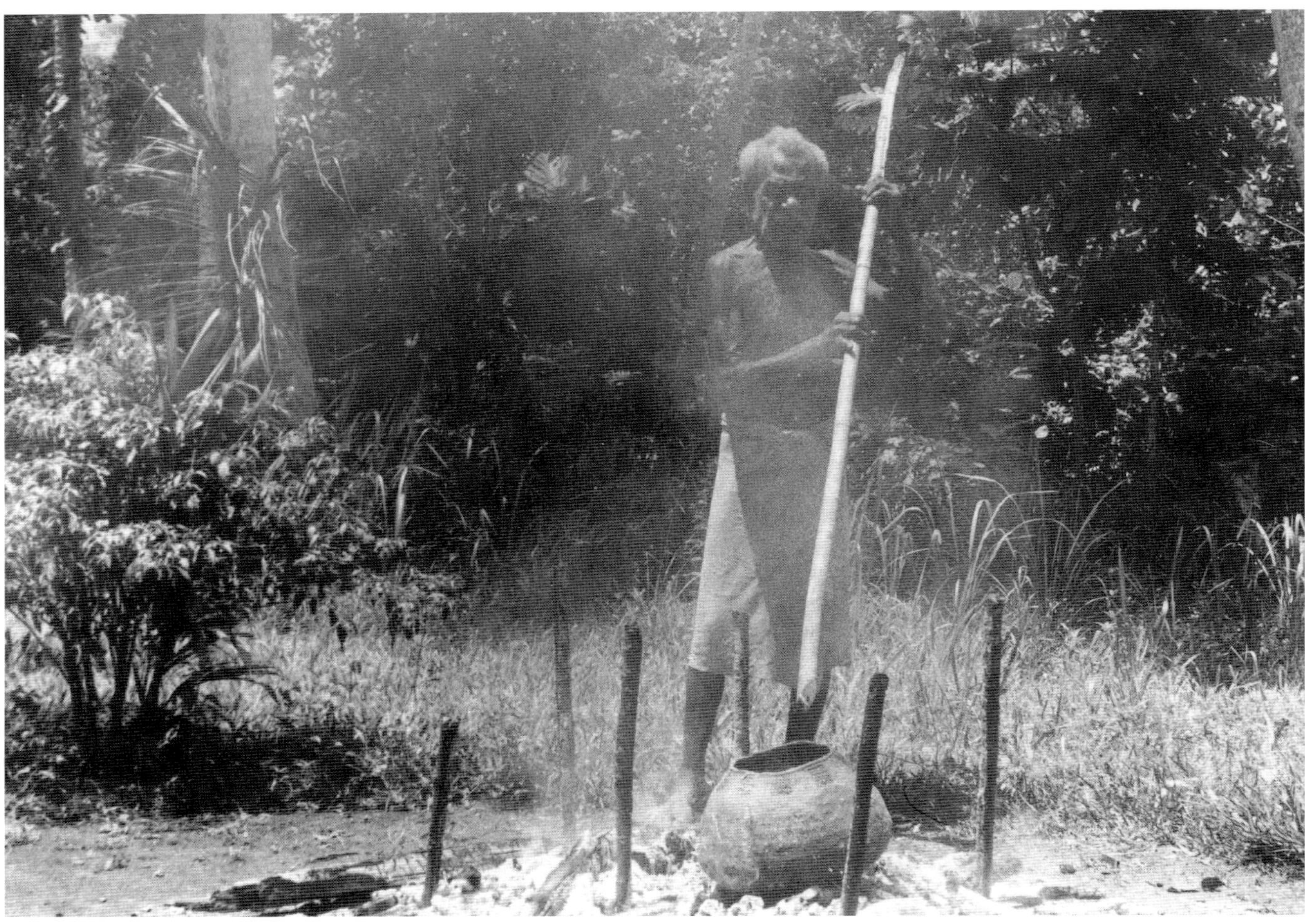

Fig. 8.30
Leaves being boiled in a newly fired pot to seal it, Gonoa.

decorations. In the past this vast area of coiling extended to most of the inland villages. There are many groups of villages as yet unresearched and where pot making might still exist.

Inland Madang south, an area including the hinterland of Astrolabe Bay and part of the Adelbert and Finisterre ranges, has many pot producing villages whose people speak a number of different languages. These are mostly mountain dwelling people and, except for two lowlands groups, are non-Austronesian speakers. The industries to be discussed are the Ham, Bau, Girawa-Bemal, Usino-Sumau-Urigina, Rawa and Mari (which is now defunct). Girawa-Bemal languages are in the Kokon family; Usino-Sumau-Urigina are in the Peka family. The first four groups are closely related: in all of them men are the potters, methods of gathering and preparing the clay are similar, production is by the coil technique, methods of firing are similar and basic form and decorating techniques are comparable. All produce only one type of vessel, the cooking pot (fig. 8.23).

These groups have never been studied in detail although one or two vessels have been described briefly in 19th century ethnographic publications. Ian Hughes (1971) has reported on the distribution and form of pots from the Sumau-Urigina industry. Schmitz (1960) briefly mentions spiral-coiled vessels found in the hinterland of Astrolabe Bay, including pots from three of the four areas. The drawings of these vessels are not accurate, however.

Ham

The first of these industries comprises a group of villages located in the low hills between the Gogol

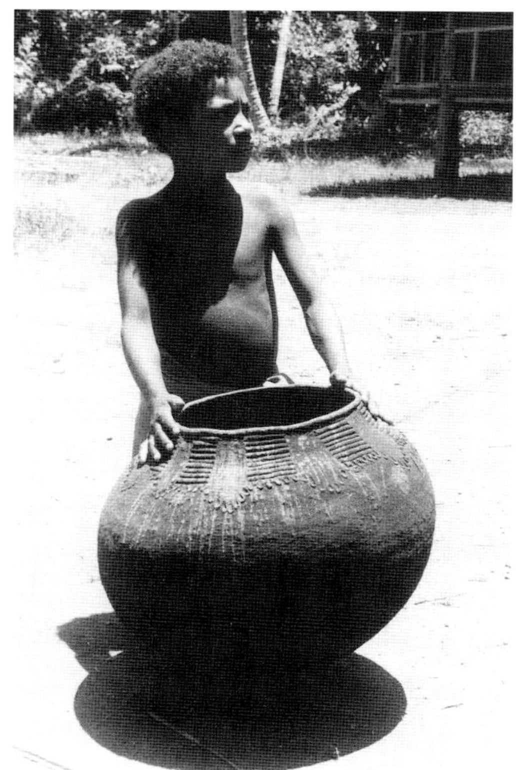

Fig. 8.31
Boy with a huge feast pot, *mis*, near Gonoa.

and Naru rivers. Access to these villages is via either the Madang-Amenob or the Utu roads by vehicle then by foot across the Gogol River and into the interior, all of the villages being on the south-western side of the river. The people are members of the Ham language group, an Austronesian language, who originated in the Bilbil clans and at some time immigrated inland (Z'Graggen 1971). They are surrounded by non-Austronesian speakers. Curiously, the pots made in this area superficially conform to the general Austronesian type of spherical vessels with wide mouth openings but they clearly display characteristics of the coil technique. They are similar to the cooking pots made by the Abelam and Arapesh women in the inland Sepik area. The Ham word for cooking pot is *mis*, a non-Austronesian word borrowed from the Kokon languages The pots from the other related areas are deeper, more bottle-shaped and with smaller, more restricted mouths. As the mountains get higher the pots seem to become longer and thinner.

Villages where pottery is produced are Atu, Barum, Buroa. Buru, Malu (a hamlet near Buru), Derin, Kuyonbon, Mair. Gonua, Tadabu and Ouba. Ato is the only village in the Ham group where pots are not made. The Ouba people are bilingual, speaking both Girawa and Ham, but informants report that Ham-style pots are made there. The exchange of pottery is mostly limited to villages belonging to the Ham language group but trading does extend north across the Gogol River to Amele and Sihan-speaking villages and northeast towards Madang and the coast.

The same basic methods of clay gathering, coil technique and firing are followed in all of the industries. The generic term for pottery is *mis* and all pots are used for cooking only. Food is eaten directly from the pots with coconut spoons. Biro (1901), quoting Hagen, describes the shapes of these vessels as a half coconut with a pointed base. They are of medium depth (usually the diameter of the largest part of the belly equals or is larger than the height of the vessel) and have pointed or nipple bases. There is usually no neck area although

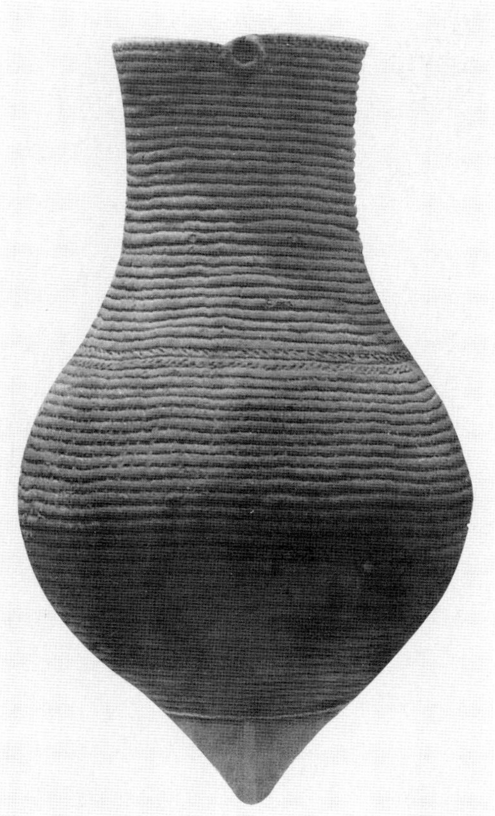

Fig. 8.32
Old Bau cooking pot, *avar*, showing typical decoration with the last coil, *h* 30 cm.

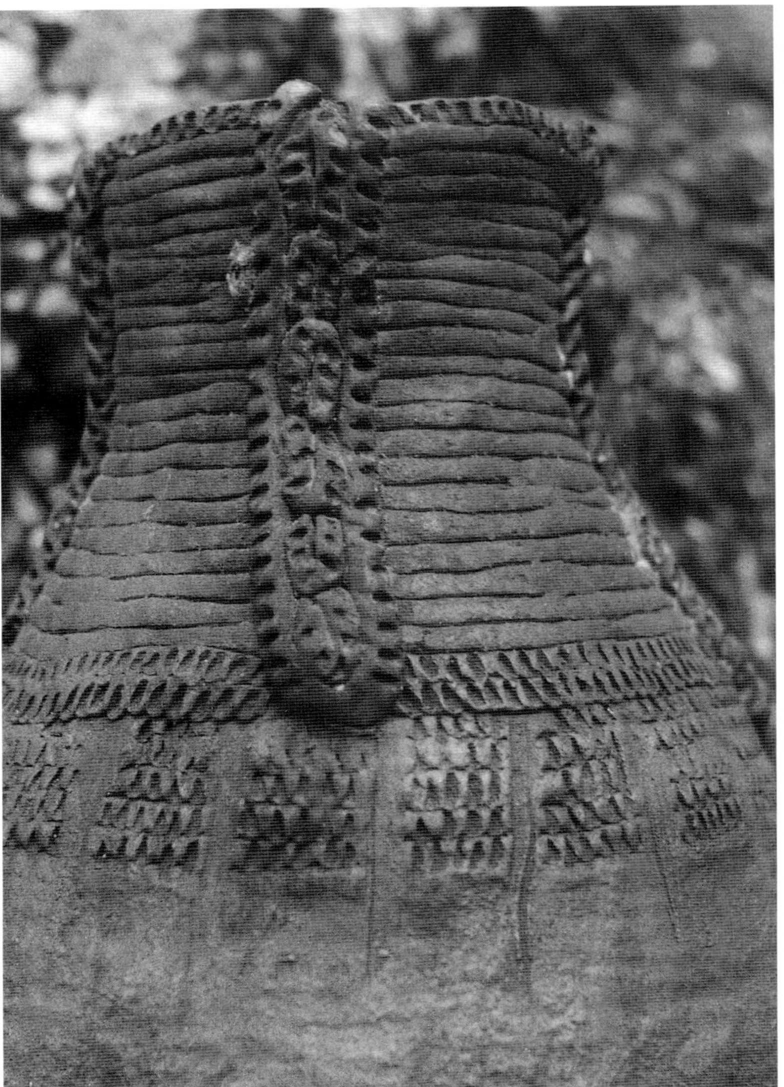

Fig. 8.33
Unusual decoration on a Bau cooking pot from Fulumu village. See typical treatment of last coil (fig. 8.32).

a few pots have a slight neck with an everted rim. Most pots have direct rims and restricted openings. Sizes range from small individual cooking vessels about 15 to 20 centimetres high to large communal pots approximately 92 centimetres high which are used for special feasts (figs 8.31-8.32).

Decoration is restricted to the upper third of the vessel, that is, the shoulder and rim area. The final coil forming the rim is left unmarked. The coils of the bottom two-thirds of the vessel walls are smoothed inside and out. The simple decorative motifs fall into three categories: in the first, the upper five to seven coils are left unbonded and are marked by vertical grooves made by the fingers or stick or bamboo tools; in the second, alternate areas of grooved and smoothed coils provide a rhythmic contrasting pattern; in the third, which is an elaboration of the second, alternating triangular-shaped areas of grooved and smoothed coils are linked beneath by a scalloped design of punctate marks made with the end of a small twig. The overall impression is of a durable rough pottery, masculine (in spite of the round shape) and simply decorated. The clay is gritty and the vessel walls are rough to the touch. The pots are surprisingly light, especially when compared to the Boiken and Abelam cooking pots which resemble the inland Madang ware and are made in the same way.

There are numerous clay pits in the area; the Gonua clay source is located within the village and other villages have easy access to their supplies. Men and boys use a pointed stick or iron bar to quarry the clay, *maper*. The Gonua clay is grey yellowish-brown and moderately plastic, with much coarse grit which must be removed. It is composed of a smectite, sodium feldspar, quartz and probably poorly crystallized kaolinite. A mottled clay which kneads to the same colour and is similar to the Gonua clay is situated between Derin, Malu and Buru and is used by all three villages. It has 45 per cent clay mineral (a smectite) with the non-plastic content made up of much quartz and some feldspar, limonite, epidote and greenolite. Despite its coarse grittiness it has good plasticity.

While clay gathering and actual manufacture of pots are men's work, the women are allowed to prepare the clay. Football-sized lumps of clay are gathered and put in rows at the clay pit. If the lumps dry before they are needed they are placed on a large piece of 'limbum' and soaked with water. The women work handfuls of clay into thin pancake shapes approximately 15 centimetres in diameter and remove the larger pieces of grit, stones and roots. Sometimes the women will prepare the clay by pounding it out on the 'limbum'. The male potter then compacts the pancakes into lumps weighing about 4 kilograms; these are wrapped in banana leaves to keep them damp. The clay is then squeezed downward to form roughly-shaped rolls about 20 to 40 centimetres long and 2 to 3 centimetres thick. A supply of these rolls is

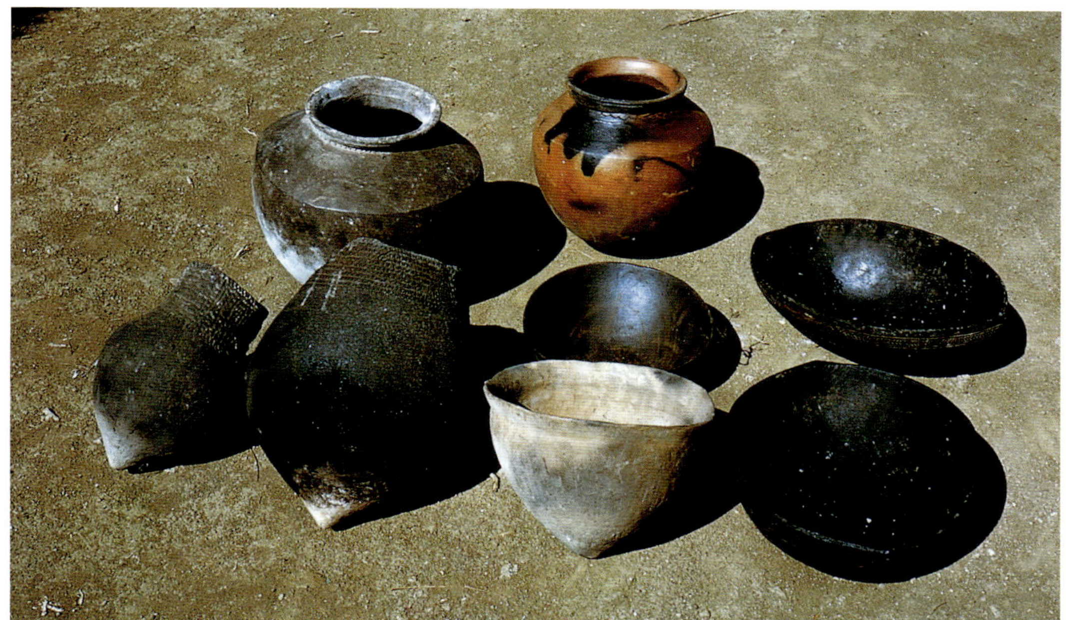

Fig. 8.34
Group of cooking pots and wooden bowls at Amron village, near the Garuh group: (left back) Bilbil; (left front) two Garuh pots; (centre front) Bosman pot.

kept moist in a green leaf. They are rolled out onto a long, slightly concave piece of 'pangal' with the palm and heel of the hand. When the coil is 60 to 120 centimetres long and about 8 millimetres in diameter the potter turns it spirally onto itself, feeding the coil directly on from its extended position on the 'pangal'. As additional coils are added and the shape grows in the potter's hands, the coils on the inside are smoothed with a downward motion of the thumb. When the vessel is about 8 to 10 centimetres high it is turned upside down and the outside coils are bonded together. The bottom coil is then shaped into a nipple-like point. At this stage the partially formed vessel is placed upright on a thickly woven ring of pandanus leaves lined with a small piece of banana leaf. The potter continues to add coils, smoothing them on the inside by turning the entire ring (for large pots he will work himself around the vessel in a squatting position, adding coils as he goes). The final coil which forms the rim is thinned down toward the end and left unbonded, often making an uneven top edge. The pot is decorated while damp or leather-hard with a pointed stick or with the fingers.

The vessel, still supported in the pandanus leaf ring, is taken into a house to dry. It may rest on a platform built near the ceiling or it can be bound

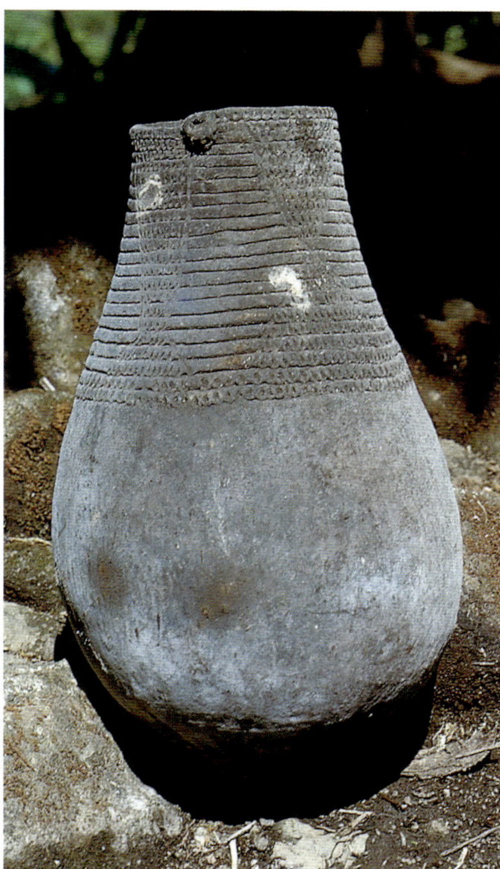

Fig. 8.35
Typical Garuh cooking pot, *hinai*, Amron village, *h* 43 cm.

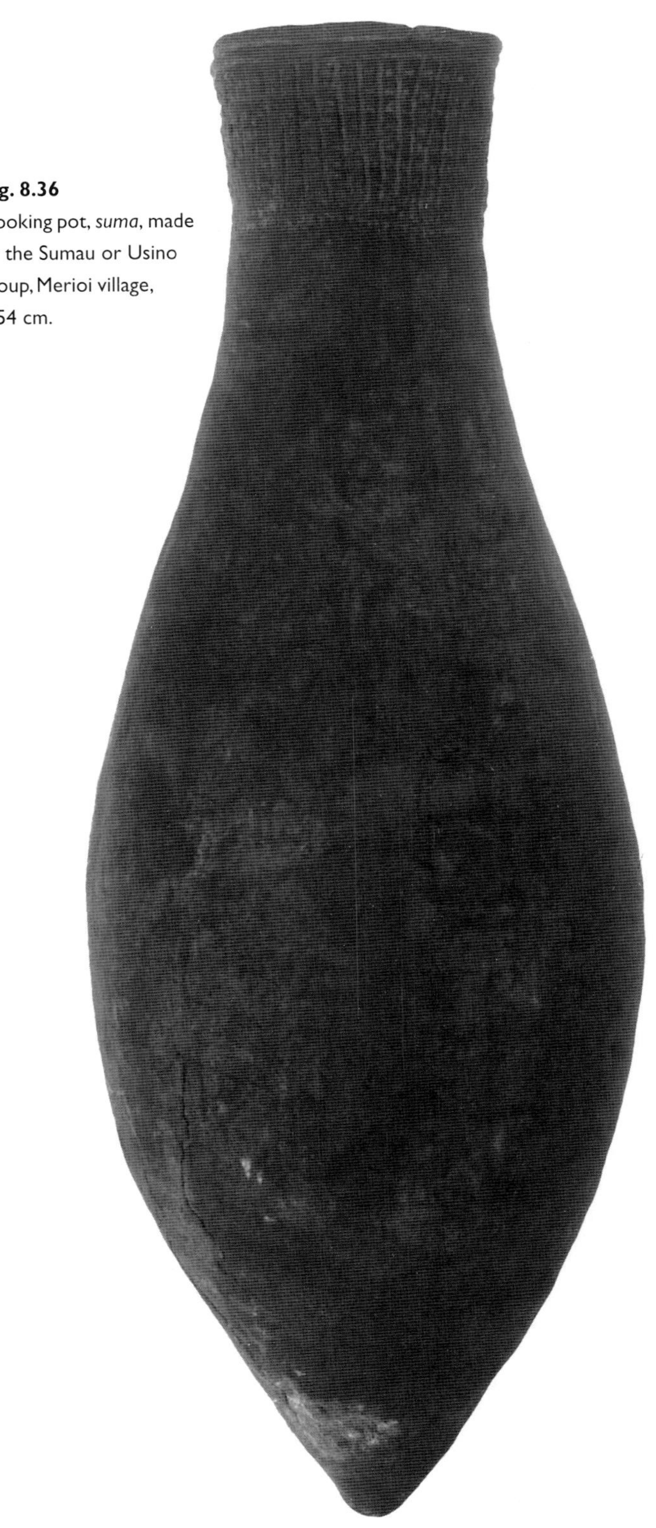

Fig. 8.36
Cooking pot, *suma*, made by the Sumau or Usino group, Merioi village, *h* 54 cm.

with split cane and hung upside down from the rafters, where it becomes blackened by smoke from the cooking fires. At Malu hamlet there were special low huts where the pots were placed on the ground to dry. Drying lasts for about three weeks.

Firing can take place any time after the pot has dried and may be put off for as long as a year. Fuel consists of whole or split pieces of wood placed overlapping each other to form a square built up to 60 to 70 centimetres high. Further pieces of fuel are leaned inside the square to fill the centre. A handful of dry leaves is placed on top; these are lit and when they are burning strongly a single pot is placed directly into the flames. Each pot has its own square and when more than one pot is being fired the pots are placed in adjoining squares. Towards the end of the firing the potter, to obtain even heat, frequently turns the vessel from side to side with a long stick. The vessel should turn red when properly fired; if it turns black it is not acceptable. The finished colour is dark red smudged with blackened reduction marks and firing takes at least thirty minutes. While the vessel still rests on the smouldering coals green leaves and water are poured inside it to seal it (fig. 8.30).

Although trade is not extensive and metal kettles are ubiquitous this homogeneous group of potters continues to produce vessels for its own use and satisfaction.

Bau

In the mountains west of Madang and starting about 5 kilometres north of the Ham potteries is another industry carried on by Bau-speaking people. Their villages are bounded on the north by the Gum River and on the south-west by the Gogol River. Within a 60-kilometre radius of the Bau group many other scattered language groups also make similar pots. To the north-west are the Gumalu, Mawan, Baimak, Gal and, possibly, the Utu people; farther north are the Garuh, Nake, Saruga, Murupi and Wamas speakers. The very diverse languages of these groups are all classified under the Mabuso stock in two different families. The Munit-speakers to the west of Bau belong to the same family as Bemal and Girawa but appear to make the same pots as the Bau. Further study is

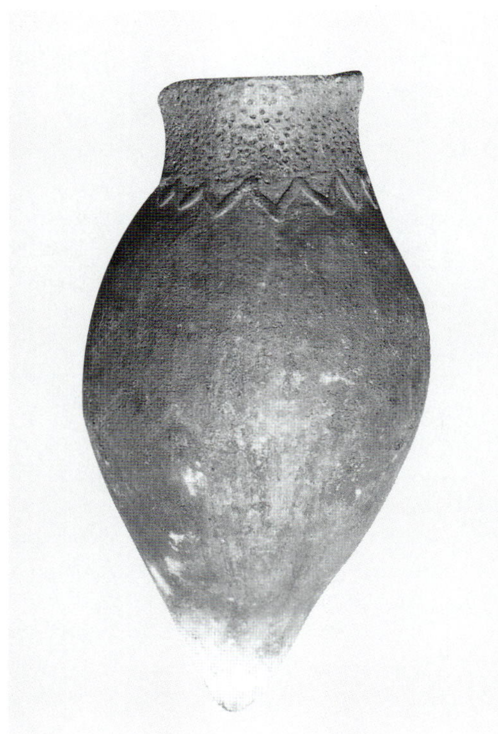

Fig. 8.37
Girawa cooking vessel, *sima*, at Begasin, *h* 28 cm.

necessary to clarify the exact boundaries of the pot making area, relationships between various groups and variations in style and technique.

The pot making activity in the villages of this area will be referred to as the Bau industry. Although the industry is gradually dying out there are still quite a few middle-aged men who continue to make pots and pots have always been valuable items of exchange with neighbouring peoples. They are used in bride price transactions along with a distinctly Bau style of wooden bowl. The wooden bowl is quite different from the Astrolabe Bay bowls which are boat-shaped; it is closer in style to the other strong competitors, the semi-spherical bowls traded across the Finisterres to the coast from the Rawa people. Bau vessels have been found in villages far to the north, almost as far as the Ramu River, and to the east until, close to the coast, the Yabob-Bilbil industry predominates. In hilly or mountainous regions where water is scarce, the tall, narrow, small-mouthed vessels are favoured because vegetables are said to cook faster in them than they do in the round-bellied, open-mouthed pots from the coast and there is less evaporation. Water is a precious commodity in mountainous regions and often must be carried great distances.

Pottery is said to be made in the following Bau villages: Bafalu, Bauk, Efu, Dolonu, Fulumu, Guman, Bemehal, Umun and Lagaha. Twenty to thirty years ago, Umun was the centre of the industry but pot making there is now defunct. The authors have no information about villages outside the Bau group which may produce a similar type of vessel. The characteristics of these cooking pots indicate certain affinities with the round-bodied Ham vessels and the longer gourd shapes of the two other industries yet to be described and might be considered a transitional type.

The Bau cooking pots, called *avar*, are composite shapes with conical bases, having knobs or points which merge into a belly that bulges to form an ellipsoid. At the shoulder the shape becomes cylindrical; sometimes a truncated neck flares out to form an everted direct rim. The remnant coil always extends down the neck to form an applied initial-like motif (tear drop, loop or circular design) which is often notched with rope-like markings along the edge. This applied design is the mark or

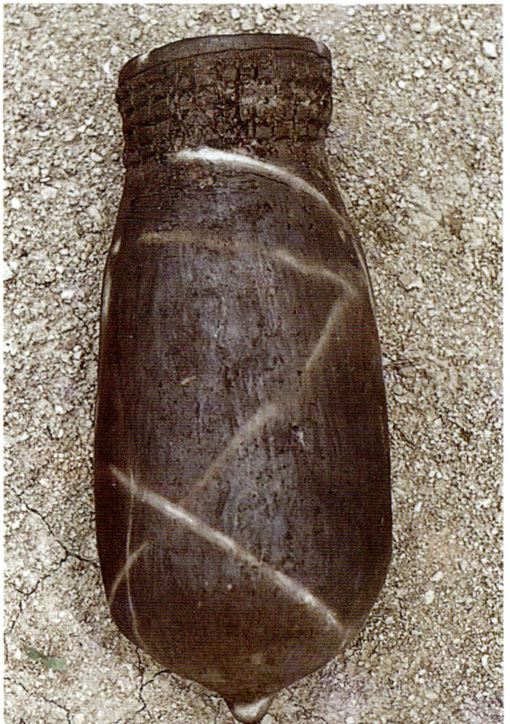

Fig. 8.38
Unfired Girawa pot with marks from the cane used to hang the pot to smoke in the house: Sanawai village.

Fig. 8.39
Urigina potter Yagume with his newly fired cooking pot, *somo*, at the new village of Korona.

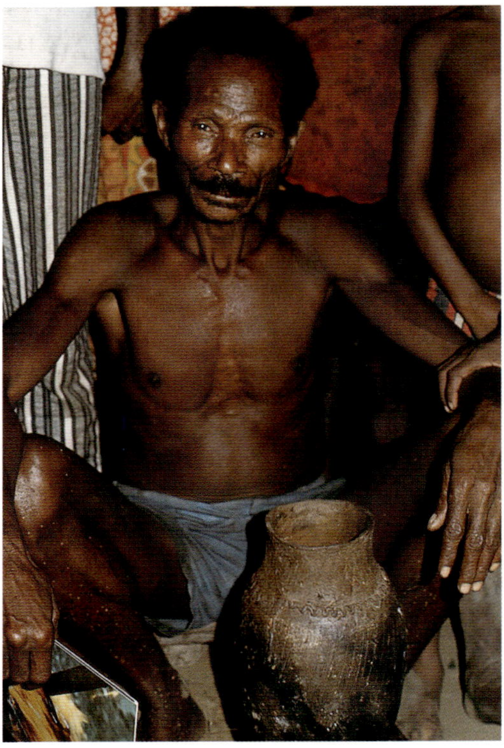

signature of the potter. Size of vessels ranges from about 17 to 50 centimetres high. The walls are very thin and vary from approximately 3 to 5 millimetres in thickness, depending upon the size of the vessel. Pots made from very fine coils, 5 millimetres in diameter, are light in weight and misleadingly fragile in appearance (figs 8.31-8.33).

The decoration, in contrast to that of the Ham vessels, is not confined to the shoulder area: the entire vessel serves as a field for a more sophisticated, homogeneous scheme of decorative elements. The Bau pots are structurally and visibly divisible into five zones – base, body, shoulder, neck and rim – which are defined by exposed and smoothed coils, incised markings, notches, appliqué, point impressions and smoothed areas lightly scored. The base area, from the end of the point to approximately 5 to 6 centimetres up the everted cone-shaped base, is always smoothed. The body area, which includes that section of greatest width (the belly) and extends to the inflection point or just above it at the shoulder, is generally defined by exposed coils which may be marked by vertical incisions; a few examples sighted had smoothed coils from base to the shoulder and one striking example consisted of triangular motifs formed by alternating impressed and smoothed coils (fig. 1.22). The shoulder is defined by one or two exposed coils impressed or incised with herringbone or hatched designs. The neck is defined by exposed coils either contrasting with (if coils below have not been smoothed) or repeating (if coils below have been bonded) the fabric of the body. The rim may have impressed, indented, notched or nicked designs, it may remain undecorated or it may have the remnant coil used as a decorative motif in the manner previously mentioned.

One unique vessel appears to be over-decorated and is probably a departure from tradition. The coils making up the base and belly area have been bonded and the decoration on the shoulder consists of a series of rectangular motifs of exposed, impressed coils inscribed within bonded areas. Above this two indented exposed coils mark the point between shoulder and neck, the neck area consisting of exposed coils. Four sausage-like coils have been applied vertically, running from the rim to the horizontal belt and dividing the neck into four vertical zones. These coils are impressed along the outer edges and form U-shaped squiggles of

Fig. 8.40
Naigo at Asas village with a Urigina cooking pot, *som* (in Asas language), made at Yagumba village.

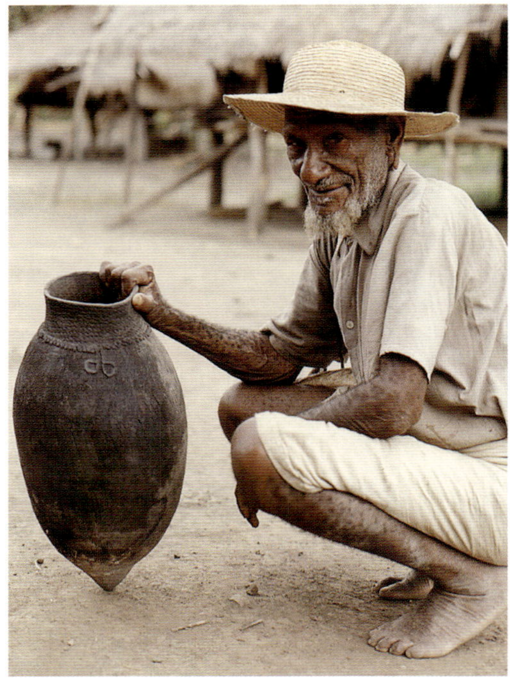

clay down the centre. The final coil of the rim has also been impressed. This was not only an eccentric example of decoration but the pot is unusually large. It was originally made as a cooking pot but when the authors saw it it was being used as a dye container (fig. 8.33).

The Bau style of making and firing pots is closely related to the Ham methods, although women do not prepare the clay. At Fulumu village, clay, *mil*, is held in the hand, not laid on the ground while it is beaten with a short stick. As the beating progresses, the grit and stones are removed and the beater is dipped into water at intervals. The only difference from the Ham method of making the pot is in the forming of the point at the base: at Fulumu, the first roll of clay is doubled over on itself for about 5 centimetres before it is coiled. This excess lump of clay is later formed into the pointed base. Vessels are decorated with sticks and fingers and firing methods are similar to those of the Ham potters.

Very little research has been carried out on Garuh and the other related language groups which are north-west of Madang and the industry appears to be almost at a standstill. In comparison to pots of the Bau region there is a subtle variation in the form of some of the larger pots sighted in this area: the neck is shorter and the shoulder less defined (figs 8.34. 8.35).

Egloff (1973) reports that the pottery of Wamas is thicker and the exteriors of the vessels are smoothed. The people of Murupi produce pots similar to those of Bau.

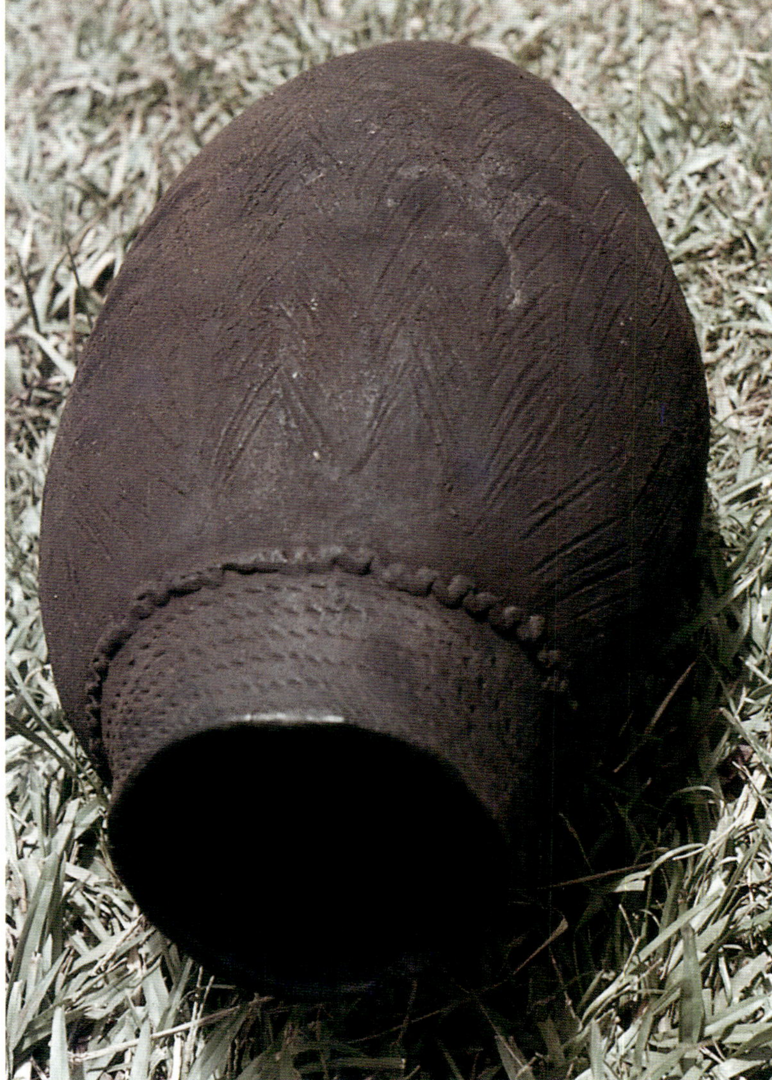

Fig. 8.41
Urigina cooking pot, *somo*, showing the scoring on the body, at Bundi, *h* 43 cm.

Kokon-Peka

In the hinterland of Madang, south-west of the Ham and Bau people, is a range of mountains covered in dense tropical rainforest. These mountains slope down to become hills which give way to the plains and wetlands that eventually merge into the Ramu River. To the south-east the high Finisterre Range borders the area. In a vast area of hills and mountains between the Nopu River (a tributary of the Ramu) to the south, the Naru River to the east and the Kokon River to the north, there are groups of potters.

The elongated gourd-shaped pots of the region received only superficial mention from researchers who penetrated the area. Biro's report (1911) of two pots having pointed bases and 'bottle gourd' shapes is one of the earliest. Schmitz (1960) has described three pots from this area, from Begasin and the Rawa and Nahu areas. The most important description to date of the distribution, techniques of production and trade of the Urigina-Sumau group has come from Hughes (1971). It is curious that it has taken about 100 years since European colonisation and the opening up of Madang Province and the Ramu River for these potting industries to be recorded. The area has been combed by explorers, birdwatchers, anthro-

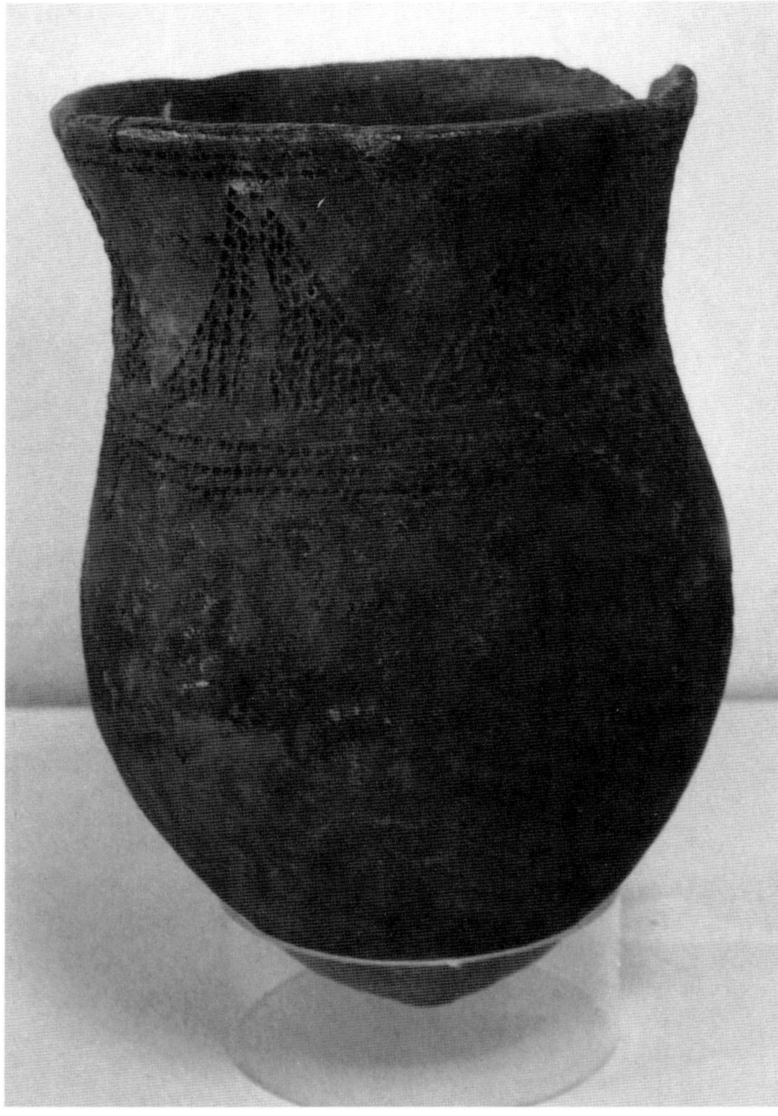

Fig. 8.42
Rawa cooking pot collected at Henganofi, Eastern Highlands, *h* 29 cm.

pologists, demographers and missionaries. Jorgen Petersen only had to travel up the Madang-Amele road for about 20 kilometres to find examples of imported mountain coil pots made by Ham and Bau men and yet he makes no mention of these in his report.

Girawa-Bemal (Kokon)

The Girawa people live in the mountains overlooking the Ramu River to the south-west and the Naru River to the east. The Kokon River lies to the north. The people of this area are comparatively poor; some coffee is grown but there is little scope for earning cash and the severe shortage of water during the dry season affects yields from subsistence crops. The men make pottery vessels which, when compared to those of their neighbours, are cruder in shape, more brittle and more simply decorated. They also carve crude bowls resembling the boat-shaped wooden vessels from the Huon Gulf. Generally, pots from this area found their way east toward the coast and few examples of these wares have been discovered across the Ramu or in the Eastern Highlands.

The villages still producing pottery are Begasin (near the Begasin Lutheran mission), Bamesos, Gomuru, Gasua, Aigut, Sanawai and Baisop. All belong to the Girawa language group. Included in the sub-industry are the villages of Jal and Bemal, where the Bemai language is spoken (Z'Graggen 1973). These villages are geographically close to the Ham and Bau potteries and trade is oriented in that direction. There is an ancient track going from Usino patrol post through Begasin, eastward through Bau country and finally through Arnele villages to the coast.

The pots, *sima*, are ovoid with pointed bases and restricted orifices; the proportions are tall and thin. There are two basic shapes: one has a slightly everted neck, the other has cylindrical walls and no neck: both have direct rims. Vessel size ranges from 24 to 60 centimetres high and most vessels have a uniform 8 to 9-centimetre orifice regardless of the size of the body. Simple decoration consists of four to six partially exposed coils defining the neck area, most of which are grooved with marks made by dragging a finger or a wooden or bamboo implement vertically down across the coils. Among the vessels sighted were a few with hatched designs running horizontally around the body of the pot at the inflection point of the neck The smoothed coils of the body are generally untextured although occasionally a pot is casually marked by finger scoring. Informants attached no significance to the decoration but, functionally, the bonded exposed coils of the neck aid in gripping since a pot is lifted from the fire by the shoulder and neck and the contents – taro, sweet potato, cooking bananas, greens, pig or fowl – are tipped into another container, an enamel plate or, during special feasts, a wooden bowl.

Sumau-Usino-Urigina (Peka)

People of these three language groups, all of the Peka language family, inhabit the low mountain ranges south-west of Madang, overlooking the Ramu River to the south-west and the Naru River to the east. The pottery of Sumau (Garia) and Urigina has been described by Hughes (1971) who refers to the potters as the 'Usur potters', after Z'Graggen's (1971) classification. This places Usino, Sumau and Urigina under the Usur group; however, in 1973 Z'Graggen revised his language map of Madang and the confusing 'Usur' languages were classified under the Rai coast stock in the Peka family.

The Sumau pot makers are very close neighbours of the Girawa, living only a few ridges to the south of them. Villages among the Sumau group where pots are produced are Sumau, Totopa, Yanipa, Uria, Igurue, Enam, Poini, Mobo, and Nugu.

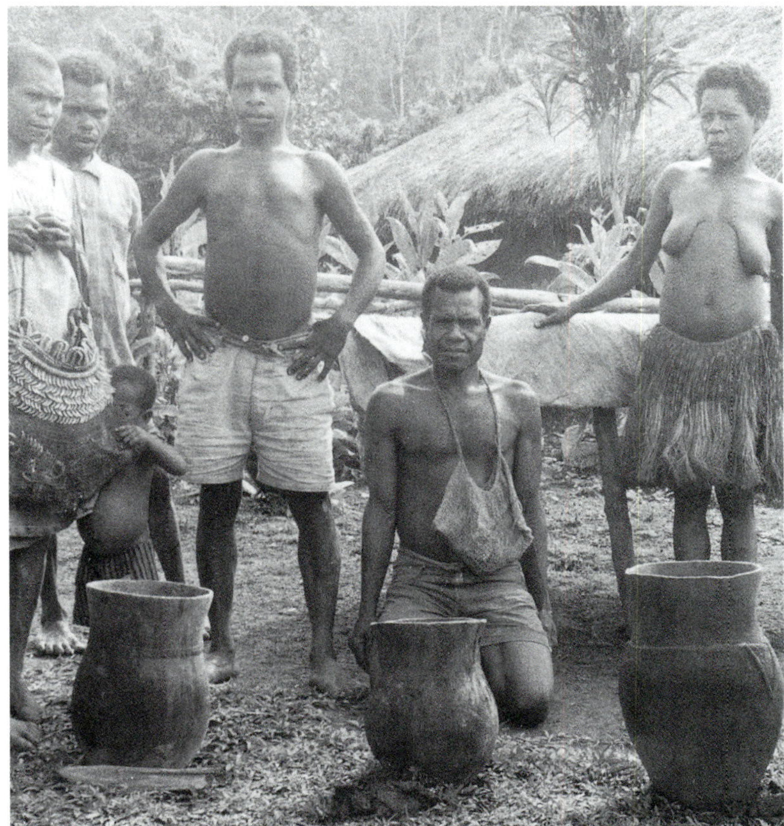

Fig. 8.43
Rawa cooking pots supported in holes in the ground, Tauta village.

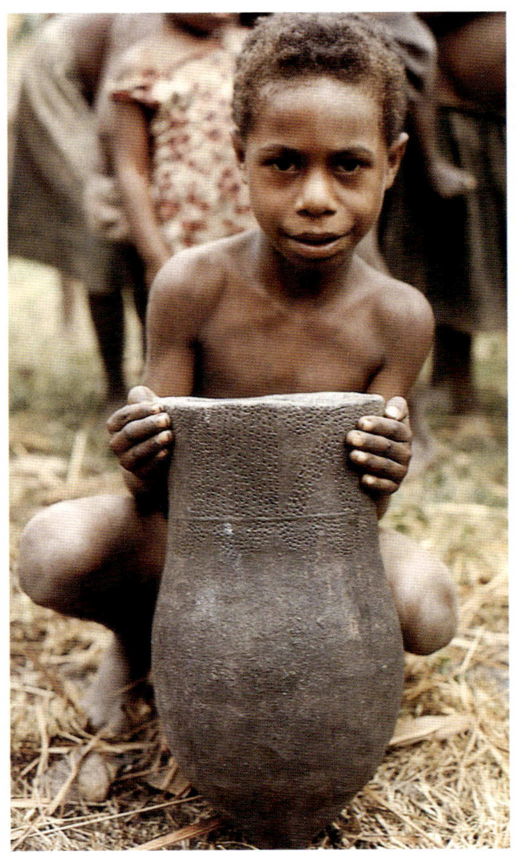

Fig. 8.44
Old Rawa cooking pot at the Mari village of Sankian, *h* 37 cm.

Some reports say that the Usino speakers have never made pots but it has been established by the authors that they are made in two of their many villages, Deini (Komas) and Beire. These two villages are geographically very close to Sumau territory so it would seem that their pot making skills have probably come about through contact with their neighbours.

The Urigina potters live south-east of the Usino patrol post, isolated in the hills near the tributaries of the Nopu River. The main pot making villages reported by Hughes are Ongoru, Kesa and Sana; farther to the east on the upper reaches of the Nopu, the villagers of Mataloi and Biri occasionally produce some pots. The authors have found that pots are also made at Yagumba, Rainbana and Wiai and that men from Ongoru, Kesa and Mataloi who have settled in a new village, Korona, are continuing with their pot making.

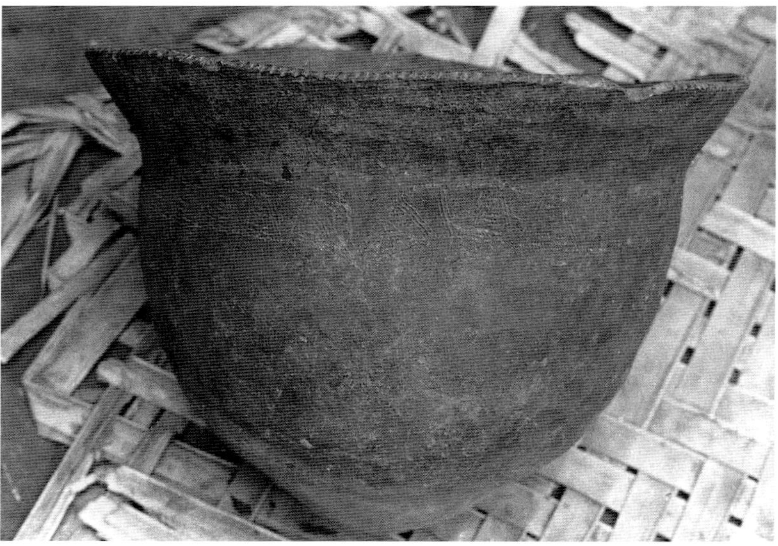

Fig. 8.45
Old Mari cooking pot, *gurr*, at Sankian village. Made by Barabarump (long since deceased) when at Wambun village, *h* 28 cm.

Similar pots are made at Sausi village in the neighbouring language group of Sausi. In the past pots were made at Danaru, an isolated village where the Danaru language is spoken, situated between Sumau and Urigina.

Many sources have reported seeing the elongated pots in the highlands, especially around Bundi. Once the pots are made by the men, they become women's possessions and examples in the Bundi area were owned by families who had received them in bride price transactions. Hughes stresses the fact that an abundance of these pots has not been found in the highlands; in fact, shells and other objects from the coast were in far greater demand than such curious items as pots, for which the highland people had little use since they traditionally cooked in wooden ovens or in holes in the ground and ate from wooden bowls. Thus, trade in ceramics was never vigorous and vessels were and are made mostly for local consumption and trade with nearby neighbours who do not make pots. Danaru and Usino serve as middle-men between the Kesa and Ongoru potters and the Faita and Garaligut people. Sumau and Urigina pots are exchanged for wooden bowls, dry meat and bows with valley and mountain people who do not make pots. The circulation of pots is still aided by their use in bride price transactions.

In basic style and form, the vessels observed by Hughes are comparable to the Girawa vessels. Pots, called *suma* (Sumau language), are deep with ellipsoid or ovoid bodies; they have everted cone-shaped bases, are restricted and have direct rims. There are forms with inflected necks or no necks; the walls of the vessels are restricted, cylindrical or everted. Decoration generally extends from the rim down to the inflection point and design motifs are more varied, using incised lines to form vertical, horizontal, zig-zag or scalloped designs. The body of the vessel can be scored (incised with long, casual vertical or horizontal lines) or decorated with point impressions inscribed within a diamond-shaped motif. One elaborately decorated vessel copies the star-and-triangle incised designs which distinguish the wooden bowls, *kogotu*, made by the Rawa men in the Finisterre Range.

In general, the Sumau and Urigina vessels show more variation in shape and decorative elements than do the pots from neighbouring areas to the north-west. Hughes admits there are problems in identifying the provenance of the vessels from these two groups. In summary he describes Garia vessels as simple unscored reckless vessels, or elaborately decorated vessels having restricted, inflected, everted or straight necks. These are decorated by applied coil patterns, incised lines, point impression and combinations of different elements. The Urigina pots are more simply decorated by light body scoring and a number of exposed coils define the rim.

Clay gathering, manufacturing techniques and firing processes of the Sumau and Urigina industries are similar to the Girawa, Usino, Ham and Bau potteries. The clay is usually gathered by women and stored in breadfruit leaves until ready for use. The coils are bonded not only with the fingers but with the aid of a piece of wood, bamboo or a knife, as in the Girawa area. Two days after the body of the vessel has been completed the point of the base is formed by the addition of a small piece of clay that supposedly strengthens it. Sometimes the outside of the pot is smoothed with a piece of coconut. Pots are dried for a comparatively long period, from six to eight weeks, before firing (Hughes 1971).

Most of the Sumau villages obtain their clay from Sumau and Yanipa. The Usino village of Deini has rights to a clay pit located about 1 kilometre from the village, just off the track leading to Sanawai.

The pit is covered with small logs and banana leaves for protection during the dry season. There appears to be no ritual surrounding the quarrying of the clay: men, women and children may gather it. It is a grey yellowish-brown clay composed of a smectite (18 per cent) and 82 per cent non-plastics which include iron-stained quartose sand grains and some igneous rock fragments. In spite of its low percentage of clay mineral and rough character, this clay is reasonably plastic. It is prepared by pounding on a 'limbum' with a heavy log approximately 90 centimetres long and 8 centimetres wide; grit and stones are removed by the women and water is added when needed. The body of the pot is then built up by the coil method, starting with the bottom coil which is pinched to form a point. The remaining methods are similar to those of the Bau and Ham industries except that the growing vessel is sometimes smoothed with a piece of bamboo. The decoration of the neck is made with a bamboo stick. When the pot is ready for drying it is bound by a woven support, taken to the men's house (a form of ritual) and suspended from the beams to dry for about one month. Hardwood from the bush is used as a fuel for firing the pots; dried pandanus leaves may also be used. The fire is built up in the same way as the Ham area although multiple firings are undertaken here.

The people still prefer to cook in their tall vertical vessels but the industry is on the decline and Yabob vessels are now imported in a small way.

Rawa

A group of Rawa-speaking villages in the foothills and along the ridges of the Finisterre Range constitutes another industry. This vast mountain range flanks the Ramu River valley to the south and runs east parallel to the Rai coast. The distribution of Rawa pots has been more widespread than that of vessels from the other industries because of trade affiliations between the Rawa and the Benabena people, who live on the other side of the Ramu River in the Benabena valley. Keil (1974) has given an account of the trading relations between these two groups, describing the preparations and hazards of the journey, the exchange of goods and the inter-cultural relations between the two groups.

Only about eight groups of Benabena habitually make the trip. They exchange pigs small enough

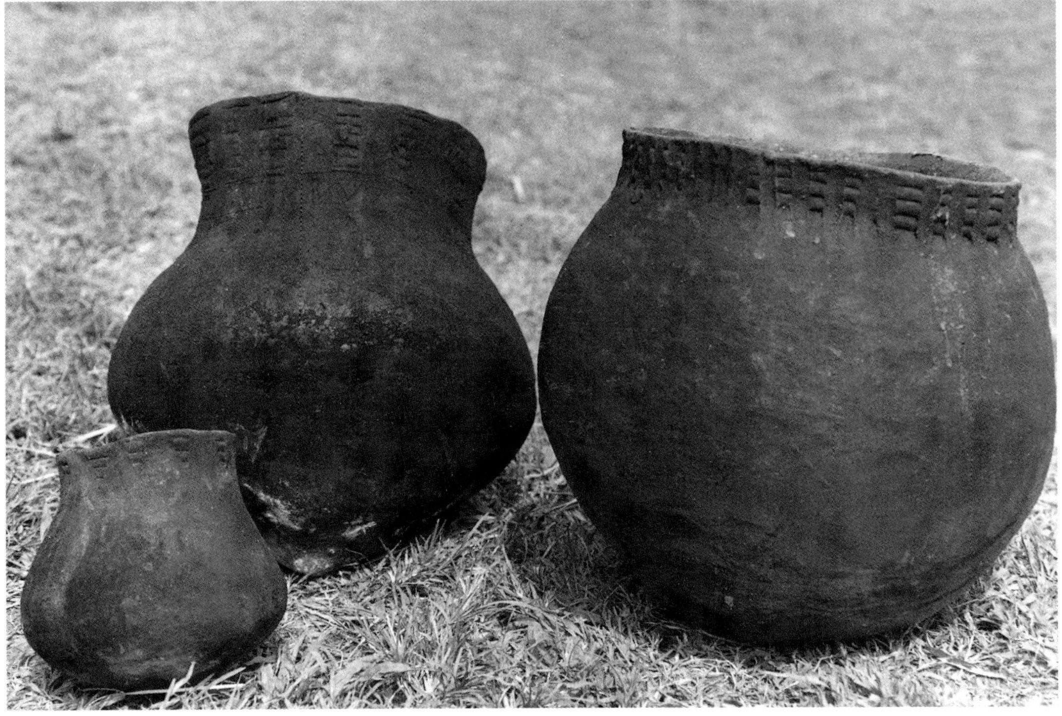

Fig. 8.46
Three cooking pots, *manou*: (left and right) made by Iwumbi; (centre) made by Lambua Ruami, Wasamb village, Tangu. Tallest *h* 35 cm.

Fig. 8.47
Mikarew feast pot made many years ago, seen at Sirin village, *h* 42 cm.

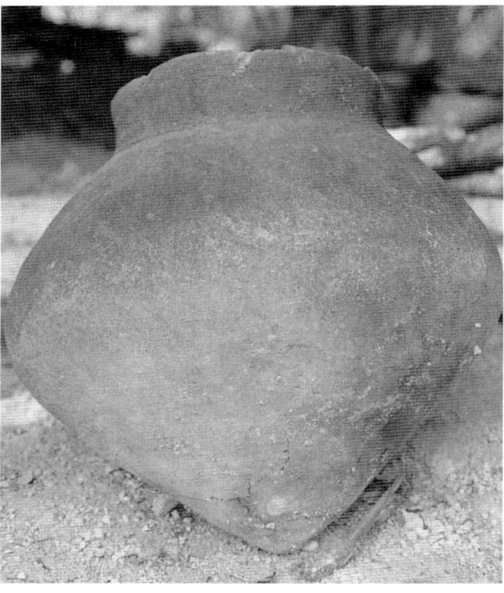

to be carried, dogs, dogs' teeth, bows, arrows, lime, string bags, salt and stone axes for pottery and wooden bowls, both made by the Rawa men, and sea shells which the Rawa acquire from neighbours to the east. Men, women and children travel in large groups; in the past this gave protection against the people living in the Ramu valley. The men carry the exchange items and the women carry heavy loads of sweet potato for food during the trip. The travellers usually make the river crossing in the morning and several trips are made across the chest-high water because the valuable goods must be carried across a little at a time in case a man slips. Once over the river, the group heads across the flat grasslands toward the Surinam River (a tributary of the Ramu) its course leading up into the foot-hills towards the Rawa hamlets.

During the actual exchange the visitors tether their pigs and dogs, sit down in a hamlet, sort out their valuables and wait for the hosts to favour them. Negotiations are between individuals. A wooden bowl and a pot are usually the first two items brought forth by the Rawa men as a bid for one of the displayed items. The Benabena people have a belief that the bowl and the pot are married, the pot being the male and the bowl being the female, a reasonable symbolism since the pot is an elongated shape and the bowl a wide open form. The Rawa, however, do not appear to share this interpretation. The visitors prefer light, medium-sized pots to larger, heavier ones because of the problems of transport. After successful negotiations the visitors are offered food and shelter. Sometimes the highland women marry the Rawa men and the highlanders value the bride price items: pots, bowls and the highly regarded shells, particularly strings of money cowry.

Fig. 8.48
Detail of Mikarew feast pot, Sirin.

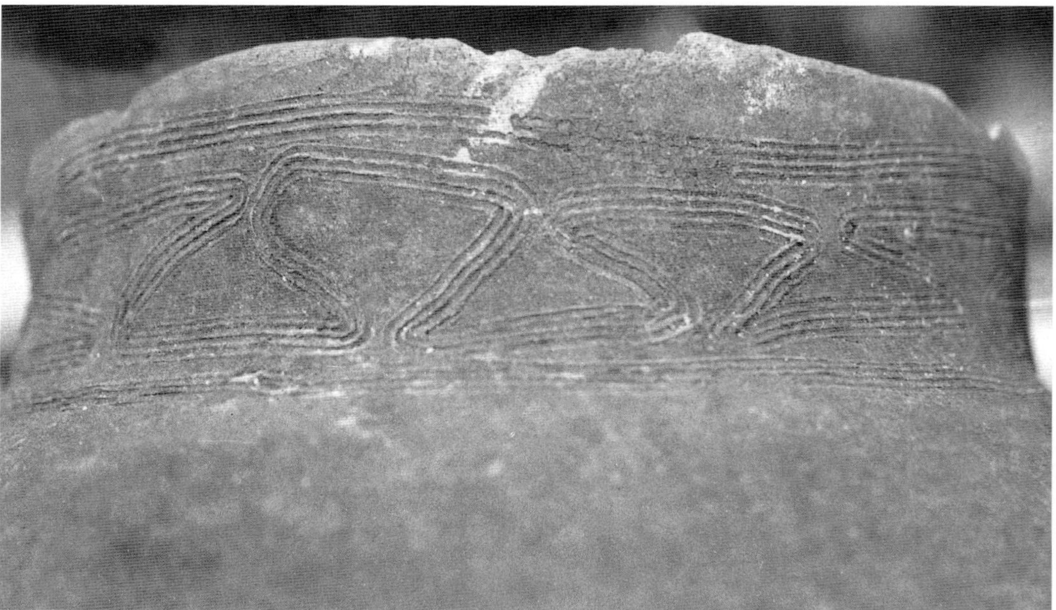

The Benabena, especially those living around Lihona (an area known locally as 'Wesan', meaning 'white sands'), act as middle-men in the further distribution of shells and pots. Rawa vessels have been found in villages around Henganofi and are occasionally displayed in local council exhibits at the Goroka show. The people who own these pots are ignorant of their origin, believing they are made at 'Wesan'. The situation is similar with the 'Usur' pots of Sumau and Urigina found in Bundi: in Bundi, all evidence indicated the Ramu River valley as their origin.

Rawa pots are poorly documented. Schmitz (1960) recorded an inaccurately drawn vessel from the 'Erawa' and Hughes collected one unidentified vessel at Sausi which he suggested originated in the Rawa area. Villages where pottery is thought to be produced are Sisimba, Kikipei, Tauta, Beringai, Mungo, Boro, Damanti, Gomumu, Seringo and Parimo (Barim); all are located in the southern part of the Rawa territory. Other Rawa villages higher in the mountains to the north apparently do not make pots. The Mari people who live along the Dumpu-Markham road say that the Rawa are no longer making pots, at least for trade. The Rawa, on the other hand, insisted that pots are still being made and young men who display aptitude and motivation are being trained in pot

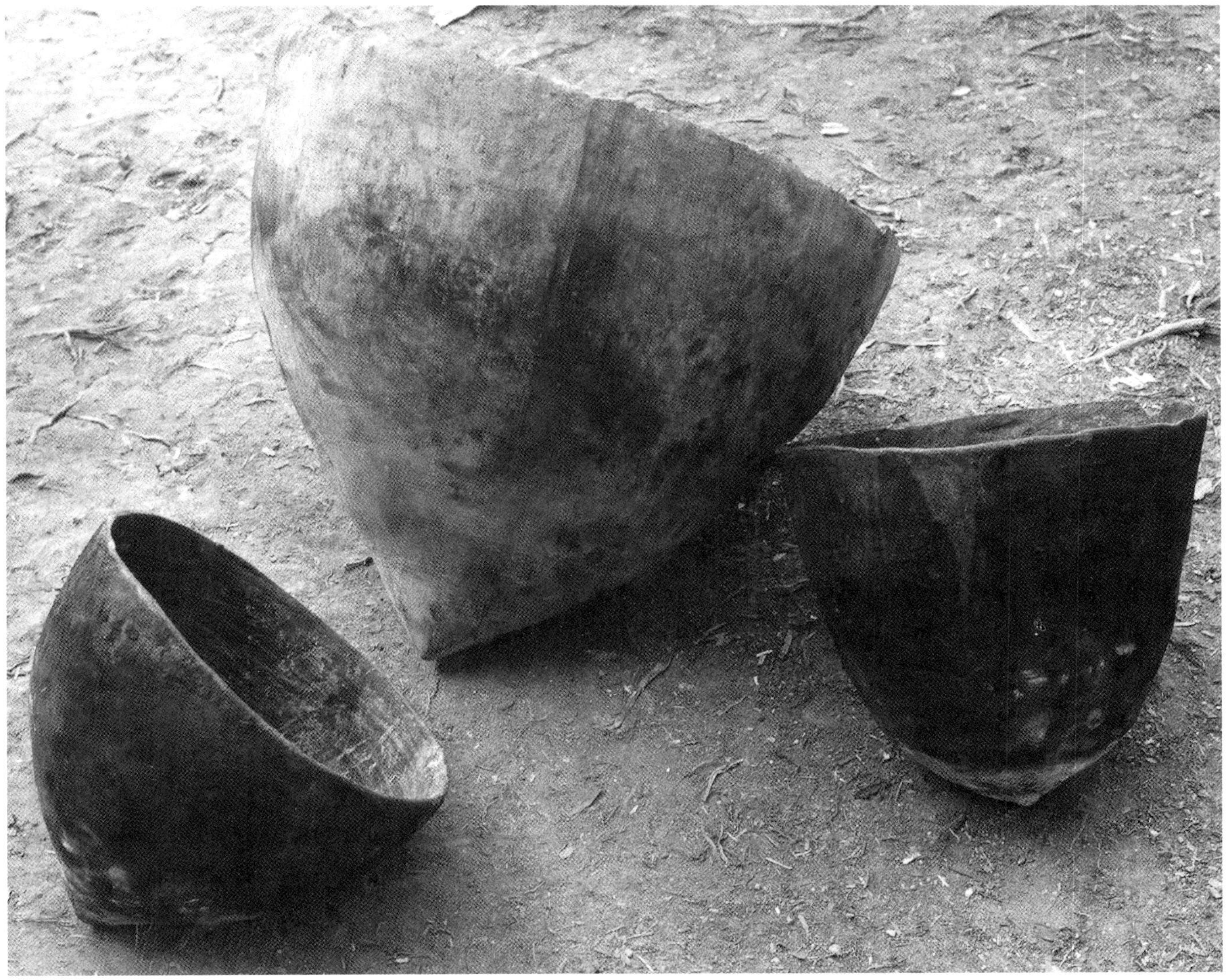

Fig. 8.49
Three cooking pots: (left) made at Pondoma; (centre) made at Tumbunduwi; (right) made at Simba. Tumbunduwi village, Josephstaal area. Tallest *h* 46 cm.

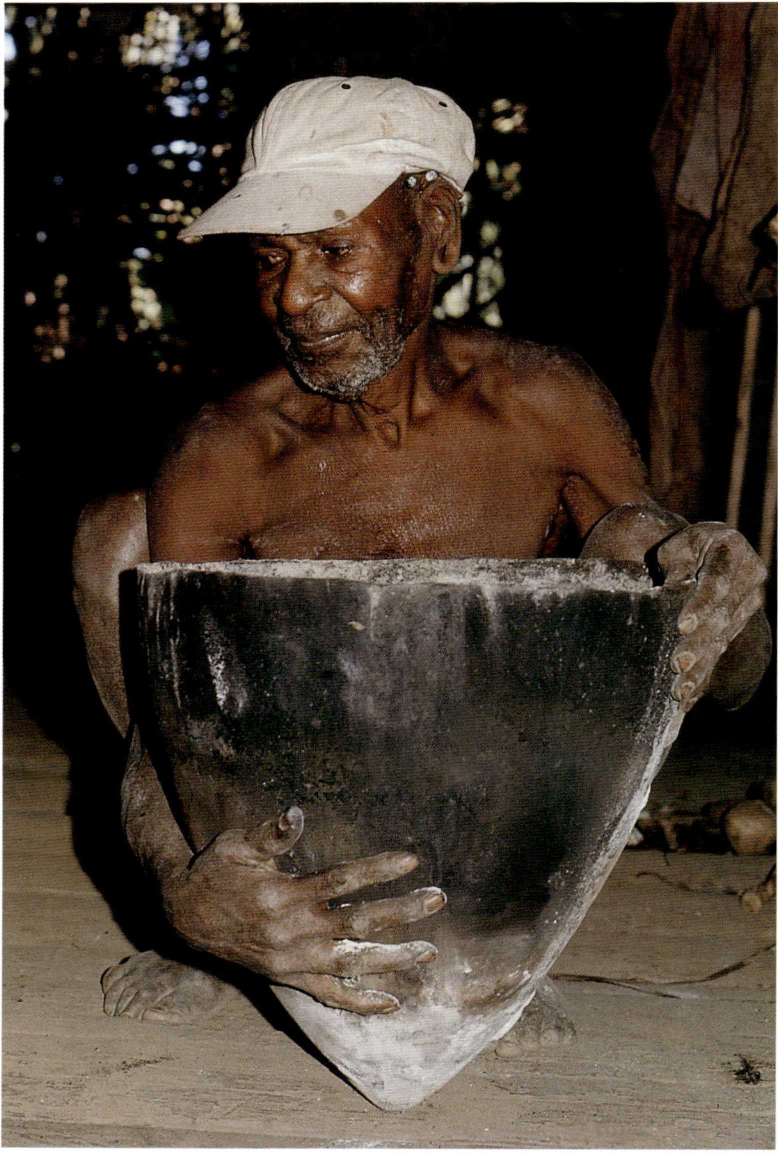

Fig. 8.50
Yavaki with his tallest pot, Waititangu village, Josephstaal area, *h* 41 cm.

making. There were eighteen named potters living in Tauta in 1973.

Rawa pots are composite in shape, with an inverted cone for the base, an ovoid body and a rather widely flaring everted neck which forms a corner point with the body and always has a direct rim. Vessels come in all sizes: small pots measure about 25 centimetres high and large pots are about 52 centimetres high. It was said that very large vessels are sometimes made, 'large enough to hold six little pigs!' (fig. 8.43).

The neck area usually serves as the field for decoration, which comprises incised patterns of cross-hatching, chevrons and herringbone motifs, applied coils marked by incised and punctate marks which define the joint of the neck and the body and applied nodules encircling the vessel below the inflection point. The rim is sometimes incised. Decorating by exposed coils, as found in the pots to the north-west, is not used here.

Although informants initially said that the marks had no particular meaning it was later claimed that they were representations of certain objects found in nature. On one vessel a design of five triangular-shaped areas extending from the rim down to the inflection point was said to represent peaks of mountains. Another vessel from Sisimbo had a design of triangles outlined by incised markings and filled in with gouged dashes; this was said to represent the belly of a small black bird which lives in the bush. A herringbone pattern was said to represent the bones of a fish. The same explanations were given, independently, for more complex designs on bamboo lime containers. Informants from the other industries in Madang did not proffer explanations of marks on their vessels.

The mountains of this area abound with clay deposits. The clay is blue-grey and may only be collected by the women, who also prepare it by picking out large pieces of grit and beating it with a large stick. The potters roll the coils on a long flat piece of any type of bark. Coiling is started on the palm of the hand; when a large vessel is about 15 to 16 centimetres high it is transferred to a ring of pandanus leaves. From then on the method of production is similar to that described in previous industries. Bamboo and flying fox bones are used to mark the vessels and when they are ready for drying they are placed in a string bag and suspended from the roof of a house to hang for about four weeks. Firing methods correspond to those of the other industries and fuel is wood or bark. A platform of firewood is constructed, the pot is placed right side up in the middle of the burning fuel and burning pieces of bark are placed inside the vessel. The pot is turned several times with a stick

In Tauta a story was told about the introduction of pottery:

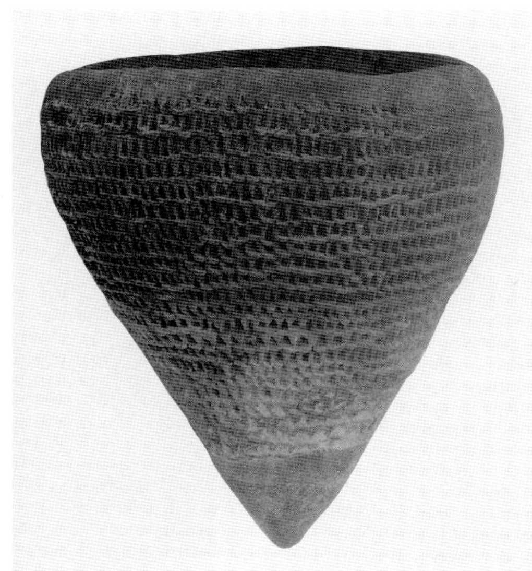

Fig. 8.51
Wanuma cooking pot.

> Before, our people came from behind the Nambai mountains [Saidor]: they did not have pots and cooked in wood, putting hot stones and leaves into hollowed out sections of tree trunks. One day they came down to the Ramu River. The people from there have pots and our grandfathers tasted food cooked in pots and it was good. Then our people came and settled at Sambo. They worked a 'rope' [a trade link] from the top of the mountain to the bottom. They sent pots from this rope and pulled up string bags, bows and arrows, lime and salt. The people from Bena came to trade with the Rawa people. The Rawa people gave them pots and the Bena people sent women. A lot of Rawa men married Bena girls.

Nahu

There is another industry yet to be recorded, that of the Nahu-speaking neighbours of the Rawa who live in the Finisterre Range near the Gusap River. The Rawa people say that their neighbours make pots similar to their own.

Mari

The Mari people live in villages along the Ramu River plains, beneath the foothills of the Finisterres. They are linguistically related to the Azera and were once potters, too, but the industry has been defunct for at least twenty years, probably due to the predominance of Azera vessels. The generic name for pots is *gurr*. One old man from Bumbu, a potter named Lasus, described the technique to us. The women gathered the clay, which came from the vicinity of the Ramu River, and the men prepared it. The form was started as in the Eastern Highlands: a shallow depression was made in the ground and the coiling was started in this. A bamboo scraper was used to smooth the coils and refine the walls. Designs running around the neck, just under the outward flaring rim, were made by the serrated edge of a shell and punctation marks were made by a sharp pointed tool, probably bamboo. The authors located one Mari vessel in Sankian village. The base is slightly pointed, the body ovoid and the neck flares outward forming a flange and a wide mouth (fig. 8.45).

Tangu

In the north-west of Madang Province, some 25 kilometres inland from the coast in the hills and forested mountains of the Bogia region, is an

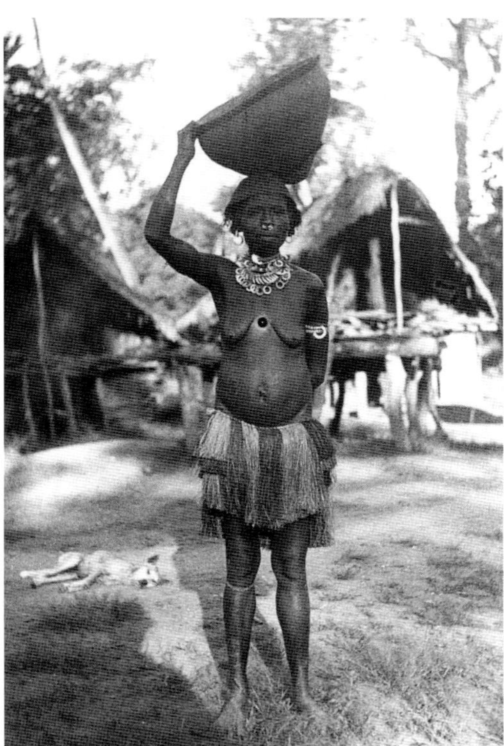

Fig. 8.52
Woman carrying a newly fired Bosman cooking pot, *gun*.

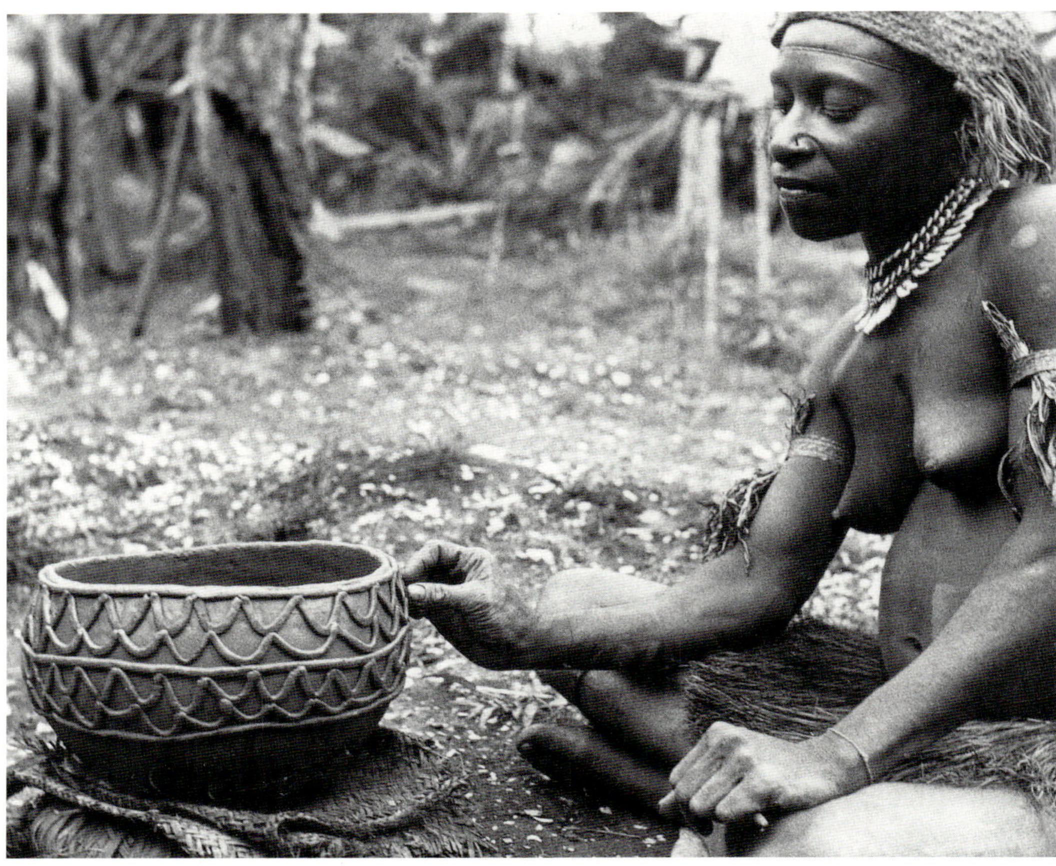

Fig. 8.53
Decorating a cooking pot: a new style, imitating a brass bowl.

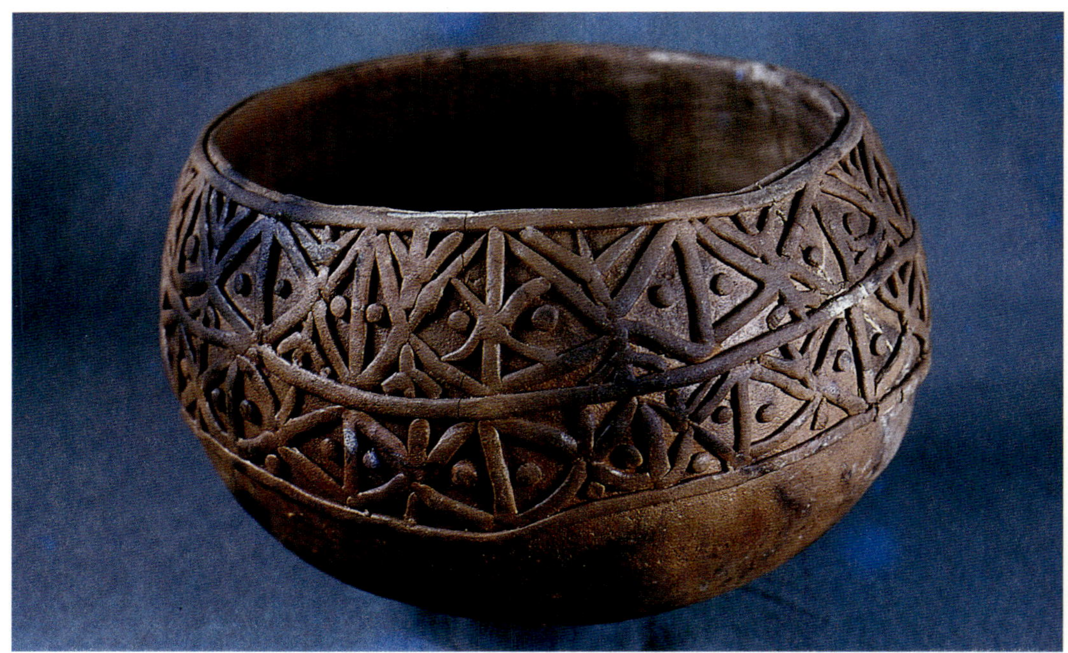

Fig. 8.54
A new style Bosman pot, collected by Beatrice Blackwood for the Pitt Rivers Museum.

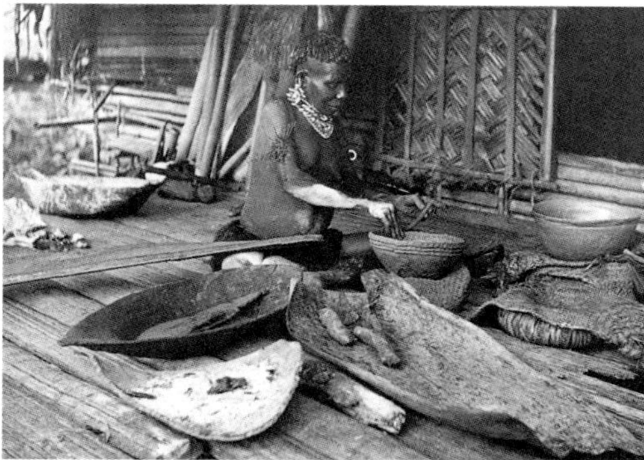

Fig. 8.55

association of four small communities related by kinship ties, trade alliances and language. The loosely grouped communities are Wanitzir, Biampitzir (Beiamp), Mangigumitzir and Riekitzir. 'Tangu' has been adopted as the name for this group by K.O. Burridge who has written extensively of the area.

The Tangu people are mainly agriculturalists and hunters although a number of males work as labourers along the coast. The main foodstuffs consist of taro, yam, sago, sweet potato, bananas and coconuts. Trade between the Tangu communities helps to unify the areas, solidify relationships and distribute resources. The two pot producing groups are Wanitzir and Biampitzir. They supply the other Tangu people with pots in exchange for commodities they lack, such as sago, string bags, tobacco, betel nut and pandanus. People outside the Tangu region come to the area for pots and social exchange. The Tangu in turn journey to the coast for salt, lime, dogs and manufactured goods (Burridge 1969). The main demand for pots was from people who came to Tangu from as far afield as Manam Island on the traditional trade route from the coast and from the Mikarew people among whom pot making has almost ceased.

Since Burridge wrote, pottery activity has declined rapidly and what used to be a regular occupation is now at best spasmodic. In some villages only one or two pot makers remain. The villages in Biampitzir (Beiamp) where pots are produced are Riknang'tien, Ruonganan, Barein and Wanar, and, in Wanitzir, Wasamb and Ni'out. Both men and women make pots by the coil technique and sometimes they work together on the same pot. Young girls may join in and help work the coils.

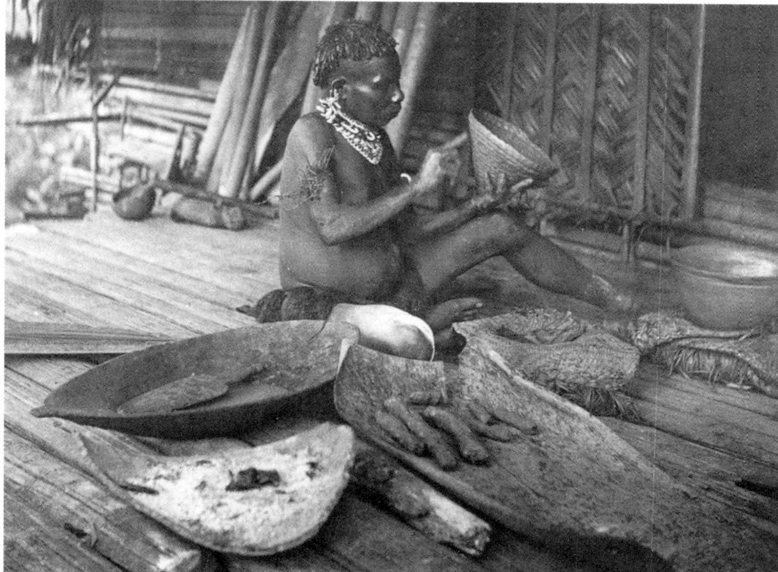

Fig. 8.56

The only taboo noted is against menstruating women, who are not allowed to make pots or even go near them lest they break.

Only cooking pots, *manou*, are produced. They are all of a similar type; some are not unlike the Bau pots but more irregularly shaped. The vessels have pointed or knobbed bases and are restricted in form, with very wide belly areas, necks and everted rims. Decoration is mostly confined to the neck and consists of alternating zones of smoothed and marked coils. Some vessels combine finger drag

Figs 8.55 to 8.62
Bosman potters, 1937.

Fig. 8.55
Applying a coil.

Fig. 8.56
Bonding the coils on the outside of the pot.

Fig. 8.57
Rolling up the coil to form the pointed base.

Fig. 8.57

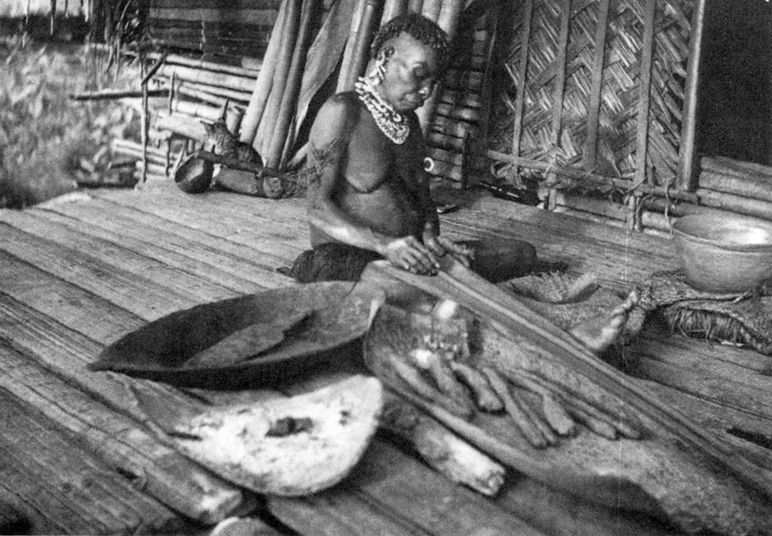

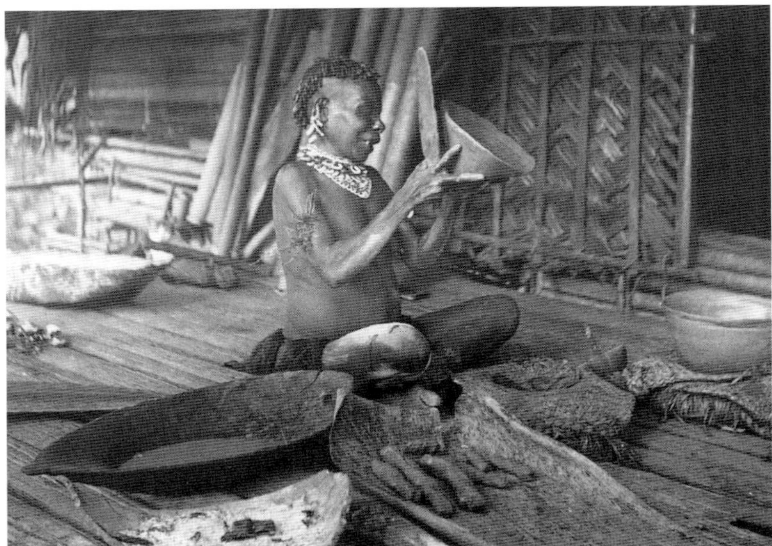

Fig. 8.58

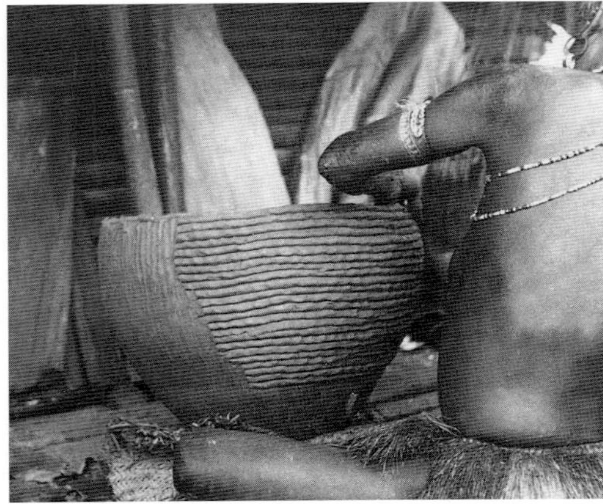

Fig. 8.59

Fig. 8.58
Beating the outside with a wooden paddle.

Fig. 8.59
Large pot – potter bonding coils.

Fig. 8.60
Potter with her finished vessel.

Fig. 8.61
Firing – potter adding more 'pangal'.

marks with combed zig-zag and wavy lines which extend below the neck (fig. 8.46).

The mountains abound in clay and all of the villages have their own source. At Riknang'tien a hole is dug near the bottom of a small bank, topsoil cleared away and the clay removed from the wet pit with a pointed stick. Small roots are removed and the clay is patted into coconut-sized balls and carried back to the village in baskets. Usually the clay is left for three days or so before it is used. It is a grey yellowish-brown colour with good plasticity and is of fairly sandy texture.

The potter pulls a lump of clay, *manav*, off the ball and presses it out between thumb and fingers, removing stones and roots. It is then squeezed into a rough thick roll and the palm of the hand is used to roll it out on a 'pangal' to pencil thickness. The vessel is then made in the spiral coil technique. As the pot grows in size it is transferred to a banana leaf ring-cushion. Final smoothing with wet hands immediately precedes the decorating, which is most commonly done by dragging the finger down at intervals across the top five or six coils from the lip to the neck area; sometimes, however, the marks are made with a small stick or comb. Pots are dried

Fig. 8.60

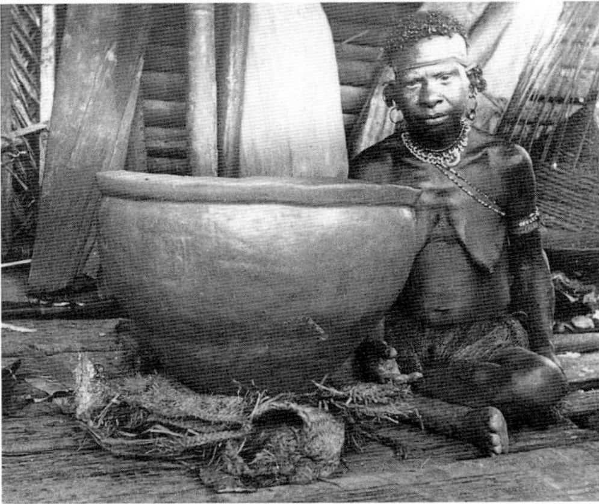

Fig. 8.61

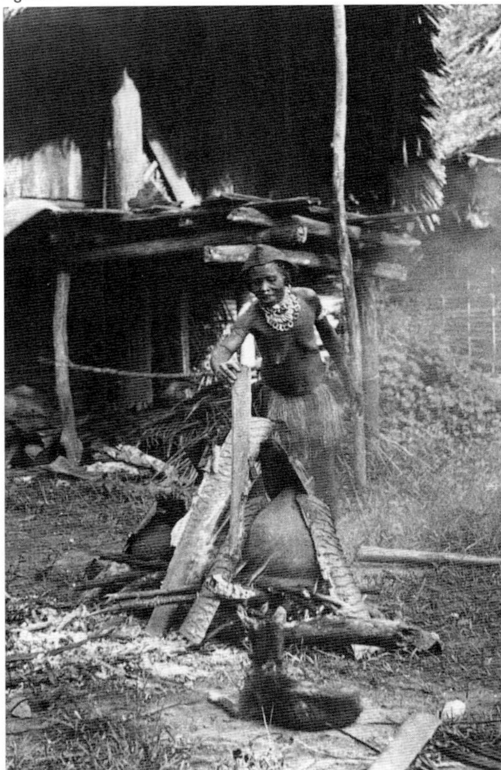

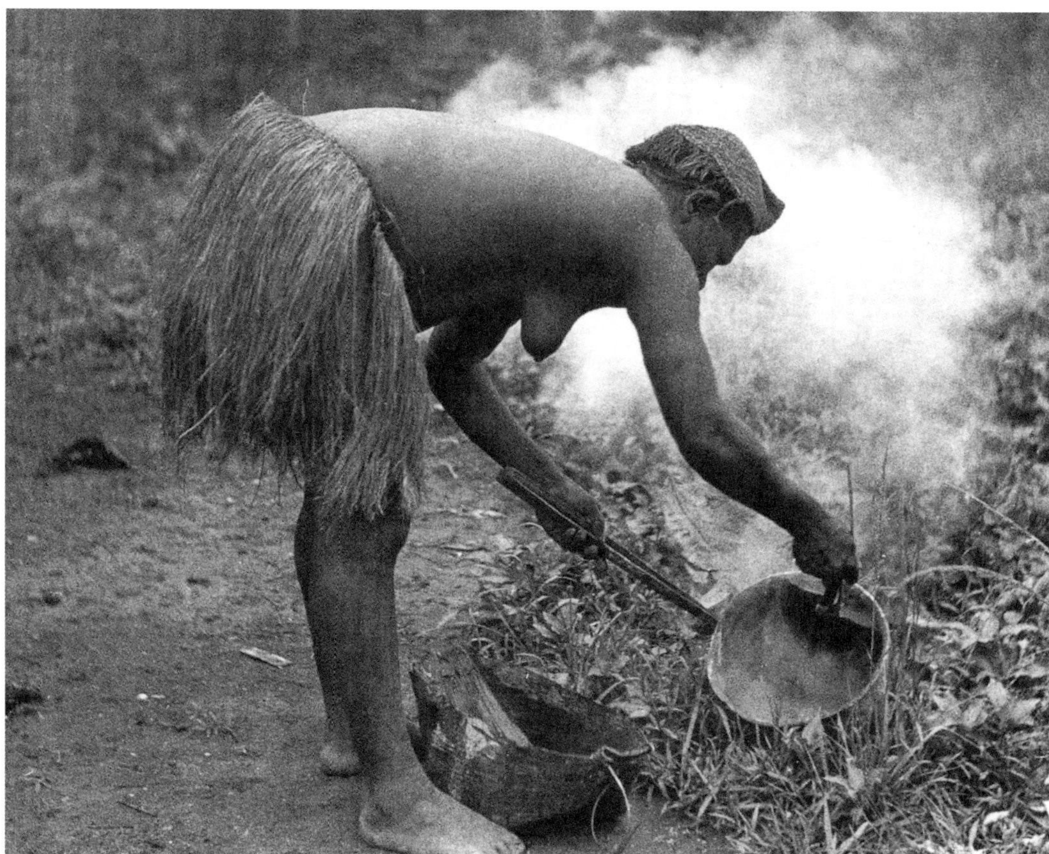

Fig. 8.62
Bosman potter sealing a pot, hot from the firing, with sago solution, 1937.

inside the house for one or two months and then fired with coconut fronds as fuel.

Mikarew

The widespread Mikarew language group includes some thirty villages north and north-west of Tangu and reaches the coast just north of Bogia. It includes some pot makers but the number and distribution, style and technique have not been fully recorded. It is said they make pots similar to those of the Tangu, and they also are made by men and women. Confirmation of these points is only available for the villages around Ariangong mission and the village of Makarup. Makarup potters have to collect their clay from Tiap and Tongbur, some distance to the east, and only make pots when they are needed.

One pot observed had a wavy line decoration, produced by a four-pronged comb, just below the rim on the neck area. This was a very old pot which had a finer finish and different character from those seen today in the Tangu area. (figs 8.47, 8.48).

Josephstaal

Three groups of people who produce the same type of pottery are located inland in a vast area which lies between the Adelbert Range and the Ramu River and is drained by the tributaries of the Guam and Sogeram rivers, which flow into the Ramu. These are the Pondoma who live near the Josephstaal patrol post, the Katiati to the south-east and the Ikundun to the north-west. It is said that pots were once made in every village of the area but now only a few are still producing them. Among these are Katiati, Kisila and Angasa (Katiati language) and Pondoma (Pondoma language).

Large conical, unrestricted and restricted cooking vessels are made in the coil technique by both men and women. They are undecorated. These

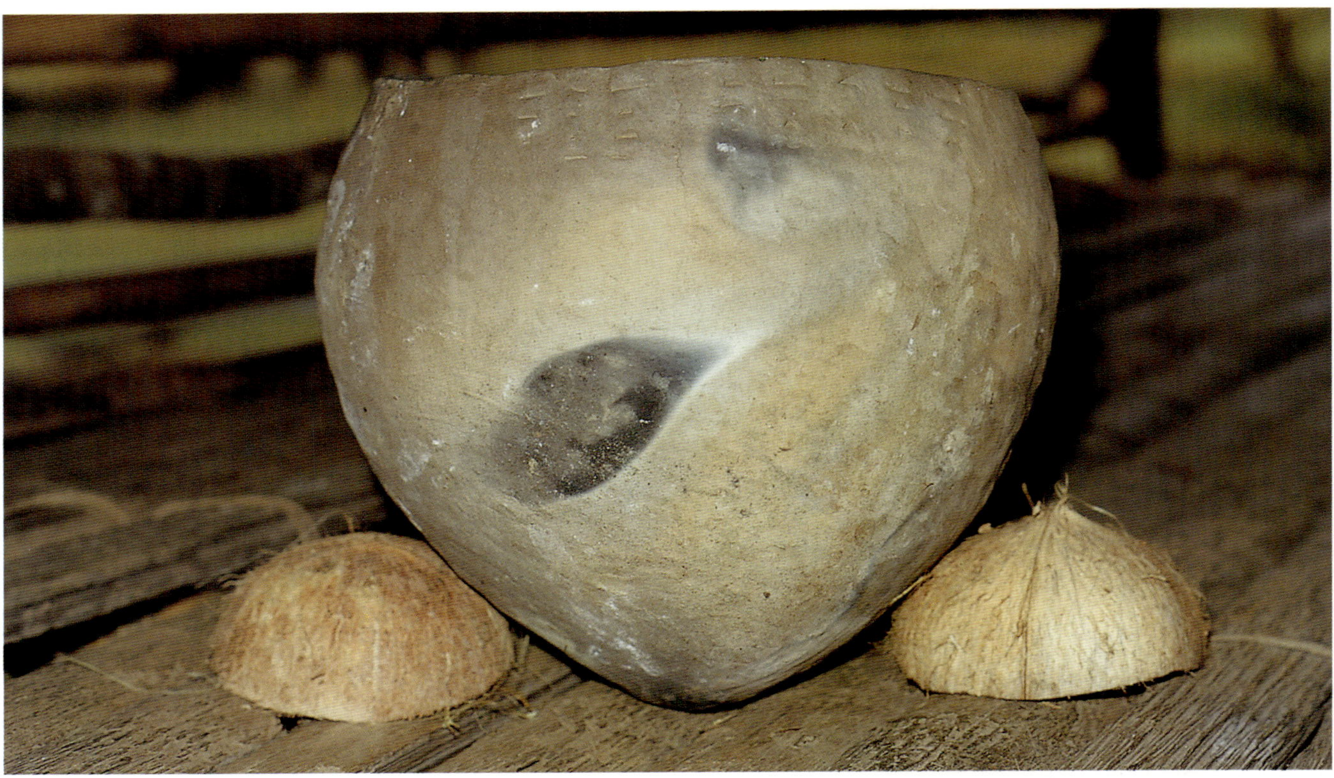

Fig. 8.63
Rao cooking pot, *n'ge*, showing a smudge mark from the firing, Nodabu village, Middle Ramu River.

pots, used for all general cooking purposes and feasts, are called *hunan* in Pondoma and *sangu* in Katiati. Size ranges from pots 34 centimetres high with 38-centimetre mouths to large ones 46 centimetres high with mouth diameters of 48 to 54 centimetres. Broken pieces of cooking pots are used for frying sago cakes. Clay, *pelai* (Katiati), is prepared by mixing it with water and treading it with the feet. Pencil thin coils are rolled out onto a 'pangal', they are spiral coiled from the point upwards and joined with the fingers. The surface is smoothed by gently beating the outside of the pot with a wet wooden paddle against a hand held inside. There is no information concerning firing. When used for cooking, the pointed-based vessels are placed in a hole in the ground and a fire is built up around the base (figs 8.49, 8.50).

Midsivindi

To the west of the Ikundun language group are the people who speak the Midsivindi language and are said to be potters. The area requires investigation.

Wanuma

To the east of Josephstaal, about half way between the coast and the Ramu River, live the Wanuma people whose men make cooking pots by the coiling technique. Several of the villages around the Wanuma mission station, including Sengrusengru and Wabriatau, have the right to make pots. Women are allowed to make pots if they so desire but usually only help the men with clay gathering and preparation and organising the firing.

The Wanuma pots are conical with pointed bases and have restricted and unrestricted orifices (fig. 8.51). Most vessels have smooth surfaces but some can be decorated with exposed coils marked by a square-ended stick in a 'stab and drag technique. In the past, huge pots as high as 75 centimetres were reported to be made but now smaller pots, approximately 28 to 40 centimetres high, are made. All the pot makers collect their clay from one source at the foot of a mountain. The clay is beaten until it attains the proper consistency and then it is formed into long thin coils. The vessel is built up

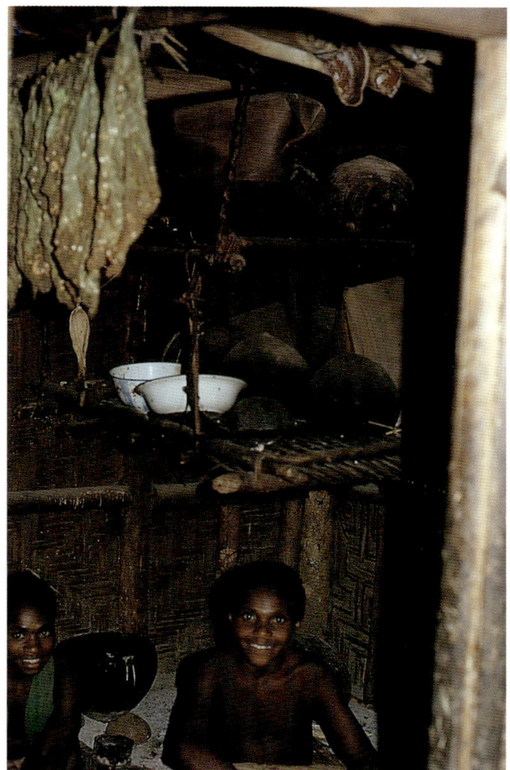

spirally, supported on a pandanus leaf ring. It is dried in a house for up to eight months before it is fired.

Yaben and Parawan

Several other pot making areas are reported to exist south-east of Wanuma. Yaben villages cited as centres of pot production are Ikarinagra and Komiarum; Parawan villages mentioned are Ilebeguma, Ilima, Kosilanta and Magila. As is the case with the Wanuma industry, the need for further studies in these areas is urgent: the craft is in danger of extinction.

Bosman

Three villages belonging to the Bosman language group are located about 18 kilometres inland from the mouth of the Ramu River, on a small tributary leading off the main river. These villages, always referred to as the 'Bosman' villages, are now named separately as Mangai, Dongon and Goinbang. Pots are made by the Awar-speaking people in two other villages located on the coast at Awar and Nubia. Beatrice Blackwood (1951), an anthropologist from the Pitt Rivers Museum, Oxford, lived in the centre of the Bosman group in 1937 and recorded pot making there. Georg von Höltker (1965) has also written a detailed report on pottery in the area. At the time of Blackwood's sojourn pottery making was one of the principal industries of the women but today the industry is declining.

Pots, *gun*, are made in the coiling technique, with paddle-and-anvil finish. Two types of cooking

Fig. 8.64
Interior of a house showing typical rack for storing pots over the fire, Watabu village, middle Ramu.

Fig. 8.65
Rao potter Gravagim coiling, Nodabu village, middle Ramu.

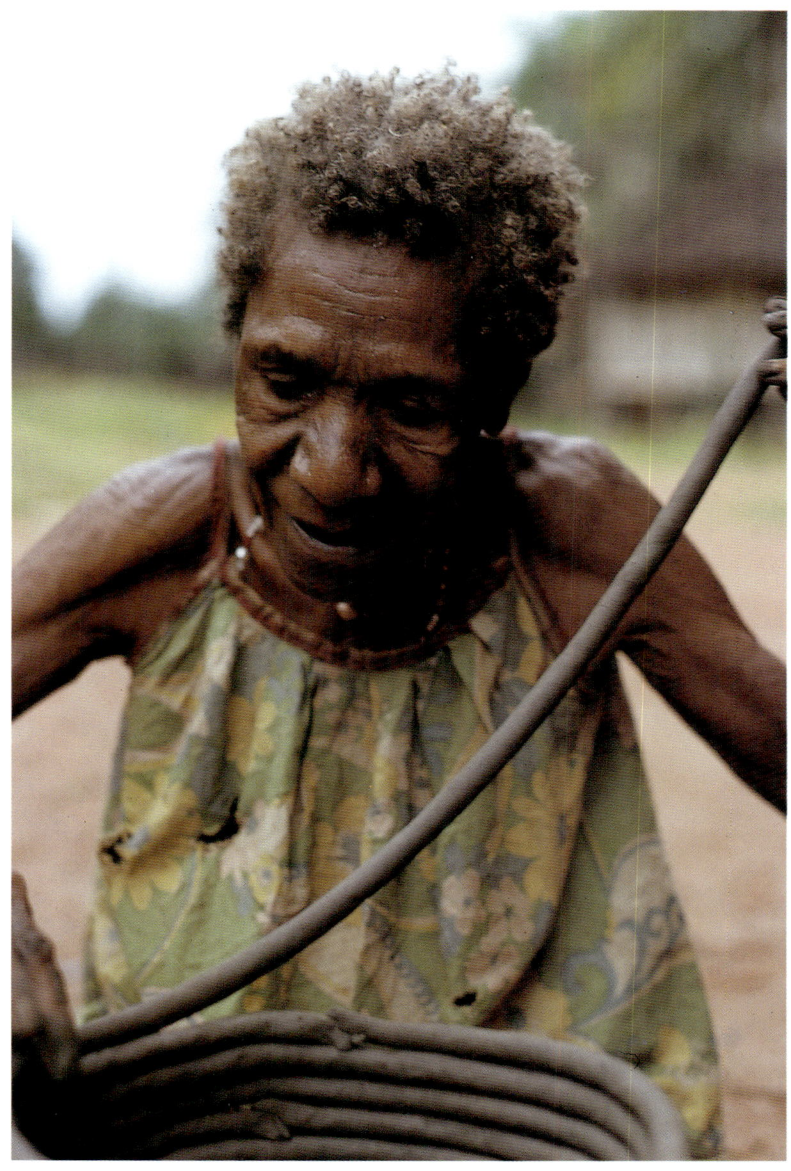

vessel are made. The first is a wide-mouthed, ovoid vessel with a pointed base and everted rim ranging in size from 28 to 40 centimetres high. This type is not decorated. The second is a semi-spherical pot with a rounded or slightly pointed bottom. It can be restricted or straight-sided and the top rim is bevelled. Size varies greatly, from small bowls 8 centimetres high to taller pots 23 centimetres high. Decoration consists in coils applied in wavy, scalloped bands running around the top third portion of the vessel or in a series of straight horizontal bands with other coils forming short vertical registers, crosses and angled lines offset by random dots. This type of decoration, and possibly the rounded version of the base, were said by Blackwood to be recent innovations inspired by a metal bowl some of the potters saw in a European's house at Awar plantation (Figs 8.52, 8.53).

Apart from the cooking pots a curious doll-like figurine is fashioned from scrap pieces of clay. These dolls are said to be made purely for pleasure and are used as toys by the young girls. Höltker suggests they are made by young girls who are learning to pot and are used to practise firing technique. The figurines are roughly modelled, with squarish bodies and stumps for arms and legs. The head and face are clearly rendered, with a prominent nose, a mouth and pierced ears through which tufts of fibre are tied. The only close analogy to these figures is the modelled figures made at Dimiri-Marawat-Yaul, off the Yuat River in the Sepik Province.

There is some evidence that clay objects were used in ritual. Höltker describes a kind of water drum, a pot filled with water which is blown into it from a hollow bamboo tube. The noise this makes is associated with the spirits and it is used to frighten the women and children. After the ceremony the pots were buried in one of the old men's houses. Another clay object, shaped like a penis and undoubtedly made by men, is unknown to the women and Höltker suspects it was used in fertility rites.

Clay, *teschin*, is found close to the villages and collected by groups of women. The forming technique is coiling, similar to the other methods but with some variations. The coils are quite long, about 100 centimetres. The first coil is started on a narrow 'pangal' until half the coil is fed around on itself and bonded; then the potter picks up the pot and holds it in her hand while continuing the coiling. When the first coils are in place the pot is placed on a grass ring covered by green leaves. The pot is turned on this and further coils are added. The end of the previous coil is left dangling while a new one is rolled; the joining is then completed and the next coil added. This use of the dangling coil is, to the authors' knowledge, unique in Papua New Guinea. At various stages the coils are joined together, smoothed with wet hands and beaten with a flat wooden beater until all traces of coiling have been removed. The top edge is trimmed with a shell or indented with the forefinger. The pot is finally smoothed with the paddle and the everted bevelled rim is formed with the thumb and first finger.

Two or three pots may be fired at one time. Fuel, pieces of wood and dry coconut palm fronds, is stacked together and set alight. The pots are then set upside down on the burning fuel and more dry coconut fronds are stacked against them, completely covering them. Firings are reported to last for about ten minutes, making this one of the most rapid firings in Papua New Guinea. The pots are lifted off the embers with a long stick and splashed with a sago solution for sealing and strengthening.

No information regarding trading is given by Blackwood but sightings by the authors of Bosman pots in distant villages and reports by informants suggest that they were traded over a wide area in the past and that some are still exchanged or sold. They were traded to the Mikarew and Tangu people, south to Pir near the Ramu River and up into the Porapora country to the west. The authors saw Bosman pots as far afield as Rurunat on the Bogia coast, at Amron inland from Alexishafen and at Usino patrol post near the source of the Ramu, close to the Morobe-Madang border.

Rao

Some members of the widespread Rao language group, the middle Ramu and upper Keram rivers, are pot makers. The pot making is now carried out only by a few older women in the villages of Nodabu, Sabu, Watabu, Pakingabu, Kragabu, Balbu and Moibu on the Ramu, at Nagrabu and

Bamfu on the Keram where it flows close to the Ramu and, possibly, at Litibu in the foothills of the Schrader Range. The clay source for the Keram villagers and some of the Ramu people is close to the Ramu, in the Tsumba area; the Keram women come over to camps on the Ramu at Brambido and nearby to gather clay and make pots.

Only rough cooking pots, *n'ge*, are now made; flat frying pans are occasionally manufactured but more often large broken pieces of cooking pots are used for frying sago cakes.

The cooking pots may also be used for stirring sago. They are slightly round-based, hemispherical and with restricted or unrestricted orifices. Most pots are not decorated but occasionally two to four coils are left unjoined, forming casual decoration along the top rim (fig. 8.63).

Women from the villages near the Annaberg mission collect clay, also called *n'ge*, from the western side of the Ramu in the foothills of the Schrader Range. The brownish-grey clay is relatively free of rubble but is quite sandy and has very good plasticity. It is squeezed into thick sausages about 15 centimetres long and rolled out on 'pangal' into pencil thin coils about 60 centimetres long. Coiling is started on the 'pangal'; when the pot is about 15 centimetres high the potter transfers it to her hand and supports it against her knee. Later she lifts it onto a ring. Only now does the potter bond the coils and shape the vessel by working and smoothing the coils downwards from the inside, swelling the shape as it is smoothed. The top is levelled by pushing the high areas along between thumb and forefinger to fill in the lower areas. It is reported that the potters in the Tsumba area sometimes use a wooden paddle for smoothing the pot. Any kind of wood is used for firing but sago palm leaves and coconut fronds are not used here. The pots, hot from the fire, are sealed with a thin sago solution.

From the Tsumba area pots used to be traded north to Bingo, east to the Guam River villages, west into the Porapora country and south into the middle Keram area and to some villages on the Ramu; this trading has almost ceased now. Nodabu seems to be one of the main potting villages and people come there from great distances to trade yam, fish, betel nut, string bags, bows, arrows and tobacco for pots. The people of Jitibu obtain pots from all of the villages mentioned in exchange for the usual trading items as well as canoes and the bark of the tulip tree (*Gnetum gnemon*) which is used in making string for string bags. Twenty pots could be obtained for one canoe, four for a large fish and from five to ten pots for a large bundle of bark. The Rao who live in the Schrader Range foothills act as middle-men between the river people and the people of the mountains. Kasprus (1973) reports that these mountain groups wanted sago, salt and pots from the lower areas. The foothill group provided pandanus fruit and the mountain people sent tobacco, string bags, sweet potatoes, stone axes and bird of paradise feathers. The pygmy mountain people were particularly keen to acquire money cowries from the river people and in return supplied them with lumps of clay-like earth which was used as a 'medicine' for dogs, being added to their food and supposedly turning them into ferocious hunters of bush pigs.

Breri

Intruding into the Rao area is the Breri language group, which occupies a 20-kilometre length of the Ramu River from south of Tsumba to just north of Nodabu. The only report of pot making among the Breri is from Kasprus (1973), who records that the Ormon-ke Breri make cone-shaped pots which have the great disadvantage of not being watertight. The Breri themselves prefer the Rao vessels.

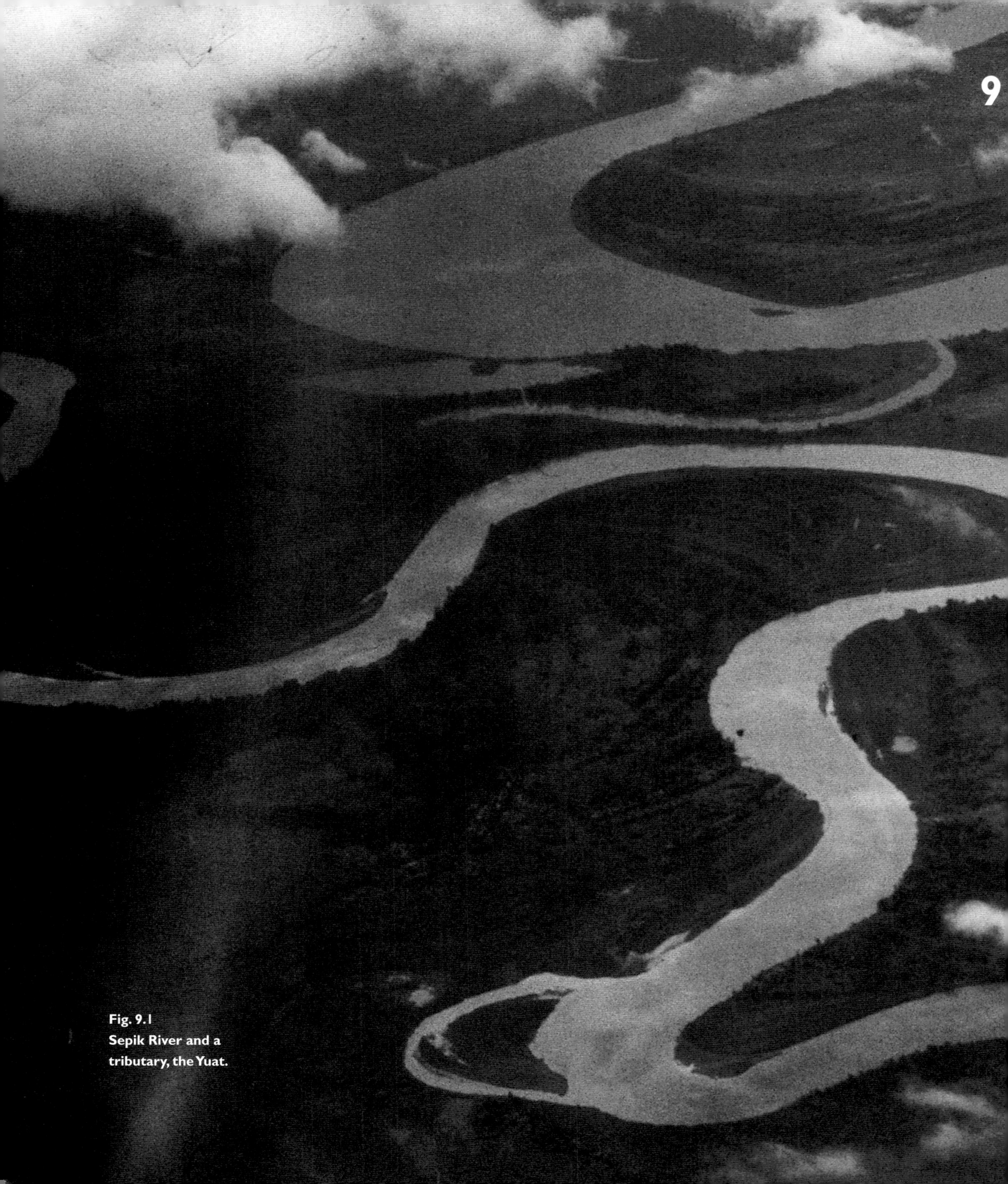

9

Fig. 9.1
Sepik River and a tributary, the Yuat.

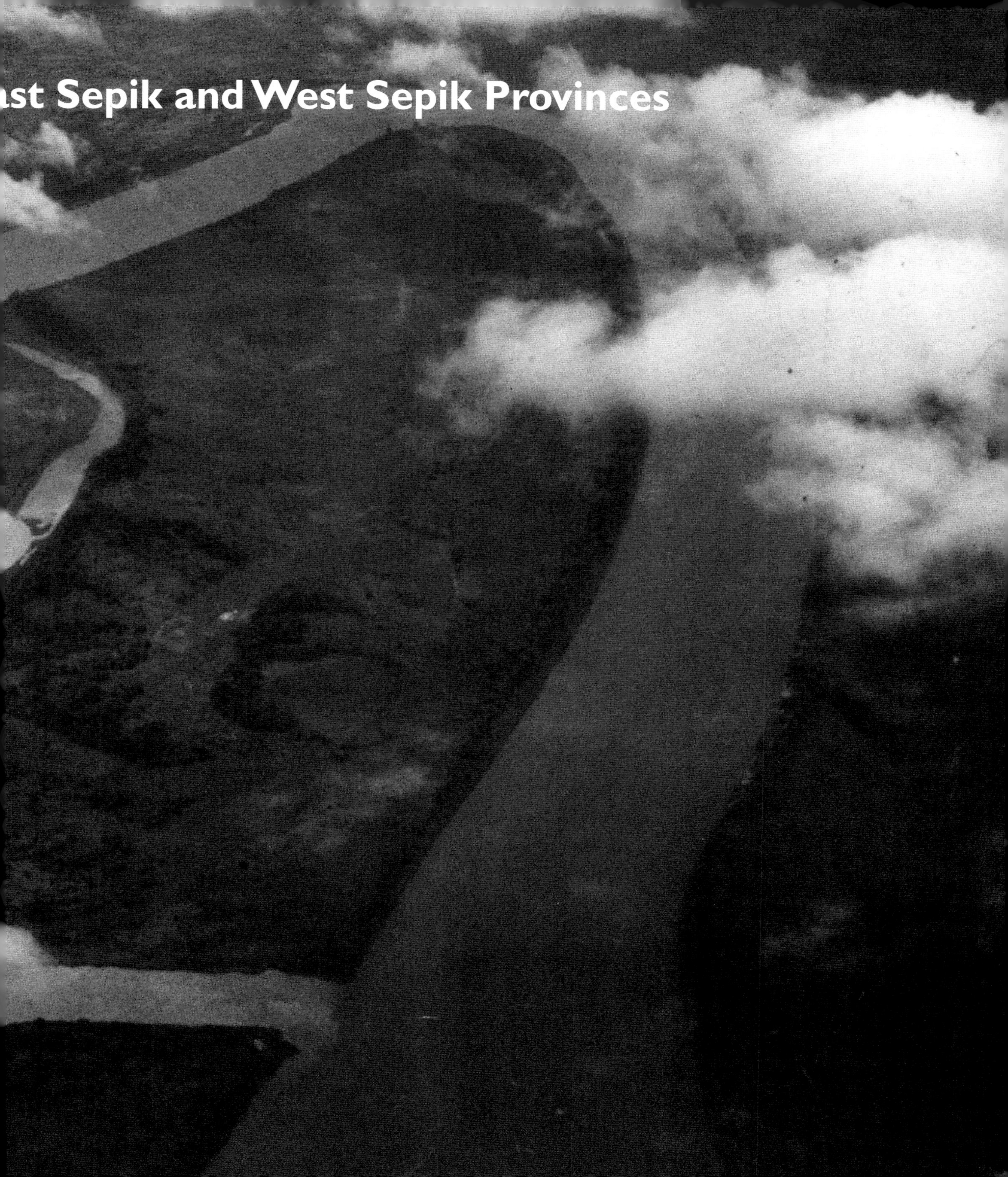
ast Sepik and West Sepik Provinces

MAP 10

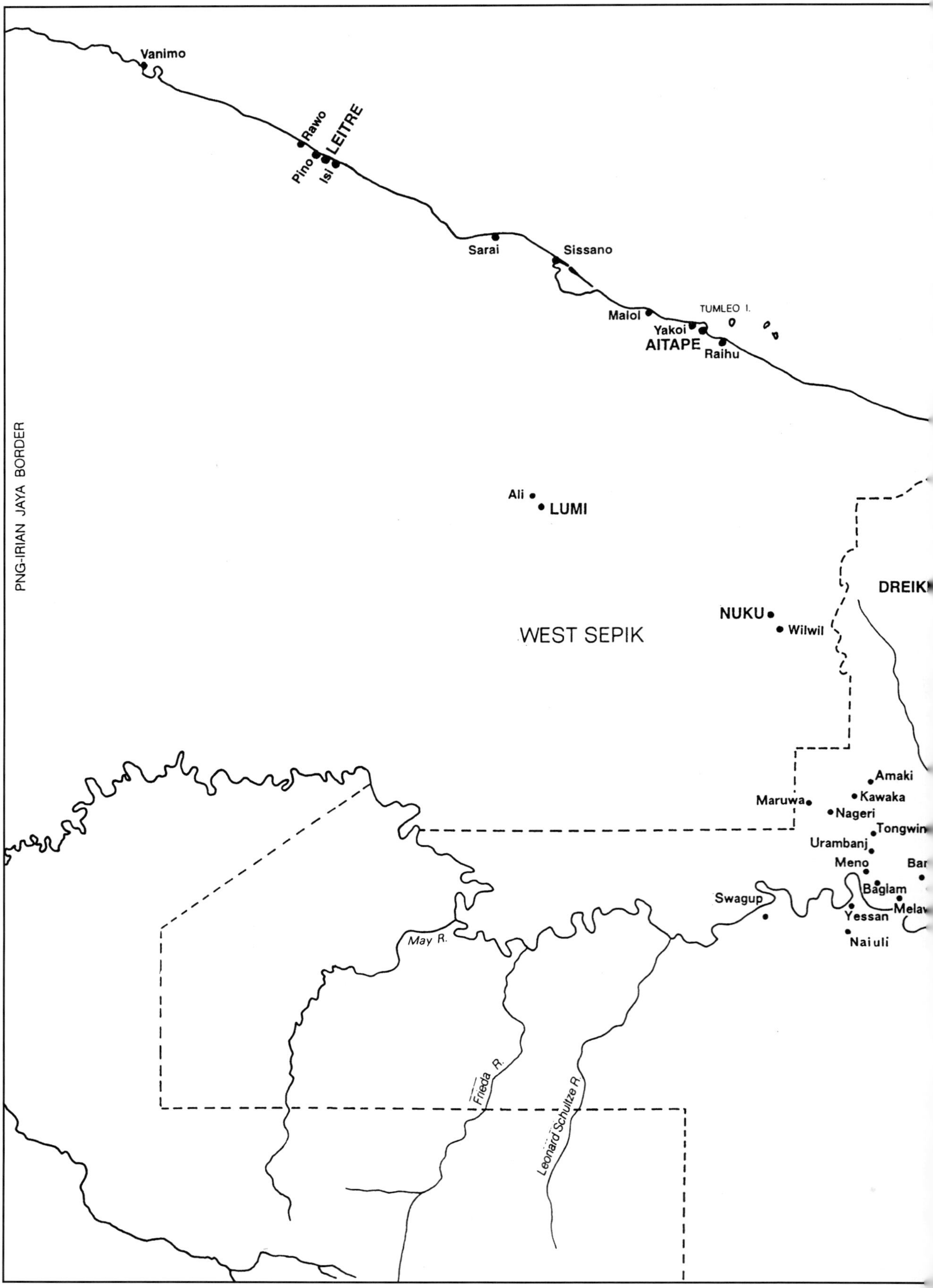

Vanimo
Rawo
LEITRE
Pino
Isi
Sarai
Sissano
Maloi
TUMLEO I.
Yakoi
AITAPE
Raihu
PNG-IRIAN JAYA BORDER
Ali
LUMI
DREIK
NUKU
Wilwil
WEST SEPIK
Amaki
Kawaka
Maruwa
Nageri
Tongwin
Urambanj
Meno
Bar
Baglam
Swagup
Melav
Yessan
Naiuli
May R.
Frieda R.
Leonard Schultze R.

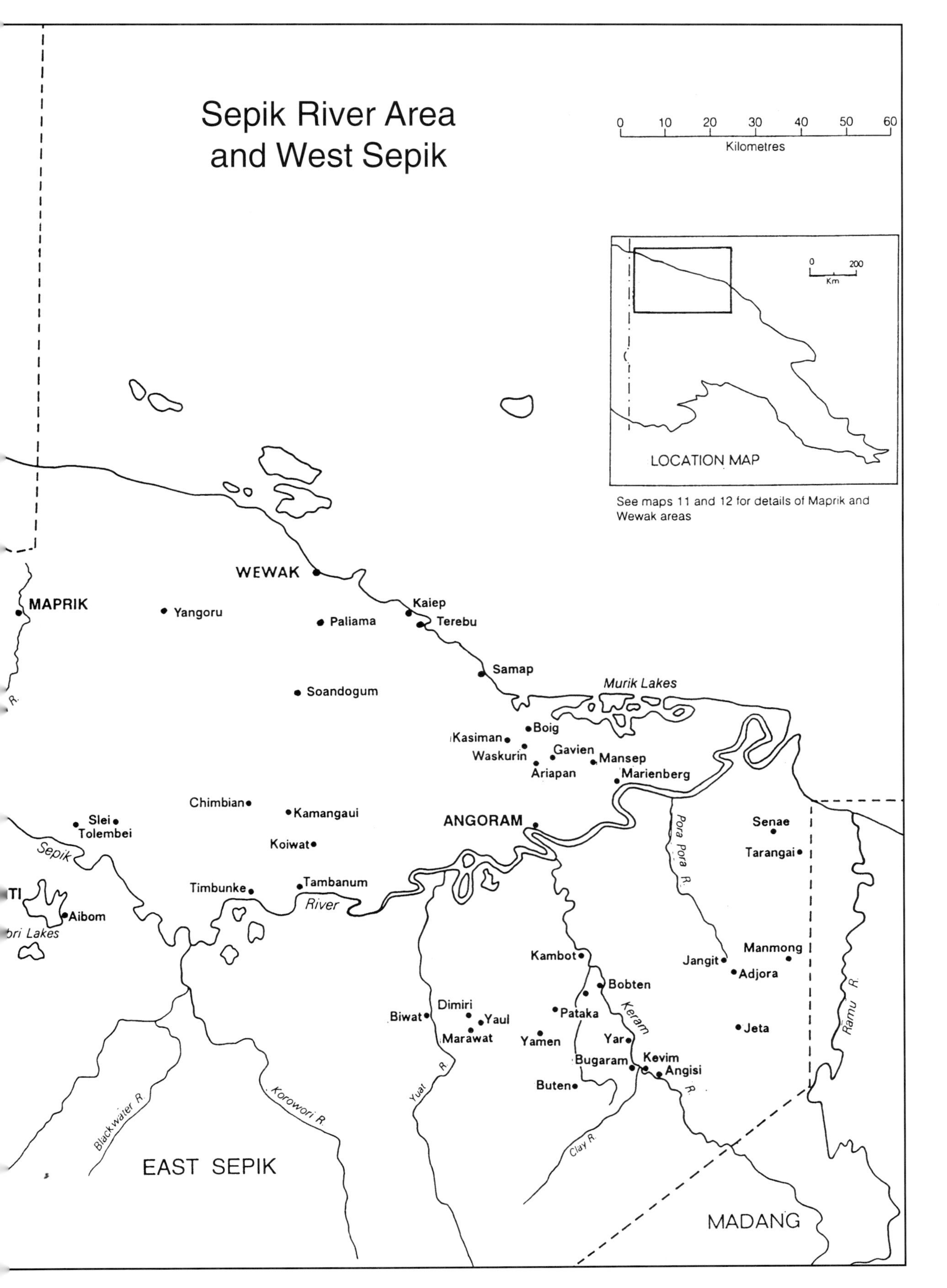
Sepik River Area
and West Sepik
0
10
20
30
40
50
60
Kilometres
0
200
Km
LOCATION MAP
See maps 11 and 12 for details of Maprik and Wewak areas
WEWAK
MAPRIK
Yangoru
Paliama
Kaiep
Terebu
Samap
Soandogum
Murik Lakes
Boig
Kasiman
Waskurin
Gavien
Mansep
Ariapan
Marienberg
Chimbian
Kamangaui
Slei
Tolembei
Sepik
ANGORAM
Koiwat
Senae
Tarangai
Pora Pora R.
Timbunke
Tambanum
River
Aibom
Kambot
Jangit
Manmong
Adjora
Bobten
Dimiri
Biwat
Yaul
Pataka
Keram
Jeta
Marawat
Yamen
Yar
Bugaram
Kevim
Angisi
Buten
R.
Ramu R.
Yuat R.
Blackwater R.
Korowori R.
Clay R.
EAST SEPIK
MADANG

The authors have classified pottery from the East and West Sepik provinces into three broad categories based on geography rather than art styles: the Sepik River and its tributaries; the inland Sepik area, including the Sepik plains and grasslands stretching north and north-west of the main river and the foothills and mountains of the Torricelli and Prince Alexander ranges; and the coastal area.

Up to the end of World War I the Sepik area was governed by the Germans and early exploration and mapping of the river, its tributaries and the hinterland were carried out by them. The area came under Australian trusteeship in 1920 and in 1966 it was divided by the administration into two districts (now provinces), East and West Sepik. At present very little is known about the early settlement of the Sepik provinces and it would be presumptuous to theorise about the art styles and pottery traditions. While Laycock and other linguists from the Summer Institute of Linguistics have contributed valuable data, prehistorians, archaeologists and art historians have yet to come to grips with the vast amount of data the area affords.

The general pattern of settlement indicates early waves of migration of people from South-East Asia who pushed their way up the Sepik River and its tributaries and up the Ramu River. These people were displaced by later migrations and the older inhabitants gradually found their way into the interior away from the river and toward the north and north-west. Recent geomorphological and archaeological research has shown that several thousand years ago the north-east coast of New Guinea was much further south than it is today, and that the Sepik Basin was once a deep salt water bay. Migrations into the Sepik may thus have proceeded along the coast and coastal cordillera, and later northwards into what is now the Prince Alexander and Torricelli ranges. Such movements, and the likelihood of exchange partnerships, help explain the high degree of linguistic and cultural diversity in the Sepik region. The inland Sepik people are all non-Austronesians. The Austronesians, true to form, have settled along the coast at Kaiep-Samap-Terebu and north of Wewak to beyond the border of Irian Jaya and New Guinea.

SEPIK RIVER

From its mouth 90 kilometres south-east of Wewak the Sepik stretches almost 1100 kilometres in a westerly direction to the border with Irian Jaya where it turns south, crossing back into Papua New Guinea and disappearing into the mountain range which runs down the centre of the island. The river has numerous tributaries including the Porapora, Keram, Yuat, Korewori, Blackwater, Korosemeri, Leonhard-Schultze, Frieda and May rivers. The main tributary in the middle Sepik is the Screw River. To the north is a mixture of savannah and forest vegetation which gradually merges into the hills and mountains of the Prince Alexander, Torricelli and Bewani ranges.

Sago and other swamp areas are located between the mouth of the May River and the Washkuk hills, along the Keram, Yuat, and Porapora rivers and between the Ramu River and the lower Sepik. The Sepik River terrain is a flood area and the embankments often change as a result of the build-up of solid land by sand and mud and by the erosion of the banks during high water.

There is no pottery making along the Sepik River itself; industries exist inland along the tributaries and lakes off the main stream. Industries in the Sepik River area are restricted to a few villages in the Porapora swamplands, along the Keram River and its 'baret', east of the Yuat River village of

Biwat, on Lake Chambri at Aibom village, behind Ambunti in the Washkuk hills, behind Timbunke in the forest and grasslands of the Sawos people, and in the hills and grasslands of the Marienberg area. Any area north of these regions will be discussed as 'inland Sepik' but this is not intended to detract from their relationship with the 'river' industries. The region between the Keram and Korosemeri rivers has yielded sherds indicating pottery activity in the past and the Korewori River has been named by local informants as an area of pottery activity but the area is yet to be surveyed.

The Sepik River is a great unifying factor in the exchange, between widespread groups, of foodstuffs, utilitarian objects such as pottery, weapons, ritual paraphernalia and personal adornment. The religious life, the complex relationship between man and the supernatural, has induced a diversity of art forms used in ceremonies centring around the men's societies and the 'haus tambaran'. The entire Sepik area is known for its intense cult activities.

The diversity of art forms is also reflected in the pottery. The clay itself has magic properties as well as material value: in many areas it is equated with the process of creation which is symbolised by fertility and blood. The functions of clay vessels and objects are manifold. Not only are there containers for the preparation and storage of food but clay objects have evolved which are used in ceremony, ritual and magic. These are generally elaborately decorated with curvilinear or figurative designs similar to the designs on the carved wooden objects and bark paintings. Women as a rule produce the purely utilitarian vessels while men dominate the manufacture of objects and vessels that are used in cult activities or in the preparation of magic. Paint, another magical substance, is applied by the men to many of these objects, not only to enliven the surface but to give them additional magical properties. The phenomenon of modelled three-dimensional clay objects and their use in ritual makes this area unique in Papua New Guinea.

The technique of production is that of spiral coiling. The Aibom potters constitute the single exception: they use the ring building method. Decoration consists of incising, scratching, notching, chip carving, appliqué, punctation and modelling. The division of labour is very complex and varies from industry to industry; one cannot generalise.

Kwoma, Nukuma and Mayo

A definite style of pottery comes from groups located behind Ambunti on the Sepik River, in and around the hills and waterways of the Ambunti Mountains. The three primary sources of data on these groups are Whiting and Reed (1938-39) who have done an anthropological study of the area,

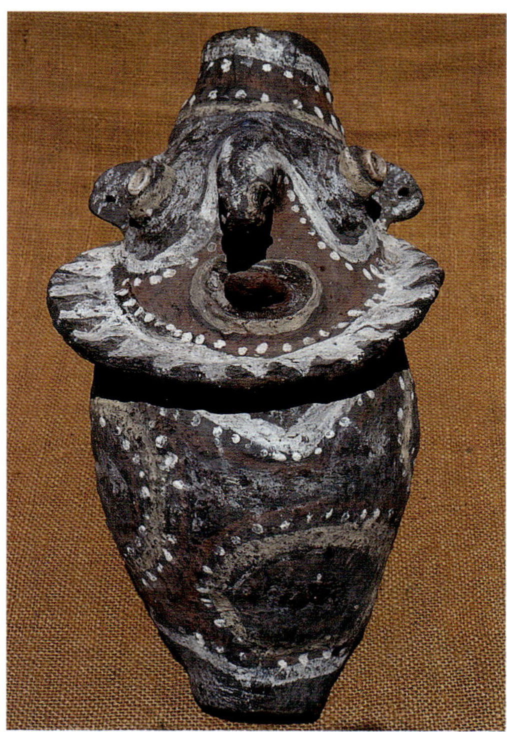

Fig. 9.2
Kwoma cult object, *h* 36 cm.

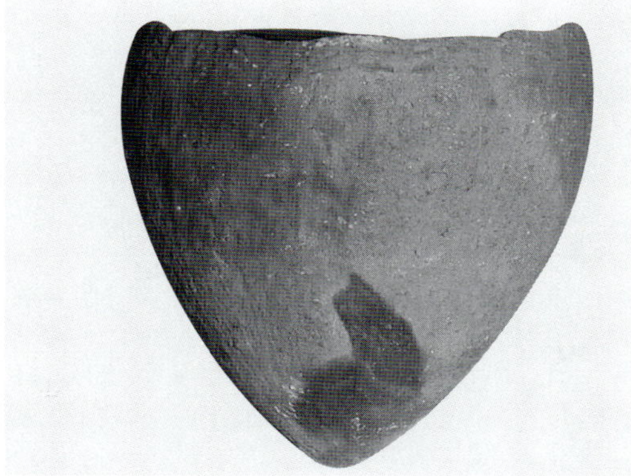

Fig. 9.3
Kwoma cooking pot, *poilau*, *h* 26 cm.

Fig. 9.4
Bagliam village tree oil container, *h* 33 cm.

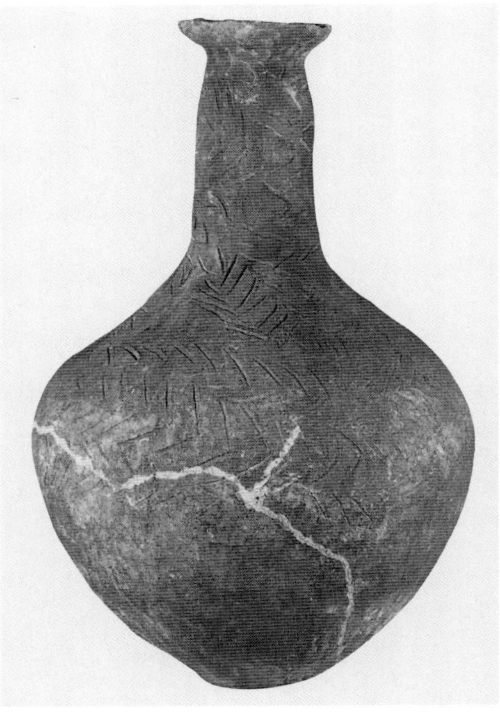

Fig. 9.5
Ceremonial vessel, *aumar*, made in Nukuma area, *h* 28 cm.

Douglas Newton (1971) who has written on the use of art, carvings and cult objects in ceremonies and Christian Kaufmann (1972) who has completed a thorough art historical and ethnographical study of the pottery.

The three main pot producing groups have been defined as the Kwoma, Nukuma and Mayo. The above studies of these groups were all completed prior to new language classifications by Laycock (1973) in which the Kwoma and Nukuma are classified under the Kwoma language in the Nukuma family. Although the authors have standardised language groupings and villages according to Laycock's 1973 classifications and the listings of villages in the *Village Directory* (1973) they have used Kaufmann's groupings for the Kwoma and Nukuma potters.

Examples of Kwoma and related pottery types were collected by a Basel museum expedition in the 1960s. The Museum für Völkerkunde, Berlin, has some fine examples of pots and cult objects (see Kelm 1966: Vol. II, figs 94-117) and Newton shows examples of cult objects, many of which are owned by private collectors. The Papua New Guinea Museum in Port Moresby has many examples of pottery from this area and it is hoped that a comprehensive museum catalogue will be produced. Much of the following data has been taken from Kaufmann's study. The authors have made several short field trips in this area.

The Kwoma and Nukuma groups, although separate 'tribes', are closely related by language and cultural elements. Neighbouring Kwoma and Nukuma villages have always had closer ties with each other than with the more remote villages of their own linguistic group (Kaufmann, pers. comm.). Commonly called 'Washkuk' after the Washkuk hills of the Ambunti Mountains, the Kwoma (mountain men) who live in hamlets on the ridges of mountains are divided into four separate subgroups. These are the Tanggwishempi (Togugwinshempi) at Tongwinjamb village, the Honggwama at Washkuk, Melawei and Bangwis villages, the Koriyasi (Koaryassi) at Meno and Baglam (previously Saseriman village) and the Worombandji (Urumbandj) at Urambanj village (Newton 1971).

The Nukuma ('people at the headwaters') who live to the north-west and north-east of the Kwoma

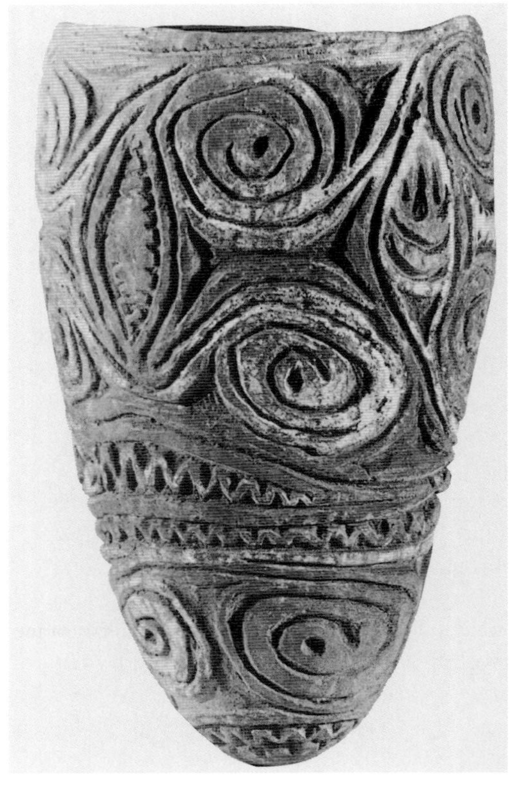

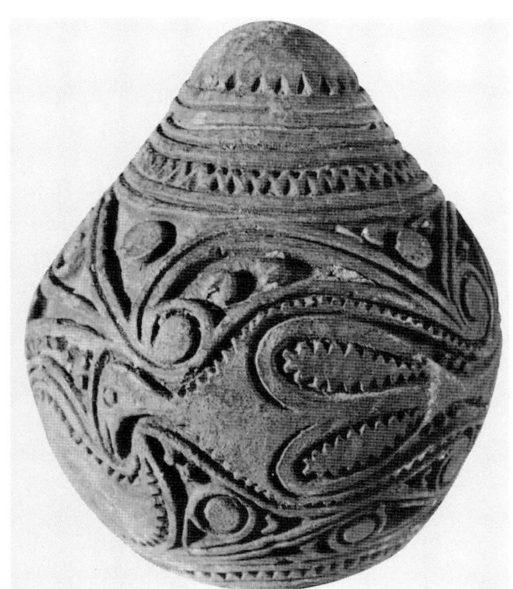

inhabit the waterways and bush. The pottery making villages of the Nukuma are Amaki, Kawaka and Nageri.

Kwoma

Pottery is significant to the Kwoma society because it is still used for cooking and storing of sago and plays an important role in ritual and ceremony. It is now an important source of cash as well, clay pots being sold to dealers, collectors and tourists. Trading partners are the Meno and Begilam people who trade clay pots with the Mayo villagers for mussel shells. At one time the Mayo, who did not own much of their own clay, had digging rights with the Kwoma but now they prefer to procure ready-made pots and the Kwoma enjoy the lime they extract from the mussel shells, which is chewed with betel nut. Traditionally the Manambu, especially the villages of Avatip and Malu, were clearing houses for clay pots from the 'Washkuk hills' area; these were traded to the Sepik River villages in return for mussel and snail shells (used for decoration) and Aibom pottery.

The ability to produce well-made sago storage pots and finely decorated ceremonial and ritual clay objects gives a man a degree of status within the society. Only very successful men who have been favoured by the supernatural in all aspects of their achievements – carving, pot making, hunting, planting, dancing and singing – can rise to the fourth and highest stage of initiation. For women, pot making does not present the same avenue to high status but they must be able to make good sturdy pots as well as care for the children, provide food from the gardens and fetch water and firewood.

Kaufmann records that the Meno Kwoma classify types of pots according to shape and function. He also warns that since most of his research was undertaken in Meno village, variations and details of other aspects of the Kwoma pottery in other villages could differ in minor respects. Types of

Fig. 9.6
Kwoma ceremonial pot, *aumar*, *h* 23 cm.

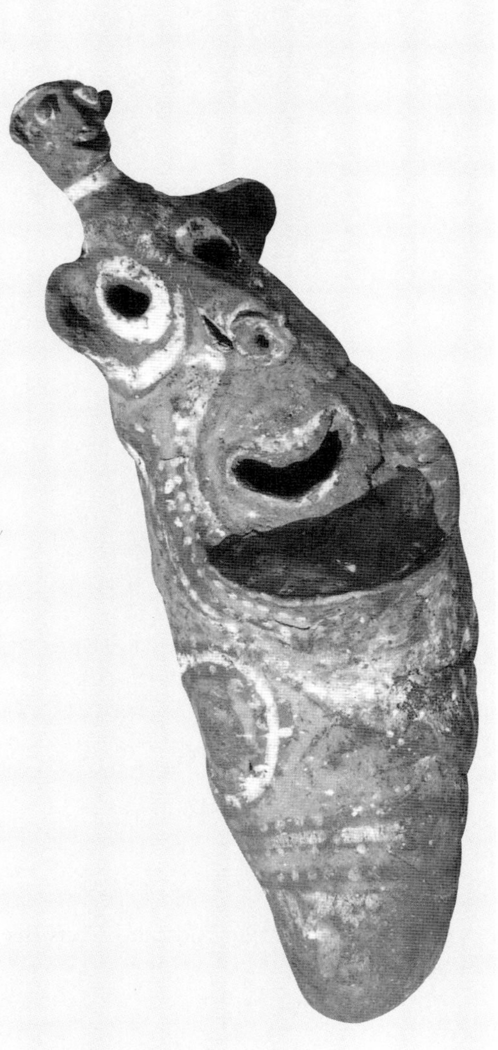

Fig. 9.7
Ceremonial object made by Guskein, Meno village, *h* 56 cm.

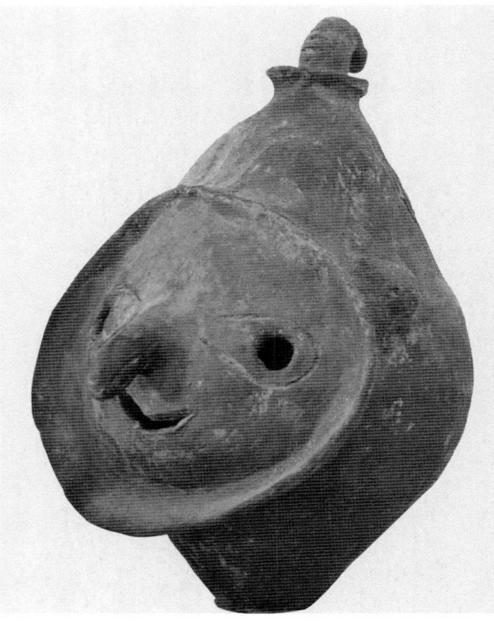

Fig. 9.8
Kwoma cult object, *h* 33 cm.

ceramic objects produced are sago storage vessels, common cooking pots, pots used for cooking special foods (taro, yam, meat and birds), sago stirring vessels, sago frying pans, tree sap storage vessels, cult objects and magic and ceremonial pots.

Noukitjau are sago storage vessels. These are large pots 40 to 75 centimetres high, with pointed bases. They are cylindrical or sometimes shaped like the Aibom sago storage pots, with a belly and a long, truncated, slightly inverted neck area. The openings are usually oval, wide enough to allow room for removing sago and narrow enough to be covered to protect the contents from vermin. Decoration comprises scratched patterns along the top portion of the vessel or modelled faces and applied wavy lines and nubbins. In general the shape is rather roughly formed. Because of their great size these storage vessels have to be supported upright in the houses, bound with cane to two poles which flank them on either side.

Poilau is a large common cooking pot, about 30 to 50 centimetres high. Kaufmann shows two types: one has a pointed base and a hemispherical shape with a large opening; the other is more cone-shaped and curves in at the top. These are more carefully formed than the *noukitjau*. The decoration, scratched into the top portion, is casual and consists of lozenge, circular and diamond patterns or sometimes marked coils decorate the rim. Large and more elaborate cooking pots of this type are used in the men's house during special feasts and ceremonies. According to one of Kaufmann's informants, after a successful pig kill or hunt several pots are brought to the men's house; the pig is cut up and parts of it are boiled in the pots. After the pig has been cooked, a thick gluggy dish (porridge) is made from yam. The pig is then fried or roasted over the fire. The initiated men arrive and everyone eats. Meanwhile, the wives have brought sago packages which are collected by the men, taken into the house, divided into packets and later distributed. These pots are also used during initiation and other cult activities.

Polok poilau are medium-sized, about 18 centimetres high and the same shape as the *poilau*. They are used for cooking yam, taro and porridge (gruel with pandanus and sago). They are simply decorated with incised or punctate patterns.

Huau, the sago stirring vessel (also used for cooking pandanus and other vegetables) is tall, with a wide mouth and a pointed base. An average-sized vessel is about 30 centimetres high.

Wugi huau is a small cooking pot, about 13 centimetres high, used for vegetables, meat of small animals, birds, turtles and fish. Its shape is comparable to that of the *poilau* but it has a wider opening and is usually undecorated.

Haranggoil au, the sago frying pan, is shaped like the sago frying pans from the Slei/Sawos area. It is an oval, shallow dish which has one or two projections at the ends which are formed into birds' or animals' heads. These are relatively scarce because flat sago cakes are usually eaten only when a member of the family dies.

Dor-poilau, an unusual pot used for cooking different foods at the same time while keeping them separate, is divided by a partition.

Warkiromba is a cooking pot which has an indirect everted rim and can be decorated by small nodules applied at intervals around the underside of the rim.

Kwar'au (meaning 'tree oil') is a pot which is used in different ways, most especially to care for the wounds inflicted when cutting the decorative marks into the skin of young men and women. Some *kwar'au* are sacred, others like the container

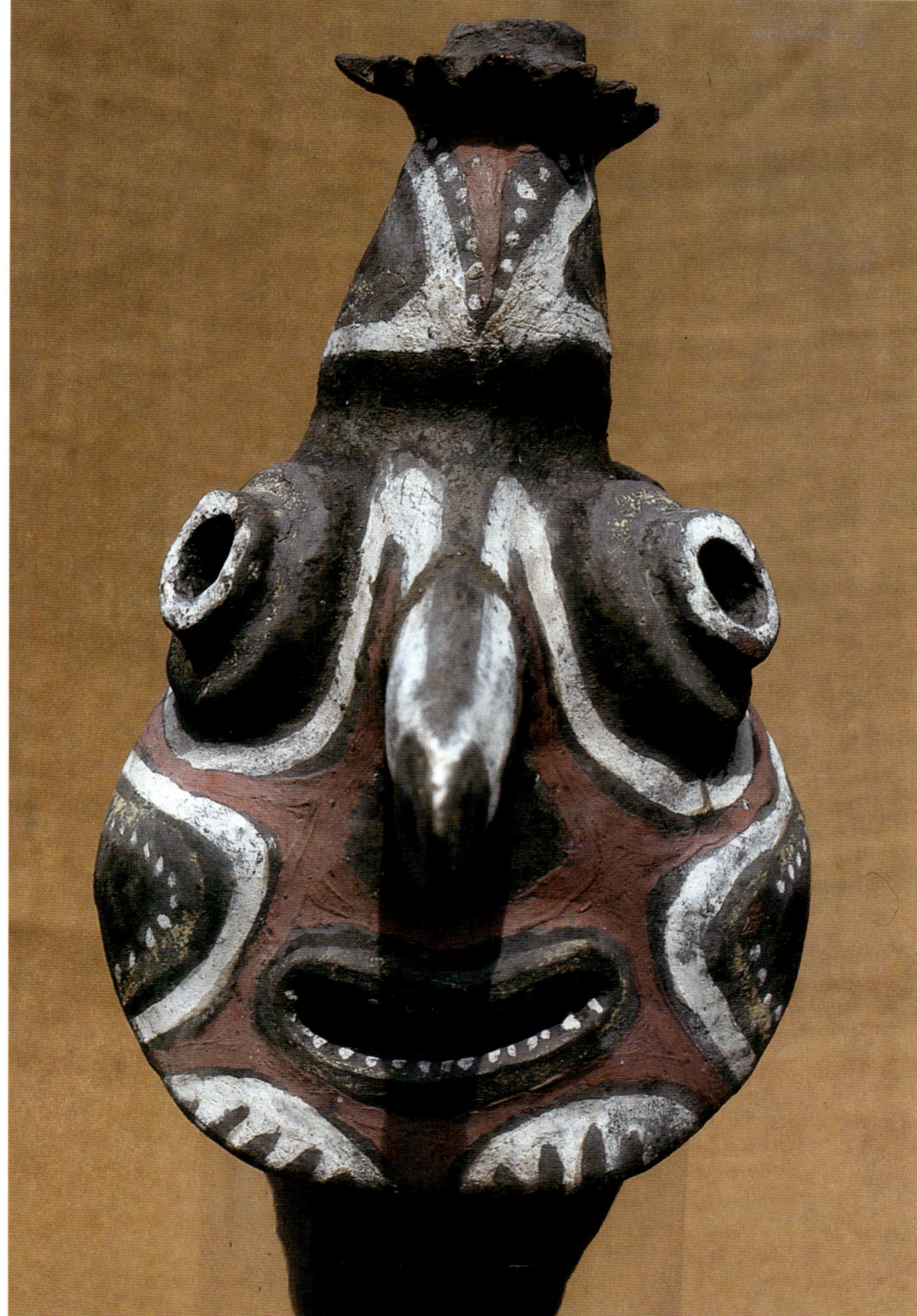

Fig. 9.9
Kwoma cult object,
h 35 cm.

Fig. 9.10
Kwoma cult ojbect.

Fig. 9.11
Kwoma cult ojbect.

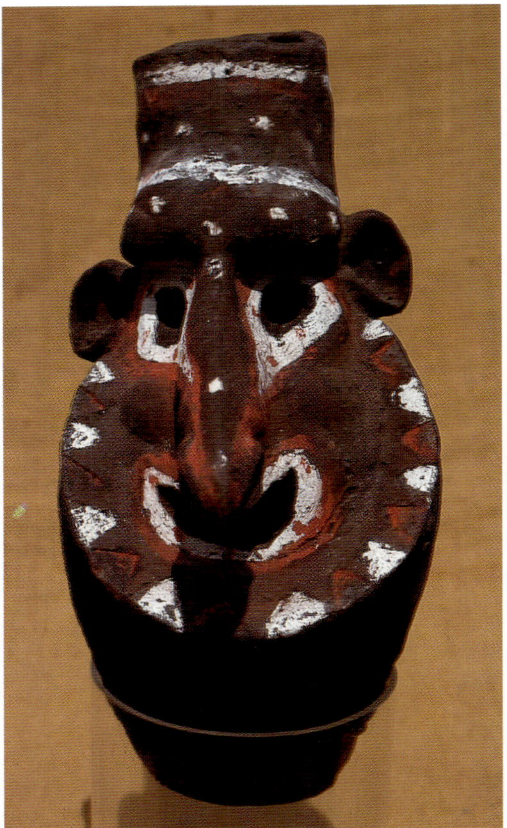

Fig. 9.10

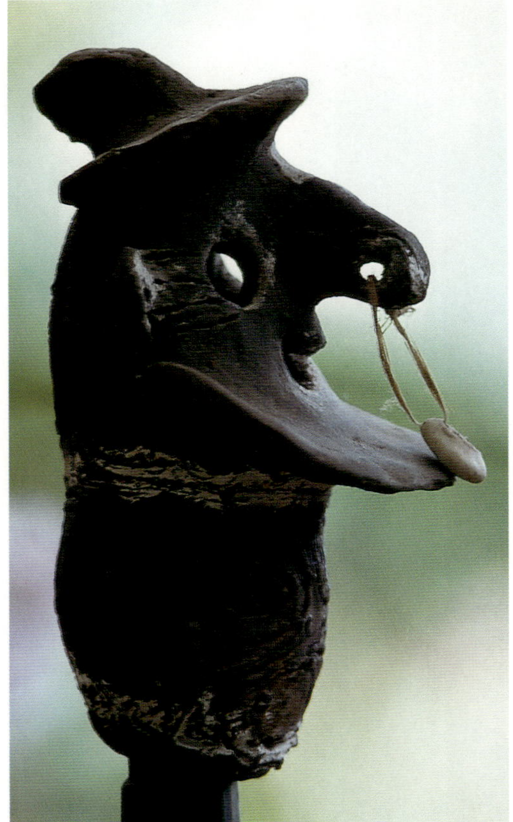

Fig. 9.11

(fig. 9.4) probably used to store tree oil for healing the wounds, are more profane (Kaufmann, pers. comm.). *Kwar'au* were observed being used at a cult feast in Orambanj village – the feasts are held for the highest initiation group, the yam planters. The pots are placed in the men's house and are filled with uncooked yam and coconuts. The feasting goes on for two nights. Yam, the flesh of coconuts and pig are cooked in the *kwar'au*. The food is eaten in the morning from open palm leaf containers. At Meno during this feast a clay head is erected in the men's house. This vessel can be variously shaped and often has a rim which flares outward. It is usually rather elaborately decorated with applied lugs, nipple-like projections, wavy coils and circular and curvilinear patterns: it can also have incised or scratched designs. Some examples have an indirect, slightly everted rim.

Sengasu'au is a magic pot. Kaufmann saw only one example, which was 14.5 centimetres high, with a flattish base and a concave belly area extending into an attenuated trunk with an everted rim. It was decorated on the exterior walls and the inner rim with incised patterns. Whiting and Reed (1938) record the use of these pots by sorcerers. The sorcerer is hired by a person who intends to bring harm to another. After collecting sorcery material (that is, exuviae, food scraps or something which has come into direct contact with the victim), the employer presents this to the sorcerer who

> retires to a secluded spot with the sorcery material and a special, narrow-necked, clay pot. The pot with the materials in it is placed on a fire and allowed to become very hot. Cold water is then poured in, causing a burst of steam. The sorcery material must disappear completely to bring death to the victim; if some scraps remain the latter will merely become very sick. [Whiting and Reed 1938; 214]

The authors know of at least three other areas where vessels are used as sorcery or magic pots: at Yule

Island, amongst the Azera of the Markham Valley and in the Porapora River area.

Aumar or *au'maka* are ceremonial pots which are quite distinctive because of the carefully conceived, rich decorative patterns used and the perfect shaping of each vessel (as opposed to the sometimes crudely-shaped vessels previously described). These pots (and the cult objects made in the form of heads) are regarded as very exotic and are eagerly sought after by collectors, dealers and museums. The shapes are basically ovoid but a pronounced belly area gives the profile a stretched or bulbous look. Decoration covers the entire outer surfaces from the rim to the pointed base (only the base point is left unmarked) and consists of chip-carved designs. The rim and base portions are distinguished by a series of sawtooth, wavy or scalloped running bands alternating with unmarked bands. Although the carving is more boldly executed and differs in design motifs, the overall use of design elements resembles that of the Wosera and the Yambes-Kombio vessels (figs 1.10, 9.5, 9.6, 9.141, 9.159).

These pots are never used for cooking; they are used exclusively as containers for food (eating bowls) during initiation stages for Kwoma men. Apparently, a 'ceremonial father', a man who is fully initiated into all the grades, becomes an initiation father to an initiate. He gives the younger man an *aumar* that he has made and decorated himself and presents it filled with a yam soup he has cooked himself. The relatives are allowed to be present during the presentation of the *aumar*. The next day the initiate has to go to the gardens and plant his first yam.

Ap'au means 'bird pot' in the Kwoma language and it is a vessel used in ceremony. It is oval or conical and has two handle-like projections on either side of the widest portion of the mouth. These projections, or 'continuations', are formed into heads of crocodiles, birds, snakes or men; sometimes one projection represents the head and the other the tail of the depicted creature. Other decoration covering the sides consists of applied, pricked and chip-carved designs.

Wasau are cult objects shaped like pots, with pointed closed bases and open orifices. They are distinguished by modelled faces or heads. These faces consist of an applied ridge which forms a jutting angle in the shape of the outline of a head, a projecting long or beaked nose, cutaway round eyes and a cutaway bow-shaped mouth (this typical Kwoma face is also found on the carvings used in ceremony). The remaining surface can be covered with scratched, incised or chip-carved patterns. Related to this container-like anthropomorphic form is another clay cult object which is really a sculptured form, not a vessel. These come in many forms but in general are hollow inside, open at the bottom and with a rounded or modelled clay head which is capped off by a topknot. These are used in cult house activities and are surmounted on wooden sticks and displayed around the cult altar. A third category of cult object is a solid modelled clay head with a small hollow opening in the trunk by which it is held aloft on a narrow stick.

Kaufmann gives a thorough description of various cults and the uses of the clay heads in the ceremonies. Here follows a summary of data from Kaufmann and Newton on cults and the use of clay heads.

> In general with the clay heads one is dealing with the representation of the sacred spirit beings, *sikilawas*, who are closely related to yams and happenings in the primeval age (thus pot = head = yam = the spirits of ages past). [Kaufmann 1973: 182]

Kaufmann is quick to point out the difficulties in attaching a meaning to each clay head; informants give totally different reports. But a few of the legends recorded by him are worth repeating since they cast some light on the origins of the clay heads within the religion of the people and their use in ceremony. A condensed version of the Meno story of Sopermel and his mother follows:

> Sopermel carried a pot, *wasau*, in his belly. When he died he was laid out by his relations on a scaffold in a tree deep in the forest. The body decayed and the belly opened up and the pot fell out onto the ground where it lay undamaged. Sopermel's mother found the pot and together with Kwasei, Sopermel's son, they took it home and showed it to all the people. The people agreed that the pot should be kept in the house so that descendants could tell the story.

The Tongwinjamb version is more detailed and relates the pot to a ceremony where taboos were broken and the ceremony discontinued.

A feast, *nawa*, was held and all the men dressed up in mask costumes made of wicker-work and grasses. The food, pork, bananas, sago grubs and yam, was cooked in a *poilau* and distributed. Two men, Nagusu and Kalawar, broke taboos forbidding intercourse during feasts, and left the ceremony to visit a woman. They were unable to have real intercourse but only spat and breathed heavily. But the woman became pregnant and had a boy called Sopermel who in turn became pregnant (that is, he carried something in his belly that made it swell up and grow bigger).

Sopermel, foreseeing his forthcoming death, asked his mother to build an elevated platform and to lay him down on it and to be sure to obey him. When he died and was laid out on the platform, his belly opened and a clay vessel fell out onto the ground. The next morning the mother opened up the fence surrounding the platform and saw a *wasau*, red all over. She picked it up and carried it home where it was viewed by all the relatives. The mother wanted to break it but the pot said to her, 'You must not kill me, you have to take care of me and look after me'. The pot then punished the woman by giving her a serious illness. The pot was then packed in the sheath of a betel palm, laid on a storage shelf inside the house and carefully guarded. It stayed there forever, carefully guarded until it was broken during World War II.

To go back to the time of the feast, Nagusu and Kalawar returned to finish eating but found they could not remove their mask costume. Other men (their relations) sent them out to find shelter in the bush. They walked until they came to a river (between Tongwinjamb and Meno) where they lay down to sleep and then changed into crocodiles. The other men finished the feast and decided never to conduct it again so that the same misfortune wouldn't fall on them. They destroyed their costumes and hid them in the bush. Then they washed themselves and started a new dancing feast.

Kaufmann was told about two feasts held in Tongwinjamb where the clay heads are used: the Hamayo feast, held during the high water period after the yam creepers have been tied up, and the Yinamu feast held during the dry season, when the clay head is placed on a platform (altar) and different species of yam corms are piled up around it. The heads are supported on sticks, stood upright and secured with bush twine. They are then decorated with leaves and human hair. In Kaufmann's opinion the clay heads and yam tubers are of similar importance. 'If this interpretation is valid, the clay heads were equivalent to especially powerful and durable yam tubers' (Kaufmann 1972: 181).

Thus there are two broad categories of clay objects produced by the Kwoma and Nukuma: the functional container vessels and objects used for cult activities. The only other groups in the country known to use clay objects (non-containers) in ritual or magic are the Bosman people whose men make a penis-shaped clay object, the Dimiri-Marawat men who made a hermaphroditic or male three-dimensional clay object and the Aibom men who make a type of gable decoration. As well, there are the clay ocarinas used in cult activities by the Wosera and Dimiri-Marawat groups and the clay drums made and used by the men in the Markham Valley.

The absence of common eating bowls is noteworthy. The Kwoma-Nukuma are surrounded by cultures that make and use everyday eating bowls, including the Kwanga, the Yambes-Kombio, the Abelam, all three Boiken groups and the Koiwat (Sawos). The Kwoma usually ate out of coconut shells or spoons; sago pudding is eaten from special leaves or from a container made from palm sheath rather than a clay bowl (Kaufmann, pers. comm.).The eating bowls here, *aumar*, are used only in a ceremonial context.

Both men and women make pots in the spiral coil technique. The women are responsible for making and decorating the functional vessels. The men, of course, make and decorate the ceremonial vessels and cult objects and occasionally the sago storage jars. Women will also customarily decorate the large cooking and sago storage pots but here we have an unusual occurrence: if a woman seems to be in difficulty with the design a man will take over and complete it for her or, in the case of shaping, he will interrupt her work and complete a rim or help with the large sago storage jars. Children and other adults may help the potter work; children will roll out coils for their mothers or a wife will roll them out for her husband. Kaufmann observed a man and his wife working in shifts to complete a vessel. Cooperation is necessary if the woman is

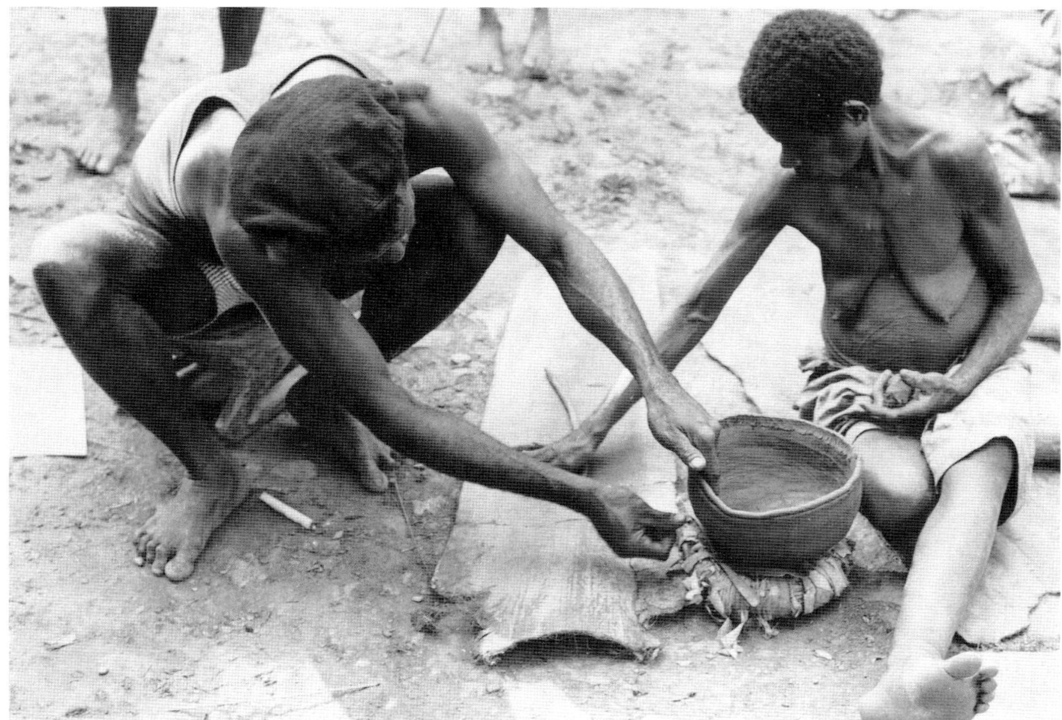

Fig. 9.12
Wasolanda and Wandamari, Kwoma language group, working together on a cooking pot at Meno village.

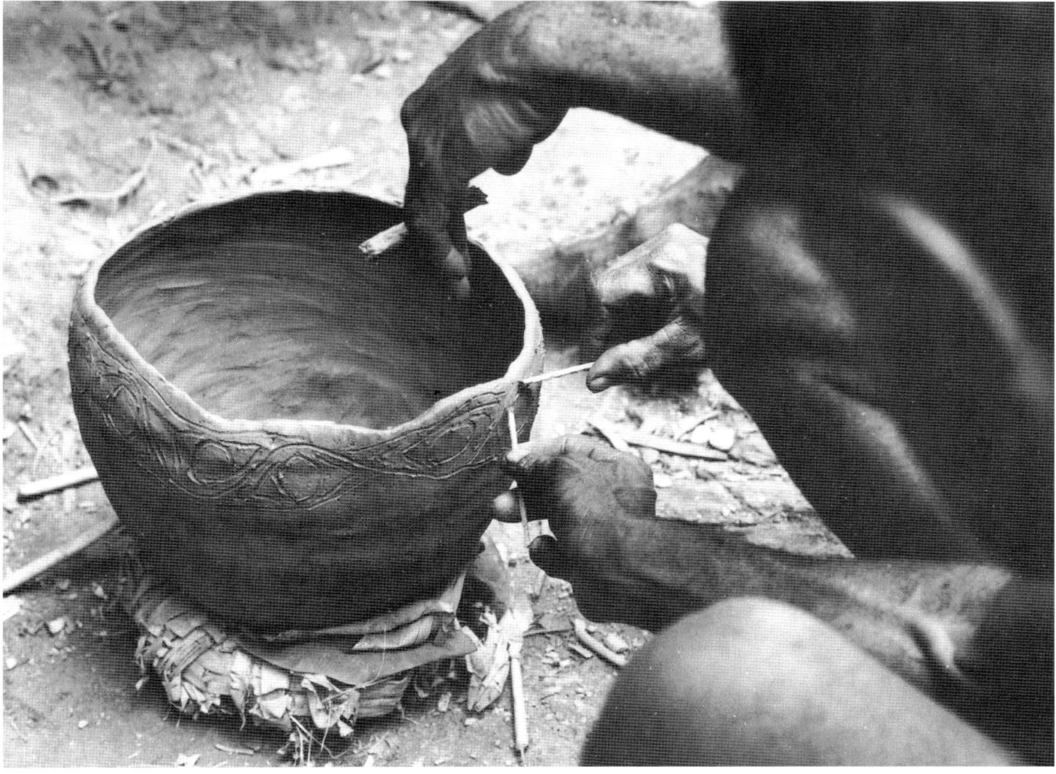

Fig. 9.13
Wandamari and Yessomari decorating-incising soft clay, Meno.

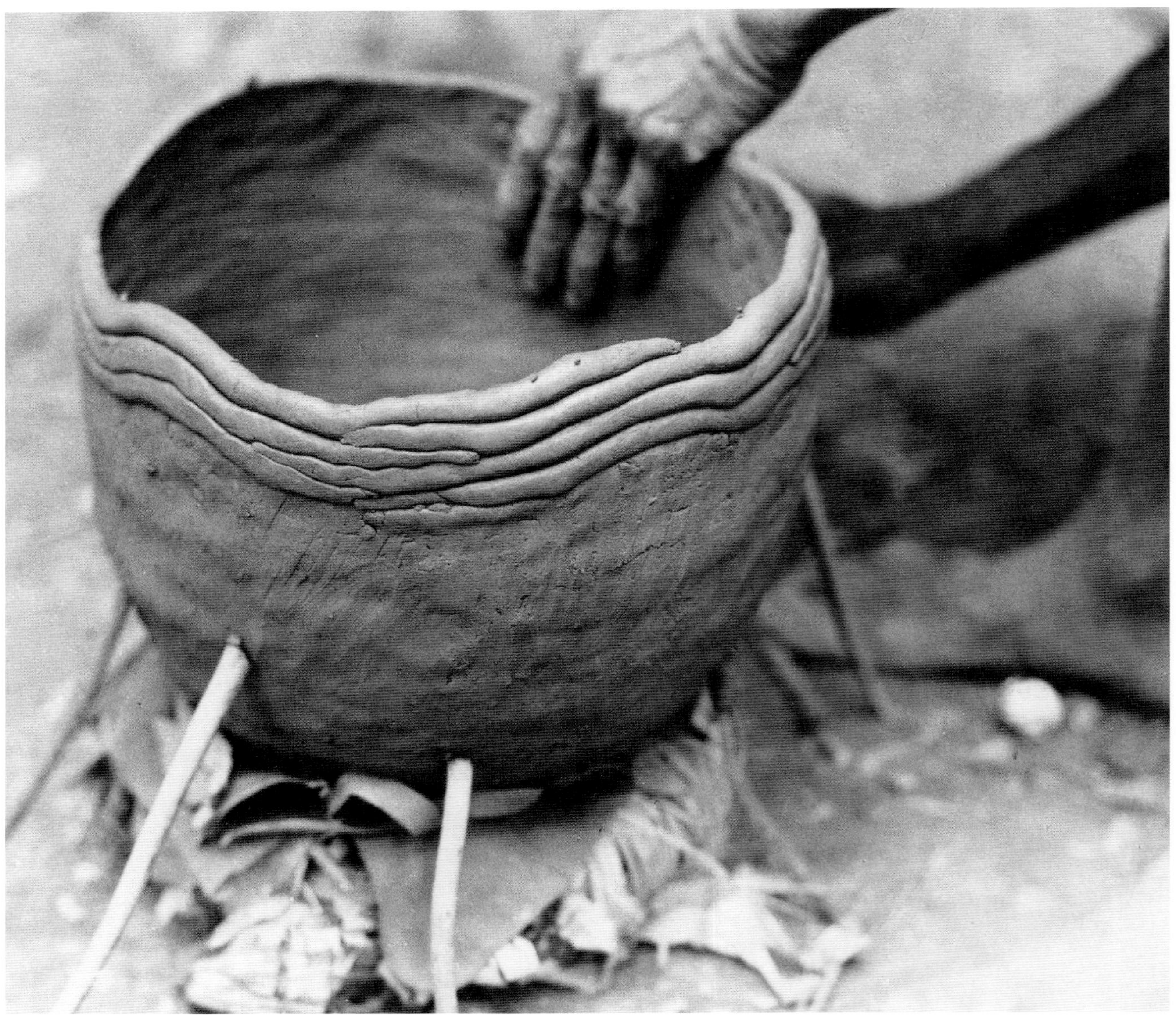

Fig. 9.14
Taro stalks propping up the sagging pot, Meno village.

inexperienced and a large pot must be completed before the sun goes down.

The number of pots an experienced woman can make in a day depends upon a number of factors: the size of the vessels, her work duties, the condition of the clay and the weather. She will be helped during the day by children who watch over her baby and by relatives who will prepare food for her household. Small children, boys and girls, learn about pot making by watching the adults and helping to make the rolls. Before puberty children are allowed to make small pots and if these pots seem strong enough they are fired and used as toys. It is especially important for the men to know how to decorate pots and young boys scratch designs on their 'toy' pots. Later on, their father or a male relative will supply them with a ready-made vessel upon which the design has been scratched. The young man must then convert this preliminary sketch into a deeply carved design using the chip-carving method. The application of design is learned by the potters by watching, copying and practising.

The Kwoma believe that there is a connection between clay and religious life and there are sanctions and taboos governing all aspects of pot making, from the division of labour and the age at which the potters are allowed to make pots to clay gathering and the use of certain ceremonial vessels. Children up to the time of puberty are allowed to play at pot making but women may not make pots until they have married and borne two or three children. Men are not allowed to pot until they have reached the third stage of initiation at about thirty-five years. For the duration of pot making, neither sex may engage in intercourse and menstruating and pregnant women may not go near the clay. While building the large vessels men and women are not allowed to wash themselves before their work is finished and loud talking and loud noises are forbidden. Wood must not be chopped, sago palms felled or sago pulp beaten and yam and taro must not be dug out of the ground. Patience, quiet and respect for the making of the pots must be observed at all times. Men are not allowed to pot during the yam planting season for fear the yams will dry up and women who build the large sago jars must work inside a fenced area and are only permitted to eat or drink warm food and water. Kaufmann was assured by his informants that disobedience would be catastrophic for future pot making: not only would the clay revert back to soil and the pot break at firing but the clay pits themselves would be affected.

Clay gathering is limited to fully initiated men and their wives. The Meno clay pits are located in the bush close to the rivers. The pits are owned by particular clans but members of other related clans are given permission to gather clay. The best time for digging the clay is in the dry season (June to November) and the pits are worked to form a square about 60 to 1 00 centimetres deep and 40 to 60 centimetres wide. The clay is excavated with a digging stick *ya'amba*. After the women have separated the clay and earth they put the clay into string bags and carry it back to the village (each woman can carry up to about 30 kilograms of clay). There are different varieties of clay. One, a yellowish colour, is used for the ceremonial vessels and the large sago containers. It is comparatively free of coarse foreign matter and thus provides a smooth surface suitable for elaborate decorations. Another sort, a black-brown variety, is used for the cooking pots. Tests show this to be a coarse-grained clay with reasonable plasticity and low shrinkage. It contains quartz, some biotite and muscovite mica. Usually the woman prepares the clay. She works on her verandah in the shade and places the clay on a piece of 'limbum'. Sometimes it needs very little preparation, sometimes two varieties are mixed together. Grit is casually removed, the potter moistens the clay by pouring water (stored in bamboo sections) over it and leaves it for at least an hour, often overnight. When the clay has absorbed the correct amount of moisture it is pounded on the 'limbum' with the wet end of a short stick or pounder, about 50 centimetres long and 6 centimetres in diameter. A flat pancake shape is made, the leaf-base is folded over and the cake inside is compacted again. Pounding is resumed and the process is repeated for about an hour. The clay is then set aside to dry for as long as the potter deems necessary, its degree of wetness being a matter of preference.

The potter gathers together the tools to be used in forming the pot. These are a flattened palm leaf stalk, a ring made from banana leaves, several green taro leaves to put over the ring and a coconut shell filled with water. The potter sits and takes a lump of the prepared clay and makes a sausage about 30 centimetres long and 2 to 3 centimetres thick. This shape is then divided into five to eight equal lengths. From each of these, a coil about 30 to 60 centimetres long and 0.5 to 1 centimetre thick is formed by rolling out a length on a 'pangal'; the potter rolls the coil on itself from where it lies and as she rolls it her thumb joins the coils to form the base. She then picks up this form in her left hand and, while supporting it against a knee, she joins another coil spirally with her right hand. In this way coils are added and the walls of the vessel are gradually built up. The pot achieves its final shape by smoothing which is done with the tip of the index finger, the thumb or a knuckle. Bonding the coils does not begin until the pot is about 10 centimetres high, when it is transferred to the banana leaf ring which has the soft green taro leaves resting over it.

The pot is then left to dry for several hours, this time supported by taro stalks which are propped up around the outside to prevent it from sagging.

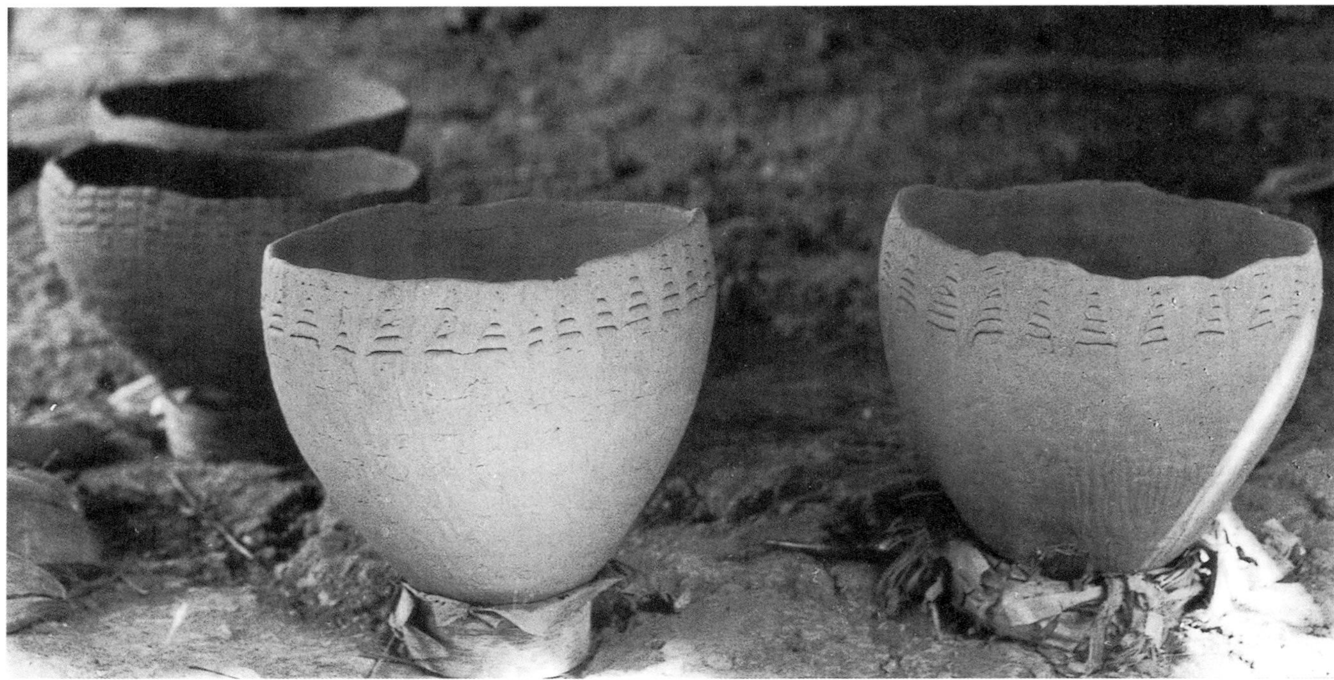

Fig. 9.15
Kwoma cooking pots, *poilau,* drying.

Decoration is applied when the pot has become firmer and consists in combinations of scratching, incising, pricking and chip-carving techniques and the application of three-dimensional forms and patterns onto the various types of vessels. The simplest decoration is used on common cooking pots, which are decorated by the women. It consists of areas of smoothed and unsmoothed coils marked by finger drag marks and is found throughout the inland Sepik Province industries.

The women or men will also scratch or incise designs into large and small cooking pots. Simple decorations consist of parallel bands of horizontal or vertical zig-zag lines running round the top edge of the pot. This pattern is called *uku wandja*, meaning waves of water. Another popular motif, *egel yat*, the track of a bush rat, is a series of running triangles scratched or incised with pricked patterns filling the interior space of the triangle; there are also pricked lines running down from the apex.

The decorating tools are splinters of bamboo, pieces of the rib of a palm leaf or a small stick. More complicated patterns undertaken by the men require extreme concentration and may involve erasures and restarts of scratched or incised patterns. Chip carving, used on ceremonial and cult objects, is done in two stages by experienced men who also instruct younger, less experienced men. Tools used are sticks made of bamboo, palm or wood and a knife. The potter begins work on a leather-hard vessel by scratching in his design, starting with the horizontal zig-zag lines defining the tip and bottom of the pot. The circular, spiral and curvilinear patterns are prescratched into the main body of the vessel. After this the potter will use a knife to chip-carve his scratched zig-zag and sawtoothed band patterns; then the elaboration of the main body is undertaken. The potter carves his patterns by cutting the clay (about 2 to 4 millimetres deep) from the wall in small chips; this produces a fine curling remnant of clay that is either wiped away with the hand or blown away.

Kaufmann divides the motifs used into four groups: those taken from fauna, those taken from flora, those representing more normal spirits present in natural phenomena, i.e. rocks, water, trees, and those representing sacred spirits. They are not arbitrary depictions but are selected from objects or things which appear in mythology. Each element of a pattern is given a descriptive name: a circle inscribed around three or more horizontal lines is named *nggumasak*, the fruit from a nut tree;

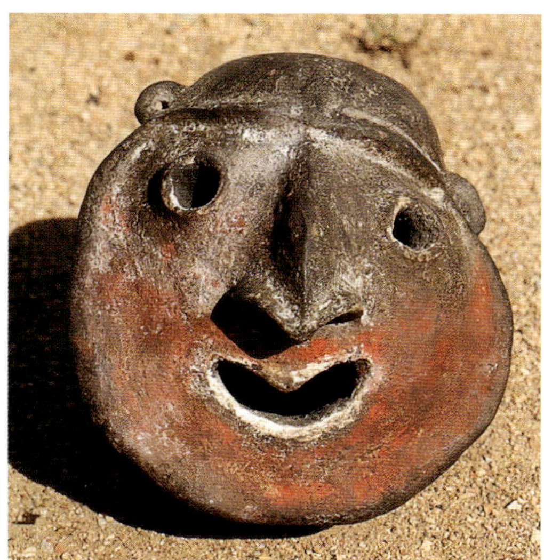

Fig. 9.16
Nukuma cult object from Amaki village, *h* 20 cm.

a series of three curvilinear designs surrounding the circle (which is inscribing parallel lines) represents a creeper or vine and its fruit; an oval-shaped motif set off by two connecting open triangles is named *nggrisa*, the body of a frog; a face-like motif with two round circles and a nose is named *wailerekwa*, a small black bird. Kaufmann has collected about sixty different chip-carved patterns taken from local flora and fauna. Some of the motifs representing objects in nature or the spirit world are *nggalanggalar*, the spiked edge of the leaf of a species of pandanus; *mepoko*, the pupa stage of an insect; *mandanggaranggara*, a poisonous spider; *manggaliko*, a long caterpillar; *watjou*, a grub which feasts on felled breadfruit trees; *manal*, a bright red gliding possum equated by the Kwoma with meteorites and comets; *argunjaulum*, an insect that glides across the water; *abungimbi*, a flying fox; *aragumaka*, the generic term for the faces of 'masalai'.

This description of patterns does not necessarily reflect the apparent nor the hidden meaning of the composite image in the clay body surface. However, in the samples given *manggeliko* is such a definite reference to an important mythological character for whom a story exists (Kaufmann, pers. comm.).By studying myths, taboos, names and stories connected to the pottery, he concludes that:

> A certain connection seems to exist between good blood, good health, good potters' clay (as long as it is wet), the human ability for procreation, the successful growing of yam tubers, and the religious meaning of sago starch on the one hand, and bad blood, sickness, common ground unsuitable for pottery work etc. on the other hand. The main point is that the importance of sago pudding in mythical times seems to be equal to the importance of yams today. [Kaufmann 1972: 215]

Plastic decoration can be used independently or in combination with scratched, incised or chip-carved patterns. Wet fingers are used to shape coils into heads of animals and birds; eyes are formed by applying small lumps of clay and details such as the mouth are incised in the clay with a knife or other tool.

The pots are dried under the houses or on a rack in the 'cook house', a small structure made of bush materials. Drying time is from one to five days, depending on the size of the vessel and the weather. Sometimes the pots are put out into the sun after a few hours of drying. The clay does not shrink much in the process.

Firing can take place about the fourth or fifth day after the pot is made but it is preferable to wait about three weeks. A woman and her husband will

Fig. 9.17
Nukuma cult object, Amaki, *h* 18 cm.

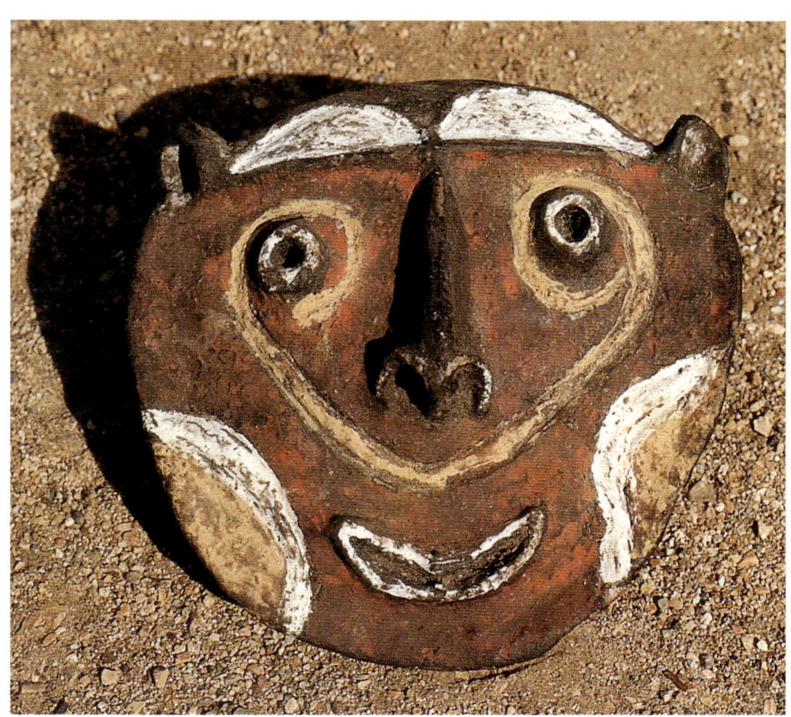

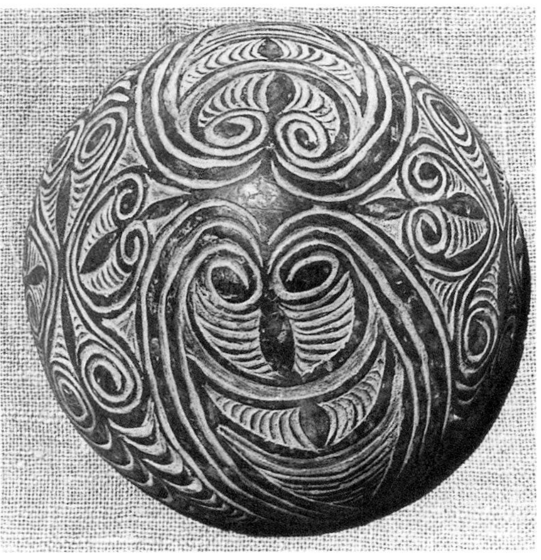

Fig. 9.18
Koiwat eating bowl, *kamana*, *h* 19 cm.

fire from about five to nine pots at a time during the day when the sun is strong. Fuel consists of dried sago fronds which are laid in a grill shape. Small branches are then spread over the grill and another level of 'pangal' is put on top. These layers form a square platform about 20 centimetres high; the pots will be set on top of this and covered completely by more 'pangal'. The fuel is lit by a burning bunch of dry leaves and a large crackling fire is the result. This burns for about ten minutes; the flames then diminish and more 'pangal' is added to portions of the pots that need it; the fire dies down until it is reduced to glowing embers. After the pots have been left on the embers for one to two hours they are removed by hand if they are cool enough or with sticks if they are still hot. They are placed close to the dying fire to enable them to cool slowly.

The degree of variation in actual techniques used by different potters is small but the degree of expertise and concept of the finished product seems to vary considerably. Some potters hardly bother to smooth the outside walls while others, especially the men, are meticulous in creating a smooth even surface. This concern for perfection is undoubtedly due to motivation: a male potter gains special status through his pot making while the woman potter's role is to make functional pots as quickly and efficiently as possible. Also, the male is usually concerned with the aesthetic appearance of his pots which will be used in ceremony and care must be taken to ensure the surface is smooth enough to afford a suitable field for elaborate decoration.

Nukoma

Although very similar to those of the Kwoma, the vessels of the Nukuma usually have slightly thicker walls and are more robust. Cooking pots, *huau*, are larger and sago storage vessels, *noukwitje'au*, are taller and thinner. The ceremonial vessels, *aumaka aumar*, are more crudely shaped and decorated. The homogeneous flow of curvilinear design and curve of the walls found on the Kwoma *aumar* is lacking on the Nukuma types and their decoration is more stilted and linear. The clay heads are usually hollow and have a hole in the bottom where they are stuck on sticks and affixed to an altar. The faces are painted for ceremonies in red, white and yellow pigments; feathers are glued to the chin and the nose and ears can be adorned with jewellery (nose bones, shell earrings and so on).

In the initiation rites the Nageri 'big men' use the *aumaka* to serve special food to the initiates. In Kawaka village the *aumar* are not used for food bowls as they are in the Kwoma villages; they are used to display yam and coconuts on the altar during cult feasts.

The older men gather the clay from deposits near one of the hills. The techniques of production seem to conform to those of the Kwoma.

Mayo

Kaufmann describes the pottery of two groups: Yauangget pottery made in the village of Maruwa and Yassean-Mayo pottery from the villages of Nau'ali and Yessan. Laycock has now classified these villages under the Mayo language. The Mayo were trading partners (and enemies) to the Kwoma.

Information concerning Yauangget (Yaunget or Yauget) pottery is limited. Clay is fetched from the north and men make all the pots, these being only sago storage and cooking vessels. No cult objects or ceremonial pots appear to be made and decoration is very simple, consisting in incising, stab marks and areas of smoothed and unsmoothed coils. Pots made by both men and women in Yessan and Nau'ali are very similar to those of the Kwoma.

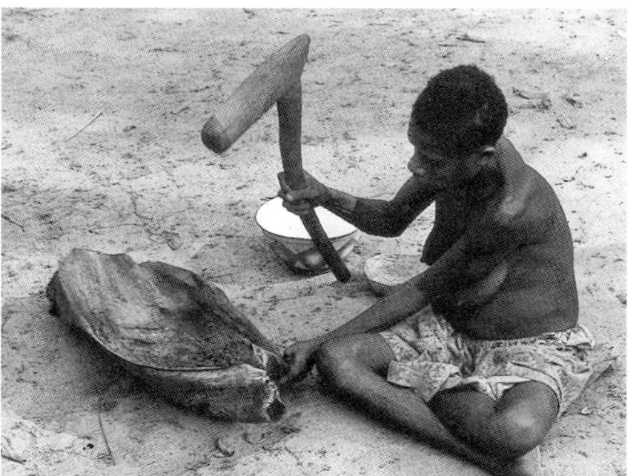

Fig. 9.19

Cooking pots, sago storage vessels, eating vessels and cult heads are produced.

Ngala

In this area another village where sago storage jars and cooking pots are produced is Swagup, an Ngala-speaking village located on a small tributary off the Sepik River. This village is occupied by speakers of a language directly belonging to the Ndu family, related to the Manambu, Sawos, Iatmul and Abelam. The women use the spiral coiling technique and are unique in the area in mixing a sand temper with their clay. Simple decoration consists of alternating smoothed and unsmoothed coils forming triangular motifs. Kaufmann suggests that these pots are similar to the cooking and sago storage vessels of the Sawos.

Sawos

Koiwat and Kamanggaui are the two most important pot producing villages of the Sawos language group, otherwise called Tshuosh, Sepik Plains or Kwongai. They lie about 10 kilometres to the north-east of the middle Sepik village of Timbunke, between the Sepik flood area and the grasslands of the Plains Boiken villages to the north. Timbunke is situated on the river, about half way between Tambanam and Ambunti. In the past it was a powerful warlike contender to Tambanam and Kanganaman but today it is a sad and depressed settlement, having never fully recovered from the Japanese occupation in 1942 and the massacre of about 100 occupants who betrayed the Japanese position to the Australian forces. The Koiwat area is either swampy or covered with long grass. Food staples are sago, taro and yam; fish is obtained from Timbunke and the bush and grasslands supply small

Fig. 9.21

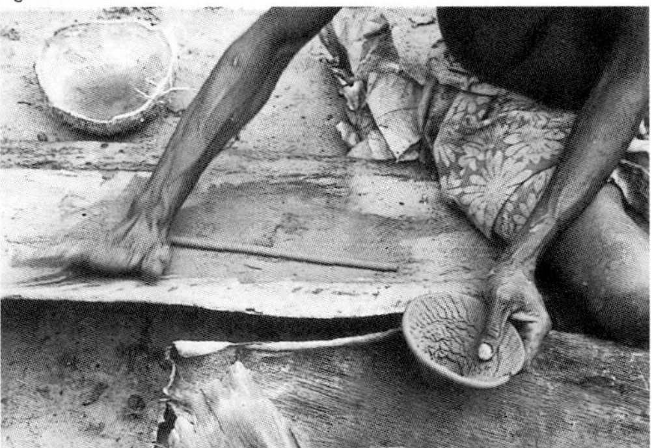

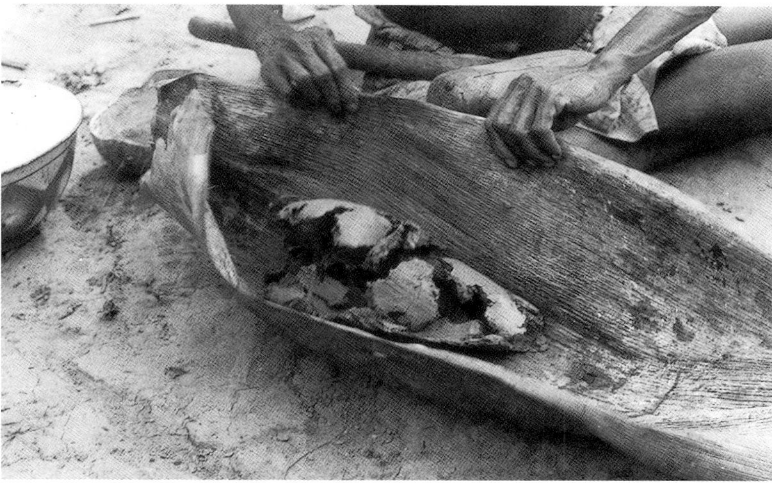

Fig. 9.20

Fig. 9.22

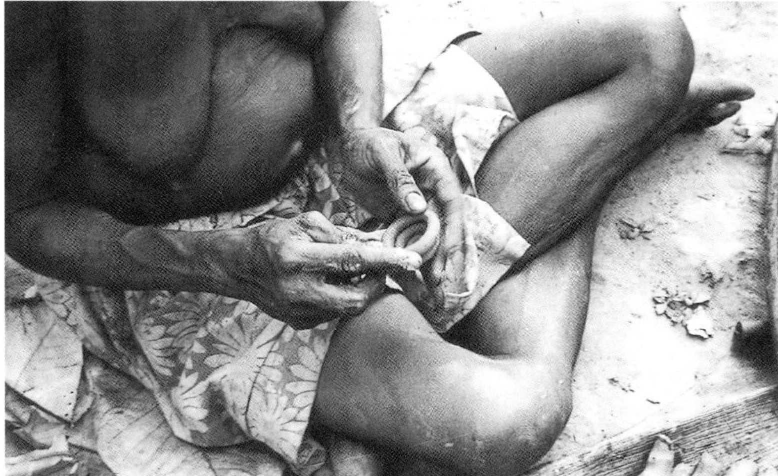

Figs 9.19 to 9.22
Coiling series, Koiwat.
The potter is Laugwe.
Fig. 9.19
Pounding clay with a wooden mallet.
Fig. 9.20
Compacting the clay in a 'limbum' for further pounding.
Fig. 9.21
Rolling a coil of clay on a smooth surfaced 'pangal'.
Fig. 9.22
Spiral coiling: forming the base of the pot.

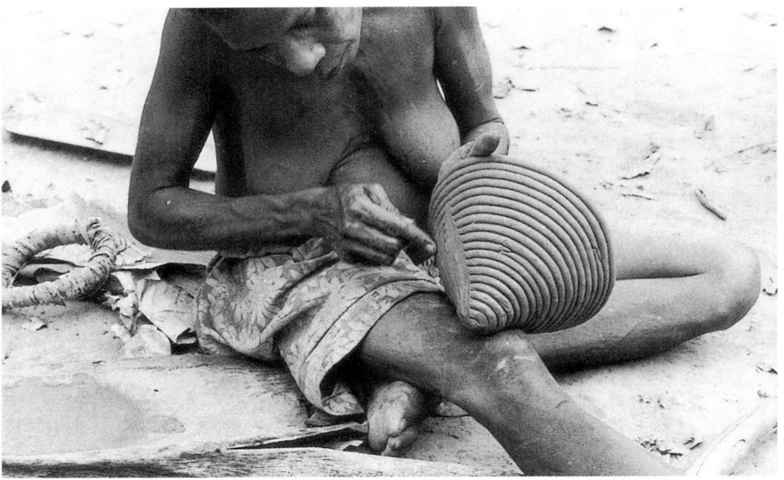

Fig. 9.23

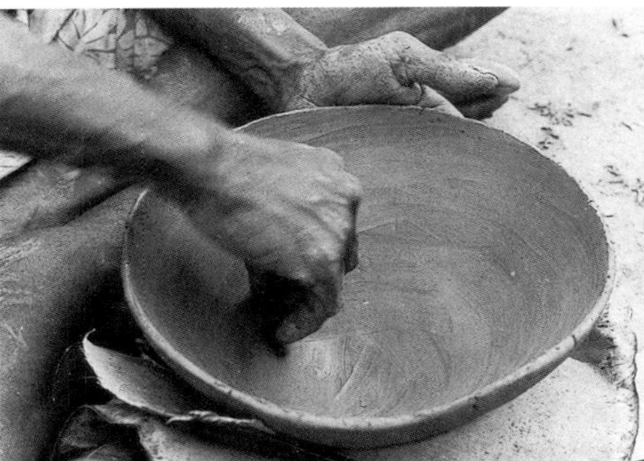

Fig. 9.24

Fig. 9.23
Bonding coils on the outside.

Fig. 9.24
Smoothing and shaping the inside with a mussel shell.

game. Cooking pots and sago storage vessels are bartered with villages to the north in exchange for tobacco, tubers and dogs. Pottery (decorated sago eating bowls) and artifacts are produced for barter and cash sales to Timbunke, Tambanam and Kanduanam, their inhabitants acting as intermediaries for the distribution of Sawos vessels to villages as far away as Angoram downstream and Ambunti upstream and to tourists and dealers. This is another area like Aibom and Dimiri-Marawat, inaccessible to any but the most diligent and fit.

Examples of the exquisitely decorated conical eating bowls were collected by early European expeditions. The Museum für Völkerkunde in Berlin has a large selection dating from 1912-13, all of which were collected on the Sepik River, some as far down as the Murik Lakes (see Kelm 1966: Vol. I, Plates 322-48). A comparison of these early vessels with those produced today shows little variation in design motif and no loss of quality in either design elements or technique. The same high quality of production has been sustained for some sixty years, in remarkable contrast to many of the other recorded pottery traditions.

To date the most thorough study of this pottery area has been undertaken by Kaufmann of Basel Museum in Switzerland; he has recorded on film (Kaufmann 1974) the uses of the pots, clay gathering, clay preparation, the manufacture of an eating bowl, the application of decorations, firing and the subsequent painting process. Information concerning the Sawos pottery has been taken from Kaufmann's film supplemented by the authors' field trips.

Generically, pots are called *au*. There are five types of vessels: *ling-au*, the common cooking pot; *nyam-au*, a sago preparation vessel; *yani*, a sago baking dish; *nangulagacowi-au*, a sago storage vessel; and *kamana*, the sago eating dish, of which there are two variations, a conical open-rimmed bowl and a conical bowl with a more rounded belly, more vertical walls and a slightly inverted mouth. The coiling technique is used and all vessels are made by women but decorated by men.

Fig. 9.25

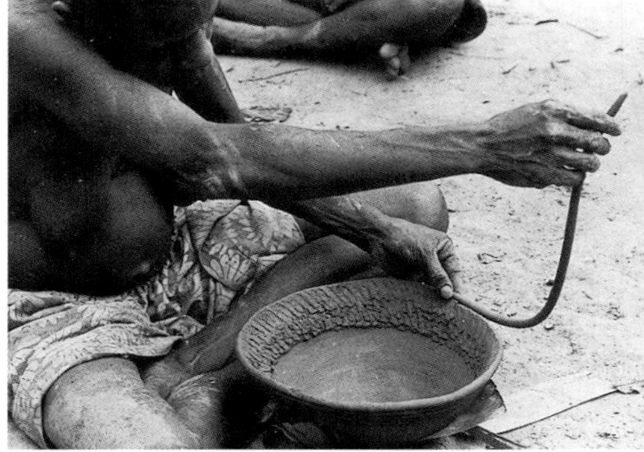

Fig. 9.26

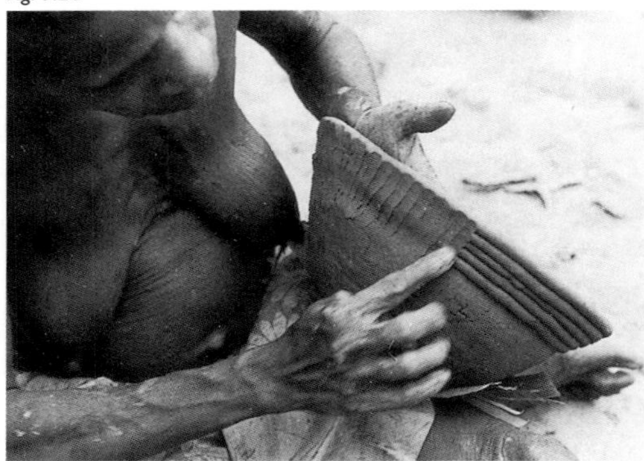

Fig. 9.25
Adding second layer of coils, pressing down across the coils with the thumb.

Fig. 9.26
Bonding the final layer of coils on the outside.

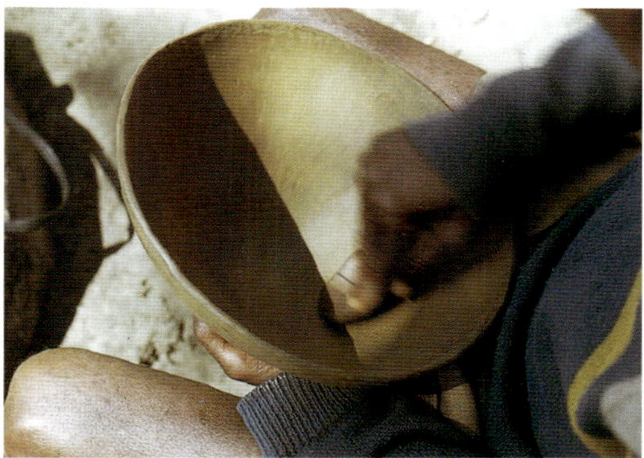

Fig. 9.27

There are two types of clay. One, *kamana kapma*, is used to make the decorated eating bowls. It is an alluvial smectite clay and the deposits are located in the flood area towards the Sepik. It is dark yellowish-brown, fine-grained and completely free of coarse grit. It contains 77 per cent non-plastics. The other, *au kapma*, is rougher in texture and found in the villages. It is used to make cooking pots and sago storage and baking vessels.

The clay is gathered by the women. Lumps of clay are carried back to the village where they are

Fig. 9.28

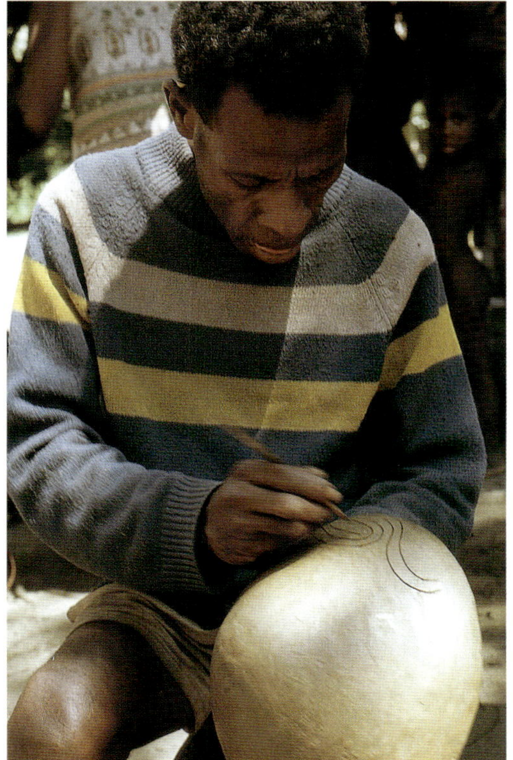

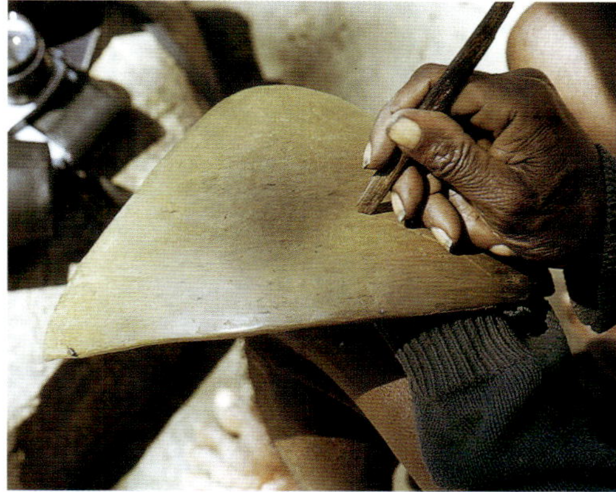

Fig. 9.29

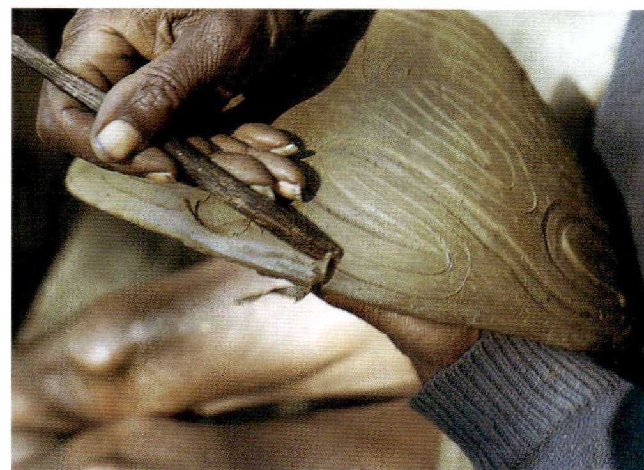

Fig. 9.30

Figs 9.27 to 9.31
Decorating techniques, Koiwat village. The potter Levetmeri is decorating the pot made by Laugwe.

Fig. 9.27
Burnishing the inside of the eating bowl with a small, round piece of coconut shell.

Fig. 9.28
Incising the double outlines of the decoration.

Fig. 9.29
Starting to incise on the outside burnished surface.

Fig. 9.30
Chip-carving between the incised lines.

Fig. 9.31
Nicking the cutaway areas.

Fig. 9.31

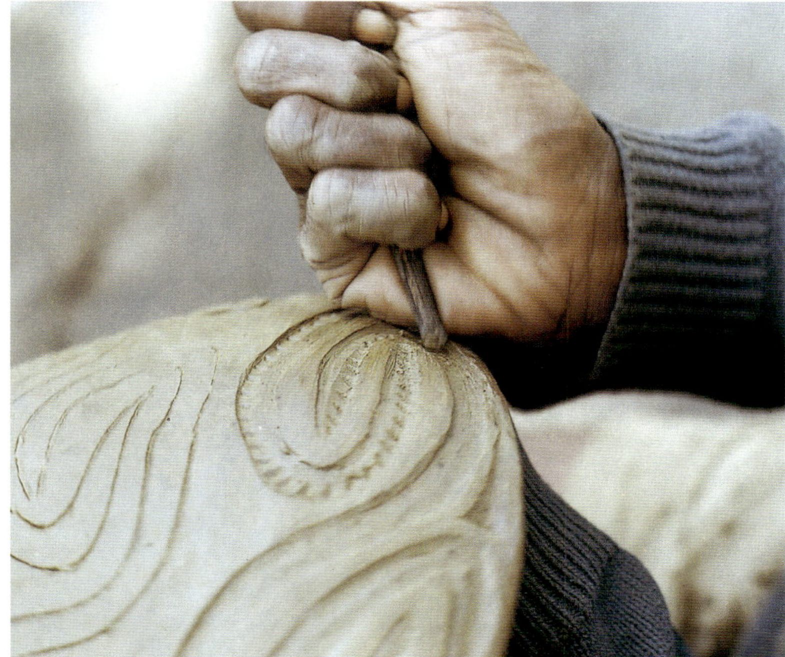

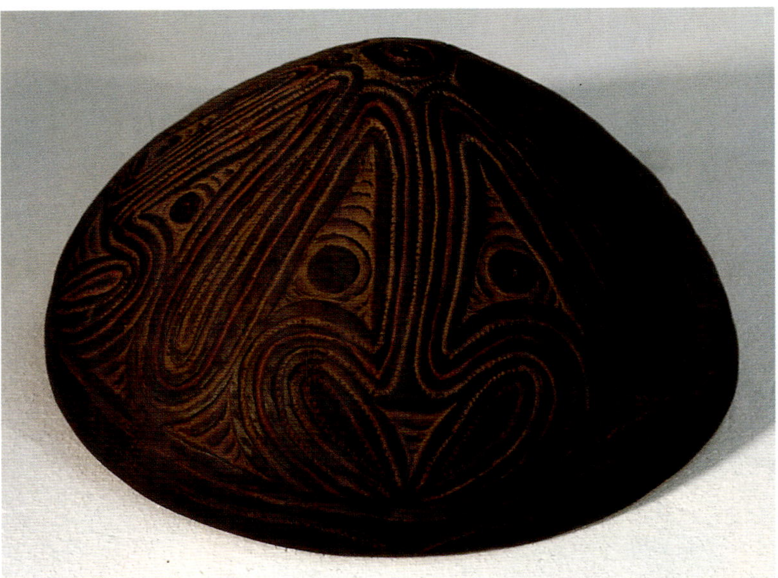

Fig. 9.32
Eating bowl, *kamana,* showing traces of red and yellow ochre, Koiwat village, *h* 16 cm.

Fig. 9.33
Koiwat eating bowl, *kamana;* painted after firing, *h* 15 cm.

stored under a house. When preparing the clay, the potter spreads it onto a large 'limbum' and beats it regularly with a special adze-shaped tool, *kamogwi*, adding water stored in a coconut shell in the process. After the clay is flattened it is folded over by doubling up and rocking the 'limbum' back and forth and then beaten again. The potter prepares enough clay in one sitting to make two or three sago eating bowls and it is generally worked during the next day or so. Water is added to restore plasticity and a portion of clay is separated from the pug and squeezed out in the hands, making short thick rolls. These are rolled out onto a 'pangal' in the normal manner until they form a coil about 40 centimetres long and 5 to 8 millimetres thick. The potter starts her spiral coiling on the 'pangal' or in her hand. She joins each coil onto the one below with a rhythmic downward pressure of her thumb while turning the pot around on her lap. After about twenty coils have been added, the outside coils are bonded with the index finger in either an upwards or downwards motion, depending upon the potter's fashion. For the final joining and smoothing the vessel is supported on a leaf ring-cushion, *ndagu*. As the pot walls grow vertically the potter shapes the vessel with a freshwater shell, *wudi*. While the outside is supported by the palm of the hand the inner surface is smoothed and the walls are gently pushed outward. When the vessel attains a height of about 14 centimetres and a characteristic convex form it is smoothed all over with a dampened index finger. The rim is trimmed by cutting away a portion of the top edge with a plant fibre. The vessel is left on its ring-support and taken inside the house for a few days to dry (figs 9.19-9.26).

The men decorate all the vessels by the chip-carving method. When the pot is leather-hard the man burnishes the surface with a small circular section of coconut shell, *kwainga*. He has several other burnishing and cutting tools of various sizes made from the hard vein of the sago leaf and he uses these to incise the basic design into the pot. He works away from himself and adjusts the position of the pot as the design progresses. This basic design is drawn into two parallel lines; later the wedge-shaped cutting edge of the tools is used to cut into the clay (between the lines) and the clay is then removed in chips and longer curling bits leaving patterns which have been engraved into the surface. Different tools are used for different decorative effects. The vessel is then burnished again on the outside to smooth the cut edges of the design (figs 9.27-9.31).

Firing is generally done by the women and takes place after the pot has been left to dry for about two weeks. A square framework is fashioned from lengths of coconut palm leaves and 'pangal' sections are laid over this to form a grid upon which the vessel is placed right side up. The hottest part

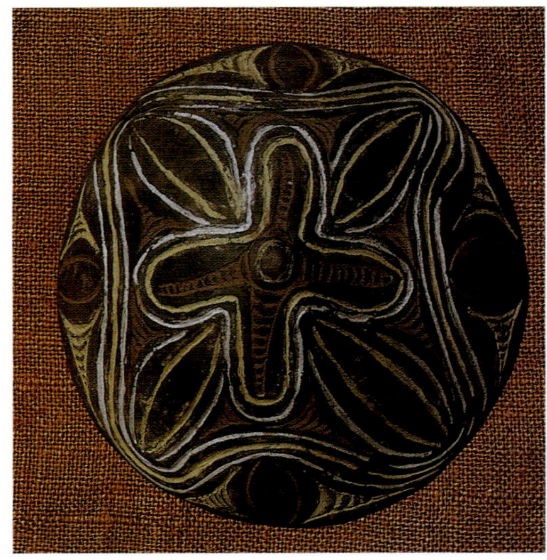

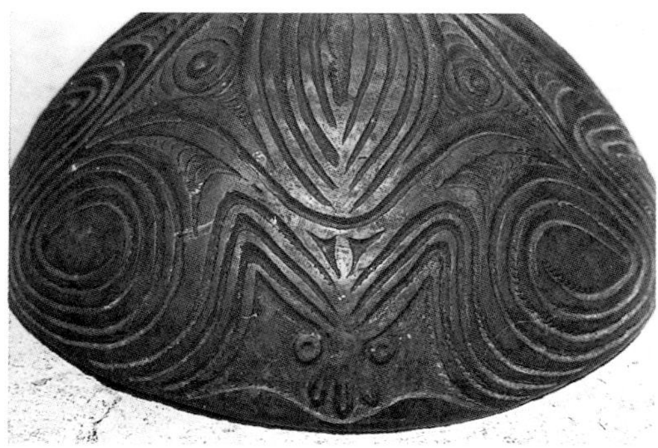

of the firing lasts for about fifteen minutes. The pot is then removed from the ashes with two sticks and sprinkled with a sago and water solution. All newly-fired cooking pots, in order to strengthen them and make them waterproof, must be smoked over a fire until black before being used for cooking food.

The painting of the vessel is done by a man, who uses red, yellow, white and black earth pigments taken from a creek bed and mixes them with water. The artist uses a brush made from the chewed ends of a leaf stem to apply the pigments to the negative cutaway parts of the decoration. Then the vessel is left to stand inside a house to become smoked or covered with soot before it is used or traded. When in use the conical *kamana* are placed in cane rings (plaited by men from split liana vines) and set around the cooking pots ready to receive the sago brew.

The Sawos sago eating dishes are among the most attractive decorated pots of the Sepik area because of the variety and exactness of design elements, the suitability of these designs to the shape of the vessel and the cohesive qualities of the clay, which produces a tightly knit fabric free of rubble or grit and takes on a highly polished surface when burnished or handled. In the Sawos area, and Papua New Guinea as a whole, analysis of both connotative and formal aspects of pottery decoration has been sadly neglected. The sole exceptions to this are prolonged field studies carried out by the Schusters in Aibom and Kaufmann in the Kwoma area. There are many criteria for classifying design as Shepard points out:

> The problems of classification can be simplified by distinguishing the connotative and the formal aspects of design and by recognizing that they can be studied independently. By connotative I refer not only to what is represented, but also to its meaning in the culture ... By formal aspects I refer to those qualities that define style ... adaptation to vessel shape, composition or structure, use of elements and motifs and such characteristics as symmetry, relation of figure to ground and balance of dark and light. [Shepard 1971: 259-60]

The Sawos vessels offer rich material for thorough study of the more formal aspects of design but a connotative study will be more difficult. This is so for two reasons. First, although exquisitely decorated, they are not thought of as ceremonial vessels, unlike the male-decorated eating bowls of the Kwoma, Wosera, Abelam, Boiken and Kwanga industries which serve a ceremonial or semi-religious function. Second, although the patterns cut into the clay are given specific names indicating their significance, Kaufmann suggests that:

> Unfortunately almost nothing can be said about the numerous individual patterns distinguished by the potters. The names for the separate forms refer probably to this or that object in nature supposedly evoked in the pattern – above all to animals and also

Fig. 9.34
Koiwat eating bowl, *kamana*. Decoration is said to represent an ant-lion, *h* 13 cm.

Fig. 9.35
Koiwat eating bowl, *kamana*, collected at Chimbian, *h* 12 cm.

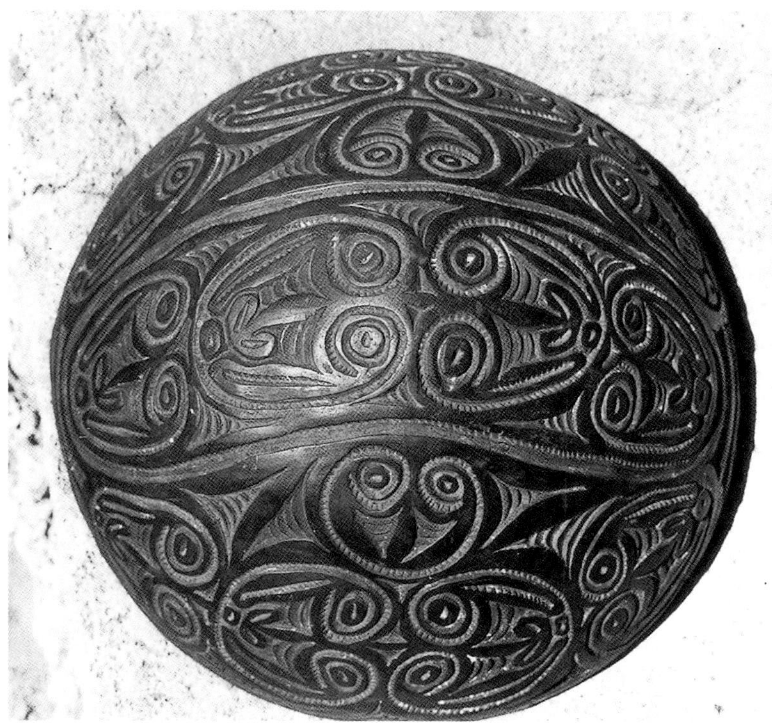

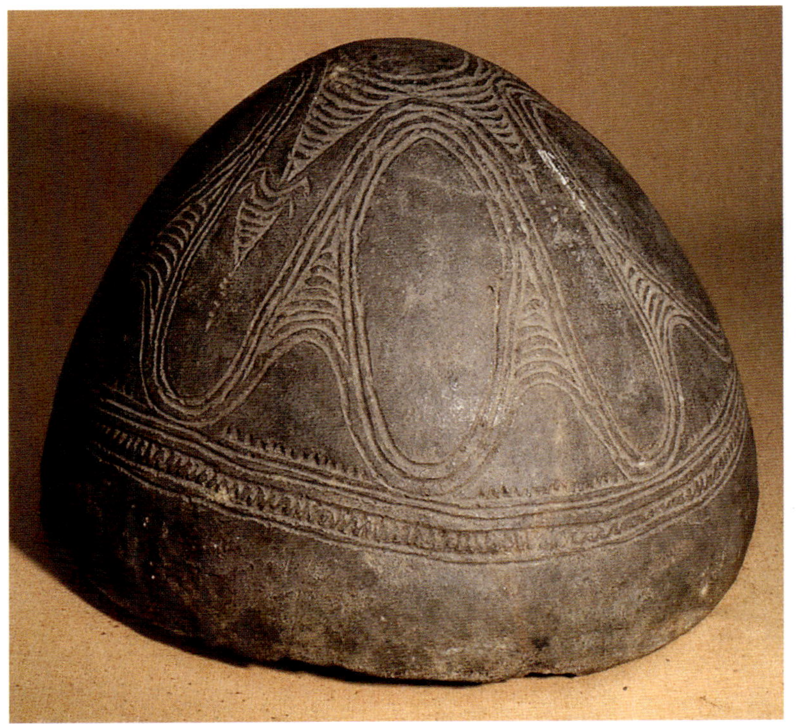

> to parts of plants from the local environment: fish, reptiles, wood and grassland birds as well as the pig. According to all the evidence, however, there is no question of actual representation of these objects. [Kaufmann 1974: 10]

From the wide repertoire of motifs used today and the evidence of designs on vessels collected sixty years ago one can conclude that the artists are drawing upon a reservoir of patterns and combinations of elements prescribed as formulae within the social structure of the Sawos people. There is no evidence of recent artistic licence or innovation of design or form as has occurred amongst the Aibom, Dimiri-Marawat and Wosera industries.

The adaptation of design to vessel shape is of particularly high aesthetic quality. The conical vessel, with its gently curved concave walls, offers no angles which limit visibility. The total surface of the outside walls from the wide open rim to the pointed base is used as the field of decoration. The design can be completely visualised and understood by viewing the everted vessel from the base. Contrary

Fig. 9.36
Eating bowl from Mangul village, probably made long ago at Tolembei, a Sawos village, *h* 18 cm.

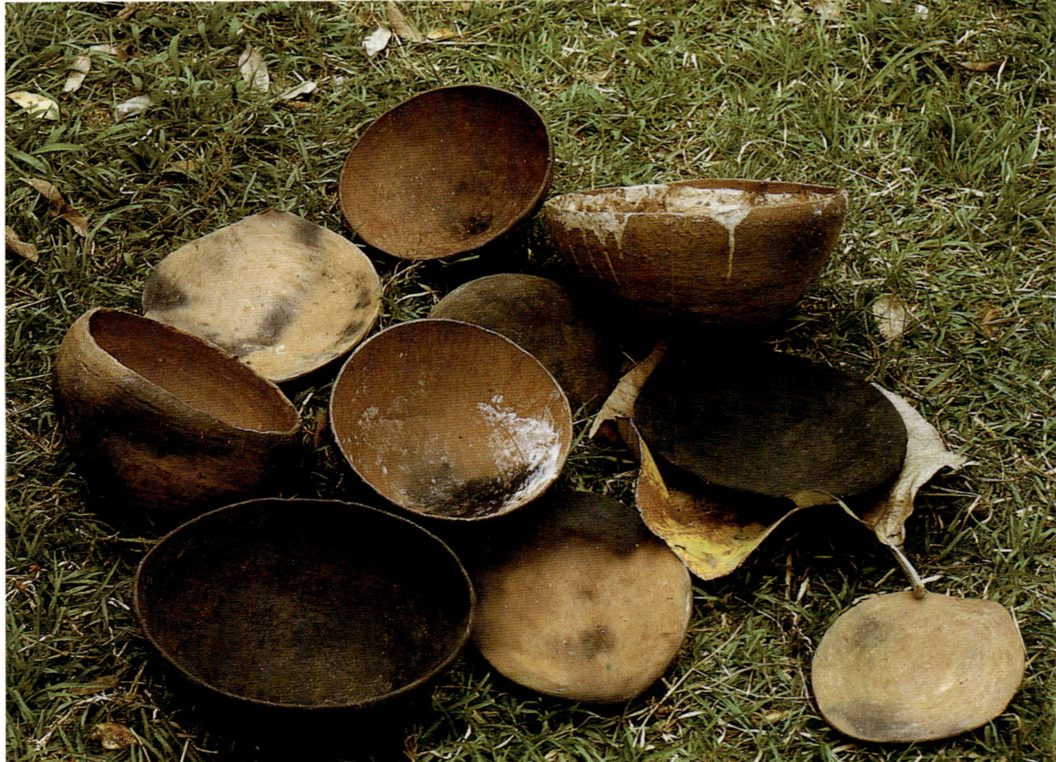

Fig. 9.37
Cooking pots and new sago frying pans made at Chimbian, a Sawos village.

to use, the vessel design is meant to be seen with the vessel in an inverted position. This can be accounted for by the technique of carving, in which the artist supports the upturned bowl on his lap and over one hand (figs 9.28-9.30).

The overall decorative scheme is curvilinear and a rhythmic effect is achieved by the repetition of certain elements: volutes, scrolls, arabesques and series of inscribed concentric circles. A figurative design having the appearance of a 'spirit face' is sometimes used as the primary element or as a series of repeated motifs. Its form is made up of volute-shaped eyes and the outline of a face and a bow-shaped nose with a circular, crescent or lozenge-shaped mouth. This 'spirit face' can be repeated two, three or four more times, depending on its size and proportions. The repetition of elements enlivens the surface and imparts a sense of dynamic motion comparable to designs seen on Celtic, Islamic and Art Nouveau objects. The rim is sometimes given emphasis by longitudinal scalloped designs extending around the circumference but in most cases these rim elaborations flow with the overall design instead of acting as definite borders. In some examples the base point is emphasised by circles engraved around it; when this occurs the overall pattern generally consists of radial or rotational designs made up of scrolls, starfish or lozenge-shaped elements (fig. 9.33).

The addition of paint to the carved, cutaway surface of the design enhances the contrast between dark and light values of the paint and the vessel surface. Indeed, it is difficult to determine whether the cutaway areas or the relief areas are background or figure, positive or negative elements in the design. Painting the cutaway surface of the vessel to enliven it is unnecessary and is evidenced by examples of pots whose paint has long since worn away: the burnished relief surface serves as sufficient contrast to the carved away area to effectively furnish a dominant pattern. The painting of objects and people in many Sepik societies is associated with the magical qualities of the paint.

Although Koiwat and Kamanggaui form the centre of the Sawos pottery industry pots of a different style are made in four other Sawos-speaking villages: Tolembei 1 and 2 and Slei 1 and 2 lie to the west of Koiwat-Kamanggaui, towards the Pagwi road which links Maprik to the river. They are some 10 to 15 kilometres north of the river. Only brief references have been made to these villages by Kaufmann (1972) and no other reports are available. According to him, pots were still made at Slei in 1966 but production had ceased at Tolembei. Some very old Tolembei pots are in the museum collections in Rotterdam and Basel; the notch patterns differ considerably from those of the more recent Slei pots. The authors saw vessels from this area at Mangul and Kupmabit, villages to the north of Slei. They are deep bowl-shaped pots with curvilinear designs not usually representing human or animal forms. They are probably made by women and decorated by men. The carving is more narrow and shallow than that of Koiwat-Kamanggaui (fig. 9.36).

Chimbian

Vessels used for cooking only are made at Chimbian, a Sawos village about 5 kilometres north of Koiwat on the road to Soandogum. Half way to Soandogum and a little to the west is the village of Peringa, also a Sawos village. In 1976 it was listed by village informants as being one of the 'plains Boiken' pot producing places and therefore the pots are probably more akin to the Soandogum type. At Chimbian men and women make simple coiled cooking pots, sago stirring vessels and sago frying pans. The cooking pots and sago stirring vessels, called *au*, have rounded to pointed bases and can be restricted or unrestricted. The frying pans are leaf-shaped, similar in form to Aibom frying pans but not decorated.

It seems that there is no suitable clay, *kupma*, for making refined carved bowls but there is a good quality reddish-grey cooking pot clay. It is medium to fine grained but has a reasonably open texture and few discardable pieces of rubble. No lime-bearing materials are present, the chief non-plastic component being fine quartz. The clay may be fairly dry when collected from the pit, which is very close to the village. Water is sprinkled on it and it is then pounded with the same wooden tool, *kowie*, as used at Koiwat. Clay preparation and forming techniques are similar to those of Koiwat. The area needs further study.

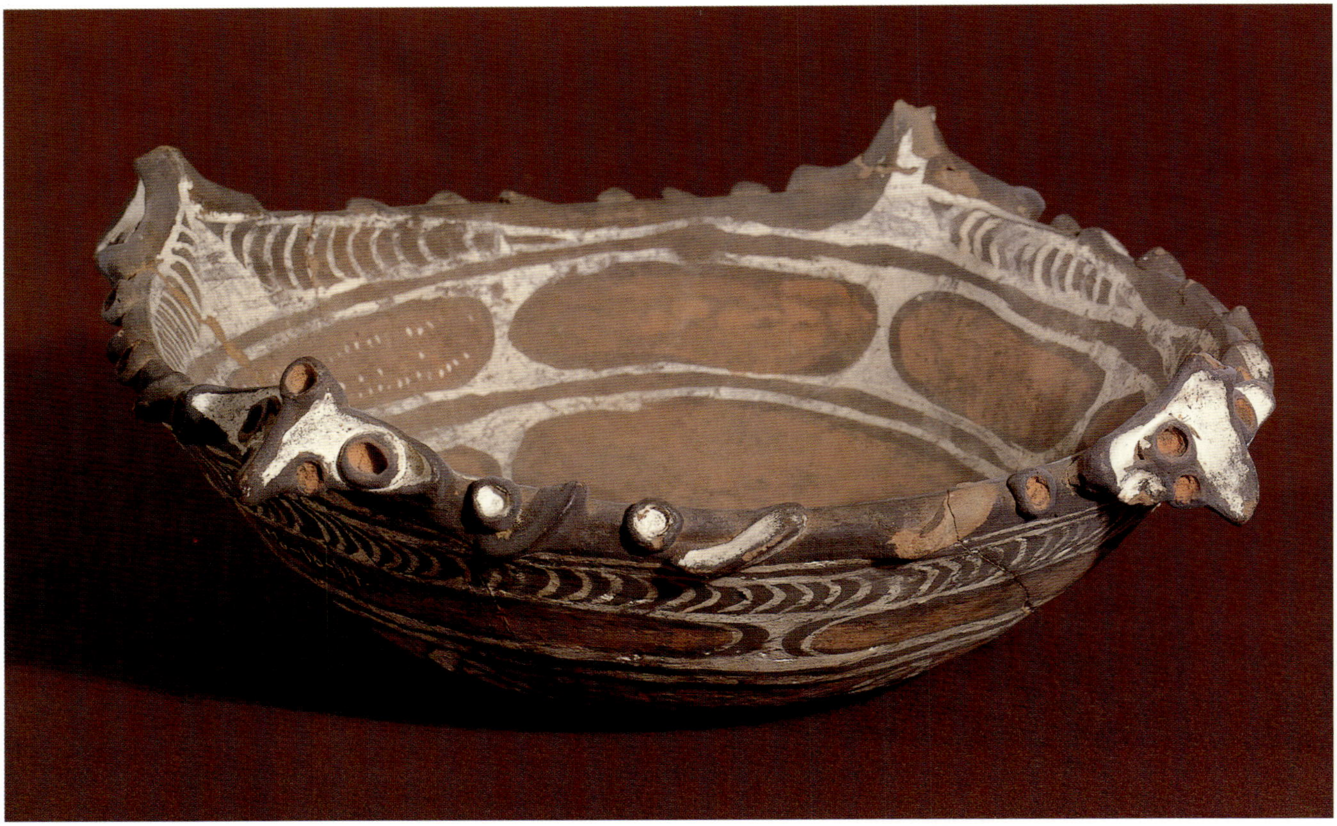

Fig. 9.38
Aibom ceremonial food bowl, *ntshangguigo*, collected early 1900s, *h* 12 cm.

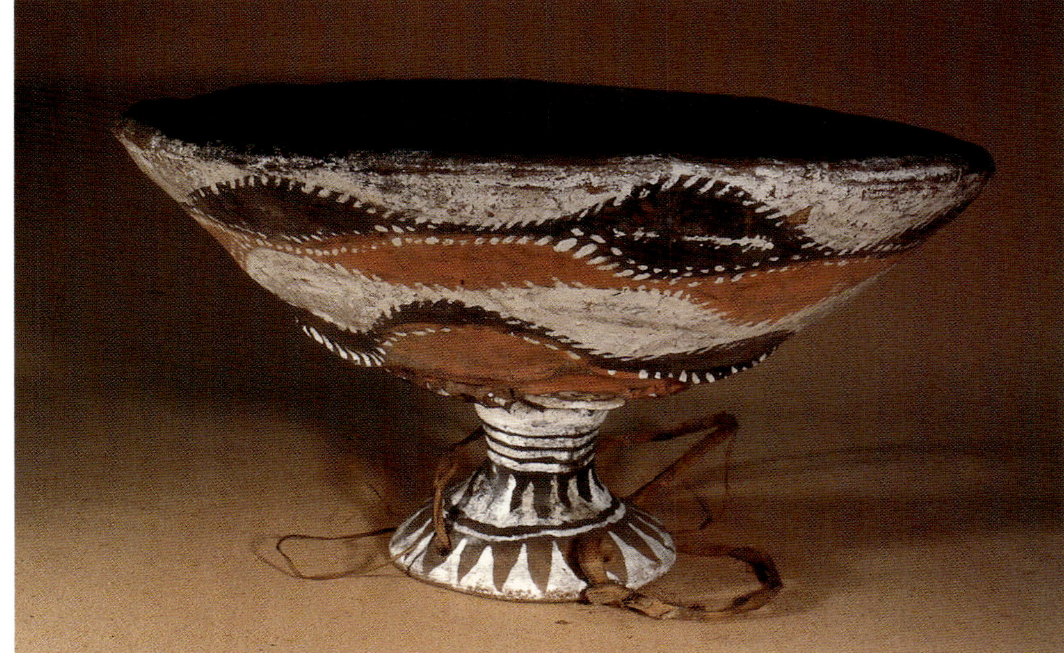

Fig. 9.39
Aibom ceremonial food bowl, *sembuk au*, collected 1936, *h* 20 cm.

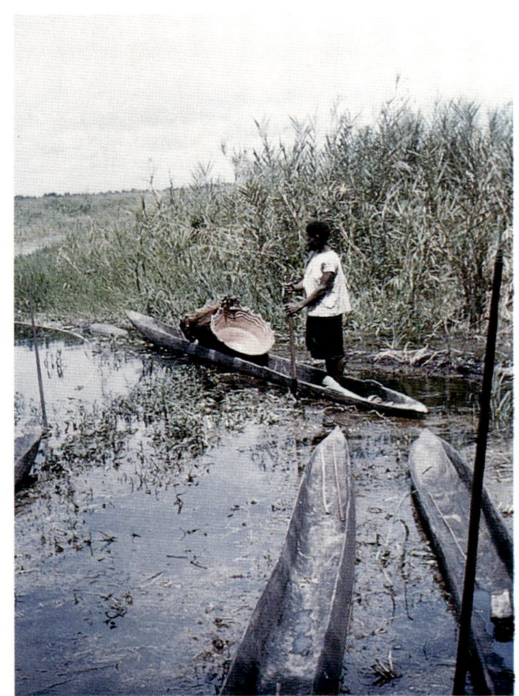

Aibom

The best known and most universally recognisable pottery from Papua New Guinea is made at Aibom village, on the edge of the Chambri Lakes. The Aibom people live in the central Sepik region and speak a dialect of the Iatmul language (Laycock 1973). In the past pottery was also manufactured at the neighbouring village of Chambri and at Wombun, a village located to the north-east of Chambri but Aibom has now assumed a monopoly over the craft. The lakes are located inland off the middle Sepik River and are reached by narrow waterways fringed with jungle and often choked by logs and floating islands of grass which break away during high water from larger islands in the lagoons and float down the Sepik and out to sea. The lakes are accessible by canoe only: canoes with outboard motors can navigate the waterways in high water but it is often necessary to jump overboard and push and pole the canoes through the islands of grass. The remoteness and inaccessibility of Aibom account for the lateness of European contact, in contrast to the large middle Sepik villages.

Margaret Mead's published account of the Lake Tchambuli (Chambri) villages (Mead 1936) unfortunately fails to describe, other than in asides, the Aibom village groups and the important role pottery played both in the economy and rituals of the villages. Fortunately, in 1967, Basel Museum sent to Aibom a study team headed by Meinhard Schuster; his resultant publication *Die Töpfergottheit von Aibom* (1969) records systematically the types of vessels produced, their distinctive decoration and tales of the pottery deities. The Basel team also made a number of documentary films recording techniques and use of pottery at Aibom. Collecting expeditions by museum personnel, private collectors and dealers have dispersed the bizarre sago storage jars, gable adornments and other vessels decorated with the distinctive zoomorphic and

Fig. 9.40
Two Aibom hearths in a canoe being taken home after trading.

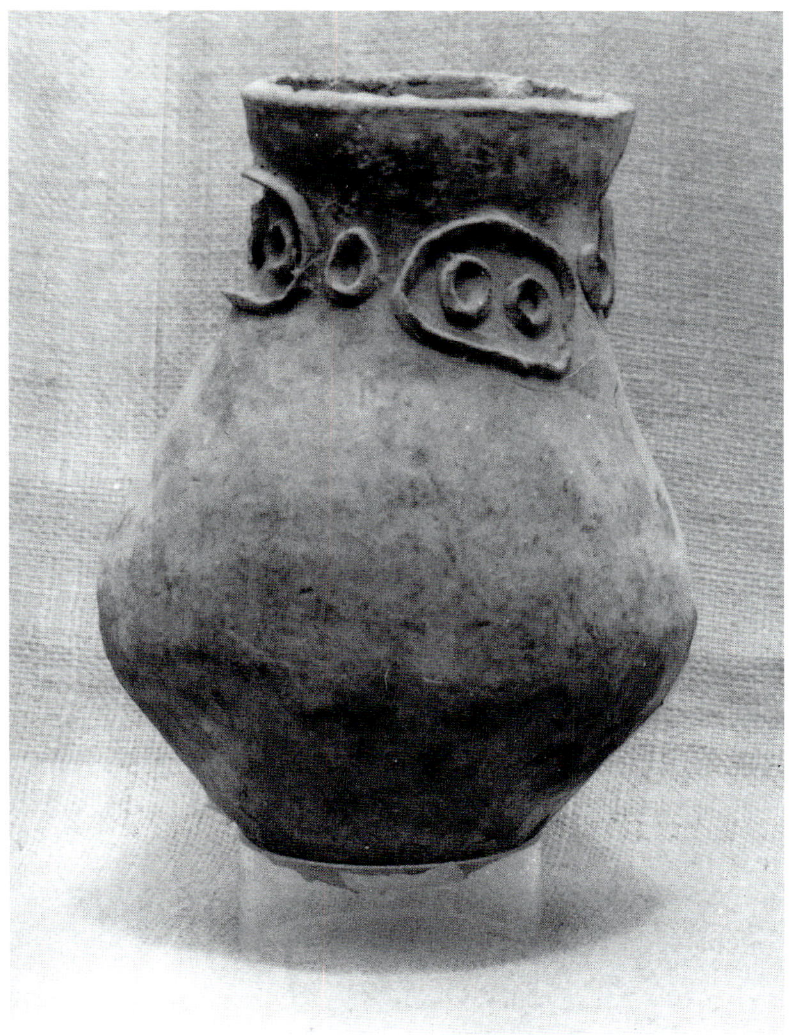

Fig. 9.41
Old jar, collected on the April River, claimed to have been imported from Aibom village.

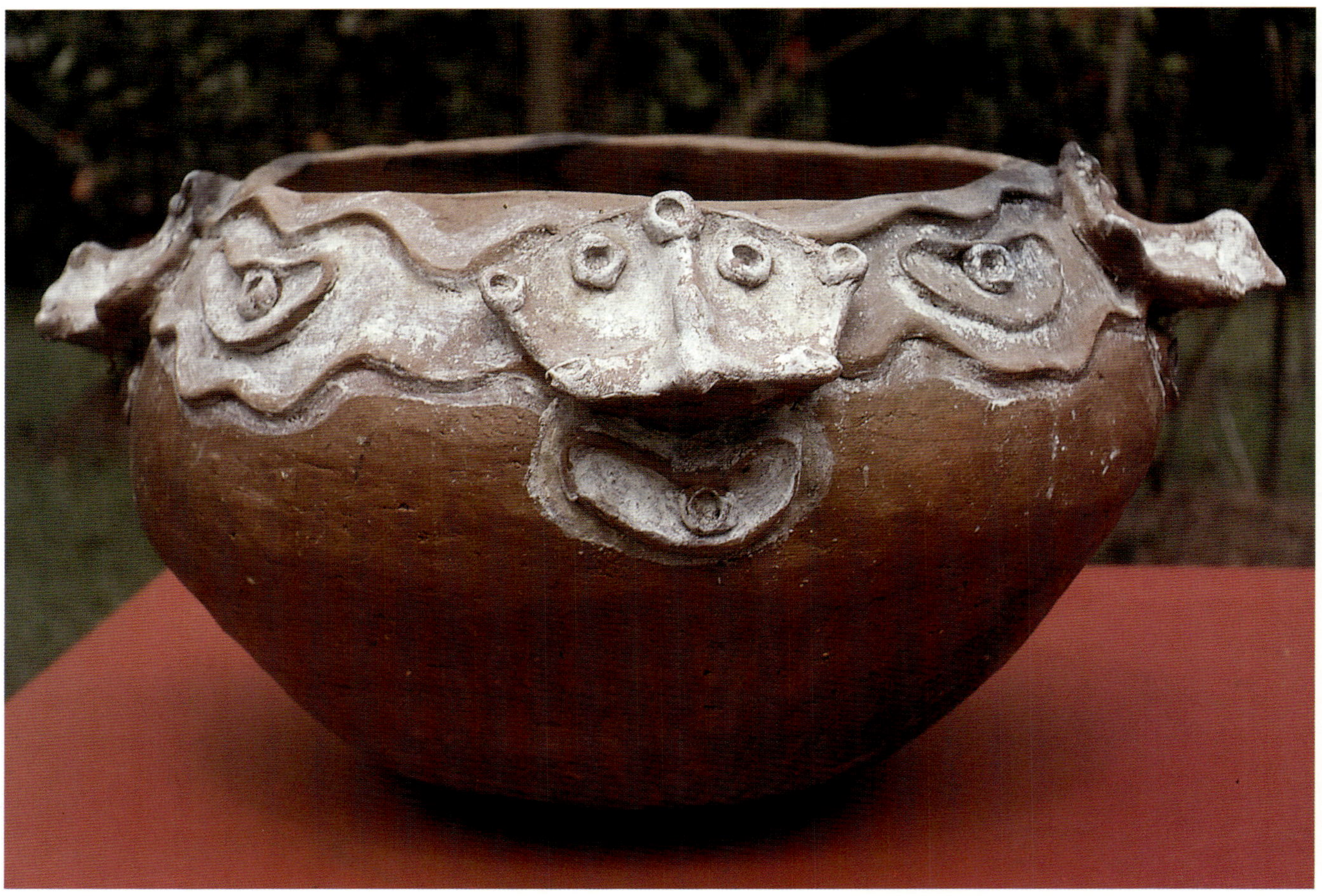

Fig. 9.42
Large Aibom feast pot, *kombio*, *h* 28.5 cm.

anthropomorphic relief depictions of mythological spirits throughout Europe, America, Australia and, more recently, Japan. The Museum für Völkerkunde in Berlin has an excellent selection of Aibom vessels, some dating from the first decade of the 20th century and most of which were collected from villages along the Sepik River.

Aibom pottery was traditionally and still is a precious item of exchange. Sago and fish form the staple diet of the Aibom people and in order to secure sago, which they do not gather or process themselves, they depend upon trade with the bush people living in the hill country behind the lakes. Now that government has been imposed upon the middle Sepik villages and headhunting and warfare are things of the past, the Aibom people have extended their trading activities up and down the river with the help of middle-men, particularly from the villages of Tambanam and Maringei.

Tambanam, located in the middle reaches of the Sepik, retains a pronounced belief in ceremonial and 'tambaran' practices in spite of intense mission activity and constant exposure to anthropologists, dealers, collectors and tourists. The Tambanam people, characteristically keen to acquire imported objects of ritual significance, collect masks, ceremonial carvings, personal adornment and pots. Practically every household has sago storage jars and cooking pots from Aibom and Dimiri and fire hearths from Aibom, most of which are in everyday use. Also in abundance are the conical serving bowls made in the Sawos area. These are not generally used but are offered for sale.

While Tambanam villagers act as middle-men for the exchange of artifacts and pottery from all the neighbouring regions the Maringei people, who live on the Sepik close to the 'baret' leading to Chambri Lakes, are the chief local middle-men

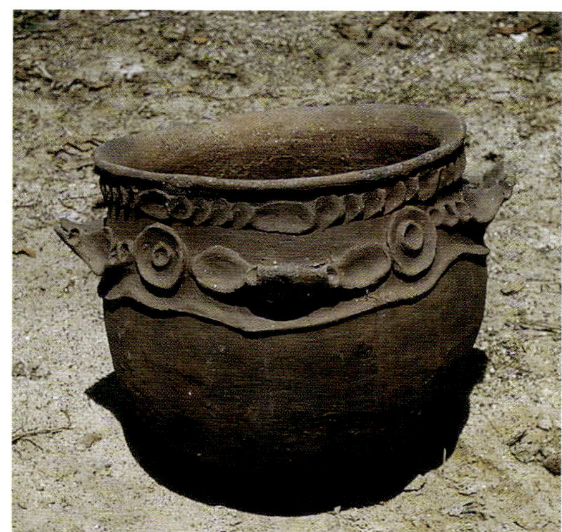

responsible for the distribution of Aibom pottery. Maringei women take their canoes full of sago, grass skirts from the April River and betel nut to Aibom to exchange for pottery and smoked fish. From Maringei the pottery is traded up and down the river. Aibom pottery of recent manufacture has been sighted as far south as the Murik Lakes and as far north as the April River. One example of an older Aibom vessel, sighted in the upper reaches of the Sepik, was presumably an exchange item between intermediaries or a captured spoil from fights between warring groups (fig. 9.41).

Ceramic objects produced at Aibom include sago storage jars, cooking pots, gable ridge ornaments, fire dishes or hearths, sago frying dishes, serving bowls, eating dishes which also serve as lids for covering sago storage jars and food preparation dishes. Although Aibom pots seem to cover a great variety of shapes and serve many functions there are actually only a few basic shapes, the forms of which are modified and decorated with applied and modelled adornments. The types of objects produced are as follows. Sago storage jars, called *au* have two variations, the *damarau* and the *noranggau*. The *damarau* is a larger jar, 60 to 120 centimetres high with a rounded base, globular belly and long slender neck with an everted rim. It can be used for cooking, for storing smoked sago and for serving food at ceremonies. Also characteristic of the *damarau* (*dama* = nose, face) is its decoration, which always consists of one modelled face applied in relief on the painted cylindrical neck area. There are five different faces representing humans, animals and spirits: a pig's face with two eyes and a protruding snout; a human face; a bush spirit face with a prominent nose, a slightly protruding mouth, a bow-shaped arch extending from the forehead to the chin and decorated with strips applied in a scalloped design; a bird's face (probably that of an eagle), disc-shaped, with a sharply defined beak and mouth; and a mask or abstraction of a human skull (figs 1.16, 1.17).

The *noranggau* is smaller than the *damarau*, more squat in proportion and with a shorter, wider neck and larger mouth opening. It is used to store freshly prepared sago before it is smoked or cooked. It can also be used as a cooking vessel. Its decoration consists of relief sculpture depicting animal or human faces although neither the skull nor the pig's face is ever used. Unlike the *damarau*, the *noranggau* usually has two or four faces applied to the shorter neck area, which extends further down the body of the vessel. These forms have been simplified and reduced to protruding noses which can serve as handles (fig. 9.44).

Fig. 9.43
Large Aibom cooking vessel, *sero*, at Marienberg.

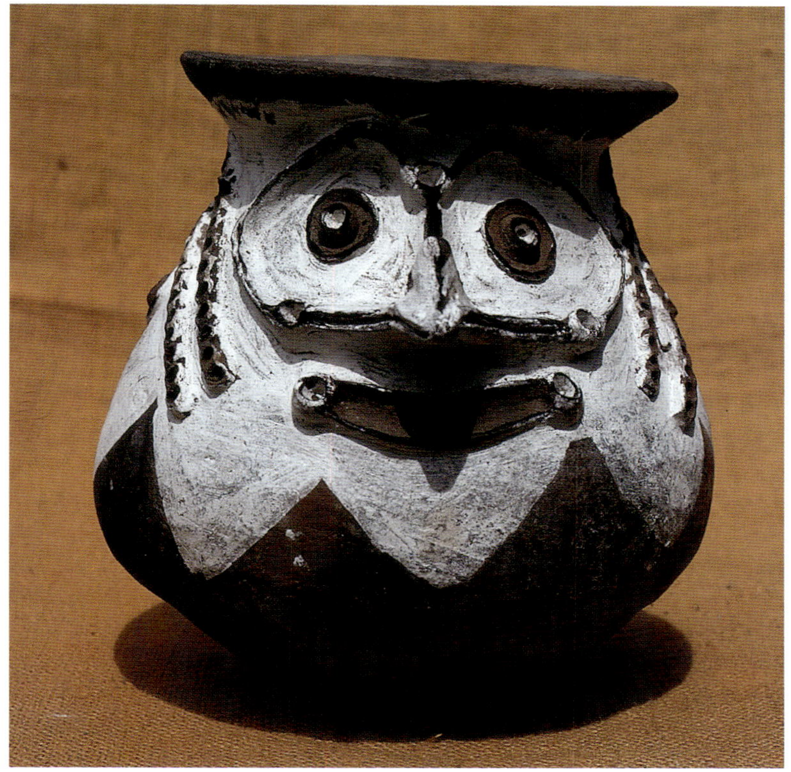

Fig. 9.44
Squat sago storage jar, *noranggau*, from Aibom village, *h* 21 cm.

Fig. 9.45
Aibom gable decoration.

Fig. 9.46
Hearth, *gugumbe,* in use in a house at Tambanan, Sepik River.

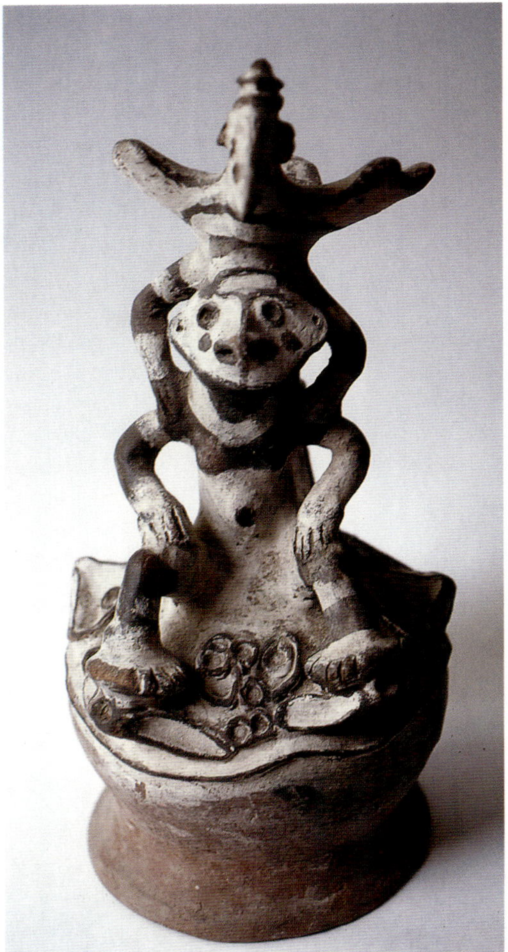
Fig. 9.45

A second basic type related by technique of manufacture to the sago storage jars but more bowl-shaped with little or no neck and a slightly restricted orifice is the *sero*, a common cooking pot usually about 20 centimetres high. The *kombio*, a larger, wider version, is used only for cooking meats: crocodile, pig and, in the past, man. The decoration used on the *sero* type cooking vessels is distinctive because of its simplicity and use of geometric designs. A *sero* will often have two or four handles, or lugs, of roughly flattened triangular shapes marked by a scallop design; rondels may be applied which are made with coils about 7 centimetres long formed into a circle, applied to the wall of the vessel and then flattened in the centre by the thumb. Further elaboration involves applied coils meandering around the pot and possible decoration

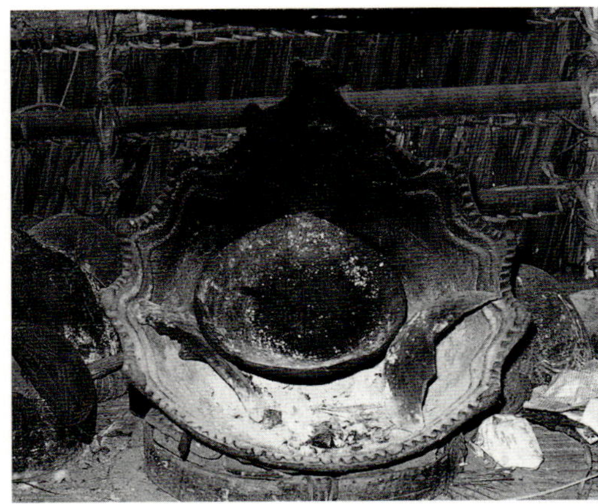
Fig. 9.46

with finger indentations. (See Kelm 1966: Vol. I, Catalogue Nos. 295-98, for examples of pots with incised designs.) The *kombio* with its distinctive outward flaring sides, is decorated with rondels, or faces, applied in intervals around the top portion and with undulating scalloped strips. Gable decorations, sometimes referred to as 'ridge tiles', are inverted *sero* type vessels. They are made by women then taken over by the men who affix a modelled three-dimensional representation of a human head with a long protruding trunk-like nose, a seated hermaphroditic figure surmounted by an eagle or, recently, a rooster with outspread wings. The base of the *sero* type is generally covered with the rondels and is always painted in white lime and ochres. These ceramic sculptures are placed on top of the gables of the men's house and resemble the huge wooden sculptures of the cannibal eagle mounted with outspread wings over the shoulders of a man, which traditionally guards the 'haus tambaran' and village. Today the ridge decoration is manufactured mainly for commercial reasons but is occasionally used and probably retains a symbolic and ritual purpose as a protective talisman.

Gugumbe is a fire dish or hearth used inside the house: it sits on stones, crudely fashioned clay supports, broken pieces of pottery or bark rings (fig. 9.46). Measuring 60 to 160 centimetres in diameter, it has a round base and open flaring walls, one edge of which is raised higher than the other sides to form a peak that is always decorated in applied relief with the face of a bush spirit, a bird or a pig. The rim of the fire dish is fashioned in undulating, rhythmic peaks, valleys and/or loops and the inner

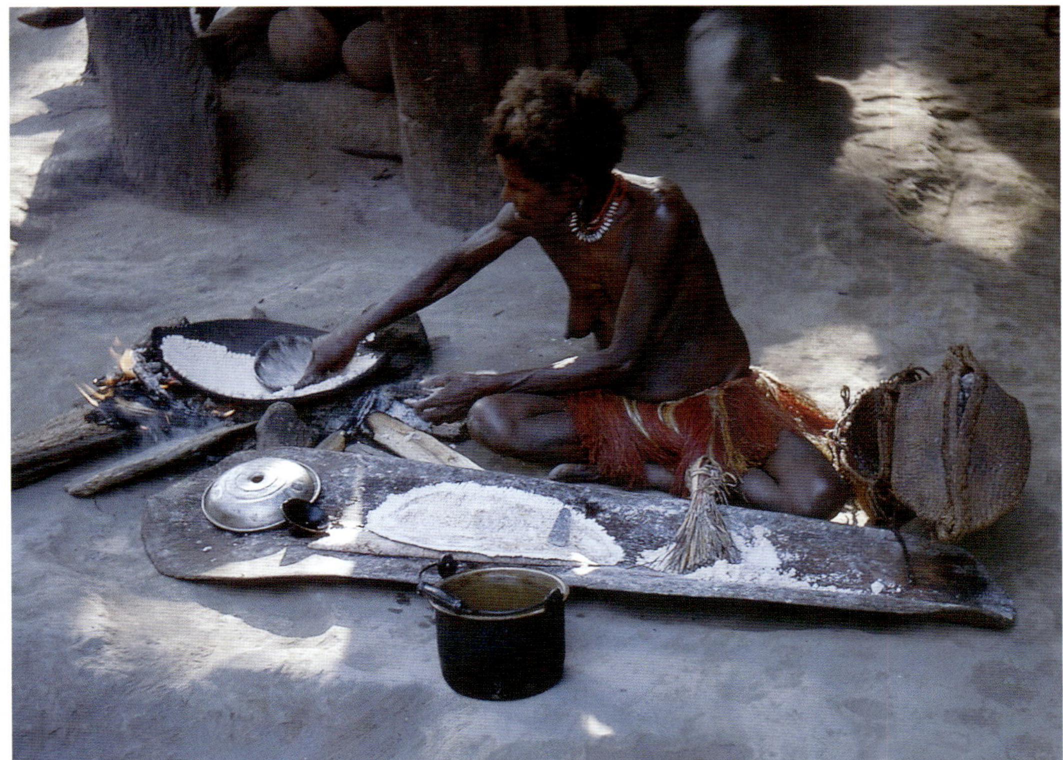

Fig. 9.47
Sago cakes cooking in an Aibom frying pan, *yaintshe*, Tambanam, Sepik River.

edge is enlivened with decorated coiled strips applied in sympathetic agreement with the undulating rim. It is never painted (fig. 9.55). The fire dish is placed against the wall of the house in a slightly uptilted direction. A fire is lit in it and cooking pots and frying pans are placed on clay supports, stones or sherds over the fire. Some foods may be placed directly in the embers: smoke serves as a deterrent to mosquitoes and the glowing embers ensure a light for tobacco smoking. Fish and meat are smoked on racks above the fire. Smaller, portable versions of the fire dish are made for use in canoes. As well as being used for cooking they give warmth in the cool of the early morning and protection from mosquitoes. This smaller *gugumbe* is often made with an attached base for support.

Yaintshe, a sago frying dish, is oval or leaf-shaped, shallow, about 50 centimetres long and 35 centimetres wide and with its two ends forming handle-like protuberances, or peaks. In most examples these vessels are simply decorated with stick or finger impressions made on the last 10 centimetres of the sides and on the end points. Sometimes the handles resemble creatures. Further decoration may include applied undulating strips edging the rim, depicting the scalloped borders of the bush spirit's face.

Ntshangguigo, a serving or eating bowl, is a shallow dish, either round or oval and with a wide unrestricted mouth. The walls of the vessel are sometimes drawn up to form triangular peaks along the rim and modelled birds' heads may extend over the edge (figs 9.38, 9.48).

Sembuk au has its three primary functions reflected in its shape. It is a bowl with walls flaring outward, a wide mouth opening and a cylindrical

Fig. 9.48
Aibom food bowl, *ntshangguigo, h* 8 cm.

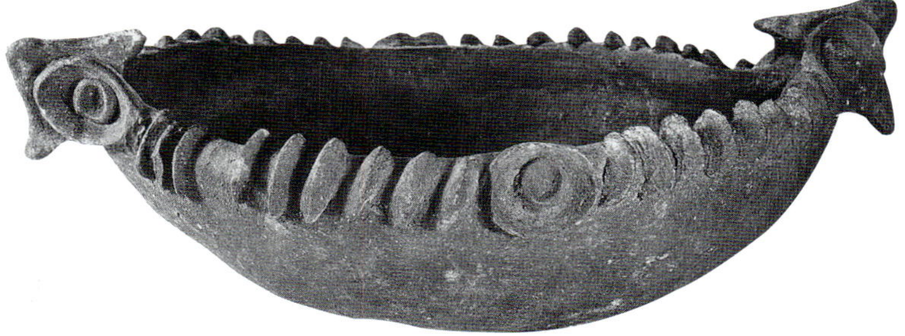

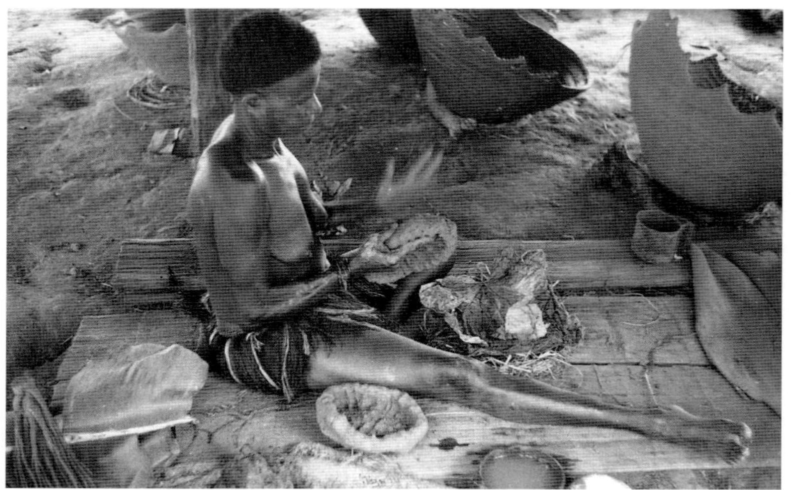

Figs 9.49 to 9.54
Techniques at Aibom village, 1965.

Fig. 9.49
Two pinched bases which will be bashed together to form the base of a pot.

base. It can be inverted to serve as a lid for sago storage jars, it can be used as an eating dish or soup container, and larger versions may be used for the preparation of food (fig. 9.39).

Tshisiran are pot stands, small simple dishes which are placed upside down in the fire dish and used for supporting cooking pots and frying pans.

The range of traditional manufactured ceramics has recently been increased due to mission influence to include commercial objects, mostly figurines, vases, candle holders and cups. On the whole these objects are crudely made and by 1975 this 'airport art' seemed to be dying a natural death (fig. 1.23). On the other hand, there has been increased production of the gable decorations and small sago storage jars that are popular with tourists and collectors. Highly innovative and bizarre lizard, bird and zoomorphic figures now surmount the inverted *sero*. Quality remains high although the painting is often applied in a crude and untidy manner.

The method of manufacture of Aibom pottery is ring building, unique in Papua New Guinea. The women make the vessels and apply the decoration but men specialise in forming and decorating the faces and figures on the ridge sculptures applied to vessels used in ceremonies and in modelling the faces on the large sago storage jars. Almost all the adult women from the age of fifteen years know how to make pots. There is no particular specialisation in the types of vessels made; all women can and do produce all kinds. Pottery is made mainly during the wet season.

Aibom is the only Iatmul village with clay suitable for producing ceramics. None of the villages situated on the banks of the Sepik makes pots; in most cases this is due to lack of raw material. If women of Aibom marry out of the village they

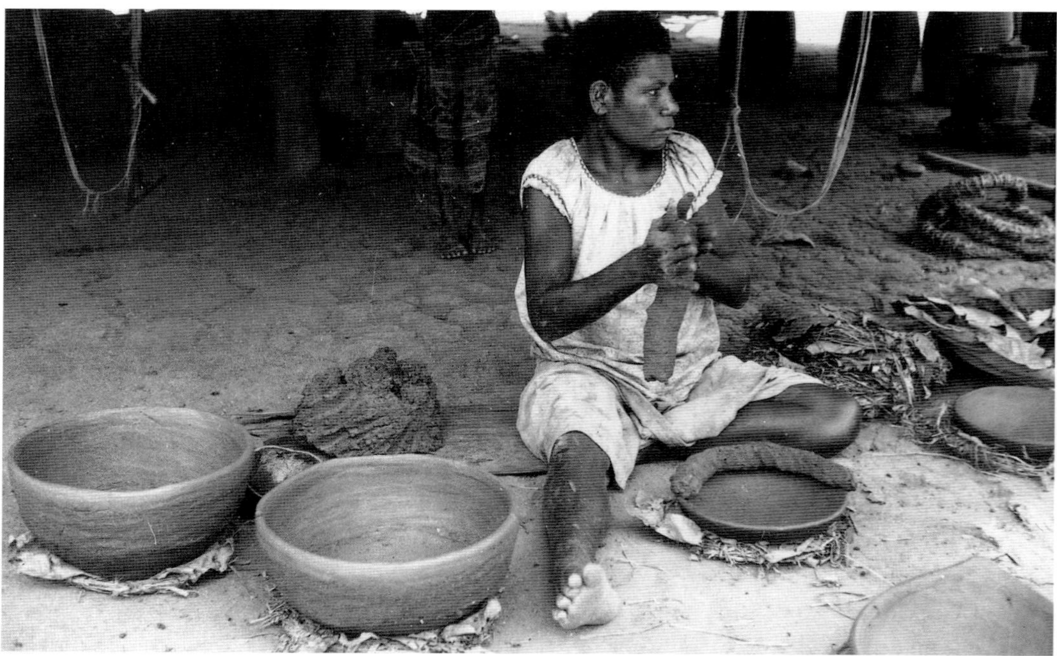

Fig. 9.50
Aibom potter making thick roll of clay to build up the walls.

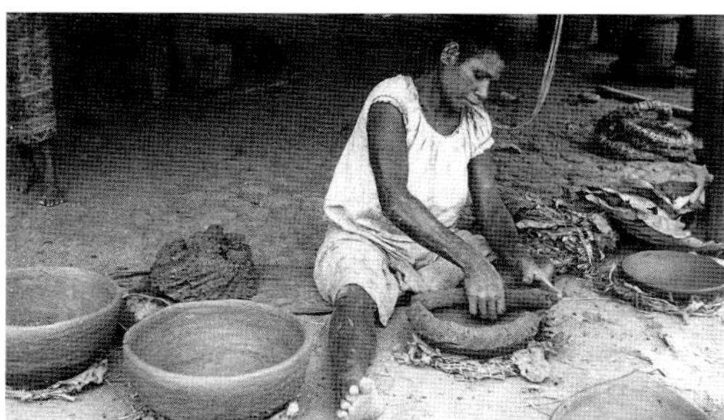
Fig. 9.51

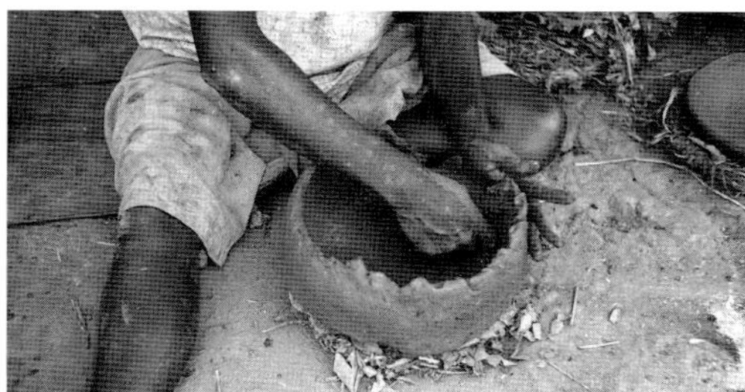
Fig. 9.52

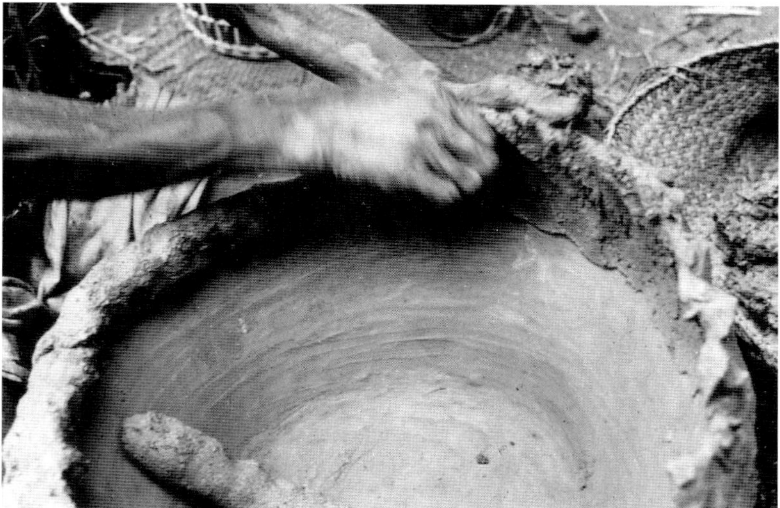
Fig. 9.53

forfeit the rights to their clay pits but they do not have to relinquish their right to make pots.

Clay deposits are numerous on the slopes of the hill behind Aibom village. Different kinds of clay come from many pits: most women mix two, a few add a third type. One clay reported is whitish and relatively free of grit. The two most often used are a mottled, very gritty, sandy, grey yellowish-brown clay, and a blackish, more compact clay. Usually several women related by kinship ties share a pit; they dig the clay with bush knives and digging sticks and carry it in plaited bags back to the houses, where it is kept moist and stored in old dugout canoes. While the clays are being mixed and kneaded together and water added if necessary stones and roots are removed. The resultant amalgam is most often dark brown and moderately plastic but it still retains a coarse gritty texture. Tests show that most of the gravel-sized pieces of disintegrating rock found in the clay break up on becoming wet and become part of the finer non-plastics.

The potter sits under the house and begins to form the base from very soft clay. She pinches out a ball of clay and models a shallow rough dish. She makes a second one and then bashes the two together, one inside the other, thus gaining a larger mass which she consolidates by pounding on the inside with her fist. This base is now supported on a grass ring, *entagu*, reinforced with liana vine that has a green banana leaf placed over it. The woman turns the vessel around on the ring while she shapes and smooths the base with her fingers and knuckles. A round or an oval dish may be produced, as desired. The potter makes several of the basic shapes and puts them aside to become firmer. If the vessel is to be a frying pan the shaping is finished quickly by adding extra clay to the oval dish to form the peaks at each end. To make cooking pots or sago storage jars, the walls of the original round base must be raised. The potter squeezes and rolls out a thick cylinder of clay between her hands

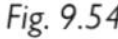

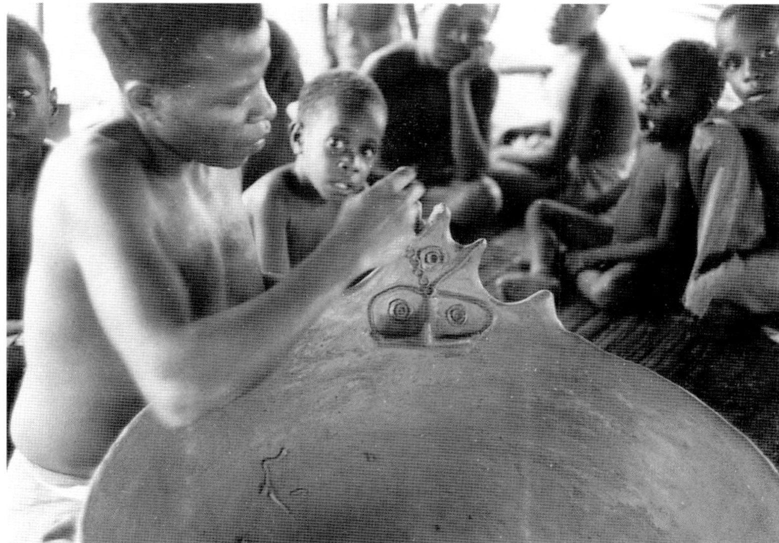
Fig. 9.54

Fig. 9.51
Applying the roll of clay.

Fig. 9.52
Dragging clay up with the knuckles to form the walls.

Fig. 9.53
Dragging soft clay up with the fingers.

Fig. 9.54
Forming the face on a hearth with small rolls of clay.

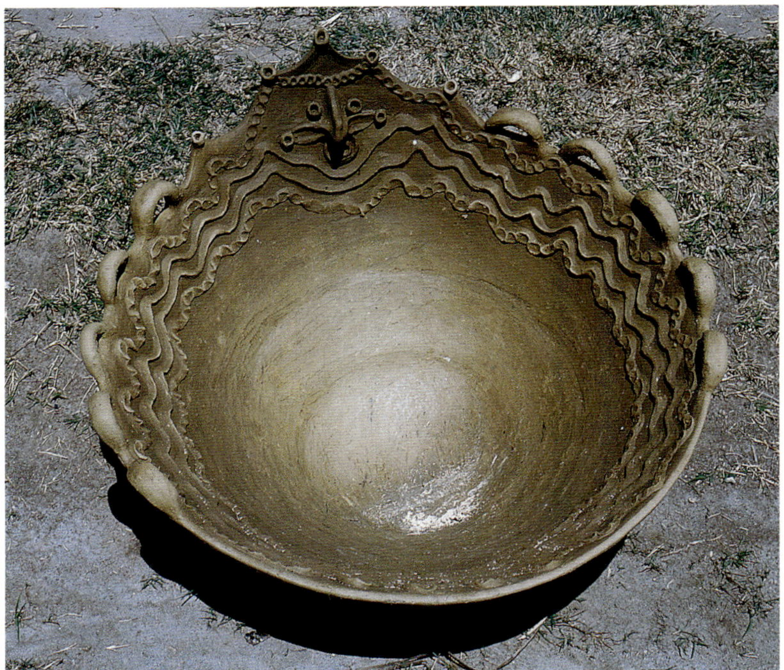

Fig. 9.55
Finished hearth, *gugumbe,* drying in the sun, Aibom village.

held at shoulder height. When it is about 4 centimetres in diameter it is joined to the top edge of the base and overlapped on the inside. The clay is dragged upwards with the fingers in a rhythmic movement, raising the walls by some 10 centimetres. Two to three rolls usually complete a circle. Any unevenness of the top edge is corrected by filling in low areas with clay from the high spots. The joined area is now smoothed and the vessel is placed in the sun to become firmer. When more rolls of clay have been added and smoothing and shaping are accomplished the left hand supports the exterior walls and a smooth moistened piece of coconut shell is worked around the inside to further round out the shape, to thin it and to raise the walls.

When a newly formed base is firm enough it is planed down with an ingenious tool, a freshwater mussel shell which has in the middle a hole formed by rubbing it against a rock. The sharp inner edge cuts away the thick rough clay until the walls are even, leaving a very open texture which shows all the non-plastic inclusions. The surfaces of the frying pans, sago jars and fire bowls are left like this but the cooking pots are smoothed once again by pressing in the grit and filling up the holes with bits of clay. Wet hands are now rubbed over the surface and final smoothing inside and out is done with the smooth bit of coconut shell.

Decoration is applied to the leather-hard vessels after they have dried under the house. There are four basic types of decoration: applied strips or coils, finger or tool impressed (the end of a battery cone is now sometimes used); applied rondels, thumb pressed or garnished with small round balls, called *popop*, impressed in the middle with the end of the battery cone or a smooth-ended stick; modelled relief sculpture built up from lumps of clay applied to wetted areas of the pot; painting (after firing) with lime and natural ochres. Examples of pottery collected in 1912-13 show incised markings but these are rarely seen today.

Drying time lasts from one to several weeks and women often prefer to leave firing until just before a big market day. Pots must be put in the sun for a few hours before being fired. A square frame of four dried ribs of coconut palm is used as a platform, supported over four large rocks placed at the corners. A grid of interlacing split bamboo, dried twigs, or slats of 'limbum' is then constructed over the frame and dried grasses, coconut shells and dried coconut fronds are placed over the grid. The pots are placed in the middle of the stack, with larger vessels in the centre and smaller objects arranged around them. Dried sago palm fronds are then stacked on top of and around the pots in several layers. Reported firing times are from about thirty minutes to one hour. Fuel is added when needed. Black firing marks are not acceptable and whenever possible the black patch is quickly covered with burning or glowing fuel; sometimes a pot has to be refired to eliminate these marks. Bamboo tongs are used to remove the vessels from the ashes. Pots are considered to be properly fired when they turn orange. Fire hearths and cooking vessels are treated with a sealing mixture of starchy sago water which is spattered over the warm pots with a leafy twig. Figurines and three-dimensional gable ornaments are often not properly fired because of their thickness. They tend to break easily and cross-sections reveal a core of brown unfired clay.

The decorations and modelled forms and faces used on the ceramics are representative of cultural deities within the mythology of the tribe and totems of different clans. Basically there are two deities: a male figure, Meintumbangge, and a female, Kolimangge, both of whom are depicted as animal and bush spirits. There are many versions of the myth of the female deity, called variously Kolimangge, Yuman-Wusmangge, Ntshambeyaintshe, Wiremangge and Mempintshaua. In one version Kolimangge created pottery for the tribe and taught the women to pot. The little stick used by potters to press designs into the relief decorations is Kolimangge's 'pencil' and the water in the coconut shell which keeps the clay from sticking is her 'ink'. She subsequently transformed herself into earth and clay and is thus called *kolimangge*.

In another story, Yuman made pots which were her children, created by her own hands without a father. She was raped and disappeared. The ancestors tried to make a mask of her face but they were unsuccessful until they killed an enemy, cut off his head, boiled it, over-modelled it with clay and painted it. This became a 'tumbuan's' head. At one time Yuman had killed a man and used his thigh and upper arm bones to make music in a dance; now, cassowary bones are used in this dance. The human bones, the cassowary bones and the hand drums used in this ceremony are called *yaintshe,* the name given to the sago frying dish. This mask, a human skull over-modelled with clay, is depicted in clay and appears on the sago storage pots; it represents Yuman.

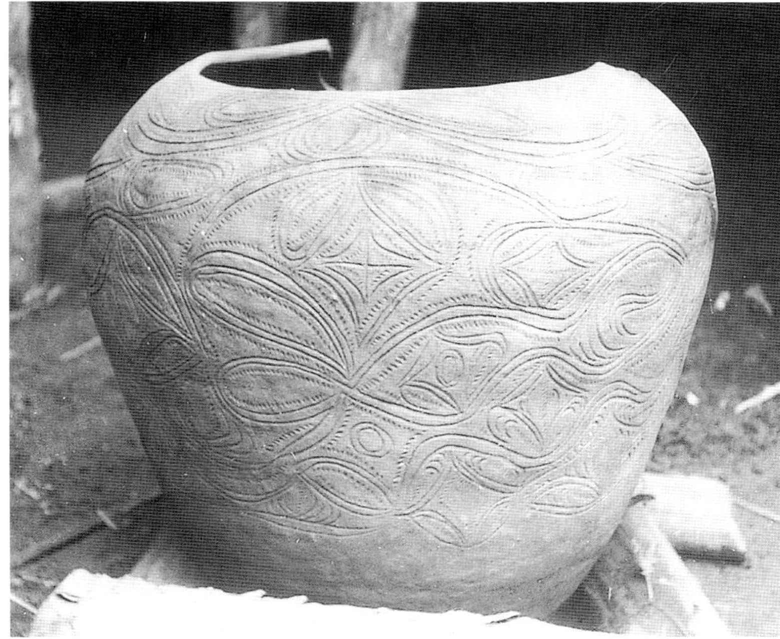

Fig. 9.56
Yaul sago storage jar, *h* 63 cm.

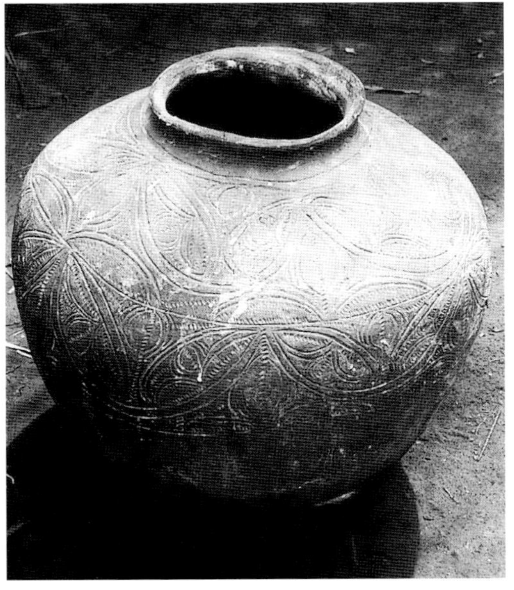

Fig. 9.57
Yaul sago storage jar, *mangumbu, h* 64 cm.

A different Kolimangge story tells how the clay, fuel and the sago sealing solution all came to her when she called them. On her command, the fuel prepared itself for a firing, the pots settled themselves on the fuel and later took themselves to market and stood in a row. After marrying a man called Korumblaban she lost her command over the raw materials and pots and since then all women potters must carry their own clay, build their own fires and take their own pots to market.

The mythological female figure, Ntshambeyaintshe, associated with Kolimangge, had two faces: a human face and the face of a duck. In one story she was eaten by the pigs, Suie and Weintu; from her blood originated the red coconut palm and from her brain the black palm issues. Her body is thus accredited with the creation of two of the most useful plants in the region. Meintu is mentioned in the mythology as son, brother and creator of Kolimangge. He is identified as a cannibal eagle and a pig and appears on the pottery as a bush spirit, a pig and an eagle.

The faces of the duck, the bush spirit, the pig and the eagle appear on the pottery and represent cultural heroes of the clans or the totems of these clans. Sometimes these faces are abstracted or schematised into simple elements that are recognised

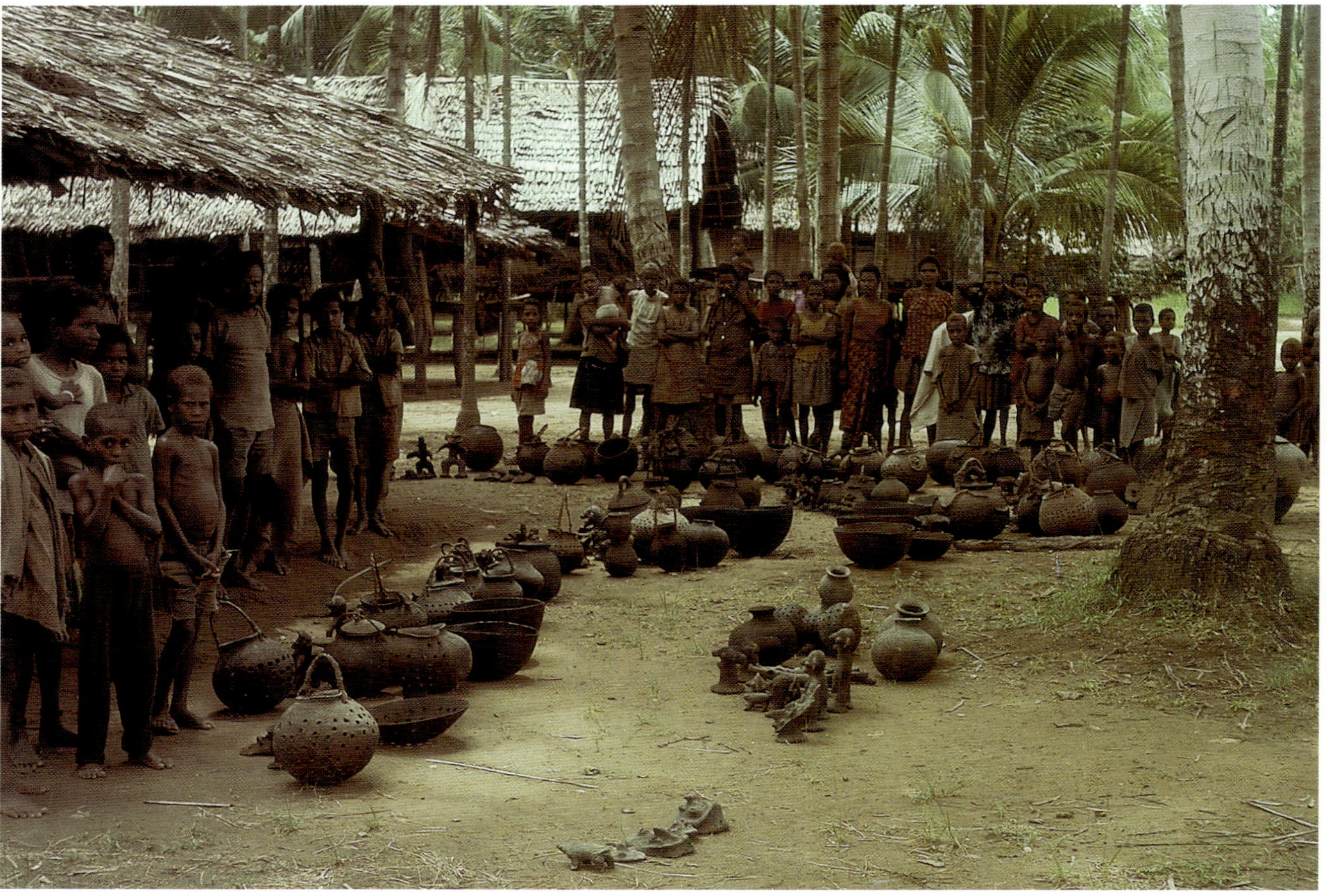

Fig. 9.58
Impromptu market, Dimiri.

by the people as the whole face of which they are a part.

In the past, painting the vessels was done exclusively by the men. Almost all pots were painted, sometimes on the inside as well as the outside. Recently women have painted pots made to sell to tourists, with considerable loss of quality. Natural earth colours, red, black and white, are mixed with water in coconut shells and applied to the pots with a brush made from the chewed end of bamboo or cane. The paint follows the plastic modelled decorations but also is applied freely to the walls of the pots in undulating and scalloped designs, giving the surfaces a sense of movement and dynamism comparable to Minoan and South-East Asian Neolithic pottery.

Aibom pottery has often been compared to the Jomon Neolithic pottery of Japan and there are some remarkable similarities of form and decoration. Kidder (1952), in summarising one of the Jomon styles, makes a statement which could be applied to Aibom pottery.

> The unusually wide range of shapes, increase in vessel size, diversity of ornamentation, new concept of the importance of decoration and its glorification, sculptural attitude, belief that the manufacture of pottery and its use should reach beyond the satisfaction of mere physical necessities into the mystic realm of spiritual needs, and thus the greater integration of the art of the ceramicist with the beliefs and precepts of the people – these are the major bequests of the Katsusaka potters.

Yaul

A complex of three villages where pottery is produced, Dimiri-Marawat-Yaul, is located about one and a half hours' walk inland from the Yuat River village of Biwat in an easterly direction through mosquito-infested sago swamps. The Yuat River, a tributary of the Sepik, is fast flowing and treacherous. In 1936 Margaret Mead stayed with the Mundugumor (also known as the Biwat) people who live along the Yuat River: she described them as headhunters and cannibals. They were originally bush people but the swelling of the river, which only several generations back was a meandering stream, changed their way of life, eventually cutting hamlets and villages in half and dividing and alienating a once united group. The inland group of pottery producing people, who speak the Yaul language, supplied the Biwat with cooking and sago storage pots, carrying baskets, mosquito bags and carved flutes. In German times they also supplied small clay masks which were tied to the knees and bodies of ancestor figures (Kaufmann, pers. comm.).

> For these miserable swamp people the Mundugumor preserved a contempt tinged with a sense of their usefulness as makers of pots and baskets. They said they were careful not to kill all of them for then there would be no makers of pots left alive. [Mead 1935: 170-71]

As a result of their specialisation in the manufacture of traceable and saleable commodities the swamp people now have a more viable economy than their historically famous river neighbours. Hundreds of ceramic objects are produced for local consumption, for trade with Yuat, Sepik and Keram river people and for cash sales to dealers and collectors. However, marketing is a major problem and to sell their pottery the villagers depend upon visits by Europeans and the occasional trip by canoe to Angoram.

Next to Aibom pottery the repertoire of shapes, functions and forms of the ceramic vessels made by this group is the most diversified in the Sepik. Objects produced now are sago storage vessels, sago stirring vessels, water carrying pots, sago frying pans, plates for cooking meat, vessels used for smoking meat and fish, cooking pots, eating plates, dishes used for scraping coconut and making soup, hearth supports, ocarinas and modelled objects depicting heads of mythological beings, animals and other creatures, and upright three-dimensional forms of a hermaphroditic mythological culture hero.

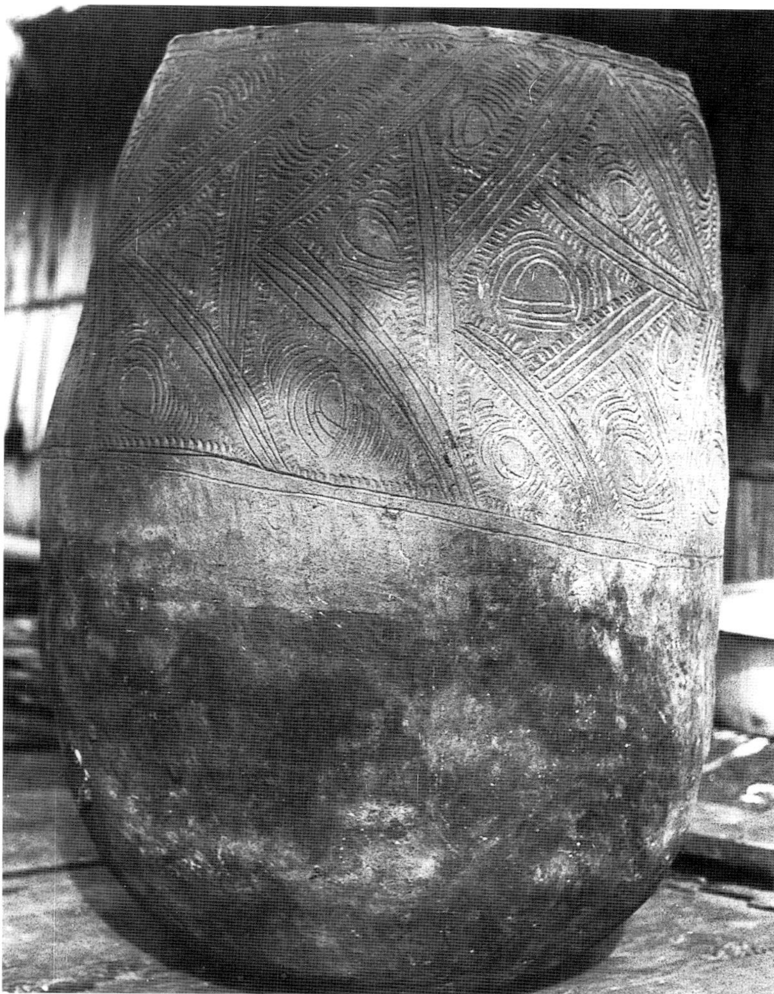

Fig. 9.59
Yaul sago storage jar, *h* 100 cm.

Mangumbu is one of two varieties of sago storage vessel. Often a very large pot (on average the circumference of the belly is 175 centimetres and the height 38 centimetres), it is globular or ovoid with either a wide unrestricted mouth or a smaller restricted one. *Vini*, the other sago storage vessel, is a smaller spherical vessel with a neck and everted rim. The top portion of both forms is decorated with freely executed incised flora and fauna designs. Sago storage jars are much sought after by neighbouring peoples; plastic and metal containers and plates can be purchased at trade stores but it is difficult to find containers as large as these (figs 9.56, 9.57, 9.59, 9.62).

Lamana and *lamanaka* are two vessel types unique to this area; they are distinguished by small

Fig. 9.60
Yaul smoking pot, *lamana*, *h* 28 cm.

Fig. 9.61
Yaul eating dish, *urat*, *h* 8 cm.

Fig. 9.62
Yaul sago storage jar, *mangumbu*, *h* 38 cm.

Fig. 9.63
Yaul pot or hearth stand, *lamu*, with the addition of a bird.

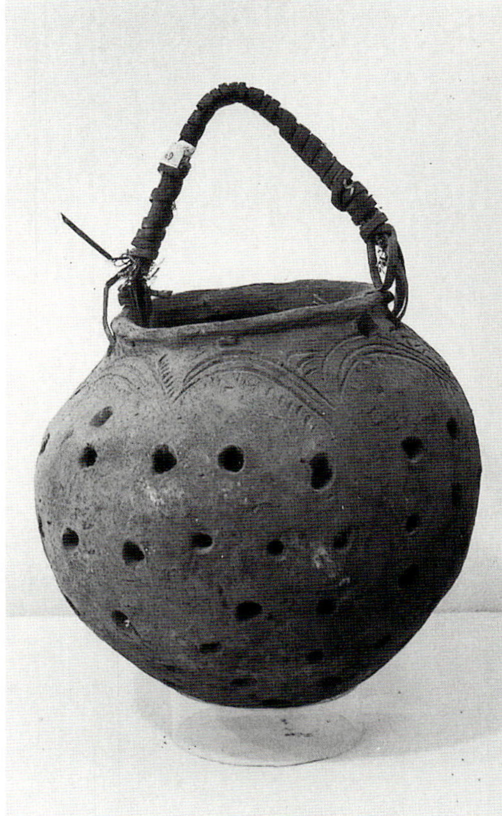

Fig. 9.60

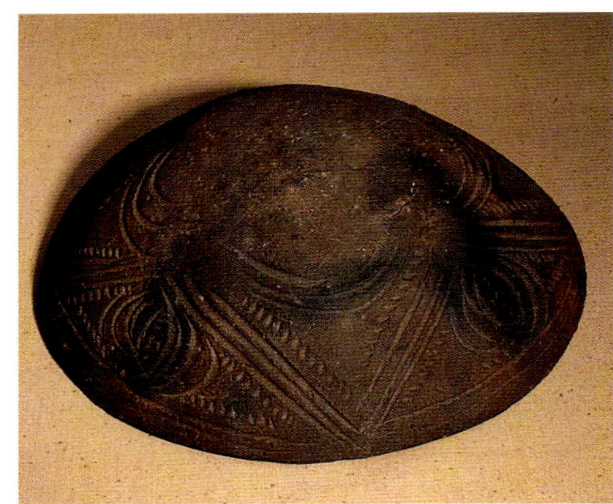

Fig. 9.61

perforations in the walls. *Lamana* is used for smoking meat or fish. It is globular, with a neck, restricted mouth and everted rim. The pot is suspended over the fire from a cane handle attached by two holes to the neck; it is sometimes decorated along the upper half by a characteristic casual floral design. The holes, evenly distributed, puncture the lower half of the vessel, leaving the base intact (fig. 9.60). Potters have recently introduced modelled forms of faces, frogs or tortoises; these are not traditional

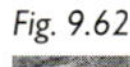

Fig. 9.62

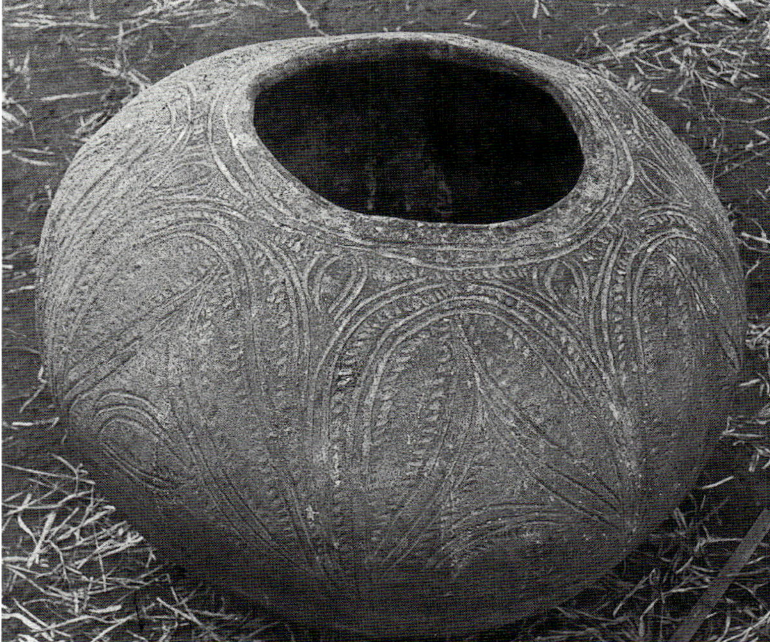

Fig. 9.63

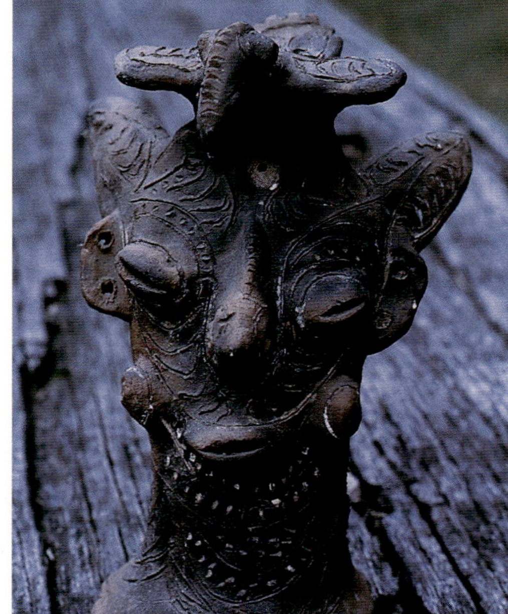

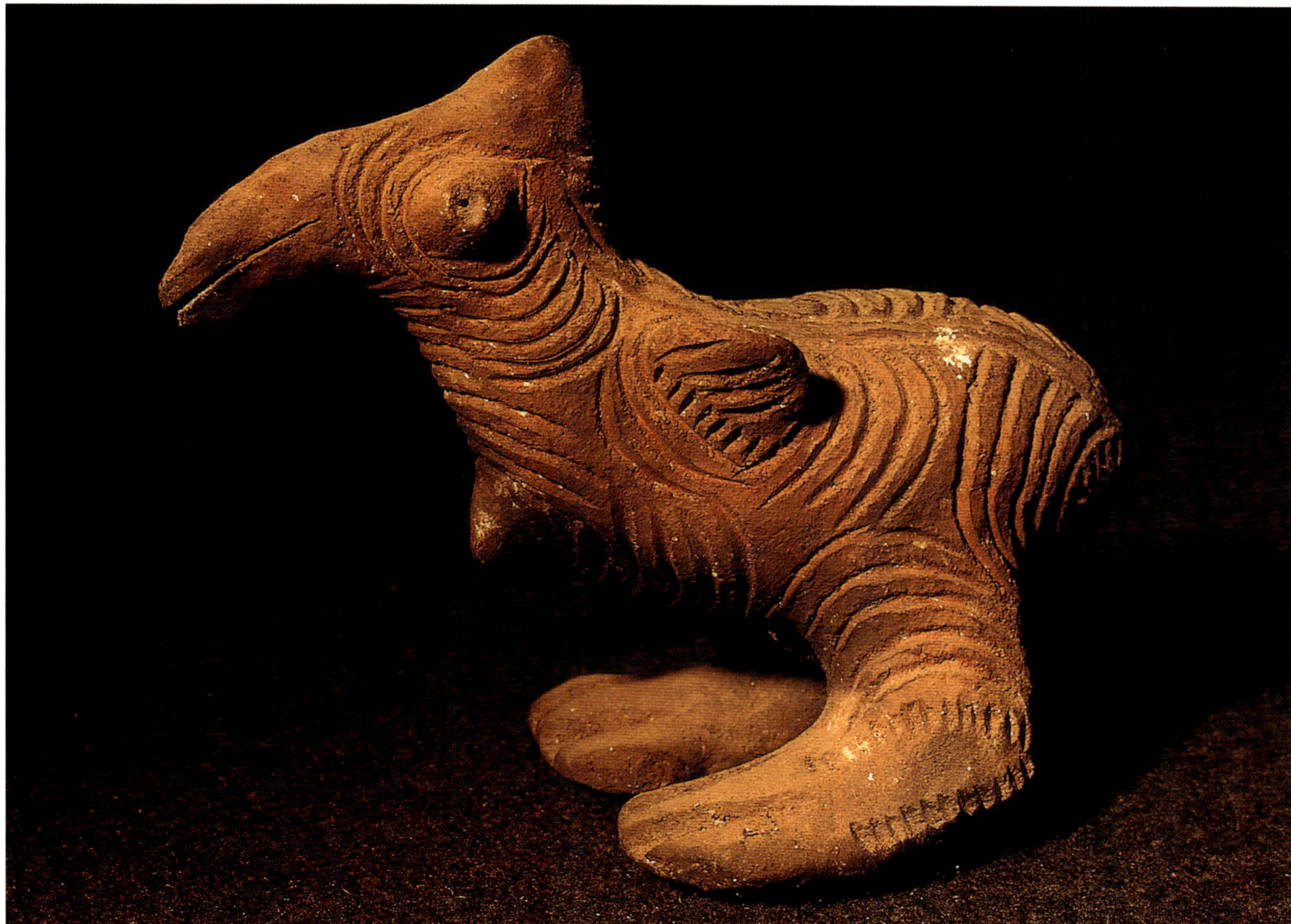

Fig. 9.64
Yaul bird, *h* 17 cm.

and do not add to the aesthetic value of the vessel since they appear additive. *Lamanaka* is a disc or crescent-shaped dish with slightly upturned walls; it is rimless and very shallow. The holes start just below the rim. It is used for cooking meat and is placed directly into the embers of the fire.

Walambatu, or *latambu*, is a water container, spherical, with a neck, restricted mouth and everted rim; average size is 24 centimetres high. Decoration is applied to the upper half of the vessel (fig. 1.14). *Karum* (*kurum*) is a common cooking pot, spherical in shape and with a restricted rim. It is generally not decorated. *Bimari*, used for stirring sago, is bowl-shaped, with wide outward facing sides and unrestricted mouth. It is always decorated. *Urat* is a flattish plate with outward flaring walls; it is used as an eating dish. Usually it is decorated along the upper sides. *Potum* is a deeper plate than the *urat*; it is used for making soups and as a container for scraping coconut. *Bosanga* is a flat oval plate used for frying sago cakes.

Lamu is an upright hearth stand used to support cooking, smoking and sago stirring vessels; it is modelled in a bizarre representation of the head of a mythological creature called *moran*. The surface area is decorated with meander designs. The average height of these supports is 22 centimetres but smaller replicas are made for sale to Europeans. The *lamu* depicted in fig. 9.63 has been made for the tourist market; the addition of a bird on the top renders it impractical as a pot stand. *Awu* is a curious cylindrical ocarina with two holes; it is decorated with faces and symbols and is always made by men. Today these musical instruments are

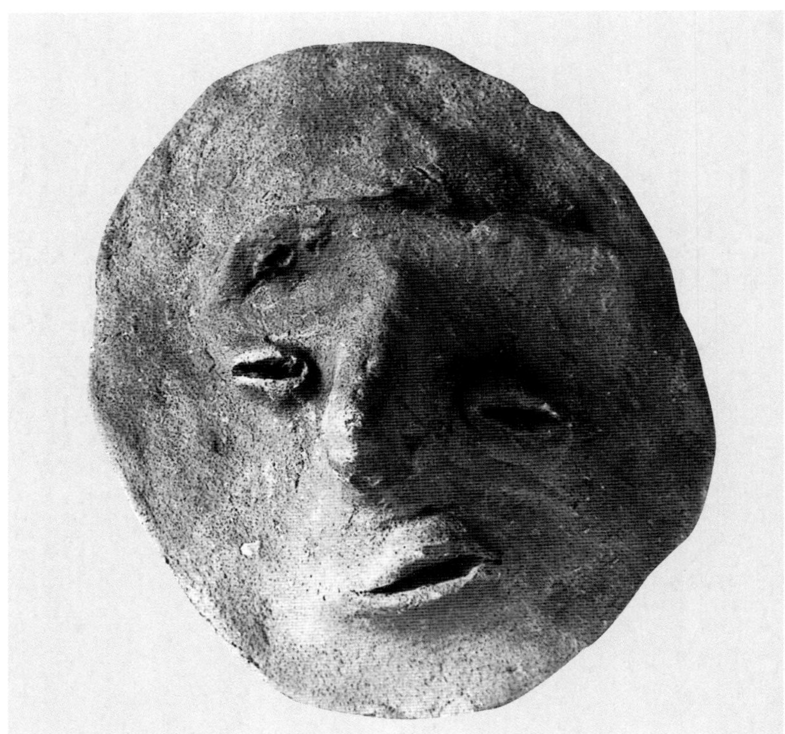

Fig. 9.65
Yaul modelled face, *h* 18 cm.

sold to Europeans but in the past they were exclusively used by the men in cult activities, initiations, headhunting excursions and in the bush to communicate positions to other members of the hunt.

A series of figurines, heads, animals and mythological creatures is made by both men and women for the European market. Realistic and whimsical depictions of frogs, lizards, crocodiles, catfish, cassowaries, cockatoos, hornbills, tortoises, pigs and dogs are easily identified and indicate a remarkable freedom of individual creative expression (fig. 9.64). Although made for sale these sculptures are not wholly innovative since three-dimensional modelled heads (derived from the custom of over-modelling skulls), the curious fire hearth stands and an upright hermaphroditic figure that refers to a mythological ancestor of the clan were all made before European contact. Two objects shown to the authors were purported to have been excavated from the old village site, located deeper in the bush and abandoned several generations ago, and to have been made before the memory of present villagers. The first object, a modelled head, is far superior in quality of form, expression and durability to present models. The second, a fragment of a larger sculpture, appears to be a rendering of a dog-like creature. An archaeological study of the area is necessary to facilitate understanding of the stylistic and formal traditions of present-day pottery.

Both men and women make pots but there is a high degree of specialisation. Women work the functional vessels which are made by coiling, although only a few women have mastered the technique of making the large sago storage jars. A few women are allowed to make the ceramic hearth stands which are usually decorated by the men. Only men make objects used in ritual.

Clay is abundant in all three hamlets and is generally excavated by the men. It is bluish-grey and fine sand from the creek banks is added to it. Apart from those at Swagup on the upper Sepik these are the only coil makers who add sand to their clay.

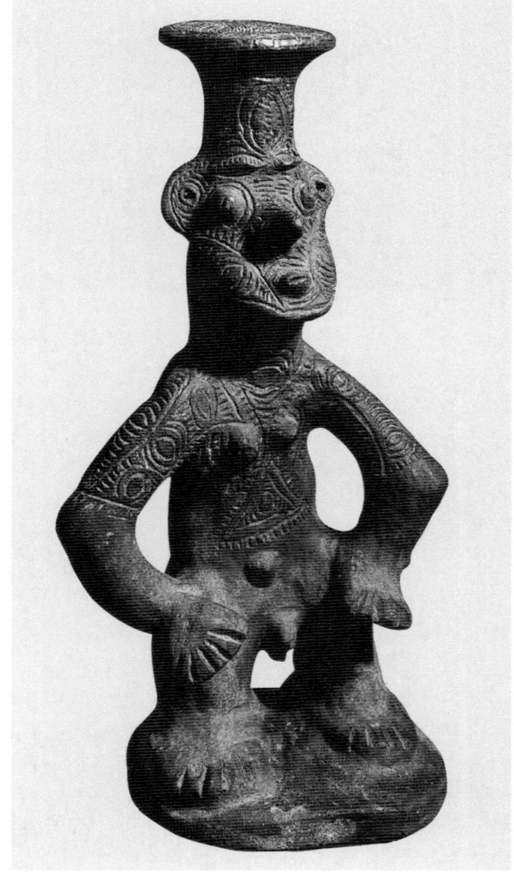

Fig. 9.66
Yaul mythological figure, *h* 48 cm.

Pots are made in the rainy season, October to May. Pots are never made when a 'big man' dies and it can be several months while funeral and mourning rites are conducted before manufacture is resumed. The women prepare the clay by beating it with a wooden paddle and water is added to make it pliable. Roughly shaped coils about 46 centimetres long are then squeezed out and placed in bundles. The coils are rolled out on a 1.5-metre plank of timber or a piece of 'pangal' until they measure about 2 centimetres in diameter. All vessels are started in the same manner: a cone shape is built up with coils, smoothed and joined with the fingers, first on the inside, from the top down to the base and then further shaped and smoothed by a piece of coconut, called *sivata*. The cone shape is then transferred to a grass ring covered by a banana leaf. The walls of the vessel are extended outward with a smooth piece of coconut shell which is dipped in water and rubbed on the inside in swirling motions and gently supported on the outside with the other hand.

A report by Kaufmann (pers. comm.) describes the cutting away of the excess clay from the wall with a wooden knife in order to obtain a semi-spherical pot for preparing sago pudding and for cooking, in comparison to the more widespread method of thinning the wall with the fingers or by beating. The unfinished pots are then put aside to dry until they become firm enough to support the addition of further coils. When the vessel has dried sufficiently decoration is applied with a bamboo implement. The outside surface is polished and smoothed with a section of grass called *parum*. The vessel is left in the house for two to three days then put outside to dry although larger vessels are left in the house for up to four or five weeks. Firing is multiple and orderly and each woman fires her own pots. The vessels are heaped over a framework of broken pots and dried grasses, more grass is piled on top of the vessels and strips of 'pangal', the only fuel, are carefully distributed in 'teepee' fashion over and around the vessels. Pots are removed from the ashes with bamboo tongs, called *nungan*.

The modelling of figurines, traditionally a special skill held only by some men and women, is now carried on by everyone, even children and non-potters; as a result, quality varies greatly. The figurines are fashioned from lumps of clay and bamboo sticks are used to decorate them. Improper firing due to uneven heat distribution is a possible cause of fragility; many figurines are so thick that the core is not exposed to a sufficiently high temperature. However, the hearth stands and larger figurines apparently are still made only by skilled potters and the durability of the sago storage jars, water jugs and traditional vessels is in remarkable contrast to that of many of the items made for sale.

The Yaul people say that in the past they carried out extensive trade with distant groups, especially villages along the Keram River and those bordering the grasslands. A few older Yaul pots were sighted in villages on the Keram and informants said that they used to buy pots from Biwat in exchange for dogs, bows and arrows, string bags and aprons. Dimiri informants say they traded pots and string bags with the Keram people for stone rings, tobacco and yam. At present in most of the middle Sepik

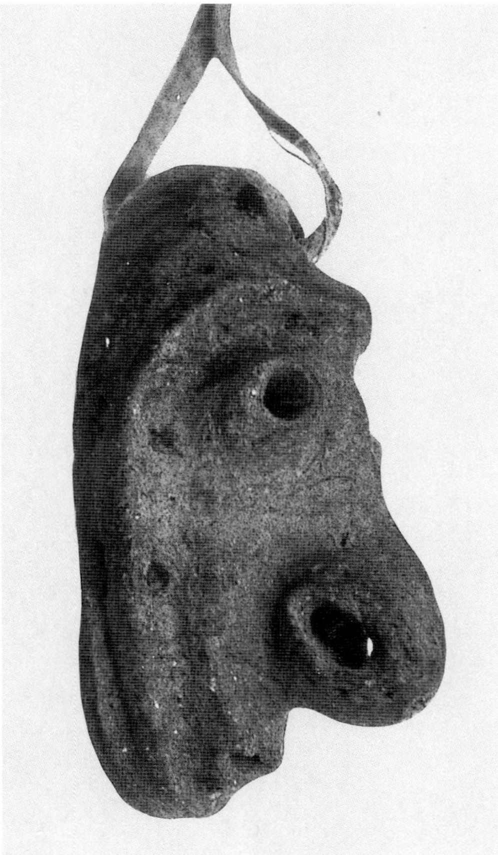

Fig. 9.67
Small Yaul clay head, *h* 8 cm.

Fig. 9.68
Ritual object, possibly Keram or Porapora River, *h* 18 cm.

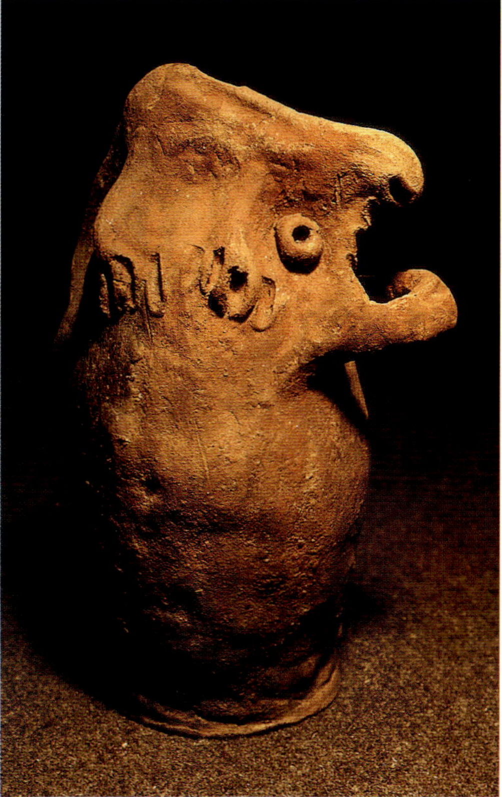

Fig. 9.69
Rare example of an elaborately incised platter used for frying sago cakes, Yar village, Keram River.

Fig. 9.70
Keram River sago storage jar, collected at Yar village.

villages, sago storage jars and an occasional smoking pot can be found. Amicable economic and social relations exist with the Yuat River people. The Biwat people exploit their advantageous location on the river and act as middle-men in selling the Yaul wares. It is a difficult and uncomfortable trek inland to the pottery villages and the majority of Europeans never get farther than Biwat hamlet. Prices are inflated along the river and choice is limited.

Keram River and its tributaries

At one time there were potting industries in most villages along the Keram River, from Kambot village near the Sepik River to the headwaters of the Keram. Smaller industries were located along the Clay River and the Korogopa 'baret', tributaries of the Keram. These Keram industries were related to those of the Rao people of the Ramu River and to the Porapora industries and those of the Dimiri-Marawat-Yaul complex.

The Keram River, mapped and explored by Behrmann and Thurnwald in 1912-13, was named by them 'Töpferfluss' (pottery river) because of the abundance of pottery industries. The lower Keram

Fig. 9.69

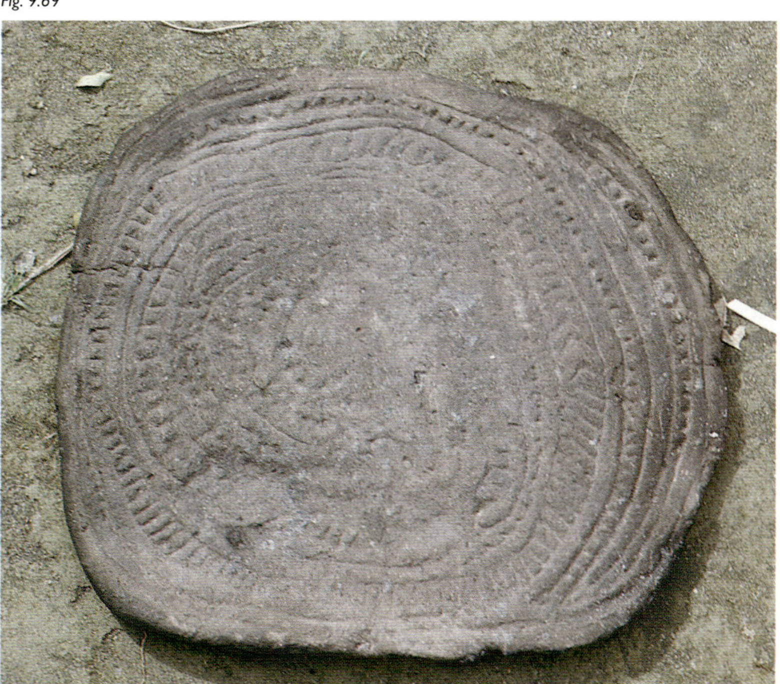

Fig. 9.70

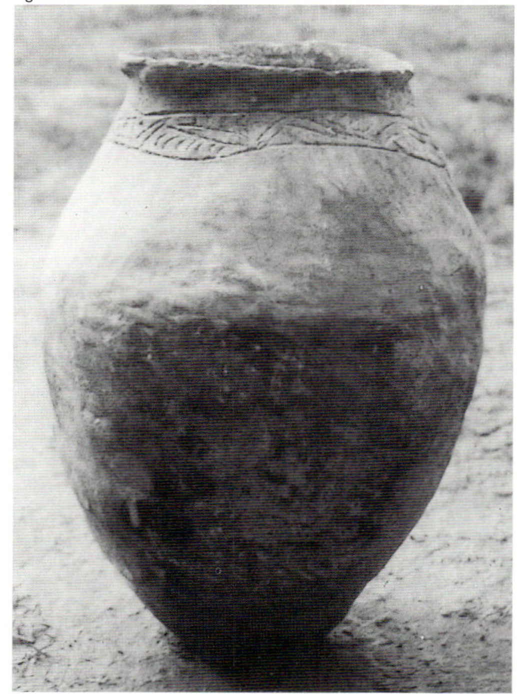

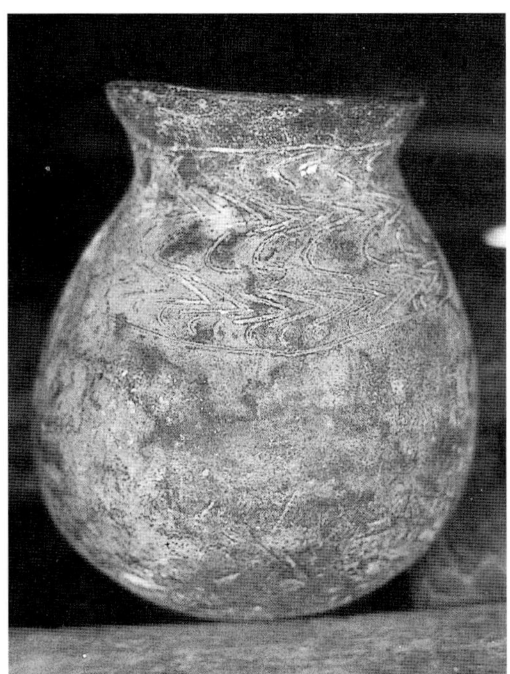

Fig. 9.71
Keram River sago storage jar at Lake Imbuando, Sepik River.

was the chief centre of pot making and there was lively trading between the pot making villages and the Sepik River people.

Today, industries along the Keram and its tributaries are almost extinct, although they still manufacture crude cylindrical pot supports and flat sago frying platters, neither of which requires much skill to manufacture. Along the Keram itself, pottery is made by the Kambot-speaking women of Bobten but, although there are still a few old potters alive, the young women are not learning the skill. Kambot village informants say pots were made 'a long time ago but the clay is a long way from the village and women no longer care to make the trip'. Aibom and Dimiri-Marawat-Yaul pots and European metalware have replaced the home-made variety.

Arbitrary household inventories in villages along the Keram up as far as the Clay River revealed a few examples of old Keram vessels still in use. These were mainly large, strong sago storage jars and sago stirring vessels. Also sighted were some examples of Dimiri-Marawat-Yaul ware, especially the *bimari* type (an open bowl-shaped sago stirring vessel). It was established that there were, and are, strong trade links with the Yaul people via the middle-men of the Korogopa 'baret'. The forms and decorative aspects of the Keram River and the subsidiary Korogopa industry vessels are similar to those of the Yaul.

Korogopa 'baret'

Kambot-speaking villagers of the Korogopa 'baret' live at Pataka and Dorum (a new camp settled by the Yamen people who deserted their old village site, located about a thirty-minute walk inland through sago swamps, to take advantage of the waterway now that raiding parties are a thing of the past). Pots are still produced on a small scale in these two villages. The women make all the pots but the men decorate certain vessels used in cult activities. Types of pots produced are *nom*, a common cooking pot, *bang*, a sago stirring vessel, *not*, an eating bowl used in ceremonies, *nat*, a sago storage jar, *naga*, a sago frying platter, and *tan*, a cylindrical pot support. It was difficult to distinguish these pots from the Yaul types, so close are they in form and design elements, but in general they are cruder in shape and decoration and rougher in texture.

The clay deposit is located at the old village of Yamen and the clay contains much grit and rubble. It is excavated by the women and beaten with a black palm stick about 1 metre long and 5 centimetres thick. The technique of pot making is spiral coiling. The first spiral is started in the palm of the hand, after which it is moved to an old canoe board and further coils are added. A coconut spoon is used to smooth the coils. The decorations are applied with pig or flying fox bones while the vessel is still slightly wet; it is then set under a house to dry. Drying takes from four to six weeks and pots are fired singly. Dried 'pangal' is the only fuel used.

Banaro

Yar village, located on the Clay River, was previously one of the major pot producing areas. The people belong to the Banaro language group. Other villages where pots are said to be produced are Buten, Bugaram, Angisi and Kevin. The villagers say they used to trade pots with villagers from places such as Kambot in exchange for pigs.

Pots are made by the women and decorated by both men and women. Clay is generally gathered by the women and deposits are fairly abundant and

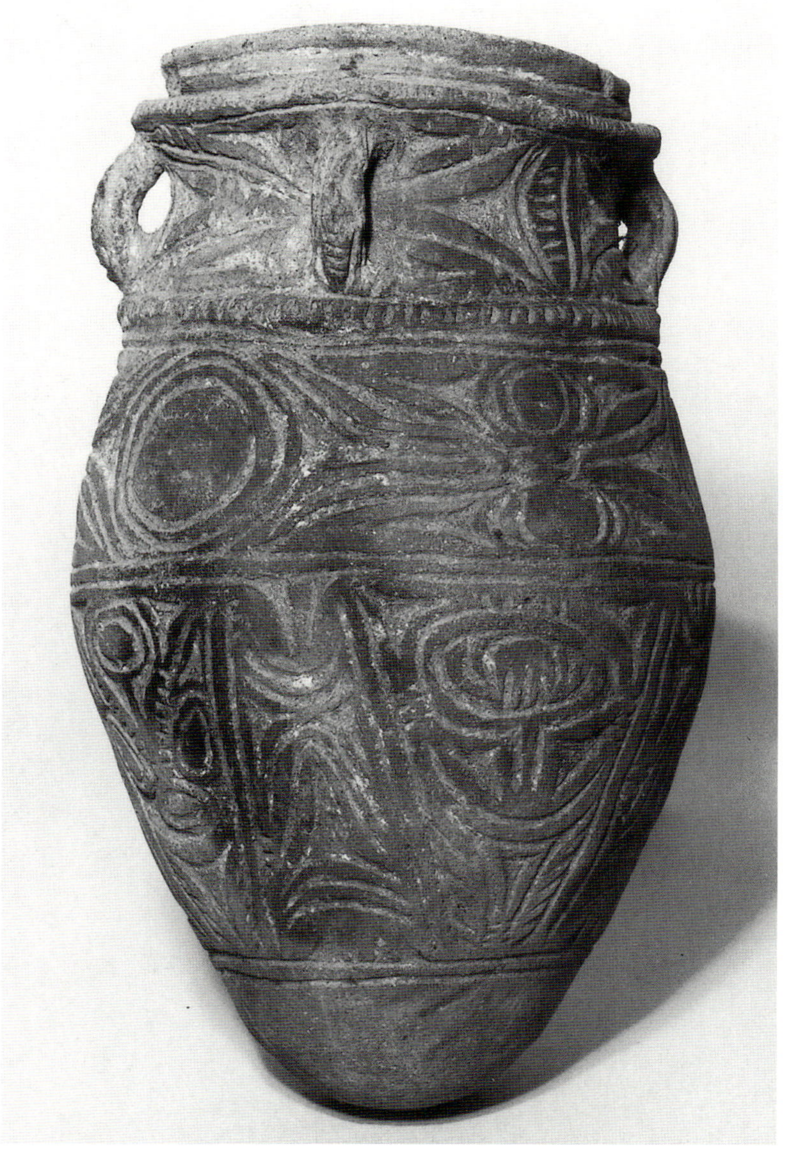

Fig. 9.72
Porapora River sorcery pot, *h* 28 cm.

close to the villages. The technique of manufacture is spiral coiling. A black palm club-shaped tool is used to beat the clay and water is added to make it plastic because it is always collected during the dry season. Roughly shaped coils about 46 centimetres long and 3 centimetres in diameter are rolled out on an inverted section of 'limbum'. Coils are smoothed together by the thumb while the index finger supports the vessel walls on the outside. The vessel is finally smoothed with a piece of coconut. A bamboo knife is used to trim the top edge, forming a neat and clearly defined rim. The decorations are then applied with bamboo tools or flying fox teeth. The pot is wrapped in green sago leaves and set aside under the house to dry for three or four weeks. Firings are multiple and fuel consists in various kinds of hardwood and softwood. The vessels are placed upright over pieces of wood and longer sections of fuel are stacked around in a pyramid fashion. Scissor-like tongs are used to turn the pots on the fire and to add burning faggots to the insides. A sealing mixture of sago gruel is splashed over the pots when they are still warm.

Objects manufactured are sago frying platters, pot supports, sago storage jars, sago stirring vessels and cooking pots for vegetables and meat. *Beng* is a flat sago frying plate which can be oval, square or round and has an upturned rim. *Kwid* is a cylindrical pot support, very rough and crudely formed. *Werpiru*, the sago storage jar, comes in various shapes: a round-based, globular-bellied type with a neck area that flares outward and a wide mouth; a type very similar to the Yaul *mangumbu*, globular or ovoid with a restricted orifice; a tall, round-based pot with a truncated neck and everted rim which resembles the Aibom storage jar. Decoration on these three types is very similar to decoration seen on Yaul vessels. It is confined to the top neck area and consists of casually incised curvilinear patterns. *Kagot*, the sago stirring vessel, has a slightly pointed base and a round open form with an unrestricted rim. It can be decorated along the rim by simple incised designs or left unmarked. *Werdepru*, a cooking pot used for feasts, is shaped like the kagot but is always decorated. *Ngingbru*, the common cooking pot, is used for cooking both meat and vegetables. As a rule, it is not decorated.

Women from Buta village, also on the Clay River, still make and use two types of clay object: the *kitura*, which is a pot support like the Keram River *kwid* and the *beng*, the sago frying platter. Sago storage jars are not used here; sago is stored in 'limbum' baskets. In the past the Buta people traded with Dimiri-Marawat-Yaul, exchanging dogs, bows and arrows, string bags and aprons for pots.

The authors received a report from a missionary that women from the village of Buten, located on a tributary of the Keram and running parallel to the Clay River, are still actively making pots and

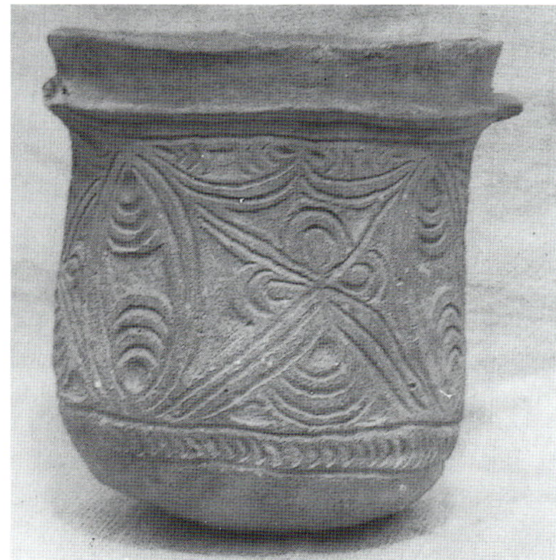

Fig. 9.73
Serving vessel sighted at Nangumarum village (provenance unknown). Compare the decoration with Porapora pots, *h* 18 cm.

that older men made pottery; this information has not been confirmed. The above description of the Keram River and its related industries is sketchy. When the authors visited the area it was the wet season; no pots were being made and there was no clay available. The area needs further investigation.

Porapora River

The Porapora lies to the south of the Sepik River, between the Keram and Ramu rivers; it joins the Sepik between the Marienberg mission and the Sepik mouth. Many narrow waterways which become clogged with grass and weeds link the river and its tributaries. It is a very swampy environment and in the wet season movement can only be achieved by canoe. Most of the villages speak the Adjora language but a group on the lower Porapora speaks the Aion language. Both are in the Grass family which also includes the Kambot language of the Keram River villages.

Little is known about the pottery from the Porapora area but evidence already collected suggests that perhaps the most interesting ceramic ware in the country was once made here. The difficulties of collecting information are substantial: the population is small and scattered; historically there appears to have been little trade or movement of people; the terrain is formidable; and archaeologists were only able to work in the dry season when they would have to contend with myriad stagnant waterways, submerged village sites, clouds of mosquitoes and relentless sun.

Strange pottery sherds have been described by an artifact collector. He reports sherds covered with frieze-like depictions of animals and faces, a description which is more reminiscent of decorations on Islamic or Indonesian metalwork than of pottery from Papua New Guinea. The late Father Lehner of the Catholic Mission, Marienberg, a renowned Sepik character, collected what he called 'poison pots' from somewhere in the Porapora region. Unfortunately, his collection has been dispersed; one notable pot is now in the Art Gallery of New South Wales, Sydney (fig. 9.72). There are three or four similar vessels in the Basel Museum collection in Switzerland.

According to Father Lehner, these pots were sorcery pots. Sacred objects were stored in them and brews to be used by sorcerers were cooked in them. These sorcerers' concoctions were smeared on objects which a victim might touch; in this way

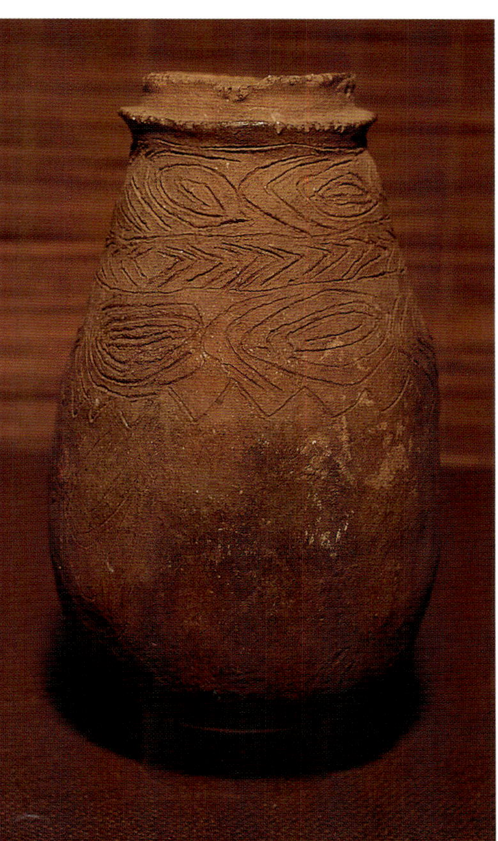

Fig. 9.74
Porapora River sorcery pot, *h* 24 cm.

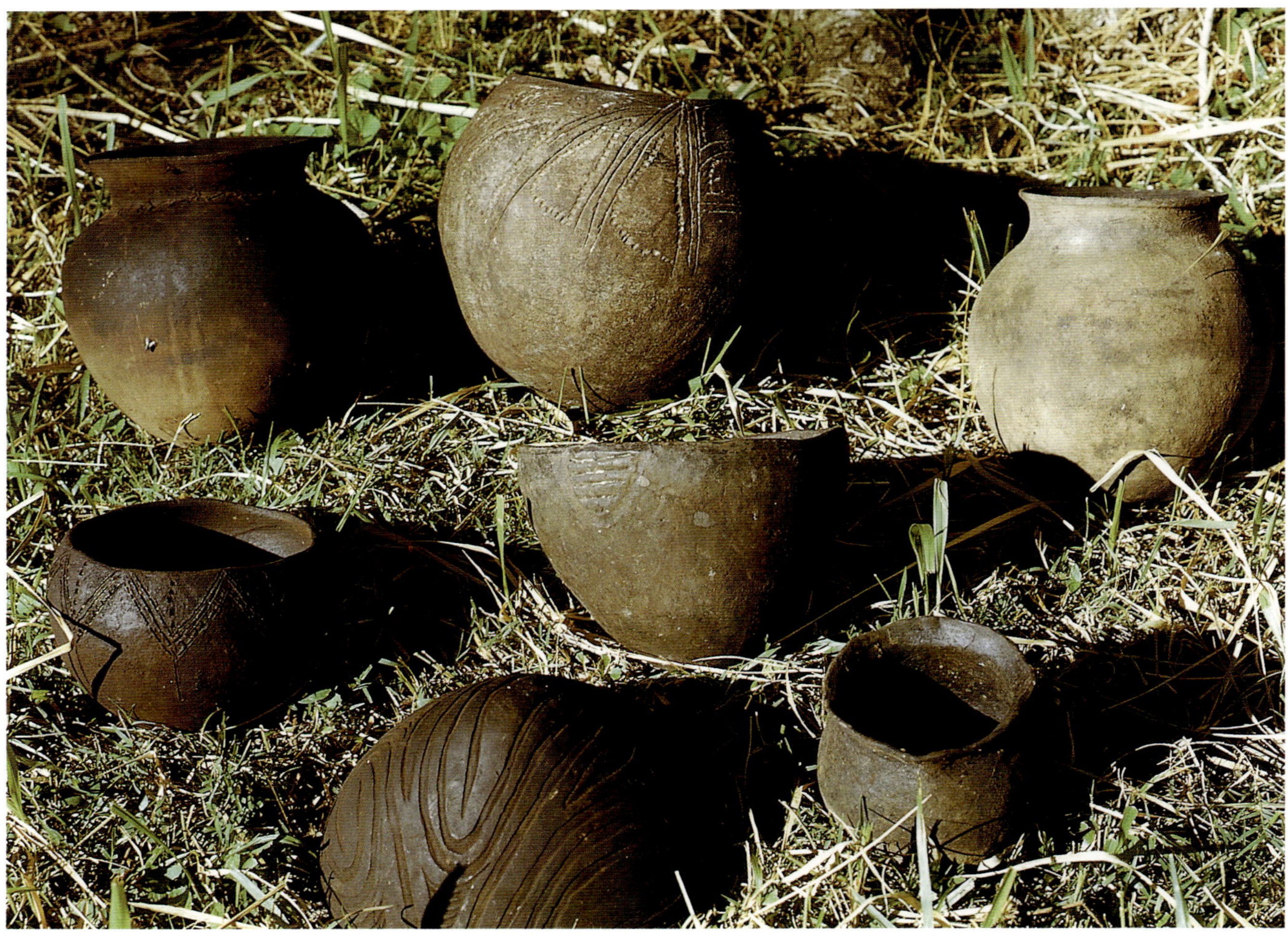

Fig. 9.75
Pots from several areas sighted at Mansep village: (top) Kaiep, Dimiri-Marawat-Yaul; (middle) Mansep; (front) Sawos.

his death would be assured. One informant told Father Lehner that fingernails, hair or exuviae from a victim would be collected, put in the pot and buried and a fire made over it. The sorcerer also used the pot to make magic to enable himself to become invisible. It is said, further, that the pots were used for cooking pigs to be dedicated to the spirits and for boiling heads taken in headhunting raids; this seems unlikely since it is not the usual practice to use elaborately decorated pots for cooking.

The Porapora pots are very different from any other vessels known in Papua New Guinea. They are mostly ellipsoid with everted necks and indirect rims. The vessel illustrated has a composite rim made up of a ridge, above which rises a second rim. There are four handles around the neck, presumably used for hanging in the 'haus tambaran'. This pot has never been used for cooking and its carved decoration is also unusual. The vessel has been divided into five horizontal zones. The base is smoothed but defined by two horizontal lines. The zone including the sides and slight belly area has been decorated with vertical directed motifs inscribed in triangles (pie-shaped wedges). Two lines separate this zone from the next, which includes the area above the belly. The decoration here is horizontally oriented; the motifs are seen on artifacts and clay pots throughout the Sepik area: inscribed circles and the 'butterfly' or spider design. The next register, also defined by horizontal lines and a slight ridge-like projection that has been notched with parallel vertical lines, includes the neck and the four handles which extend vertically from the slight ridge up to the final, more prominent ridge. This

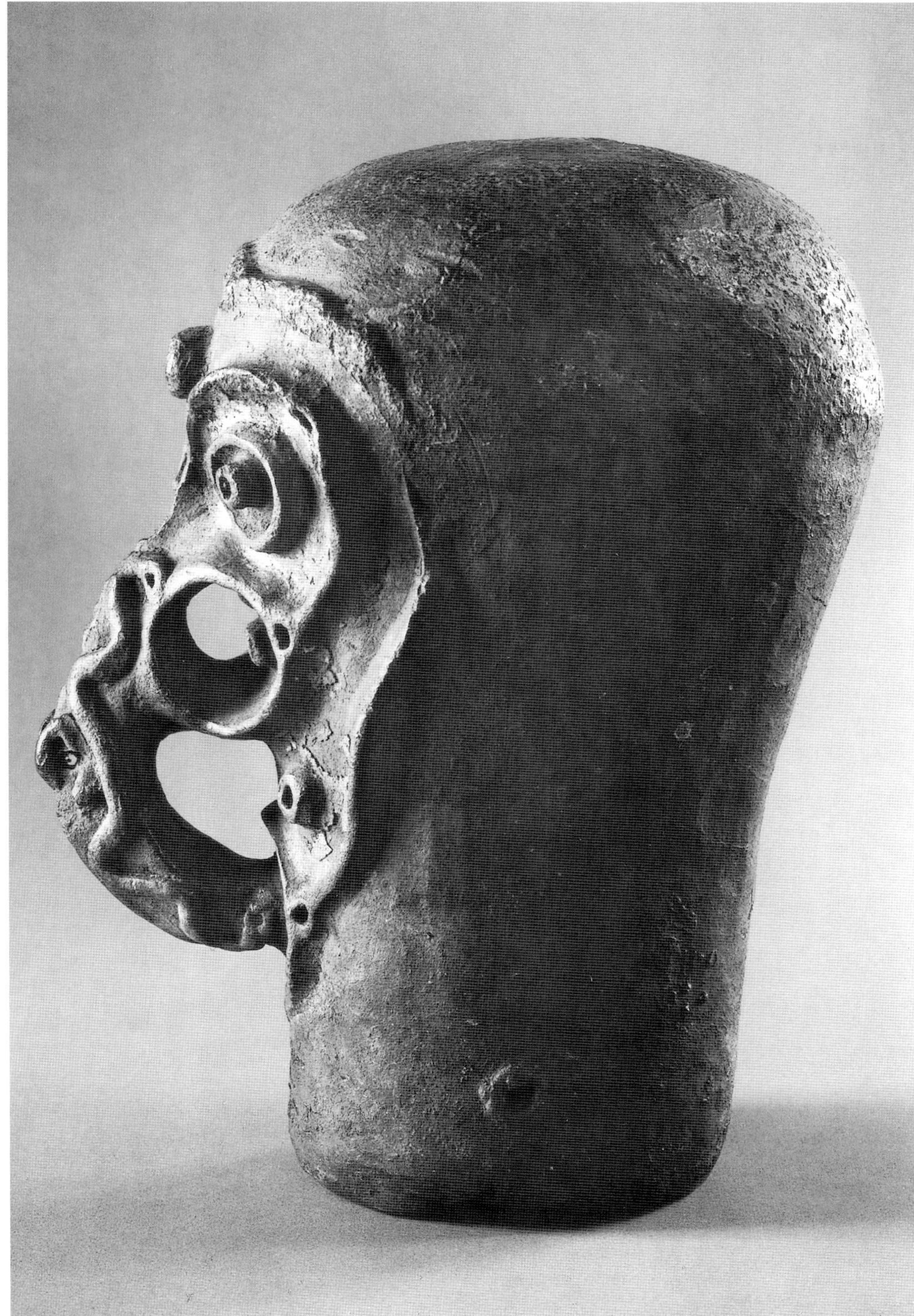

Fig. 9.76
Cult object collected from the Porapora River area, *h* 26 cm.

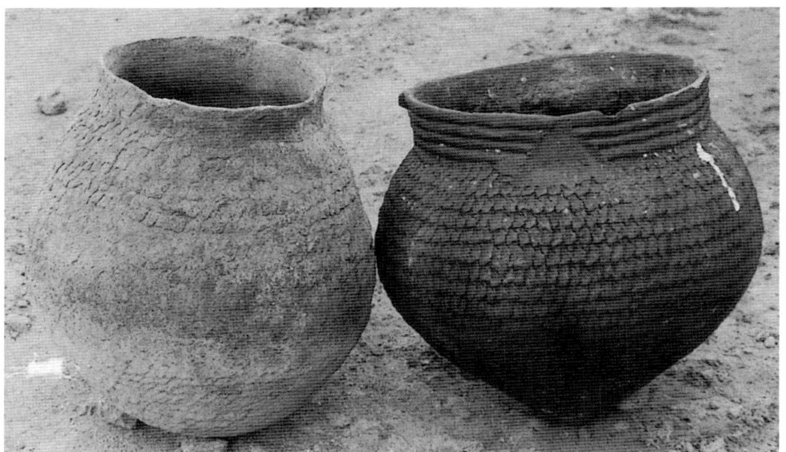

Fig. 9.77
Bungain pot used for cooking or storing sago, *mono*, Wangain village.

area is marked by lozenge-shaped motifs. The nearest parallel in design is that seen on the Yaul water pots, sago storage jars and smoking pots. The repertoire of motifs is similar but the Yaul vessels are not divided into zones as are the Porapora pots.

Another vessel to be compared to the 'poison pot' is one collected by the authors from Nangumarum along the Maprik-Wewak road in 1972. The villagers had a variety of pots from the plains Boiken, Toanumbu, Yangoru Boiken and the Abelam areas. They did not know where this vessel originated. It has some affinity with the Porapora vessel. It is hyperboloid, a most unusual feature, with a ridge just below the 3 centimetres or so of smoothed rim area and two lugs (one broken) projecting from the ridge. It has not been used for cooking. The field of decoration is that area a few centimetres above the base to the ridge around the neck. The design has been chip-carved and incised and features the 'butterfly' and lozenge motifs not uncommon in the Abelam ceremonial vessels, and certainly not uncommon to the whole Sepik region (fig. 9.73).

At Angoram the authors collected a vessel which had been brought in for sale by people from Jeta on the Porapora; it led them to believe that the 'poison pots' are or were made at Jeta. It is newly made and has not been used for cooking. The shape is more ovoid than ellipsoid but there is the characteristic incised, or scratched, decoration covering the upper third portion of the vessel.

Jeta is also believed to be the source of bizarre clay faces (inverted pots with applied faces). The authors have been able to gather little data concerning their use except that they are cult objects and probably made by the men. They have been made with clay that has been mixed with tree oil to prevent cracking. One clay head has been illustrated in Felix von Luschan's ethnography of the Sepik River (1911); he collected it at a place he called Kambrini on the Sepik River. Kelm also pictures one of these heads collected by Neuhauss in 1909 (see Kelm 1966: Vol. I, fig. 366). A Sydney-based dealer came across one in 1968 at the village of Wom, one of the villages near Angoram, up the 'baret' from Kambaramba. The villagers told him it was a 'poison pot'. These clay heads are strongly reminiscent of Aibom ware; they are shaped like the Aibom gable ridge adornments (inverted *sero* types) and the faces on the Jeta heads are formed with applied strips of clay, a long curved trunk-like nose and rondels very similar to the decorative elements used on Aibom vessels. Thus these cult objects, poison pots and clay heads, appear to have links with both Yaul and Aibom pottery and it is imperative that archaeologists and other researchers examine the Porapora industry as soon as possible before the knowledge of the older people is lost. Kaufmann (pers. comm.) believes the inverted clay heads are of Aibom origin and a type of specific gable decoration. If this is the case then the Porapora people would have acquired these through trade and adapted them to usage in ritual (fig. 9.76).

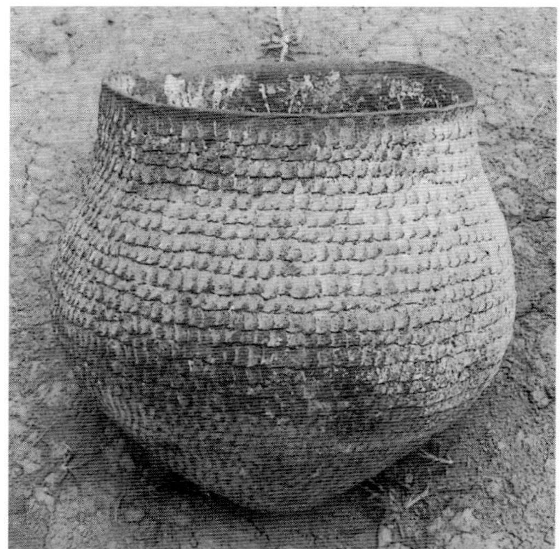

Fig. 9.78
Kamasau cooking pot, *aus*.

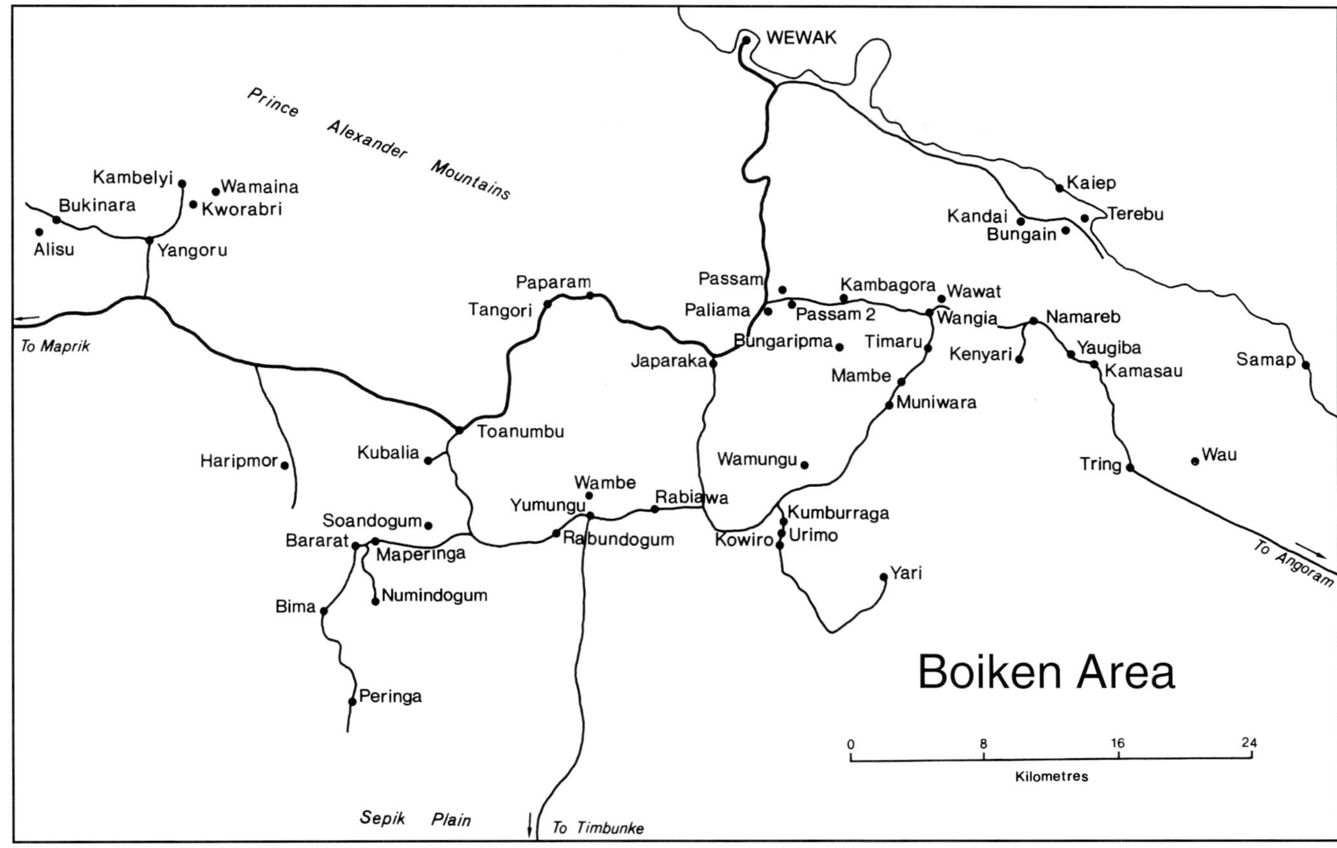

MAP 11

Cooking pots are still made in a few villages: Manmong, Senae, Tarangai, Adjora and Jangit. Previously, they were also made at Ogomania and at Ombos and Akaian in the Aion group. No written reports on pottery are available for the area and the authors have neither surveyed it nor been able to find any examples of the present-day cooking pots. They are said to be crudely made, mostly free of decoration but sometimes having a simple line decoration along the top edge.

Marienberg hills

In the Marienberg hills north of Angoram the women of the Buna language group occasionally make spiral-coiled cooking pots, called *yu*. These cooking pots are ellipsoid with pointed to rounded bases; some are tall. Villages named by informants as producing pots in the past are Mansep, Gavien, Ariapan, Waskurin, Boig and Kasiman. Laycock (1973) lists five other villages in the language group but they were not cited as being centres of pot making. However, there seems to be confusion about which vessels were traded in and which were made locally. Pots seen at Mansep and Gavien included examples from Dimiri-Marawat-Yaul, Koiwat-Kamanggaui, Kaiep-Samap-Terebu and a type the authors think was made locally (fig. 9.75).

The clay source is some distance from the village and the reddish-brown clay is of medium-fine grain with low non-plastic shrinkage. The clay minerals are halloysite and smectite. A wooden beater, *tagem*, similar to the Koiwat clay beater, is used in preparing the clay. Rough rolls of clay are squeezed in the hands and rolled out on a 'pangal'. Spiral coiling is started on the 'pangal', then the vessel is held in the hand and finally transferred to a banana leaf ring. The decoration consists of simple incised geometric patterns and rim markings formed by unsmoothed finger drag marks.

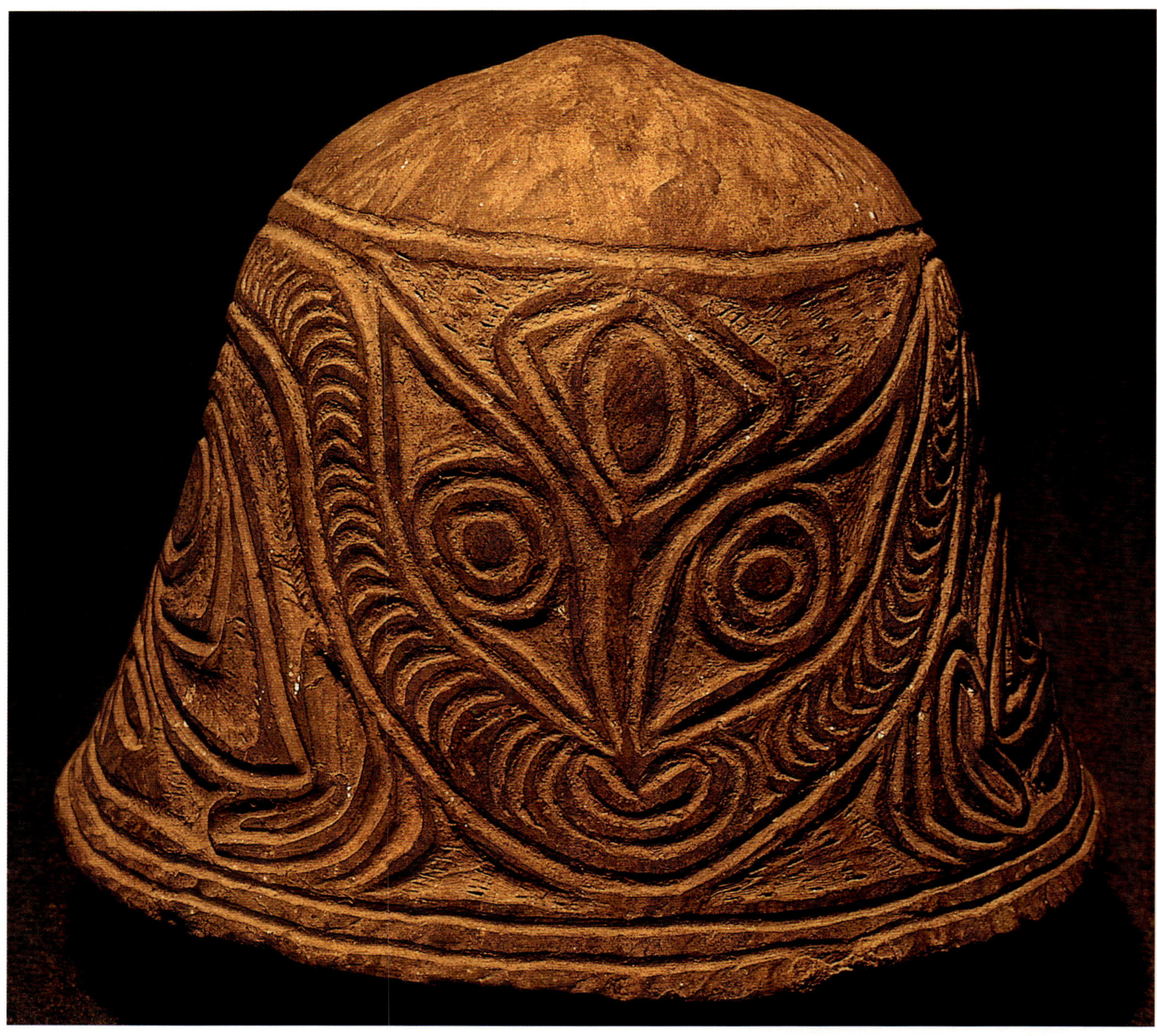

Fig. 9.79
Muniwara type serving vessel, collected at Paliama village, *h* 27 cm.

In this area, which is close to the Murik Lakes wooden plate and bowl industries, wooden plates for use as food containers are also made.

INLAND SEPIK

The inland area of the East Sepik Province, extending from Wewak on the coast to the border of the West Sepik Province and including the Sepik plains, Prince Alexander Mountains and Torricelli Mountains, is honeycombed with potting industries. This area presents many problems for the classification of pottery. Firstly, population density among the Abelam, Boiken, Kwanga and Arapesh people is among the highest in Papua New Guinea and field work is made difficult by the fact that people live in widely separated groups of small hamlets. Secondly, there is a great degree of variation in form and decoration on vessels found in a given area, which indicates complex trading and infusion of borrowed cultural styles. Thirdly, a great number of regional industries appears to have died out within the last twenty years. Other difficulties are posed by confusion and often total loss of memory on the part of informants as to the origins of vessels and meanings of design elements, lack of archaeological evidence and dispersal of vessels collected by dealers, museums and missions who often neglected to record adequate data.

Despite the difficulties of categorisation of some industries, especially among the widespread and densely populated Abelam speakers, it is still possible to describe several strong centres of activity and to attempt to distinguish several mixed industries, which may indeed have always been hybrid. In some areas, where categorisation is impossible because of incomplete or confused data, the authors give a brief description of available data in the hope of attracting future study.

Bungain, Kamasau, Muniwara-Urimo

On the grass-covered Sepik plains, between the coast and the foothills of the Prince Alexander Mountains, live people belonging to a number of small language groups; they made pottery in the past and now have either declining or defunct industries. A road adjacent to the Maprik-Wewak road and originating at Paliama winds over the plains to the east and south-east and leads to the village of Wandemi, about 50 kilometres away in the Sepik grasslands. The road system feeds almost every hamlet in this sparsely settled region and people from all villages claim knowledge of pottery making. There are numerous clay deposits throughout the area. Men make the pots.

The Bungain villagers of Wawat, Namareb and Yaugiba are said to make pots. Two types of vessels are manufactured. *Mono(k)* is a cooking and sago stirring vessel, ovoid with an everted neck and pointed, or nipple, base. Decoration consists in texturing the outside walls with finger drag marks and occasionally marking the neck with five to nine exposed coils. *Dieni* is an eating bowl, shaped like

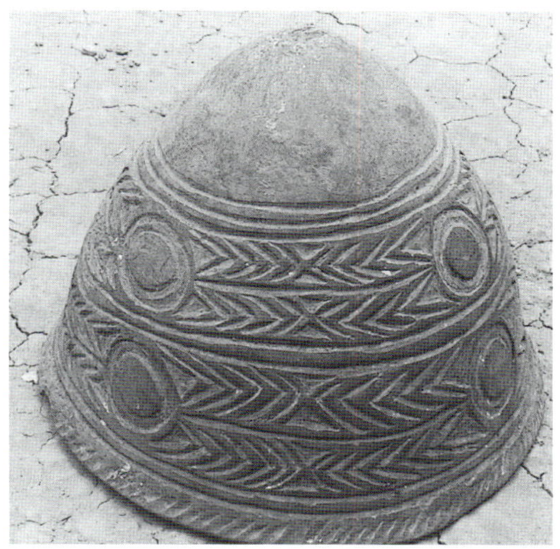

Fig. 9.80
Muniwara-Urimo eating vessel, *komogi,* made at Wamango village, *h* 27 cm.

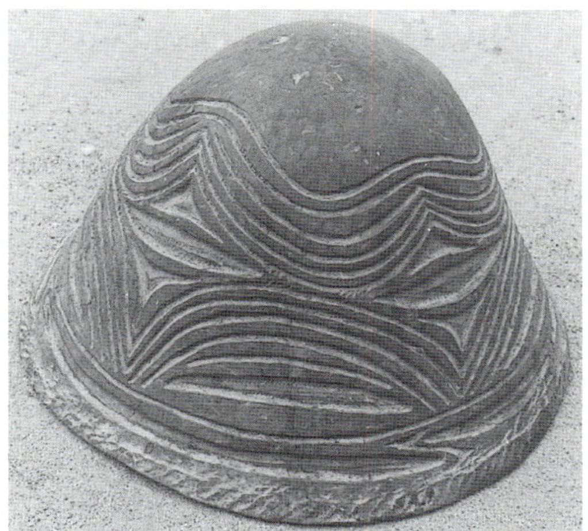

Fig. 9.81
Muniwara eating bowl, 1976. Compare with fig. 9.82.

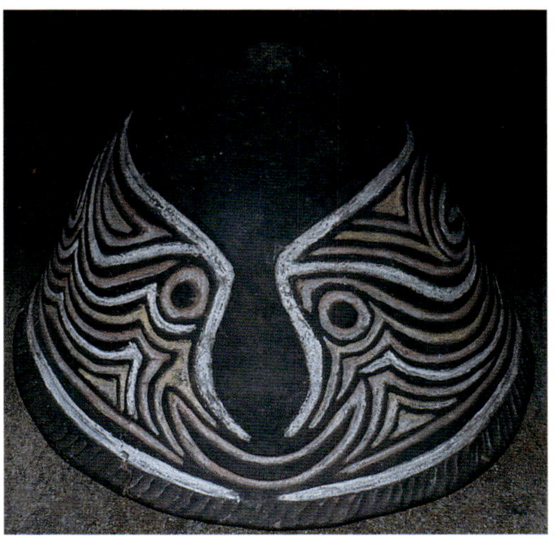

Fig. 9.82
Serving and/or eating vessel, probably Muniwara, collected at Mendam, near Murik Lakes, 1909-13, *h* 19 cm.

Fig. 9.83
Paparam village children with sago storage pots.

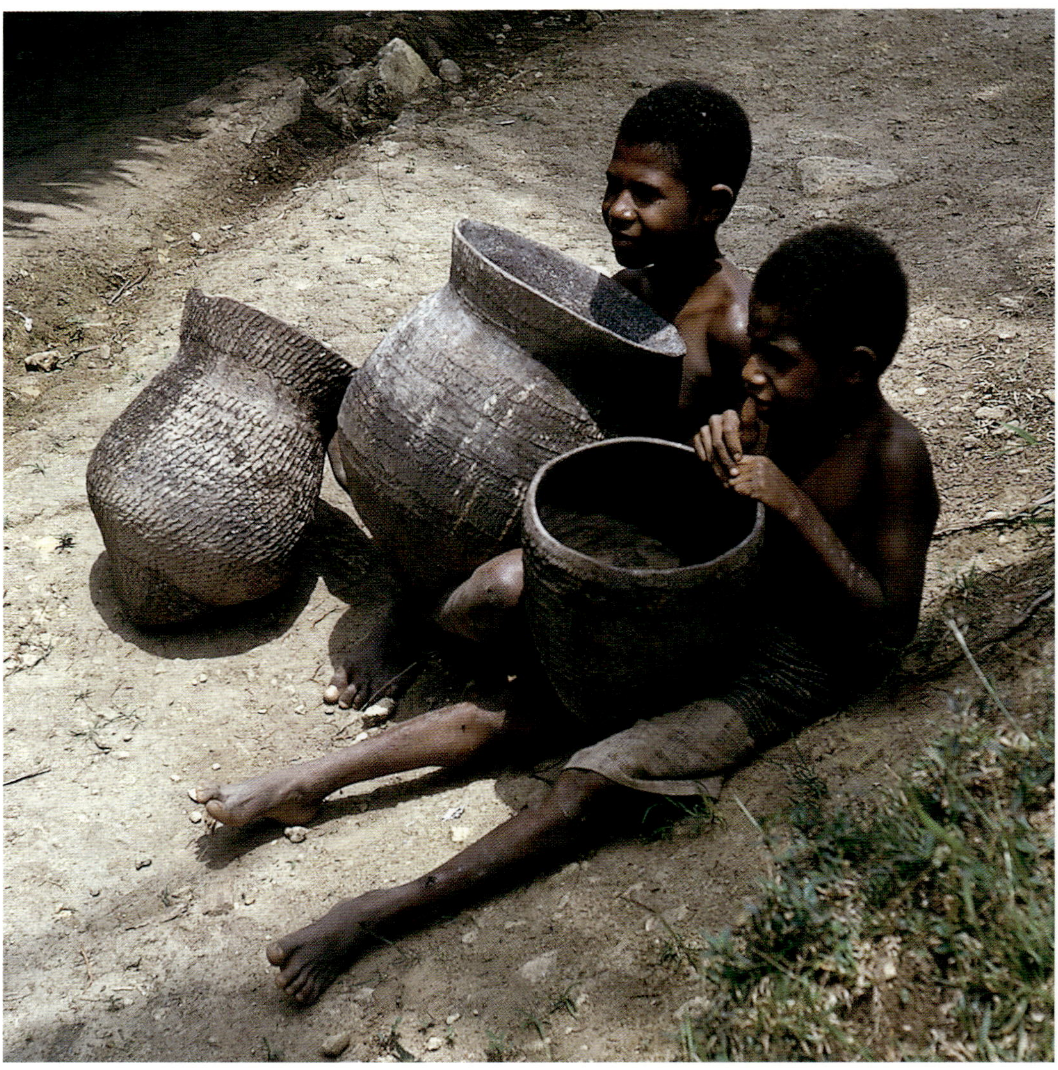

the cooking pots but thinner-walled and undecorated. Highly decorated eating dishes from the Muniwara-Urimo people, *komoa* were acquired by the Bungain and used for special feasts but informants deny that these vessels had any ritual value. The villages also make and use a wooden plate for eating, called *bagai*.

South of the Bungain villages live the Kamasau-speaking people. In Tring, Wau and Kenyari two types of vessel similar to those of the Bungain were produced: *aus*, a cooking pot textured with finger drag marks, and *opiai*, an eating bowl distinguished by a band of exposed coils along the outer rim. Although pot making is now defunct, in the past many vessels were made and used as trade commodities with the Angoram people on the Sepik River. The Angoram came up to the plains with crocodile meat and tobacco to exchange for pots and wooden plates, *yeng*. There was also considerable trade between the Kamasau and Bungain villages and Kaiep and Terebu on the coast, but the situation was reversed because the paddle-and-anvil ware of the coastal people was highly valued and used in bride price transactions. The Bungain villages situated to the east (Forok, Haregin, Kandai and others) were not cited as pot producing places. This area needs further study but close proximity to the coastal pottery villages and easy access to the

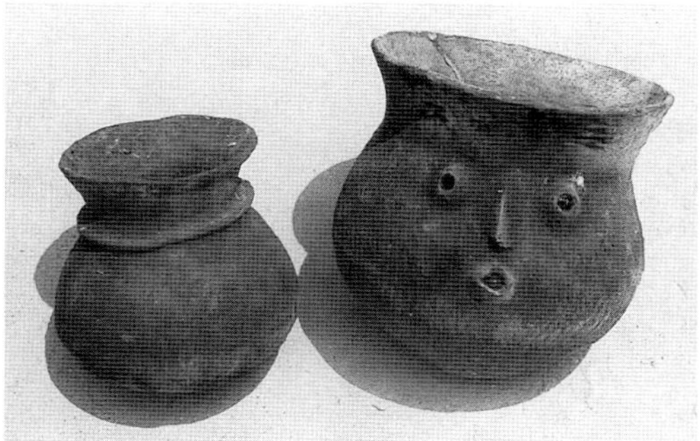

Fig. 9.84

superior thinner-walled vessels would suggest that they did not produce their own pottery but acquired it by traditional exchange.

An interesting and important pottery tradition emerges south and south-west of the Kamasau-Bungain speakers. It is exemplified by elaborate serving dishes and eating bowls made by men belonging to the Muniwara and Urimo language groups. The tradition is carried on westwards to the remaining centres of activity in the East Sepik Province and has already been discussed in the Sawos and Kwoma industries. Unfortunately, the Muniwara-Urimo people have stopped making pots. Most of the villages and hamlets belonging to the two language groups, Timaru, Muniwara, Kowiro, Wamango, Kumburraga, Yari , Mambe and Pitan, are reputed to have been pot making centres in the past. This is an area little 'raided' by collectors of pots since the road has only recently been upgraded and many households still retain fine examples of the serving and eating dishes. These vessels found their way either through direct trade or through middle-men to the Bungain, Kamasau and Boiken villages along the road near Paliama-Passam. There is a general lack of knowledge amongst informants as to the provenance of their pots although they admit they were trade pots acquired ten to twenty years ago.

There were two types of vessel made. The first, *tau*, is a small to medium (30 to 50 centimetres high) cooking and sago stirring pot similar to those made by the neighbouring Boiken, Kamasau and Bungain people. The second, *komogi*, is a decorated eating serving bowl used as an individual eating dish and in ceremonies and cult activities. Only selected *komogi* find their way to the 'haus tambaran' and it has not yet been determined whether

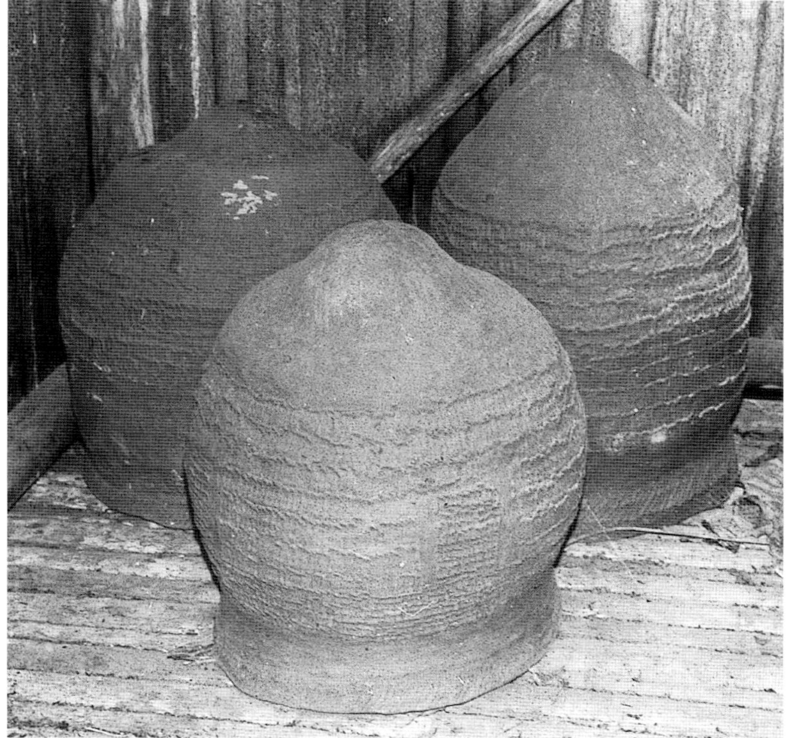

Fig. 9.85

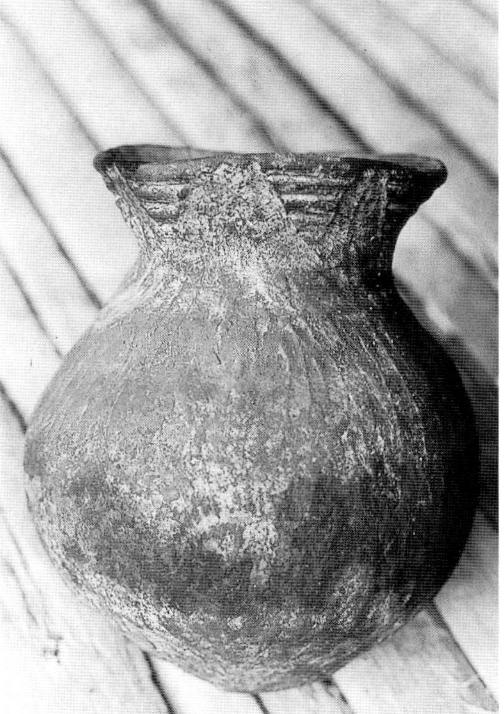

Fig. 9.86

Fig. 9.84
Unusual cooking pots from Japaraka village : (left) *h* 17 cm; (right) *h* 23 cm.

Fig. 9.85
Sago storage jars drying for many months before being fired, Paliama village, *h* 70 cm.

Fig. 9.86
Small cooking or storage pot, Paliama.

Fig. 9.87
Kasper Hananumbo completing a coiled pot, Paliama village.

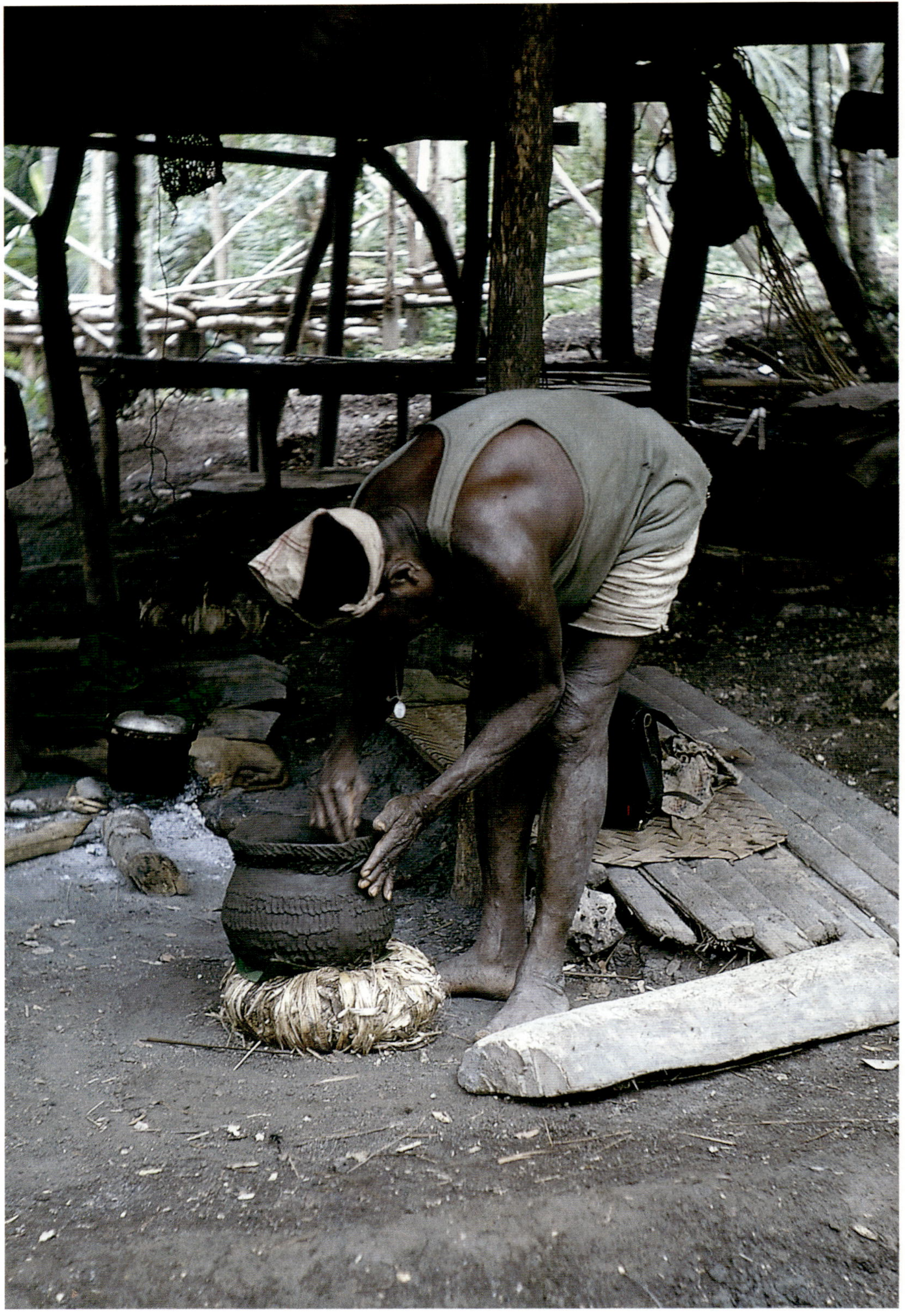

they were made specifically for use in ceremony. The shape of the *komogi* is basically an unrestricted ellipsoid with rounded base, slightly rounded belly and outward flaring mouth or a straight-sided rim. The diameter of the orifice is always greater than the height of the vessel which ranges from approximately 22 to 34 centimetres. While the *komogi* is similar to the eating bowls of the Sawos in form and decorative elements it is nonetheless typical of this area in its variation in shape and design patterns. One of its most characteristic features is the undecorated area around the base. Sometimes a decorative band is found around the outside of the rim (Dennett, pers. comm.). This is usually 2 to 3 centimetres wide, with markings that look as if they were made into fairly soft clay rather than carved or gouged into leather-hard clay. These marks appear different from the remainder of the decoration and this particular effect is not found on any other plains Boiken or Sawos vessels.

The technique of forming is coiling and designs are chip-carved and gouged into the leather-hard vessels. Women make the cooking pots and the men make and decorate the eating/serving bowls. Only the old men can remember stories about decorative techniques and meanings of designs since there has been little potting activity in the last ten years. This is yet another area that warrants further study.

Boiken industries

The people belonging to the Boiken language group numbered about 31 000 in the early 1970s (*Village Directory*, 1973). They occupy the area stretching west from Wewak, the southern foothills of the Prince Alexander Mountains and the grasslands of the Sepik plains. Laycock (1973) suggests a tentative seven groupings of dialects, some of which are of immediate concern because of their pottery activities.

Central Boiken

Boiken villages (no dialect affiliation except for Japaraka which is assigned to the eastern dialect) where a distinctive type of cooking pot is produced or has been produced in the recent past are spread out along the Maprik-Wewak road, about 15 to 40 kilometres outside Wewak. These are Passam, Paliama, Bungaripma, Kumbagora, Paparum, Tangori, Nangumarum, Japaraka, Nagusempo and Toanumbu. This group will be referred to as the Central Boiken industry, not to be confused with Laycock's terms. The villagers of Paliama, Paparum and Japaraka are the most active. In Tangori pots are no longer made and Toanumbu will be described separately because the potters specialise in

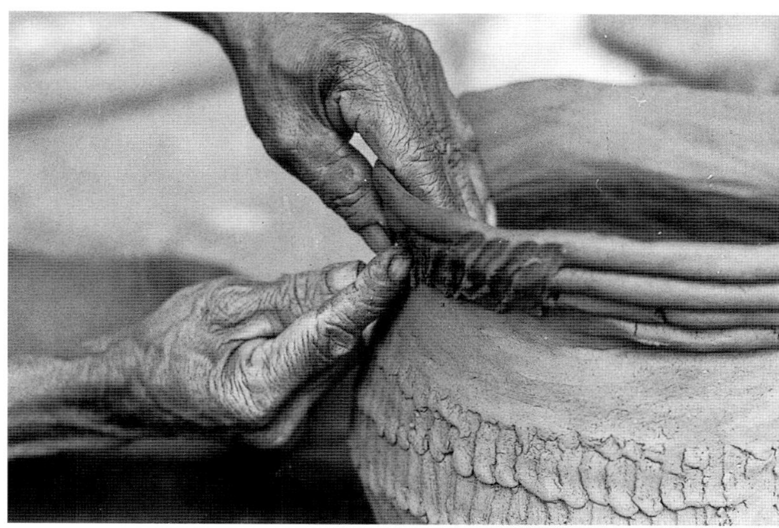

Fig. 9.88
Kasper Hananumbo making finger drag decoration, Paliama.

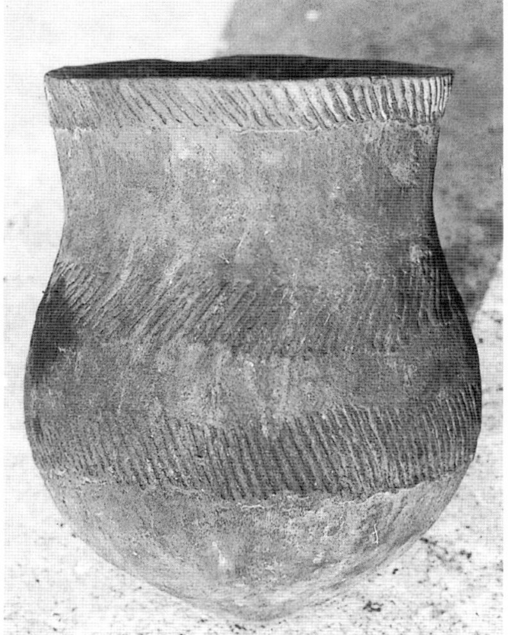

Fig. 9.89
Sago storage vessel from Paparam with three bands of finger drag decoration, *h* 36 cm. Compare with Bau pot (fig. 1.22).

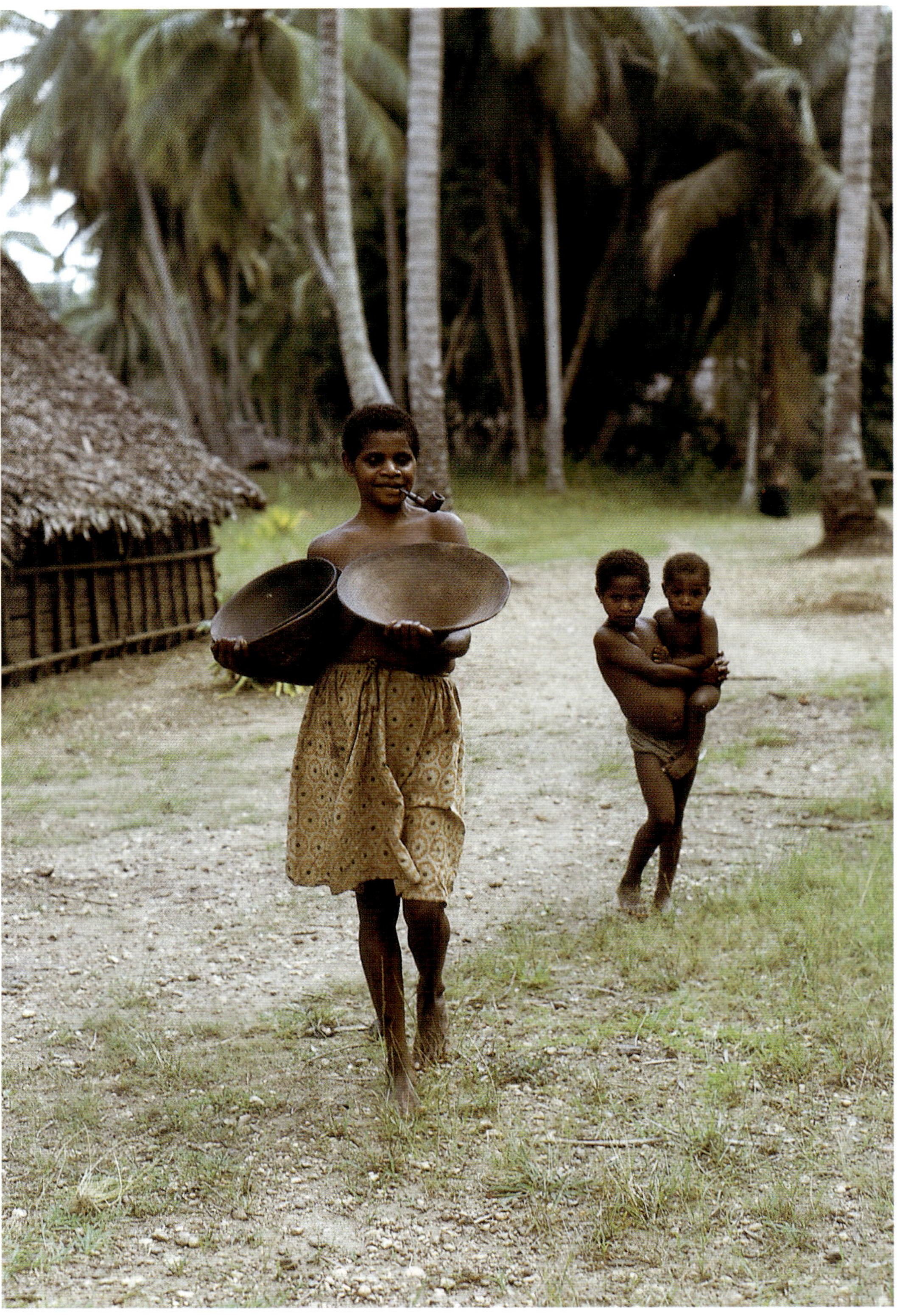

Fig. 9.90
Rabundogum woman bringing pots to show the authors, Plains Boiken.

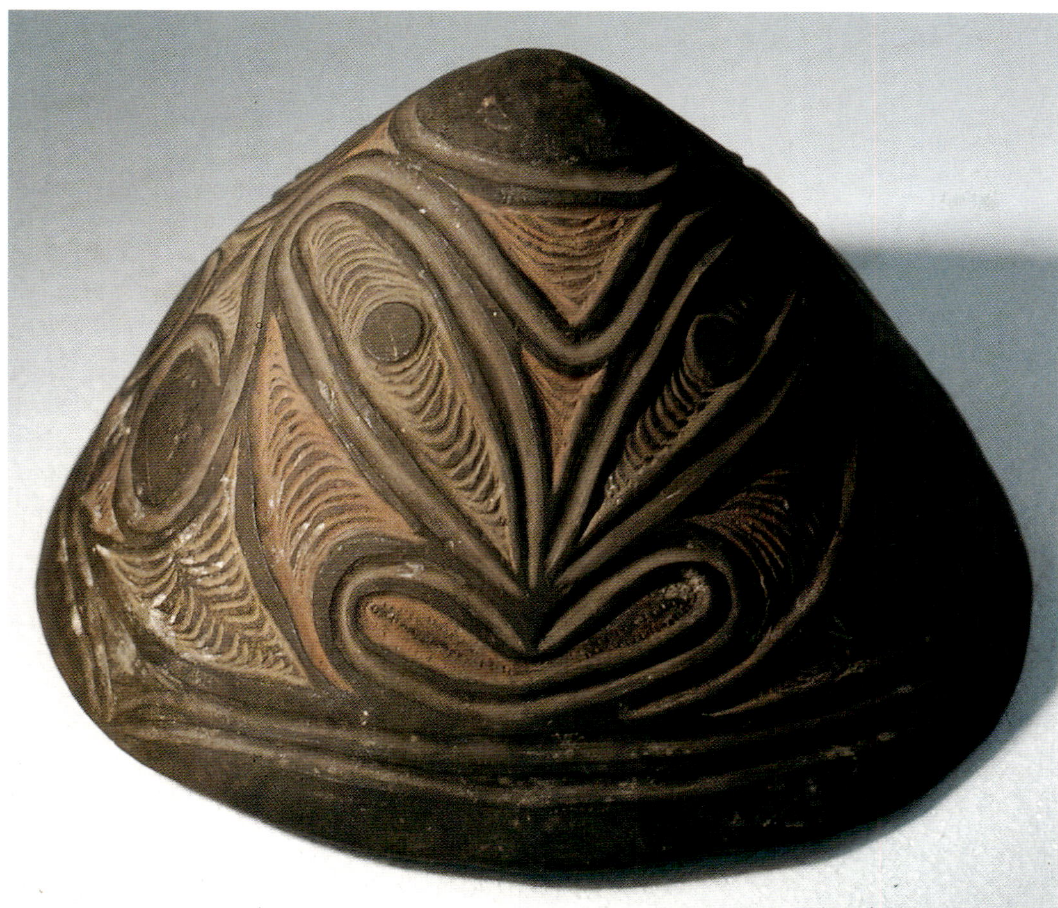

Fig. 9.91
Eating vessel, *khomongu*, from Soandogum village, Plains Boiken, *h* 18 cm.

making eating dishes whereas only cooking and sago stirring and storage vessels are made in the other villages.

Sago storage jars and cooking pots are called *au*. There are two basic vessel shapes but varying depths and proportions cause the repertoire of types to appear greater than it is. First the vessels are all coil made, deep and with pointed or nipple bases; some have curved sides, others vertical sides; all have direct rims and one variety has an outward flaring neck. Others are neckless. Some are more shallow and ovoid. The tallest cooking pot seen was 52 centimetres high and the tallest sago storage jar was 60 to 70 centimetres high; the average size is 27 to 44 centimetres high.

Decoration consists of either texturing the entire surface of the vessel with fingernail or finger drag marks across the unbonded coils or marking zones creating a rhythmic pattern of alternating smoothed and impressed bands. Ridges are sometimes formed by accumulations of dragged-down clay. On some pots the bands of finger marks are done at different angles, alternately, giving a zigzag effect. With these decorations all the unbonded coils are obliterated. A few of the vessels have drag-marked diamond-shaped patterns along the top or diamond-shaped remnant coil patterns resembling the rim decorations of cooking pots made in inland Madang in the Gogol River region.

It is difficult to determine function on the grounds of shape but in general pots with wide openings are used for stirring and storing sago and those with narrower necks and restricted openings are used for cooking. There are no sanctions regarding cooking. Meats and vegetables are cooked in the same vessel.

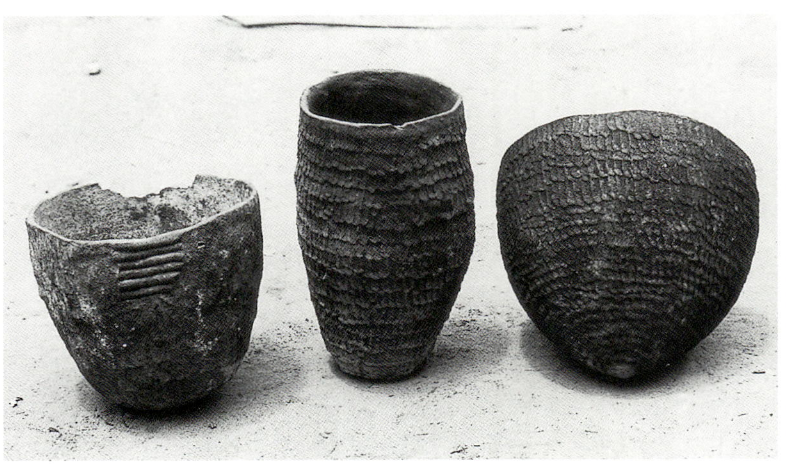

Fig. 9.92
Yumungu village cooking pots, *au*, Plains Boiken.

There are several active male potters in Paliama village. Two different clays are used for making pots; one, which is gathered close to the village, is grey and a superior red-brown variety comes from farther away. The clay is excavated during the wet season. The potter spreads it out on a 'limbum' and beats it with a wooden club, *mi*, the head of which is the natural knot formation of a branch or root of a tree with the handle the narrower extension (fig. 2.10). When ready, the clay is patted with the *mi* into a compact lump weighing 2 to 3 kilograms which is sliced into sections with a length of coconut fibre. These sections are squeezed out between the hands (held aloft) into rolls, *malanke*, about 16 centimetres long and 1 centimetre thick. The coils, *kwambe*, are rolled out on a long 'pangal' using the palm of the hand only. The coil is held in the hands at chin level until a small cone is formed by the spiral coiling technique. The first four to six coils are thoroughly bonded inside and out. After the next six or more coils are added the potter bonds them inside and starts decorating the outside by dragging his dry forefinger (held at an angle) down so that finger and nail mark across two coils at a time. The other hand supports the wall of the pot from the inside. The pot is then set down on a banana leaf ring, *jabu*. The potter sits on the ground and turns the vessel as he builds it. Later, he stands and walks around the vessel as more coils are added and bonded. Any stones in the clay are removed with a fine flying fox bone sliced to a point at one end. When the pot is completed the potter wipes it on the outside with wet hands and smooths the rougher edges of the decoration. Very large pots are said to need one or two years to dry, which seems

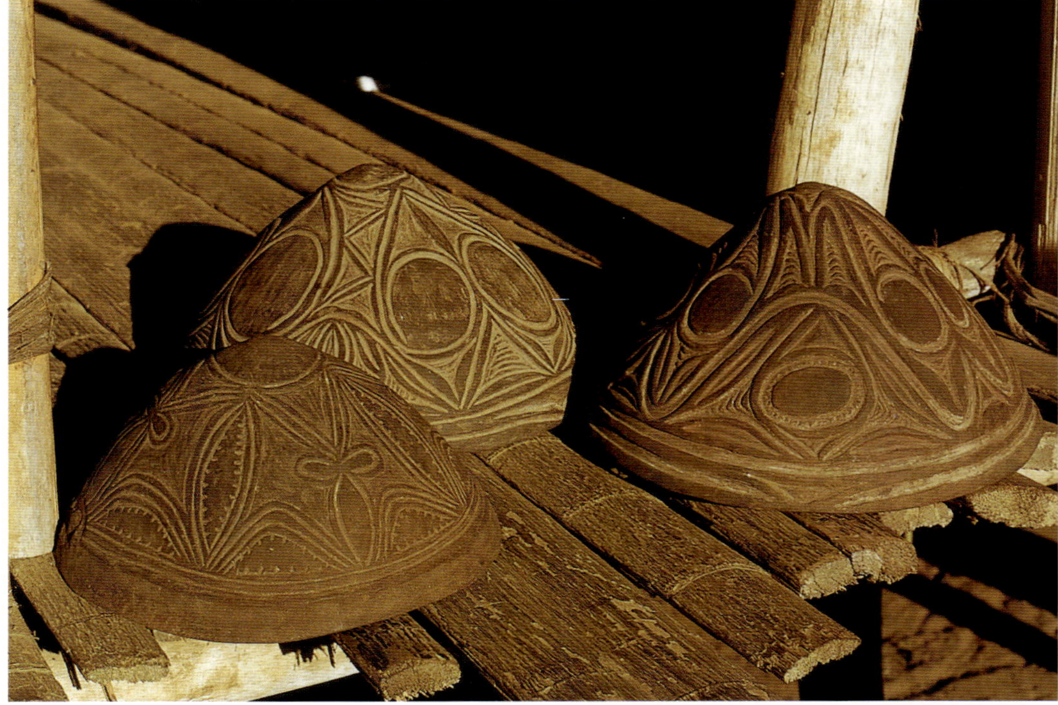

Fig. 9.93
Three eating vessels, *khomongu*, in the doorway of a village house, Soandogum, Plains Boiken.

an excessive amount of time (fig. 9.85). Any wood is used for fuel and after firing a cut yam is rubbed on the pots to seal them. Firings may be multiple.

A curious aspect of some of these pots is their affinity in form and certain simple design elements with pots produced in Madang Province. This lends credence to prehistorians' theories that an agricultural people colonised the foothills and plains of the Prince Alexander and eastern Finisterre mountains before settlement by the Sepik River people and that there are still small pockets in the inland Sepik Province of cultures that have remained inviolate to the strong influence of the Sepik River art styles (fig. 1.22).

Notably absent among these Boiken speakers are decorated eating or serving bowls. A few isolated ceremonial eating bowls imported from the Muniwara-Urimo area are owned by some households but this is an area which traditionally uses wooden plates. The distribution of wooden plates occurs along the Wewak coast, in the pottery making villages of Kaiep-Samap-Terebu, in the Murik Lakes and to the west of Wewak. Ceramic eating and/or serving bowls become dominant the further one goes from Wewak and the closer one gets to the Sawos and Abelam/Wosera spheres of influence. The use of individual pots as eating dishes is particularly strong north-west of Maprik in the Dreikikir-Torricelli mountain region.

Plains Boiken

South-west of the Muniwara-Urimo group, located deep in the Sepik plains, are about ten settlements belonging to the Boiken language group, where pottery was made in the recent past. Now there are only a few potters alive in the villages of Maperinga, Soandogum, Rabundogum, Rabiawa, Bararat,

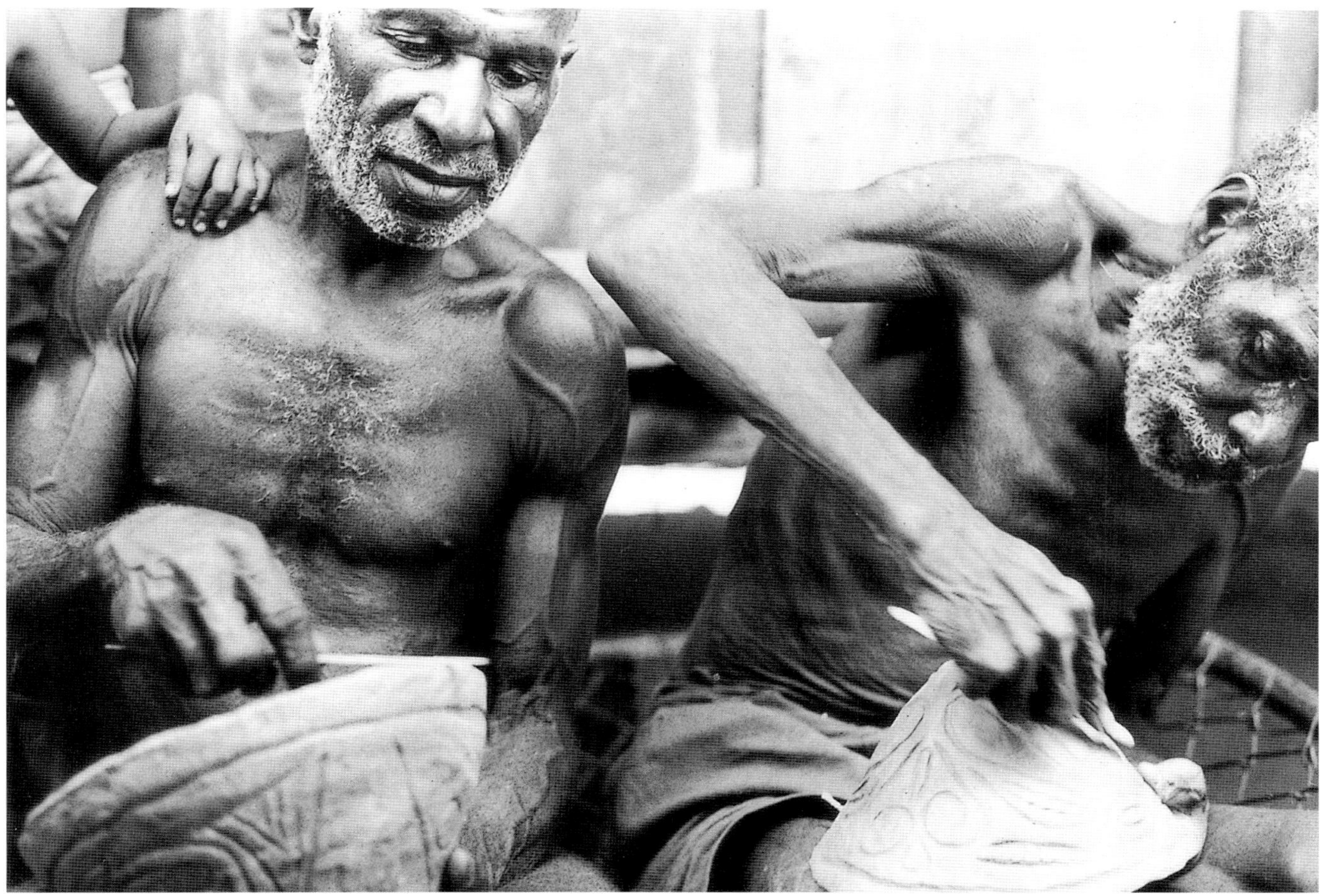

Fig. 9.94
Nanguiama and Boliabi, the last two potters in Soandogum, Plains Boiken, in 1972, burnishing pots made for the authors.

Fig. 9.95
Eating bowl, *khomongu,* recently fired and not yet in use, Rabundogum village, 1973.

Figs 9.96 to 9.101
Typical eating bowls, *khomongu,* from the Plains Boiken villages.

Fig. 9.96
h 9 cm.

Fig. 9.97
h 11 cm

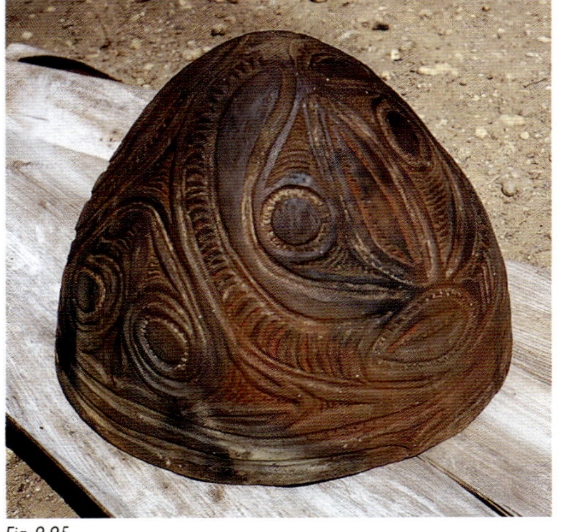

Fig. 9.95

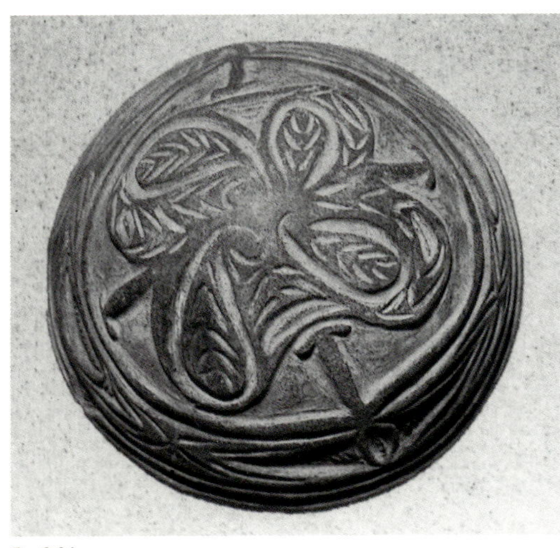

Fig. 9.96

Bima, Yumungu (all belonging to the 'plains' Boiken dialect), Kiniambu (Haripmor dialect) and Numindogum (Yangon dialect) (Laycock 1973). For classification purposes, the pottery from this region is referred to as 'plains Boiken'.

These villages are geographically close to the Sawos pottery makers and the eating bowls of both groups are similar in technique of production, form and application of design elements, although there are slight variations in shape and iconography. They are also related to the Muniwara-Urimo wares. Indeed, informants listed several Muniwara-Urimo villages as making the same pots but there is a definite style boundary between the two groups.

Three formal variants of the eating bowl, *khomongu*, can be distinguished: a deep or shallow conical bowl with a wide mouth, a shallow, round-based bowl and a deep slightly restricted ellipsoid bowl, very similar to the *komogi* of Muniwara-Urimo but lacking the everted rim. Many of the *khomongu* have a knob at the base point which is formed by the beginning coil. (Sawos vessels do not usually have knobs.) The cooking and sago storage vessels (one and the same), called *au,* are made in the varying sizes and shapes of the central Boiken potters. It is the same tradition. They are generally decorated with finger or thumb drag marks executed in bands running longitudinally around the entire surface of the vessel. The final two or three coils can be drag-marked or bonded.

Unlike the Sawos pottery, which is made by women and decorated by men, the plains Boiken pots are manufactured in the coil technique entirely by men; in fact, the manufacture of all Boiken pottery, including common cooking vessels, is a male occupation. This specialisation is observed in only a few other areas: the Markham Valley, Madang, Agarabi, Ole and Lumi in the West Sepik Province; Kamasau and Bungain in the East Sepik Province; and among the Siwai in Bougainville.

Pottery was made mostly for local consumption and was not traded widely because most of the neighbouring groups had their own industries or other traditional trade partners. It would seem that the Sawos villagers captured the Sepik River trade and, because of the extent of their sphere of influence, their pottery industry is still a viable economic concern while the plains Boiken industry is dying out and will soon be defunct. In Soandogum,

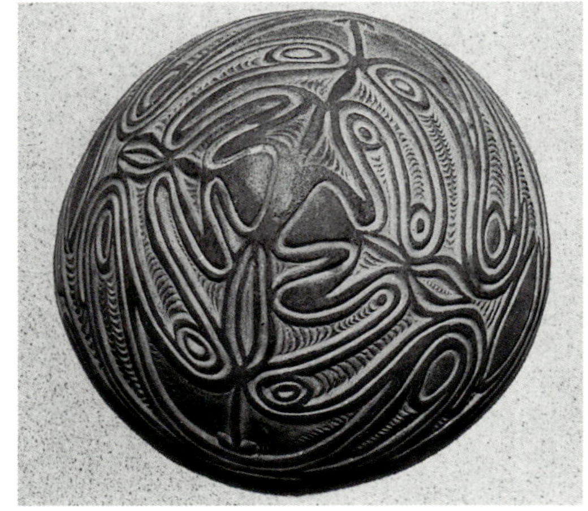

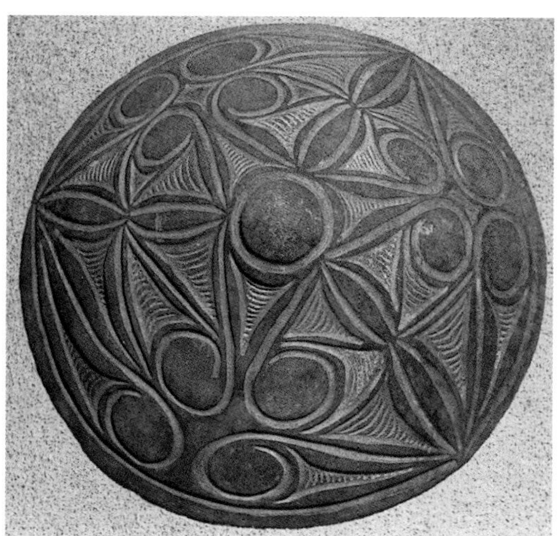
Fig. 9.98

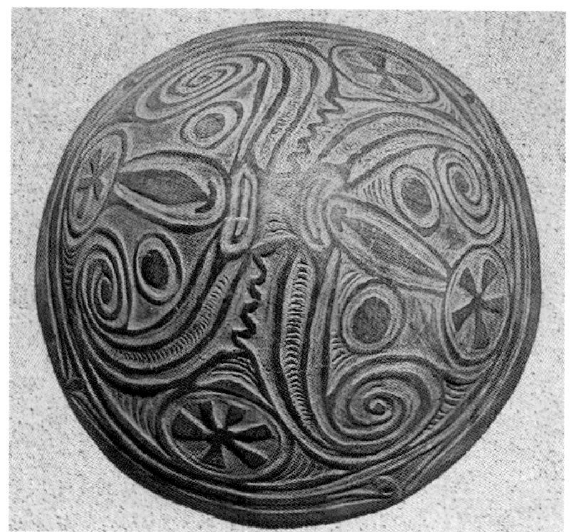
Fig. 9.99

Fig. 9.98
h 14.5 cm.

Fig. 9.99

Rabundogum, Yumungu and Rabiawa were sighted dozens of eating bowls made several years ago and now stored in or under the houses, unused and dusty. In 1976 only one potter, now an old man, was left in Soandogum and the young men are not taking up the techniques. There are no living potters in Yumungu.

Clay, called *kupma*, is abundant throughout the area. There are two varieties in Soandogum: one, a grey-yellow to orange clay, free of gravel but with plenty of fine sand, mostly quartz and of open texture, is used for eating bowls, called *belikupma*; the other is a reddish-brown clay used for cooking pots, called *winkupma*. Men collect the clay in the rainy season and prepare it on a 'limbum' board. A traditional adze-shaped tool (like that from Kolwat) is used to beat the clay, which is then kneaded and rolled into a sausage-shaped pug; stones are removed when the potter prepares the clay for coiling. Coils are rolled out on 'pangal' and started in the hand; the vessel is smoothed outside with a finger dragged down across the coils. When the pot is about 4 centimetres high it is transferred to the ground and supported by the potter's feet. At 8 centimetres it is placed in a shallow hole lined with banana leaves and coiling is continued until the vessel attains the desired height. The top edge is then cut and levelled with a coconut fibre tool and the rim is smoothed with wet fingers. The inside is smoothed with wet knuckles and fingers.

After drying overnight the vessel is decorated by the chip-carving and gouging technique. Traditional tools are fashioned from wild betel nut. Vessels are rubbed with wet hands after carving and

Fig. 9.100
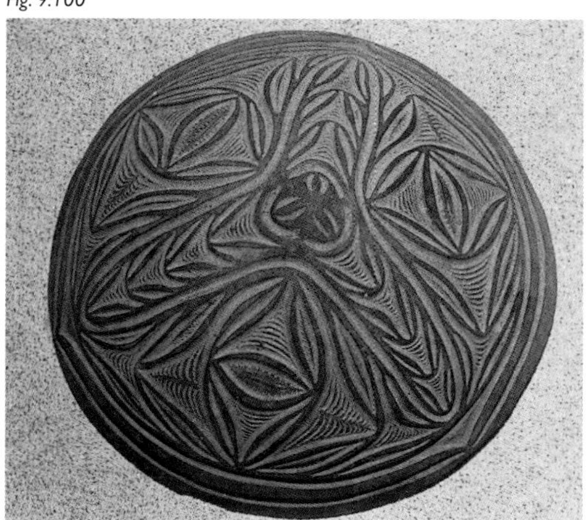

Fig. 9.101
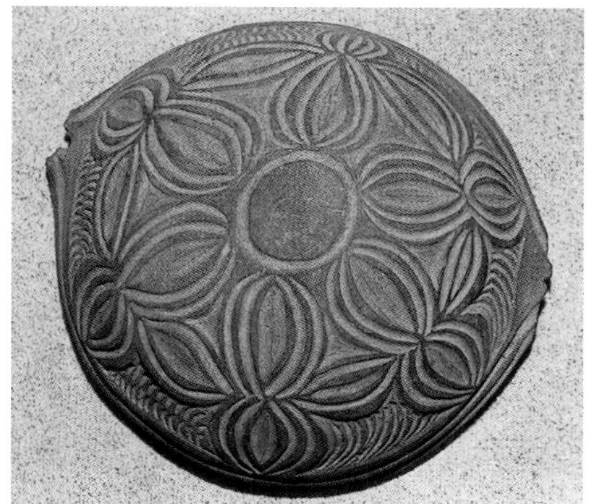

Fig. 9.100
h 14 cm.

Fig. 9.101
h 10 cm.

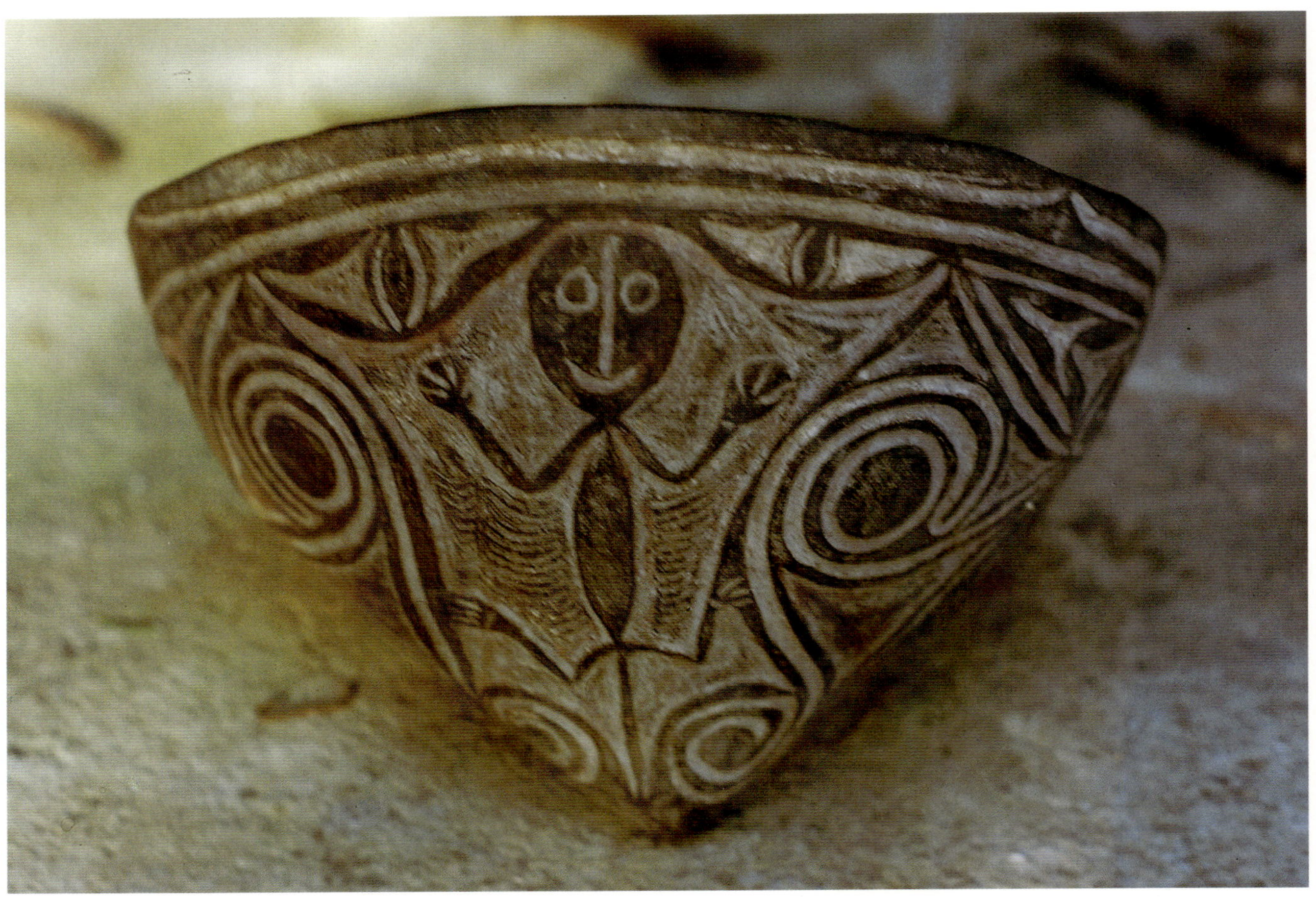

Fig. 9.102
Eating bowl, *khomongu,* with unusual decoration – figure said to be a lizard, Rabundogum village, *h* 22 cm.

burnished inside and outside with the rounded back edge of a bamboo knife. The pot is dried for about a week and only one vessel is fired at a time. Several varieties of wood are used for fuel. For ceremonial occasions the *khomongu* is painted after firing; all colours – red, yellow, white and black are derived from either crushed or rubbed stones mixed with water. A length of betel nut stem, the end of which has been chewed, is used as a brush (figs 9.91, 9.95).

The designs on the *khomongu* represent 'masalai' or stories about them. A 'masalai' is a supernatural being which inhabits waterholes, trees and places in the bush; it can be embodied in animals, reptiles or birds and is greatly feared and respected. Each patrilineal clan has its own 'masalai' and consequently a design on a *khomongu* represents the 'masalai' of that particular potter's clan. This leads to ambiguity when attempting an analysis of the connotative aspects of design because two vessels decorated by the same potter will have the same name (after a 'masalai') even if the designs are totally different. Conversely, two pots having the same design but made by different potters will have different names. The individual design elements represent characteristics of particular 'masalai'. Eyes are a common motif, as are tracks, marks of feathers or skin attributes belonging to the 'masalai'. Designs are applied to the vessel with an eye towards viewing it in an inverted position, that is, with the orifice facing downward. The entire decorative scheme can be seen by looking upon the base point although some of the more representational motifs, the eyes, nose and mouth of the 'masalai' appear upside down. Other vessels which have repeated motifs of abstracted elements connoting the attributes of creatures are visually understood from either position. To understand fully a given unit or

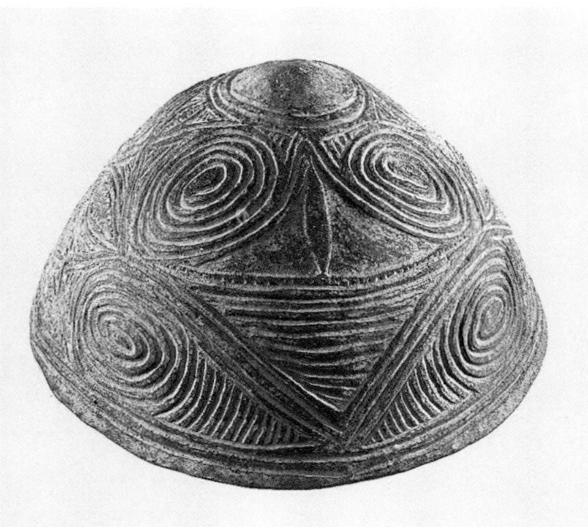

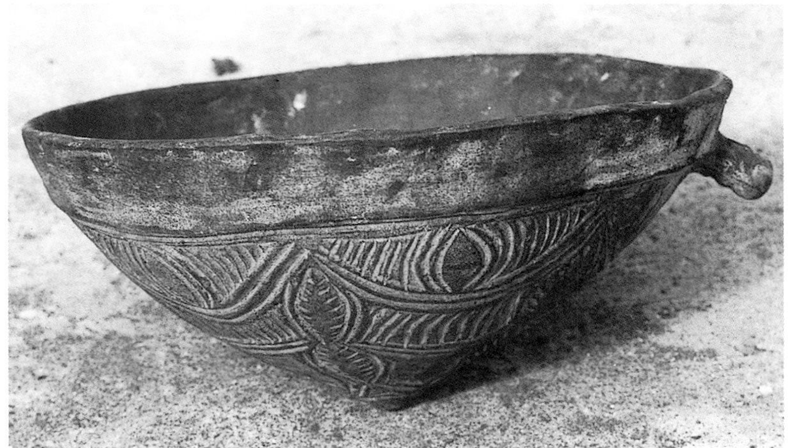

dominant element the vessels must be placed face down and viewed from the side. The field of decoration extends from the base point to the rim and the entire area serves as the decorative zone. The base point is the fulcrum for the design which is made up of primary and secondary elements that rotate about the centre point. These elements are curvilinear and form volutes, circles, scrolls and lozenge motifs. Fillers (lines used to fill in the background field) add texture and contrast to the larger, more dominant elements. When paint is applied to the bowls it covers the cutaway portions only. The raised portion of the design is darker (the burnished surface is low in tone value) than the painted areas.

It is difficult to distinguish between Sawos and plains Boiken eating bowls unless one acquires a familiarity with the characteristic iconography from each area. Sawos pots are more polished in appearance and greasy to the touch, probably because they are still being used.

While the *khomongu* are owned individually (every man and woman has his or her own eating bowl) a communal *au* is kept in the 'haus tambaran' and used ceremonially for cooking the ubiquitous 'white soup', a gruel made from yam, taro and green vegetables, which is used in cult activities, especially in the men's initiation stages. This custom is observed throughout the inland Sepik Province, as is the use of a special cooking pot and eating dishes. A rare *au* from Rabundogum (now in the Wewak cultural centre) is a deep vessel with straight sides and adorned by two faces representing a 'masalai' applied on opposite sides of the neck. It is called *khamanunguin*. Several isolated examples of similar cooking pots with applied faces originating from the plains Boiken have appeared in central Boiken villages. An eating bowl from Washkuk with a similar applied face is now in the Australian Museum, Sydney, and suggests a related tradition.

A unique vessel from Soandogum indicates the existence of a neighbouring group of people who practised an expert tradition of pot making. Both the people and their industry are now extinct, according to Soandogum informants but the story relating to the pot is now part of the oral tradition of Soandogum.

Fig. 9.103
Unusual large serving bowl, *khomongu,* from Toanambu village, Plains Boiken, *h* 21 cm.

Fig. 9.104
Eating bowl, *khomongu,* with one lug, Toanambu.

Fig. 9.105
Ceremonial vessel made by a Kubalia man, at Soandogum, a Plains Boiken village, *h* 22 cm.

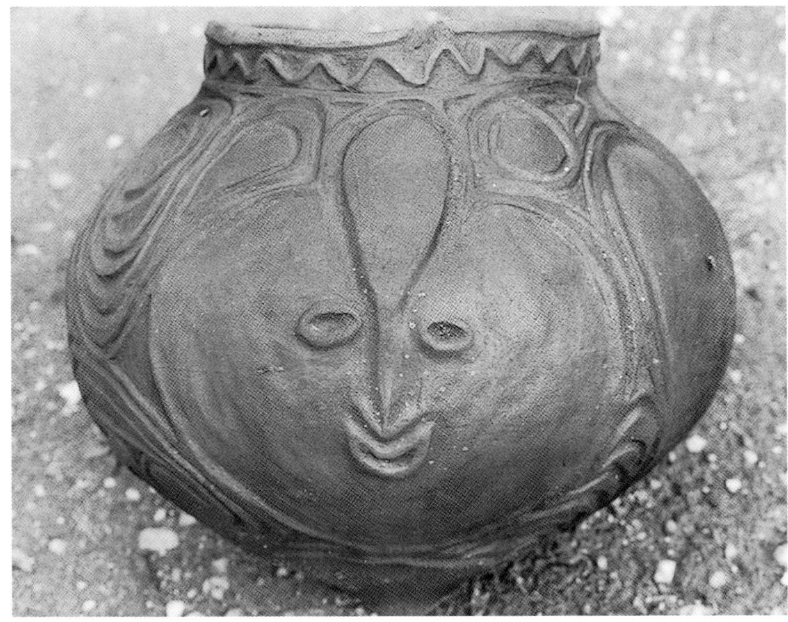

Fig. 9.106
Large ceremonial vessel used in cult activity (provenance unknown, but owned by Toanambu village).

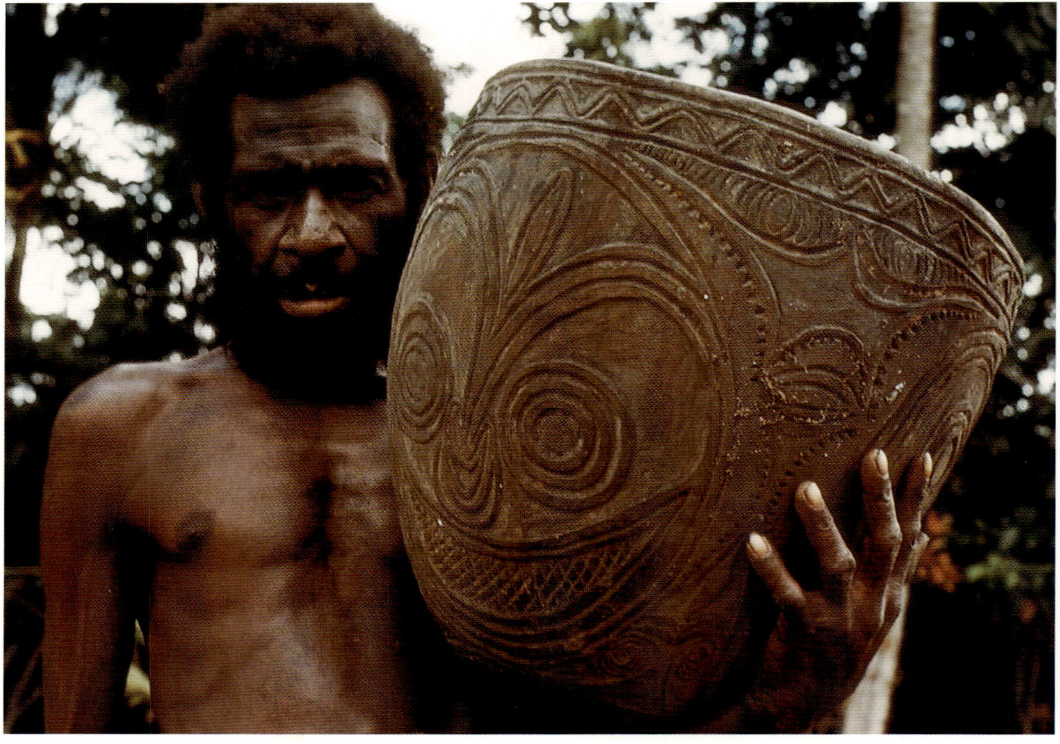

> Before, there were other people who lived at Kubalia. These were the original settlers. The people from Soandogum went to Kubalia to fight them. Everyone was killed from there except one man, called Wabihawa, who was a potter. He was brought back to Soandogum as a captive and continued to make many pots but during fights and the passage of time most of these vessels were broken. When Wabihawa died, his skills and craft died with him, and there were no longer any pots like his made again.

The two faces represent a Kubalia 'masalai'. The vessel is an *au* and, although very old, it has never been used for cooking. It is different in form and decoration from any pot the authors have seen made by the plains Boiken although the faces on the *khamanunguin* seen at Rabundogum might be derived (albeit rather crudely) from the 'masalai' faces of the Kubalia vessel (fig. 9.105).

Toanumbu

One other area notable for its specialisation in making eating bowls similar to those of the plains Boiken and Muniwara-Urimo groups is Toanumbu, one of the largest village complexes in the province. It is spread out along both sides of the Wewak-Maprik road and consists of numerous connected hamlets ranging along a series of ridges. The Kubalia road leading across the plains to the south and connecting the plains Boiken villages has its source at Toanumbu. Yangoru and Mount Turu are also close to these hamlets. While the people speak the Boiken language, they do not belong to the plains dialect affiliation (Laycock has not yet assigned them a dialect).

Cooking vessels are obtained from the eastern Boiken villages, Paparam and Japaraka and although the male potters are able to make cooking pots they tend to produce only serving dishes, called *khomongu*. These eating dishes may be categorised as hybrid rather than as extensions of the plains Boiken type because variations in style reveal formal and decorative influences from the Yangoru Boiken as well as the plains Boiken pots. Shape mostly resembles the plains Boiken pots: eating dishes are either shallow and conical with a knob on the base or more bowl-shaped with rounded bottoms, lacking knobs. In contrast to the large Yangoru communal serving bowls, the smaller size of the Toanumbu vessels indicates that they are used as individual eating dishes. There are no large communal *khomongu*. Many of the vessels contain one lug, as do those from Yangoru (fig. 9.104). The designs tend to repeat some of the plains Boiken designs but there are many that are not used (the repertoire of motifs is more limited) and some are derived from the typical Yangoru type of 'masalai' face formed by concentric circles. In appearance some of the Toanumbu pots are rougher and cruder and this is possibly due to the clay which is coarser in texture.

In 1973 there were said to be ten potters still working in the hamlets; sadly, this is consistent with the other Boiken pottery producing areas: only the only older men still pot and the industries are dying out.

Toanumbu techniques are similar to those of the plains Boiken speakers. Apparently clay resources here are not plentiful and gathering involves a walk of many kilometres. The vessels are decorated in the leather-hard stage by chip carving and gouging methods. They are placed inside the houses on cane rings to dry for two to three months before firing. Firings can be multiple and many kinds of fuel are used. While the pot is still hot from the firing the surface is rubbed with cut raw yam to strengthen it.

It is customary to paint the *khomongu* in preparation for ceremonial occasions. Paint is always applied to the cutaway areas and the colours used are white made from white clay or coral rubble, yellow made from yellow stones, red made from a paste of red seeds, called *kou waringa*, and grey made from clay. A binder added to the pigments comes from the sap of the breadfruit tree.

Yangoru Boiken

A distinctive style of pottery is made by the Boiken speakers (Central Yangoru dialect: Laycock 1973) who live in a string of hamlets situated above the Yangoru patrol post and along the lower slopes of Mount Turu in the Prince Alexander Mountains, the centre in the early 1970s of one of the largest cargo cults in the country's history. This industry will be referred to as 'Yangoru Boiken'. Yangoru Boiken vessels were traditionally widely traded; examples have been found at Urip, Dagua and Kopi on the coast north-west of Wewak, along the Maprik-Wewak road close to Yangoru and in the plains villages. The centre of the industry is located at Wamaina; Kworabri and Mambuk also make pots. In the past not all the Yangoru villages produced pottery but they all acquired it from the Wamaina complex of hamlets. There is no evidence that they used vessels from the other Boiken industries. There has been no attempt to commercialise the industry and, from the evidence of sightings of mostly older vessels and the fact that the young men are not learning the techniques, it seems that pottery making here is dying out.

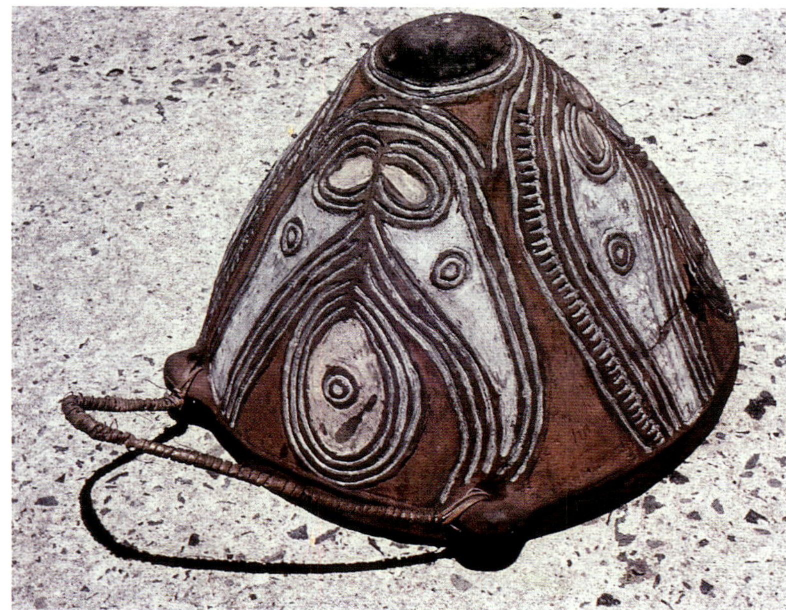

Fig. 9.107
Yangoru Boiken serving vessel , *khomongu,* with cane handle, collected 1930-40, *h* 23 cm.

The word for pots is *awo* and there are three types of vessels made. *Gelawo*, or *kibeawo*, is a cooking vessel, round-bottomed, deep and either conical or straight-sided. Size ranges from small pots about 20 centimetres high with a mouth diameter of 22 to 24 centimetres to large vessels about 40 centimetres high and with a 42 to 43-centimetre diameter mouth. These pots are simply decorated at the outside top rim with a band of two to six exposed coils, some of which have been impressed with a thumb and fingernail or marked with either a stick or an animal's bone, usually a pig's

Fig. 9.108
Large cooking pot, *gelawo,* Wamaina village.

Fig. 9.109
Detail of fig. 9.108. Peto demonstrating how he made the decoration on the cooking pot, Wamaina.

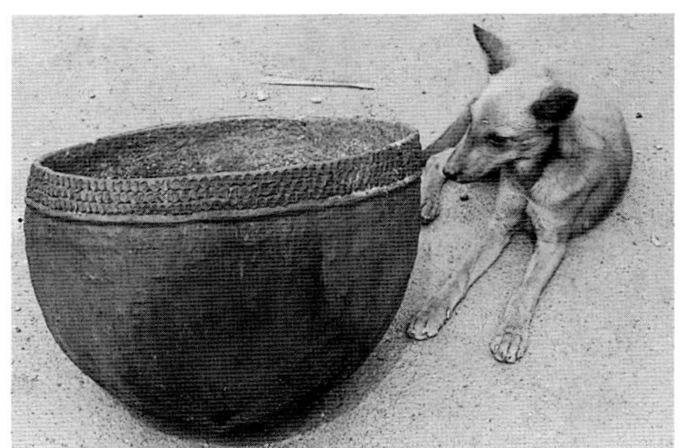

Fig. 9.108

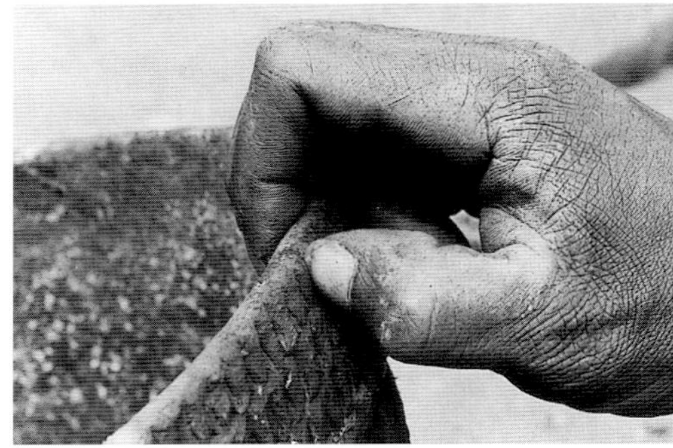

Fig. 9.109

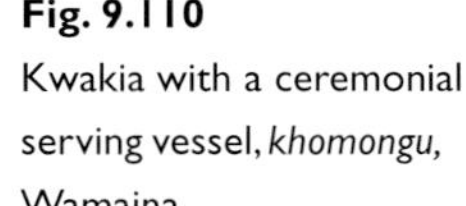

Fig. 9.110
Kwakia with a ceremonial serving vessel, *khomongu,* Wamaina.

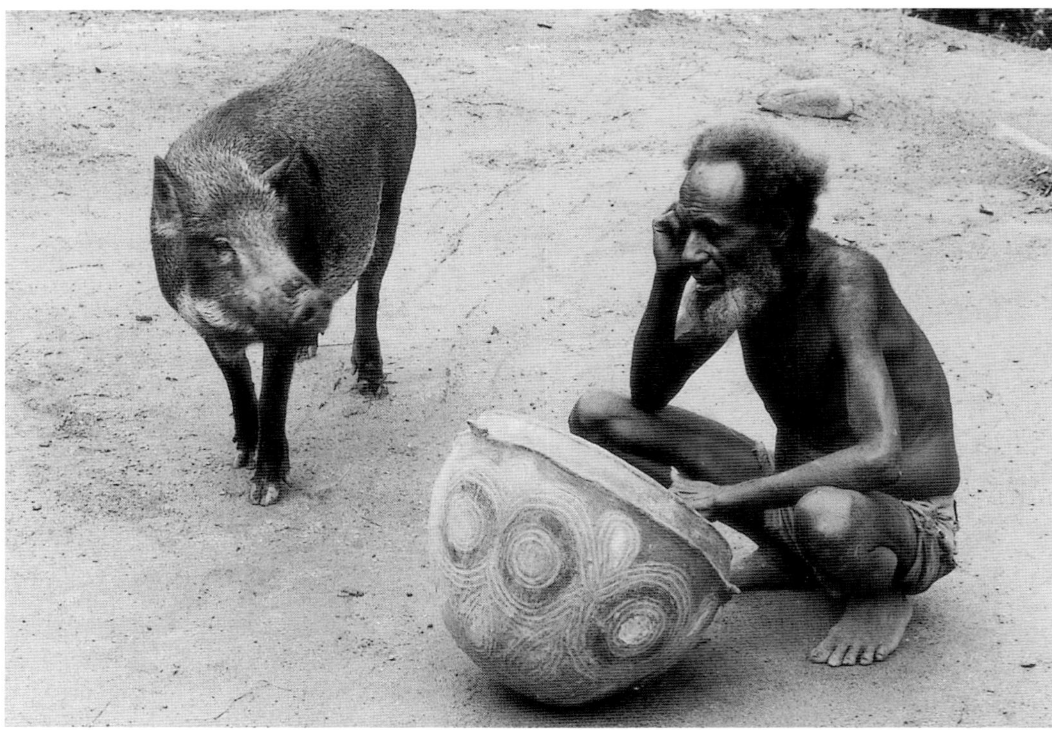

Fig. 9.111

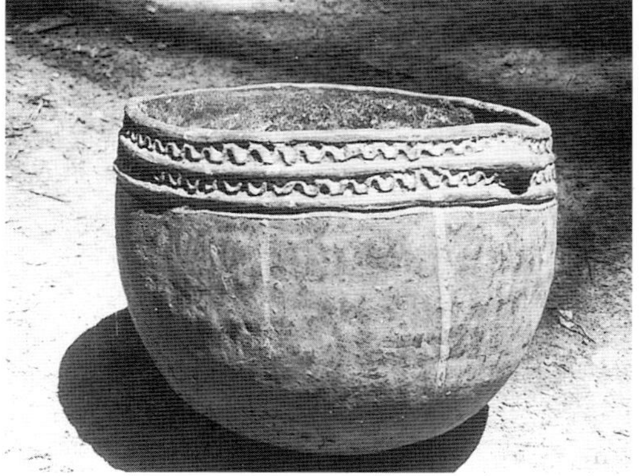

Fig. 9.112

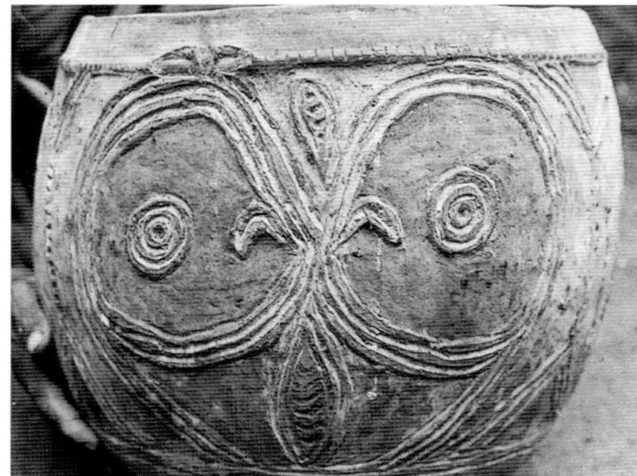

Fig. 9.111
Serving vessel, *khomongu,* from Wamaina.

Fig. 9.112
Ceremonial serving vessel, *khomongu,* Kworabri village; the lug has been broken off, *h* 41 cm.

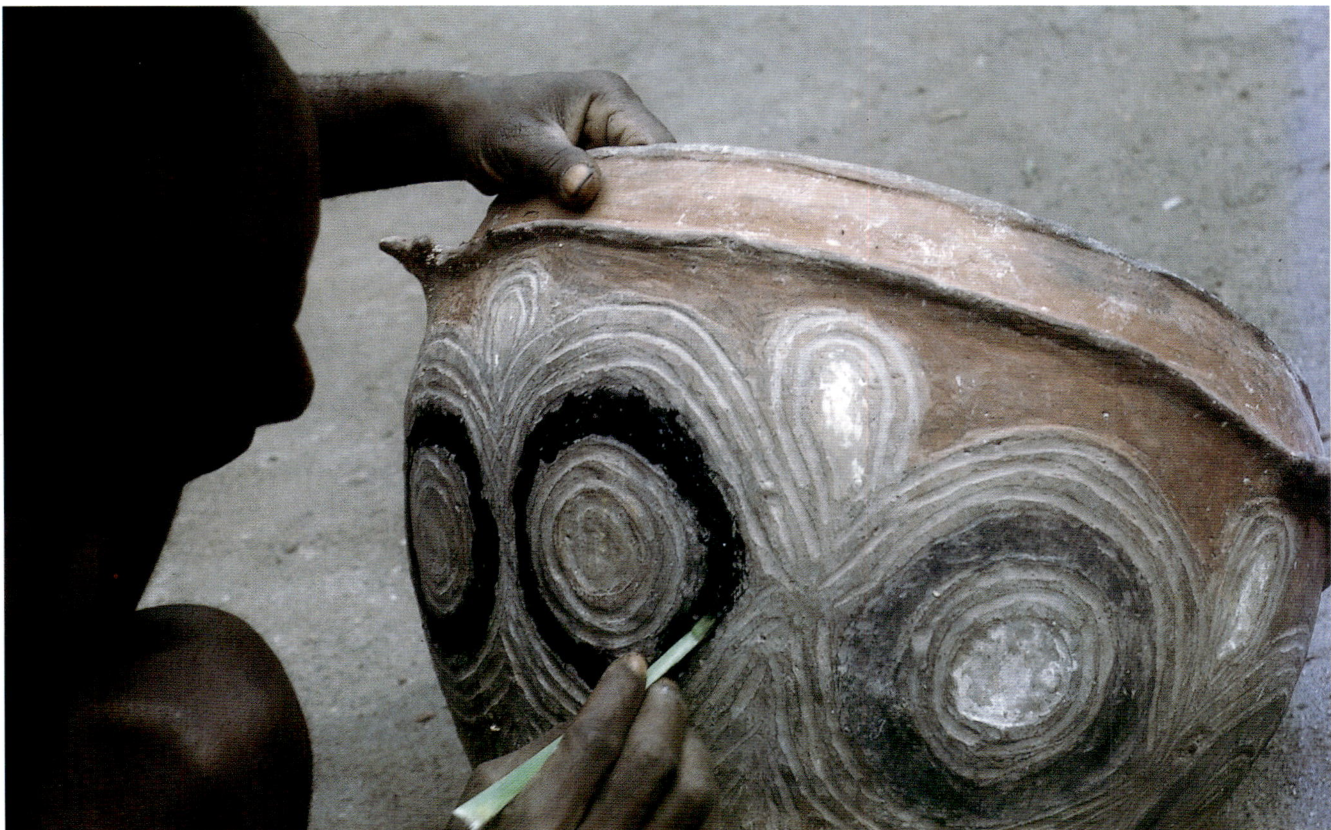

Fig. 9.113
Kwakia painting a ceremonial vessel, *khomongu*, Wamaina Village.

rib. The bottom coil is often left unmarked (figs 9.108, 9.109).

Khomongu is a serving bowl of which there are two varieties, classified by design elements, size and shape. One is a rather small eating bowl (average height 20 to 27 centimetres) used by a family or individual; it is semi-spherical with a rounded base, a globular belly, a slightly restricted mouth and one lug. The principal characteristic of this everyday eating bowl is the simplicity of the decoration, which is confined to the top third portion around the rim and extending down the walls, in comparison to the other more richly decorated *khomongu*. The top rim coil is always left unmarked; underneath there are either one or two applied bands of zig-zag design, scallops or diamonds running horizontally around the edge and separated by an unmarked coil. These patterns are often painted with white lime (fig. 9.111).

The second type of *khomongu*, always elaborately decorated, is reserved for feasts and used communally. It is quite large, about 25 to 40 centimetres high, round-based and either semi-spherical or ellipsoid in shape with a slightly restricted mouth. The top inverted direct rim is always defined by one or two unbonded coils which form a horizontal band, cutaway in appearance. Curvilinear designs are cut into the walls of the vessel and the cutaway portion is painted with red, white, black and yellow pigments. The design motifs, characteristic of most Sepik art, are derived from the flora and fauna of the environment. The most commonly repeated motif of concentric circles is said to represent the face of a 'masalai'. Most of these vessels have one or two lugs with a hole pierced in the middle. The eating bowls are hung in the houses with bush string fitted through the hole in the lug.

Men make the pots by the coil method. There are some clay pits around the ridges but when striking a new source it is necessary for the potter to give the clay a trial by making a small model pot. There are two types of clay, one used for cooking

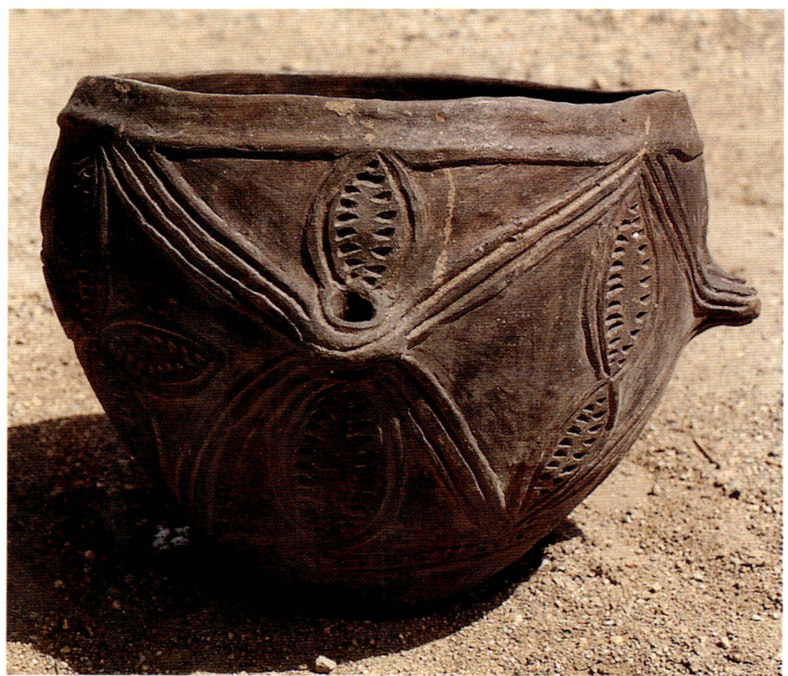

Fig. 9.114
Yangoru Boiken serving vessel, *khomongu*, *h* 26 cm.

vessels and one for serving bowls. Kworabri village owns a clay pit and sells clay to men from other villages. Traditionally, polished shell rings were traded for clay but nowadays it is purchased with money.

The clay close to Kunyik hamlet is yellowish-brown and contains gravel and coarse sand composed of unaltered rock fragments and some schist grains. The men dig the clay themselves; there appear to be sanctions against women's participation in various aspects of pot making but the women may transport the clay back to the village, where it remains for about a week; they may also help prepare it by beating it with sticks. Water is added during the beating, which is carried out on a flat rock at a river or creek After this. the rubble is removed by hand, small pieces of clay are removed from the lump and individually felt and picked over. Coils are then rolled out on 'pangal' and the first coil is started in the hand.

Pots are dried alternately in the house and in the sun for several days. When the vessels are leather-hard (after about a week) they are decorated in the chip-carving method. Before firing the surfaces are burnished with a small flat stone. Firing can be multiple and several varieties of wood, which is plentiful in the hilly bushy area, are used for fuel.

Khomongu type vessels are painted for ceremonial occasions in red, yellow, black and white but only the cutaway portions are coloured. Red is derived from stones, black is made from a combination of charcoal and lime bound with the chewed sap of the 'tulip' tree leaf, white comes from a whitish clay. The colours, mixed in a coconut shell, are brushed onto the pot with the chewed end portion of a 'tanket' leaf stem.

Mountain Arapesh

To the north-east of the main concentration of Abelam villages, further up in the foothills of the Prince Alexander Mountains, live the mountain Arapesh. Their neighbours to the east are the central Boiken speakers (Yangoru Boiken). Some villages straddling the border between these two groups speak both languages and have cultural affinities with both the Boiken and Abelam people. This is readily seen in the pots made in the villages of Malapaiem, Alisu, and Kaboibus and in many of the mountain Arapesh villages themselves.

Similar vessels have been seen by the authors in the following villages: Alisu (Boiken/mountain Arapesh), Bukinara (Boiken/mountain Arapesh) and Nimbihu (mountain Arapesh). The remaining mountain Arapesh villages are as yet unsurveyed. In Nimbihu informants said that all the surrounding places make their own pots but cited Kuragamon as specialising in large ceremonial 'haus tambaran' serving bowls which are bought by or traded to the other mountain Arapesh villagers.

There are three kinds of vessels produced in Nimbihu. *Malep* is a cooking pot similar in shape and appearance to Abelam vessels and with a decoration of triangles formed by exposed coils running around the top outer rim. *Sahin*, the individual eating bowl which can also be used by households, comes in a variety of shapes and designs, all of which resemble the Yangoru Boiken *khomungu*; they are small to medium-sized, about 20 centimetres high. *Bitap*, the 'haus tambaran' ceremonial vessel, is a large (about 30 centimetres high) vessel with a pointed base, curved walls, restricted opening and everted lip. Designs boldly executed in the chip-carving method are in some examples similar to those found on Yangoru Boiken types, namely, patterns of concentric circles set around the belly of the vessel, offset by parallel scalloped lines marking the circumference at the top and bottom (fig. 9.118). In the pot seen in Nimbihu, the design elements are more akin to those found on Kwimbu and Yenigo vessels (fig. 9.119). A *bitap* seen at Bukinara is closer in shape to the *khomongu* of the Yangoru Boiken than are the Alisu and Nimbihu examples (fig. 9.120).

The authors were told that only the men make the pots in this area. There are two types of clay, *magus*, a coarse red gritty-textured variety used for cooking pots and eating bowls, and a yellow finer-textured clay used for making the *bitap*. While women dig for and collect the clay in the wet season, certain sanctions are followed: they are not allowed to smoke or chew betel nut while they collect and prepare the clay. The authors have no information or details of the spiral coiling technique used in this area or of firing methods. The men paint the ceremonial vessels in red, yellow, white and black pigments for special occasions. This area needs further study.

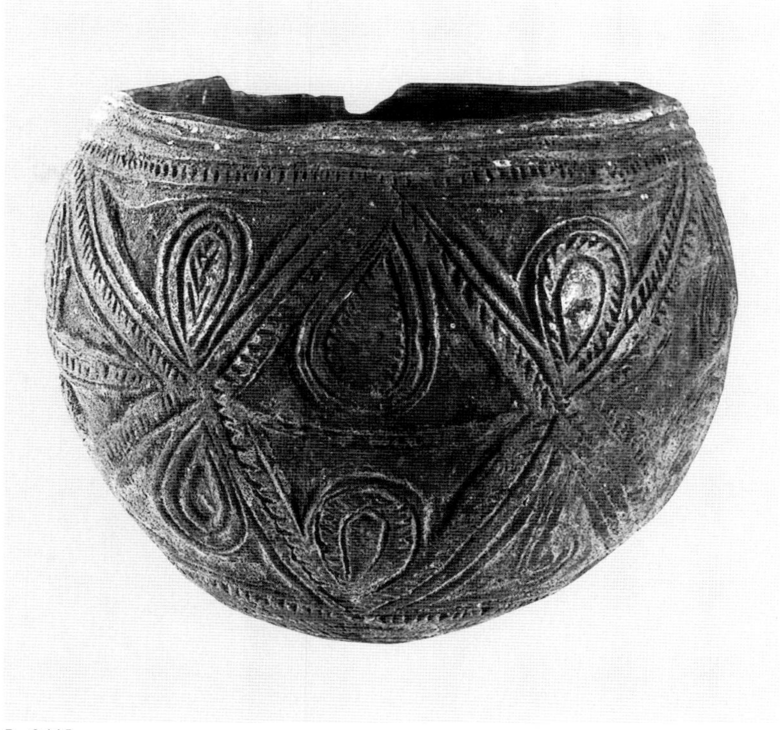

Fig. 9.115

Fig. 9.116

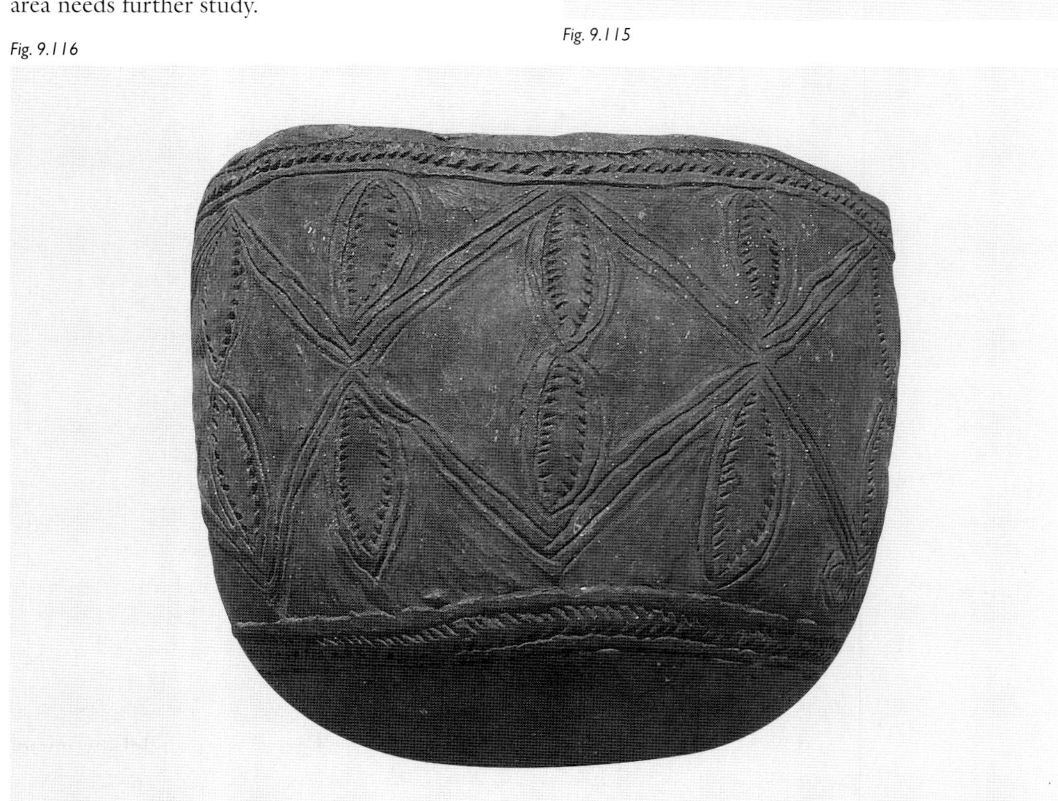

Figs 9.115, 9.116
Compare the decoration on the Kombio and Abelam pots with that of the Yangoru pot in fig. 9.114.

Fig. 9.115
Kombio eating bowl, *kudruk, h* 13 cm.

Fig. 9.116
Abelam serving bowl, *amagat,* at Wagupma, an Abelam village.

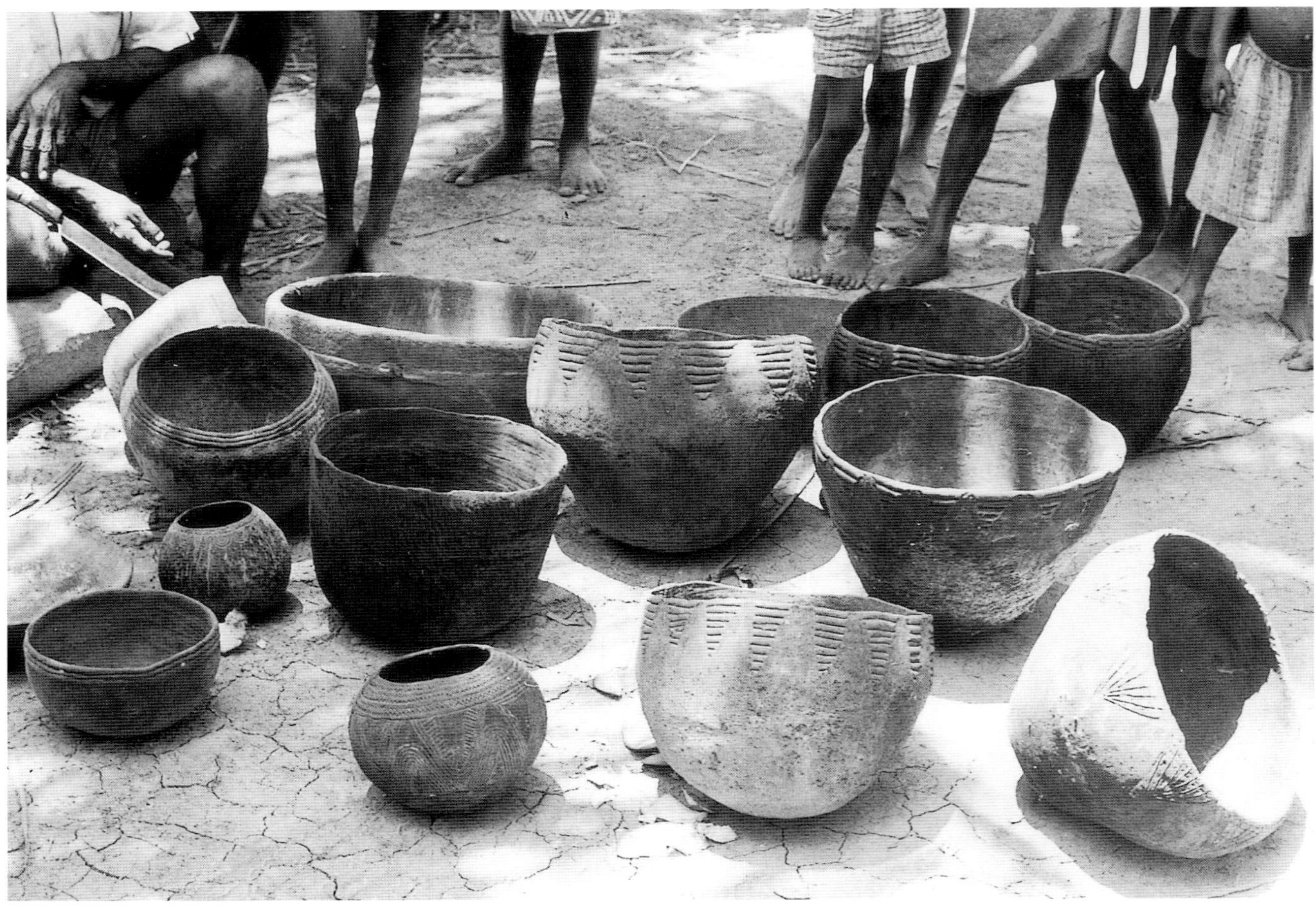

Fig. 9.117
Cooking and serving pots and two eating bowls, Malapaiem, Mount Arapesh.

Abelam

The Abelam tribe, numbering in the early 1970s about 40 000, lives entirely within the Maprik district. Neighbours to the east are the Boiken, to the west the Kwanga and to the north the Arapesh. The Sepik plains people (the Sawos and Iatmul) inhabit the far southern boundaries. The Abelam are the largest group in the Sepik region and the most densely populated group on the mainland. They occupy the southern slopes of the Prince Alexander Mountains and the northern portion of the Sepik plains.

The Abelam are culturally and socially distinct from their neighbours but linguistic and ethnographic evidence relates them most clearly to the people of the Sepik River where they probably originated, migrating to the north and pushing the original inhabitants, the Arapesh and Kwanga, farther north and west. The movement was caused by depletion of the once fertile Sepik plains, now a sparsely populated grassland between the river and the densely populated foothills (Forge 1963). Linguistically, the Abelam are divided into four major dialects: Wingei, Wosera, west Wosera and Maprik (Laycock 1973).

Abelam society is one of the most ritualistic in Papua New Guinea, its activities centering around the yam and 'tambaran' cults.

> The tambaran cult assured the benevolence of the spirits, provided opportunities for display and magnificence, and a means of expression for artistic talents, as well as a demonstration of the individual's pride in his clan and village ... The yam cult is concerned with the cultivation and display of long yams, and in the Wosera, of the *asagwa mami* variety as well. [Forge 1963]

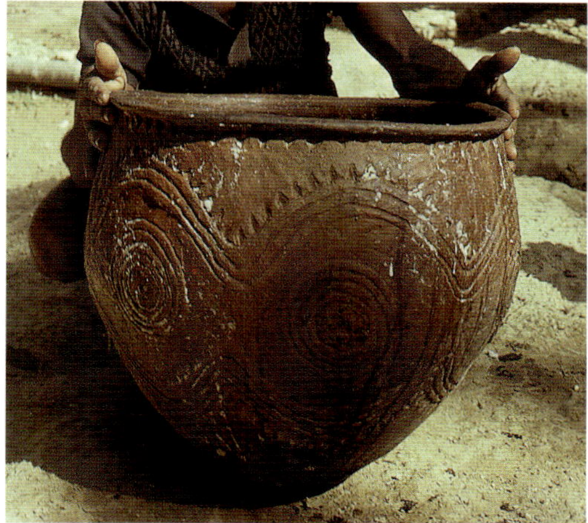

Fig. 9.118

In spite of intense mission activity and administration influence almost every village engages in 'tambaran' activities. New 'haus tambaran' are being constructed all over the district, young men are still initiated, the yam harvest and exchange is still celebrated by cult activities. Cult and religious objects used ceremonially reflect vigorous artistic expression. Taboos centering around the yam cult are rigorously practised. Yam cultivation is solely the man's responsibility: he plants, cultivates and harvests the staple crop and prepares the magic used to ensure the yam's growth. Women are forbidden access to the yam gardens, storehouses and, of course, the 'haus tambaran'. Artistic endeavours are also the male responsibility. The Abelam repertoire of carved, woven and painted objects is wide. Carvings and painted 'pangal' panels adorn the facades of the A-frame 'haus tambaran', carvings of human figures, pigs and birds are made for use in cult activities, and small masks and headdresses are woven from dried grasses and used to adorn the yams during their display and distribution. Women are responsible for the manufacture of clay cooking pots, many of which are unremarkable and crudely shaped. In some villages the women make a common eating bowl while men make and decorate ceremonial vessels.

There is no evidence that sago storage vessels have ever been made or used. Sago, although not a staple crop, is sometimes eaten. It is stored hanging in the houses, carefully wrapped in leaves. Cooking pots are used in a unique manner in this area: a hole is pierced through the base and they are inverted and stacked over the protruding centre post of the A-frame 'haus tambaran'. Informants say their function is simply to stop the rain from dripping down into the building (figs 1.18, 9.121-9.123).

The primary pottery producing area of the Abelam is located in the south-west, commonly called the Wosera, an area of high population density and acute land shortage, where soil fertility is decreasing and the bush is being depleted. Protein intake is low. The staple root crop is the yam, supplemented

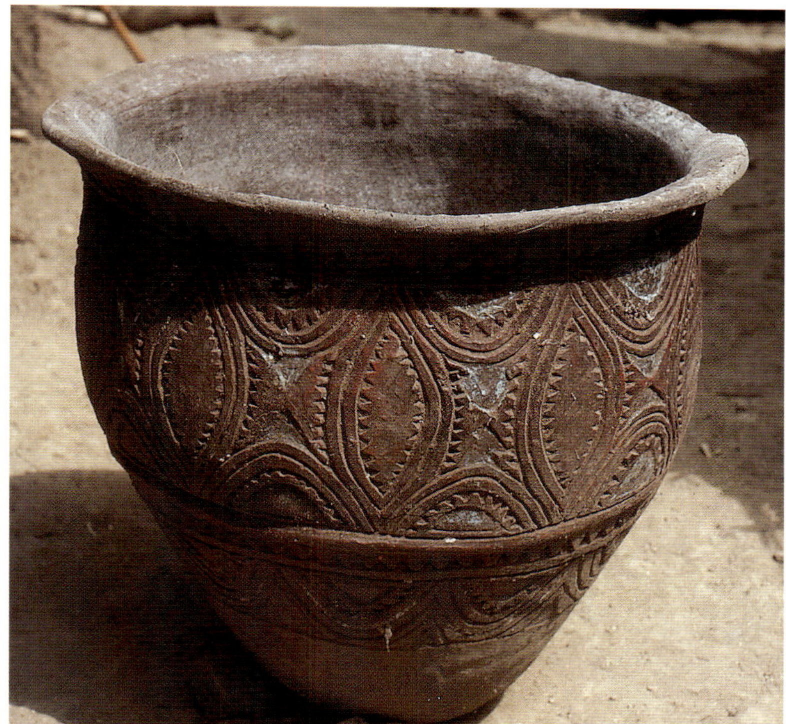

Fig. 9.119

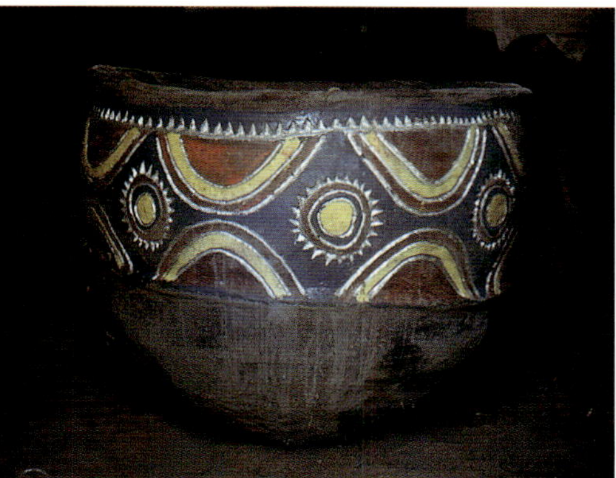

Fig. 9.118
Ceremonial serving vessel, *bitap*, from Alisu, Mount Arapesh.

Fig. 9.119
Bitap seen at Nimbuhu, probably traded from Yabominu, Mount Arapesh.

Fig. 9.120
Bitap from Bukinara, Mount Arapesh, *h* 36 cm.

Fig. 9.121
Cooking pots being placed over the central post of a new 'haus tambaran' at the Abelam village of Gwynyingi.

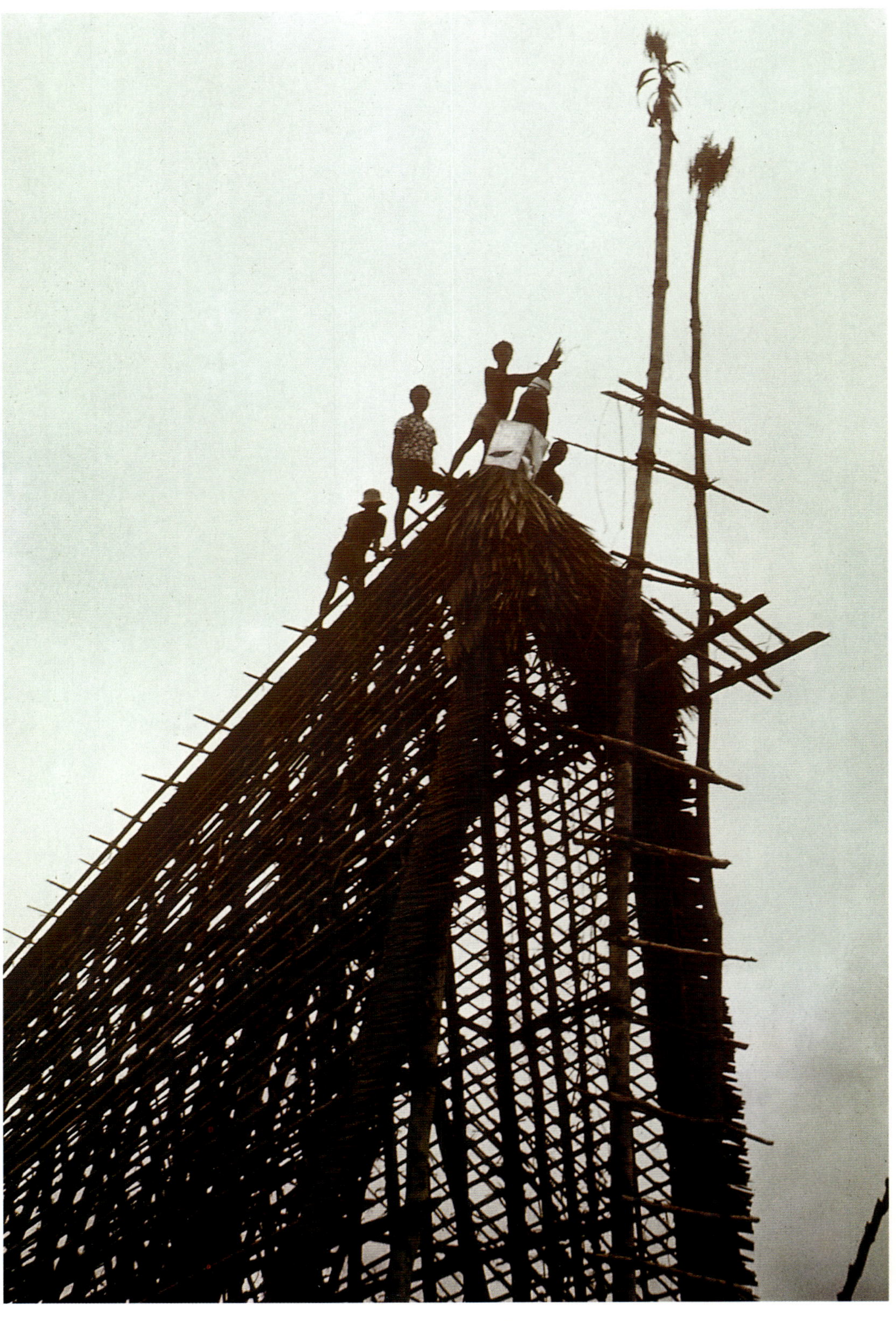

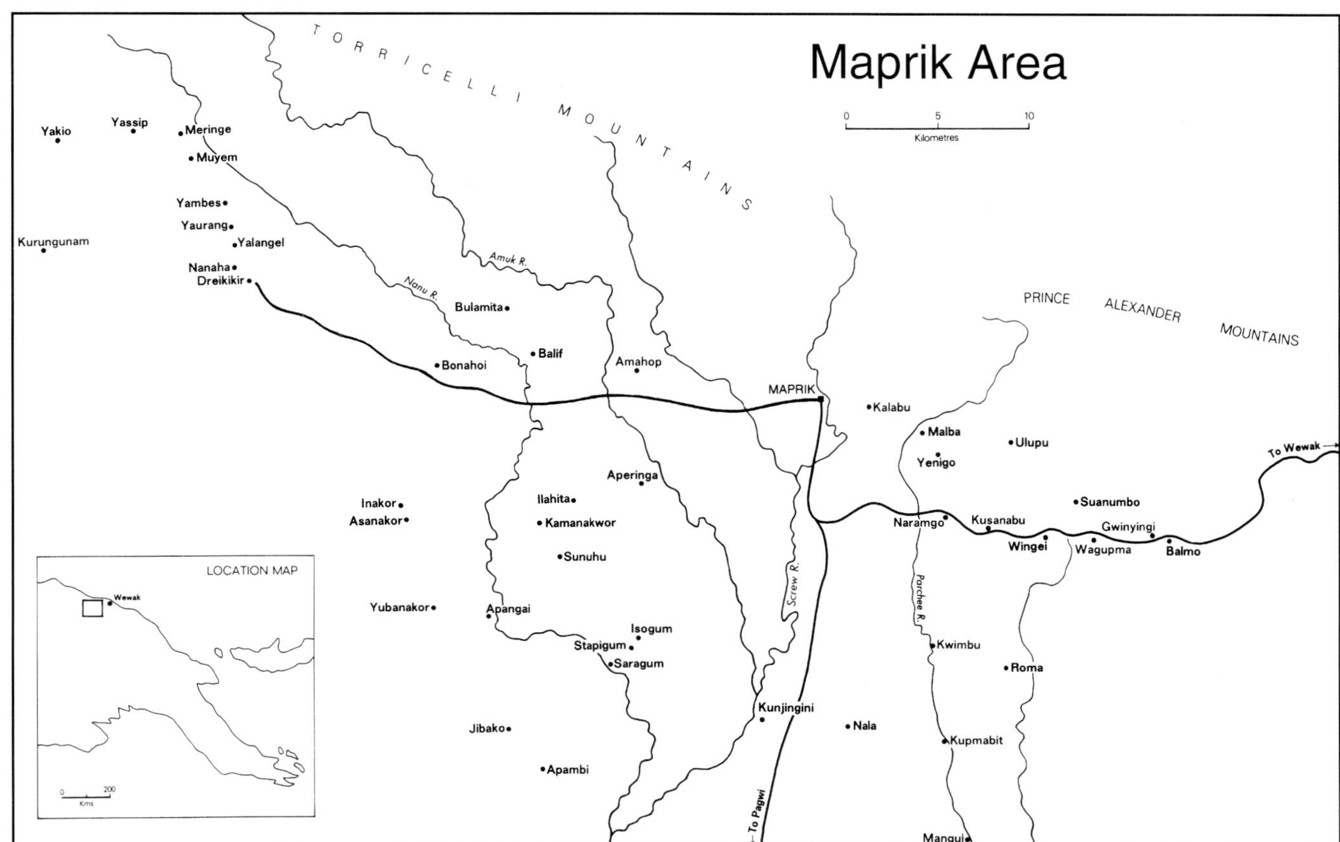

MAP 12

by taro and sago. There is little bush to shelter small mammals and birds although dried fish are sometimes obtained from the Sepik River in exchange for clay pots. Tinned fish and rice have become the major foodstuffs when cash is available.

Wosera pot making, unlike the neighbouring Abelam industries, is increasing due to economic necessity (the sale of clay pots brings in a much needed source of cash) and the abundance and high quality of the clay. That Wosera vessels are an item of exchange with neighbouring people is evidenced by examples of pots found in villages in the Sepik plains and in the Boiken, Kwanga and Wingei-Maprik areas. Resident expatriates and tourists purchase these pots from the Maprik market, at the Maprik High School, along the Maprik-Wewak road and in Wewak township.

In the north Abelam area, almost all villages produced pottery in the recent past. Notable amongst these are Yenigo, Gwinyingi, the Nanglangria hamlets, Suanumbo, Wagupma, Kusanabu, Naramgo, Ulupu, Malba 1 and 2, Wingei, Balmo and Kalabu. The problems of classifying pot styles or designating particular types as being from particular places are manifold. Village sightings of vessels in some households reveal a variety of cooking, eating and serving bowls which have in common few characteristics of shape or design. Since informants insist that all varieties are made in their village it must be assumed (until further extensive field work is carried out and archaeological evidence is uncovered) that indeed the area's pottery making is a mixed industry, where a hybridisation of styles influenced by the Wosera, Sepik plains, Boiken (Yangoru) and the Sepik River has taken place and that each village has adopted its own style of decoration and form. Common features of the pottery are that the spiral coil technique is used and decoration consists of incised, punctated or chip-carved curvilinear, geometric or figurative motifs. Most ceremonial vessels are customarily painted before use.

Fig. 9.122
'Haus tambaran' facade with ceramic toilet on top at Bugita, an Abelam village.

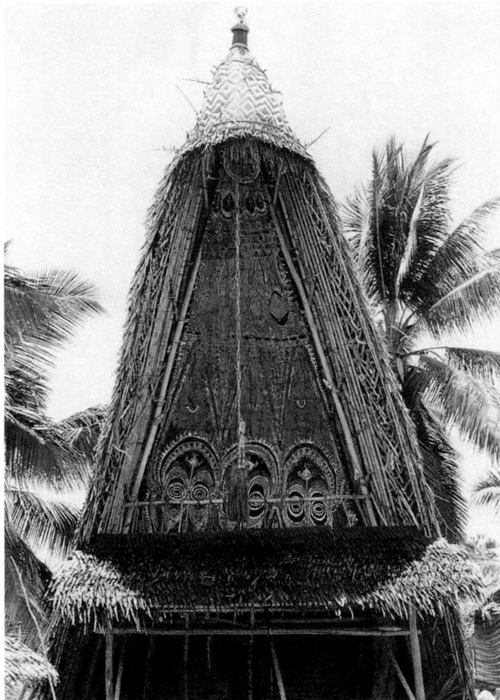

Fig. 9.123
Detail of fig. 9.122.

Fig. 9.124
Abelam ceremonial vessel, collected on the Roma road, 1969 (provenance unknown), *h* 30 cm.

Fig. 9.123

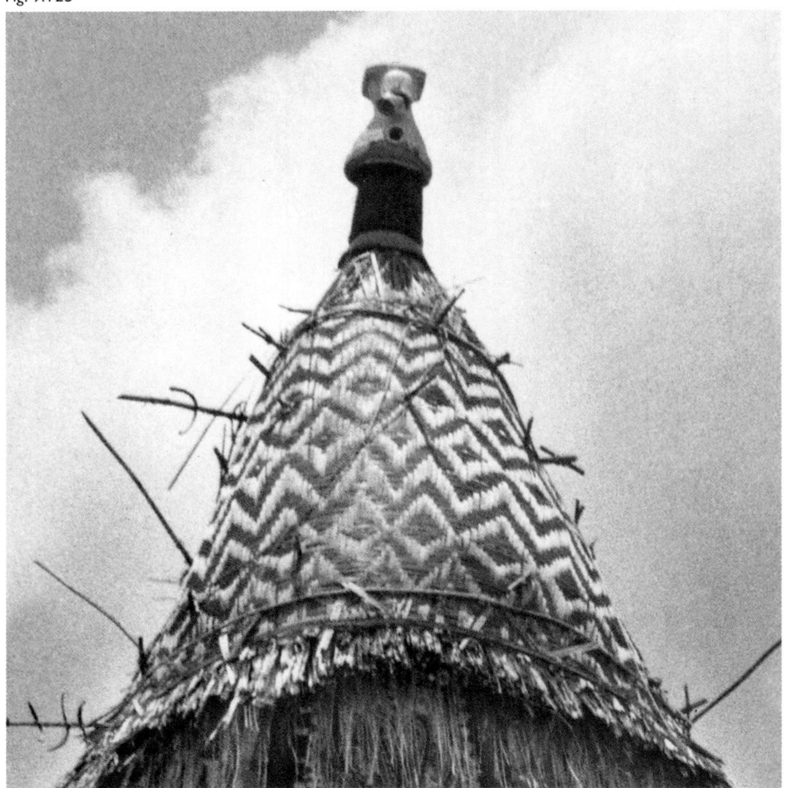

Abelam (Wingei and Maprik dialects)

Gwinyingi (Wingei dialect) is a large village complex made up of several hamlets. Pottery making has died out here; in recent years there has been no evidence of the elaborately decorated ceremonial vessels that were customarily made by the men in the past. A few women potters are still alive but they claim they have not made any pots for 'a long time'.

Three types of vessels were produced. A common, roughly-shaped cooking pot, called *au*, is similar to but rougher in texture than those made throughout Abelam villages. Its walls may be plain or textured by finger or thumb sloughing. A serving bowl was made in two typical shapes: one round-based, restricted, semi-spherical; the other, a larger, deeper version with a round bottom, straighter sides and a direct rim. These serving bowls, called *amagat*, are always simply decorated with three exposed coils at the top rim and have a shiny surface caused by burnishing. Food is ladled from the cooking pot into the serving bowl with a half coconut shell attached to a long handle. Villagers then use half coconut shells, plain or decorated with intricate incised designs, as individual eating dishes which they fill from the serving bowl.

The third type of vessel, also called *amagat*, of which there are only a few examples remaining, was used in the 'haus tambaran' cult activities. This was always made and decorated by men. One such ves-

Fig. 9.124

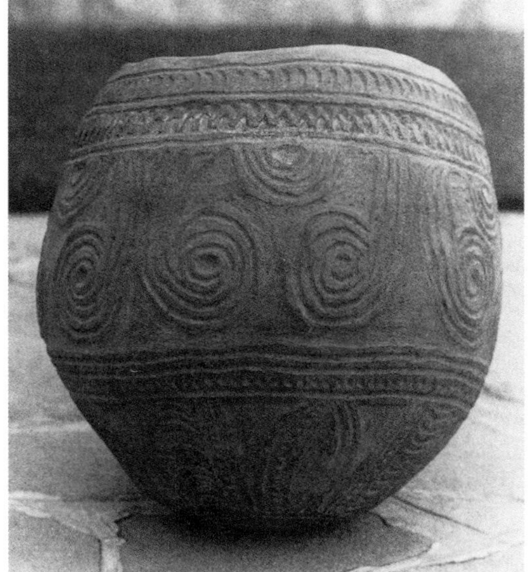

sel is wide-mouthed with a rounded base and vertical sides. The decorative scheme is unusual in that familiar elements or motifs – lozenge shapes and simplified 'faces' – are arranged longitudinally around the vessel in a chain-like sequence carved in a casual freehand manner (fig. 9.132).

Another example is roughly cylindrical; it has been crudely formed and the top rim is uneven. The decoration is casual and consists of a longitudinal series of unevenly shaped lozenges running around the middle, offset by bilateral vertical elements that form a quatrefoil arrangement strong enough to give the overall design a vertical movement. The decorative elements on these two vessels are used by both Yangoru Boiken and Wosera industries in varying schematic designs (figs 9.116, 9.129).

Vessels sighted in Suanumbu and a nearby hamlet in the foothills north of Gwinyingi revealed cooking pots, *au*, and simple serving bowls, *amagat*, similar to those seen in other Abelam villages. A variation of the Abelam type, with three exposed coils decorating the rim, has six vertical ladders of exposed coils alternating around the top half of the vessel, or, as in one case, extending down the entire visible wall of the pot to the base. These also have a burnished surface (fig. 9.130).

The cooking vessels with triangular-shaped remnant coil patterns are typical of the Abelam. There were no examples of decorated 'haus tambaran' vessels; there certainly would have been some in the past but they have either been broken or sold.

Potters from the Kalabu hamlets in the southern foothills of the Torricelli Mountains, at the northern boundary of the Abelam tribe and about 6 kilometres from Maprik, used to make cooking pots and serving bowls of the type seen in Gwinyingi and Suanumbu. The serving bowls are typical semi-spherical shapes, decorated with three or four exposed coils at the top. Phyllis Kaberry, an anthropologist who carried out field work in Kalabu in 1939, mentions that pot making was women's work but does not describe the pots. In 1968, the Museum für Völkerkunde, Berlin, organised a collecting expedition and the pottery illustrated in a subsequent catalogue (Koch 1978: Plates 231-48) is described as being collected at Kalabu although the catalogue does not attempt to pinpoint its origins. All of the decorated vessels (Plates 238-48) are of Wosera manufacture.

A variation of the three-coiled serving bowl made at Kalabu, Gwinyingi and Suanumbu is a speciality of the Yenigo area. These pots have a casual overall design of carved circles and lozenges, distinctively defined by prick marks made with a sharp pointed tool (bamboo or bone) or the end of a plant stem.

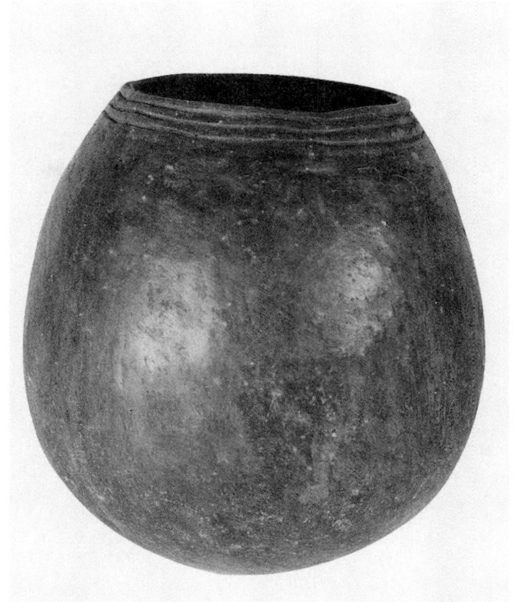

Fig. 9.125
Burnished Abelam serving bowl, *amagat*: typical three coils unbonded at the rim, *h* 21 cm.

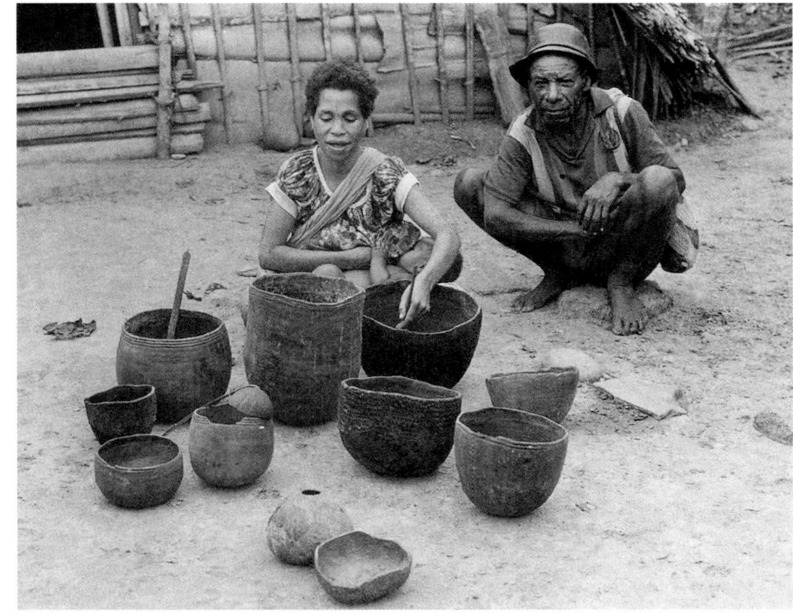

Fig. 9.126
Group of Abelam cooking pots and serving bowls, Gwynyingi village. The woman is demonstrating how food is ladled from one to the other.

Fig. 9.127
Abelam serving bowls, *amagat,* seen in a market on the Maprik-Wewak road near Balmo village.

Fig. 9.128
Abelam serving bowl, *amagat,* probably from Yenigo area.

Fig. 9.129
Amagat inside a new 'haus tambaran', Gwynyingi village.

Fig. 9.130
Large feast pot and small eating bowl, *amagat,* seen at Suanumbo village. Large pot *h* 34 cm.

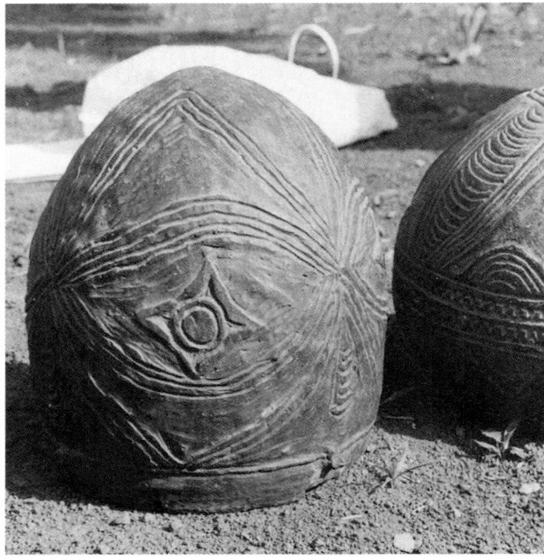

Fig. 9.127

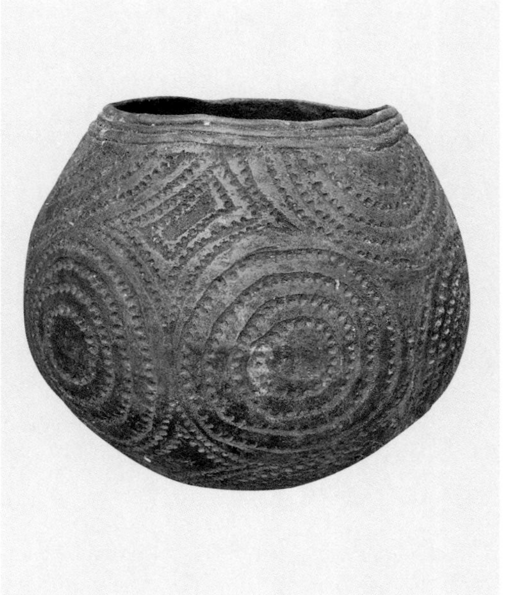

Fig. 9.128

Two, three or four coils always distinguish the top outer rim. Distribution occurs throughout the north Abelam area, especially near Malba, Yenigo and Ulupu. The shape is similar to that of Wosera vessels (fig. 9.128).

Several *amagat,* individual eating vessels made at Yenigo, are similar in shape and design to the *amagat* seen in the Kwimbu area. These eating bowls are round-bottomed, with wide mouths and rather straight sides with direct rims. A few examples, deeper in proportion, have walls that curve inward at the shoulder. The designs are essentially vertically directed. The direct rim is marked by horizontal or zig-zag scallops; the base is unmarked but defined by several concentric circles. The walls of the vessels are decorated with design elements representing flora and fauna of the area, chevrons, herringbone patterns, circles, lozenge shapes and ellipsoids. The application is more curvilinear than geometric and freely and casually executed (fig. 9.134).

Kwimbu village and several related hamlets are located south of the Maprik-Wewak road, along a track opposite Yenigo which leads to the Sepik

Fig. 9.129

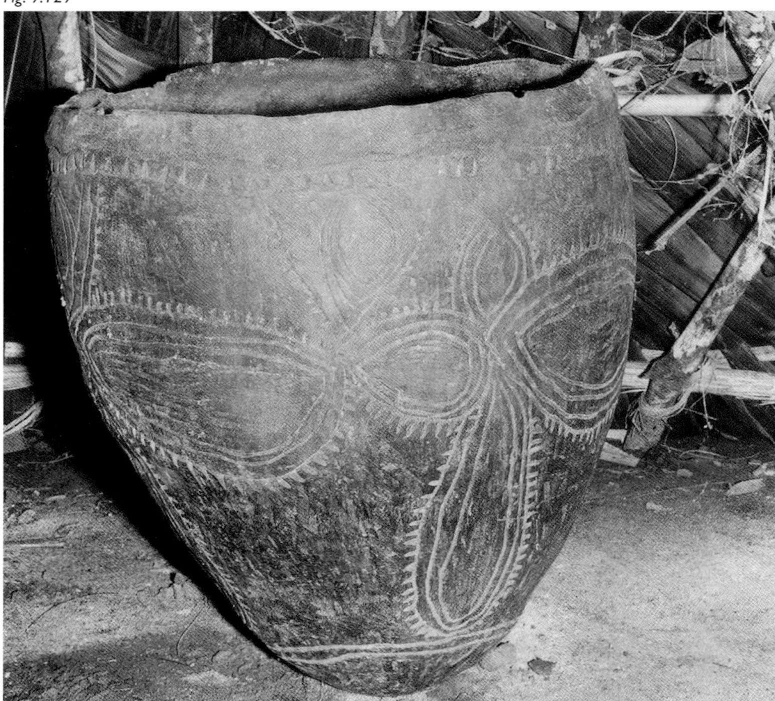

Fig. 9.130

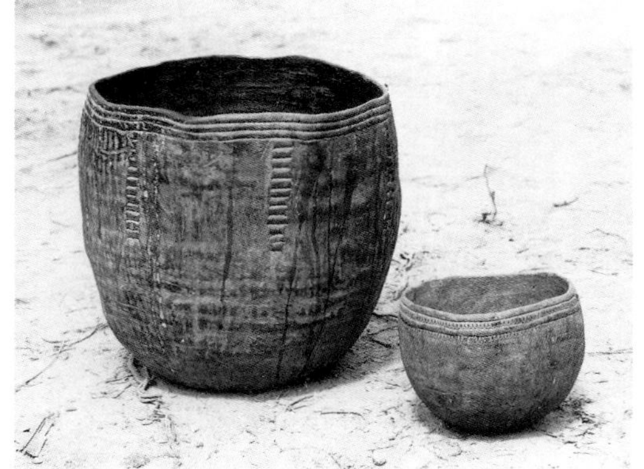

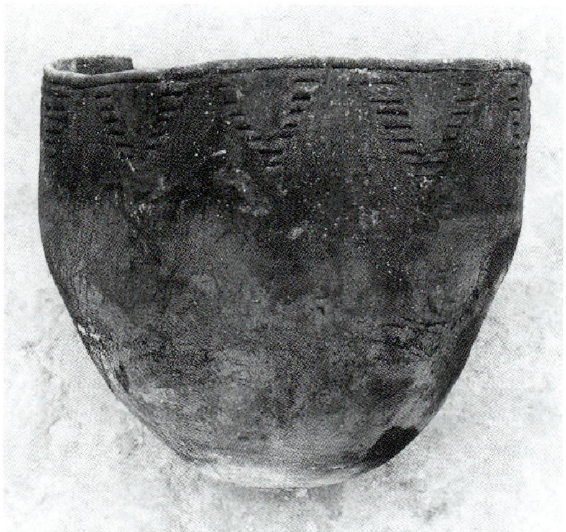

Fig. 9.131

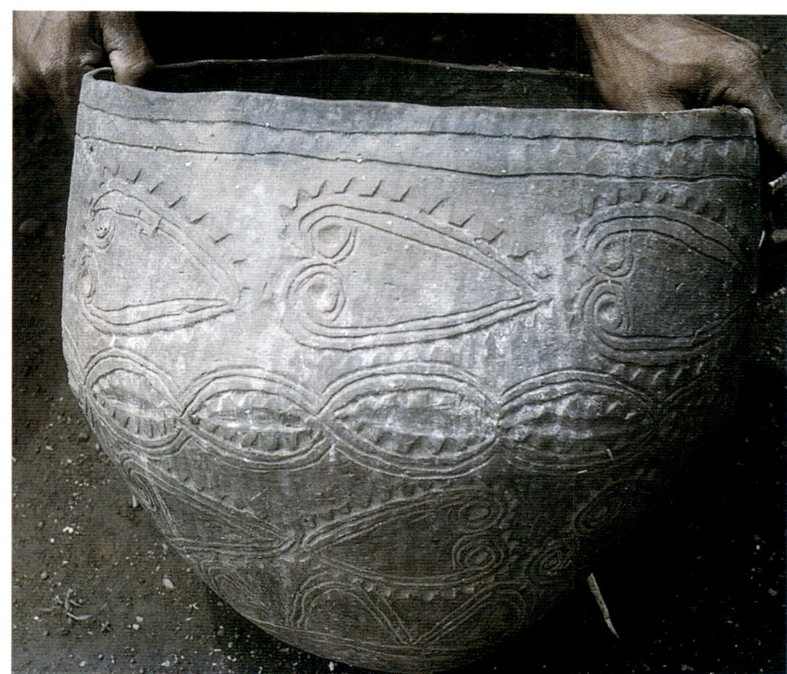

Fig. 9.132

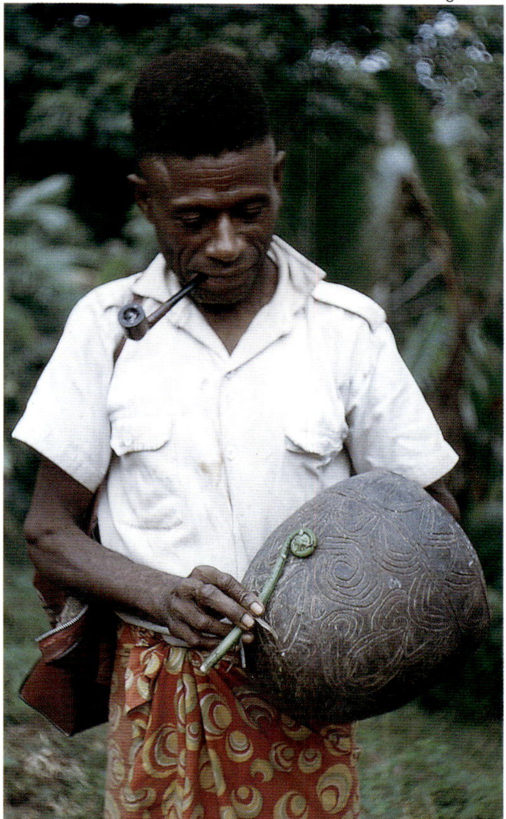

Fig. 9.133

plains. The people speak the Maprik dialect but they are geographically close to the Wosera area to the south-west. The potters claim to have made many pots in the past. Both men and women made pots and the men decorated vessels used in cult activities. Clay is available but can be worked only in the wet season. As in the rest of the Abelam area, the coil method is used and coils are started on a small piece of 'pangal'; when the vessel attains a particular height, the sides are bound by a string tied around the top for support. Designs are carved with a sharp piece of wood or a pig's tooth. They are painted for special feasts, not only yam displays but now also Christian holidays such as Easter and Christmas.

Types of vessels found at Kwimbu and nearby hamlets include an Abelam type wide-mouthed, rough, blackened cooking vessel; ceremonial vessels, round-based, ellipsoid or straight-sided, tall and with design elements similar to those of vessels seen at Yenigo; and serving bowls or cult vessels shaped and decorated like the Wosera *kwam* (serving bowl).

The village people readily identified two pots traded across from the Wosera and confirmed that the other Wosera type vessels were copied by them down to the last detail. On the other hand, a distinctive type of face found carved on the ceremonial vessels is said to be a Kwimbu type and the Wosera people copied it.

At Wagupma village a survey revealed five 'haus tambaran' pots reported to have been made there

Fig. 9.131
Typical decoration of an Abelam cooking pot.

Fig. 9.132
Abelam serving bowl, *amagat,* seen at Gwynyingi village.

Fig. 9.133
Ramus, from Yenigo village, showing a fern frond, a model for one of the typical decorations of this area.

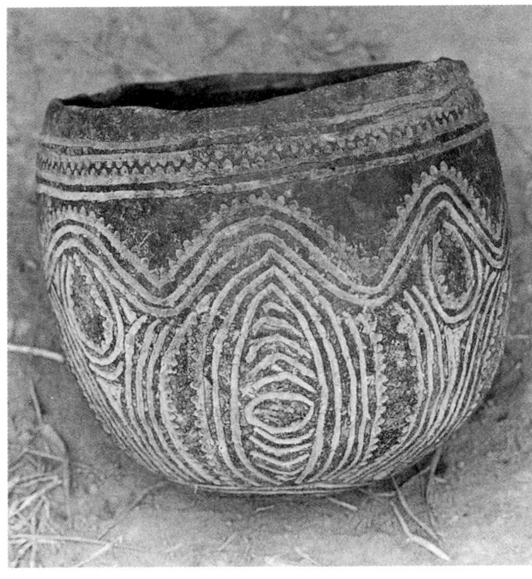

Fig. 9.134
Abelam serving bowl, *amagat,* said to be made at Yenigo, collected at Yangisagu.

in the past. Three of the vessels have a common design element: a geometric pattern of opposed triangles forming a diamond shape, inscribed within which are the face of a 'masalai', a herringbone lozenge shape possibly representing 'a man's belly' or a larva (this motif is used throughout the inland Sepik area), and a series of circles. While two of the vessels are similar in shape – open bowls – the third example is most unusual and is similar to one of the major 'problem' pots found in this area (fig. 9.139). This pot was collected in the early 1970s at Paparam by a Sydney dealer travelling along the Maprik-Wewak road. It is now in the Basel Museum collection. Although the Wagupma example has many similar characteristics one example does not offer enough data to assign a provenance to the Basel vessel (figs 9.137-9.139).

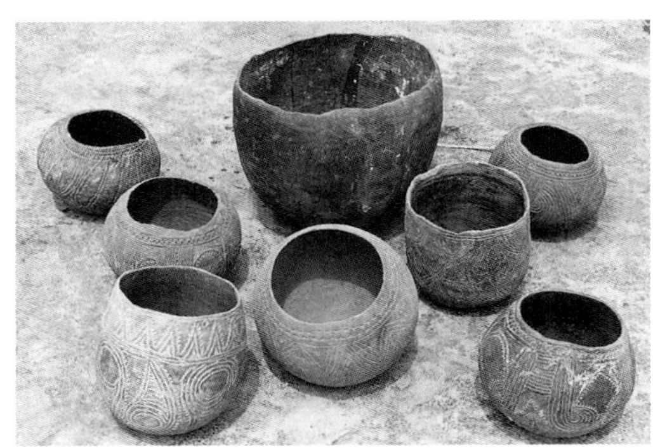

Fig. 9.135
Group of local and traded pots, Kwimbu village.

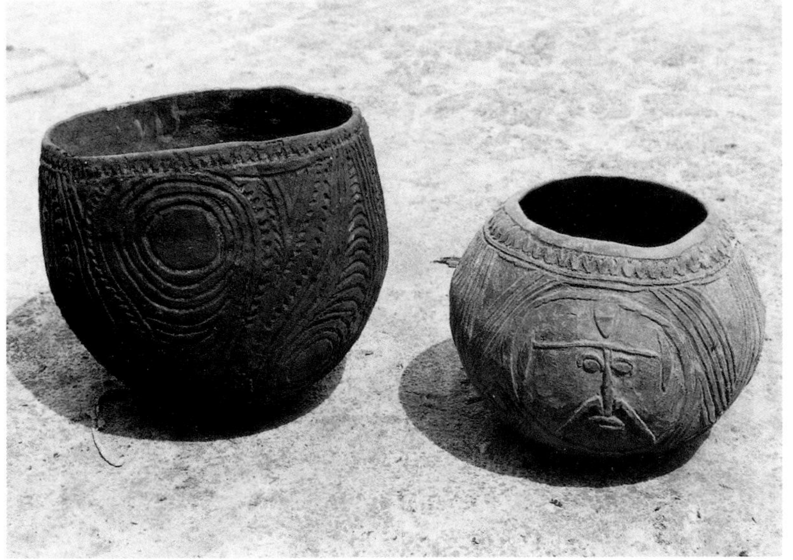

Fig. 9.136
Two serving bowls, *amagat,* one with the 'Kwimbu face'. Largest *h* 23 cm.

Abelam (Wosera)

The main pot producing villages of the Wosera are Saragum, Stapigum (two of the largest villages), Isogum and Numbungai. Cooking pots only are also made from local clay by women at Apambi and Jibako in the west Wosera. At one time pots were made in most of the Wosera villages. Saragum village owns extensive clay deposits and sells clay to potters from other villages.

The clay, *kupma*, is naturally sandy in texture and may be gathered by men or women. Traditionally women made the cooking pots, called ake, and the ceremonial vessels, *kwam*, while men carved designs and painted the *kwam*. The spiral coil technique is used. The decorated vessels were used in 'tambaran' and yam cult activities and for feasts and social ceremonies. Young male initiates, during their initiation period, ate only the 'white soup' made from coconut, taro and yam, served in the *kwam* which were kept in the 'haus tambaran'. Strict sanctions and distinctions relating to the *kwam* have died out because this highly decorated type of vessel is now made for commercial sale but taboos concerning its manufacture are respected and men still decorate and paint the vessels. Another clay object traditionally used in cult activities and made, decorated and painted by the men is a small (about 9 to 12 centimetres in diameter) whistle, *kutagwa*, with two holes in the top and

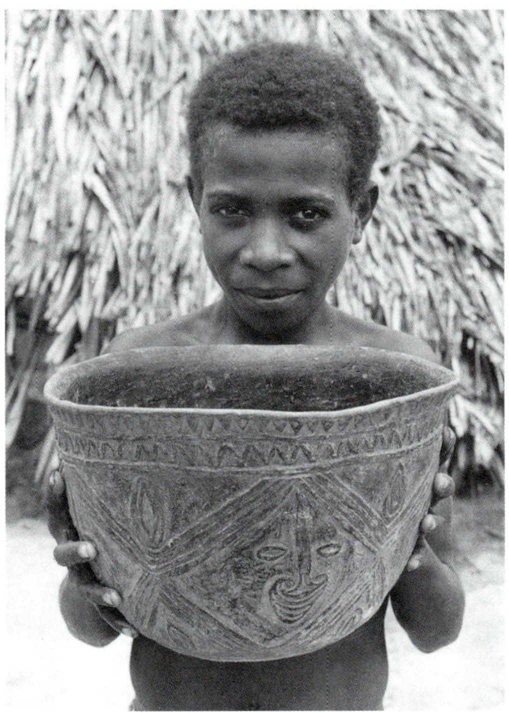

Fig. 9.137

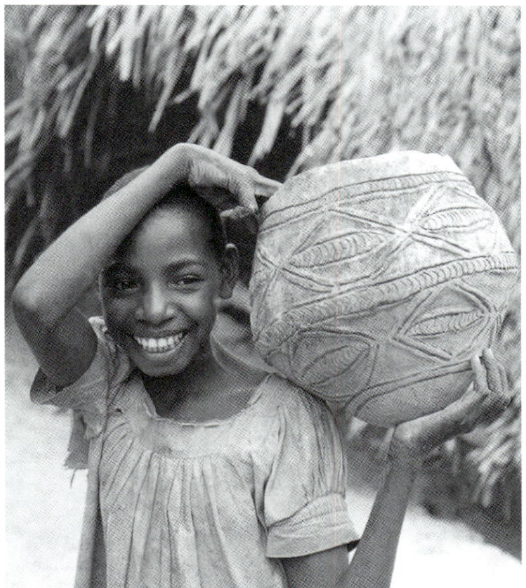

Fig. 9.138

Figs 9.137, 9.138
Two large Abelam serving bowls, *amagat*, Wagupma village. Compare with fig. 9.139.

Fig. 9.137

Fig. 9.138

side. The neighbouring Abelam people use a similar object made from a nut and richly decorated. These whistles can be round or oval. They are now made commercially but also are still used ceremonially (fig. 9.142). Sago storage vessels are not made here; sago is stored in a disused cooking pot which is called *djamba* ('an old pot').

The cooking pots are undecorated, rough in shape, round-based and of medium depth. They have wide openings and direct rims. The *kwam* are all the same shape but vary in size; the average height is 15 centimetres and the diameter of the mouth always measures less than the height. They are spherical or ovoid with narrow mouths. Men decorate the vessels in the leather-hard stage and use either a bamboo implement or flying fox bone, *kwa'antz*, to carve and incise designs which cover the entire visible surface of the pot. The base, which is not seen, is left uncarved and is generally defined by a simple circular band. The rim is always distinctly defined by a formal border consisting of a contrasting final smoothed coil followed by a longitudinal zig-zag line offset by one or more longitudinal running bands.

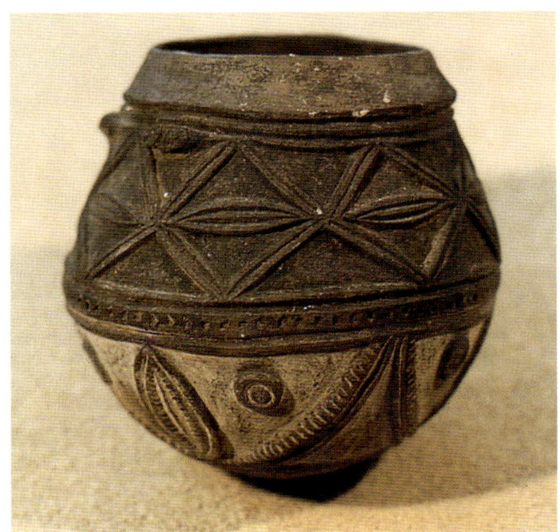

Fig. 9.139
Ceremonial vessel from Paparam village, *h* 22 cm.

The fundamental part of the design generally consists of figurative elements in a bifold or quatrefold arrangement, offset by scrolls, ovals, diamonds or triangular elements, giving the surface a static quality. The figurative motif represents the face of 'man', or of the spirit *ngwalandu* (butterfly) or a bird, usually the white cockatoo, *wama*, or the black cockatoo, *mange*. When questioned, different potters will identify the oval 'face' as man. Scrolls and geometric elements are used both to frame the 'face' design and to fill space. Interpretations of these motifs differ but the repertoire includes various types of insects, insect tracks, insect larvae, stars, moons and leaves of various trees

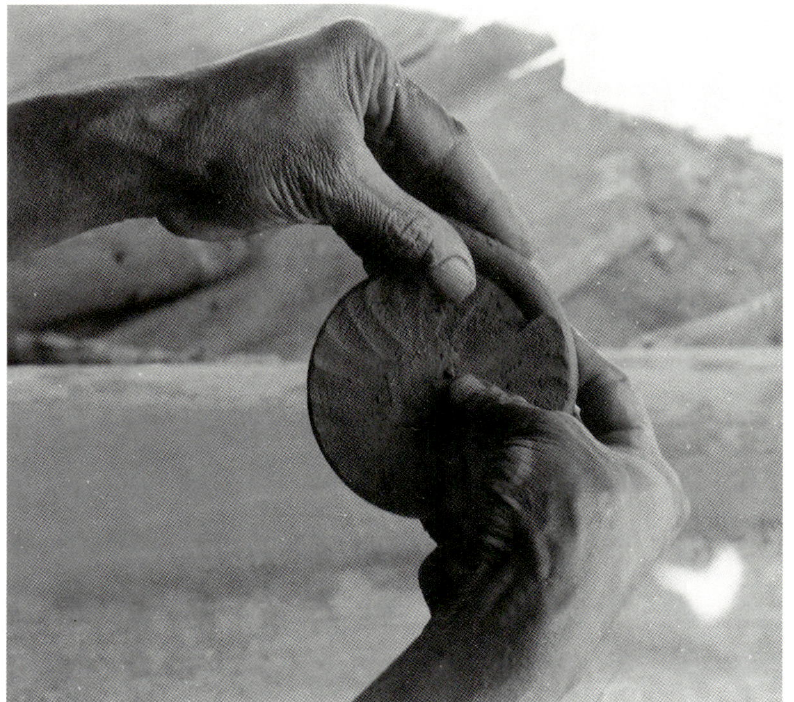

Fig. 9.140

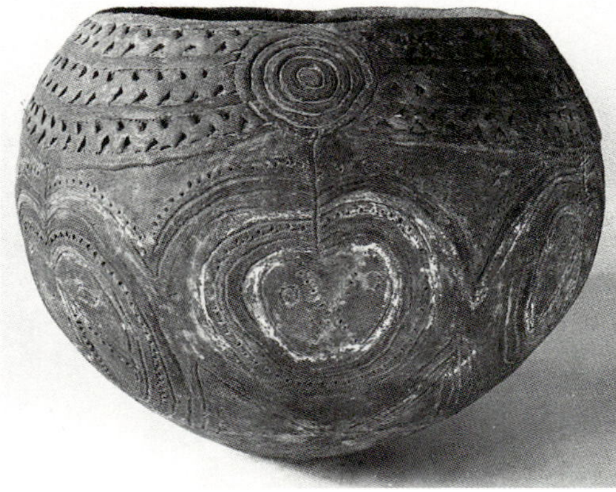

Fig. 9.141

Now, commercial paints are obtained from trade stores. The frayed end of a strong plant fibre is used as a brush. The entire surface of Wosera pots is coloured; the natural ground colour is not used as an element in the colour scheme as is done in other Sepik areas where only the portion carved away is painted (figs 9.144, 9.147).

Fig. 9.140
Wosera potter bonding coils at the base of a pot.

Fig. 9.141
Kwam, an eating bowl from the Wosera area, *h* 13 cm.

Fig. 9.142
Ocarina, *kutagwa,* made by Bengamali of Saragum village, North Wosera area, *h* 17 cm.

Fig. 9.143
Cooking pots, *ake*. The one on the right is drying.

Fig. 9.144
Typical north Wosera area serving bowl, *kwam, h* 19 cm.

and plants. One interesting version of the *kwam* which is very popular with tourists is decorated with applied disc-shaped 'faces', usually two, placed bilaterally; these have prominent beak-like noses, mouths, holes for eyes and a horizontal ridge depicting a headdress defining the forehead. It is believed that this type of *kwam* is a recent innovation, possibly influenced by Aibom. Innovative decorative features have multiplied in the last three to four years due to increased interest by expatriate buyers. An example shows the rendering of four figures, male and female, with exposed genitalia and head, arms, torso, legs and feet carved horizontally around the middle of the pot. The vessel must be rotated fully in order to view the complete design; in more traditional patterns two or four viewpoints are sufficient (figs 9.145, 9.146).

Kwam are always painted in red, black, yellow and white. Traditionally, black came from charcoal with a leaf binder added, white from river stones; red from various sources – a paste from the red seeds of a shrub, *Bixa orellana*, from river stones and from the burned stem of a tree that grows in the bush near water; and yellow from lumps of clay.

Southern Wosera

In the grass country to the south-east of the Wosera pottery area are some isolated villages which also belong to the Abelam (Wosera) language. Nala is about 12 kilometres from Stapigum; further south

Fig. 9.142

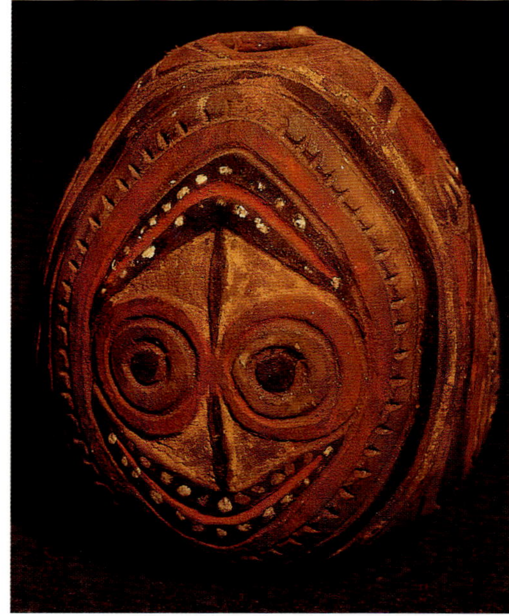

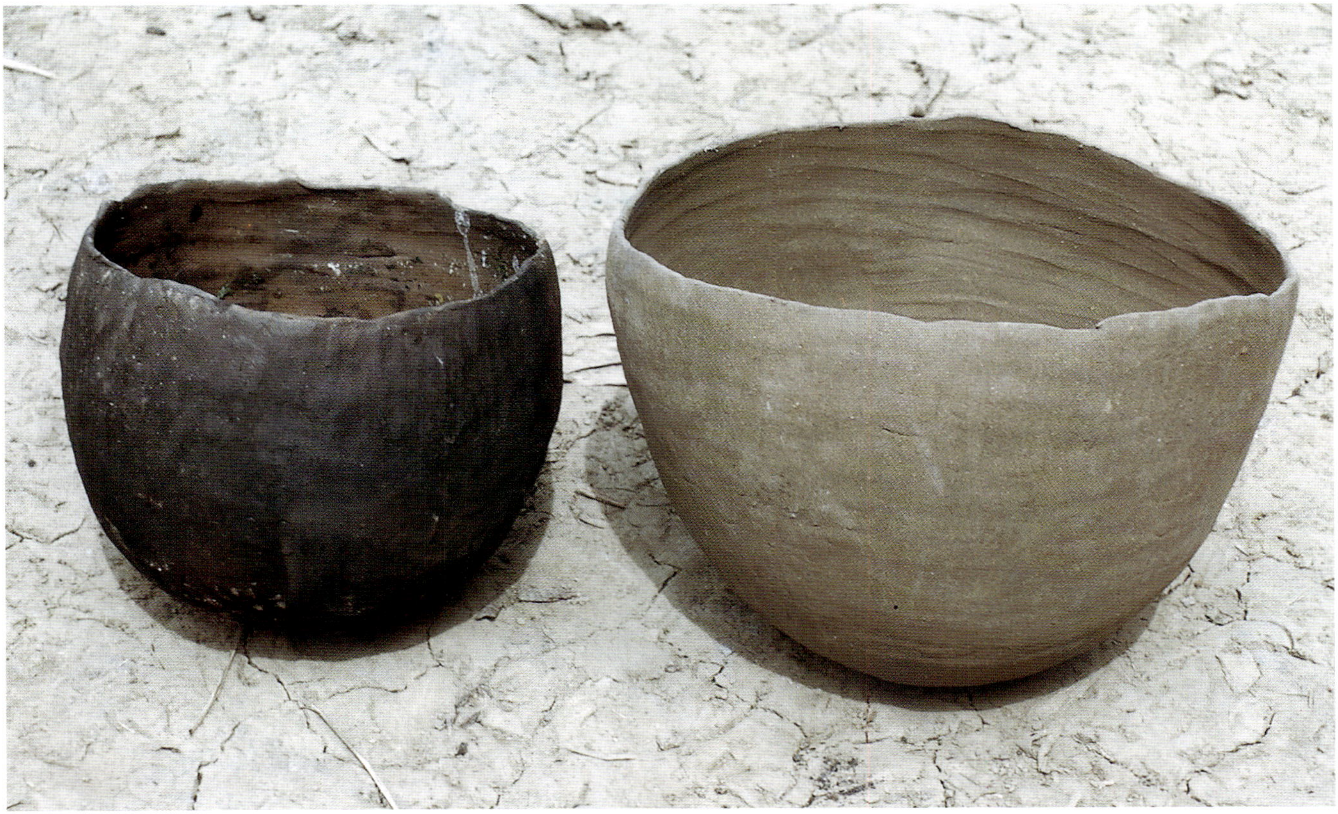

Fig. 9.143

are Kupmabit 1 and 2; Mangul 1 and 2 are further south again, close to the Sawos people. Informants in the Wosera cited Nala and Kunjingini as making pottery in the past but claimed their pots were unfortunately inferior because the clay used was a red earth containing white flecks which produced flaws and thus weak pots.

A wide range of pots was seen; several different types were said to have been made here, making it (as with other Abelam areas) difficult to establish a definite style. At Kupmabit there was one type of vessel, a deep conical pot with lugs, which has not been seen elsewhere. Decoration covers the pot from about 3 centimetres from the top to near the base, which finishes in a smoothed circular area; a ridge marks the start of the decoration at the top and above this the outside rim is smooth. The decoration of geometric and curvilinear elements is similar to that seen on other Abelam and Yangoru Boiken pots. Two lugs are placed about 3 centimetres below the top ridge and about 12 centimetres

Fig. 9.144

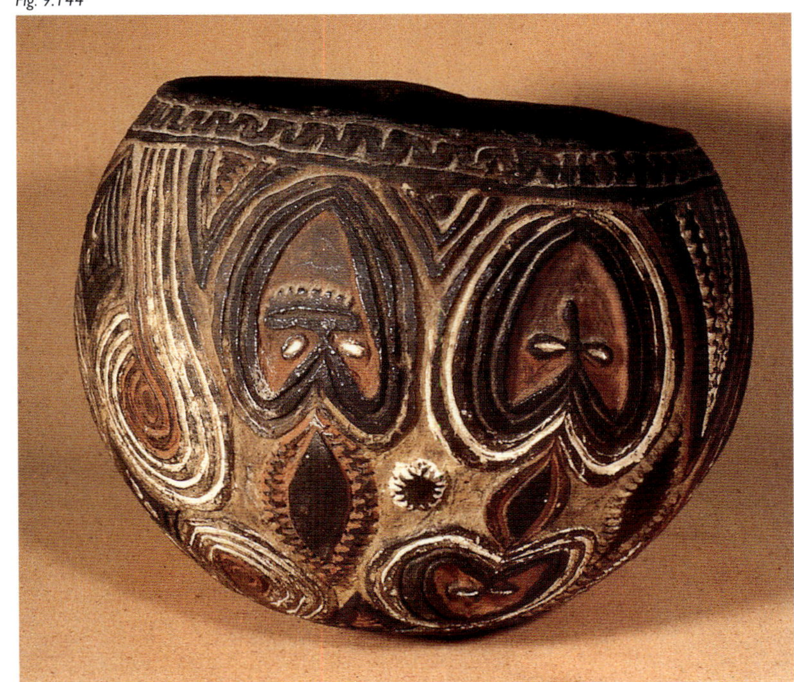

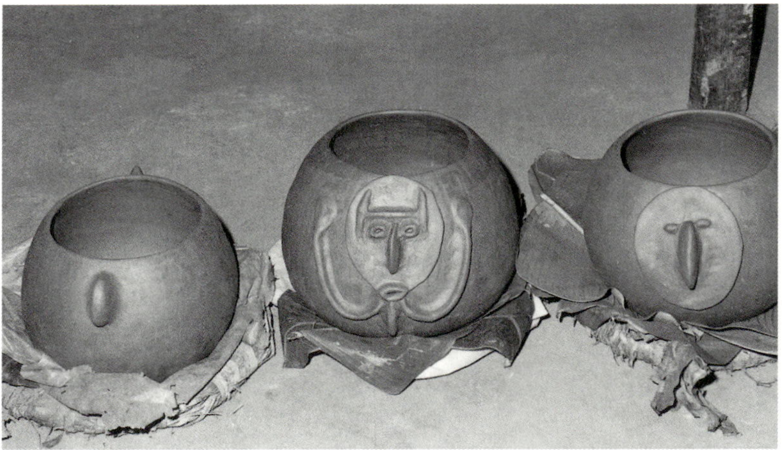

Fig. 9.145

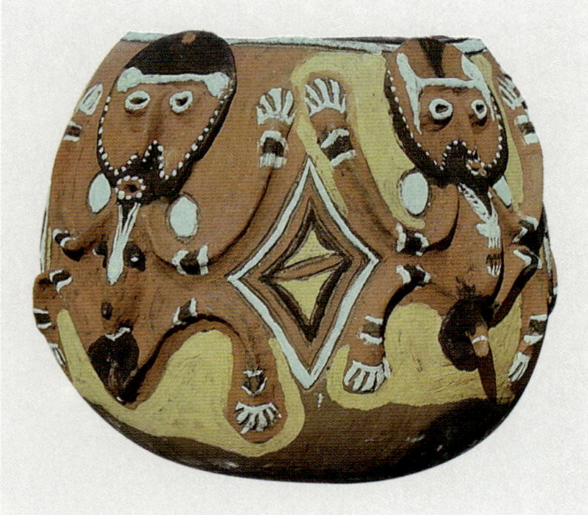

Fig. 9.146

Fig. 9.145
Pots made by Bangamali and his wife at Maprik High School.

Fig. 9.146
Innovative decoration of applied figures on *kwam*, Wosera area, *h* 28.5 cm.

apart; there is a hole through the centre of each. The Yangoru Boiken vessels had lugs that sprang directly from the ridge but here they are placed below the ridge (fig. 9.149).

Two or three pots in the Wosera style were also claimed to have been locally made. These could have been locally made either in the traditional style or as copies of Wosera pots or they could have been traded in from the Wosera. It was acknowledged that other Wosera pots in use here had come from the Wosera. There were some Aibom pots which had been purchased at Membei, near the Tolembi Catholic mission. Other pots of interest were two bowls, fairly deep, round-based, open-mouthed, covered with curvilinear designs and believed to have come from Slei, the Sawos pot making village to the south.

The Mangul people claim to have made pots in the past but the variety of types found makes it difficult to draw any conclusions at this stage.

Fig. 9.147
Detail of ceremonial *kwam*, Mikau village, Wosera area.

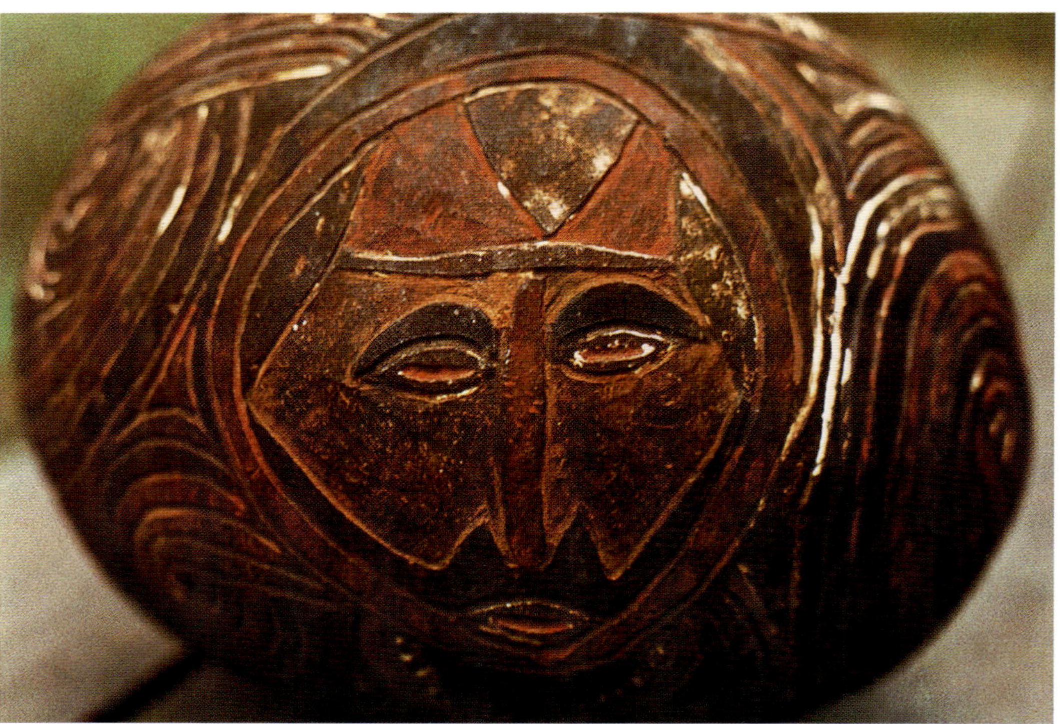

Kwanga

Beyond the territory of the Abelam and the Wosera, to the north-west and occupying the Torricelli foothills and mountains live a number of distinct dialect groups who have been pushed steadily north-west by the proliferating Abelam people. The Kwanga group is notable for its nucleus of pot producing villages located several kilometres north of Saragum. While Kwanga pots share many formal aspects with pots from the Wosera and Abelam they are nonetheless sufficiently distinctive to be classified as a definite style province. Kwanga pots are made in the following villages: Kamanakwor, Sunuhu, Apangai, Asanakor, Inakor and Yubanakor, all belonging to the Yubanakor dialect. Other dialect groups within the Kwanga language do not produce pots. Donald Tuzin, an American anthropologist, has made a thorough study of pot making at Kamanakwor village during a prolonged period of field work in the region. The Abelam culture has had an impact on neighbouring groups and this can be seen in cultural affinities, especially artistic expression and vocabulary of forms and design motifs seen on paraphernalia used in the 'tambaran' and yam cults.

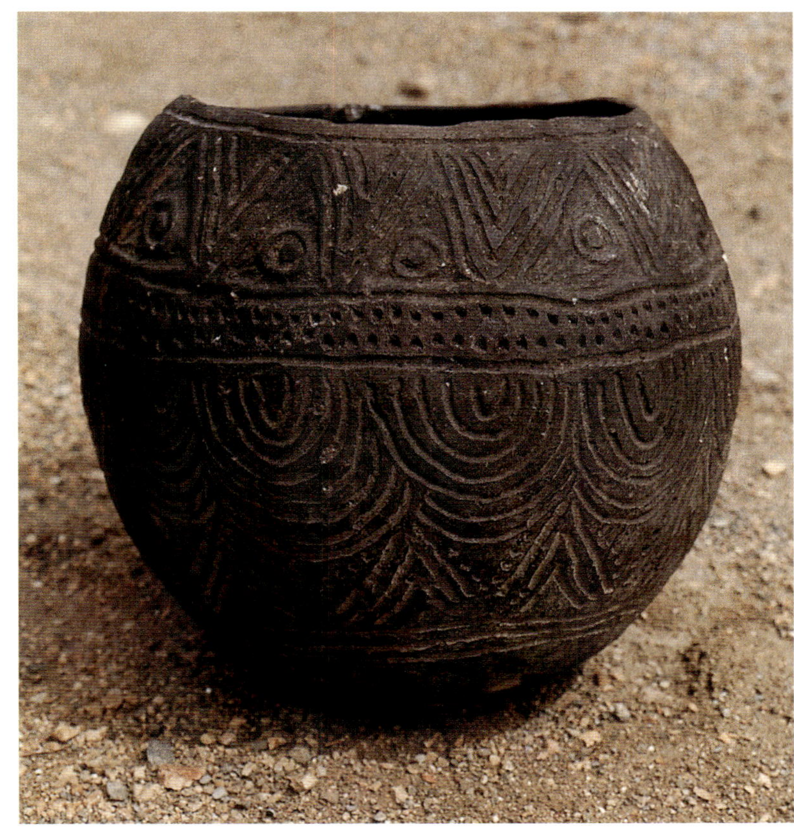

Fig. 9.148
Serving bowl, *kwam*, collected at Mangul village (provenance unknown), *h* 23 cm.

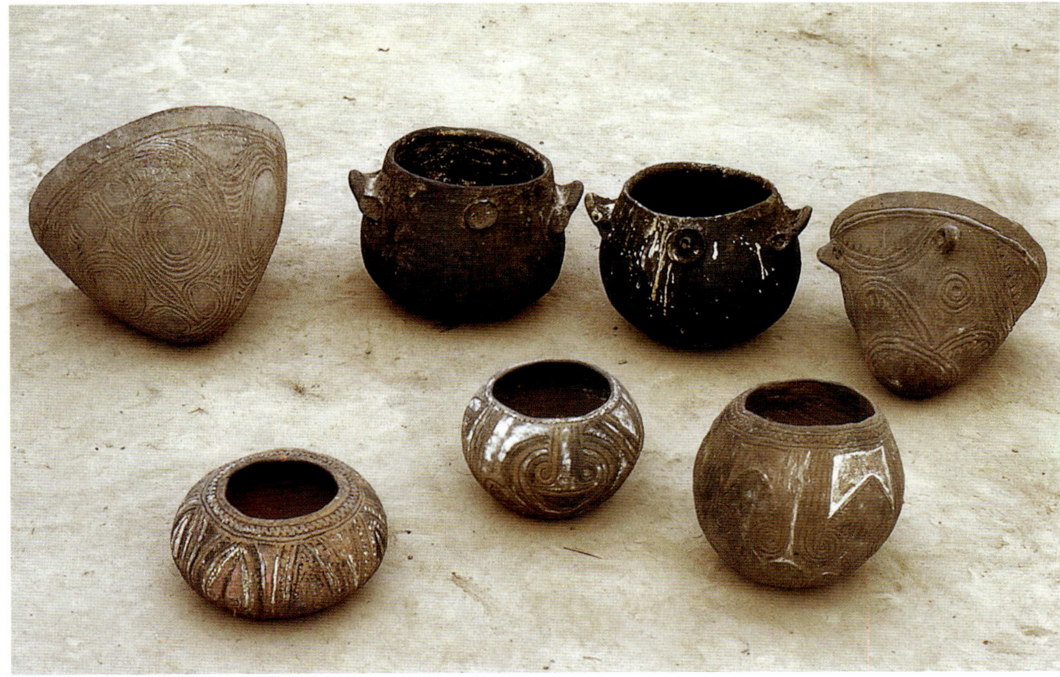

Fig. 9.149
Two Aibom cooking pots; (left) one old Kupmabit serving bowl, *kwam*, *h* 22 cm; (front) three north Wosera pots, Kupmabit village.

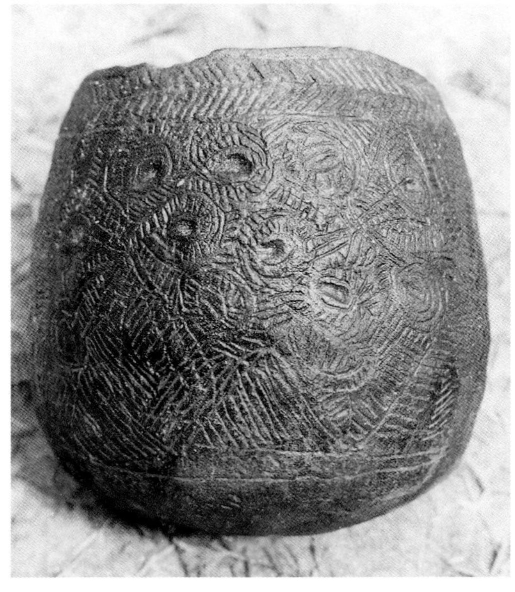

Fig. 9.150
Kwanga serving vessel from Sunuhu, seen at the Southern Arapesh village of Amahop.

The southern Arapesh live in the mountains north of the Kwanga. They do not make pottery but serve as middle-men, especially the villagers of Ilahita, for the distribution of Kwanga and Wosera vessels. Many 'Yubanakor' pots have been seen in the households of the Arapesh villages, Aperinga, Amahop, Balif, Bulamita and Wamsak. While most informants attributed their provenance to Ilahita or the direction of Ilahita, a few recognised the pots as originating in the Kamanakwor-Sunuhu region. On the other hand, informants in Bumbita and Bonahoi (Bumbita Arapesh language) claim to have made pots in the past. Examples of decorated serving/eating bowls seen in these villages have stylistic affinities with vessels from the Kwanga but are on the whole thicker-walled, more crudely shaped and less expertly decorated. A few older, very fine vessels were said to have come originally from the Kwanga. More information is required to determine whether the southern and Bumbita Arapesh ever did have a pot industry and, if so, to what extent. It is the authors' contention from the evidence of arbitrary household surveys that pot making techniques were adopted from neighbouring people (Abelam, Wosera and the Kwanga). There is an abundance of local clay deposits but the craft never really developed into a viable industry and eventually gave way to the importation of the superior, thinner-walled ware.

The Kamanakwor people manufacture two types of vessels. *Hungwe* is a cooking pot with a pointed base, outward-flaring walls and a wide mouth. The decoration is crude and simple, usually consisting in a few exposed coils along the outer rim. Each household owns several *hungwe*, which are medium-sized (about 30 centimetres high). Larger pots (about 60 centimetres high) are kept in the 'haus tambaran' and used to cook the 'white soup' made during initiation and other cult activities. The second type of vessel, called a *papi*, is an eating bowl. It is a simple, ellipsoid vessel, with a pointed or rounded base and a restricted orifice. An average-sized bowl (about 15 centimetres high) used by one person is generally shaped like a coconut. This eating bowl becomes predominant as a style north-west of Maprik, the Abelam-Sepik style boundary. The ellipsoid shape is introduced by the Wosera pots but they are larger and heavier and thus have less affinity with the coconut form than do the lighter, thinner-walled and smaller versions of the Kwanga and Kombio-Yambes examples. The eating bowls of these two groups are similar to the intricately incised coconut bowls made by the Abelam. Both types of vessels are used as individual eating bowls.

The Kwanga *papi*, a large version approximately 30 centimetres high, is used by men in the haus tambaran'. A *papi* has no innate distinction as a

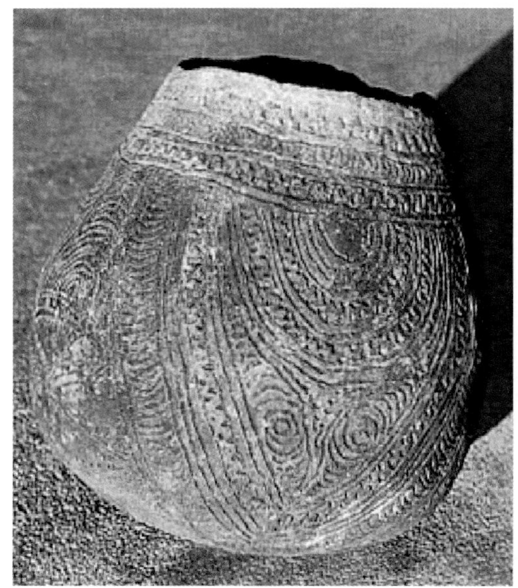

Fig. 9.151
Old Kwanga serving vessel, said to come from Sunuhu, at Amahop, *h* 22 cm.

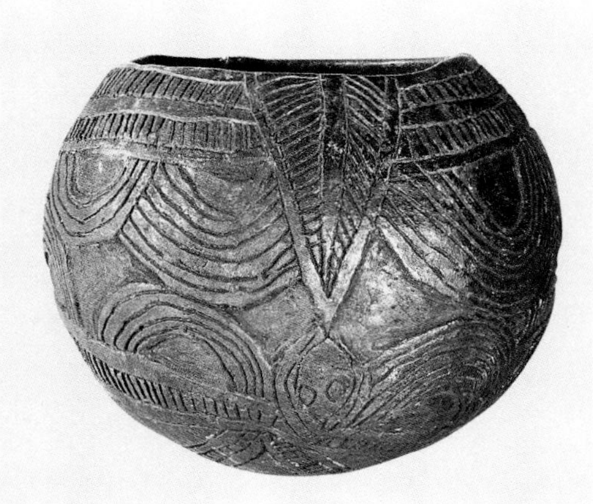

Fig. 9.152

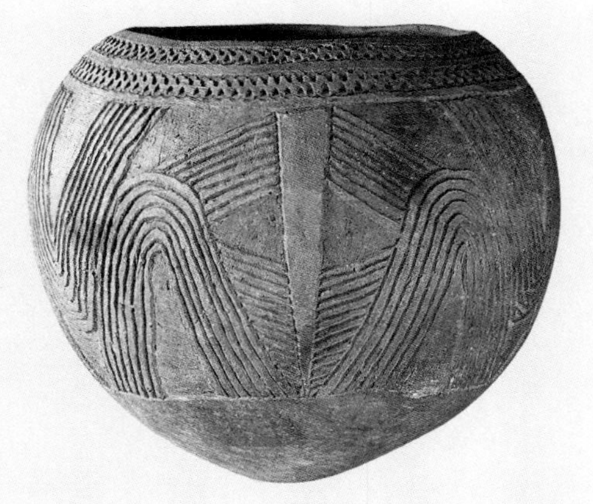

Fig. 9.153

Fig. 9.152
Eating vessel made at a Kwanga village, collected at Amahop, *h* 11 cm.

Fig. 9.153
Pot from Amahop, said to be made in the Ilahita area, *h* 19 cm.

ritual object until it has been used ceremonially, when it is painted in white, yellow and red and then set aside for future use in the cult house. It is always richly decorated in geometric, as opposed to curvilinear, patterns. The field of decoration covers the rim and the visible contour of the pot and generally stops where it will not be appreciated by a direct view. The base is not marked although it is defined by a horizontal band of repeated herringbone, waffle or scalloped patterns. The rim is bordered by a series of repeated patterns: herringbone, scallop or zig-zag. Between the rim and base area is a central zone which is decorated by triangular, diamond or spherical panels. A connotative analysis of these motifs is limited to naming separate elements of representation within the culture. Some of the major motifs were described as follows: the leaf-like motif inscribed in a triangle or oval, placed just under the direct rim and extending down the neck for 3 to 4 centimetres is called *mesgahape* which is the name of a tree with a long leaf (Kamanakwor pots are noted for this mark); a group of parallel lines called *obuarakawe* represents the wings of a black bush fowl; bands of parallel semicircular lines called *tebekumbo* represent the profile view of a man's leg. All of these designs are either clan markings or are connected to the 'tambaran'.

Women are the potters and the men mark the *papi* with a bamboo knife. The method of manufacture is coiling. After marriage women are taught to make pots by their husband's mother; men can make pots after they have gone through several grades of initiation. Clay is plentiful and there are two varieties, a yellow kind used for making the *bungwe* and a dark red rubble-free clay used for the *papi*. There are no taboos associated with gathering the clay except that it is woman's work

The coils measure about l centimetre in diameter and about 36 to 46 centimetres long and are started in the palm of the hand. As more coils are applied, the woman supports the growing pot in her lap; later it is transferred to a pandanus or banana leaf ring, still supported in her lap. Coils are smoothed from the top down. The knob or nipple base is not smoothed on cooking pots and serves as a distinctive feature. While the pots are drying they are carefully inspected for cracks, which are mended by a mixture of clay and the sticky milky sap from the breadfruit tree. Firings are multiple, four or five pots being fired together. Sago fronds are the only fuel used. These are laid in a criss-cross grid pattern,

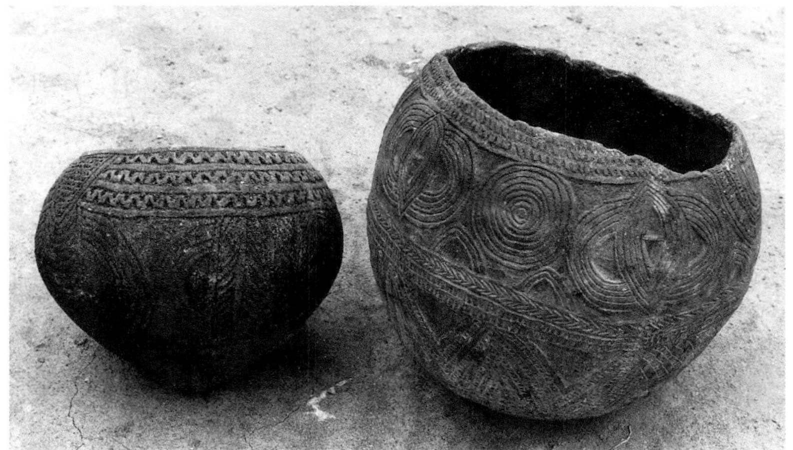

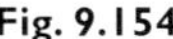

Fig. 9.154
Two pots, Bulamita village: (left) probably made at Kamanakor, *h* 16 cm; (right) possibly made at the Southern Arapesh village of Bulamita, *h* 24 cm.

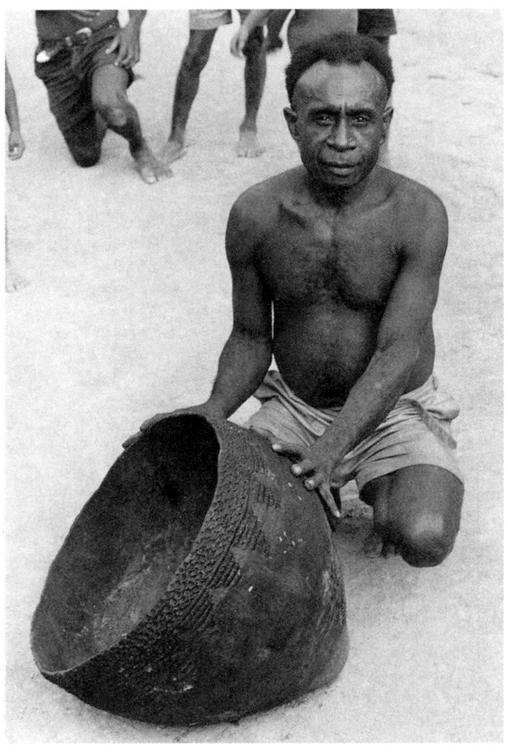

Fig. 9.155
Cooking vessel, *wil,* made by Nyiram Manggeyam, Meringe village, Kombio, *h* 43 cm.

the pots are placed on this and then more sago fronds are stacked around them. While the pots are still warm from the firing a sealing starch of yam and banana soup is rubbed over the surfaces. The vessels are then washed with a mixture of turmeric juice and ash, which leaves a slight reddish stain. The *papi* are painted by the men for ceremonies and the pigments are applied by finger.

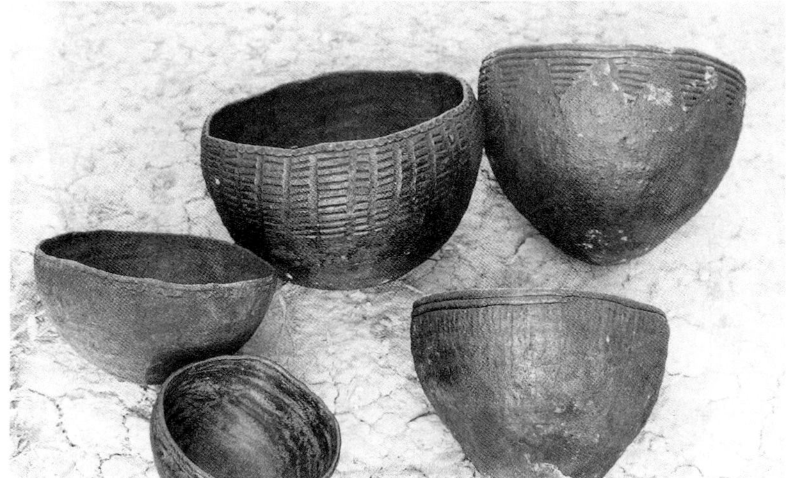

Fig. 9.156
Cooking pots, *malup* and *wil*, made in the Torricelli Mountains by the Kombio-Yambes-Urat people.

Pot making has decreased alarmingly in the last three years and informants say that, while all the older women know how to make pots, none of the younger wives has learned the craft. Also, there are only a few surviving older men who can still decorate the *papi*. Distribution of the Kwanga ware outside its own language group is limited to the Arapesh villages and does not appear to extend to the Abelam and Wosera peoples. To the north in the Torricelli Mountains, another style area becomes dominant, that of the Kombio-Yambes-Urim-Urat people.

Kombio-Yambes-Urim-Urat

Some of the most exquisite pots made in Papua New Guinea come from the people living in the foothills of the Torricelli Mountains north of Dreikikir. Positively identified as centres of pot making are the Kombio-speaking villages of Muyem, Meringe, Yaurang, Yalangel and Yakio, the Yambes-speaking village of Yambes and the Urim-speaking village of Kurungunam. The villagers of Musingwa and Nanaha who speak the Urat language live in close proximity to the Kombio people and make the same type of pottery. Informants claim that the Yambes people adopted the technique of pot making from their Kombio neighbours, as perhaps did the Urat people. There are about twenty-two more villages in the Kombio language group that have not been surveyed.

Pot making is declining although the efforts of a European living in Wewak have brought about a revival of activity in the Kombio villages near the Yassip Catholic mission. The potters are eager to sell the decorated eating bowls to collectors and dealers but marketing and packaging remain a problem. Also, the men who carve the designs are older now; they suffer from poorer eyesight and less surety of skill necessary for incising the intricate patterns.

There are only two types of vessel, a cooking pot, *malup* (Yambes language) or *wil* (Kombio-Urim language), made and decorated by women, and a serving/eating bowl, *kadruk* (Kombio-Urim language), made and decorated by men. The spiral coil technique is used. Very fine, thin coils about 30 centimetres long are rolled out on the thigh to form the *kubrak*; the coils used for the cooking vessels are slightly thicker. Different clays, *malup* (Yambes language), are used for making the cooking and eating bowls and this is readily visible; the fabric of the *kadrak* walls is fine, free of grit and always highly polished in appearance; the *malup* vessels are rougher in texture, with gravel-sized pieces of rubble showing. There are two characteristic shapes of the *malup*: a pointed-based, wide-mouthed conical pot, and a more rounded-based, hemispherical pot usually shallower than the pointed-base variety. There are modifications to each of these shapes. Generally the decoration of the *malup* consists of a border around the top edge formed from several exposed coils marked by finger or stick drags and creating alternating longitudinal, smoothed lines with the horizontal patterns formed by the coils. The unbonded coils can also be marked with rows of indentations formed by the fingertips or smoothed to form triangular or zig-zag patterns, *mutuangai*, around the top. When fingertip impressions are combined with finger drag marks the decoration is called *aikuarel*. In a few examples, especially on larger cooking pots, these decorations are combined in rows which extend almost half way down the vessel. Coils themselves, whether used to form the pot or to decorate it, are called *malupipman*. (All are Kombio language terms.) The shape and style of decoration on the pots having three or four exposed coils and marked by finger drag marks closely resemble the *gelatau* of the Yangoru Boiken. It is probably that there has been some cross influence in the past but only archaeological evidence will be able to elucidate the true origin.

The serving/eating bowls are remarkably light thin-walled and spherical with rounded bases and restricted mouths. Usually the diameter of the mouth is the same as the height of the vessel. An average-sized soup bowl is about 13 centimetres high. They repeat the shape of a coconut and some of the decorative motifs and overall schemes are used on the intricately incised coconut bowls made by the Abelam people. Designs are incised on the leather-hard vessel with a flying fox bone, a sago thorn or a piece of wire, thus accounting for the fineness and precision of the draughtsmanship.

Among those pots surveyed there were few exceptions to the rule that no two schematic designs are repeated. The repertoire of design motifs and elements is limited but the ingenious handling of various combinations by the individual potters makes each vessel unique. There is as much variety amongst the Yambes-Kombio eating serving bowls as there is amongst the Sawos vessels.

In general, the field of decoration extends from the rim to the centre point of the base; in other words, the entire area of the vessel serves as the decorative zone, as at Kolwat. The curvature of the bowl has not been a major consideration of the artist. The vessel must be viewed from the side, the top and the bottom to take in the full subtlety of its design (unlike the Koiwat vessels, where the entire decorative scheme can be understood by everting the cone-shaped pot and viewing it from its base point). The overall decorative scheme is both linear and curvilinear; major elements of offset

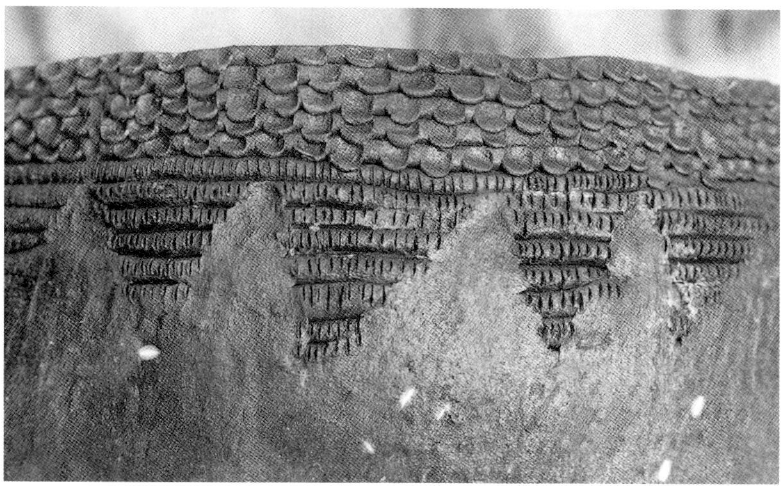

Fig. 9.157
Detail of decoration on the Meringe cooking vessel (fig. 9.155).

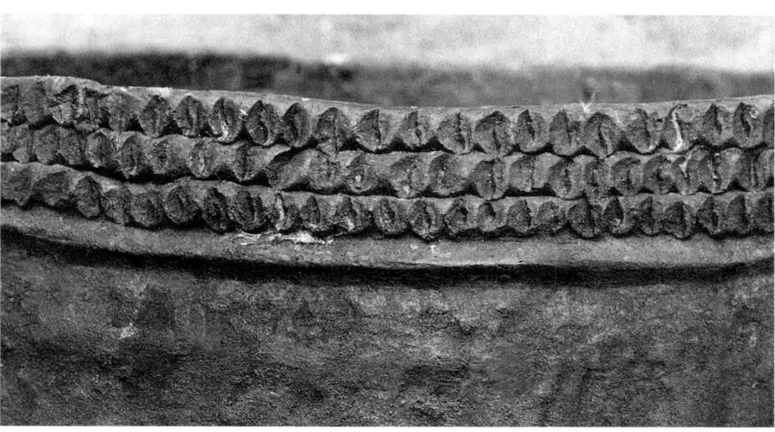

Fig. 9.158
Detail of decoration on a Yangoru Boiken cooking pot, *gelawo*. Compare with fig. 9.157.

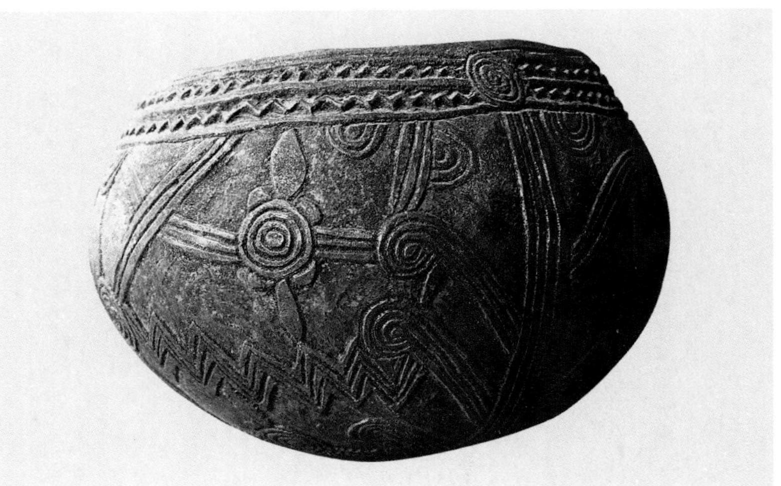

Fig. 9.159
Urim eating bowl, *kudruk*, collected at Kurungunam village. Compare decoration with Kwoma pot (fig. 9.6) and Wosera pot (fig. 9.141).

Fig. 9.160
A very thin walled Kombio eating bowl, *kudruk*, from Yaurang village, *h* 17 cm, diam. of mouth also 17 cm.

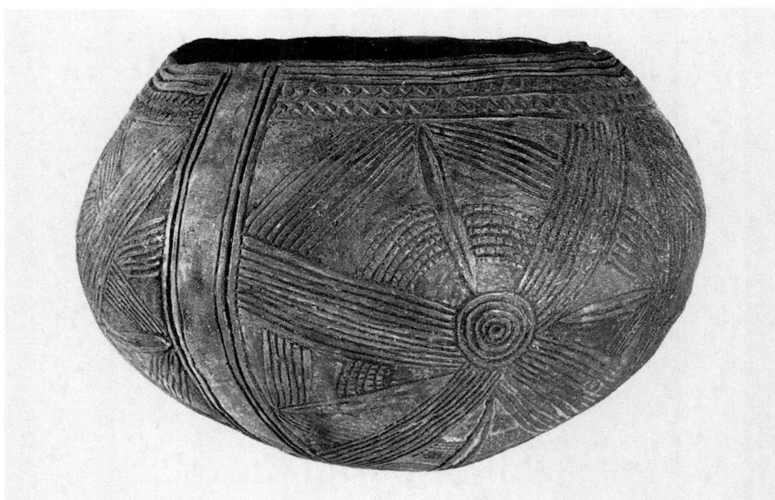

bands of parallel lines radiate from the base and extend to the bottom edge of the linear band bordering the rim. Tangential bands dissect the major bands, forming a series of minor complex areas where the fields are filled with motifs in the forms of multiple circles, ovals, volutes and scrolls.

The motifs, other than the positive bands of parallel lines, were named as follows: a bean shape with zig-zag outlines is a kind of insect, *tikinan*; a multi-circle, *yambap*, is described as an eye or the leaf of a tree; a scroll formed from parallel lines, *sombanggl*, is the unfurled, newly formed frond of a fern (this form has universal interpretation on Abelam and Boiken pots). In all but a few examples, the linear division of the vessel into rough geometric panels – parallelograms, triangles, diamonds – provides fields for these motifs. The subdivision of space is complex, the symmetry of the main elements is oblique. A feeling of motion is imparted by the use of parallel linear elements which seem to rotate with the shape of the vessel, by the unbalanced quality resulting from the oblique position of minor linear elements and by the repetition of elements and motifs. Most examples have elaborate rim borders, usually 3 to 4 centimetres wide, made up of combinations of longitudinal bands, ticked lines, herringbone designs, notched sawtooth designs or bands of running scallops or zig-zags. The base view often shows a circle or rough parallelogram with radiating linear elements which form the principal panels or zones, similar to a starfish form.

A brief analysis of the elements of design is attempted using two vessels as examples. The first vessel, found at Yaklik hamlet (close to Kurungunam) in the Urim group, is unusual in the symmetrical arrangement of elements in a geometrical overall pattern. Viewed from the base, a perfect circle made up of four linear elements is inscribed within a five-pointed star, the apex of which is the circle and the points of which extend half way up the vessel walls. Each of the five points of the star, actually five triangular fields, contains a separate motif including three circular forms, *yambap*, one oval-shaped, *tikinam*, and one bar made up of seven pricked longitudinal lines. This schematic pattern can be seen to be repeated when the vessel is viewed from the top. The border rim, made up of six longitudinal lines, repeats the circle of the base and the points of a five-pointed star, containing five triangular fields, extend down to within 2 centimertres of the base star. Thus the space between the emergence of the two stars becomes a plain dark area of a longitudinal running band (2 centimetres wide); the triangular spaces are filled by simple geometric and curvilinear motifs, but three of them are subdivided by linear bands forming a diamond in the centre and two triangles at the top (figs 9.161-9.166).

In contrast to the Yaklik vessel's precise geometric and symmetrical design is a vessel from Yambes, illustrating a more casual and less orderly handling of spatial relations between primary elements and

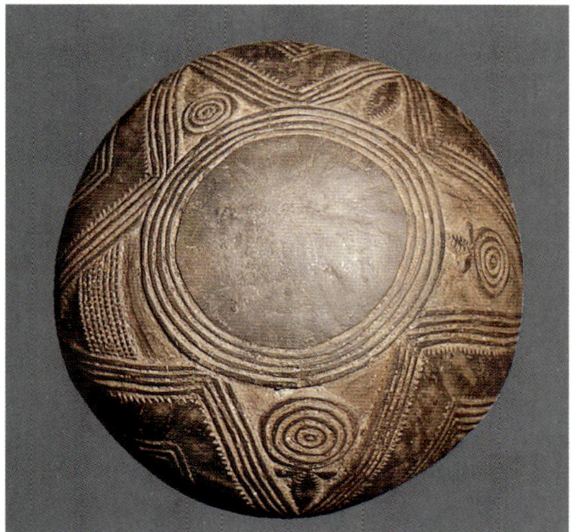
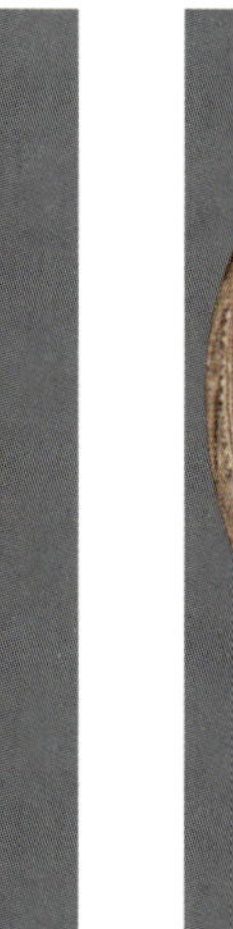

Fig. 9.161

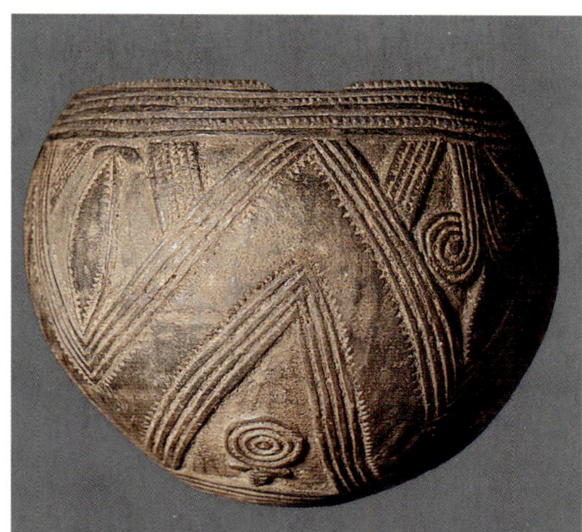
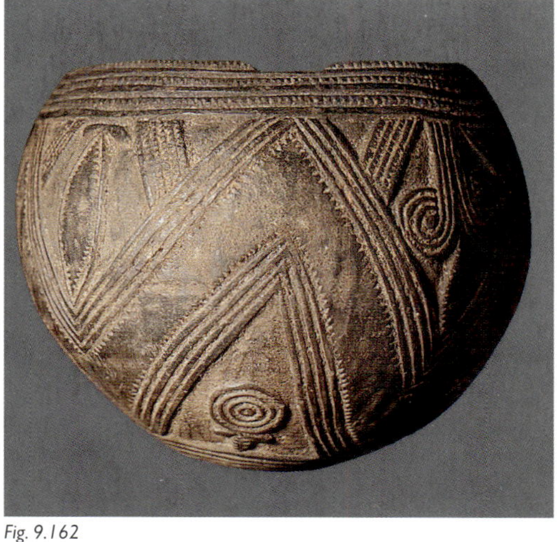

Fig. 9.162

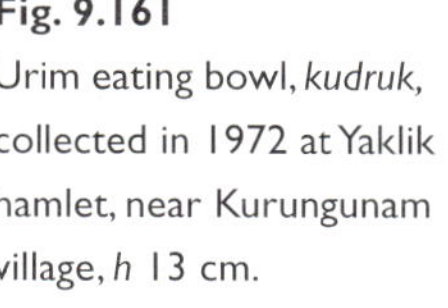

Fig. 9.161
Urim eating bowl, *kudruk*, collected in 1972 at Yaklik hamlet, near Kurungunam village, *h* 13 cm.

Figs 9.162 to 9.166
Details of fig. 9.161: fig. 9.163 shows *sambanggal* and *tikinan* designs; fig. 9.164 shows *yambap* design.

Fig. 9.162

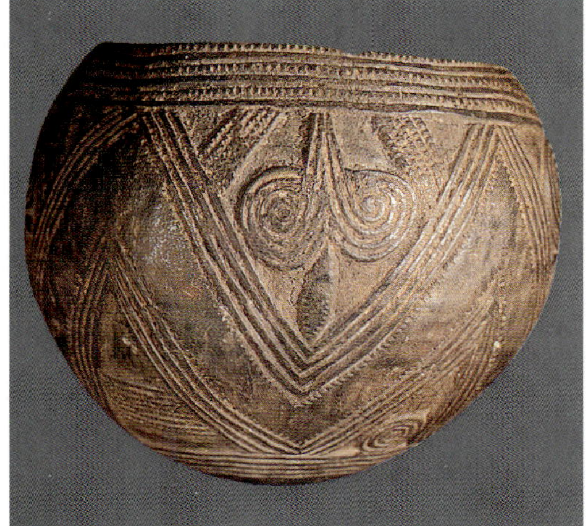

Fig. 9.163

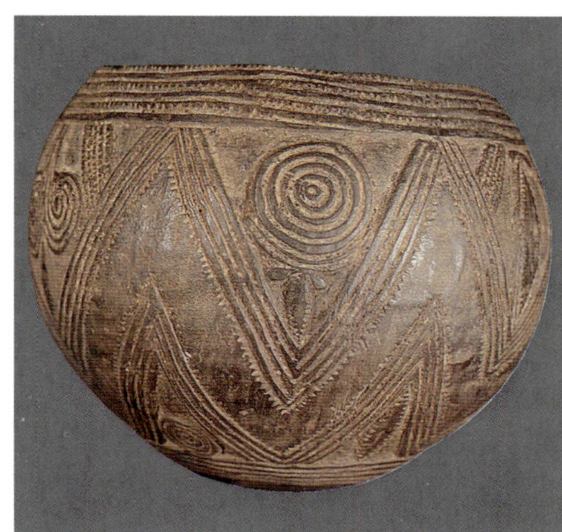

Fig. 9.164

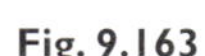

Fig. 9.163

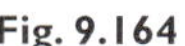

Fig. 9.164

Fig. 9.165

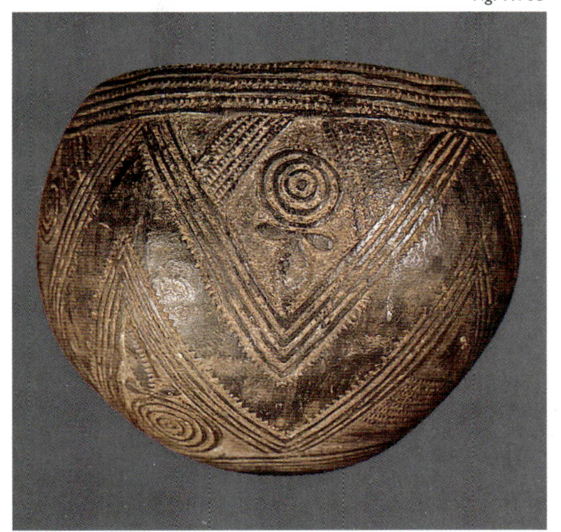

Fig. 9.166

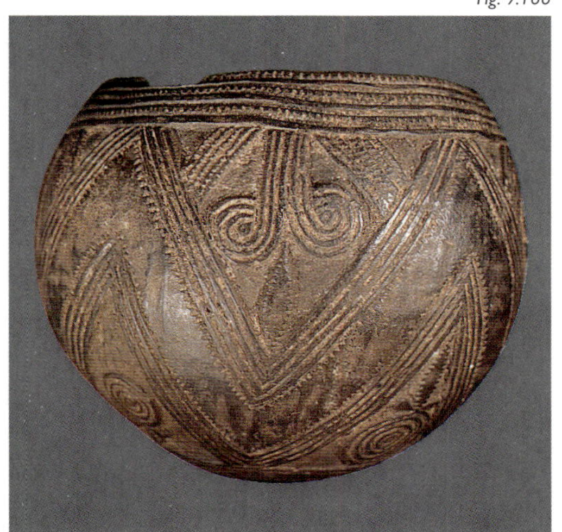

Fig. 9.165

Fig. 9.166

Fig. 9.167
A very thin-walled eating bowl from Yambes village, *h* 20 cm.

Figs 9.168 to 9.169
Compare decoration of shields and pot (fig. 9.167).

Fig. 9.168
Detail of decoration on shield from Dreikikir area.

Fig. 9.169
Shield, collected near Dreikikir, 1972.

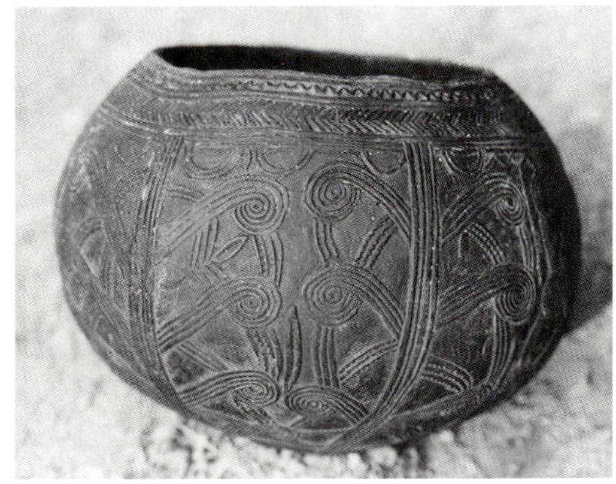

Fig. 9.167

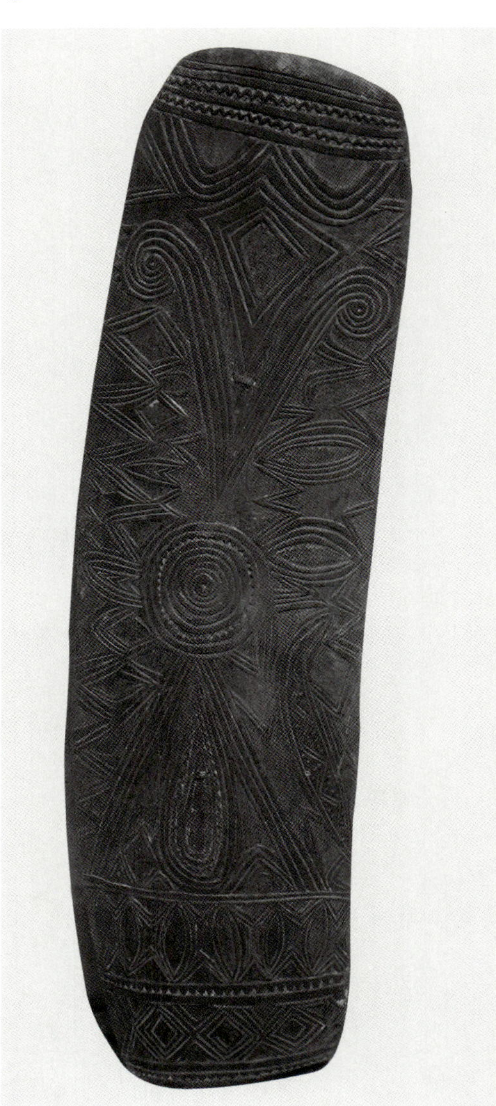

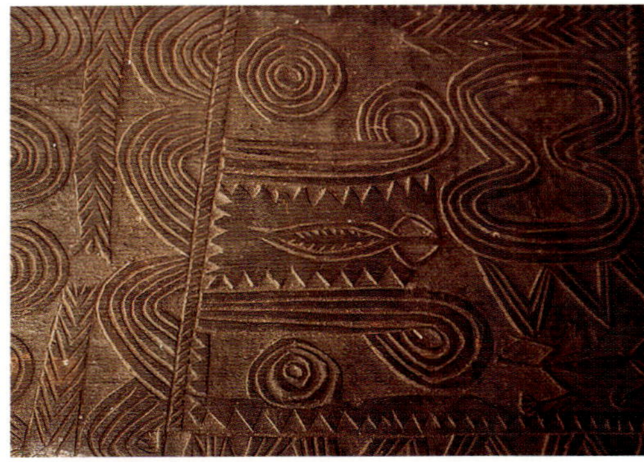

Fig. 9.168

motifs. In the Yaklik pot, geometric elements define the space into zones or panels, each containing a separate geometric motif, and the areas of pattern and negative spaces have equal emphasis. In the Yambes vessel, space is defined geometrically by five bars of parallel lines running from the base around the curve up to the rim band. This divides the field into five pie-shaped panels. Within each of the panels a series of three opposing fern-shaped, curvilinear designs grows out of the vertical bands; oblique and tangential bands then connect fern to fern. The overall effect is of a jungle of tendrils; the impact is of floral motifs used in naturalistic and asymmetric patterns. The surface design of this vessel is less static than that of the Yaklik pot. Curvilinear, volute and scroll forms tend to enliven the surface, with implications of a writhing movement. The top band of decoration gives a longitudinal movement to the border; it consists of longitudinal lines and herringbone and sawtooth patterns (fig. 9.167). The similarity of design on the Abelam carved coconut cups, *sanguan*, can be attributed to the use of the same motifs, the fern and the oval. But the definition of space by the use of bands of longitudinal parallel lines is a unique iconographic expression of the Kombio potters.

The only other evidence found of the style of Kombio artistic expression can be seen on spear shafts and shields. Shields in the inland Sepik regions are unusual and are not generally seen until the Lumi district in the West Sepik Province. In 1969 the Catholic mission at Wewak was selling shields collected north of Dreikikir. Since then a few newly carved shields have surfaced again around Dreikikir but the authors have as yet been unable to trace their origin. Design elements used on the shields are similar to those used in the Kombio-Yambes pots, especially the use of a series of inscribed circles radiating from linear fern motifs (figs 9.168, 9.169).

Nuku

In the densely populated area around the Nuku patrol post, in the west of the Torricelli Mountains, are a number of villages where pottery is made. Nuku is in the Lumi district of the West Sepik Province, inland from Aitape and close to the border with East Sepik Province. Only two of the many pot making villages were visited by the authors; these were the Mehek-speaking villages of Wilwil and Nuku. Additional information about pottery making in the area has been supplied by local mission personnel.

At Wilwil and Nuku, simple rough cooking pots like those of the Abelam and Kwoma are made by spiral coiling. Women are the principal pot makers but some old men are also potters. Cooking pots and sago stirring vessels are made. The general purpose cooking pot, *au*, is an ovoid, simple restricted or unrestricted form with either a rounded, slightly pointed or flattish base. Heights range from 17 to 25 centimetres (fig. 9.170). A small cooking pot, *nanglu au*, is used for cooking greens only; it is usually about 12 centimetres high. The sago stirring vessel, *nakun garfu*, comes in a variety of shapes but always has a wide mouth.

The clay source for Wilwil potters is close to their village. Clay, *sul*, is placed on a 'limbum' sheet and prepared for use by beating with a heavy stick. The clay is squeezed into thick rolls which are then rolled out on a 'pangal'. The pot, which rests in a pandanus leaf ring, *au silki*, is built up by spiral coiling and smoothed inside and out with wet hands. Finished pots are covered with green leaves and left to dry slowly in the house. The firing process seems to be very similar to that used at Lumi. Simple finger or stick-drag decoration across the top few coils or simple short line incisions appear to be the only forms of decoration.

Other Mehek villages reported to make pots are Ifkindu, Mantsuku, Yiminim, and Klapei 1, 2 and 3 (Kafle). Pots are also made in a group of six villages known as Nambulo, south of Nuku, and at Leiku and Libuat women and young boys are making pots infrequently. At Brugap (Au language) pots were made in the recent past but are not now made. According to informants, among the Ningil and Alu language groups of this area men used to make pots. It has not been determined whether all

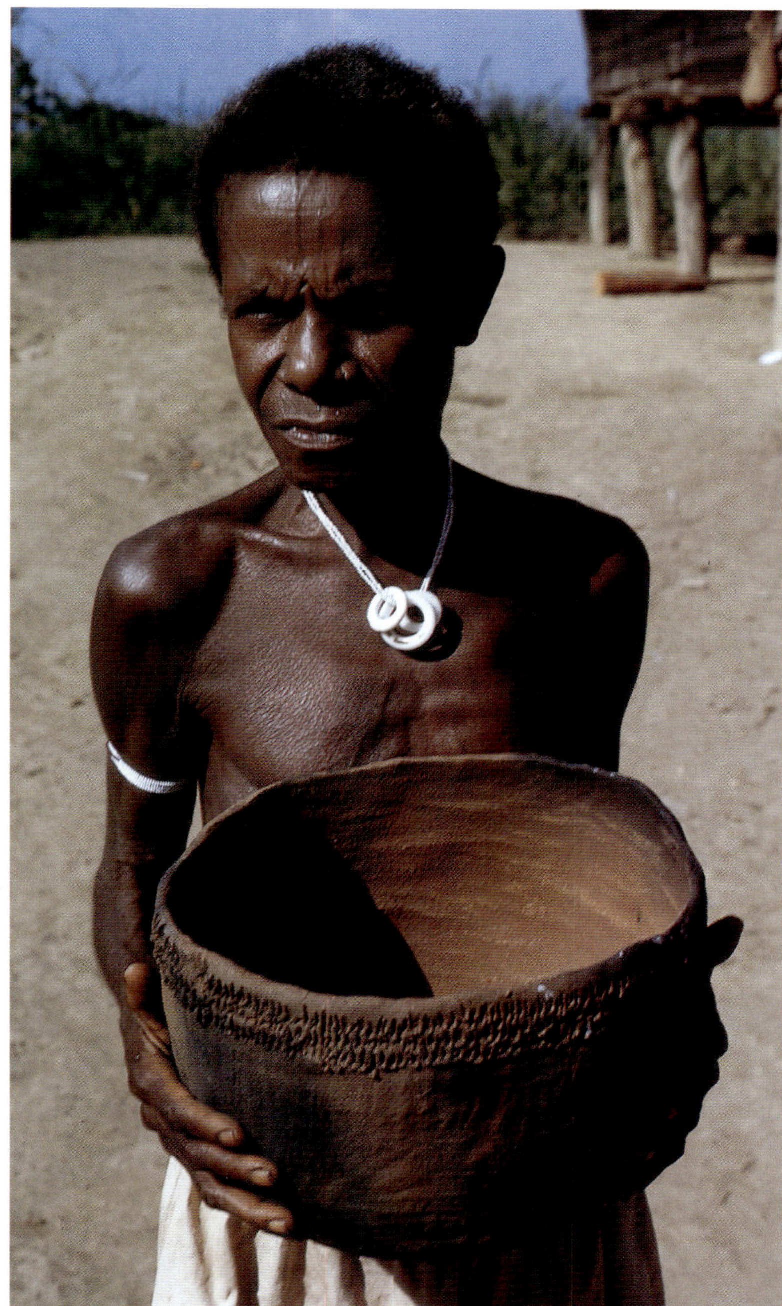

Fig. 9.170
Wilwil village woman with typical cooking pot, *au*, from Nuku area, *h* 18 cm.

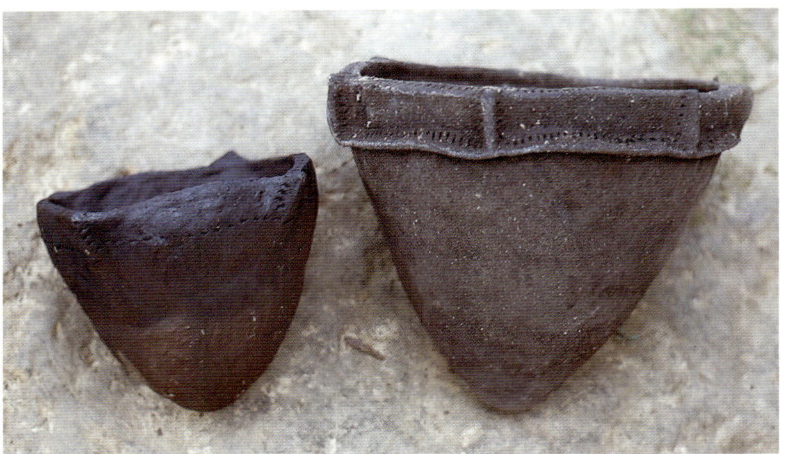

Fig. 9.171
The larger pot, *melef ulu,* was made by Malisa, Ali village, Lumi area, *h* 33 cm.

Fig. 9.172
Telefi coiling: the coil, which was supported around his neck, now rests on his arm, Ali.

these groups make pots similar to those made at Wilwil and Nuku but information suggests a common style.

Kaufmann reports that neighbours of the Kwoma and Mayo people in the Nuku hill country build tall conical pots with pointed bases using the spiral coil technique. It is notable that although the Mayo and Mehek languages are in the same family and the cooking pots of the two groups are similar, there is no sign in the Nuku area of the elaborate ceremonial ware made by the Mayo.

Lumi

To the west of Nuku, around the district headquarters of Lumi, there are a number of villages where pots are made which are quite distinct from those of Nuku: Ali, Orutei, Eretei, Buru'um, Karaitem, Pail, Waiteli, Amaitem and Tofungu. Villages which are said to have made pots in the recent past are Otemgi, Klelbuf, Mauwi, Wabuf, Miliom, Talbipi, Wilikli and Lumi. All of these villages are of the Olo language group. Some 20 kilometres to the north of Lumi in the One village of Goiniri and its hamlet Malili pots are made in the same style. Pots were also traded to the Sepik River plains in the south and north to the coast but the flourishing Tumleo industry now supplies most of the northern villages. In the villages of Siaute, Wauningi and Pes, 15 kilometres inland from Aitape, pots from both Tumleo and Lumi were seen.

Pots are made by men although old women occasionally make them. Cooking pots only are made. The pots of Lumi differ from any other inland Sepik cooking pots in having applied decoration. They are particularly thick and heavy but of good proportion and handsomely decorated. The most common shape is conical but there are variations. Recently made pots are often cruder than those made in the past.

The generic term for cooking pots is *melef.* A large cooking pot is *melef ulu*, a small one, *melef kumbus.* Three types were observed in this area. One is a conical, thick-walled variety with a pointed base and 11 to 34 centimetres high. It is decorated with a heavy applied ridge around the top third of the pot, handle-like additions between the ridge and the rim, sometimes three or four triangular lugs just below the rim, and punctation marks along the top of the rim and often also on the applied portions. One vessel had an applied snake-like form curving around the top two-thirds of the pot. The

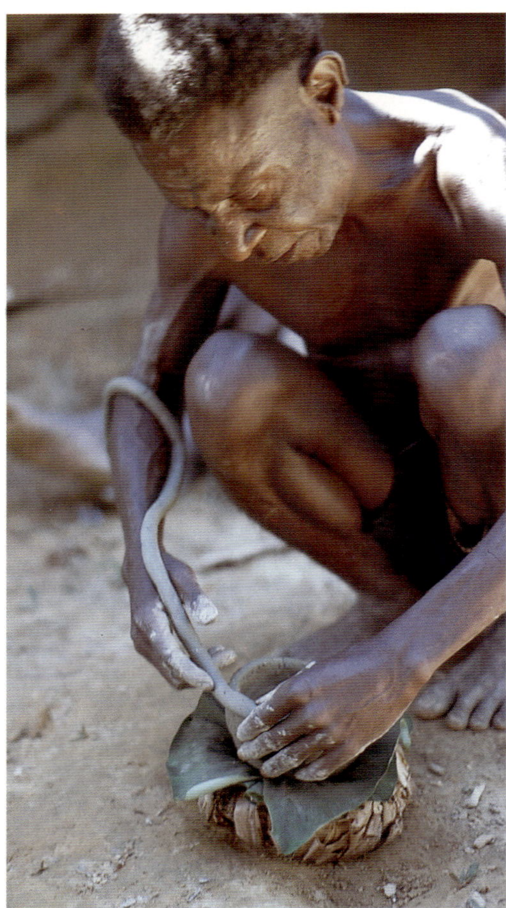

second type is more ovoid, with a moderately pointed base and a high shoulder and slight neck area. The third type is a round-based, ovoid, restricted form decorated by an applied ridge with punctation marks.

Clay, also called *melef* can only be gathered at special times of the year, when the root vegetables are ready for harvest; the people say that at that time the ground 'breaks open' and the clay can be found easily. A greenish-grey clay used at Ali village but collected some distance away is coarse-grained with good plasticity and low firing shrinkage. The non-plastics in the clay are mostly unweathered granitic material. Another clay used sometimes by Ali potters is found by the side of the road to Karaitem. It is finer-grained, has moderate shrinkage and contains a mixture of sandstone, schist and igneous rock fragments as its non-plastic content.

Clay is prepared by the men and young boys. It is squeezed into short thick rolls and then rolled out on a 'limbum' or 'pangal' into coils, *rofril melef,* approximately 60 to 80 centimetres long and 1 to 1.5 centimetres thick. Spiral coiling is started on the 'pangal'; the vessel is placed on a banana leaf ring, *melef wi*, for the rest of the forming. Coils are joined by pinching downward with the left thumb. (The authors observed one potter who fed coils on to the pot from around his neck and down his right arm.) Young boys sometimes help with the coils. Smoothing is done with wet fingers both inside and out and the applied decoration is formed from added coils smoothed on with the fingers. Punctations are made with a stick or piece of bamboo.

Pots are bound up with split cane and hung over the fire in the house for several weeks before they are fired. This period of smoking is considered essential to make them strong. They are placed on the firing platform with the cane still in place (it is quickly burned off). The fuel for firing is 'pangal' and hardwood. Firings take place close to the potter's house; in one instance the fire was first used for cooking breadfruit. A fire is lit and allowed to die down. The embers are spread out and sticks of 'pangal' are placed to form a platform of three or four criss-crossed layers. The pots are placed on this, on their sides and more 'pangal' is built up over and around them. Meanwhile the fire smoulders and the pots are gradually warmed. This is one of the more efficient methods of preheating. When the added fuel catches alight it takes about twenty minutes to flare up and burn to soft ash. The pots are then lifted out and left to cool. Inedible leaves are always boiled in them to test them before use. Vessels are first heated before water is poured in for cooking because the villagers believe the pots would crack if water were put in before the pot was properly heated.

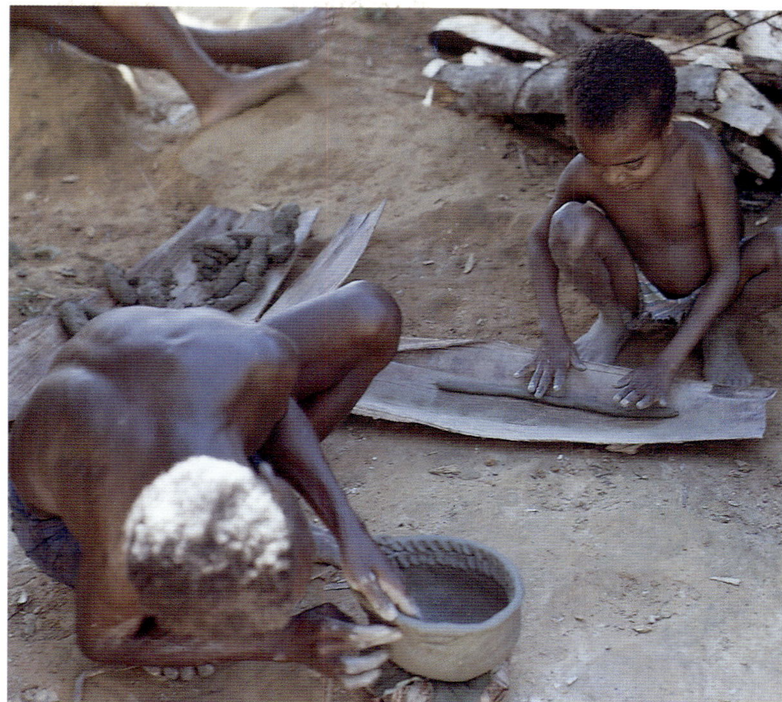

Fig. 9.173
Boy rolling coils for Telefi, Ali village, Lumi area.

In the 125 kilometres or so of country between Lumi and the Irian Jaya border there is no pottery making. However, Douglas Miles, an anthropologist who worked in this area in 1964, has reported an unusual fireplace in use around Telefomin, Green River and Amanab. It is a clay column built on the ground and protruding up into the floor of the house. Miles has suggested the possibility that such hearths might be precursors of the large portable fireplaces made at Aibom.

COASTAL SEPIK

Along the north coast of New Guinea, from Irian Jaya to the Murik Lakes, are several pot making

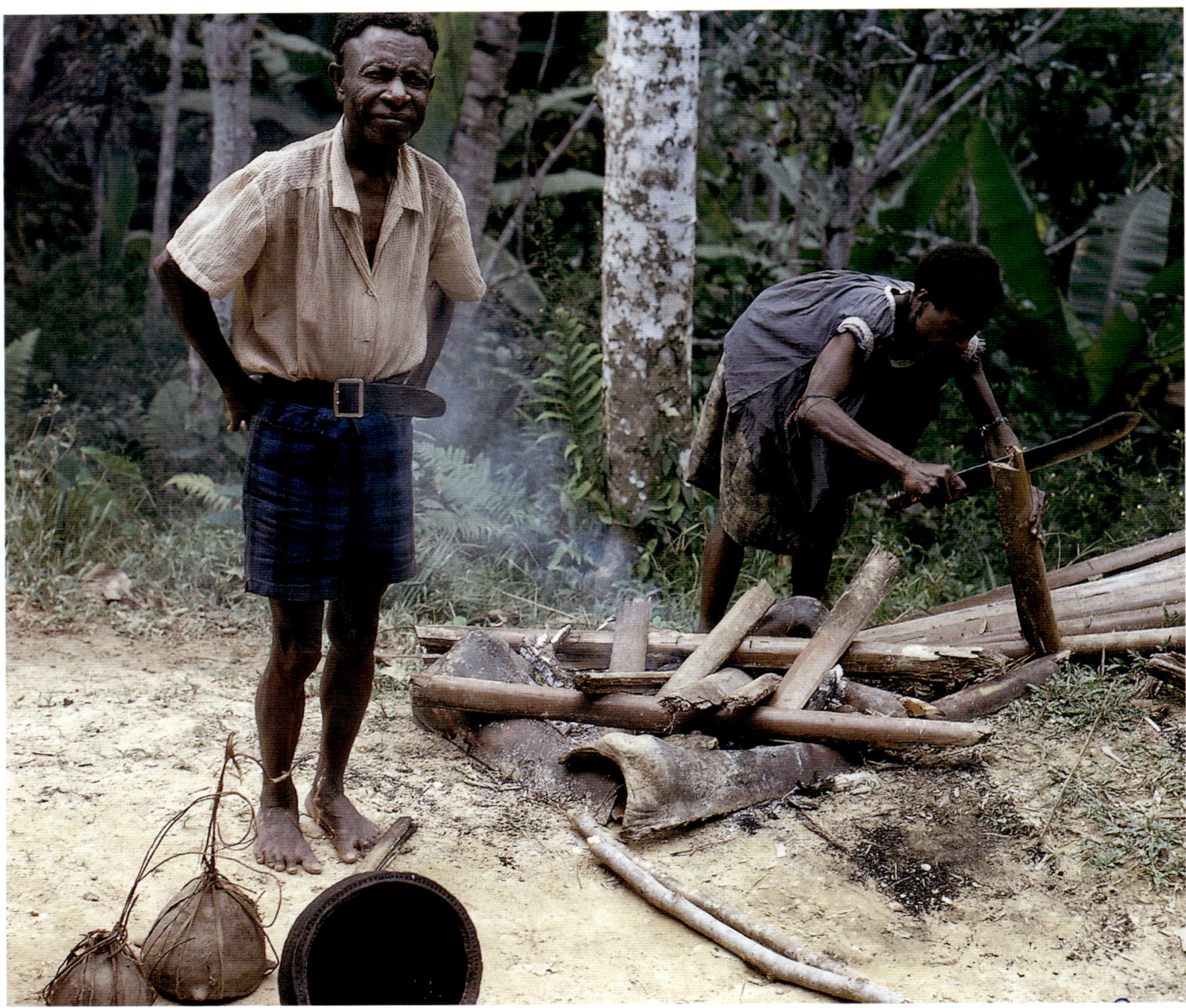

Fig. 9.174
Telefi and his wife firing: 'pangal' are laid over the warm ashes of a cooking fire, Ali village, Lumi area.

centres where women make the pottery using predominantly the paddle-and-anvil technique. About 30 kilometres east from the border, near the township of Vanimo, is Vanimo village where spherical beaten pots are still made, although not prolifically. Further east is a string of coastal villages near Leitre, some peopled by previous mountain dwellers; this mixture of races (all non-Austronesian, as at Vanimo) has produced a motley of pottery traditions with a variety of techniques: coiling, paddle-and-anvil and piece technique. The activity is, however, spasmodic.

In the Sissano area (Austronesian) pot making was known in the past but appears to have died out completely except for one village a short way inland which belongs to a different language group. On Tumleo Island and at two coastal villages close to Aitape where Tumleo people have settled the women are actively using the paddle-and-anvil method to produce a wide range of spherical pots. The next centre of pot making is at villages just east of Wewak: Kaiep, Terebu and Samap. The people here, mostly Austronesian like the Tumleo people and using a related potting method, are associated with them, too, through a legend telling of the origins of pot making at the Wewak villages. They are still producing pots.

Vanimo, Leitre, Sissano and Tumleo are all within West Sepik Province while the Wewak villages are in East Sepik Province.

Margarete Schurig (1930) shows on her map several other pottery centres in this area but they seem to be unknown to present-day Papua New Guineans. In some cases, no doubt, it is because pot making has since died out but in others, places of collection seem to have been taken as production centres. Schurig's information comes from secondary sources. Tagai, shown close to Aitape, must have given its name to the airstrip but there is no village of this name now. Jakamul (Yakamul), on the coast east of Aitape, has never been a pot making village in the memory of Aitape or Boiken/Dagua people but would have acquired pots from both Tumleo and from the Torricelli Mountains area inland. Seleo Island has always been a recipient of Tumleo pots and has probably retraced many of them but the islanders are not known as potters. Nearer Wewak, the Dalmanhafen area has no tradition of pot making but the people would have acquired their supply of pots from the Wewak coastal villages and from Tumleo, and no doubt coiled pots from inland as well. According to Otto Finsch's (1914) description of the forms and the colourfully painted pots, they acquired pots from as far away as Vanimo and Humboldt Bay. Finsch also saw pots which he likened to some from Bilbili in Krauel Bay – so many pots in the houses 'that one imagines a village of potters must be nearby'. In this he was correct because Samap, one of the Wewak coastal villages, is in the bay that was formerly known as Krauel Bay.

The Austronesian pot makers of the Admiralty Islands at Hus and M'Buke (see Chapter 11) should be mentioned here as their techniques are closely related to those of Vanimo although their spherical pots are much thinner and lighter than any of the New Guinea coastal pots. Also, the pots of the Humboldt Bay and Lake Sentani people of Irian Jaya must be compared stylistically and technically with both the Admiralty Islands pots and those of Vanimo. These potters are not described fully here because this country is outside the authors' survey area but it is interesting to note that, although belonging to the same language family as the Vanimo people and making similar pots by fairly similar techniques, the decoration of the vessels is entirely different. The Humboldt Bay pots seen in museums in the Netherlands and Germany have swirling creature motifs painted around and under the round-based pots whereas Vanimo vessels have only simple incised decoration under the lip (fig. 9.175).

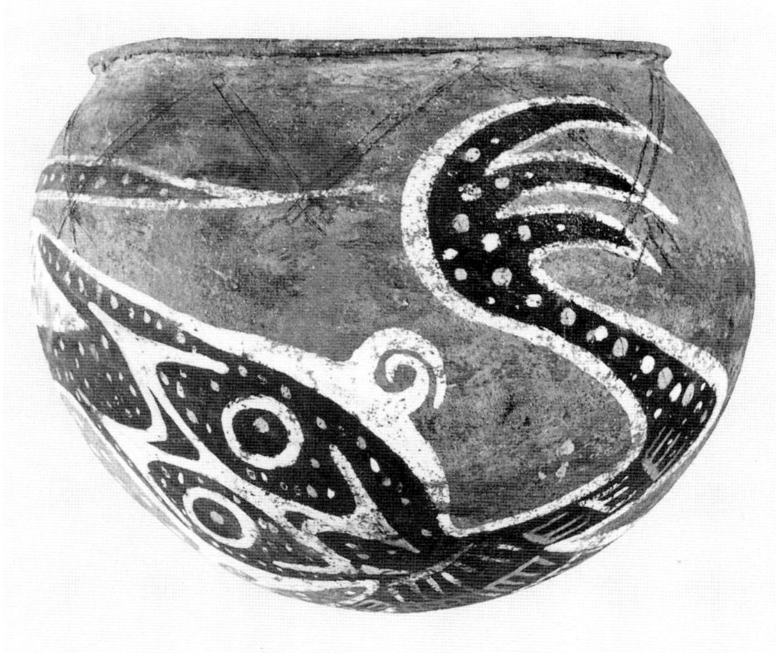

Fig. 9.175
Irian Jaya vessel from Humboldt Bay, decorated with black and white painted design.

Nowhere in Papua New Guinea do the potters decorate with painted motifs except where combined with carved or applied decorations. At Humboldt Bay the painted vessels are used as serving bowls but cooking pots have been made at Kajo Jenbi. People of the Lake Sentani village of Abar also produced pots with simple applied coil decorations. It is not certain whether these villagers are still producing pots. Another link between this part of Irian Jaya and Vanimo is the elaborate cane pot holders made by the young men in the spirit houses; these must be used only in this sacred area and are not to be seen by women. The loops and curved ends of cane represent snakes and dogs' tails. One other noteworthy point concerning Irian Jaya is that at Doreh, on the western end of the island of New Guinea, is the only reported example

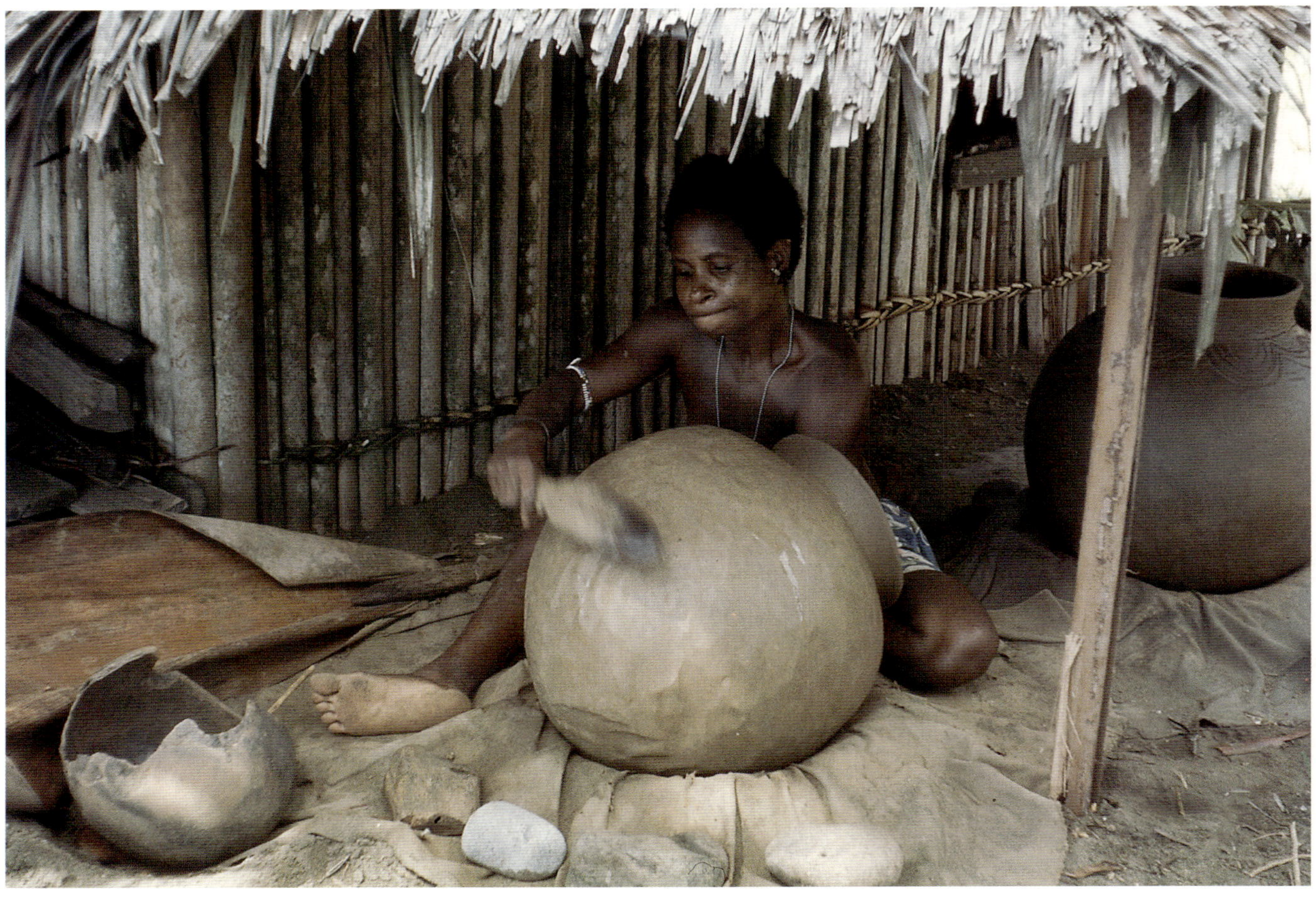

Fig. 9.176
Final beating at Kaiep village.

of a stone beater (paddle) for pot making: one stone, the anvil, is held inside the pot as usual while on the outside another smooth stone is used instead of a wooden beater. This is recorded by Forrest (1779).

Kaiep, Terebu and Samap

The coastal villages of Kaiep, Terebu (Turubu) and Samap are located 25 to 40 kilometres east of Wewak. Kaiep, the nearest to Wewak is at the mouth of the Riau River. Terebu is 6 kilometres to the east in Nightingale Bay and Samap is further east, only 26 kilometres from Murik Lakes. Two hamlets of Samap, Kapak 1 and 2, just west of the main village, are also centres of pot making.

According to Laycock (1973) the people used to speak an Austronesian language, now known as the Kaiep language, but both Terebu and Samap have been infiltrated by non-Austronesian speakers from inland and the nearby coast. Terebu is now predominantly Bungain-speaking but some Kaiep language speakers still live there. The language at Samap is still under review; Elipi is the name currently given to it but there are some Kaiep speakers there also.

Pottery is very important in the economy of these villages. Cooking and sago storage pots are in everyday use and they are traded for some distance up and down the coast and inland. They are also taken to Wewak market for cash sale. They are exchanged with the Murik Lakes people for baskets, pearl shells and fish; with the Wogeo islanders for 'galip' nuts (*Canarium* sp.), fishing nets and woven baskets; with the Kairiru people for native tobacco; and with the Wewak people (located in the villages west of Wewak in the foothills of the Prince Alexander Mountains) for wooden plates.

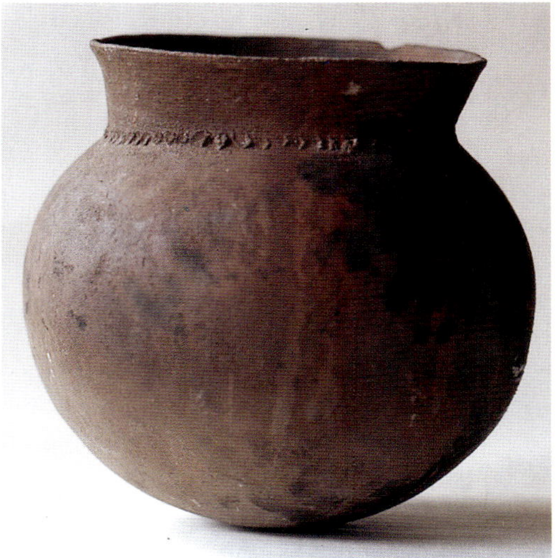

Fig. 9.177

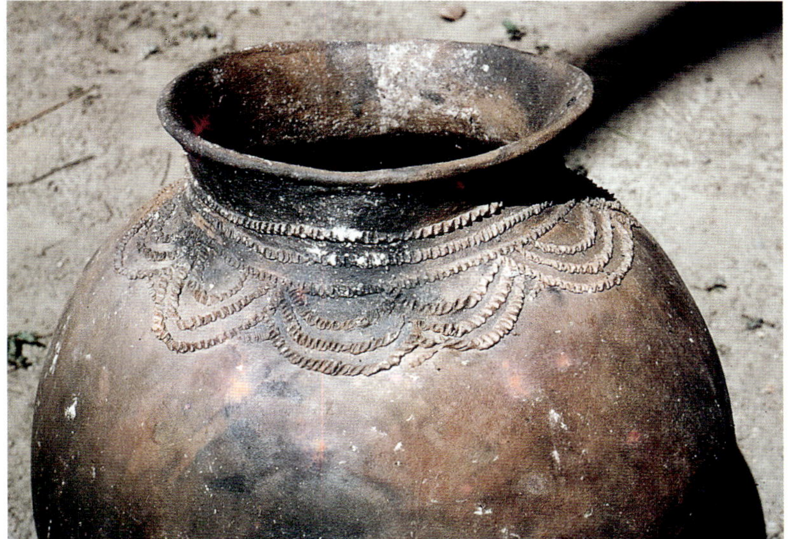

Fig. 9.178

On the other hand, sago stirring vessels, are imported from Tumleo because they are considered particularly strong.

The Kaiep people claim that their ancestors came originally from Tumleo and two versions of a story of the beginnings of pot making at Kaiep, told differently by two inhabitants, relate how their knowledge of it came from Tumleo people.

The first version tells of a woman called Walisbanui who came from Tumleo to the Wewak area to get sago but a big tide came up and she could not get home so she tested clays and sat down and made pots. She taught a Kaiep woman, Waisop, how to make pots that were the same shape as the Tumleo pots; previously, the Kaiep pots had been long pots. In the second version, a woman, Walisbam, went from Tumleo to Aitape to get sago but a big wind blew up and she was washed down the coast to Kaiep; she came ashore near the Riau River. Walisbam found clay there, made pots and taught two Kaiep women how to make them. Then many people came in canoes to watch the women making pots and they took pots home and were happy and cooked good food.

The pots made at all three villages are similar to Tumleo pots, basically spherical with round bases. The generic word for pots in the Kaiep language is *biar*, or *pier*, which is also the Tumleo word for pot. The common cooking pot, *pier*, has a short neck and everted rim. The rim on some examples was as wide as or wider than the belly. They may be decorated with incised markings. The sago stirring pot, called *tububun*, is neckless and often decorated around the top portion with incised markings defined by a ridge underneath. The sago storage jar, *kanaf*, has a short neck and everted rim and is larger than the cooking pot. It can have incised or applied decoration around the neck and shoulder and, in older pots, on the belly area. The double cooking pot, *sulu*, has the same use as the *pier*. It is a composite vessel with a double-bellied ver-

Fig. 9.177
Old cooking pot from Terebu village, *h* 27 cm.

Fig. 9.178
Sago storage jar, *kanaf*, showing applied decoration, Kaiep village.

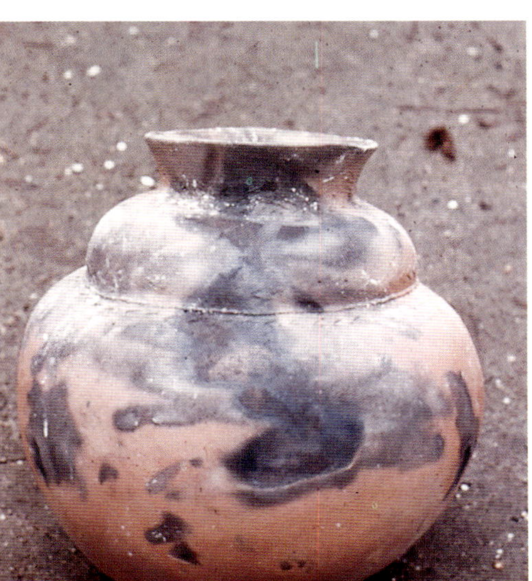

Fig. 9.179
Double cooking pot, Kaiep, *h* 43 cm.

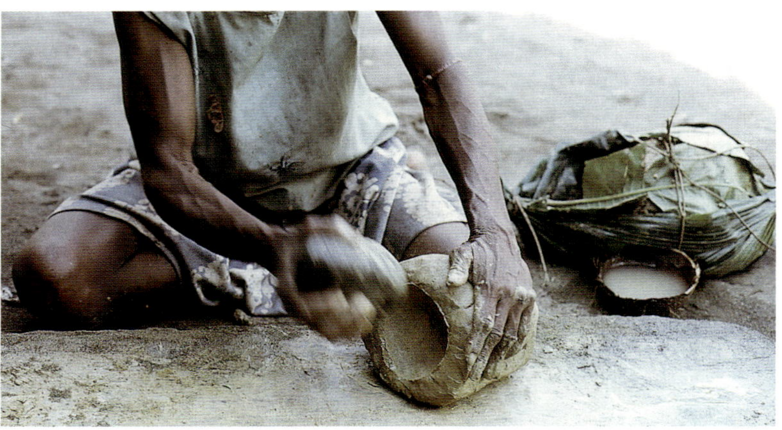

Fig. 9.180
Potter thumping open the ball of clay, Terebu village.

tical axis. A small cooking pot, *wias sol*, is a smaller version of the sago storage vessel and is used for cooking leafy greens. A round-based, half ellipsoid dish, *kambu*, is used as a lid for the sago storage jar and as a sago frying pan. Finally, there is a hanging pot, used to keep food away from rats and dogs. It has an outward flaring rim which is pierced by three holes; these are used to hang it from the rafters of the house.

The pots which are most readily comparable to those of Tumleo are the cooking pots, sago stirring pots, some of the sago storage pots and the lids, which are exactly the same as the undecorated frying pans or support dishes of Tumleo. Both industries have hanging pots but those at Tumleo have handles over the top. According to the Kaiep people water pots have never been made at these villages, they say that water used to be collected, carried and stored in bamboo tubes and coconut shells. But Finsch (1914) reports wide-mouthed water pots in Dalmanhafen which could very probably have come from Kaiep.

Some potters have specially built workshops, low buildings with earth floors where they can work out of the sun and store their tools, clay and pots for drying.

Pot making was observed at both Kaiep and Terebu and descriptions were given at Samap. Identical techniques are used. There are several clay sources available for the people of Kaiep. One is located in the jungle, on top of a steep hill immediately behind the beach. From this pit the women dig a yellowish-brown fine-grained plastic clay containing a small amount of gravel (weathered rock fragments), fine quartz and some plant debris. Clay from a site to the south of the village is similar but darker and very sticky. The potters say that both clays are equally good. Terebu's clay source is on the headland (Cape Terebu) between Kaiep and Terebu, where there are three pits containing the same clay and where Kaiep women sometimes also get their clay.

Tools used, collectively called *tenekur*, include a long stone, narrow at the holding end and wide and flat at the beating end, used to pound the clay; a narrower stone used for opening out the ball of clay in the preliminary stage of forming; and a round smooth stone used as an 'anvil'. There are three different beaters (paddles), collectively called *linak*, made by the men from any hard wood. They are paddle-shaped, with a handle which has a knob at the end for better gripping, and are sometimes decorated with carving on the backs. They vary in shape and weight. A heavy beater, *mutul*, rounded on both sides, is used in the preliminary stages of beating; a narrower lightweight beater, *manak*, is used for shaping; a wider, flatter, lightweight beater, *linak*, is used for finishing. Other tools are a smooth thin stick, *nuinyou*, used for shaping and smoothing the neck of the pot, a piece of thin split cane used to cut and level the top and a small thin pointed stick for incised decoration. Potters may wear a flexible 'limbum' apron to protect themselves from splashes while working the clay.

A lump of fairly stiff clay, about 5 kilograms, is taken from the bundle and placed on a wooden board which is first sprinkled with grey beach sand. This clay is pounded with the flat wide end of the stone and more sand is sprinkled on while it is pounded and flattened. Water is trickled down the stone beater to moisten the clay sand mixture. Periodically the clay is lifted (thumbs pushing into it to help fold it over and pick it up) and bashed down on the board. More sand is sprinkled on the board and on the clay and the pounding is repeated. Throughout this process stones and roots are removed but, of course, some are also crushed up by the pounder (fig. 2.2). When deemed ready, the clay is patted into a firm ball, covered with green leaves and put aside in the potter's workshop.

The first stage of forming is carried out with the potter squatting or sitting beside the board. A ball

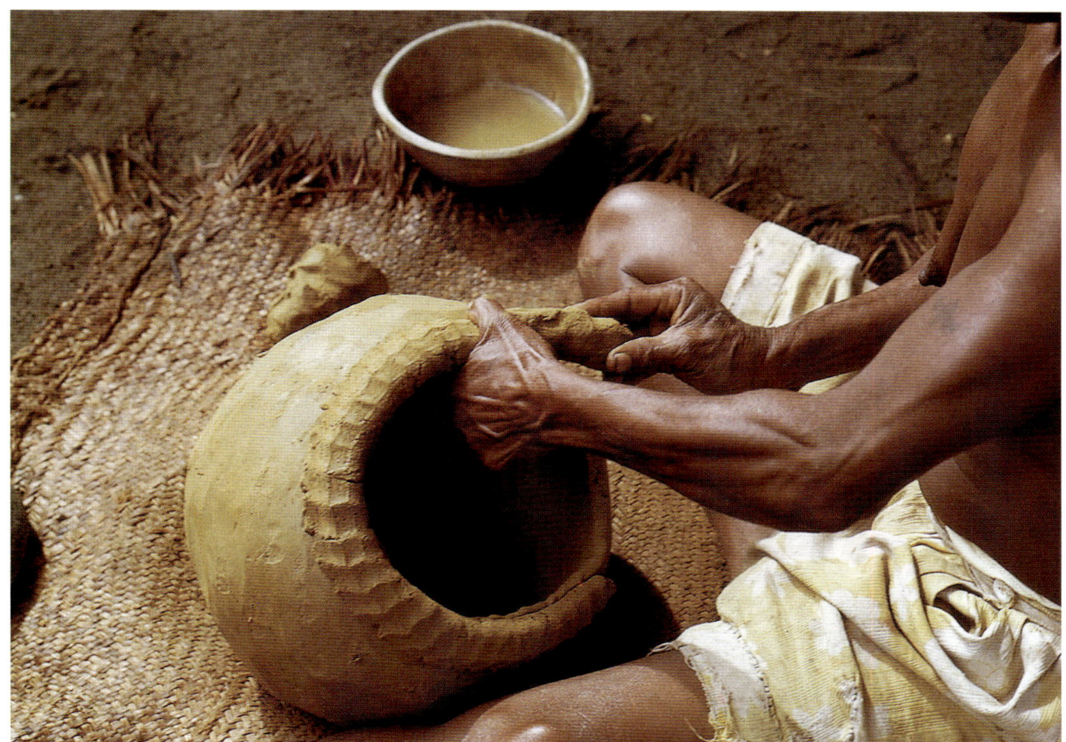

Fig. 9.181
Kaiep village potter Monica joining a roll of clay to form the neck.

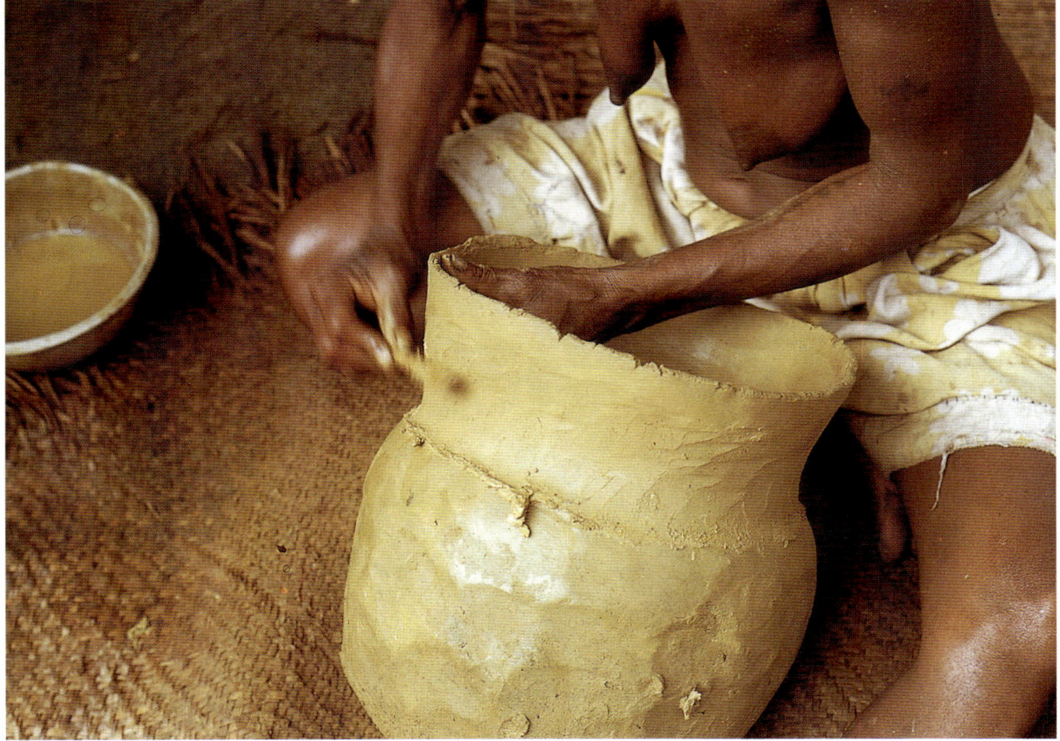

Fig. 9.182
Monica smoothing and shaping the neck with a smooth stick, Kaiep.

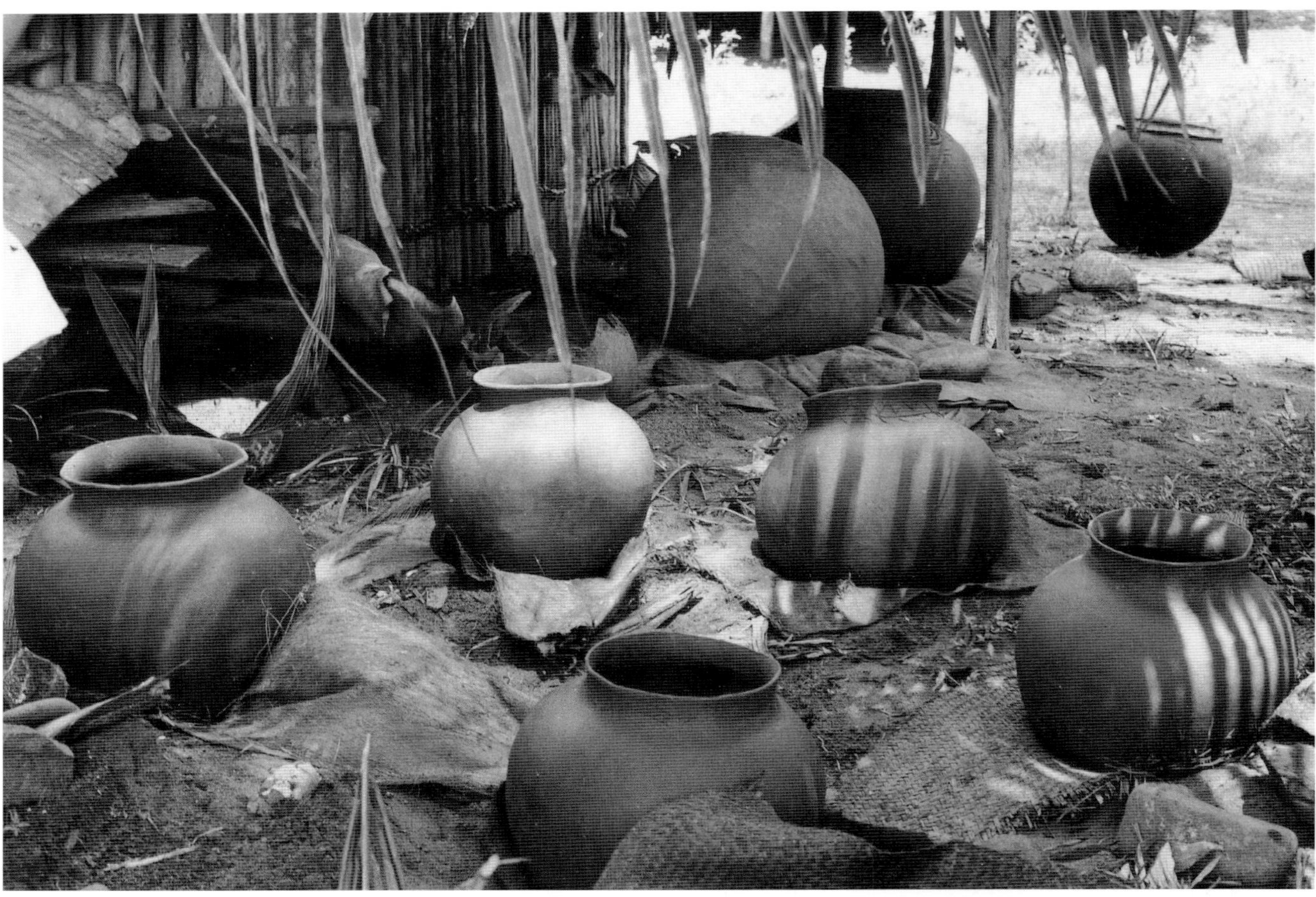

Fig. 9.183
Cooking and sago storage pots drying in mat-lined hollows on the sand, Kaiep village.

of clay is placed on the board and the potter taps firmly into the top of the ball with the narrow stone, opening it up but leaving the centre unbeaten until a stalk of clay remains sticking up in the middle. She puts down the beater and removes this piece of clay, setting it aside until it is needed for the neck. After pounding the opening a little more the potter consolidates the edge of the thick round shape, moving it around with her thumbs inside and fingers outside, working over any cracks which have appeared while it was pounded open. Next, the potter makes a depression in the sand with her foot and spreads a soft woven mat or a piece of cloth or sack over the hole, forming a bed to accommodate the growing bellied-out pot during further beating.

The neck is formed by adding a thick roll of clay (fashioned from the clay kept aside from the centre of the original lump) to the top outer edge of the form. This is then partially shaped by beating with a paddle and anvil. The beating process results in a convex neck marked by a ridge where the join occurs; a moistened smooth stick is worked down from the top of the pot over the join while a thumb, held on the inside, pushes out the top edge, giving the neck a concave shape and eradicating the ridge. Small bits of clay which gather on the stick are wiped off and kept inside the vessel. A thin strip of cane is then used to cut and level the edge of the neck, the cut pieces falling into the pot later to be compacted with other scraps and used for patching. After the top edge is smoothed with wet fingers the pot is set aside in one of the mat-covered hollows to become firmer before final beating.

Simple decorations of incised or slashed lines, zig-zags or chevrons are applied to the outside of the neck while the clay is still soft enough, sometimes before the final beating of the base. Pots with

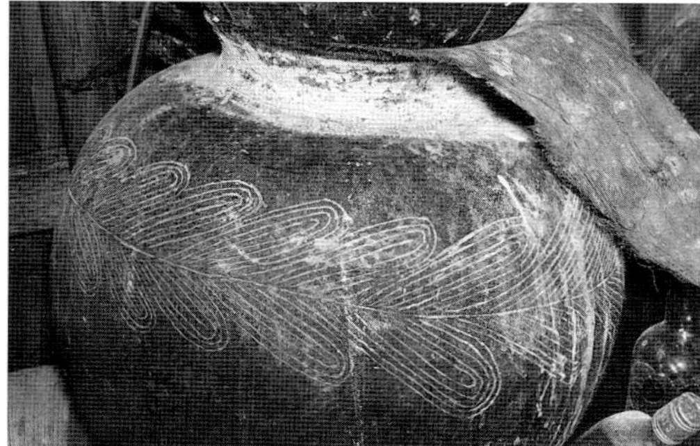

Fig. 9.184

Fig. 9.184
Large old sago storage jar with unusual incised decoration which has probably become filled with sago flour, Samap village.

wide everted rims are often decorated along the interior of the rim only. More elaborate incising covering the neck and shoulder area can be seen on some older sago storage pots. At Samap one example, said to have been made many years ago, had a very different decoration. The vessel was incised around the widest part of the belly with a multilined, paired, leaf-like pattern which was filled in with white (most likely caused by sago flour spilling over the edge of the pot for years) (fig. 9.184).

Some sago storage jars are decorated with applied lines on the neck and shoulder areas. Groups of straight parallel lines can be combined with groups of curved lines. They are made by working small pieces of clay onto the neck of the pot with wet fingers. Stick impressions are made into this soft clay (fig. 9.178).

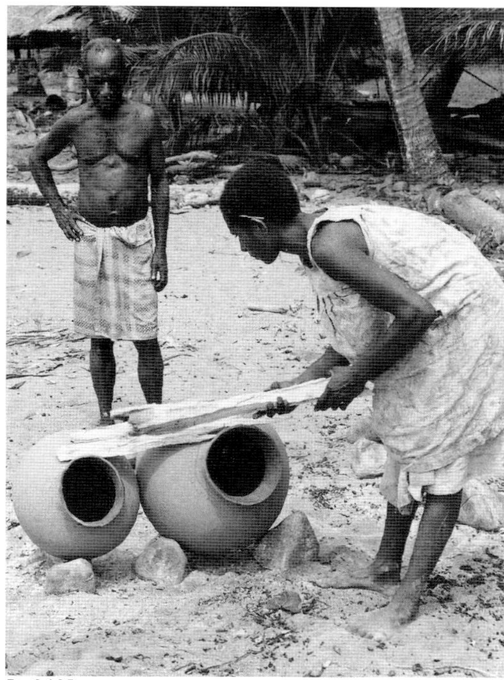

Fig. 9.185

Fig. 9.185
Regina Teraku placing wood across two pots for firing on the beach, Kaiep village.

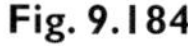

Pots are warmed in the sun all day on the beach before being fired in the cool of the evening. To preheat them, a bundle of dry coconut palm leaves is burnt inside the pots while they are lying on their sides on the beach facing into the wind. After about ten minutes the ashes and unburnt remains are

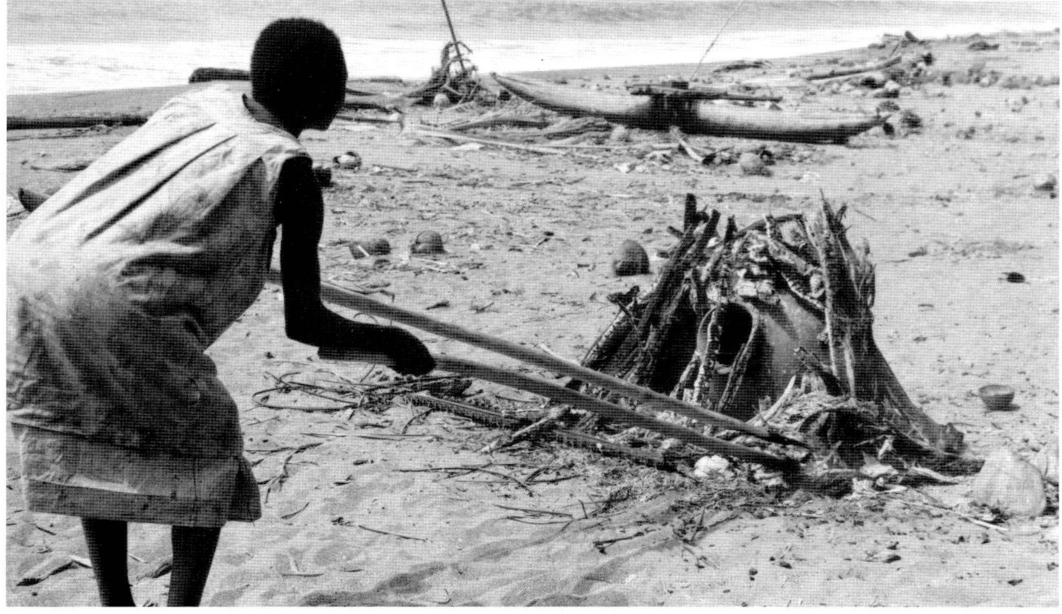

Fig. 9.186
Regina placing unburnt fuel against the pots, Kaiep.

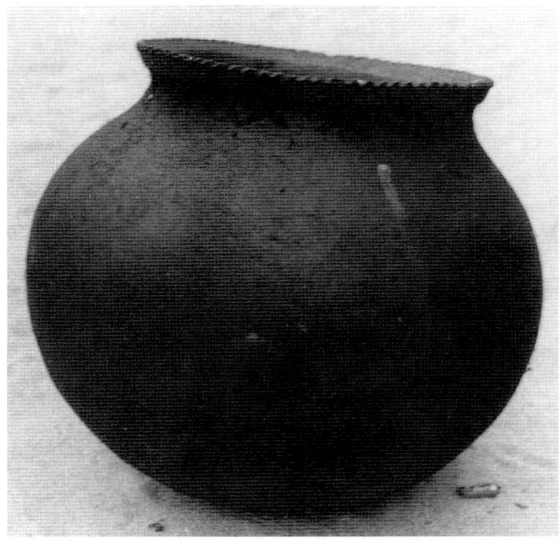

Fig. 9.187
Tumleo Island cooking pot, *pier*, *h* 31 cm.

tipped out. About twenty pots can be fired at a time. Each one is placed on three rocks so that it is about 8 centimetres above the sand, with its mouth facing into the wind. Various fuels are used: coconut and sago palm fronds, black palm, driftwood, neat bundles of split logs and smaller sticks. Fuel is placed across the top of the pots and against the mouths, leaning in at the top; extra fuel is stacked on the windward side. The solid timber is placed nearest the pots and the palm fronds are arranged along the outside. Finally, leafy fronds are laid down in front on the windward side and set alight. The palm pieces ignite quickly and gradually set fire to the thicker pieces so that, in effect, the pots receive a second preheating. After ten minutes the whole mass is burning fiercely. As the fire dies down the potter picks up burning pieces and props them against and inside the pots.

Pawpaws, bananas or breadfruit are cooked inside cooking pots to seal them before use. Sago storage jars receive no further treatment; their porosity probably helps the sago to 'breathe' and remain fresh. The people in this area had been storing their sago in metal containers but had returned to using clay pots because the sago was going sour in the metal ones.

Tumleo

Tumleo Island, once known as Tamara, is a small island about 2 kilometres long and 1 kilometre wide, located off the mainland near Aitape. Part of the same limestone-volcanic sequence as the mainland, it lies with a group of small coral islands, Ali, Angel and Seleo. All four islands are peopled by Austronesian speakers but the Tumleo people belong to a different subgroup of the language and are the only pot makers. Some Tumleo people now live at two villages on the mainland, one, Yakoi, just north of Aitape and one a little south of Aitape, Raiyu, sometimes referred to as 'Tumleo-Raiyu'. Pot making is still flourishing at all three locations.

Two early German ethnographers described the pot making of Tumleo Island: Parkinson in 1900 and Erdweg in more detail in 1902. Father Joseph Erdweg, a linguist, was among the first missionaries to settle on Tumleo Island.

The population of Tumleo Island is grouped in small hamlets mostly on the south-eastern end of the island, the main ones being Sepij, Ainamul, Alii, and Anup'pius. There are between two and five women potters in each hamlet. Many different types of pots with specific uses are made by the women. Descriptions and drawings of some of

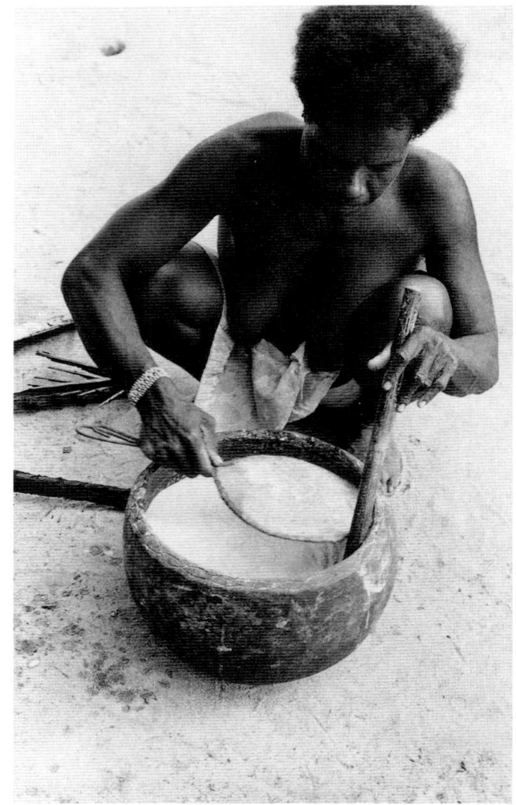

Fig. 9.188
Sago stirring pot, *sal*. Straining shreds off the sago.

these, made by Parkinson and Erdweg and, subsequently, Schurig, show some differences but all the pots illustrated by them are still made today.

Traditionally, the trading of pots for sago with the mainland was necessary to ensure sufficient food to last for the period of the north-west winds (November to May) when it was unsafe to travel by canoe. The population, in fact, was so dependent on the production of pottery that the men only married local women who could make pots. Now, with trade store foods available, the stockpiling of sago is not necessary but some trading continues. Tumleo people still exchange pots and sweet potato for fish and tobacco with Ali, Seleo and Angel islanders, although much of the exchange is now done through the Aitape markets. Pots are sometimes sold outright to the people. The coastal villages east of Aitape – Yakamul, Ulau and Suain – traditionally exchanged sago for Tumleo pots as well as the thin, finely carved coiled pots from the inland Kombio area. Farther east the people of Urip and Dagua use many Tumleo pots which have been traded for tobacco, yam and baskets. They favour sago stirring pots because they get cooking pots from the mountains in the Yangoru area.

Tumleo pots are sometimes taken in boatloads to Wewak markets and also as far west as the Sissano villages. Ali Island people, who are especially good boatmen, act as middle-men in the distribution of Tumleo pots and the pots are found in the villages inland from Aitape, at Siaute, Wom and Salongo. Traditionally Tumleo pots found their way well up into the Torricelli Mountains in exchange for food and pigs' teeth among other items.

Pots are named by the people according to their function. Cooking pots, sago stirring pots, sago storage jars, food storage vessels, sago frying pans, pot support dishes, lids and babies' wash pots are all made. *Pier*, or *pier ahin* (*ahin* means 'lip'), is one of two types of cooking pots. It is used for cooling vegetables and meat and for boiling water for the 'hot-water sago'. It is spherical and round-based, with a short neck and everted rim which is often indented. The second type of cooking pot, the *takum* has similar uses to the *pier* but is smaller; it may be ellipsoid or spherical and has no neck.

Sal is the sago stirring vessel. Sago flour is stirred to a paste in this pot and then boiling water is ladled into it from the *pier*; the mixture is stirred until it thickens and becomes translucent. *Sal* has thicker walls than the cooking pot (due to function); it is round-bottomed and spherical or straight-sided, with a thick composite inwardly sloping edge which is often incised.

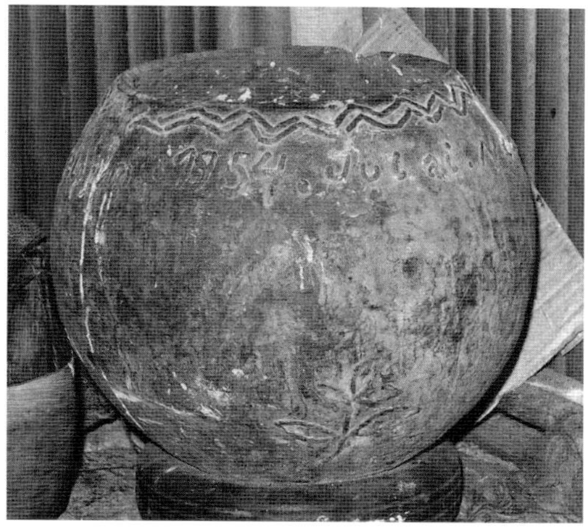

Fig. 9.189
Sago storage jar, *suyanu*, Tumleo Island, *h* 28 cm.

Suyanu, the sago storage jars, are usually very large (about 60 centimetres high) and are used for storing wet sago flour. In the past a special *suyanu* was used for storing water which had been collected in 'limbum' baskets. Finsch (1914) reports being given drinking water at Dalmanhafen from large, low, wide-mouthed pots with a coconut shell ladle. The pots he describes were probably made either at Tumleo or at Kaiep-Terebu. Now water is collected from roofs or wells and stored in 44-gallon

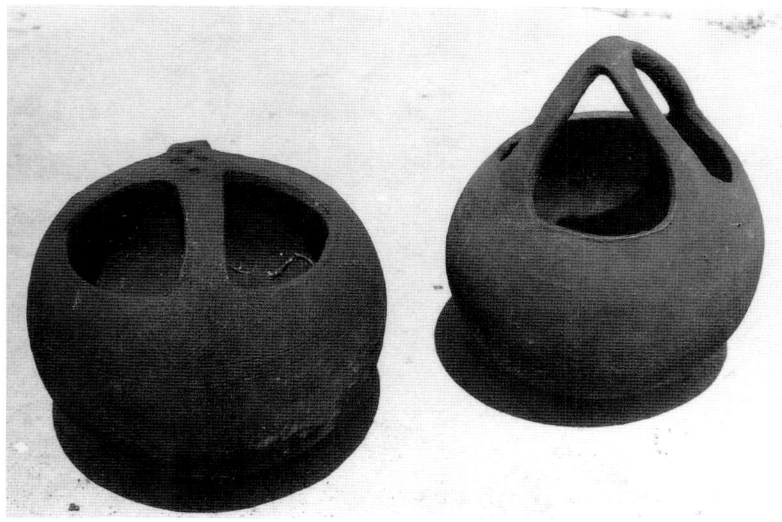

Fig. 9.190
Food storage pots, *pier atjek vol*, Sapij hamlet, Tumleo Island: (left) *h* 19 cm; (right) *h* 26 cm.

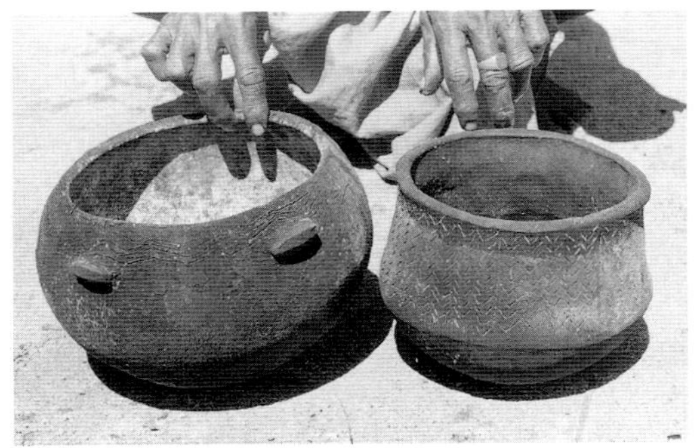

Fig. 9.191
Tumleo Island sago stirring pot, *sal*, and baby's wash pot, *su lapij puak*.

drums. *Lup mlangon*, another sago storage jar, is round-based, spherical and has no neck area; some have applied decoration.

Pier atjek vol, the spherical food storage pot, comes in varying sizes and has three or four handles over the top of the opening or two to six holes around the top rim which allows the sections between the holes to be used as handles. It is hung in the rafters of the house to store small amounts of food away from rats and dogs. Erdweg claims that it was made mainly as an object to be admired and Parkinson suggests that the pots were used to store coconut oil or water. Perhaps the use has changed over the years but they would be very awkward water pots.

Tapel, the sago frying pans, are round-based, semi-ellipsoid bowls that are sometimes decorated on the outside or along the top rim. Sago flour is mixed with grated coconut and fried in the *tapel*. The crumbly mixture is spread over the inside of one heated frying pan while another heated *tapel* is placed over it (the same way up) thus sandwiching the sago cake and cooking the top of it at the same time.

Karap is a pot support made in the range of sizes necessary to support the different types and sizes of pots during manufacture. It is the same shape as the *tapel* but more roughly finished and never decorated or blackened on the outside.

Tapel tjup, or *karap tjup*, is a lid used on cooking pots and sago storage jars. It has scalloped edges which, Parkinson suggests, allow the steam to escape and thus prevent the lid being pushed off by the pressure. It is the same shape as the *tapel* and *karap*.

Su lapij puak, a baby's wash pot, is used to hold water for the ritual washing of a newborn baby. These pots are given to pregnant girls by female relatives or friends. They are also sometimes used to leave prepared food in the house for old people who have been left on their own for the day.

Erdweg does not mention either of these functions. He states merely that the wash pots have a practical use and that he has seen them hanging upside down outside a 'haus tambaran' (which is presumably why Schurig illustrates it upside down). Erdweg's illustration is of a bell-shaped pot taller than that seen today. Meyer and Parkinson, in their album of excellent old photographs, show a 'haus tambaran' on Tumleo Island with small painted pots hanging upside down under the eaves but they do not say which type of pots these are. This vessel is usually round-bottomed with slightly concave or convex sides and is covered over the top portion with incised decoration.

Tumleo Island, like the nearby mainland, is mainly formed from volcanic agglomerates and tuffaceous spiroclypeus limestones. It is a flat island with only two small hills on the north-western end. Some of the potters' raw materials are found on the hill but one clay, a red one, has always been collected from the mainland. All varieties of clay are available on the mainland and are now mostly collected from there because, being less stony, they are considered superior.

Three different materials are considered essential for the Tumleo clay body and traditionally a fourth was also included. A dark brown clay, *peitj njotj*, is found on the island as well as on the mainland near Aitape. This is a rough sandy material

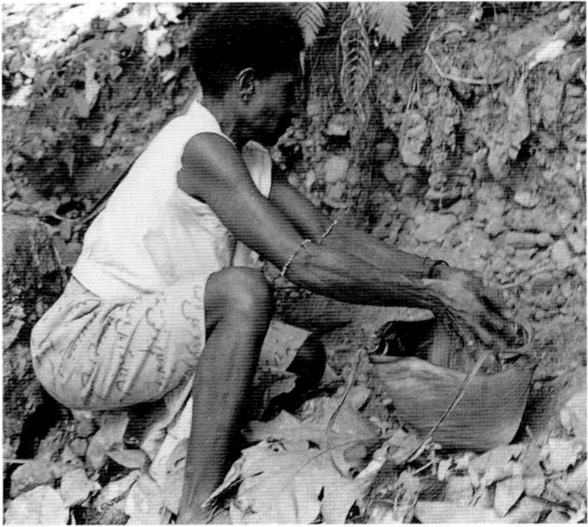

Fig. 9.192
Juliana Paisom digging temper from the slopes of a hill on Tumleo Island.

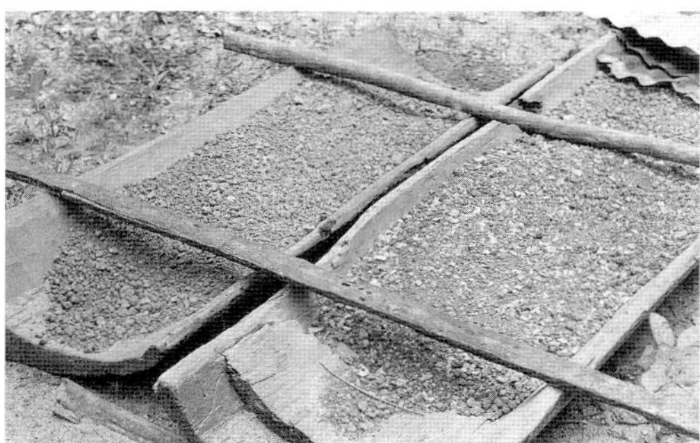

Fig. 9.193

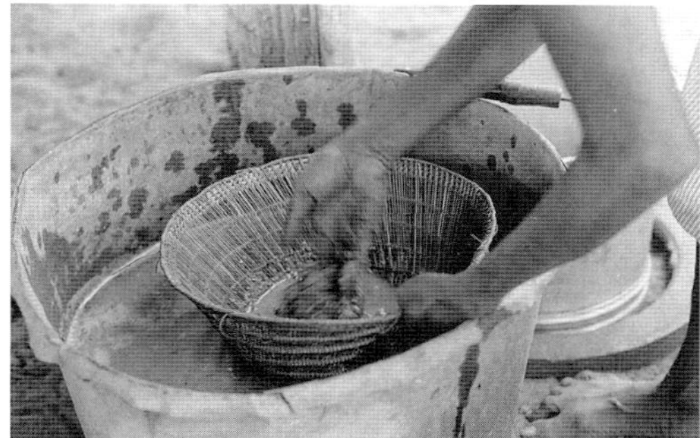

Fig. 9.194

Fig. 9.193
Red and brown clay drying in sections of dug-out canoes, Sapij hamlet.

Fig. 9.194
Nona sieving wetted clay, Tumleo-Raiya village.

with a very low clay mineral (montmorillonite) proportion. It could be classed as a temper. A brown (known locally as 'red') clay, *peitj raiy* (*par-ret*) is usually collected on the mainland not far from Raiyu village. This is the main plastic ingredient of the clay body; it contains 63 per cent clay minerals which include halloysite as well as montmorillanite. The non-plastic element includes quartz and calcite as well as shell fragments. The third material, *peitj rarun*, another temper, has an even lower clay mineral content than the dark brown clay; it is a light yellow brownish-grey and is an unusual material, containing a particularly large amount of inter-layer water, which causes high non-plastic shrinkage. It is difficult to understand the necessity for this ingredient as well as the brown low plasticity clay. The optional addition of the fourth material, *peitj rien*, is even more surprising but it was only ever used sparingly; it is said that an excess of it could cause breaking. Although the potters refer to it as a clay it is not one and is mostly limestone and weathered rock found both on the island and on the mainland.

The preparation of the clay here is a far more elaborate process than anywhere else in Papua New Guinea and even includes the use of a specially made cane sieve, unique in the country. Pot manufacturing processes are carried out in cycles; enough clay is collected and prepared, perhaps over a period of weeks, before pot making is begun.

At the village, the potters spread the brown and 'red' clays out to dry separately on old canoe boards; in recent years it has been found that the clay dries more quickly on sheets of corrugated iron. The dry brown clay is spread on a board with a layer of the 'red' clay on top in the rough proportion of one to five; the mixture is then put into a sieve and agitated under water in a 44-gallon drum (previously a broken *sayanu*). Sea water was used but the potters now use fresh water and claim it makes stronger pots. The *peitj rarun* is sun dried, pounded with a large stone on a board and when dry sieved into a separate container, usually an old pot. The residue from the first sieving is re-pounded and sieved into the pot.

Approximately one week before it is needed some of the now brownish-grey sandy slip is taken from the drum and poured into a large old clay pot to become firmer. The porous pot soaks up the excess water. When ready, the dry *peitj rarun* is first sprinkled in a layer approximately 2 centimetres deep on a wooden board; a 10-centimetre or so thickness of the still sloshy clay mixture is spread on it and more of the dry material sprinkled on top of that. The mixture is now kneaded with the fingers, more temper being added until it is felt to be the right consistency, still very soft. If the fourth material is to be used (only a few potters use it now) it is added dry with the *peitj rarun*. Finally, the mixture is divided into lumps of approximately 3 kilograms which are individually kneaded and thumped on the board and patted into elongated balls.

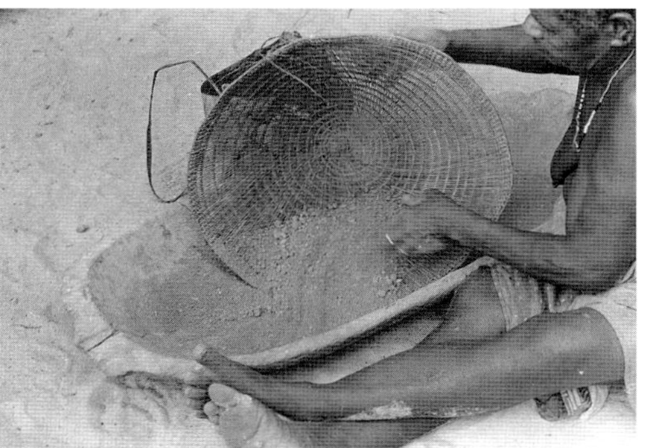

Fig. 9.195
Yetcinta Wakom sieving dry temper in a *wo'uapin*, Sapij hamlet.

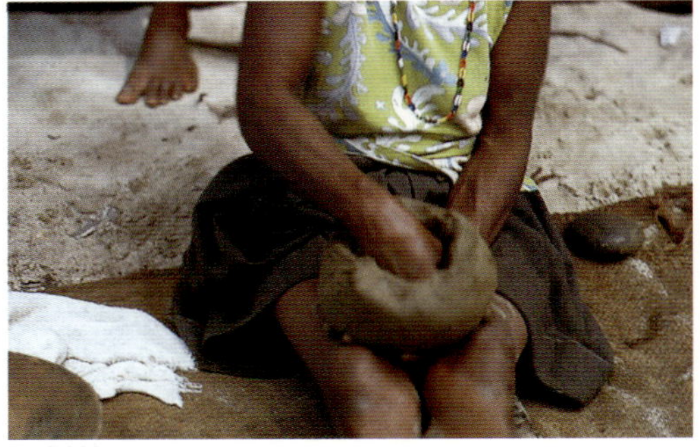

Fig. 9.196

Fig. 9.196
Tanmaok Aijakiel thumping open the lump of clay with her fist, Sapij hamlet, Tumleo Island.

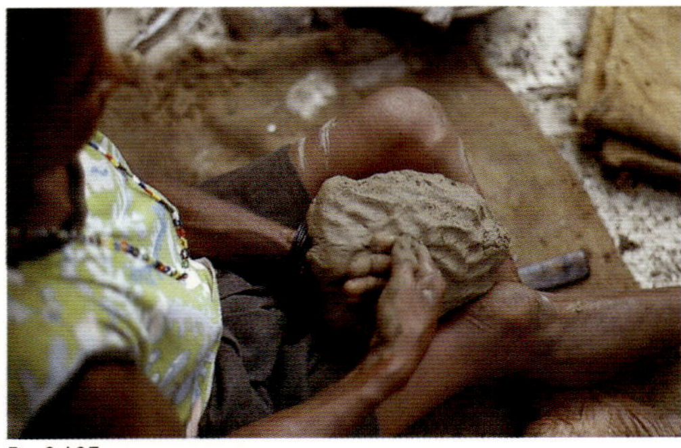

Fig. 9.197

Fig. 9.197
Tanmaok thinning the outside by thumping the wall with her knuckles, Sapij.

The traditional sieves, *wo'uapin*, used for all these potters' materials, are also used for sieving sago and coconut milk. They are made from thin strips of split cane and woven in a conical shape, 30 to 60 centimetres across the mouth and often with scalloped patterns woven in the top portion. The women of Mallol and Arop, the river and lagoon people on the coast west of Aitape, make the sieves; they are one of the trade items with Tumleo although today the Tumleo people often purchase them. Now the Tumleo potters frequently use wire sieves made from a double thickness of fly wire on wooden frames (fig. 9.195).

Tools used in making pots are beaters (paddles) and round stones used as anvils. *Anaarakun* is a narrow beater used for general forming. It is made from hard black palm wood, is about 30 centimetres long and 2 to 4 centimetres wide and is sometimes tapered at one or both ends. *Valak rakun*, a spoon-shaped beater about 30 centimetres long and 8 to 10 centimetres at the widest part, is used in later stages of manufacturing the large *supanu*. *Ai tatun* are smooth round beach stones collected by the potters on the coast near Suain. They are collected only when the seas are calm. Their size depends on the size of the potter's hand; the stone must fit comfortably and be large enough so that the potter's fingertips do not extend past its surface.

For a small pot, one lump of prepared clay will be used. Two to four lumps are needed for larger pots such as sago storage jars. During the first stage, the lump of clay is either held in the left hand or put down on a board while the right fist is punched into the centre of it to form a hole. Erdweg reports a stone being used to pound open the hole, which is the method used at Kaiep. A patrol report in 1950 also tells of the use of a smooth stone to punch a cavity first before the fist is thrust in. The potter sits on the ground with the left leg bent and the left foot tucked under the right knee to form a cradle for the pot which is next gently beaten with the knuckles of the right hand against the supporting left hand inside. When the walls are about 4 to 5 centimetres thick and the rough shape about 20 to 25 centimetres high it is placed upright in the support dish, which acts as a turntable, and is pinched and smoothed with the fingers. In the past broken pot necks were sometimes used to support the pot.

The potter now beats the sides of the pot above the rim of the support dish using the stone, *ai tatun*, and the beater, *anaarakun*, moistening both by dipping the beater into fresh water and trickling the water onto the stone. At this stage the support dish is balanced at a slight angle between the sole of the left foot and the inside of the right knee. The dish's round bottom facilitates easy swivelling of the pot as each section at 'three o'clock' position is completed. Some of the women can achieve this turning of the dish with their feet and without the aid of their hands. When the top half of the sides has been evened to approximately 2 to

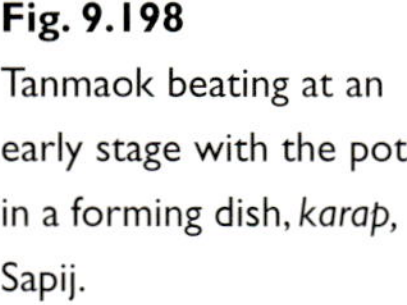

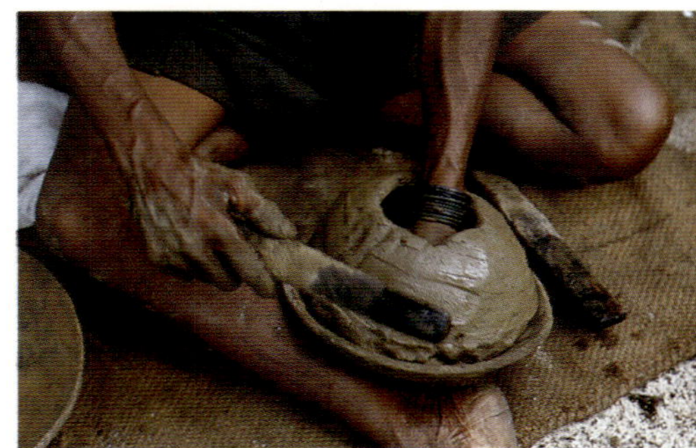

Fig. 9.198
Tanmaok beating at an early stage with the pot in a forming dish, *karap*, Sapij.

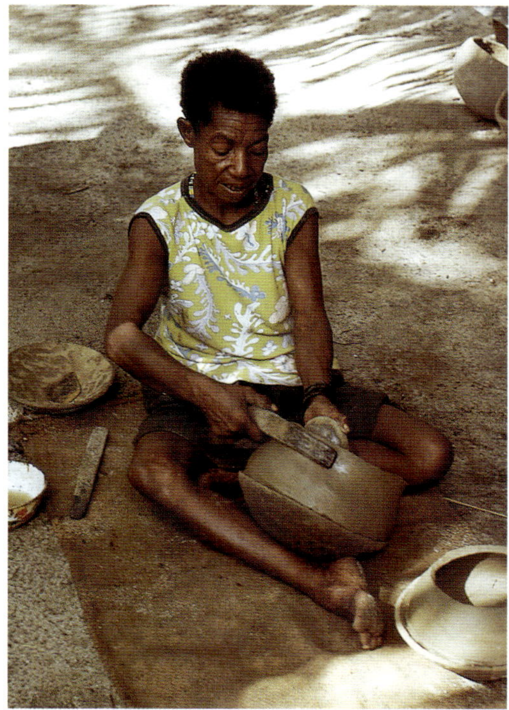

Fig. 9.199
Tanmoak Aijakiel beating the neck into shape with a narrow beater, Sapij hamlet.

3 centimetres the rim is either tapped to flatten and consolidate it or trimmed by cutting with a strip of coconut fibre or wire and then tapped. At this stage the general shape of the pot, and thus its eventual function, is established. Up to this point several pots are made at one sitting, with eight to ten minutes spent on each one. They are then left to firm under the house or in the workshop for half a day or overnight.

For the second stage, the pot is taken out of the support dish and the base is rounded, thinned and smoothed a little by beating. It is now returned to its support in the same upright position, the walls are beaten to a thickness of about 1 to 2 centimetres and the final shape is started; a rough lip is formed or the rim is enlarged for a *sal* or narrowed for a *takam*. If making a *su lapij puak*, the small pot with concave sides, instead of beating from the rim of the support dish upwards the potter beats from the rim of the pot down and inwards to form a hump between the concavity and rounded bottom. The pot is set aside to stiffen again and often while it is drying large cracks appear in the base.

After several hours the pot is gently beaten until all cracks disappear and it is rounded. The potter must choose carefully the ideal time to do this; the rim must be dry enough to hold its shape while the base must be soft enough for the cracks to be closed over. By now the spherical shape has often been enlarged to the extent that it no longer fits in its original support dish and if this is the case it is placed in a larger one. The large *suyanu* may require three such changes. All the smaller pots are beaten with the dish supported on top of the sole of the left foot and balanced against the inside of the right knee. This is not possible with the larger pots, which are beaten with the dish resting on the ground but still supported with the sole of the foot and the knee. At this stage the sides and rim are completed by beating, trimming and decorating. The schedule is changed a little when making a *pier atjek vol* (those pots with handles over the top). Usually these are finished and decorated but left without the handles at the second stage. Then, after beating the base as described in the third stage, the handle is added: a coil is roughly made and attached inside. This is then gently beaten into shape with stone and paddle and decorated as desired.

Water is now rubbed gently over the upper exposed areas and pots are left to become leather-hard

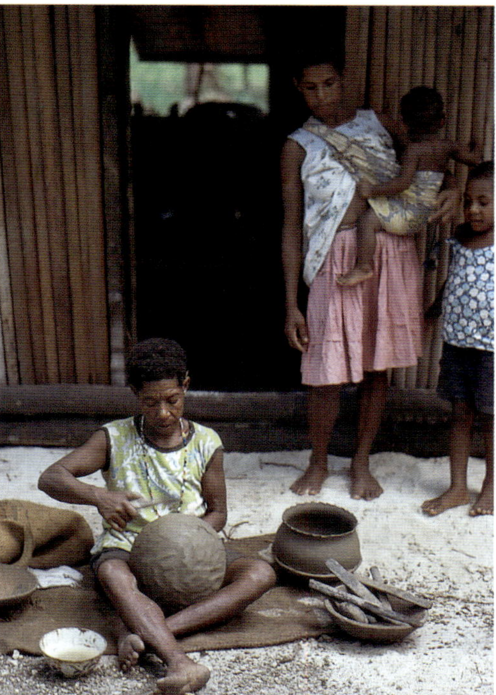

Fig. 9.200
Tanmaok beating the base of the pot, Sapij.

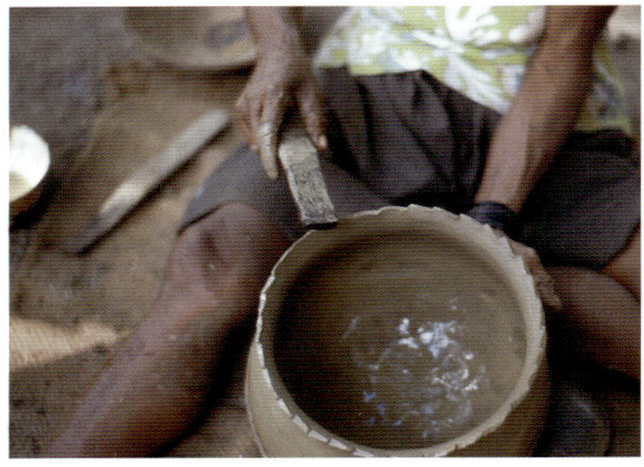

Fig. 9.201
Tanmaok Aijakiel notching the rim, Sapij hamlet, Tumleo Island.

above the dish. In the final stage the pot is removed from the dish and the base gently beaten with a slightly smaller beater to smooth and check cracks. It is important that the top half is very firm before finishing off the base or the rim will crack from pressure. The potter must take care to arrange her legs so that the maximum amount of rim is given support; the pot is almost inverted in her lap with her left arm bent up inside. This process is particularly difficult when making the pots with handles.

Except for those pots with handles, which are left lying on their sides in the sand to dry, the pot is at last inverted in the sand and the base is gently tapped with a lightweight beater. After a quick wipe with water the pot is left for a few days upside down under the house. When it seems dry it is often taken into the house to sit on its side or base until it is completely dry and the potter is ready to fire it.

Apart from his brief description of what he calls the normal method on Tumleo Island, Parkinson (1900) reports an extraordinary technique that he suggests is probably only used to produce a larger amount of pots quickly. The potters make a semispherical bowl shape from grass and coconut leaves. This is lined with clay and the clay is brought out over the edge to form a rim. When it is dry the clay, in its 'mould', is fired; the grass and leaves naturally burn away and the clay bowl remains, showing the impression of the leaves on the outside.

Schurig (1930) describes what she calls the Stückchentechnik (piece technique) at Tumleo: 'a technique in which they [pots] are put together from little pieces' but she then gives almost word for word Parkinson's description of pot making in the northern Solomons (Parkinson 1907). There is no evidence or memory among Tumleo people today of either of these two methods although some potters in the Leitre area do use a piece technique.

During World War II much of this coast suffered damage from bombing and the Tumleo islanders were forced to flee to the mainland after their homes had been destroyed. When the potters came to start up their industry again they were at first lost without a support dish and made use of a rounded metal lightshade left behind by troops.

For firing the potters carry their pots down to the beach or to a clearing in the village. Most potters preheat their pots, especially the larger ones. But first a kind of ritual is carried out which is considered most important by the potters: each pot is rubbed carefully all over with the hands either before or after preheating. No reason can be ascertained for this ritual but the women believe that the pots will break if it is not done.

Preheating is achieved by placing the pots close together on their sides in the sand and putting a bunch of burning coconut palm leaves in their mouths; the pots are turned regularly to ensure even heating. When they are too hot to hold easily they are ready. Now they are set in about three rows, facing outwards with openings upwards; an average of twenty pots is fired at one time. Coconut fronds are spread on the sand, one in between each two pots and radiating outwards; more are placed across them and on top of the pots and then leafy fronds on top again. Some bamboo and coconut leaf bases are used, too, and occasionally some driftwood. The dry leaves are lit in several different places and the fire flares up quickly; more fronds are immediately put on any uncovered spots. After about fifteen minutes, when the fire has died down, the pots are manoeuvred onto their other sides with the aid of long flexible sticks. More fuel is piled over them and they are left for another ten minutes or so. The potter now checks for pots with too much black marking and turns these over into hot spots. They are then lifted off onto the sand and left to cool. The main firing takes about thirty minutes. Erdweg reports firings taking three times as long but perhaps he counted the time for preheating and moving the pots to the main firing area.

At some time, either immediately after firing or later (sometimes just before pots are traded), the outsides of the pots are blackened over a small fire of coconut leaves; it is believed that this makes them stronger. After being blackened over the fire the still hot pot is sealed with sago solution rubbed over the outside and splashed on the inside with a piece of coconut husk.

Sissano

On the coast about half way between Leitre and Aitape is the Sissano lagoon and the group of villages known as the Sissano villages is found on the western shores of the lagoon and on the nearby coast. The coastal village of Sarai (previously Sia, Sera or Serra) is further to the north-west. About 10 kilometres to the south-east of Sissano, on the other side of the lagoon and on the coast, are the Arop villages, now grouped as Arop 1 and Arop 2. The people of these villages are all Austronesians. Inland, some 12 kilometres from Sissano, is Ramo village which is part of a group of a non-Austronesian language in the same family as that under which most of the Leitre villages are grouped. These villages will be referred to collectively as the Sissano area.

Very little information is available about this area. Neuhauss (1911) mentions eight Sissano villages but says that pottery was made in only one of them; he gives no village name but probably refers to the group known as the Sissano villages. He adds that coils are rolled on a firm base and are therefore very smooth. Some description of pot making in Sissano has been given by Lewis (1945), who also reports that the potters are coil builders but names no villages. He describes the pots as being thin and fragile and showing the thumb pressure marks made while joining the coils. The first coil is tightly spiralled in a forming dish and the walls built up in what sounds like a normal coiling technique.

It was reported that pots used to be made at Arop a long time ago. The only villages said to be making pots now are Ramo and Sarai. No information was obtained concerning the Ramo manufacturing techniques, pottery style or types. The Sarai people make sago frying pans and cooking pots of a rough sort similar to those from Leitre. They also used to make sago storage pots. Some of their larger cooking pots have simple applied groups of line motifs placed below the rim or sometimes a series of small holes punctured into the top of the rim. Neuhauss speaks of frying pans made by the Sarai people and used by the Sissano. He describes the method of cooking flat sago cakes with two clay bowls as 'peculiar' but it is probably the same method as that used by the Tumleo people. The Sissano villagers are now supplied with pots by Ramo, Sarai and Tumleo and there are reports of trading between Arop and Lumi. This area needs further study.

Leitre

Forty kilometres to the south-east of Vanimo there is a mission settlement at Leitre. There are several villages on the coast within 10 kilometres or so of Leitre; these will be referred to as the Leitre villages. Some of the people of these villages used to live in the inland mountain areas and migrated to the coast, in some cases intermarrying with coastal dwellers; thus, there tends to be an amalgam of several languages, all, however, non-Austronesian.

People of some of the Leitre villages used to make pots in the past, some still do. The villages display a variety of techniques and could not be said to constitute a single industry or tradition although in all cases women are the potters. The villages have been collected together here solely because of their geographical proximity. The people of Isi, the village

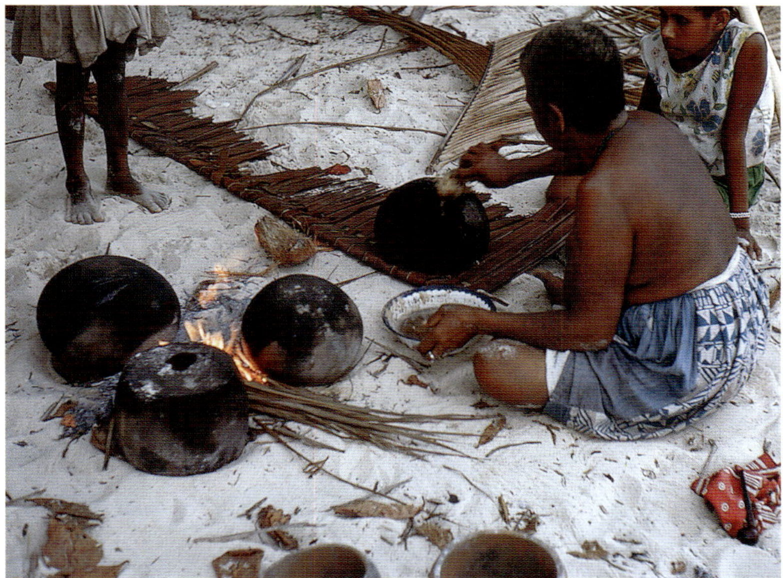

Fig. 9.202
Yetcinta Wakom applying sago solution to seal the pot after blackening it over a small smoky fire, Sapij.

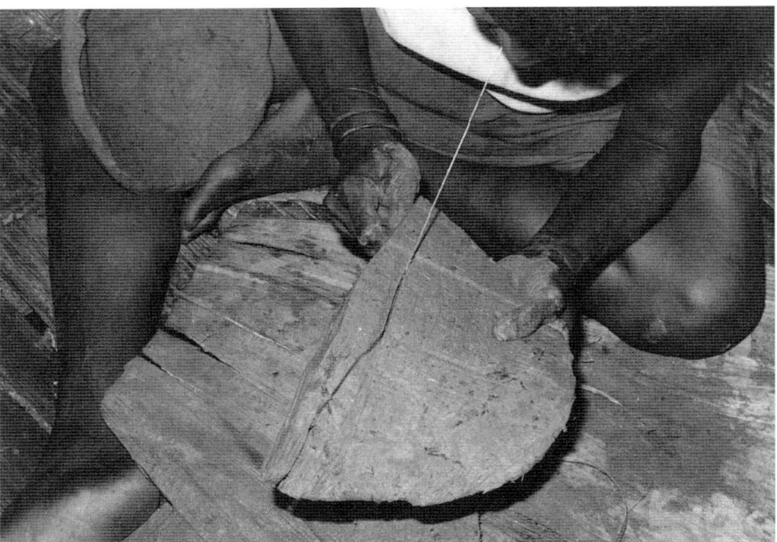

Fig. 9.203
Victoria Bobi slicing off strips of clay ready to build up the walls of a pot, Isi village, Leitre.

nearest to Leitre, still make pots. Always coastal dwellers, they speak the same language as Vanimo. The other groups who still make pots belong to a different family of languages but of the same stock. Some of the people who have moved from inland to the coast used to make pots in their former mountain villages where they had good clay. Very little information about these people was obtainable but it seems that they probably made coil pots; now, with only inferior clay on the coast, they have mostly ceased pot making, the exception being the Rawo people who still occasionally make coiled pots. Some of the Pino people were always on the coast and make pottery with their traditional paddle-and-anvil technique.

Pot making was briefly observed by the authors at Isi village. Clay is collected from a swamp a little less than 1 kilometre inland and there is a plentiful supply. The brown clay is free of stones but full of roots, some of which are removed. It is a fine-grained clay which packs tightly. The non-plastics are mostly quartz and a little magnetite. The clay is prepared for use by pressing it between thumbs and fingers, removing any roots before banging it into balls weighing about 2 kilograms. The potter sits on the floor in her house. She flattens two balls of clay using a long flat wooden beater, with the clay resting on a thick slice of tree trunk covered by a 'limbum' mat. Both pieces of clay are beaten out to about 30 centimetres diameter and 2 to 3 centimetres thick. The edges are tapped with the beater to thicken and consolidate them. First one slab is held against the inside of the potter's right knee and with a stone held on the inside of the pot she quickly beats it with a wider wooden beater into a shallow dish shape, using her left foot to help move the dish around. The potter now slices the other slab into strips of varying lengths up to 30 centimetres and about 2 to 3 centimetres thick by holding a thread of 'limbum' fibre between her teeth and one hand and holding the disc of clay in the other hand. She slices towards herself through the slab. The slices of clay are overlapped on the outside and beaten with the wide beater onto the top edge of the basic shape. After the first row of slices is added the pot is moved to a banana bark ring where more slices are added and beaten into place. With further beating the shape is gradually brought into a restricted form. Finally, wet fingers and hands smooth the whole pot (figs 2.22, 9.203).

Sago storage jars used to be made, but seldom are now, by this piece technique that is very similar to the method used for sago storage pots at Vanimo. Frying pans are made by the same method, without slices being added. Pots are dried in the banana bark rings in the house; firing was not observed or recorded. The cooking pots made at Isi have a much rougher finish than those made at Vanimo and range from simple unrestricted to restricted forms. Pots are mostly undecorated but some have simple, rough incised markings, similar to Vanimo but not as precise, and some have applied knobs.

At Pino cooking pots similar to Vanimo pots are made by the paddle-and-anvil method. Their tools are smaller than the Vanimo ones but the pots are well made, with more decoration than at the other Leitre villages: incised motifs, some similar to Vanimo's, some more swirling.

At Rawo village a half coconut shell is used to beat a lump of clay into a concave shape. The shaping is then completed with fingers only: the right forefinger is crooked and scraped around the inside of the pot, raising the walls; it is supported on the outside with the left hand. In the past larger pots were coiled. Pots are rarely made here now and then only small cooking pots and frying pans.

Another group of people who made coil pots were the Puarri, also migrants from the mountains, but they lack suitable clay on the coast and are not making pots any more. Ningera and Taris-Nowage, a combined village, contains some former hill people who used to make pots but no longer do.

There is no longer very active trading from the Leitre villages but Waterstone village, near Vanimo, and Rawo get some cooking pots and frying pans from Isi. Most of the Leitre villagers still get some pots from Vanimo, especially the big sago storage jars which they no longer make themselves. Leitre people still have the old glass beads to use as money for their trading but they are not as important to them as they are to the Vanimo people. A more vigorous material culture seems to have existed between Vanimo and the border area than along the Leitre coast.

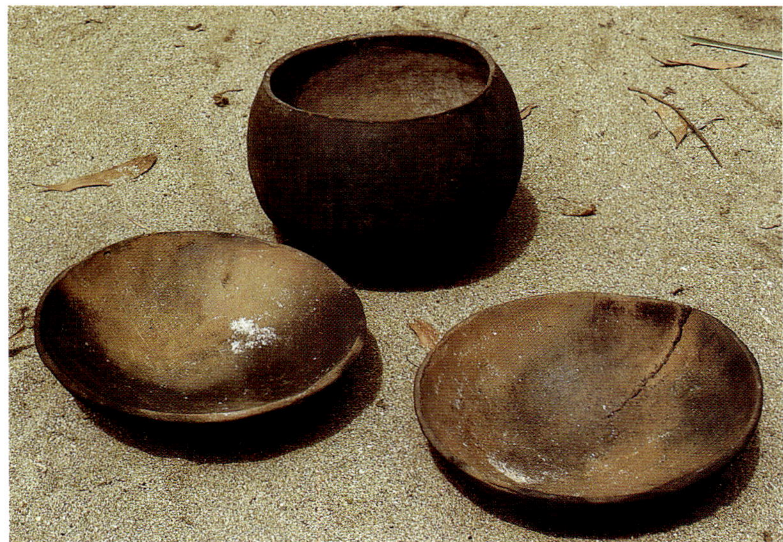

Fig. 9.204
Leitre sago frying pans at Waterstone village, Vanimo.

Vanimo

Vanimo, an isolated pot making village on the north coast, is about 3 kilometres west of the town of Vanimo, known in the past by the Germans as Angrishafen. This non-Austronesian group speaks the Vanimo language which is in the same language family as neighbouring villages up to and over the border into Irian Jaya.

Vanimo women make a variety of cooking pots, storage jars and, occasionally, frying pans. The sago jars sit in rows against the walls of the houses, supported on cane rings and with pots resting on top as lids. Water is collected in bamboo tubes and used to be stored in cooking pots; it is now kept in kettles or saucepans.

The *eda*, a simple round-based spherical vessel is used for general cooking and sago stirring. A variation has an everted rim and incised decoration and is slightly larger, 20 to 23 centimetres high. The sago storage jar, *hlu*, used to store wet sago flour, comes in two forms: a round-based spherical vessel with an everted rim and about 40 centimetres high and an ellipsoid vessel about 50 centimetres high. Both forms are decorated with applied or incised decorations (fig. 9.205). Vessels used in ceremonies and 'tambaran' activities are called *lan*. They are cooking pot types covered with cane and may be incised or left undecorated. Frying pans, *hawe*, are used to cook cakes made of sago flour and grated coconut.

The Vanimo people have never in their memory made clay plates or serving bowls and do not use wooden plates. Food was served from the cooking pot into small 'limbum' baskets, about 25 centimetres square and 7 centimetres deep, made in a similar fashion to the carrying baskets: folded at the ends and tied together with vines. These are sometimes still used but have been mostly replaced by enamel bowls. Finsch (1888) records the use of a large potsherd serving as a fireplace on large boats along the coast.

Each Vanimo family used to own several ceremonial cooking pots, *fan*, one for each 'tambaran'. If a pot needed to be replaced, the 'tambaran', knowing its pot by the attributes woven into the cane, would set about replacing it, putting the old broken pot outside the house of the family to which it belonged. A new pot would be placed outside the house and the name of the 'tambaran' for whom it was intended was called out. He would come in the night, take the pot to the men's house and decorate it. When ready, it was returned to the woman's house where she stored it for special occasions. For these it was filled with the food appropriate for that particular 'tambaran': if he came from the sea it would be filled with fish, if from an area east of the village, it would be filled with the root vegetable 'mami', a type of yam. The men would then collect the pot and take it to the men's house, where the food was eaten by the men, who

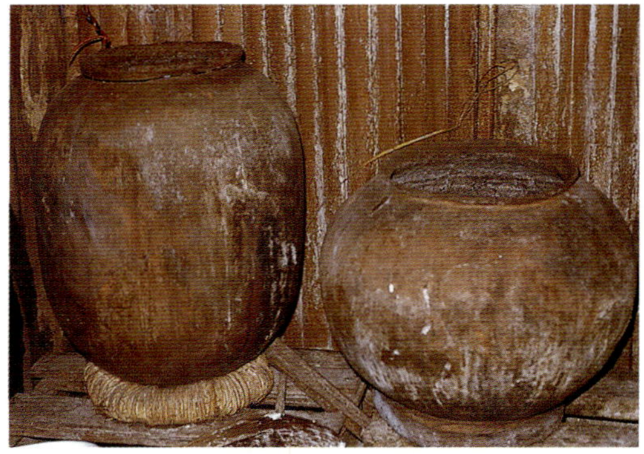

Fig. 9.205
Vanimo sago storage pots in an Isi village house, Leitre.

said that the 'tambaran' ate the food. A similar custom existed just west of Vanimo, at Warimo village, where pots are imported from Vanimo and Opitei Island.

Vanimo pots are traded west to Warimo, Yako, Musu and Wutung on the Irian Jaya border. In Dutch colonial times there was a great deal of contact between the people of these villages and the people across the border at Jayapura and farther west; now, with border controls, this has almost ceased. The people are interrelated and movement across the border is a source of political contention. Traditionally glass beads were used in all trading to the west. None of today's people seems to know the origin of these blue, green and sometimes spirally striped beads. Researchers have suggested that the beads are of Venetian origin and came with the first Portuguese or Spanish navigators or that they originated in India; Dutch ethnographer van der Sande (1907) claims that they are of Chinese derivation. The beads are now becoming scarce but are still used in bride price and ceremonial payments and play an important role in other village transactions.

People inland from Vanimo – the Bewani, Sossi and others – were never pot makers nor did they use clay pots. Kuaso, Mandi and Mondal (1998) have recorded an additional pottery industry at Krisa village, 17 kilometres south of Vanimo, Kilimeri Census Division, West Sepik Province which was already defunct in 1980 but where women potters made 'generally undecorated' cooking pots within living memory. Now a new road gives them good access to the coast and they come down from the mountains and buy, for cash, pots as well as trade store saucepans from Vanimo village. Vanimo pots are also traded to Waterstone village on the coast east of Vanimo and to Ningere and other Leitre villages. These people especially like to acquire the big sago storage jars which are rarely made now.

The Vanimo women have a song which they call 'stori bilong sospen'.

> A woman called Yavwu lived long long ago and was the first woman in Vanimo village to make pots. No one had taught her; she made up the method of using stone and paddle and it was she who taught the other women, who in turn passed the craft on to their daughters.
>
> She married a man from Mallol (a village on a lagoon about 110 kilometres east of Vanimo in the Aitape district). She went to live there with him and after a while became pregnant. But when her time came she found herself in the village without another woman to help her – everyone was away working in their gardens and only her husband was near. He witnessed the birth, which is forbidden by traditional law. This gave Yavwu great shame so that she felt she could no longer stay in Mallol. She placed the newborn baby in a basket and pushed him off from the beach out to sea. Gathering her belongings, including her potting tools, she set off to walk back to Vanimo, her home village. One of her brothers was standing on the beach at Vanimo some time later when the basket containing the baby floated in. He recognised the child and took it to his house. Later Yavwu walked in herself and settled down in Vanimo

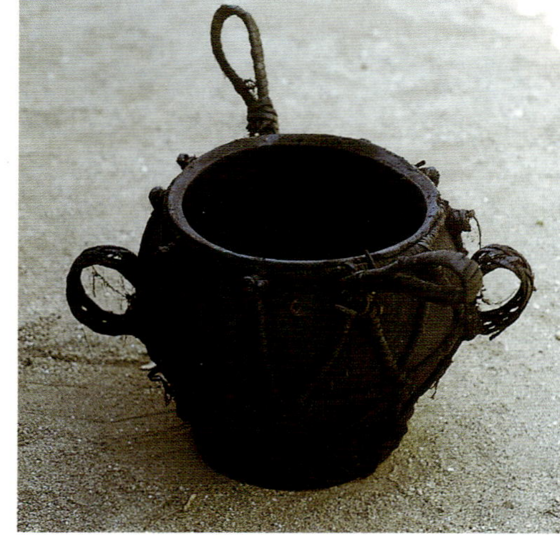

Fig. 9.206
Old ceremonial vessel, *lan*, Warimo village, near Vanimo, *h* 34 cm.

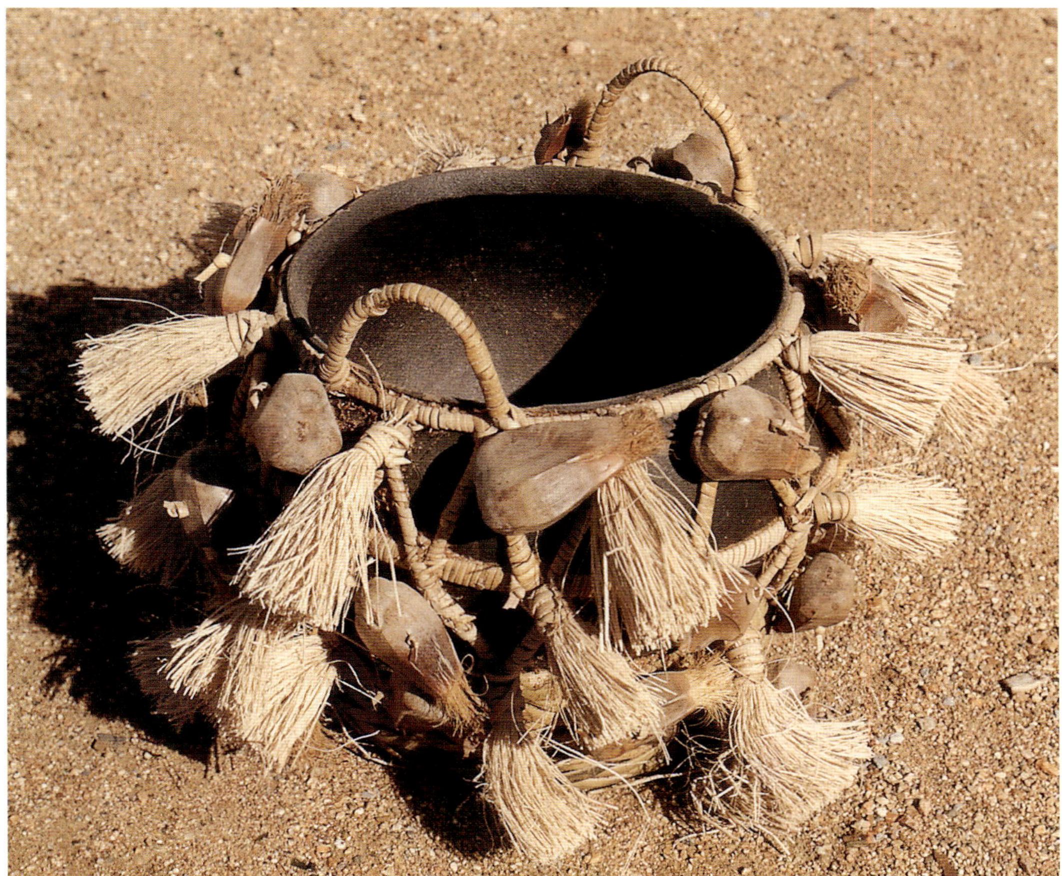

Fig. 9.207
Ceremonial pot, *lan,* newly covered with cane by Nanuku, Warimo.

for the rest of her life. She then taught the women how to make pots.

A yellowish-brown clay, *eda edayino*, is prised out of small pockets in a limestone cliff above the Dadi River, about 3 kilometres from Vanimo village. It is moderately plastic, fine-grained and contains quartz and limestone among the non-plastic components. The women press pieces of the clay between fingers and thumbs to remove small pieces of coral before loading the lumps into 'limbum' baskets to carry them back to the village. The clay is kept in covered baskets for some weeks. During sunny weather it is kept under the house but it is exposed to the rain at times and if it dries out salt water is sprinkled over it (fresh water is used during clay preparation). Sand collected from the Dadi River is sieved through coconut fibre (the flexible part found between the leaf-base and the trunk). The wet sand, in the proportion of roughly one to three parts of clay, is kneaded in, folded and re-folded for thirty to forty-five minutes and any remaining stones and sticks are removed. Lumps of 1 to 3 kilograms are prepared about a week before the pots are made. The clay is patted into balls and stored uncovered under or in the house for up to a week until it is sufficiently firm for the potter to use.

Tools are sentimentally valued and often handed down through generations. Flattish, rounded, smooth stones are collected from a river many kilometres up the coast. They vary in size according to the potter's hand but average about 10 centimetres in diameter and are used for pounding the clay at the first stage of manufacture and later as an anvil. For the smoothing and finishing stages potters use paddles, *himli*, of varying shapes which are made of heavy fine-grained 'kwila' (*Intsia bijuga*) wood. Although made of a heavy timber these

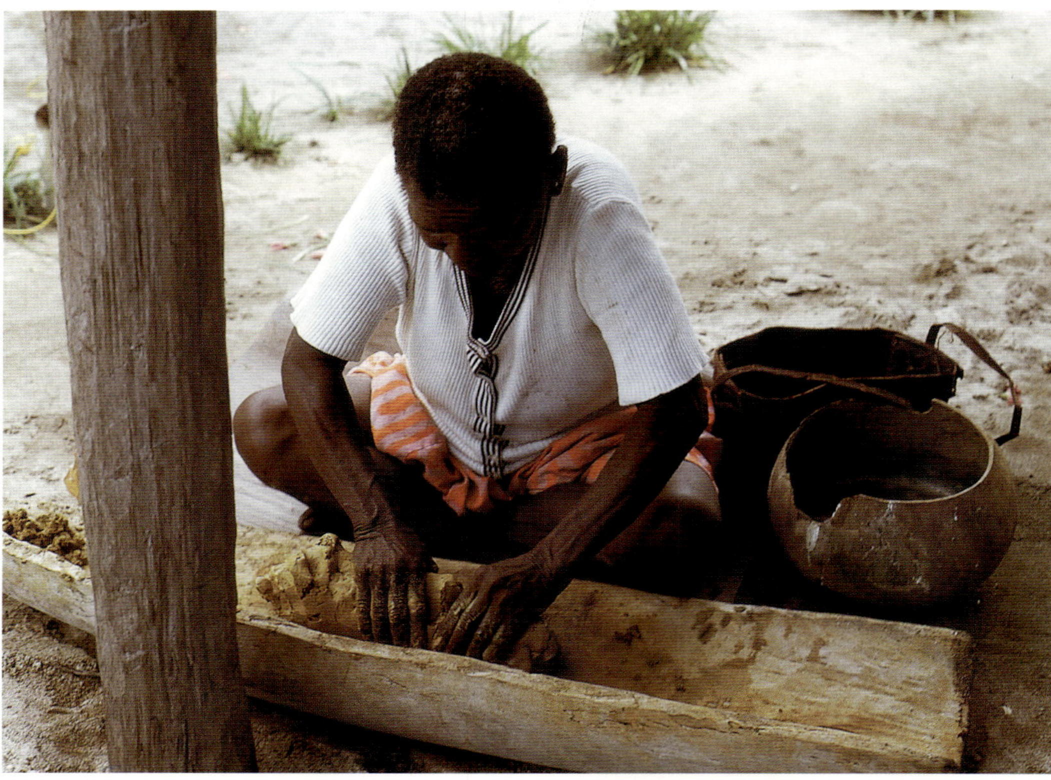

Fig. 9.208
Oma kneading clay in part of an old dug-out canoe, Vanimo village.

smooth paddles are thinly carved and light. The general shape is triangular, with either a slight or deep waist close to the thinner end. The surface is slightly convex and both ends are used. The beaters vary from 22 to 25 centimetres long and 6 to 11 centimetres wide and taper to a rounded point or have a knobbed end. A sliver of thin bamboo or a piece of coconut fibre, more commonly now a knife, is used to level the top edge of the pot.

The potter works sitting on the 'limbum' with legs spread out and the pot on the ground between them. A ball of clay is first flattened out into a disc about 30 centimetres in diameter and 3 centimetres thick by pounding it with the stone (fig. 2.21). The edge of the disc is firmed by tapping with a wooden beater. Next she holds the disc flat on her hand and shapes it into a shallow dish by tapping the stone into the centre. This dish is supported on its side in the ring-cushion while the potter beats it against the anvil stone with the narrow-ridged paddle, thus forcing the clay upwards and thinning the walls. The pot is then placed upright in the ring while the top edge is tapped gently with the narrow end of the 'kwila' beater to strengthen and thicken it. Beating is resumed with the pot resting sideways in the support.

As the walls grow, they are bellied out and brought in a little at the top to form a full, rounded shape. When satisfied that the walls are thinned as much as is practical – to approximately 6 millimetres – the potter uses the smooth, thin paddle for finishing. This is moistened and used very lightly in conjunction with the stone to smooth the outside of the pot by removing the texture left by the ridged paddle. The rim is now moistened with wet fingers and, with the narrow end of the tapered paddle held firmly against the inside top edge and her left hand supporting outside, the potter forms an outward sloping lip by using brisk sweeping movements towards her body. For final smoothness she passes her wet hands quickly all over the pot, inside and out. Vanimo potters use fairly stiff clay at the start and this enables them to finish the pots in one sitting. If for some reason the clay were softer the pot would be put aside to become firmer at any stage of its production.

A different method is used to build the large sago storage pots. The base is formed as usual by the paddle-and-anvil technique until it becomes a wide dish. At that stage the walls are built up layer by layer using the piece technique, as at nearby Leitre villages. Pieces sliced off a lump of clay with a big knife are flattened between thumbs and fingers and then draped over the rim and beaten on with stone and paddle. Three or four cooking pots can be made in one day but the storage jars take three days to complete and are made infrequently.

If the pot is to be decorated, this is done while it is still damp. A small pointed stick is used for incising or applied motifs are added. Simple geometric patterns are used, sometimes combined with family clan designs in the form of stylised lizards and other motifs. The simple spherical cooking pots without rims are never decorated; cooking pots or storage jars with rims can be left undecorated, too, but most have motifs placed just below the rim, either concentrated in one area or scattered around the pot. The women of Vanimo, traditionally and some still today, have cicatrices cut on their shoulders; these motifs are the same clan designs as are used on the pots and are similar in character to tattoo designs in the Humboldt Bay area.

At Vanimo village special small houses are built for storing firewood and these are also used as pot drying houses. A small verandah with overhanging roof gives access to the high level floor where pots are stored to dry, some upside down on their rims, some sitting in thick padded rings. They may also be dried sitting on the sandy floor. They are left for months before firing and this is carried out in the dry season only. The large storage pots are sometimes left to dry for over two years and often get damaged by rain from leaky roofs.

Well-dried coconut fronds are used as fuel for firing, which must not take place for about a fortnight after rain. The pieces of coconut fuel are carried to a place near the beach where a bed of thin fronds is laid in two layers. The number of pots fired will depend on size; an average firing could be about six cooking pots. Pots are placed on a platform of sticks in two rows on their sides, bottoms touching and openings facing outwards. More fronds and leaf-bases are leant up against the pots, sloping in towards the top. During the firing fuel may be added or pieces pushed back onto the pots with a long stick. Within about thirty minutes the fire has burnt away to ashes and the pots are rolled aside and immediately splashed with cold fresh water. The women believe that unless this is done the pots will not turn red. They sizzle and steam for a few minutes after this drastic treatment which does not, however, appear to cause cracking. They are a warm rich red with some patches of yellow or grey.

Sometimes sago solution is rubbed on the pots with a piece of coconut husk after firing and this

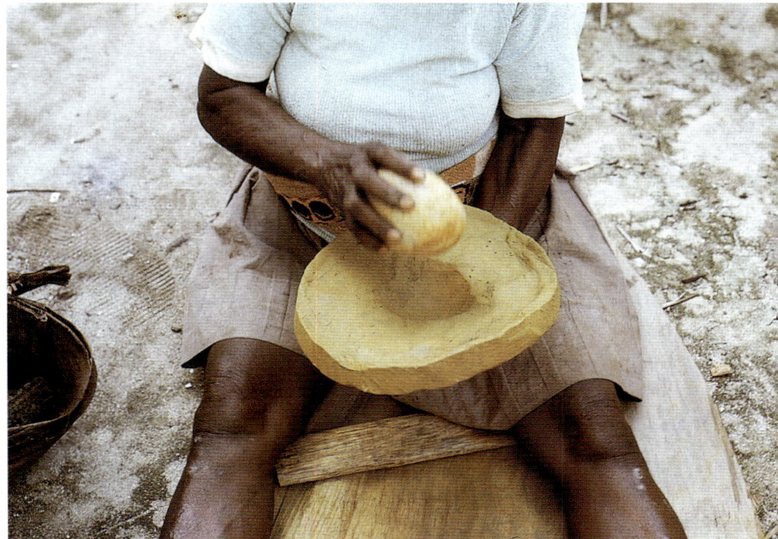

Fig. 9.209
A stone is tapped into the centre of the base to form a dish shape, Vanimo.

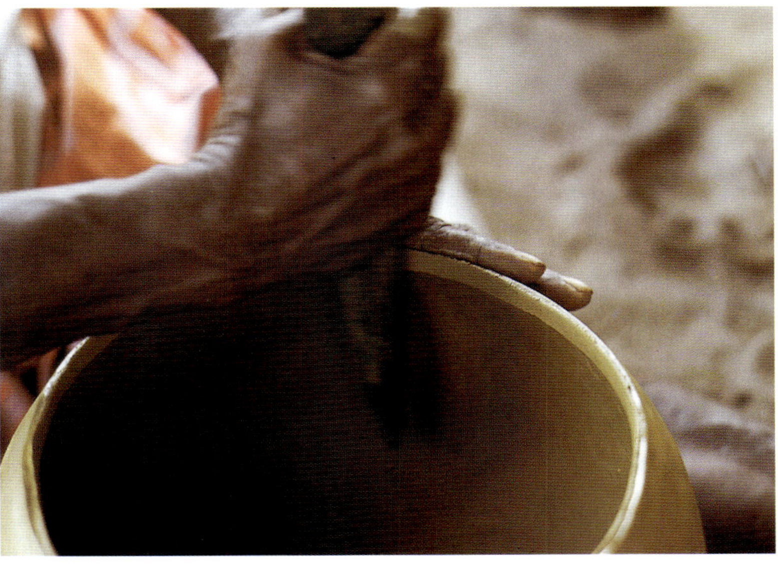

Fig. 9.210
Forming the rim with the narrow end of a triangular paddle, Vanimo.

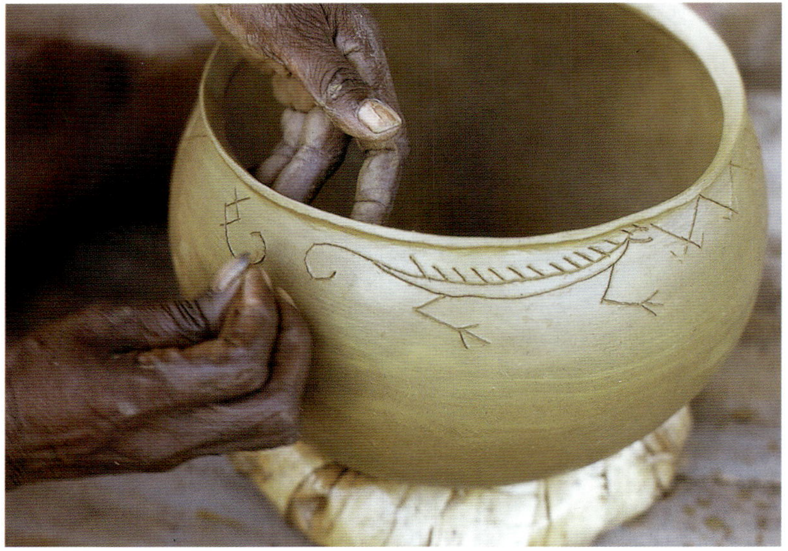

Fig. 9.211
Oma incising a lizard decoration on a cooking pot, Vanimo village.

gives them a glossy finish. This is only for aesthetic reasons, according to the potters, who claim that the pots are made stronger by keeping them on racks over the fireplaces in the houses before use. The combination of these two treatments leaves the Vanimo pots with a more shiny black finish than any other pots seen by the authors in Papua New Guinea (fig. 9.214). After use as cooking pots the sago sheen is naturally burnt away and the pot takes on the normal sooty appearance.

The skill of weaving the basket carrier used around the ceremonial pot, *lan*, is still known by the men of Warimo. One was made by Nanuku at Warimo in 1973 for the Papua New Guinea Museum in Port Moresby. A split cane ring about 5 centimetres high is first woven; the pot is placed in this and a strong cane ring is fixed around it immediately under the turned-out rim. Flexible split cane is bound up and down in a triangular pattern from rim to base. One more circle of cane is placed around the widest circumference of the pot, handles are made from the top ring and then all are bound with extra cane to thicken each part. Tufts of thinly split cane and nuts and seeds are attached at regular intervals around the pot in three layers (figs 9.206, 9.207).

At Opitei Island off the coast of Irian Jaya pots are made which are similar to those from Vanimo but the authors have no information concerning techniques of production.

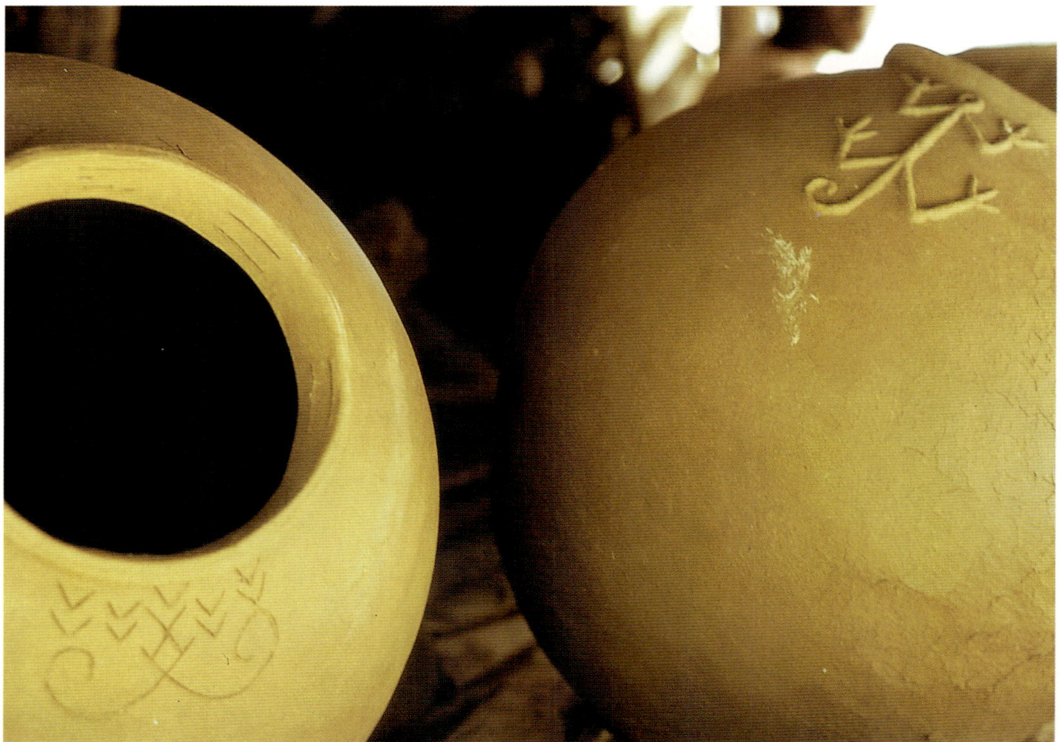

Fig. 9.212
Sago storage jars, with applied and incised decoration, damaged by a storm while drying, Vanimo village.

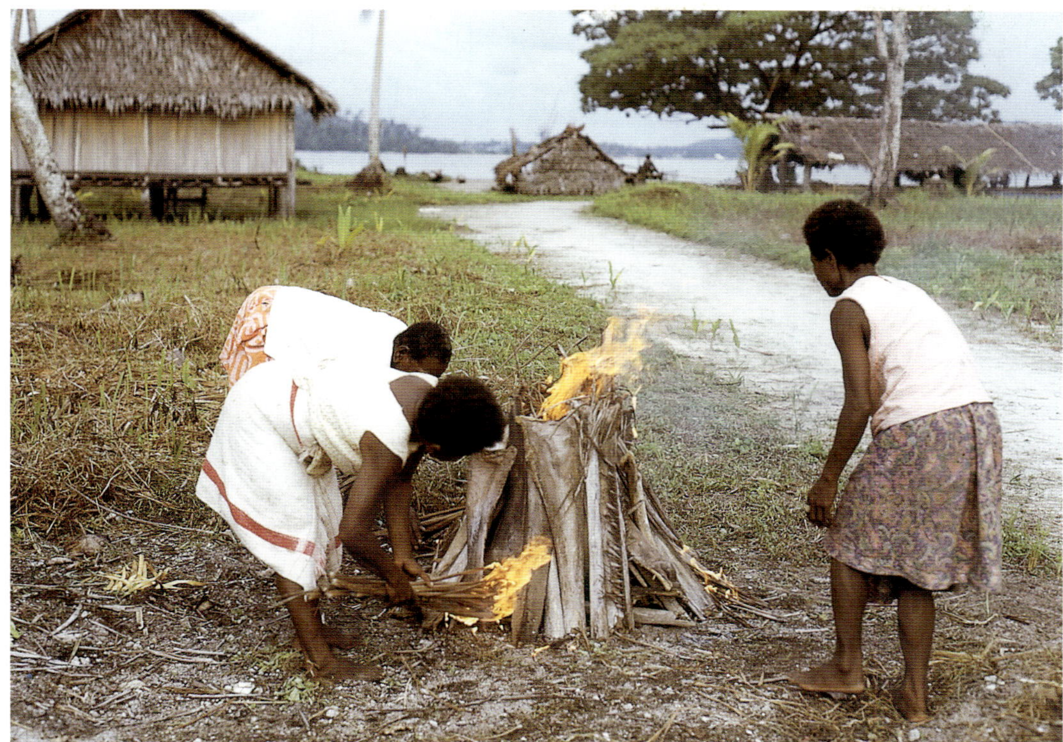

Fig. 9.213
Oma and friends beginning a firing, Vanimo village.

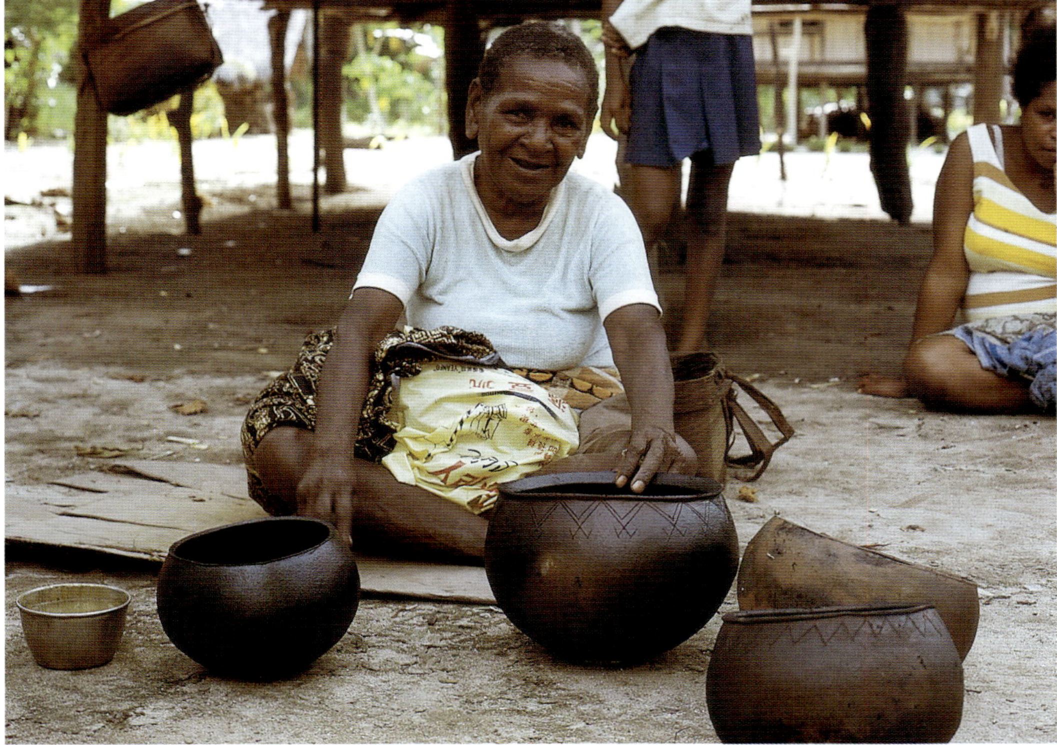

Fig. 9.214
Oma with her pots at Vanimo village. They are black from smoking in the house and shiny from sago coating.

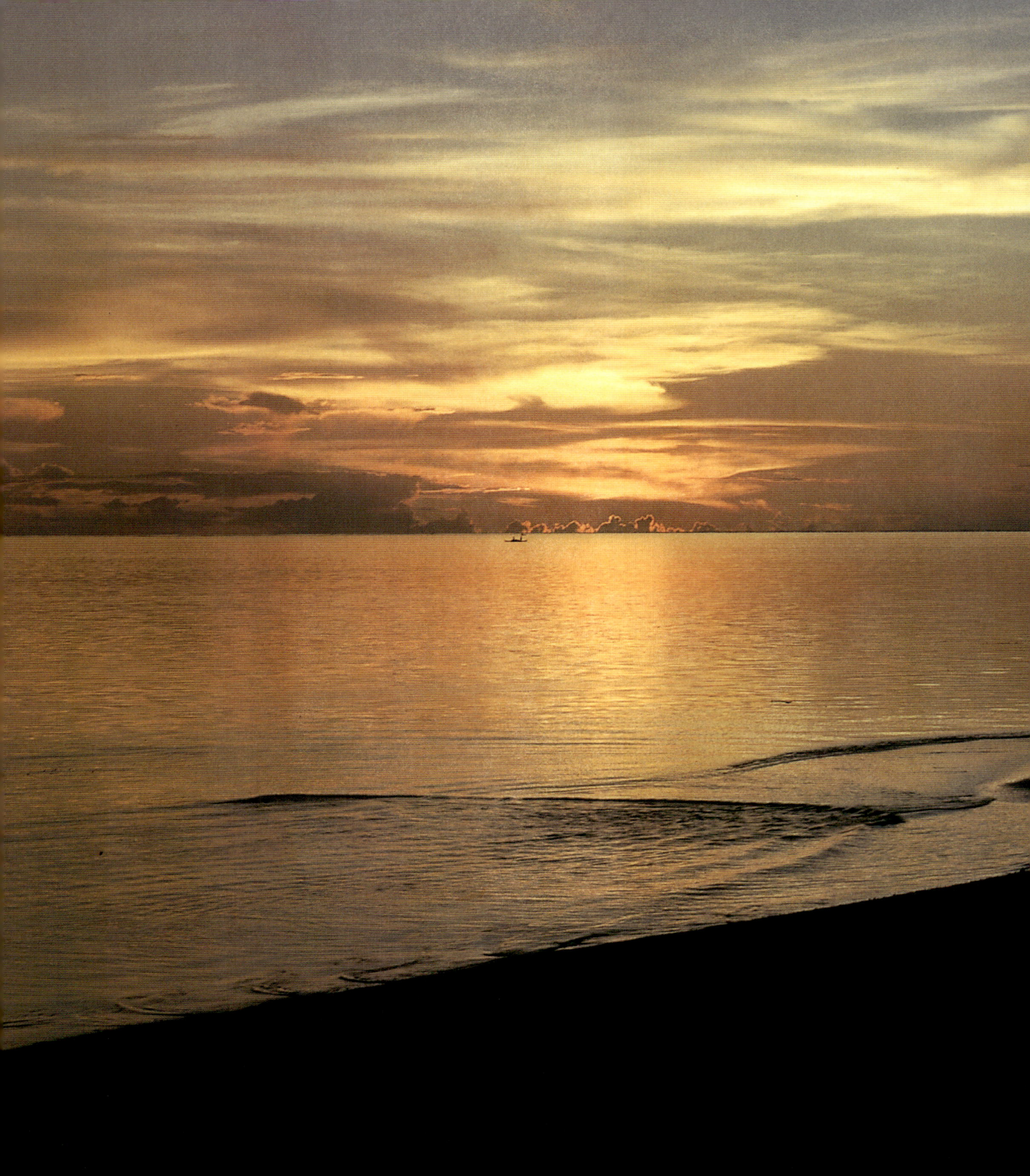

10 Manus Province

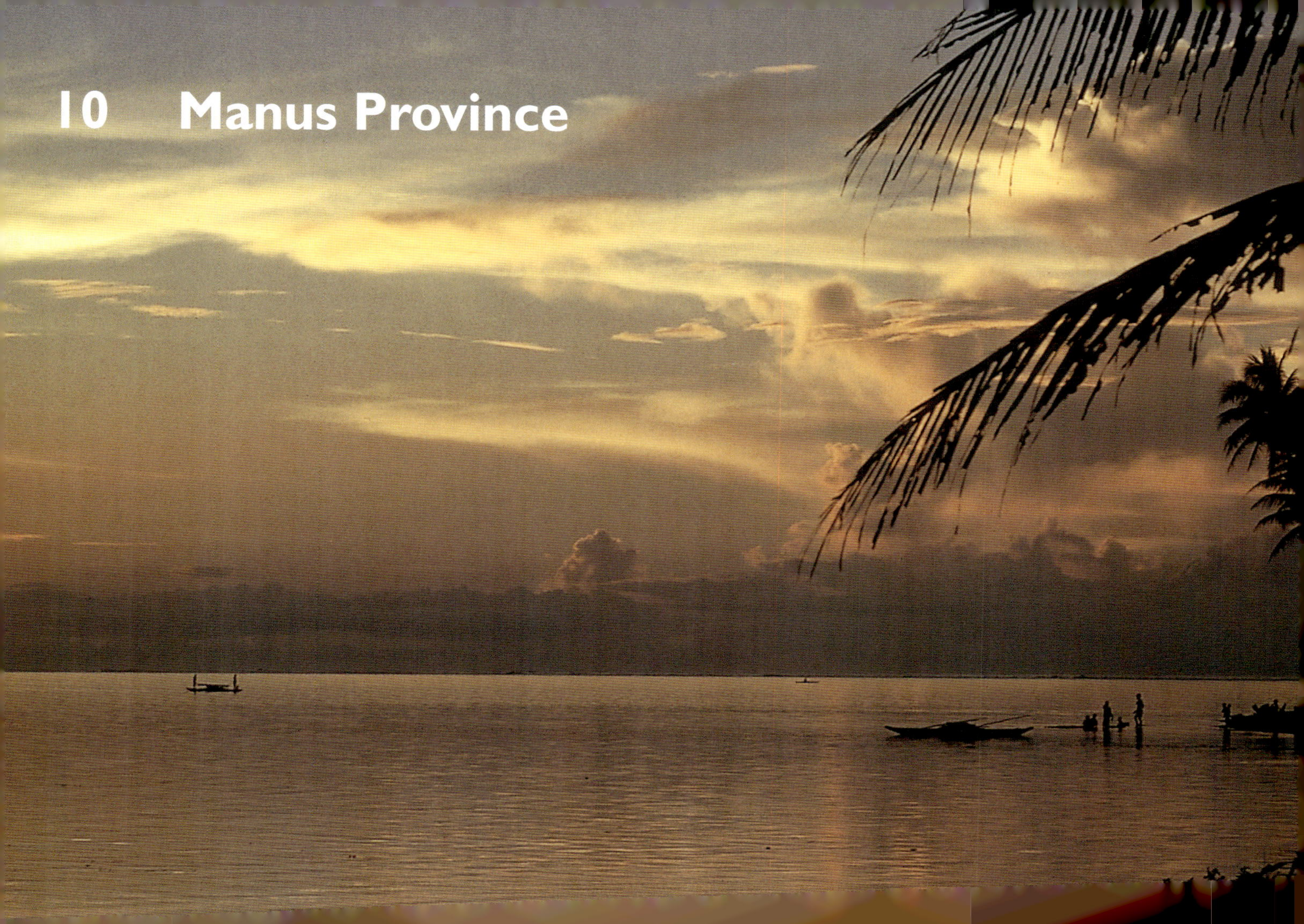

Manus Province consists of the Admiralty Islands and small island groups to the west. The Admiralty Islands are part of the Bismarck Archipelago and the only islands of this large group where pots are produced. The largest islands of the Bismarck Archipelago are New Britain and New Ireland; no pot making has been recorded on these islands since European contact; however, important archaeological sites on Watom Island, at Talasea in New Britain and in New Ireland have yielded Lapita-style pottery sherds.

Manus Island (previously known as Greater Admiralty) is the largest of the Admiralty group, with numerous small islands, nearly all of which are low-lying atolls, scattered around its coast. One of these atolls, Hus, lying in the coral reef north of Manus, is the home of a group of women potters and at nearby Pityliu Island some of the older women remember making pots in the past. Other potters live on another small island, M'Buke, which is about 25 kilometres south of Manus Island. The women of Timoenai (Moenai) on the south coast of Manus are also pot makers. Previously they lived on the Tawi Islands, about 8 kilometres to the east of Timoenai and originally they came from the even smaller Johnston Islands between M'Buke and Lou

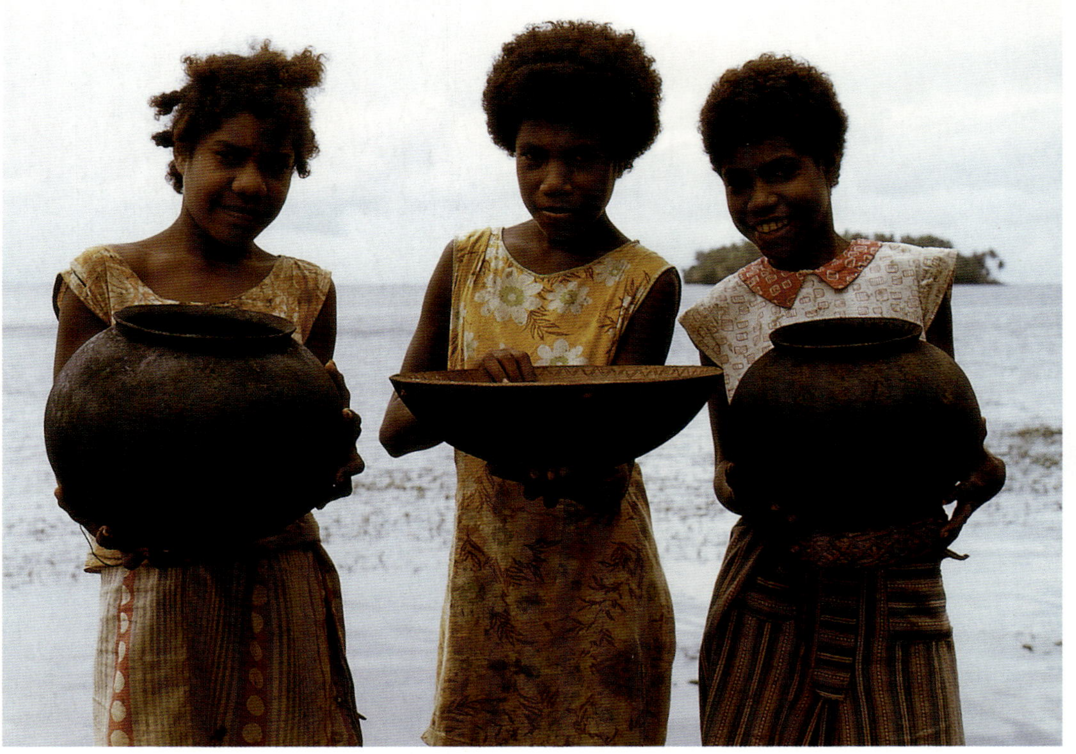

Fig. 10.2
Three M'Buke Island girls with cooking and water pots and a frying pan.

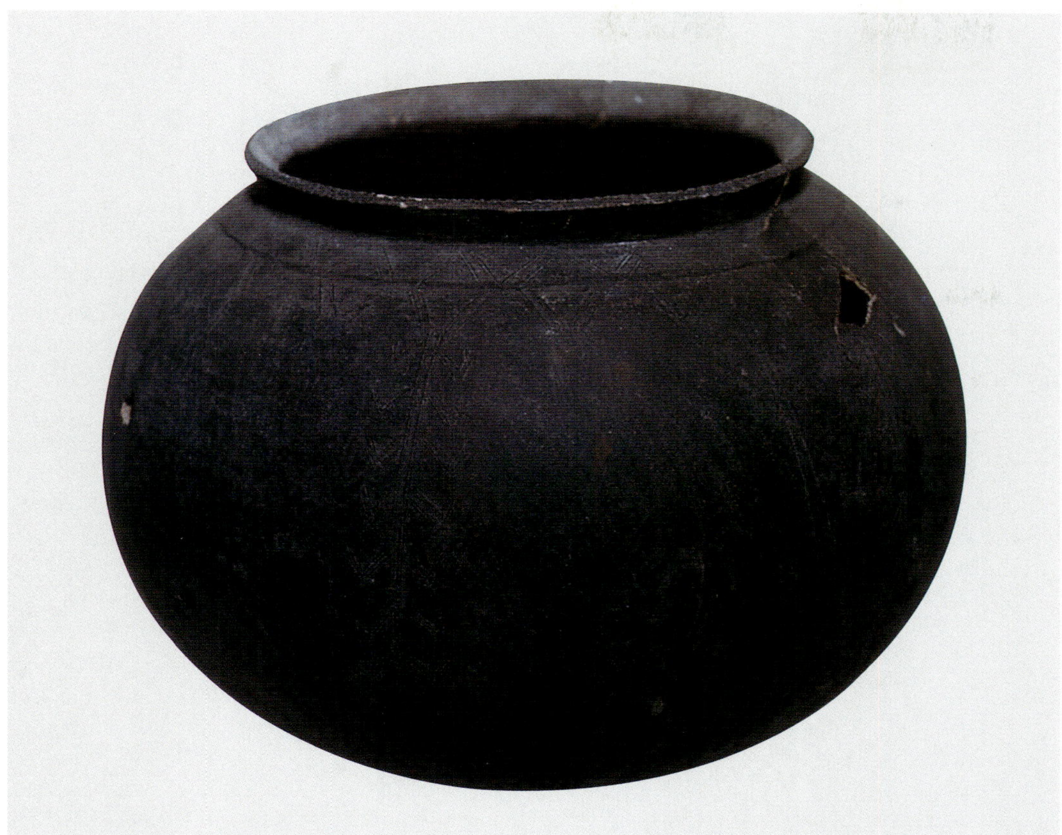

Fig. 10.3
Manus cooking or water pot. The hole shows the amazing thinness of the wall of the pot.

Fig. 10.4
Adding coils to the base, M'Buke Island.

islands. The small Tawi Islands became over-populated and the people were continually fighting with the Usiai from inland Manus over sago, which they obtained from them in exchange for fish and pots. They moved to Timoenai where they could grow their own sago as well as obtain fish and carry on with their pot production.

The German anthropologist, Nevermann, published the results of the Hamburgische Südsee Expedition 1908-10, using descriptions of pot making from Vogel (1911), Parkinson (1907) and Alfred Bühler (unpublished). Nevermann (1934) reports two other pottery centres on the mainland of Manus Island: Tjapale and Lala. It seems that these were M'Buke people who in the early 1900s migrated to the coast from their island because they feared European contact but pot making did not flourish there and today it is difficult to find anyone who remembers its existence. By 1930 M'Buke was again the centre of pot making.

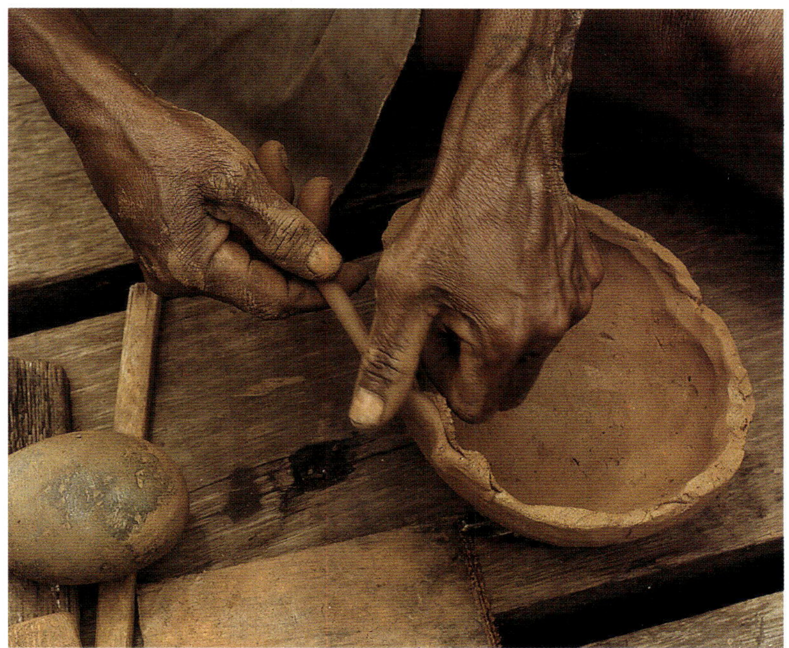

The earliest report of pots in the Admiralty Islands, in fact probably of any pots in Papua New Guinea, was from Carteret (1766-69). He saw in a captured canoe

> Two Earthen pots, as hard, and as well baiked as our common Earthen Utensils ... they were made like a round Jug, with a large mouth & no handles; one of these they had over a fire, as I supposed to boil their Victuals.

In the Hakluyt Society's re-editing of Carteret's account, in 1965, a footnote agrees that they are cooking pots but also gives the surprising information that 'men in some areas make special highly ornamented pots'. It goes on to say that 'In most tribes the ordinary pots are made by women'. There have been no other reports of men making pots anywhere in the Admiralties nor of highly ornamented pots.

The Admiralty islanders are an Austronesian-speaking group. According to Parkinson they are a mixed race divided into three tribes: the Moanus, who inhabit the coast and islands and build their villages on the beaches and often in shallow water on reefs entirely surrounded by the sea; the Matankor, who live on small islands; and the Usiai who lived in the hinterland of Manus. Robert Blust, a linguist at the Australian National University, Canberra, reports that none of these early 'tribe' names is a significant linguistic division. The 'Moanus' of M'Buke Island call their language 'Titan'. Titan speakers are found on M'Buke and Mok islands, are scattered along the south coast of Manus Island and include the people of Timoenai. The Hus islanders, previously called 'Matankor', are now classified under the Hus-Andra linguistic group. The term 'Usiai' was a derogatory Titan reference to the 'bushies' in the interior of Manus Island.

Cooking pots and water pots are made infrequently by the women in all three of the pot making centres but frying pans are now only made at M'Buke and Timoenai. On Hus much the same technique as that of Vanimo is used but on M'Buke and Timoenai an addition, surprising in this Austronesian area, is the use of coiling in conjunction with paddle-and-anvil for producing larger pots (fig. 10.4). All the vessels in the Admiralty Islands are light and have walls which are almost paper thin (fig. 10.3). Forms are spherical but there are variations. The only decoration is simple nicked and incised marks on the shoulders, neck or lip. Margaret Mead (1931) states in her brief references to pots of the Admiralty Islands that the pots of Hus Island are white and those of M'Buke are black. M'Buke pots are sometimes blackened with the fruit of a mangrove, likewise some Hus pots are also stained. Her comment was possibly the result of having seen only pots which were black from use at M'Buke and only newly fired ones at Hus although before use the Hus pots could only be described as brown, red-brown or perhaps buff, never 'white'.

Coconut oil in big basketwork containers used to be traded between the islands. On Hus and Pityliu these containers were known as *kuru hilegai*. As tall as 130 centimetres, they were made by a coiled rattan technique and smeared all over with a paste made from grated putty nut which seals them. The nut, which is the size of a small pear, has a hard skin that must first be peeled off. The paste, which looks like plastic wood, is used for other purposes as well, notably caulking outrigger canoes. These baskets have been mistaken for clay pots at times and because they were unbreakable they were considered superior to the pots. If damaged in any way they were easily repaired by re-weaving or applying more coatings of paste. Some were made with extra-thick coatings of the putty nut and decorated by scratching away areas of the paste and painting on designs. These basket containers are unique to the Admiralty Islands but unfortunately have not been made for many years.

The shell money used by all Admiralty Island people in the past for trading was strings of small white shell discs. They were made by the Matankor people of Ponam and Sori islands on the north coast and traded all around the mainland and islands. Whole aprons of shell money were made and armbands and anklets were ornamented with it as well as with black and red seeds. Unfortunately, when trade store beads were introduced they took over but beadwork is still produced. Dogs' teeth were also an important medium of exchange. All groups except the Moanus people, who were mainly fishermen, specialised in some particular manufacture, such as the wooden bowls of Balowan and Lou and the pots of Hus, M'Buke and Timoenai.

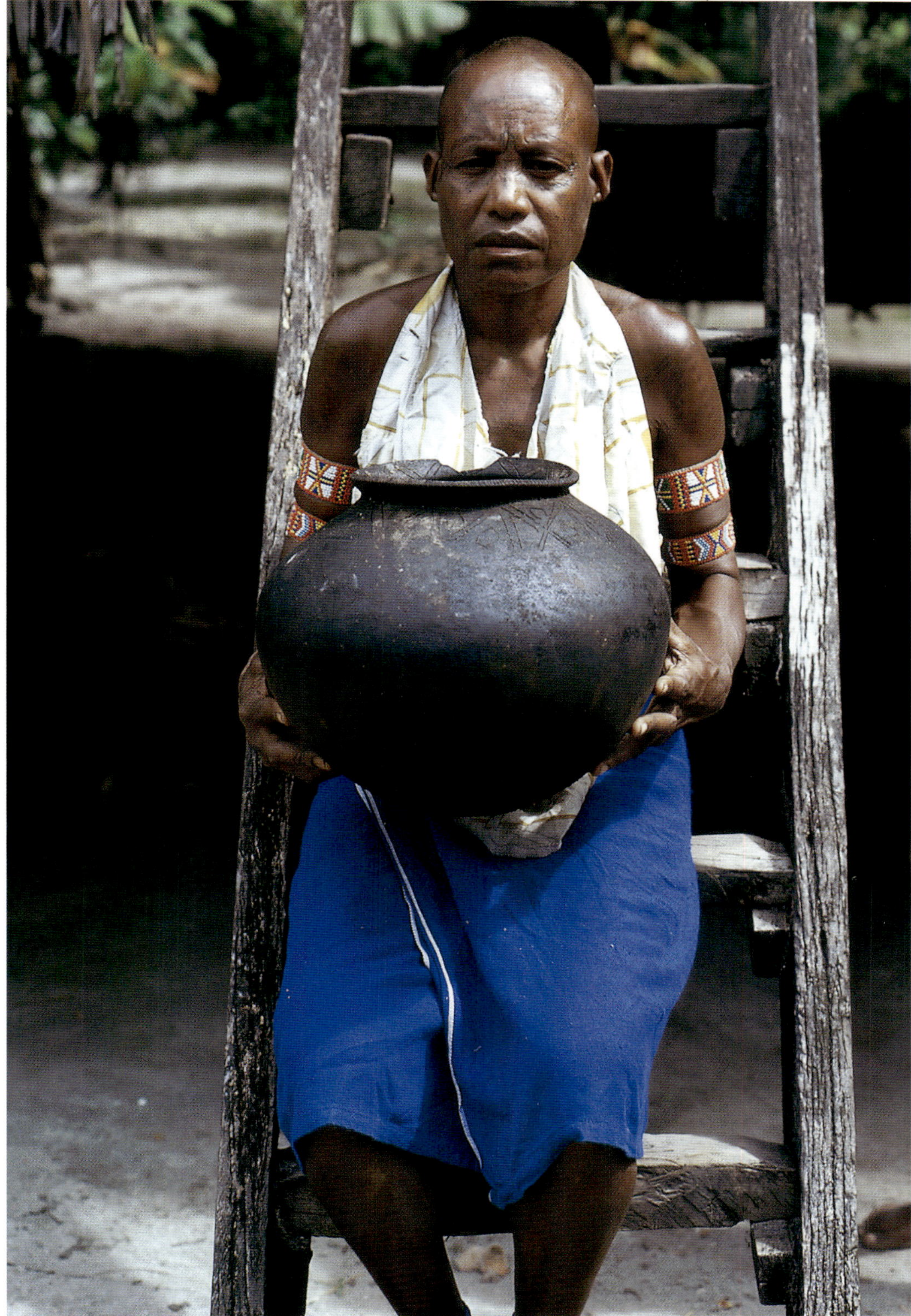

Fig. 10.5
Wide-necked water pot, *porkwat,* or cooking pot, *kur,* Hur.

Hus Island

Hus Island lies 2 to 3 kilometres north of the Manus coast and about 25 kilometres west of Lorengau, the administrative capital of the Admiralties. It is a small, round and flat coral island roughly 2 kilometres across; it has no clay and the potters must go to the mainland of Manus to get it. About ten to fifteen middle-aged and older women occasionally make pots and a few younger people do as well.

The spherical pots all have necks and everted lips, whereas at M'Buke and Timoenai the neck is missing. Hus cooking pots and water pots can be almost identical in shape. The cooking pot, *kur* or *kurr* is used for general cooking and is 20 to 28 centimetres high. It is spherical with a short neck and everted rim. There are generally rows of nicks around the neck and some vessels are indented along the top edge. The water pots, *porkwat*, are used for storing water in the houses, their porosity helping to keep the water cool. They can be wide-mouthed, in which case water is dipped out with a ladle, or narrow-mouthed, which aids in pouring. Their size range has not been established. These pots are the same shape as the *kur*. Decoration consists of incised lines and circles or a combination of incised lines and nicks. Some are indented on the top edge. Another type of water pot has two openings. It is called *chepoung* or *japon*. According to Nevermann, the openings can be either both the same size or one is sometimes larger, presumably to pour water into while the smaller one is used to pour water from or perhaps to drink from. A plug of banana leaf or wood can stop up the openings. These vessels are spherical, with two small-necked openings with everted rims placed on top of the sphere. Decoration consists of incised lines and nicks (fig. 1.15).

The frying pan, *haporlong*, was used in the past for frying sago-coconut pancakes but is no longer made. Sheets of tin are used instead or pieces of broken pots, which were being used as long ago as 1931. It is round-based, quatro-spherical and is never decorated. A bowl, *poinchukuru*, is a vessel with a wide mouth which is used as a container for water or soup. It is spherical, has no decoration and is possibly no longer made. Another bowl, which has two handles and three feet, *puengwai*, is not manufactured now. It is an unusual form in Papua New Guinea and still recognised by very old people on Hus Island. Its function is not known but it was probably used for serving food at feasts. Wooden bowls with feet and inward curving handles are also called *puengwai* so perhaps the potters copied the shape of the wooden bowl. There is a clay *puengwai* in the British Museum; it was collected in 1885 on Wild Island (now Sori Island) in the Admiralties by the Challenger Expedition. Wild Island has not been reported as a pot making centre and presumably the pot had been made at Hus or M'Buke and traded. It is an unrestricted vessel with four feet made from applied short stalks of clay and two handles curving inwards over the top edge of the pot.

The traditional clay source is at Kali Bay on Manus Island, directly opposite Hus. The potters and sometimes male helpers paddle over in outrigger canoes. The clay is in swamps on the eastern side of the bay and there is a plentiful supply from holes scattered over a wide area. About 60 centimetres of topsoil is first removed from a new hole and the clay loosened with a pointed stick. Discarded roots are carefully returned to one of the clay holes because the people think that they revert back into good clay (carbonaceous matter does help plasticity).

Large balls of surplus clay are stored under the houses and clay is prepared for use by hand. It is a fine-grained but open-textured clay containing some quartz and a significant amount of magnetite. The predominant clay mineral is halloysite. An unusual component is tubes of indurated clay which are presumed to have formed around roots; some are removed but they are soft and disintegrate easily to become part of the clay body. Fine coral beach sand is kneaded in; a test of this mixture showed a low 19 per cent of clay mineral, giving only a fair plasticity. It is a strong yellowish-brown, close in colour to the Vanimo clay body.

Potters sit and prepare their clay on sacks and sheets of tin. A large breadfruit tree leaf may also be used for preparation and fresh water for moistening the clay is kept in a half coconut shell. A thick pandanus leaf ring is used to support the pot during beating. Four different beaters are used: a round thick stick, *kerung*; a heavy ridged stick, *sayuran*; a flat wider beater, *kabup*; and a narrow beater, pointed at one end, *hanesan*. A round, smooth, flattish stone, *pat*, is used as the anvil.

A disc of clay 20 to 25 centimetres in diameter and 2 to 3 centimetres thick is prepared in a similar manner to that used at Vanimo. Sitting on the ground supporting this sheet of clay with her feet, the potter thumps the centre of it with the stone while her left hand tilts the edges up into a shallow bowl shape, which is then further shaped by beating with paddle and anvil. The belly of the pot swells out and the neck starts to take shape. The potter shapes the neck further with her fingers, by pleating the top edge to bring it inwards, then pinching and smoothing this and wetting and beating it with the narrow, pointed beater. This is repeated until the desired shape is attained, at which stage the potter finally taps around the top edge with the same pointed beater, supporting under the lip with her left index finger. Final smoothing and shaping of the main body of the pot is done with the widest beater. Now the pot is left to get firmer; the base is then beaten for the last time and the pot is left upright in the ring until strong enough to be inverted for final drying. Pots must dry in the sun for three or four days before they are ready for firing; the potters say that they keep turning them around until they feel light and then they are ready.

Nevermann and Parkinson describe different techniques; the variations are possibly those of different potters or perhaps there has been a change over the years. In Nevermann's description the potter opens out the ball of clay with her thumb and then enlarges the hole with both hands by pressing the clay from both inside and outside, making the walls higher. He also describes the addition of coils to the base but does not make it clear whether this is referring to M'Buke technique only. Parkinson says the method of manufacture is the same as that employed in the Solomon Islands and in New Guinea and goes on to describe pieces of clay joined to a disc, which are then beaten on; this is certainly the technique used in some parts of the Solomons but is not currently used in the Admiralties.

A firing was not observed but a description of it was given by several potters. Between one and ten pots are fired at a time; they are supported on three stones about the size of oranges, sitting almost upright. During the firing the potters turn them in all directions with two long sticks. Coconut fronds are heaped all around them and more fuel is added if necessary. After approximately thirty minutes they are left to cool, then washed in the sea and put in the house to dry. Before the pots are used water must be boiled in them. Sometimes pots are sealed by rubbing over the outside with putty nut; the pot becomes stained a darker colour where the nut is applied.

In the past Hus Island pots were carried to other islands and to the mainland but now only enough pots are made for local use and for trading to the mainland in exchange for sago, taro, greens and coconut oil.

M'Buke Island

M'Buke Island, south of Manus, is surrounded by coral reefs and belongs to the Moanus. It is about twice the size of Hus Island and is dominated by a small volcanic mountain which gives it the alternative name of Sugarloaf Island. The name M'Buke means 'tridacna shell'. About ten women on the

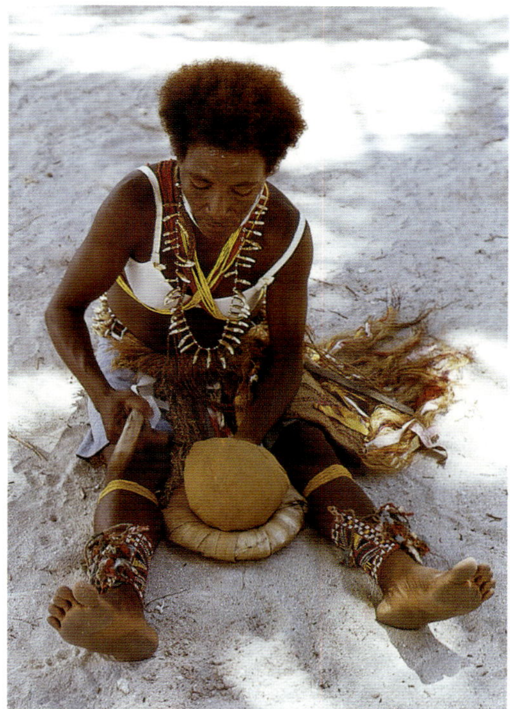

Fig. 10.6
Hedwig, dressed ready for a 'singsing' on Hus Island, demonstrating paddle-and-anvil technique.

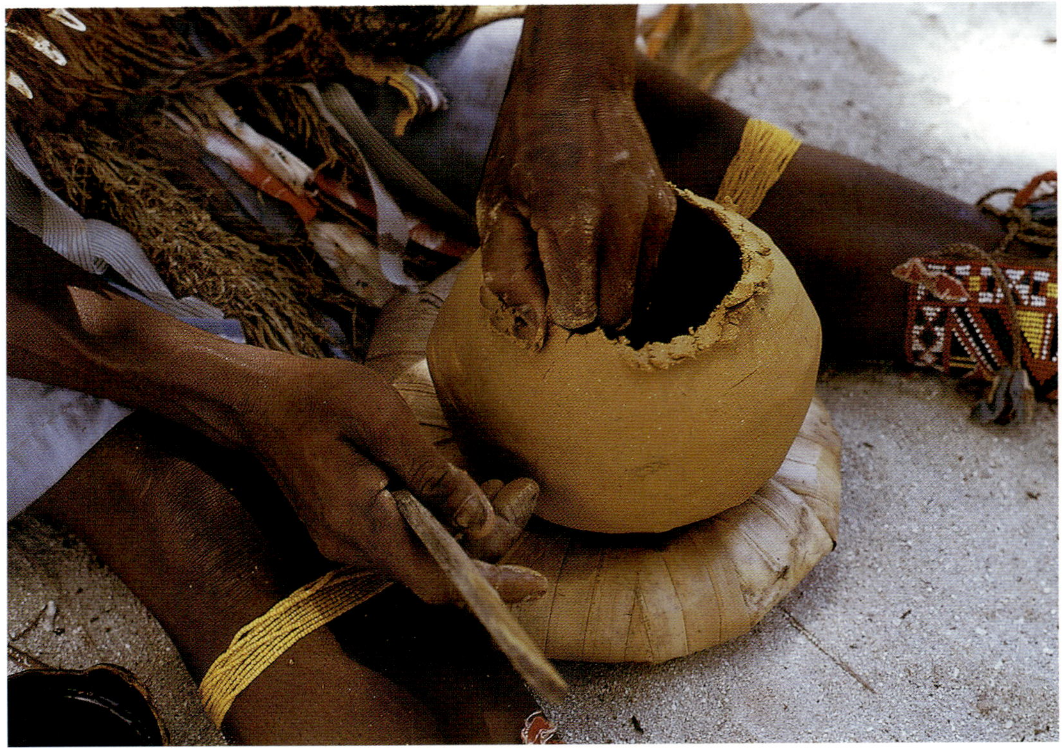

Fig. 10.7
Hedwig doubling over the top edge to thicken it, Hus Island.

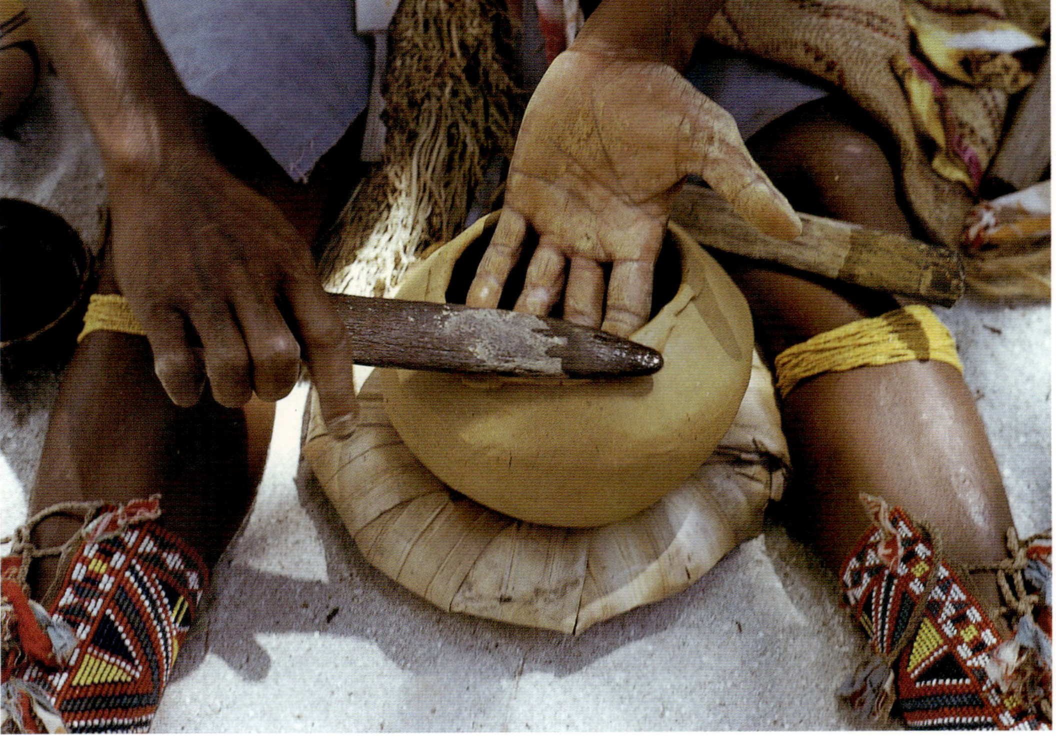

Fig. 10.8
Hedwig beating the thickened rim, Hus Island.

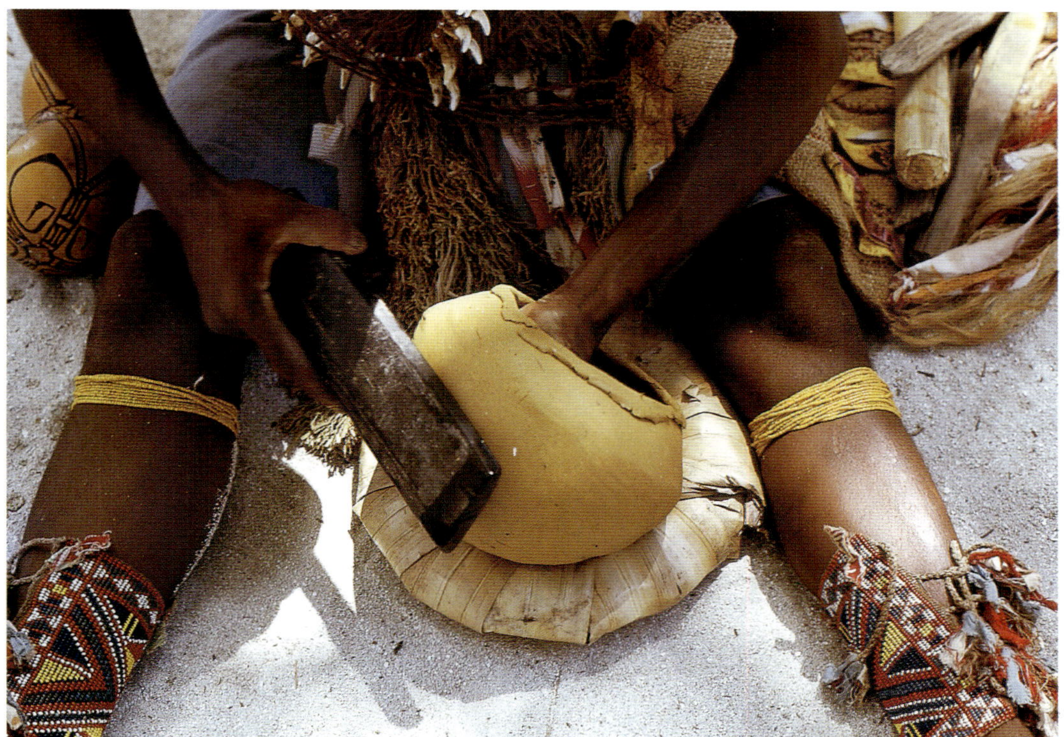

Fig. 10.9
Hedwig beating with a wide smooth paddle, Hus Island.

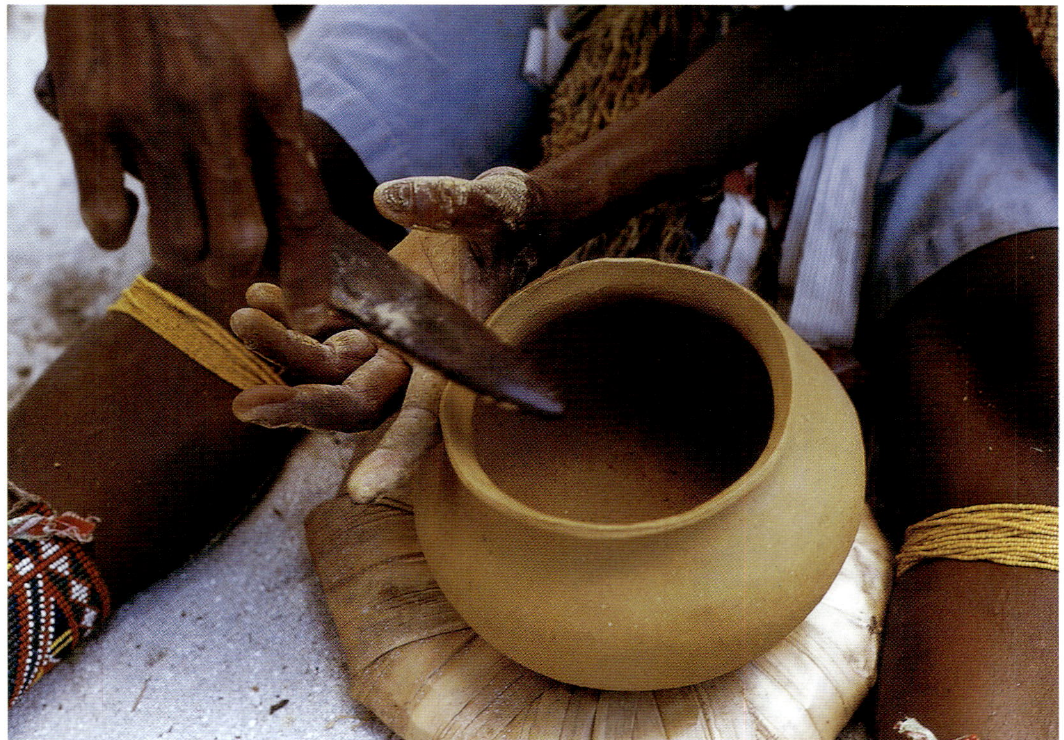

Fig. 10.10
Hedwig shaping the neck, Hus Island.

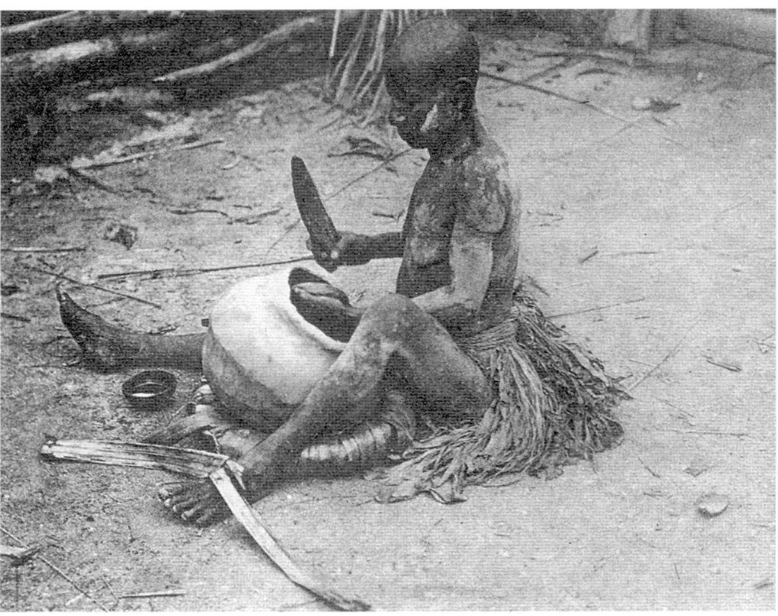

Fig. 10.11
Hus potter, early 20th century.

Fig. 10.12
Hus potter, early 20th century.

island still make pots and they are encouraged by a women's club which helps with marketing and sales to visitors.

The M'Buke pots are even thinner and lighter than the Hus pots. The cooking pot, *matapwei*, is used for general cooking. It is spherical, neckless and has an everted rim. It measures 20 to 30 centimetres high, with a mouth opening 15 to 20 centimetres wide. It can be undecorated or incised on the shoulder and/or lip and decoration is confined to simple fine-lined incising. Water pots, *pwentung*, are used for storing water in the houses. As at Hus, a water pot can be the same shape as a cooking pot, it can have a much narrower mouth, in which case it is used as a pouring vessel, or it can have a wider mouth from which water is ladled. These vessels are the same shape as the cooking pots and have a similar decoration. Some examples have inscriptions relating to the women's club and dates incised on them. Double-mouthed water pots are also used and water is sometimes drunk directly from one of the narrow mouths. They are spherical, have two small-necked openings with everted rims and are incised. Frying pans, *kaol*, are used for frying sago or coconut pancakes. Some are the usual sub-spherical shallow bowls, others are deeper and have a slightly everted lip. They are not decorated (fig. 10.2).

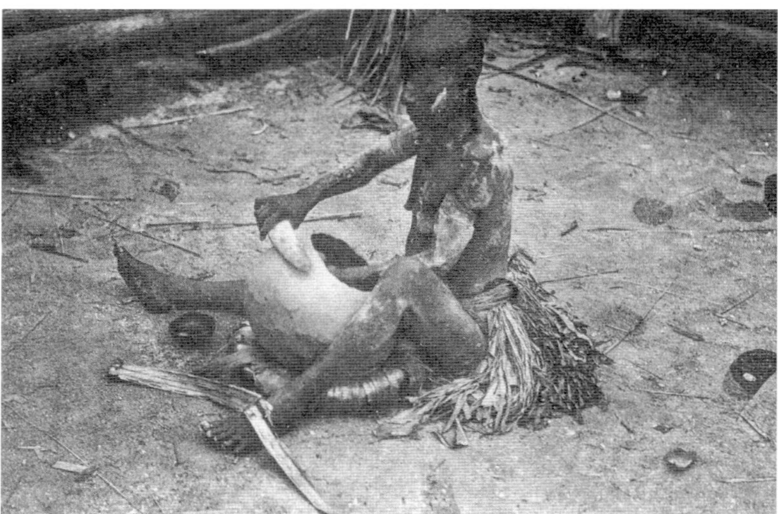

Thilenius (1902) mentions cooking pots made of wood but gives no further description of them. Mead tells of tall black pots containing a coconut soup, *bulukol*, which was heated by dropping hot stones into it. This, without doubt, would be a wooden vessel.

Clay from the volcanic mountain on M'Buke is sometimes used but there are several other sources: Chepuwai River on the coast west of Pelikawa, Boyalimo River and Boymao near Tawi Island, and Vogali Island close to M'Buke. They are all fine-grained clays. Two different clays, such as the Chepowai River and Vogali clays, are mixed together with a volcanic beach sand while wet, banged into large balls and stored in the pottery sheds (not often used now) or under the houses until needed. Then they are soaked in sea water until soft and kneaded ready for use. The clay body is a dark reddish-brown.

The equipment and tools are similar to those used on Hus Island. The basic bowl shape is formed in exactly the same manner as at Hus; coils are then rolled on a board with the palm of the hand and added to the top edge of the pot and beaten into place with the paddle-and-anvil method. Frying pans and small pots for the tourist trade are made without the addition of coils.

The authors have no information about the drying and firing methods. Pots are sometimes blackened after firing by rubbing with the cut-open fruit of a mangrove. Probably the putty nut is also used.

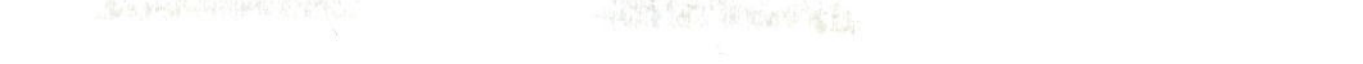

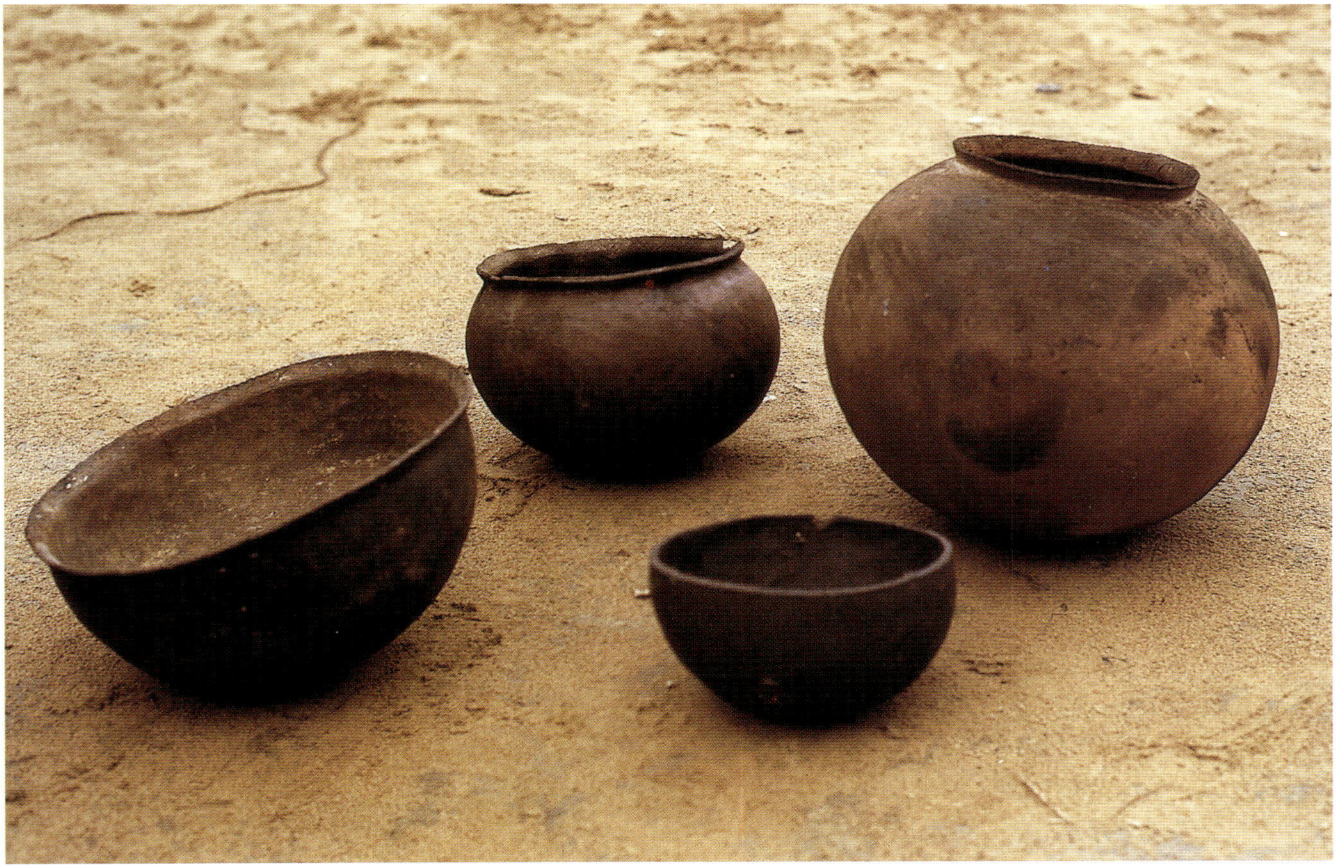

M'Buke pots are still traded for sago with Manus Island villagers in the Malai Bay area and east along the coast, and for taro, bananas, sugar cane, pumpkins, pawpaw and sweet potato with the people of Lou, Baluan and Rambutjo islands to the east of M'Buke.

At the time Mead was working on Manus (1930) the Moanus, acting as middle-men, controlled the trade in the whole area and helped distribute the material culture of the Usiai and Matankor people. In Peri (Perre) pottery played an important role in social and economic exchanges and was valued highly. Mead relates details of a marriage during which the bride, led by her mother-in-law, enters the house where her bridegroom awaits her. Inside, female members of the husband's family are fashionably critical of the bride's dowry, including pots, which are said to be too small and broken. She also describes a relative hastily paddling away with a canoe load of pots from a house where a woman had just died. This was to rescue them before the mourners arrived and broke them.

Fig. 10.13
Cooking pots, *tjako,* and a deeper frying pan made at Timoenai village, Manus Island.

Timoenai (Moenai)

Pots identical to M'Buke pots are made at Timoenai, on Manus Island, using the same techniques. Clay comes from the headwaters of Watani River and from the eastern side of Tawi Island.

11 North Solomons Province and Solomon Islands

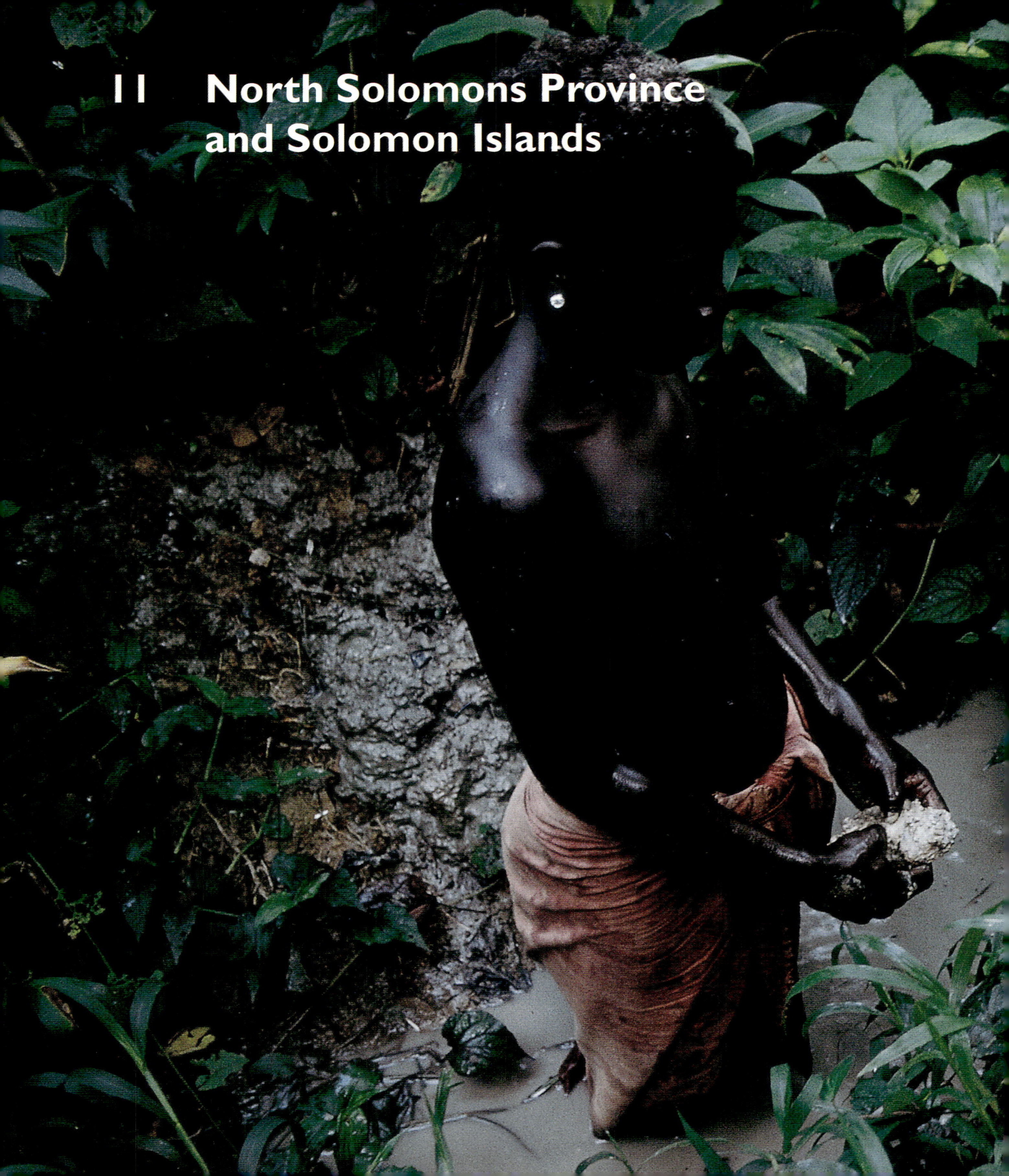

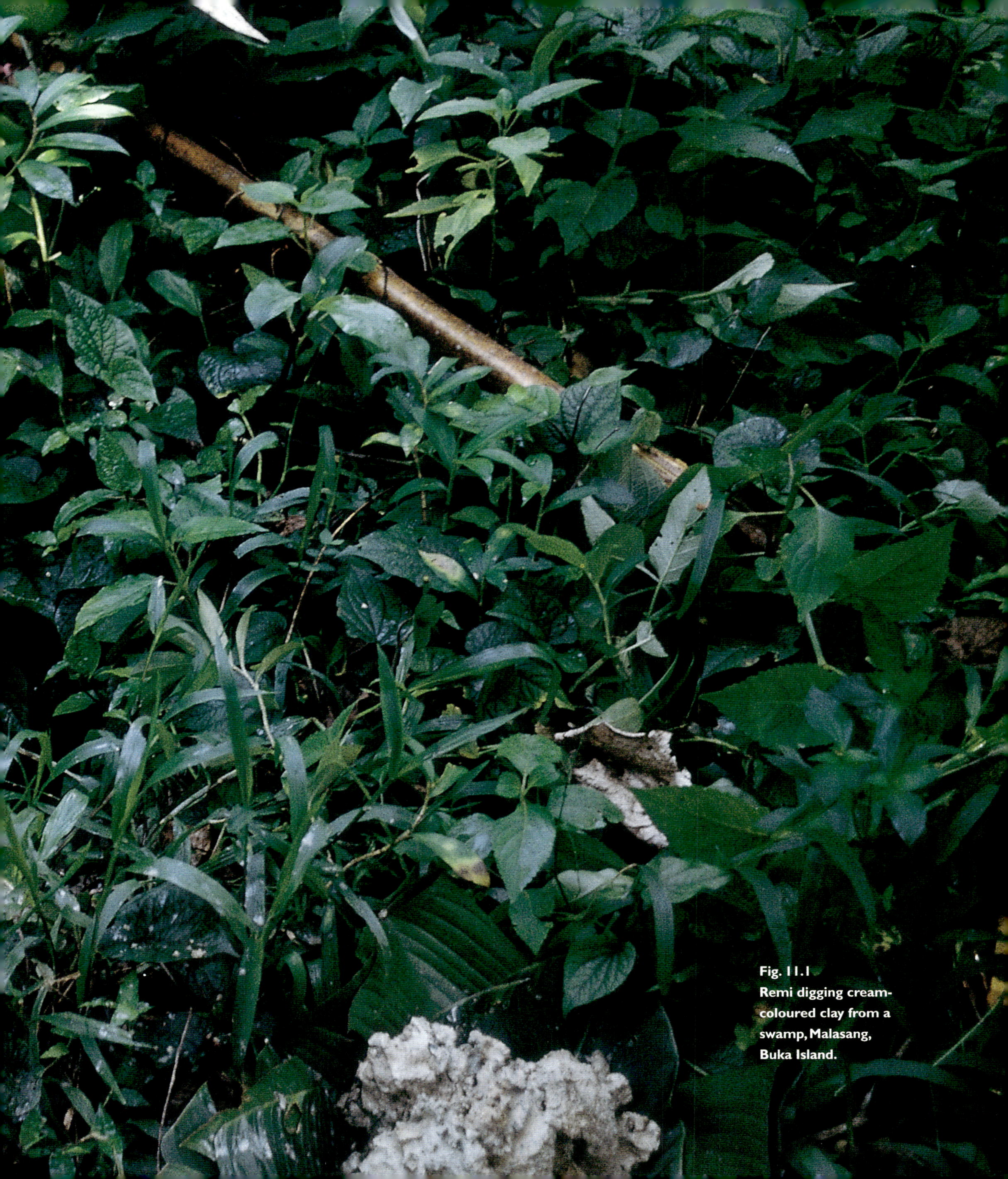

Fig. 11.1
Remi digging cream-coloured clay from a swamp, Malasang, Buka Island.

The Solomon Islands lie to the extreme east of Papua New Guinea. The two northern most islands of Buka and Bougainville are part of Papua New Guinea (North Solomons Province) while the long string of smaller islands to the south-east comprises the (formerly British) Solomon Islands. The pottery industries in the Bougainville Strait islands and Choiseul Island in the Solomons are closely related to those of Bougainville and they have therefore been included in this survey in spite of the fact that other Melanesian pottery industries in Vanuatu, New Caledonia and Fiji have not been described (Maps 1, 3).

Pot making occurs in the southern part of Bougainville. Buka Island has an isolated pottery tradition different from that of both Bougainville and the other groups mentioned. Linguistic studies by Allen and Hurd (n.d.) classify the Buka Island people as Austronesians, and, in southern Bougainville, the Nasioi, Siwai, and Buin as non-Austronesians.

Buka Island

Beatrice Blackwood described the pottery industry of Buka in *Both Sides of Buka Passage* (1935). Specht (1972) has made a more recent study. The authors have drawn on both these sources.

The pot making village of Malasang is located on the south-east coast; at two nearby villages, Lonahan and Hangan, pots were made in the past. In the 1930s Blackwood reported a flourishing industry at Malasang but by the time of Specht's research in 1967 the industry had declined there and had ceased at Lonahan and Hangan. A 1976 report tells of Malasang potters still producing just enough pots for themselves and a few nearby villages. The village of Tung on the west coast is said to have been a traditional centre but the authors have been unable to verify this.

Men are not involved in any stage of the pot making. The people of Malasang have the rights over the clay materials but the Lonahan and Hangan women are allowed access to the pits. Women of the three villages forfeit their right to make pots if they marry into any other village.

The following description of form and function has been taken from Specht (1972). The generic name for pots is *tabeli*, which term may also refer to the everyday cooking pot. The *tabeli* are tall conical pots with pointed to slightly rounded bases. The mouth may be restricted or unrestricted and the upper walls incline inwards. The average height is 32 centimetres and the mouth 45 centimetres; the tallest pot recorded by Specht was 46 centimetres high. The thin lip is notched and there is a narrow decorated band around the outside top portion. The base of the vessel is quite thick.

Huge cooking pots, *abonon*, measuring up to 100 centimetres high were described by the people

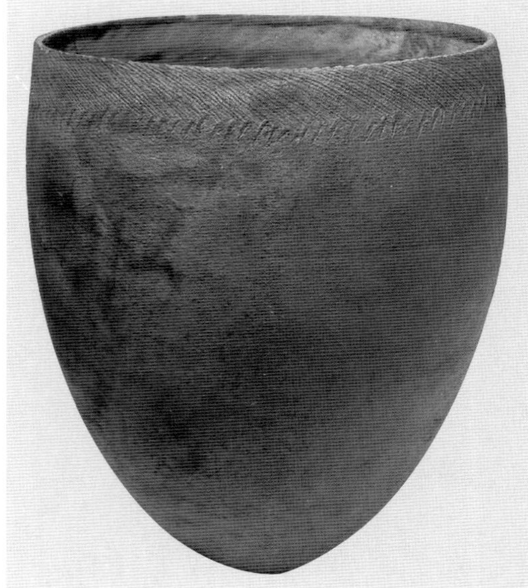

Fig. 11.2
A cooking pot, *tabeli*, from Malasang village, Buka Island, *h* 36 cm.

but not observed by Specht or Blackwood. They were made only when needed for cooking pig for feasts.

Three other pots, all called *kolo*, have different functions and two are of special interest. One, a smaller *tabeli* seen by Specht, was being used for storing ceremonial currency of porpoise or flying fox teeth. The inside of the pot was coated with red ochre, red being a sought-after colour. The other, a more squat pot with a flattish base, is used mostly for water collection and storage. The third is related because it is similar in shape to the previous one and is probably used for storage.

Twin vessels, called *hipuna*, which means 'two-of-a-kind', are rare; they are found only in the men's house and seem to be used for storing shell money. Two *kolo* are joined by a cylinder of clay or they may rest directly against each other. This is the only Buka pot ever to be painted (usually with red vertical stripes).

A vessel unique to Buka is the *kepa*, used for boiling coconut cream in order to thicken it. Mashed taro is added to make a ceremonial dish, *menak*, provided for such occasions as marriages, funerals and the launching of new canoes. Men prepare the *menak* and usually are the only ones to use the *kepa* but recently they have been used for cooking fish and rice. *Kepa* are generally oval but may be round; they have pouring lips, one on each side, which is rare in Papua New Guinea.

Larger vessels are notched on the lip and have thin incised decorations made with a stick, the edge of a shell or a two-pronged comb. The decoration is either in the form of a narrow band 3 to 5 centimetres wide around the outside of the rim or it covers most of the body down to or below the widest point. Motifs are simple lines and zig-zags – single and double – combined with combed wavy lines and rows of diamonds. Apparently any motif may be used by any of the women but it is probable that clan and rank marks were used by particular people in the past.

On her first visit to the clay pit a woman is prevented by taboo from approaching until one of the other women sprinkles pig fat on the ground and hands her some clay. The light yellowish-grey clay, *petako*, is located in a swamp area about thirty minutes' walk from Malasang and is removed from under the water in one of the many small pits. After roots and other rough stuff have been discarded the wet clay is wrapped in banana leaves. Buka potters add a temper to attain a good clay body and this is found on top of the Hahan hills, about another thirty minutes' walk away from the clay source. This material, *mimia*, is a semi-consolidated lithic tuff and is scraped out with a shell. After quarrying, the potter must strike the pit entrance with a banana leaf to ward off evil spirits. At the clay pits the temper is kneaded with the sticky clay, about one part to three by volume. Extra water from the swampy clay holes is added to ensure that the dry temper is thoroughly wet and will bond better with the damp clay. Although beach sand is more easily procured it is never used, nor is sea water.

Blackwood (1935: 396-98) describes in great detail the techniques used for pot making:

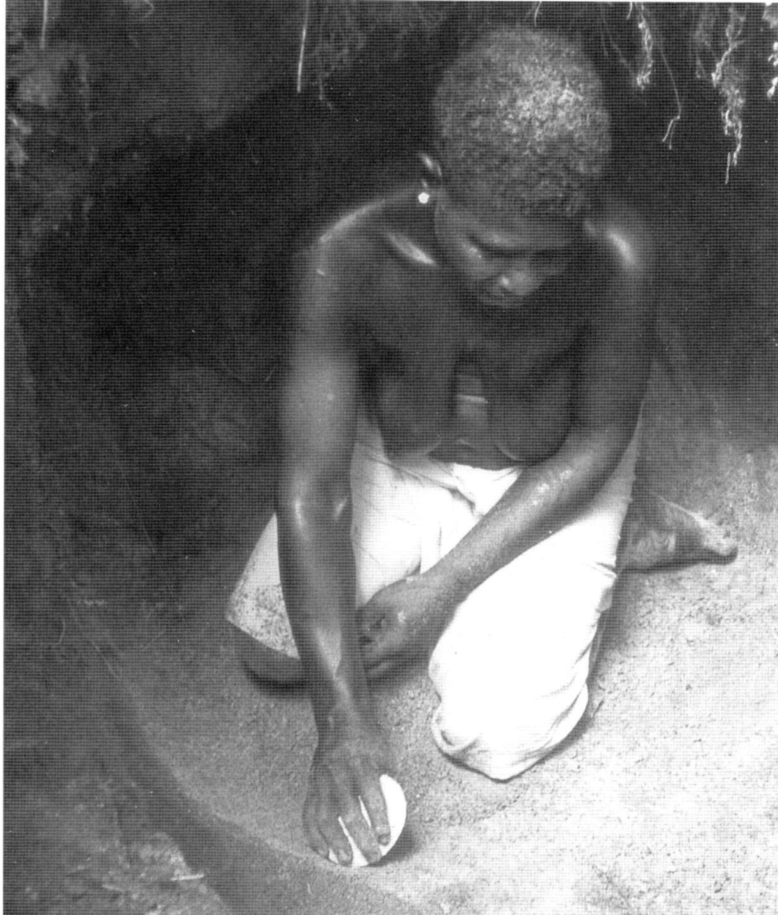

Fig. 11.3
Remi scraping out *mimia* with a shell, Malasang.

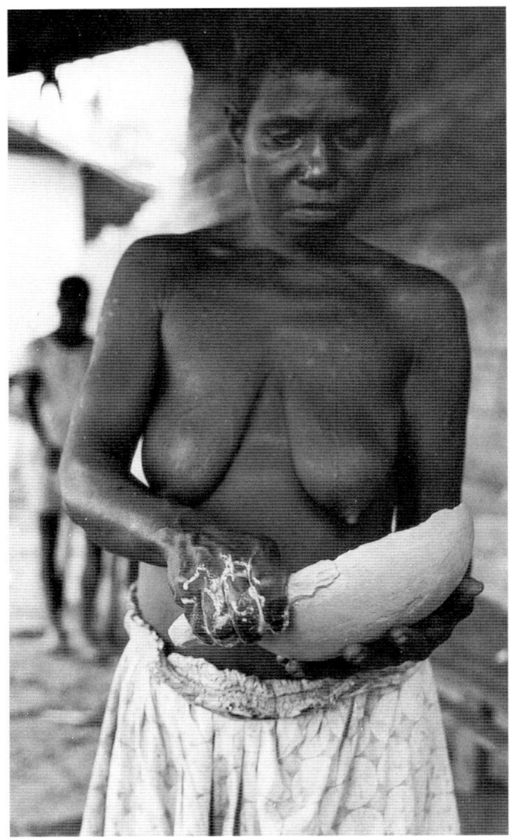

Fig. 11.4
Remi squeezing a handful of clay on to the top edge of the growing pot, Malasang, Buka Island.

The potter sits on the ground, but some women prefer a low stool, made by fixing a plank upon a couple of small logs. Her legs are stretched out in front of her, with the knees slightly bent, the pot resting on them.

In beginning a new pot, a lump of the mixture is taken in the hand, and worked into a ball about the size of a tennis ball. The potter then lays it in her palm, takes up a smooth flat stone (*rako*) in the other hand and holding the stone with her four fingers on the inside of the lump, and her thumb on its outside, she hollows the ball into a bowl shape with quick short sweeps of the stone, turning the clay in her hand as she runs round the edge. This base is then put aside to dry, and another is begun.

At the next session the potter takes a handful of clay in her wet palm, and kneads it with the fingers of the same hand. One of the bases prepared at the previous session is then picked up, and the clay very quickly and deftly applied all round its edge, adding about an inch to its height. No attempt is made to construct a sausage-shaped roll before applying it to the pot; the amount required is squeezed out between thumb and first finger. The thumb is kept inside the pot, and the four fingers curled round the outside. The first finger is pressed down as the clay

Fig. 11.5
Remi forming the base with a round flat stone, Malasang.

The potter works at her craft in the early morning and in the late afternoon. The sound of the tapping is heard almost at dawn. When she is not working, the half-finished pots rest on a low platform of thin logs placed slightly apart, between which the pots are set, the logs providing sufficient support to keep them upright. The platform runs down one side of the hut, and the small girls of the family are kept busy fetching and carrying pots for the worker who sits at the far end. There may be a couple of dozen on the platform at one time, with very little space between them. Setting them up is a ticklish business, but woe betide the child who lets one fall over, injuring its delicate edge. I watched one unlucky little girl to whom this happened trying, with more optimism than judgement, to repair the damage with her own unskilful fingers. The result was disastrous. All the operations, except the firing, are carried on indoors. If the work is done outside, the sun spoils the clay. As a very special favour, one potter brought her work outside so that I could take photographs.

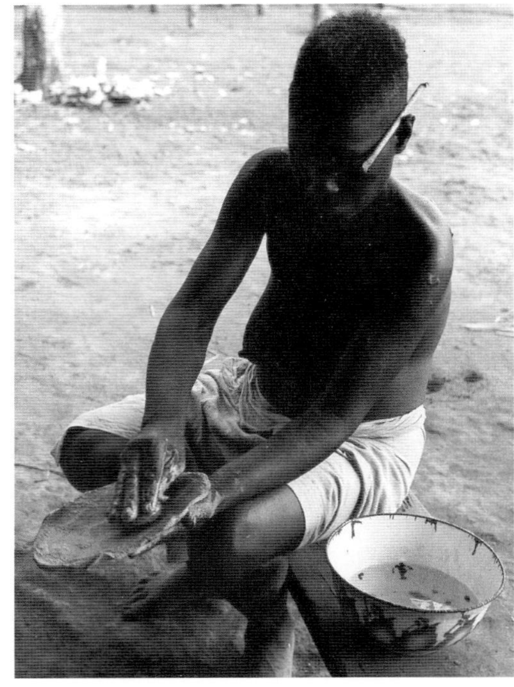

fits round the pot, leaving a crinkled appearance which is afterwards smoothed out with the hand dipped in the broken pot full of water which stands by the worker's side. One handful of clay went round a pot about 12 inches in diameter. On a larger pot, if the first handful is not enough to go round, a second lump is taken, the ends are made to overlap the first strip for a couple of inches or so, and the joins completely smoothed out. The result of this process is to provide the pot with an edging about an inch deep and from 1/2 to 3/4 of an inch thick at the top, projecting slightly on the outside and smooth inside, like the rim of an ordinary flowerpot. The pot is then put aside again to dry. The potter will keep a dozen or more going at once, at two or three different stages of construction, putting another layer on each in turn.

At the next session the potter takes up the pot and lays it across her knees. She then takes the flat stone in her left hand, and in her right a small wooden spatula or beater; *saksak*, which she dips into the pot of water beside her. With quick light strokes she flattens out the rim of clay, holding the stone underneath and beating the clay down on to it, turning the pot round as required. After every few strokes the beater is dipped into the water, and a tap is given to the stone with the wet beater before the beating is resumed; this has the effect of keeping the stone moistened. The work is done very rapidly. A band which when first applied was about an inch in height and 1/2 to 3/4 of an inch thick, adds, when flattened out, between 2 and 3 inches to the height of the pot, and has a thickness of about an eighth of an inch. It is very flexible, bending under the hand of the woman as she smooths it over after the flattening with the beater is finished. It is then put aside again. Both inside and outside are now perfectly smooth, with no sign whatever of the joins between the layers.

Special care is taken with the last layer, which is to form the rim of the pot. After it has been flattened out the potter runs round it with first finger inside and thumb outside, pinching off tiny pieces to make it even, and then smoothing the edge with thumb inside and all four fingers extended on the outside. During this process she will stop several times to look at it, and when she has finished she will ask the opinion of those standing by as to whether it is symmetrical. Not till every one has expressed satisfaction does she proceed to the next process, which is to put the ornamentation round the edge. This is done with the fluted edge of a shell (*katsibélo*, a species of *Arca*). The pattern is not intended simply as an ornament. It was carefully explained to me that it also serves as a mark of identification, so that a woman would recognize her pot if anyone stole it. There are several designs in general use, differing slightly from each other, but a potter will put the same one on several pots in succession. On the pot I saw being made, a line of diagonal scratches was put on nearest the rim, extending about three inches down the sides of the pot. These were made with the fluted edge of the shell. Over these lines, about an inch from the rim, a horizontal line of wavy marks was made with one corner of the shell. The edge of the pot was then very lightly fluted by a succession of quick impressions made with the edge of the shell. Frequently however, the edge is merely pricked or it may be left smooth.

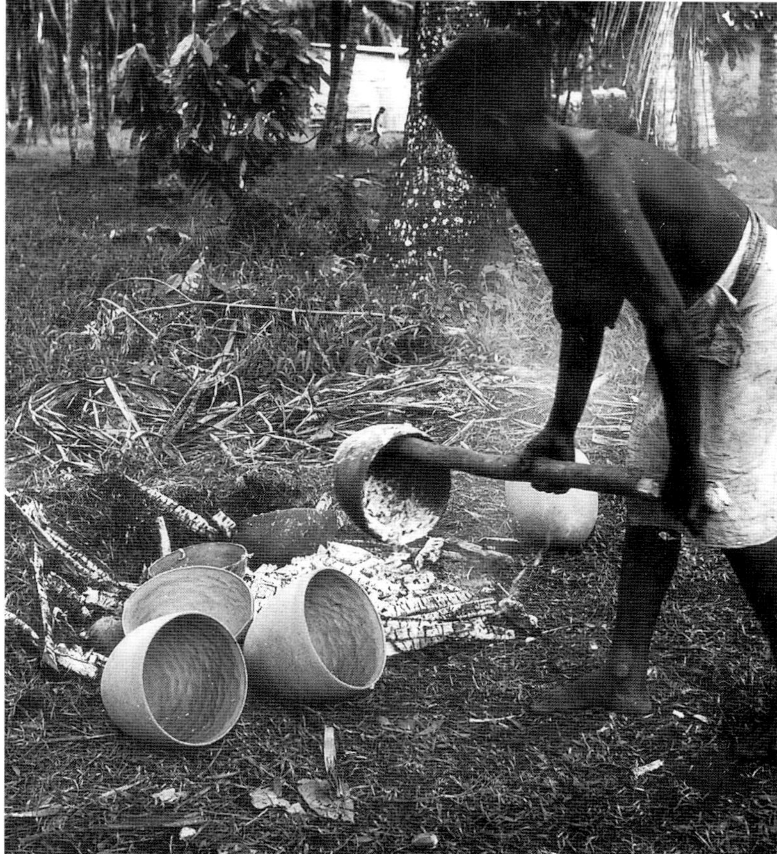

Fig. 11.6
Remi firing pots and preheating some with their thick bases close to the fire, Malasang, Buka Island.

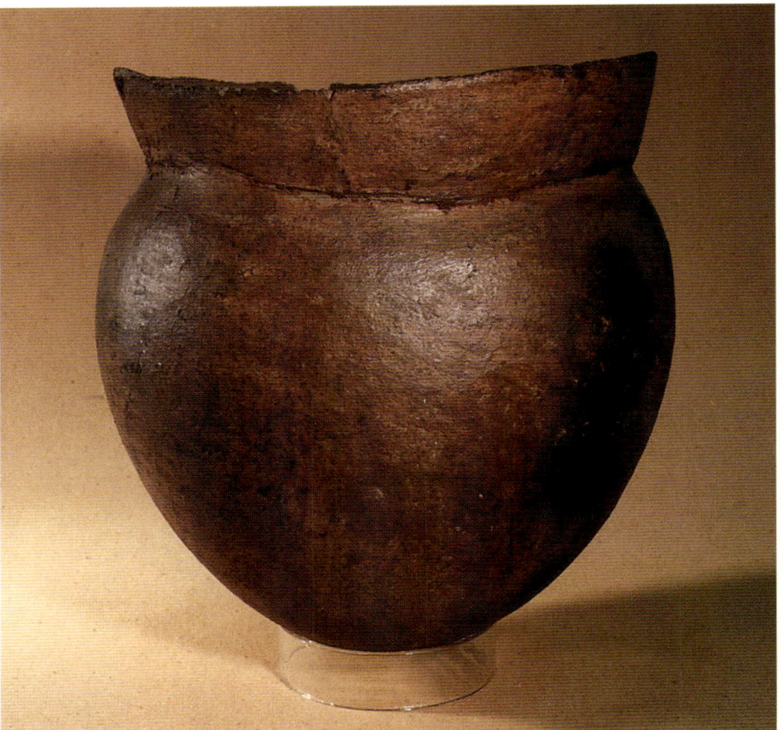

Fig. 11.7
Nasioi cooking pot showing the stains from putty nut sealing, Bougainville Island, *h* 26 cm.

Firing details have been compiled from Specht and Blackwood. After drying in the house for some days the pot must be dried in the sun for at least several hours. The firing takes place in the late afternoon. Preheating is achieved in a practical way by setting the pots around a small fire with their thick bases towards the heat. This preliminary heating would be of special importance for pots with such uneven walls. They are soon laid on their sides on the warm ashes with their top edges propped up a little on sticks. More sticks (no information is given on fuel type) are leaned against the pots and gradually the embers ignite the wood and a fierce fire burns for ten to twenty minutes. The pots are removed while still hot on the end of two long sticks. Smudging marks do not appear to bother the potters; the pots will be finally smoked black in the rafters of the house. But first water is boiled in them to test them before they are traded or sold.

In the 1930s Buka pots were in great demand all over Buka Island, in north Bougainville and on smaller islands. The main trading voyage of the Buka people was to north Bougainville, especially to Teop in the north-east and sometimes further south to Wakunai. Red ochre for ceremonial use was the important exchange item on these voyages. Traders came also to Malasang with many different products including lime, taro, tobacco, pandanus capes and pigs. Buka pots reached Nissan Island, across the Pacific to the north, by a succession of trading activities and passing through Lontis, on the north-west tip of Buka. Pots were packed in areca palm baskets for transport.

Bougainville

The form of the southern Bougainville pottery is similar in all three groups but there is an interesting variation in method. The women at Nasioi and women and some men at Buin employ a technique of adding slabs to a beaten base but Siwai men add coils to a beaten base. All finish in the paddle-and-anvil manner. It should be noted here that the techniques used by the southern Solomons groups are similar to those of the Nasioi and Buin. The only other place in Melanesia where slabs are joined onto a beaten base is Fiji. Pot making appears to be dying out in most of southern Bougainville and it ceased long ago on the islands of the Bougainville Strait.

As far as is known, only cooking pots are made. They have pointed to rounded bases, high shoulders and necks and everted rims. Noticeable features of these pots are the marks left by the beater at the angle of the neck and flaring rim and the curious stained surface texture which comes from sealing with putty nut.

Nasioi

The people of the Nasioi language group live on the coast and inland in the mountains. They occupy a large area of south-eastern Bougainville. Ogan (1970) says that it is possible that the Nasioi only became potters in fairly recent times and two early ethnographers suggest that the women of Alu (Shortland Islands) moved to the area of Kieta, the main town of Bougainville, during the late 1800s and brought the art of pot making to Nasioi, a fact which concurs with the similarity in forming methods. Ogan recounts a legend of a boy named Kii who looked on the newly made pots as humans and called to them to come in out of the rain to avoid getting spoilt. It is said that the art of pottery was invented by his mother, a woman of Shortland Islands origin.

Villages where it is reported that pots have been made in the last ten years or so are Rumba village, Pidia on the east coast just north of Kieta, Popok in the Bay of Kieta, Toboroi 32 kilometres south of Kieta, Lonsiro near Arawa and Pavairi at the top of Okorova Mountains.

Nasioi pots differ, it would seem, only in proportion and size. Frizzi (1914) lists three different shapes (or possibly sizes): *aroa*, a large pot; *kodeu*, of medium size; *kakazi*, a small one. Ogan's description of the technique used at Rumba and reports from Lonsiro show the methods to be almost identical. Reports of Pidia and Pavairi pot making also tally. The following description has been taken mainly from Ogan.

The women of Rumba village gather the clay, *kansi*, from a deposit not far from Kieta, called, since European contact, Point Saucepan. The women believe they must take great care not to drop any clay on the ground because a pot, *otao*, might later say to the potter, 'You dropped me and now I know your pubic hair, *sitapu*'. The clay is usually wrapped in wet banana leaves and left to mature for a week or two. When needed it is spread on a board and pounded with a rock. A little fresh water is poured on the clay from a bamboo tube. It must not be salt water; in fact the women must have no contact with sea water or it is thought the pot will be fragile. At Pidia it is known that sand is sometimes added to the clay if necessary but it is not known how the potters judge this. Foreign matter is removed with the fingers during preparation of the clay.

When it is ready the clay is patted into a solid cylindrical shape and with a ruler-shaped stick, *baako*, the potter cuts it into five pieces. One section is patted into a flat disc with the *baako*, sometimes on a wooden box or board, sometimes on a big slab of stone. This round piece is pressed down into a banana leaf ring-support, *bapiua*, to become the dish-shaped base. The other pieces are beaten into slabs roughly 25 centimetres square or, more often, oblongs 1 to 2 centimetres thick. They are placed upright and joined to the base to form the walls; the overlaps are beaten firmly with a paddle and anvil. Two slabs complete a circle. Often the pot is rested sideways on the ring to enable the potter to beat the base piece upwards over the join. She walks around the pot, beating it until it is an even thickness, except for the top edge which is left thick so that the next layer of slabs can be joined to it. After a period of drying the final two slabs are joined. A second person helps hold the slabs in place on the higher walls. Strips of bark are sometimes tied around the bottom half of the pot to support

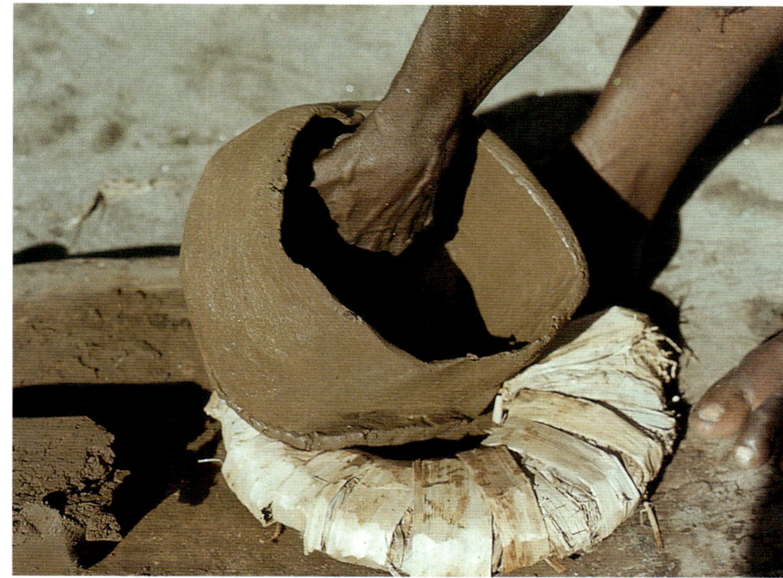

Fig. 11.8
Slab building at Pidea village, Nasioi, group. Slabs are welded with paddle and anvil.

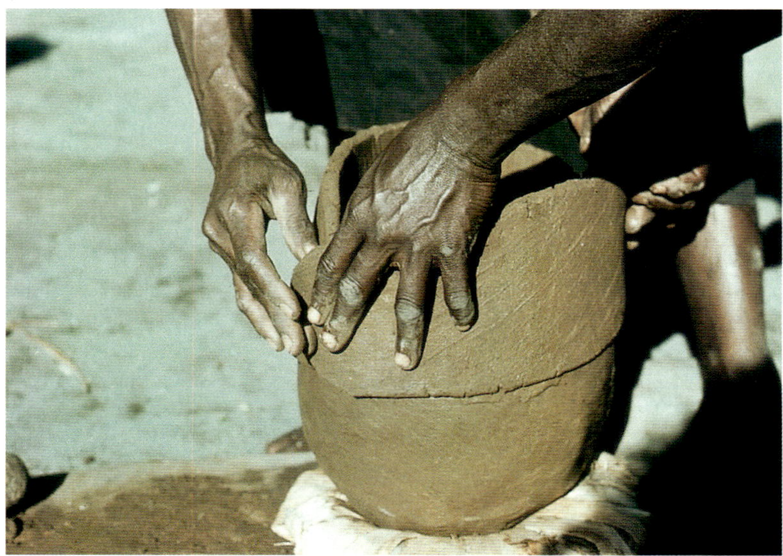

Fig. 11.9
Another person helps place the second layer of slabs, Pidea.

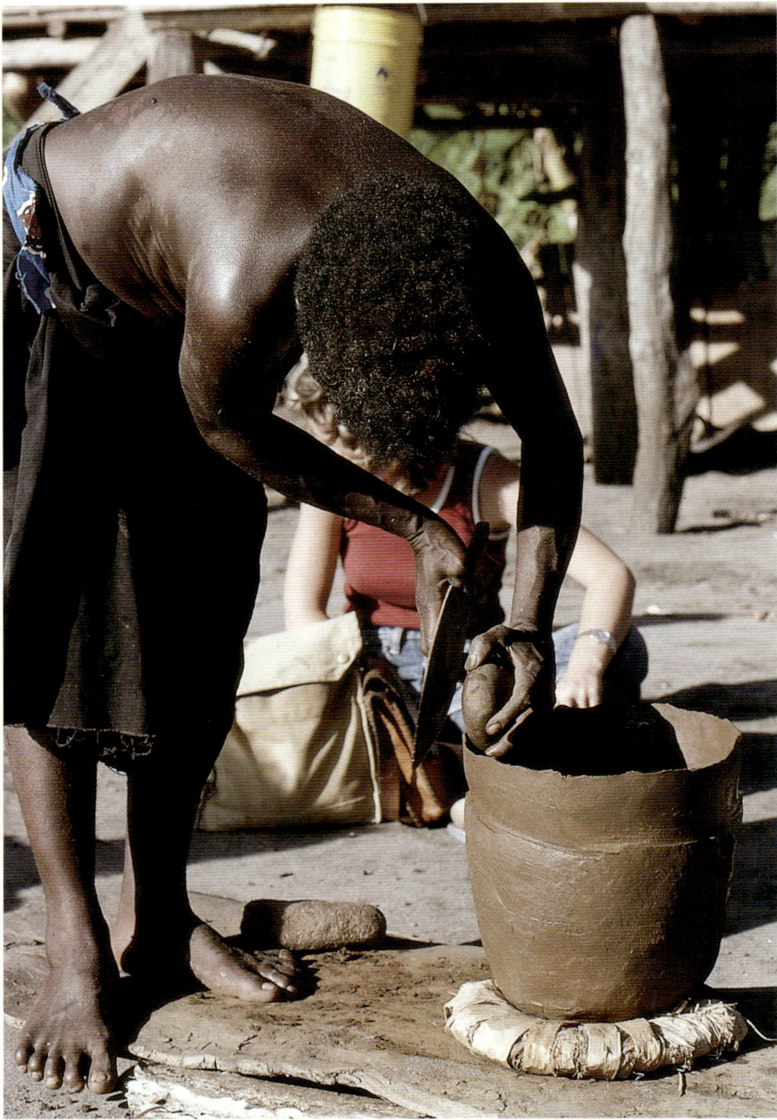

Fig. 11.10
The vessel takes shape: final beating at Pidea village, Nasioi group.

it. When the last two slabs are thoroughly joined the top edge is sliced level, using a thread of coconut fibre, and smoothed with a damp stone. The typical neck of Bougainville pots is formed by beating with a leaf-shaped beater, *tabi*, but first a narrow stick is used to mark where the neck will start, leaving distinct ridged marks around the angle of inflection. This is surprising because it is hardly a decorative feature and normally all ridges on any part of a pot are later smoothed. The pot is set aside to become firmer before the final beating; the base is beaten with the vessel supported on the potter's lap. The only form of decoration on Nasioi pots is the occasional serration of the rim with a shell. Occasionally, on small cooking pots at Pidia, coils of clay about 5 centimetres long are placed in groups on one side just under the rim. This is similar to the decoration on the pots of Shortland and Treasury islands. The pots are dried for about one week, some of the time in the sun but also in the house.

The fire is constructed from logs laid to form a rough platform on which the pots are rested on their sides. At Rumba, *taruai* wood (*Macaranga tanavius*) is split for this purpose. More fuel is roughly stacked around the pots in a pyramid and it is lit at the base. Wood is replaced over the pots if it falls away. The pots are lifted out of the still glowing fire after fifteen to thirty minutes. Ash is brushed off and the split-open fruit of the putty nut, *asita*, is rubbed over the still hot pots. Any cracks are filled with this plastic wood-like substance. When coated, the pots are put back into the hot coals to destroy toxic substances from the nut.

Pottery was traded widely in the Nasioi area. Pots were exchanged, together with fish and salt from the coast, for labour, coconuts, sago and tubers with the Aropa valley people. The pots were passed on from them to the mountain Nasioi in exchange for bows and arrows, mats and small game.

Buin

The Buin language speakers live on the southernmost part of Bougainville; the coastal Buin people have mostly moved inland. Three villages where pots are made are reported by Terrell (1976): Moro, Luaguo and Mamaromino.

Women are the potters but Terrell reports that a woman of Moro village was taught to make pots by an old man. Her activities ceased soon after World War II. Cooking pots for everyday use and larger ones for cooking pigs at feasts were produced. Some vessels are similar to those of Nasioi, with rounded bases, high shoulders and everted rims; some have more pointed bases; some are conical with a rounded base and everted rim. The generic term for clay pot is *igupo* and clay is sometimes referred to by the same name. At Moro, however, the clay is called *didiai*; the preparation is much the same as at Nasioi.

The following description of technique is taken from Terrell's observations and photographs of a special demonstration. What Terrell describes as a coil in the case of Buin will be called a slab or strip.

The potter forms a ball of clay which she pounds into a 'bluntly pointed but rounded pile'. She then taps the stone into the flat side to form a hollow and pushes up the sides with the stone to make a dish shape. Next she turns the rudimentary pot upside down, with the stone inside it resting on her hand, and beats the outside of it with a wooden paddle, *karibai*. With the frequently dampened beater she taps the edges until the clay stretches almost around the stone. This is the base of the pot and it is now rested in a banana leaf support. The potter next forms a long piece of clay which she flattens with the stone until it is about 30 centimetres long, 3 to 4 centimetres wide and 0.7 centimetres thick. After thinning the top edge of the shape by the paddle-and-anvil method she lays the narrow slab of clay around, overlapping it by 1 to 2 centimetres, and proceeds in the same manner as the Nasioi. The slabs used here are much narrower than those of the Nasioi and so may be termed strips. The forming of the neck by beating with the paddle forms ridges which are retained, as at Nasioi. With the edge of the paddle the potter further elaborates the lip by beating in little impressions or notches.

The pot is decorated before firing by what Terrell calls 'thin painting'. The potter prepares a yellowish-tan clay slip, *ugula*, and paints marks on the 'by then quite hard' surface of the pot with her finger. She subdivides the field of decoration into areas marked by thin horizontal bands which are filled in with vertical, diagonal or curvilinear motifs. The pot is then fired. This technique of decorating by painting and then firing is unique in the authors' study area although archaeological evidence indicates a continuing tradition of pottery decorated with paint and subsequently fired.

The firing at the Buin village of Moro is similar to that of the Nasioi and again there is no mention of the type of fuel used. The decoration of applied yellowish-tan clay paint becomes red-brown after the firing, suggesting that the raw material is coloured by limonite. This still shows up on the lighter brown fired pot, which has some smudging but does not appear to hide the patterns.

In the past the southern Bougainville areas were closely associated with the people of Bougainville Strait. The widespread trading network included Choiseul Island, all the small islands and the coast; it was disrupted by a customs barrier imposed by the Europeans between Bougainville and the southern Solomons. Oliver (1955) reports that the Siwai traded pots and spears for shell money, fish, lime and other commodities through middle-men on the coast to the Bougainville Strait islands. Buin carried on similar trading.

Siwai

The Siwai (Siuai) people live in the south-western part of Bougainville. Oliver states that the north-east of Siwai is the pot making centre but gives no village names. Friedlaender (1975) shows a man making pots at Moronei village. This is the only industry in the Solomon Islands where men are exclusively the potters although a few men make pots in the Buin area.

Pots, *hiuwo* (Chinnery 1931), are basically the same shape as those from both Nasioi and Buin but according to Oliver's illustrations some are very tall, up to 100 centimetres high. Also, judging by Friedlaender's photo, they appear to have wider flaring rims; that is, the width of the mouth seems greater than the belly. They have the same paddle indentations at the neck but these are less pronounced than on the Nasioi-Buin pots. Chinnery calls the large vessels *tanamasa*; these are for feasts in the clubhouse, for cooking pigs. Small pots are called *kunisa*. Cooking pots only are made. Water is carried and stored in bamboo tubes and coconut shells and this is probably true for all the Solomons since no water pots appear to have been made. Clay preparation is the same as at Nasioi and Buin. The best clay is found in the north-east of the potting area and other scattered pot making villages must buy their clay from there.

Terrell proposes that the forming technique can be compared closely with that of Buin but both Whitney (n.d.) and Chinnery (1931) describe the rolling out of coils on a piece of smooth bark, probably a 'pangal'. Whitney says that the coil technique is used in 'concentric circles'. This seems to be a case of straightforward coiling in contrast to the

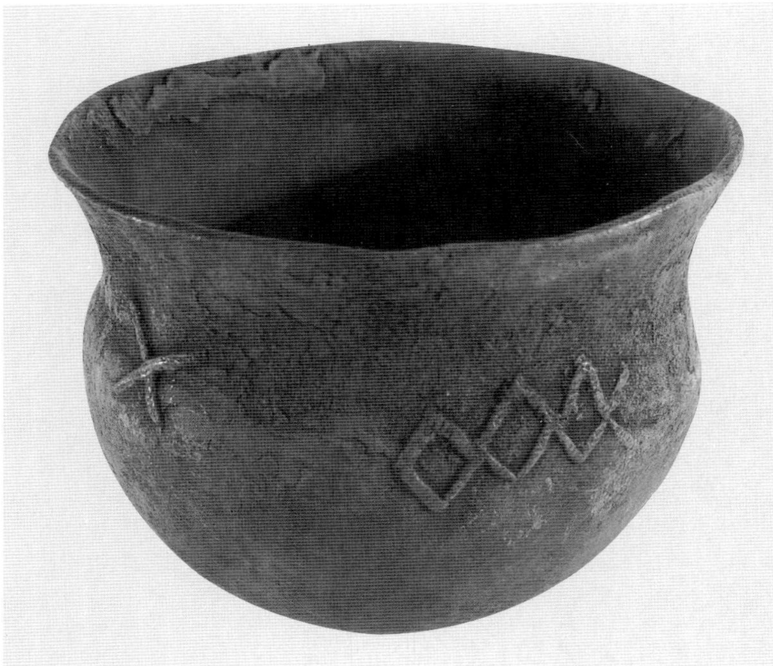

Fig. 11.11
Cooking pot made about 1896, from Falamai village, Mono Island (Treasury Islands), *h* 121 cm.

Fig. 11.12
Old cooking pot showing carved paddle marks, Shortland Island, *h* 11cm.

slab or strip construction of Buin, Nasioi, Bougainville Strait islands and Choiseul. As with the other industries, shaping and smoothing are done with a paddle but the hand rather than a stone anvil is used. The paddle is spear-shaped.

Whitney reports two unusual aspects. Firstly, a base is beaten out over a piece of woven matting, which leaves an imprint on the bottom of the pot. Secondly, what seems to be a unique technique is employed: the base is warmed and so partly dried by holding a bunch of burning palm fronds near it. After each coil is pinched and pressed into place the same treatment is repeated.

Sometimes a few incised lines are added as decoration. Firing is the same as at Nasioi and Buin. Much cracking during firing is reported, perhaps due to too much drying during construction. The putty nut is not used here.

Specht (1975) and others have written on the clay pipe making of Buka and Bougainville; the following is compiled from Specht's report. He concludes that the industry was almost certainly introduced by Europeans in the 18th or 19th centuries. Familiarity with clay pipes for smoking probably started at the time of the first whaling activities in the area in the 1820s or during the time of 'blackbirding', in the 1870s, when Buka men were taken to Queensland as plantation workers. Soon European clay pipes were sold from trade stores on Buka. By 1886 Parkinson (1888) observed a local pipe making industry when visiting Buka and Bougainville.

Specht lists three, possibly four, main centres of manufacture: on Buka and the small islands off its west coast, in the Kunua area of north-west Bougainville, in southern Bougainville and possibly also along the central eastern coast of Bougainville. The village of Sapani in central Buka and the west coast Buka islands became active in this craft but the traditional pot makers of the east coast did not participate. This was perhaps because men had through contact become the craftsmen in this case.

Clay came from sources different from those used by the potters and it seems that no temper was added. It could be expected that the bowl of the pipe would be made by the 'pinch pot' method but it is said to have been moulded over the maker's finger. Clay was folded around a thin straight stick or grass stem to produce the stem of the pipe and this was either withdrawn or burnt out later. The stem and bowl were joined and a heel, or spur, was formed where they met. Some simple incised decoration was used.

Clay pipes became included in the trade items both within Buka and to the east coast of Bougainville and Nissan Island to the north. During Blackwood's visit in 1929-30 they were popular both for trading and for monetary returns. In 1967 they were not being made but by 1976 the craft seems to have had at least a small revival on Buka Island; pipe making is reported at Gagan and even at Malasang. The pipes at Gagan, *nikasan*, are made from two cream-coloured clay materials collected

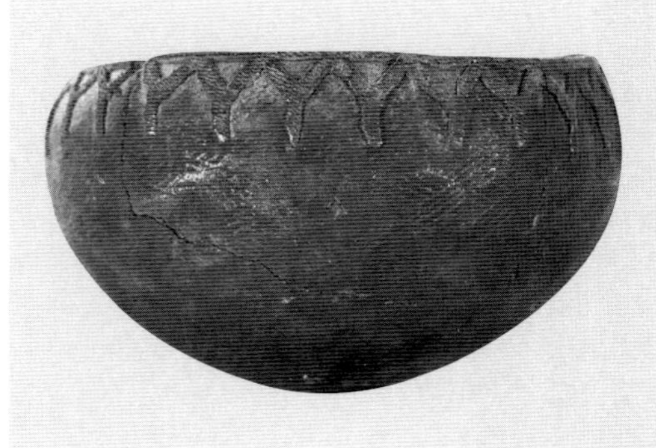

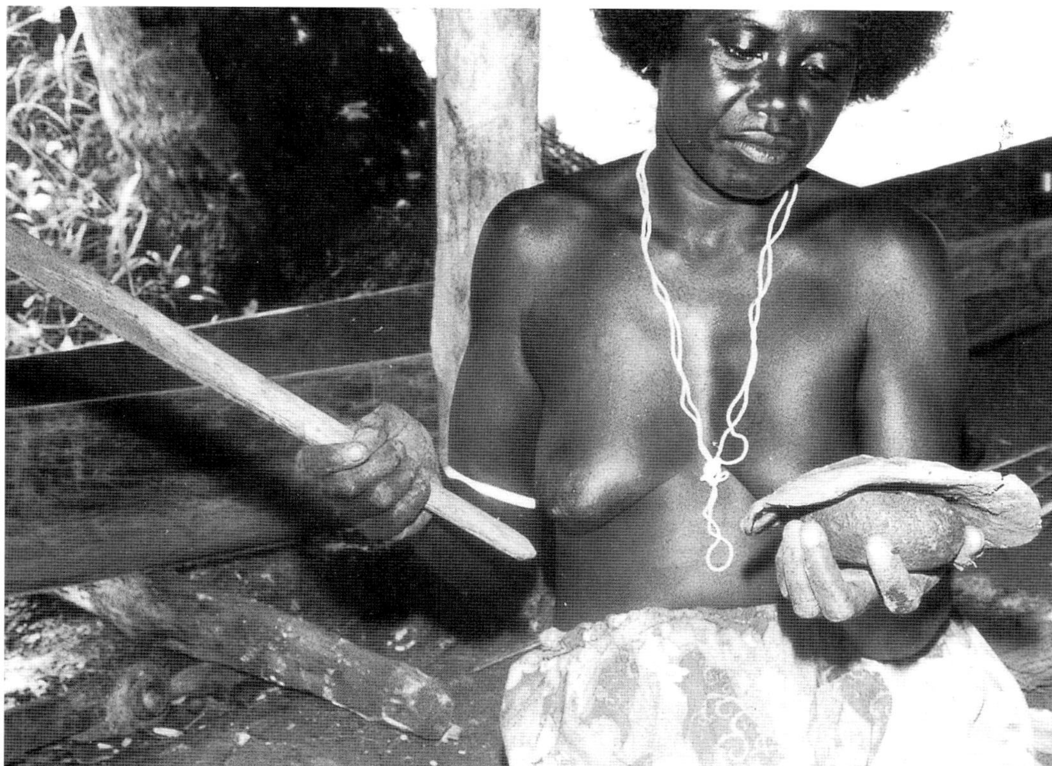

Fig. 11.13
Emma forming the base of a pot at Tarasidoko village, Choiseul Island.

from far away and are sold for a few dollars each. At Malasang they are made from the pot making clay body and are called *simuk* (pidgin for 'smoke'). In both cases the pipes have bamboo mouthpieces. They are placed in the cooking hearth for a few weeks instead of being fired in a traditional manner.

Solomon Islands

To the south of Bougainville Island, in what was before 1976 the British Solomon Islands, pottery is or was made at three islands in the Bougainville Strait and on Choiseul Island. All the potters are Austronesian speakers.

In the Bougainville Strait the pot making islands of the past were Alu (now known as Shortland Island) and Mono, which, with a smaller nearby island, are known as the Treasury Islands (Guppy 1887). To the north-east of Shortland is Fauro, the third of the larger islands between Bougainville and Choiseul. Ribbe (1903) records pot making at only one village on Fauro Island, Gisu. Batley (1968) describes a Mono Island pot after Guppy.

It seems that the method of making the wares (Wheeler 1928) was similar on all three islands and close to that used by the Nasioi and Buin potters. Pots on Fauro Island are placed in baskets to dry and they retain the woven pattern of the basketry, which is pressed into the undried clay. Treasury and Shortland islanders are noted for their use of a carved wooden paddle which also imparts a pattern to the outside of the pot. Irwin (1974) discusses carved paddle impressions on prehistoric sherds in this area and suggests that each potter had her own individual paddle and that the study of these decorations is invaluable in establishing distribution and chronology.

Old pots are still seen on the islands. As far as can be determined from a limited number of illustrations, the people of Mono made round-bottomed pots, some with a neck and outward-flaring rim but of much squatter proportions than the mainland pots. Shortland Island pots have no neck or outward-turning rim and are wide open shallow bowls. One Fauro Island vessel illustrated by Ribbe is similar to the others but a second is quite

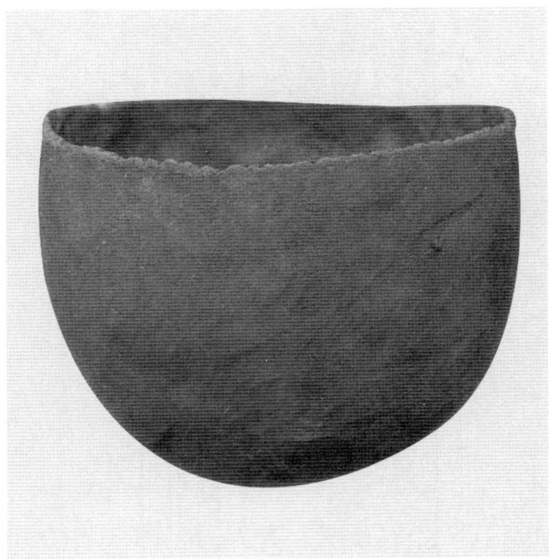

Fig. 11.14
Cooking pot from the Chirovanga area, Choiseul Island, *h* 13 cm.

different; it is shaped like the vessels made by the Bau people of Madang Province and looks strangely out of place. Taller than other vessels of the area, it has a slightly pointed base, a round belly, a neck and outward-flaring rim; applied decoration is used around the outer top edge or around the neck.

On Choiseul Island there are very few pot makers left. The main activity centre seems to have been on the north-east coast but possibly there was also a centre on the north-west coast. Villages on the north-east coast where pots are made are Tarasidoko, Sirovanga, Penetare and Vuranggo.

Whitney (n.d.) and Rattliff (1967) give accounts of the potting of Choiseul Island. Women make the pots in this area by the same slab or strip techniques and with paddle-and-anvil finish as at Nasioi and Buin. The only variation from place to place seems to be in the length and breadth of the slabs. Choiseul Island is the only place in the Solomon Islands, apart from Buka, where a temper, in this case sand, is added to the clay. Present-day Choiseul Island vessels are simple, undecorated, roughly spherical forms with a wide mouth and no neck or flaring rim. After firing they are finished with the putty nut sealer.

Appendix A
TERMINOLOGY

A number of terms are used to describe vessel profile, shape and structure. The authors have adopted the classification set out in Shepard (1965) but in the interest of simplicity and because the range of shapes occurring in Papua New Guinea is not as diverse as those for which Shepard has attempted to provide a classificatory system the authors have used only part of her terminology. The principal structural elements are illustrated in Diagram 1, showing corner point and inflection point, and Diagram 3, showing restricted and unrestricted and composite vessels. Of course, the forms selected for illustration are not exhaustive of the range of forms found in Papua New Guinea.

The authors have also resorted to visually descriptive terms: neck, shoulder, belly and base. 'Neck' can be defined without ambiguity in terms of corner or inflection points (see Glossary); many Papua New Guinea pots do not have necks.

'Shoulder' is more difficult to define. Shepard defines the shoulder, or upper body area, as the area above the point of maximum diameter on a restricted vessel. However, the authors have found this term too inclusive and have generally restricted the use of the term 'shoulder' to vessels which have a marked convexity between the belly and the neck. The authors have used the term 'belly' somewhat loosely to describe the area around the point of maximum diameter of the body (equator) of a restricted vessel. On some pots, notably those where the inflection point occurs low on the body, the boundary between neck-shoulder-belly is not clearly distinguishable. In using these terms to describe characteristics (particularly areas of decoration) on different pots, the authors are aware that their usage may not be entirely consistent. They have used the term 'base' to describe loosely the area around the bottom end point (see Diagram 2).

The principal terms used to describe rim characteristics are illustrated in Diagram 4.

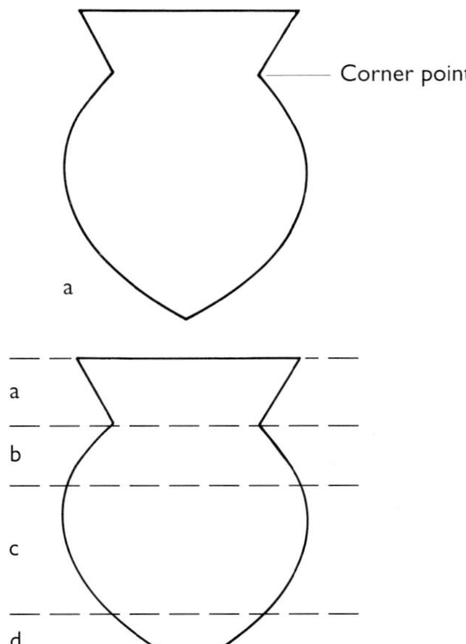

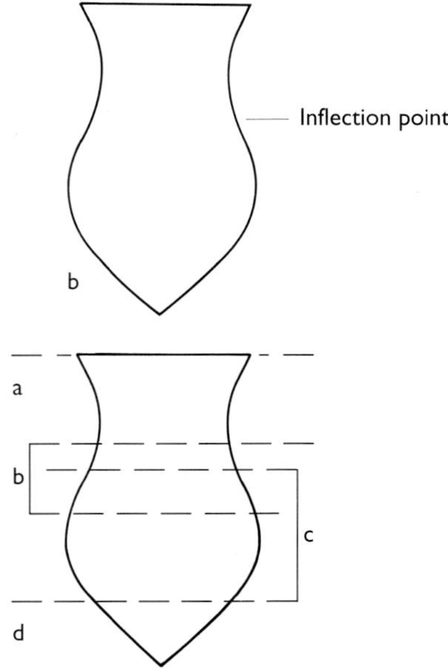

Diagram 1
Points of vessel profile:
a. corner point;
b. inflection point.

Diagram 2
Components of vessel profile:
a. neck;
b. shoulder;
c. belly;
d. base.

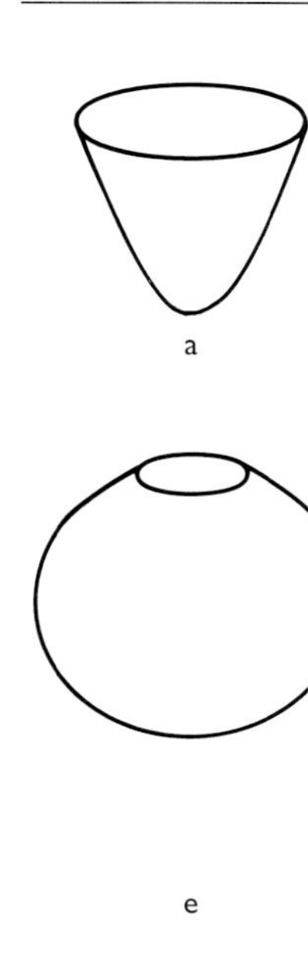

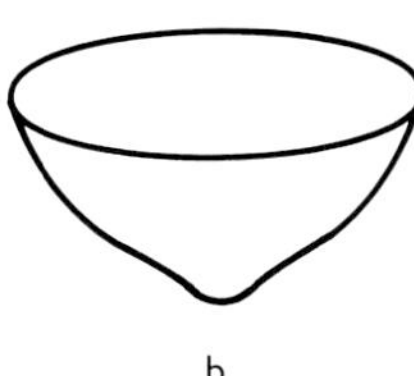

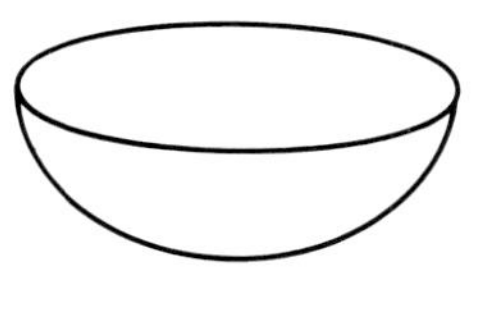

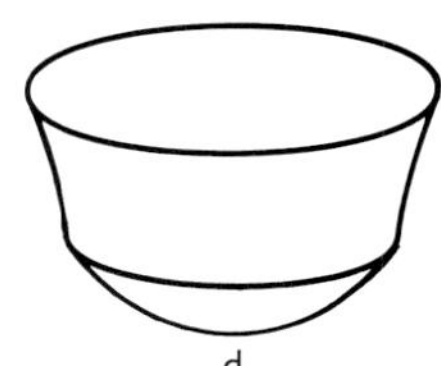

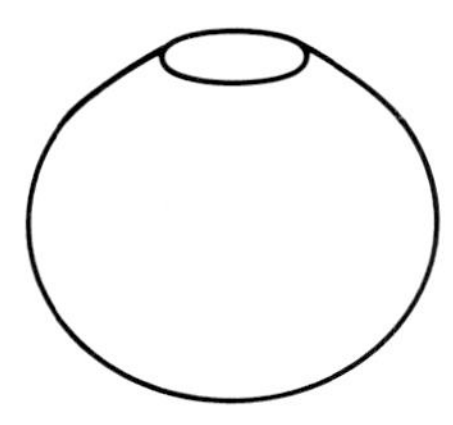

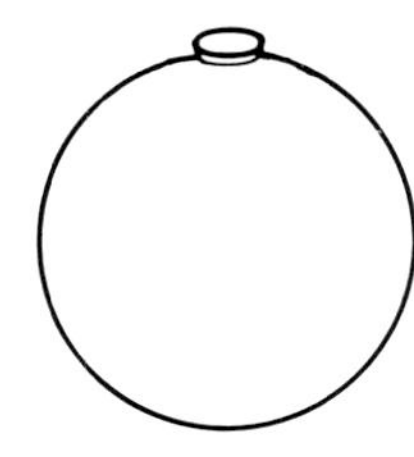

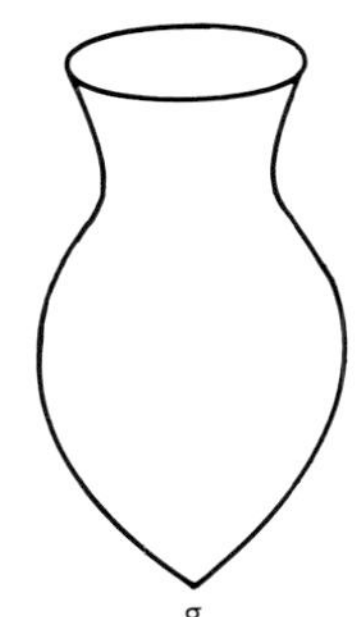

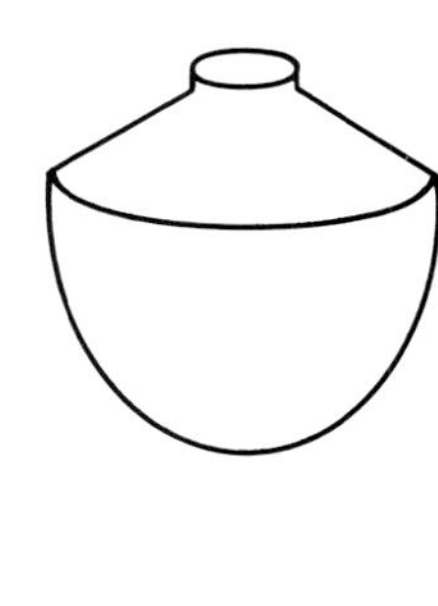
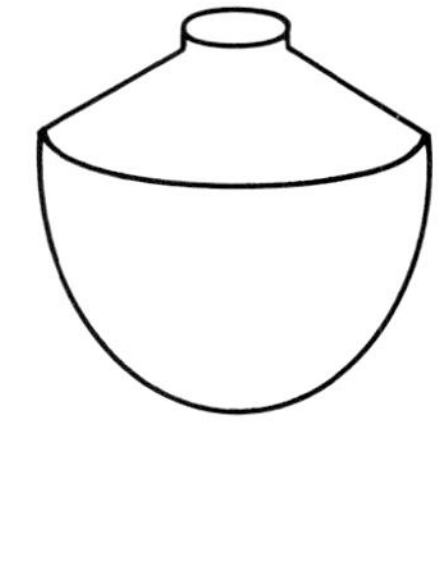

Diagram 3

Classification of vessel shape:

a-d. unrestricted vessels;

e-h. restricted vessels;

d. and h. composite vessels.

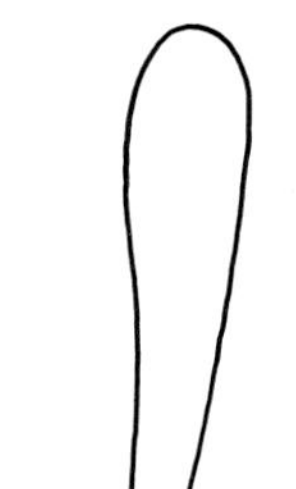

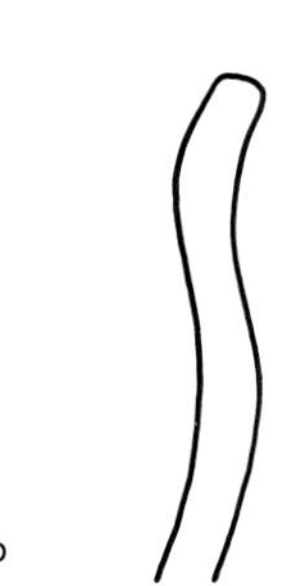

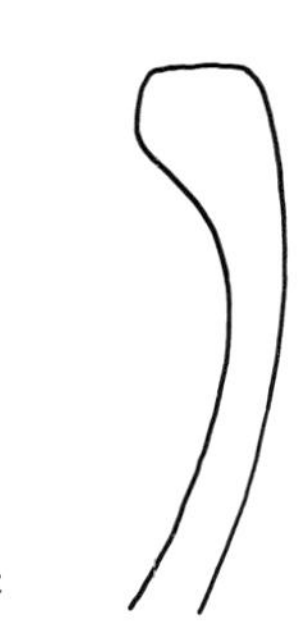

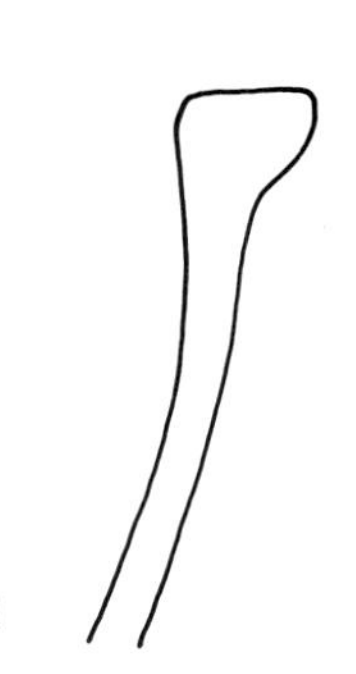

Diagram 4

Examples of rim types:

a. direct;

b-d. indirect;

a. thickened;

c. inverted;

d. everted.

Appendix B
CLAY ANALYSES

Sixty-five samples of clay and temper, collected by Margaret Tuckson in the field, have been analysed. The authors' thanks go to the following individuals and organisations: Russell Hill, Commonwealth Scientific and Industrial Research Organisation (CSIRO), Australia, for industrial analyses of thirty-two samples at the laboratories in Port Moresby, showing grit (gravel) size, water content values, rupture angles, ignition loss, fired colour, vitrification temperatures, softening points and impurities; Lloyd Hamilton, at the University of Papua New Guinea and at CSIRO, Ryde, Sydney, for X-ray diffraction of seventeen samples; Dr R.G. Anthony, University of New South Wales, for X-ray diffraction of two samples; Lindsay Anderson, Sydney, for analyses of nine samples and further testing of ten of the CSIRO samples, showing grain size distribution (sieve and pipette), petrographic microscope examination of the coarse fractions and X-ray diffraction of the clay minerals and some also tested for water content and drying, shrinkage and firing characteristics.

Copies of all the results of the above May-Tuckson clay tests will be lodged at the National Museum and Art Gallery, Port Moresby, the University of Papua New Guinea, the Australian Museum, and the School of Pacific Studies at the Australian National University, Canberra. The remaining clay samples will be deposited at the National Museum and Art Gallery in Port Moresby.

GLOSSARY

Acid rocks Igneous rocks containing more than 65 per cent of silica.

Adze A tool the working edge of which is set at an angle to the handle and curving towards it.

Allophane A clay mineral having a similar structure and composition to kaolinite. It is mostly amorphous (very poorly or not crystallised) and difficult to detect by X-ray diffraction.

Alluvium Gravel, sand, silt and clay deposited by water, especially rivers.

Andesite An intermediate volcanic rock characterised by plagioclase.

Anvil A smooth, rounded and hard object, usually a stone, which is held inside a vessel to resist the impact of a beating tool against the outside walls.

Appliqué Applied decoration. Clay decoration applied to or on the surface of a vessel or clay object.

Arkose A rock of the sandstone type in which feldspar and quartz predominate.

Baret (pidgin) A narrow waterway.

Basalt A basic black volcanic rock having pyroxene, calcic plagioclase and sometimes olivine as the main minerals.

Base The bottom portion of a pot.

Basic rocks Dark-coloured igneous rocks containing less silica than either intermediate or acid rocks: 45 to 55 per cent silica.

Belly The area of greatest diameter between the mouth or neck of a restricted vessel and its base.

Betel nut The fruit of *Areca catechu*, used as a stimulant.

Bi-fold Pertaining to decoration; the field of decoration is divided into two symmetrical elements.

Bonding The technique of joining coils to each other along their longitudinal surfaces either by sliding or pushing the clay across the join with the thumb, finger or a tool, or by exerting firm pressure downwards on the top coil with a finger or thumb.

Burnishing A surface finishing technique. A newly made vessel in the leather-hard stage is polished by rubbing the walls with a hard, preferably rounded surface, such as a pebble, the back of a shell, a piece of coconut shell or a bean seed.

Calcareous Composed of calcium carbonate ($CaCO_3$).

Calcite A mineral and the dominant constituent of limestone.

Calcium hydroxide $Ca(OH)_2$ is formed from calcium oxide (CaO) by the absorption of water.

Calcium oxide CaO can result from the firing of calcium carbonate ($CaCO_3$) which decomposes between red heat (600°C) and 950°C.

Carbon An element which is combined in nearly all organic compounds.

Carbonate Mostly referring to calcium carbonate ($CaCO_3$), but could be magnesium carbonate ($MgCO_3$). Chief component of shells and limestone.

Chip-carving A decorating technique in which a knife or sharp wooden tool is used to cut small chip-sized pieces from vessel walls. A fine curling remnant of clay results and must be discarded by brushing or blowing away. Kaufmann (1975) introduced the term.

Chlorite A clay mineral group. $(OH)_4\ (SiAI)_8\ (Mg\ Fe)_6\ O_{20}\ (MgAl)_6\ (OH)_{12}$. Green hydrous silicates in which iron and magnesium atoms are prominent. Related to the micas.

Clay A sediment or soil, an assemblage of one or more clay minerals with accessory minerals. The term 'clay' is also used to refer to the smallest size range in the scale of Grain Size Distribution (less than 0.002 millimetres). This scale has been used throughout the work.

Clay body Prepared clay ready for use. The term

is used particularly when additions have been made to the clay.

Clay minerals A group of minerals, hydrous aluminium silicates, which occur as extremely small particles. The principal ones are kaolinite, smectites, halloysite and illites.

Coil A rolled-out length of clay.

Coiling The process of building up the vessel walls by superimposing lengths of coils.

Colloidal carbon Carbon in a range of particle sizes between microscopic and molecules, too fine to be visible with a microscope.

Combing A decorating technique where groups of parallel lines are made with the teeth of a tool by dragging it across the still damp clay.

Communal firings A firing at which a number of potters fire their pots on a common fire.

Composite vessels Vessels, the profiles of which show two or more distinct contours separated by one or more corner points.

Corner point A point on a vessel at which there is a sharp change in contour.

Decomposition of calcium carbonate Occurs between 600°C and 950°C and results in calcium oxide (CaO).

Dehydration Loss of chemically combined water.

Dentate stamping A decorating technique in which tooth-like indentations are made in the clay with a multi-pronged tool.

Direct rim (*see* **Rim**)

Disintegrated Broken up from the mass by weathering and reduced to particles.

Drag marking A decorating technique. The surface of the vessel is marked by dragging a finger or thumb through the clay or across unbonded coils.

Eating bowl A bowl from which food is eaten and which is not used for cooking.

Ellipsoid vessel A vessel, the shape of which approximates an ellipsoid.

Epidote A family of minerals. A silicate containing calcium and occurring mainly in metamorphic rocks.

Family Linguistic. A group of interrelated languages that generally share 28 per cent or more basic vocabulary cognates.

Feldspar A family of minerals, one of the most important of the rock-forming mineral groups. Plagioclase, a sodium and calcium feldspar ($NaAlSi_3O_8 - CaAl_2Si_2O_8$), and orthoclase, a potassium feldspar ($KAlSi_3O_8$), are common in igneous rocks and arkose.

Ferric oxide Red iron oxide (Fe_2O_3) from the mineral hematite or from limonite. Used as a colouring agent.

Fine sand fraction Sand within the range of grain size distribution 0.2 millimetres to 0.02 millimetres.

Forming dish A shallow, round-bottomed bowl of fired clay in which the bases of pots are formed in some areas. They are also used as turntables.

Globular A term used to describe vessels which are roughly spherical, bulbous or squat in shape.

Goethite A mineral, $FeO(OH)_2$. Hydrous iron oxide, a crystalline form of limonite.

Gouging A decorating technique. A cutting tool is held at an angle and pushed through the clay by cutting into it and forming a channel. The lines formed are free from burr. Excess clay is discarded.

Grain size distribution Statistical expression of the abundance and range of grain sizes of sediments, soils and clays determined by mechanical analysis. The scale used for the purposes of this work is as follows:

over 2.00 millimetres = fine gravel or grit
2.00 to 0.2 millimetres = sand
0.2 to 0.02 millimetres = fine sand
0.02 to 0.002 millimetres = silt
less than 0.002 millimetres = clay

Greenalite A mineral. Hydrous iron silicate.

Grooving A decorating technique in which grooves or continuous channels are cut into the clay with a tool. The edge of the line is sharp and clean and there is an abrupt break at the end of the stroke.

Gypsum A mineral. Natural hydrated calcium sulphate, $CaSO_4 2H_2O$. A chemical sediment.

Halloysite A clay mineral. Two varieties are known, one having the same formula as kaolinite. The other form is hydrated and is thought to have tubular structure. In comparison with kaolinite it does not slake easily in water and has a higher drying shrinkage.

Haus tambaran (pidgin) A building used in conjunction with men's secret cults.

Hematite A mineral, ferric oxide (Fe_2O_3), known

as red ochre in its earthy form but can also be grey or black in its hard form. It is the pigment of red clays.

Hemispherical vessel A vessel the shape of which approximates a hemisphere, that is, a round shape of which the ratio of height to diameter at the mouth is 0.5.

Hornblende A mineral of the Amphibole family, having a dark elongate form. A silicate of aluminium, calcium, magnesium and iron with sodium.

Hospitality gifts Presentations made by visitors to their hosts.

Hot-water sago A gluggy gruel made by adding cold water and then hot water to sago flour.

Hydrated minerals Those containing chemically combined water.

Hyperboloid vessel A vessel the shape of which approximates a hyperboloid.

Igneous rocks Rocks which have been forced up into or through the earth's crust in the form of molten magma and which have then cooled, crystallised or vitrified.

Illites A clay mineral group having a composition close to that of the micas but with a higher silica alumina ratio. They have substantially no expanding lattice characteristics. Potassium is a distinctive component of illites.

Impressing A decorating technique in which depressed patterns or marks are made in the clay.

Incising A decorating technique in which fine lines are made in the clay by means of a pointed tool which can either be pushed or pulled along, forming a trough and a raised edge. The excess clay is either depressed or displaced to the side.

Independent Applies to restricted vessels. Indicates that the diameter at the corner or inflection point is independent of, or distinct from, the diameter at the widest part of the belly. Shepard introduced the term (Shepard 1971: 230).

Indirect rim (*see* **Rim**)

Inflection point A point on a vessel at which there is a change in contour from concave to convex. This is not a sharp change. (*See also* **Corner point**.)

Intermediate rocks Igneous rocks containing less silica than acid rocks but more than basic rocks, 55-65 per cent silica.

Intrusion Igneous rocks formed from molten magma which has been forced into the upper regions of the earth's crust but not through the surface.

Jasper A mineral. An opaque form of cryptocrystalline silica (minute crystals), usually red, brown or yellow.

Kaolin China clay. A white firing clay, sometimes almost pure kaolinite, formed from the decomposition of feldspar. Used in the production of stoneware and porcelain.

Kaolinite The 'ideal' clay mineral, $(OH)_8Si_4Al_4O_{10}$.

Knead To mix and work clay into a homogeneous plastic mass by pressing, rolling and folding.

Kwila (pidgin) The ironwood tree. It has dark reddish grained wood and is so heavy it will not float.

Leather-hard The condition of a newly made vessel when it is firm but not yet dry.

Limbum (pidgin) Several species of palm, most commonly various types of black palm, whose timbers and leaf-bases are used by the villagers. In this work, limbum usually refers to the flexible leaf-base which is cut to a roughly rectangular shape, flattened out and then employed as a rough surface on which to prepare clay and, rarely, to roll out coils.

Limonite A mineral. Hydrous iron oxide, $2Fe_2O_33H_2O$. When soft and earthy it is known as yellow ochre and is often the colouring pigment in yellowish clays.

Lip The term is commonly used to describe the end point of the pot at the mouth. To avoid confusion the authors have used the term 'mouth', or 'orifice', to refer to the opening of the vessel and the term 'rim' to refer to the margin around the mouth (see **Rim**).

Lug A piece of clay applied to or modelled onto the wall of a vessel mostly for use as a handle and often having a hole for a vine or plaited bush string from which to hang the vessel.

Magnetite A mineral. Iron oxide, Fe_3O_4. Black or dark red in colour, it occurs in igneous and metamorphic rocks, sandstones and sands.

Mami (pidgin) A species of yam: *Dioscorea esculanta*.

Masalai (pidgin) Term for a spirit which usually resides in the bush or near water.

Massim A term used to describe the eastern part of Milne Bay Province, including the tip of the mainland and the islands north to the Trobriand Islands, and east to Rossel Island. The term is also used for the art style characteristic of this region.

Metamorphic rocks Those that have been formed by the action of great heat and/or pressure on sedimentary, igneous or other metamorphic rocks.

Mica A mineral group having a distinctive sheet-like structure similar to clay minerals and a metallic lustre. It occurs in many clays. Biotite mica is black and common in some granites; muscovite mica is white and is more common in sedimentary rocks.

Modelling Hand manipulation of clay. Used to make free-standing or applied representations of zoomorphic or decorative forms.

Montmorillonite A clay mineral, $(OH)_4Si_8(Al_{3.34}Mg_{0.66})0_{20}$. The name is also used for a group of clay minerals but the term 'smectite' is now usually preferred. They are noted for having an expanded lattice which takes up water, giving rise to the term 'swelling clays'. The specific mineral montmorillonite is high in alumina compared with others of the group.

Multiple firings A firing at which more than one pot is fired simultaneously.

Neck The area between a corner point or point of inflection and the mouth of the vessel.

Non-plastic Referring to materials which do not become plastic on mixing with water.

Notched A decorating technique of V-shaped indentations or incisions across the surface of a vessel. May also refer to nicks made along an edge.

Nubbin A small, usually oval, round or oblong projection of clay either raised from the surface of the clay by finger pinching or applied to it. Used as decoration.

Obsidian Volcanic glass. A rock which breaks in smooth, curved, sharp-edged surfaces and has silica as its main component.

Olivine A mineral family. A silicate containing iron and magnesium and occurring in most basic igneous rocks.

Oxidising Firing under conditions in which there is sufficient free oxygen for the iron compounds and carbonaceous matter in the clay body to be brought to their highest state of oxidation and thus remain red, buff or orange.

Paddle A wooden beater used to shape and thin out vessel walls.

Pangal (pidgin) Term used for various parts of the leaf of the sago palm, *Metroxylon* spp. In this work it specifically refers to the leaf-base which is cut to a roughly rectangular shape and flattened for use as a surface on which to roll coils and, rarely, to prepare clay. Also used as fuel for firings.

Pigment A colouring matter or substance.

Plasticity The property which enables moistened clay to be deformed by pressure and to retain its shape when the pressure is withdrawn.

Polishing (*see* **Burnishing**)

Poorly crystalline Having a less regular crystal lattice. It is not easy to identify a poorly crystalline mineral by X-ray diffraction.

Poorly sorted When referring to sediments, having a wide range of grain sizes.

Porosity The ratio of the volume of pore spaces in a material to the volume of that material.

Preheating A preliminary gentle heating of vessels before firing.

Pug An uncommon term for a lump of clay (not a ball of clay) derived from the cylindrical section of clay produced by a pug-mill, a machine for mixing and softening clay which extrudes clay in a continuous thick cylinder. The authors have adopted the term 'pug' for their own uses, despite the fact that Papua New Guineans do not have machines for processing clay.

Pumice An acid volcanic rock with numerous gas bubble holes making it very light in weight.

Punctate A decorating technique in which indentations (punctures) are made in the clay by a wooden, bamboo or shell tool.

Pyrite A mineral: iron sulphide, FeS_2, often called 'fool's gold'.

Pyrometer A device for measuring high temperatures.

Pyroxene A family of ferro-magnesium minerals, augite being the principal member.

Quartz A mineral: silicon dioxide, SiO_2 (silica). Quartz is the most common mineral in the earth's crust, making up a large proportion of acid igneous rocks such as granite and also sandstones and quartzites.

Quartzose sand Sand largely or entirely composed of quartz.

Quatrefoil A decorative scheme consisting of four elements radiating from a common centre.

Quatrefold Pertaining to decoration where the field of decoration is divided into four symmetrical elements.

Reducing Firing under conditions in which there is insufficient free oxygen for full combustion of the fuel. The iron in the clay body is reduced to its lowest state and is grey in colour.

Remnant coil The remaining piece of coil at the top of a vessel which is brought down from the rim and formed into an applied decoration or is left to form an uneven rim.

Restricted vessel A vessel with a mouth the diameter of which is less than the maximum diameter of the vessel; that is, the walls of the vessel converge towards the top.

Rib Midrib. The central vein of a leaf extending from the petiole, or leaf-stem, to the apex.

Rim The margin of the mouth (lip) of the vessel. It may be elaborated in many ways but there are two main variables: direction in relation to the contour of the vessel side and thickness. When the vessel wall extends to the margin without change in direction or thickness it is referred to as a direct rim. An indirect rim is set off by direction or thickness as a distinct part of the vessel. If it deviates from the vessel walls in an inward direction it is inverted; if it turns outwards it is everted. (*See* "Appendix A", p. 349).

Ring building The process of building up the walls of a vessel with coils that complete a circle for each level. The length of coil needed may be judged exactly or may be pinched off if too long.

Ring-cushion Ring-support. Made from either banana leaves or pandanus leaves by first forming a ring of several layers and then binding over and over this until a thick padded ring is formed. It accommodates the round or pointed bases of the pots during forming and also acts as a turntable.

Sago Palm trees (*Metroxylon* spp.) of lowland swampy areas. The pith of the palm yields sago flour, the leaf-bases and stalks are used as building materials and for other purposes (*see* **Pangal**), the leaves are used for thatching and basketry, and the midrib is used as a decorating tool by potters.

Sago frying pan Flat or shallow dishes used for cooking 'pancakes' of sago flour, grated coconut and water, usually without grease.

Schist A metamorphic rock with a 'platy' texture. Varieties are named after the dominant mineral in them, often mica.

Scoring A surface finishing technique in which the surface of the vessel is marked by casual and random striations. Used to give texture to the body of the vessel.

Scraping Thinning and smoothing the vessel walls of excess clay.

Scratching A decorating technique in which shallow superficial 'scratch' marks are made in the clay by a sharp tool or fingernail.

Sealing The process in which a pot is sealed by the application of a vegetable sealing agent. The main one used is sago solution.

Sedimentary rocks Rocks formed, usually by a hardening process, from materials deposited by wind, water, ice or organisms.

Seger cone A device in the form of a small pyramid made of glaze/clay materials, numbered and proportioned to 'squat' at given temperatures.

Semi-consolidated lithic tuff Slightly hardened fine non-quartzose material (ash) deposited from a volcanic eruption.

Serving vessel A vessel into which food is ladled after being cooked; the food may be eaten from this vessel individually or communally, or may be redistributed from it into individual eating bowls.

Shoulder The area below the neck of a restricted vessel, marked by pronounced convexity or curvature. Shepard (1971) refers to this as 'upper body'.

Slab building The process of building up the walls of a vessel with slabs of clay which are beaten out or sliced off.

Slip A smooth mixture of clay and water of creamy consistency used to coat a vessel inside and/or outside for the purpose of changing its colour or imparting a smoother surface.

Slurry A thick, rough mixture of clay and water of fairly creamy consistency used for joining clay parts.

Smectite A clay mineral group, the members of which have an expanding lattice. Smectite is the alternative, and now preferred, name for the montmorillonite group. Unlike kaolinite, this group contains atoms of either magnesium, sodium, iron or lithium in the crystal lattice.

Smoothing A surface finishing technique in which the still plastic clay is evenly distributed to achieve a smooth texture with wet hands, fingers or tools (shells or paddles).

Smudging Localised black and grey areas on fired pots, caused by colloidal carbon penetrating the pores of the clay during firing.

Sponge spicules Skeletal elements of the marine animal, the sponge.

Stippling A decorating technique in which small indentations (holes) are made in the clay, usually with a pointed tool.

Stock Linguistic. A group of interrelated families in which, in general, member languages of one of the families share 12 to 28 per cent basic vocabulary cognates with member languages of the other families. The member families of a stock may contain a single language only.

Talc A mineral family: hydrous magnesium silicate, white and soapy in texture. Occurs most commonly in schist.

Tambaran (pidgin) A supernatural guardian spirit associated with male cults.

Tanget (pidgin) A shrub, *Cordyline* spp.

Taro Several members of the Araceae family which produce edible corms and leaves.

Temper Any non-plastic material, vegetable or mineral, added to a clay to decrease its shrinkage and improve its ability to withstand sudden changes of temperature during firing.

Texturing Altering the texture of the walls of a ceramic object by scratching, scoring, scraping or drag marking.

Thermal shock resistance The ability of a clay body to withstand recurring sudden changes of temperature without cracking or shattering.

Thermocouple The activating part of a pyrometer, made of two wires of dissimilar alloys fused together at one end. They are attached outside the kiln or bonfire to the pyrometer indicator. (*See also* **Pyrometer**.)

Tulip (pidgin) A tree, *Gnetum gnemon*, the leaves, fruit, and bark of which are used for a variety of purposes.

Tumbuan (pidgin) A masked dancer or the mask worn by him.

Turntable A studio potters' device, a wheel-head which can be turned or spun by hand, used for working on hand-built pots or for decorating.

Unrestricted vessel A vessel with a mouth the diameter of which is equal to or greater than the maximum diameter of the vessel; that is, the walls of the vessel are vertical or diverging.

Vitrification The point at which clay starts to become glassy by fusion during heating.

X-ray diffraction A technique used to determine the identity of clay minerals. The crystals are 'bombarded' by an X-ray beam which is diffracted by the crystal structures. The diffraction through each crystal structure results in a characteristic pattern of bands on a photographic film placed behind the crystal.

Yam An edible tuber (*Dioscorea* spp.). In several parts of the country, notably the Sepik area and parts of Milne Bay, the cultivation of the long yam, mostly *D. alata* is associated with male cults.

Zircon A mineral: Zirconium silicate, $ZrSiO_4$.

Bibliography

Abramson, J. 'A Preliminary Archaeological Survey of the Tami Islands, Territory of New Guinea.' *Archaeology and Physical Anthropology in Oceania* IV(2), 1969.

Allen, J. 'A Pottery Collection from the Madang District T.P.N.G.' *Records of the Papua and New Guinea Museum and Art Gallery* 1(2), 1971.

Allen. J. and Littlewood, H. 'Funerary Cave Pottery from the Cape Rodney Area, Central Papua.' *Records of the Papua New Guinea Museum and Art Gallery* 4, 1974.

Allen, J. and Hurd, C. *Languages of the Bougainville District.* Ukarumpa, Summer Institute of Linguistics, n.d.

Aufenanger, H. *The Passing Scene in North-East New-Guinea: a documentation.* Monograph vol. 2. St Augustin, Germany, Anthropos Institute, 1972.

Barclay, B. 'A Comparison of Primitive Pottery Techniques in four Papua New Guinea Villages.' *Pottery in Australia* 10(2), 1971.

Bateson, G. *Naven.* Stanford, Stanford University Press, 1936.

Batley, R.A. 'A Pottery Cooking Vessel from Mono Island.' *Journal of the Polynesian Society* 77, 1968.

Beck, C. von 'Neu Guinea.' *Das überseeische Deutschland* 2, 1911.

Behrmann, W. *Das Westliche Kaiser Wilhelms-Land in Neu-Guinea.* Ergänzungsheft I zur Zeitschrift der Gesellschaft für Erdkunde zu Berlin, 1924.

Beier, G. 'Wosera Pottery Collection for the Wewak Pottery Museum.' *Gigibori* 3(1), 1976.

Belshaw, C. 'In Search of Wealth.' *American Anthropologist* 57(1) Part 2, American Anthropological Association, memoir 80, 1955.

Berde, S. *Melanesians as Methodists: Economy and Marriage on a Papua New Guinea Island.* Ann Arbor, Michigan: University Microfilms (Xerox), 1974.

———. 'Missionizing a Melanesian Society: Religious Syncretism and Exchange on Panaeati Island.' Unpublished manuscript, n.d.

Biro, L. *Beschreibender Catalog der Ethnographischen Sammlung Ludwig Biro's aus Deutsch-Neu-Guinea.* Ethnographische Sammlungen des Ungarischen Nationalmuseums I. Budapest, 1899.

———. *Beschreibender Catalog der Ethnographischen Sammlung Ludwig Biro's aus Deutsch-Neu-Guinea (Astrolabe Bai).* Ethnographische Sammlungen des Ungarischen Nationalmuseums III, Budapest, 1901.

Blackwood, B. *Both Sides of Buka Passage.* Oxford, The Clarendon Press, 1935.

———. 'Life on the Upper Watut, New Guinea.' *The Geographical Journal* 94(1), 1939.

———. 'Some Arts and Industries of the Bosman, Ramu River, New Guinea.' *Südseestudien, Gedenkschrift zur Erinnerung an F Speiser.* Basel, Museum für Völkerkunde, 1951.

Bodrogi, T. 'New-Guinea Style Provinces. The Style Province of Astrolabe Bay.' *Opuscula Ethnological Memoriae Ludevici Biro Sacra.* Budapest, Akadémiai Kiadó, 1959.

———. *Art in North-east New Guinea.* Budapest, Hungarian Academy of Sciences, 1961.

Broadhurst, H. 'Oma, Potter of Vanimo.' *Pottery in Australia* 14(1), 1975.

Brown, H.A. *Elema Traditions and Art.* London Missionary Society, 1959.

Buhler, A. *Kunststile am Sepik. Führer darch das Museum für Völkerkunde Basel.* Sonderausstellung, 1960.

Bulmer, R. and Davidson, J. *Notes on a Visit to the East Sepik District, 28 August - 11 September 1970.* Mimeograph, University of Papua New Guinea, 1970.

Bulmer, S. 'The Historic and Prehistoric Pottery of New Guinea, with remarks on the external relationships of the pottery of the Port Moresby region.' Paper presented to ANZASS Congress, Port Moresby, August 1970.

———. 'Archaeological Investigations at the Koigen site, near Wewak, East Sepik District.' *Records of the Papua and New Guinea Museum and Art Gallery* I(2), 1971*a*.

———. 'Two Old Sepik Pots Presented to the Museum.' *Records of the Papua and New Guinea Museum and Art Gallery* I(2), 1971*b*.

———. 'Prehistoric settlement patterns and pottery in the Port Moresby area.' *Journal of the Papua and New Guinea Society* 5(2), 1971*c*.

Burridge, K.O. *Tangu Traditions: a study of the way of life, mythology and developing experience of a New Guinea People.* Oxford, Clarendon Press, 1969.

Capell, A. *The Linguistic Position of South-Eastern Papua.* Sydney, Australasian Medical Publishing Co., 1943.

———. *A Survey of New Guinea Languages.* Sydney, Sydney University Press, 1969.

Cardew, M. *Pioneer Pottery.* London, Longman's, Green & Co. Ltd., 1969.

Carteret, P. *Carteret's Voyage round the World, 1766-69.* Hakluyt Society, Cambridge University Press, 1965.

Chalmers, J. and Gill, W. *Work and Adventure in New Guinea.* London, The Religious Tract Society, 1885.

———. 'History and Description of the pottery trade.' *Picturesque New Guinea-Land*, edited by J.W. Lindt. London, Longman's, 1887.

Chatterton, P. 'The Story of a Migration.' *Journal of the Papua and New Guinea Society* 2(2), 1969.

Chauvet, S. *Les Arts Indigènes en Nouvelle-Guinée.* Paris, Société d'Éditions geographiques, maritimes et coloniales, 1930.

Chick, John and Sue. *Grass Roots Art of the Solomons: Images and Islands.* Sydney, Pacific Publications, 1978.

Chinnery, E.W. 'Notes on Natives of Certain Villages of the Mandated Territory of New Guinea, visited during the Voyages of the Government Steam Yacht "Franklin" January-March 1925.' *Territory of New Guinea Anthropological Report No. I.* Melbourne, 1931.

Christensen, R. (ed.) *Madang and Siassi: Traditional Art and Craft.* Madang Teachers' College, 1975.

Churchill, W. *Sissano, Movements of Migration within and through Melanesia.* Washington, The Carnegie Institution of Washington, 1916.

Clarke, W.C. *Place and People.* Canberra, Australian National University, 1971.

Cochrane, P. *Vagi and Varo, Children of Papua.* Melbourne, Oxford University Press, 1961.

Cochrane, R. 'The Potter is a Woman.' *Pottery Quarterly* 20, 1958.

Coutts, P. 'Pottery of Eastern New Guinea and Papua.' *Mankind* 6(10), 1967.

Davenport, W. 'Preliminary Excavations on Santa Ana Island, Eastern Solomon Islands.' *Archaeology and Physical Anthropology in Oceania* 7(3), 1972.

Dempwolff, O. 'Sagen und Märchen aus Bilibili.' *Baessler Archiv.* I, 1905.

Department of the Chief Minister and Development Administration. *Village Directory.* Konedobu, Papua New Guinea, 1973.

Dickinson, W. and Shutler, R. 'Temper Sands in Pre-Historic Pottery of the Pacific Islands.' Unpublished manuscript, 1971.

Douglas, J. 'Honpain, the Yabob Potter's Legend.' *Pottery in Australia* 9(2), 1970.

Dow, D.B. 'The Geological Evolution of Papua New Guinea.' *Australian National History* 17(12), 1973.

Du Toit, B. *Akuna: A New Guinea Village Community.* Rotterdam, A.A. Balkema, 1975.

Dutton, T.E. 'The Peopling of Central Papua: Some Preliminary Observations.' *Pacific Linguistics* Series B(9). Canberra, Australian National University, 1969.

———. 'A Checklist of Languages and Present-day Villages of Central and South-East Mainland Papua.' *Pacific Linguistics* Series B(24). Canberra, Australian National University, 1973.

Dye, W. and Townsend, P. 'The Sepik Hill Languages: a Preliminary Report.' *Oceania* 39(2), 1968.

Edge-Partington, J. *An Album of the Weapons, Tools, Ornaments. Articles of Dress of the Natives of the Pacific Islands.* Manchester, privately published, 1890-98.

Egloff, B. 'Collingwood Bay and the Trobriand

Islands in Recent Prehistory.' Ph.D. thesis, Australian National University, 1971.

———. 'The Sepulchral Pottery of Nuamata Island, Papua.' *Archaeology and Physical Anthropology in Oceania* 7(2), 1972.

———, 'Archaeological Researches in the Collingwood Bay Area of Papua.' *Asian Perspectives* XIV, 1973*a*.

———. *Contemporary Wanigela Pottery.* Occasional Papers 2, Anthropology Museum, University of Queensland, 1973*b*.

———. 'Report on Fieldwork in the Madang District 26 April 1973 – 3 June 1973.' Unpublished manuscript for Papua New Guinea Public Museum and Art Gallery, 1973*c*.

———. 'Archaeological investigations in the coastal Madang area and on Eloaue Island of the St Matthias Group.' *Records of the Papua New Guinea Public Museum and Art Gallery* 5, Port Moresby, 1975.

———. 'A Comment on Pottery from Melanesia: The Block Collection.' Unpublished paper, n.d.

Egloff, B. (ed.) *Pottery of Papua New Guinea: The National Collection.* Port Moresby, The Trustees Papua New Guinea National Museum and Art Gallery, 1977.

Ehrich, R.W. 'Ceramics and Man: A Cultural Perspective.' *Ceramics and Man.* Edited by F.R. Matson. Viking Fund Publications in Anthropology 41, 1965.

Ehrich, W. 'Die Kaumuskulzatur von 14 Papua und Melanesiern.' *Zeitschrift für Morphologie und Anthropologie* 25(3), 1962.

Ellen, R.F. and Glover, I. 'Pottery Manufacture and Trade in the Central Moluccas, Indonesia: The Modern Situation and the Historical Implications.' *Man* 9(3), 1974.

Erdweg M. J. 'Die Bewohner der Insel Tumleo, Berlin-hafen, Deutsch-Neu Guinea.' *Mitteilungen der Anthropologischen Gesellschaft in Wien* 32, 1902.

Finsch, O. *Samoafahrten. Reisen in Kaiser Wilhelms-land und Anglisch Neu-Guinea in den Jahren 1884 und 1885.* Leipzig, F. Hirt and son, 1888*a*.

———. 'Exploring Cruises of the "Samoa".' *Ethnological Atlas.* Leipzig, 1888*b*.

———. 'Papua-Töpferei Aus dem Wiegenalter der Keramik.' *Globus* 84, 1903.

———. *Südseearbeiten. Gewerbe und Kunstfleiss, Tauschmittel und 'Geld' der Eingeborenen auf Grundlage der Rohstoffe und der geographischen Verbreitung.* Hamburg, L. Friederichsen, 1914.

Fischer, H. 'Oberflächenfunde und rezente Töpferei am unteren Watut River (Ost-Neuguinea).' *Abhandlungen und Berichte des Stoatliches Museum für Völkerkunde zu Dresden* 21, 1962.

Forge, A. 'Art and Environment in the Sepik.' *Proceedings of the Royal Anthropological Institute of Great Britain and Ireland*, 1965.

———. 'The Abelam Artist.' *Social Organization: Essays Presented to Raymond Firth*, edited by M. Freedman. London, F. Cass, 1967.

Forrest, Capt. T.A. *Voyage to New Guinea and the Moluccas.* London, G. Scott, 1779.

Fortune, R.F. *Sorcerers of Dobu.* New York, E.P. Dutton & Co., 1932.

———. *Arapesh.* New York, American Ethnological Society Publication, 1942.

Fournier, R. *Illustrated Dictionary of Practical Pottery.* Melbourne, Van Rostrand Reinhold Company, 1967.

Friedlaender, J.C. *The Demography, Genetics and Phenetics of Bougainville Islanders.* Cambridge, Harvard University Press, 1975.

Frizzi, E. *Ein Beitrag zur Ethnologie von Bougainville und Buka mit spezieller Berücksichtigung der Nasioi.* Baessler-Archiv Beiträge zur Völkerkunde: Beiheft 6, 1914.

Frobenius, L. 'Die Kulturformen Ozeaniens.' *Petermanns GeographischeMitteilungen* 46, 1900.

Fujihira Industry Co. Ltd. *Standard Soil Colour Chart.* Tokyo, n.d.

Garanger, J. 'Incised and Applied-relief Pottery, its Chronology and Development in Southeastern Melanesia, and Extra Areal Comparisons', in R.C. Green and M. Kelly (eds.), Studies in Oceanic Culture History, vol. 2, *Pacific Anthropological Records*, 1971.

Gardi, R. *Tambaran.* London, Constable, 1960.

Gardin, J.C. 'Four Codes for the Description of Artifacts: An Essay in Archeological Technique and Theory.' *American Anthropologist* 60, 1958.

Girard, F. 'The Buang of the Snake River.' *Antiquity and Survival* 5, 1956.

———. 'Tessons et poteries recueillis chez les Buang, District de Morobe, Nouvelle Guinée orientale.'

Journal de la Société des Oceanistes 31(47), 1975.

Glasgow, D. and Loving, R. *Languages of the Maprik Sub-Division*. Port Moresby, Department of Information and Extension Services, 1964.

Glover, I. 'Pottery Making in Oralan Village, Portuguese Timor.' *Australian National History* 16, 1968.

Golson, J. 'Both Sides of the Wallace Line: New Guinea, Australia and Island Melanesia.' *Early Chinese Art and its Possible Influence in the Pacific Basin*, edited by N. Barrard, vol. 2. New York, Intercultural Arts Press, 1972.

———. 'Lapita Ware and its Transformations', in R.C. Green and M. Kelly (eds.) Studies in Oceanic Culture History, vol. 2, *Pacific Anthropological Records* 12, 1971.

Grim, R.E. *Clay Minerology*. London, McGraw-Hill Book Co., 1953.

Groves, M.C. 'Motu Pottery.' *Journal of the Polynesian Society* 69(1), 1960.

Groves, W.C. 'The Natives of Sio Island, South-Eastern New Guinea: A Study in Culture Contact.' *Oceania* V(1), 1934-35.

Guppy, H.B. *The Solomon Islands and their Natives.* London, Swan Sonnenschein, 1887.

Hanntzens, H.A. *Lands of the Wewak Lower Sepik Area, New Guinea*. Canberra, CSIRO, Division of Land Research and Regional Survey, Divisional Report 61/2, 1961.

Haberland, E. 'Tasks of Research in the Sepik Region, New Guinea.' *Bulletin of the International Committee on Urgent Anthropological and Ethnological Research* 7, 1965.

———. 'Die Töpfergottheit Korimangge im Männerhaus Wolimbit in Kanganamum (Mittlerer Sepik).' *Paideuma* 15, 1969.

Haddon, A.C. *The Decorative Art of British New Guinea: A Study in Papuan Ethnography*. Dublin, Royal Irish Academy, 1894.

———. 'Studies in the Anthropogeography of British New Guinea.' *Geographical Journal* 16, 1900.

———. 'A Prehistoric Sherd from the Mailu District, Papua.' *Man* 32, 1932.

Hagen, B. *Unter den Papuas.* Weisbaden, C.W. Kreidel, 1899.

Harding T.G. *Voyagers of the Vitiaz Strait. A Study of a New Guinea Trade System*. Seattle, University of Washington Press, 1967.

Hill, R. *Ceramic Clays of Papua New Guinea*. Melbourne, CSIRO, Australian Division of Building Research Technical Paper, Second Series (20), 1977.

Hill, R. and Tauber, E. 'Investigation of the Drying Process of Clays and Ceramic Bodies with a Barelattograph.' *Journal of the Australian Ceramic Society* 5(1), 1969.

Hogbin, I. 'Trading Expeditions in Northern New Guinea.' *Oceania* 5(4), 1935.

———. 'Native Culture of Wogeo: report of field-work in New Guinea.' *Oceania* 5(1), 1934-35.

———. 'Native Trade around the Huon Gulf North-Eastern New Guinea.' *Journal of the Polynesian Society* (3), 1947.

———. *Transformation Scene: the changing culture of a New Guinea village*. London, Routledge & Kegan Paul Ltd, 1951.

———. *Kinship and Marriage in a New Guinea Village*. London, The Athlone Press, 1963.

Holdsworth, D.K. 'Caves, Bores and Customs in the Trobriands.' *Pacific Islands Monthly* December, 1959.

Höltker, G. 'Töpferei und irdene Spielpuppen bei den Bosngun in Nordost-Neuguinea.' *Jahrbuch des Museums für Völkerkunde zu Leipzig* 21, 1965.

———. *Menschen und Kulturen in Nordost-Neu Guinea*. Monograph vol. 29. St Augustin, Germany, Anthropos Institute, 1975.

Holzknecht, H. 'Anthropological Research and Associated Findings in the Markham Valley of Papua New Guinea.' *Department of Agriculture, Stock and Fisheries Research Bulletin* 15, Port Moresby, 1974.

Holzknecht, K. 'Über Töpferei und Tontrommeln der Azera in Ost-Neuguinea.' *Zeitschrift fur Ethnologie* 82, 1957.

———. 'On the Pottery and Clay Drums of the Adzera of Eastern New Guinea.' *Journal of the Morobe Province Historical Society* 4(1), 1977.

Hooley, B.A. and McElhanon, K.A. 'Languages of the Morobe District, New Guinea.' *Pacific Linguistic Studies in Honour of Arthur Capell* Series C(13). Canberra, Australian National University, 1970.

Hosking, L. and Dikuwola, K. 'Pottery in Silosilo Bay, Milne Bay.' *Oral History* VI(8), 1978.

Hosking, L and Tuckson, M. 'Report on Fieldwork in Milne Bay, Northern Morobe and Madang Districts, Papua New Guinea.' Unpublished paper, 1975.

Hughes, I. 'Recent Neolithic Trade in New Guinea.' Ph.D. thesis, Australian National University, 1971.

Hurley, F. *Pearls and Savages: Adventures in the Air, on Land and Sea in New Guinea.* New York, Putnam, 1926.

Irwin, J. 'Carved Paddle Decoration of Pottery and its Capacity for Inference in Archaeology: An example from the Solomon Islands.' *Journal of the Polynesian Society* 83, 1974.

———. 'The Emergence of Mailu as a Central Place in the Prehistory of Central Papua.' Ph.D. thesis, Australian National University, 1977.

Jenness, D. and Ballantyne, A. *The Northern D'Entrecasteaux.* Oxford, Clarendon Press, 1919.

Johnston, G.A. 'Collection of Contemporary Pottery from Papua New Guinea for the Auckland Institute and Museum, New Zealand.' Unpublished report of field work, 1974.

Kaberry, P.M. 'The Abelam Tribe, Sepik District, New Guinea. A Preliminary Report.' *Oceania* XI(3), 1940-41.

———. 'Law and Political Organization in the Abelam Tribe, New Guinea.' *Oceania* XII(1,3,4), 1941-42.

Kasprus, A. 'The Tribes of the Middle Ramu and the Upper Keram Rivers.' *Anthropos* 17, 1973.

Kaufmann, C. *Das Töpferhandwerk der Kwoma in Nord-Neuguinea.* Basel, Pharos-Verlag Hansrudolf Schwabe AG, 1972.

———. 'Kwaiwat (Neuguinea Mittlerer Sepik) Töpferei und Verzieren einer Sago-EßS'chale.' Film script. *Encyclopaedia Cinematographica.* Göttingen, Institut für den Wissenschaftlichen, 1974.

———. *Papua Niugini: Ein Inselstoadt in Werden.* Basel, Museum für Völkerkunde und Schweizerische Museum für Volkskunde Basel, 1975.

Keil, D. 'The Inter-Group Economy of the Nekematigi, Eastern Highlands District, New Guinea.' Ph.D. thesis, Northwestern University, 1974.

Kelm, H. *Kunst vom Sepik I (Mittellauf).* Berlin, Veröffentlichungen des Museums für Völkerkunde, 1966*a*.

———. *Kunst vom Sepik II (Oberlauf).* Berlin, Veröffentlichungen des Museums für Völkerkunde, 1966*b*.

———. *Kunst vom Sepik III (Unterlauf und Nachträge).* Berlin, Veröffentlichungen des Museums für Völkerkunde, 1968.

Key, C. 'Pottery Manufacture in the Wanigela area of Collingwood Bay, Papua.' *Mankind* 6(12), 1968.

———. 'Pottery Manufacturing Techniques in Papua New Guinea.' *Asian Perspectives* 14, 1971.

———. 'Modern and Prehistoric Pottery in the South-west Pacific.' Unpublished manuscript, n.d.

———. 'Ceramic Technology and Ceramic Analyses in Melanesia.' Unpublished manuscript, n.d.

Kidder, J. E. *Prehistoric Japanese Arts: Jomon Pottery.* Tokyo, Kodansha International Ltd, 1976.

Koch, G. *Kultur der Abelam. Die Berliner 'Maprik' Sammlung.* Berlin, Veröffentlichungen des Museums für Völkerkunde, 1968.

Krieger, M. *Neu Guinea.* Berlin, Schall, 1899.

Kunze, G. *Im Dienst des Kreuzes auf Ungebahnten Pfaden.* 2nd edition. Gütersloh, Bertelsmann, 1901.

———. *Bilder aus dem Leben der Papua.* 3rd edition. Barmen, Verlag des Missionshauses, 1926.

Lampert, R J. 'Some Archaeological Sites of the Motu and Koiari Areas.' *Journal of the Papua and New Guinea Society* 2(2), 1969.

Lasaro, I. 'History of Bonarua Island.' *Oral History* III(7), 1975.

Lauer, P.K. 'Sailing with the Amphlett Islanders.' *Journal of the Polynesian Society* 79(4), 1970*a*.

———. 'Amphlett Islands Pottery Trade and the Kula.' *Mankind* 7(3), 1970*b*.

———. 'The Changing Patterns of Pottery Trade to the Trobriand Islands.' *World Archeology* 3(2), 1971.

——. A Neglected Aspect of New Guinea Pottery Technology: Firing.' *Pottery in Australia* II(1), 1972.

———. 'Preliminary Report on Ethnoarchaeological Research in the Northwestern Massim T.P.N.G.' *Asian Perspectives* 14, 1971.

———. 'Miadeba Pottery.' *Records of the Papua New Guinea Museum and Art Gallery* 3, 1973*a*.

——. 'The Technology of Pottery Manufacture on

Goodenough Island and in the Amphlett Group Southeast Papua,' Occasional Papers 2, Anthropology Museum, University of Queensland, 1973*b*.

———. 'Pottery Traditions in the D'Entrecasteaux Islands of Papua,' Occasional Papers 3, Anthropology Museum, University of Queensland, 1974.

Lawrence, P. *Road Belong Cargo: A Study of the Cargo Movement in the Southern Madang District, New Guinea.* Melbourne, Melbourne University Press, 1964.

Laycock, D. 'The Sepik and its languages.' *Australian Territories* I(4), 1961.

———. *The Ndu Language Family (Sepik District, New Guinea).* Linguistic Circle of Canberra Publications Series C(1), Canberra, Australian National University, 1965.

———. 'Languages of the Lumi Subdistrict (West Sepik District), New Guinea.' *Oceanic Linguistics* 7(1), 1968.

———. *Sepik Languages Checklist and Preliminary Classification.* Pacific Linguistics Series B(25), Canberra, Australian National University, 1973.

Lea, D. 'The Abelam: A Study in Local Differentiation.' *Pacific Viewpoint* 6, 1965.

Lewis, A.B. *The Melanesians: People of the South Pacific.* Chicago, Natural History Museum Press, 1951.

Luschan, F. von. *Zur Ethnographie des Kaiserin Augusta-Flusses.* Leipzig/Berlin, Baessler-Archiv. I(1910/11), 1910.

Lyons, A.P. 'Sepulchral Pottery of Murua, Papua.' *Man* 22, 1922.

Maahs, A. 'Village of Saucepans.' *Walkabout* 15(6), 1949.

McElhanon, K.A. 'Towards a Typology of the Finisterre-Huon Languages New Guinea.' Series B(22), Canberra, Australian National University, 1973.

McGregor, W. *British New Guinea: Country and People.* London, J. Murray, 1897.

Maclachlan, R. 'Native Pottery from Central and Southern Melanesia and Western Polynesia.' *Journal of the Polynesian Society* 47, 1938.

———. 'Native Pottery of the New Hebrides.' *Journal of the Polynesian Society* 48, 1939.

McMeekin, I. *Notes for Potters in Australia. Vol. I: Raw Materials and Clay Bodies.* Sydney, University of New South Wales, 1967.

Malinowski, B. 'The Natives of Mailu', *Transactions and Proceedings of the Royal Society of South Australia* 39, 1915.

———. 'Kula: the circulating Exchange of Valuables in the Archipelagoes of Eastern New Guinea.' *Man* 20(51), 1920.

———. *Argonauts of the Western Pacific.* London, Routledge & Kegan Paul, 1922.

———. *Coral Gardens and their Magic.* London, Allen & Unwin, 1935.

Matson, F.R. *Some Aspects of Ceramic Technology.* New York, Basic Books, 1963.

May, P. and Tuckson, M. 'Coastal Pottery Villages, Wewak, New Guinea.' *Pottery in Australia* 12(1), 1973.

Mead, M. *Growing Up In New Guinea.* New York, Blue Ribbon Books, 1931.

———. 'The Marsalai Cult among the Arapesh with special reference to the rainbow serpent beliefs of the Australian Aborigines.' *Oceania* 4(1), 1933-34.

———. 'Tambarans and Tumbuans in New Guinea.' *Journal of the American Museum of Natural History* 34(3), 1934.

———. *Sex and Temperament in Three Primitive Societies.* London, Routledge & Kegan Paul, 1935.

———. The Mountain Arapesh. New York, The Natural History Press, 1968.

———. *The Mountain Arapesh: Arts and Supernaturalism.* New York, The Natural History Press, 1970.

———. *The Mountain Arapesh: Stream of Events in Alitoa.* New York, The Natural History Press, 1971.

Mihalic, F. *The Jacaranda Dictionary and Grammar of Melanesian Pidgin.* Brisbane, Jacaranda Press, 1971.

Miklouho-Maclay, N. *Miklouho-Maclay: New Guinea Diaries 1871-1883.* Translated by C.L. Sentinella, Madang, Kristen Press, 1975.

Monckton, C.A. *Last Days in New Guinea.* New York, Dodd Mead and Co., 1922.

Moore, D. and Tuckson, M. 'Melanesian Art in the Australian Museum.' *Pottery in Australia* 7(2), 1968.

Morauta, L. *Beyond the Village*. Canberra, Australian National University, 1974.

Moseley, H. N. 'On the Inhabitants of the Admiralty Islands.' *Royal Anthropological Institute of Great Britain and Ireland Journal* 6, 1877.

Murphy, J. *Sepik District Patrol Conducted in the Aitape Island Group 16-28 August*. Department of District Administration, Sepik District Patrol Report 7, September, 1950.

Neuhauss, R. *Deutsch Neu-Guinea*. 3 vols. Berlin, Dietrich Reimer, 1911.

Nevermann, H. *Admiralitäts-Inseln*. Hamburg, L. Friederichsen. 1934.

Newton, D. *Crocodile and Cassowary*. New York, Museum of Primitive Art, 1971.

———. *Art of the Massim Area*. New York, Museum of Primitive Art, 1975.

Ogan, E. 'Nasioi Pottery-Making.' Journal of the Polynesian Society. 79(1), 1970.

Oliver, D.L. *A Solomons Island Society*. Cambridge, Harvard University, 1955.

Oram, N. 'Taurama: Oral Sources for a study of recent Motuan Prehistory.' *Journal of the Papua and New Guinea Society* 2(2), 1969.

———. *Colonial town to Melanesian City: Port Moresby 1884-1974*. Canberra, Australian National University, 1976.

O'Reilly, P. 'Description Sommaire d'une Collection d'objets ethnographiques de l'île de Bougainville.' *Annali Lataranensi* 4, 1940.

Palili, P. 'Coiling Pottery in Mambuk Village (Yangoru area).' *Oral History* 2(8), 1974.

Parkinson, R. 'Die Berlinhafen-Sektion Ein Beitrag zur Ethnographie der Neu-Guinéa-Kuste.' *Internationales Archiv für Ethnographie* 13, 1900.

———. *Dreissig Jahre in der Südsee*. Stuttgart, Strecker and Schroeder, 1907.

Petersen, J. *Pottery in Papua New Guinea*. Sydney, International Labour Organisation, 1970.

Peterson, N. 'Notes on Pot Making Equipment from Wari Island, Milne Bay.' Catalogue Notes. Australian National University, Anthropology Department, 1971.

Price, N. 'Development of Handicraft Activities at the Kaugere Community Centre, Port Moresby.' *South Pacific Bulletin*, Second Quarter, 1968.

Ratliff, D. 'A Report on Pottery Making on Choiseul Is., British Solomons.' *Pottery in Australia* 15(2), 1976.

Reche, O. *Der Kaiserin-Augusta-Fluss. Ergebnisse der Südsee Expedition 1908-1910*. Hamburg, L. Friederichsen, 1913.

Reisenfeld, A. *The Megalithic Culture of Melanesia*. Leiden, E.J. Brill, 1950.

Ribbe, C. *Zwei Jahre unter den Kannibalen der Saloma-Inseln*. Dresden, Beyer, 1903.

Ryan, D. 'Rural and Urban Villages: A Bi-local Social System in Papua.' Ph.D. thesis, University of Hawaii, 1970.

Rye, O. 'Keeping your temper under control: Materials and the Manufacture of Papuan Pottery.' *Archaeology and Physical Anthropology in Oceania* 11(2), 1976.

Rye, O. and Evans, C. 'Traditional Pottery. Techniques in Pakistan. Field and Laboratory Studies.' *Smithsonian Contributions to Anthropology* 21, 1977*a*.

———. 'Pottery Manufacturing Techniques: X-ray Studies.' *Archaeometry* 19, 1977*b*.

Rye, O. and Tuckson, M. 'Comments on Modern and Prehistoric Pottery in the South-west Pacific.' Unpublished paper.

Sack P. *The Bloodthirsty Laewomba*. Canberra, Australian National University, 1976.

Sande, G.A van der 'Nova Guinea. Resultats de L'Expedition Scientifique Néderlandaise à la Nouvelle-Guinée en 1903.' *Ethnography and Anthropology* III, 1907.

Saville, W. *In Unknown New Guinea*. London, J.B. Lippincott Co., 1926.

Schafroth, M. M. *Südsee-Welten vor dem grossen Krieg*. Bern, A. Francke, 1916.

Schlaginhaufen, O. *Eine Ethnographische Sammlung Von Kaiserin – Augustafluss in Neuguinea*. Abhandlungen und Berichte des Königal. Leipzig, Zoologisches und Anthropologisch-Ethno Graphischen Museums Zu Dresden, 1910.

Schmitz, C.A. 'Style Provinces and Style Elements: A Study in Method.' *Mankind* 5, 1956.

———. 'Historische Probleme in Nordost-Neuguinea, Huon Halbinsel.' *Studien zur Kultur-Kunde* 16, 1960*a*.

———. 'Beitrage Zur Ethnographie des Wantoat Tales Nordost – Neu Guinea.' Kölner ethnologische Mitteilungen. Köln, Kolner Universitäts Verlag, 1960*b*.

Schurig, M. *Die Südseetöpferei*. Leipzig, Schlindler, 1930.

Schuster, M. 'Die Töpfergottheit Von Aibom.' *Paideuma* 15, 1969.

Schuster, M. and Haberland, E. *Sepik Kunst aus Neuguinea*. Aus den Sammlungen der Neuguinea-Expedition des Städt, Museums für Völkerkunde, Frankfort/Main, 1964.

Schuster, M. and Schuster, G. 'Aibom (New Guinea, Middle Sepik District) Pottery (Frying Pan, Fire Bowl, Sago Jar).' Film script. *Encyclopaedia Cinematographica*. Institut für den Wissenschaftlichen, 1975.

Schwimmer, E. *Exchange in the Social Structure of the Orokaiva*. London, C. Hurst and Co., 1973.

Schwimmer, Z. 'Reports of Handcrafts of the Northern District.' Department of Business Development, unpublished report, 1967.

Scott, S.D. and Segman, P. 'Pottery from Melanesia: The Black Collection.' *Bulletin of the Buffalo Society of Natural Sciences* 24, 1968.

Seligmann, C. *The Melanesians of British New Guinea*. Cambridge, Cambridge University Press, 1910.

Shepard, A.O. *Ceramics for the Archaeologist*. Washington, Carnegie Institute, 1965.

Shutler, M.E. 'Pottery-Making at Wusi New Hebrides.' *South Pacific Bulletin* 18(4), 1968.

Shutler, M.E. and Shutler, R. 'Origins of the Melanesians.' *Archaeology and Physical Anthropology in Oceania* 11(2), 1967.

———. 'Potsherds from Bougainville Island.' *Asian Perspectives* 8(1), 1964.

———. *Oceanic Prehistory*. Menlo Park, California, Cummings Publishing Co.: Ontario, Don Mills, 1975.

Shutler, R. and Marck, J. 'On the Dispersal of the Austronesian Horticulturalists.' *Archaeology and Physical Anthropology in Oceania* X(2), 1975.

Smith, J. 'Report on Pottery Making at Aibom Village, Sepik District.' Unpublished mimeograph, 1966.

———. 'The Potter of Yabob.' *Australian Territories* 7(1-3), 1967.

Solheim, W.G. 'Pottery of Oceania.' MA thesis, University of California, 1949.

———. 'Oceanian Pottery Manufacture.' *The University of Manila Journal of East Asiatic Studies* I(2), 1952*a*.

———. 'Paddle Decoration of Pottery.' *The University of Manila Journal of East Asiatic Studies* II(1), 1952*b*.

———. 'Further relationships of the Sa-Huynh-Kalanay Pottery tradition.' *Asian Perspectives* 8(1), 1964*a*.

———. 'The Archaeology of the Central Philippines: a study chiefly of the Iron Age and its Relationships.' *Journal of the Siam Society Bangkok* 52(2), 1964*b*.

———. 'The Functions of Pottery in Southeast Asia: from the Present to the Past.' *Ceramics and Man*. Edited by F.R. Matson. Viking Fund Publications in Anthropology 41, 1965.

———. 'Possible Routes of Migration into Melanesia as shown by Statistical Analysis of Methods of Pottery Manufacture.' *Asian and Pacific Archaeology* Series 2, 1968.

Specht, J. 'A Prehistoric Pottery Site in Coastal New Guinea.' *Antiquity* XLI, 1967*a*.

———. 'Archaeology in Melanesia: A Suggested Procedure.' *Mankind* 6, 1967*b*.

———. 'Preliminary report of excavations on Watom Island.' *Journal of the Polynesian Society* 77(2), 1968.

———. 'Prehistoric and Modern Pottery Industries of Buka Island.' Ph.D. thesis, Australian National University, 1969.

———. 'The Pottery Industry of Buka Island. Territory of Papua New Guinea.' *Archaeology and Physical Anthropology in Oceania* 7(2), 1972.

———. 'Prehistory Poses Many Problems.' *Australian Natural History* 17(2), 1973.

———. 'Of Menak and Men: Trade and the Distribution of Resources on Buka Island, Papua New Guinea.' *Ethnology* XIII(3), 1974.

———. 'Smoking Pipes and Culture Change on Buka Island, Papua New Guinea.' *Journal of the Polynesian Society* 84(3), 1975.

Specht, J. and Holzknecht, H. 'Some archaeological sites in the Upper Markham Valley, Morobe District.' *Records of the Papua and New Guinea Museum and Art Gallery* 1(2), 1971.

Swadling, P., Aitsi, L., Trompf, G. and Kari, M. 'Beyond the Early Oral Tradition of the Austronesian Speaking People of the Gulf and Western Central Provinces.' *Oral History* V(1), 1977.

Terrell, J. *Perspectives on the Prehistory of Bougainville Island Papua New Guinea: a study in the human geography of the South-western Pacific.* Cambridge, Harvard University, 1976.

Thurnwald, R. 'Social Organization and Kinship System of a Tribe in the Interior of New Guinea, Banaro Society.' *Anthropological Association* 3(4), 1916.

———. *Die Gemeinde der Bánaro.* Stuttgart, Verlag von Ferdinand, 1921.

Tiesler, F. *Die intertribalen Beziehungen an der Nordost Küste Neuguineas im Gelbiet der Kleinen Schouten-Inseln.* Berlin, Abhandlungen und Berichte des Staatlichen Museums für Völkerkunde, 1969-70.

———. *Töpferei Zeugnisse Aus Dem Torricelli-Gebirge Sepik-Distrikt (Nord-Neuguinea).* Dresden, Abhandlungen und Berichte des Staatlichen Museums für Völkerkunde, 1975.

Tindale, N.B. 'Some Polychrome Incised Pottery Ware from Mt Turu, New Guinea.' *Records of the South Australian Museum* 6(4), 1941.

Tindale, N. B. and Bartlett, H.K. 'Notes on Some Clay Pots from Panaeati Island, South-East of New Guinea.' *Transactions and Proceedings of the Royal Society of South Australia* 61, 1937.

Tuckson, M. 'Pottery in New Guinea.' *Pottery in Australia* 5(1), 1966. Reprinted in *Craft Horizons* 28(4), 1968 and 29(1), 1969 (corrected captions).

———. 'Pottery Project in Papua New Guinea.' *Pottery in Australia* 10(2), 1971.

Tuckson, M. and May, P. 'Pots and Potters of Papua New Guinea.' *Australian Natural History* 18(5), 1975.

Tuelting, L.T. *Native Trade in Southeast New Guinea.* Occasional Papers 11(15), Bernice P. Bishop Museum, 1935.

Tuzin, D. 'Yam Symbolism in the Sepik: An Interpretive Account.' *Southwestern Journal of Anthropology* 28(3), 1972.

Vanderwal, R.L. 'Prehistoric Ceramic Styles. Hall Sound. Papua New Guinea.' Unpublished paper, 1970.

———. 'Prehistoric Studies in Central Coastal Papua.' Ph.D. thesis, Australian National University, 1973.

Vogel, H. *Eine Forschungsreise im Bismark Archipelago.* Hamburg, L. Friedrichsen, 1911.

Waddell, E.W. and Krinks, P.A. 'The Organisation of Production and Distribution among the Orokaiva.' *New Guinea Research Bulletin* 24, 1968.

Ward, J. and Lea, D. (eds.) *An Atlas of Papua New Guinea.* Glasgow, University of Papua New Guinea, 1970.

Watson, V. 'Pottery in the Eastern Highlands of New Guinea.' *Southwestern Journal of Anthropology* 11, 1955.

———. 'Pottery in the Eastern Highlands of New Guinea: Postscript.' *Mankind* 11(1), 1977.

Werner, E. *Kaiser-Wilhelms-Land.* Freiburg in Breisgau, Herder, 1911.

Wheeler, G.C. 'On some pottery from Alu, Bougainville Strait. Solomon Islands.' *Man* 28, 1928.

White, J.P. and Hamilton, D. 'Anthropology.' *New Guinea Barrier Reefs: preliminary results of the 1969 coral reef expedition to the Trobriand Islands and the Louisiade Archipelago, Papua New Guinea.* Edited by W. Manser. Occasional Papers I, University of Papua New Guinea, Geology Department, 1973.

Whiteman, J. 'A Comparison of Life, Beliefs and Social Changes in Two Abelam Villages.' *Oceania* XXXVII(1), 1966.

Whiting, J. *Becoming a Kwoma.* Yale University, Institute of Human Relations, 1941.

Whiting, J. and Reed, S. 'Kwoma Culture: Report on Field Work in the Mandated Territory of New Guinea.' *Oceania* IX(2), 1938/39.

Whitney, H. 'Two Styles of Pottery Making Currently in Use in the British Solomons and in Bougainville.' Unpublished manuscript, 1968.

Williams, F.E. *Orokaiva Society.* London, Oxford University Press, 1930.

———. 'Trading Voyages from the Gulf of Papua.' *Oceania* III(2), 1932/33.

Wirz, P. 'Die Töpferei der Buka.' *Bulletin der Schweizerischen Gesellschaft für Anthropologie und Ethnologie* 31, 1954-55.

Z'Graggen, J. 'Classificatory and Typological Studies in Languages of the Madang District.' *Pacific Linguistics* Series C(19), Canberra, Australian National University, 1971.

———. 'The Languages of the Madang District, Papua New Guinea.' *Pacific Linguistics* Series

D(25), Canberra, Australian National University, 1973.

ADDENDUM TO THIS EDITION

Bowden, R. *Yena: Art and Ceremony in a Sepik Society.* Oxford, Pitt Rivers Museum, 1983.

Dennett, H. Report of a field trip to the Muniwara and Urimo villages in the East Sepik Province. Unpublished report, 1990.

Kaufmann, C. Kwoma (New Guinea, Sepik) – 'Töpfern und Verzieren eives Zeremonial – gefasses.' ['Construction and Decoration of a Ceremonial Vessel.'] Film E2188 des TWF Göttingen, 1979. Publikation von C. Kaufmann, *Publikationen zu Wissenschaftlichen Filmen, Sektion Ethnologe* [ISSN 0341-5910], Ser. 10, Nr. 25/E2188 (1980), 35s (with English text).

———. Review of *Yena: Art and Ceremony in a Sepik Society* by Ross Bowden. *Pacific Arts Newsletter*, 19, 1984.

———. Kwoma (New Guinea, Sepik) – 'Zubereiten einer Pandanus Suppe.' ['Preparing a pandanus soup.'] Film F2104 des IWF, Göttingen, 1983. Publikation von C. Kaufmann, *Publ wiss. Film, Sekt Ethnol.*, Ser. 12, Nr. 24/E2164 (1982), 30s (with English text).

———. 'Research on Sepik pottery traditions and its implications for Melanesian prehistory,' read at the International Conference 'The Western Pacific, 5000 to 2000 BP: Colonisations and Transformations.' Port Vila, Vanuatu, 1996.

Kirch, P.V. *The Lapita Peoples: ancestors of the Oceanic World.* Oxford, Blackwell, 1997.

Kuaso, A.F., Mandui, H.S. and R.T. Mondal. *Report on Kilimeri Achaeological Reconnaissance Survey, West Sepik Province.* Port Moresby, Papua New Guinea Museum and Art Gallery, 1998.

Ohnemus, S. *An Ethnology of the Admiralty Islanders. The Alfred Bühler Collection, Museum der Kulturen, Basel.* 1996 (German language ed.). Bathurst, Crawford House Publishing, 1998.

Spriggs, M. *The Island Melanesians.* Oxford, Blackwell, 1997.

Swadling, P. and G. Hope. 'Environmental change in New Guinea since human settlement' in *The Native Lands: Prehistory and environmental change in Australia and the Southwest Pacific*, edited by J. Dodson. Melbourne, Longman Cheshire, 1992.

Swadling, P., Chappell, J., Francis, G., Araho, N. and B. Ivuyo. 'A late quantennary Inland Sea and Early Pottery in Papua New Guinea.' *Archaeology in Oceania* 24, 1989.

Terrell, J.E. and R.L. Welsch. 'Lapita and the temporal geography of prehistory.' *Antiquity* 71, 1997.

Sources of and acknowledgements for photographs

Museum collections

The listings below are in the following format:
Fig. no. Year collected, Registration no., Photographer

The Australian Museum, Sydney

1.4	Late 1800s, E8556, Gregory Millen
1.5	1975, E67035, authors
1.7	1973, E65569, Gregory Millen
1.13	1975, E67041, Yutta Malnic
1.15	1887, E757, Gregory Millen
3.8-3.13	Early 1900s, E63286, C.V. Turner
3.16	Early 1900s, E23316, authors
4.15	1975, E67003, authors
4.16	1975, E67004, authors
4.18	1975, E67007, authors
4.55	1975, E66999, Gregory Millen
4.56	1975, E66994, Gregory Millen
5.4	1975, E67017, authors, by courtesy of the museum
5.9	1904-7, E12955, authors
5.10	1904-7, E17179, authors
5.11	1904-7, E17178, authors
6.22	1975, E67018,[1] Lynne Hosking, for the museum
6.33	1972, E65497, Gregory Millen
6.35	1972, E65413, Gregory Millen
8.5	1969, E64578, Gregory Millen
8.17	1975, E67023(1)[2] E67024(5), authors E67025(6)
8.39	1975, E67038, authors
8.41	1971, E65221, John Parker
9.6	1964, E62356, authors, by courtesy of the museum
9.7	1972, E67185, Gregory Millen
9.32	1973, E65612, authors, by courtesy of the museum
9.34	1973, E65611, authors
9.36	1973, E65601, authors, by courtesy of the museum
9.39	1936, E46078, authors, by courtesy of the museum
9.91	1973, E65610, authors, by courtesy of the museum
9.107	1930-40, E62891, authors, by courtesy of the museum
9.125	1964, E62333, authors, by courtesy of the museum
9.149	1973, E65603, authors, by courtesy of the museum
11.2	early 1800s, E22425, Gregory Millen
11.7	c.1916, E25130, authors

Papua New Guinea National Museum and Art Gallery, Port Moresby

3.17	1975, 75.2.3, photo provided by the museum
4.36	1973, E12000, authors
4.62	1973, E11990, authors
5.7	1975, 75.1.13, Lynne Hosking
7.7	1975, 75.1.29, authors
8.7	1973, E11983, authors
8.17	1975, 75.1.31(2),[2] authors 75.1.18(3)
8.34	1973, E11897t,[3] authors
9.4	1973, E11892, photo provided by the museum
5.5	1972, E10585, photo provided the museum
5.16	Pre-1975, n.a., authors
9.17	Pre-1975, n.a., authors
9.84	1972, E11317(left), authors
9.89	1972, E11318, authors
9.102	1973, E11264, authors
9.114	1972, E10539, authors

1. Pot second from back only.

2. Pots numbered 1 to 6 from left to right.

3. Pot centre front

9.115 n.a., E16261, photo provided by the museum
9.148 1973, E11282, authors
9.154 1972, E10962(left), authors
9.170 1973, E11265, authors
9.171 1973, E11292, authors
9.179 1973, E11270, authors
9.187 1973, E11034?, authors
9.190 1972, E11303(1eft), authors E 11302 (right)
9.191 1973, E11256(right), authors
9.206 1973, 76.17.1, authors
9.207 1973, 76.17.2, authors
9.214 1973, E11259(1eft), authors

Museum für Völkerkunde und Schweizerisches Museum für Volkskunde Basel (now Museum fur Kulturen)

9.38 Pre-1914, Vb 1907, photo provided by the museum
9.139 Pre-1972, Vb 27078, authors (in the field)
9.151 1972, Vb 27508, authors (in the field)
9.167 1972, Vb 27501, authors (in the field)

Art Gallery of New South Wales, Sydney

9.66 1965, cat. no.32, Douglas Thompson
9.72 1965, cat. no.21, photo provided by the Gallery
9.103 1965, cat. no.101, Kerry Dundas

The Macleay Museum, University of Sydney

3.2 1875, D701, authors by courtesy the museum
3.15 1875, D689a, authors
8.4 1877, D705, photo provided by museum

Linden Museum, Stuttgart, Staatliches Museum für Völkerkunde, Germany

6.18 Pre-1935, 114013, photo provided by the museum

9.175 Pre-1910 , 63151, photo provided by the museum

Ceramics Department, East Sydney Technical College

3.5 1964, n.a., authors
10.3 n.a., n.a., authors

National Museum of New Zealand

11.11 1960s, deposit no. 1968/19 (on loan), photo provided by the museum

Field Museum of Natural History, Chicago

9.82 1909-13, 138022, authors, by courtesy of the museum

Pitt Rivers Museum, Oxford

8.54 1937, 111378, photo provided by the museum

South Australian Museum

4.42 1935, A19137, authors, by courtesy of the Trustees of the South Australian Museum

Solomon Islands Museum

11.14 1972, 72.127, Dale Ratliff

Queensland Museum

5.12 1883-87, Mac 3402, photo provided by the museum

The Australia Council

4.14 1975, n.a., authors

National Ethnographic Collection, Australian Institute of Anatomy, Canberra

11.12 Early 1900s, M-DCe2, photo provided by the Institute

Museum für Völkerkunde Staatliche Museum Preußischer Kulturbesitz, Berlin

9.76 1909, VI31.180, photo provided by the museum

Private collections

May collection

Fig. no.	*Year collected*
1.11	1972
1.14	1975
1.16	1973
1.17	1973
3.4	1976
7.1	1969
7.2	1969
7.3	1972
8.32	1969
8.44	1970
9.2	1976
9.8	Pre-1969
9.9	1976
9.10	1976
9.18	1969
9.41	1975
9.42	1976
9.44	1976
9.60	1969
9.61	1975
9.64	1975
9.67	1976
9.68	Pre-1969
9.70	1975
9.74	1976
9.79	1976
9.96-9.101	1976
9.142	1975
9.147	1976
9.161-9.166	1972
9.168	1970
9.169	1970

Tuckson collection

Fig. no.	*Year collected*	*Registration no.*
1.6	1973	MT90
1.22	1971	MT45
1.23	1966	MT 12
2.33	1966	MT25
3.24	1965	MT3
		MT4
4.27	1973	MT84[4]
4.59	1973	MT85
5.8	1975	MT91
7.5	1967	MT35
8.36	1971	MT50[5]
9.3	1972	MT62
9.35	1973	MT76
9.48	1973	MT15
9.62	1965	MT 17
9.65	1965	MT22
9.84	1972	MT59
9.141	1965	MT24
9.144	1966	MT26
9.146	1972	MT61
9.152	1972	MT67
9.153	1972	MT68
9.159	1972	MT52
9.160	1972	MT54
9.177	1972	MT82

Where no acknowledgement has been made, the photograph was taken by the authors.

Photographed from publications

Fig. no. *Year photographed, photographer*

3.6 and 3.7 1921, Frank Hurley, from *Pearls and Savages* (see "Bibliography"). By courtesy of the Australian Museum.

3.14 Early 1900s, from C. Seligmann, *The Melanesians of British New Guinea* (see "Bibliography"), by courtesy of the Australian Museum.

8.2 1905, H. Bethke, from *Papua Niugini*, by courtesy of the Museum für Völkerkunde, Basel.

10.11 and 10.12 Early 1900s, Fr Fülleborn, from H. Nevermann, *Admiralitäts-Inseln* (see "Bibliography").

Photographs held by the Australian Museum and other sources

3.3 Late 1800s, Charles Kerry, courtesy of Tyrell's Book Shop, Crows Nest, NSW.

3.18 1964, courtesy of Extension Services,

4. Photograph provided by the Australian Museum.

5. Photographed by Jim Molloy.

Administration of Papua and New Guinea.

3.25 1921, Frank Hurley, courtesy of the Australian Museum.

5.2 Early 1900s, Frank Hurley, courtesy of the Australian Museum.

6.30-6.32 Early 1900s, Albert B. Lewis, courtesy of the Field Museum of Natural History, Chicago.

Photographs taken in the field

Fig. No.	*Photographer*
2.26	Lynne Hosking
4.54	Lynne Hosking
5.6	Lynne Hosking
5.7	Lynne Hosking
6.21	Francoise Girard
6.22	Lynne Hosking
6.29	Lynne Hosking
7.4	Muriel Larner
8.1	John Parker
8.11	Robin Smith
8.20	Lynne Hosking
8.37	Gabrielle Johnston
8.38	John Parker
8.46-8.48	Lynne Hosking
8.52	Beatrice Blackwood
8.53	Beatrice Blackwood
8.55-8.62	Beatrice Blackwood
9.40	Douglas Miles
9.53	Douglas Miles
9.59	Frank Hodgkinson
9.83	Sonia Farley
9.87	Sonia Farley
9.95	Sonia Farley
9.178	Sonia Farley
9.202	Sonia Farley
11.1	Jim Specht
11.3-11.6	Jim Specht
11.8-11.10	Paul Greenaway
11.13	Dale Ratliff

Photographs by authors

Fig. no.	*Year collected, owners*
1.19	n.a., Tim Ward
1.20	n.a., Tim Ward
2.31	1975, Lynne Hosking
4.18	1975, Lynne Hosking
8.51	c. 1970, Bob Willis
9.11	n.a., Geoffrey Ellworthy (photographed by owner)
9.45	n.a., John Henshaw (photographed by owner)
9.63	n.a., Wallace Thornton
9.124	1968, Barbara Perry

Index

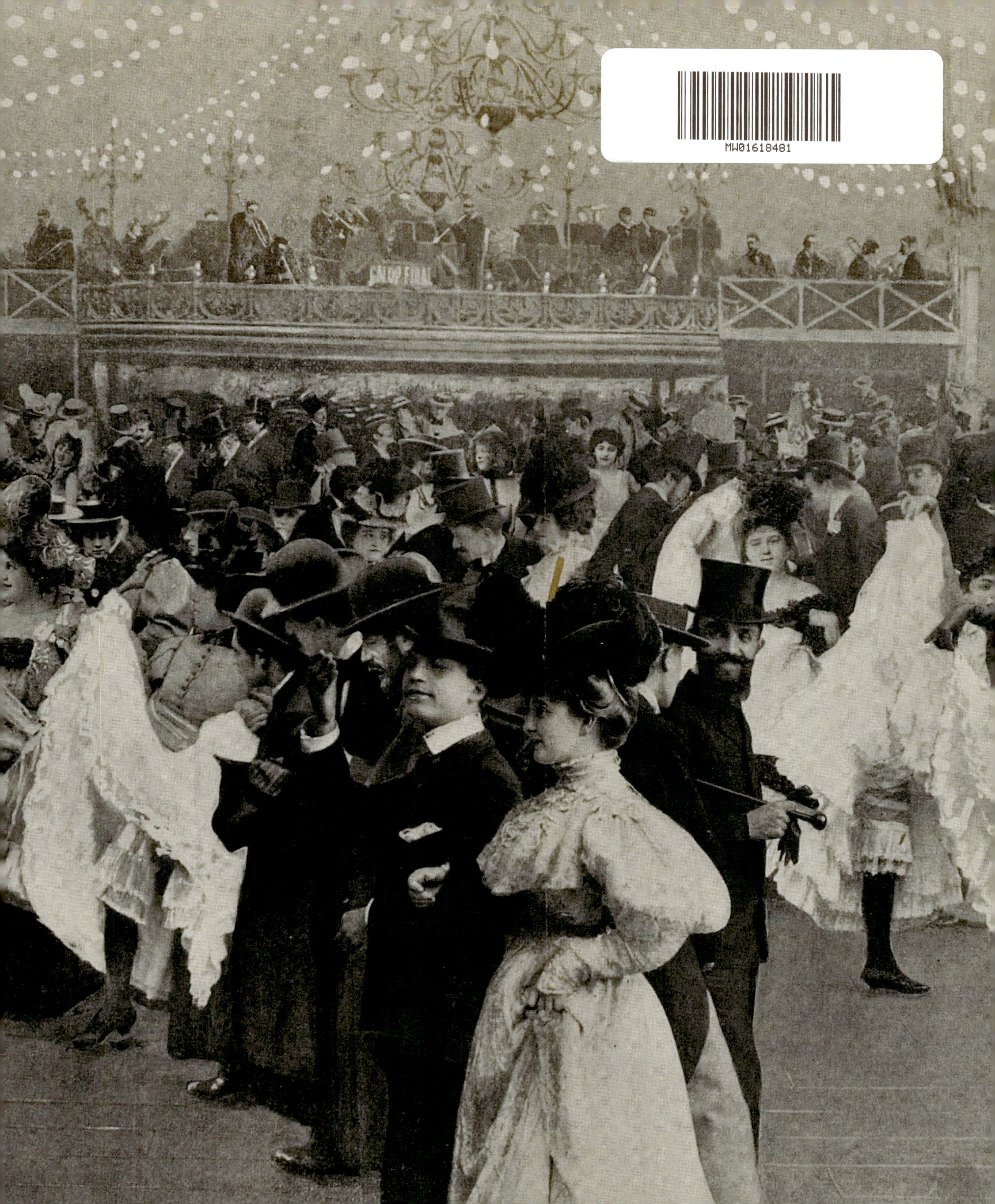

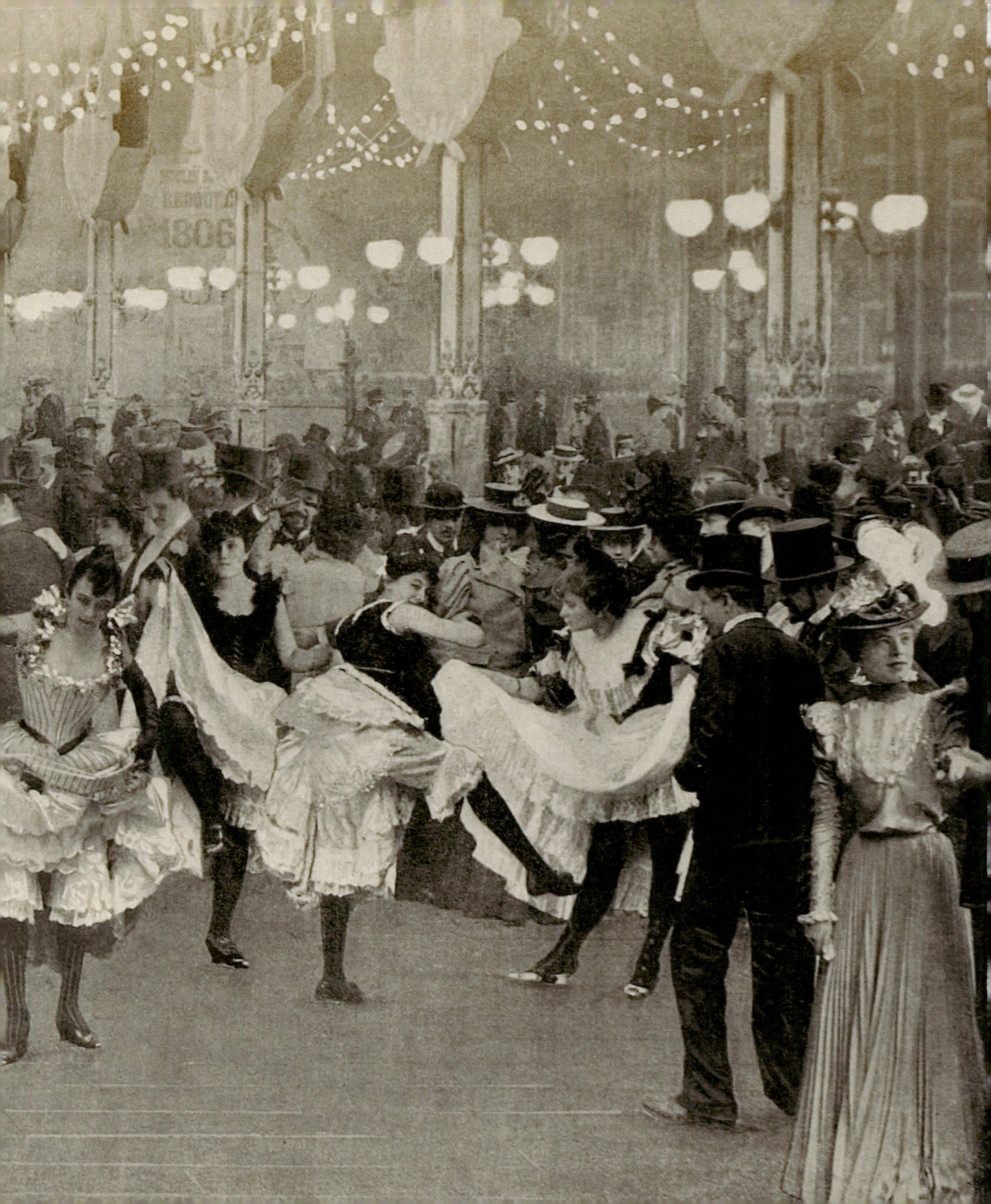

THE PARIS OF TOULOUSE-LAUTREC

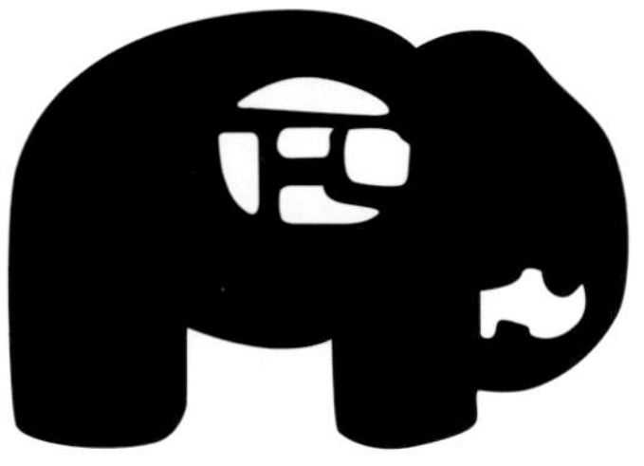

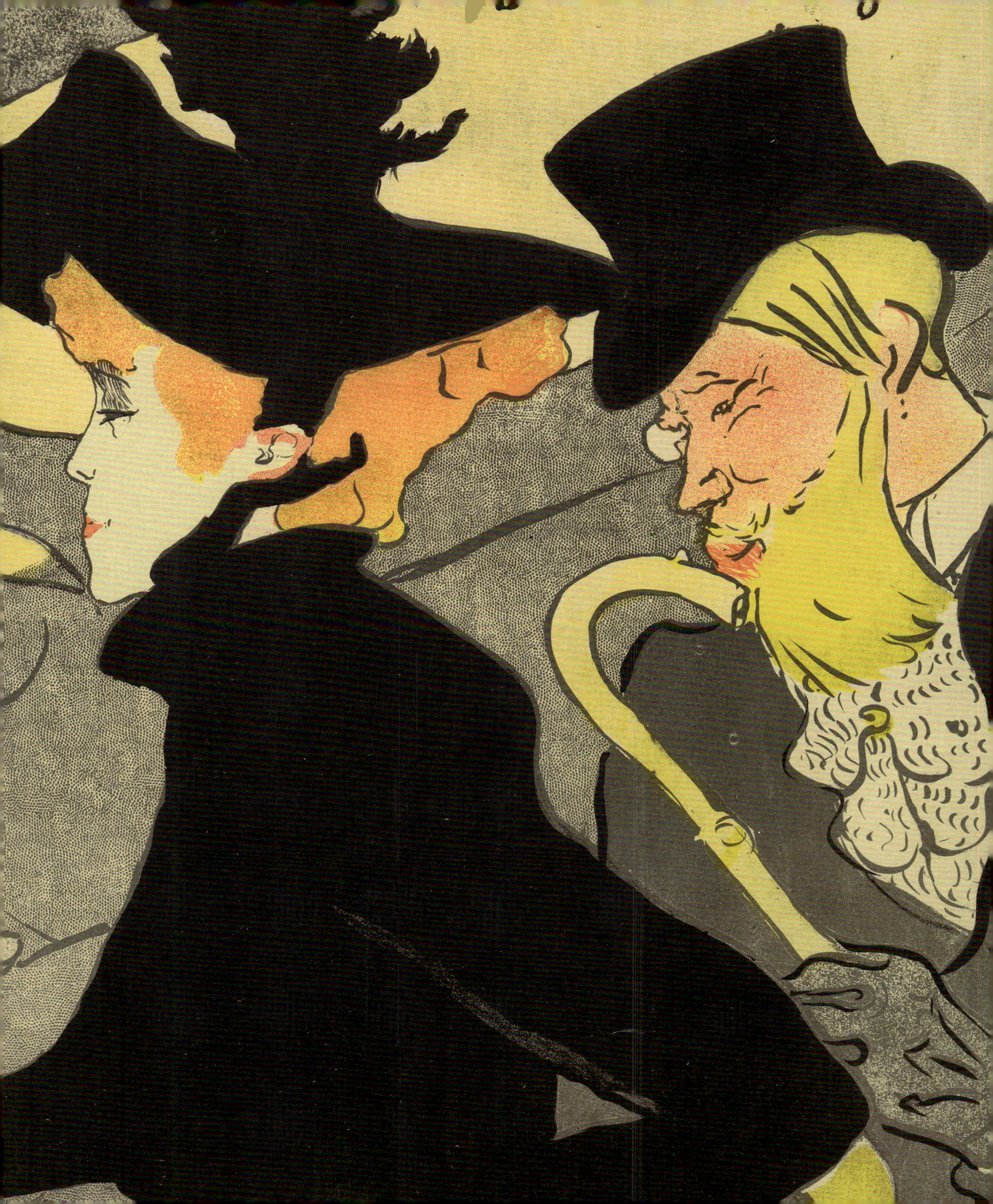

THE PARIS OF

TOULOUSE-LAUTREC

PRINTS AND POSTERS

FROM THE MUSEUM OF MODERN ART

SARAH SUZUKI

THE MUSEUM OF MODERN ART, NEW YORK

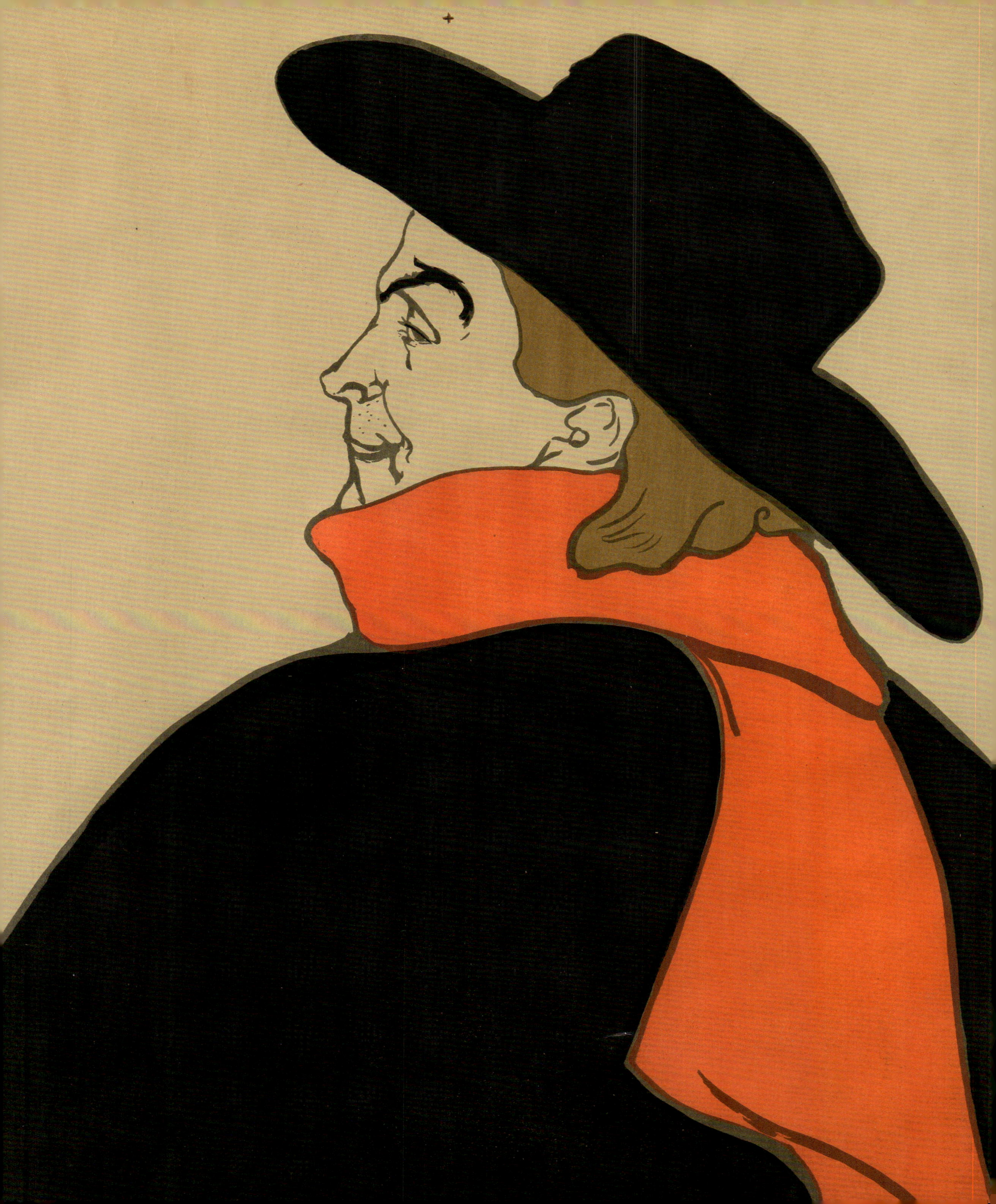

CONTENTS

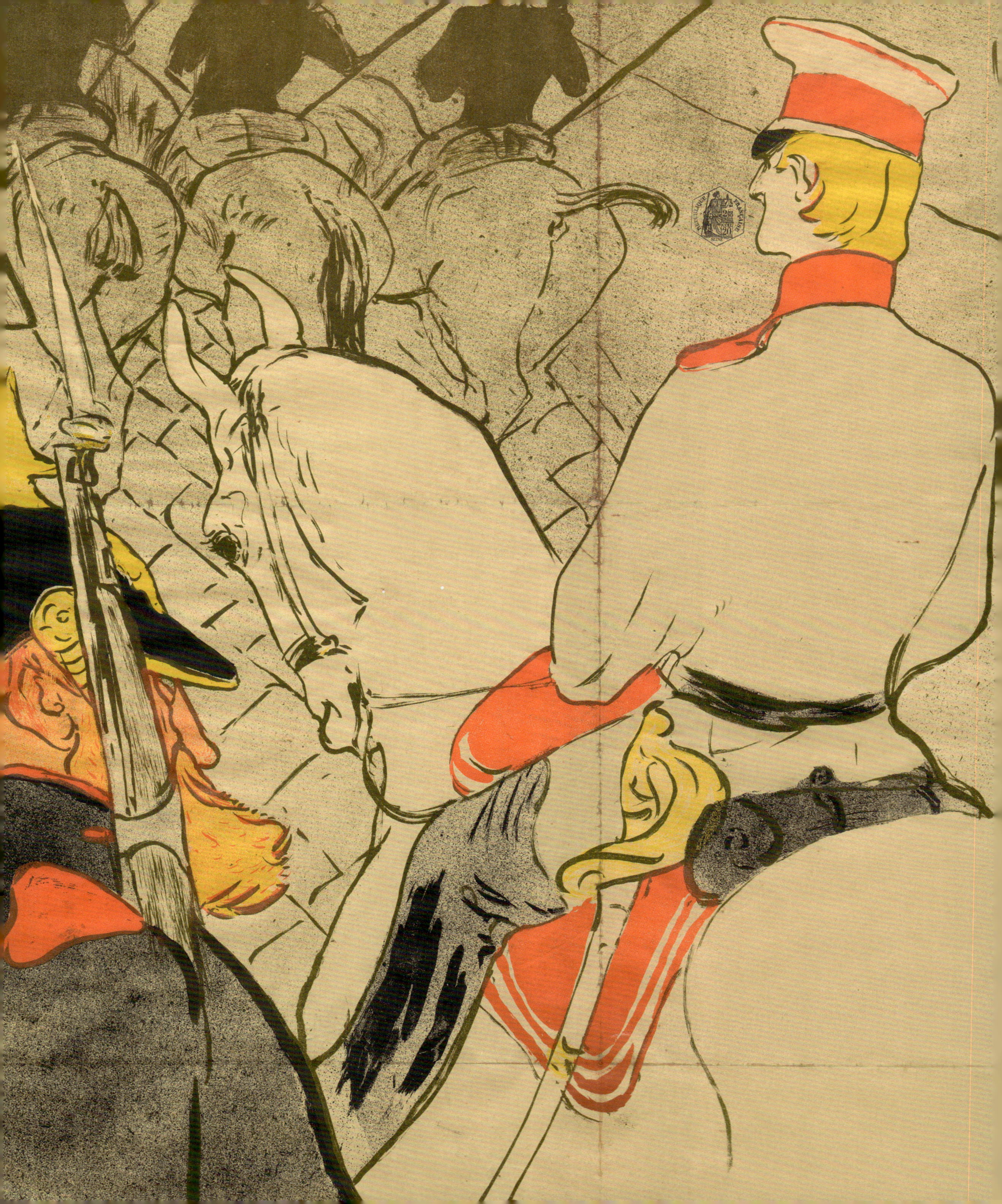

FOREWORD

The connection between Henri de Toulouse-Lautrec and The Museum of Modern Art dates back to the institution's earliest days. In 1931, just two years after it was founded, the Museum presented *Toulouse-Lautrec, Redon*, an exhibition that recognized Lautrec as a fundamental figure in the history and development of modern art. Since that time, he has been the subject of several important monographic exhibitions at MoMA, culminating in a landmark retrospective in 1985. As the Museum deepens its commitment to the artists of the present, it continues to recognize its responsibility to reexamine the artists of the past. Thus, it is with great pleasure that we present *The Paris of Toulouse-Lautrec: Prints and Posters from The Museum of Modern Art*, the first monographic exhibition devoted to Lautrec's work at MoMA in almost thirty years.

This project celebrates the Museum's outstanding collection of approximately two hundred prints and posters by Lautrec. In lithography—the cornerstone of his practice—Lautrec demonstrated intrepid experimentation and utter mastery, making both posters for the streets of Paris and editions for the collector's living room, as well as *livres d'artiste* and illustrations for magazines, journals, menus, theater programs, books, and song sheets. The works by Lautrec in the Museum's collection, spanning the breadth of the artist's decade-long mature career, both exemplify this range and brilliantly evoke Lautrec's milieu and central preoccupation: fin-de-siècle Paris—high and low, onstage and off, at work and at play.

The Museum's collection owes much to Abby Aldrich Rockefeller, one of the institution's three co-founders and a dedicated print enthusiast. By 1932 her own collection included three of Lautrec's most important posters—*Babylone d'Allemagne* (1894), *L'Aube* (1896), and *La Troupe de Mademoiselle Églantine* (1896). These were included in her monumental 1940 gift to MoMA of 1,600 etchings, woodcuts, and lithographs by various artists, which formed the core of the print collection. Mrs. Rockefeller's subsequent gift of sixty-one lithographs by Lautrec, in 1946, made MoMA's holdings of works by the artist among the best in the country. David Rockefeller, himself a great champion of The Museum of Modern Art, has honored his mother's legacy by generously lending four works from his collection to this exhibition.

Sarah Suzuki, Associate Curator of Drawings and Prints, has created a thoughtful and lively exhibition and catalogue that beautifully showcase Lautrec's prints and posters while also exploring their relationship to the time and place of their creation. I extend my gratitude to her and to MoMA's exceptional staff for their dedication and professionalism in realizing this project.

Glenn D. Lowry
Director, The Museum of Modern Art

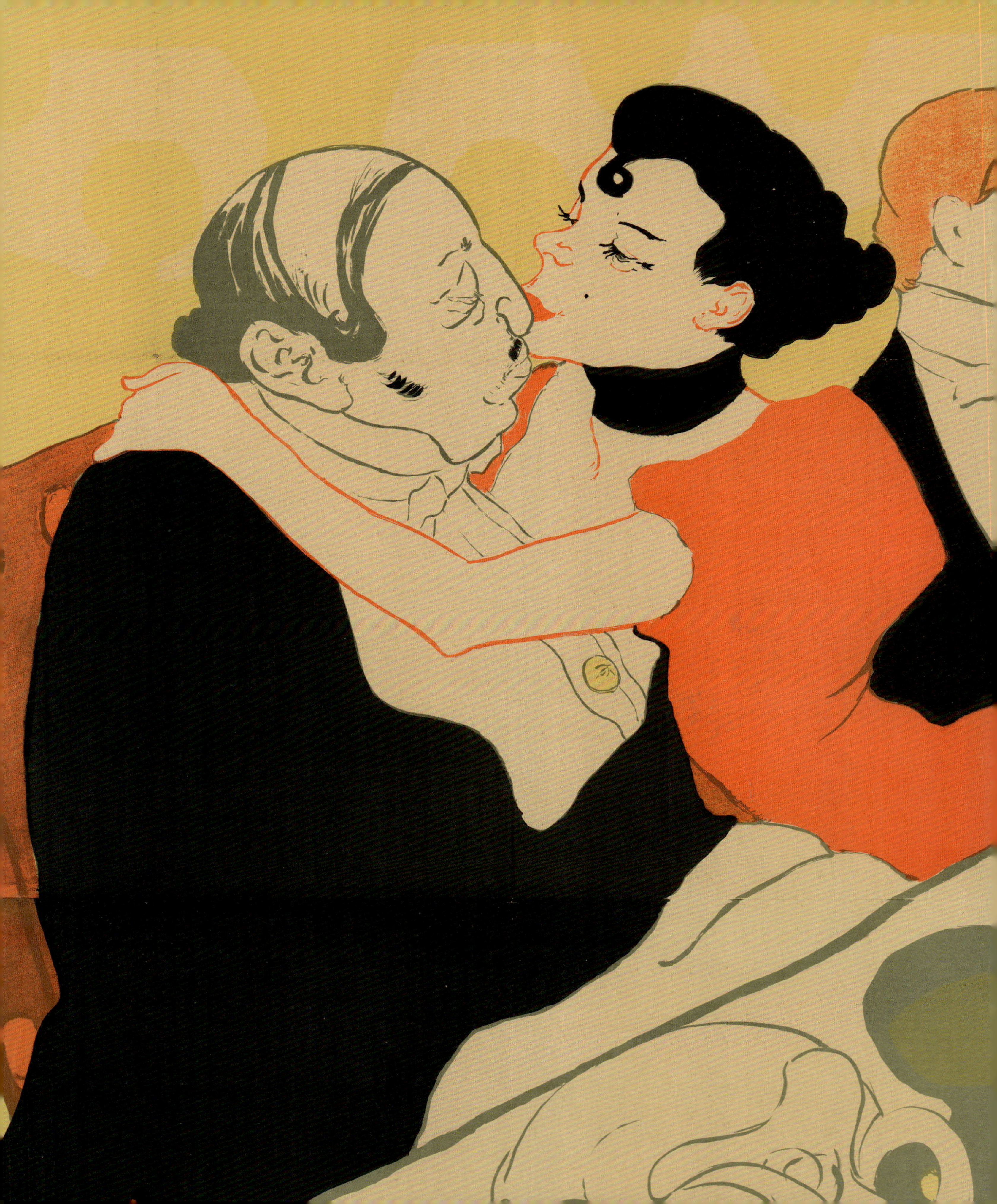

TOULOUSE-LAUTREC
LIFE AND LITHOGRAPHY

SARAH SUZUKI

Henri de Toulouse-Lautrec, who captured the public imagination from the moment his first poster hit the streets of Paris in 1891, continues to be a subject of fascination today, 150 years after his birth. His story seems to come straight from the pages of fiction: the only son of aristocratic first cousins, Lautrec was physically disabled and artistically gifted, finding fame depicting bohemian Belle Époque Paris, fueled by a steady diet of absinthe and women that eventually contributed to his tragically early death. His was a bifurcated existence, as he moved seamlessly from the châteaux and expansive estates of his birthright and the elite salons of his friends in creative circles to seedy Montmartre café-concerts, lesbian bars, brothels, and city streets. In its totality, his oeuvre creates a portrait of fin-de-siècle Paris at all levels.

Lautrec's work was a chronicle of the modern, a depiction of contemporary people, places, and events, relying on the resurgent medium of lithography in a visual language that drew on diverse sources—from Post-Impressionist painting to Japanese woodcuts—but that ultimately was entirely his own. His oeuvre forms something of a diary, recording the places he visited; the performances, plays, and operas he saw; the songs he heard. In his dogged documentation, he was a paparazzo without a camera and a harbinger of our celebrity-obsessed culture. He was also a performer, playing one part for his aristocratic family and another, as the outrageous drunken genius dwarf of bohemian Paris. His personal and professional obsessions, which he termed *furias*,[1] often focused on figures in whom he saw similar, successfully created and executed public personae. He paid special attention to those who, like him, truly inhabited their roles.

Despite his aristocratic origins, Lautrec was resolutely a populist. Although quite intelligent, he eschewed intellectual snobbism in favor of what he found entertaining, scandalous, or funny, and his taste was very much in line with that of the general public. The most important aspect of Lautrec's artistic production—namely, his prints and posters—was intended for public consumption, displayed on the streets outside cabarets and café-concerts or made in editions so that twenty-five collectors might be able to enjoy the same image in their living rooms. Such anti-elite forms of production and distribution were purposeful and powerful choices on the part of this august heir of noble pedigree.

Descended from three lines of French aristocrats—the ruling families of Toulouse, Lautrec, and

Monfa—Henri Marie Raymond de Toulouse-Lautrec Monfa (November 24, 1864–September 9, 1901; fig. 1) was born to Adèle and Count Alphonse ("Alph"). Their conservative, royalist, Catholic families saw their union as a means of keeping the lineage undiluted and the family wealth concentrated, and thus they sanctioned the marriage even though the two were first cousins. The downside of this practice, which extended beyond Lautrec's parents, would become apparent in the next generation, as Lautrec and one-quarter of his cousins suffered from genetic birth defects.

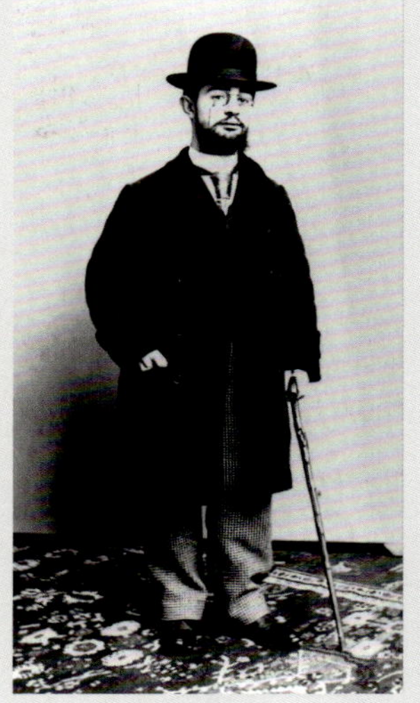

1. Lautrec. n.d. Musée Toulouse-Lautrec, Albi, France

While their relationship began as a passionate affair, Adèle and Alph soon discovered that their personalities were diametrically opposite. Adèle was unfailingly pious, almost irrationally frugal, and deeply, perhaps unhealthily, devoted to her only son.[2] She shared a bed with him until he was eight years old,[3] rented an apartment near his when he moved to Paris, dined with him almost every night, and, when they were apart, maintained a regular (and mostly affectionate) correspondence.

Alph was an aristocratic eccentric of the highest order. While Adèle was devoted to God, Alph was devoted to the hunt and lavished his attention not on his wife and child but instead on his birds, dogs, horses, and even the prey he relished pursuing (fig. 2). Strapping and bearded, he had a reputation as a womanizer (with a particular taste for barmaids), an excellent cook and gourmet, a skilled equestrian, and an adept draftsman. Lautrec's grandmother wrote that when her son "kills a woodcock, the bird affords [him] three pleasures: those of the gun, the pencil, and the fork."[4] Lautrec once remarked to her, "If Papa is there, one is sure not to be the most remarkable."[5] Agreeing that both life together and divorce were impossible, Alph and Adèle peacefully lived apart, with Adèle wholly present in their son's life, and Alph mostly absent.

2. **HENRI DE TOULOUSE-LAUTREC**. *The Count of Toulouse-Lautrec Falconning*. 1881. Oil on wood, 9¼ x 5½ in. (23.4 x 14 cm). Musée Toulouse-Lautrec, Albi, France

It was expected that Lautrec, as heir to Alph's title, would follow in his father's footsteps, and by the time he was a young man, he had either inherited or emulated many of his traits: a love of gastronomy, a passion for animals, and, above all, an artistic gift that greatly surpassed that of the dilettante patriarch. Yet unlike his hardy, athletic father, Lautrec was stricken with respiratory problems, headaches, and terrible leg pains. The serious blow came at thirteen, when an innocuous slip resulted in his breaking a femur—the strongest bone in the body. As he recuperated, he remained steadfast and cheerful. He never complained; sent regular correspondence to grandparents and cousins that displayed his characteristic charm, sharp wit, and self-effacing sense of humor; and sketched endlessly. The following year, he fell into a dry riverbed and broke the other thighbone. With these traumas, Lautrec stopped growing. He would remain four feet eleven inches tall and walk with a cane for the rest of his life. As he entered adolescence, Lautrec suffered further genetic abnormalities: the growth of his nose and lips outpaced that of the rest of his face, causing him to drool and lisp, and his chronic sinus problems resulted in an incessant sniffle.

With an aristocratic sporting life out of the question, Lautrec's parents encouraged their son's artistic pursuits. He moved to Paris to study—first with René Princeteau, a deaf-mute family friend who specialized in equestrian paintings, and then in the academic ateliers of Léon Bonnat and Fernand Cormon. Lautrec experienced his first taste of freedom and, popular among his classmates, made lasting friendships with his fellow artists. At night the students would head out to explore the bars, and before long Lautrec, though of the noblest stock, had firmly established himself as "of Montmartre," the rundown neighborhood on the outskirts of Paris. This pseudo-rural hill, or *butte*, was a haven not only for the poor who struggled to eke out a living but also for criminals and prostitutes as well as artists and bohemians. Nightclubs opened that drew toughs from the neighborhood as well as "slumming aristocrats and *demi-mondaines*, bourgeois tourists, and now and then a representative from the police morals squad, on the watch to be sure the *chahuteuses* (cancan dancers) were wearing underwear."[6]

While Lautrec first went to these night spots to sketch at the suggestion of his teachers, he soon became a fixture, with a reserved table awaiting him. It was in this milieu that he found both his greatest artistic inspiration and his greatest fame. When his poster *Moulin Rouge, La Goulue* (fig. 3) went up in fall 1891, he became an overnight sensation. He started exhibiting widely in Paris and beyond. Pursuing the success he had with his lithographed poster, he often visited the printshop in the morning, painted in the afternoon, had dinner with his mother, and then headed to the bars. By 1895 his fame had spread internationally, and he was featured prominently in a British publication about the history of the poster, which noted that, while Jules Chéret was perhaps the more famous poster artist, Lautrec was "more fascinating. . . . He . . . compel[s] your attention by the force of his realism or the curiosity of his grotesqueness."[7]

Lautrec's mature career lasted only ten years. As he became entrenched in Montmartre's debauched lifestyle, his days and nights were soaked in alcohol (including the hallucinogenic wormwood-based absinthe), which he used as both a physical and a psychological analgesic. His regular dalliances with prostitutes led to his contracting syphilis. Though he joked, "I can paint until I'm forty. After that, I intend to dry up,"[8] it was a tragic overestimation. In 1899 he was confined to a psychiatric hospital in the suburb of Neuilly for several months. After his release, his health dete-

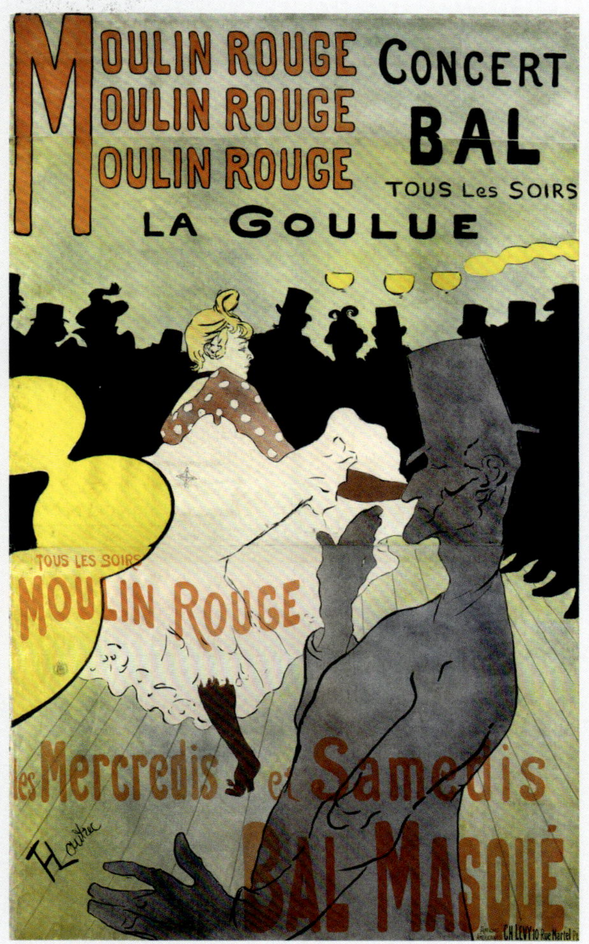

3. **HENRI DE TOULOUSE-LAUTREC**. *Moulin Rouge, La Goulue*. 1891. Lithograph, 6 ft. 2 13/16 in. x 45 7/8 in. (190 x 116.5 cm). The Metropolitan Museum of Art, New York. Harris Brisbane Dick Fund, 1932

riorated rapidly, and he died following a stroke on September 9, 1901. He was thirty-six years old.

Lautrec left behind a voluminous body of work, including 368 prints and posters[9] that offer the most lasting testament to his innovation, influence, and success. While many artists saw printmaking as a secondary or reproductive activity, for Lautrec it was equal in importance to his painting and drawing. Throughout his short career as a printmaker, he worked almost exclusively in lithography, a medium in which his unique skill was immediately appreciated. He often included his prints when submitting work for an exhibition, signaling his conviction that they should represent him not only in the public eye but also in the rarified milieu of the art world.

In André Mellerio's treatise on color lithography published in 1898, Lautrec is the first and foremost artist he cites in making the case for the medium's potential.[10] Invented in Germany in 1789, it involves a complex chemical process based on the simple principle that oil and water do not mix. A drawing, made with greasy crayons or liquids on a specially prepared slab of limestone, is bonded to the stone using a chemical solution. The stone is then inked and put through a printing press to make multiple impressions of the image. In the early nineteenth century, Paris was a hotbed of printing activity, with more than 280 lithographic presses producing advertisements, magazines, and broadsides.[11] It was toward the end of the century that the medium was adopted for artistic purposes. Once Lautrec was introduced to lithography in 1891, it became one of his *furias*. He enjoyed the collaborative workaday air of the printshop in contrast to the isolation of his studio. A visit became part of his daily routine, as he checked the colors of stones and supervised the printing. Of printmaking, he said, "It's fun; I had the feeling of being in control of an entire shop, and it was a new feeling for me."[12] He befriended the craftsmen in the shop, mining their knowledge and experimenting with new techniques and processes.

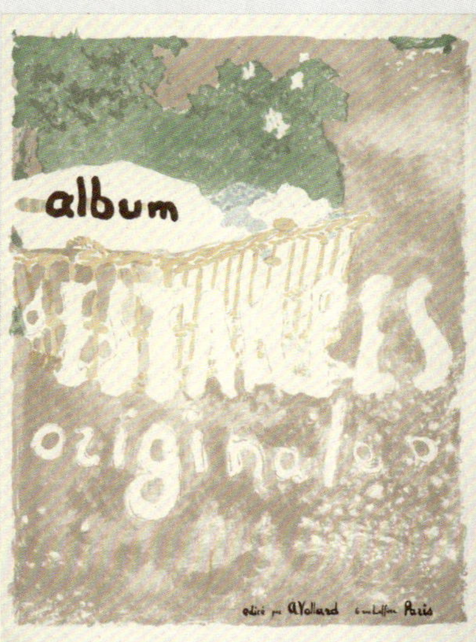

4. **ÉDOUARD VUILLARD** (French, 1868–1940). Cover for the portfolio *L'Album des peintres et graveurs*. c. 1899. Lithograph, 25 3/16 x 18 11/16 in. (64 x 47.5 cm). The Museum of Modern Art, New York. Abby Aldrich Rockefeller Fund, 1951

Lithography allows for an incredible range of mark-making with a wide array of tools, and Lautrec became particularly well-known for his *crachis*, a splatter effect that he achieved by raking the bristles of a toothbrush or shooting ink from a gun.[13] Even while hospitalized, he had the urge to work on his lithographs, asking his friend Maurice Joyant, who would become the executor of his estate and the caretaker of his legacy, "Send me some grained stones and a box of watercolors with sepia, brushes, litho crayons, and good-quality India ink and paper."[14]

Lautrec's prints and posters reflected the version of himself that he wanted to put forward into the world. He declared, "*L'affiche y a qu'ça!*" (The poster, that's all there is!).[15] His paintings and drawings often served as preparatory studies for prints or posters. He sketched in bars and café-concerts on napkins or notebooks, frequently leaving them behind, using those sessions only to commit the gestures to memory. What mattered and what lasted was what he fixed on the lithographic stone. As a fan of popular entertainment, he had an eye for public taste and understood what made a poster successful. He stripped away unnecessary detail, presenting striking, pared-down images that were unmistakably his. He also understood the pace of modern life and the speed and immediacy with which an image had to grab the viewer's attention. A friend later recalled, "I still remember the shock I had when I first saw the Moulin Rouge poster . . . carried along the avenue de l'Opéra on a kind of small cart, and I was so enchanted that I walked alongside it on the pavement."[16]

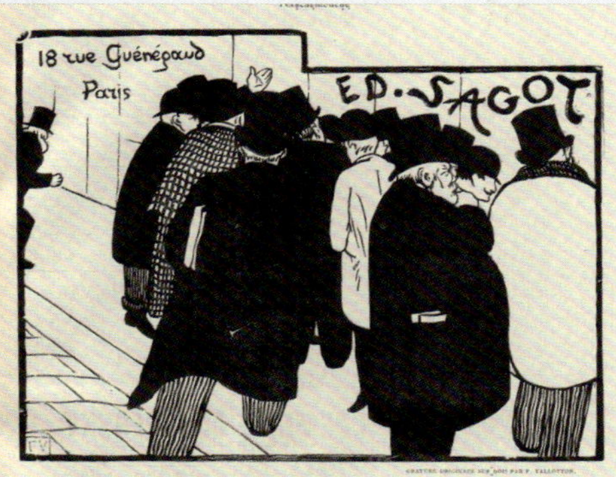

5. **FÉLIX VALLOTTON** (French, 1865–1925). *The Print Lovers*, advertisement for Edmond Sagot from the journal *L'Escarmouche* (November 26, 1893). Halftone relief, page: 15 3/8 x 11 3/4 in. (39 x 29.9 cm). The Museum of Modern Art, New York. The Louis E. Stern Collection, 1964

The 1890s in Paris were a high point in the history of lithography, as France was experiencing a surge in artistic printmaking. Established artists, including Pierre Bonnard, Maurice Denis, and Édouard Vuillard (fig. 4), ushered in the era of the *peintre-graveur*, in which artists embraced both mediums with equal enthusiasm, and lithography became a technique of choice. This surge was furthered in part by technological developments. The preceding decades had seen the introduction of machine presses, in addition to hand-cranked ones, to facilitate more expansive production; improvements in registration techniques to align images for printing; the accommodation of larger sizes and formats; and experiments with separations and overlays, spearheaded by the artist Jules Chéret, that made color printing easier.[17] Also supporting the increase in popularity of the medium was a network of publishers, printers, dealers, and collectors. André Marty, of the *Journal des artistes*, decided to capitalize on the rise in print production and of collecting by the middle class with *L'Estampe originale*, planned as a quarterly portfolio comprising ten original prints by leading artists of the day, at a price of 150 francs per year. The first issue, published in March 1893, included a text by the influential critic Roger Marx and original prints by Bonnard, Denis, Félix Vallotton, and others. The cover for this issue, designed by Lautrec (pl. 38), is a love letter to contemporary print culture. We are transported inside the workshop of Edward Ancourt, where the aged printer Père Cotelle dutifully works the arm of his Brisset press, rollers and inks and other tools of his trade at the ready, the wall behind him lined with lithographic stones. In the foreground, the dancer Jane Avril inspects a freshly pulled impression with the eye of a budding connoisseur. Printers like Cotelle, who specialized not in commercial production but rather in artistic collaboration, also facilitated artistic efforts in printmaking. After Cotelle's death, Henri Stern filled the role of Lautrec's trusted printer and omnipresent drinking partner.

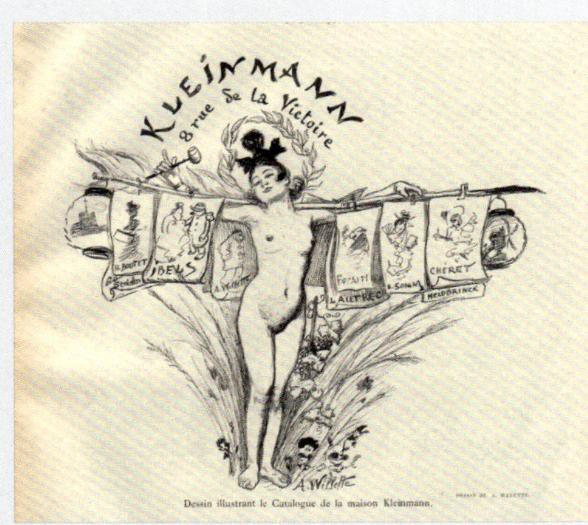

6. **ADOLPHE WILLETTE** (French, 1857–1926). Advertisement for Maison Kleinmann from the journal *L'Escarmouche* (November 12, 1893). Halftone relief, page: 15 3/8 x 11 3/4 in. (39 x 29.9 cm). The Museum of Modern Art, New York. The Louis E. Stern Collection, 1964

Distribution networks were also taking shape. Edmond Sagot opened the first gallery devoted specifically to posters, collecting and selling examples by Chéret, Vallotton (fig. 5), and others. The dealer and publisher Édouard Kleinmann (fig. 6), known for having a good eye and a love for printed material, was lauded

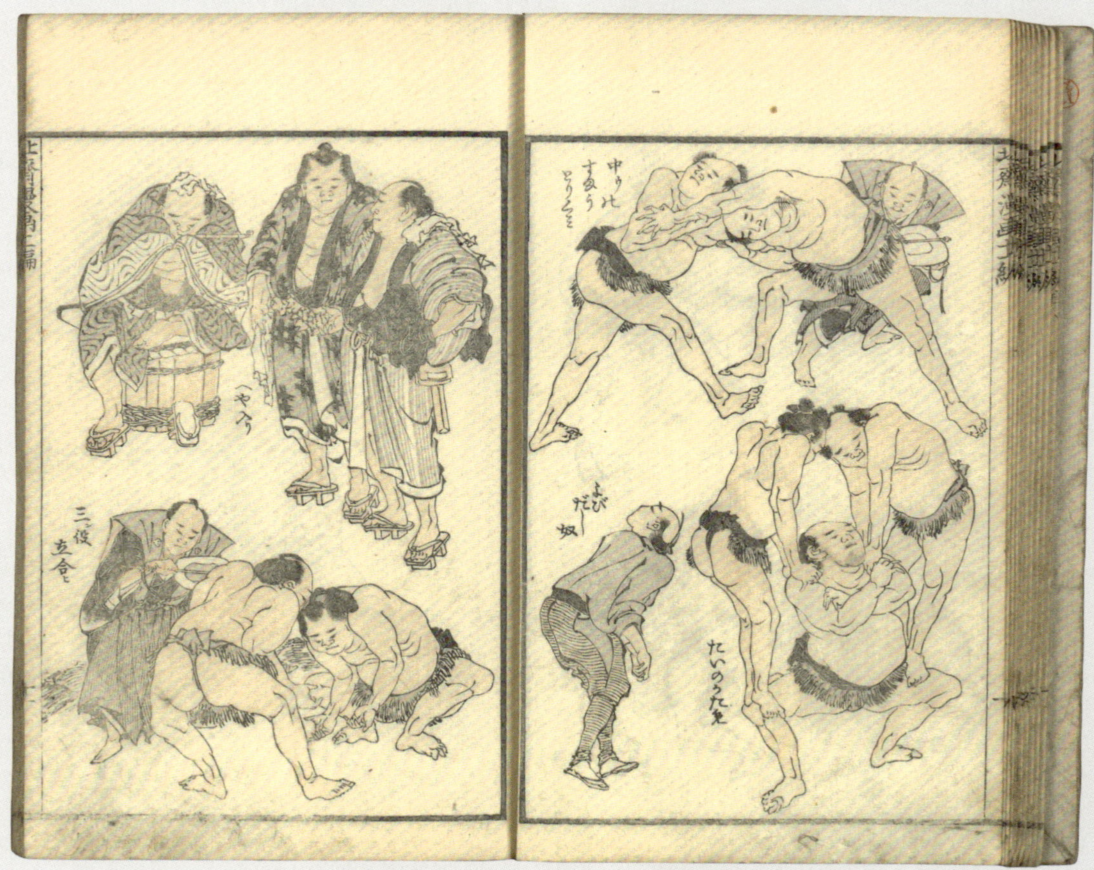

7. **KATSUSHIKA HOKUSAI** (Japanese, 1760–1849).
Sumo Wrestlers. n.d. Woodcut, page: 7¼ x 10 in.
(18.4 x 25.4 cm). The New York Public Library

for having "ardently advocated for Lautrec from the beginning."[18] Gustave Pellet rapidly became an important dealer, specializing in erotic material, and publishing and distributing work by Lautrec, Félicien Rops, and others.

The taste for Japanese prints was another major factor in the rise of color lithography.[19] First introduced in France in the early nineteenth century, Japanese art and aesthetics had a profound influence on artistic vision in Paris and beyond. There were exhibitions, themed cafés (pl. 39), specialized dealers, art-historical studies, monographs, rapturous art critics, and proselytizing collectors such as Edmond de Goncourt, who wrote in 1884 that this material was "in the process of revolutionizing the vision of the European peoples . . . [bringing] a new sense of *color*, a new *decorative system*, and, if you like, a *poetic imagination* in the invention of the *objet d'art*, which never existed even in the most perfect medieval or Renaissance pieces."[20]

In particular, collectible eighteenth-century *ukiyo-e* woodcuts and manga (sketchbooks featuring multiple studies or views of a single figure, form, or theme; fig. 7) had taken Paris by storm; the records of one midrange dealer document the importation of approximately 160,000 *ukiyo-e* prints during a nine-year period. Literally translated as "pictures of the floating world," *ukiyo-e* woodcuts of cosmopolitan Edo Japan depicted life's fleeting pleasures: "In practice, *ukiyo-e* became the world of entertainment and daily pastimes: the theater and the café, picnics and boating parties, busy streets and private households—a celebration of ordinary scenes and events."[21] The making of *ukiyo-e* prints required a series of experts: an artist to create the drawing, craftsmen to cut the blocks, and master printers to align, register, and print them. Commercial in nature, they were produced in large quantities, intended for wide distribution.

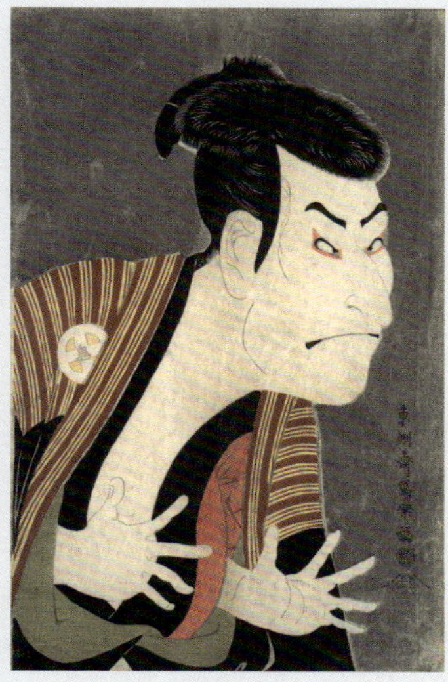

8. **TŌSHŪSAI SHARAKU** (Japanese, active 1794–95). *Ōtani Oniji III as Yakko Edobei in the Play "Koinyôbô Somewake Tazuna."* 1794. Woodcut with mica additions, 15 x 9 ⅞ in. (38.1 x 25.1 cm). The Metropolitan Museum of Art, New York. Henry L. Phillips Collection, Bequest of Henry L. Phillips, 1939

French artists of Lautrec's period began to adopt the formal lessons of these earlier prints, using muted, secondary color palettes; bird's-eye perspectives; flattened spaces; strong, raking diagonals; complex compositions that required the eye to navigate into the picture; unmodulated areas of color; interlocking sections of clashing pattern; simple, flowing lines; and quotidian subjects. Lautrec absorbed these precepts avidly and integrated them into his work.

Lautrec's interest in Japan, which extended beyond printed matter, began around 1883, when he and fellow artists Tristan Bernard and Louis Anquetin visited the *Exposition Rétrospective de l'Art Japonais*, where they saw the work of Katsushika Hokusai, Utagawa Kuniyoshi, and Utagawa Hiroshige. Lautrec had many opportunities to see, study, buy, and trade Japanese prints and books; one friend recalled the collection of prints—some of them erotic—that the artist kept in his studio.[22] A fan of masquerade balls, he dressed up in Japanese costumes and mimicked the dramatic postures of Tōshūsai Sharaku's portraits of actors (figs. 8, 9). According to his friend François Gauzi, "Lautrec considered the Japanese like his brothers, the same size that he was. Alongside them, he appeared normal. All his life, he wanted to visit the land of the *mousmés* and bonsai trees, of which he had formed a marvelous picture based on Hokusai's prints."[23] Proof of his allegiance, he adopted the use of a Japanese-style remarque (small, personalized marginalia, which he used to sign his prints) in about 1892, compressing his initials, HTL, into a single character contained within a circle (fig. 10).

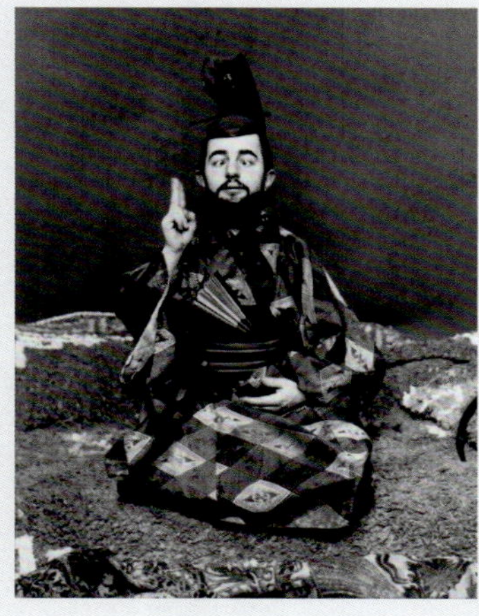

9. Lautrec posing in a samurai costume. c. 1892. Photograph by Maurice Guibert (French, 1856–1913). Musée Toulouse-Lautrec, Albi, France

A link between Lautrec, in particular his prints and posters, and The Museum of Modern Art has existed since MoMA's earliest days, a testament to his esteemed position in the history of modern art. The three pioneering women who founded the institution—Lillie P. Bliss, Abby Aldrich Rockefeller, and Mary Quinn Sullivan—all acquired work by the artist for

10. Lautrec's monogram remarque

their private collections even before the Museum was founded, in 1929. In 1931, while still in its original location in the Heckscher Building at 730 Fifth Avenue, The Museum of Modern Art mounted an exhibition devoted to the work of Odilon Redon and Lautrec (fig. 11), presented as two of the unique European voices of modern art. Of the sixty-six works by Lautrec on view, at least one-third were prints, signifying that there was already an understanding of the central role printmaking played in his practice. Another exhibition followed in 1956 (fig. 12), and a 1985 retrospective sought to highlight the artist's "virtuoso printmaking and its influence on modern art."[24]

The Museum of Modern Art's holdings of more than one hundred prints and posters, as well as dozens of illustrated books, journals, song sheets, and theater programs by Lautrec make it one of the best institutional collections of the artist's work in the United States, a position due almost solely to Mrs. Rockefeller. A philanthropist and advocate for progressive social issues, from public housing to women's causes, she was deeply interested in bringing modern art to the public's attention and saw prints as a democratic medium able to reach a wider audience.

She herself collected prints extensively, focusing both on Europe, as she "firmly believed that modernism originated with avant-garde painting in France in the late nineteenth century,"[25] and the United States, where she saw the opportunity to support young artists in New York. According to the art historian Russell Lynes, "Her tastes in art were definite, even unyielding. She knew precisely what she liked and what she did not like; she was not easily persuaded to alter her judgments. The pictures and prints which she bought, first of all for herself, reflect her own inclinations and enjoyments."[26] An informal catalogue of her collection, maintained between 1925 and 1935, includes stellar works by Hilaire-Germain-Edgar Degas, Paul Gauguin, and of course Lautrec, whose three brilliant posters *La Troupe de Mademoiselle Églantine* (pl. 36), *L'Aube* (pl. 59), and *Babylone d'Allemagne* (pl. 64) she purchased at New York's Kraushaar Gallery in 1932. These three works were included in Mrs. Rockefeller's monumental 1940 gift to the Museum, which, comprising 1,600 etchings, woodcuts, and lithographs by various artists, formed the core of the print collection.

Mrs. Rockefeller accelerated her print collecting with the Museum in mind, and in 1946 she made another major gift, which included sixty-one lithographs by Lautrec, making MoMA's holdings of his work among the best in the world. She had

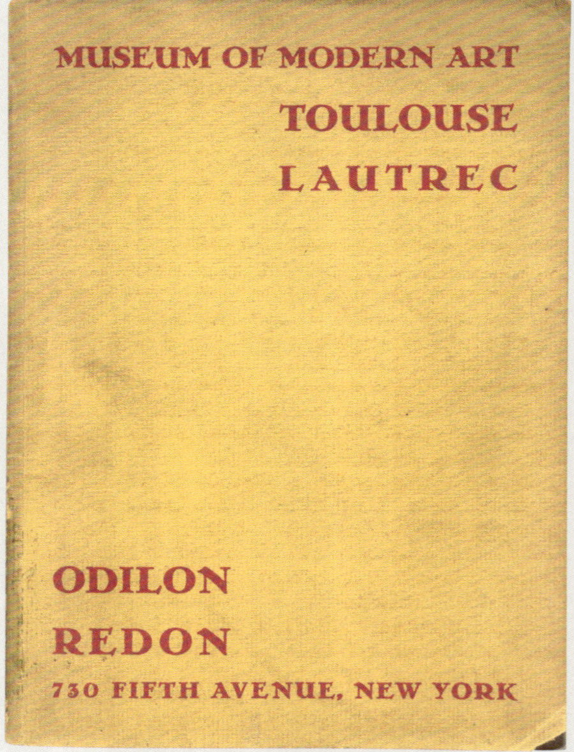

11. Cover of the catalogue *Toulouse-Lautrec, Redon*, published by The Museum of Modern Art, New York. 1931. The Museum of Modern Art Library, New York

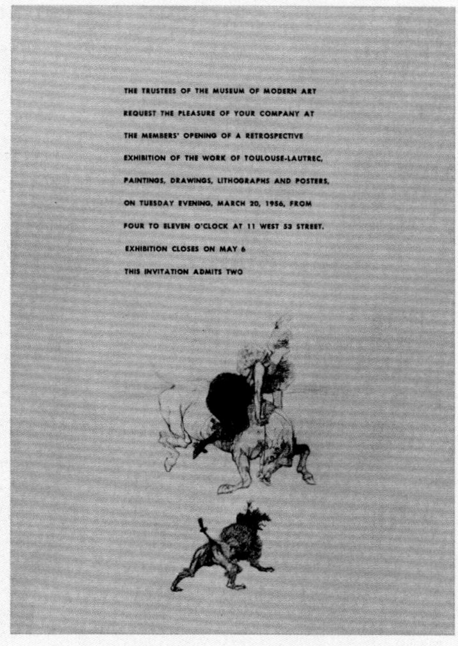

12. Invitation to the opening of the exhibition *Toulouse-Lautrec*, March 20, 1956. The Museum of Modern Art Archives, New York

assembled a spectacular collection, fearlessly recognizing Lautrec's radically unromantic depiction of modern life and not shying away from his more risqué subjects. "Here are the vignettes of the boulevards, the begoggled automobilist, the black-stockinged little girl, glimpses of the racecourse, the courtroom, and the salon," wrote Alfred H. Barr, Jr., the Museum's founding director, of her 1946 gift.[27]

MoMA's collection of printed material by Lautrec is explored in these pages, becoming a guide to fin-de-siècle Paris as seen through the eyes of the man who once said, "*J'ai deux vies*"[28]—an artist who lived a dual life as the dutiful son of aristocrats and a wild bohemian. His prints and posters take us from the elite salons of the Champs-Élysées to the Bois de Boulogne to the stages and orchestra pits of Paris. As a chronicler of his day, he depicted performers, playwrights, and prostitutes with the same gimlet eye, and earned his reputation as a poster pioneer, a titan of lithography, and one of the great artists in the history of printmaking.

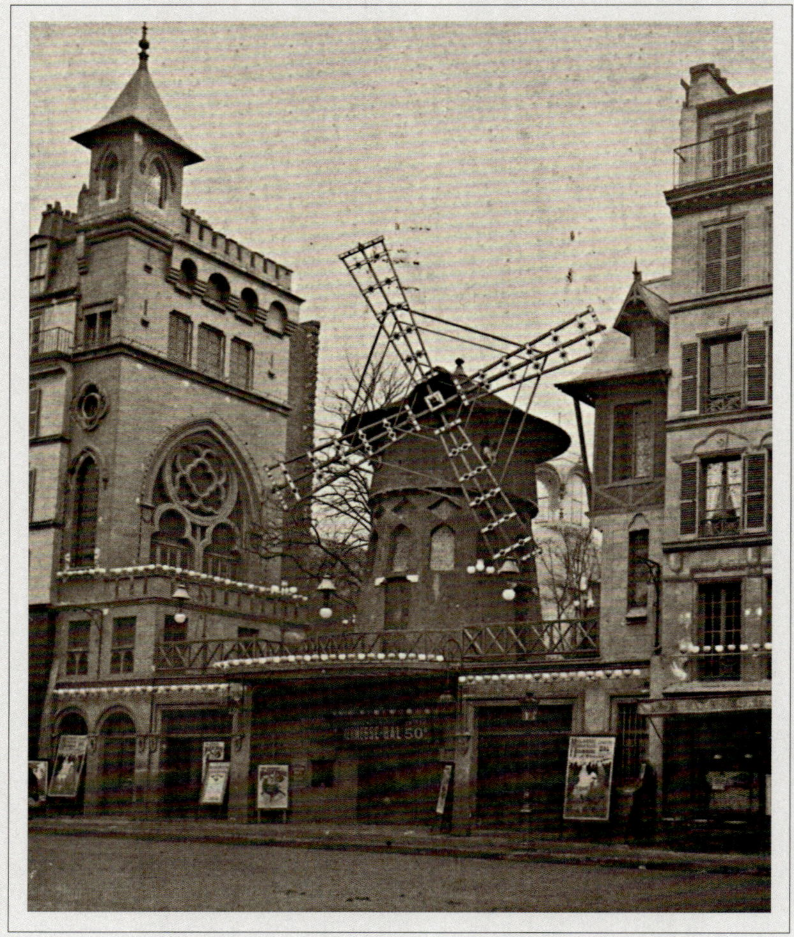

THE CAFÉ-CONCERT

The second half of the nineteenth century saw an explosive rise of nightlife culture in Paris, as genres multiplied and subcultures sprang up with entertainments to suit every taste and every stratum of society. Establishments ranged from *cabarets artistiques* (such as Le Chat Noir, with its literary crowd and published journal) to theaters (such as the Comédie-Française, in which highbrow classics by Molière and Jean Racine were performed by Sarah Bernhardt) to dance halls (from the rough and rowdy Moulin de la Galette to the deluxe, decadent Moulin Rouge; fig. 13) to circuses such as the Medrano, where "the frequenters are drawn from the middle- and working-class population, amongst which mingle the pretty maidens of Montmartre at la Butte."[29]

Paris had developed an international reputation as a party town, and rightfully so. Although the culture of the café—a kind of public living room for eating, reading, and conversing—had long been

13. The Moulin Rouge on the boulevard de Clichy, with Lautrec's poster *Moulin Rouge, La Goulue* in front. 1891. Bibliothèque Nationale de France, Paris

ingrained in French life, drinking culture was new. Formerly confined to feast days, drinking proliferated in the mid-1850s as the price of liquor dropped dramatically and the occasional indulgence became commonplace. By the 1890s France had the highest per capita consumption of alcohol in the world.[30]

Lautrec was a nightly visitor to the theater, the circus, and the opera, finding tremendous freedom and inspiration in those milieus. Among the costumed performers and outlandish entertainers, his physical appearance marked him not as odd but rather as one of the gang. He used these settings for his most celebrated pictures, in what became a symbiotic relationship: Lautrec made these venues and performers famous through his posters and prints, and in turn, it was his work for them that brought him the greatest acclaim.

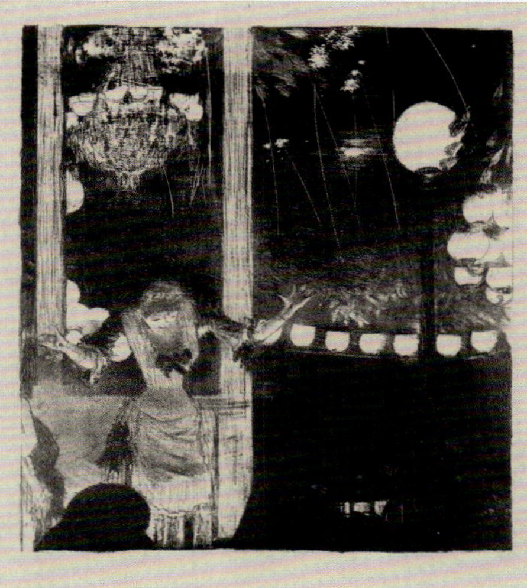

14. **HILAIRE-GERMAIN-EDGAR DEGAS** (French, 1834–1917). *Mademoiselle Bécat at the Ambassadeurs.* c. 1877. Lithograph, 13 ½ x 10 ¾ in. (34.3 x 27.3 cm). The Museum of Modern Art, New York. Gift of Abby Aldrich Rockefeller, 1940

Chief among these new types of entertainment was the café-concert, where men and women could meet to smoke, eat, drink, and listen to live music. By 1896 there were nearly three hundred such spots in Paris, many of which were suspected to be havens of prostitution, where shopgirls, farm girls, and models went in the hopes of finding stardom. Instead, they often found themselves indebted to theater directors for the cost of costumes and training, and encouraged to make more money by fraternizing with customers at "private" dinners.[31]

Lautrec created an ode to this muse in 1893: a portfolio of twenty-three lithographs called *Le Café concert* (pls. 1–6, 8, 34) produced jointly with artist Henri-Gabriel Ibels and including an introductory text by writer Georges Montorgueil. Montorgueil (a pseudonym for Octave Lebesgue) argued that the café-concert was not a den of iniquity but rather a tonic for modern life, a cure for all that ails, and a place to relax and to commune for people from all walks of life, a sentiment reiterated by Georges Clemenceau the following year: "For the audience of the café-concert is really everyone. From the dinner jacket adorned with a white chrysanthemum to the overalls of a workman from the suburbs, the whole hierarchy meets and mixes here."[32] Lautrec captured a cross section of café-concert culture: dancers (his beloved Jane Avril, Edmée Lescot); comedians (the portly Caudieux); singers (Yvette Guilbert, the somber "Daumier-esque" Madame Abdala, the coarse Aristide Bruant); monologists (the British male impersonator Mary Hamilton); spectators; and staff (Pierre Ducarré, the highly respected talent scout, booker, and manager of the elegant Ambassadeurs).

The Ambassadeurs was the height of sophistication, occupying a prime spot on the Champs-Élysées since the late 1700s, with a twinkling garden space described in a contemporary guide:

The visitor may easily imagine himself to be a guest at some Royal fête; on so grand a scale is everything carried out, that there remains simply nothing to desire—everything seems to be anticipated and is ready to hand [sic]. *All the lady singers and performers at the Ambassadeurs are star artistes . . . no second-rate talent is tolerated. . . . At the concerts it is the custom of the audience to take up the refrain of the popular melody of the day, and the heartiness with which this refrain is sung gives unmistakable evidence of the pleasure afforded by the opportunity in thus assisting or taking part in the harmony of the evening.*[33]

The Ambassadeurs was a landmark, and it had already captured the interest of many artists, including Lautrec's idol, Hilaire-Germain-Edgar Degas, in whose thematic footsteps he followed. In a lithograph made nearly twenty years earlier (fig. 14), Degas presented a gesturing chanteuse in a formfitting costume, seen from the audience, in a carefully described interior with an ornate chandelier and the glow of gaslights.

Lautrec's take on the same scene (pl. 7), made for *L'Estampe originale*, differs radically from that of his predecessor. The composition employs a tripartite division frequently found in *ukiyo-e* woodcuts and is almost bisected horizontally, with nearly all the action taking place within just one panel that has been pressed into two-dimensional flatness, with unmodulated, abutting areas of cool blue and soft pink. Only vague efforts were made to establish the specificity of place: chandelier, leafy trees, clouds of smoke billowing through the air. Rather than being among the audience, we see the performer from behind, as though we were in the wings, watching her gesture in her low-backed dress to the unseen mass of spectators.

Across town, in the slums of Montmartre, was another of Lautrec's favorite spots, the Mirliton, the creation of Aristide Bruant (fig. 15). A domineering figure of the café-concert, Bruant was a proprietor, performer, lyricist, and sometime publisher who, in his youth, had moved from rural France to Paris to find work. He absorbed the rhythms and slang of the lower classes and became intimate with the local hardscrabble laborers, petty criminals, and working girls. He began to write songs and stories about the Parisian poor, their trials and woes, presenting himself as one of them—the voice of the underclass.

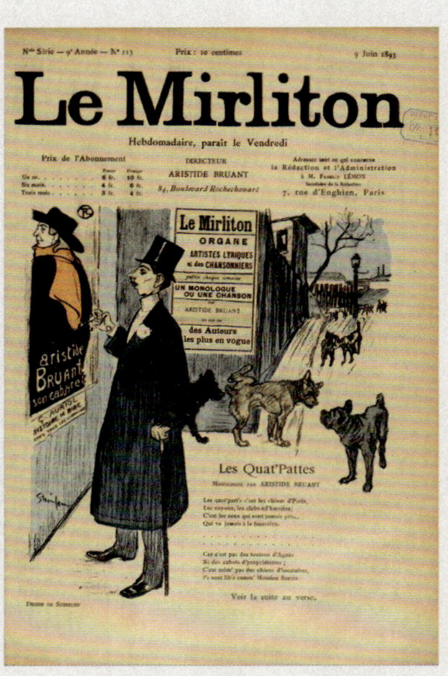

Prix : 10 centimes

9 Juin 1893

Le Mirliton

Hebdomadaire, paraît le Vendredi

Prix de l'Abonnement

DIRECTEUR

ARISTIDE BRUANT

84, Boulevard Rochechouart

la Rédaction et l'Administration

7, rue d'Enghien, Paris

Les Quat'Pattes

ARISTIDE BRUANT

Voir la suite au verso.

15. **THÉOPHILE-ALEXANDRE STEINLEN** (French, 1859–1923). *Lautrec's Poster of Aristide Bruant on a Fence*, cover for the journal *Le Mirliton* (June 9, 1893). Halftone relief, page: 15 1/16 x 11 in. (38.3 x 28 cm). Bibliothèque Nationale de France, Paris. Cabinet des Médailles

Bruant carried this idea through all aspects of his persona. He adopted an unusual and distinctive costume: a "large soft felt hat, corduroy trousers, a double-breasted waistcoat, a velvet hunting coat with brass buttons, and a red belt."[34] He designed the Mirliton to have a purposefully rough working-class air. He brayed from the stage about pimps and prostitutes, mocking the bourgeoisie who flocked to the club, in a kind of poverty tourism, for the novelty of being maltreated by the one and only Bruant. The sign on the facade read, "The Mirliton—rendezvous for those seeking to be abused," and he enjoyed torturing patrons with his exclusionary door policy: "Bruant ran the Mirliton on the principle that the more difficult a pleasure was to obtain, the more it was valued. One could not just go inside as one did at an ordinary café or pay for a seat as one could upstairs at the Chat Noir. On the contrary, Bruant enjoyed leaving people outside, standing in the street, while he examined them from behind a little barred window."[35]

Bruant recognized Lautrec's talent, decorating the place with the young artist's work and calling out to him from the stage as he entered at night, "Silence, Messieurs, here's the great painter Toulouse-Lautrec with a friend, and a bastard I don't know."[36] He commissioned several posters from him. By the time Lautrec portrayed Bruant in the 1893 portfolio *Le Café concert* (pl. 8), Bruant's costume and persona were firmly established: with hat and scarf in place, he looks down his nose with a haughty, intimidating sneer, affecting the attitude he would if the person who acquired this print turned up at the door of the Mirliton. The small poster *Aristide Bruant* (pl. 9), depicting Bruant full-length from behind, testifies to the height of his fame—his silhouette was so renowned that one need not see his face to identify him. Lautrec depicted him standing on the cobblestone streets of his district, literally *dans la rue*—a man of the people, of the community whose woes and triumphs he popularized in song. The large poster (pl. 10) from the same year is perhaps the most daring, as Bruant—composed of the unmodulated blocks of color that form his coat, hat, and scarf—takes on a monumental presence. His profile peeks out in emulation of the powerful depictions of Japanese actors in *ukiyo-e* woodcuts (fig. 16). An iconic and unforgettable image, it was so synonymous with the performer that Bruant used it again in 1912 to advertise his retirement tour.

Lautrec was always drawn to performers like Bruant, who had developed an unmistakable public persona, and he probably also recognized his own "double life" in him. While playing the abusive proprietor, mocking the bourgeoisie, and lamenting the lot of the poor, Bruant was also commanding a handsome sum for his performances and becoming quite wealthy.

Perhaps no other venue has inspired as much interest, speculation, and historical reimagining as the Moulin Rouge. Now shorthand for the raucous, drunken, sex-soaked, cancan-filled nights of the Belle Époque, the Moulin Rouge opened in 1889, aspiring to be the best, most luxurious, and most exuberant nightclub in all of Paris. The owner, Charles Zidler, and the manager, Joseph Oller, spared no expense, adding both a dance hall and a cabaret, and booking salacious sideshow acts,

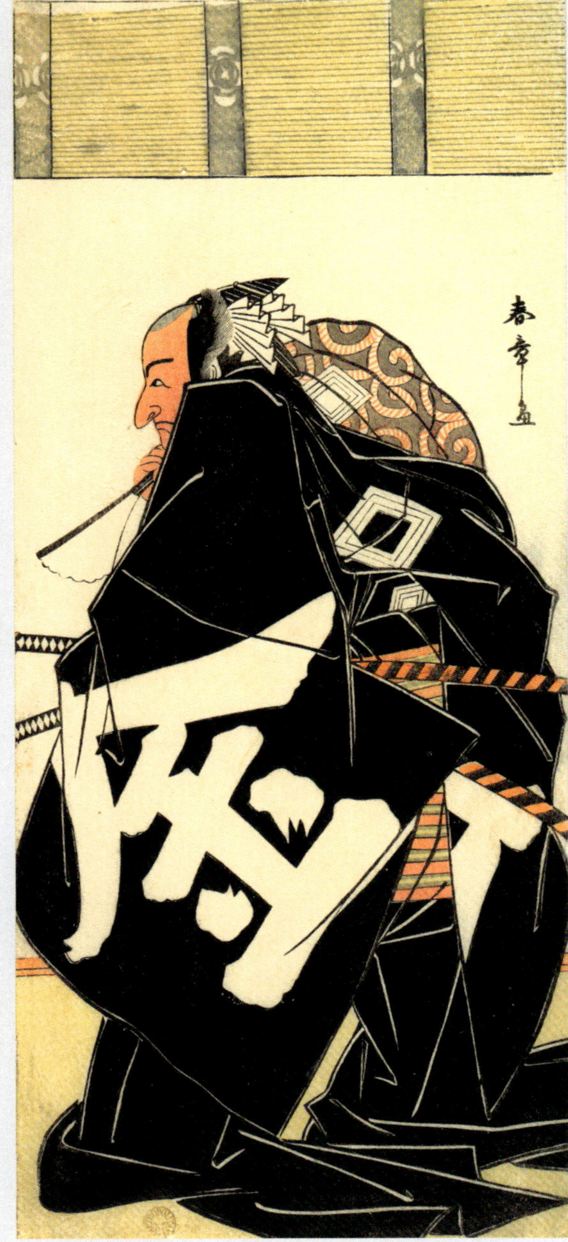

16. **KATSUKAWA SHUNSHŌ** (Japanese, 1726–92). *Ichikawa Danjuro V in the Role of Sakata Kintoki from the Play "Shitenno tonoi no kisewata."* 1781. Woodcut, 12 5/16 x 5 1/2 in. (31.3 x 14 cm). The Metropolitan Museum of Art, New York. Purchase, Joseph Pulitzer Bequest, 1918

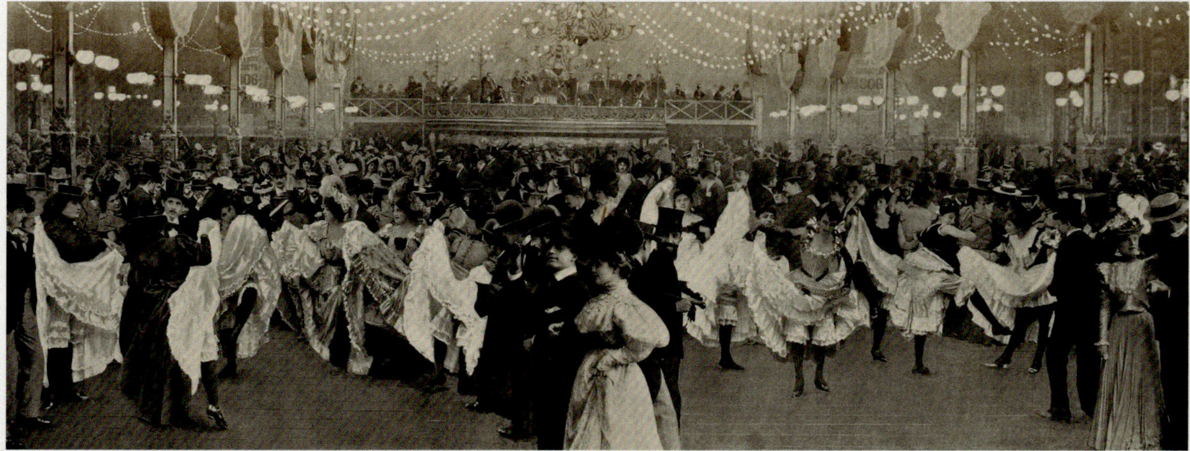

17. **E. LAGRANGE** (French, dates unknown). *The Dance Hall of the Moulin Rouge*, illustration in *Le Panorama: Paris la nuit*, published by Ludovic Baschet, Paris. c. 1898. Collection Zimmerli Art Museum at Rutgers University, gift of Phillip Dennis Cate and Lynn Gumpert

fortune-tellers, and clowns. One of Lautrec's favorites was the clown Cha-U-Kao, whom he depicted numerous times. Her Japanese-inspired persona included her name—adapted from *chahut-chaos*, a high-stepping dance and the frenzy it unleashed—a geisha-inspired topknot, and a low-necked ruffled bodice. In *La Clownesse au Moulin Rouge* (pl. 19), she is arm in arm with her lover, Gabrielle, who was also a model for Lautrec; they may also be the couple in *La Danse au Moulin Rouge* (pl. 15).[37]

The Moulin Rouge hired the most famous dancers to perform the *quadrille naturaliste* (cancan), which delighted spectators with its swish of petticoats and flashing flesh as legs flew high—knickers optional (fig. 17). In the garden, Zidler installed the enormous papier-mâché elephant he bought from the Exposition Universelle that year (a symbol that became Lautrec's most common remarque) and also had trained monkeys and donkey rides (fig. 18). Out front, the signature windmill—a reference to Montmartre's recent rural past—beckoned pleasure-seekers to "a beautiful factory which provided those always-appreciated commodities: amusement and pleasure."[38]

Zidler and Oller created a social space where anything was possible. Men and women drank and socialized openly (pl. 17); Lautrec's *L'Anglais au Moulin Rouge* (pl. 16) captures the lively pickup scene. In the print, a dandy (Lautrec's friend the British painter William Tom Warrener) is deep blue, perhaps in response to the risqué conversation in which the two women have engaged him. In another work (pl. 12), depicting Lautrec's cousin Gabriel Tapié de Céleyran and the photographer Paul Sescau, the men lasciviously eye two strolling women. Lovers could meet clandestinely, and revel-

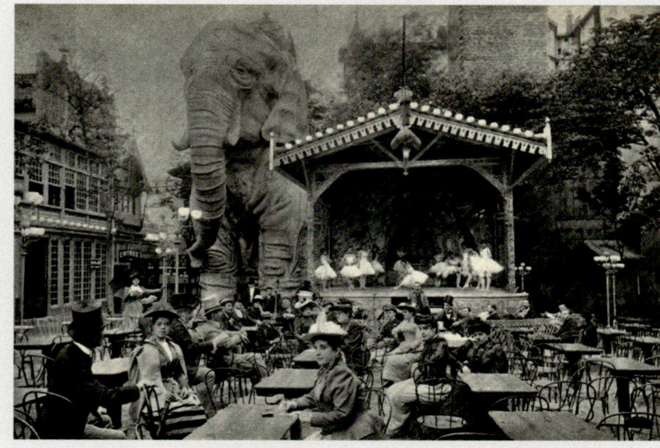

18. The Moulin Rouge. c. 1889–90. Private collection

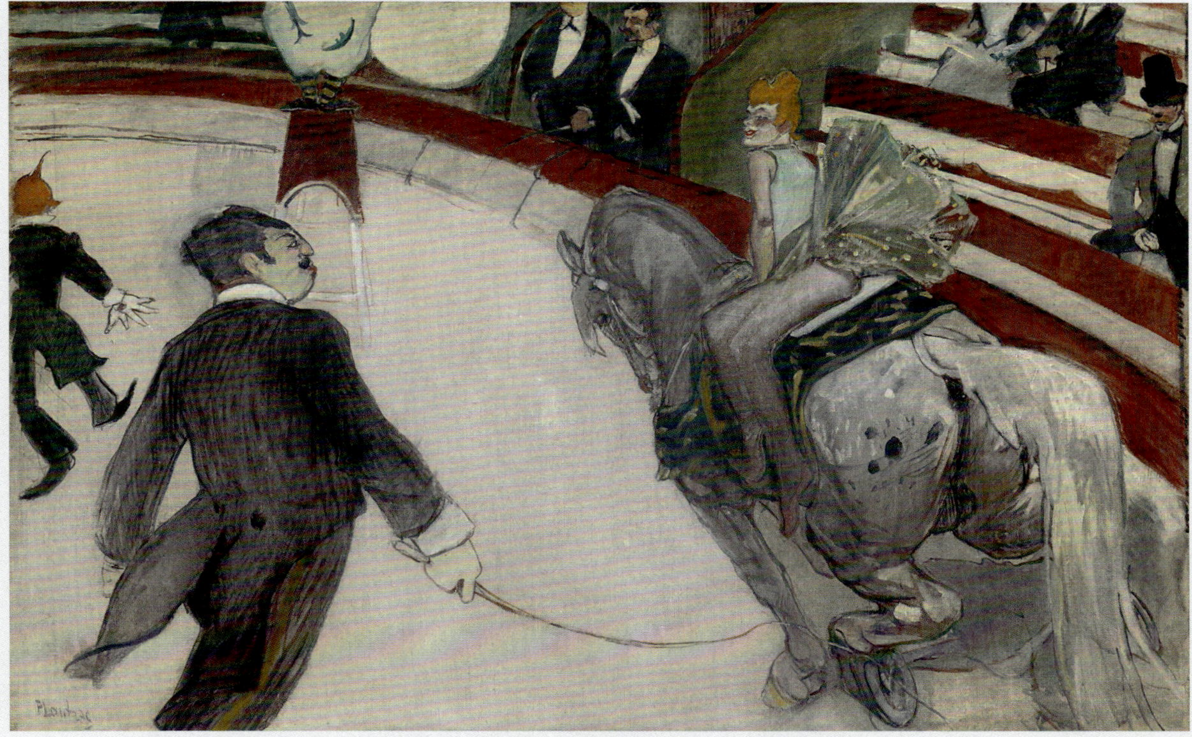

19. **HENRI DE TOULOUSE-LAUTREC**. *Equestrienne (At the Cirque Fernando).* 1887–88. Oil on canvas, 39 ½ x 63 ½ in. (100.3 x 161.3 cm). The Art Institute of Chicago. Joseph Winterbotham Collection, 1925

ers could let loose, concealed by masks at parades (pl. 21) and costume balls.

The Moulin Rouge was Lautrec's from the start. At the grand opening, guests were greeted in the entry hall by one of his large circus paintings (fig. 19), purchased by Zidler.[39] His first poster (fig. 3), which launched his career into the stratosphere, was commissioned by the Moulin Rouge. The poster advertised the performance of La Goulue (The Glutton), an ambitious country laundress made famous by the cancan. Born Louise Weber and nicknamed for her insatiable appetite for both life and food, the strawberry blonde aggressively courted fame, dancing in transparent muslin knickers, posing topless in publicity photos, and cultivating a bawdy, sexually adventurous reputation.

Her signature costume consisted of a low-cut gown, a distinctive and much-copied high chignon, and a black ribbon choker. The look became so clearly hers that in Lautrec's most famous images of her, he did not need to show her from the front. In a lithograph of 1894 (pl. 14), La Goulue is easy to identify even from the back by her updo, side curls, and protruding belly. She is dancing with another popular performer, known as Valentin-le-Désossé (Valentin the Boneless), famous for his flexibility on the dance floor and often identified in Lautrec's work by his top hat and aquiline profile. Like Lautrec, Valentin lived a double life—mild-mannered clerk Jacques Renaudin by day, and dance hall celebrity by night—and he prevented the two from overlapping. A friend once said that if any acquaintances

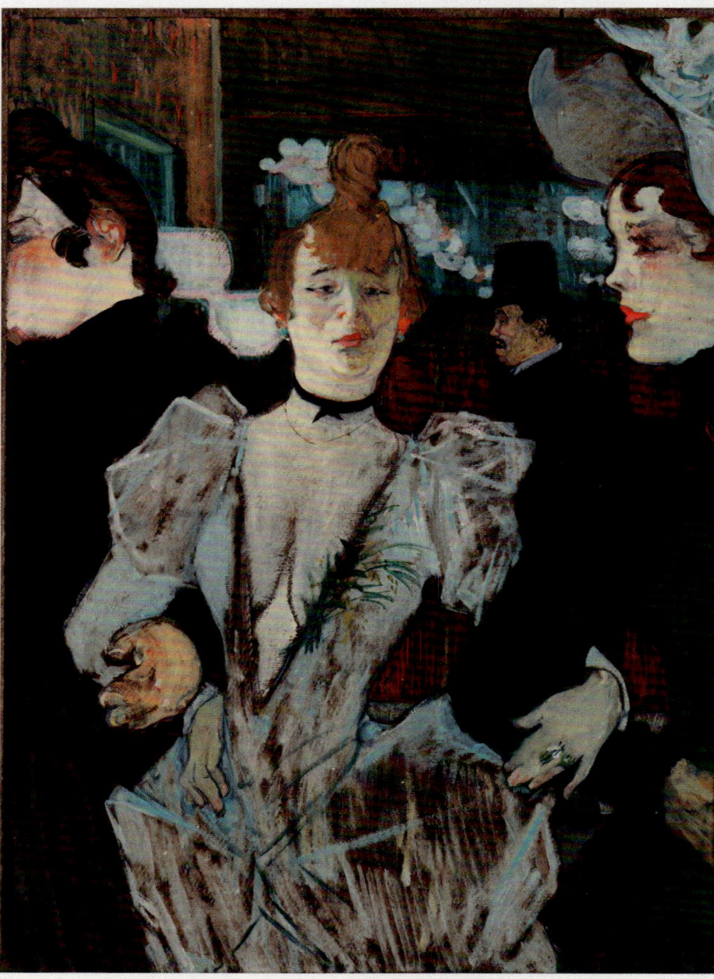

20. **HENRI DE TOULOUSE-LAUTREC**. *La Goulue at the Moulin Rouge*. 1891–92. Oil on board, 31¼ x 23¼ in. (79.4 x 59 cm). The Museum of Modern Art, New York. Gift of Mrs. David M. Levy, 1957

ran into Jacques during the day, he pretended not to recognize them.[40]

These images clearly reveal Lautrec's debt to depictions of actors in Japanese *ukiyo-e* woodcuts. Often unconcerned with trying to create a specific likeness, the Japanese artists instead used signs and symbols—a specific gesture, an accessory or accoutrement, a hairstyle—to indicate their subject. The art critic Gustave Geffroy, with whom Lautrec collaborated on multiple occasions, wrote eloquently of Japanese artists, "To represent figures, too, they have found specific lines, which summarize the movement. . . . They constantly seek and find one single significant detail that can stand for all the others. They have even contrived to form the human body out of a single wavy line."[41] His comments could also describe the work of Lautrec, who used the low-cut dress of La Goulue, the high-stepping posture of Jane Avril, the gloves of Yvette Guilbert, and the profile of Valentin, rather than traditional portrait likenesses. Lautrec himself was quoted telling Guilbert, "Ma chère, I don't *detail* you. I *totalize* you!"[42]

A lithograph from 1892 depicts La Goulue entering the Moulin Rouge with a woman on her arm (pl. 13). Identified as the performer's "sister," the figure is more likely the dancer Môme Fromage, with whom she had a romantic relationship. At the time, lesbians often explained their cohabitation by saying they were sisters. Avril later recalled that La Goulue lived with Môme Fromage, "a basset hound made woman . . . who had the air of a laundry woman. . . . One day, an eavesdropper wanted to know the truth about their relationship. . . . La Goulue, taking modesty, denied being lesbian," and Môme Fromage threw a fit, shouting, "Louise, how can you deny that you love me!"[43] In the painting *La Goulue at the Moulin Rouge* (fig. 20), made contemporaneously with the lithograph, we are spun around to the front of the same scene and see La Goulue linking arms with the rotund Môme Fromage, on her right, and May Milton, a well-known and openly lesbian performer, on her left, further suggesting that the "sister" in the lithograph is actually her lover.

Lautrec socialized with a number of lesbian performers on the café-concert circuit, including Milton, an Irish actress who had come to Paris with a British dance troupe and who performed a popular "naughty little girl" routine. In Lautrec's work, Milton is often marked by her pug nose and a peculiar kind of hat, described as having two protruding "antennae,"[44] as seen on the cover of the song sheet *Eros vanné* (pl. 11). One of many examples of sheet music illustrated by Lautrec, it depicts two women in hats at a bar, accompanied by a worse-for-wear Eros, put out of work by the prevalence of lesbian relationships: "*J'assiste aux amours Saphiques/ Des femmes qui n'ont point d'amants.*"[45] Stripped of his mythological accoutrements—his wings and bow and arrow—he appears comically wounded, balanced on a crutch, his broken leg protruding phallically and his head wrapped in bandages. The song, performed by Guilbert, told of a jaded, injured cupid. Milton is identifiable by her unusual insect hat,[46] which is again referred to obliquely in a poster Lautrec made to advertise her United States tour (fig. 21), with the letters "l" and "t" protruding from her head like antennae.

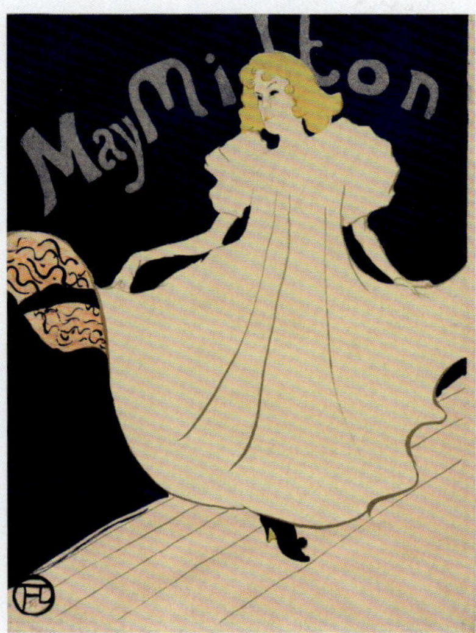

21. **HENRI DE TOULOUSE-LAUTREC**. *May Milton*. 1895. Lithograph, 31⅝ x 23 11/16 in. (80.3 x 60.1 cm). The Art Institute of Chicago. Mr. and Mrs. Carter H. Harrison Collection, 1948

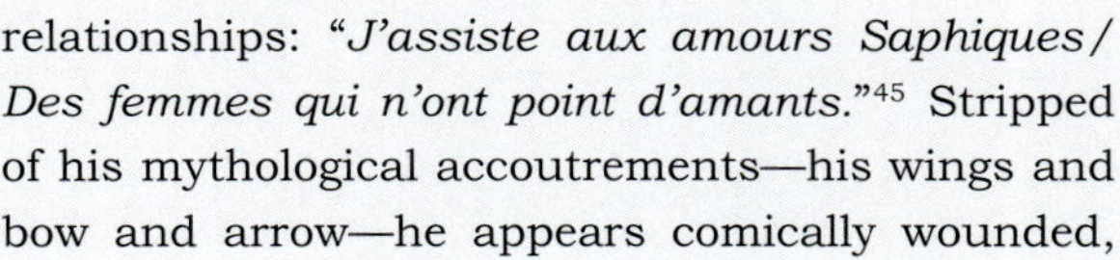

La Goulue's career was short-lived. After unsuccessfully attempting to update her act by working with trained animals[47] and later taking a booth at a Parisian fair, she descended into obscurity and poverty. In 1928 she was said to be selling peanuts and cigarettes, and a year later she died, forgotten. La Goulue was the first of Lautrec's professional *furias*, but she would not be the last.

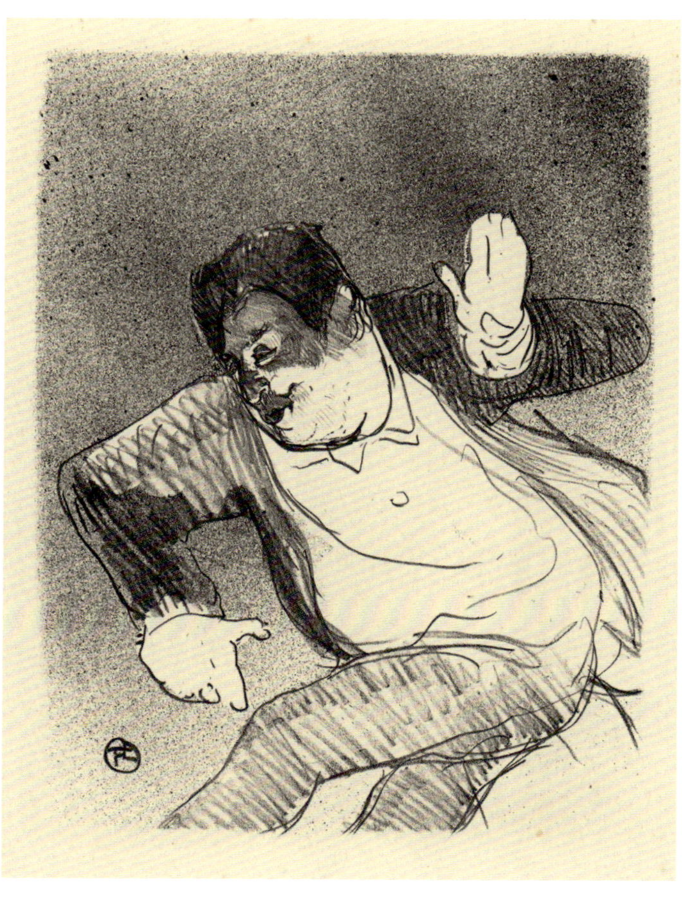

Plate 1
CAUDIEUX, PETIT CASINO (**CAUDIEUX AT THE PETIT CASINO**)
from the portfolio **LE CAFÉ CONCERT**. 1893
Lithograph, sheet: 17 5/16 x 12 5/8 in. (44 x 32 cm)
The Louis E. Stern Collection, 1964

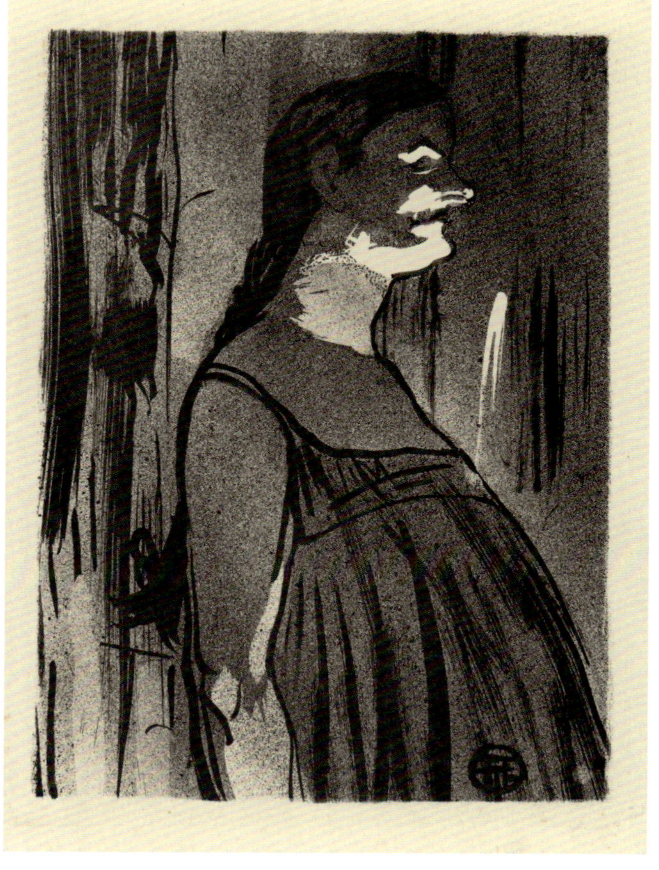

Plate 2
MADAME ABDALA from the portfolio **LE CAFÉ CONCERT**. 1893
Lithograph, sheet: 17 5/16 x 12 9/16 in. (44 x 31.9 cm)
The Louis E. Stern Collection, 1964

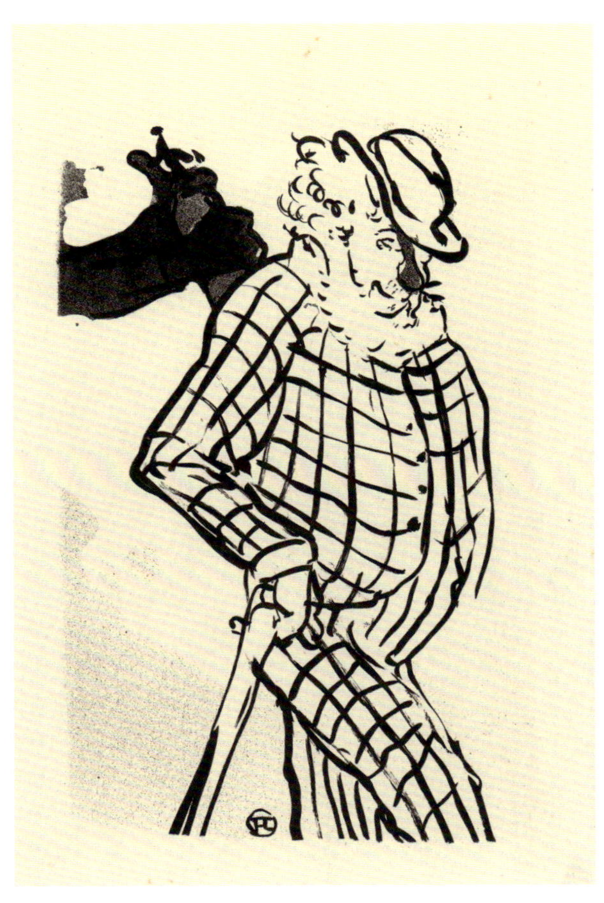

Plate 3
COMIQUE EXCENTRIQUE ANGLAIS (**ECCENTRIC ENGLISH COMEDIAN**) from the portfolio **LE CAFÉ CONCERT**. 1893
Lithograph, sheet: 17 5/16 x 12 5/8 in. (44 x 32 cm)
The Louis E. Stern Collection, 1964

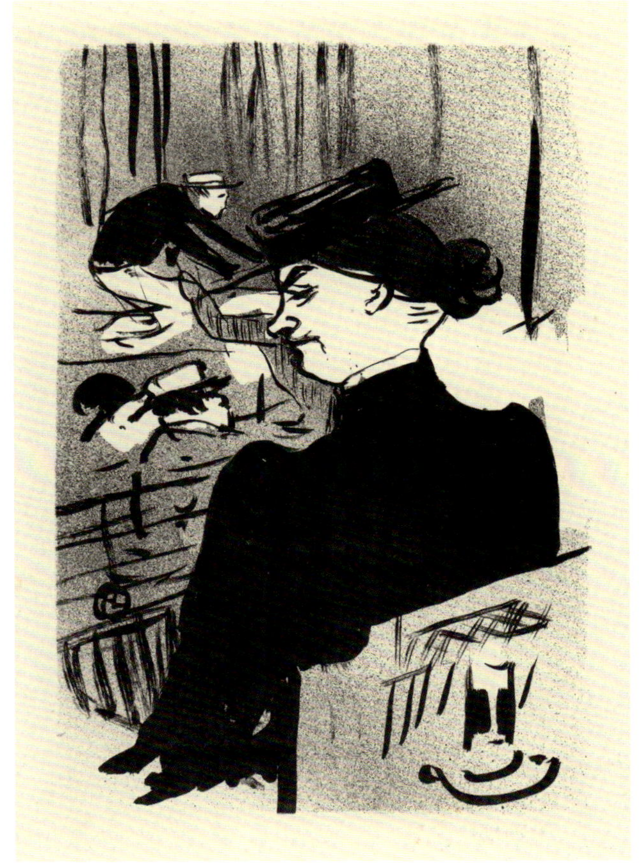

Plate 4
UNE SPECTATRICE (**A SPECTATOR**)
from the portfolio **LE CAFÉ CONCERT**. 1893
Lithograph, sheet: 17 1/16 x 12 11/16 in. (43.3 x 32.2 cm)
The Louis E. Stern Collection, 1964

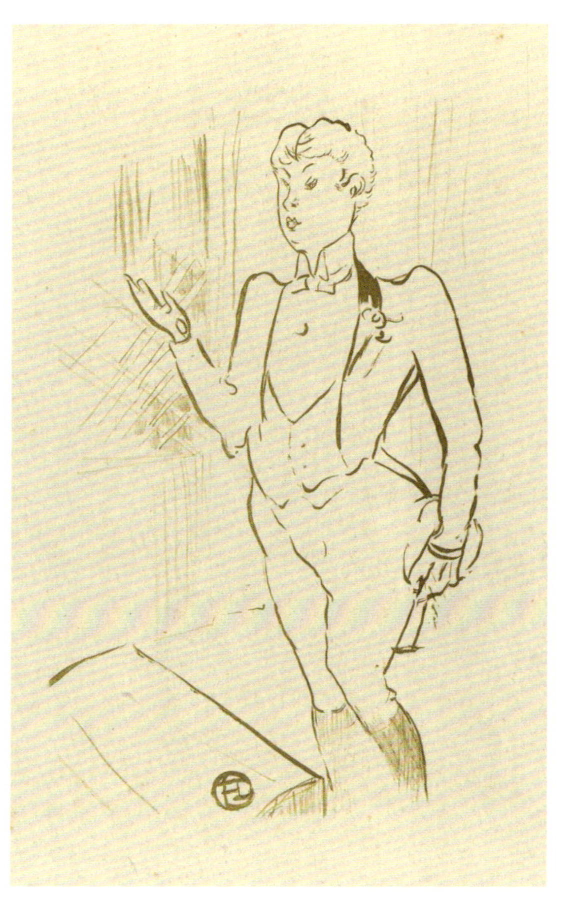

Plate 5
MARY HAMILTON from the portfolio
LE CAFÉ CONCERT. 1893
Lithograph, sheet: 17 3/16 x 12 5/8 in. (43.7 x 32.1 cm)
The Louis E. Stern Collection, 1964

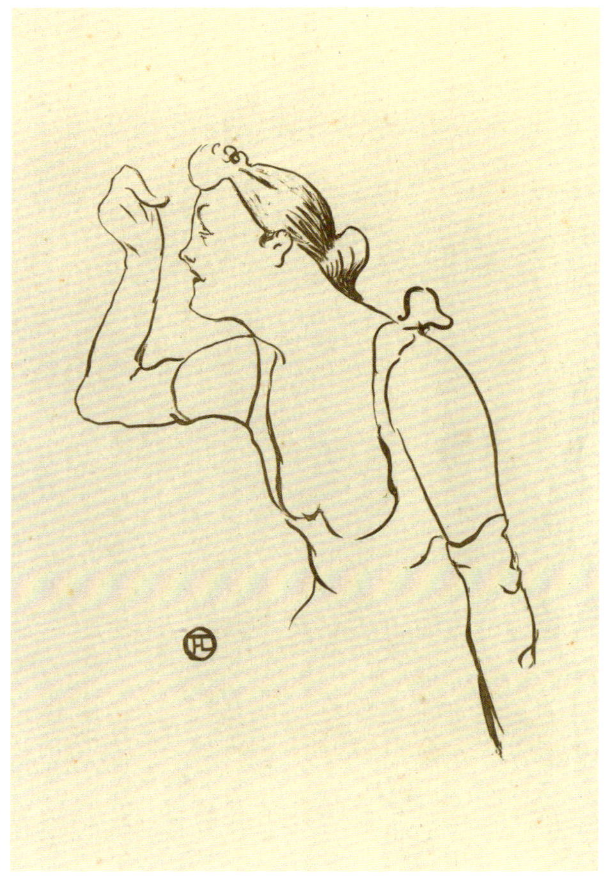

Plate 6
PAULA BRÉBION from the portfolio
LE CAFÉ CONCERT. 1893
Lithograph, sheet: 17 3/16 x 12 5/8 in. (43.7 x 32.1 cm)
The Louis E. Stern Collection, 1964

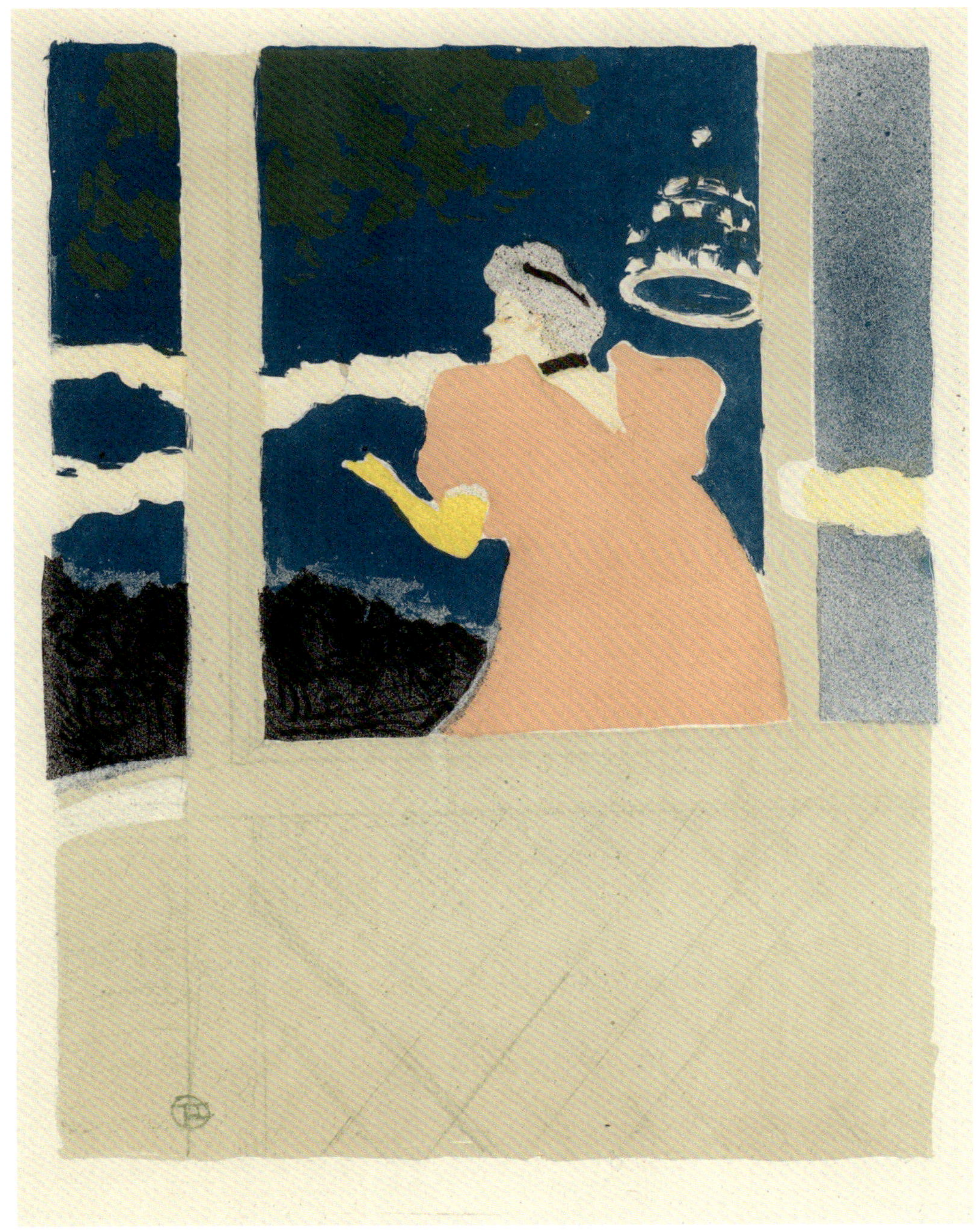

Plate 7
AUX AMBASSADEURS (AT THE AMBASSADEURS). 1894
Lithograph, sheet: 24 3/16 x 16 15/16 in. (61.4 x 43 cm)
David and Peggy Rockefeller Collection

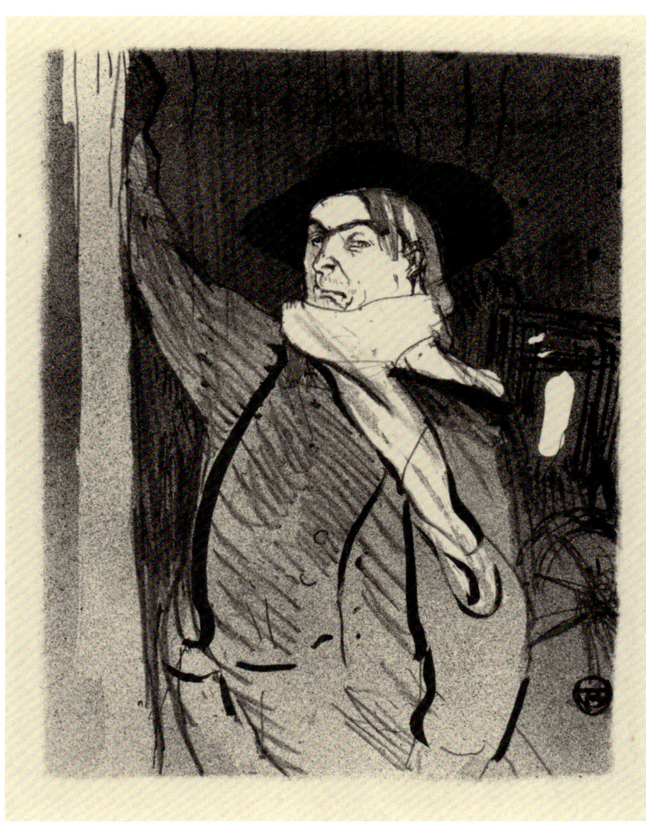

Plate 8
ARISTIDE BRUANT from the portfolio **LE CAFÉ CONCERT**. 1893
Lithograph, sheet: 17 1/4 x 12 11/16 in. (43.8 x 32.3 cm)
The Louis E. Stern Collection, 1964

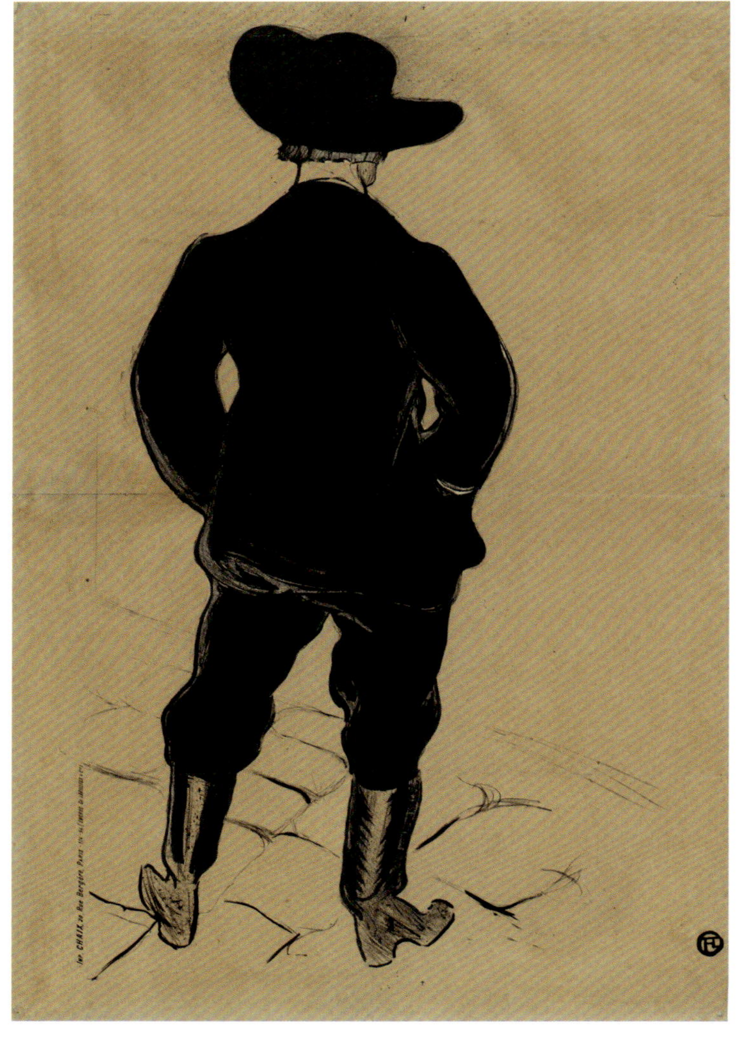

Plate 9
ARISTIDE BRUANT. 1893
Lithograph, sheet: 33 1/4 x 23 3/4 in. (84.5 x 60.3 cm)
Grace M. Mayer Bequest, 1997

Plate 10
ARISTIDE BRUANT DANS SON CABARET
(**ARISTIDE BRUANT IN HIS CABARET**). 1893
Lithograph, sheet: 53 9/16 x 37 15/16 in. (136 x 96.3 cm)
Gift of Emilio Sanchez, 1961

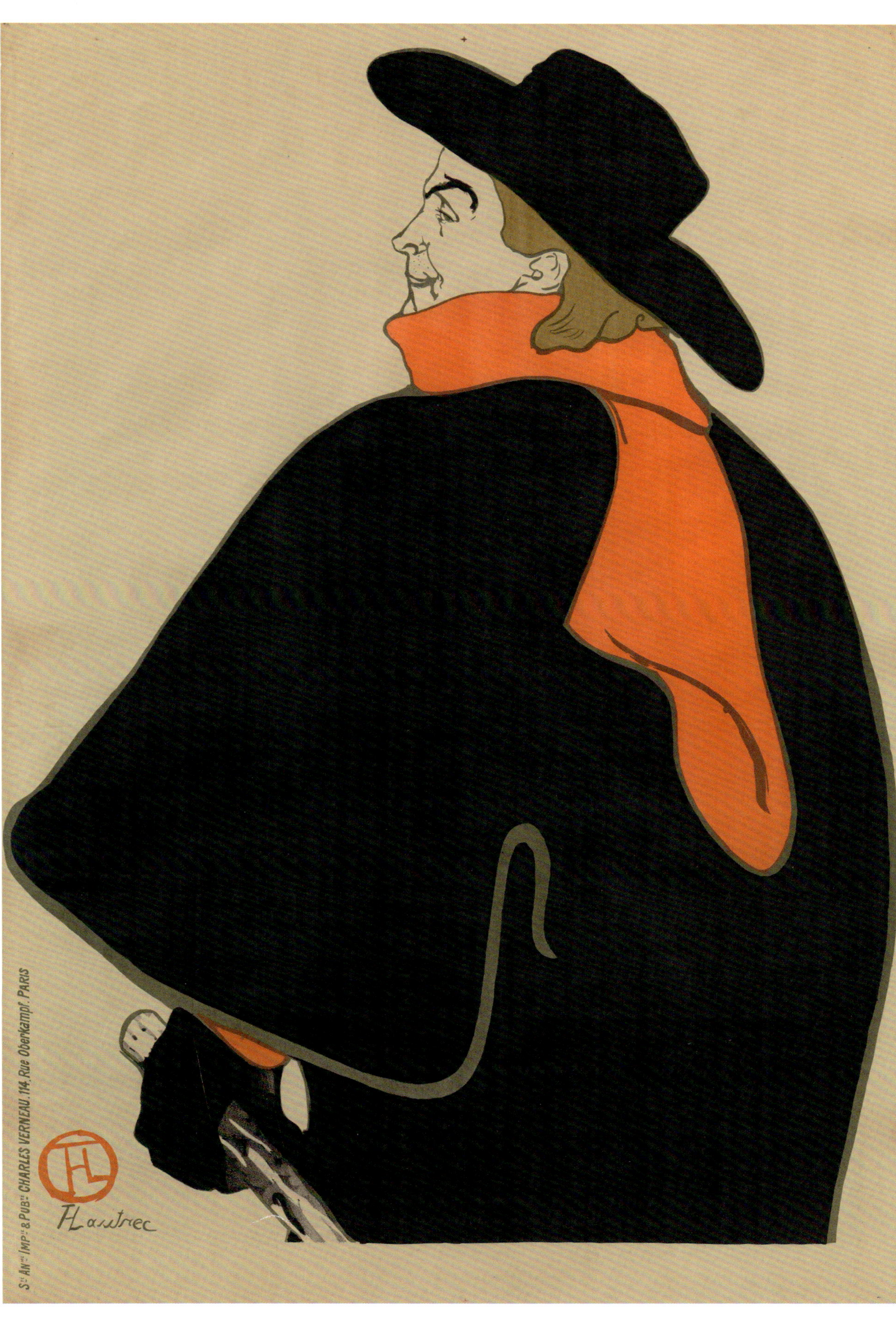
CHARLES VERNEAU. 114, Rue Oberkampf. PARIS
HLautrec

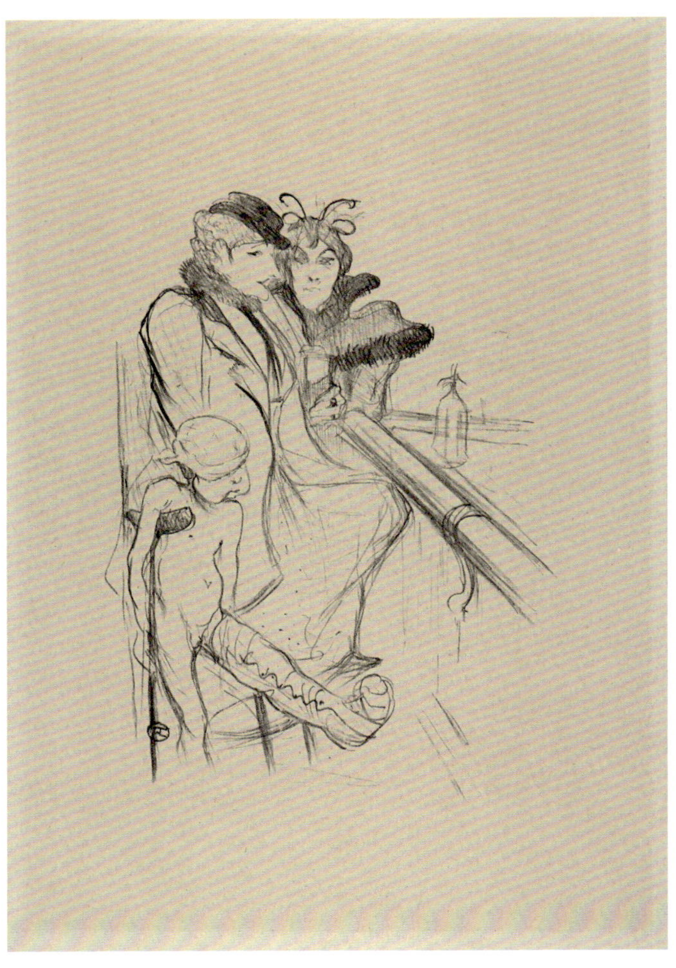

Plate 11
EROS VANNÉ (EROS VANQUISHED). 1894, published before 1910
Lithograph, sheet: 17 13/16 x 12 11/16 in. (45.2 x 32.3 cm)
Grace M. Mayer Bequest, 1997

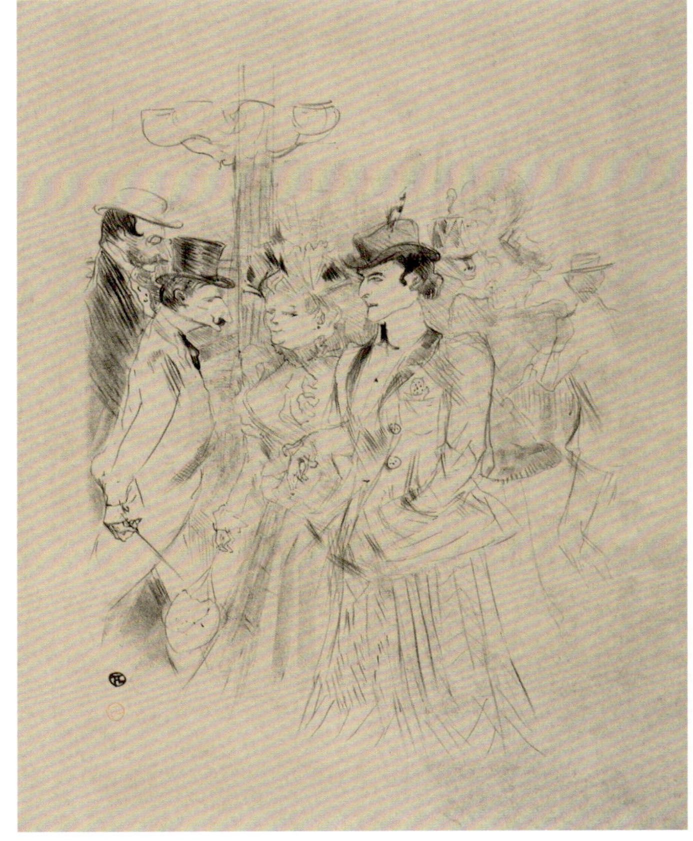

Plate 12
PROMENOIR (THE FOYER). 1898
Lithograph, sheet: 27 3/4 x 21 1/4 in. (70.5 x 54 cm)
Gift of Abby Aldrich Rockefeller, 1946

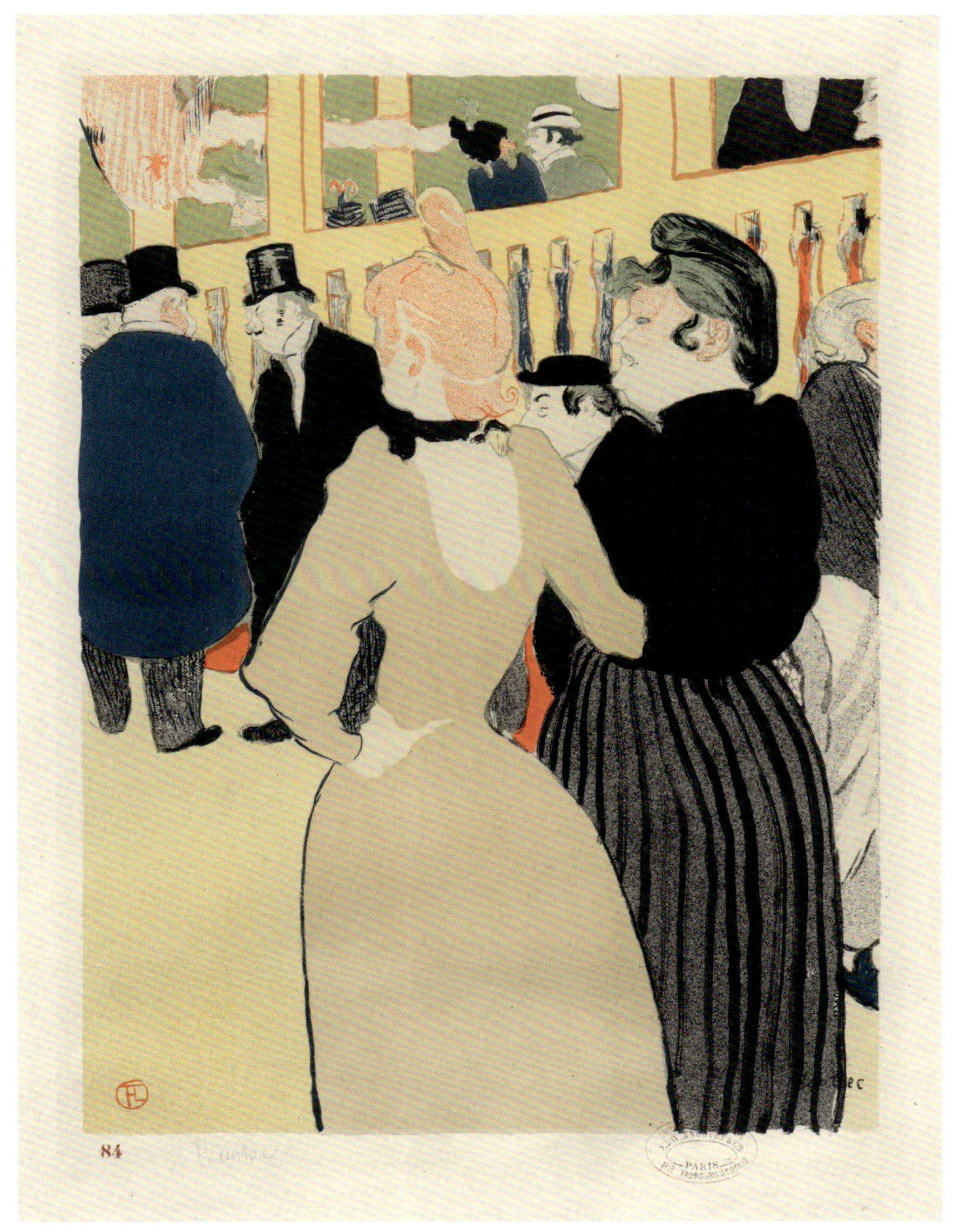

Plate 13

AU MOULIN ROUGE, LA GOULUE ET SA SŒUR
(**AT THE MOULIN ROUGE, LA GOULUE AND HER SISTER**). 1892

Lithograph, sheet: $25\frac{1}{4}$ x $19\frac{7}{16}$ in. (64.2 x 49.3 cm)

Gift of Abby Aldrich Rockefeller, 1946

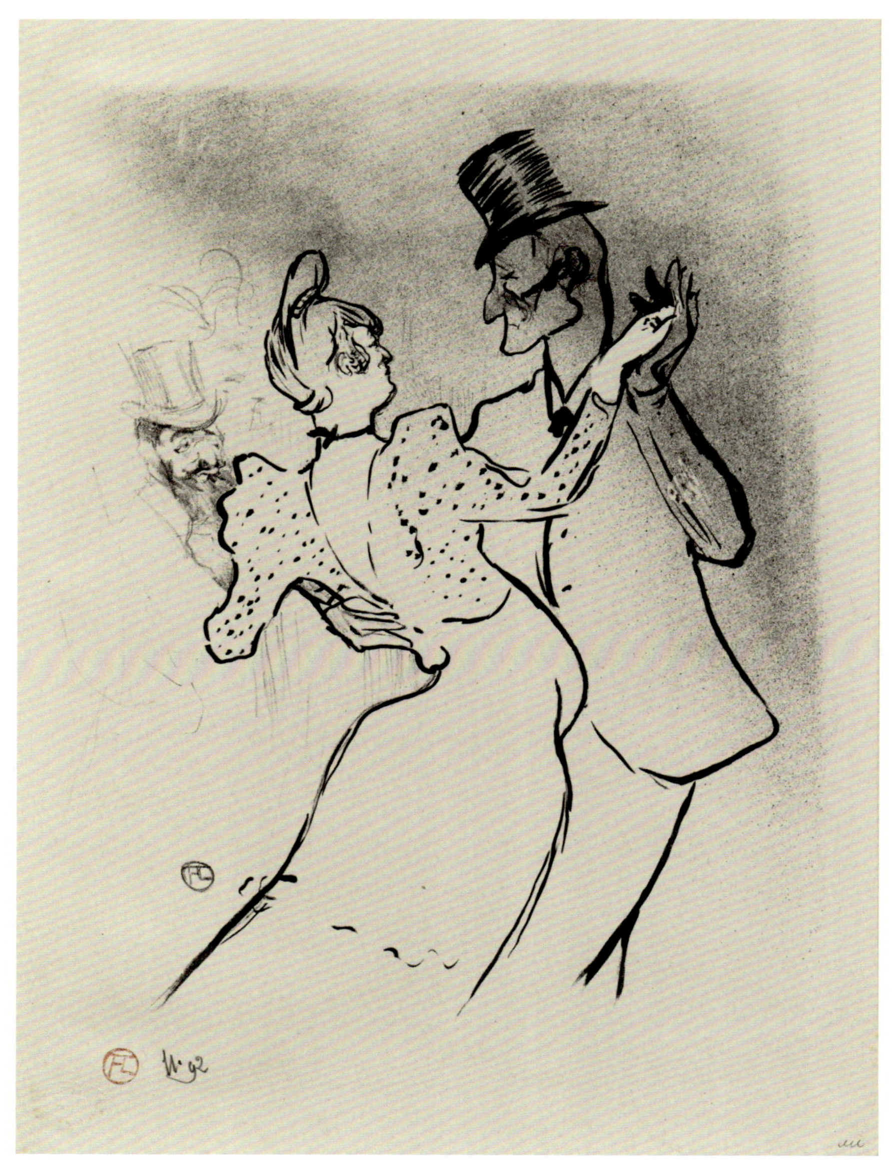

Plate 14

LA GOULUE. 1894

Lithograph, sheet: 14 15/16 x 11 in. (37.9 x 28 cm)

Gift of Abby Aldrich Rockefeller, 1946

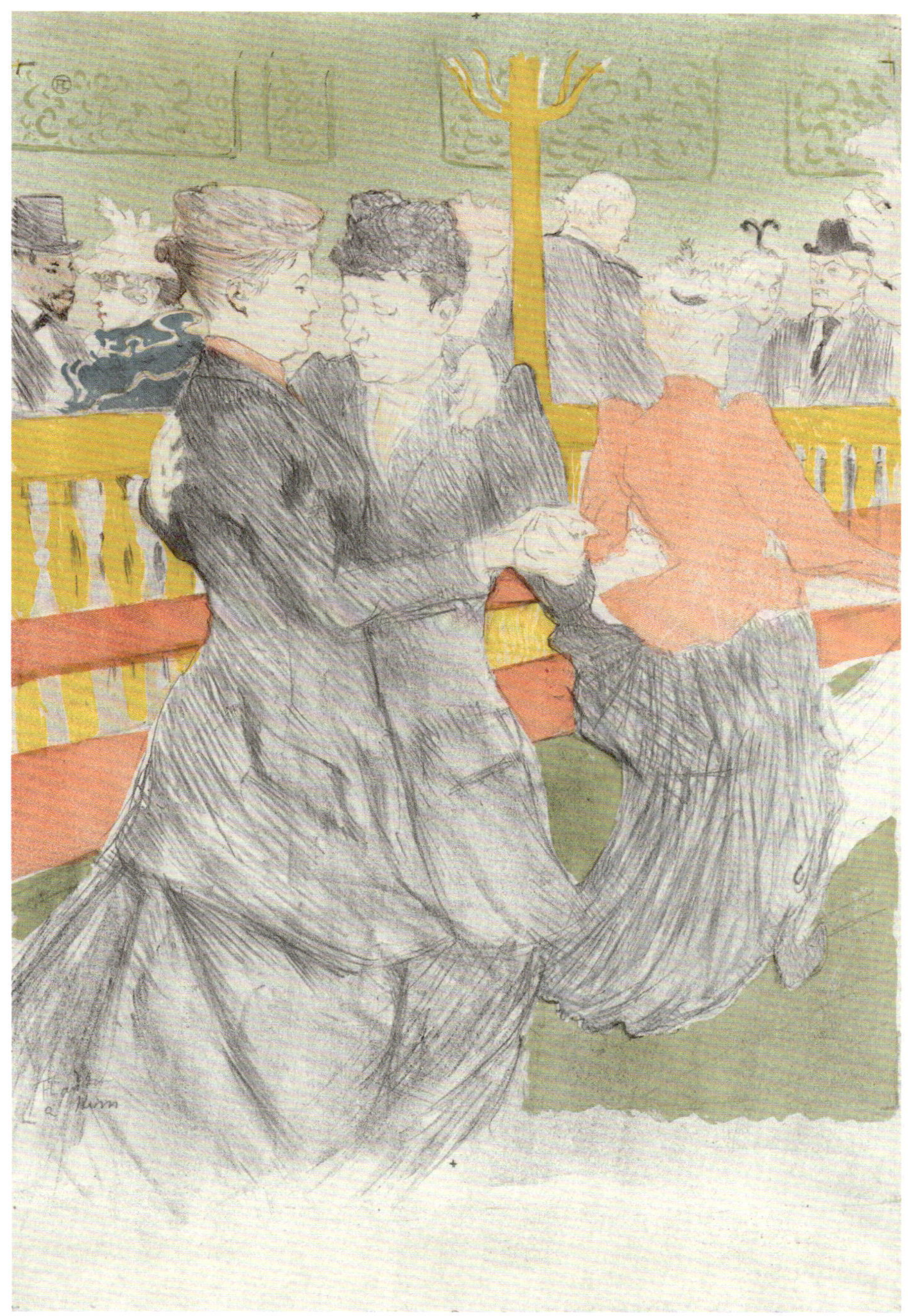

Plate 15
LA DANSE AU MOULIN ROUGE
(**THE DANCE AT THE MOULIN ROUGE**). 1897
Lithograph, sheet: 20½ x 14 in. (52.1 x 35.5 cm)
David and Peggy Rockefeller Collection

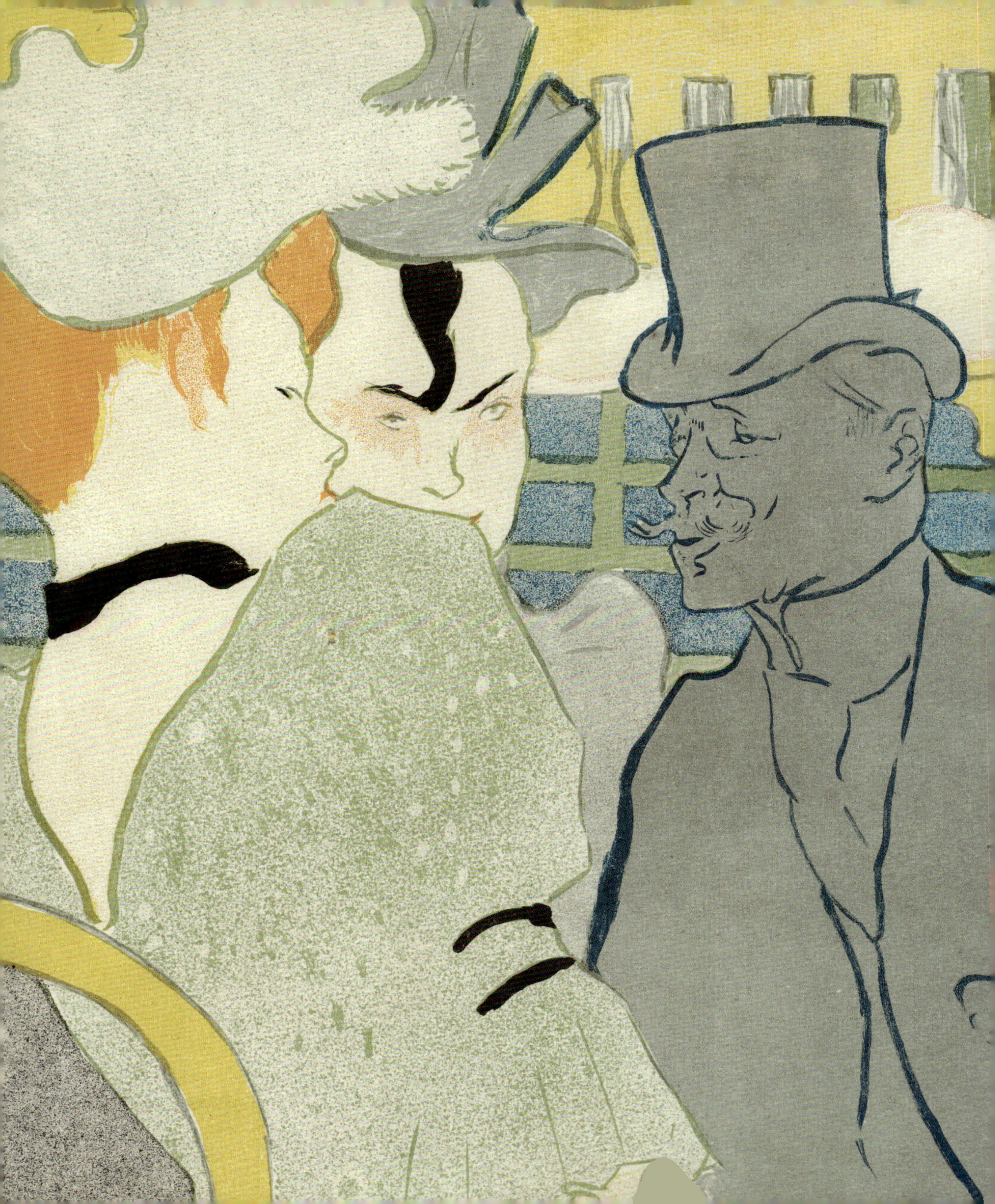

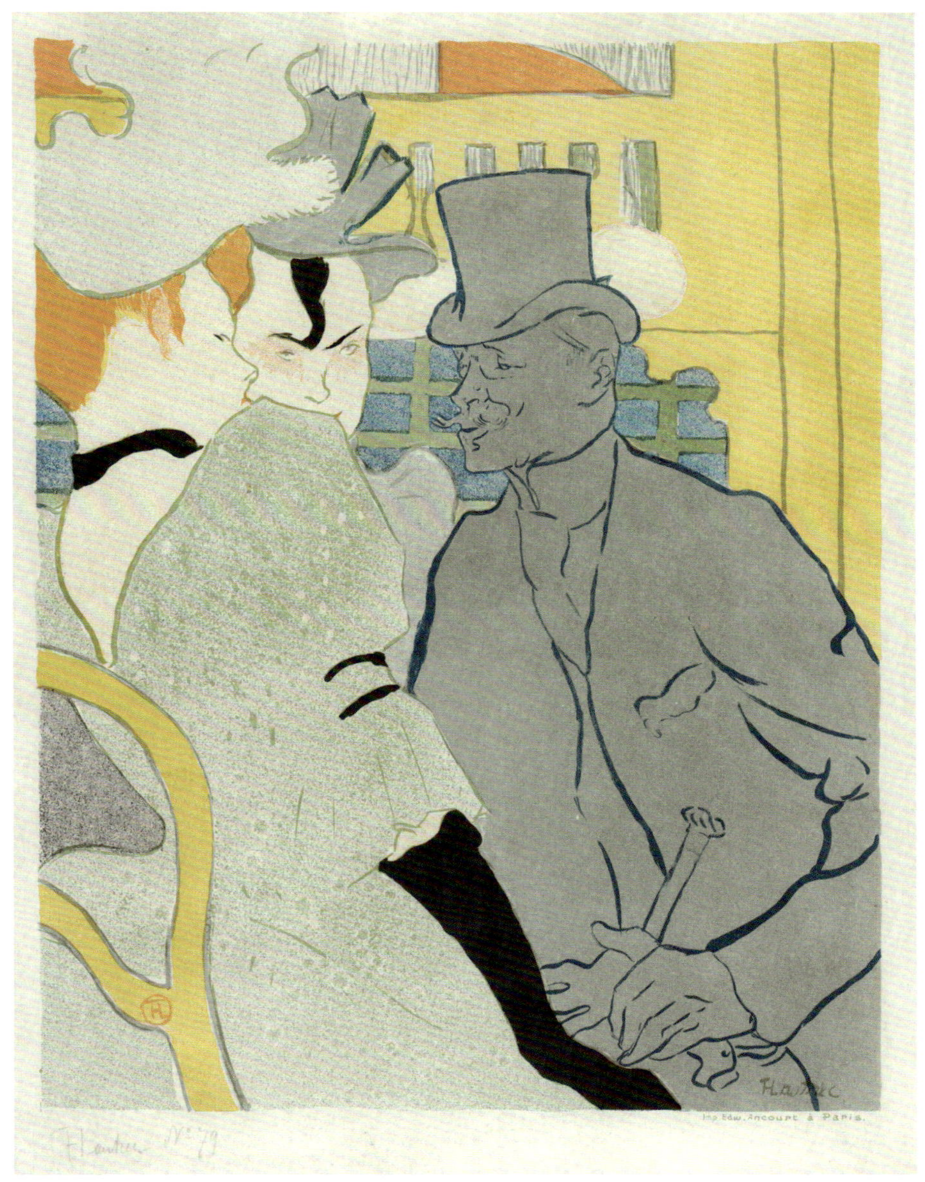

Plate 16

L'ANGLAIS AU MOULIN ROUGE
(**ENGLISHMAN AT THE MOULIN ROUGE**). 1892
Lithograph, sheet: 23½ x 19⅛ in. (59.7 x 48.5 cm)
David and Peggy Rockefeller Collection

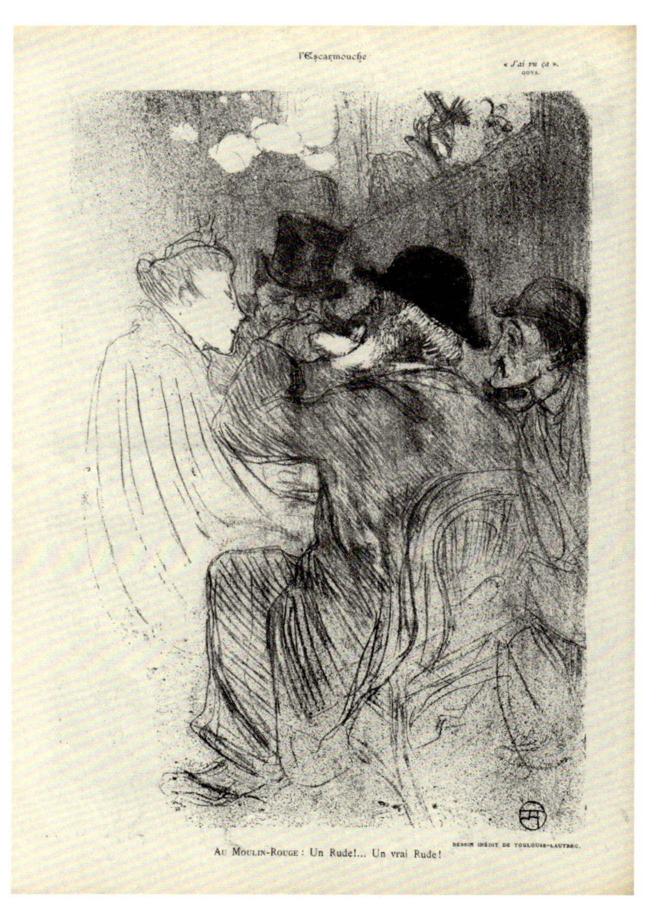

Plate 17
AU MOULIN ROUGE: UN RUDE! UN VRAI RUDE!
(AT THE MOULIN ROUGE: A RUFFIAN! A REAL RUFFIAN!)
from the journal **L'ESCARMOUCHE** (December 10, 1893)
Halftone relief, page: 15⅜ x 11¾ in. (39 x 29.9 cm)
The Louis E. Stern Collection, 1964

l'Escarmouche
« J'ai vu ça ».
Goya.
Au Moulin Rouge : L'Union franco-russe
Dessin inédit de Toulouse-Lautrec

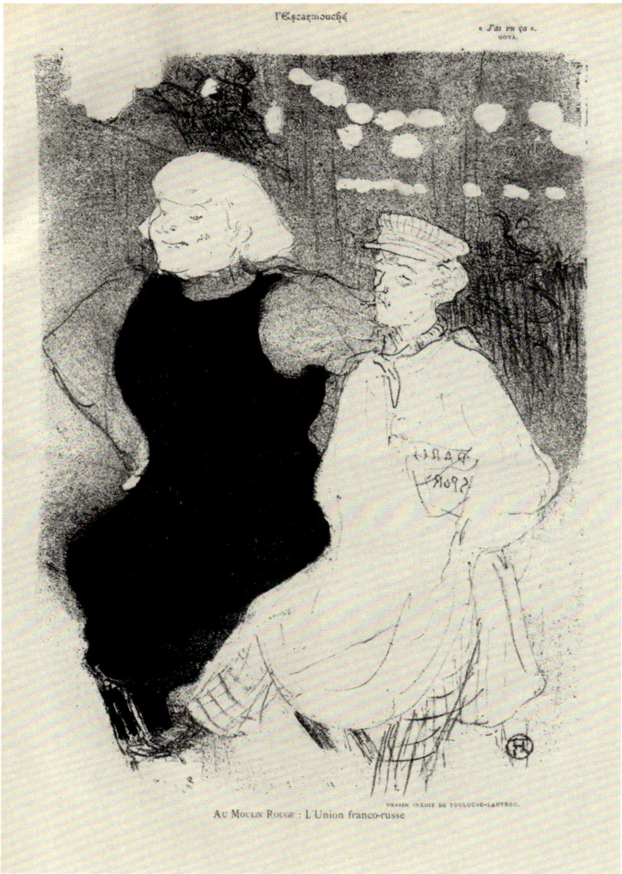

Plate 18
AU MOULIN ROUGE: L'UNION FRANCO-RUSSE
(AT THE MOULIN ROUGE: THE FRANCO-RUSSIAN UNION)
from the journal **L'ESCARMOUCHE** (January 7, 1894)
Halftone relief, page: 15⅜ x 11¾ in. (39 x 29.9 cm)
The Louis E. Stern Collection, 1964

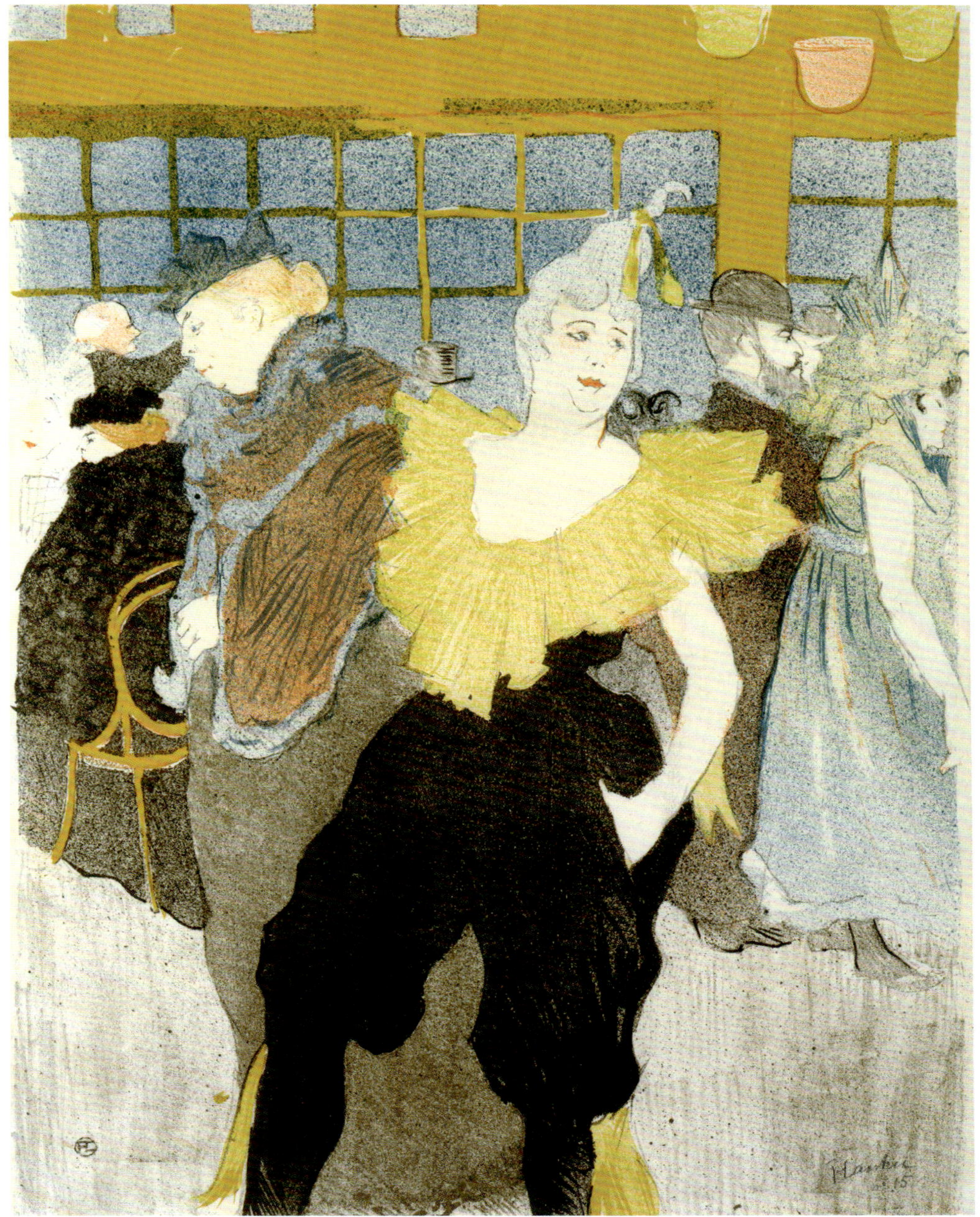

Plate 19

LA CLOWNESSE AU MOULIN ROUGE

(**THE CLOWNESS AT THE MOULIN ROUGE**). 1897

Lithograph, sheet: $15\frac{7}{8}$ x $12\frac{11}{16}$ in. (40.4 x 32.3 cm)

Gift of Abby Aldrich Rockefeller, 1946

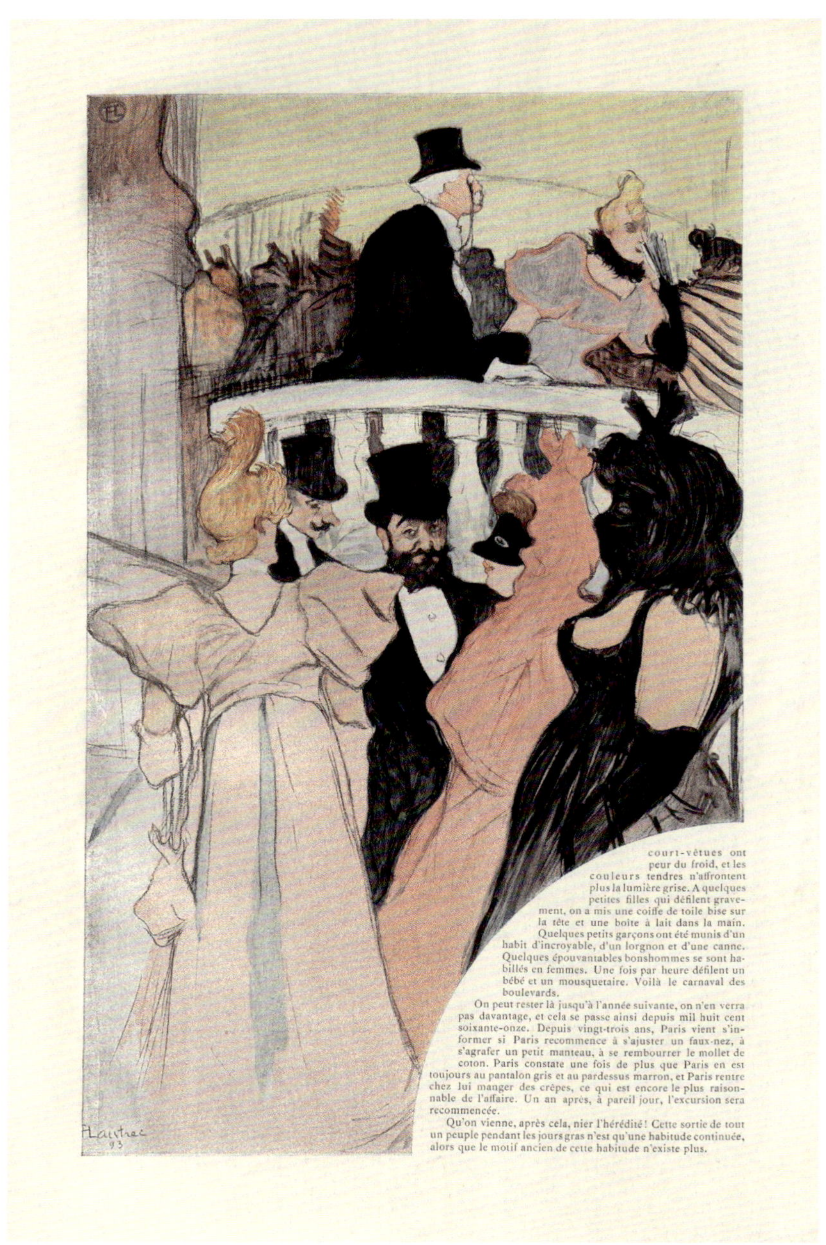

court-vêtues ont peur du froid, et les couleurs tendres n'affrontent plus la lumière grise. A quelques petites filles qui défilent gravement, on a mis une coiffe de toile bise sur la tête et une boite à lait dans la main. Quelques petits garçons ont été munis d'un habit d'incroyable, d'un lorgnon et d'une canne. Quelques épouvantables bonshommes se sont habillés en femmes. Une fois par heure défilent un bébé et un mousquetaire. Voilà le carnaval des boulevards.

On peut rester là jusqu'à l'année suivante, on n'en verra pas davantage, et cela se passe ainsi depuis mil huit cent soixante-onze. Depuis vingt-trois ans, Paris vient s'informer si Paris recommence à s'ajuster un faux-nez, à s'agrafer un petit manteau, à se rembourrer le mollet de coton. Paris constate une fois de plus que Paris en est toujours au pantalon gris et au pardessus marron, et Paris rentre chez lui manger des crêpes, ce qui est encore le plus raisonnable de l'affaire. Un an après, à pareil jour, l'excursion sera recommencée.

Qu'on vienne, après cela, nier l'hérédité! Cette sortie de tout un peuple pendant les jours gras n'est qu'une habitude continuée, alors que le motif ancien de cette habitude n'existe plus.

Plate 20

LE PLAISIR À PARIS: LES BALS ET LE CARNAVAL
(PLEASURE IN PARIS: BALLS AND CARNIVAL)
from the journal **LE FIGARO ILLUSTRÉ** (February 1894)
Halftone relief and line block, page: 16⅛ x 11 15/16 in. (41 x 30 cm)
The Museum of Modern Art Library, New York

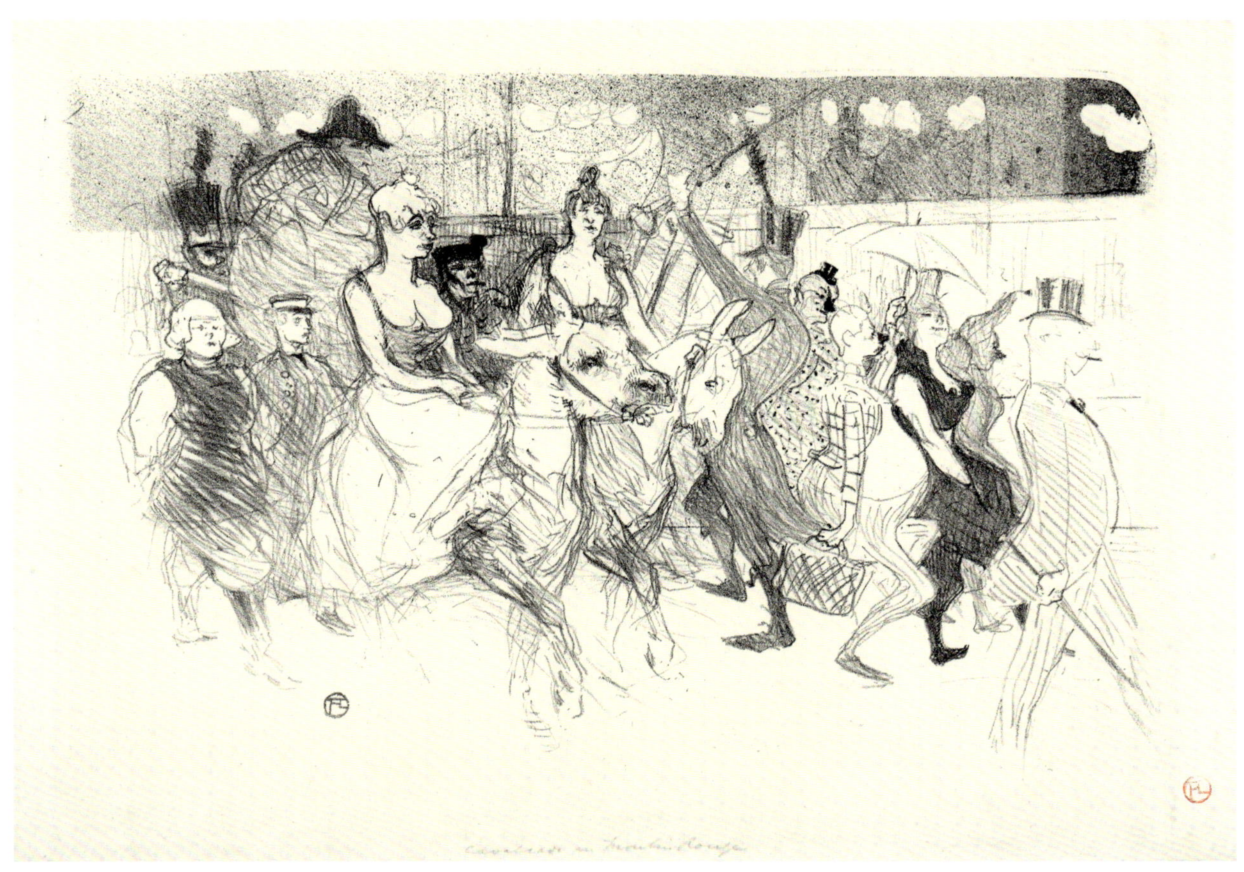

Plate 21
UNE REDOUTE AU MOULIN ROUGE
(**A GALA EVENING AT THE MOULIN ROUGE**). 1893
Lithograph, sheet: 14 13/16 x 21 7/8 in. (37.7 x 55.6 cm)
Gift of Abby Aldrich Rockefeller, 1946

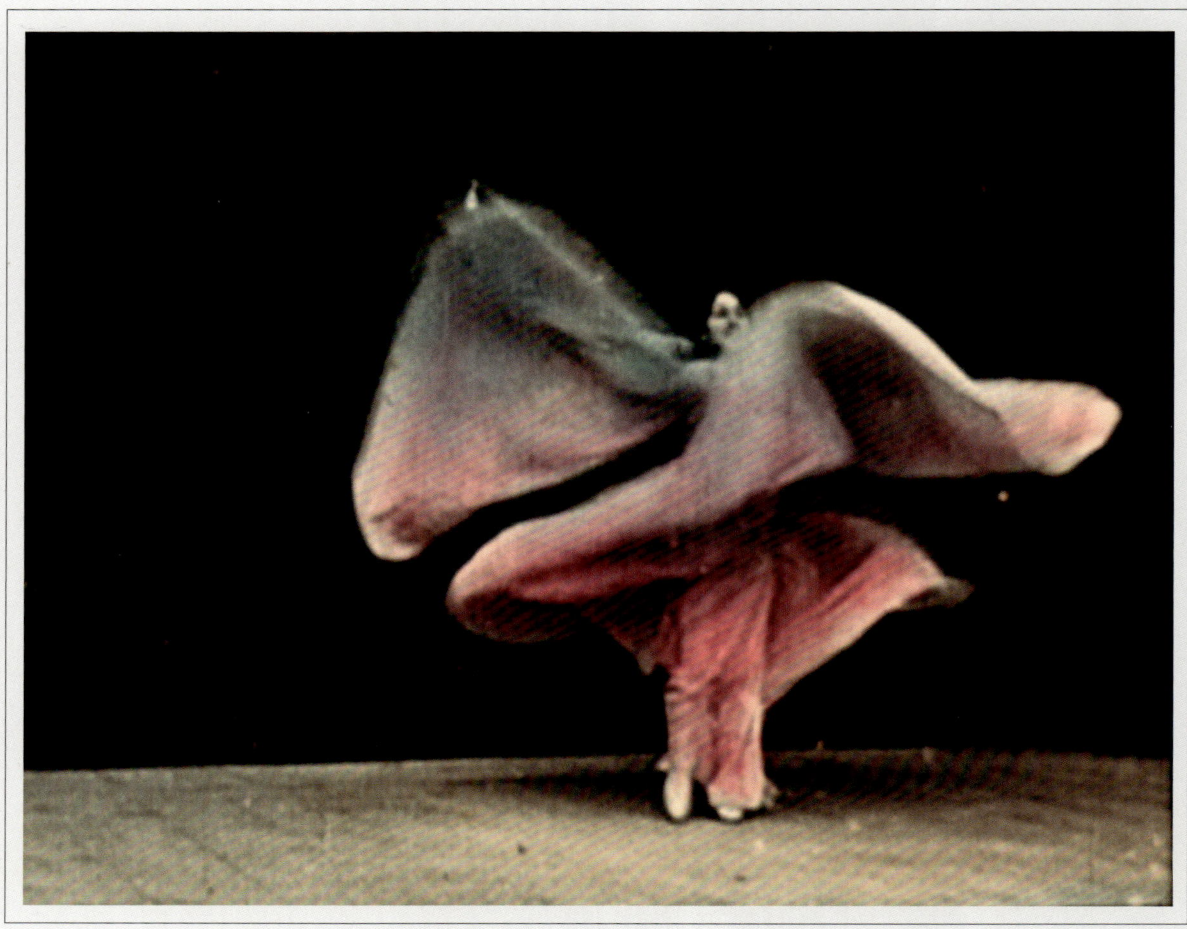

ON STAGE

Lautrec's fascination with a performer could manifest itself in a single image or in many, and while some of his *furias* did not inspire lasting legacies, others had an enduring impact. Loïe Fuller, an innovative American performer (and mentor to modern dance's Isadora Duncan), took Paris by storm in 1893. In Fuller's own words, she "created something new, something composed of light, color, music, and the dance,"[48] incorporating innovations in costume (dozens of yards of lightweight silk that she manipulated on bamboo poles so that it billowed and flowed around her), early electric lighting (with hand-turned colored gels over footlight bulbs that created ever-changing effects), and production design (dancing on a darkened stage in an unlit hall). In her debut at the Folies-Bergère in late 1892, her set included her signature serpentine dance as well as the violet dance, the butterfly dance, and the so-called white dance, in which fabric whirled magnificently around her, bathed in the glow of lights,

22. **AUGUSTE LUMIÈRE** (French, 1862–1954) and **LOUIS LUMIÈRE** (French, 1864–1948). A dancer imitating Loïe Fuller's serpentine dance. 1897. Film still (detail). Musée National d'Art Moderne, Centre Georges Pompidou, Paris

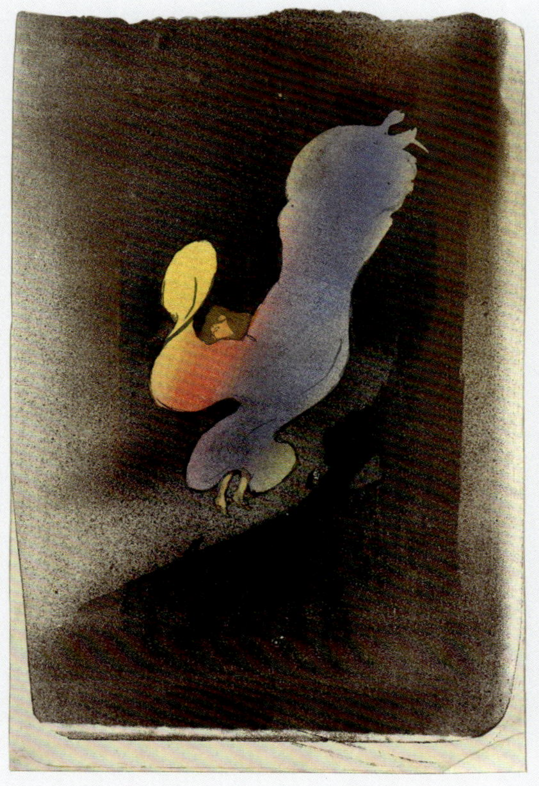

23. **HENRI DE TOULOUSE-LAUTREC**. *Miss Loïe Fuller*. 1893. Lithograph, 14½ x 10$\frac{9}{16}$ in. (36.8 x 26.8 cm). Bibliothèque Nationale de France, Paris

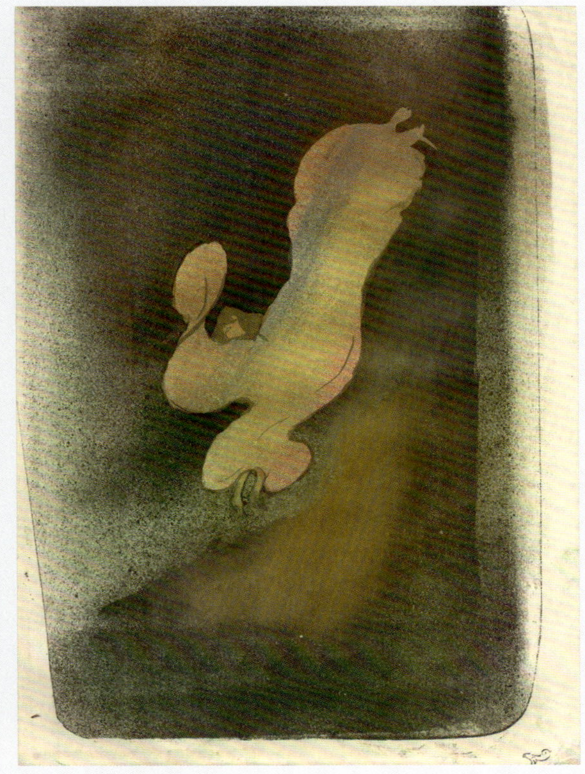

24. **HENRI DE TOULOUSE-LAUTREC**. *Miss Loïe Fuller*. 1893. Lithograph, 14½ x 10$\frac{9}{16}$ in. (36.8 x 26.8 cm). Boston Public Library, Print Department. Collection of Albert H. Wiggin

which were continually shifting in color. The audience was spellbound; one critic described her as "the marvelous dream-creature you see dancing madly in a vision swirling among her dappled veils, which change ten thousand times a minute."[49]

Artists were also enthralled, as the Lumière brothers attempted to capture her style of dance on film (fig. 22); James McNeill Whistler, Jules Chéret, and Emmanuel-Joseph-Raphael Orazi (fig. 25) to depict her on paper; and Théodore Rivière and Raoul François Larche to portray her in marble and bronze. But no one described the essence of Fuller as brilliantly as Lautrec in his masterful color lithograph of 1893 (pl. 22). A flowing, seemingly abstract form floats at the center of the rectangular picture plane. Only on closer examination does the scene come into focus: the neck of a double bass emerges from the shadowy foreground, suggesting the depth of the stage beyond, and the subject becomes discernible as that of the dancer, her head thrown back, her dainty feet peeking out from under her billowing gown. Each of the sixty impressions of this lithograph is inked in a unique combination of colors—green, yellow, orange, mauve, violet, blue, and rose—many of them dusted with metallic pigments to give a mysterious luster (figs. 23, 24). The image is daring in its simplicity and radical in its near abstraction, capturing flickering instants of Fuller's fluid appearance. If there is a precedent, it is the Japanese *ukiyo-e* tradition (an affinity noted

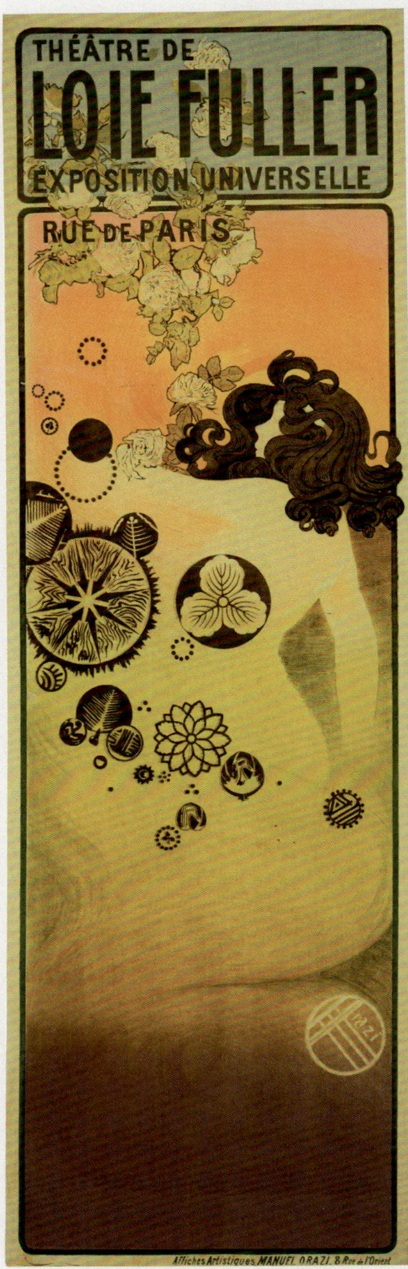

25. **EMMANUEL-JOSEPH-RAPHAEL ORAZI** (French, born Italy. 1860–1934). *Theater of Loïe Fuller: World's Fair*. 1900. Lithograph, 6 ft. 6¼ in. x 25¼ in. (198.7 x 64.1 cm). The Museum of Modern Art, New York. Gift of Mr. Joseph H. Heil, 1967

almost immediately in a *Figaro illustré* article[50] in February 1893), apparent in the blocked entry to the pictorial space, the isolation of the figure, the metallic accent, and even the subsummation of the performer to her costume.

Other *furias* inspired a flurry of depictions. In 1895 Lautrec was said to have seen Marcelle Lender in the revival of the operetta *Chilpéric* at the Théâtre des Variétés twenty times. His friend and collaborator Romain Coolus, who could stand to accompany Lautrec only six of those times, asked him what the attraction was. "I only come to see Lender's back," Lautrec said of the redhead. "Look carefully, you will rarely see anything as splendid."[51] Interestingly enough, only one of the twelve editioned lithographs that resulted from this burst of theatergoing depicts Lender from behind. Instead, she is seen frontally, with hands on hips, dancing the bolero (pl. 24), or fully costumed (pl. 25). The most ambitious depiction is an elaborate multicolored bust-length portrait, in which Lender, surrounded by areas of interlocking pattern that recall *ukiyo-e* portraits of courtesans, has massive poppies ornamenting her hair (pl. 23). This work was also a testament to Lautrec's growing international reputation, as the editor Julius Meier-Graefe included it in his German art magazine, *Pan*. This example of the new French art, which had so enchanted Meier-Graefe, was met with dismay and incredulity in Germany, where critics derided it as "decadentpoisonous."[52]

One of Lautrec's longtime muses was the acclaimed stage performer Yvette Guilbert, described as "the most brilliant star in the café-concert firmament today, [who has] completely revolutionized the style of presentation of songs. She is a master of the art of declaiming harmless obscenities in a nonchalant manner."[53] Guilbert was unique not only in her delivery but also in her look. Rather than adopting one of the popular costumes of the day—the frothy petticoats of the quadrille or the naughty baby gowns of May Milton or May Belfort—she modeled her style after the luminous wax head of a woman, once attributed to Raphael, from the Lille museum.

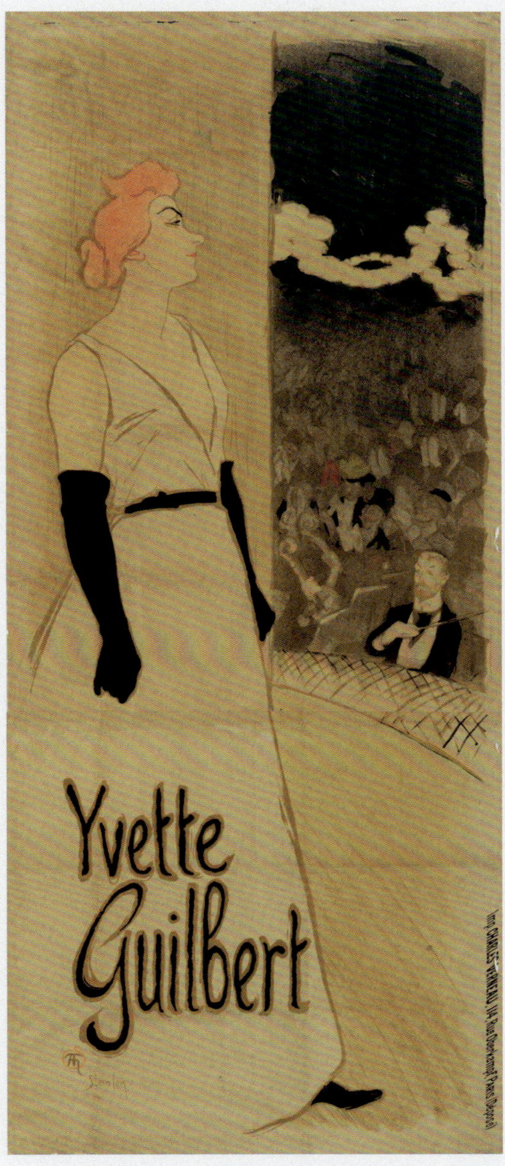

26. **THÉOPHILE-ALEXANDRE STEINLEN** (French, 1859–1923). *Yvette Guilbert*. 1894. Lithograph, 60 x 31½ in. (152.4 x 80 cm). The Museum of Modern Art, New York. Gift of Bates Lowry, 1968

As she said, her "pallor, her crown of red hair . . . in my opinion, her distinction came from her perfect simplicity."[54] Guilbert created a stage look that was markedly different from that of her contemporaries: ginger hennaed hair, pale skin, a formfitting and low-cut gown that accentuated her slender figure, and elbow-length black gloves. More of a *diseuse* than a chanteuse, she spoke her songs in a low tone: "Each syllable comes to us like an arrow shot from the throat, teeth and tongue, borne on a wave of clear, transparent sound, at once firm and frail, like a vibrating crystal."[55] She stood stock-still as she performed, extending her neck to emphasize its length, without gesturing or winking or mincing to further convey the often bawdy content of her material.

While Lautrec was deeply taken with Guilbert, it is unclear to what extent she returned his devoted admiration. To describe her first reaction to him, at a lunch with her lyricist Maurice Donnay, as unkind would be an understatement. She did not mince words in her description of his "oily, greasy skin," mouth like "a large open wound," and "flabby, flattened lips." She did, however, see something remarkable in his eyes—"Ah! They were beautiful, wide, warm, sparkling, so luminous"[56]—but she was conflicted about what Lautrec saw through them. Of an 1894 sketch of her, she wrote, "For the love of heaven don't make me so atrociously ugly! Just a little less!"[57] Certainly, she was the subject of many other posters at the time, by Théophile-Alexandre Steinlen (fig. 26), Henri-Gabriel Ibels, and others, all of them remarkably more flattering than those by Lautrec.

Lautrec's apotheosis of Guilbert may be seen in the 1894 album of seventeen lithographs, with an accompanying text by Gustave Geffroy that goes into great detail about the performer's character and, more generally, the milieu of the cabarets and café-concerts (pls. 26–33). As is so often the case in Lautrec's oeuvre, the images are not portraits but rather summations of the performer, with the silhouette of her gown, extended neck, and black gloves signaling her identity more than any direct likeness.

The book functions like a manga, with a series of sketched studies of different on- and offstage postures: arriving at the theater, powdering her face, meeting with admirers. The volume was met with some derision, from critiques of the unflattering nature of the depictions to the color in which it was printed, described by one critic as "goose-shit green"[58] (a color choice that may have been inspired by the green gown that Guilbert wore in the winter). One fan of the book rapturously declared it "a step in the history of publishing. . . . Nothing could be more seductive than the union of Toulouse-Lautrec's lithographs and Gustave Geffroy's text."[59]

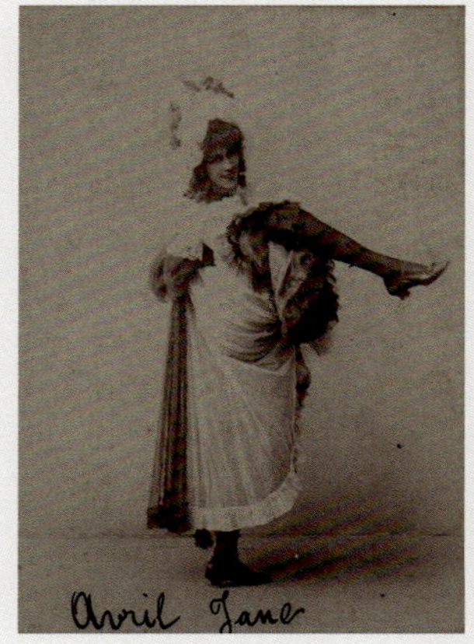

27. Jane Avril. c. 1893. Photograph by Paul Sescau (French, 1858–1926). Biblioteca Nacional de España. American Board of the Colección Fernández Ardavín/Leonard Parish

The performer with the greatest long-term presence in Lautrec's work was the dancer Jane Avril, whom he depicted many times between 1892 and 1899. Also known as La Mélinite (the name of an explosive used by the French government), Avril was born in 1868 to an unwed mother. She suffered an unhappy childhood before being diagnosed with chorea, a neurological disorder that causes rolling spasmodic bodily movements, and admitted to Pitié-Salpêtrière Hospital for two years of treatment. Avril found her "cure" in dance and her calling in a high-kicking, frenzied quadrille, ironically enough mining her own illness for her distinctive movements. Lautrec perhaps saw a kindred spirit in this untraditional redhead: Avril had a facial tic, an unremarkably endowed figure, and a chronic illness, and yet she found success, satisfaction, acceptance, and even public adoration.

In 1893, when Avril returned to the stage after suffering a flare-up of chorea, Lautrec depicted her with an elegant economy of means in *Le Café concert* (pl. 34) and in an elaborate color poster she commissioned for her stint at the Jardin de Paris (pl. 35). In this unusual and inventive composition, Lautrec extended the neck of the double bass up and around to follow the slightly irregular outline of the lithographic stone. Contained within the resulting bubble is the performer in her reverie, her signature bonnet atop her head, petticoats flashing as she clasps her hands beneath her raised knee in a posture that she made famous in her publicity photos (fig. 27). At lower right, the bass player appears as a flattened caricature, his brow furrowed in concentration as his hairy fingers clasp the neck of his instrument. With its striking flat panels of secondary color and *ukiyo-e*–inspired vertiginous diagonals, the poster found many admirers on the streets of Paris, and Lautrec fielded press requests from *L'Art français* and *Courrier français*, among others, to reproduce it on their pages.

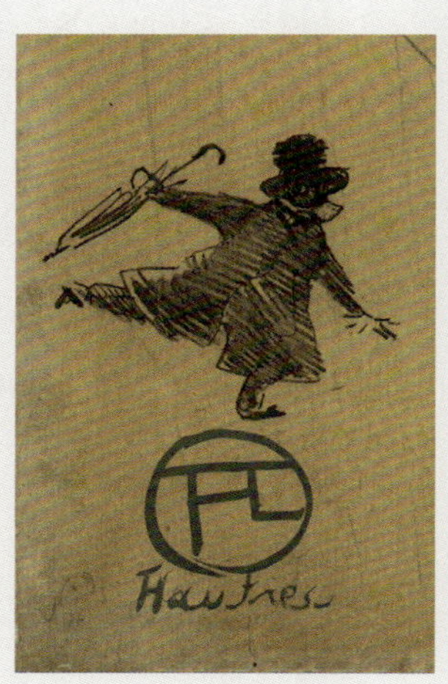

28. Lautrec's remarque featuring a figure with an umbrella

Avril prevailed on the artist to help advertise her London tour in 1896, when she performed as part of a troupe led by Mademoiselle Églantine (pl. 36). In the poster, he pays special attention to her—the redhead with legs akimbo stepping out of line from the other dancers. A remarque on an earlier state shows a figure in a trench coat, holding an umbrella (fig. 28), likely a reference to London's notoriously rainy weather and to Avril's rough sea passage from Paris for the tour.[60]

Lautrec's final commission from Avril, which was never used publicly, came in 1899, when the artist had entered his final decline. Clad in her customary hat, Avril is shown as a simplified flat shape, determined by a single, flowing contour. A snake wraps around her dress and she throws up her hands in mock horror at the sight (pl. 37).[61] Lautrec often worked from a combination of photography and what he committed to memory during his sketching sessions, particularly during this period of deterioration and hospitalization.[62] He might have recalled a recently rediscovered publicity photo showing Avril in a serpent-motif dress in 1892 (fig. 29)[63]—the time Fuller was attempting to trademark her serpent dance to prevent the many imitations that had sprung up. Usually, a multicolored motif such as this one would have required several stones, but working closely with his friend, drinking partner, and printshop sidekick Henri Stern (whose name appears in the right margin), Lautrec found an inventive and economical way to combine several colors in a kind of rainbow roll.

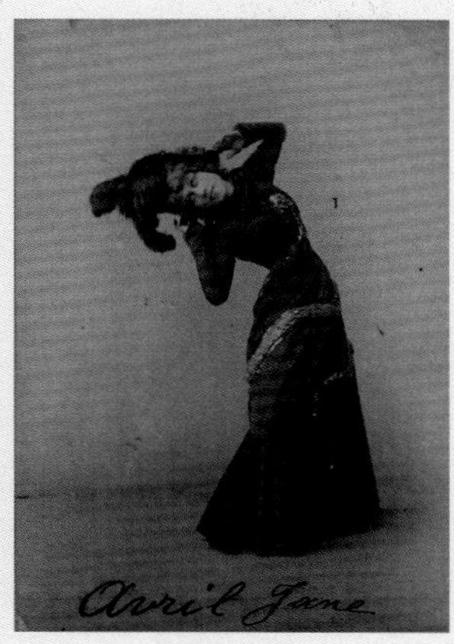

29. Jane Avril. 1892. Photograph by Paul Sescau (French, 1858–1926). Biblioteca Nacional de España. American Board of the Colección Fernández Ardavín/Leonard Parish

Lautrec and Avril were friends as well as artist and muse. He once dressed as her for a costume ball, donning her signature coat, hat, and feather boa (fig. 30). He also invited her into his daytime universe—his second home, at the printshop—perhaps even soliciting her opinion. In 1893 he depicted Avril in decidedly offstage dress, dwarfed by a massive coat, at the Ancourt printshop, inspecting a print while Père Cotelle mans the lithographic press (pl. 38). She is the only performer that he also portrayed offstage, in her everyday life. In an 1893 poster for Divan Japonais (pl. 39), a café-concert that had been recently refurbished with a Japanese-themed decor, Avril is off duty at the bar. A brutally cropped Guilbert, easily identifiable by her long black gloves and distinctive posture, performs on the stage. Approaching Avril is Édouard Dujardin, an intellectual, music critic, and co-editor, with Avril's onetime lover Téodor de Wyzewa, of the *Revue Wagnérienne.* Lautrec's sophisticated image works on multiple levels. Effectively serving as an engaging advertisement for Parisian nightlife, it shows one performer relaxing at a bar while another well-known singer is onstage, and also makes a nod to artistic circles with the inclusion of Dujardin, an advocate of *japonisme*—the style to which both the poster and the café owed a debt.

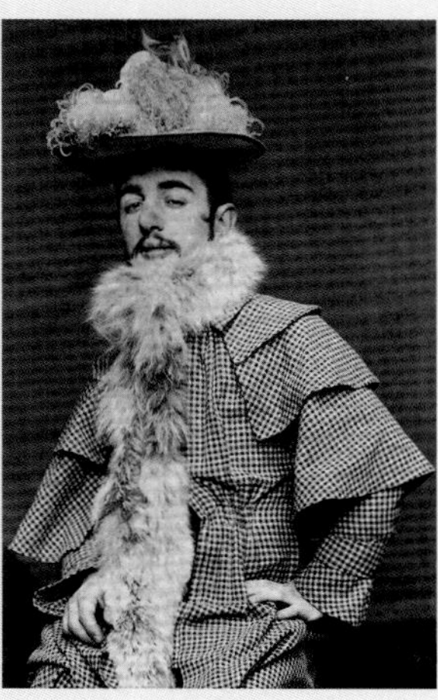

30. Lautrec dressed in a woman's hat and boa. c. 1894. Musée Toulouse-Lautrec, Albi, France

Lautrec and Avril were bound together as much by his depictions of her and their lasting resonance as by their friendship. The art critic Arsène Alexandre wrote in 1893, "A woman who knows perfectly how to find and to announce her unique character with the right formula and the right clothes is a true work of art. They've existed in every era, these unrecognized artists; but they don't always find a painter like Lautrec to keep their memory alive for those who, later, wish to understand the raffish charms of the subtlety they possessed."[64] Avril was one of the few performers who understood what Lautrec had done for her career: "It is more than certain that I owe him the fame that I enjoyed, dating from his first poster of me."[65]

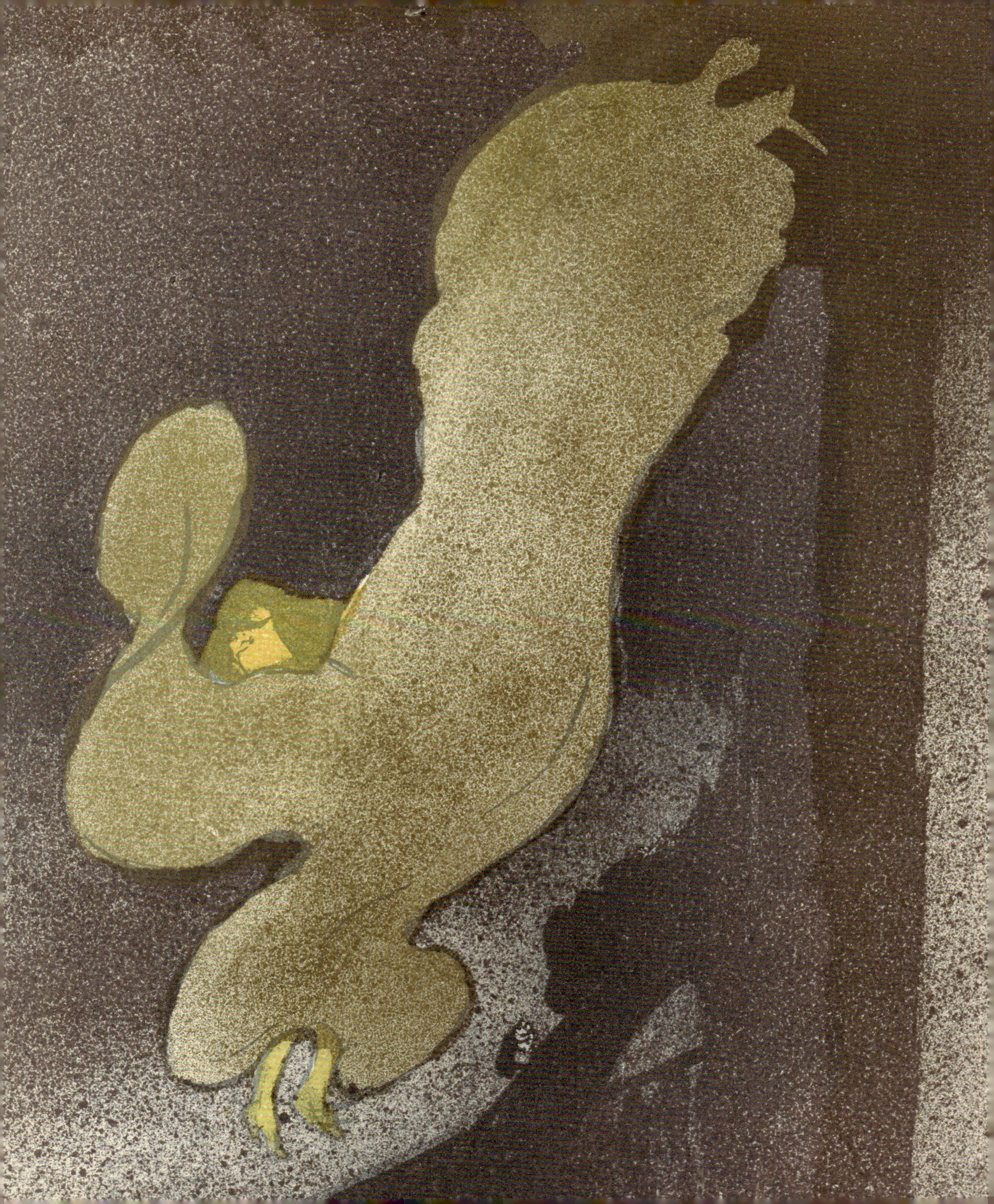

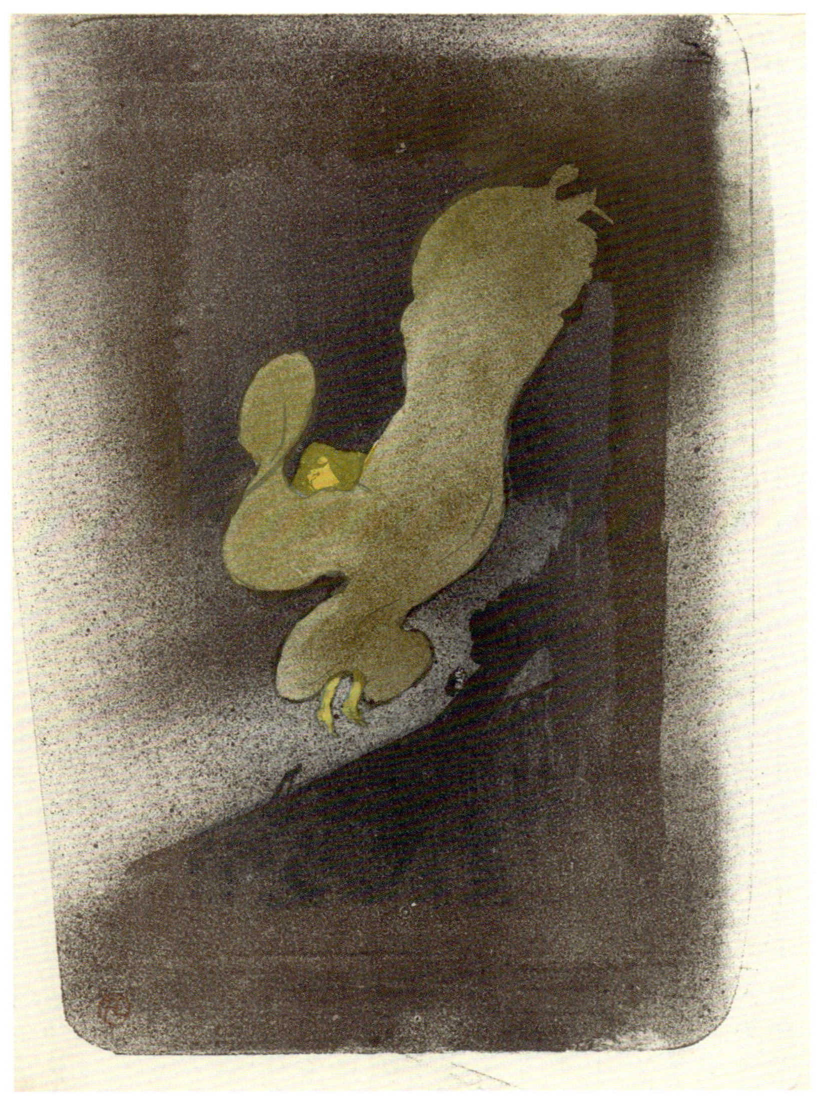

Plate 22
MISS LOÏE FULLER. 1893
Lithograph, sheet: 14 15⁄16 x 11 1⁄8 in. (38 x 28.2 cm)
General Print Fund, 2006

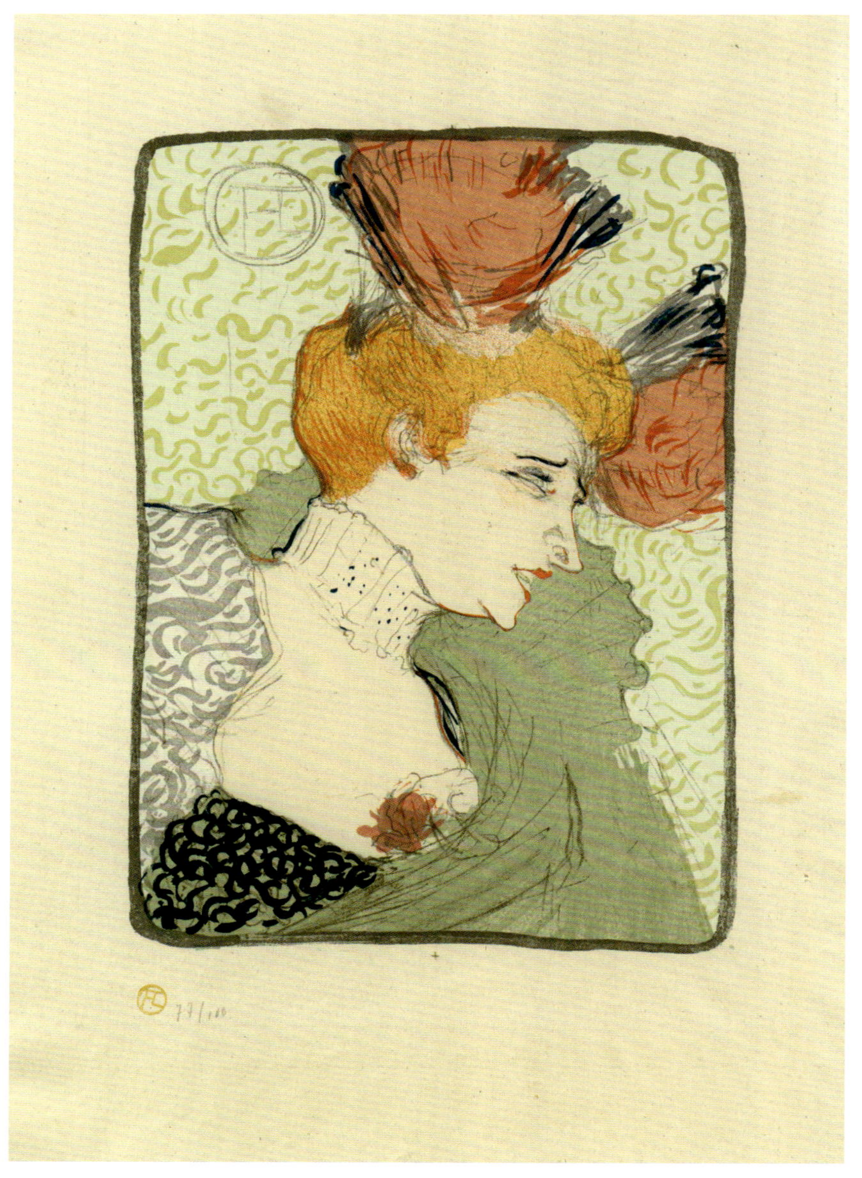

Plate 23

MADEMOISELLE MARCELLE LENDER, EN BUSTE
(**MADEMOISELLE MARCELLE LENDER, HALF-LENGTH**). 1895
Lithograph, sheet: 21 7/16 x 15 11/16 in. (54.5 x 39.8 cm)
Gift of Abby Aldrich Rockefeller, 1946

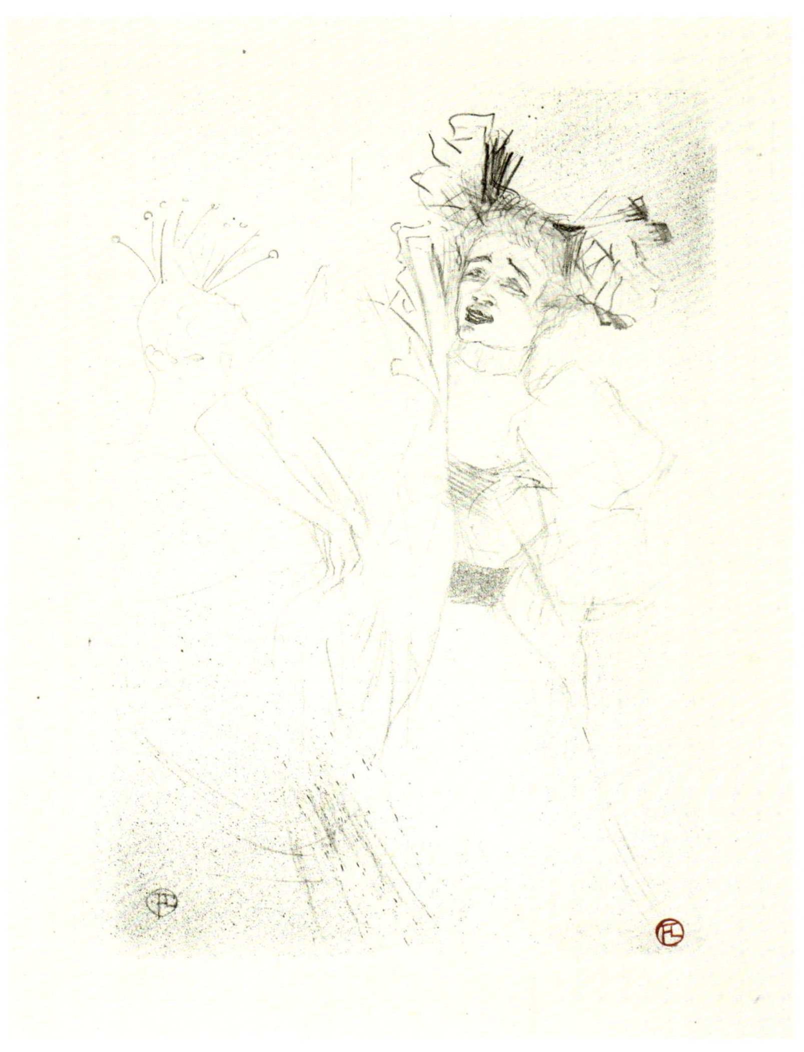

Plate 24

LENDER DE FACE, DANS "CHILPÉRIC" (LENDER, FRONTAL VIEW, IN "CHILPÉRIC"). 1895

Lithograph, sheet: 21 7/16 x 11 7/8 in. (54.5 x 30.1 cm)

Gift of Abby Aldrich Rockefeller, 1946

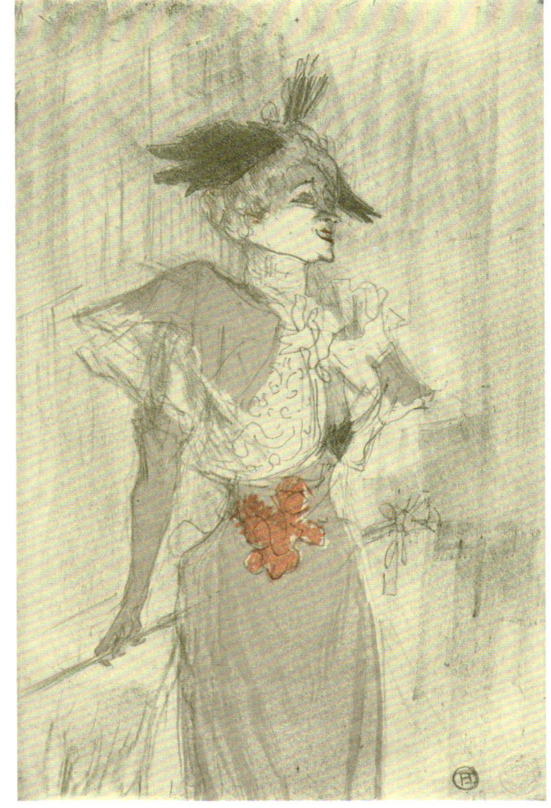

Plate 25

MADEMOISELLE MARCELLE LENDER, DEBOUT (MADEMOISELLE MARCELLE LENDER, STANDING). 1895

Lithograph, sheet: 14 3/8 x 9 1/2 in. (36.5 x 24.2 cm)

Gift of Abby Aldrich Rockefeller, 1946

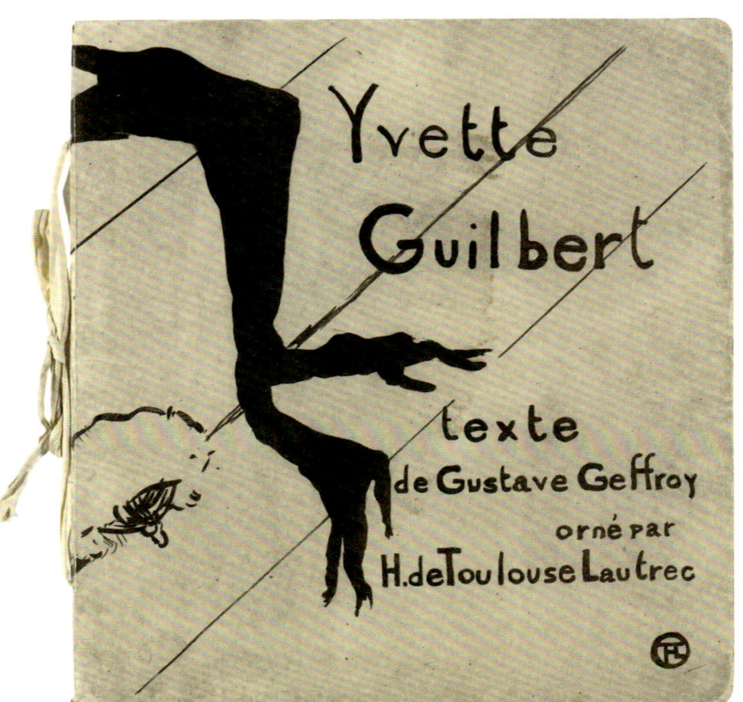

Plate 26
Cover for the illustrated book
YVETTE GUILBERT by Gustave Geffroy. 1894
Lithograph, page: 15 1/16 x 15 3/16 in. (38.3 x 38.5 cm)
The Louis E. Stern Collection, 1964

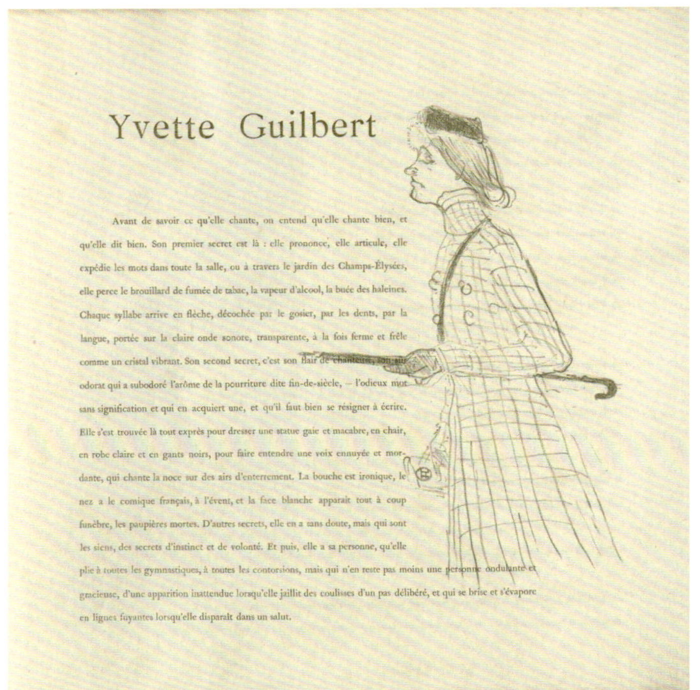

Yvette Guilbert

Avant de savoir ce qu'elle chante, on entend qu'elle chante bien, et qu'elle dit bien. Son premier secret est là : elle prononce, elle articule, elle expédie les mots dans toute la salle, ou à travers le jardin des Champs-Élysées, elle perce le brouillard de fumée de tabac, la vapeur d'alcool, la buée des haleines. Chaque syllabe arrive en flèche, décochée par le gosier, par les dents, par la langue, portée sur la claire onde sonore, transparente, à la fois ferme et frêle comme un cristal vibrant. Son second secret, c'est son flair de [illegible] odorat qui a subodoré l'arôme de la pourriture dite fin-de-siècle, – l'odieux mot sans signification et qui en acquiert une, et qu'il faut bien se résigner à écrire. Elle s'est trouvée là tout exprès pour dresser une statue gaie et macabre, en chair, en robe claire et en gants noirs, pour faire entendre une voix ennuyée et mordante, qui chante la noce sur des airs d'enterrement. La bouche est ironique, le nez a le comique français, à l'évent, et la face blanche apparait tout à coup funèbre, les paupières mortes. D'autres secrets, elle en a sans doute, mais qui sont les siens, des secrets d'instinct et de volonté. Et puis, elle a sa personne, qu'elle plie à toutes les gymnastiques, à toutes les contorsions, mais qui n'en reste pas moins une personne ondulante et gracieuse, d'une apparition inattendue lorsqu'elle jaillit des coulisses d'un pas délibéré, et qui se brise et s'évapore en lignes fuyantes lorsqu'elle disparait dans un salut.

Plates 27–29
Pages from the illustrated book
YVETTE GUILBERT by Gustave Geffroy. 1894
Lithograph, page: 15 1/16 x 15 3/16 in. (38.3 x 38.5 cm)
The Louis E. Stern Collection, 1964

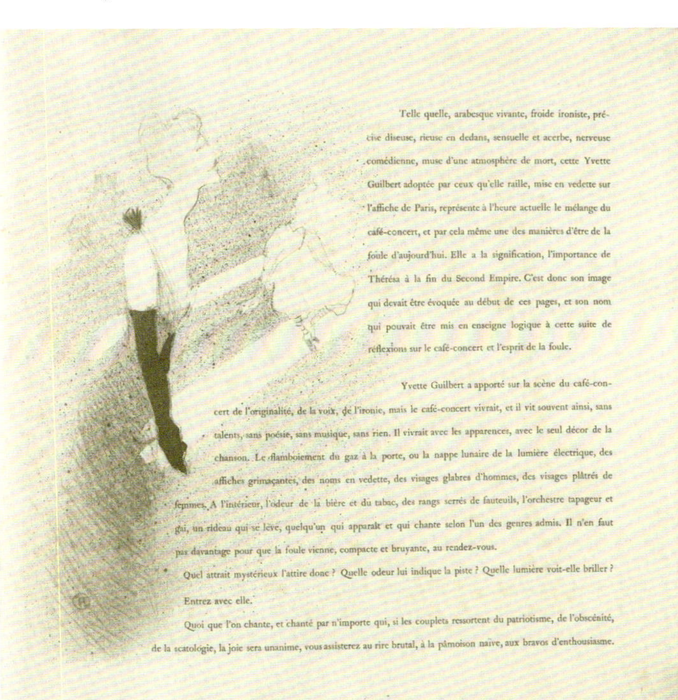

Telle quelle, arabesque vivante, froide ironiste, précise diseuse, rieuse en dedans, sensuelle et acerbe, nerveuse comédienne, muse d'une atmosphère de mort, cette Yvette Guilbert adoptée par ceux qu'elle raille, mise en vedette sur l'affiche de Paris, représente à l'heure actuelle le mélange du café-concert, et par cela même une des manières d'être de la foule d'aujourd'hui. Elle a la signification, l'importance de Thérésa à la fin du Second Empire. C'est donc son image qui devait être évoquée au début de ces pages, et son nom qui pouvait être mis en enseigne logique à cette suite de réflexions sur le café-concert et l'esprit de la foule.

Yvette Guilbert a apporté sur la scène du café-concert de l'originalité, de la voix, de l'ironie, mais le café-concert vivrait, et il vit souvent ainsi, sans talents, sans poésie, sans musique, sans rien. Il vivrait avec les apparences, avec le seul décor de la chanson. Le flamboiement du gaz à la porte, ou la nappe lunaire de la lumière électrique, des affiches grimaçantes, des noms en vedette, des visages glabres d'hommes, des visages plâtrés de femmes. A l'intérieur, l'odeur de la bière et du tabac, des rangs serrés de fauteuils, l'orchestre tapageur et gai, un rideau qui se lève, quelqu'un qui apparaît et qui chante selon l'un des genres admis. Il n'en faut pas davantage pour que la foule vienne, compacte et bruyante, au rendez-vous.

Quel attrait mystérieux l'attire donc ? Quelle odeur lui indique la piste ? Quelle lumière voit-elle briller ?

Entrez avec elle.

Quoi que l'on chante, et chanté par n'importe qui, si les couplets ressortent du patriotisme, de l'obscénité, de la scatologie, la joie sera unanime, vous assisterez au rire brutal, à la pâmoison naïve, aux bravos d'enthousiasme.

choisissent les pièces dont ils veulent se donner les représentations de lecture à eux-mêmes, sans décors et sans acteurs, sur la scène de l'imagination.

Pour les autres, l'important, qu'ils l'avouent donc, est de sortir de chez eux où ils s'ennuient, et de s'en aller n'importe où chercher la lumière, le bruit, et la complicité tacite de la foule, des êtres semblables à eux, de la cohue des ennuyés.

En venir là, à cette constatation, c'est en venir, non à la défense du café-concert, — le monstre est vivace, et nul ne défendrait son insolente santé, — mais à la défense, ou plutôt, à l'explication du public du café-concert.

On n'a pas tout dit quand on a dit l'abjection du spectacle, le bas-fond remué, la montée de ruisseau, la débâcle de fange. Le réquisitoire a souvent été fait, et il est facilement fait, il se formule de lui-même.

Mais cette masse riante, qui applaudit les niaiseries et les cochonneries, pourquoi est-elle là ? Tous ces gens qui pourraient donner leurs cinquante sous au Drame, à la Comédie, ou à l'Opéra...

Comment dites-vous cela ?

Quelle erreur est la vôtre ! Ces cinquante sous, ils pourraient les porter ailleurs, mais savez-vous bien à quelles conditions ? Avez-vous réfléchi aux misères et aux vexations de la vie, à tout ce qui poursuit le misérable homme, la pauvre unité sociale, jusque dans ses plaisirs ? Ces cinquante sous, pris sur le nécessaire, sur la paie de la semaine, sur les appointements du mois, sur les bénéfices de la boutique, on n'est pas

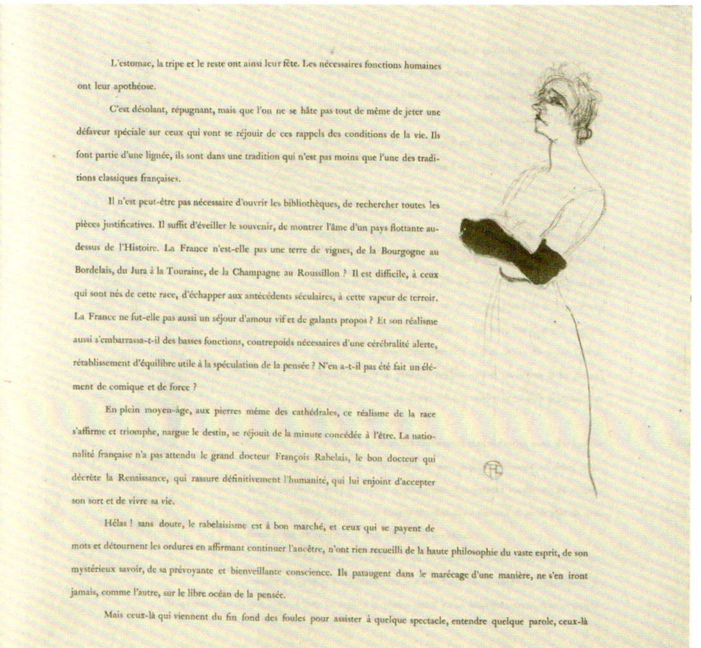

L'estomac, la tripe et le reste ont ainsi leur fête. Les nécessaires fonctions humaines ont leur apothéose.

C'est désolant, répugnant, mais que l'on ne se hâte pas tout de même de jeter une défaveur spéciale sur ceux qui vont se réjouir de ces rappels des conditions de la vie. Ils font partie d'une lignée, ils sont dans une tradition qui n'est pas moins que l'une des traditions classiques françaises.

Il n'est peut-être pas nécessaire d'ouvrir les bibliothèques, de rechercher toutes les pièces justificatives. Il suffit d'éveiller le souvenir, de montrer l'âme d'un pays flottante au-dessus de l'Histoire. La France n'est-elle pas une terre de vignes, de la Bourgogne au Bordelais, du Jura à la Touraine, de la Champagne au Roussillon ? Il est difficile, à ceux qui sont nés de cette race, d'échapper aux antécédents séculaires, à cette vapeur de terroir. La France ne fut-elle pas aussi un séjour d'amour vif et de galants propos ? Et son réalisme aussi s'embarrassa-t-il des basses fonctions, contrepoids nécessaires d'une cérébralité alerte, rétablissement d'équilibre utile à la spéculation de la pensée ? N'en a-t-il pas été fait un élément de comique et de force ?

En plein moyen-âge, aux pierres même des cathédrales, ce réalisme de la race s'affirme et triomphe, nargue le destin, se réjouit de la minute concédée à l'être. La nationalité française n'a pas attendu le grand docteur François Rabelais, le bon docteur qui décrète la Renaissance, qui rassure définitivement l'humanité, qui lui enjoint d'accepter son sort et de vivre sa vie.

Hélas ! sans doute, le rabelaisisme est à bon marché, et ceux qui se payent de mots et détournent les ordures en affirmant continuer l'ancêtre, n'ont rien recueilli de la haute philosophie du vaste esprit, de son mystérieux savoir, de sa prévoyante et bienveillante conscience. Ils pataugent dans le marécage d'une manière, ne s'en iront jamais, comme l'autre, sur le libre océan de la pensée.

Mais ceux-là qui viennent du fin fond des foules pour assister à quelque spectacle, entendre quelque parole, ceux-là

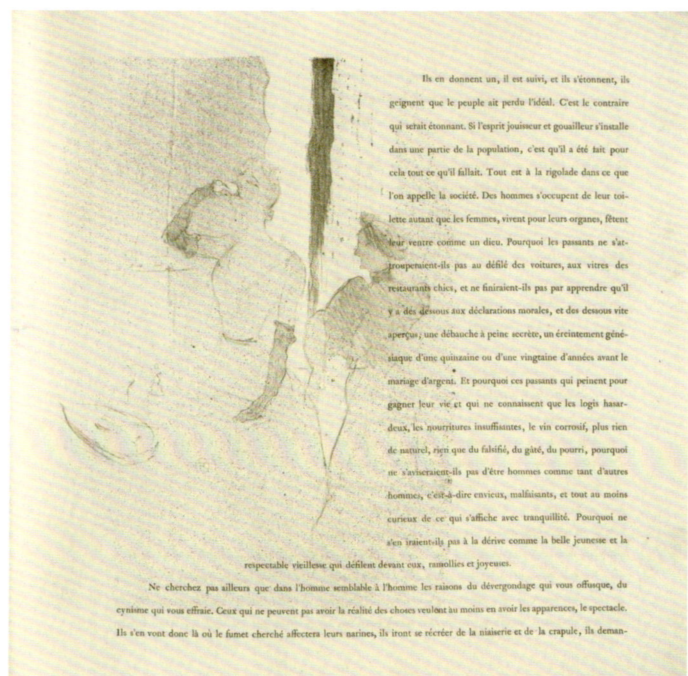

Ils en donnent un, il est suivi, et ils s'étonnent, ils geignent que le peuple ait perdu l'idéal. C'est le contraire qui serait étonnant. Si l'esprit jouisseur et gouailleur s'installe dans une partie de la population, c'est qu'il a été fait pour cela tout ce qu'il fallait. Tout est à la rigolade dans ce que l'on appelle la société. Des hommes s'occupent de leur toilette autant que les femmes, vivent pour leurs organes, fêtent leur ventre comme un dieu. Pourquoi les passants ne s'attrouperaient-ils pas au défilé des voitures, aux vitres des restaurants chics, et ne finiraient-ils pas par apprendre qu'il y a des dessous aux déclarations morales, et des dessous vite aperçus, une débauche à peine secrète, un éreintement génésiaque d'une quinzaine ou d'une vingtaine d'années avant le mariage d'argent. Et pourquoi ces passants qui peinent pour gagner leur vie et qui ne connaissent que les logis hasardeux, les nourritures insuffisantes, le vin corrosif, plus rien de naturel, rien que du falsifié, du gâté, du pourri, pourquoi ne s'aviseraient-ils pas d'être hommes comme tant d'autres hommes, c'est-à-dire envieux, malfaisants, et tout au moins curieux de ce qui s'affiche avec tranquillité. Pourquoi ne s'en iraient-ils pas à la dérive comme la belle jeunesse et la respectable vieillesse qui défilent devant eux, ramollies et joyeuses.

Ne cherchez pas ailleurs que dans l'homme semblable à l'homme les raisons du dévergondage qui vous offusque, du cynisme qui vous effraie. Ceux qui ne peuvent pas avoir la réalité des choses veulent au moins en avoir les apparences, le spectacle. Ils s'en vont donc là où le fumet cherché affectera leurs narines, ils iront se récréer de la niaiserie et de la crapule, ils deman-

Plates 30–33
Pages from the illustrated book
YVETTE GUILBERT by Gustave Geffroy. 1894
Lithograph, page: $15\frac{1}{16}$ x $15\frac{3}{16}$ in. (38.3 x 38.5 cm)
The Louis E. Stern Collection, 1964

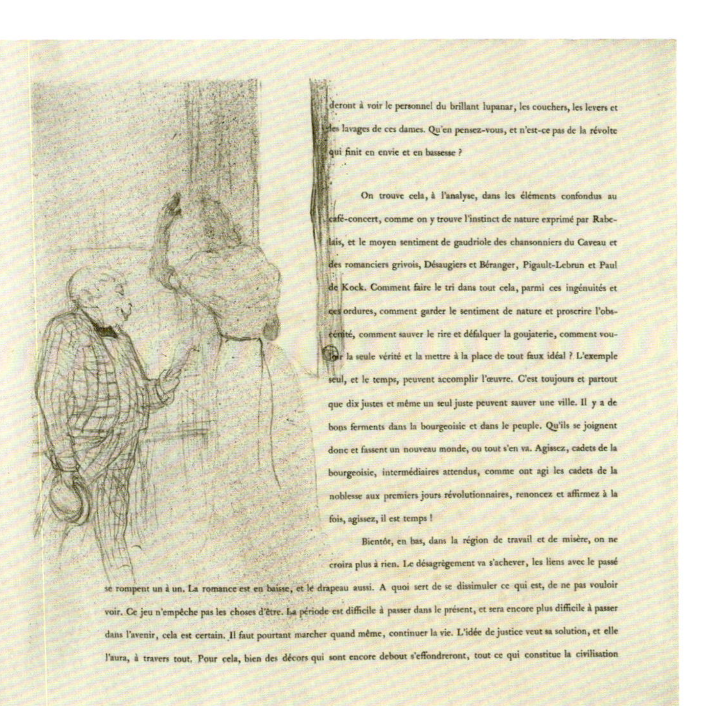

deront à voir le personnel du brillant lupanar, les couchers, les levers et les lavages de ces dames. Qu'en pensez-vous, et n'est-ce pas de la révolte qui finit en envie et en bassesse ?

On trouve cela, à l'analyse, dans les éléments confondus au café-concert, comme on y trouve l'instinct de nature exprimé par Rabelais, et le moyen sentiment de gaudriole des chansonniers du Caveau et des romanciers grivois, Désaugiers et Béranger, Pigault-Lebrun et Paul de Kock. Comment faire le tri dans tout cela, parmi ces ingénuités et ces ordures, comment garder le sentiment de nature et proscrire l'obscénité, comment sauver le rire et défalquer la goujaterie, comment vouloir la seule vérité et la mettre à la place de tout faux idéal ? L'exemple seul, et le temps, peuvent accomplir l'œuvre. C'est toujours et partout que dix justes et même un seul juste peuvent sauver une ville. Il y a de bons ferments dans la bourgeoisie et dans le peuple. Qu'ils se joignent donc et fassent un nouveau monde, ou tout s'en va. Agissez, cadets de la bourgeoisie, intermédiaires attendus, comme ont agi les cadets de la noblesse aux premiers jours révolutionnaires, renoncez et affirmez à la fois, agissez, il est temps !

Bientôt, en bas, dans la région de travail et de misère, on ne croira plus à rien. Le désagrègement va s'achever, les liens avec le passé se rompent un à un. La romance est en baisse, et le drapeau aussi. A quoi sert de se dissimuler ce qui est, de ne pas vouloir voir. Ce jeu n'empêche pas les choses d'être. La période est difficile à passer dans le présent, et sera encore plus difficile à passer dans l'avenir, cela est certain. Il faut pourtant marcher quand même, continuer la vie. L'idée de justice veut sa solution, et elle l'aura, à travers tout. Pour cela, bien des décors qui sont encore debout s'effondreront, tout ce qui constitue la civilisation

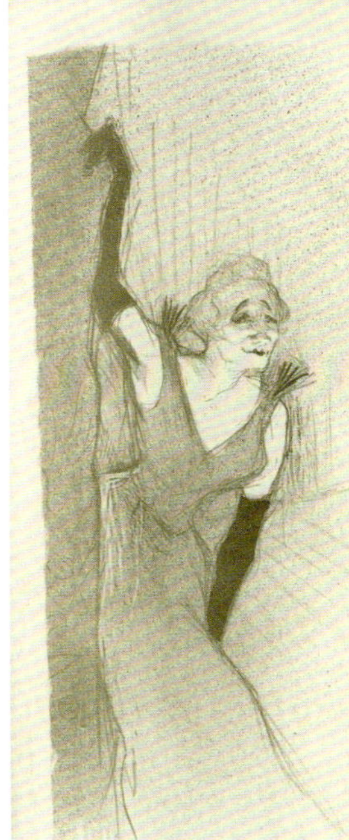

héritée, l'Eglise et la Bourse, le Palais et la Caserne. Mais qui ne consentira, dans l'avenir, à l'effritement et à l'écroulement des monuments, si chacun peut enfin jouir de sa maison et de son jardin, de ses fleurs, de sa ruche et de son arbre ? Le fameux idéal invoqué comporte trop de truffes et de champagne pour les uns, et pas assez même de pain sec pour les autres. Ce sera tout bénéfice pour l'humanité si elle entend et comprend d'une certaine façon ce qui lui sera crié : « Il n'y a pas d'idéal, il y a la soupe et le bœuf, il faut vivre d'abord, créer de la vie, posséder la Terre, lui faire donner son maximum de bonheur. » Ce sera là le commencement de l'action.

Ce sera la conclusion de ces feuilles, si vous le voulez bien. La chanteuse Yvette Guilbert, lorsqu'elle a fini sa chanson, et qu'elle se sauve, la gorge âcre de la fumée respirée, toute sa personne imprégnée de l'atmosphère chaude, où va-t-elle ? Elle saute dans un train, quitte Paris, se rafraîchit à l'air sain de l'espace, retrouve son jardin et sa rivière de Vaux. Humanité tombée au café-concert, fais comme ta chanteuse, aussitôt que tu le pourras, quitte les grandes villes, retourne à la nature avec ce que tu as appris d'histoire et de civilisation, cherche l'ombre de l'arbre, le chant de la branche et du sillon, contente-toi du petit jardin autour duquel il y a l'espace, vis ta propre existence, unis-toi à la Terre enfin dominée par la Pensée.

GUSTAVE GEFFROY.

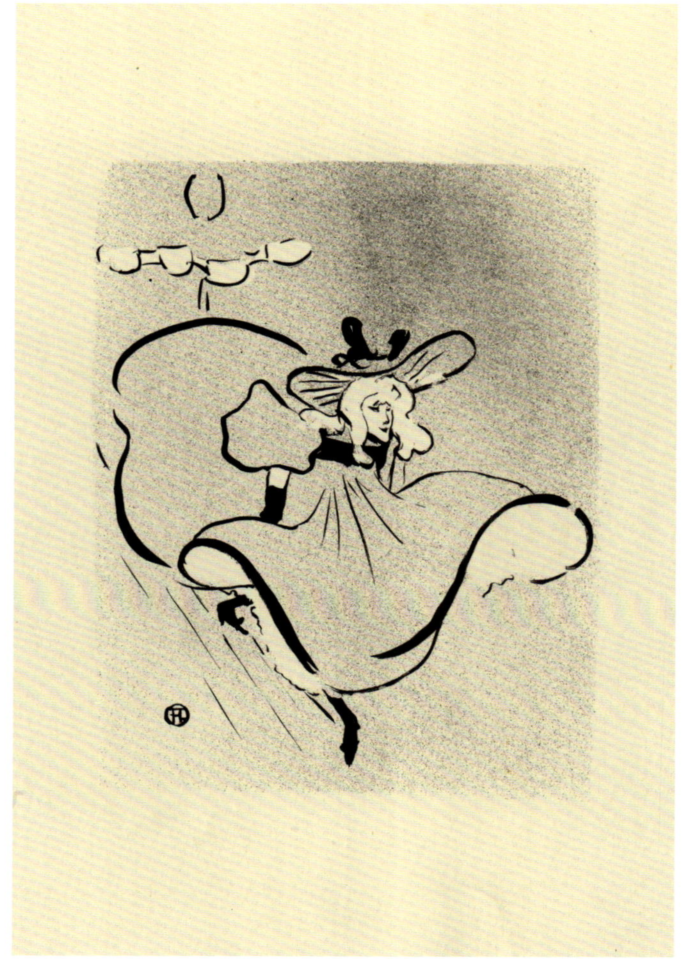

Plate 34
JANE AVRIL from the portfolio **LE CAFÉ CONCERT**. 1893
Lithograph, sheet: 17 1/8 x 12 1/2 in. (43.5 x 31.7 cm)
The Louis E. Stern Collection, 1964

Plate 35
JANE AVRIL. 1893
Lithograph, sheet: 49 5/8 x 36 1/8 in. (126 x 91.8 cm)
Gift of A. Conger Goodyear, 1954

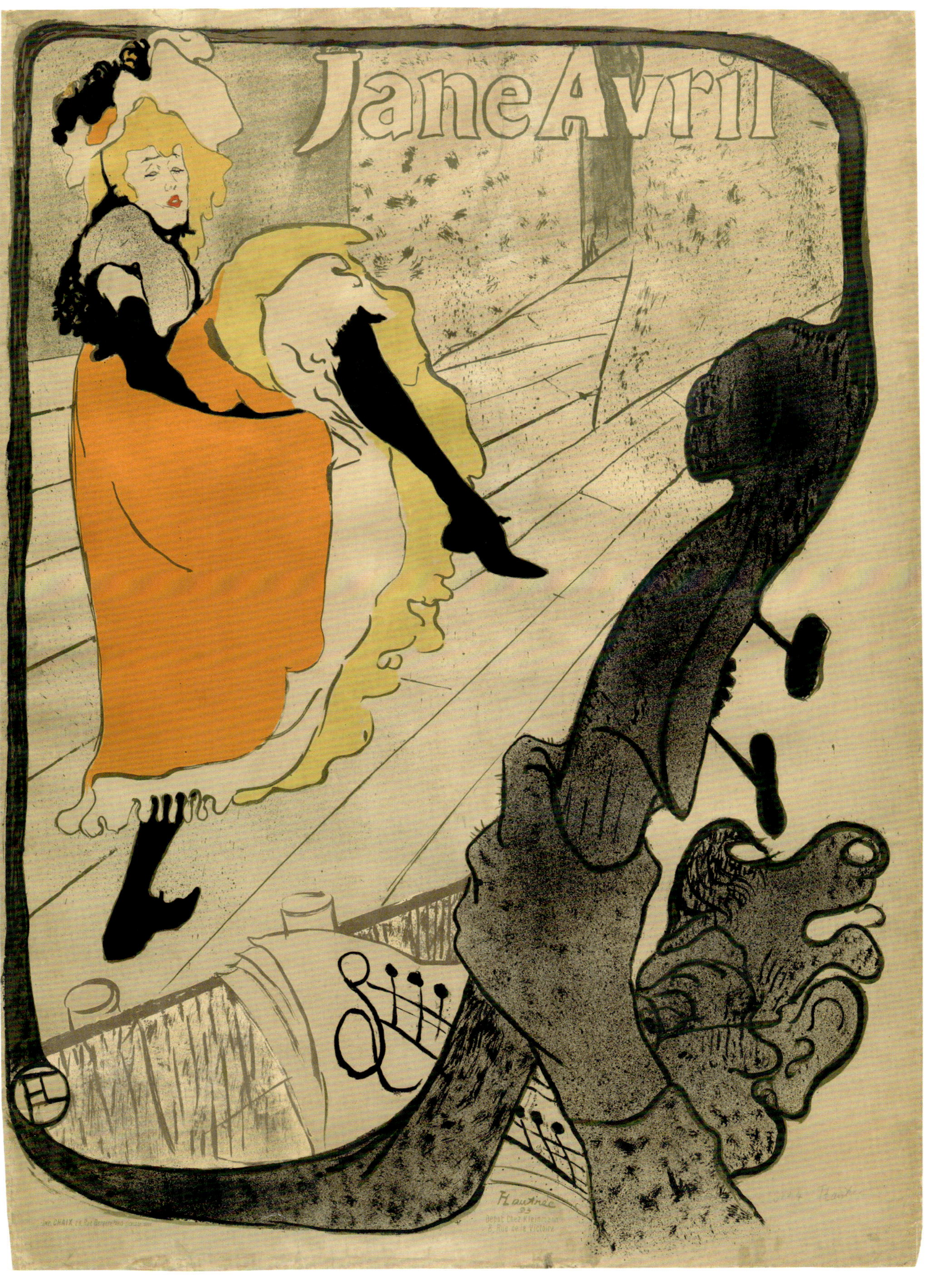
Jane Avril
HLautrec
93
Dépôt Chez Kleinmann
8, Rue de la Victoire

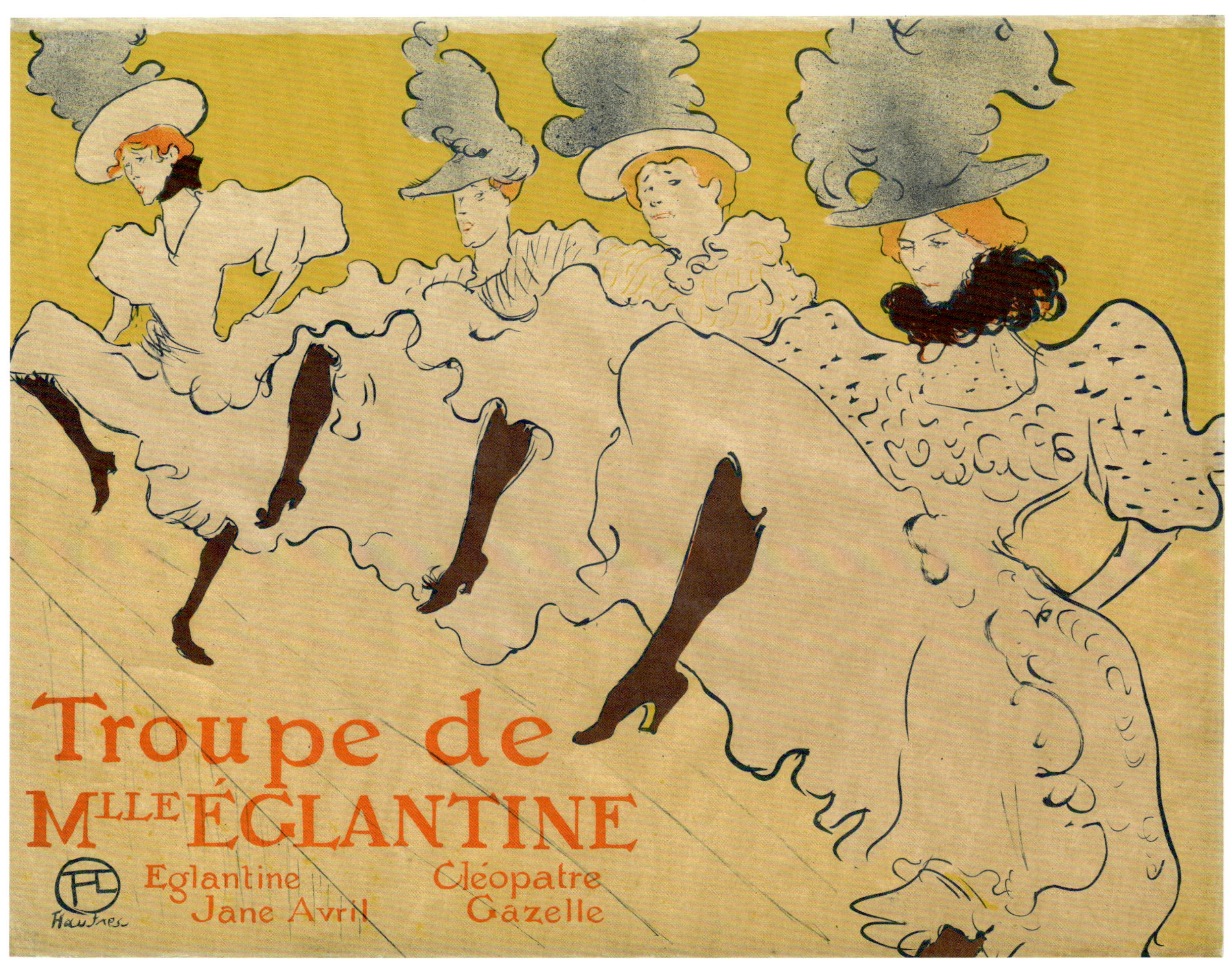

Plate 36

LA TROUPE DE MADEMOISELLE ÉGLANTINE
(**MADEMOISELLE ÉGLANTINE'S TROUPE**). 1896
Lithograph, sheet: 24¼ x 31¼ in. (61.6 x 79.4 cm)
Gift of Abby Aldrich Rockefeller, 1940

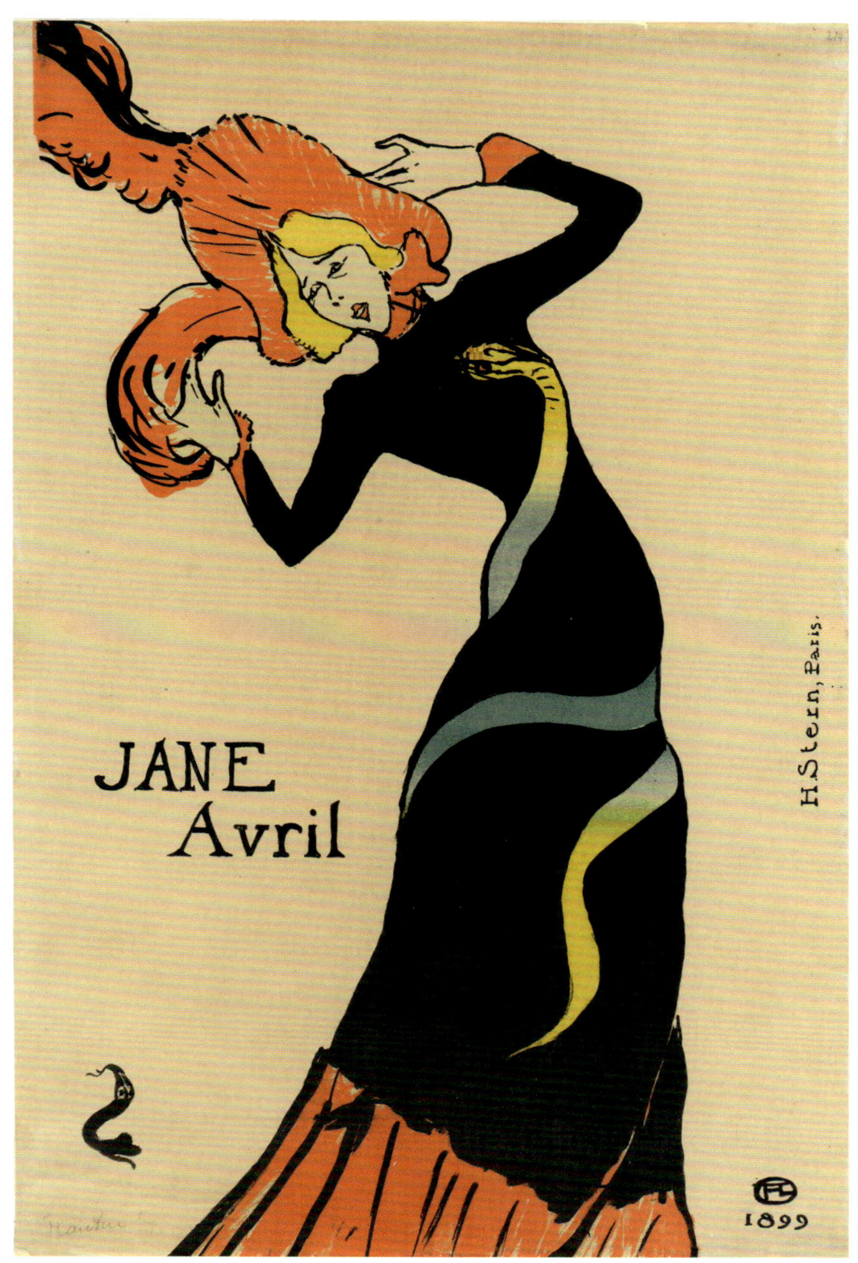

Plate 37
JANE AVRIL. 1899
Lithograph, sheet: 22 1/16 x 15 in. (56 x 38.1 cm)
Gift of Abby Aldrich Rockefeller, 1946

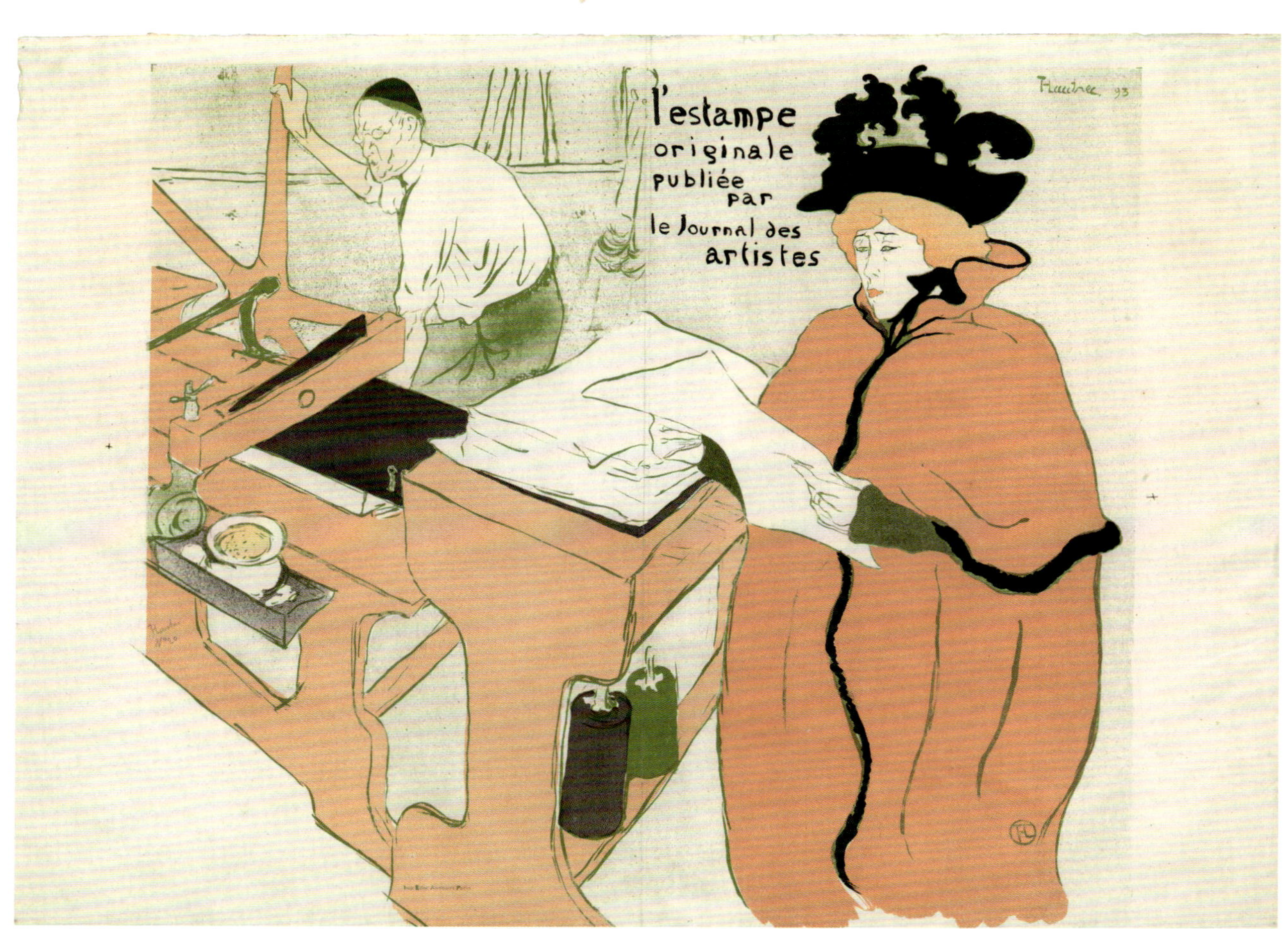

Plate 38
Cover for the journal **L'ESTAMPE ORIGINALE**. 1893
Lithograph, sheet: 23 1/16 x 32 3/4 in. (58.5 x 83.2 cm)
Grace M. Mayer Bequest, 1997

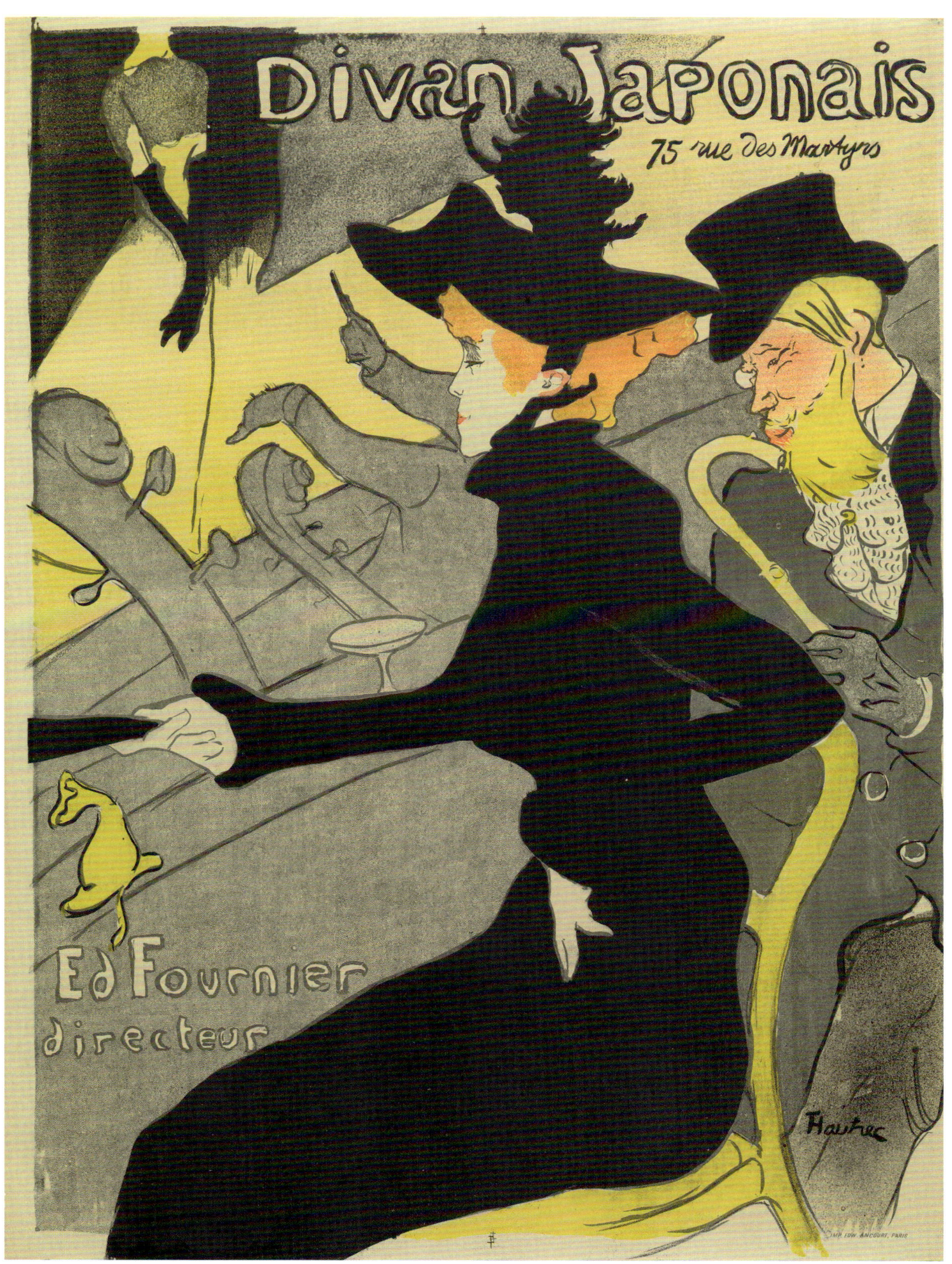

Plate 39
DIVAN JAPONAIS, 1893
Lithograph, sheet: 31 15/16 x 24 1/2 in. (81.2 x 62.2 cm)
Abby Aldrich Rockefeller Fund, 1949

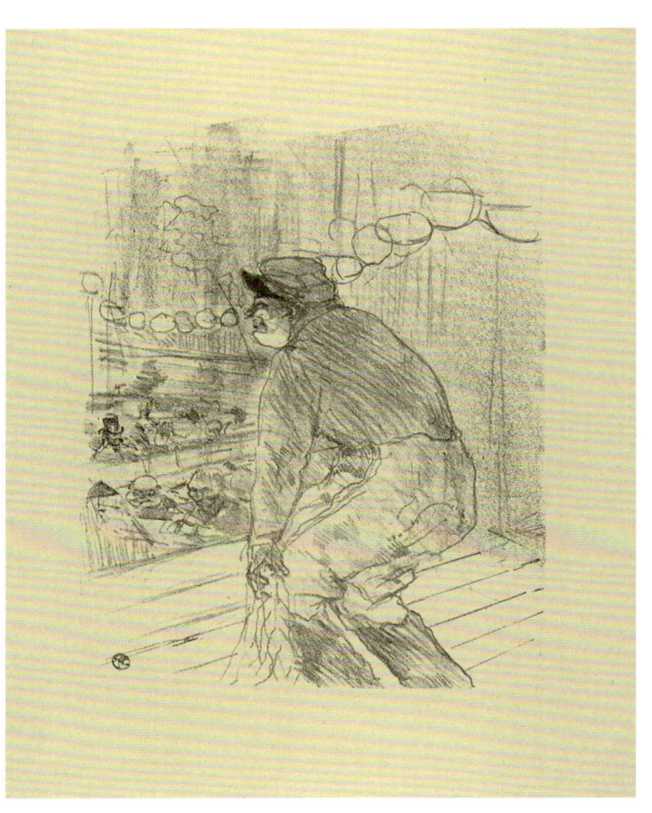

Plate 40
POLIN from the portfolio **PORTRAITS D'ACTEURS & ACTRICES: TREIZE LITHOGRAPHIES (PORTRAITS OF ACTORS & ACTRESSES: THIRTEEN LITHOGRAPHS)**. 1898, published c. 1906
Lithograph, sheet: 15⅜ x 12⅝ in. (39.1 x 32.1 cm)
Gift of Abby Aldrich Rockefeller, 1946

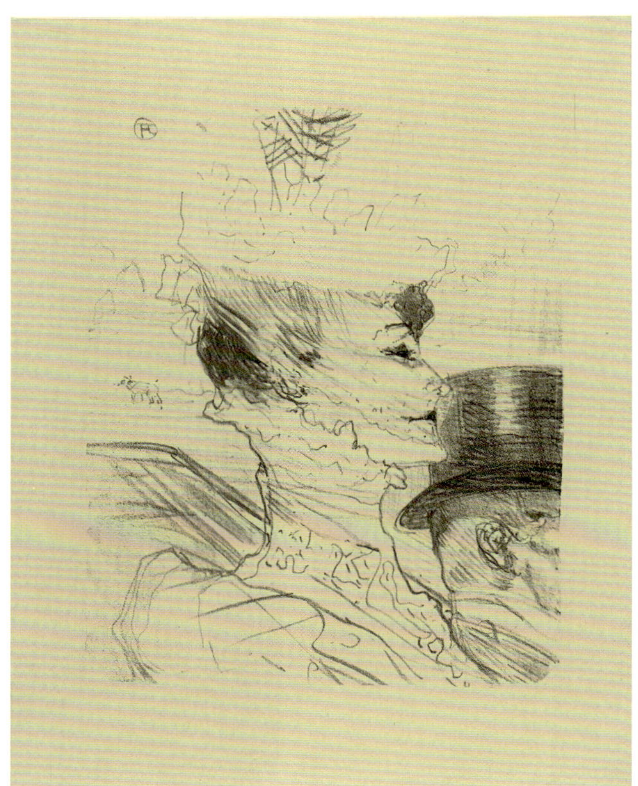

Plate 41
LOUISE BALTHY from the portfolio **PORTRAITS D'ACTEURS & ACTRICES: TREIZE LITHOGRAPHIES (PORTRAITS OF ACTORS & ACTRESSES: THIRTEEN LITHOGRAPHS)**. 1898, published c. 1906
Lithograph, sheet: 15 7/16 x 12⅝ in. (39.2 x 32.1 cm)
Gift of Abby Aldrich Rockefeller, 1946

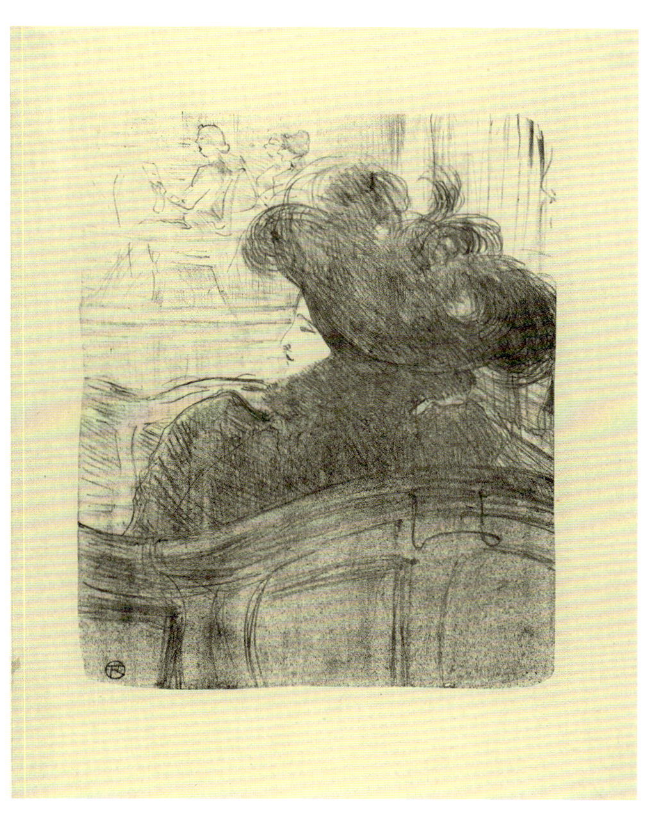

Plate 42
CLÉO DE MÉRODE from the portfolio **PORTRAITS D'ACTEURS & ACTRICES: TREIZE LITHOGRAPHIES** (**PORTRAITS OF ACTORS & ACTRESSES: THIRTEEN LITHOGRAPHS**). 1898, published c. 1906
Lithograph, sheet: 15⅜ x 12⅜ in. (39 x 31.5 cm)
Gift of Abby Aldrich Rockefeller, 1946

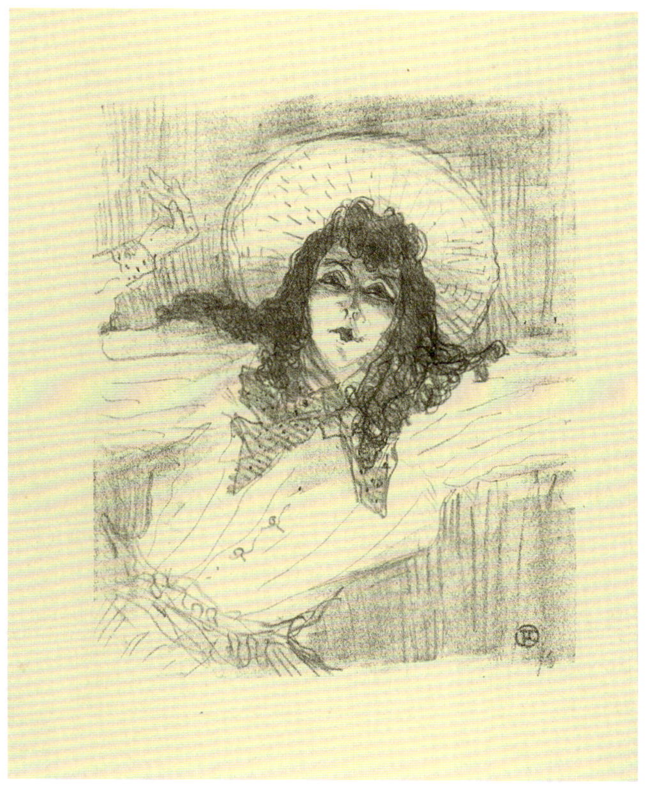

Plate 43
MAY BELFORT from the portfolio **PORTRAITS D'ACTEURS & ACTRICES: TREIZE LITHOGRAPHIES** (**PORTRAITS OF ACTORS & ACTRESSES: THIRTEEN LITHOGRAPHS**). 1898, published c. 1906
Lithograph, sheet: 15 7/16 x 12 7/16 in. (39.2 x 31.6 cm)
Gift of Abby Aldrich Rockefeller, 1946

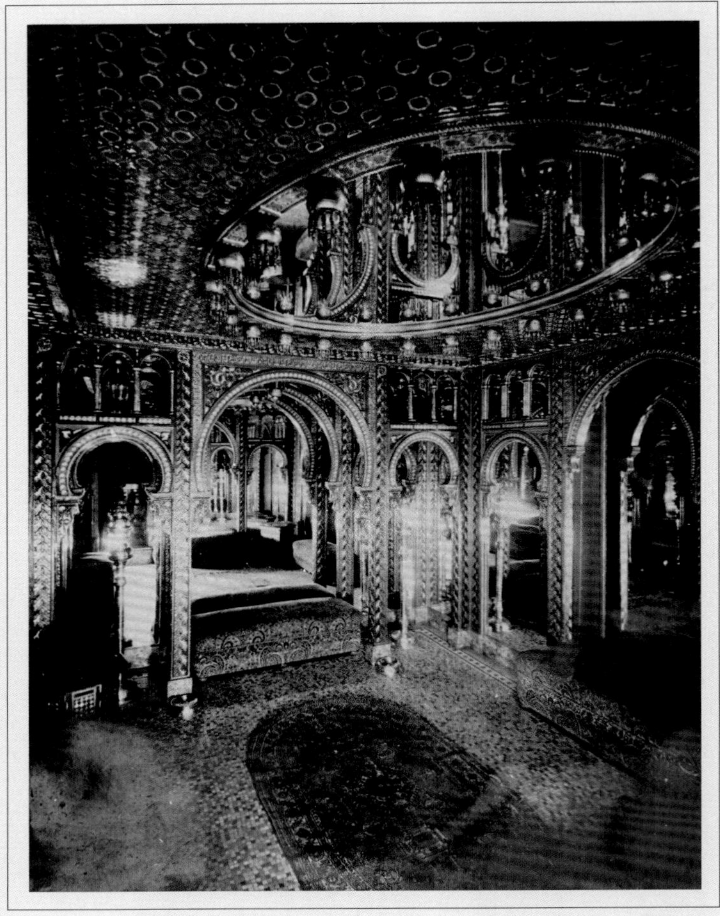

FEMMES, FILLES, ELLES

Lautrec's fascination with women was all-encompassing, from shopgirls and demi-mondaines to the performers with whom he socialized and the prostitutes he paid to model for him. He preferred redheads, he said, "because they had a particular odor that he found arousing."[66] His personal relationships with women, however, were complex and conflicted. Lautrec often admired them from afar or allowed potential romantic relationships to become friendships instead: "The feeling he experienced for his women friends was a curious mixture of jovial comradeship and restrained desire. And as he was fully conscious of his physical inferiority, and, like Cyrano, did not suffer from petty jealousy; when he appreciated a woman to whom he refused to show it, his greatest joy was for her also to be appreciated—but more fully—by a friend."[67] Such was probably the case with the milliner Renée Vert, who trafficked in one of Lautrec's favorite accessories. Hats are a distinguishing char-

31. Moorish room in a Parisian brothel. c. 1890–99.
Ludwig Charell Collection on Henri de Toulouse-Lautrec,
II.13. The Museum of Modern Art Archives, New York

acteristic of the artist's portraits, often drawn with more detail and attention than his subjects' faces. Although he may have been attracted to Vert, he happily gave her away when she married his friend Adolphe (Dodo) Albert in September 1893.[68]

Lautrec depicted Vert on a menu he designed for the summer banquet of the Société des Indépendants, with whom he had exhibited earlier that year. In one impression (pl. 45), in which the menu text has been removed, Vert is seen from a distance, arranging her wares, a large hatbox at her feet. The box is labeled with Lautrec's monogram remarque, perhaps a reference to his affection for her or to a purchase he had made. The olive color corresponds to her last name, the French word for "green." Louise Blouet, a luxuriant blonde with the face of an "alert squirrel,"[69] whom Lautrec nicknamed "*croques-y-margouin*" (the "good-enough-to-eat model"), worked for Vert and also became a friend. She was the subject of several of Lautrec's late pictures (pl. 44).

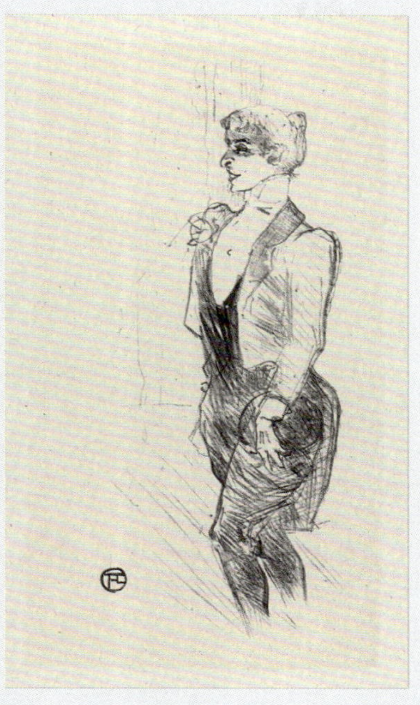

32. **HENRI DE TOULOUSE-LAUTREC**. *Mary Hamilton*. 1894, published 1925. Lithograph, 14 5/16 x 10 3/4 in. (36.4 x 27.3 cm). The Museum of Modern Art, New York. Purchase Fund, 1949

Lautrec's physical handicaps made him an unlikely heartthrob, but rumors of his sexual prowess and endowment (one friend described him as a "penis with legs"[70]) abounded. Nevertheless, it is believed that the artist's sole romantic relationship was with the painter Suzanne Valadon and that all his other sexual encounters were with prostitutes at the brothels where he was a frequent visitor and sometime resident. Prostitution was common and widely accepted in Paris at the time, and even regulated with weekly medical checkups. Lautrec and his male friends visited brothels often, frequenting all varieties, from low-class to deluxe, as on the rue des Moulins, where the wealthy could live out their sexual fantasies in rooms lavishly decorated with different themes (fig. 31).

While Lautrec's images set in brothels, such as *Étude de femme* (pl. 46), are rarely lurid or titillating, there are plenty of explicit caricatures among his drawings, sketches, and doodles. In his print oeuvre, however, *Débauché* (pl. 47), is unusual. Here, a man modeled on Lautrec's close friend the painter-engraver Maxime Dethomas (see pls. 95 and 96 for examples of Dethomas's work) reaches around to grab the bare breast of the woman lounging in front of him. The image was used on the cover of a sales catalogue for posters.

Lautrec had a circle of close male friends from his days in the ateliers and his nights of carousing. They included the artist Louis Anquetin, Moët & Chandon representative Maurice Guibert, photographer Paul Sescau, childhood friend and art dealer Maurice Joyant, Paul Leclercq of *La Revue blanche,* and Lautrec's cousin Gabriel Tapié de Céleyran. But he also had a circle of female friends, many of whom were performers and many of whom were lesbians: Yvette Guilbert, May Milton, Mary Hamilton (fig. 32), Jane Avril, La Goulue, Môme Fromage, Gabrielle, and the clown Cha-U-Kao among them. Same-sex female relationships were common and, unlike male homosexuality, not actively persecuted in the 1890s. One author goes so far as to declare Paris at this time "the undisputed capital of world lesbianism."[71] Lautrec created sympathetic depictions of his gay female friends, avidly attended their performances, and patronized their bars and nightclubs, where he was warmly welcomed when other men were barred from entry. Leclercq noted, "One could often find Lautrec in some little bar where the Tout-Lesbos of Montmartre found themselves between the end of their day and dinnertime. But it was Palmyre's, at La Souris, that he frequented most readily."[72] The one-eyed Madame Palmyre presided over the popular bar, often accompanied by her naughty French bulldog, Bouboule. The dog was a subject of Lautrec's on multiple occasions, including on a menu for a dinner given by Palmyre, on which both the dog and a *souris* (mouse) are depicted, making sly reference to the name of the venue (fig. 33). Madame Armande Brazier owned another of Lautrec's favorite spots, the Brasserie du Hanneton, on the rue Pigalle. A contemporary guidebook describes it:

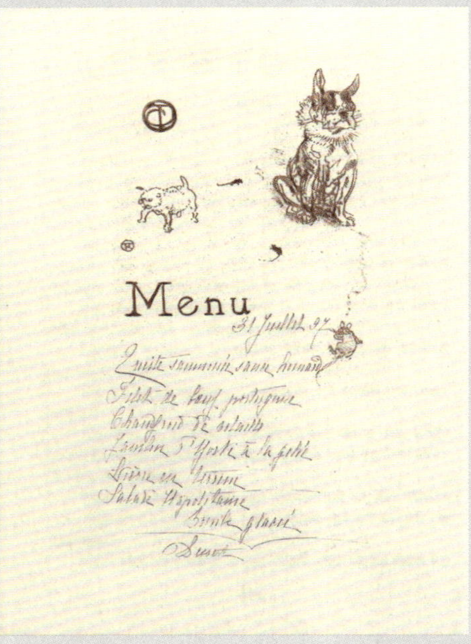

33. **HENRI DE TOULOUSE-LAUTREC**. Menu from *La Cuisine de Monsieur Momo Célibataire* by Maurice Joyant. c. 1880, published 1930. Photogravure, page: 9¼ x 7¼ in. (23.5 x 18.4 cm). The Museum of Modern Art, New York. The Louis E. Stern Collection, 1964

This is a very small and low kind of house. The red curtains are at once a sign that it is one of the women restaurants, and it is in reality a refreshment place for women, differing somewhat from the Rat-Mort and the Abbaye de Thélème. During the evening it rarely happens that men are present. Sometimes not even a single representative of the male sex puts in an appearance. The women frequenters are of the "masculine order," mistresses of the neighborhood, dining together at small tables, and afterwards indulging in the fragrant weed in the shape of cigarettes. The sight presented is a pathological curiosity.[73]

Women are also the singular focus of *Elles* (1896; pls. 48–58), a portfolio of twelve works that marks Lautrec's greatest achievement in lithography. The series of carefully observed brothel scenes runs counter to the expectation of the titillating and the tawdry, instead presenting quiet moments of mundane intimacy. Scholarship suggests that *Elles* is about the relationship of a lesbian couple, in part because the series opens with an image set not in the *maison close*, or brothel, but rather in the Moulin Rouge, with a portrait of Cha-U-Kao (pl. 49). The *clownesse*, portrayed by Lautrec on numerous occasions, including with her lover Gabrielle (pl. 19), faces out in an unabashedly masculine posture in an unguarded moment backstage. In the doorway, the lights of the dance hall are visible, along with the scene of a masked ball.[74]

What follows are quotidian scenes: having coffee in the boudoir, the final moments before waking, rumpled sheets and unmade beds, hair to be repinned and corsets to be relaced. In *Femme qui se lave, la toilette* (pl. 53), a woman washes before a basin, her bare breasts reflected in the mirror, contrasted with the eroticized picture of seduction that hangs above. The brilliant *Femme au tub* (pl. 52), with its studies in pattern and texture,[75] is set in an elaborately decorated room. There is nothing erotic in the scene, save the image of Leda and the Swan displayed on the wall, and no sense that the subject knows she is being watched, for a lock of hair slips out of her chignon.

Elles was likely inspired by Kitagawa Utamaro's twelve-part masterpiece *The Twelve Hours of the "Green Houses"* (c. 1794), depicting a day in the life of a courtesan in Edo's Yoshiwara pleasure district. Lautrec's references to Utamaro are

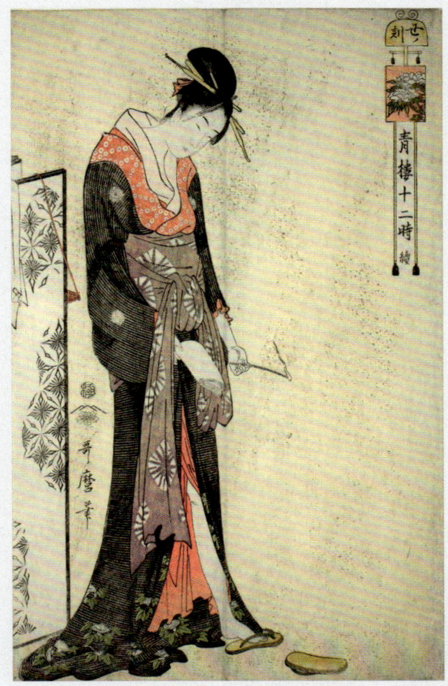

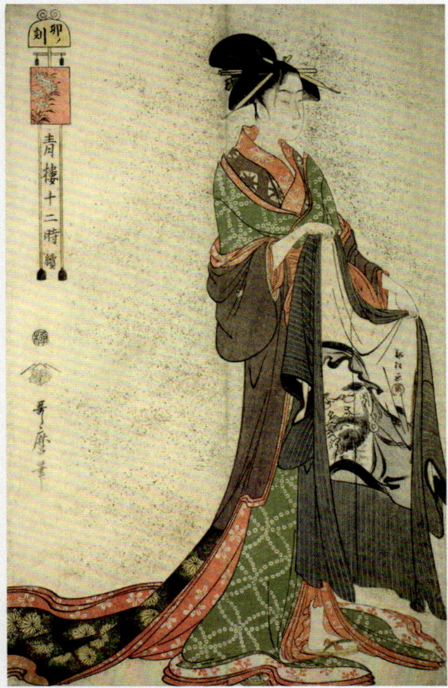

34 and 35. **KITAGAWA UTAMARO** (Japanese, 1753?–1806). *Hour of the Ox (2 a.m.)* and *Hour of the Hare (6 a.m.)* from the series *The Twelve Hours of the "Green Houses."* c. 1794. Color woodcuts, each: $14\frac{13}{16} \times 9\frac{9}{16}$ in. (37.6 x 24.3 cm). The Art Institute of Chicago. Clarence Buckingham Collection, 1925

sometimes specific: the slippers in *Femme à glace, la glace à main* (pl. 54) echo those in his *Hour of the Ox (2 a.m.)* (fig. 34); the comb in the *Femme qui se peigne, la coiffure* (pl. 57) appears in *Hour of the Horse (noon to 2 p.m.)*; and the presentation of tea in *Femme au plateau, petit-déjeuner* (pl. 50) recalls that in *Hour of the Snake (10 a.m. to noon).* In other instances Lautrec uses the same device as Utamaro: compare the unseen male presence represented by the empty coat in the *Hour of the Hare (6 a.m.)* (fig. 35) and the top hat in Lautrec's frontispiece to *Elles* (pl. 48). Also compelling is the shared tone of the two series. While there were plenty of explicit, erotic Japanese prints (or *shunga*), *The Twelve Hours* is quite chaste and focuses on the relationships between the courtesans and other women while still obliquely acknowledging the male presence.

Gustave Pellet, a dealer and publisher who specialized in erotic material, commissioned *Elles* and spared no expense in its production. The series includes several full-color prints that required multiple stones and it was printed on a paper made specifically for the occasion, watermarked with both Pellet's and Lautrec's initials. It was, however, a commercial flop. Lautrec did not deliver an erotic fantasy but rather an intimate portrayal of women whom he knew firsthand and the milieu in which they lived and worked.

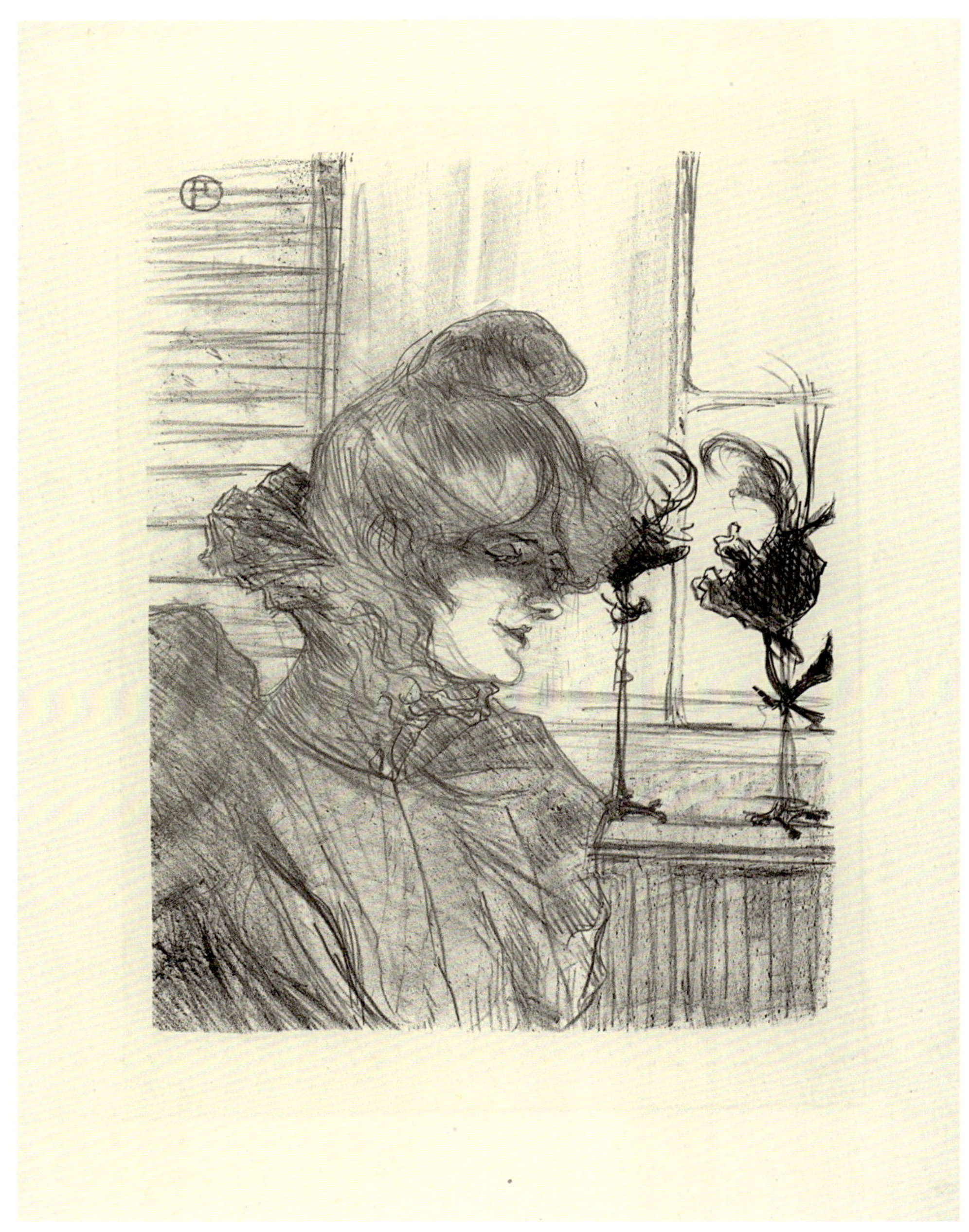

Plate 44
LE MARGOUIN (MADEMOISELLE LOUISE BLOUET). 1900
Lithograph, sheet: 19¾ x 14 in. (50.2 x 35.5 cm)
Gift of Abby Aldrich Rockefeller, 1946

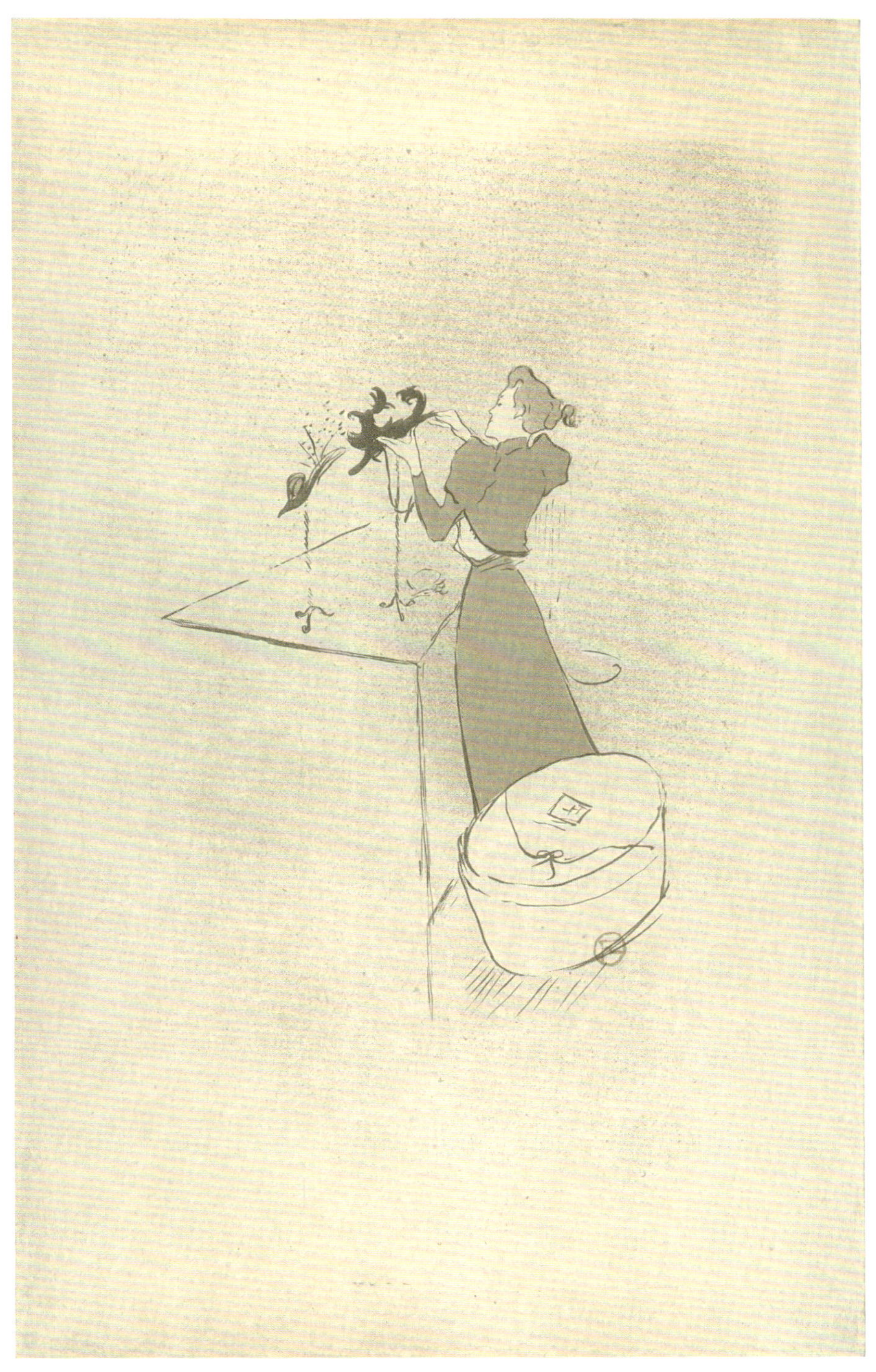

Plate 45
LA MODISTE, RENÉE VERT (THE MILLINER, RENÉE VERT). 1893
Lithograph, sheet: $21\frac{5}{8}$ x $13\frac{3}{4}$ in. (55 x 35 cm)
Grace M. Mayer Bequest, 1997

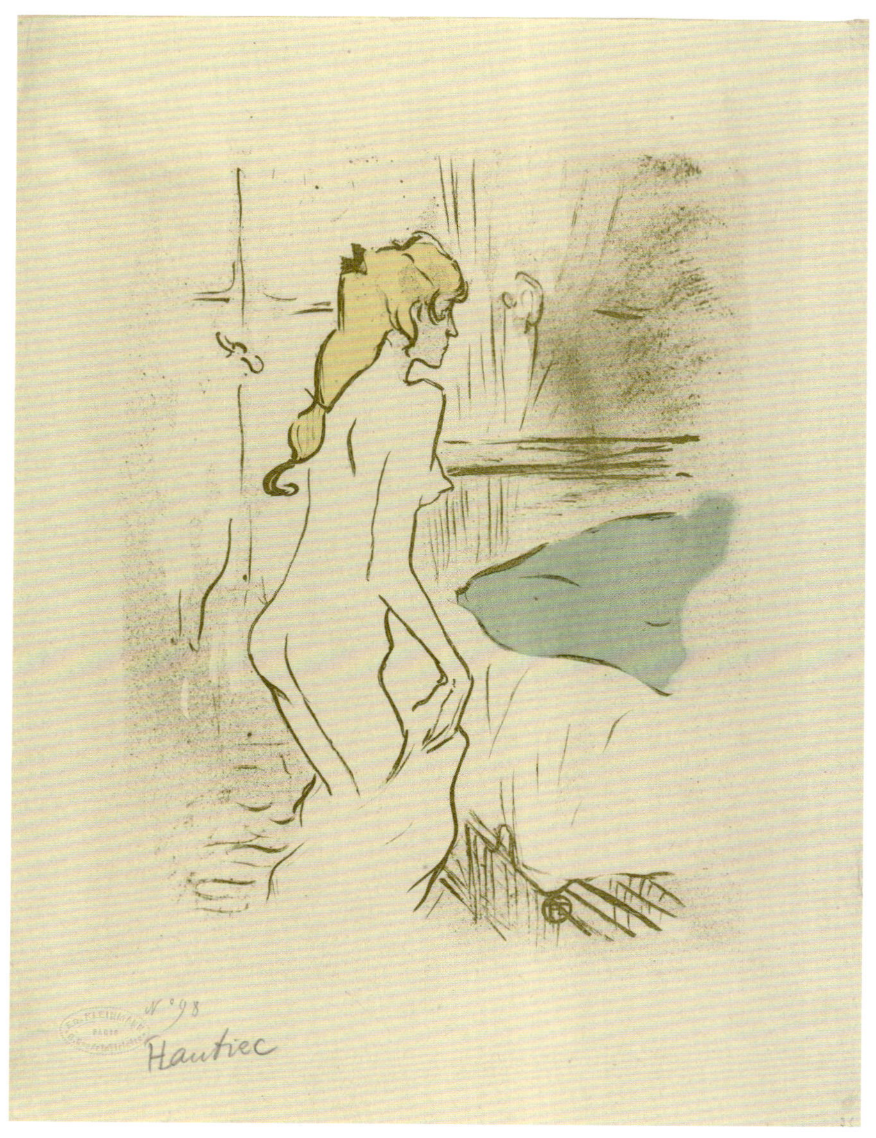

Plate 46

ÉTUDE DE FEMME (STUDY OF A WOMAN). 1893

Lithograph with stencil additions, sheet: 13 13/16 x 10 11/16 in. (35.1 x 27.2 cm)

Gift of Abby Aldrich Rockefeller, 1946

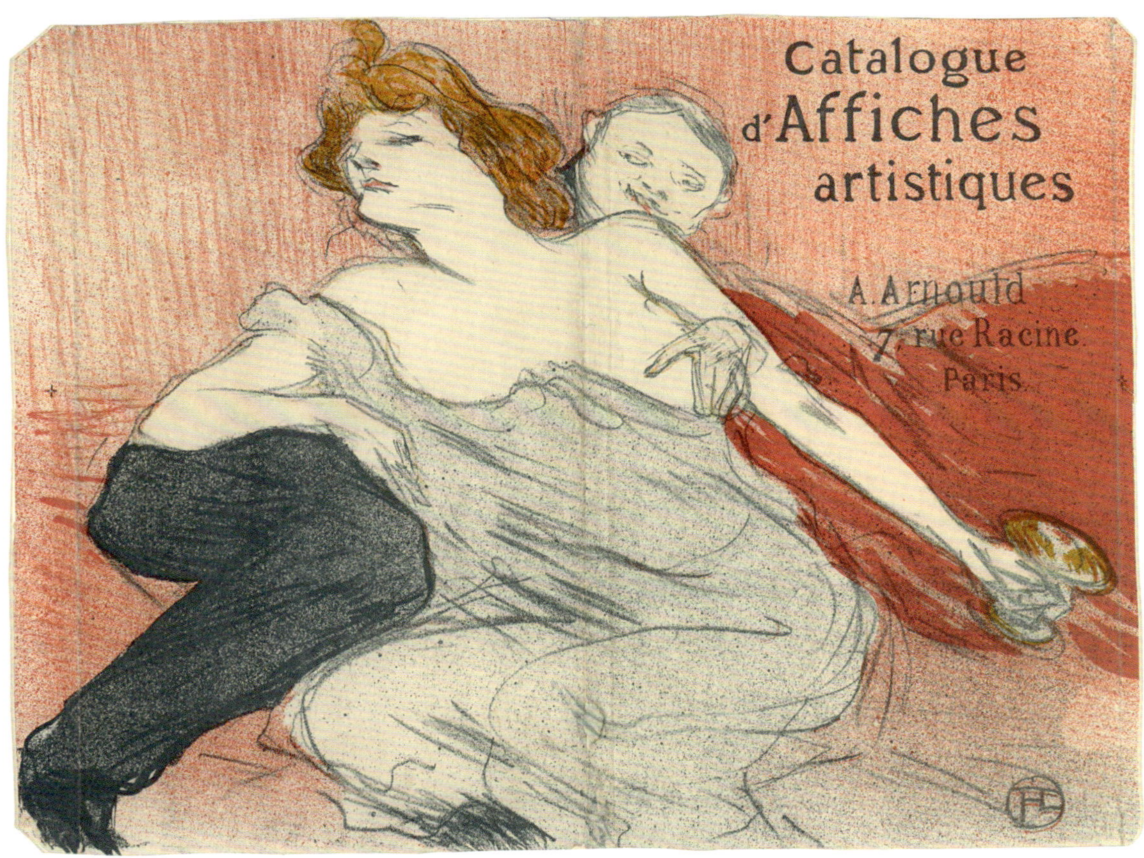

Plate 47
DÉBAUCHÉ (THE DEBAUCHER). 1896
Lithograph, sheet: 9 3/16 x 12 5/16 in. (23.3 x 31.3 cm)
Gift of Louise Bourgeois, 1997

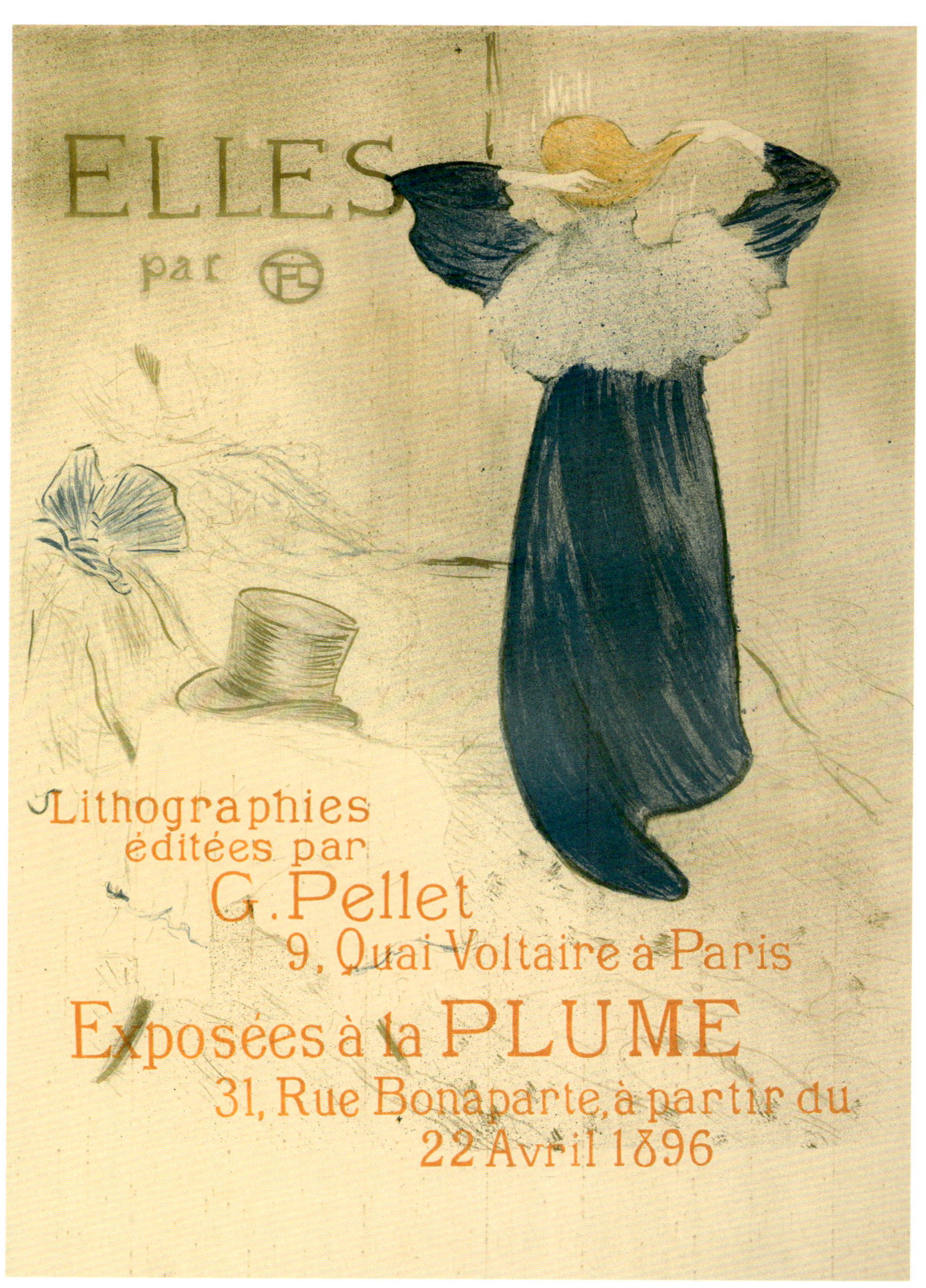

Plate 48
Poster for **ELLES**. 1896
Lithograph, sheet: 26¾ x 19⅝ in. (68 x 49.8 cm)
Gift of Mr. and Mrs. Richard Rodgers, 1961

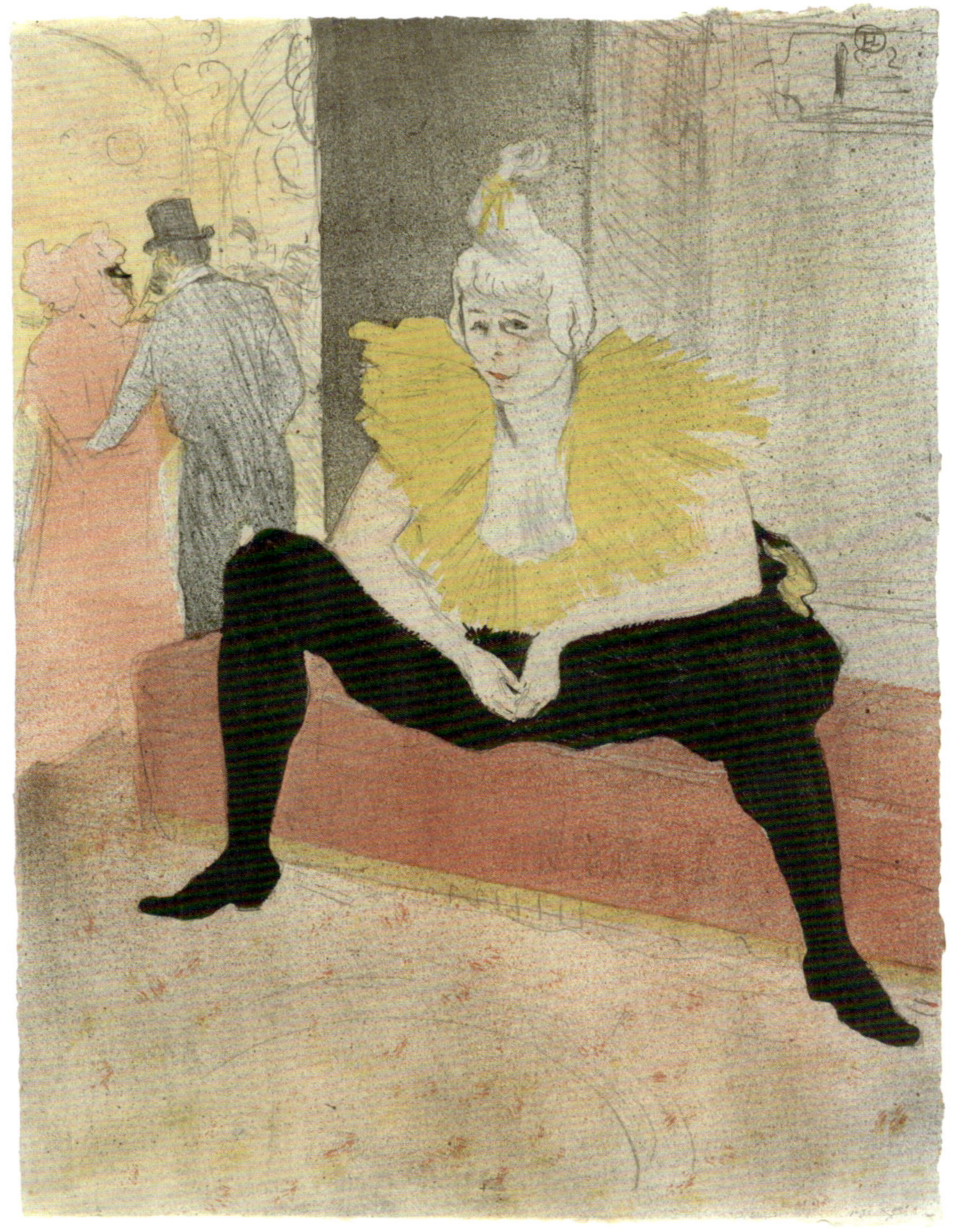

Plate 49

MADEMOISELLE CHA-U-KAO, LA CLOWNESSE ASSISE
(MADEMOISELLE CHA-U-KAO, THE SEATED CLOWNESS)

from the portfolio **ELLES**. 1896

Lithograph, sheet: 20⅞ x 15 13/16 in. (53 x 40.2 cm)

Gift of Abby Aldrich Rockefeller, 1946

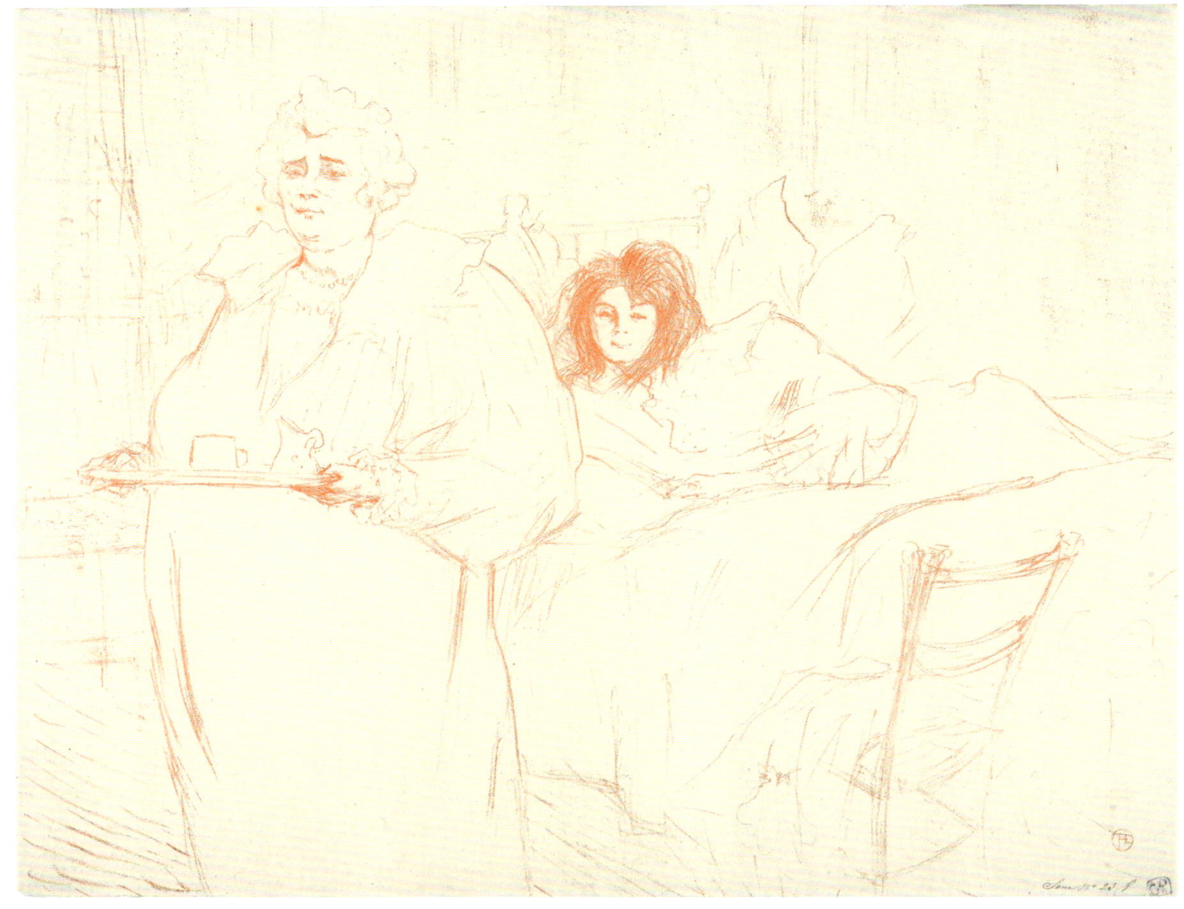

Plate 50
FEMME AU PLATEAU, PETIT-DÉJEUNER
(**WOMAN WITH A TRAY, BREAKFAST**) from the portfolio **ELLES**. 1896
Lithograph, sheet: 15 3/8 x 20 1/16 in. (39 x 51 cm)
Gift of Abby Aldrich Rockefeller, 1946

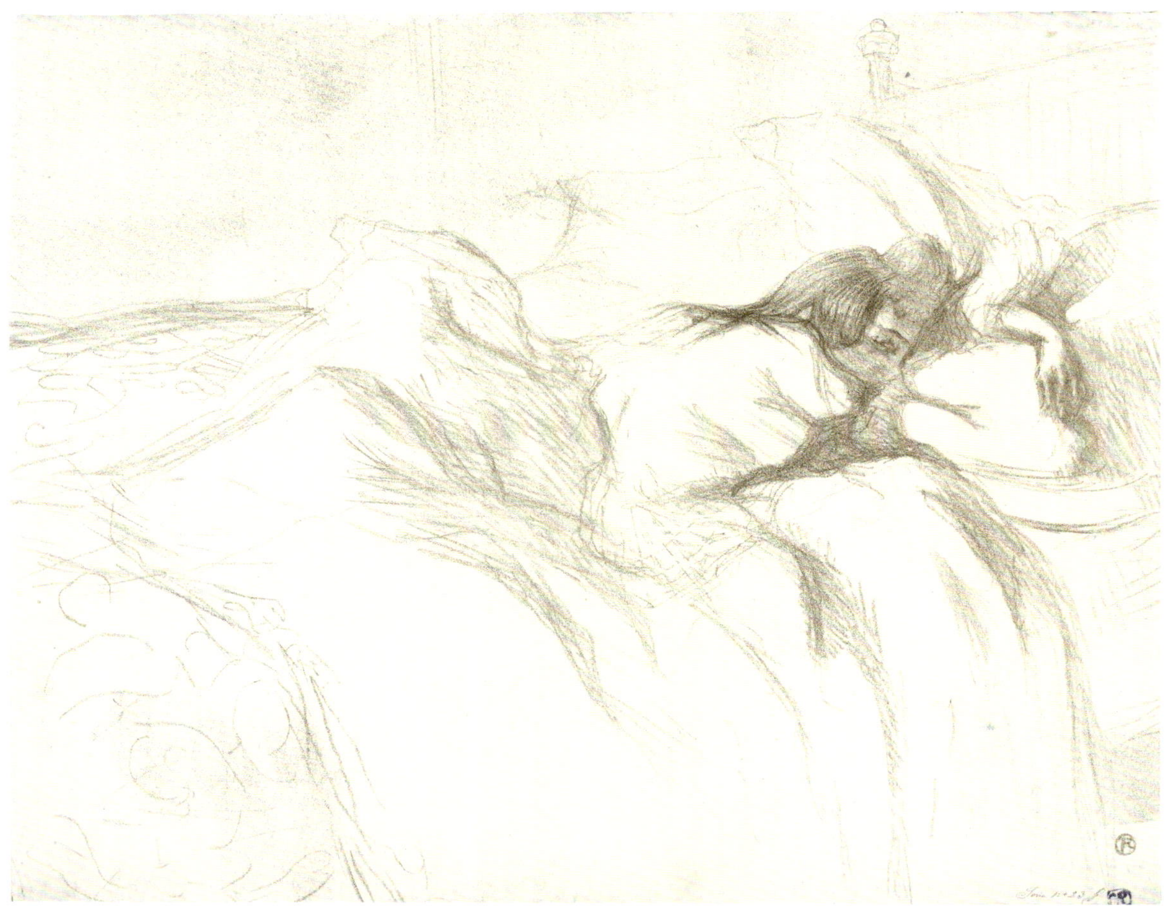

Plate 51
FEMME COUCHÉE, RÉVEIL (**WOMAN WAKING UP IN BED**)
from the portfolio **ELLES**. 1896
Lithograph, sheet: 15¾ x 20$\frac{5}{16}$ in. (40 x 51.6 cm)
Gift of Abby Aldrich Rockefeller, 1946

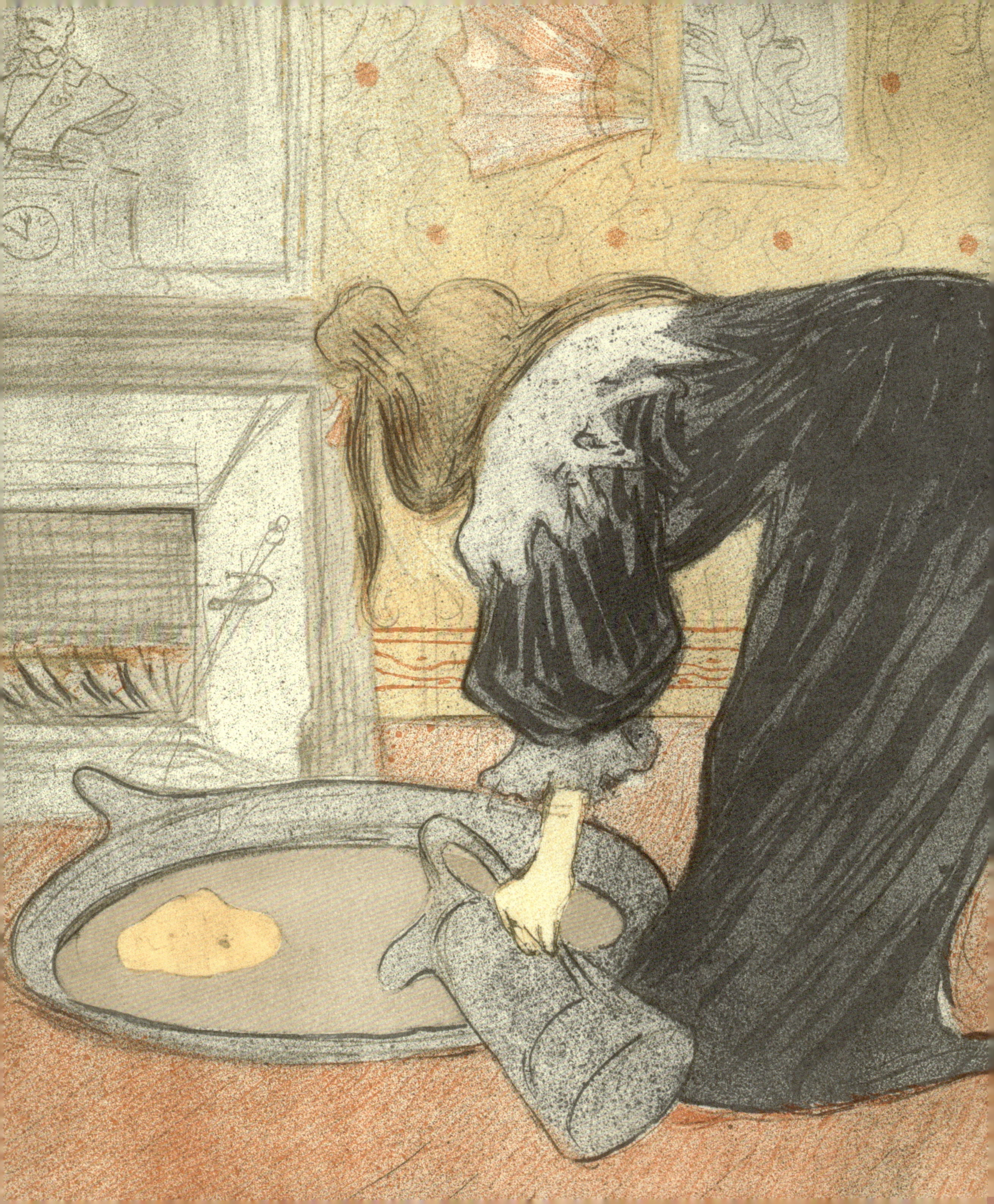

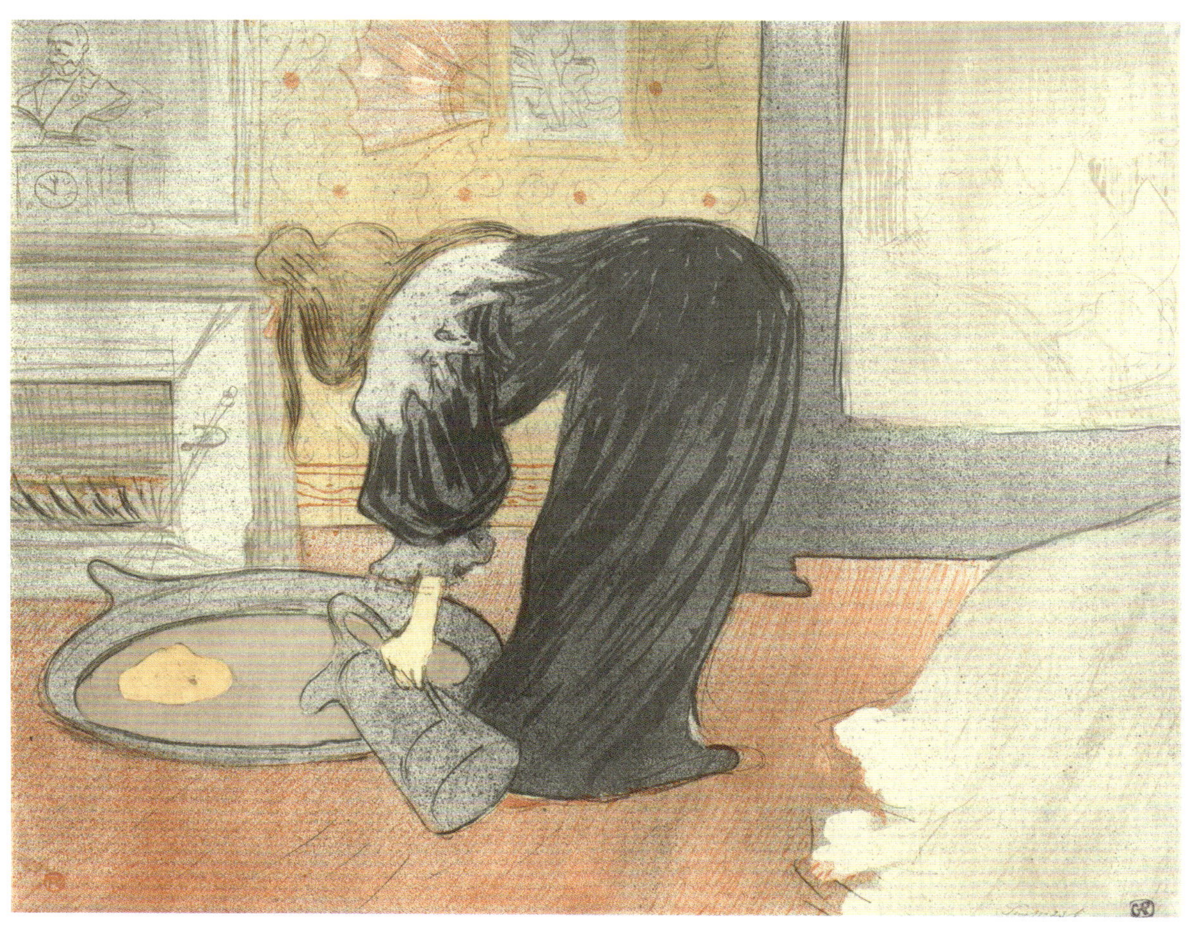

Plate 52
FEMME AU TUB (**WOMAN AT THE TUB**) from the portfolio **ELLES**. 1896
Lithograph, sheet: 15½ x 20¼ in. (39.4 x 51.4 cm)
Gift of Abby Aldrich Rockefeller, 1946

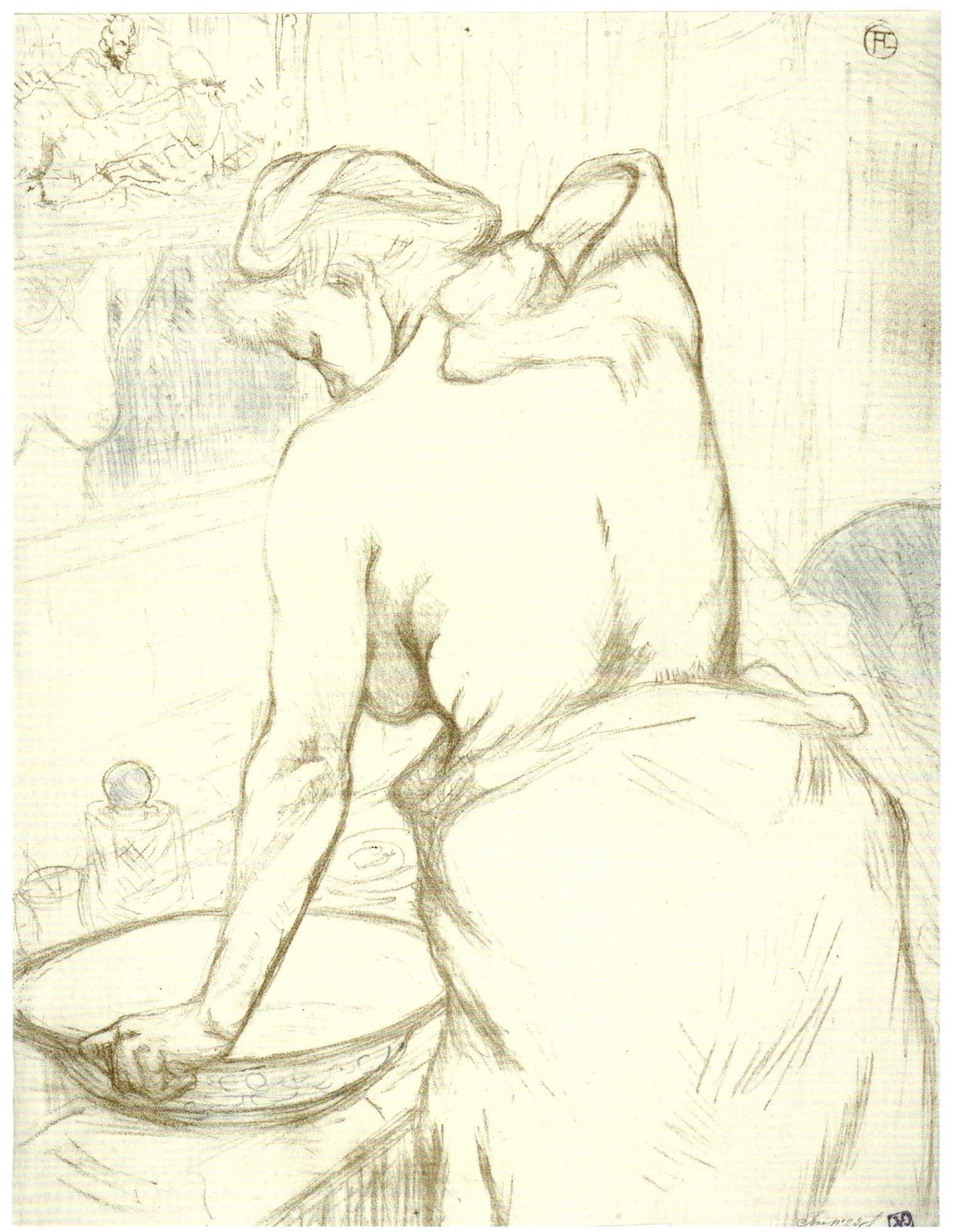

Plate 53

FEMME QUI SE LAVE, LA TOILETTE (WOMAN AT HER TOILETTE, WASHING HERSELF) from the portfolio **ELLES**. 1896

Lithograph, sheet: $20\frac{5}{16} \times 15\frac{1}{2}$ in. (51.6 x 39.4 cm)

Gift of Abby Aldrich Rockefeller, 1946

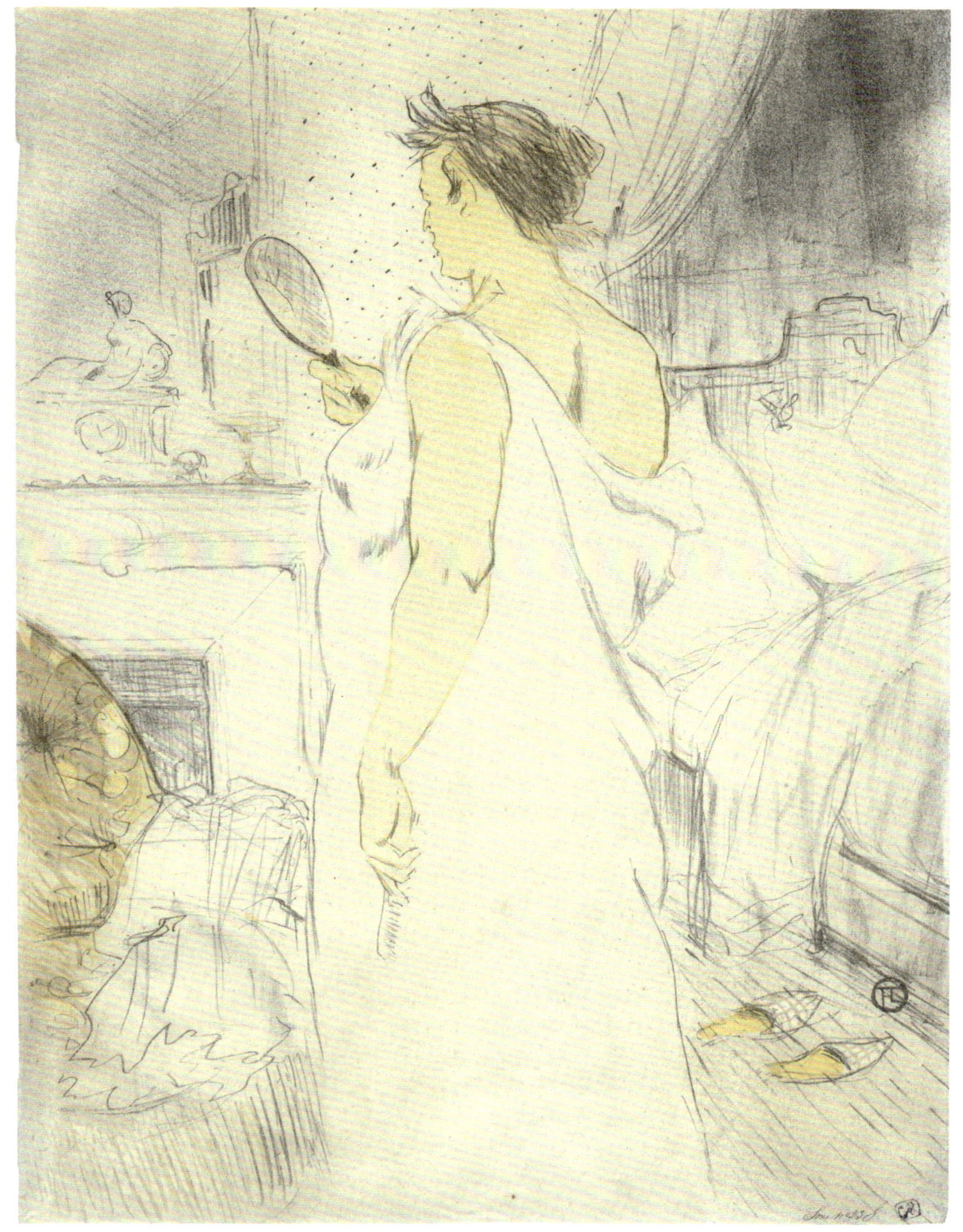

Plate 54
FEMME À GLACE, LA GLACE À MAIN
(**WOMAN WITH A HAND MIRROR**) from the portfolio **ELLES**. 1896
Lithograph, sheet: 20⅜ x 15 11/16 in. (51.7 x 39.8 cm)
Gift of Abby Aldrich Rockefeller, 1946

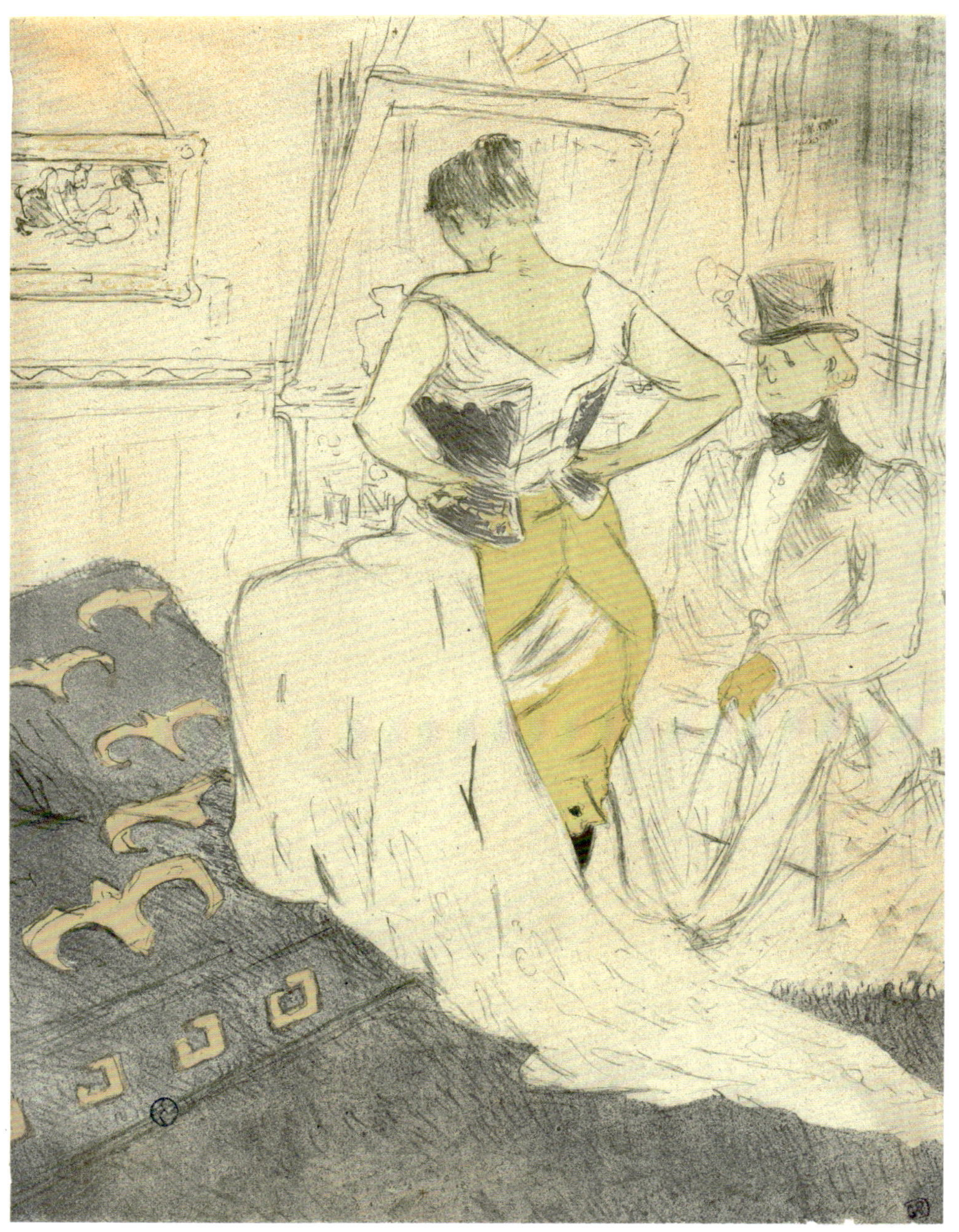

Plate 55

FEMME EN CORSET (WOMAN IN CORSET)

from the portfolio **ELLES**. 1896

Lithograph, sheet: 20 x 15½ in. (50.8 x 39.4 cm)

Gift of Abby Aldrich Rockefeller, 1946

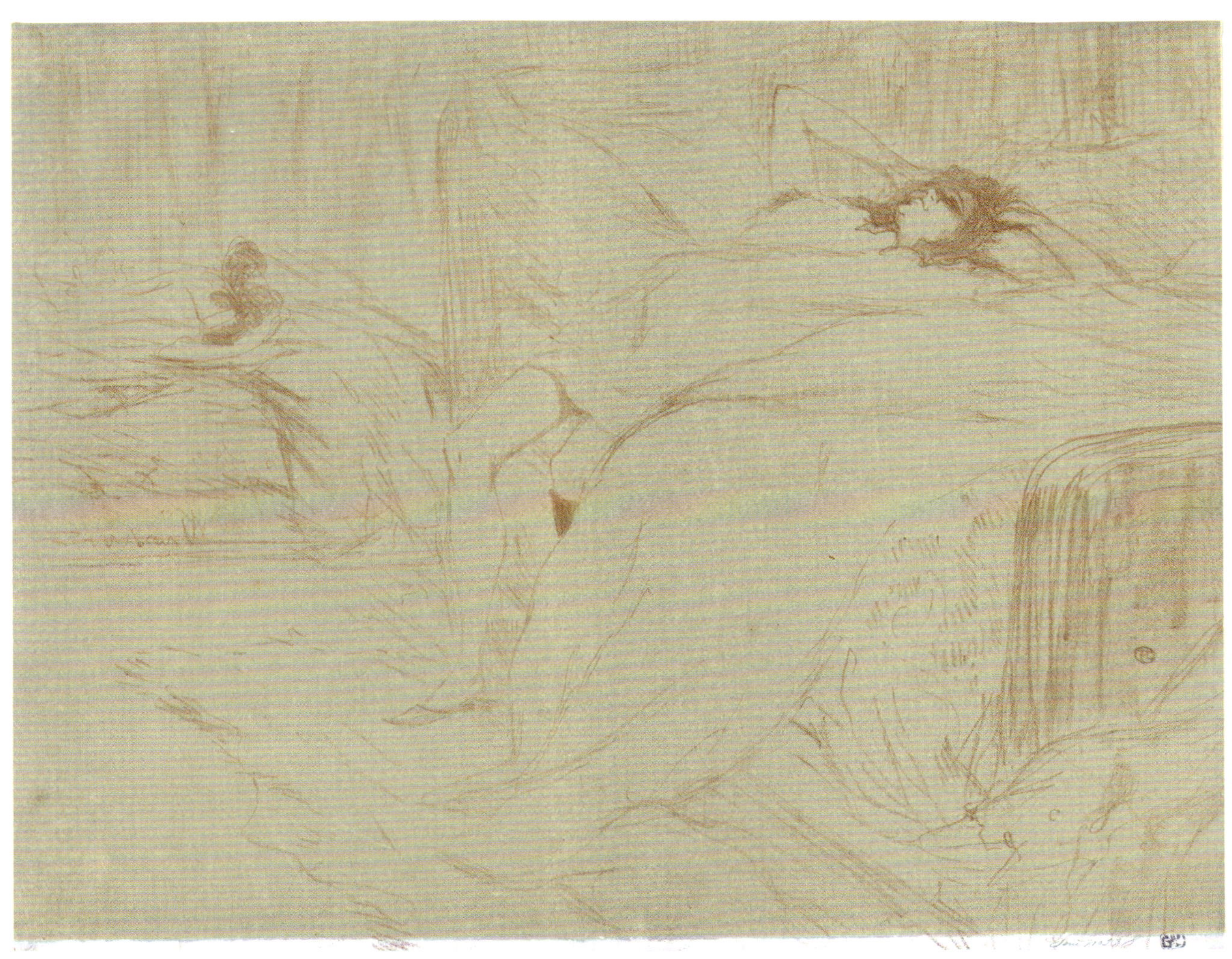

Plate 56
FEMME SUR LE DOS, LASSITUDE (RECLINING WOMAN, LASSITUDE)
from the portfolio **ELLES**. 1896
Lithograph, sheet: 15⁹⁄₁₆ x 20¼ in. (39.5 x 51.5 cm)
Gift of Abby Aldrich Rockefeller, 1946

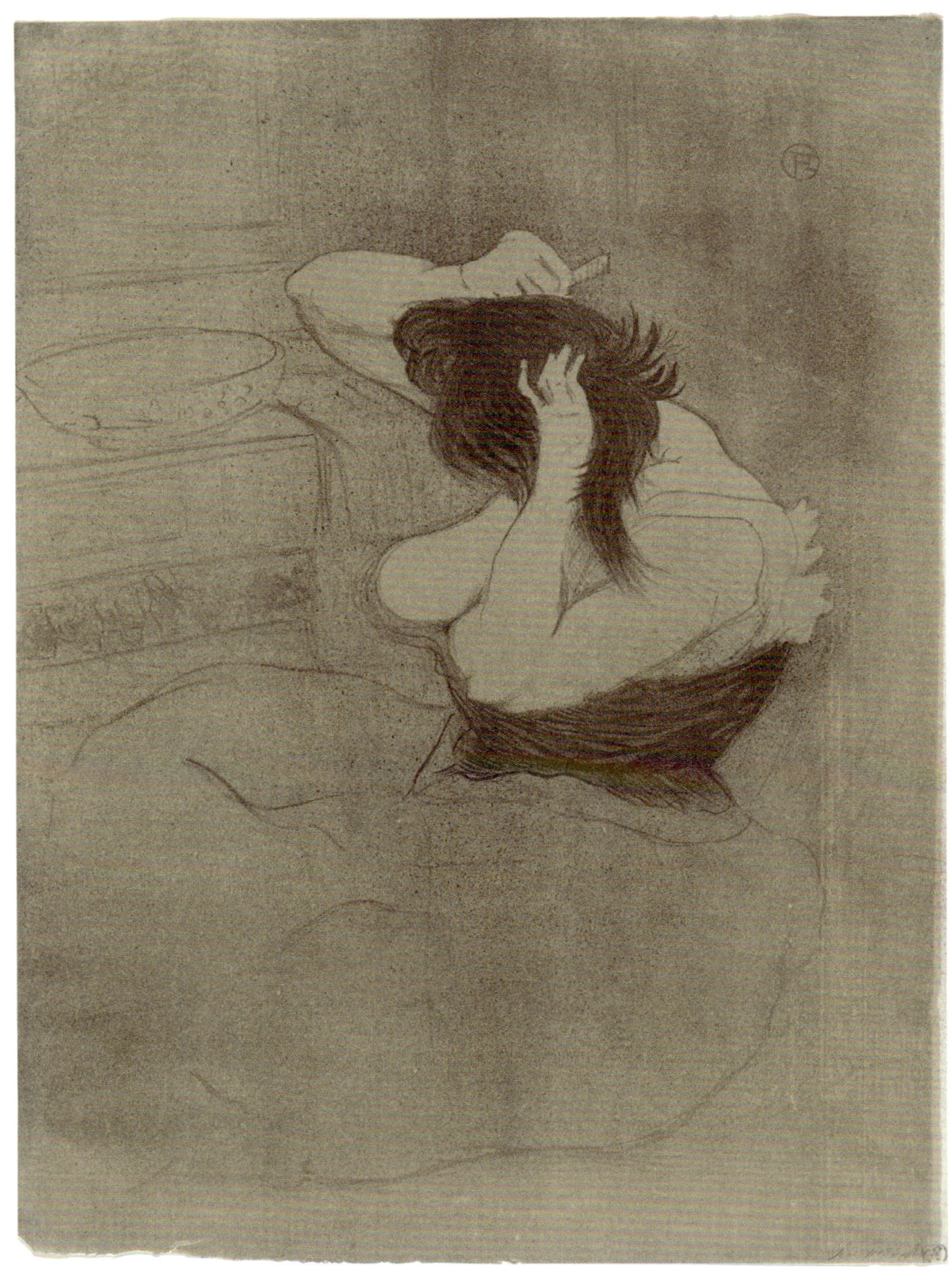

Plate 57

FEMME QUI SE PEIGNE, LA COIFFURE

(**WOMAN COMBING HER HAIR**) from the portfolio **ELLES**. 1896

Lithograph, sheet: 20 7/16 x 15 3/16 in. (51.9 x 38.5 cm)

Gift of Abby Aldrich Rockefeller, 1946

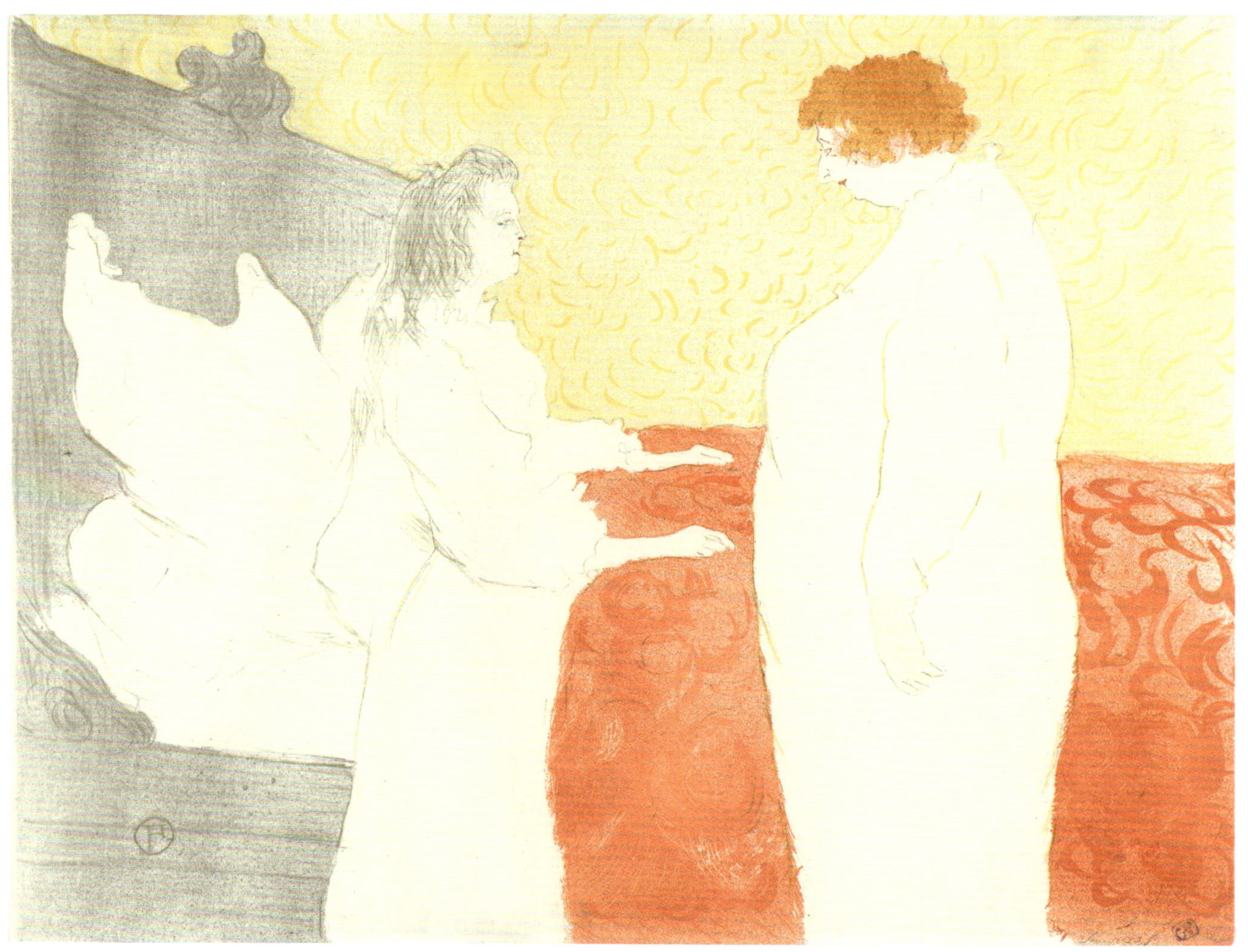

Plate 58

FEMME AU LIT, PROFIL, AU PETIT LEVER

(**WOMAN IN BED, PROFILE, AWAKENING**) from the portfolio **ELLES**. 1896

Lithograph, sheet: 15½ x 20$\frac{7}{16}$ in. (39.3 x 51.9 cm)

Gift of Abby Aldrich Rockefeller, 1946

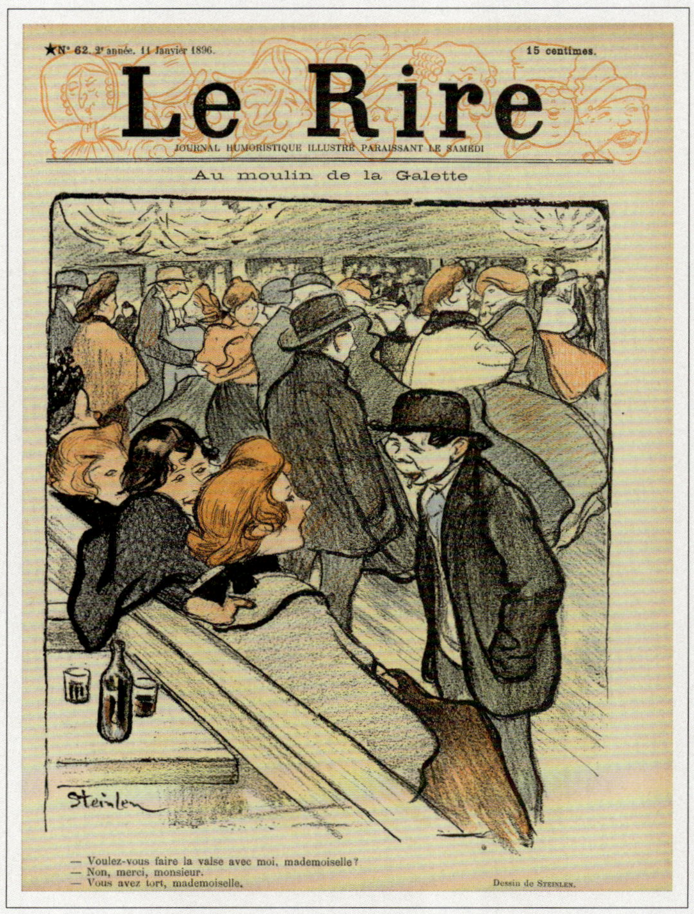

★N° 62. 2e année. 11 Janvier 1896.

15 centimes.

Le Rire

JOURNAL HUMORISTIQUE ILLUSTRÉ PARAISSANT LE SAMEDI

Au moulin de la Galette

— Voulez-vous faire la valse avec moi, mademoiselle?
— Non, merci, monsieur.
— Vous avez tort, mademoiselle.

Dessin de Steinlen.

CREATIVE CIRCLES

While Lautrec socialized with the stars of the café-concerts, he was also part of a creative circle of authors, editors, and composers who commissioned him to publicize their work. Lautrec was not one for theory; the writings he left are primarily pithy, chatty letters rather than artistic treatises, essays, or articles stating a position or philosophy. He was most interested in things that entertained him. He contributed illustrations to humorous magazines such as *Le Rire* (fig. 36) and *L'Escarmouche* (pls. 17, 18), soft-core erotica like *La Fin de siècle*, chronicles of Paris pleasures like *Courrier français*, and newsy journals such as *Le Figaro illustré*. He made posters to advertise reviews, including the American magazine *The Chap Book*, *La Revue blanche* (pl. 107), and *L'Aube* (pl. 59), a short-lived publication remembered exclusively for Lautrec's elegant lithograph. The monochrome image suggests the journal's title—the blue light of dawn. Two women, trudging behind a cart loaded

36. **THÉOPHILE-ALEXANDRE STEINLEN** (French, 1859–1923). *At the Moulin de la Galette* from the journal *Le Rire* (January 11, 1896). Halftone relief, page: 11⅞ x 9 ⅛ in. (30.2 x 23.2 cm). The Museum of Modern Art, New York. Linda Barth Goldstein Fund, 1997

perhaps with laundry, are contained within a triangle formed by the strong rays of light cast by the streetlamp, which illuminates the horse leading the group up the hill.

Lautrec designed one of his most arresting posters for his hometown newspaper, *La Dépêche de Toulouse*. Commissioned by the editor, Arthur Huc, *Le Pendu* (pl. 60) publicized the serialization of *Les Drames de Toulouse*, novelized accounts of three moments in the city's history: the family drama of the notorious Calas case of the 1760s, the peasant insurgency at Pech-David in 1799, and the assassination of the suspected Napoleonic loyalist General Jean-Pierre Ramel in 1815. These sensationalist tales of violence and revenge appealed to Lautrec. The Calas case was one of familial estrangement, wrongful accusation, assumed filicide, suicide, religious intolerance, execution, and redemption that came too late. Lautrec's poster depicts the macabre moment when Jean Calas discovers that his son has hanged himself, dramatically illuminating the body in the glow of candlelight.

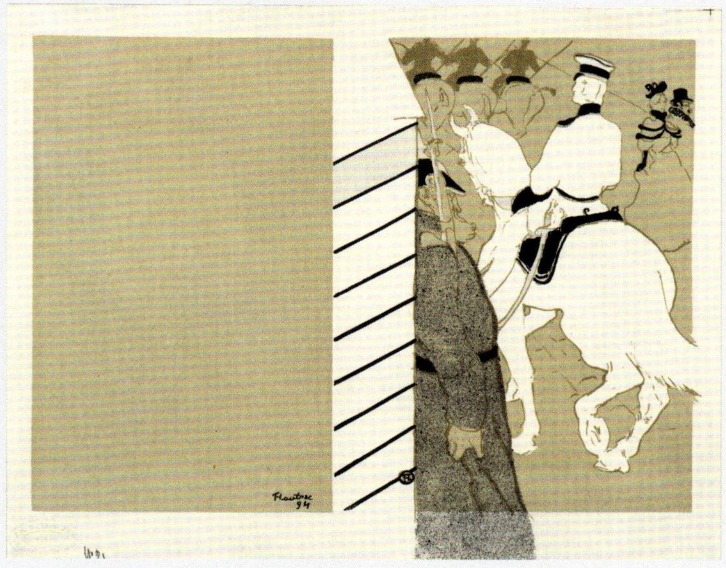

37. **HENRI DE TOULOUSE-LAUTREC**. Cover for the book *Babylon d'Allemagne* by Victor Joze. 1894. Lithograph, 8 11/16 x 11 in. (22 x 28 cm). The Museum of Modern Art, New York. Gift of Abby Aldrich Rockefeller, 1946

Lautrec's taste in most things was resoundingly populist. On several occasions, the artist's friend and drinking partner Victor Joze (the pen name of the Polish author Victor Joze Dobrski de Zastzebiec) commissioned him to help publicize *La Ménagerie sociale*, his semi-trashy series of *romans de gare*[76] that capitalized on the general public's hunger for tawdry tales. In *Reine de joie* (1892), Joze focuses on the Parisian demimonde, describing the relationship between a beautiful woman, Alice Lamy, and her wealthy patron, Olizac, the Baron de Rozenfeld. Joze describes the arrangement between them as quite clear—sexual gain for him and material gain for her. The public was engrossed not only by these salacious details but also by the scandal that followed. The Parisian financier Baron Alphonse de Rothschild believed the story to be a defamatory (and anti-Semitic) satirization of himself and sued to stop the distribution of both the book and the poster.

The fabulous image Lautrec created to publicize the novel (pl. 62)—hard to miss on the streets of Paris, with its bright red, yellow, and black—confirmed the public's worst fears about the relationship between the young woman and her portly patron with his greasy comb-over. The physical mismatch of the couple is played out against the tableware, the curvilinear cruet meeting the round plate bearing the baron's coat of arms. Thadée Natanson, the Jewish editor of *La Revue blanche*, wrote admiringly of the poster in a review of Lautrec's work: "It . . . especially, makes us thrill: the delicious *reine de joie*, bright, pretty, and exquisitely perverse."[77]

Another title in the series, *Babylone d'Allemagne* (1894), compares the social and sexual mores of Germany to those of the biblical city of Babylon, locus of debauchery and indulgence. The

German ambassador considered Joze's novel denigrating to the Prussians, who had defeated the French just a few years earlier, and in protest, he nearly set off a diplomatic incident. Lautrec's poster for the book (pl. 64) is a study in dynamic movement. As riders glide diagonally across the page, the guardhouse stands firm, manned by a caricature of the German emperor Wilhelm I. Unable to stay attentive to politics for too long, Lautrec also included a pretty passerby, who admires the elegant horseman with a sidelong glance, ignoring her shorter companion. Lautrec's cover design for the volume (never realized) emphasizes the central figures of horse and rider, unified to create a single form. The striped guardhouse is wrapped inventively around the spine (fig. 37).

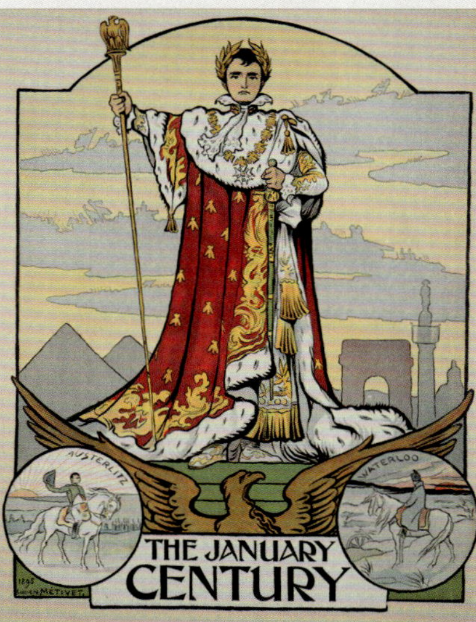

38. **LUCIEN MÉTIVET** (French, 1863–1930). *The January Century*. 1895. Lithograph, 25½ x 20½ in. (64.8 x 52.1 cm). Collection Zimmerli Art Museum at Rutgers University, David A. and Mildred H. Morse Acquisition Fund

In 1897 Joze tapped Lautrec again as he revisited the Rozenfeld family he had introduced in *Reine de joie*. *La Tribu d'Isidore* is the first in a series of novels tracing several generations of a Jewish family "in the process of conquering Europe, thanks to these four qualities: intelligence, energy, guile and patience."[78] Lautrec's cover for the book (pl. 100) works on multiple levels: as a depiction of three generations of Rozenfelds (Judas, Isidore, and Abraham); as a manga-esque evocation of portrait sketches; and as one of his contemporary scenes of carriage promenades with canine passengers. In the preface, Joze specifically denies any prejudicial intent: "One would be greatly wrong to believe that my end is to make a series of pamphlets against the Jews. First, I am an enemy of novels with a thesis, and then I am not an anti-Semite in any precise sense of the word."[79]

The then still-unfolding Dreyfus Affair—a political scandal hinging on anti-Semitism—had divided Paris and seen a rise in anti-Jewish sentiment. Lautrec's position on the matter is difficult to assess, as he came from a staunchly conservative Catholic family and yet had many Jewish friends. He worked with Joze to publicize his arguably prejudiced novels but also with Georges Clemenceau on illustrations for *Au pied du Sinaï* (pls. 65–68), the writer's collection of short stories sympathetic to the Jewish experience. In preparation for illustrating these comic tales about the rich Baron Moïse von Goldschlammbach and the poor Ukrainian tailor Solomon Fuss, Lautrec, ever the observer, spent time sketching in the Jewish quarters of Paris. The resulting images have been judged "accurate and artistic," containing "none of the viciously anti-Semitic caricature that prevailed in the daily and weekly Parisian artistic journals."[80] It is likely that Lautrec, apolitical and relatively uninterested in current events, found the texts to be amusing stories rather than endorsements of a political philosophy.

Lautrec often failed in attempts at cerebral projects. Highbrow literary collaborations seemed to elude him, and history generally did not interest him: "I . . . moreover have never done any *current events*. It's not my style."[81] When he was nineteen, drawings he made for his first commission, to illustrate a volume of Victor Hugo's work, were rejected. In 1895 he submitted a poster, again unsuccessfully, for a competition held to advertise William Milligan Sloane's four-volume biography *The Life of Napoleon Bonaparte* (pl. 63). In typical Lautrec fashion, Napoleon is distinguished by his hat rather than by a careful likeness. He is accompanied by figures that suggest the global vision and expansive nature of his campaigns. In an elegant touch, the three horses embody the colors of the French flag, with Napoleon on his white steed conveying a sense of isolation and loneliness that evokes his sad exile and end on Elba. Undeterred by losing the competition to a traditional academic depiction by Lucien Métivet (fig. 38), Lautrec published his own edition of one hundred impressions, paying for the printing of the poster himself.

Edmond de Goncourt was a generation older than Lautrec and had a firmly established reputation as an art critic, historian, and ardent collector of Japanese art who wrote monographs on Kitagawa Utamaro and Katsushika Hokusai. His *Journal Goncourt,* written with his brother Jules, chronicled the literary and artistic life of Paris. His naturalist novels inspired authors such as Émile Zola and Paul Verlaine, and he established the Prix Goncourt, an annual prize for outstanding French literature that is still awarded today. Goncourt's tragic 1877 novel *La Fille Élisa* followed the miserable life of the title character from a childhood marked by poverty, through a life of prostitution, to death in prison following a murder conviction. Lautrec was a tremendous fan of the tale and hoped to illustrate a new edition. His friends, including Gustave Geffroy, Thadée Natanson, Romain Coolus, and Maurice Joyant, all encouraged him, but Goncourt rejected Lautrec's drawings, perhaps deterred by the artist's associations with lowbrow, populist material. Although the publication was never realized, Joyant held onto Lautrec's own 1877 copy of the book, in which the artist had made a series of sketches. It was published as a facsimile in 1931 (pls. 69–72).[82]

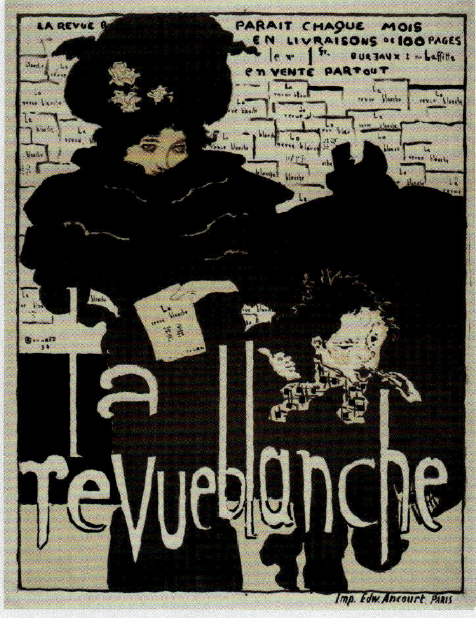

39. **PIERRE BONNARD** (French, 1867–1947). *La Revue blanche.* 1894. Lithograph, 31¾ x 24⅜ in. (80.7 x 61.9 cm). The Museum of Modern Art, New York. Abby Aldrich Rockefeller Fund, 1949

The one exception to Lautrec's lack of success with intellectual projects was his work with *La Revue blanche,* the premier Parisian literary and artistic review, whose circle of contributors included the editors Alexandre, Thadée, and Alfred Natanson; the authors Romain Coolus, Paul Leclercq, and Jules Renard; and the artist Tristan Bernard. Many of them became close friends with Lautrec, accompanying him on his nightly prowls or traveling with him to the country on weekends. In addition to fiction, essays, and art criticism, the *Revue* commissioned artists to make posters (fig. 39), and briefly published original prints, a selection of which was issued in 1894 as *L'Album de la Revue blanche.* Enthusiastic supporters of Lautrec's work, the editors wrote encouragingly of him on their pages, published several of his lithographs, and commissioned one of his best-loved posters (pl. 107).

The booming café-concert scene demanded a constant supply of new musical material, and Lautrec made numerous cover illustrations for song sheets sung or written by his friends. Among them was Désiré Dihau, a distant cousin who played bassoon with several Paris orchestras, including the Opéra and the El Dorado.[83] Dihau was also friendly with Hilaire-Germain-Edgar Degas and was the subject of a major painting by the artist (fig. 40). Lautrec used to visit Dihau specifically to gaze at the painting, and it is likely

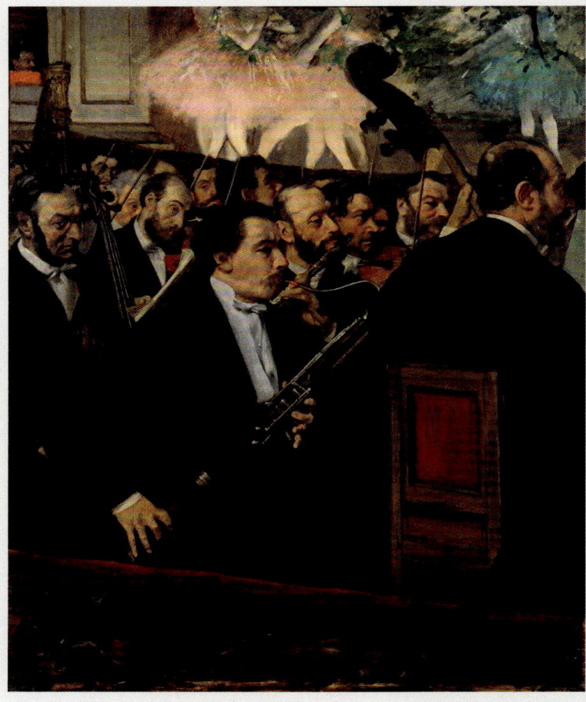

40. **HILAIRE-GERMAIN-EDGAR DEGAS** (French, 1834–1917). *The Orchestra at the Opera*. c. 1870. Oil on canvas, 22¼ x 17 11/16 in. (56.5 x 45 cm). Musée d'Orsay, Paris

through him that the two artists met. Lautrec revisited Degas's depiction of the musician in the orchestra pit for the cover of *Pour Toi!* (fig. 41) and offered another take on the cover of *Les Vieilles Histoires* (pl. 73), a collection of songs popularized in working-class café-concerts, with poetry by Jean Goudezki set to music by Dihau. Here the mustachioed Dihau is seen leading a leashed and muzzled bear—the incorrigible misanthrope Goudezki—across the Pont des Arts. Lautrec offers us an unusually long view of Paris, perhaps inspired by Hokusai's *Thirty-Six Views of Mount Fuji* (1831–33), with the Eiffel Tower and Les Invalides in the background and a lone hot-air balloon floating above.

The standout among Lautrec's musical material is the cover of the song sheet for "Carnot malade!" (pl. 61), by Eugène Lemercier and popularized by the composer at the Chat Noir in 1893. That summer the French president, Marie François Sadi Carnot, was taken ill. According to a report in the *New York Times*, Carnot's condition was serious—he was suffering from either liver trouble or an intestinal obstruction.[84] His ailment was parodied in Lemercier's lyrics, in which the president's poor health is likened to that of the French Republic: "Ah! Heck! If Carnot is sick, it's probably to be like the government!" Carnot recovered but was assassinated in 1894 by an Italian anarchist, who stabbed him near the liver. In Lautrec's image, the helpless official is tucked in bed like a sick child, his face and hands yellowed by jaundice, the tricolor of the French flag featured on his folded bedclothes. At his bedside a minister takes his pulse and a nurse bears a bowl of broth. His papers, unattended, are in danger of falling to the floor.

Lautrec loved the theater, and he became involved as more than a spectator. The Théâtre Libre, run by his friend André Antoine (who would later establish the eponymous Théâtre Antoine), was one among several companies with which he was especially close. Antoine's avant-garde company brought the work of Émile Zola and August Strindberg to the French stage, with productions so radically realistic that they would include live chickens or a side of beef for a scene set in a butcher shop. Lautrec was a season ticket holder and made a number of posters and programs for the company.[85] In a particularly brilliant program for *Le Missionnaire* (pl. 79), he inverted the spectacle of the theater, depicting the audience instead of the performers, as if to indicate that they were as much a part of the action as what occurred onstage.

The Théâtre de l'Oeuvre, managed by Thadée Natanson's school friend Aurélien Lugné-Poë,[86] presented intellectually challenging Symbolist plays by Henrik Ibsen, Stéphane Mallarmé, Alfred Jarry, and others. Among the programs Lautrec produced for the company was one for a double bill featuring Oscar Wilde's *Salomé* (pl. 84) and Romain Coolus's *Raphaël* (pl. 83). *Salomé* was making its debut in

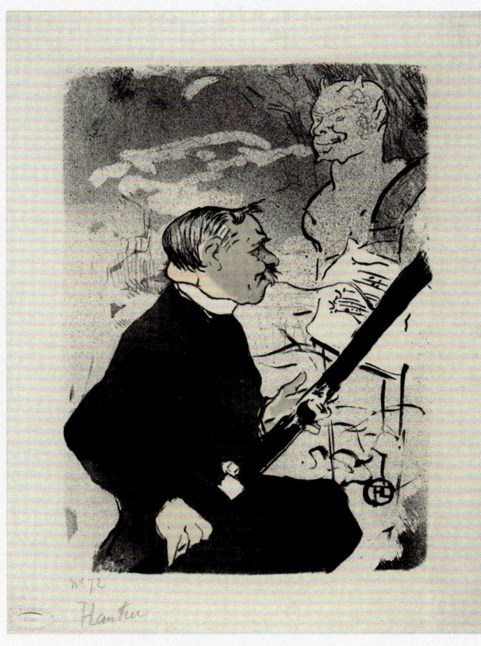

41. **HENRI DE TOULOUSE-LAUTREC.** *Pour Toi!* 1893. Lithograph, 10 9/16 x 7 9/16 in. (26.9 x 19.2 cm). The British Museum, London

Paris after being banned during rehearsals in London. Wilde, like Lautrec, a notorious bon vivant, was in jail in London at the time, having been convicted of homosexual practices.

The work of these avant-garde theater companies was closely intertwined with that of like-minded artists such as Lautrec, Pierre Bonnard, Henri-Gabriel Ibels, and Édouard Vuillard, who collaborated with them on designs for posters, programs, and sets. This unique history is captured in a remarkable album of theater programs assembled by the French bibliophile, print collector, and theatergoer Henri Beraldi, which is now in the collection of The Museum of Modern Art (pls. 79–98). These programs document major cultural events, including the premier of Alfred Jarry's scandalous, scatological, paradigm-shifting comedy *Ubu roi* in 1896 (pl. 85). Comprising fifty pristine impressions of the most esteemed late-nineteenth-century examples, including several by Lautrec (pls. 79, 80), the volume is a testament to the cross-fertilization of art and theater in Paris in this period.

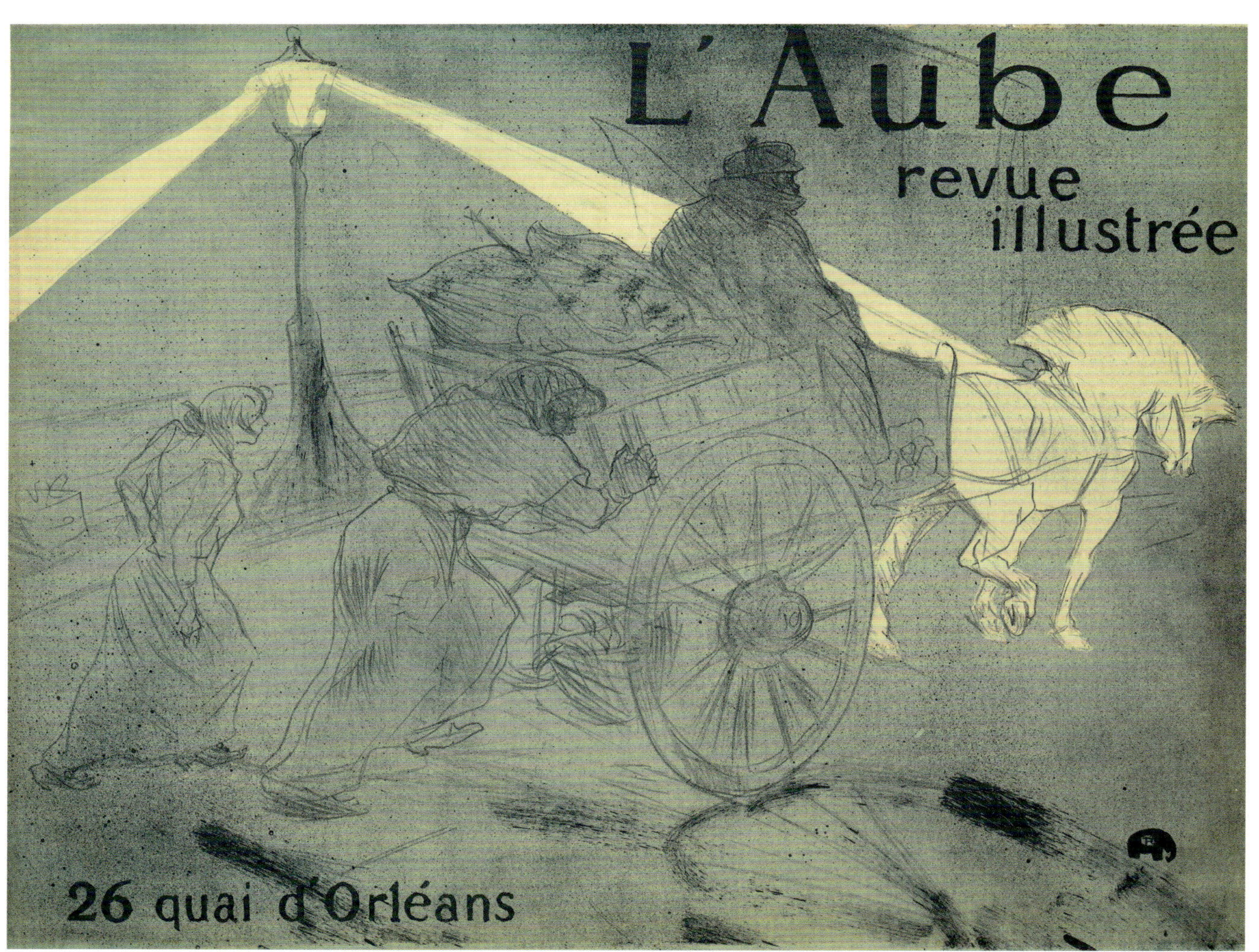

Plate 59
L'AUBE (THE DAWN). 1896
Lithograph, sheet: 23 13/16 x 31 3/4 in. (60.5 x 80.6 cm)
Gift of Abby Aldrich Rockefeller, 1940

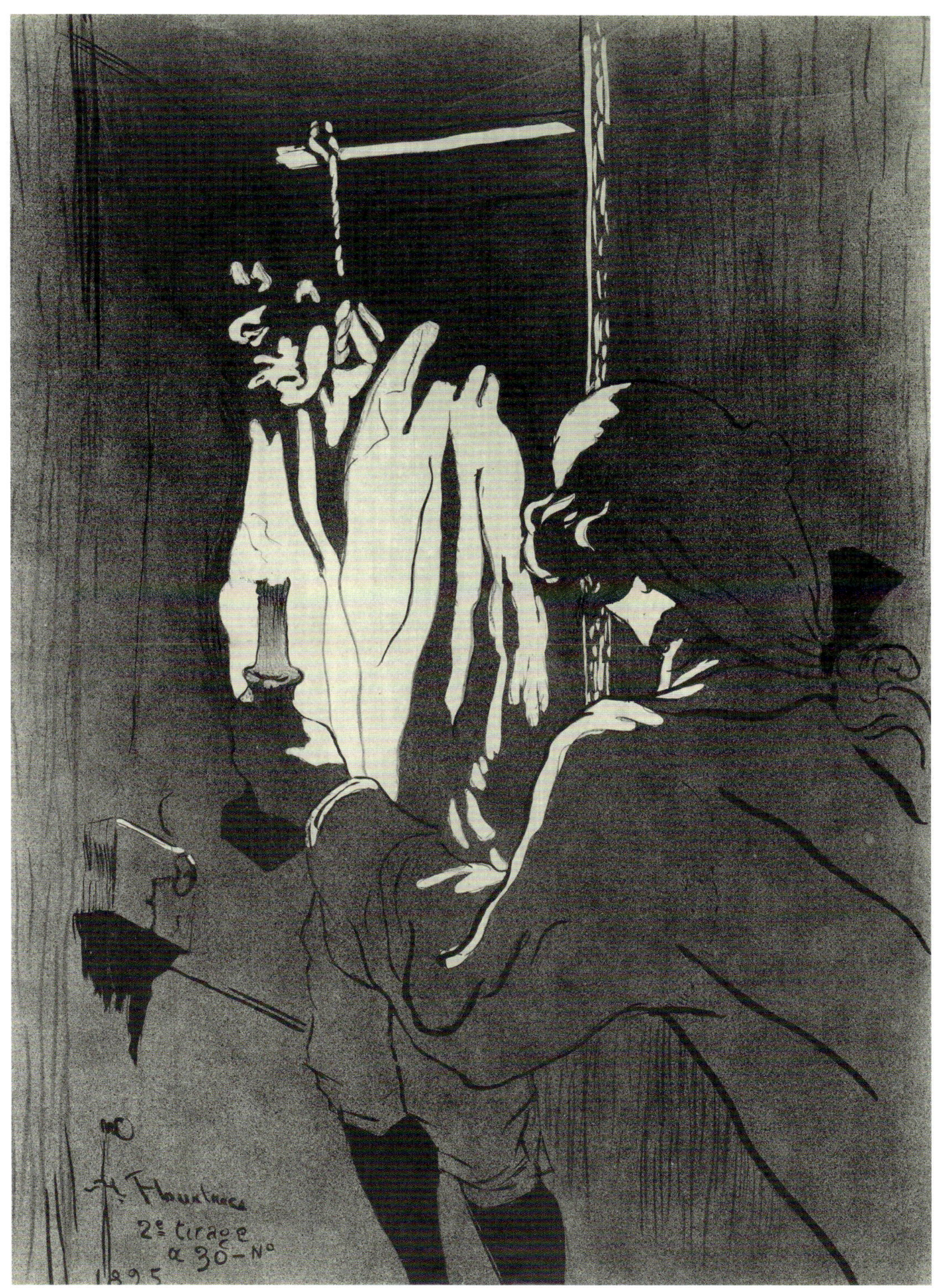

Plate 60

LE PENDU (HANGING MAN). 1895

Lithograph, sheet: 30¼ x 21 15/16 in. (76.8 x 55.7 cm)

Purchase, 1949

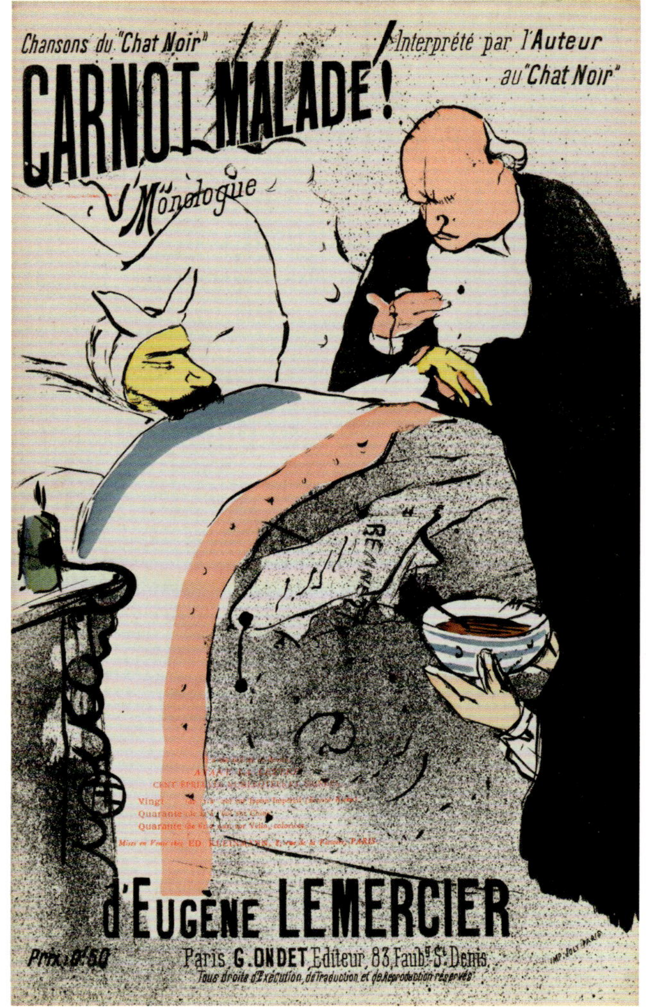

Plate 61
CARNOT MALADE! (SICK CARNOT!). 1893
Lithograph with stencil additions, sheet: $10\frac{15}{16}$ x $6\frac{7}{8}$ in. (27.8 x 17.5 cm)
Gift of Emilio Sanchez, 1967

Plate 62
REINE DE JOIE (QUEEN OF JOY). 1892
Lithograph, sheet: $59\frac{7}{16}$ x $39\frac{7}{16}$ in. (151 x 100.1 cm)
Gift of Mr. and Mrs. Richard Rodgers, 1961

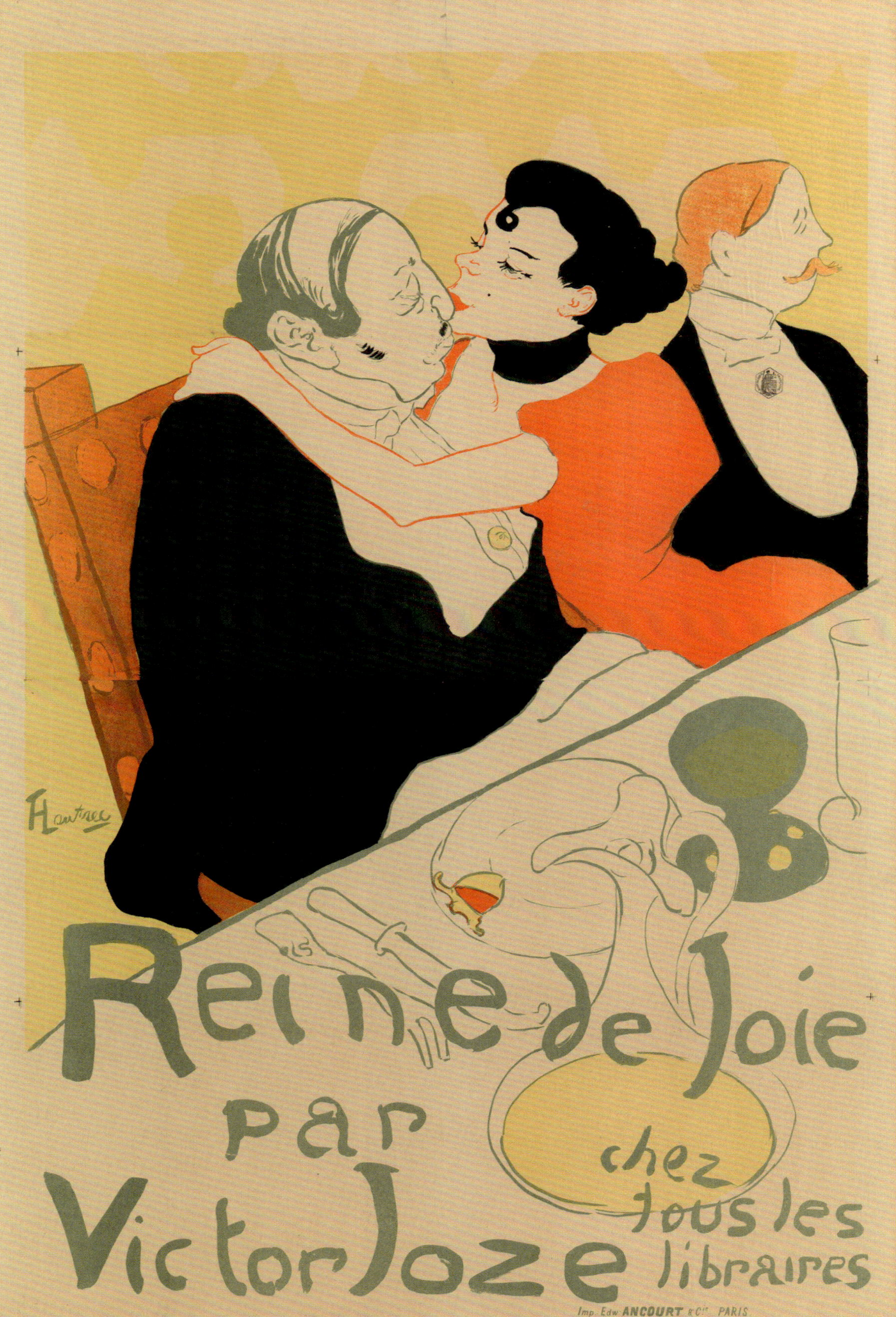
Reine de Joie
par
Victor Joze
chez tous les libraires
Imp. Edw. ANCOURT &Cie PARIS

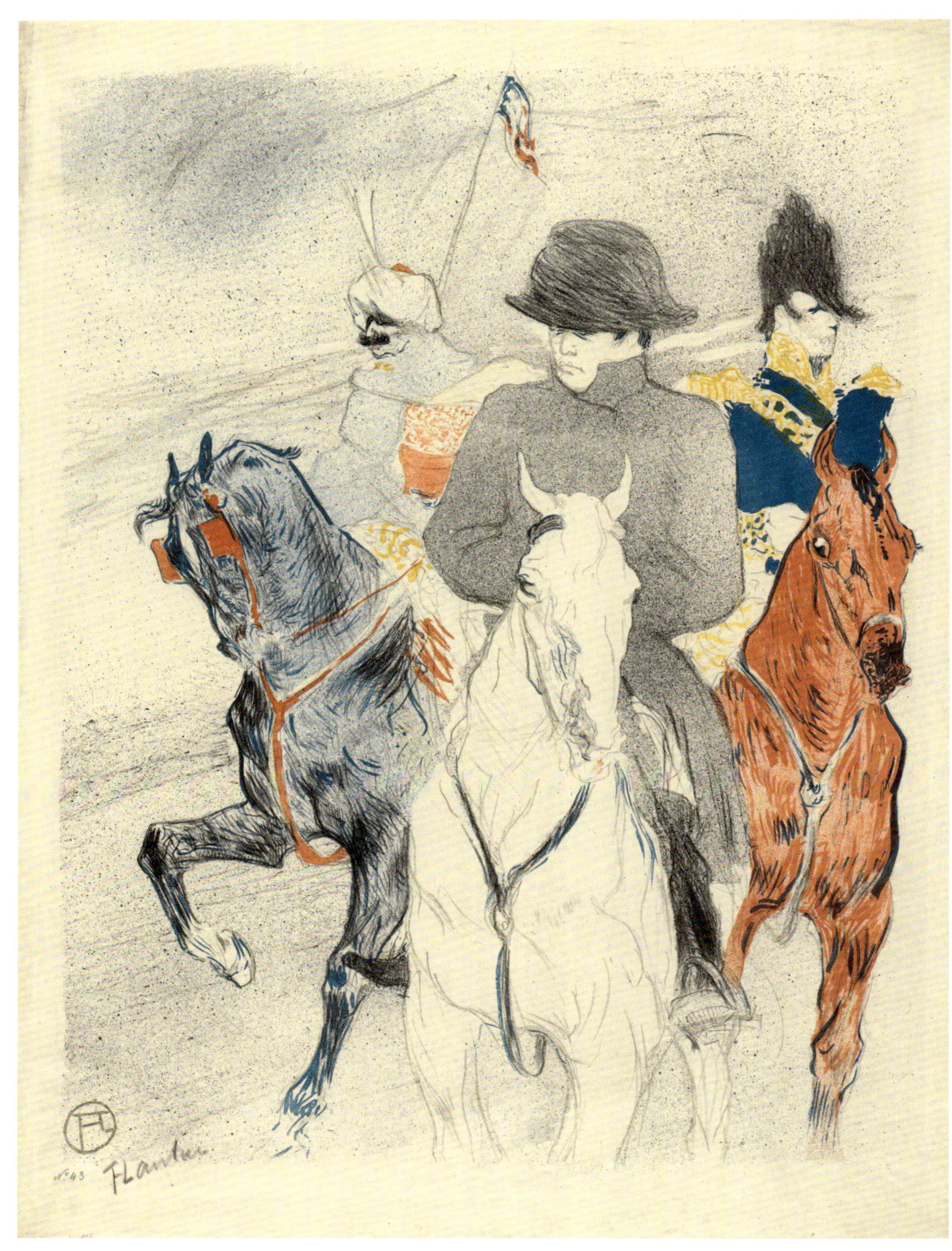

Plate 63
NAPOLEON. 1895
Lithograph, sheet: 25 11/16 x 19 5/8 in. (65.3 x 49.8 cm)
Gift of Abby Aldrich Rockefeller, 1946

Plate 64
BABYLONE D'ALLEMAGNE (**GERMAN BABYLON**). 1894
Lithograph, sheet: 46 9/16 x 33 3/16 in. (118.3 x 84.3 cm)
Gift of Abby Aldrich Rockefeller, 1940

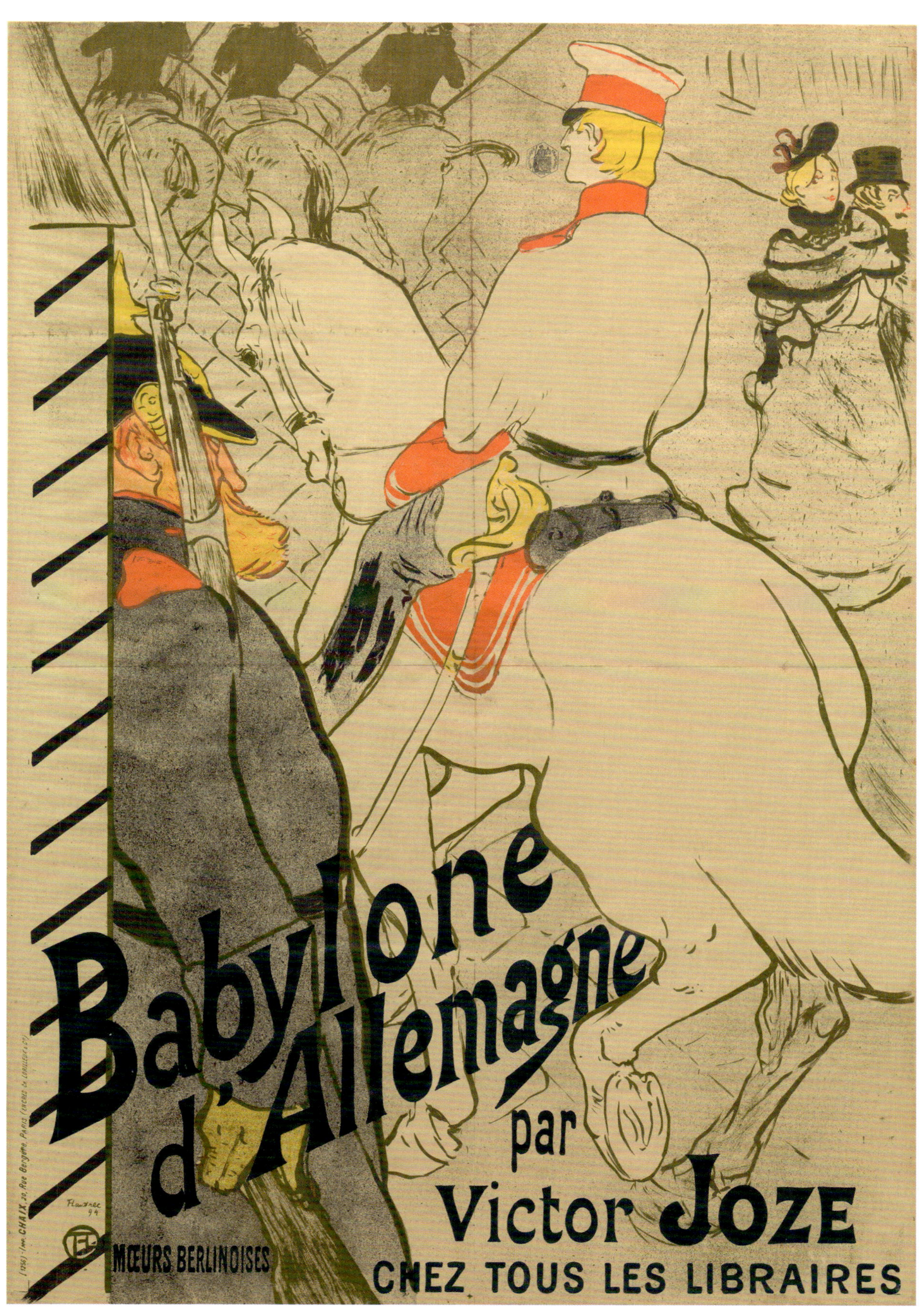

Babylone d'Allemagne
par
Victor JOZE
CHEZ TOUS LES LIBRAIRES
MŒURS BERLINOISES

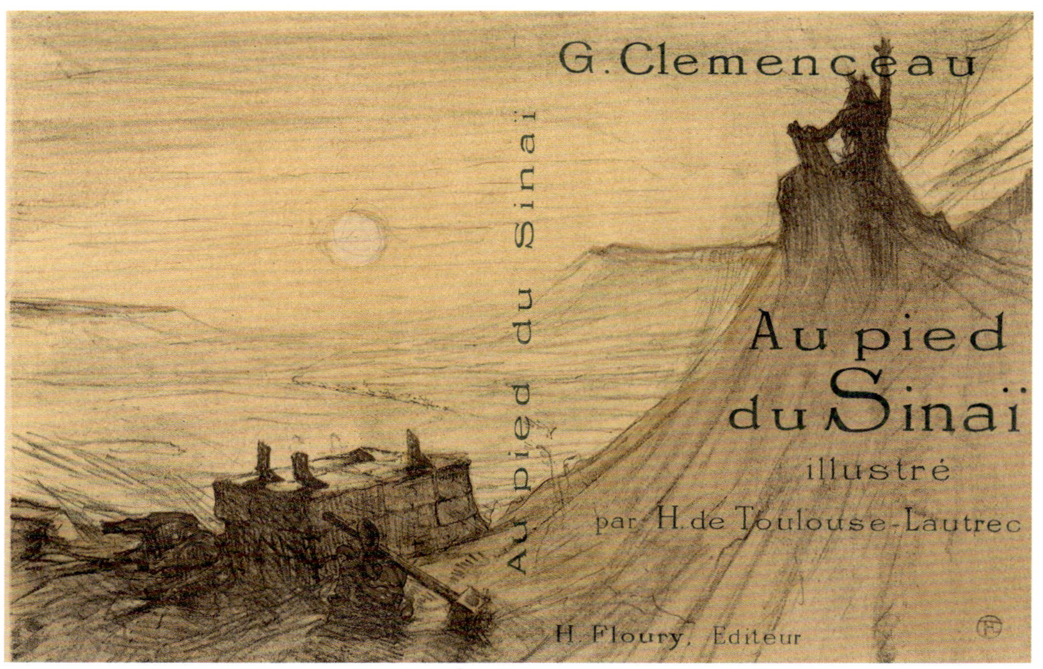

Plate 65
Cover for the illustrated book **AU PIED DU SINAÏ**
by Georges Clemenceau. 1897, published 1898
Lithograph, sheet: 14 15/16 x 21 15/16 in. (37.9 x 55.7 cm)
Gift of Mr. and Mrs. Herbert D. Schimmel, 1996

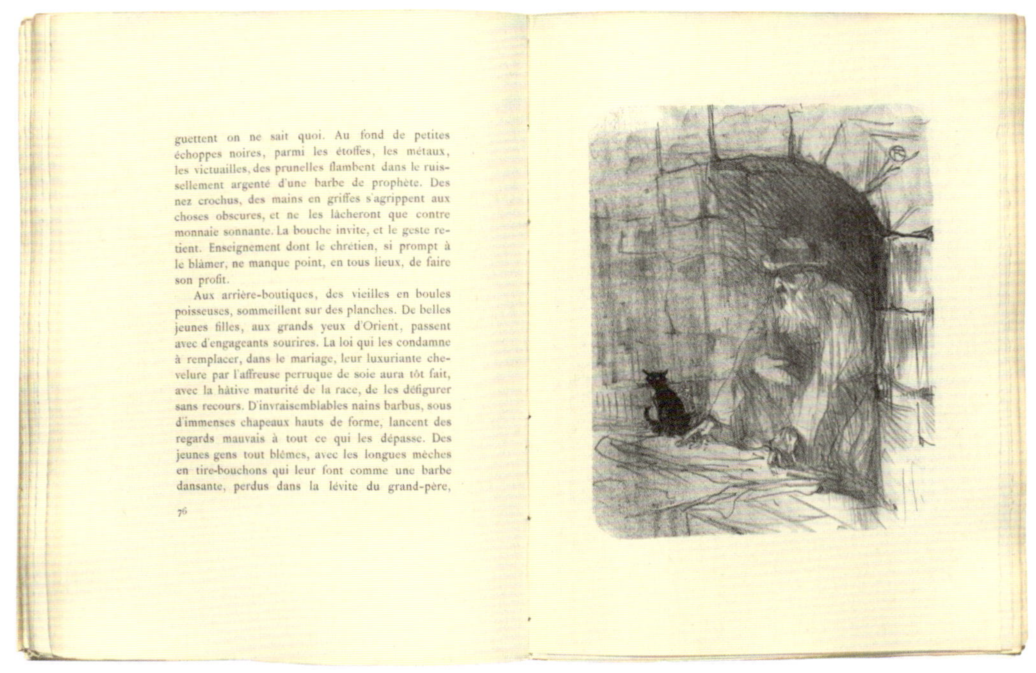

guettent on ne sait quoi. Au fond de petites échoppes noires, parmi les étoffes, les métaux, les victuailles, des prunelles flambent dans le ruissellement argenté d'une barbe de prophète. Des nez crochus, des mains en griffes s'agrippent aux choses obscures, et ne les lâcheront que contre monnaie sonnante. La bouche invite, et le geste retient. Enseignement dont le chrétien, si prompt à le blâmer, ne manque point, en tous lieux, de faire son profit.

Aux arrière-boutiques, des vieilles en boules poisseuses, sommeillent sur des planches. De belles jeunes filles, aux grands yeux d'Orient, passent avec d'engageants sourires. La loi qui les condamne à remplacer, dans le mariage, leur luxuriante chevelure par l'affreuse perruque de soie aura tôt fait, avec la hâtive maturité de la race, de les défigurer sans recours. D'invraisemblables nains barbus, sous d'immenses chapeaux hauts de forme, lancent des regards mauvais à tout ce qui les dépasse. Des jeunes gens tout blêmes, avec les longues mèches en tire-bouchons qui leur font comme une barbe dansante, perdus dans la lévite du grand-père,

76

Plate 66
UNE ARRIÈRE-BOUTIQUE À CRACOVIE
(**A BASEMENT SHOP IN KRAKOW**) from the illustrated book
AU PIED DU SINAÏ by Georges Clemenceau. 1897, published 1898
Lithograph, page: 10 1/4 x 7 7/8 in. (26 x 20 cm)
The Louis E. Stern Collection, 1964

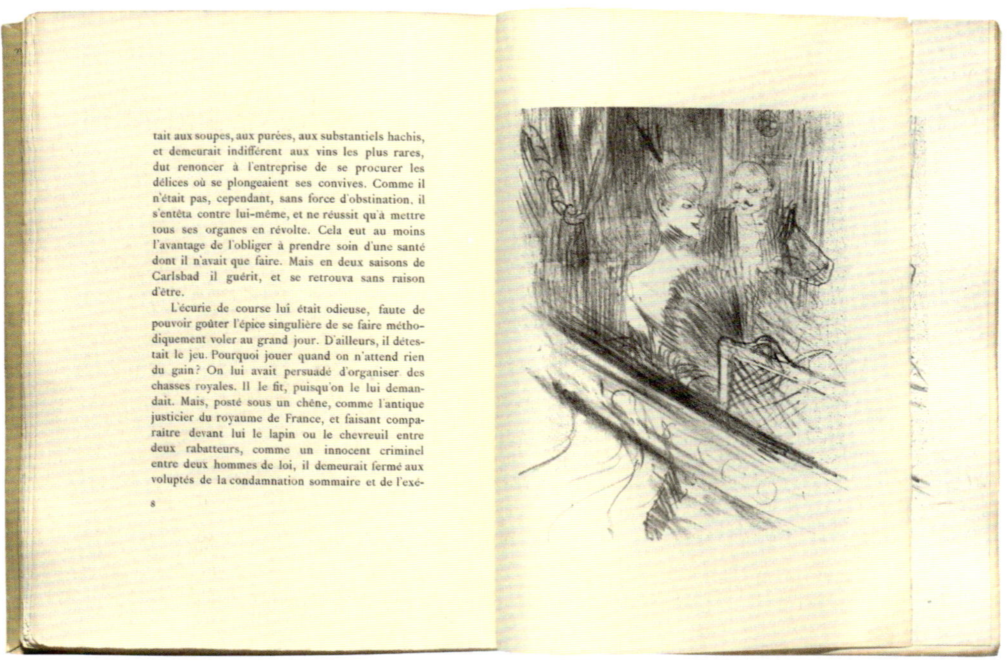

tait aux soupes, aux purées, aux substantiels hachis, et demeurait indifférent aux vins les plus rares, dut renoncer à l'entreprise de se procurer les délices où se plongeaient ses convives. Comme il n'était pas, cependant, sans force d'obstination, il s'entêta contre lui-même, et ne réussit qu'à mettre tous ses organes en révolte. Cela eut au moins l'avantage de l'obliger à prendre soin d'une santé dont il n'avait que faire. Mais en deux saisons de Carlsbad il guérit, et se retrouva sans raison d'être.

L'écurie de course lui était odieuse, faute de pouvoir goûter l'épice singulière de se faire méthodiquement voler au grand jour. D'ailleurs, il détestait le jeu. Pourquoi jouer quand on n'attend rien du gain? On lui avait persuadé d'organiser des chasses royales. Il le fit, puisqu'on le lui demandait. Mais, posté sous un chêne, comme l'antique justicier du royaume de France, et faisant comparaitre devant lui le lapin ou le chevreuil entre deux rabatteurs, comme un innocent criminel entre deux hommes de loi, il demeurait fermé aux voluptés de la condamnation sommaire et de l'exé-

8

Plate 67

LE BARON MOÏSE, LA LOGE (**BARON MOÏSE, THE BALCONY**) from the illustrated book **AU PIED DU SINAÏ** by Georges Clemenceau. 1897, published 1898

Lithograph, page: 10¼ x 7⅞ in. (26 x 20 cm)

The Louis E. Stern Collection, 1964

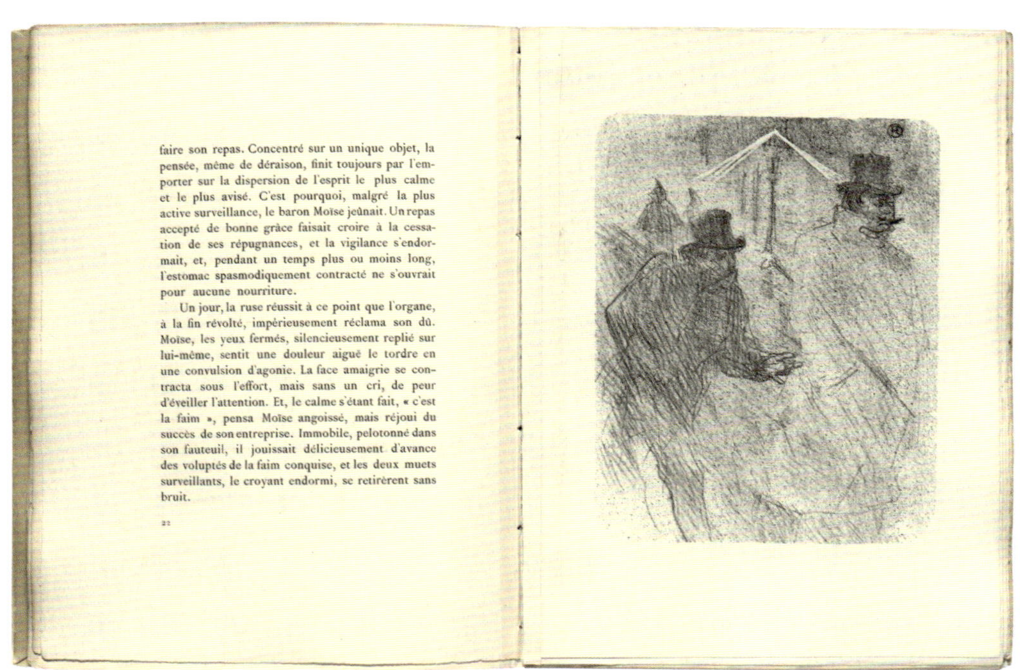

faire son repas. Concentré sur un unique objet, la pensée, même de déraison, finit toujours par l'emporter sur la dispersion de l'esprit le plus calme et le plus avisé. C'est pourquoi, malgré la plus active surveillance, le baron Moïse jeûnait. Un repas accepté de bonne grâce faisait croire à la cessation de ses répugnances, et la vigilance s'endormait, et, pendant un temps plus ou moins long, l'estomac spasmodiquement contracté ne s'ouvrait pour aucune nourriture.

Un jour, la ruse réussit à ce point que l'organe, à la fin révolté, impérieusement réclama son dû. Moïse, les yeux fermés, silencieusement replié sur lui-même, sentit une douleur aiguë le tordre en une convulsion d'agonie. La face amaigrie se contracta sous l'effort, mais sans un cri, de peur d'éveiller l'attention. Et, le calme s'étant fait, « c'est la faim », pensa Moïse angoissé, mais réjoui du succès de son entreprise. Immobile, pelotonné dans son fauteuil, il jouissait délicieusement d'avance des voluptés de la faim conquise, et les deux muets surveillants, le croyant endormi, se retirèrent sans bruit.

22

Plate 68

LE BARON MOÏSE MENDIANT (**BARON MOÏSE BEGGING**) from the illustrated book **AU PIED DU SINAÏ** by Georges Clemenceau. 1897, published 1898

Lithograph, page: 10¼ x 7⅞ in. (26 x 20 cm)

The Louis E. Stern Collection, 1964

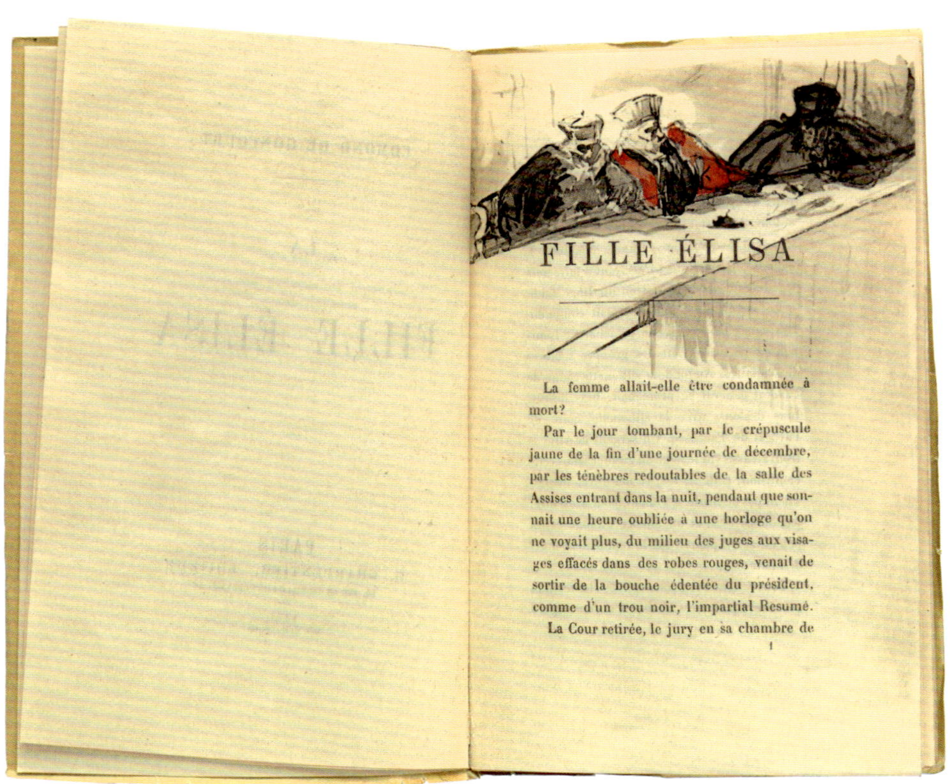

FILLE ÉLISA

La femme allait-elle être condamnée à mort?

Par le jour tombant, par le crépuscule jaune de la fin d'une journée de décembre, par les ténèbres redoutables de la salle des Assises entrant dans la nuit, pendant que sonnait une heure oubliée à une horloge qu'on ne voyait plus, du milieu des juges aux visages effacés dans des robes rouges, venait de sortir de la bouche édentée du président, comme d'un trou noir, l'impartial Resumé.

La Cour retirée, le jury en sa chambre de

1

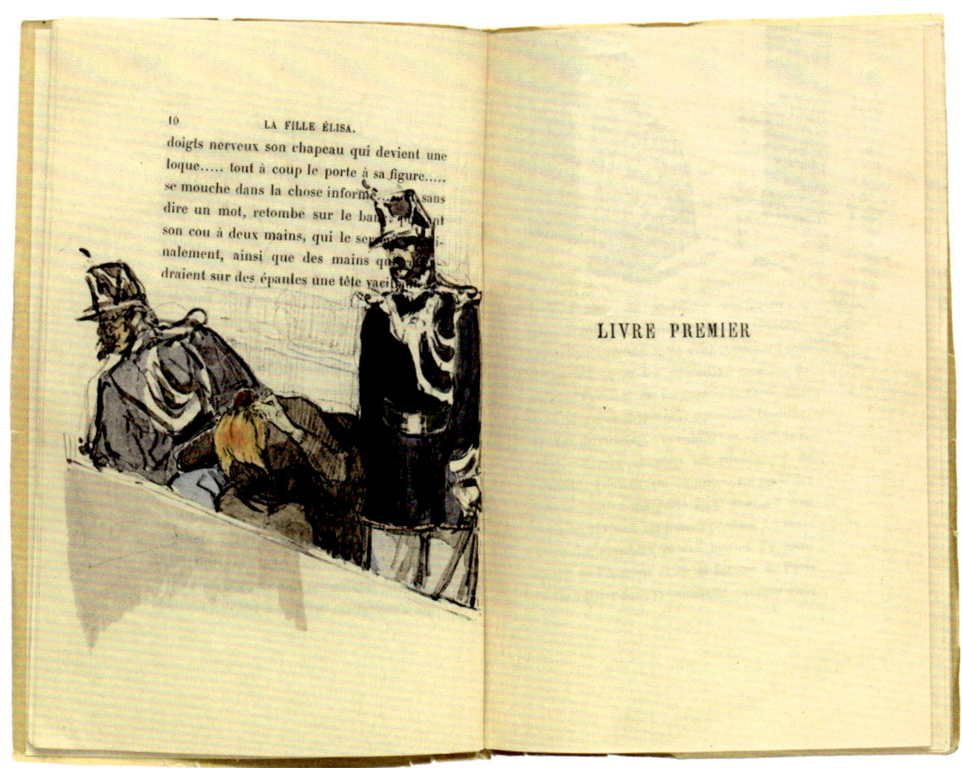

doigts nerveux son chapeau qui devient une loque..... tout à coup le porte à sa figure..... se mouche dans la chose informe sans dire un mot, retombe sur le ba son cou à deux mains, qui le se nalement, ainsi que des mains q draient sur des épaules une tête

LIVRE PREMIER

Plates 69–72

Pages from the illustrated book **LA FILLE ÉLISA** by

Edmond de Goncourt. 1896, published 1931

Collotype reproductions with pochoir, page: 7 3/16 x 4 5/8 in. (18.2 x 11.7 cm)

The Louis E. Stern Collection, 1964

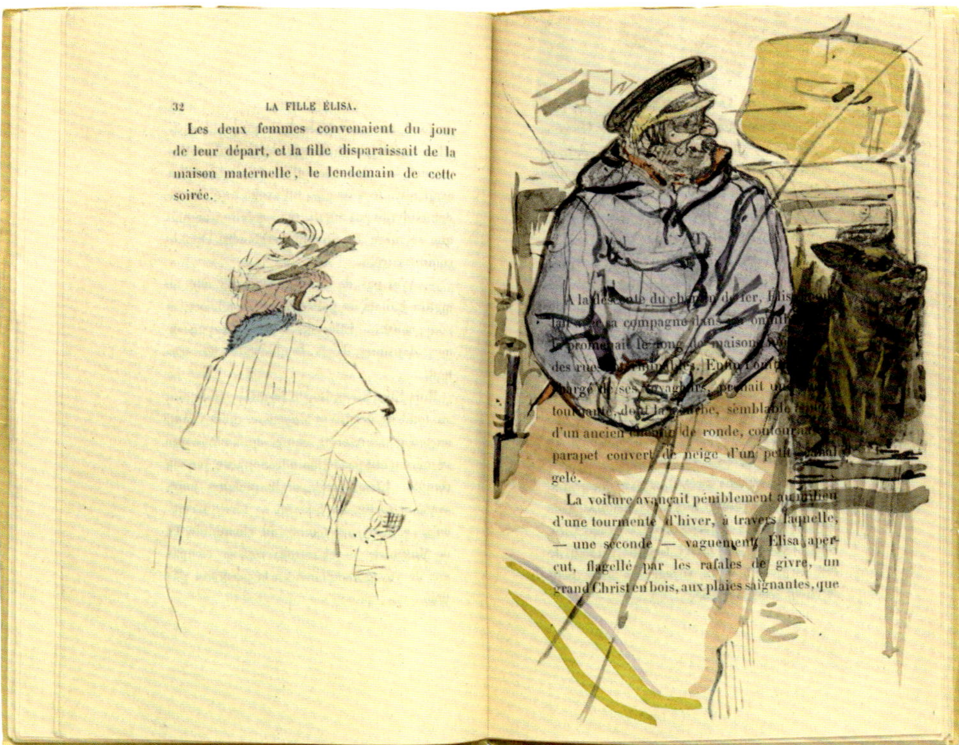

32 LA FILLE ÉLISA.

Les deux femmes convenaient du jour de leur départ, et la fille disparaissait de la maison maternelle, le lendemain de cette soirée.

À la [illegible] du ch[illegible] de fer, [illegible] [illegible] sa compagne [illegible] le promen[illegible] le long [illegible] maison[illegible] des rue[illegible]. En[illegible] [illegible]argé de ses [illegible] [illegible]ait u[illegible] tou[illegible], do[illegible] [illegible]e, semblab[illegible] d'un ancien [illegible] de ronde, contour[illegible] parapet couvert de neige d'un peti[illegible] gelé.

La voiture avançait péniblement au milieu d'une tourmente d'hiver, à travers laquelle, — une seconde — vaguement, Élisa aperçut, flagellé par les rafales de givre, un grand Christ en bois, aux plaies saignantes, que

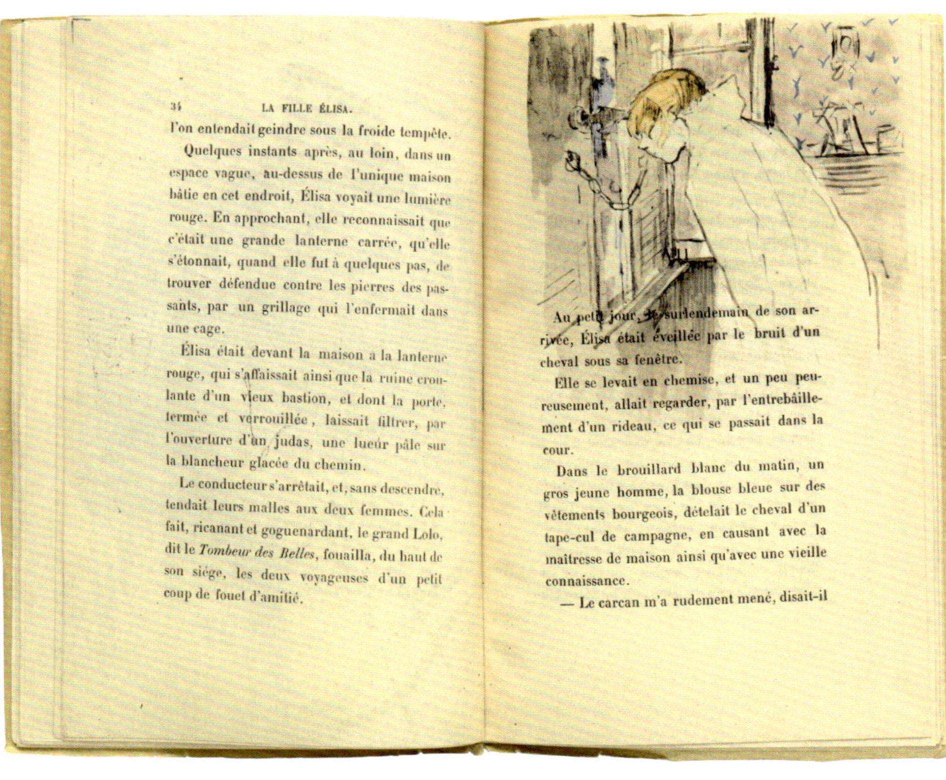

34 LA FILLE ÉLISA.

l'on entendait geindre sous la froide tempête.

Quelques instants après, au loin, dans un espace vague, au-dessus de l'unique maison bâtie en cet endroit, Élisa voyait une lumière rouge. En approchant, elle reconnaissait que c'était une grande lanterne carrée, qu'elle s'étonnait, quand elle fut à quelques pas, de trouver défendue contre les pierres des passants, par un grillage qui l'enfermait dans une cage.

Élisa était devant la maison a la lanterne rouge, qui s'affaissait ainsi que la ruine croulante d'un vieux bastion, et dont la porte, fermée et verrouillée, laissait filtrer, par l'ouverture d'un judas, une lueur pâle sur la blancheur glacée du chemin.

Le conducteur s'arrêtait, et, sans descendre, tendait leurs malles aux deux femmes. Cela fait, ricanant et goguenardant, le grand Lolo, dit le *Tombeur des Belles*, fouailla, du haut de son siége, les deux voyageuses d'un petit coup de fouet d'amitié.

Au petit jour, le surlendemain de son arrivée, Élisa était éveillée par le bruit d'un cheval sous sa fenêtre.

Elle se levait en chemise, et un peu peureusement, allait regarder, par l'entrebâillement d'un rideau, ce qui se passait dans la cour.

Dans le brouillard blanc du matin, un gros jeune homme, la blouse bleue sur des vêtements bourgeois, dételait le cheval d'un tape-cul de campagne, en causant avec la maîtresse de maison ainsi qu'avec une vieille connaissance.

— Le carcan m'a rudement mené, disait-il

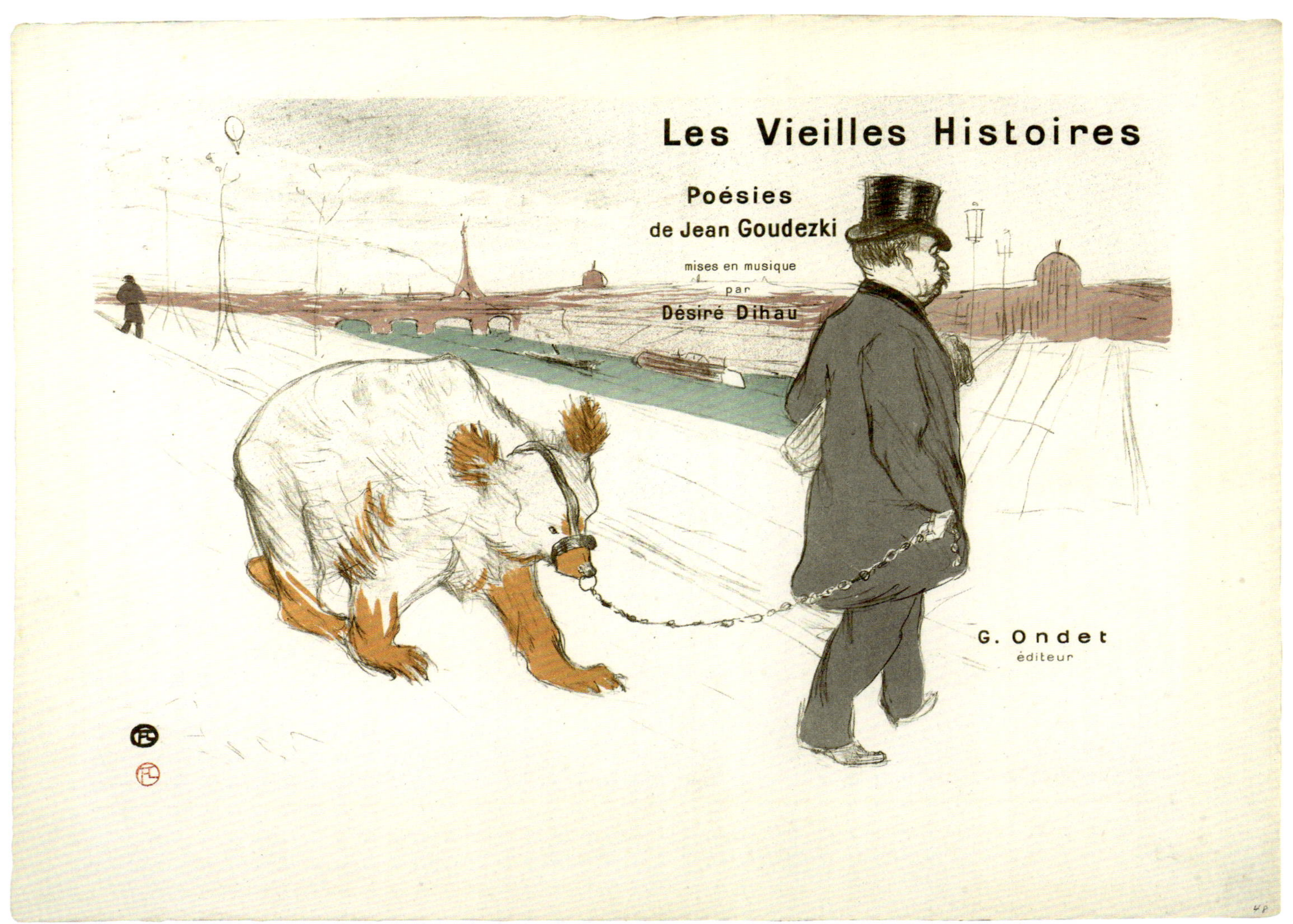

Plate 73
Cover for the portfolio **LES VIEILLES HISTOIRES** (**OLD STORIES**),
poetry by Jean Goudezki, with music by Désiré Dihau. 1893
Lithograph, sheet: 17 13/16 x 25 in. (45.2 x 63.5 cm)
Gift of Abby Aldrich Rockefeller, 1946

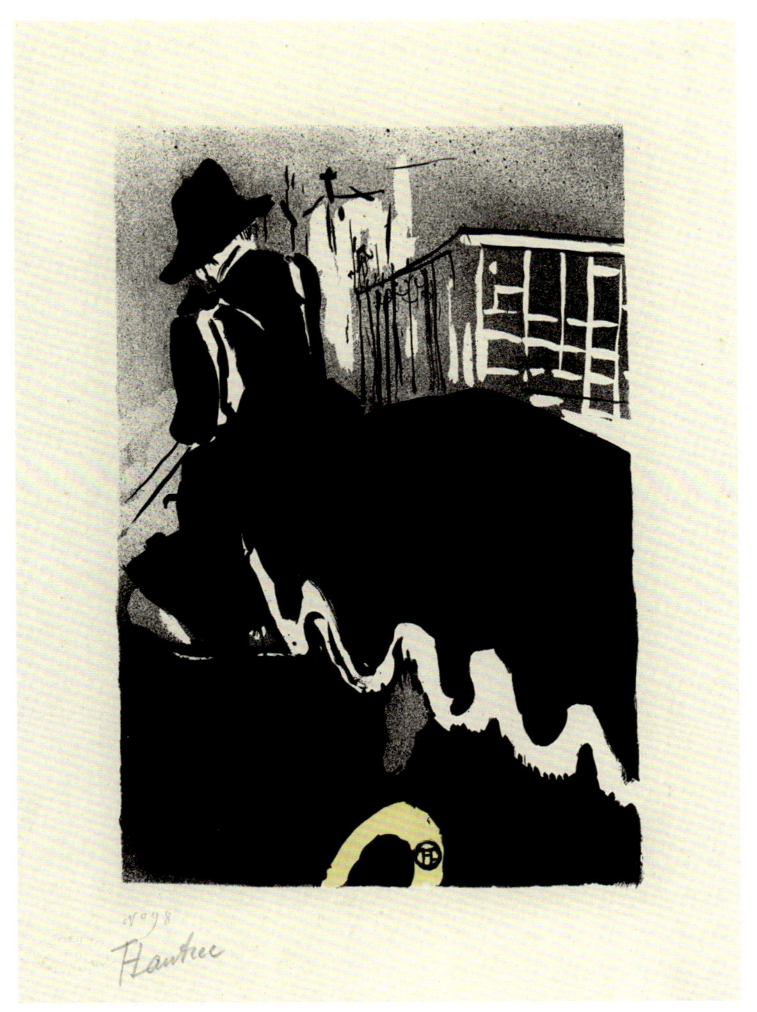

Plate 74

ULTIME BALLADE (LAST BALLAD). 1893

Lithograph with stencil additions, sheet: $13\frac{3}{4}$ x $10\frac{3}{4}$ in. (34.9 x 27.3 cm)

Gift of Abby Aldrich Rockefeller, 1946

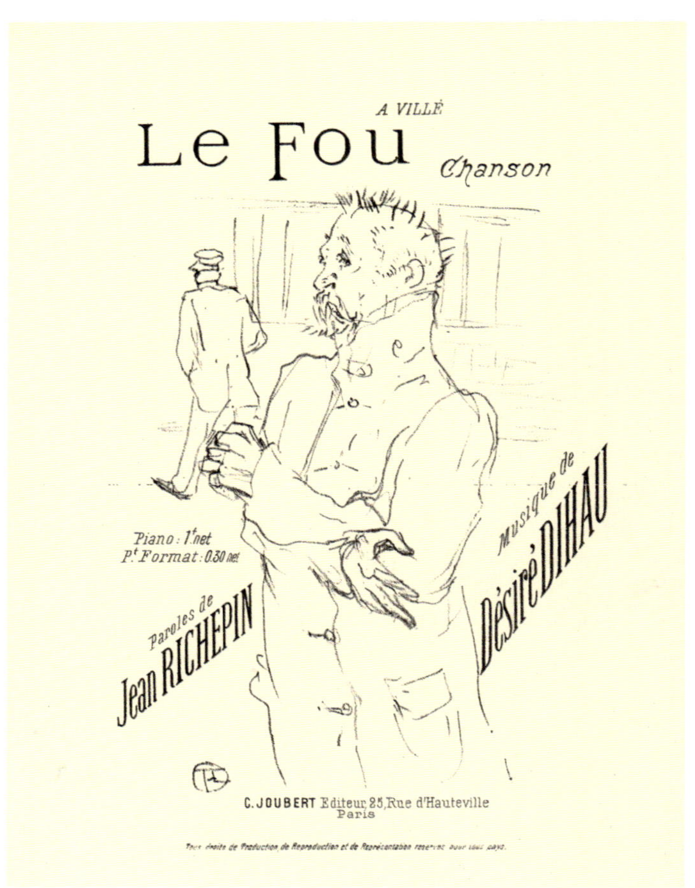

Plate 75
LE FOU (THE MADMAN) from **MÉLODIES DE DÉSIRÉ DIHAU (SONGS BY DÉSIRÉ DIHAU)**. 1895, published 1935
Lithograph, sheet: $13\frac{11}{16}$ x $10\frac{9}{16}$ in. (34.8 x 26.9 cm)
The Louis E. Stern Collection, 1964

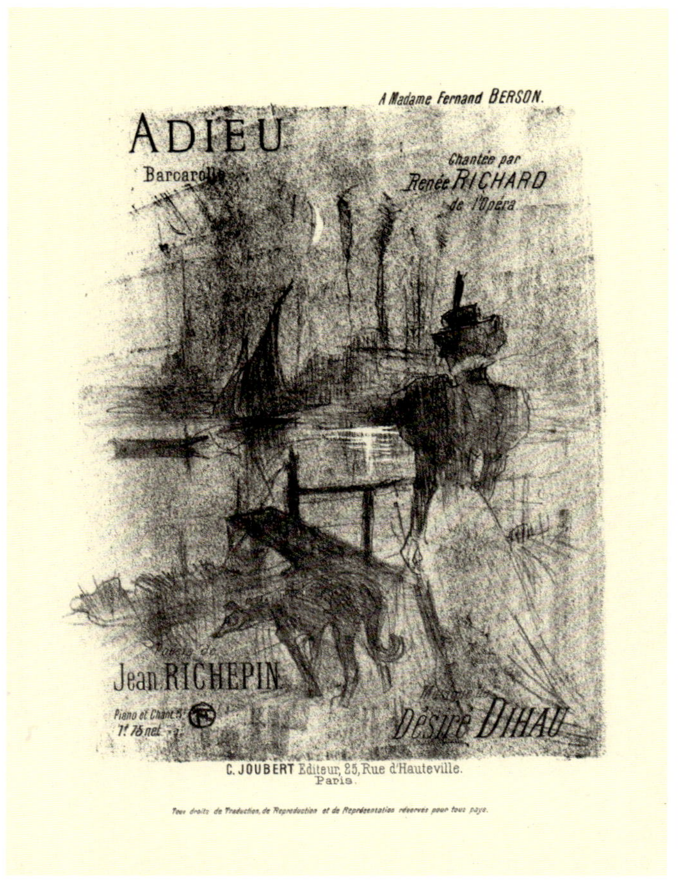

Plate 76
ADIEU (FAREWELL) from **MÉLODIES DE DÉSIRÉ DIHAU (SONGS BY DÉSIRÉ DIHAU)**. 1895, published 1935
Lithograph, sheet: $12\frac{13}{16}$ x $9\frac{13}{16}$ in. (32.5 x 25 cm)
The Louis E. Stern Collection, 1964

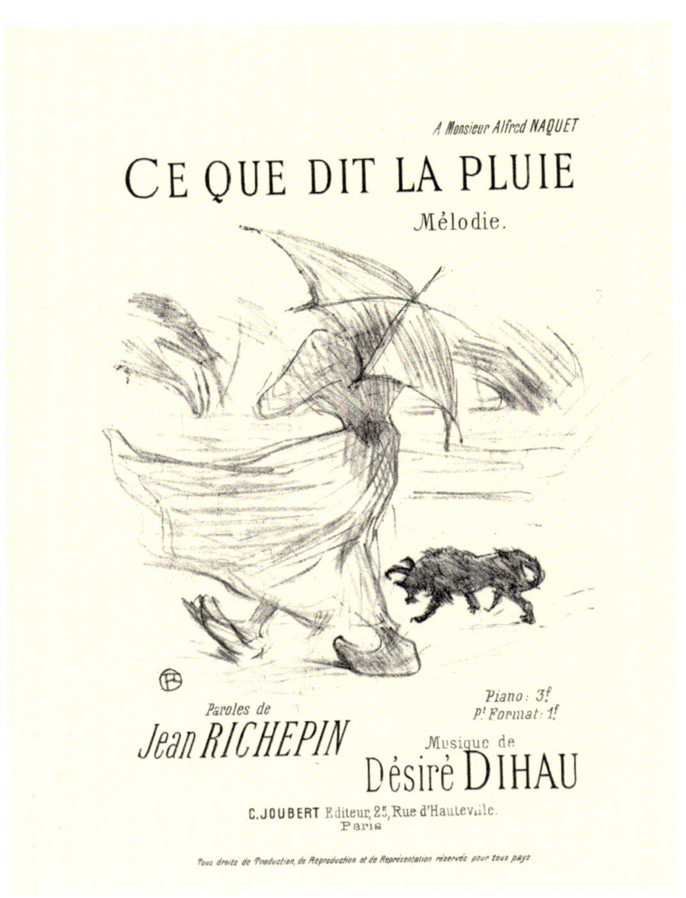

Plate 77

CE QUE DIT LA PLUIE (**WHAT THE RAIN SAYS**) from **MÉLODIES DE DÉSIRÉ DIHAU** (**SONGS BY DÉSIRÉ DIHAU**). 1895, published 1935

Lithograph, sheet: 12$\frac{3}{4}$ x 9$\frac{13}{16}$ in. (32.4 x 25 cm)

The Louis E. Stern Collection, 1964

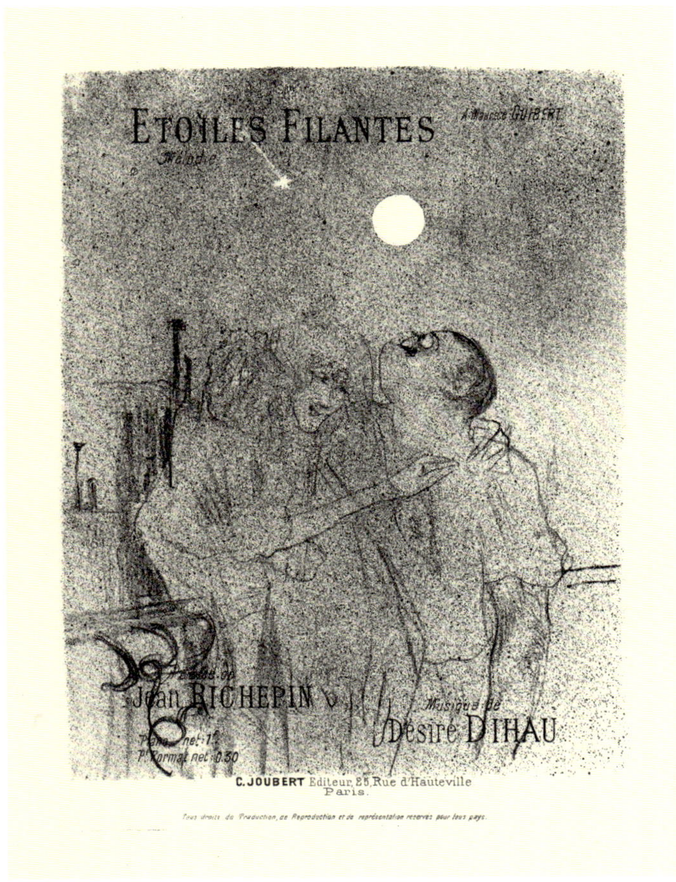

Plate 78

ÉTOILES FILANTES (**SHOOTING STARS**) from **MÉLODIES DE DÉSIRÉ DIHAU** (**SONGS BY DÉSIRÉ DIHAU**). 1895, published 1935

Lithograph, sheet: 12$\frac{3}{4}$ x 9$\frac{13}{16}$ in. (32.4 x 25 cm)

The Louis E. Stern Collection, 1964

THE BERALDI ALBUM OF THEATRE PROGRAMS. 1887–98

Selections from an album of fifty lithographs assembled by Henri Beraldi,
page: 18 5/16 x 13 3/8 in. (46.5 x 34 cm)
Johanna and Leslie J. Garfield Fund, Mary Ellen Oldenburg Fund,
and Sharon P. Rockefeller Fund, 2008

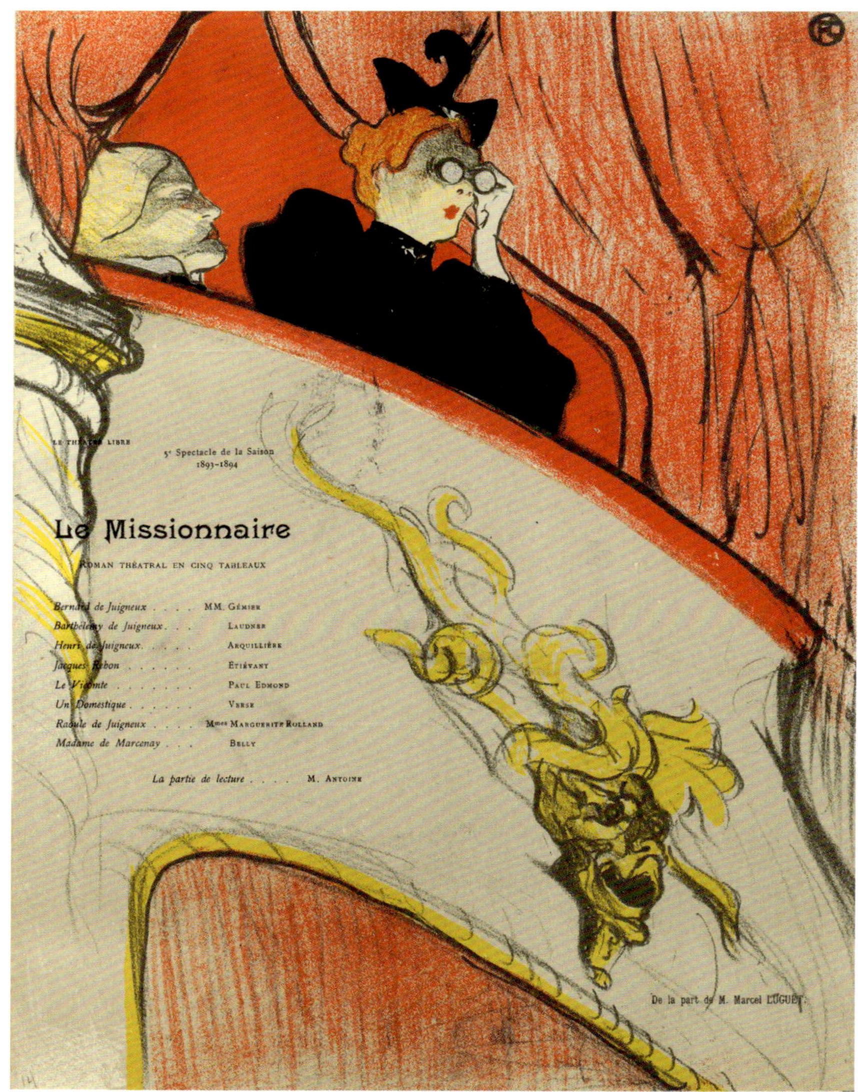

Plate 79
LA LOGE AU MASCARON DORÉ (**THE BOX WITH THE GILDED MASK**),
program for **LE MISSIONNAIRE** (**THE MISSIONARY**) at the Théâtre Libre. 1894
Lithograph, sheet: 12 1/16 x 9 7/16 in. (30.6 x 24 cm)

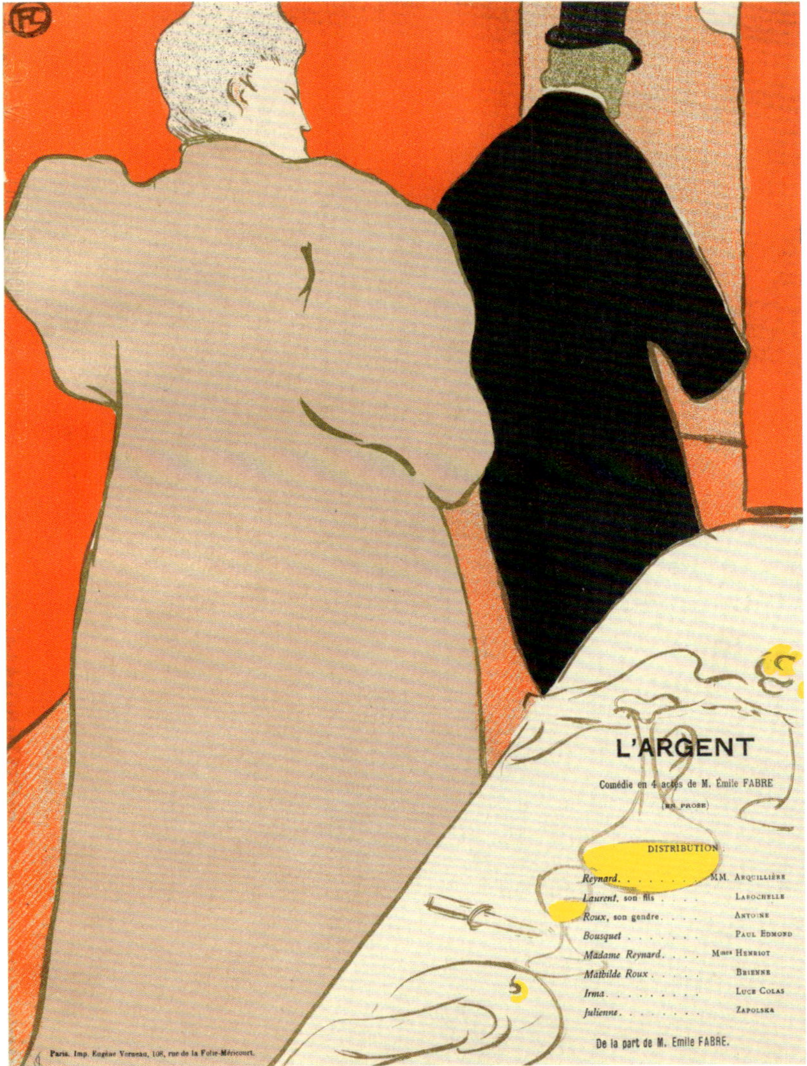

Plate 80

UN MONSIEUR ET UNE DAME (**A GENTLEMAN AND A LADY**),
program for **L'ARGENT** (**MONEY**) at the Théâtre Libre. 1895
Lithograph, sheet: 12½ x 9⅜ in. (31.8 x 23.8 cm)

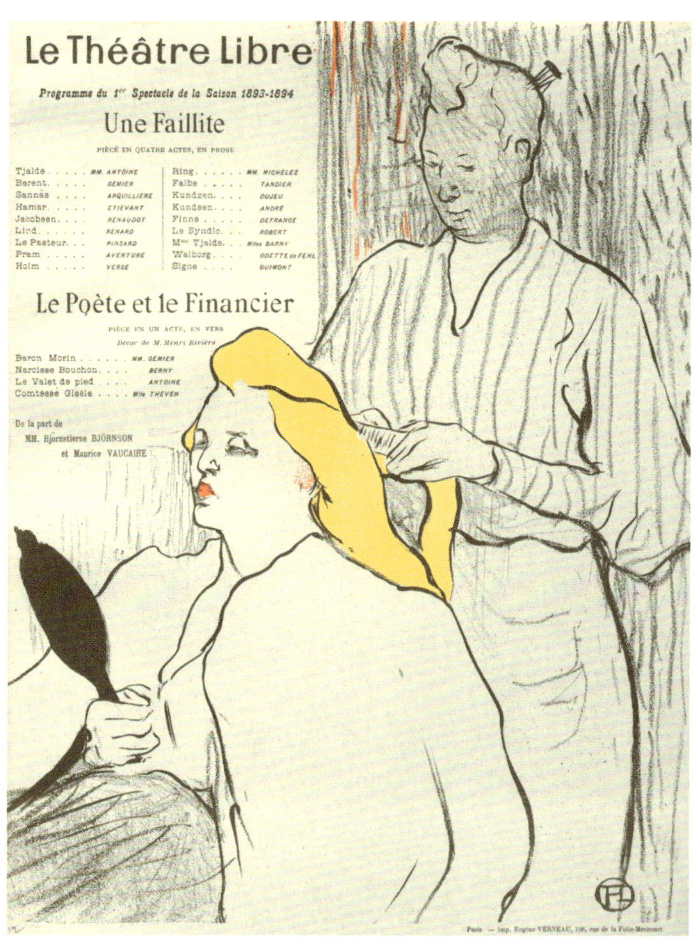

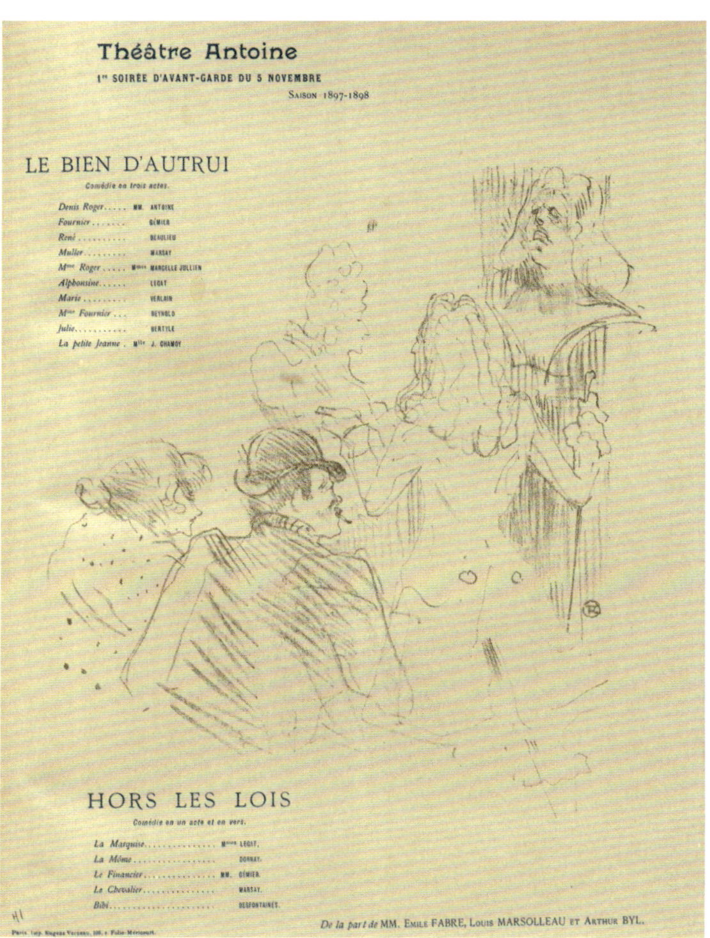

Plate 81

LA COIFFURE (THE HAIRDRESSER), program for **UNE FAILLITE (BANKRUPTCY)** and **LE POÈTE ET LE FINANCIER (THE POET AND THE FINANCIER)** at the Théâtre Libre. 1893

Lithograph, sheet: 12⅝ x 9 7/16 in. (32 x 23.9 cm)

Plate 82

HOMMAGE À MOLIÈRE (HOMAGE TO MOLIÈRE), program for **LE BIEN D'AUTRUI (OTHER PEOPLE'S PROPERTY)** and **HORS LES LOIS (OUTSIDE THE LAW)** at the Théâtre Antoine. 1897

Lithograph, sheet: 12½ x 9⅝ in. (31.7 x 24.4 cm)

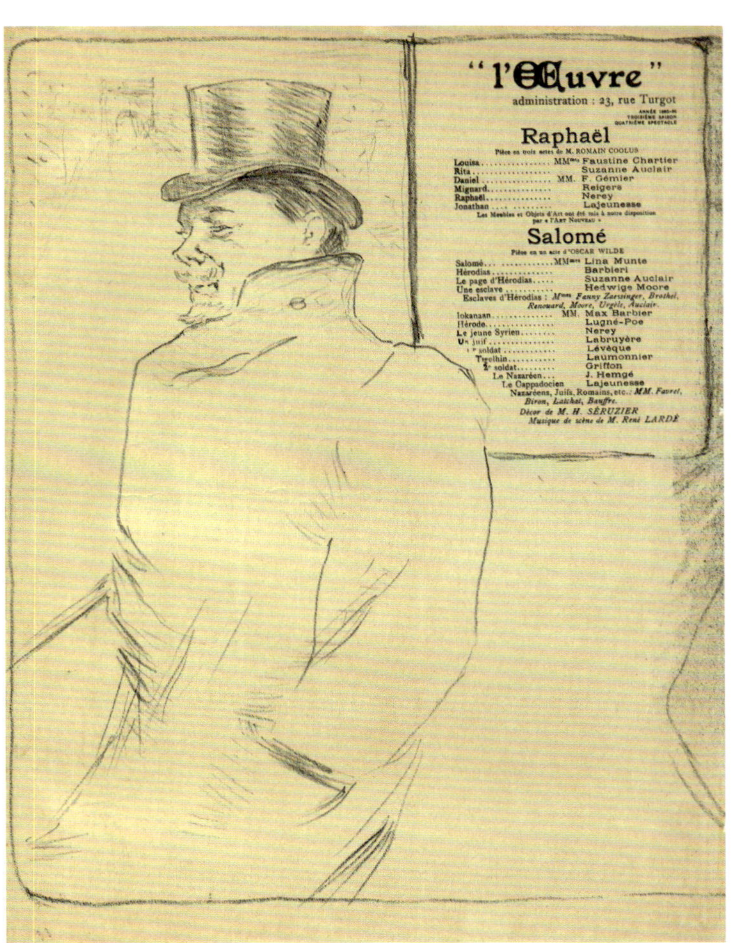

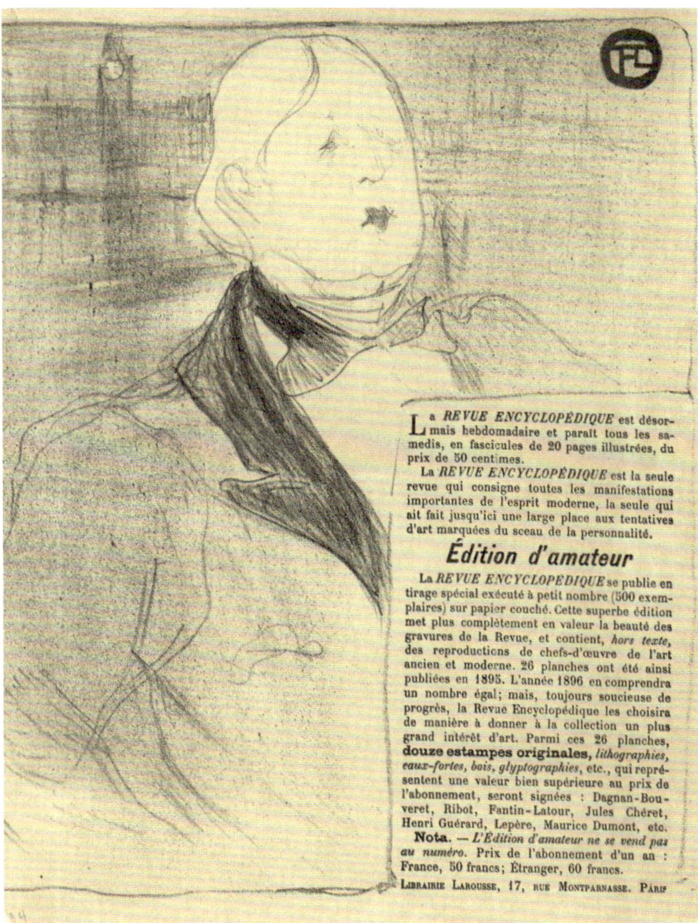

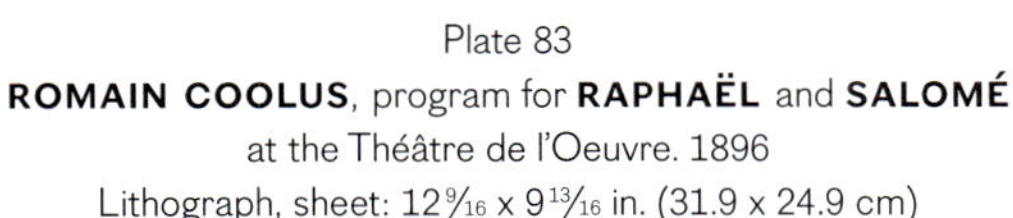

Plate 83
ROMAIN COOLUS, program for **RAPHAËL** and **SALOMÉ**
at the Théâtre de l'Oeuvre. 1896
Lithograph, sheet: $12\frac{9}{16} \times 9\frac{13}{16}$ in. (31.9 x 24.9 cm)

Plate 84
OSCAR WILDE, program for **RAPHAËL** and **SALOMÉ**
at the Théâtre de l'Oeuvre. 1896
Lithograph, sheet: $12\frac{7}{16} \times 9\frac{7}{16}$ in. (31.6 x 24 cm)

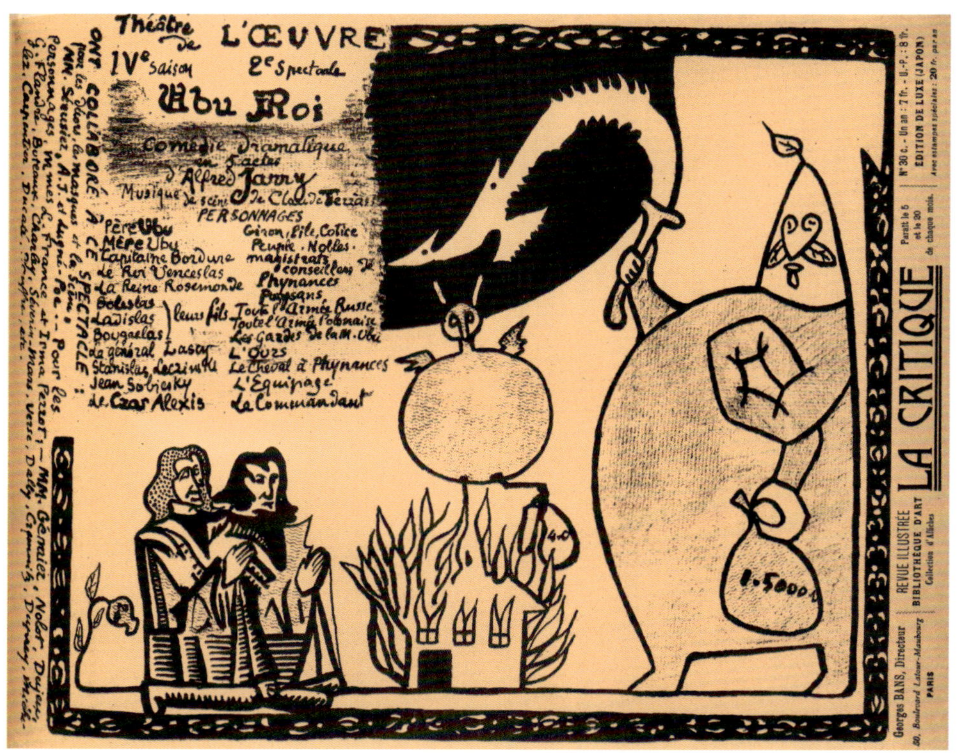

Plate 85
ALFRED JARRY (French, 1873–1907)
Program for *Ubu roi* (*King Ubu*) at the Théâtre de l'Oeuvre. 1896
Lithograph, sheet: 9 11/16 x 12 11/16 in. (24.6 x 32.3 cm)

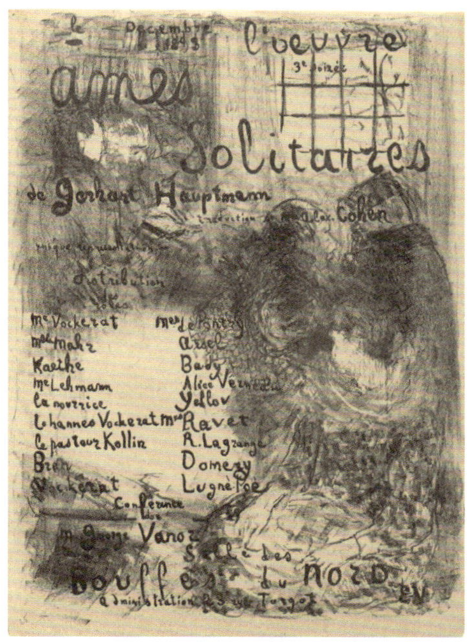

Plate 86
ÉDOUARD VUILLARD (French, 1868–1940)
Program for *Âmes solitaires* (*Lonely Souls*)
at the Théâtre de l'Oeuvre. 1893
Lithograph, sheet: 12 15/16 x 9 1/2 in. (32.8 x 24.1 cm)

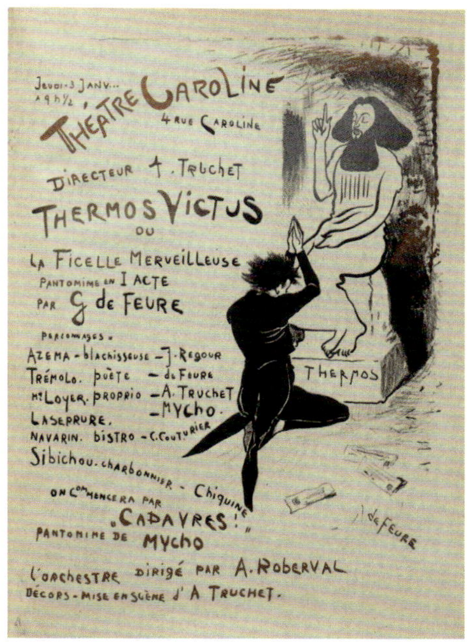

Plate 87
GEORGES DE FEURE (French, 1869–1928)
Program for *Thermos victus ou La Ficelle merveilleuse*
(*Thermos Victus or The Marvelous String*)
at the Théâtre Caroline. 1895
Lithograph, sheet: 12 11/16 x 9 5/16 in. (32.3 x 23.7 cm)

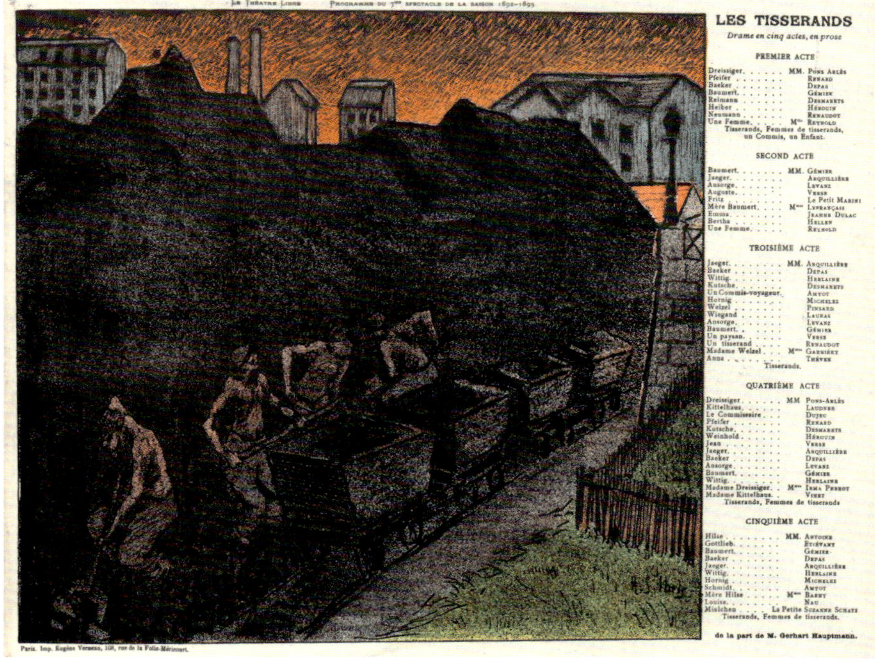

Plate 88
HENRI-GABRIEL IBELS (French, 1867–1936)
Program for *Les Tisserands* (*The Weavers*) at the Théâtre Libre. 1893
Lithograph, sheet: 9 3/8 x 12 7/16 in. (23.8 x 31.6 cm)

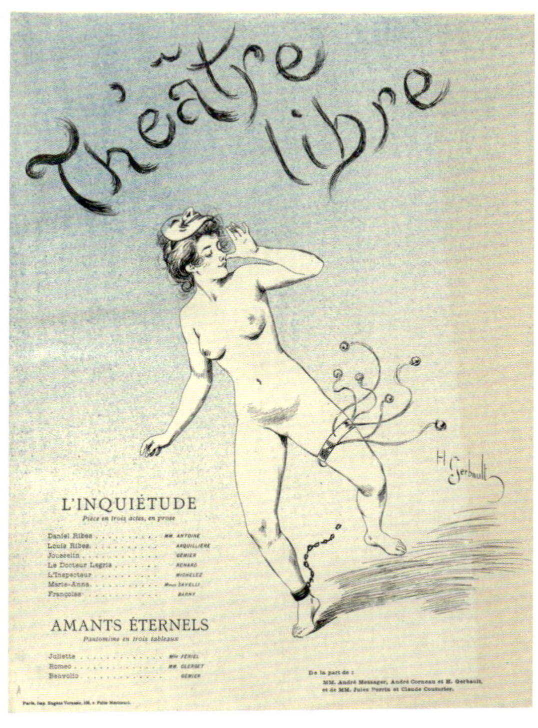

Plate 89
HENRI GERBAULT (French, 1863–1930)
Program for *L'Inquiétude* (*Anxiety*) and *Amants éternels* (*Eternal Lovers*) at the Théâtre Libre. 1893
Lithograph, sheet: 12 9/16 x 9 1/2 in. (31.9 x 24.2 cm)

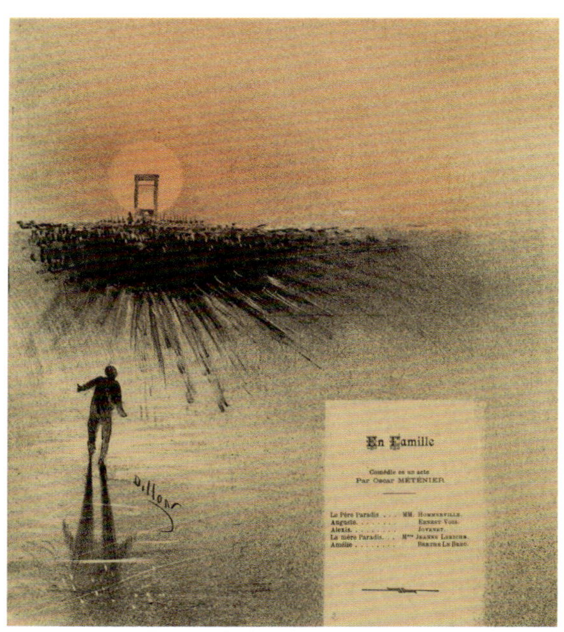

Plate 90
HENRI-PATRICE DILLON (French, born United States. 1851–1909)
Program for *En famille* (*In the Family*) at the Théâtre Libre. 1887
Lithograph, sheet: 9 5/8 x 8 3/4 in. (24.4 x 22.2 cm)

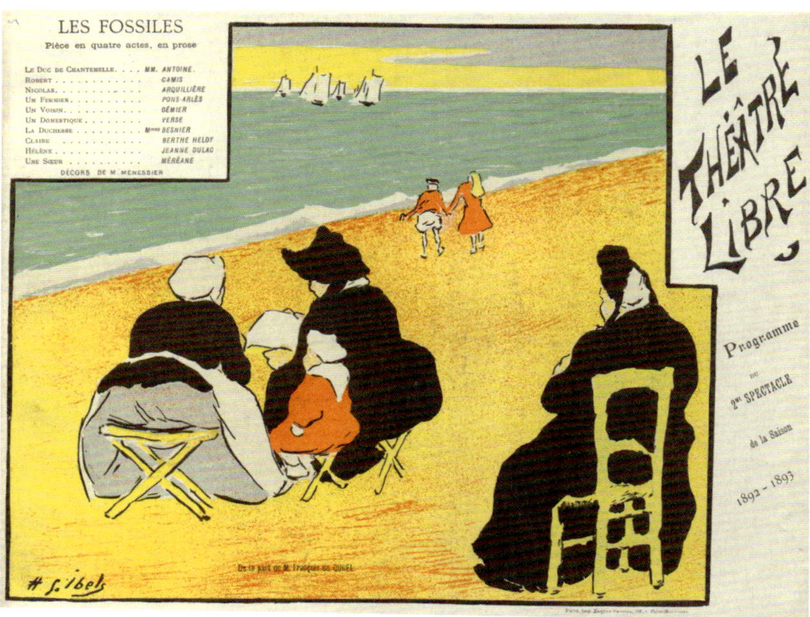

Plate 91
HENRI-GABRIEL IBELS (French, 1867–1936)
Program for *Les Fossiles* (*The Fossils*) at the Théâtre Libre. 1892
Lithograph, sheet: 9 3/8 x 12 11/16 in. (23.8 x 32.2 cm)

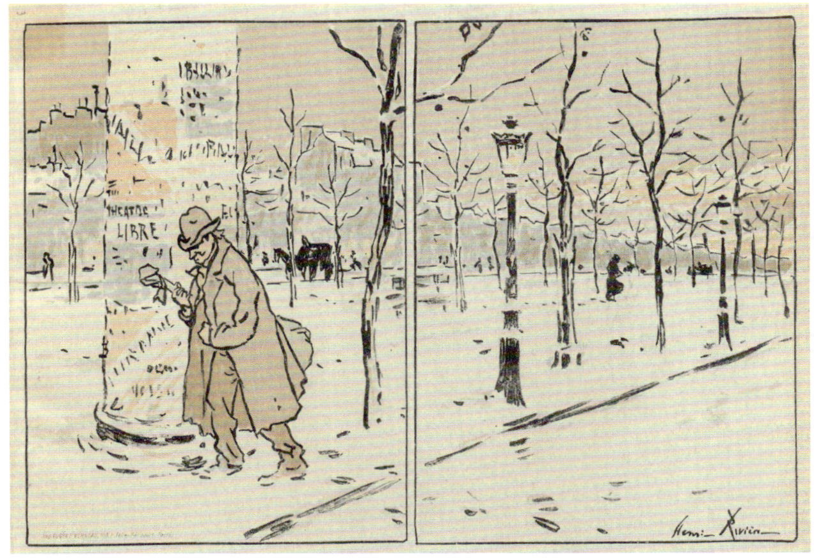

Plate 92

HENRI RIVIÈRE (French, 1864–1951)

Paris en hiver (*Paris in Winter*), program for *Les Frères Zemganno* (*The Zemganno Brothers*) and *Deux Tourtereaux* (*Two Lovebirds*) at the Théâtre Libre. 1890

Lithograph, sheet: 8⁵⁄₁₆ x 12¹⁄₁₆ in. (21.1 x 30.7 cm)

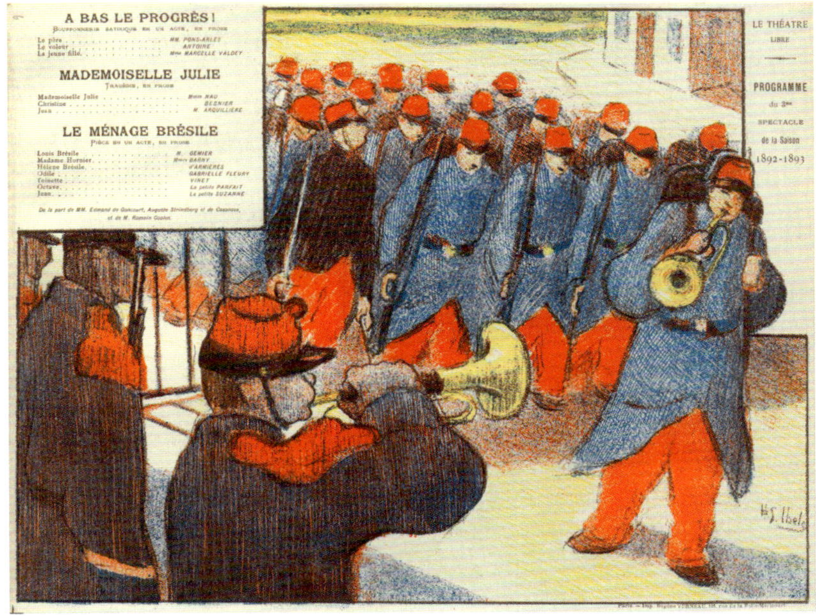

Plate 93

HENRI-GABRIEL IBELS (French, 1867–1936)

Program for *À bas le progrès!* (*Down with Progress!*), *Mademoiselle Julie* (*Miss Julie*), and *Le Ménage brésile* (*The Brazilian Household*) at the Théâtre Libre. 1893

Lithograph, sheet: 9⁷⁄₁₆ x 12½ in. (24 x 31.8 cm)

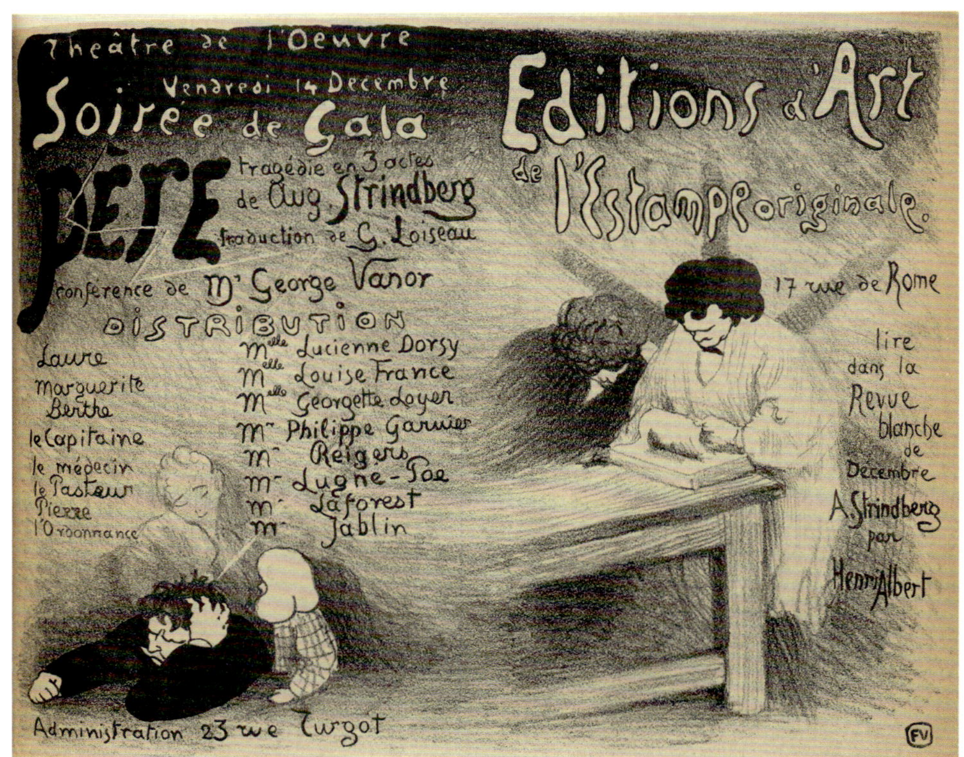

Plate 94
FÉLIX VALLOTTON (French, 1865–1925)
Program for *Père* (*Father*) at the Théâtre de l'Oeuvre. 1894
Lithograph, sheet: 9 13/16 x 12 7/8 in. (24.9 x 32.7 cm)

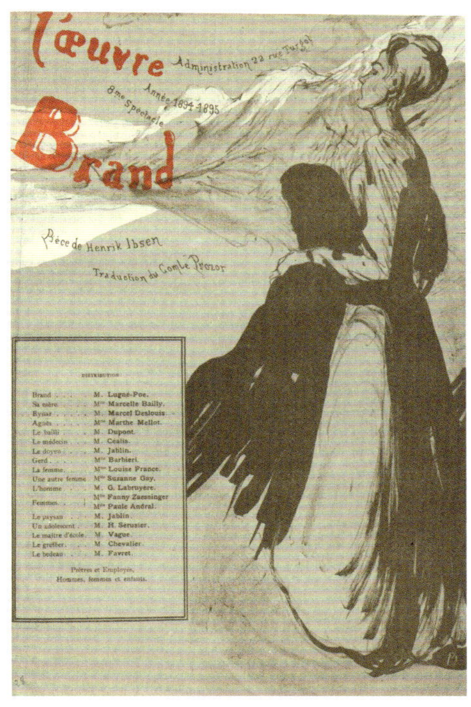

Plate 95
MAXIME DETHOMAS (French, 1867–1929)
Program for *Brand* at the Théâtre de l'Oeuvre. 1895
Lithograph, sheet: $13\frac{1}{4}$ x $8\frac{15}{16}$ in. (33.7 x 22.7 cm)

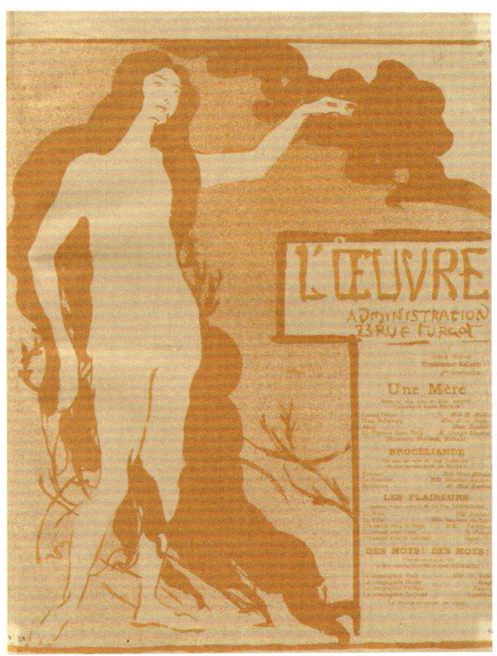

Plate 96
MAXIME DETHOMAS (French, 1867–1929)
Program for *Une Mère* (*A Mother*), *Brocéliande*, *Les Flaireurs* (*The Sniffers*), and *Des Mots! Des Mots!* (*Words! Words!*) at the Théâtre de l'Oeuvre. 1896
Lithograph, sheet: $12\frac{5}{8}$ x $9\frac{5}{8}$ in. (32.1 x 24.4 cm)

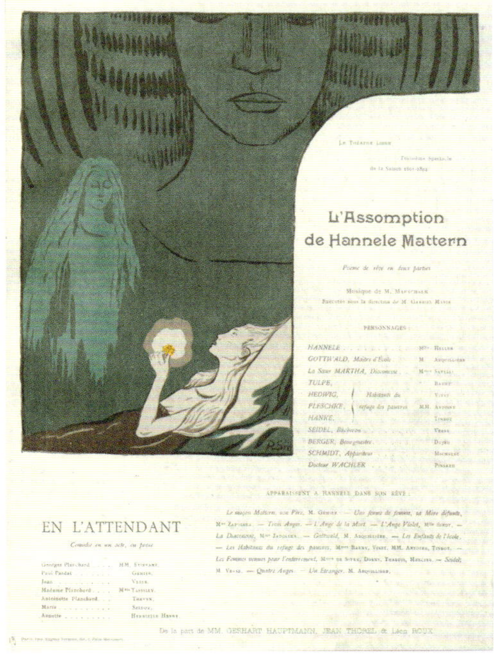

Plate 97
PAUL SÉRUSIER (French, 1864–1927)
Program for *L'Assomption de Hannele Mattern* (*The Assumption of Hannele Mattern*) and *En l'attendant* (*Waiting for Him*) at the Théâtre Libre. 1894
Lithograph, sheet: $12\frac{5}{16}$ x $9\frac{3}{16}$ in. (31.2 x 23.3 cm)

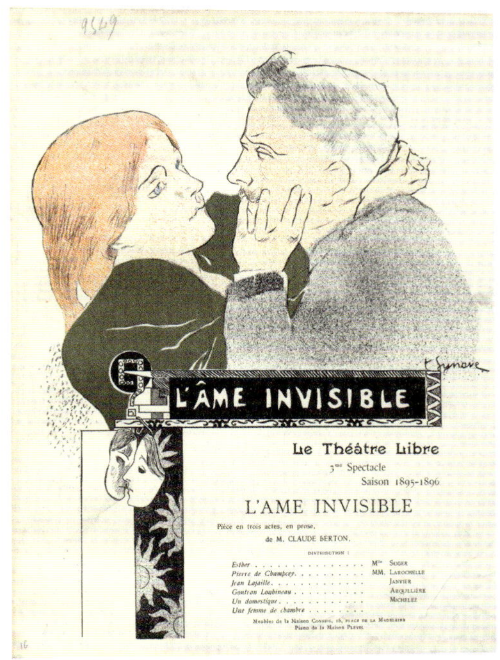

Plate 98
TANCRÈDE SYNAVE (French, 1860–1936)
Program for *L'Âme invisible* (*The Invisible Soul*) at the Théâtre Libre. 1896
Lithograph, sheet: $12\frac{5}{8}$ x $9\frac{1}{2}$ in. (32 x 24.2 cm)

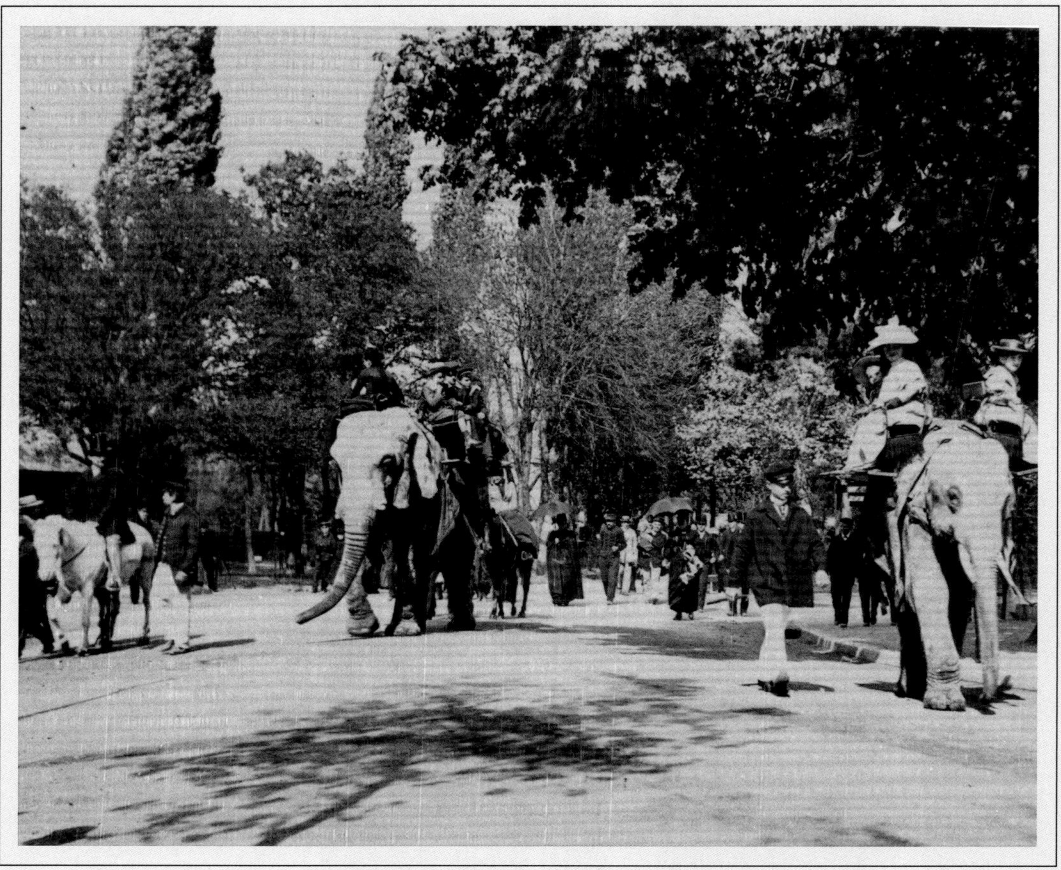

PLEASURES OF PARIS

Lautrec was an avid traveler, journeying to Amsterdam, Brussels, and Madrid, as well as throughout France, to family estates and friends' country homes. He frequently visited London, where he was able to speak his excellent English and where, as his friend the dancer Jane Avril pointed out, there was a greater sense of freedom: "I remarked that over there, one lives freely without bothering others, or making fun of them as happens so often at home."[87]

But Paris was Lautrec's city, the site of his studio, his printers and publishers, his friends, his beloved nightlife, and his muses. He passed many hours in the Bois de Boulogne, the cultivated wilderness that was one of the city's great meeting places and which presented an ever-changing cross section of society for observation (fig. 42). A contemporary guidebook claimed, "There are some scenes on this earth of ours that reach the high-water mark of our ideal, and possess a beauty and charm far

42. People and elephants in the Bois de Boulogne. 1894–1900. Photograph by Henri Lemoine (French, 1848–1924). Musée d'Orsay, Paris

and above our highest conception. Amongst these may be placed the Bois de Boulogne."[88] The park was the place to promenade—whether on foot or horseback, by bicycle, carriage, or motorcar—where people went to see and be seen and Lautrec frequently went to sketch.

Lautrec's drawing of his cousin Aline de Rivières walking with her little dog (pl. 99), a rider silhouetted in the background, is set in the Bois de Boulogne, as is *L'Automobiliste* (pl. 101), which depicts his cousin Dr. Gabriel Tapié de Céleyran. Céleyran, perhaps Lautrec's most constant companion, was a physician and assistant to the preeminent French surgeon Jules-Émile Péan. He introduced Lautrec to scenes in the operating room, while Lautrec introduced him to Parisian nightlife. Céleyran was thought at the time to be one of the first motorists in the city.[89] Depicted in a fur coat, cap, and goggles, he tightly grips the wheel and stick shift; trailed by a plume of smoke, the doctor is so engrossed that he is oblivious to the shapely female passerby at his left.

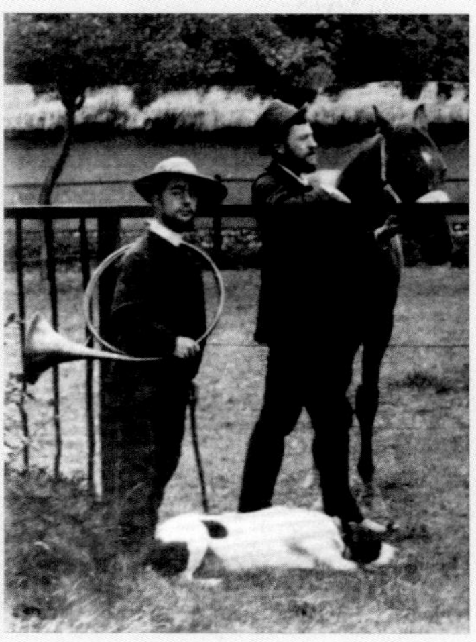

43. Lautrec and Louis Anquetin on an outing with horse and dog. n.d. Musée Toulouse-Lautrec, Albi, France

Lautrec's love of animals was well-known; even in youthful letters he always sent hugs and kisses not only to cousins and grandmothers but also to canaries and dogs (fig. 43). Some of his earliest drawings are of horses, and he depicted them carefully and lovingly throughout his life, often paying more attention to them than to his human sitters. *Le Cheval et le colley* (pl. 103) shows a horse, Philibert, that belonged to the heavy-drinking stable owner Édouard Calmèse, a controversial late arrival in Lautrec's life whom his family saw as a bad influence.[90] Berthe Sarrazin, his mother's maid, who was dispatched to Lautrec's household when the artist's mental state deteriorated and who reported to her employer nearly daily, certainly was not a fan: "That pig Calmèse, they should put him in jail. He's going to be the death of poor Monsieur."[91] The writer Paul Leclercq described Philibert as "a little horse with sharp eyes that bounced like a fat sausage," qualities neatly conveyed in Lautrec's lithograph.[92] According to Leclercq, Lautrec had a true connection with Philibert, slipping him sugar cubes in his paddock and walking with him along the Bois de Boulogne in the mornings.[93]

The park was also home to the famous Longchamp racetrack. In one of his final lithographs, *Le Jockey* (pl. 104), Lautrec depicted a race with great dynamism. The viewer is not a spectator confined to the sidelines but rather is placed amid the action, as the horses speed by with a great diagonal thrust, hooves flying. As a teenager, Lautrec was aware of Eadweard Muybridge's pioneering photographs of a horse at gallop (fig. 44),[94] which definitively settled the debate about whether or not all four feet are ever off the ground simultaneously. Lautrec's depiction reflects Muybridge's findings, as all of the horse's feet are drawn up at the apex of its gait.

There were other amusements to be had at the park, such as bicycling, which Lautrec could not participate in but enjoyed watching and made several posters promoting. Indoor ice skating had arrived in Paris in 1890, as technological advancements made artificially frozen ice possible. The park's Gran Plaza de Toros, once home to bullfights, was converted into a massive skating rink,[95] and a rage for the activity swept Paris—even Lautrec's cousin Céleyran learned how to skate.[96] People came in full costume to watch and be watched, creating a kind of Moulin Rouge on ice. Lautrec illustrated the scene for an 1896 issue of *Le Rire* (pl. 106), showing the professional skater Liane de Lancy pausing at the side of the rink to chat with a male spectator.

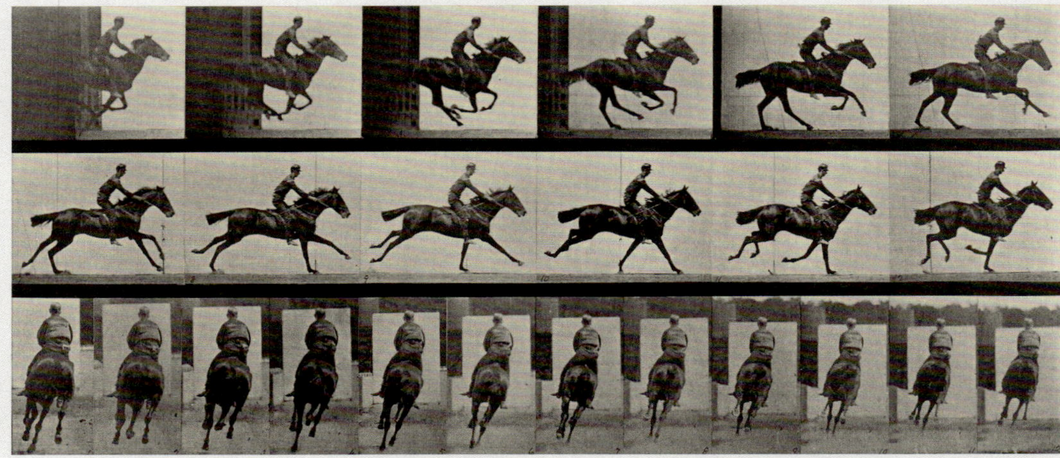

44. **EADWEARD MUYBRIDGE** (American, born England. 1830–1904). *"Bouquet" Galloping, Saddled.* 1884–86. Collotype, 7 3/16 x 16 7/16 in. (18.3 x 41.7 cm). The Museum of Modern Art, New York. Gift of the Philadelphia Commercial Museum, 1937

In 1895 Lautrec prepared a large poster to be used as an advertisement for the literary review *La Revue blanche* (pl. 107) featuring the aristocratic redhead Misia Godebska, the editor Thadée Natanson's wife, who had become Lautrec's close friend and confidante. Her beloved younger brother, Cipa, had been born with a physical disability,[97] which perhaps predisposed her to like Lautrec. Witty, beautiful, a brilliant pianist, and the queen of Paris's premier intellectual salon, Godebska symbolized *La Revue blanche* for Lautrec. Against a nearly blank background, with only the barest sense of the ice rink, she is shown clad in a polka-dot dress, fur muff and capelet, and veiled hat with elaborate plumage. While her skates are not depicted, she seems to glide by and we catch a glimpse of her in passing. The connection to skating is made stronger in an earlier state of the poster that includes a remarque (fig. 45) at lower left depicting a second skater, Liane de Lancy, her skates clearly visible.

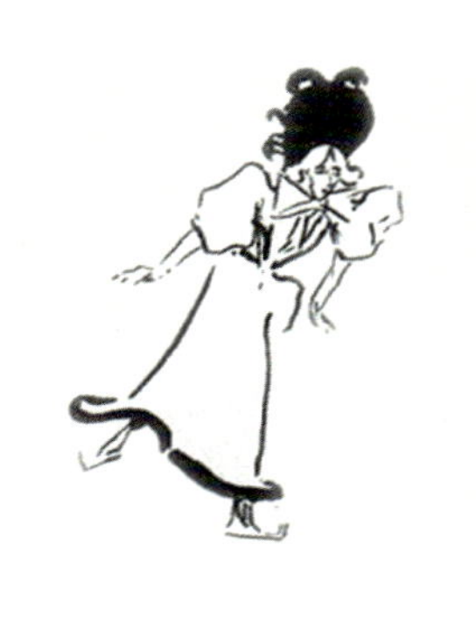

45. Lautrec's remarque featuring Liane de Lancy

The zoo in the Bois de Boulogne had suffered during the siege of Paris but was prospering in Lautrec's day, home to thousands of animals, including the elephants Romeo and Juliet, tapirs, aardvarks, and more. Lautrec visited often and had special favorites among the animals that amused him and sometimes seemed to recognize him. According to Leclercq, he had long conversations with the keepers about the animals' habits and gestures, asking after their health "as he would an old friend."[98]

It was there and from memory[99] that he worked on images to accompany a proposed bestiary by Jules Renard, depicting animals of field and farm, floating unanchored in white space (pls. 108–119). The rabbits (pl. 115) appear in several poses, as in a Japanese manga study (fig. 46), munching away on some hay, sitting alert with ears pricked, and bounding into the distance. A fourth rabbit has been added to the composition in the form of the bunny

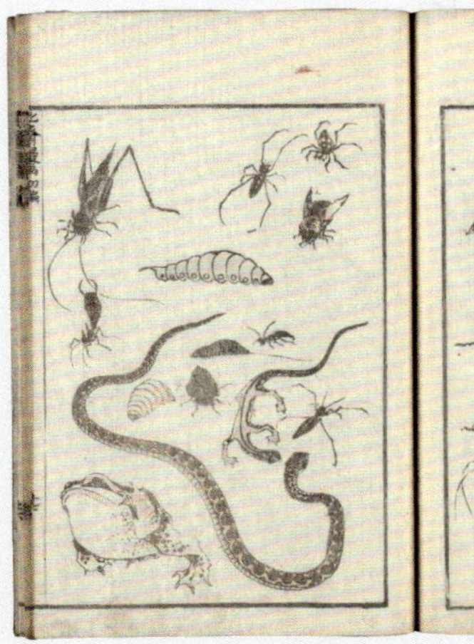
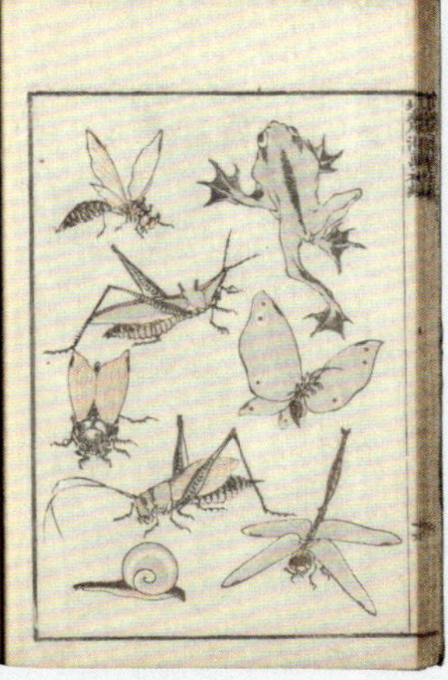

46. **KATSUSHIKA HOKUSAI** (Japanese, 1760–1849). *Insects, Snake, and Frogs.* 1814. Woodcut, page: 7¼ x 10 in. (18.4 x 25.4). The New York Public Library

ears in Lautrec's monogram remarque. The working animals are shown at labor: the bulls hitched to a wagon, the donkey with the windmill visible behind, and the horse bridled, with a lone chicken pecking about behind it.

Outside the park, Lautrec found inspiration in the city's urban character. These streets were the artist's gallery walls. *The Chestnut Vendor* (fig. 47) is a crowded street scene of the intersecting circles of Parisian society: the swaying hourglass shape of a woman viewed from behind, the silhouette of the vendor opening the top of his roasting pot, a laborer slouching against the wall with his hands in his pockets, and a little black bulldog.

Confetti (pl. 120) is one of the few posters Lautrec made to advertise a consumer product. According to several accounts, paper confetti was introduced to the city in 1892 by the stage manager of the Casino de Paris. Previously, confetti was either sugarcoated bonbons or bits of colored plaster, and throwing it became a serious safety hazard, as it stung the skin and eyes of those hit by it.[100] Lautrec knew that all too well. As a boy, he spent one Mardi Gras in Nice with his mother, who recalled, "Everybody has to wear a mask made out of metal screening to be protected from the confetti . . . with which people have furious battles."[101] In Lautrec's poster, the model's eyes are closed in delight, as she turns up her face to enjoy the flutter of the confetti, happy to be freed from having to wear a protective mask. Lautrec used his signature *crachis* technique to great effect, his colored splatter mimicking the round form of the product, which was already big business. The fifty thousand kilos sold annually in France at this time was worth 250,000 francs,[102] and the English paper manufacturer J. & E. Bella, who was quite interested in the flourishing art of poster design, commissioned Lautrec in hopes of expanding its product line.

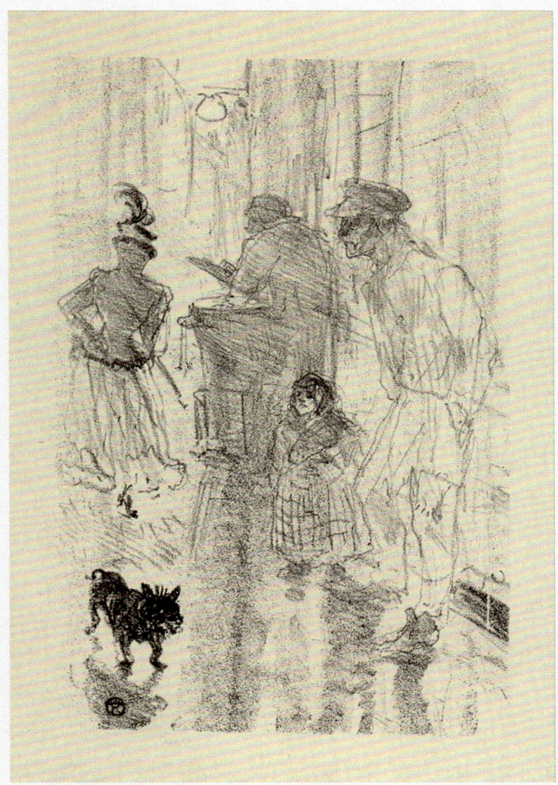

47. **HENRI DE TOULOUSE-LAUTREC**. *The Chestnut Vendor.* 1897, published 1925. Lithograph, 14$\frac{13}{16}$ x 11 in. (37.6 x 27.9 cm). The Museum of Modern Art, New York. Gift of Louise Bourgeois, 1997

Lautrec also made a promotional poster for his friend the photographer Paul Sescau. Like Lautrec, Sescau was from the upper class yet deeply engaged in the bohemian milieu of Montmartre. Tall and thin with a drooping mustache, he had a reputation as a ladies' man and used his studio not just for posed portraits but also for erotic photographs. This suggestion is borne out in Lautrec's design (pl. 122), in which the tripod of the camera is echoed by that formed by Sescau's legs and the cloth dangling suggestively between them. There is a general air of titillation—even Lautrec's little elephant remarque is excited, its tail raised instead of lowered. The subject of Sescau's priapic lens appears ready to dart out of the picture. In this rare first state, she still wears a yellow mask, indicating that she's dressed for a costume ball and linking her to a depiction of a similarly dressed Jane Avril in an illustration for *Le Figaro illustré* (pl. 20) as well as in the background of *Mademoiselle Cha-U-Kao, La Clownesse assise* (pl. 49). Sescau certainly knew Avril, as he took publicity shots for her, including one in the serpent dress that Lautrec depicted in 1899 (see fig. 29 and pl. 37).[103] The first state also retains a playful nude in sadomasochistic regalia with a trained pig, perhaps a reference to Félicien Rops's *Pornokrates*, a drawing recently translated into lithography, published by Gustave Pellet and available at the same time as Lautrec's *Elles* (fig. 48),[104] but also resembling a photograph of the dancer Môme Fromage taken in Lautrec's studio (fig. 49).

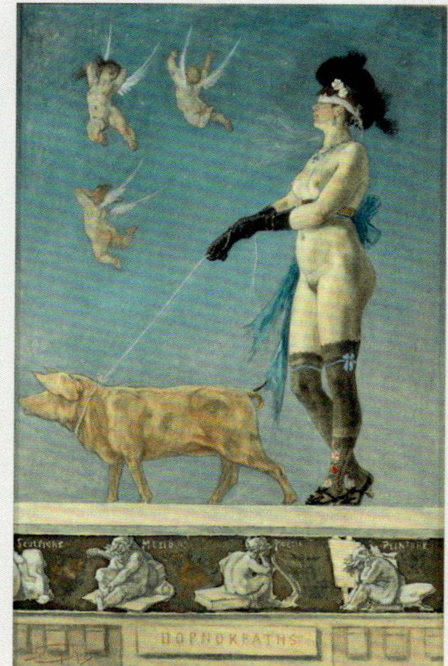

48. **FÉLICIEN ROPS** (Belgian, 1833–1898). *Pornokrates*. 1879. Pastel and gouache on paper, 27 9/16 x 17 11/16 in. (70 x 45 cm). Musée Provincial Félicien Rops, Namur, Belgium

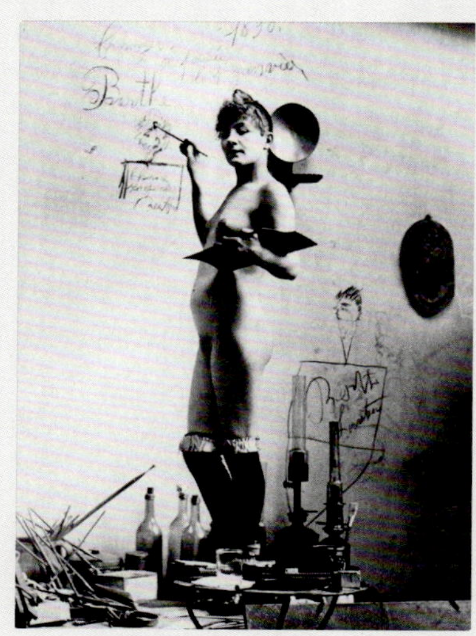

49. Môme Fromage posing in Lautrec's studio. c. 1890

Like his father, Lautrec was a gourmet and, reportedly, an excellent chef. His biographer reports, "All his life, two of Henry's [*sic*] favorite haunts would be zoos and restaurants."[105] Many of the artist's scenes, including *Reine de joie* (pl. 62) and the program for *L'Argent* (pl. 80), are set at the dinner table. He chronicled restaurants for *Le Figaro illustré* (pl. 125), and depicted, at the table, his friend Charles Conder, a British-born artist and fellow student of Fernand Cormon, described as "often without a sou, but . . . never without a lady,"[106] who died quite young from syphilis.

When Lautrec found a bar or a restaurant that he liked, he often ate there nightly, making it an extension of his living room. The Irish and American Bar on the chic rue Royale was a hangout for British expatriates, jockeys, trainers, grooms, and racing fans (pl. 128).[107] Lautrec dined there on British cuisine, eating Welsh rarebit and sighing to his mother that he was "living on roast beef."[108] He controlled the door policy much as Aristide Bruant did across town at the Mirliton, goading the staff to deny service to those he disliked. As he became a regular there, the restaurant and its cast of characters became a steady presence in his work. Lautrec paid homage to his fellow patrons, including Tom (pls. 126, 128), the burly coachman for Baron Rothschild, who appears in another image with May Milton's lover, May Belfort (pl. 127); Ralph, the Chinese–American Indian bartender; and the boss, Achille.

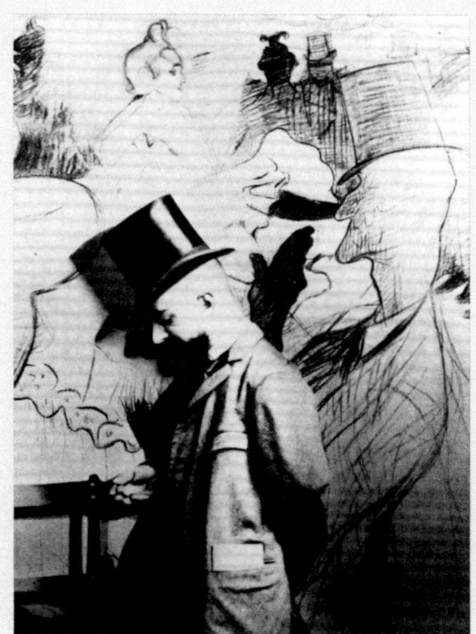

50. Lautrec in front of a sketch for his poster *Moulin Rouge, La Goulue*, in a photograph taken after he shaved his head. n.d.

Himself a legendary bartender, Lautrec presided over an infamous party thrown by Alexandre Natanson. On February 16, 1895, at 8:30 p.m., the Natansons welcomed three hundred guests to their home at 60, avenue du Bois de Boulogne (today avenue Foch) to celebrate the unveiling of the multipanel mural *Jardins publics* that Édouard Vuillard had painted for their dining room (some panels are now in the collection of the Musée d'Orsay, Paris). The invitation was designed by Lautrec (pl. 123) and written in English, promising "American and other drinks," hinting at the American flavor of the evening. When guests arrived, they found Lautrec dressed as a bartender in a short white jacket, his head and beard shaved to properly suit the role of working-class barman—a part to which he committed fully (fig. 50). He concocted legendarily strong drinks for all the guests, including his inventive "solid cocktails"—for example, sardines, juniper, and port.[109] Everyone except Lautrec got wildly drunk, and Thadée Natanson recalled "chambermaids and English governesses act[ing] as nurses for the growing number of casualties. In no time all horizontal surfaces were occupied . . . Vuillard was barely conscious . . . Bonnard, dead drunk, fell stiffly into bed."[110]

Lautrec was at the center of this notorious evening and at many other events that are now recalled as the golden age of Belle Époque Paris. As he watched from his table at the Moulin Rouge, his seat in the carriage in the Bois de Boulogne, and his box at the Opéra or the Théâtre Libre, he committed to memory—and later to lithographic stone—the sights of his city. These depictions of the many facets of Paris—at work and at play, bucolic and urbane, in commerce and at leisure, its artists and actors onstage and off, its aristocrats and demimondaines—create an enduring portrait of a place and a time as seen through the eyes of the city's premier artist-observer.

1. Julia Frey, *Toulouse-Lautrec: A Life* (New York: Viking Press, 1994), p. 112.
2. A second son, Richard, born in 1867, did not survive beyond his first birthday; see ibid., p. 26.
3. Frey, "Henri de Toulouse-Lautrec: Life as Art," in *Toulouse-Lautrec: The Baldwin M. Baldwin Collection*, ed. Nora Desloge (San Diego: San Diego Museum of Art, 1988), p. 22.
4. Frey, *A Life*, p. 46.
5. Frey, "Life as Art," p. 22.
6. Ibid., p. 26.
7. Charles Hiatt, *Picture Posters: A Short History of the Illustrated Placard, with Many Reproductions of the Most Artistic Examples in All Countries* (London: George Bell and Sons, 1895), pp. 61–62.
8. Frey, *A Life*, p. 472.
9. As well as more than 700 paintings, nearly 300 watercolors, and 4,700 drawings.
10. André Mellerio, *La Lithographie originale en couleurs* (Paris: Publication de l'Estampe et l'Affiche, 1898), p. 7.
11. For more on printmaking in Paris in this period, see Sarah Suzuki, *What Is a Print?: Selections from The Museum of Modern Art* (New York: The Museum of Modern Art, 2011), p. 85.
12. Lautrec, letter to Adèle de Toulouse-Lautrec, November–December 1891, in *The Letters of Henri de Toulouse-Lautrec*, ed. Herbert D. Schimmel (Oxford and New York: Oxford University Press, 1991), pp. 154–55, letter 209.
13. Edmond de Goncourt and Jules de Goncourt, *Journal: Mémoires de la vie littéraire: 1892–1895* (Paris: G. Charpentier et E. Fasquelle, 1896), vol. 3, pp. 248–49. In a journal entry from August 30, 1894, the Goncourt brothers recall how Gustave Geffroy told them about a painter (Lautrec) using a revolutionary technique—the *crachis*.
14. Lautrec, letter to Maurice Joyant, March 17, 1899, in Schimmel, *Letters*, p. 349, letter 564.
15. Frey, *A Life*, p. 327.
16. Frey reports this remark by Francis Jourdain, in translation, in ibid., p. 296.
17. For more on this subject and on Chéret's experiments, see Phillip Dennis Cate, "The 1880s: The Prelude," in Phillip Dennis Cate and Sinclair Hamilton Hitchings, *The Color Revolution: Color Lithography in France, 1890–1900* (New Brunswick, N.J.: Peregrine Smith and Rutgers University Art Gallery, 1978), pp. 1–15.
18. Mellerio, *Lithographie originale*, p. 23. Translation by the author.
19. Ibid., pp. 3–4.
20. Goncourt, *Journal*, April 19, 1884, p. 334.
21. Colta Feller Ives, *The Great Wave: The Influence of Japanese Woodcuts on French Prints* (New York: Metropolitan Museum of Art, 1974), p. 15.
22. Paul Leclercq, *Autour de Toulouse-Lautrec*, rev. ed. (Geneva: Pierre Cailler, 1954), p. 60.
23. François Gauzi, *Lautrec et son temps* (Paris: David Perret, 1954), p. 53. Translation by the author. A *mousmé* is a Japanese girl.
24. "Henri de Toulouse-Lautrec," press release, The Museum of Modern Art, New York, September 1985, MoMA Archives, Curatorial Exhibition Files, Exh. #1408, available online, http://www.moma.org/pdfs/docs/press_archives/6224/releases/MOMA_1985_0078_75.pdf?2010.
25. Deborah Wye and Audrey Isselbacher, *Abby Aldrich Rockefeller and Print Collecting: An Early Mission for MoMA.* Exh. brochure (New York: The Museum of Modern Art, 1999).
26. Russell Lynes, *Good Old Modern: An Intimate Portrait of The Museum of Modern Art* (New York: Atheneum, 1973), p. 343.
27. Barr, quoted in "Mrs. John D. Rockefeller, Jr., Gift of Toulouse-Lautrec Print Collection Exhibited by Museum of Modern Art," press release, The Museum of Modern Art, New York, November 18, 1946, MoMA Archives, CUR, Exh. #598, available online, http://www.moma.org/pdfs/docs/press_archives/1182/releases/MOMA_1946-1948_0056_1946-11-18_461118-55.pdf?2010.
28. Frey, *A Life*, p. 6.
29. George Day, *Pleasure Guide to Paris: Illustrated by Photographs* (London and Paris: Nilsson & Co., 1903?), p. 60.
30. Susanna Barrows, "Nineteenth-Century Cafés: Arenas of Everyday Life," in *Pleasures of Paris: Daumier to Picasso*, ed. Barbara Stern Shapiro (Boston: Museum of Fine Arts, Boston, 1991), pp. 17–19.
31. For more on women workers in cafés-concerts in this period, see Geraldine Harris, "But Is It Art? Female Performers in the Café-Concert," *New Theatre Quarterly* 5, no. 20 (November 1989).
32. Georges Clemenceau, *La Justice* (September 15, 1894), cited in Götz Adriani, *Toulouse-Lautrec: The Complete Graphic Works: A Catalogue Raisonné: The Gerstenberg Collection* (London: Royal Academy of Arts, in association with Thames and Hudson, 1988), p. 117.
33. Day, *Pleasure Guide*, p. 73.
34. Ibid., p. 95.
35. Frey, *A Life*, p. 186.
36. Ibid., p. 187.
37. For more on the women depicted in these works, see David Sweetman, *Explosive Acts: Toulouse-Lautrec, Oscar Wilde, Félix Fénéon and the Art & Anarchy of the Fin de Siècle* (New York: Simon & Schuster, 1999), pp. 366–67.
38. Jacques Lassaigne, *Toulouse-Lautrec and the Paris of Cabarets* (Paris: Tête de Feuilles, 1976), p. 9.
39. Frey, *A Life*, p. 260.
40. Jean Adhémar, *Toulouse-Lautrec: His Complete Lithographs and Drypoints* (New York: Harry N. Abrams, 1965), cat. no. 1.
41. Gustave Geffroy, *La Vie artistique* (Paris: E. Dentu, 1892), vol. 1, pp. 117–18, quoted, in translation, in Klaus Berger, *Japonisme in Western Painting from Whistler to Matisse*, trans. David Britt (Cambridge and New York: Cambridge University Press, 1992), p. 192.
42. This remark by Lautrec is quoted, in translation, in Daniel C. Rich, *Henri de Toulouse-Lautrec "Au Moulin Rouge," in the Art Institute of Chicago* (London: Percy Lund Humphries & Company, 1949?), p. 10.
43. Catherine van Casselaer, *Lot's Wife: Lesbian Paris, 1890–1914* (Liverpool: Janus Press, 1986), p. 59.
44. Sweetman, *Explosive Acts*, p. 354.
45. "I assist in Sapphic loves / Of women who are not quite lovers," quoted, in translation, in Desloge, ed., *The Baldwin M. Baldwin Collection*, p. 112.
46. Reinhold Heller, "Rediscovering Henri de Toulouse-Lautrec's 'At the Moulin Rouge,'" *Art Institute of Chicago Museum Studies* 12, no. 2 (1986): 120, available online, http://www.jstor.org/stable/4115937.
47. Lautrec later depicted La Goulue with her trained dog testifying before the senator René Béranger's *Ligue Morale* (Moral League), which brought charges of immoral conduct against artists and models in attendance at the masquerade *Bal des Quatr'z' Arts* (Four Arts' Ball) in 1893. It is likely a composite image, as Lautrec made it six years after the trial, while institutionalized, and in 1893 La Goulue had not yet begun her work with performing animals.
48. Loïe Fuller, *Fifteen Years of a Dancer's Life: with Some Account of Her Distinguished Friends* (New York: Dance Horizons, 1978), p. 62.
49. Arsène Alexandre, "Le Théâtre de la Loïe Fuller," *Le Théâtre* 4 (August 11, 1900): 24, quoted, in translation, in Carolyn Sinsky, "Loïe Fuller," *The Modernism Lab*, Yale University, 2010, available online, http://modernism.research.yale.edu/wiki/index.php/Loie_Fuller.
50. C. D., "Japonisme d'art," *Le Figaro illustré* 33 (April 1893), cited in Ives, *The Great Wave*, p. 87.

51. M. G. Dortu and Philippe Huisman, *Lautrec by Lautrec*, trans. Corinne Bellow (New York: Viking Press, 1964), p. 173.
52. This term appears in English, as presented, in Kenworth Moffett, "Meier-Graefe and Jugendstil" in *Meier-Graefe as Art Critic* (Munich: Prestel, 1973), pp. 16–18.
53. Victor Joncières, *Le Figaro* (June 1896), quoted, in translation, in *Toulouse-Lautrec, 1864–1901* (Montreal: Musée des Beaux-Arts de Montréal, 1968), p. 17.
54. Yvette Guilbert, *La Chanson de ma vie (Mes Mémoires)* (Paris: B. Grasset, 1927), p. 63.
55. Gustave Geffroy, *Yvette Guilbert*, trans. Barbara Sessions (New York: Walker and Company, 1968), n.p.
56. Guilbert, *La Chanson*, p. 225.
57. This story is recalled in Theodore B. Donson and Marvel M. Griepp, *Henri de Toulouse-Lautrec: Performers of the Stage and the Boudoir, 1891–1899* (New York: Theodore B. Donson, 1980), cat. no. 22.
58. Jean Lorrain, *L'Écho de Paris* (October 15, 1894), quoted, in translation, in Claire Frèches-Thory and José Frèches, *Toulouse-Lautrec: Painter of the Night* (London: Thames and Hudson, 1994), p. 313.
59. Gaston Davenay, "From Day to Day: Yvette Guilbert," *Le Figaro* (August 16, 1894), quoted, in translation, in Peter Wick, "Introduction," in Geffroy, *Yvette Guilbert*, n.p.
60. For more on her stormy voyage, see Jane Avril, *Mes Mémoires* (Paris: Phébus, 2005), p. 86.
61. In the first state, reproduced here (see pl. 37), the snake motif is echoed in a remarque at bottom left.
62. Lautrec was not much of a photographer, but many of his friends were. He also made extensive use of publicity photographs.
63. This photograph was recently rediscovered by Steven F. Joseph, and published in Stephen F. Joseph, "Paul Sescau: Toulouse-Lautrec's Elusive Neighbor," *History of Photography* 37, no. 2 (May 2013): 156, 158.
64. Arsène Alexandre, "She Who Dances," supplement to *L'Art français* (July 29, 1893), quoted, in translation, in Nancy Ireson, *Toulouse-Lautrec and Jane Avril: Beyond the Moulin Rouge* (London: The Courtauld Gallery in association with Paul Holberton Publishing, 2011), p. 133.
65. Avril, *Mes Mémoires*, p. 61.
66. Frey, *A Life*, p. 171.
67. Leclercq, *Autour*, p. 24.
68. Frey, *A Life*, p. 330.
69. This comment by Leclercq appears in ibid., p. 482.
70. This description by Thadée Natanson appears in ibid., p. 379.
71. Van Casselaer, *Lot's Wife*, p. 5. Several contemporary studies—among them, Alexandre Parent-Duchâtelet's *De la prostitution dans la ville de Paris* (Paris: Baillière, 1836); A. Coffignon's *Paris vivant: La Corruption à Paris* (Paris: Librairie illustrée, 1898); and Gabriel Antoine Jogand-Pagé's *La Corruption fin-de-siècle* (Paris: G. Carré, 1894)—examine the practice as it pertained to their investigations into prostitution, detention centers, contemporary morality, and social mores. Julien Chevalier presented a pseudo-scientific study, *Inversion sexuelle* (Lyon: A. Storck, 1893), and fiction writers such as Émile Zola followed suit, chronicling pickup strategies, bars, and neighborhoods of lesbian activity.
72. Leclercq, *Autour*, p. 69.
73. Day, *Pleasure Guide*, p. 128.
74. The woman in the red gown bears a marked resemblance to the woman in the Sescau poster (pl. 122) and the *Figaro illustré* article (pl. 20).
75. Lautrec's emulation of the wood grain along the baseboard may have been inspired by Edvard Munch's woodcut *The Scream*, reproduced in *La Revue blanche* in 1896. Munch owned *Elles*. See Frey, *A Life*, pp. 417–18.
76. Ibid., p. 307.
77. Thadée Natanson, *La Revue blanche* 16 (February 1893): 146, quoted, in translation, in Desloge, ed., *The Baldwin M. Baldwin Collection*, p. 204.
78. Victor Joze, *Les Rozenfeld, histoire d'une famille juive. La Tribu d'Isidore* (Paris: Antony, 1897), p. vii, quoted, in translation, in Phillip Dennis Cate, "The Paris Cry: Graphic Artists and the Dreyfus Affair," in *The Dreyfus Affair: Art, Truth, and Justice*, ed. Norman L. Kleeblatt (Berkeley: University of California Press, 1987), pp. 70–71.
79. Ibid., p. 71.
80. Phillip Dennis Cate, "*Treize Lithographies* and Yvette Guilbert: The Actors and Actresses of Henri de Toulouse-Lautrec," in *The Henri de Toulouse-Lautrec, W. H. B. Sands Correspondence*, ed. Herbert D. Schimmel and Phillip Dennis Cate (New York: Dodd, Mead & Company, 1983), p. 21.
81. Lautrec, letter to A. Berthier, November 17, 1897, in Schimmel, *Letters*, p. 309, letter 489.
82. Edmond de Goncourt, *La Fille Élisa* (Paris: G. Charpentier, 1877), n.p.
83. For more on Dihau and his work, see Mindy Keyes, "Degas, Toulouse-Lautrec and Désiré Dihau: Portrait of a Bassoonist and His Bassoon," *Double Reed* 13, no. 2 (Fall 1990): 54–57.
84. "Carnot Seriously Ill: Anxiety about the Condition of the President of France," *New York Times*, June 17, 1893.
85. Frey, *A Life*, p. 368.
86. Arthur Gold and Robert Fizdale, *Misia: The Life of Misia Sert* (New York: Morrow Quill Paperbacks, 1981), p. 43.
87. Avril is quoted, in translation, in Ireson, *Beyond the Moulin Rouge*, p. 18.
88. Day, *Pleasure Guide*, p. 199.
89. Adriani, *The Complete Graphic Works*, p. 355.
90. Desloge, ed., *The Baldwin M. Baldwin Collection*, p. 186.
91. Sarrazin, letter to Mlle Adeline Cromont, January 17, 1899, in Schimmel, *Letters*, p. 396, letter 4.
92. Leclercq, *Autour*, p. 72.
93. Ibid., pp. 72–73.
94. Frey, *A Life*, p. 123–24.
95. For a contemporary description of the rink and its technical workings, see "The New Parisian Skating Rink, with Artificial Ice," *Manufacturer and Builder* 22 (April 1890): 84.
96. Lautrec, letter to Adèle de Toulouse-Lautrec, November–December 1895, in Schimmel, *Letters*, p. 285, letter 442.
97. Gold and Fizdale, *Misia*, p. 20.
98. Leclercq, *Autour*, pp. 71–72.
99. Printer Henri Stern saw him drawing two images from memory while in the psychiatric hospital, in Neuilly, in 1899; see Adhémar, *His Complete Lithographs and Drypoints*, cat. nos. 333–55.
100. See "Paper Confetti: History of Its Use," *Star* 9538 (May 10, 1909): 2; "The History of Paper Confetti," *Bathurst Free Press and Mining Journal* (May 20, 1897): 1; and Christian Roy, *Traditional Festivals: A Multicultural Encyclopedia*, vol. 2. (Santa Barbara: ABC-CLIO, 2005), p. 53.
101. Adèle de Toulouse-Lautrec is quoted, in translation, in Frey, *A Life*, p. 102.
102. "Paper Confetti:" 2.
103. This is the recently rediscovered publicity photograph of Avril, published in Joseph, "Paul Sescau," pp. 156–58 (see note 63 and pl. 37).
104. Ibid., p. 166.
105. Frey, *A Life*, p. 32.
106. William Rothenstein, *Men and Memories. A History of the Arts, 1872–1922, Being the Recollections of William Rothenstein* (New York: Tudor Publishing Co., 1937), vol. 1, p. 115.
107. Another version of this image, with added text, served as an advertisement for *The Chap Book*, an American magazine published between 1894 and 1898.
108. Lautrec, letter to Adèle de Toulouse-Lautrec, November–December 1895, in Schimmel, *Letters*, p. 285, letter 442.
109. Leclercq, *Autour*, p. 113.
110. Natanson is quoted, in translation, in Gold and Fizdale, *Misia*, p. 54.

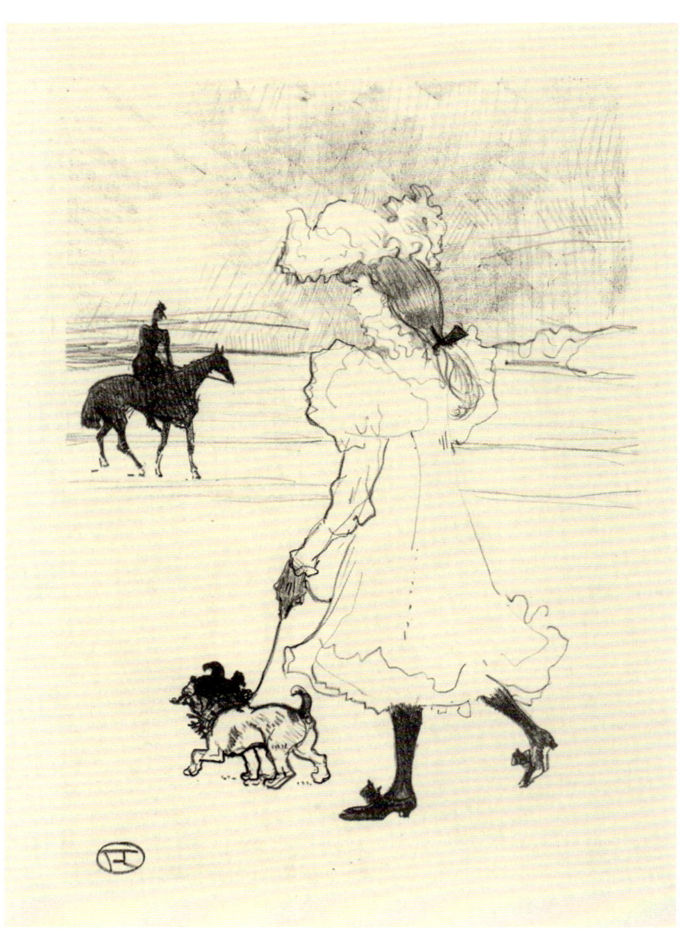

Plate 99
AU BOIS (IN THE BOIS DE BOULOGNE). 1897
Lithograph, sheet: 22 × 14⅝ in. (55.9 × 37.2 cm)
Gift of Abby Aldrich Rockefeller, 1946

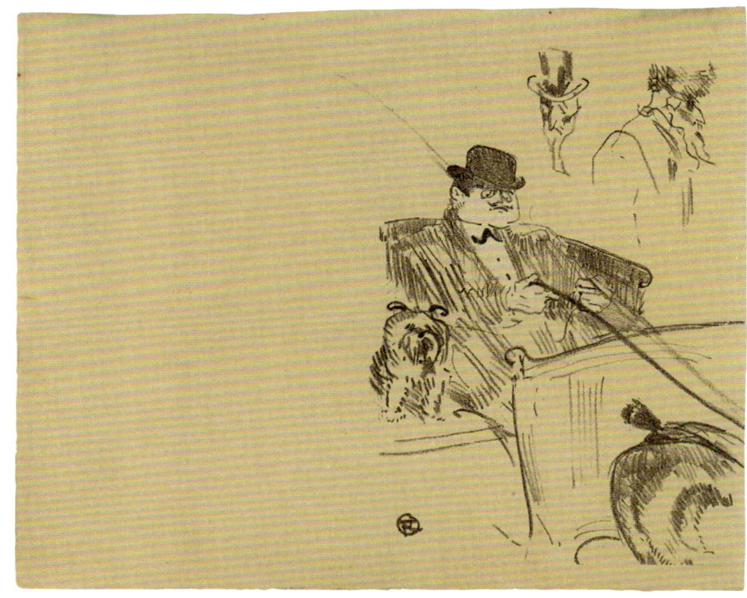

Plate 100
Cover for the book **LA TRIBU D'ISIDORE** by Victor Joze. 1897
Lithograph, sheet: 7 15/16 × 9⅝ in. (20.1 × 24.4 cm)
Gift of Abby Aldrich Rockefeller, 1946

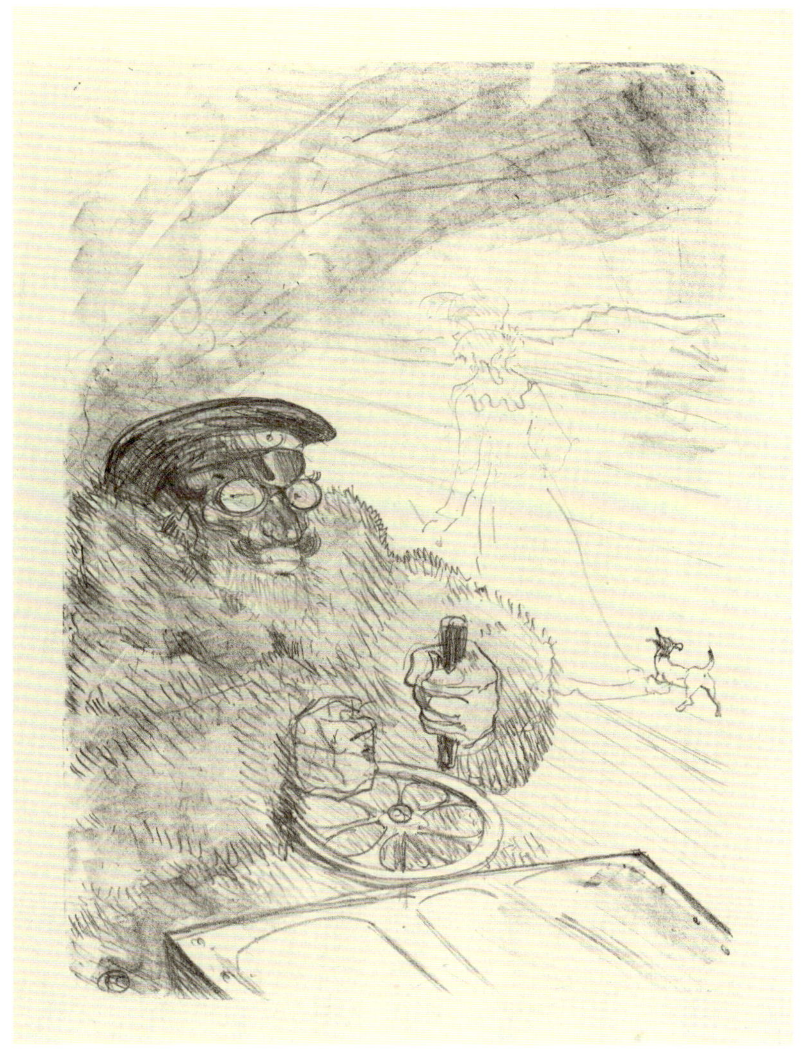

Plate 101
L'AUTOMOBILISTE (THE AUTOMOBILE DRIVER). 1898
Lithograph, sheet: 19¾ × 14 in. (50.1 × 35.5 cm)
Gift of Abby Aldrich Rockefeller, 1946

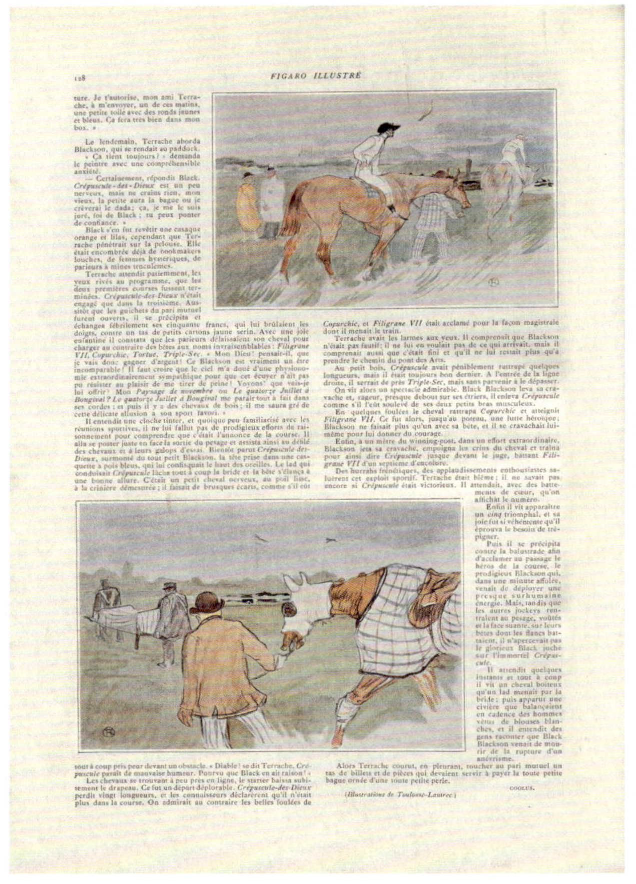

128 FIGARO ILLUSTRÉ

ture. Je t'autorise, mon ami Terrache, à m'envoyer, un de ces matins, une petite toile avec des ronds jaunes et bleus. Ça fera très bien dans mon box. »

Le lendemain, Terrache aborda Blackson, qui se rendait au paddock.

« Ça tient toujours? » demanda le peintre avec une compréhensible anxiété.

— Certainement, répondit Black. *Crépuscule-des-Dieux* est un peu nerveux, mais ne crains rien, mon vieux, la petite aura la bague ou je crèverai le dada; ça, je me le suis juré, foi de Black; tu peux ponter de confiance. »

Black s'en fut revêtir une casaque orange et lilas, cependant que Terrache pénétrait sur la pelouse. Elle était encombrée déjà de bookmakers louches, de femmes hystériques, de parieurs à mines truculentes.

Terrache attendit patiemment, les yeux rivés au programme, que les deux premières courses fussent terminées. *Crépuscule-des-Dieux* n'était engagé que dans la troisième. Aussitôt que les guichets du pari mutuel furent ouverts, il se précipita et échangea fébrilement ses cinquante francs, qui lui brûlaient les doigts, contre un tas de petits cartons jaune serin. Avec une joie enfantine il constata que les parieurs délaissaient son cheval pour charger au contraire des bêtes aux noms invraisemblables: *Filigrane VII, Copurchic, Tortue, Triple-Sec*. « Mon Dieu! pensait-il, que je vais donc gagner d'argent! Ce Blackson est vraiment un être incomparable! Il faut croire que le ciel m'a doué d'une physionomie extraordinairement sympathique pour que cet écuyer n'ait pas pu résister au plaisir de me tirer de peine! Voyons! que vais-je lui offrir? Mon *Paysage de novembre* ou *Le quatorze Juillet à Bougival*? *Le quatorze Juillet à Bougival* me parait tout à fait dans ses cordes; et puis il y a des chevaux de bois; il me saura gré de cette délicate allusion à son sport favori. »

Il entendit une cloche tinter, et quoique peu familiarisé avec les réunions sportives, il ne lui fallut pas de prodigieux efforts de raisonnement pour comprendre que c'était l'annonce de la course. Il alla se poster juste en face la sortie du pesage et assista ainsi au défilé des chevaux et à leurs galops d'essai. Bientôt parut *Crépuscule-des-Dieux*, surmonté du tout petit Blackson, la tête prise dans une casquette à pois bleus, qui lui confisquait le haut des oreilles. Le lad qui conduisait *Crépuscule* lâcha tout à coup la bride et la bête s'élança à une bonne allure. C'était un petit cheval nerveux, au poil lisse, à la crinière démesurée; il faisait de brusques écarts, comme s'il eût tout à coup pris peur devant un obstacle. « Diable! se dit Terrache, *Crépuscule* paraît de mauvaise humeur. Pourvu que Black en ait raison! »

Les chevaux se trouvant à peu près en ligne, le starter baissa subitement le drapeau. Ce fut un départ déplorable. *Crépuscule-des-Dieux* perdit vingt longueurs, et les connaisseurs déclarèrent qu'il n'était plus dans la course. On admirait au contraire les belles foulées de *Copurchic*, et *Filigrane VII* était acclamé pour la façon magistrale dont il menait le train.

Terrache avait les larmes aux yeux. Il comprenait que Blackson n'était pas fautif; il ne lui en voulait pas de ce qui arrivait, mais il comprenait aussi que c'était fini et qu'il ne lui restait plus qu'à prendre le chemin du pont des Arts.

Au petit bois, *Crépuscule* avait péniblement rattrapé quelques longueurs, mais il était toujours bon dernier. A l'entrée de la ligne droite, il serrait de près *Triple-Sec*, mais sans parvenir à le dépasser.

On vit alors un spectacle admirable. Black Blackson leva sa cravache et, rageur, presque debout sur ses étriers, il enleva *Crépuscule* comme s'il l'eût soulevé de ses deux petits bras musculeux.

En quelques foulées le cheval rattrapa *Copurchic* et atteignit *Filigrane VII*. Ce fut alors, jusqu'au poteau, une lutte héroïque; Blackson ne faisait plus qu'un avec sa bête, et il se cravachait lui-même pour lui donner du courage.

Enfin, à un mètre du winning-post, dans un effort extraordinaire, Blackson jeta sa cravache, empoigna les crins du cheval et traîna pour ainsi dire *Crépuscule* jusque devant le juge, battant *Filigrane VII* d'un septième d'encolure.

Des hurrahs frénétiques, des applaudissements enthousiastes saluèrent cet exploit sportif. Terrache était blême; il ne savait pas encore si *Crépuscule* était victorieux. Il attendait, avec des battements de cœur, qu'on affichât le numéro.

Enfin il vit apparaître un *cinq* triomphal, et sa joie fut si véhémente qu'il éprouva le besoin de trépigner.

Puis il se précipita contre la balustrade afin d'acclamer au passage le héros de la course, le prodigieux Blackson qui, dans une minute affolée, venait de déployer une presque surhumaine énergie. Mais, tandis que les autres jockeys rentraient au pesage, voûtés et la face suante, sur leurs bêtes dont les flancs battaient, il n'apercevait pas le glorieux Black juché sur l'immortel *Crépuscule*.

Il attendit quelques instants et tout à coup il vit un cheval boiteux qu'un lad menait par la bride; puis apparut une civière que balançaient en cadence des hommes vêtus de blouses blanches, et il entendit des gens raconter que Black Blackson venait de mourir de la rupture d'un anévrisme.

Alors Terrache courut, en pleurant, toucher au pari mutuel un tas de billets et de pièces qui devaient servir à payer la toute petite bague ornée d'une toute petite perle.

COOLUS.

(*Illustrations de Toulouse-Lautrec*.)

Plate 102

LE BON JOCKEY: CONTE SPORTIF (THE GOOD JOCKEY: A SPORTS STORY) from the journal **LE FIGARO ILLUSTRÉ** (July 1895)

Halftone relief and line block, page: 16⅛ × 11¹⁵⁄₁₆ in. (41 × 30.4 cm)

The Museum of Modern Art Library, New York

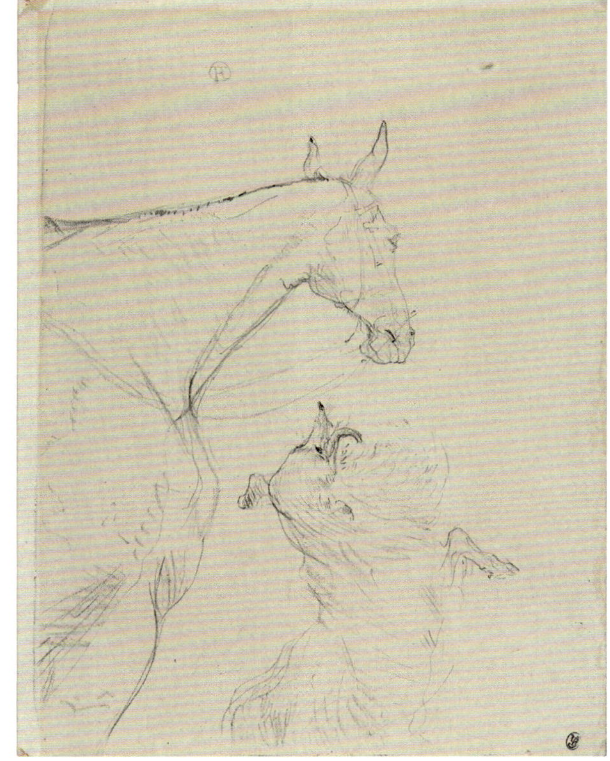

Plate 103

LE CHEVAL ET LE COLLEY

(THE HORSE AND THE COLLIE). 1898

Lithograph, sheet: 14³⁄₁₆ × 11 in. (36.1 × 27.9 cm)

Gift of Jeanne C. Thayer, 1991

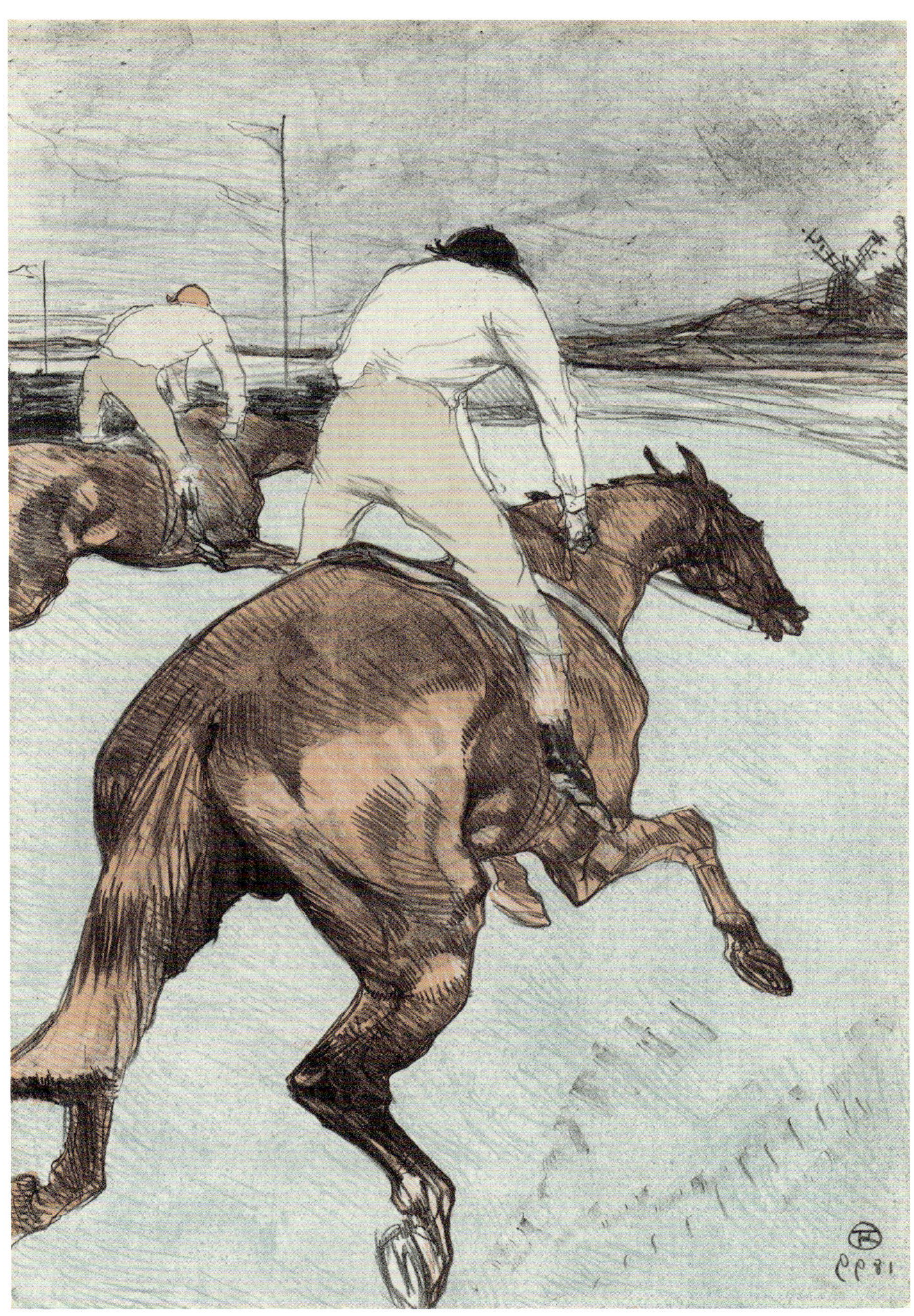

Plate 104
LE JOCKEY. 1899
Lithograph, sheet: 20⁵⁄₁₆ × 14¼ in. (51.6 × 36.2 cm)
David and Peggy Rockefeller Collection

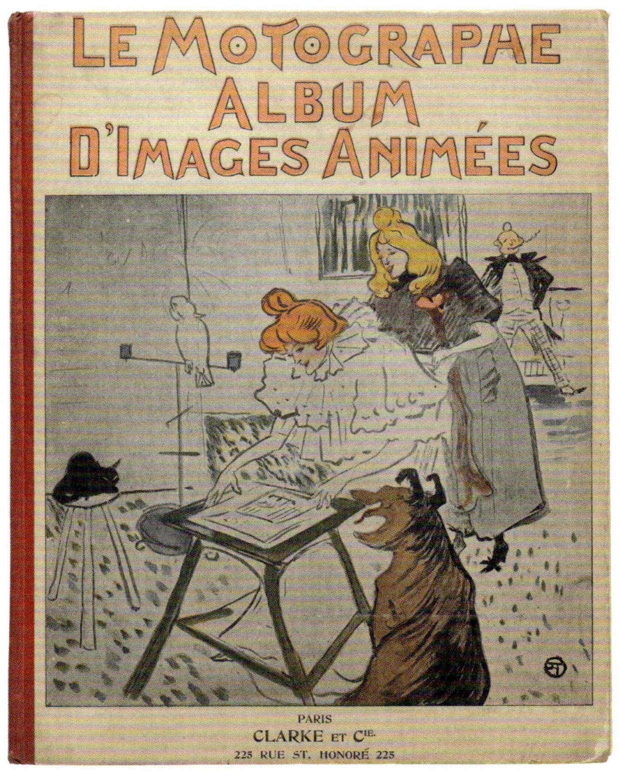

Plate 105
Cover for the book **LE MOTOGRAPHE: ALBUM D'IMAGES ANIMÉES**. 1899
Halftone relief and line block, page: $11\frac{7}{16} \times 9\frac{3}{16}$ in. (29 × 23.3 cm)
The Museum of Modern Art Library, New York

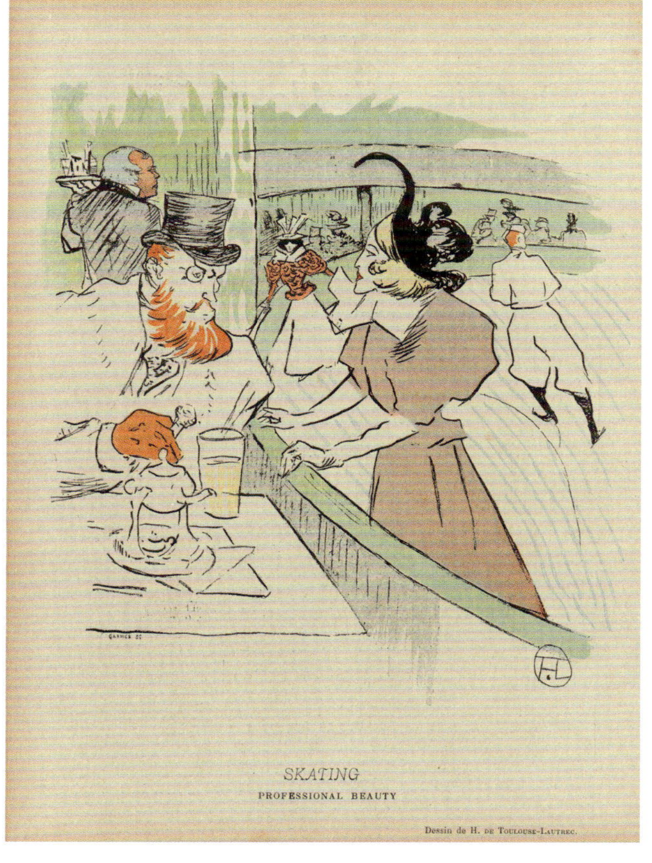

Plate 106
SKATING, PROFESSIONAL BEAUTY from the journal **LE RIRE** (January 11, 1896)
Halftone relief, page: $11\frac{7}{8} \times 9\frac{1}{8}$ in. (30.2 × 23.2 cm)
Linda Barth Goldstein Fund, 1997

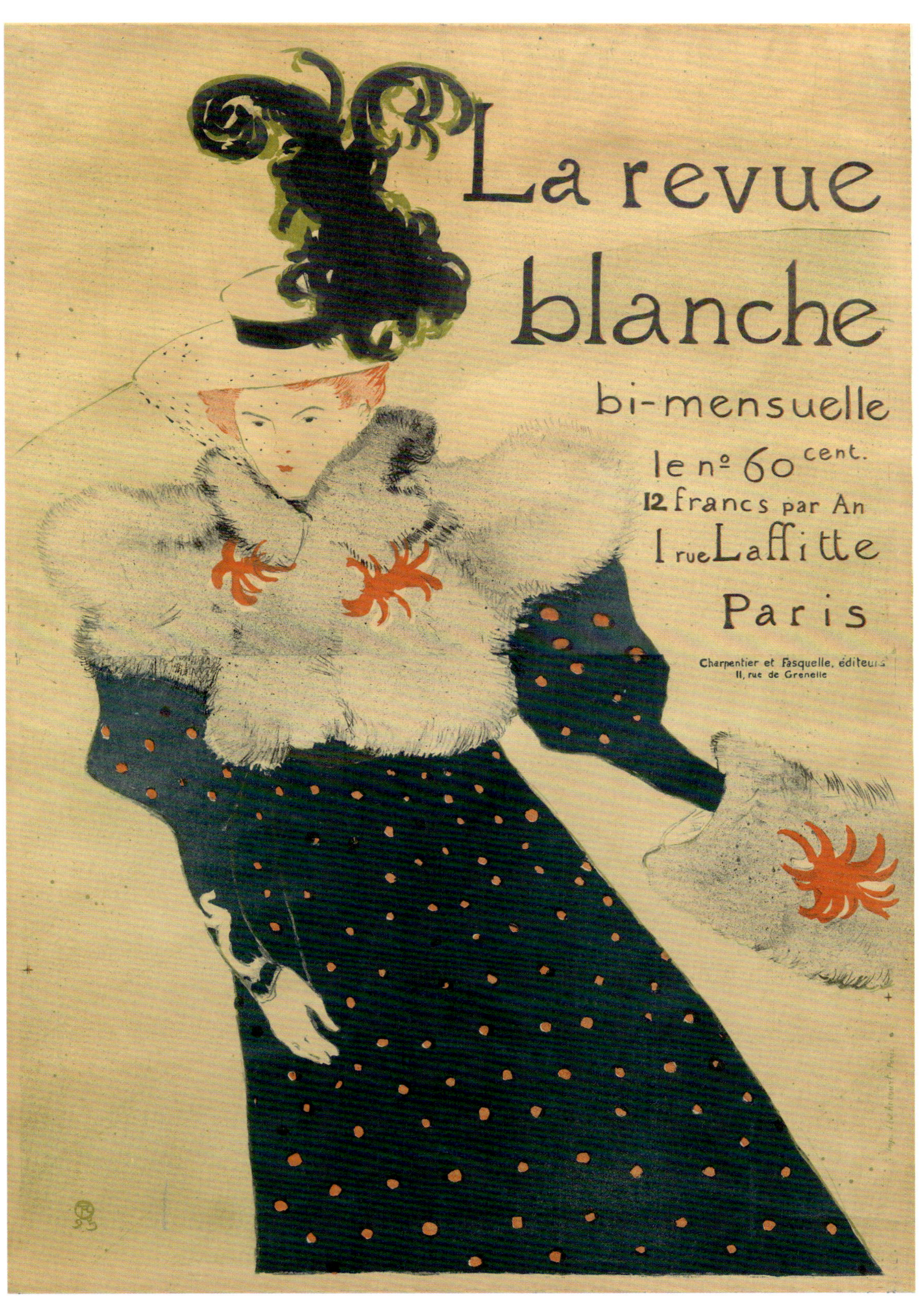

Plate 107
LA REVUE BLANCHE. 1895
Lithograph, sheet: 51 x 36 11/16 in. (129.6 x 93.2 cm)
Purchase, 1967

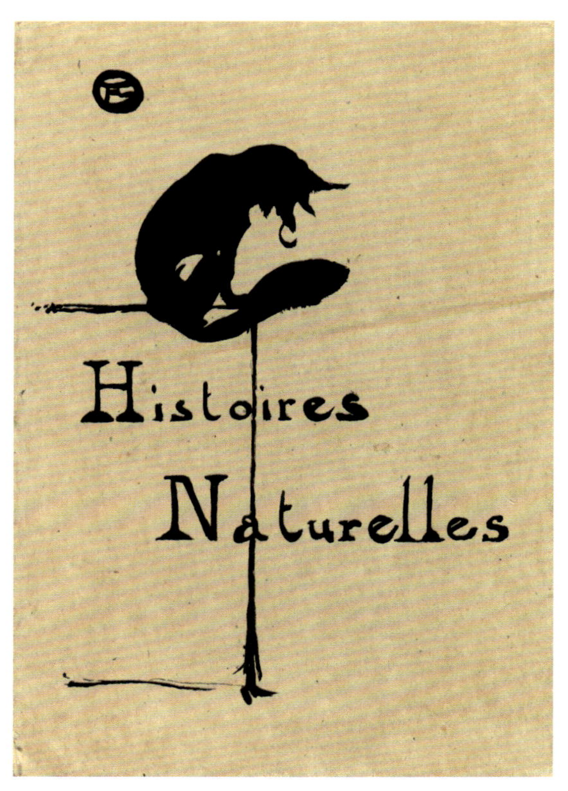

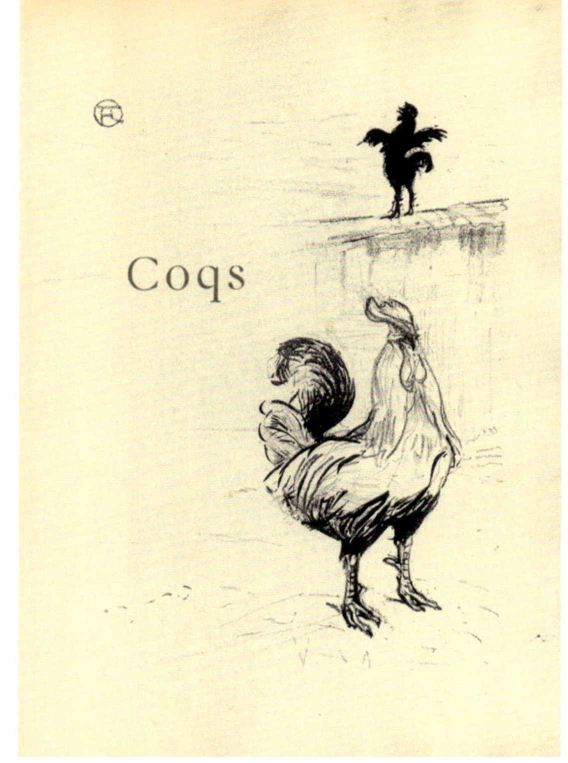

Plates 108–119
Cover for and pages from the illustrated book
HISTOIRES NATURELLES
by Jules Renard. 1897, published 1899
Lithograph, page: 12⅜ x 8⅞ in. (31.5 x 22.5 cm)
The Louis E. Stern Collection, 1964

Plate 109
COQS (**ROOSTERS**)

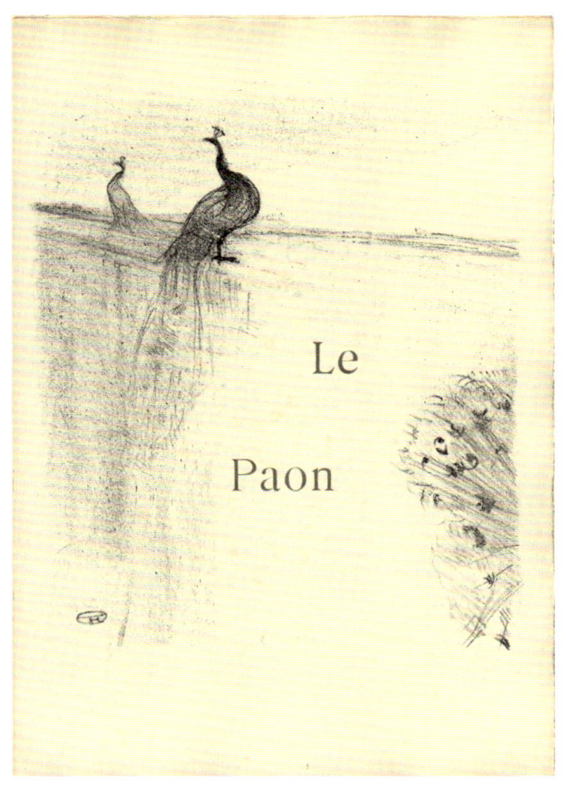

Plate 110
LE PAON (THE PEACOCK)

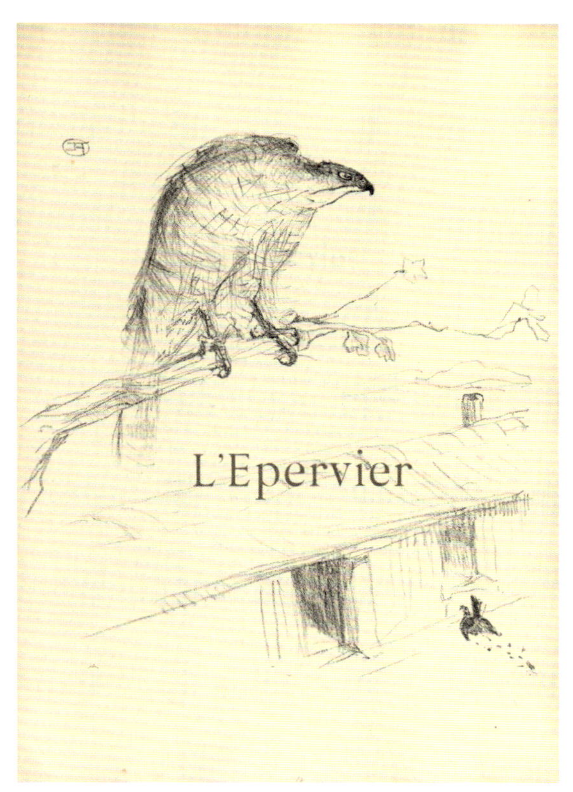

Plate 111
L'ÉPERVIER (THE SPARROW HAWK)

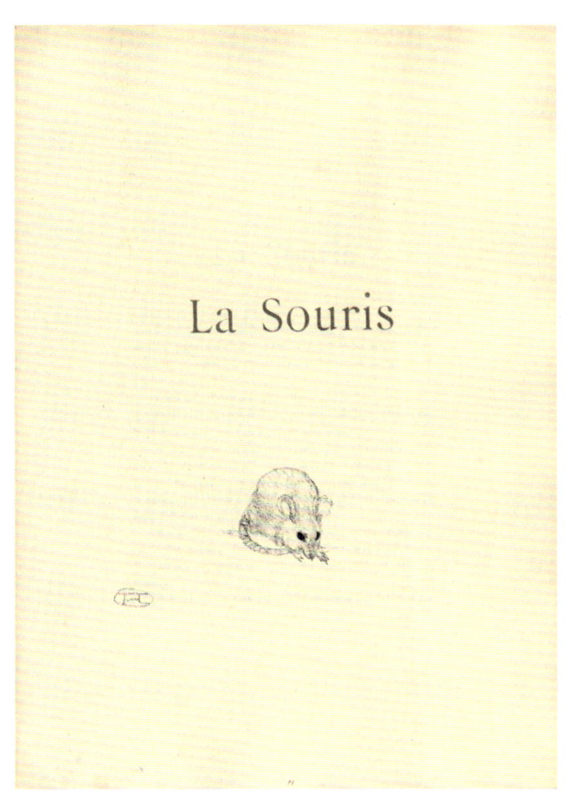

Plate 112
LA SOURIS (THE MOUSE)

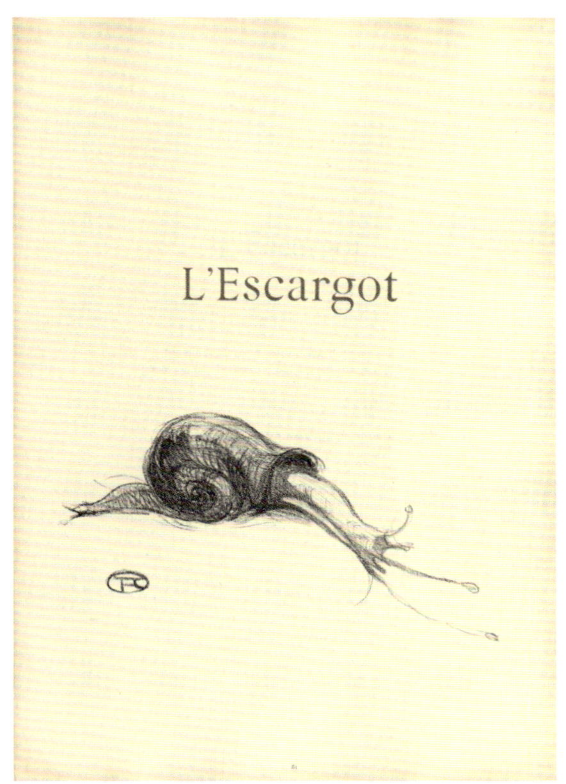

Plate 113
L'ESCARGOT (THE SNAIL)

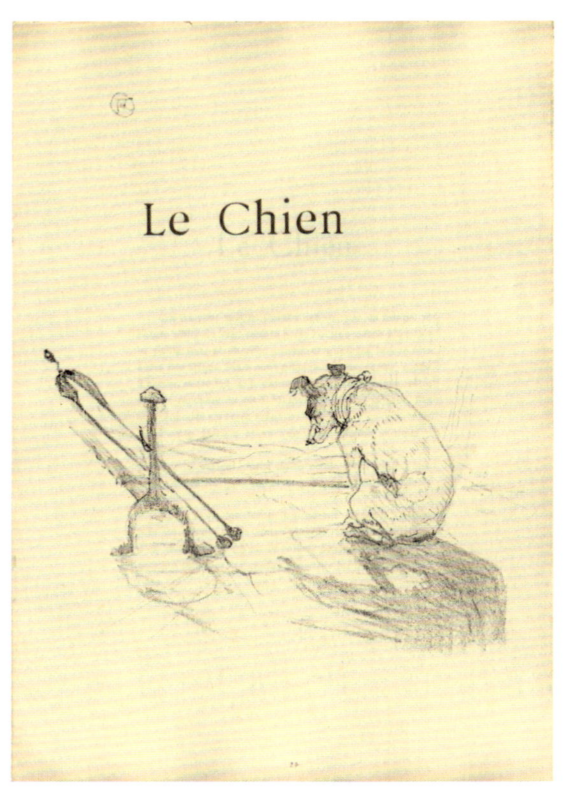

Plate 114
LE CHIEN (THE DOG)

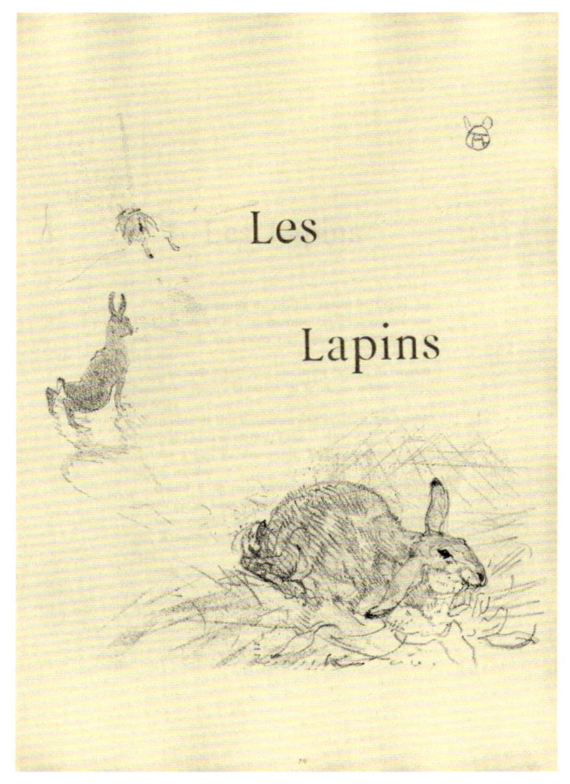

Plate 115
LES LAPINS (THE RABBITS)

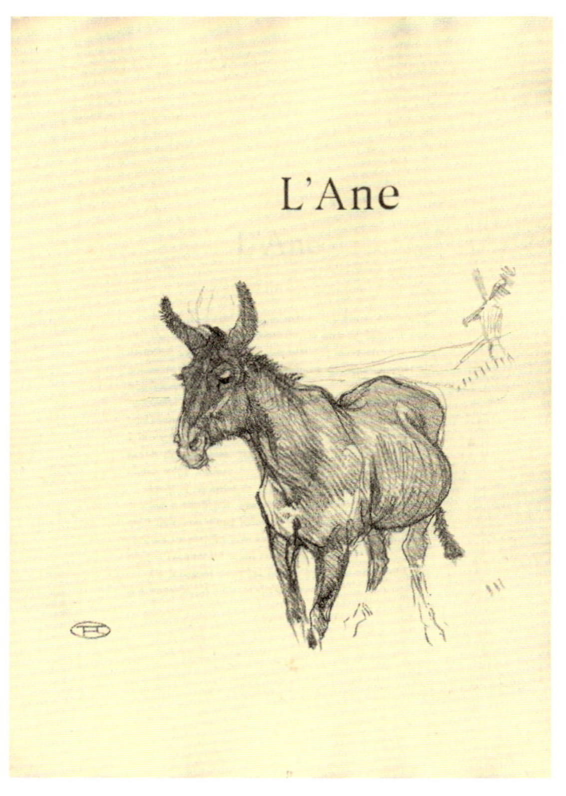

Plate 116
L'ÂNE (THE DONKEY)

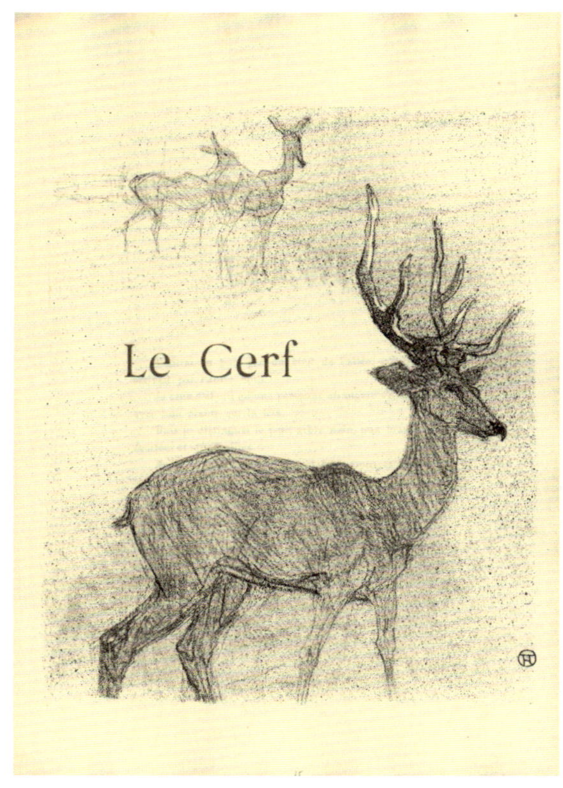

Plate 117
LE CERF (THE STAG)

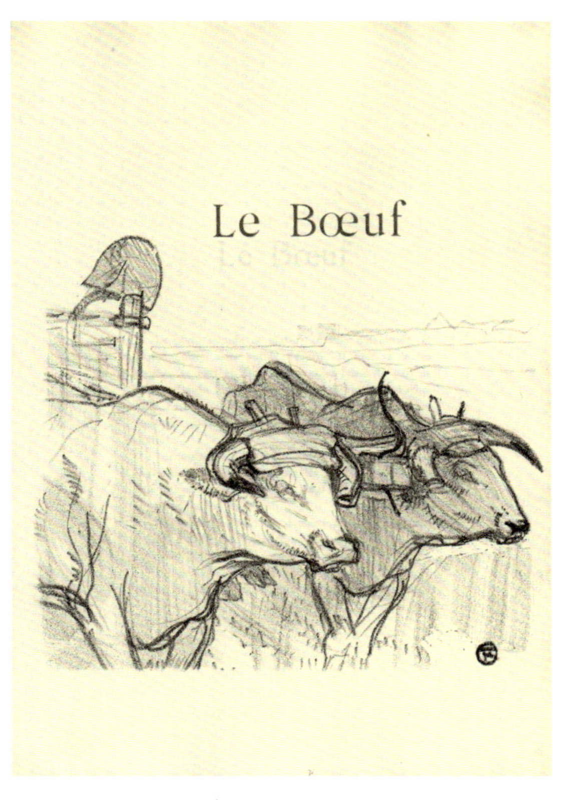

Plate 118
LE BŒUF (THE OX)

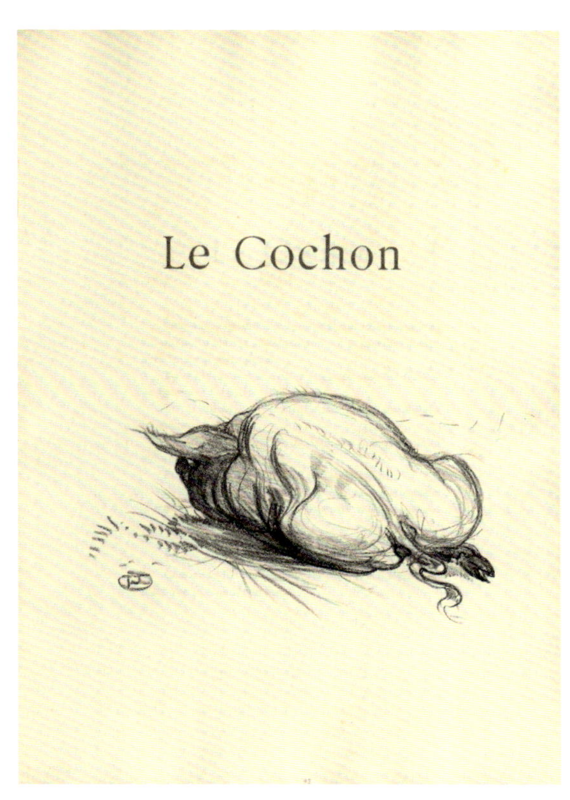

Plate 119
LE COCHON (THE PIG)

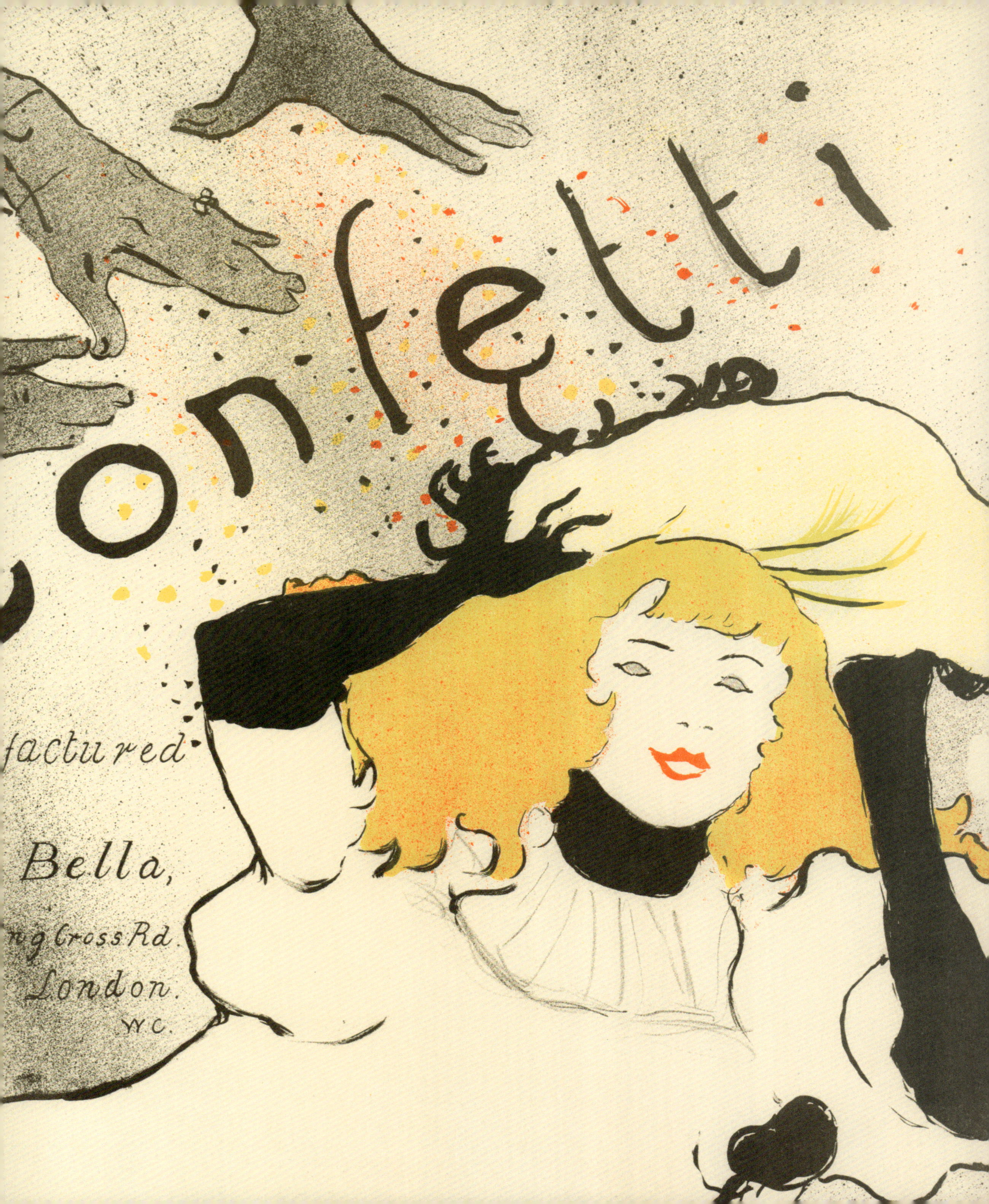
Confetti
facturred
Bella,
ng Cross Rd
London.
W.C.

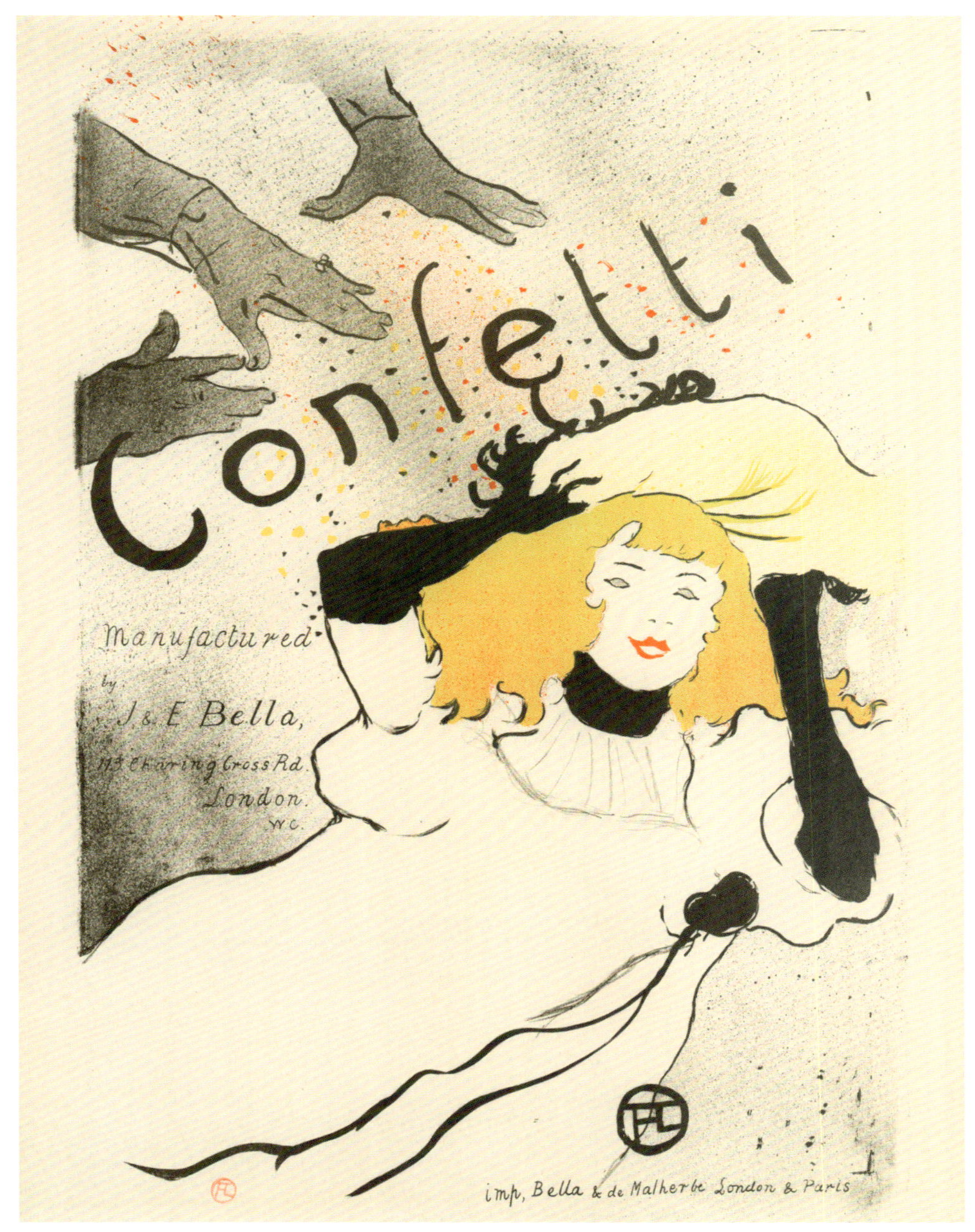

Plate 120
CONFETTI. 1894
Lithograph, sheet: 22⅝ x 17 9/16 in. (57.4 x 44.6 cm)
Acquired in honor of Joanne M. Stern by the Committee on Prints and Illustrated Books
in appreciation for her contribution as Committee Chair, 1999

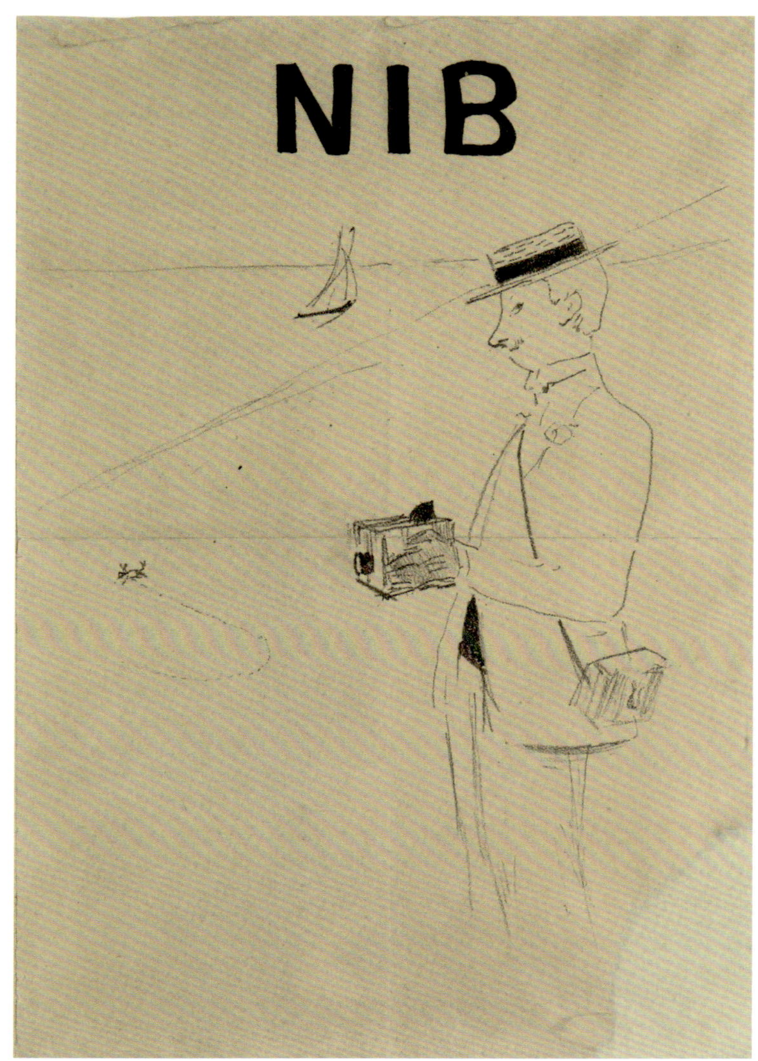

Plate 121
LE PHOTOGRAPHE-AMATEUR (THE AMATEUR PHOTOGRAPHER)
from the journal **NIB**, supplement to **LA REVUE BLANCHE**. 1894, published 1895
Lithograph, page: 19½ × 13¾ in. (49.6 × 35 cm)
Gift of Eastman Kodak Company, 1951

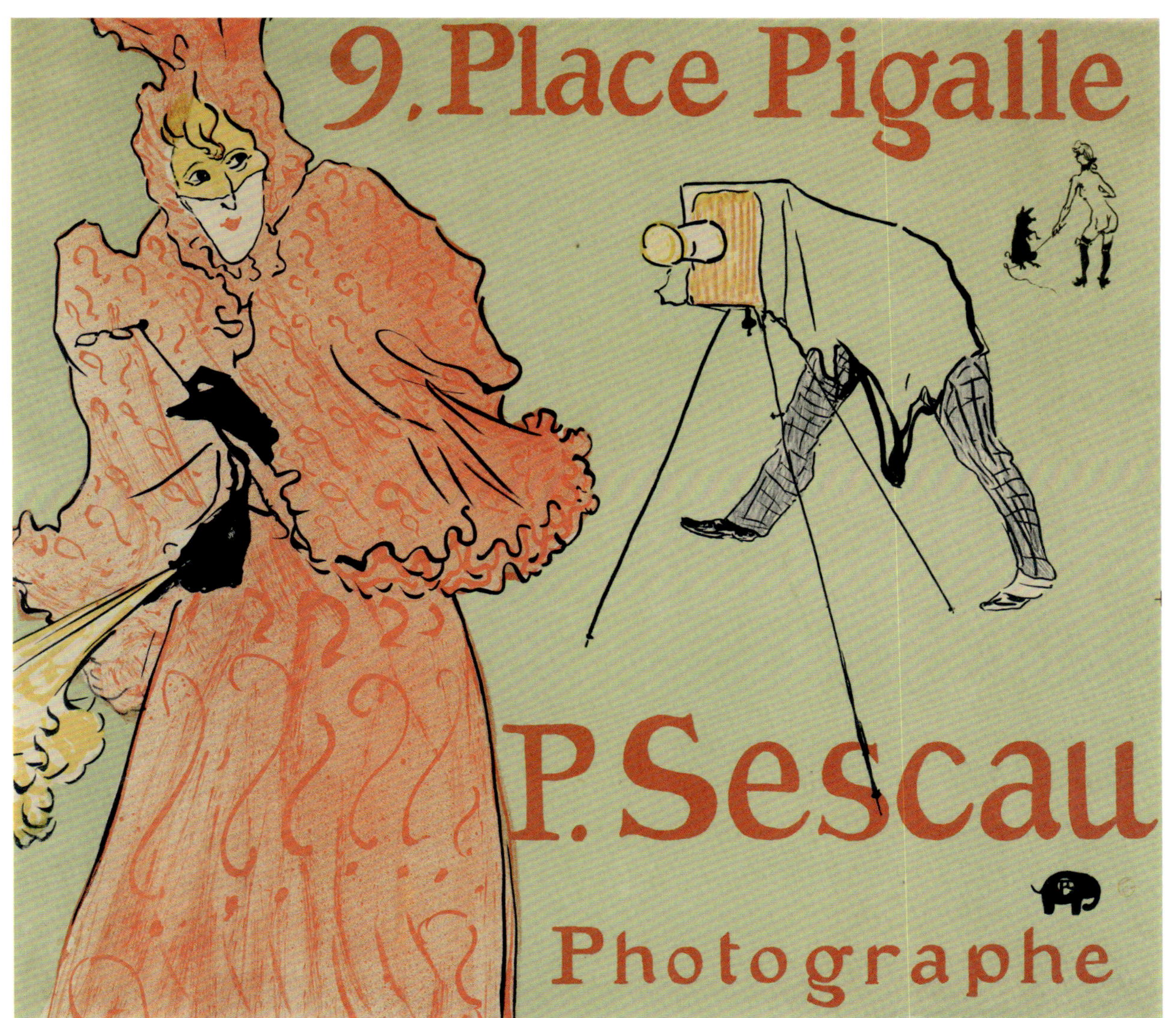

Plate 122
LE PHOTOGRAPHE SESCAU (THE PHOTOGRAPHER SESCAU). 1894
Lithograph, sheet: 24 7/8 × 31 1/8 in. (63.2 × 79 cm)
Grace M. Mayer Bequest, 1997

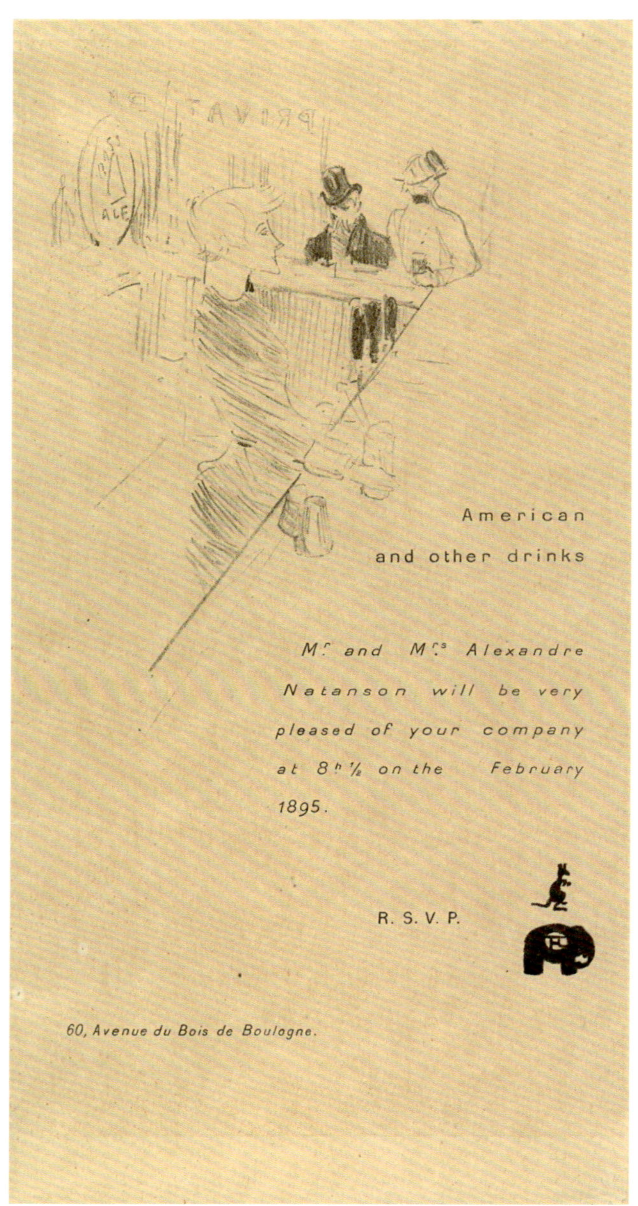

Plate 123
INVITATION CARD FOR ALEXANDRE NATANSON. 1895
Lithograph, sheet: 13⅜ × 7 in. (33.9 × 17.8 cm)
Gift of Mr. and Mrs. Herbert D. Schimmel, 1996

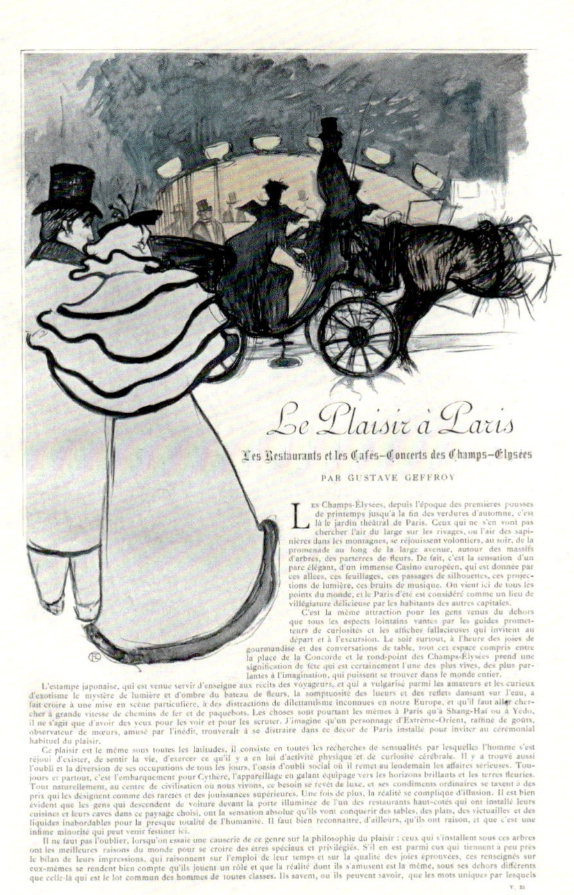

Le Plaisir à Paris

Les Restaurants et les Cafés-Concerts des Champs-Élysées

PAR GUSTAVE GEFFROY

Les Champs-Élysées, depuis l'époque des premières pousses de printemps jusqu'à la fin des verdures d'automne, c'est là le jardin théâtral de Paris. Ceux qui ne s'en vont pas chercher l'air du large sur les rivages, ou l'air des sapinières dans les montagnes, se réjouissent volontiers, au soir, de la promenade au long de la large avenue, autour des massifs d'arbres, des parterres de fleurs. De fait, c'est la sensation d'un parc élégant, d'un immense Casino européen, qui est donnée par ces allées, ces feuillages, ces passages de silhouettes, ces projections de lumière, ces bruits de musique. On vient ici de tous les points du monde, et le Paris d'été est considéré comme un lieu de villégiature délicieuse par les habitants des autres capitales.

C'est la même attraction pour les gens venus du dehors que tous les aspects lointains vantés par les guides prometteurs de curiosités et les affiches fallacieuses qui invitent au départ et à l'excursion. Le soir surtout, à l'heure des joies de gourmandise et des conversations de table, tout cet espace compris entre la place de la Concorde et le rond-point des Champs-Élysées prend une signification de fête qui est certainement l'une des plus vives, des plus parlantes à l'imagination, qui puissent se trouver dans le monde entier.

L'estampe japonaise, qui est venue servir d'enseigne aux récits des voyageurs, et qui a vulgarisé parmi les amateurs et les curieux d'exotisme le mystère de lumière et d'ombre du bateau de fleurs, la somptuosité des lueurs et des reflets dansant sur l'eau, a fait croire à une mise en scène particulière, à des distractions de dilettantisme inconnues en notre Europe, et qu'il faut aller chercher à grande vitesse de chemins de fer et de paquebots. Les choses sont pourtant les mêmes à Paris qu'à Shang-Haï ou à Yédo, il ne s'agit que d'avoir des yeux pour les voir et pour les scruter. J'imagine qu'un personnage d'Extrême-Orient, raffiné de goûts, observateur de mœurs, amusé par l'inédit, trouverait à se distraire dans ce décor de Paris installé pour inviter au cérémonial habituel du plaisir.

Ce plaisir est le même sous toutes les latitudes. Il consiste en toutes les recherches de sensualités par lesquelles l'homme s'est réjoui d'exister, de sentir la vie, d'exercer ce qu'il y a en lui d'activité physique et de curiosité cérébrale. Il y a trouvé aussi l'oubli et la diversion de ses occupations de tous les jours, l'oasis d'oubli social où il remet au lendemain les affaires sérieuses. Toujours et partout, c'est l'embarquement pour Cythère, l'appareillage en galant équipage vers les horizons brillants et les terres fleuries. Tout naturellement, au centre de civilisation où nous vivons, ce besoin se revêt de luxe, et ses condiments ordinaires se taxent à des prix qui les désignent comme des raretés et des jouissances supérieures. Une fois de plus, la réalité se complique d'illusion. Il est bien évident que les gens qui descendent de voiture devant la porte illuminée de l'un des restaurants haut-cotés qui ont installé leurs cuisines et leurs caves dans ce paysage choisi, ont la sensation absolue qu'ils vont conquérir des tables, des plats, des victuailles et des liquides inabordables pour la presque totalité de l'humanité. Il faut bien reconnaître, d'ailleurs, qu'ils ont raison, et que c'est une infime minorité qui peut venir festiner ici.

Il ne faut pas l'oublier, lorsqu'on essaie une causerie de ce genre sur la philosophie du plaisir : ceux qui s'installent sous ces arbres ont les meilleures raisons du monde pour se croire des êtres spéciaux et privilégiés. S'il en est parmi eux qui tiennent à peu près le bilan de leurs impressions, qui raisonnent sur l'emploi de leur temps et sur la qualité des joies éprouvées, ces renseignés sur eux-mêmes se rendent bien compte qu'ils jouent un rôle et que la réalité dont ils s'amusent est la même, sous ses dehors différents que celle-là qui est le lot commun des hommes de toutes classes. Ils savent, ou ils peuvent savoir, que les mots uniques par lesquels

V. 35

se représentent et se réduisent leurs occupations plaisantes sont les mots qui désignent le manger, le boire, le repos, la galanterie, tout ce qui s'adresse en flatterie directe à la vue, à l'ouïe, à l'odorat, au goût, au toucher, et à toutes les subdivisions naturelles ou artificielles et supplémentaires, qui peuvent nuancer les satisfactions des sens.

Précisément, ce plaisir particulier qu'ils éprouvent est un plaisir artificiel, mais ils ne l'en goûtent pas moins vivement, et pour eux, c'est bien l'essentiel. Ils ne font que se nourrir, comme tous les autres êtres, dans les restaurants et les cafés où ils s'installent, et ils seraient également nourris dans l'humble établissement, bouillon, brasserie ou boutique de marchand de vin où l'on trouve les aliments nécessaires : pain, viandes, légumes, vin, eau, bière et café. Ils pourraient aussi fumer du tabac dans une pipe, et leur désir d'engourdissement et de fumée serait également satisfait. Mais ce qu'ils recherchent et qu'ils exigent, c'est la mise en scène de ces utilités alimentaires.

Ils ne peuvent se satisfaire que dans certaines conditions apparentes où leur goût fatigué et leur vanité toujours en éveil trouvent leur compte. C'est la grande raison d'être des maisons où ils fréquentent. Le besoin physiologique qui les y amène semble disparaître dans les arrangements d'élégance et les dispositions d'accessoires. Le prix de la note à payer est considérable, et il doit être considérable en effet, puisque ce qui n'y figure pas, et qu'ils paient, n'a pas de prix fixe, n'a de valeur que la valeur consentie. C'est une atmosphère de satisfaction qui est soldée par ceux qui accomplissent les rites de cette fête. Leur offrande est le signe de leur reconnaissance pour la haute idée que l'on a réussi à leur donner d'eux-mêmes. Ils s'enorgueillissent du prix que l'on attribue à la possibilité de se trouver dans un lieu de délices pareil, et ils affirment avec enthousiasme, par le tribut qu'ils consentent, qu'ils se regardent en effet comme des favoris du sort pour avoir pris un repas dans de telles conditions, dans un tel jardin, sous de tels arbres, servis par de tels garçons conscients de la mission qu'ils ont assumée de servir de tels clients.

C'est la même opération d'esprit qui leur fait accepter comme un bienfait inestimable le tête-à-tête avec les princesses de la haute noce. La partie ne serait pas complète sans la présence enorgueillissante au suprême degré de la femme connue de tous et estimée à sa valeur comme la sauce du poisson, le légume et le fruit en primeur, la bouteille de vin datée d'il y a un quart de siècle. Ces partenaires indispensables sont aussi, très souvent, datées et très datées, mais la bonification est aussi bien pour elles que pour les crus célèbres, et le fait est facilement compréhensible. On n'arrive jamais que tardivement à la réputation et à la situation. C'est vrai dans le royaume de l'esprit, dans la littérature, dans l'art, dans la philosophie, dans la science. C'est également vrai dans le royaume de la galanterie.

Il faut avoir fait ses preuves, là comme partout, avoir montré ce dont on était capable. Il faut surtout avoir duré. La renommée des grands penseurs et des grands artistes s'accroît à mesure que s'accumulent les œuvres et les années. C'est lorsqu'ils sont arrivés aux approches de la vieillesse que l'on commence à reconnaître que, décidément, ils existent, que l'on commence à les louer, à les célébrer, selon leurs mérites. Lorsqu'ils sont à la période éteinte qui précède l'agonie, lorsqu'ils en sont enfin à leur agonie et à leur mort, l'impartialité ne connaît plus de bornes et devient véritablement frénétique. Lorsqu'enfin ils sont morts, la louange prend une ampleur, une sérénité, une universalité dignes de ceux qui ont disparu. A mesure que le temps passe, que les années s'écoulent, l'œuvre des grands hommes s'aperçoit mieux, prend des proportions, s'élève au-dessus des choses et se voit de loin comme le monument qui domine la ville et la plaine.

Il n'y a dans cette constatation nulle pensée d'ironie, nulle intention de reproche, les choses étant ainsi, et ne pouvant réellement pas être autrement. Mais il importait d'indiquer cet ordre d'idées et de faire ce rapprochement pour aider à comprendre le rôle joué dans la galanterie par les femmes relativement âgées. C'est peu à peu que l'on a connu leur valeur, apprécié la sûreté de leur commerce. Elles n'ont pu plaire, aux heures de leurs débuts, qu'à de très experts et très anciens personnages, devinant les ressources des nouvelles venues, distinguant les purs sangs qui fourniront les longues courses de celles qui échoueront au premier détour du chemin. Ces prévisions sont rares, et il arrive, le plus souvent, que celles qui acquerront les réputations les mieux méritées doivent vivre de longues années de triste obscurité et de misérables aventures. On les découvre lentement, et elles n'arrivent à la célébrité que sur le tard, exactement comme les grands artistes. Sans doute aussi, de même que ceux-ci ont grandi en intelligence et en compréhension, de même les facultés de celles-là se sont-elles développées avec les années.

Plates 124 and 125

LE PLAISIR À PARIS: LES RESTAURANTS ET LES CAFÉS-CONCERTS DES CHAMPS-ÉLYSÉES (PLEASURE IN PARIS: RESTAURANTS AND CAFÉS-CONCERTS ON THE CHAMPS-ÉLYSÉES)

from the journal **LE FIGARO ILLUSTRÉ** (July 1893)

Halftone relief and line block, page: 16 1/8 × 11 15/16 in. (41 × 30.4 cm)

The Museum of Modern Art Library, New York

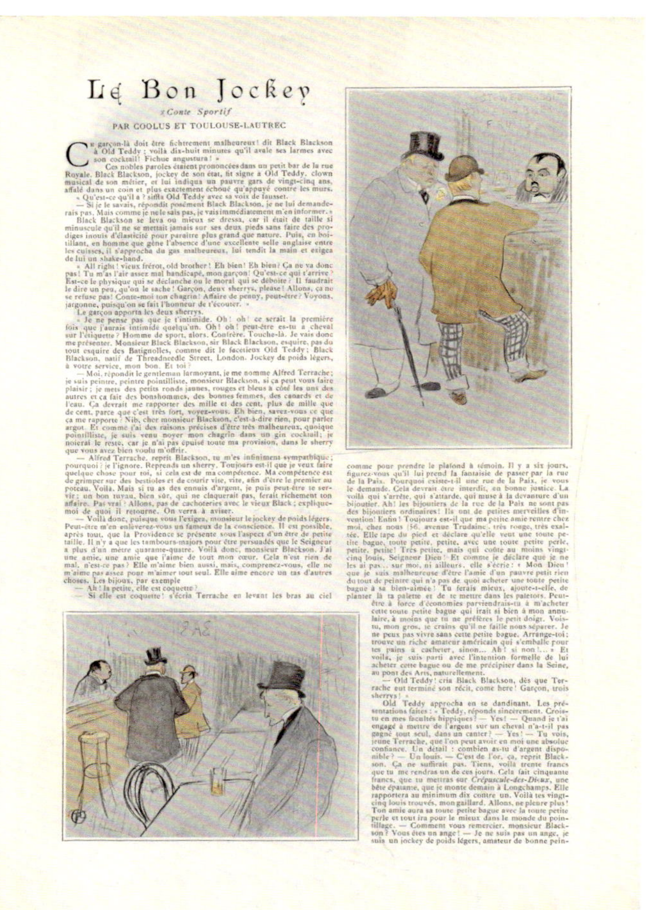

Le Bon Jockey

Conte Sportif

PAR COOLUS ET TOULOUSE-LAUTREC

« Ce garçon-là doit être fichtrement malheureux ! dit Black Blackson à Old Teddy ; voilà dix-huit minutes qu'il avale ses larmes avec son cocktail ! Fichue angustura ! »

Ces nobles paroles étaient prononcées dans un petit bar de la rue Royale. Black Blackson, jockey de son état, fit signe à Old Teddy, clown musical de son métier, et lui indiqua un pauvre gars de vingt-cinq ans, affalé dans un coin et plus exactement échoué qu'appuyé contre les murs.

« Qu'est-ce qu'il a ? siffla Old Teddy avec sa voix de fausset.

— Si je le savais, répondit posément Black Blackson, je ne lui demanderais pas. Mais comme je ne le sais pas, je vais immédiatement m'en informer. »

Black Blackson se leva ou mieux se dressa, car il était de taille si minuscule qu'il ne se mettait jamais sur ses deux pieds sans faire des prodiges inouïs d'élasticité pour paraître plus grand que nature. Puis, en boitillant, en homme que gêne l'absence d'une excellente selle anglaise entre les cuisses, il s'approcha du gas malheureux, lui tendit la main et exigea de lui un shake-hand.

« All right ! vieux frérot, old brother ! Eh bien ! Eh bien ? Ça ne va donc pas ! Tu m'as l'air assez mal handicapé, mon garçon ! Qu'est-ce qui t'arrive ? Est-ce le physique qui se déclanche ou le moral qui se déboîte ? Il faudrait le dire un peu, qu'on le sache ! Garçon, deux sherrys, please ! Allons, ça ne se refuse pas ! Conte-moi ton chagrin ! Affaire de penny, peut-être ? Voyons, jargonne, puisqu'on se fait l'honneur de t'écouter. »

Le garçon apporta les deux sherrys.

« Je ne pense pas que je t'intimide. Oh ! oh ! ce serait la première fois que j'aurais intimidé quelqu'un. Oh ! oh ! peut-être es-tu à cheval sur l'étiquette ? Homme de sport, alors. Confrère. Touche-là. Je vais donc me présenter. Monsieur Black Blackson, sir Black Blackson, esquire, pas du tout esquire des Batignolles, comme dit le facétieux Old Teddy ; Black Blackson, natif de Threadneedle Street, London. Jockey de poids légers, à votre service, mon bon. Et toi ?

— Moi, répondit le gentleman larmoyant, je me nomme Alfred Terrache ; je suis peintre, peintre pointilliste, monsieur Blackson, si ça peut vous faire plaisir ; je mets des petits ronds jaunes, rouges et bleus à côté les uns des autres et ça fait des bonshommes, des bonnes femmes, des canards et de l'eau. Ça devrait me rapporter des mille et des cent, plus de mille que de cent, parce que c'est très fort, voyez-vous. Eh bien, savez-vous ce que ça me rapporte ? Nib, cher monsieur Blackson, c'est-à-dire rien, pour parler argot. Et comme j'ai des raisons précises d'être très malheureux, quoique pointilliste, je suis venu noyer mon chagrin dans un gin cocktail ; je noierai le reste, car je n'ai pas épuisé toute ma provision, dans le sherry que vous avez bien voulu m'offrir.

— Alfred Terrache, reprit Blackson, tu m'es infiniment sympathique ; pourquoi ? je l'ignore. Reprends un sherry. Toujours est-il que je veux faire quelque chose pour toi, si cela est de ma compétence. Ma compétence est de grimper sur des bestioles et de courir vite, vite, afin d'être le premier au poteau. Voilà. Mais si tu as des ennuis d'argent, je puis peut-être te servir ; un bon tuyau, bien sûr, qui ne claquerait pas, ferait richement ton affaire. Pas vrai ? Allons, pas de cachoteries avec le vieux Black ; explique-moi de quoi il retourne. On verra à aviser.

— Voilà donc, puisque vous l'exigez, monsieur le jockey de poids légers. Peut-être m'en enlèverez-vous un fameux de la conscience. Il est possible, après tout, que la Providence se présente sous l'aspect d'un être de petite taille. Il n'y a que les tambours-majors pour être persuadés que le Seigneur a plus d'un mètre quarante-quatre. Voilà donc, monsieur Blackson. J'ai une amie, une amie que j'aime de tout mon cœur. Cela n'est rien de mal, n'est-ce pas ? Elle m'aime bien aussi, mais, comprenez-vous, elle ne m'aime pas assez pour m'aimer tout seul. Elle aime encore un tas d'autres choses. Les bijoux, par exemple

— Ah ! la petite, elle est coquette ?

— Si elle est coquette ! s'écria Terrache en levant les bras au ciel comme pour prendre le plafond à témoin. Il y a six jours, figurez-vous qu'il lui prend la fantaisie de passer par la rue de la Paix. Pourquoi existe-t-il une rue de la Paix, je vous le demande. Cela devrait être interdit, en bonne justice. La voilà qui s'arrête, qui s'attarde, qui muse à la devanture d'un bijoutier. Ah ! les bijoutiers de la rue de la Paix ne sont pas des bijoutiers ordinaires ! Ils ont de petites merveilles d'invention ! Enfin ! Toujours est-il que ma petite amie rentre chez moi, chez nous (56, avenue Trudaine), très rouge, très exaltée. Elle tape du pied et déclare qu'elle veut une toute petite bague, toute petite, petite, avec une toute petite perle, petite, petite ! Très petite, mais qui coûte au moins vingt-cinq louis, Seigneur Dieu ! Et comme je déclare que je ne les ai pas... sur moi, ni ailleurs, elle s'écrie : « Mon Dieu ! que je suis malheureuse d'être l'amie d'un pauvre petit rien du tout de peintre qui n'a pas de quoi acheter une toute petite bague à sa bien-aimée ! Tu ferais mieux, ajoute-t-elle, de planter là ta palette et de te mettre dans les paletots. Peut-être à force d'économies parviendrais-tu à m'acheter cette toute petite bague qui irait si bien à mon annulaire, à moins que tu ne préfères le petit doigt. Vois-tu, mon gros, je crains qu'il ne faille nous séparer. Je ne peux pas vivre sans cette petite bague. Arrange-toi ; trouve un riche amateur américain qui s'emballe pour tes pains à cacheter, sinon... Ah ! si non !... » Et voilà, je suis parti avec l'intention formelle de lui acheter cette bague ou de me précipiter dans la Seine, au pont des Arts, naturellement.

— Old Teddy ! cria Black Blackson, dès que Terrache eut terminé son récit, come here ! Garçon, trois sherrys ! »

Old Teddy approcha en se dandinant. Les présentations faites : « Teddy, réponds sincèrement. Crois-tu en mes facultés hippiques ? — Yes ! — Quand je t'ai engagé à mettre de l'argent sur un cheval n'a-t-il pas gagné tout seul, dans un canter ? — Yes ! — Tu vois, jeune Terrache, que l'on peut avoir en moi une absolue confiance. Un détail : combien as-tu d'argent disponible ? — Un louis. — C'est de l'or, ça, reprit Blackson. Ça ne suffirait pas. Tiens, voilà trente francs que tu me rendras un de ces jours. Cela fait cinquante francs, que tu mettras sur *Crépuscule-des-Dieux*, une bête épatante, que je monte demain à Longchamps. Elle rapportera au minimum dix contre un. Voilà tes vingt-cinq louis trouvés, mon gaillard. Allons, ne pleure plus ! Ton amie aura sa toute petite bague avec la toute petite perle et tout ira pour le mieux dans le monde du pointillage. — Comment vous remercier, monsieur Blackson ? Vous êtes un ange ! — Je ne suis pas un ange, je suis un jockey de poids légers, amateur de bonne pein-

Plate 126

LE BON JOCKEY: CONTE SPORTIF (THE GOOD JOCKEY: A SPORTS STORY) from the journal **LE FIGARO ILLUSTRÉ** (July 1895)

Halftone relief and line block, page: 16 1/8 × 11 15/16 in. (41 × 30.4 cm)

The Museum of Modern Art Library, New York

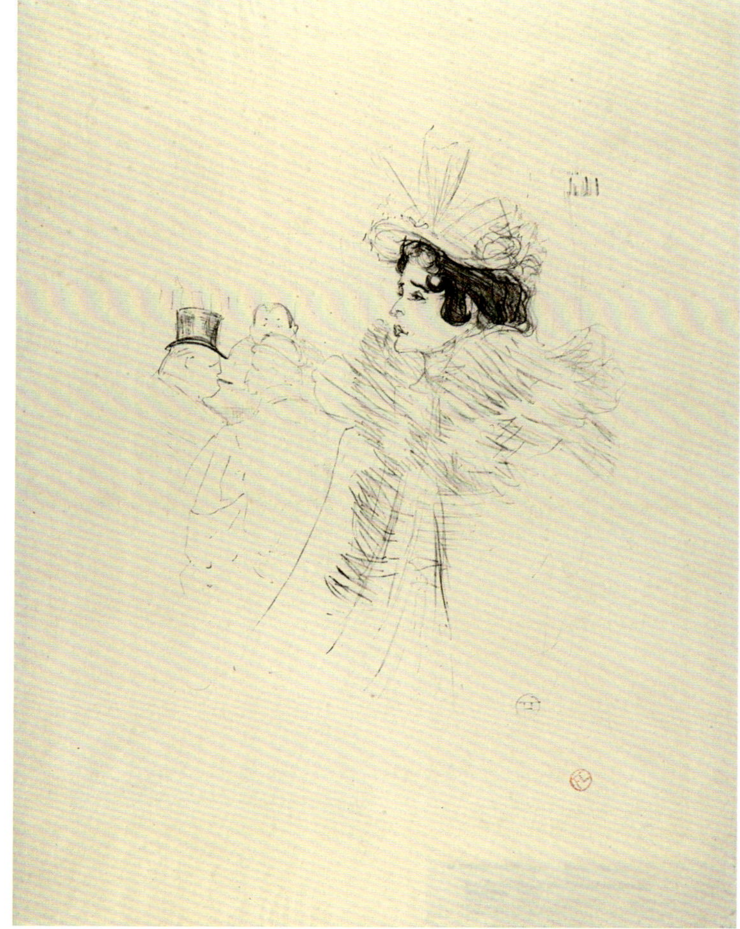

Plate 127

MISS MAY BELFORT AU IRISH AMERICAN BAR, RUE ROYALE (MISS MAY BELFORT AT THE IRISH AMERICAN BAR, RUE ROYALE). 1895

Lithograph, sheet: 20 1/16 × 15 1/2 in. (51 × 39.4 cm)

Gift of Abby Aldrich Rockefeller, 1946

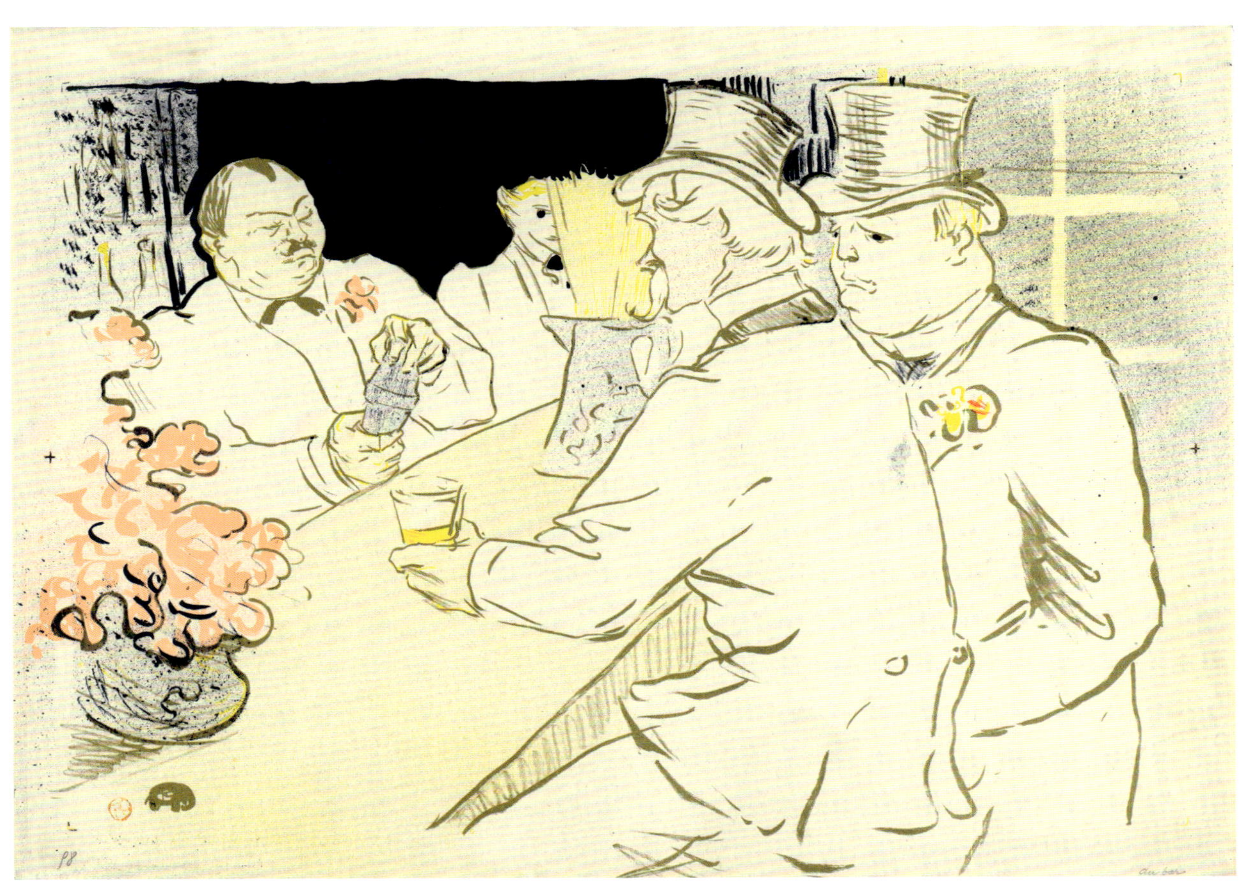

Plate 128
IRISH AMERICAN BAR, RUE ROYALE. 1895
Lithograph, sheet: $16\frac{15}{16} \times 24\frac{5}{16}$ in. (43.1 × 61.7 cm)
Gift of Abby Aldrich Rockefeller, 1946

CHECKLIST

This checklist of The Museum of Modern Art's collection of prints, posters, illustrated books, drawings, and paintings by Henri de Toulouse-Lautrec is organized chronologically, by medium. Not included are duplicates of works listed, works in The Museum of Modern Art Library, and the few works from private collections that appear in the plates. This information is followed by a list of the fifty prints that comprise *The Beraldi Album of Theatre Programs*—an album of prints by various artists, including Lautrec, that the Museum acquired in 2008—organized alphabetically, by artist. Each checklist entry includes French and English titles, with dates taken directly from the object or from a catalogue raisonné. The Museum's accession numbers, which include the year the object was acquired, are noted after the credit line in each entry. Definitive catalogue raisonné numbers are also provided. Note that Wittrock numbers including a P are from the poster section of the raisonné.

CATALOGUES RAISONNÉS

Adhémar, Jean. *Toulouse-Lautrec: His Complete Lithographs and Drypoints.* New York: Harry N. Abrams, 1965.

Adriani, Götz. *Toulouse-Lautrec: The Complete Graphic Works: A Catalogue Raisonné: The Gerstenberg Collection.* London: Royal Academy of Arts, in association with Thames and Hudson, 1988.

Delteil, Loÿs. *H. de Toulouse-Lautrec.* Paris: Chez l'auteur, 1920.

Wittrock, Wolfgang. *Toulouse-Lautrec: The Complete Prints.* 2 vols. Ed. and trans. Catherine E. Kuehn. London: Philip Wilson Publishers Limited, 1985.

PRINTS AND POSTERS

BEFORE 1892

LA CUISINE DE MONSIEUR MOMO CÉLIBATAIRE by Maurice Joyant. c. 1880, published 1930. Illustrated book with twenty-five photogravure reproductions (seven with pochoir), page: 9¼ x 7¼ in. (23.5 x 18.4 cm). Publisher: Éditions Pellet, Paris. Printer: Padovani, Paris. Edition: 250. The Louis E. Stern Collection, 1069.1964. Figure 33

SUBMERSION. 1881, published 1938. Illustrated book with forty-nine collotype reproductions, page: 9$\frac{1}{16}$ x 7$\frac{1}{16}$ in. (23 x 17.9 cm). Publisher: Arts & Métiers Graphiques, Paris. Printer: Duval, Paris. Edition: 200. The Louis E. Stern Collection, 1071.1964.1–49

1892

AU MOULIN ROUGE, LA GOULUE ET SA SŒUR (AT THE MOULIN ROUGE, LA GOULUE AND HER SISTER). 1892. Lithograph, composition: 18 x 13$\frac{9}{16}$ in. (45.7 x 34.5 cm); sheet: 25¼ x 19$\frac{7}{16}$ in. (64.2 x 49.3 cm). Publisher: Boussod, Valadon et Cie., Paris. Printer: Edward Ancourt, Paris. Edition: 100. Gift of Abby Aldrich Rockefeller, 139.1946. (Wittrock 1; Delteil 11; Adhémar 2; Adriani 6). Plate 13

REINE DE JOIE (QUEEN OF JOY). 1892. Lithograph, composition: 53⅞ x 36¾ in. (136.8 x 93.3 cm); sheet: 59$\frac{7}{16}$ x 39$\frac{7}{16}$ in. (151 x 100.1 cm). Publisher: Victor Joze, Paris. Printer: Edward Ancourt, Paris. Edition: unknown, approx. 1,000–3,000. Gift of Mr. and Mrs. Richard Rodgers, 73.1961. (Wittrock P3; Delteil 342; Adhémar 5; Adriani 5). Plate 62

1893

À LA GAIETÉ ROCHECHOUART: NICOLLE (AT THE GAIETÉ ROCHECHOUART: NICOLLE) from the journal **L'ESCARMOUCHE**, December 31, 1893. Halftone relief, page: 15⅜ x 11¾ in. (39 x 29.9 cm). Publisher: *L'Escarmouche*, Paris. Printer: Gaston Roussel, Paris. Edition: unknown. The Louis E. Stern Collection, 1108.1964. (Wittrock 38; Delteil 48; Adhémar 51; Adriani 53)

À LA RENAISSANCE: SARAH BERNHARDT DANS "PHÈDRE" (AT THE RENAISSANCE: SARAH BERNHARDT IN "PHAEDRA") from the journal **L'ESCARMOUCHE**, December 24, 1893. Halftone relief, page: 15⅜ x 11¾ in. (39 x 29.9 cm). Publisher: *L'Escarmouche*, Paris. Printer: Gaston Roussel, Paris. Edition: unknown. The Louis E. Stern Collection, 1108.1964. (Wittrock 37; Delteil 46; Adhémar 49; Adriani 52)

ARISTIDE BRUANT. 1893. Lithograph, composition: 32$\frac{5}{16}$ x 21$\frac{7}{16}$ in. (82 x 54.5 cm); sheet: 33¼ x 23¾ in. (84.5 x 60.3 cm). Publisher: Aristide Bruant, Paris. Printer: Chaix, Paris. Edition: proof before lettering. Grace M. Mayer Bequest, 590.1997. (Wittrock P10; Delteil 349; Adhémar 71; Adriani 57). Plate 9

ARISTIDE BRUANT DANS SON CABARET (**ARISTIDE BRUANT IN HIS CABARET**). 1893. Lithograph, composition: $50\frac{1}{8}$ x $37\frac{1}{2}$ in. (127.3 x 95.2 cm); sheet: $53\frac{9}{16}$ x $37\frac{15}{16}$ in. (136 x 96.3 cm). Publisher: Aristide Bruant, Paris. Printer: Charles Verneau, Paris. Edition: unknown. Gift of Emilio Sanchez, 52.1961. (Wittrock P9; Delteil 348; Adhémar 15; Adriani 12). Plate 10

AU MOULIN ROUGE: UN RUDE! UN VRAI RUDE! (**AT THE MOULIN ROUGE: A RUFFIAN! A REAL RUFFIAN!**) from the journal **L'ESCARMOUCHE**, December 10, 1893. Halftone relief, page: $15\frac{3}{8}$ x $11\frac{3}{4}$ in. (39 x 29.9 cm). Publisher: *L'Escarmouche*, Paris. Printer: René Meunier, Paris. Edition: unknown. The Louis E. Stern Collection, 1108.1964. (Wittrock 35; Delteil 45; Adhémar 48; Adriani 50). Plate 17

AU THÉÂTRE LIBRE: ANTOINE DANS "L'INQUIÉTUDE" (**AT THE THÉÂTRE LIBRE: ANTOINE IN "ANXIETY"**) from the journal **L'ESCARMOUCHE**, December 17, 1893. Halftone relief, page: $15\frac{3}{8}$ x $11\frac{3}{4}$ in. (39 x 29.9 cm). Publisher: *L'Escarmouche*, Paris. Printer: Gaston Roussel, Paris. Edition: unknown. The Louis E. Stern Collection, 1108.1964. (Wittrock 36; Delteil 46; Adhémar 49; Adriani 56)

AUX VARIÉTÉS: MADEMOISELLE LENDER ET BRASSEUR (**AT THE VARIÉTÉS: MADEMOISELLE LENDER AND BRASSEUR**) from the journal **L'ESCARMOUCHE**, November 19, 1893. Halftone relief, page: $15\frac{3}{8}$ x $11\frac{3}{4}$ in. (39 x 29.9 cm). Publisher: *L'Escarmouche*, Paris. Printer: René Meunier, Paris. Edition: unknown. The Louis E. Stern Collection, 1108.1964. (Wittrock 31; Delteil 41; Adhémar 44; Adriani 46)

LE CAFÉ CONCERT. 1893. Portfolio of twenty-three lithographs, eleven by Lautrec and twelve by Henri-Gabriel Ibels (French, 1867–1936), including wrapper front and duplicate on box, sheet (each approx.): $16\frac{15}{16}$ x $12\frac{1}{2}$ in. (43 x 31.8 cm). Publisher: *L'Estampe originale* (André Marty), Paris. Printer: Edward Ancourt, Paris. Edition: 500. The Louis E. Stern Collection, 1107.1964.1–23. (Wittrock 18–28; Delteil 28–38; Adhémar 28–38; Adriani 16–26). Plates 1–6, 8, 34

CARNOT MALADE! (**SICK CARNOT!**). 1893. Lithograph with stencil additions, composition and sheet: $10\frac{15}{16}$ x $6\frac{7}{8}$ in. (27.8 x 17.5 cm). Publisher: G. Ondet, Paris. Printer: Joly, Paris. Edition: unknown. Gift of Emilio Sanchez, 519.1967. (Wittrock 12; Delteil 25; Adhémar 24; Adriani 34). Plate 61

LA COIFFURE (**THE HAIRDRESSER**), program for **UNE FAILLITE** (**BANKRUPTCY**) and **LE POÈTE ET LE FINANCIER** (**THE POET AND THE FINANCIER**) at the Théâtre Libre, Paris, from **THE BERALDI ALBUM OF THEATRE PROGRAMS**. 1893. Lithograph, composition: $8\frac{5}{8}$ x $6\frac{7}{16}$ in. (21.9 x 16.3 cm); sheet: $12\frac{5}{8}$ x $9\frac{7}{16}$ in. (32 x 23.9 cm). Publisher: Théâtre Libre, Paris. Printer: Eugène Verneau, Paris. Edition: unknown (several hundred). Johanna and Leslie J. Garfield Fund, Mary Ellen Oldenburg Fund, and Sharon P. Rockefeller Fund, 289.2008.12. (Wittrock 15; Delteil 14; Adhémar 40; Adriani 40). Plate 81

DIVAN JAPONAIS. 1893. Lithograph, composition: $31\frac{15}{16}$ x $23\frac{3}{4}$ in. (81.2 x 60.3 cm); sheet: $31\frac{15}{16}$ x $24\frac{1}{2}$ in. (81.2 x 62.2 cm). Publisher: Édouard Fournier, Paris. Printer: Edward Ancourt, Paris. Edition: unknown. Abby Aldrich Rockefeller Fund, 97.1949. (Wittrock P11; Delteil 341; Adhémar 11; Adriani 8). Plate 39

EN QUARANTE (**IN THEIR FORTIES**) from the journal **L'ESCARMOUCHE**, November 26, 1893. Halftone relief, page: $15\frac{3}{8}$ x $11\frac{3}{4}$ in. (39 x 29.9 cm). Publisher: *L'Escarmouche*, Paris. Printer: René Meunier, Paris. Edition: unknown. The Louis E. Stern Collection, 1108.1964. (Wittrock 32; Delteil 42; Adhémar 45; Adriani 47)

Cover for the journal **L'ESTAMPE ORIGINALE**. 1893. Lithograph, composition: $22\frac{1}{4}$ x $25\frac{13}{16}$ in. (56.5 x 65.5 cm); sheet: $23\frac{1}{16}$ x $32\frac{3}{4}$ in. (58.5 x 83.2 cm). Publisher: *L'Estampe originale* (André Marty), Paris. Printer: Edward Ancourt, Paris. Edition: 100. Grace M. Mayer Bequest, 587.1997. (Wittrock 3; Delteil 17; Adhémar 10; Adriani 9). Plate 38

ÉTUDE DE FEMME (**STUDY OF A WOMAN**). 1893. Lithograph with stencil additions, composition: $10\frac{1}{4}$ x $7\frac{13}{16}$ in. (26 x 19.9 cm); sheet: $13\frac{13}{16}$ x $10\frac{11}{16}$ in. (35.1 x 27.2 cm). Publisher: Édouard Kleinmann, Paris. Printer: unknown. Edition: 100. Gift of Abby Aldrich Rockefeller, 142.1946. (Wittrock 11; Delteil 24; Adhémar 26; Adriani 33). Plate 46

FOLIES-BERGÈRE: LES PUDEURS DE MONSIEUR PRUDHOMME (**FOLIES-BERGÈRE: THE MODESTY OF MONSIEUR PRUDHOMME**). 1893. Lithograph, composition: $14\frac{13}{16}$ x $10\frac{9}{16}$ in. (37.6 x 26.9 cm); sheet: $15\frac{1}{8}$ x 11 in. (38.4 x 27.9 cm). Publisher: *L'Escarmouche*, Paris. Printer: Edward Ancourt, Paris. Edition: 100. Gift of Abby Aldrich Rockefeller, 144.1946. (Wittrock 36; Delteil 46; Adhémar 49; Adriani 51)

FOLIES-BERGÈRE: LES PUDEURS DE MONSIEUR PRUDHOMME (**FOLIES-BERGÈRE: THE MODESTY OF MONSIEUR PRUDHOMME**) from the journal **L'ESCARMOUCHE**, December 17, 1893. Halftone relief, page: 15⅜ x 11¾ in. (39 x 29.9 cm). Publisher: *L'Escarmouche*, Paris. Printer: Gaston Roussel, Paris. Edition: unknown. The Louis E. Stern Collection, 1108.1964. (Wittrock 36; Delteil 47; Adhémar 50; Adriani 51)

JANE AVRIL. 1893. Lithograph, composition: 48 13/16 x 34 15/16 in. (124 x 88.8 cm); sheet: 49⅝ x 36⅛ in. (126 x 91.8 cm). Publisher: Jardin de Paris, Paris. Printer: Chaix, Paris. Edition: 20. Gift of A. Conger Goodyear, 456.1954. (Wittrock P6; Delteil 345; Adhémar 12; Adriani 11). Plate 35

MADEMOISELLE LENDER ET BARON (**MADEMOISELLE LENDER AND BARON**) from the journal **L'ESCARMOUCHE**, December 3, 1893. Halftone relief, page: 15⅜ x 11¾ in. (39 x 29.9 cm). Publisher: *L'Escarmouche*, Paris. Printer: René Meunier, Paris. Edition: unknown. The Louis E. Stern Collection, 1108.1964. (Wittrock 33; Delteil 43; Adhémar 46; Adriani 48)

MISS LOÏE FULLER. 1893. Lithograph, composition: 14⅜ x 10⅝ in. (36.5 x 27 cm); sheet: 14 15/16 x 11⅛ in. (38 x 28.2 cm). Publisher: André Marty, Paris. Printer: Edward Ancourt, Paris. Edition: approx. 60, each unique. General Print Fund, 513.2006. (Wittrock 17; Delteil 39; Adhémar 8; Adriani 10). Plate 22

LA MODISTE, RENÉE VERT (**THE MILLINER, RENÉE VERT**). 1893. Lithograph, composition: 17 11/16 x 11 7/16 in. (45 x 29 cm); sheet: 21⅝ x 13¾ in. (55 x 35 cm). Publisher: Édouard Kleinmann, Paris. Printer: Edward Ancourt, Paris. Edition: 50. Grace M. Mayer Bequest, 589.1997. (Wittrock 4; Delteil 13; Adhémar 17; Adriani 13). Plate 45

POURQUOI PAS?. . . UNE FOIS N'EST PAS COUTUME (**WHY NOT?. . . ONCE IS NOT TO MAKE A HABIT OF IT**) from the journal **L'ESCARMOUCHE**, November 12, 1893. Halftone relief, page: 15⅜ x 11¾ in. (39 x 29.9 cm). Publisher: *L'Escarmouche*, Paris. Printer: René Meunier, Paris. Edition: unknown. The Louis E. Stern Collection, 1108.1964. (Wittrock 30; Delteil 40; Adhémar 43 ; Adriani 45)

UNE REDOUTE AU MOULIN ROUGE (**A GALA EVENING AT THE MOULIN ROUGE**). 1893. Lithograph, composition: 11½ x 18½ in. (29.2 x 47 cm); sheet: 14 13/16 x 21⅞ in. (37.7 x 55.6 cm). Publisher: probably the artist, Paris. Printer: unknown. Edition: 50. Gift of Abby Aldrich Rockefeller, 146.1946. (Wittrock 42; Delteil 65; Adhémar 54; Adriani 42). Plate 21

RÉPÉTITION GÉNÉRALE AUX FOLIES-BERGÈRE—ÉMILIENNE D'ALENÇON ET MARIQUITA (**DRESS REHEARSAL AT THE FOLIES-BERGÈRE—ÉMILIENNE D'ALENÇON AND MARIQUITA**) from the journal **L'ESCARMOUCHE**, December 3, 1893. Halftone relief, page: 15⅜ x 11¾ in. (39 x 29.9 cm). Publisher: *L'Escarmouche*, Paris. Printer: René Meunier, Paris. Edition: unknown. The Louis E. Stern Collection, 1108.1964. (Wittrock 34; Delteil 44; Adhémar 47; Adriani 49)

ULTIME BALLADE (**LAST BALLAD**). 1893. Lithograph with stencil additions, composition: 10½ x 7 3/16 in. (26.6 x 18.2 cm); sheet: 13¾ x 10¾ in. (34.9 x 27.3 cm). Publisher: Édouard Kleinmann, Paris. Printer: unknown. Edition: 100. Gift of Abby Aldrich Rockefeller, 141.1946. (Wittrock 10; Delteil 23; Adhémar 22; Adriani 32). Plate 74

Cover for the portfolio **LES VIEILLES HISTOIRES** (**OLD STORIES**), poems by Jean Goudezki, with music by Désiré Dihau. 1893. Lithograph, composition: 13⅜ x 21 7/16 in. (34 x 54.5 cm); sheet: 17 13/16 x 25 in. (45.2 x 63.5 cm). Publisher: G. Ondet, Paris. Printer: unknown. Edition: 100. Gift of Abby Aldrich Rockefeller, 140.1946. (Wittrock 5; Delteil 18; Adhémar 19; Adriani 27). Plate 73

1894

À L'OPÉRA: MADAME CARON DANS "FAUST" (**AT THE OPÉRA: MADAME CARON IN "FAUST"**) from the journal **L'ESCARMOUCHE**, January 14, 1894. Halftone relief, page: 15⅜ x 11¾ in. (39 x 29.9 cm). Publisher: *L'Escarmouche*, Paris. Printer: Gaston Roussel, Paris. Edition: unknown. The Louis E. Stern Collection, 1108.1964. (Wittrock 41; Delteil 51; Adhémar 55; Adriani 54)

AU MOULIN ROUGE: L'UNION FRANCO-RUSSE (**AT THE MOULIN ROUGE: THE FRANCO-RUSSIAN UNION**) from the journal **L'ESCARMOUCHE**, January 7, 1894. Halftone relief, page: 15⅜ x 11¾ in. (39 x 29.9 cm). Publisher: *L'Escarmouche*, Paris. Printer: Gaston Roussel, Paris. Edition: unknown. The Louis E. Stern Collection, 1108.1964. (Wittrock 40; Delteil 50; Adhémar 53; Adriani 55). Plate 18

BABYLONE D'ALLEMAGNE (**GERMAN BABYLON**). 1894. Lithograph, composition: 46 9/16 x 32⅞ in. (118.3 x 83.5 cm); sheet: 46 9/16 x 33 3/16 in. (118.3 x 84.3 cm). Publisher: Victor Joze, Paris. Printer: Chaix, Paris. Edition: unknown, approx. 1,000–3,000. Gift of Abby Aldrich Rockefeller, 590.1940. (Wittrock P12; Delteil 351; Adhémar 68; Adriani 58). Plate 64

Cover for the book **BABYLONE D'ALLEMAGNE** by Victor Joze. 1894. Lithograph, composition: $8\frac{1}{8}$ x $10\frac{3}{8}$ in. (20.7 x 26.4 cm); sheet: $8\frac{11}{16}$ x 11 in. (22 x 28 cm). Publisher: unknown. Printer: unknown. Edition: unknown. Gift of Abby Aldrich Rockefeller, 148.1946. (Delteil 76; Adhémar 67). Figure 37

BRANDÈS ET LELOIR, DANS "CABOTINS" (**BRANDÈS AND LELOIR IN "CABOTINS"**). 1894. Lithograph, composition: $15\frac{7}{8}$ x $11\frac{13}{16}$ in. (40.3 x 30 cm); sheet: $20\frac{7}{8}$ x $15\frac{3}{16}$ in. (53.1 x 38.5 cm). Publisher: probably the artist, Paris. Printer: unknown. Edition: 50. Gift of Abby Aldrich Rockefeller, 145.1946. (Wittrock 53; Delteil 62; Adhémar 66; Adriani 68)

CONFETTI. 1894. Lithograph, composition: $22\frac{5}{8}$ x $15\frac{5}{8}$ in. (57.4 x 39.7 cm); sheet: $22\frac{5}{8}$ x $17\frac{9}{16}$ in. (57.4 x 44.6 cm). Publisher: J. & E. Bella, London. Printer: Bella & de Malherbe, London and Paris. Edition: approx. 100. Acquired in honor of Joanne M. Stern by the Committee on Prints and Illustrated Books in appreciation for her contribution as Committee Chair, 74.1999. (Wittrock P13; Delteil 352; Adhémar 9; Adriani 101). Plate 120

EROS VANNÉ (**EROS VANQUISHED**). 1894, published before 1910. Lithograph, composition: $11\frac{7}{16}$ x $8\frac{9}{16}$ in. (29 x 21.8 cm); sheet: $17\frac{13}{16}$ x $12\frac{11}{16}$ in. (45.2 x 32.3 cm). Publisher: Éditions Pellet, Paris. Printer: unknown. Edition: approx. 45. Grace M. Mayer Bequest, 592.1997. (Wittrock 56; Delteil 74; Adhémar 81; Adriani 92). Plate 11

LA GOULUE. 1894. Lithograph, composition: $11\frac{13}{16}$ x $9\frac{15}{16}$ in. (30.3 x 25.2 cm); sheet: $14\frac{15}{16}$ x 11 in. (37.9 x 28 cm). Publisher: probably the artist, Paris. Printer: unknown. Edition: 50. Gift of Abby Aldrich Rockefeller, 147.1946. (Wittrock 65; Delteil 71; Adhémar 77; Adriani 95). Plate 14

LA LOGE AU MASCARON DORÉ (**THE BOX WITH THE GILDED MASK**), program for **LE MISSIONNAIRE** (**THE MISSIONARY**) at the Théâtre Libre, Paris, from **THE BERALDI ALBUM OF THEATRE PROGRAMS**. 1894. Lithograph, composition and sheet: $12\frac{1}{16}$ x $9\frac{7}{16}$ in. (30.6 x 24 cm). Publisher: Théâtre Libre, Paris. Printer: Edward Ancourt, Paris. Edition: unknown (several hundred). Johanna and Leslie J. Garfield Fund, Mary Ellen Oldenburg Fund, and Sharon P. Rockefeller Fund, 289.2008.14. (Wittrock 16; Delteil 16; Adhémar 72; Adriani 69). Plate 79

MARY HAMILTON. 1894, published 1925. Lithograph, composition: $10\frac{3}{8}$ x $4\frac{3}{16}$ in. (26.4 x 10.6 cm); sheet: $14\frac{5}{16}$ x $10\frac{3}{4}$ in. (36.4 x 27.3 cm). Publisher: Edmond Frapier, Paris. Printer: unknown. Edition: 625. Purchase Fund, 175.1949.3. (Wittrock 67; Delteil 175; Adhémar 215; Adriani 142). Figure 32

NIB, supplement to **LA REVUE BLANCHE**. 1894, published 1895. Three lithographs on folded sheet, page: $19\frac{1}{2}$ x $13\frac{3}{4}$ in. (49.6 x 35 cm). Publisher: Éditions de *La Revue blanche*, Paris. Printer: Edward Ancourt, Paris. Edition: approx. 2,000. Gift of Eastman Kodak Company, 210.1951.a–c. (Wittrock 86–88; Delteil 98–100; Adhémar 106, 108, 112; Adriani 102, 103). Plate 121

LE PHOTOGRAPHE SESCAU (**THE PHOTOGRAPHER SESCAU**). 1894. Lithograph, composition: $24\frac{1}{16}$ x $31\frac{1}{8}$ in. (61.1 x 79 cm); sheet: $24\frac{7}{8}$ x $31\frac{1}{8}$ in. (63.2 x 79 cm). Publisher: Paul Sescau, Paris. Printer: unknown. Edition: few known impressions. Grace M. Mayer Bequest, 594.1997. (Wittrock P22; Delteil 353; Adhémar 69; Adriani 60). Plate 122

YVETTE GUILBERT by Gustave Geffroy. 1894. Illustrated book with seventeen lithographs (including cover), page: $15\frac{1}{16}$ x $15\frac{3}{16}$ in. (38.3 x 38.5 cm). Publisher: *L'Estampe originale* (André Marty), Paris. Printer: Edward Ancourt, Paris. Edition: 100. The Louis E. Stern Collection, 1066.1964.1–17. (Wittrock 69–85; Delteil 79–95; Adhémar 85–102; Adriani 73–89). Plates 26–33

1895

INVITATION CARD FOR ALEXANDRE NATANSON. 1895. Lithograph, composition: $12\frac{1}{4}$ x $6\frac{7}{8}$ in. (31.1 x 17.4 cm); sheet: $13\frac{3}{8}$ x 7 in. (33.9 x 17.8 cm). Publisher: Mr. and Mrs. Alexandre Natanson, Paris. Printer: unknown. Edition: approx. 300. Gift of Mr. and Mrs. Herbert D. Schimmel, 698.1996. (Wittrock 90; Delteil 101; Adhémar 123; Adriani 109). Plate 123

IRISH AMERICAN BAR, RUE ROYALE. 1895. Lithograph, composition: $16\frac{1}{8}$ x $24\frac{5}{16}$ in. (41 x 61.7 cm); sheet: $16\frac{5}{16}$ x $24\frac{5}{16}$ in. (43.1 x 61.7 cm). Publisher: *The Chap Book*, Chicago. Printer: Chaix, Paris. Edition: 100. Gift of Abby Aldrich Rockefeller, 166.1946. (Wittrock P18; Delteil 362; Adhémar 189; Adriani 139). Plate 128

LENDER DE FACE, DANS "CHILPÉRIC" (**LENDER, FRONTAL VIEW, IN "CHILPÉRIC"**). 1895. Lithograph, composition: $14\frac{5}{16}$ x $10\frac{5}{8}$ in. (36.4 x 27 cm); sheet: $21\frac{7}{16}$ x $11\frac{7}{8}$ in. (54.5 x 30.1 cm). Publisher: probably the artist, Paris. Printer: Edward Ancourt, Paris. Edition: 25. Gift of Abby Aldrich Rockefeller, 151.1946. (Wittrock 104; Delteil 105; Adhémar 129; Adriani 113). Plate 24

MADEMOISELLE MARCELLE LENDER, DEBOUT (MADEMOISELLE MARCELLE LENDER, STANDING). 1895. Lithograph, composition and sheet: 14⅜ x 9½ in. (36.5 x 24.2 cm). Publisher: probably the artist, Paris. Printer: unknown. Edition: 12. Gift of Abby Aldrich Rockefeller, 150.1946. (Wittrock 101; Delteil 103; Adhémar 134; Adriani 116). Plate 25

MADEMOISELLE MARCELLE LENDER, EN BUSTE (MADEMOISELLE MARCELLE LENDER, HALF-LENGTH). 1895. Lithograph, composition: 13 x 9⅝ in. (33 x 24.5 cm); sheet: 21 7/16 x 15 11/16 in. (54.5 x 39.8 cm). Publisher: *Pan*, Paris. Printer: Edward Ancourt, Paris. Edition: 100. Gift of Abby Aldrich Rockefeller, 149.1946. (Wittrock 99; Delteil 102; Adhémar 131; Adriani 115). Plate 23

MÉLODIES DE DÉSIRÉ DIHAU (SONGS BY DÉSIRÉ DIHAU). 1895, published 1935. Portfolio of fourteen lithographs, duplicate transfer lithograph, and song sheet, sheet (each approx.): 12 13/16 x 9 13/16 in. (32.5 x 25 cm). Publisher: A. Richard, Paris. Printer: unknown. Edition: 100. The Louis E. Stern Collection, 1072.1964.A–B. (Wittrock 124–37; Delteil 129–42; Adhémar 151–65; Adriani 145–58). Plates 75–78

MISS MAY BELFORT AU IRISH AMERICAN BAR, RUE ROYALE (MISS MAY BELFORT AT THE IRISH AMERICAN BAR, RUE ROYALE). 1895. Lithograph, composition: 12 13/16 x 10⅜ in. (32.5 x 26.3 cm); sheet: 20 1/16 x 15½ in. (51 x 39.4 cm). Publisher: probably the artist, Paris. Printer: unknown. Edition: 25. Gift of Abby Aldrich Rockefeller, 152.1946. (Wittrock 119; Delteil 123; Adhémar 124; Adriani 140). Plate 127

UN MONSIEUR ET UNE DAME (A GENTLEMAN AND A LADY), program for **L'ARGENT (MONEY)** at the Théâtre Libre, Paris, from **THE BERALDI ALBUM OF THEATRE PROGRAMS**. 1895. Lithograph, composition and sheet: 12½ x 9⅜ in. (31.8 x 23.8 cm). Publisher: Théâtre Libre, Paris. Printer: Eugène Verneau, Paris. Edition: unknown (several hundred). Johanna and Leslie J. Garfield Fund, Mary Ellen Oldenburg Fund, and Sharon P. Rockefeller Fund, 289.2008.18. (Wittrock 97; Delteil 15; Adhémar 148; Adriani 133). Plate 80

NAPOLEON. 1895. Lithograph, composition: 23⅜ x 18⅛ in. (59.3 x 46 cm); sheet: 25 11/16 x 19⅝ in. (65.3 x 49.8 cm). Publisher: probably the artist, Paris. Printer: Edward Ancourt, Paris. Edition: 100. Gift of Abby Aldrich Rockefeller, 165.1946. (Wittrock 140; Delteil 358; Adhémar 150; Adriani 135). Plate 63

LE PENDU (HANGING MAN). 1895. Lithograph, composition and sheet: 30¼ x 21 15/16 in. (76.8 x 55.7 cm). Publisher: probably the artist, Paris. Printer: unknown. Edition: 30. Purchase, 519.1949. (Wittrock P15; Delteil 340; Adhémar 4; Adriani 2). Plate 60

LA REVUE BLANCHE. 1895. Lithograph, composition: 49 7/16 x 36 5/16 in. (125.5 x 92.2 cm); sheet: 51 x 36 11/16 in. (129.6 x 93.2 cm). Publisher: *La Revue blanche* (G. Charpentier & E. Fasqualle), Paris. Printer: Edward Ancourt, Paris. Edition: unknown. Purchase, 298.1967. (Wittrock P16; Delteil 355; Adhémar 115; Adriani 130). Plate 107

1896

L'AUBE (THE DAWN). 1896. Lithograph, composition and sheet: 23 13/16 x 31¾ in. (60.5 x 80.6 cm). Publisher: *L'Aube*, Paris. Printer: Edward Ancourt, Paris. Edition: unknown. Gift of Abby Aldrich Rockefeller, 592.1940. (Wittrock P23; Delteil 363; Adhémar 220; Adriani 184). Plate 59

DÉBAUCHÉ (THE DEBAUCHER). 1896. Lithograph, composition and sheet: 9 3/16 x 12 5/16 in. (23.3 x 31.3 cm). Publisher: A. Arnould, Paris. Printer: unknown. Edition: 100. Gift of Louise Bourgeois, 267.1997. (Wittrock 167; Delteil 178; Adhémar 212; Adriani 187). Plate 47

ELLES. 1896. Portfolio of twelve lithographs, composition and sheet (each approx.): 20¼ x 15 11/16 in. (51.5 x 39.8 cm) or 15 11/16 x 20¼ in. (39.8 x 51.5 cm). Publisher: Éditions Pellet, Paris. Printer: probably Auguste Clot, Paris. Edition: 100. Gift of Abby Aldrich Rockefeller, 170.1946.1–12. (Wittrock 155–65; Delteil 179–89; Adhémar 200–211; Adriani 171–81). Plates 49–58

Poster for **ELLES**. 1896. Lithograph, composition: 22¾ x 18⅜ in. (57.8 x 46.6 cm); sheet: 26¾ x 19⅝ in. (68 x 49.8 cm). Publisher: Éditions Pellet, Paris. Printer: unknown. Edition: unknown, approx. 1,000. Gift of Mr. and Mrs. Richard Rodgers, 74.1961. (Wittrock 155; Delteil 179; Adhémar 200; Adriani 171). Plate 48

LA FILLE ÉLISA by Edmond de Goncourt. 1896, published 1931. Illustrated book with fifteen collotype reproductions, eleven with pochoir, page: 7 3/16 x 4⅝ in. (18.2 x 11.7 cm). Publisher: Librairie de France, Paris. Printer: Daniel Jacomet, Paris. Edition: 200. The Louis E. Stern Collection, 1070.1964.A–B. Plates 69–72

OSCAR WILDE, program for **RAPHAËL** and **SALOMÉ** at the Théâtre de l'Oeuvre, Paris, from **THE BERALDI ALBUM OF THEATRE PROGRAMS**. 1896. Lithograph, composition: $11\frac{3}{4}$ x $9\frac{5}{16}$ in. (29.8 x 23.7 cm); sheet: $12\frac{7}{16}$ x $9\frac{7}{16}$ in. (31.6 x 24 cm). Publisher: Théâtre de l'Oeuvre, Paris. Printer: unknown. Edition: unknown. Johanna and Leslie J. Garfield Fund, Mary Ellen Oldenburg Fund, and Sharon P. Rockefeller Fund, 289.2008.34. (Wittrock 146; Delteil 195; Adhémar 186; Adriani 163). Plate 84

OSCAR WILDE ET ROMAIN COOLUS, program for **RAPHAËL** and **SALOMÉ**. 1896. Lithograph, composition: $11\frac{7}{8}$ x $19\frac{7}{16}$ in. (30.2 x 49.4 cm); sheet: $12\frac{15}{16}$ x $19\frac{13}{16}$ in. (32.8 x 50.3 cm). Publisher: Théâtre de l'Oeuvre, Paris. Printer: unknown. Edition: unknown. Given anonymously, 205.1966. (Wittrock 146; Delteil 195; Adhémar 186; Adriani 163)

PROCÈS ARTON (**THE ARTON TRIAL**). 1896. Series of three lithographs, sheet (each): $18\frac{1}{16}$ x $24\frac{1}{2}$ in. (45.8 x 62.3 cm). Publisher: Édouard Kleinmann, Paris. Printer: Edward Ancourt, Paris. Edition: 100. Gift of Abby Aldrich Rockefeller, 168.1946.1–3. (Wittrock 149–151; Delteil 191–93; Adhémar 192–94; Adriani 168–70)

LE RIRE. January 11, 1896. Journal with halftone reliefs, page: $11\frac{7}{8}$ x $9\frac{1}{8}$ in. (30.2 x 23.2 cm). Publisher: Arsène Alexandre and Félix Juven, Paris. Printer: unknown. Edition: unknown. Linda Barth Goldstein Fund, 256.1997.1–2. Plate 106

ROMAIN COOLUS, program for **RAPHAËL** and **SALOMÉ** at the Théâtre de l'Oeuvre, Paris, from **THE BERALDI ALBUM OF THEATRE PROGRAMS**. 1896. Lithograph, composition and sheet: $12\frac{9}{16}$ x $9\frac{13}{16}$ in. (31.9 x 24.9 cm). Publisher: Théâtre de l'Oeuvre, Paris. Printer: unknown. Edition: unknown. Johanna and Leslie J. Garfield Fund, Mary Ellen Oldenburg Fund, and Sharon P. Rockefeller Fund, 289.2008.33. (Wittrock 146; Delteil 195; Adhémar 186; Adriani 163). Plate 83

SOUPER À LONDRES (**SUPPER IN LONDON**). 1896. Lithograph, composition: $12\frac{5}{16}$ x $15\frac{1}{2}$ in. (31.2 x 39.4 cm); sheet: $13\frac{9}{16}$ x $18\frac{1}{2}$ in. (34.4 x 47 cm). Publisher: Le Livre vert (*L'Estampe originale* [André Marty]), Paris. Printer: Lemercier et Cie., Paris. Edition: 100. Gift of Abby Aldrich Rockefeller, 154.1946. (Wittrock 169; Delteil 167; Adhémar 190; Adriani 192)

LA TROUPE DE MADEMOISELLE ÉGLANTINE (**MADEMOISELLE ÉGLANTINE'S TROUPE**). 1896. Lithograph, composition: $24\frac{1}{8}$ x $31\frac{1}{4}$ in. (61.2 x 79.4 cm); sheet: $24\frac{1}{4}$ x $31\frac{1}{4}$ in. (61.6 x 79.4 cm). Publisher: Jane Avril, Paris. Printer: unknown. Edition: unknown. Gift of Abby Aldrich Rockefeller, 591.1940. (Wittrock P21; Delteil 361; Adhémar 198; Adriani 162). Plate 36

1897

AU BOIS (**IN THE BOIS DE BOULOGNE**). 1897. Lithograph, composition: $13\frac{3}{8}$ x $9\frac{5}{8}$ in. (34 x 24.4 cm); sheet: 22 x $14\frac{5}{8}$ in. (55.9 x 37.2 cm). Publisher: probably the artist, Paris. Printer: unknown. Edition: approx. 20. Gift of Abby Aldrich Rockefeller, 163.1946. (Wittrock 185; Delteil 296; Adhémar 255; Adriani 349). Plate 99

AU PIED DU SINAÏ by Georges Clemenceau. 1897, published 1898. Illustrated book with twenty-one lithographs, page: $10\frac{1}{4}$ x $7\frac{7}{8}$ in. (26 x 20 cm). Publisher: Henri Floury, Paris. Printer: Chamerot et Renouard, Paris. Edition: 380. The Louis E. Stern Collection, 1067.1964.1–21. (Wittrock 188–201; Delteil 235–49; Adhémar 240–50; Adriani 213–27). Plates 66–68

Cover for the illustrated book **AU PIED DU SINAÏ** by Georges Clemenceau. 1897, published 1898. Lithograph, composition: $10\frac{1}{4}$ x $16\frac{1}{8}$ in. (26 x 41 cm); sheet: $14\frac{15}{16}$ x $21\frac{15}{16}$ in. (37.9 x 55.7 cm). Publisher: Henri Floury, Paris. Printer: Chamerot et Renouard, Paris. Edition: 355. Gift of Mr. and Mrs. Herbert D. Schimmel, 699.1996. (Wittrock 188; Delteil 235; Adhémar 240; Adriani 213). Plate 65

LE CIMETIÈRE DE BUSK (**BUSK CEMETERY**). 1897, published 1898. Lithograph, composition: $7\frac{3}{8}$ x $6\frac{3}{16}$ in. (18.8 x 15.7 cm); sheet: $11\frac{1}{4}$ x $10\frac{9}{16}$ in. (28.6 x 26.9 cm). Publisher: Henri Floury, Paris. Printer: Chamerot et Renouard, Paris. Edition: 25. Gift of Mr. and Mrs. Herbert D. Schimmel, 702.1996. (Wittrock 201; Delteil 249; Adriani 227)

UN CIMETIÈRE EN GALICIE (**A CEMETERY IN GALICIA**). 1897, published 1898. Lithograph, composition: $7\frac{5}{16}$ x 6 in. (18.5 x 15.2 cm); sheet: $11\frac{15}{16}$ x $10\frac{3}{16}$ in. (30.3 x 25.8 cm). Publisher: Henri Floury, Paris. Printer: Chamerot et Renouard, Paris. Edition: 25. Gift of Mr. and Mrs. Herbert D. Schimmel, 703.1996. (Wittrock 200; Delteil 248; Adhémar 239; Adriani 226)

LA CLOWNESSE AU MOULIN ROUGE (**THE CLOWNESS AT THE MOULIN ROUGE**). 1897. Lithograph, composition: $15\frac{7}{8}$ x $12\frac{1}{2}$ in. (40.4 x 31.8 cm); sheet: $15\frac{7}{8}$ x $12\frac{11}{16}$ in. (40.4 x 32.3 cm). Publisher: Éditions Pellet, Paris. Printer: Edward Ancourt, Paris. Edition: 20. Gift of Abby Aldrich Rockefeller, 156.1946. (Wittrock 178; Delteil 205; Adhémar 231; Adriani 203). Plate 19

Cover for the book **LES COURTES JOIES**. 1897, published 1925. Lithograph, composition: $7\frac{3}{16}$ x $9\frac{13}{16}$ in. (18.3 x 24.9 cm); sheet: $10\frac{5}{8}$ x $14\frac{7}{16}$ in. (27 x 36.6 cm). Publisher: Edmond Frapier, Paris. Printer: unknown. Edition: 625. Gift of Emilio Sanchez, 53.1961. (Wittrock 236; Delteil 216; Adhémar 228; Adriani 233)

FIRMIN GÉMIER, program for benefit performance for Firmin Gémier at the Théâtre Antoine, Paris, from **THE BERALDI ALBUM OF THEATRE PROGRAMS**. 1897. Lithograph, sheet (folded): $12\frac{3}{8}$ x $9\frac{11}{16}$ in. (31.5 x 24.6 cm). Publisher: Théâtre Antoine, Paris. Printer: Eugène Verneau, Paris. Edition: unknown. Johanna and Leslie J. Garfield Fund, Mary Ellen Oldenburg Fund, and Sharon P. Rockefeller Fund, 289.2008.40. (Wittrock 235; Delteil 221; Adhémar 268; Adriani 238)

LE GAGE. 1897. Lithograph, composition: $11\frac{7}{16}$ x $9\frac{11}{16}$ in. (29 x 24.6 cm); sheet: 14 x $12\frac{9}{16}$ in. (35.5 x 31.9 cm). Publisher: probably the artist, Paris. Printer: Henri Stern, Paris. Edition: 9 known impressions. Gift of Abby Aldrich Rockefeller, 157.1946. (Wittrock 237; Delteil 212; Adhémar 264; Adriani 234)

HISTOIRES NATURELLES by Jules Renard. 1897, published 1899. Illustrated book with twenty-three lithographs, page: $12\frac{3}{8}$ x $8\frac{7}{8}$ in. (31.5 x 22.5 cm). Publisher: Henri Floury, Paris. Printer: Henri Stern, Paris. Edition: 100. The Louis E. Stern Collection, 1068.1964.1–23. (Wittrock 202–24; Delteil 297–320; Adhémar 333–55; Adriani 321–43). Plates 108–119

HOMMAGE À MOLIÈRE (**HOMAGE TO MOLIÈRE**), program for **LE BIEN D'AUTRUI** (**OTHER PEOPLE'S PROPERTY**) and **HORS LES LOIS** (**OUTSIDE THE LAW**) at the Théâtre Antoine, Paris, from **THE BERALDI ALBUM OF THEATRE PROGRAMS**. 1897. Lithograph, sheet: $12\frac{1}{2}$ x $9\frac{5}{8}$ in. (31.7 x 24.4 cm). Publisher: Théâtre Antoine, Paris. Printer: Eugène Verneau, Paris. Edition: several hundred. Johanna and Leslie J. Garfield Fund, Mary Ellen Oldenburg Fund, and Sharon P. Rockefeller Fund, 289.2008.41. (Wittrock 231; Delteil 220; Adhémar 272; Adriani 235). Plate 82

LE MARCHAND DE MARRONS (**THE CHESTNUT VENDOR**). 1897, published 1925. Lithograph, composition: $10\frac{3}{16}$ x $6\frac{15}{16}$ in. (25.8 x 17.6 cm); sheet: $14\frac{13}{16}$ x 11 in. (37.6 x 27.9 cm). Publisher: Edmond Frapier, Paris. Printer: unknown. Edition: 625. Gift of Louise Bourgeois, 265.1997. (Wittrock 232; Delteil 335; Adhémar 254; Adriani 211). Figure 47

SCHLOMÉ FUSS À LA SYNAGOGUE (**SCHLOMÉ FUSS IN THE SYNAGOGUE**). 1897, published 1898. Lithograph, composition: $6\frac{7}{8}$ x $5\frac{11}{16}$ in. (17.5 x 14.4 cm), sheet: $11\frac{9}{16}$ x $10\frac{1}{16}$ in. (29.3 x 25.5 cm). Publisher: Henri Floury, Paris. Printer: Chamerot et Renouard, Paris. Edition: 25. Gift of Mr. and Mrs. Herbert D. Schimmel, 701.1996. (Wittrock 199; Delteil 247; Adhémar 238; Adriani 217)

Cover for the book **LA TRIBU D'ISIDORE** by Victor Joze. 1897. Lithograph, composition: $7\frac{15}{16}$ x $5\frac{3}{16}$ in. (20.1 x 13.1 cm); sheet: $7\frac{15}{16}$ x $9\frac{5}{8}$ in. (20.1 x 24.4 cm). Publisher and printer: unknown. Edition: 50. Gift of Abby Aldrich Rockefeller, 158.1946. (Wittrock 234; Delteil 215; Adhémar 235; Adriani 232). Plate 100

1898

AU HANNETON (**AT THE HANNETON**). 1898. Lithograph, composition: $14\frac{1}{8}$ x $10\frac{1}{16}$ in. (35.8 x 25.6 cm); sheet: $18\frac{11}{16}$ x $13\frac{13}{16}$ in. (47.5 x 35.1 cm). Publisher: Boussod, Manzi, Joyant & Cie, Paris. Printer: unknown. Edition: 100. Gift of Abby Aldrich Rockefeller, 160.1946. (Wittrock 296; Delteil 272; Adhémar 290; Adriani 303)

L'AUTOMOBILISTE (**THE AUTOMOBILE DRIVER**). 1898. Lithograph, composition: $14\frac{3}{4}$ x $10\frac{1}{2}$ in. (37.4 x 26.6 cm); sheet: $19\frac{3}{4}$ x 14 in. (50.1 x 35.5 cm). Publisher: probably the artist, Paris. Printer: unknown. Edition: 25. Gift of Abby Aldrich Rockefeller, 155.1946. (Wittrock 293; Delteil 203; Adhémar 295; Adriani 290). Plate 101

LE CHEVAL ET LE COLLEY (**THE HORSE AND THE COLLIE**). 1898. Lithograph, composition: $12\frac{15}{16}$ x 9 in. (32.9 x 22.8 cm); sheet: $14\frac{3}{16}$ x 11 in. (36.1 x 27.9 cm). Publisher: probably the artist, Paris. Printer: Henri Stern, Paris. Edition: 9 known impressions. Gift of Jeanne C. Thayer, 128.1991. (Wittrock 285; Delteil 283; Adhémar 259; Adriani 299). Plate 103

LE PONEY PHILIBERT (**PHILIBERT THE PONY**). 1898. Lithograph, composition: $14\frac{3}{4}$ x $10\frac{7}{16}$ in. (37.5 x 26.5 cm); sheet: $21\frac{15}{16}$ x $14\frac{1}{8}$ in. (55.8 x 35.8 cm). Publisher: probably the artist, Paris. Printer: unknown. Edition: 50. Gift of Abby Aldrich Rockefeller, 159.1946. (Wittrock 284; Delteil 224; Adhémar 300; Adriani 301)

PORTRAITS D'ACTEURS & ACTRICES: TREIZE LITHOGRAPHIES (**PORTRAITS OF ACTORS & ACTRESSES: THIRTEEN LITHOGRAPHS**). 1898, published c. 1906. Portfolio of thirteen lithographs with lithographed cover, sheet (each approx.): $15\frac{7}{16}$ x $12\frac{3}{8}$ in. (39.2 x 31.5 cm). Publisher: unknown, Paris. Printer: unknown. Edition: approx. 400. Gift of Abby Aldrich Rockefeller, 169.1946.1–14. (Wittrock 249–61; Delteil 150–62; Adhémar 166–78; Adriani 260–72). Plates 40–43

PROMENOIR (**THE FOYER**). 1898. Lithograph, composition: $17\frac{1}{2}$ x $13\frac{3}{8}$ in. (44.5 x 34 cm); sheet: $27\frac{3}{4}$ x $21\frac{1}{4}$ in. (70.5 x 54 cm). Publisher: La Maison Moderne, Paris. Printer: unknown. Edition: 100. Gift of Abby Aldrich Rockefeller, 162.1946. (Wittrock 307; Delteil 290; Adhémar 324; Adriani 309). Plate 12

TRISTAN BERNARD. 1898, published 1920. Drypoint, plate: $6\frac{11}{16}$ x $4\frac{1}{16}$ in. (17 x 10.3 cm); sheet: $12\frac{11}{16}$ x $9\frac{1}{2}$ in. (32.2 x 24.2 cm). Publisher: Loys Delteil, Paris. Printer: unknown. Edition: 445. Curt Valentin Bequest, 133.1956. (Wittrock 240; Delteil 9; Adhémar 282; Adriani 249)

1899

LA GOULUE DEVANT LE TRIBUNAL (**LA GOULUE BEFORE THE COURT**). 1899. Lithograph, composition: $12\frac{9}{16}$ x $9\frac{13}{16}$ in. (31.9 x 25 cm); sheet: $14\frac{5}{8}$ x $10\frac{7}{8}$ in. (37.2 x 27.6 cm). Publisher: probably the artist, Paris. Printer: Henri Stern, Paris. Edition: 25. Gift of Abby Aldrich Rockefeller, 153.1946. (Wittrock 329; Delteil 148; Adhémar 146; Adriani 320)

JANE AVRIL. 1899. Lithograph, composition: $22\frac{1}{16}$ x $14\frac{1}{16}$ in. (56 x 35.7 cm); sheet: $22\frac{1}{16}$ x 15 in. (56 x 38.1 cm). Publisher: Jane Avril, Paris. Printer: Henri Stern, Paris. Edition: 25. Gift of Abby Aldrich Rockefeller, 167.1946. (Wittrock P29; Delteil 367; Adhémar 323; Adriani 354). Plate 37

LE JOCKEY. 1899. Lithograph, composition: $20\frac{1}{4}$ x 14 in. (51.4 x 35.6 cm); sheet: $20\frac{1}{4}$ x $14\frac{1}{8}$ in. (51.5 x 35.8 cm). Publisher: Pierrefort, Paris. Printer: Henri Stern, Paris. Edition: approx. 70. Gift of Abby Aldrich Rockefeller, 161.1946. (Wittrock 308; Delteil 279; Adhémar 365; Adriani 345)

1900

LE MARGOUIN (**MADEMOISELLE LOUISE BLOUET**). 1900. Lithograph, composition: $12\frac{1}{2}$ x $9\frac{3}{4}$ in. (31.8 x 24.8 cm); sheet: $19\frac{3}{4}$ x 14 in. (50.2 x 35.5 cm). Publisher: probably the artist, Paris. Printer: Henri Stern, Paris. Edition: 40. Gift of Abby Aldrich Rockefeller, 164.1946. (Wittrock 334; Delteil 325; Adhémar 370; Adriani 356). Plate 44

THE BERALDI ALBUM OF THEATRE PROGRAMS

THE BERALDI ALBUM OF THEATRE PROGRAMS. 1887–98. Album of fifty lithographs assembled by Henri Beraldi, page: $18\frac{5}{16}$ x $13\frac{3}{8}$ in. (46.5 x 34 cm). Publisher: the various theaters. Printer: various. Edition: varies. Johanna and Leslie J. Garfield Fund, Mary Ellen Oldenburg Fund, and Sharon P. Rockefeller Fund, 289.2008.1–50

The album includes the following works:

Louis Abel-Truchet (French, 1857–1918). Program for **CADAVRES** at the Théâtre Caroline, Paris. c. 1890. Lithograph, sheet: $12\frac{13}{16}$ x $9\frac{5}{8}$ in. (32.6 x 24.5 cm). 289.2008.49

Louis Abel-Truchet (French, 1857–1918). Program for **LA FUMÉE, PUIS LA FLAMME** (**SMOKE THEN FLAME**) at the Théâtre Libre, Paris. 1895. Lithograph, sheet: $9\frac{3}{8}$ x $12\frac{1}{8}$ in. (23.8 x 30.8 cm). 289.2008.15

Louis Anquetin (French, 1861–1932). Program for **LA FILLE D'ARTABAN** (**THE DAUGHTER OF ARTABANUS**), **LA NÉBULEUSE** (**THE NEBULA**), and **DIALOGUE INCONNU** (**UNKNOWN DIALOGUE**) at the Théâtre Libre, Paris. 1896. Lithograph, sheet: $12\frac{3}{16}$ x $9\frac{1}{4}$ in. (31 x 23.5 cm). 289.2008.19

Louis Anquetin (French, 1861–1932). Program for **LE TALION** (**THE RETALIATION**), **LA CAGE** (**THE CAGE**), **CEUX QUI RESTENT** (**THOSE WHO REMAIN**), and **FORTUNE** at the Théâtre Antoine, Paris. 1898. Lithograph, sheet: $13\frac{9}{16}$ x $10\frac{1}{16}$ in. (34.4 x 25.6 cm). 289.2008.43

Georges Bataille (French, 1897–1962). Program for **ANNABELLA** at the Théâtre de l'Oeuvre, Paris. 1894. Lithograph, sheet: $9\frac{11}{16}$ x $12\frac{1}{2}$ in. (24.6 x 31.8 cm). 289.2008.24

Pierre Bonnard (French, 1867–1947). Program for **DERNIÈRE CROISADE** (**THE LAST CRUSADE**), **L'ERRANTE** (**THE WANDERER**), and **LA FLEUR PALAN ENLEVÉE** (**THE PURLOINED PALAN FLOWER**) at the Théâtre de l'Oeuvre, Paris. 1896. Lithograph, sheet: $12\frac{1}{2}$ x $9\frac{5}{8}$ in. (31.7 x 24.4 cm). 289.2008.36

Pierre Bonnard (French, 1867–1947). Advertisement for **REVUE ENCYCLOPÉDIQUE LAROUSSE** at the Théâtre de l'Oeuvre, Paris. 1896. Lithograph, sheet: $12\frac{5}{16}$ x $9\frac{5}{16}$ in. (31.2 x 23.6 cm). 289.2008.37

Jean de Calduin (dates unknown). Program for **KERUZEL** at the Théâtre des Poètes, Paris. c. 1895. Lithograph, sheet: $12\frac{11}{16}$ x $9\frac{5}{8}$ in. (32.2 x 24.5 cm). 289.2008.47

Maurice Denis (French, 1870–1943). Program for **LA SCÈNE** (**THE SCENE**), **LA VÉRITÉ DANS LE VIN** (**TRUTH IN WINE**), **LES PIEDS NICKELÉS** (**NICKEL-PLATED FEET**), and **INTÉRIEUR** (**INTERIOR**) at the Théâtre de l'Oeuvre, Paris. 1895. Lithograph, sheet: $9\frac{9}{16}$ x $12\frac{11}{16}$ in. (24.3 x 32.2 cm). 289.2008.22

Maxime Dethomas (French, 1867–1929). Program for **BRAND** at the Théâtre de l'Oeuvre, Paris. 1895. Lithograph, sheet: 13¼ x 8 15/16 in. (33.7 x 22.7 cm). 289.2008.28. Plate 95

Maxime Dethomas (French, 1867–1929). Advertisement for **PAN** at the Théâtre de l'Oeuvre, Paris. 1895. Lithograph, sheet: 12⅝ x 8⅝ in. (32 x 21.9 cm). 289.2008.29

Maxime Dethomas (French, 1867–1929). Program for **UNE MÈRE** (**A MOTHER**), **BROCÉLIANDE, LES FLAIREURS** (**THE SNIFFERS**), and **DES MOTS! DES MOTS!** (**WORDS! WORDS!**) at the Théâtre de l'Oeuvre, Paris. 1896. Lithograph, sheet: 12⅝ x 9⅝ in. (32.1 x 24.4 cm). 289.2008.30. Plate 96

Maxime Dethomas (French, 1867–1929). Advertisement for **REVUE ENCYCLOPÉDIQUE LAROUSSE** at the Théâtre de l'Oeuvre, Paris. 1896. Lithograph, sheet: 12¼ x 9 7/16 in. (31.1 x 24 cm). 289.2008.31

Henri-Patrice Dillon (French, born United States. 1851–1909). Program for **EN FAMILLE** (**IN THE FAMILY**) at the Théâtre Libre, Paris. 1887. Lithograph, sheet: 9⅝ x 8¾ in. (24.4 x 22.2 cm). 289.2008.2. Plate 90

Georges de Feure (French, 1869–1928). Program for **THERMOS VICTUS OU LA FICELLE MERVEILLEUSE** (**THERMOS VICTUS OR THE MARVELOUS STRING**) at the Théâtre Caroline, Paris. 1895. Lithograph, sheet: 12 11/16 x 9 5/16 in. (32.3 x 23.7 cm). 289.2008.48. Plate 87

Henri Gerbault (French, 1863–1930). Program for **L'INQUIÉTUDE** (**ANXIETY**) and **AMANTS ÉTERNELS** (**ETERNAL LOVERS**) at the Théâtre Libre, Paris. 1893. Lithograph, sheet: 12 9/16 x 9½ in. (31.9 x 24.2 cm). 289.2008.1. Plate 89

Henri-Gabriel Ibels (French, 1867–1936). Program for **LES FOSSILES** (**THE FOSSILS**) at the Théâtre Libre, Paris. 1892. Lithograph, sheet: 9⅜ x 12 11/16 in. (23.8 x 32.2 cm). 289.2008.5. Plate 91

Henri-Gabriel Ibels (French, 1867–1936). Program for **LE GRAPPIN** (**THE GRAPNEL**) and **L'AFFRANCHIE** (**THE EMANCIPATED**) at the Théâtre Libre, Paris. 1892. Lithograph, sheet: 9 5/16 x 12⅝ in. (23.7 x 32 cm). 289.2008.4

Henri-Gabriel Ibels (French, 1867–1936). Program for **À BAS LE PROGRÈS!** (**DOWN WITH PROGRESS!**), **MADEMOISELLE JULIE** (**MISS JULIE**), and **LE MÉNAGE BRÉSILE** (**THE BRAZILIAN HOUSEHOLD**) at the Théâtre Libre, Paris. 1893. Lithograph, sheet: 9 7/16 x 12½ in. (24 x 31.8 cm). 289.2008.6. Plate 93

Henri-Gabriel Ibels (French, 1867–1936). Program for **LA BELLE AU BOIS RÊVANT** (**THE DREAMING BEAUTY**), **MARIAGE D'ARGENT** (**SILVER WEDDING**), and **AHASVÈRE** (**AHASUERUS**) at the Théâtre Libre, Paris. 1893. Lithograph, sheet: 9⅜ x 12⅜ in. (23.8 x 31.5 cm). 289.2008.11

Henri-Gabriel Ibels (French, 1867–1936). Program for **BOUBOUROCHE** and **VALET DE CŒUR** (**JACK OF HEARTS**) at the Théâtre Libre, Paris. 1893. Lithograph, sheet: 9½ x 12½ in. (24.1 x 31.8 cm). 289.2008.9

Henri-Gabriel Ibels (French, 1867–1936). Program for **LE DEVÔIR** (**THE DUTY**) at the Théâtre Libre, Paris. 1893. Lithograph, sheet: 9 11/16 x 12 11/16 in. (24.6 x 32.2 cm). 289.2008.7

Henri-Gabriel Ibels (French, 1867–1936). Program for **MIRÂGES** at the Théâtre Libre, Paris. 1893. Lithograph, sheet: 9 5/16 x 12 5/16 in. (23.7 x 31.2 cm). 289.2008.8

Henri-Gabriel Ibels (French, 1867–1936). Program for **LES TISSERANDS** (**THE WEAVERS**) at the Théâtre Libre, Paris. 1893. Lithograph, sheet: 9⅜ x 12 7/16 in. (23.8 x 31.6 cm). 289.2008.10. Plate 88

Henri-Gabriel Ibels (French, 1867–1936). Program for **À BAS LE PROGRÈS** (**DOWN WITH PROGRESS**) at the Théâtre Libre, Paris. 1894. Lithograph, sheet: 12 11/16 x 9¾ in. (32.3 x 24.7 cm). 289.2008.20

Alfred Jarry (French, 1873–1907). Program for **UBU ROI** (**KING UBU**) at the Théâtre de l'Oeuvre, Paris. 1896. Lithograph, sheet: 9 11/16 x 12 11/16 in. (24.6 x 32.3 cm). 289.2008.38. Plate 85

Ernest La Jeunesse (French, 1874–1917). Program for **LA COMÉDIE DE L'AMOUR** (**THE COMEDY OF LOVE**) at the Théâtre de l'Oeuvre, Paris. 1897. Lithograph, sheet: 9 13/16 x 12½ in. (25 x 31.8 cm). 289.2008.21

Henri Lebasque (French, 1865–1947). Program for **LE FILS DE L'ABBESSE** (**THE SON OF THE ABBESS**) and **LE FARDEAU DE LA LIBERTÉ** (**THE BURDEN OF LIBERTY**) at the Théâtre Antoine, Paris. 1897. Lithograph, sheet: $12\frac{1}{2}$ x $9\frac{7}{16}$ in. (31.8 x 24 cm). 289.2008.50

Gustave Le Rouge (French, 1867–1938). Program for **LE RÊVE DE THÉO** (**THEO'S DREAM**) and **L'INFIDÈLE** (**THE INFIDEL**). c. 1890. Lithograph, sheet: $12\frac{5}{16}$ x $9\frac{1}{16}$ in. (31.3 x 23 cm). 289.2008.44

Fabrice Mory. Program for **QUI L'EMPORTERA?** (**WHO WILL WIN?**), **LES INCENDIAIRES** (**THE INCENDIARIES**), and **LE PAIN DE LA HONTE** (**THE BREAD OF SHAME**) at the Théâtre Social, Paris. 1894. Lithograph, sheet: $12\frac{13}{16}$ x $9\frac{13}{16}$ in. (32.5 x 24.9 cm). 289.2008.45

Paul Ranson (French, 1862–1909). Program for **LA CLOCHE ENGLOUTIE** (**THE SUNKEN BELL**) at the Théâtre de l'Oeuvre, Paris. 1897. Lithograph, sheet: $12\frac{1}{2}$ x $9\frac{5}{8}$ in. (31.7 x 24.5 cm). 289.2008.39

Henri Rivière (French, 1864–1951). **PARIS EN HIVER** (**PARIS IN WINTER**), program for **LES FRÈRES ZEMGANNO** (**THE ZEMGANNO BROTHERS**) and **DEUX TOURTEREAUX** (**TWO LOVEBIRDS**) at the Théâtre Libre, Paris. 1890. Lithograph, sheet: $8\frac{5}{8}$ x $12\frac{1}{16}$ in. (21.1 x 30.7 cm). 289.2008.3. Plate 92

Auguste Rodin (French, 1840–1917). Program for **LE REPAS DU LION** (**THE LION'S MEAL**) at the Théâtre Antoine, Paris. 1897. Lithograph, sheet: $12\frac{5}{8}$ x $9\frac{1}{4}$ in. (32 x 23.5 cm). 289.2008.42

Joseph Sattler (German, 1867–1931). Program for an untitled play at the Théâtre de l'Oeuvre, Paris. 1895–96. Lithograph, sheet: $9\frac{1}{2}$ x $9\frac{1}{4}$ in. (24.2 x 23.5 cm). 289.2008.35

Paul Sérusier (French, 1864–1927). Program for **L'ASSOMPTION DE HANNELE MATTERN** (**THE ASSUMPTION OF HANNELE MATTERN**) and **EN L'ATTENDANT** (**WAITING FOR HIM**) at the Théâtre Libre, Paris. 1894. Lithograph, sheet: $12\frac{5}{16}$ x $9\frac{3}{16}$ in. (31.2 x 23.3 cm). 289.2008.13. Plate 97

Théophile-Alexandre Steinlen (French, 1859–1923). Program for **LA PAQUE SOCIALISTES** (**SOCIALIST SPRING**) at the Théâtre Social, Paris. 1894. Lithograph, sheet: $8\frac{1}{4}$ x $10\frac{3}{4}$ in. (20.9 x 27.3 cm). 289.2008.46

Tancrède Synave (French, 1860–1936). Program for **L'ÂME INVISIBLE** (**THE INVISIBLE SOUL**) at the Théâtre Libre, Paris. 1896. Lithograph, sheet: $12\frac{5}{8}$ x $9\frac{1}{2}$ in. (32 x 24.2 cm). 289.2008.16. Plate 98

Tancrède Synave (French, 1860–1936). Program for **MADEMOISELLE FIFI** at the Théâtre Libre, Paris. 1896. Lithograph, sheet: $12\frac{1}{2}$ x $9\frac{7}{16}$ in. (31.8 x 24 cm). 289.2008.17

Henri de Toulouse-Lautrec (French, 1864–1901). **LA COIFFURE** (**THE HAIRDRESSER**), program for **UNE FAILLITE** (**BANKRUPTCY**) and **LE POÈTE ET LE FINANCIER** (**THE POET AND THE FINANCIER**) at the Théâtre Libre, Paris. 1893. Lithograph, sheet: $12\frac{5}{8}$ x $9\frac{3}{4}$ in. (32 x 24.7 cm). 289.2008.12. Plate 81

Henri de Toulouse-Lautrec (French, 1864–1901). **LA LOGE AU MASCARON DORÉ** (**THE BOX WITH THE GILDED MASK**), program for **LE MISSIONNAIRE** (**THE MISSIONARY**) at the Théâtre Libre, Paris. 1894. Lithograph, sheet: $12\frac{1}{16}$ x $9\frac{7}{16}$ in. (30.6 x 24 cm). 289.2008.14. Plate 79

Henri de Toulouse-Lautrec (French, 1864–1901). **UN MONSIEUR ET UNE DAME** (**A GENTLEMAN AND A LADY**), program for **L'ARGENT** (**MONEY**) at the Théâtre Libre, Paris. 1895. Lithograph, sheet: $12\frac{1}{2}$ x $9\frac{3}{8}$ in. (31.8 x 23.8 cm). 289.2008.18. Plate 80

Henri de Toulouse-Lautrec (French, 1864–1901). **OSCAR WILDE**, program for **RAPHAËL** and **SALOMÉ** at the Théâtre de l'Oeuvre, Paris. 1896. Lithograph, sheet: $12\frac{7}{16}$ x $9\frac{7}{16}$ in. (31.6 x 24 cm). 289.2008.34. Plate 84

Henri de Toulouse-Lautrec (French, 1864–1901). **ROMAIN COOLUS**, program for **RAPHAËL** and **SALOMÉ** at the Théâtre de l'Oeuvre, Paris. 1896. Lithograph, sheet: $12\frac{9}{16}$ x $9\frac{13}{16}$ in. (31.9 x 24.9 cm). 289.2008.33. Plate 83

Henri de Toulouse-Lautrec (French, 1864–1901). **FIRMIN GÉMIER**, program for benefit performance for Firmin Gémier at the Théâtre Antoine, Paris. 1897. Lithograph, sheet (folded): $12\frac{3}{8}$ x $9\frac{11}{16}$ in. (31.5 x 24.6 cm). 289.2008.40.

Henri de Toulouse-Lautrec (French, 1864–1901). **HOMMAGE À MOLIÈRE** (**HOMAGE TO MOLIÈRE**), program for **LE BIEN D'AUTRUI** (**OTHER PEOPLE'S PROPERTY**) and **HORS LES LOIS** (**OUTSIDE THE LAW**) at the Théâtre Antoine, Paris. 1897. Lithograph, sheet: $12\frac{1}{2}$ x $9\frac{5}{8}$ in. (31.7 x 24.4 cm). 289.2008.41. Plate 82

Félix Vallotton (French, 1865–1925). Program for **PÈRE** (**FATHER**) at the Théâtre de l'Oeuvre, Paris. 1894. Lithograph, sheet: 9 13/16 x 12 7/8 in. (24.9 x 32.7 cm). 289.2008.23. Plate 94

Édouard Vuillard (French, 1868–1940). Program for **ÂMES SOLITAIRES** (**LONELY SOULS**) at the Théâtre de l'Oeuvre, Paris. 1893. Lithograph, sheet: 12 15/16 x 9 1/2 in. (32.8 x 24.1 cm). 289.2008.25. Plate 86

Édouard Vuillard (French, 1868–1940). Program for **UN ENNEMI DU PEUPLE** (**AN ENEMY OF THE PEOPLE**) at the Théâtre de l'Oeuvre, Paris. 1893. Lithograph, sheet: 9 7/16 x 12 5/8 in. (24 x 32 cm). 289.2008.27

Édouard Vuillard (French, 1868–1940). Program for **LA VIE MUETTE** (**THE SILENT LIFE**) at the Théâtre de l'Oeuvre, Paris. 1894. Lithograph, sheet: 12 5/8 x 9 9/16 in. (32.1 x 24.3 cm). 289.2008.26

Unknown. Program for **L'ANNEAU DE SAKUNTALA** (**THE RING OF SAKUNTALA**) at the Théâtre de l'Oeuvre, Paris. 1895. Lithograph, sheet: 12 3/8 x 9 15/16 in. (31.5 x 25.3 cm). 289.2008.32

DRAWINGS

LA GOULUE AU MOULIN ROUGE (**LA GOULUE AT THE MOULIN ROUGE**). 1891–92. Oil on board, 31 1/4 x 23 1/4 in. (79.4 x 59 cm). Gift of Mrs. David M. Levy, 161.1957. Figure 20

CARICATURE OF FÉLIX FÉNÉON. c. 1895–96. Ink on paper, 12 1/4 x 7 7/8 in. (31.3 x 20 cm). John Rewald Bequest, SC533.1994

PAINTINGS

MME LILI GRENIER. 1888. Oil on canvas, 21 3/4 x 18 in. (55.2 x 45.7 cm). The William S. Paley Collection, SPC38.1990

M. DE LAURADOUR. 1897. Oil and gouache on cardboard, 26 3/4 x 32 1/2 in. (67.9 x 82.6 cm). The William S. Paley Collection, SPC79.1990

INDEX OF PLATES

BY TOULOUSE-LAUTREC

FRENCH TITLES

INDEX OF PLATES

BY TOULOUSE-LAUTREC

ENGLISH TITLES

SELECTED BIBLIOGRAPHY

This selected bibliography is primarily focused on English-language and French references dating from the last twenty-five years; however, a selection of earlier volumes and nineteenth-century sources is also included, as are firsthand accounts by the artist's subjects, colleagues, and friends.

Adhémar, Jean. *Toulouse-Lautrec: His Complete Lithographs and Drypoints*. New York: Harry N. Abrams, 1965.

Adriani, Götz. *Toulouse-Lautrec*. New York: Thames and Hudson, 1987.

_______. *Toulouse-Lautrec: The Complete Graphic Works: A Catalogue Raisonné: The Gerstenberg Collection*. London: Royal Academy of Arts, in association with Thames and Hudson, 1988.

Alexandre, Arsène. *L'Art français* (July 29, 1893).

_______. "Le Théâtre de la Loïe Fuller." *Le Théâtre* 4 (August 11, 1900): 24.

Anderberg, Birgitte, and Vibeke Vibolt Knudsen. *Toulouse-Lautrec: The Human Comedy*. Munich, London, and New York: Prestel, 2011.

Arnold, Matthias. *Henri de Toulouse-Lautrec, 1864–1901: The Theatre of Life*. Cologne: Taschen, 2000.

Arwas, Victor. *Belle Époque Posters and Graphics*. New York: Rizzoli, 1978.

Aubert, Louis. "Harunobu et Toulouse-Lautrec." *La Revue Paris* (February 15, 1910): 825–42.

Avril, Jane. *Mes Mémoires*. Paris: Phébus, 2005.

Barrows, Susanna. "Nineteenth-Century Cafés: Arenas of Everyday Life." In Barbara Stern Shapiro, ed. *Pleasures of Paris: Daumier to Picasso*. Boston: Museum of Fine Arts, Boston, 1991.

Beauté, Georges, ed. *A Toulouse-Lautrec Album*. Salt Lake City: Gibbs M. Smith, 1982.

Berger, Klaus. *Japonisme in Western Painting from Whistler to Matisse*. Trans. David Britt. Cambridge and New York: Cambridge University Press, 1992.

Bodelsen, Merete. *Toulouse-Lautrec's Posters: Catalogue and Comments*. Copenhagen: Museum of Decorative Arts, 1964.

Boyer, Patricia Eckert. *Artists and the Avant-Garde Theater in Paris, 1887–1900: The Martin and Liane W. Atlas Collection*. Washington, D.C.: National Gallery of Art, 1998.

Byrnes, Robert F. "Antisemitism in France before the Dreyfus Affair." *Jewish Social Studies* 11, no. 1 (January 1949): 49–68. Published by Indiana University Press. Available online, http://www.jstor.org/stable/4464787.

Carey, Frances, and Antony Griffiths. *From Manet to Toulouse-Lautrec: French Lithographs, 1860–1900. Catalogue of an Exhibition at the Department of Prints and Drawings in the British Museum, 1978.* London: British Museum Publications Ltd., 1978.

"Carnot Seriously Ill: Anxiety about the Condition of the President of France." *New York Times*, June 17, 1893.

Carvalho, Fleur Roos Rosa de, and Marije Vellekoop. *Printmaking in Paris: The Rage for Prints at the Fin de Siècle*. Amsterdam: Van Gogh Museum Publications, 2012.

Casselaer, Catherine van. *Lot's Wife: Lesbian Paris, 1890–1914*. Liverpool: Janus Press, 1986.

Cassell's Guide to Paris: with Numerous Illustrations. London: Cassel, 1901. Available online, http://babel.hathitrust.org/cgi/pt?id=uc2.ark:/13960/t5m903v09;view=1up;seq=12.

Castleman, Riva. *Toulouse-Lautrec: Posters and Prints from the Collection of Irene and Howard Stein*. Atlanta: High Museum of Art, 1998.

Castleman, Riva, and Wolfgang Wittrock, eds. *Henri de Toulouse-Lautrec: Images of the 1890s*. New York: The Museum of Modern Art, 1985.

Cate, Phillip Dennis, ed. *The Graphic Arts and French Society, 1871–1914*. New Brunswick, N.J.: Rutgers University Press and the Jane Voorhees Zimmerli Art Museum, 1988.

_______. "Japonisme and the Revival of Printmaking at the End of the Century." In Yamada Chisaburō, ed., *Japonisme in Art: An International Symposium*. Tokyo: Committee of the Year 2001 and Kodansha International Ltd., 2001.

Cate, Phillip Dennis, and Patricia Eckert Boyer. *The Circle of Toulouse-Lautrec: An Exhibition of the Work of the Artist and of His Close Associates*. New Brunswick, N.J.: Jane Voorhees Zimmerli Art Museum, 1985.

Cate, Phillip Dennis, and Sinclair Hamilton Hitchings. *The Color Revolution: Color Lithography in France, 1890–1900*. New Brunswick, N.J.: Peregrine Smith and Rutgers University Art Gallery, 1978.

Cate, Phillip Dennis, and Mary Shaw, eds. *The Spirit of Montmartre: Cabarets, Humor, and the Avant-Garde, 1875–1905*. New Brunswick, N.J.: Jane Voorhees Zimmerli Art Museum, 1996.

Charell, Ludwig. *H. de Toulouse-Lautrec: das Graphische Werk. Sammlung Ludwig Charell.* Munich: Prestel, 1951.

Chisaburō, Yamada, ed. *Japonisme in Art: An International Symposium.* Tokyo: Committee of the Year 2001 and Kodansha International Ltd., 2001.

Clemenceau, Georges. *La Justice* (September 15, 1894).

Davenay, Gaston. "From Day to Day: Yvette Guilbert." *Le Figaro* (August 16, 1894).

Day, George. *Pleasure Guide to Paris: Illustrated by Photographs.* London and Paris: Nilsson & Co., 1903(?).

Delteil, Loÿs. *H. de Toulouse-Lautrec.* Paris: Chez l'auteur, 1920.

Denvir, Bernard. *Toulouse-Lautrec.* London: Thames and Hudson, 1991.

Desloge, Nora, ed. *Toulouse-Lautrec: The Baldwin M. Baldwin Collection.* San Diego: San Diego Museum of Art, 1988.

Les Dessinateurs du "Courrier français": Catalogue-album. France: publisher unknown, 1891.

Devynck, Danièle. *Henri de Toulouse-Lautrec au Musée d'Albi.* Albi, France: Grand Sud, 2009.

———. *Toulouse-Lautrec et le japonisme.* Albi, France: Musée Toulouse-Lautrec, 1991.

Donson, Theodore B., and Marvel M. Griepp. *Henri de Toulouse-Lautrec: Performers of the Stage and the Boudoir, 1891–1899.* New York: Theodore B. Donson, 1980.

Dortu, M. G. *Toulouse-Lautrec et son oeuvre.* New York: Collectors Editions, 1971.

Dortu, M. G., and Philippe Huisman. *Lautrec by Lautrec.* Trans. Corinne Bellow. New York: Viking Press, 1964.

———. *Lautrec et le Croxi-Margouin.* Paris: L'Œil, Galerie d'Art, 1964.

Du Camp, Maxime. *Paris: ses organes, ses fonctions, et sa vie.* Paris: Hachette, 1872.

Fields, Armond. *Le Chat Noir: A Montmartre Cabaret and Its Artists in Turn-of-the-Century Paris.* Santa Barbara: Santa Barbara Museum of Art, 1993.

Frèches-Thory, Claire, and José Frèches. *Toulouse-Lautrec: Painter of the Night.* London: Thames and Hudson, 1994.

Frey, Julia. *Toulouse-Lautrec: A Life.* New York: Viking Press, 1994.

Fuller, Loïe. *Fifteen Years of a Dancer's Life: with Some Account of Her Distinguished Friends.* New York: Dance Horizons, 1978.

Gauzi, François. *Lautrec et son temps.* Paris: David Perret, 1954.

Geffroy, Gustave. *La Vie artistique,* 8 vols. Paris: E. Dentu, 1892–1903.

———. *Yvette Guilbert.* Trans. Barbara Sessions. New York: Walker and Company, 1968.

Gelfer-Jørgensen, Mirjam. *Toulouse-Lautrec Posters: The Collection of the Danish Museum of Decorative Art.* Copenhagen: Rhodos International Science and Art Publishers, 1995.

Gold, Arthur, and Robert Fizdale. *Misia: The Life of Misia Sert.* New York: Morrow Quill Paperbacks, 1981.

Goldschmidt, Lucien, and Herbert D. Schimmel, eds. *Unpublished Correspondence of Henri de Toulouse-Lautrec.* London: Phaidon, 1969.

Goldstein, Charles B. "Toulouse-Lautrec's Moulin Rouge: La Goulue: Lithograph or Reproduction." *IFAR Journal* 8, no. 2 (2005–6): 24–28.

Goncourt, Edmond de. *La Fille Élisa.* Paris: G. Charpentier, 1877.

Goncourt, Edmond de, and Jules de Goncourt. *Journal: Mémoires de la vie littéraire: 1892–1895,* vol. 3. Paris: G. Charpentier et E. Fasquelle, 1896.

Groom, Gloria. "Henri de Toulouse-Lautrec's *Au Cirque: Écuyère* (At the Circus: The Bareback Rider)." *Nineteenth-Century Art Worldwide* 10, no. 2 (Autumn 2011). Available online, http://www.19thc-artworldwide.org/autumn11/henri-de-toulouse-lautrecs-au-cirque-ecuyere-at-the-circus-the-bareback-rider.

Guilbert, Yvette. *La Chanson de ma vie (Mes Mémoires).* Paris: B. Grasset, 1927.

Harris, Geraldine. "But Is It Art? Female Performers in the Café-Concert." *New Theatre Quarterly* 5, no. 20 (November 1989): 334–47.

Heller, Reinhold. "Rediscovering Henri de Toulouse-Lautrec's 'At the Moulin Rouge.'" *Art Institute of Chicago Museum Studies* 12, no. 2 (1986): 114–35. Available online, http://www.jstor.org/stable/4115937.

———. *Toulouse-Lautrec: The Soul of Montmartre.* Munich and New York: Prestel, 1997.

Hiatt, Charles. *Picture Posters: A Short History of the Illustrated Placard, with Many Reproductions of the Most Artistic Examples in All Countries.* London: George Bell and Sons, 1895.

"The History of Paper Confetti." *Bathurst Free Press and Mining Journal* (May 20, 1897): 1.

Ireson, Nancy. *Toulouse-Lautrec and Jane Avril: Beyond the Moulin Rouge.* London: The Courtauld Gallery in association with Paul Holberton Publishing, 2011.

Iskin, Ruth E. "Identity and Interpretation: Receptions of Toulouse-Lautrec's *Reine de joie* Poster in the 1890s." *Nineteenth-Century Art Worldwide* 8, no. 1 (Spring 2009). Available online, http://www.19thc-artworldwide.org/spring09?id=63:-identity-and-interpretation-receptions-of-toulouse-lautrecs-reine-de-joie-poster-in-the-1890s&catid=34:articlec.

Ives, Colta Feller. *The Great Wave: The Influence of Japanese Woodcuts on French Prints.* New York: Metropolitan Museum of Art, 1974.

_______. *Toulouse-Lautrec in the Metropolitan Museum of Art.* New York: Metropolitan Museum of Art, 1996.

Le Japonisme: Galeries Nationales du Grand Palais, Paris, 17 mai–15 août 1988: Musée National d'Art Occidental, Tokyo, 23 Septembre–11 Décembre 1988. Paris: Ministère de la Culture et de la Communication, Éditions de la Réunion des Musées Nationaux, 1988.

Jimenez, Jill Berk, ed. *Dictionary of Artists' Models.* London: Fitzroy Dearborn Publishers, 2001.

Joseph, Steven F. "Paul Sescau: Toulouse-Lautrec's Elusive Neighbor." *History of Photography* 37, no. 2 (May 2013): 153–66.

Joyant, Maurice. *Henri de Toulouse-Lautrec* (reprint ed., 2 vols.). New York: Arno Press, 1968.

Joze, Victor. *Les Rozenfeld, histoire d'une famille juive. La Tribu d'Isidore.* Paris: Antony, 1897.

Julian, Philippe. *La Belle Époque.* New York: Metropolitan Museum of Art, 1982.

Julien, Édouard. *Musée Toulouse-Lautrec: Catalogue.* Albi, France: L'Impr. coopérative du sud-ouest, 1963.

Kert, Bernice. *Abby Aldrich Rockefeller: The Woman in the Family.* New York: Random House, 1993.

Keyes, Mindy. "Degas, Toulouse-Lautrec and Désiré Dihau: Portrait of a Bassoonist and His Bassoon." *Double Reed* 13, no. 2 (Fall 1990): 54–57.

Kinsman, Jane. "Cabaret Culture." *Artonview* 72 (Summer 2012): 4–11. Available online, issuu.com/nationalgalleryofaustralia/docs/artonview_72.

_______. "Underbelly: The Art of Henri de Toulouse-Lautrec." *Artonview* 71 (Spring 2012): 10–11. Available online, http://connection.ebscohost.com/c/entertainment-reviews/80160308/underbelly-art-henri-de-toulouse-lautrec.

Kleeblatt, Norman L., ed. *The Dreyfus Affair: Art, Truth, and Justice.* Berkeley: University of California Press, 1987.

Landre, Jeanne. *Aristide Bruant.* Paris: La Nouvelle Société d'Édition, 1930.

Lassaigne, Jacques. *Toulouse-Lautrec and the Paris of Cabarets.* Paris: Tête de Feuilles, 1976.

Leclercq, Paul. *Autour de Toulouse-Lautrec.* Rev. ed. Geneva: Pierre Cailler, 1954.

Lynes, Russell. *Good Old Modern: An Intimate Portrait of The Museum of Modern Art.* New York: Atheneum, 1973.

Mack, Gerstle. "Toulouse-Lautrec." In *Posters and Colored Lithographs, Toulouse-Lautrec, Dec. 5–31.* New York: Marie Harriman Gallery, 1938.

Mellerio, André. *La Lithographie originale en couleurs. Couverture et estampe de Pierre Bonnard.* Paris: Publication de l'Estampe et l'Affiche, 1898.

Melot, Michel. *Les Femmes de Toulouse-Lautrec.* Paris: Albin Michel, 1985.

Méténier, Oscar. *Aristide Bruant: Le Chansonnier populaire.* Paris: Au Mirliton, 1893.

Moffett, Kenworth. *Meier-Graefe as Art Critic.* Munich: Prestel, 1973.

Murray, Gale Barbara. *Toulouse-Lautrec: The Formative Years, 1878–1891.* New York: Oxford University Press, 1991.

_______. ed. *Toulouse-Lautrec: A Retrospective.* New York: Hugh Lauter Levin Associates, 1992.

_______. "Toulouse Lautrec's Illustrations for Victor Joze and Georges Clemenceau and Their Relationship to French Anti-Semitism of the 1890s." In Linda Nochlin and Tamar Garb, eds., *The Jew in the Text: Modernity and the Construction of Identity.* London: Thames and Hudson, 1995.

Natanson, Thadée. *Un Henri de Toulouse-Lautrec.* Geneva: P. Cailler, 1951.

"New Parisian Skating Rink, with Artificial Ice." *Manufacturer and Builder* 22 (April 1890): 84.

Novotny, Fritz. "Drawings of Yvette Guilbert by Toulouse-Lautrec." *Burlington Magazine* 91, no. 555 (June 1949): 159–63.

Les Nuits de Toulouse-Lautrec: De la scène aux boudoirs. Paris: Somogy; Dinan, France: Musée de Dinan, 2007.

Passeron, Roger. *French Prints of the 20th Century.* New York: Praeger, 1970.

Pennell, Elizabeth Robins. *Nights: Rome, Venice, in the Aesthetic Eighties: London, Paris, in the Fighting Nineties.* Philadelphia and London: J. B. Lippincott Co., 1916.

Pleasure Guide to Paris. Paris: 8, rue Halévy. Available online, http://babel.hathitrust.org/cgi/pt?id=uc2.ark:/13960/t9q23sn90;view=1up;seq=13.

Rearick, Charles. *Pleasures of the Belle Époque: Entertainment & Festivity in Turn-of-the-Century France.* New Haven and London: Yale University Press, 1985.

Rich, Daniel C. *Henri de Toulouse-Lautrec "Au Moulin Rouge," in the Art Institute of Chicago.* London: Percy Lund Humphries & Company, 1949 (?).

Roger-Marx, Claude. *Yvette Guilbert vue par Toulouse-Lautrec.* Paris: Au Pont des Arts, 1950.

Rothenstein, William. *Men and Memories. A History of the Arts, 1872–1922, Being the Recollections of William Rothenstein.* 2 vols. New York: Tudor Publishing Co., 1937.

Roy, Christian. *Traditional Festivals: A Multicultural Encyclopedia,* vol. 2. Santa Barbara: ABC-CLIO, 2005.

Sagne, Jean. *Toulouse-Lautrec.* Paris: Fayard, 1988.

Schimmel, Herbert D., ed. *The Letters of Henri de Toulouse-Lautrec.* Oxford and New York: Oxford University Press, 1991.

Schimmel, Herbert D., and Phillip Dennis Cate, eds. *The Henri de Toulouse-Lautrec, W. H. B. Sands Correspondence.* New York: Dodd, Mead & Company, 1983.

Segawa Seigle, Cecilia. "The Courtesan's Clock: Utamaro's Artistic Idealization and Kyōden's Literary Exposé, Antithetical Treatment of a Day and Night in the Yoshiwara." In Cecilia Segawa Seigle, Alfred H. Marks, Harue M. Summersgill, Amy Reigle Newland, Monika Hinkle, et al., *A Courtesan's Day: Hour by Hour.* Amsterdam: Hotei Publishing, KIT Publishers, 2004.

Shapiro, Barbara Stern, ed. *Pleasures of Paris: Daumier to Picasso.* Boston: Museum of Fine Arts, Boston, 1991.

Shattuck, Roger. *The Banquet Years.* New York: Vintage Books, 1968.

Shercliff, José. *Jane Avril of the Moulin Rouge.* Philadelphia: Macrae Smith Company, 1954.

Showalter, Elaine. *Sexual Anarchy: Gender and Culture at the Fin de Siècle.* New York: Viking, 1990.

Sidlauskas, Susan. *Body, Place, and Self in Nineteenth-Century Painting.* Cambridge: Cambridge University Press, 2000.

Sinsky, Carolyn. "Loïe Fuller." *The Modernism Lab,* Yale University, 2010. Available online, http://modernism.research.yale.edu/wiki/index.php/Loie_Fuller.

Stuckey, Charles. *Toulouse-Lautrec: Paintings.* Chicago: Art Institute of Chicago, 1979.

Suzuki, Sarah. *What Is a Print?: Selections from The Museum of Modern Art.* New York: The Museum of Modern Art, 2011.

Sweetman, David. *Explosive Acts: Toulouse-Lautrec, Oscar Wilde, Félix Fénéon and the Art & Anarchy of the Fin de Siècle.* New York: Simon & Schuster, 1999.

Tailhade, Laurent. *Aristide Bruant: Douze Chansons & Monologues. Les Chansonniers de Montmartre.* Paris: Libr. Universelle, 1906.

Thomson, Richard. *Toulouse-Lautrec.* New Haven: Yale University Press, 1991.

Thomson, Richard, Phillip Dennis Cate, and Mary Weaver Chapin. *Toulouse-Lautrec and Montmartre.* Washington, D.C.: National Gallery of Art, 2005.

Toulouse-Lautrec, 1864–1901. Montreal: Musée des Beaux-Arts de Montréal, 1968.

Toulouse-Lautrec et l'affiche. Paris: Fondation Dina Vierny-Musée Maillol; Réunion des Musées Nationaux, 2002.

Toulouse-Lautrec: His Lithographic Work, from the Collection of Ludwig Charell. Ottawa, Ontario: National Gallery of Canada; London: Arts Council of Great Britain, 1951.

Toulouse-Lautrec: Paintings, Drawings, Posters, and Lithographs. New York: The Museum of Modern Art, 1956.

Toulouse-Lautrec: Woman as Myth. Turin: Alberto Allemandi & Co., 2001.

Les XX, Bruxelles: Catalogue des dix expositions annuelles. Brussels: Centre International pour l'Étude du XIXe Siècle, 1981.

Weisberg, Gabriel P., and Yvonne M. L. Weisberg. *Japonisme: An Annotated Bibliography.* New York: Garland Publishing, 1990.

Whitmore, Janet. "Toulouse-Lautrec and Montmartre." *Nineteenth-Century Art Worldwide* 4, no. 3 (September 2005). Available online, http://www.19thc-artworldwide.org/autumn05/59-autumn05/autumn05review/205-toulouse-lautrec-and-montmartre.

Wittrock, Wolfgang. *Toulouse-Lautrec: The Complete Prints.* 2 vols. Ed. and trans. Catherine E. Kuehn. London: Philip Wilson Publishers Limited, 1985.

Wye, Deborah, and Audrey Isselbacher. *Paris: The 1890s.* Exh. brochure. New York: The Museum of Modern Art, 1997.

———. *Abby Aldrich Rockefeller and Print Collecting: An Early Mission for MoMA.* Exh. brochure. New York: The Museum of Modern Art, 1999.

ACKNOWLEDGMENTS

This study of Lautrec's prints and posters would have been unthinkable without the support, assistance, and encouragement of colleagues, scholars, and friends. In the Department of Drawings and Prints, I thank Christophe Cherix, The Robert Lehman Foundation Chief Curator, who supported this project with enthusiasm from the start and offered sage advice along the way; Deborah Wye, Chief Curator Emerita, whose wit and wisdom have guided me for the last fifteen years and whose comments on an earlier draft of my essay in this volume helped it to take shape; and Katherine Alcauskas, Emily Edison, and Jeff White, who oversee the cataloguing and care of our collection with tremendous professionalism. My research was supported by interns Hanna Excel, Leigh Tanner, and Jennie Waldow, and I appreciate their contributions. Emily Cushman, Research Assistant, has been my indispensable partner in this effort, and I thank her for her attention to detail and omnipresent good cheer.

My colleagues in the Department of Conservation—in particular Karl Buchberg, Senior Conservator, and Scott Gerson, former Associate Conservator—offered expertise and valuable insight. In the Library, Milan Hughston, Chief of Library and Museum Archives, and Jennifer Tobias, Librarian, are wonderful research partners and tremendously generous in sharing their collection. MoMA's Archives are treasure troves, and I thank Michelle Elligott, Tom Grischkowsky, Michelle Harvey, and Elisabeth Thomas for their assistance in navigating them.

This catalogue has been realized thanks to the thoughtful editorial oversight of Pamela T. Barr and Susan Homer. In the Department of Publications, Amanda Washburn, Senior Designer, devised a beautiful volume that elegantly reflects the subject matter; Matthew Pimm, Production Manager, and Marc Sapir, Production Director, shepherded it through production; and Rebecca Roberts, Associate Editor, provided editorial guidance and coordination. The staff of MoMA's Department of Imaging and Visual Resources, directed by Erik Landsberg and managed by Robert Kastler, is responsible for the beautiful new photography by Peter Butler, Robert Gerhardt, Thomas Griesel, Robert Kastler, Jonathan Muzikar, and John Wronn that appears in these pages.

The exhibition has depended on the logistical oversight of Rachel Kim and Registrars Kathy Hill and Sydney Briggs as well as the keen and inventive eye of Betty Fisher, Senior Design Manager, Exhibition Design and Production.

In my research, I have been fortunate to meet experts and enthusiasts who have been generous with their time and insight. My special thanks go to David Rockefeller, who graciously allowed me to include several works from his collection in this exhibition. Last, I thank my friends and family for their support in this, and all, endeavors.

Sarah Suzuki
Associate Curator, Department of Drawings and Prints
The Museum of Modern Art

Published in conjunction with the exhibition *The Paris of Toulouse-Lautrec: Prints and Posters from The Museum of Modern Art*, July 26, 2014–March 1, 2015, at The Museum of Modern Art, New York, organized by Sarah Suzuki, Associate Curator, Department of Drawings and Prints.

The exhibition is supported by the MoMA Annual Exhibition Fund.

This publication is supported by the Riva Castleman Fund for Publications in the Department of Drawings and Prints, established by The Derald H. Ruttenberg Foundation.

Produced by the Department of Publications, The Museum of Modern Art, New York

Edited by Pamela T. Barr, with Susan Homer
Designed by Amanda Washburn
Production by Matthew Pimm
Printed and bound by Ofset Yapimevi, Istanbul

This book is typeset in Bookman Oldstyle, Elephant, Figgins Sans, and Gordon. The paper is 150gsm Condat Matt Perigord.

Published by The Museum of Modern Art, New York
11 West 53 Street, New York, New York 10019
www.moma.org

Library of Congress Control Number: 2014934966

ISBN: 978-0-87070-913-5

Distributed in the United States and Canada by
ARTBOOK | D.A.P.
155 Sixth Avenue, 2nd floor, New York, New York 10013
www.artbook.com

Distributed outside the United States and Canada by
Thames & Hudson Ltd
181A High Holborn, London WC1V 7QZ
www.thamesandhudson.com

Printed in Turkey

Front cover: Henri de Toulouse-Lautrec. *Jane Avril* (detail). 1899. Lithograph, sheet: 22 1/16 x 15 in. (56 x 38.1 cm). See plate 37

Back cover and page 8: Henri de Toulouse-Lautrec. *Reine de joie* (*Queen of Joy*) (detail). 1892. Lithograph, sheet: 59 7/16 x 39 7/16 in. (151 x 100.1 cm). See plate 62

Endsheets: E. LaGrange. *The Dance Hall of the Moulin Rouge* (detail), illustration in *Le Panorama: Paris la nuit*, published by Ludovic Baschet, Paris. c. 1898. See fig. 17

Frontispiece: Henri de Toulouse-Lautrec. *Divan Japonais* (detail). 1893. Lithograph, sheet: 31 15/16 x 24 1/2 in. (81.2 x 62.2 cm). See plate 39

Page 4: Henri de Toulouse-Lautrec. *Aristide Bruant dans son cabaret* (*Aristide Bruant in His Cabaret*) (detail). 1893. Lithograph, sheet: 53 9/16 x 37 15/16 (136 x 96.3 cm). See plate 10

Page 6: Henri de Toulouse-Lautrec. *Babylone d'Allemagne* (*German Babylon*) (detail). 1894. Lithograph, sheet: 46 9/16 x 33 3/16 in. (118.3 x 84.3 cm). See plate 64

Poster: Henri de Toulouse-Lautrec. *La Troupe de Mademoiselle Églantine* (*Mademoiselle Églantine's Troupe*). 1896. Lithograph, sheet: 24 1/4 x 31 1/4 in. (61.6 x 79.4 cm). See plate 36

PHOTOGRAPH CREDITS

In reproducing the images contained in this publication, the Museum obtained the permission of the rights holders whenever possible. In those instances where the Museum could not locate the rights holders, notwithstanding good-faith efforts, it requests that any contact information concerning such rights holders be forwarded so that they may be contacted for future editions.

Photography © The Art Institute of Chicago: figs. 19, 21, 34, 35
© 2014 Artists Rights Society (ARS), New York/ADAGP, Paris: figs 4, 39, and plates 86, 92
© Association Frères Lumière: fig. 22
© Biblioteca Nacional de España: figs. 27, 29
© BnF, Dist. RMN-Grand Palais/Art Resource, NY: fig. 15
Courtesy Boston Public Library, Print Department: fig. 24
© The Trustees of the British Museum. All rights reserved: fig. 41
© Gary Bruder Fine Art: fig. 45
© CNAC/MNAM/Dist. RMN-Grand Palais/Art Resource, NY: fig. 22
© Leemage/The Bridgeman Art Library: fig. 18
Erich Lessing/Art Resource, NY: fig. 48
Image © The Metropolitan Museum of Art. Image source: Art Resource, NY: figs. 3, 8, 16
The Museum of Modern Art, New York, Department of Imaging and Visual Resources: figs. 25, 26, 37, and plates 19, 61, 120, 122; Peter Butler: figs. 5, 6, 11, 28, 33, 36, and plates 7, 9, 13, 15–18, 20, 23, 25, 37, 49, 52, 54–58, 60, 63, 66–68, 79–98, 102, 104–106, 124–26, 128; Robert Gerhardt: plates 26–33; Thomas Griesel: figs. 10, 20, and plates 10, 35, 36, 38, 39, 59, 62, 64, 69–72, 107; Paige Knight: fig. 14; Jonathan Muzikar: plate 22; Mali Olatunji: fig. 39; John Wronn: figs. 4, 32, 44, 47, and plates 1–6, 8, 11, 12, 14, 21, 24, 34, 40–48, 50, 51, 53, 65, 73–78, 99–101, 103, 108–119, 121, 123, 127
The Museum of Modern Art Archives, New York: figs. 12, 31
The New York Public Library/Art Resource, NY: figs. 7, 46
Musée d'Orsay, Paris, France/Giraudon/The Bridgeman Art Library: fig. 40
© RMN-Grand Palais/Art Resource, NY: fig. 42
Scala/Art Resource, NY: fig. 23
© Musée Toulouse-Lautrec, Albi, Tarn, France: figs. 1, 2, 9, 30, 43
Courtesy Collection of The Jane Voorhees Zimmerli Art Museum, Rutgers, The State University of New Jersey. Jack Abraham: fig. 17; Peter Jacobs: fig. 38

TRUSTEES OF THE MUSEUM OF MODERN ART

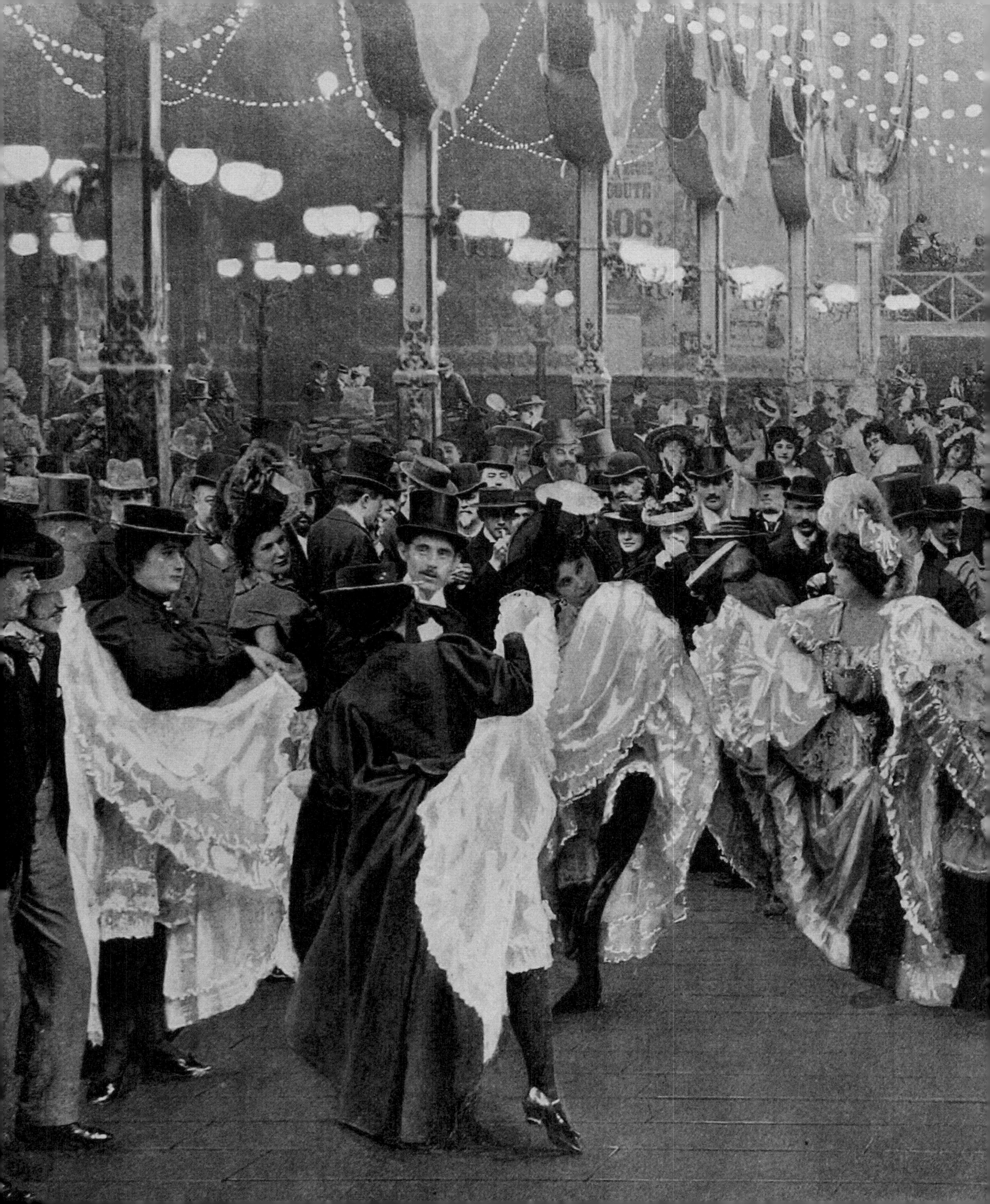

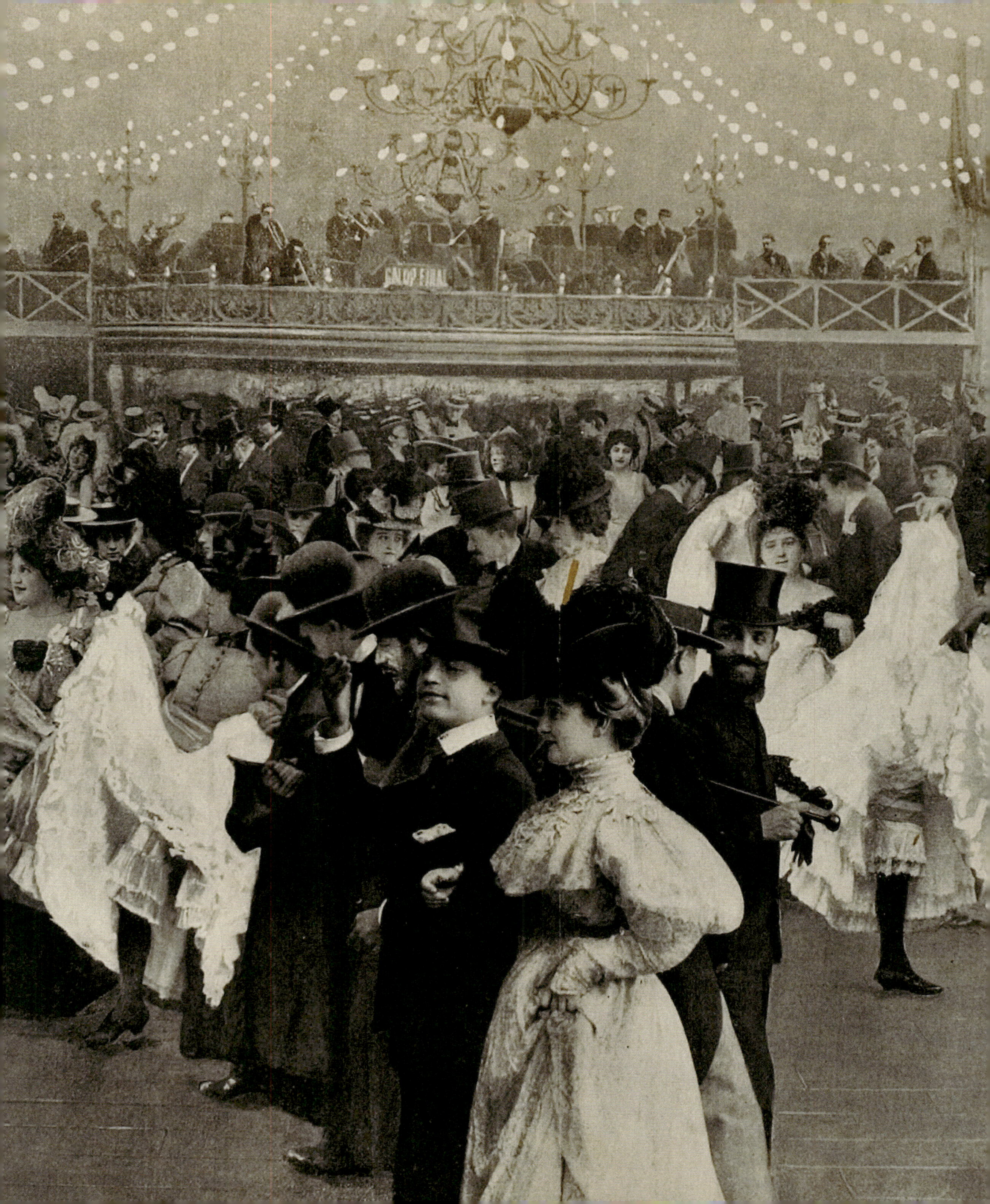